EXPLORING THE LANDS OF THE BOOK OF MORMON

SECOND EDITION

JOSEPH LOVELL ALLEN & BLAKE JOSEPH ALLEN

Book of Mormon Tours and Research Institute, LLC

Orem, Utah

2008

PO Box 970250
Orem, UT 84097
(801) 226-5200 or (888) 226-5205
www.bookofmormontours.com
email to *digest@ldstours.com*

Printed in China
Print Broker: Kevin Frye; Frye's Printing, Inc.; Napa, California
First Printing: August 2008

Design and production by Stephen Hales Creative, Inc.; Provo, Utah

ISBN 978-0-615-22171-7

About the Cover

"And it came to pass that many died in the wilderness of their wounds, and were devoured by those beasts and also the vultures of the air; and their bones have been found, and have been heaped up on the earth" (Alma 2:38).

This scripture represents one New World fulfillment of a prophecy that is recorded in several places in the standard works of the Church (see chapter 24, pages 583–86 of this second edition of *Exploring the Lands of the Book of Mormon* for details).

The front cover represents the history of the people whose lives are recorded in the Book of Mormon—that is, "their bones have been found, and have been heaped up on the earth." The Book of Mormon has come forth from the darkness of the earth and has been brought to light, "heaped upon the earth," and carried to all nations, kindreds, tongues, and people. Those who accept the gospel are gathered together and are like vultures, or eagles, or fowls of the air that devour the ancient records and, in essence, become part of the great gathering of Israel in the latter days.

Notice the distinctive Mesoamerica/Book of Mormon setting that is reflected in the design of the front cover. The Olmec head has been uncovered from the earth and represents the Jaredites, the first high civilization of the New World. The jungle background behind the Olmec head represents the east wilderness that played such a prevalent role in the lives of the second high civilization—the Nephites, Mulekites, and Lamanites. The fiery sky represents the promise of a new day as the Book of Mormon comes forth from the darkness of the earth. And the circling vultures represent all peoples of the last days who are now "devouring" the words of the Book of Mormon.

Dedicated to **Rhoda Robinson Allen,**

who forever has been—and continues to be—a dedicated wife and mother to the authors and who now is a dedicated grandmother with eyes on great-grandmotherhood. In other words, as in many homes, it's all about family and God.

Contents

Preface

ineteen years ago, we published *Exploring the Lands of the Book of Mormon*. Although it had gone through several printings and was still available in the bookstores, with the encouragement of colleagues and friends, we felt the time had arrived when we should prepare an updated version. As we got into the project, we were pleasantly surprised to discover that more than a score of vital concepts relative to our understanding the Book of Mormon had changed either because additional information had come forth or because important Book of Mormon insights had been modified.

The new content was such that we decided to leave the title the same because it precisely mirrors what the book is about: *Exploring the Lands of the Book of Mormon*, second edition. Some of the changes are minor; others are major. Interestingly, our attitude has also changed over the years. With new evidence, we have found that we should be selective and not overuse the word "proposed" in discussing insights about Mesoamerica as it relates to the Book of Mormon. If the evidence is such that it *cannot* be refuted or if the evidence is highly compelling, we feel justified in presenting the material in a more authoritative vernacular. For example, if we analyze a comparative date from Mesoamerica that deals with the same event as described in the Book of Mormon and if that date and event are associated with the same area as previously proposed, should we not reverse the burden of proof? Are we not justified in saying, "Submit evidence to the contrary to prove the concept invalid"? That evidence, or lack thereof, must therefore be subjected to the same intensity of scrutiny. We have always tried to remain true to the law of witnesses—that is, in the mouth of two or more witnesses shall the truth be established. These three witnesses are (1) the Book of Mormon, (2) archaeological evidence, and (3) historical data.

In addition, inasmuch as Mormon and the other writers used physical examples to teach spiritual messages, we should also use the same method when we write about the Book of Mormon. The change in writing style on this subject, since 1989, is greatly influenced as a result of asking the following question: "Why did Mormon include this war story, climate statement, geographical statement, and so forth in the Book of Mormon when, by his own admission, he could write only a hundredth part of the history of his people?" We have now come to believe that the study of historical geography of the Book of Mormon is supremely important because we now understand, perhaps through the shadows, that Mormon primarily uses these stories as a type and a shadow of things to come and as a means of teaching the spiritual message that is so supreme to the book itself—that of Christ our Redeemer.

The prophet Abinadi, who challenged the wicked King Noah and his equally wicked priests, is the one who said, "If ye teach the law of Moses, also teach that it is a shadow of those things which are to come—Teach them that redemption cometh through Christ the Lord" (Mosiah 16:14–15). In this new, second edition of *Exploring the Lands of the Book of Mormon*, we have tried to follow Abinadi's counsel—that is, if we are going to write about the history, culture, and geography of the Book of Mormon, then we should also present the concept of *dualism* in which the physical message is designed to emphasize the spiritual message.

As teachers of the gospel, we have been concerned at every juncture with the teaching/learning processes in connection with what we have written for the second edition of *Exploring the Lands of the Book of Mormon*. With those concerns in mind, we have intentionally employed the principle of repetition throughout the book. That is, we have written each chapter as a self-contained, standalone document. On a chapter-by-chapter basis, we have included repetitive content where appropriate to achieve that objective but have treated the repetitive subject matter from different reference points in the process.

In conclusion, as readers study, contemplate, and analyze the information in *Exploring the Lands of the Book of Mormon*, we declare that we are aware that the messages of this book are only a shadow of the marvelous work and the wonders that are contained within the pages of the Book of Mormon itself.

Joseph Lovell Allen
Blake Joseph Allen

"If ye teach the law of Moses, also teach that it is a shadow of those things which are to come—Teach . . . that redemption cometh through Christ the Lord." (Mosiah 16:14–15)

JUST A BOY

By Jessica Allen, age 14, 2005, daughter of Blake Joseph Allen, Coauthor

In commemoration of the two hundredth anniversary of the birth of the Prophet Joseph Smith

Just a boy,
only fourteen.
He prays to his Father
in a grove of trees.

He doesn't know
where to go.
He doesn't know
which teaching to follow.

Just a boy,
only fourteen.
He sees God the Father
and the Son.

They give him an answer.
They tell him,
"All these churches
are wrong."

Just a boy,
only fourteen.
He knows what he saw.
He knows God knows it.
He cannot deny it.

Just a man,
about eighteen.
Moroni visits him
and continues
for four years to come.

Just a man,
about eighteen.
He sees the golden plates
but is not allowed
to touch them.

Just a man,
about twenty-two.
He receives
the ancient records,
buried in a hill.

He finds three men
to help him:
Oliver Cowdery;
David Whitmer;
Martin Harris.

Just a man,
about twenty-four.
He begins to translate
the best book of them all.

We celebrate his birth
two hundred years ago.
Thus began his journey
to change the world.

We celebrate
the restoration
of the gospel
of Jesus Christ
as Latter-day Saints.

Just a boy?
Just a man?
Yes—but called by God
to be a prophet.

He made the world
a better place for us.
His name is Joseph Smith.

I know this truth
for myself.
I honor him
as a prophet of God.

Foreword

I am honored that coauthors Dr. Joseph L. Allen and Blake J. Allen have asked me to write the foreword to the second edition of *Exploring the Lands of the Book of Mormon.* The first edition was published in 1989 and has been an overwhelming success. It has sold over twenty-five thousand copies in fifteen printings and was the principal text used by Dr. Bruce Warren in his Brigham Young University course on archaeology and the scriptures. Its attention to detail and its descriptive maps and adherence to sound research principles have made it the authoritative reference on Book of Mormon geography, culture, and history for the past nineteen years. Yet even as the first edition was being published, new discoveries, insights, and ideas regarding the historical setting of the Book of Mormon were being presented. And although the final chapter on Book of Mormon culture will likely not be written for many years to come, the second edition of *Exploring the Lands of the Book of Mormon* is undoubtedly the most thorough text published on this subject to date.

During the past thirty years, the interest in and volume of information pertaining to the physical evidence of the Book of Mormon have escalated—at least in part because of the growth of The Church of Jesus Christ of Latter-day Saints, advances in science, and our increased ability to travel. Yet, because the central message of the Book of Mormon is spiritual and its purpose is to testify of Christ, some have questioned and even criticized the merits of this type of study and research. In respectful response to that attitude, I merely paraphrase Dr. Joseph Allen: "The more we know about the geography, history, and culture of the Book of Mormon, the more we know about the Book of Mormon."

Since the initial publication of the Book of Mormon, its readers have naturally wondered where the recorded events took place. One of the challenges of pursuing such a complex subject is to determine which method of study will be most effective. Several approaches have been employed over the years, and some of these deserve consideration and comment. One way to approach the historical study of the Book of Mormon has been to review statements attributed to leaders and other prominent historical figures of the Church of Jesus Christ and then propose a model consistent with those statements. The fundamental problem with this approach is that the only official Church statements regarding Book of Mormon geography are that the New World events took place on the American continent and that the plates upon which the Book of Mormon was written were buried in present-day New York. No other statements contain enough substance to add to our understanding of possible Book of Mormon events or locations. Another common approach has been to pick an area, usually where someone has served an LDS Church mission, and "plug in" the sites. This approach does not help but, in fact, is counterproductive because with enough imagination, a student of the Book of Mormon can propose any location as a possible Book of Mormon site despite the lack of any substantial evidence in support of that choice.

Recently, attempts have been made to use the science of DNA to provide clues to Book of Mormon locations and populations. Unfortunately, the limiting piece of this puzzle is the Book of Mormon itself. Although DNA models can be very sophisticated, the Book of Mormon contains several subcultures from over fifteen hundred years ago without enough internal detail to determine DNA origins accurately. To use this method legitimately, researchers either would have to know already with certain specificity where the Book of Mormon took place or would have to make a bold assumption regarding such locations. And because the underlying question is to discover where the Book of Mormon took place, once such an assumption is made, as each of the aforementioned study methods does, the models fall apart and lose credibility. The most objective method of studying Book of Mormon geography, history, and culture is to analyze the available information provided by the Book of Mormon and then compare this information with the scientific evidence to determine where the evidence leads. This is the most intellectually accurate approach of study and is the method used by Joseph and Blake Allen and other acknowledged scholars.

Dr. Joseph Allen began his study of Book of Mormon geography, history, and culture in the 1960s and earned a PhD from Brigham Young University in ancient scripture in 1970. Having taught seminary and institute in the LDS Church Educational System for eighteen years, he acquired knowledge and familiarity with the Book of Mormon that are extensive and second to none. In 1978, he left the formal classroom and since then has devoted his energy and time to exploring the lands of the Book of Mormon. His independent method of travel study has enabled him to do research as well as teach over five thousand "students" without the confines of a lecture hall or the constraints of an overseeing institution. Dr. Allen has spent more time on location and covered more miles exploring the lands of the Book of Mormon than any other Book of Mormon investigator. His educational background and years of on-site experience have made him one of the foremost authorities on Book of Mormon geography, history, and culture.

Blake Allen completed a two-year Spanish-speaking LDS mission to South America in 1981. Since then, he has spent much of his time working with Dr. Allen both in traveling throughout Mesoamerica and in studying archaeology, culture, and history as they relate to the Book of Mormon. Other than Dr. Allen himself, no other explorer or guide has personally organized and directed more Book of Mormon-related excursions than Blake has. His firsthand experience with locations, routes, distances, and natural landmarks and the knowledge he has acquired over the past several years have made him an indispensable contributor to this text.

The second edition of *Exploring the Lands of the Book of Mormon* is a completely revised and updated version of the original text. The second edition required about nine hundred pages and more than three hundred maps and visuals to "tell the story" adequately. It presents the most comprehensive and scientifically accurate descriptions of Book of Mormon geography, culture, and history ever published. It is sure to become the standard reference by which other publications will be compared. For almost twenty years, the fundamental goal of this text has been to increase our knowledge of the Book of Mormon. It is based on the core belief that the Book of Mormon is true and that its main purpose is to testify of Jesus Christ. The authors have successfully maintained a tradition of the first edition by forcefully asserting that the more we know about the geography, history, and culture of the Book of Mormon, the more we know about the Book of Mormon itself.

Dr. Brent J. Allen

Acknowledgments

W e give our deepest thanks to Ted D. Stoddard for his indefatigable work as editor, consultant, advocate, and friend.

We thank Todd B. Allen for his insights, humor, and expertise as a tour director for Book of Mormon Tours. He has escorted more than a hundred tour groups to Mesoamerica over a twenty-year period.

We are very much indebted to the talented photographers for their willingness to share their photos throughout the book: Nathan T. Allen, Cortney Boice, Chad Clark, George and Audrey DeLange, Boyd Hoglund, Keith Neeley, Richard Norman, Merrill C. Oaks, Phil Skousen, Mary O. Stoddard, and Sheryl Lee Wilson. We also thank Cliff Dunston for his artwork in both editions of *Exploring the Lands of the Book of Mormon;* and we thank Verl F. Morgan, now deceased, for his beautiful quetzal-bird painting that we have used in both editions of *Exploring the Lands.*

We express our gratitude to Covenant Communications and Deseret Book Company for their help with this publication and with previous publications. We thank Stephen Hales, Matt Davis, and Brad Jeppson of Stephen Hales Creative for their assistance with this second edition of *Exploring the Lands of the Book of Mormon.* We especially thank Kelly Nield of Stephen Hales Creative for his innovativeness in the design for this second edition.

We are uniquely indebted to Kevin Frye of Frye's Printing, Inc. in Napa, California, for his efforts as our print broker in arranging and supervising the printing of the second edition of *Exploring the Lands of the Book of Mormon.*

Appreciation is also given to those who have worked with Book of Mormon Tours and the *Book of Mormon Archaeological Digest* and who have, in the process, contributed to the second edition of *Exploring the Lands of the Book of Mormon,* including

Blake J. Allen II, Johannah Allen, Troy R. Allen, Joseph Gorrell, David Hadlock, Beverly Hansen, Jeff Larsen, Wendy Mendoza, Tawni LaSalle, Joseph Willard, Ryan Williams, and all contributing authors to the *Book of Mormon Archaeological Digest*.

LATTER-DAY SAINT MESOAMERICANISTS

We thank the forerunners of Book of Mormon geography and history—those who have advanced the study of geography and history of the Book of Mormon in Mesoamerica in their writing, speaking, and researching endeavors. Their efforts, in one way or another, have contributed to the content of *Exploring the Lands of the Book of Mormon*. The lists that follow are not meant to solicit an endorsement of what we have written, nor are the lists exhaustive:

1830–1930

- Joseph Smith Jr., Prophet, Seer, and Revelator: Translated the Book of Mormon by the gift and power of God; supported the location of the narrow neck of land in Central America
- John Taylor, Apostle and Prophet, The Church of Jesus Christ of Latter-day Saints: Taught that Quetzalcoatl and Christ are one and the same
- Benjamin Cluff, president of Brigham Young Academy: Led the Zarahemla Expedition to Central America

1930–80

- Brigham H. Roberts, Council of the Seventy: Favored a limited geography model for the Book of Mormon
- M. Wells Jakeman, Archaeology Department, Brigham Young University: Analyzed Stela 5 from Izapa; limited the geography of the Book of Mormon to Mesoamerica
- Thomas S. Ferguson: Founded the New World Archaeological Foundation
- Howard W. Hunter, Apostle and President of The Church of Jesus Christ of Latter-day Saints: Supported and directed the New World Archaeological Foundation
- Milton R. Hunter, Council of the Seventy: Coauthored *Ancient America and the Book of Mormon*
- Sidney B. Sperry, Dean of Religion, Brigham Young University: Endorsed the principle that the New World Book of Mormon events were confined to a limited geographical area
- John W. Welch, Brigham Young University law professor: Established the Foundation for Ancient Research and Mormon Studies; discovered chiastic structures in the Book of Mormon
- David A. Palmer: Objectively researched the geography of the Book of Mormon; authored *In Search of Cumorah: New Evidences for the Book of Mormon from Ancient America*

- John L. Sorenson, Brigham Young University emeritus professor of Anthropology: Opened the door to serious investigation of Mesoamerica as the land of the Book of Mormon; authored *An Ancient American Setting for the Book of Mormon*

SPECIAL CONTRIBUTORS

We cannot thank enough those who have contributed in any way to the second edition of *Exploring the Lands of the Book of Mormon* or who have influenced our thinking or assisted us in its coming forth, uniquely including the following individuals:

- David C. Asay: Chairman of Book of Mormon Archaeological Forum
- Don Black: Lecturer and tour director
- Ted E. Brewerton: First Quorum of the Seventy, did investigative research on ancient Guatemalan documents
- Allen J. Christenson: Translated the *Popol Vuh* from Maya to English
- F. Richard Hauck: Archaeologist and Mesoamericanist
- John L. Lund: Author and tour director
- Clate W. Mask Jr.: Second Quorum of the Seventy and tour director
- Alan C. Miner: Dentist; author and researcher, Ancient America Foundation
- V. Garth Norman: Author, archaeologist, and Mesoamericanist, Ancient America Foundation
- Francois Radzik: Dentist, author, and researcher
- Bruce W. Warren: Author, archaeologist, and Mesoamericanist, Ancient America Foundation
- Diane E. Wirth: Author, researcher, and Mesoamericanist

MESOAMERICAN ARCHAEOLOGISTS AND SCHOLARS

We recognize Mesoamerican archaeologists and scholars, both Mormon and non-Mormon, for their investigative research that has led to a greater understanding of both Mesoamerica and the Book of Mormon. We mention only a few: Ignacio Bernal, Frans Blom, Alfonso Caso, Frederick Catherwood, John E. Clark, Michael D. Coe, Miguel Covarrubias, Kent V. Flannery, Donald W. Forsyth, David Freidel, Cyrus H. Gordon, Nikolai Grube, Richard D. Hansen, Stephen D. Houston, David H. Kelley, Alfred V. Kidder, Yuri V. Knorozov, Thomas A. Lee Jr., Gareth W. Lowe, Teoberto Maler, Simon Martin, Ray T. Matheny, Peter Matthews, Sylvanus G. Morley, Tatiana Proskouriakoff, Merle Greene Robertson, Alberto Ruz, Linda Schele, Laurette Séjourné, Edwin M. Shook, John Lloyd Stephens, Matthew W. Stirling, David Stuart, J. Eric S. Thompson, Alfred Tozzer, and David L. Webster.

SPANISH CHRONICLERS AND HISTORIANS

We acknowledge the work of Spanish scholars and historians who have made major contributions to our understanding of pre-Columbian Mesoamerica. Those who have influenced us the most are the following: San Bartolome de las Casas, Bernal Diaz, Diego Duran, Fernando de Alva de Ixtlilxochitl, Diego de Landa, Bernardino de Sahagun, and Juan de Torquemada.

TOUR PARTICIPANTS

We are eternally indebted to those people who have traveled with us from all walks of life and who have a deep love for the Book of Mormon and a profound interest in discussing and gaining a further understanding of the historicity of the Book of Mormon. These individuals are laypeople and scholars, men and women, and teenagers and college students. Many have taken their families, and many have traveled with us two, three, or four times. We especially thank those who have traveled with us as tour directors between the years 1970 and 2008. A short list includes the following tour participants (the asterisks identify those who have served as tour directors or who have assembled a group to travel to the lands of the Book of Mormon): *Verle and Alyce Allred; *Richard and JoAn Berrett; *Paul R. Cheesman, Quin Cook, who baptized his son at Lake Atitlan; Kay Davenport; *Doug and Connie Earl and family; *Tom and Jennifer Ferguson; *John P. Fugal; *Webb Goodman, a travel partner; Chris Heimerdinger; *Norman and Jane Hanson; *Marion and Mary Jo Jenkins and family from Carlsbad, New Mexico; *Wendell Jones and tour group; *Irene Kopp of Switzerland; *Daniel H. Ludlow; *Gerald Lund; *John and Bonnie Lund; *Clate and Carol Mask; *Ralph and Ann McAffee, who became the equivalent of family; Don and Peggy Murray; *Hugh Nibley; *Monte Nyman; *Merrill and Jo Oaks; *Stephen B. and Dixie R. Oveson; *Alan K. Parrish; David and Julie Perry; *Mark (deceased) and Nancy Peterson and family; *Jay (deceased) and Elaine Rawlings; *Rex Reeve Jr; *Eldin Ricks; *Paul and Lael Ruffner; *Tom and Lorraine Shilton; *Darrell and Loretta Stacey; *Dale Tingey of American Indian Services; *Karen van der Werf; Niles Washburn; *S. Michael Wilcox; *Mont and Mary Wooley; *Margaret Workman, and many others. We thank these individuals and almost countless others for their contributions to *Exploring the Lands of the Book of Mormon.*

FRIENDS AND COLLEAGUES IN MEXICO AND GUATEMALA

We express our appreciation to hotel personnel; bus drivers, especially Filiberto Roca of Guatemala; tourism departments; local tour guides; museum curators; tour operators such as Sergio Navas of Guatemala, Helaman Petlecalco and siblings at Tulum, and Kim Goldsmith of Mexico City; young scholars like Enrique Romero and seasoned Church leaders like Aaron Chavez, both of Chihuahua; and friends like Harold and Lenore Herrera (deceased) Brown, Israel Perez of Guatemala, and Agricol Lozano (deceased) of Mexico. We express our unique thanks to Celia Balderas, who translated the first edition of *Exploring the Lands of the Book of Mormon* into Spanish. And we are indebted to local Church of Jesus Christ leaders and members who have received us with open arms, as brothers and sisters in the gospel, and to nonmembers who have treated us with friendship and kindness.

THE SPOKESMAN

The Lord told Joseph of Egypt that in the latter days, a seer would be raised up from Joseph's seed, that the name of this seer would also be Joseph, and that the Lord would prepare a spokesman for this seer. Although the Lord did prepare temporal spokesmen for the Prophet Joseph Smith, we are told that the Book of Mormon would be his eternal spokesman (2 Nephi 3:18–23). We revere the names and express our gratitude for those spokesmen whose names are recorded in the pages of the Book of Mormon: Nephi, Jacob, Mosiah, Benjamin, Abinadi, Alma, Helaman, Samuel, Mormon, Moroni, and the Savior Himself.

IN CONCLUSION

Be it known that we do not set ourselves up as an ensign or as the definitive scholars on the subject of Book of Mormon history and geography. We will let our credentials and research speak for us. We simply see ourselves as children of our Father in Heaven in a long line of advocates who proclaim to the world that the Book of Mormon is the word of God. We love and give thanks to our wives, Rhoda and Marion, for their love and support as we have left them at home and then returned to find them always waiting for us with open arms. We also thank our children, who have traveled with us on several occasions and who have been supportive of our endeavors. We take full responsibility for what we have written, realizing that some or many of our conclusions will be challenged as the years go by. That's good.

Joseph Lovell Allen
Blake Joseph Allen

A Note from the Editor

╚╝

D uring the years of 1987 through 1989, I worked with Dr. Joseph Allen in an editorial capacity while he wrote his manuscript about Mesoamerica as the proposed New World land of the Book of Mormon. Earlier, I had traveled extensively with Joe and his son Blake while they conducted Book of Mormon tours throughout Mesoamerica. During those occasions, I became convinced that Joe and his sons had unique Book of Mormon insights that should be shared with interested readers. Following considerable cajoling and encouragement from me, Joe eventually committed himself to writing his manuscript about Mesoamerica and the Book of Mormon.

Ted D. Stoddard, Editor

The result was a manuscript that we entitled *Exploring the Lands of the Book of Mormon*. After much thought and planning, we decided to self-publish the book so Joe could use it as he desired with his tour business, Book of Mormon Tours. We set up our own publishing company, S. A. Publishers (Stoddard and Allen Publishers), and thereafter participated in what I've labeled a "full, rich, rewarding publishing experience that taught me more lessons of life than I cared to learn." Over the years, the book has been very successful in every way—especially in reinforcing the insights given by Joe and his sons as they have conducted scores and scores of lands of the Book of Mormon tours to Mesoamerica.

In today's fast-moving world, a considerable amount of new evidence has surfaced about proposed Book of Mormon geographic locations since we first published *Exploring the Lands*. We finally accepted our fate and realized the desirability and necessity of marrying this new information with the existing content in *Exploring the Lands*. The result is the second edition of the book you are about to read, *Exploring the Lands of the Book of Mormon*.

I first read the Book of Mormon in its entirety as a young teenager. I've always believed in its truthfulness—an outcome that I consider a gift of the Spirit. Throughout the first third of my life, I devoutly believed that the New World part of its story took place according to the model I was taught—that is, the narrow neck of land is the Isthmus of Panama, South America is the land southward, North America is the land northward, and the Hill Cumorah in upstate New York is the location of the last two great battles of the book's peoples. Looking back, I freely admit that believing in such an illogical model for the geography of the Book of Mormon in no way influenced negatively my belief in the book's message and mission. That admission also reminds me that the most important message of the Book of Mormon is not a geographic message but is the one stated in its preface—to convince its readers that Jesus is the Christ.

At the same time, the issue of Book of Mormon geography "rose up and bit me" right after I returned from my two-year missionary stint for The Church of Jesus Christ of Latter-day Saints. Before my mission, I had opted not to take a Brigham Young University religion class that was dedicated exclusively to the Book of Mormon. When I returned from my mission, I decided to have that experience. I sought and received special permission to take the lower-division Book of Mormon course that had been instituted while I was on my mission.

The professor of the course was Dr. Daniel Ludlow. At the outset of the course, he announced that we would be studying the geography of the Book of Mormon as part of the course's content. I was thrilled because my testimony clearly trumpeted my feeling that the Book of Mormon is a *true* account about *real* people who lived *somewhere*.

Dr. Ludlow's teachings about the doctrines of the Book of Mormon added greatly to my knowledge and testimony of the book. His teachings about the geography of the book, however, totally frustrated me and caused me no end of grief and confusion. That is, he taught the "hourglass model" for Book of Mormon geography. The top of the hourglass is the land northward, the bottom is the land southward, and the middle of the hourglass where the sand runs through is the narrow neck of land. We spent what I thought was an inordinate amount of time *trying* to pinpoint cities, lands, and events of the Book of Mormon in relation to the top, middle, and bottom portions of the hourglass. Throughout those academic exercises, I constantly muttered to myself, "If the Book of Mormon is indeed a *true* account about *real* people, why can't we identify the *somewhere* they lived as geographic locations other than those associated with an hourglass? After all, Mormon speaks to us on most pages of the Book of Mormon as if we know the precise geographic locations in question."

The experience with Dr. Ludlow dramatically turned me off to Book of Mormon geography for most of the second third of my life, although I continued to think of geography in relation to the model I had been taught from my youth: South America is the land southward; North America is the land northward; the Isthmus of Panama is the narrow neck of land; and the Book of Mormon hill Cumorah is in upstate New York.

Toward the end of the second third of my life, I sat through a Brigham Young University course about the geography of the Book of Mormon taught by Dr. John Sorenson. As a text for the course, we used a heavily edited looseleaf version of the initial draft of his as-yet-unpublished manuscript, *An Ancient American Setting for the Book of Mormon*. I was elated with the content of the course as I listened to Dr. Sorenson's lectures because the perspectives he gave dovetailed precisely with my fundamental belief about the Book of Mormon—that is, the Book of Mormon is a *true* account about *real* people who lived *somewhere*. That *somewhere*, according to Dr. Sorenson's model, is Mesoamerica. Almost overnight, I figuratively threw into the wastebasket all the academic nonsense associated with the hourglass model for Book of Mormon geography.

I found myself hungering for additional definitive information about Dr. Sorenson's limited-geographic model for Book of Mormon geography. I spent countless hours in the library reading archaeological reports about the peoples and lands of Mesoamerica. For me, one relevant, insightful outcome of that experience was the rebuttal I intuitively made to one of my colleagues who maintained that as of the twentieth century, *nothing* archaeologically supported the Book of Mormon. I responded that he needed to read the reports I had been reading about defensive earthworks in what I had by then deduced to be the east wilderness; about the Olmec people along the Gulf Coast of Mexico, whose civilization dates precisely to the Jaredite time period in the Book of Mormon; about the radiocarbon-dated finds throughout Mesoamerica that coincide very closely with Book of Mormon dates; and about the many extant Mesoamerican ruins that had been built over other structures that dated precisely to Book of Mormon times. I further mentioned the numerous reports I had recently read that discussed the history, traditions, customs, cultures, and languages of preconquest Mesoamerican peoples from an anthropological perspective and the great similarities between the findings of these reports and the content of the Book of Mormon. For me, that discussion brought into clear focus my stance about Book of Mormon geography as I moved into the third time period of my life.

Contiguous to this same time, I landed in Mexico City as a participant in a Brigham Young University Travel Studies tour of proposed Book of Mormon lands in Mesoamerica. Upon landing, I met Dr. Joseph Allen for the first time. Because both of us were traveling alone, we roomed together. What I heard from him about Book of Mormon geography, history, culture, and language during his daytime lectures was minimal compared to what I learned during our almost-nightly conversations until one, two, and three o'clock in the mornings.

As the old saying goes, "The rest is history." A few years later, Joe and I jointly published *Exploring the Lands of the Book of Mormon*. Now, a few years after that event, we decided to self-publish a second edition of *Exploring the Lands* and to bring on Joe's son, Blake Joseph, as a coauthor because of Blake's extensive knowledge about and travels throughout Mesoamerica.

In working with Joe and Blake on the manuscript for the second edition of *Exploring the Lands,* I've found myself time and again somewhat *smugly* talking to myself and saying, "Isn't that interesting. There's a Mesoamerican city, land, valley, river, body of water, wilderness, or other geographic area that *just happens* to coincide precisely in location with what I read in the Book of Mormon."

I am so convinced that the insights of Joe and Blake about Book of Mormon geography and history are correct that I challenge any reader to find *legitimate* fault with them—keeping in mind that, in most instances in *Exploring the Lands,* Joe and Blake continue to use the word "proposed" in connection with most geographic locations. In private conversations with them, however, I've noticed that, for many Mesoamerican geographical locations and associated events, Joe and Blake have gone beyond saying "This is a *proposed* location for such and such a Book of Mormon event or landmark." After traveling throughout the geographic area of Mesoamerica on over three hundred different occasions while examining the areas in relation to what is said *in* the Book of Mormon, Joe and Blake now go beyond "proposed" in many of their comments. That is, for some geographic situations, they are now absolute in their thinking that some sites indeed *are* the geographic areas mentioned or described in the Book of Mormon.

I've always appreciated the approach to Book of Mormon geography followed by Joe Allen and his sons. They did not, as some investigators have done, develop an internal map of Book of Mormon lands based on the limited information in the Book of Mormon and then look for a place in the New World where that map seemed to fit. The Allens simply state that the Book of Mormon does not give enough evidence to develop an authoritative map following those procedures. Therefore, for example, they maintain that the so-called hourglass model is not a practical way to approach real-life Book of Mormon geography.

Neither have the Allens endorsed the idea of using a single passage of scripture to determine Book of Mormon geography—such as "isle of the sea" or "the promised land." They point out that investigators who use this approach illegitimately give themselves the liberty of arbitrarily placing Book of Mormon lands where they desire, which then allows them to create a make-believe geography of the Book of Mormon—procedures that any serious Book of Mormon student should shun.

The Allens' approach to Book of Mormon geography is as follows:

1. Based on the content of the Book of Mormon, develop criteria that *must* be satisfied by any proposed geographic area for New World Book of Mormon geography.
2. Test those criteria in connection with *any* potential geographic area for New World Book of Mormon geography.

From my perspective, the major criteria that Dr. Allen and his sons have used for almost four decades in trying to identify valid areas for New World Book of Mormon geography are derived from the content of the Book of Mormon and are four in number:

1. The area must have evidence of a high-level *written language* that was in use during the dates given in the Book of Mormon.
2. The area must reflect two *high civilizations* that show extensive evidence of major population centers, continual shifts in population demographics, and almost constant warfare among the inhabitants.
3. The *archaeology* of the proposed area must be conducive to thorough analyses of sites and artifacts with resulting radiocarbon dates that parallel the dates given in the Book of Mormon.
4. The *historical evidence* from the area must provide valid findings that dovetail with the customs and traditions associated with the peoples of the Book of Mormon.

The above criteria must be universal in nature. That is, before examining any prospective area to determine if it reflects the geography of the Book of Mormon, an investigator should be willing to apply all four criteria to the area. With that attitude in mind and with the four criteria dominating and driving the investigation, an investigator then—and only then—should feel that he or she is ready to look at a prospective Book of Mormon geographic area to see if it meets the criteria. If an area does not meet all four criteria, it should be labeled as an invalid geographic location for New World events of the Book of Mormon.

One other aspect of any Book of Mormon geography investigation is also very critical—an aspect that is often mistakenly taken for granted. That is, any geography investigator should *know* what is contained in the Book of Mormon about its geography. In fact, he or she should be intimately familiar with *precisely* what the Book of Mormon says in connection with geographic pointers. Again and again I have reached the conclusion that investigators have erred in their thinking because they evidently have *not* read the Book of Mormon carefully, and they then make geographic statements that are not supported by the content of the book itself. In other words, they either do not know what the Book of Mormon says or they ignore what it says. For example, the wording in Alma 22:32 for a day and a half's journey is *not* "from the east sea to the west sea" but rather is "from the east to the west sea." Recognition of that simple fact would have negated the illogical, unsupported thinking that the east sea is the Gulf of Mexico—a misreading of content that has set back Book of Mormon geographical studies by at least half a century.

Therefore, any serious investigation of Book of Mormon geography must exclude any misreading of geographic pointers in the Book of Mormon. Valid investigations will also avoid heartburn that is driven by previous missionary experiences, the unfounded impact of casual on-site visits to geographic areas, shallow consumption of data from archaeological or historical reports, or preconceived biases that are based on the opinions of other investigators who have not applied the criteria in their own studies.

Once the Allens applied their four criteria repeatedly for all areas being proposed as the lands of the Book of Mormon, they arrived at the conclusion that Mesoamerica—and only Mesoamerica—meets the prescribed criteria. At that point, they *then* turned their attention to geography. Trust me—no individual living today has seriously analyzed, in person over and over again via on-site visits and consumption of archaeological reports, the geographical prepositional pointers of the Book of Mormon than have Joseph Allen and his sons. They have used such Book of Mormon pointers as *into, up, up to, up out of, up into, up upon, above, down, down into, down out of, along by, away on, away by, away up beyond, near, across, around, over into, over upon, through, round about, west sea, south,* and on and on and on in proving their model. In the process, they have tromped all over Mesoamerican sites hundreds of times in their search to verify the existence of sites that match the internal geographical and topographical signals given us mostly by Mormon and that meet the predetermined criteria for verifying legitimate New World Book of Mormon geography. In short, the Allens have personally visited and analyzed sites throughout Mesoamerica in connection with Book of Mormon geographic statements in far greater depth and frequency than has any other person living today. That statement includes the Latter-day Saint archaeologists who have spent considerable time digging among the ruins of Mesoamerica as part of their profession.

One of Joe and Blake's statements in chapter 26 of this second edition of *Exploring the Lands* succinctly expresses my bottom-line assessment of Mesoamerican geography associated with the Book of Mormon. They make the argument that "we logically should survey the Mesoamerica map to determine if a 'land among many waters' that fits the prescribed Book of Mormon requirements actually exists between the proposed land of Nephi and the proposed land of Desolation." Then, with a rather casual, matter-of-fact follow-up statement, they say, "Such a place does exist." To me, that's the outcome that should be sought if we are to have valid conclusions about potential locations of Book of Mormon cities, lands, and other geographic features. That is, we must thoroughly study the internal Book of Mormon geographic pointers and then, with the four criteria in mind, ask something like, "Does an actual piece of real estate exist that fits these words and that satisfies the established criteria?" For essentially every one of the cities, lands, rivers, wilderness areas, bodies of water, and so forth mentioned in the Book of Mormon, I'm now able to say in a rather matter of fact way but with great confidence, *"Such a place does exist because it meets the established criteria."*

In summary, I have used the following imperative-mood guidelines in helping me edit the manuscript for the second edition of *Exploring the Lands of the Book of Mormon:*

- Adhere to the cardinal directions in identifying all potential Book of Mormon sites. Book of Mormon peoples used the cardinal directions in all aspects of their lives and did not rotate the compass to create an unsubstantiated, illogical "Nephite north."

- Analyze precisely what the Book of Mormon says about a site, and then search for a geographic setting that meets the criteria and that matches the wording in the Book of Mormon about that site. Don't work with a geographic site by attempting to force the Book of Mormon to fit that site.

- Accept the validity of radiocarbon dating applied to archaeological sites in helping verify the legitimacy of any proposed site.

- Examine and use historical records from both pre- and postconquest Mesoamerica in helping understand the geography, history, language, and cultural traditions of the Book of Mormon peoples.

- Stay abreast of archaeological and anthropological reports that deal with the geography, history, language, and cultural traditions of potential Book of Mormon sites and peoples.

- Maintain an appropriate distance from nineteenth-, twentieth-, and twenty-first-century "Mormon myths" that distort Book of Mormon geography, history, language, and cultural traditions.

- Extinguish the flames of heartburn that are kindled and fed by unfounded, illogically conceived perceptions about Book of Mormon geography arising from misguided teachings, unfounded hypotheses, or heartburn experiences from missionary fields of labor or casual reading of the Book of Mormon.

- Recognize that inspirational insights about Book of Mormon geography can be gained by anyone who objectively and systematically examines any premise as a reflection of what the book itself says in connection with the criteria and who then relies on the Spirit for appropriate guidance.

- Appreciate the fact that most Church instructors of religion legitimately must restrict their teachings and research largely to doctrines and history rather than to geography—a fact that should not preclude other readers from pursuing geographical studies as a valid aspect of Book of Mormon studies.

I make the same statement today about the second edition of *Exploring the Lands of the Book of Mormon* that I made in 1989 for the first edition. That statement, modified slightly, is the following: "This is good stuff. It'll bring the Book of Mormon to life for you. It'll strengthen your testimony that Jesus is the Christ. I've experienced a marvelous change in my life as a result of this material, and I can hardly wait to see what happens to you as you expose yourself to Joseph and Blake Allen's insights."

Ted D. Stoddard, Editor
Professor Emeritus of Management Communication
Marriott School of Management
Brigham Young University

Pronunciation Guide

꜠꜠꜠꜠꜠꜠꜠꜠꜠꜠꜠꜠꜠꜠꜠꜠꜠꜠꜠꜠꜠꜠꜠꜠꜠꜠꜠꜠꜠꜠꜠꜠

Spanish is the official language of both Mexico and Guatemala. However, because of the many native languages that were in existence at the time of the Spanish conquest, numerous Mesoamerican words have made it into the Spanish vocabulary. Many people today still speak their native language.

The most influential native language is the Aztec, often called the Nahuatl language. For example, the largest park in Mexico is called *Chapultepec*, which is a Nahuatl word meaning "grasshopper hill."

The word *coyote* is also a Nahuatl word that is not only used in Spanish but also has made its way into the English language. In all three languages, a coyote is the wild animal that looks like a dog. Even the word *California* is Nahuatl. *Cali* means house or home, and *fornia* means by the sea; hence, the name *California* means "their homes by the sea."

In the Yucatan area, many of the words are of Maya derivative. For example, the famous resort city of *Cancun*, pronounced *kahn KOON*, is a Maya word meaning "land of the serpents." (The solid-capital syllable is stressed in the pronunciation.)

Quetzalcoatl is Aztec for "feathered serpent," and *Kukulcan* is Maya for "feathered serpent."

Your familiarity with a few basic pronunciation skills will enable you to read *Exploring the Lands of the Book of Mormon* with ease and confidence. Although many of the words are of native Mesoamerican origin, we generally use the Spanish pronunciation. That makes the task relatively easy. In Spanish, the vowels are pronounced as follows:

A in Spanish is always pronounced *ah*, as in the word f*a*ther.
E in Spanish is always pronounced as a hard *a*, as in the word h*ay*.
I in Spanish is always pronounced as a hard *e*, as in the word h*e*.
O in Spanish is always pronounced as a hard *o*, as in the word t*o*e.
U in Spanish is always pronounced *oo*, as in the word s*oo*n.

Therefore, the Nahuatl word *Teotihuacan*, which includes all the vowels, is usually pronounced *tay oh tee wah KAHN*. Remember to pronounce each syllable distinctly and separately and to stress the syllable that is shown in solid capitals. The *h* is silent. When two vowels are together, such as *ua*, they are pronounced *oo ah*, but the result sounds like *wah* in English.

The single *r* and the double *rr* in the middle of words require a trill that is particularly difficult for some speakers. However, two "speech tricks" solve the difficulties, as follows:

Single *r* = replace with a soft *d*: *Merida* is pronounced *MED ee dah*.
Double *rr* = replace with *t* plus *r* as in *butter* or a soft *d* plus *r* as in *shudder*: *Cerros* is pronounced *SETR ohs* or *SEDR ohs*.

Some of the most difficult words to pronounce in both Spanish and English are words that contain the letters *x* or *t*, such as *Oaxaca* or *Tlatelolco*. When in the middle of the word, the *x* usually takes on the sound of the English *h* (or the Spanish *j*, which is pronounced like the English *h*). Therefore, *Oaxaca* is pronounced *wah HAH kah*. If the *x* is at the beginning of the word, such as in the Maya word *Xelha* (or *Xelja*), the *x* is pronounced *sh*. In this case, the pronunciation of the *h* is not silent. Therefore, we pronounce the word *SHEL hah*. On occasion, when the letter *x* is in the middle of the word, the sound is still *sh*. The word *Uxmal*, for example, is pronounced *oosh MAHL*. It is not pronounced *UX mahl*.

The pronunciation of some words seems to defy logic and requires speakers simply to know the correct punctuation. For example, *Dzibanche* is pronounced *see bahn CHAY* and reflects two outcomes: *d* is silent, and *z* is pronounced as an *s*.

When *t* is in front of a word, such as in the Aztec word *Tlatelolco*, the *t* has almost a clicking sound. Probably the closest sound in the English language is the word *it*, as in *it lah tay LOHL koh*.

Some individuals wonder why Aztec words show up in Maya territory, such as Quetzaltenango, Chimaltenango, and so forth. When the Spaniards conquered Guatemala, they sent surveyors from Mexico to survey the new land. As a result, many times the surveyors used Aztec (Nahuatl) words. However, natives often have continued to use the Maya word, such as Xelaju instead of Quetzaltenango. They even have used a mixture of the two, such as Xocaltenango: *Xocal* (Maya) *tenango* (Nahuatl), or "place of the fish."

Following is a pronunciation guide for selected Spanish and native words. The pronunciations are typically Spanish, which differs in some respects from Maya, Aztec, and other Mesoamerican native languages. The phonetic syllables for pronunciation purposes are our own invention. Similar sources for phonetic pronunciation of syllables vary widely in how they show syllable pronunciations, but we think you can easily follow our pronunciation directions. The syllables shown in solid capitals are emphasized during the pronunciations.

WORD	SYLLABLE PRONUNCIATION	DESCRIPTION
Abaj Takalik	ah BAH tahk ah LEEK	Archaeological site in Guatemala
Acapulco	ah kah POOL koh	Resort city in Mexico
Acayucan	ah kah YOO kahn	Modern city in Veracruz
Almolonga	ahl moh LOHN gah	Village in Quetzaltenango, Guatemala
Altun Ha	ahl TOON hah	Maya archaeological site in Belize
Amatitlan	ah mah teet LAHN	Lake south of Guatemala City
Antigua	ahn TEEG hwah	Tourist city in Guatemala
Atitlan	ah teet LAHN	Nahuatl name of lake in Guatemala
Becan	bay KAHN	Maya archaeological site in Campeche
Bonampak	boh nahm PAHK	Maya archaeological site in Chiapas
Cakchiquel	kahk chee KELL	Native Maya dialect in Guatemala
Calakmul	kah lahk MOOL	Maya archaeological site in Campeche
Campeche	kahm PAY chay	Name of state in Mexico
Cancun	kahn KOON	Maya name of resort city in Mexico
Caracol	kahr ah KOHL	Maya site in northern Belize
Catemaco	kah tay MAH koh	Village and lake in Veracruz, Mexico
Ceiba	SAY bah	Name of national tree of Guatemala
Cenote	say NOH tay	Maya word for *well*
Cerros	SETR ohs	Spanish word for *hills*
Chapultepec	chah POOL tay pehk	Nahuatl name of park in Mexico City
Chetumal	chay too MAHL	City and state in Mexico
Chiapa de Corzo	chee AH pah day KOR soh	City and site in Chiapas, Mexico
Chiapas	chee AH pahs	Name of state in Mexico
Chichen Itza	chee CHEN eet SAH	Maya name of village and site (in this case, *chen* has a soft e, as in *when*)
Chichicastenango	chee chee kahs tay NAHN goh	Nahuatl name of city in Guatemala
Chichimeca	chee chee MAY kah	Ancient tribal name in Mesoamerica
Chichonal	chee choh NAHL	Volcano south of Villahermosa
Chicuasen	chee kwah SEHN	Man-made dam along Grijalva River
Chile	CHEE lay	Country in South America
Chimaltenango	chee mahl tay NAHN goh	Nahuatl name of city in Guatemala
Chiutinamit	chee oo teen ah MEET	Ancient Maya city at Lake Atitlan
Cholula	choh LOO lah	Large pyramid in Cholula, Puebla
Chukumuk	choo koo MOOK	Ancient Maya city at Lake Atitlan
Cintalapa	seen tah LAH pah	City in western Chiapas
Cintepec	seen tay PAYK	Hill near Lake Catemaco, Veracruz
Coatepeque	koh ah tay PAY kay	Nahuatl name of city in Guatemala

WORD	SYLLABLE PRONUNCIATION	DESCRIPTION
Coba	koh BAH	Maya name of site in the Yucatan
Coban	koh BAHN	Maya name of site in the Yucatan
Comitan	koh mee TAHN	Modern city in Chiapas, Mexico
Copan	koh PAHN	Maya name of site in Honduras
Corozal	koh roh ZAHL	Maya site in northern Belize
Cuauhtemoc	kwah oo TAY mohk	Aztec ruler of Tenochtitlan; also a city
Cuchumatanes	koo choo mah TAH nays	Mountain range, Guatemala/Chiapas
Cuicuilco	kwee KWEEL koh	Ruins in Mexico City
Diego de Landa	dee YAY goh day LAHN dah	Spanish (Diego from Landa, Spain)
Dzibanche	see bahn CHAY	Maya site (writing on wood)
Dzibilchaltun	see beel chahl TOON	Archaeological site in Merida, Yucatan
Escuintla	aays KWEENT lah	Modern city in Guatemala
Grijalva	gree HAHL vah	Major river in Chiapas, Mexico
Guadalajara	gwah dah lah HAH rah	Modern city in Mexico
Guerrero	geh DETR oh	Name of state in Mexico
Huatulco	wah TOOL koh	Resort city in state of Oaxaca, Mexico
Huehue Tlapallan	WAY way it lah PAH yahn	Region in Tuxtla Mountains, Veracruz
Huehuetenango	way way tay NAHN goh	Nahuatl; very old city in Guatemala
Hueyapan	way YAH pahn	Nahuatl; very large waters
Huitzilopochtli	hweet zee loh POKHT lee	Aztec leader, fourteenth century
Iximche	ee SHEEM chay	Maya (corn-trees) Guatemala
Ixtacihuatl	eesh tah SEE wah tl	Nahuatl; volcano near Mexico City; see also Iztaccihuatl
Ixtlilxochitl	eesht leel shoh CHEE tl	Nahuatl (mother's maiden name)
Izapa	ee SAH pah	Maya site in Chiapas, Mexico
Iztaccihuatl	ees tahk see WAH tl	Nahuatl, volcano near Mexico City
Juchitan	hoo chee TAHN	City and site in Oaxaca, Mexico
Kaminaljuyu	kah mee NAHL hoo YOO	Maya (hills of dead); Guatemala
Kinichna	kee neech NAH	Maya site in Chetumal, Mexico
Kohunlich	koh hoon LEECH	Maya site in Quintana Roo, Mexico
Kukulcan	koo kool KAHN	Maya word for Quetzalcoatl
La Libertad	lah lee behr TAHD	Archaeological site; Chiapas, Mexico
Laman Ayin	lah MAHN ah YEEN	Archaeological site in Belize
La Mesilla	lah may SEE yah	Guatemala border town with Mexico
Los Encuentros	lohs ayn KWEN trohs	Spanish, crossroads in Guatemala
Maya	MAH yah	Modern name given to natives
Mayapan	mah yah PAHN	Ancient Maya tribe and site, Yucatan

WORD	SYLLABLE PRONUNCIATION	DESCRIPTION
Mazatlan	mah zaht LAHN	Resort city in Mexico
Merida	MED ee dah	Spanish, capital of state of Yucatan
Mesoamerica	may soh ah MEHD ee kah	Spanish, denoting area and time
Mexico	MAY hee koh	Nahuatl, country, state, and city
Minatitlan	mee nah teet LAHN	Nahuatl name, city in Mexico
Mirador	mee da DOHR	Spanish, "look-out" name of sites
Miraflores	mee dah FLOHR ays	Pottery style; Kaminaljuyu, Guatemala
Misolha	MEE sol HAH	Maya; waterfalls near Palenque
Mitla	MEET lah	Village and site in Oaxaca, Mexico
Mixco Viejo	MEESH koh vee AAY hoh	Maya/Spanish site in Guatemala
Mixtec	MEESH tehk	Native language name, Oaxaca
Monte Alban	MOHN tay ahl BAHN	Spanish site name, Oaxaca
Nahuatl	NAH oo ah tl	Name of Aztec language
Nicaragua	nee kahr AH gwah	Country in Central America
Oaxaca	wah HAH kah	City and state in Mexico
Ocosingo	oh koh SEEN goh	City in Chiapas, Mexico
Ocozocoautla	oh koh zoh koh AHT lah	City in Chiapas, Mexico
Olmec	OHL mayk	Name given to ancient inhabitants
Pacal	pah KAHL	Maya ruler at Palenque
Palenque	pah LAYN kay	Spanish site name, Chiapas
Panajachel	pah nah hah CHAYL	Village by Lake Atitlan, Guatemala
Papaloapan	pah pah loh AH pahn	Nahuatl for water basin/butterfly
Paredon	pah ray DOHN	Village along Pacific in Chiapas
Patzicia	paht see SEE ah	Native village in Guatemala
Pericutin	pay dee koo TEEN	City covered by volcanic eruption
Peten	pay TEHN	Department in Guatemala
Piedras Negras	pee AY drahs NAY grahs	Classic Maya site on the Usumacinta
Popocatepetl	poh poh kah tay PAY tl	Nahuatl, volcanic mountain, Mexico
Popol Vuh	poh poohl VOOH	Maya ancient record
Quetzalcoatl	kayt sahl koh AH tl	Nahuatl, feathered serpent
Quetzaltenango	kayt sahl tay NAHN goh	Nahuatl, Maya city in Guatemala
Quiche	kee CHAY	Maya language dialect, Guatemala
Quinametzin	keen ah MAYT zeen	Ancient tribe named by Ixtlilxochitl
Quirigua	kee ree GWAH	Maya site in Guatemala
Sahagun	sah ah GOON	Spanish priest from Sahagun, Spain
Siyaj K'ak'	see YAHK KAH AHK	Military leader, Teotihuacan AD 378
Soconusco	soh koh NOOS koh	Fertile valley along Pacific in Chiapas

WORD	SYLLABLE PRONUNCIATION	DESCRIPTION
Tabasco	tah BAHS koh	Name of a Mexican state
Tacana	tah kah NAH	Volcano, Chiapas/Guatemala border
Tajin	tah HEEN	Classic site near Poza Rica, Veracruz
Tajumulco	tah hoo MOOL koh	Volcano, Guatemala/Mexico
Tapachula	tah pah CHOO lah	Modern city in Chiapas, Mexico
Tecun Uman	tay KOON oo MAHN	Warrior, Guatemala/Mexico
Tehuantepec	tay WAHN tay pehk	Nahuatl, wilderness of wild beasts
Tenochtitlan	tay noch teet LAHN	Nahuatl, ancient name of Mexico City
Teotihuacan	tay oh tee wah KAHN	Nahuatl site northeast of Mexico City
Texcoco	taysh KOH koh	Suburb of Mexico City
Tikal	tee KAHL	Maya site in Peten, Guatemala
Tlaloc	it LAH lohk	Aztec rain god, Teotihuacan
Tlaxcala	it lahsh KAH lah	Name of a Mexican state
Tlatelolco	it lah tay LOHL koh	Aztec market place, Mexico City
Tlatilco	it lah TEEL koh	Preclassic site near Mexico City
Topiltzin	toh peelt SEEN	Name of priest at Tula; Quetzalcoatl
Torquemada	tor kay MAH dah	Spanish priest/historian
Totonicapan	toh toh nee kah PAHN	City in Guatemala
Tres Zapotes	trays zah POH tays	Spanish; three fruit trees; town in Veracruz, Mexico, near hill Vigia
Tuxtla Gutierrez	TOOKST lah goo tee ETTR aays	Capital of state of Chiapas
Uaxactun	wash ahk TOON	Maya, site near Tikal
Usumacinta	OO soom ah SEEN tah	Major river; divides Peten, Guatemala, from Chiapas, Mexico
Uxmal	oosh MAHL	Maya, site in Yucatan
Vigia	vee HEE ah	Hill in Veracruz, Mexico
Villahermosa	vee yah air MOH sah	Name of city in Tabasco, Mexico
Xalapa	hah LAH pah	Capital city of Veracruz, Mexico
Xela-ju	SHAY lah HOO	Maya name for Quetzaltenango, Guatemala
Xochicalco	sho chee KAHL koh	Site near Mexico City
Xunantunich	shoo nahn too NEECH	Maya, site in Belize
Yaxchilan	yash chee LAHN	Maya site along Usumacinta River
Zaculeu	sah koo LAY oo	Maya, site in Huehuetenango, Guatemala
Zapotec	sah poh TEHK	A native language of Oaxaca valley
Zocalo	SOH kah loh	Nahuatl, associated with a city square

If you say a word correctly thirty times (preferably out loud), it will be yours for life.

Exploring the Lands of the Book of Mormon

After you've practiced the above words over and over, think about names of places, people, and things in the Book of Mormon. Picture Joseph Smith and Oliver Cowdery in upstate New York in 1829 as Joseph translated and dictated the translation to his scribe Oliver. Now compare the following Book of Mormon words with the above terms. In doing so, remember that pronunciations are given for these terms in the Book of Mormon Pronouncing Guide beginning on page 432, but remember also that Joseph Smith did not give us these pronunciations. How would you pronounce the following terms from the Book of Mormon if you pronounced them with Mesoamerican pronunciation guidelines?

Caution: We need to be very cautious in attempting to equate similar-sounding Book of Mormon names or words with Mesoamerican names or words. We can usually say something like "If it sounds like a Book of Mormon name and if it feels like a Book of Mormon name, then it probably is *not* a Book of Mormon name." We think that some of the worst scholarship over the last twenty years has been to identify names that sound like Book of Mormon names and then create a geographical statement about the Book of Mormon. We can even be fooled if the names sound the same and are in the same area where a Book of Mormon scholar proposes that such and such an event took place—so the name must be a Book of Mormon geographical location.

Therefore, the logical and safe approach as you pronounce and think about the Book of Mormon names below is merely to muse to yourself that the exercise involves a fun "game" because the names "sort of" sound like Maya names—they distinctively do not sound like native upstate New York names. The fact that a word sounds like and looks like a Maya word is certainly justification for further research about the word.

Ahah	Curelom	Moriantum	Ripliancum	Shimnilon
Ammonihah	Helam	Mormon	Seantum	Shiz
Amnihu	Jacom	Moroni	Sebus	Shule
Antionum	Jarom	Moronihah	Senum	Shum
Antipara	Kishkumen	Muloki	Shem	Shurr
Antum	Korihor	Onihah	Shemlom	Teancum
Chemish	Kumen	Orihah	Shemnon	Teomner
Cohor	Kumenonhi	Paanchi	Sherem	Zeezrom
Corianton	Lachoneus	Pachus	Sheum	Zeram
Coriantum	Mathoni	Pacumeni	Shiblom	
Cumenihah	Mathonihah	Pekah	Shiblon	
Cumom	Mocum	Riplah	Shiblum	
Cumorah	Morianton	Riplakish	Shim	

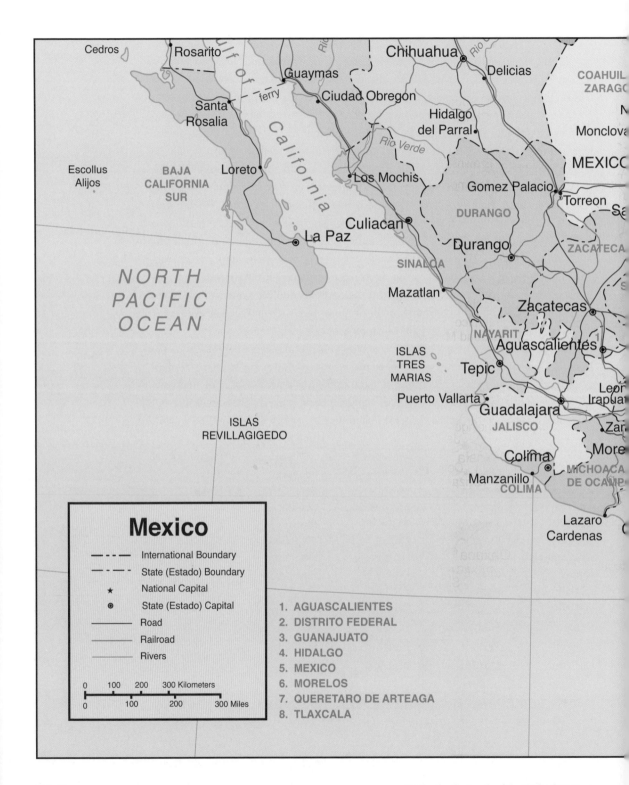

Cedros
Rosarito
Gulf of
Chihuahua
Delicias
COAHUIL
ZARAGO
Guaymas
Ciudad Obregon
N
Rio
Monclova
MEXICO
Santa
Rosalia
ferry
California
Hidalgo
del Parral
Rio Verde
Escollus
Alijos
BAJA
CALIFORNIA
SUR
Loreto
Los Mochis
Gomez Palacio
Torreon
Sa
DURANGO
ZACATECA
NORTH
PACIFIC
OCEAN
Culiacan
La Paz
Durango
SINALOA
Mazatlan
Zacatecas
NAYARIT
Aguascalientes
ISLAS
TRES
MARIAS
Tepic
Puerto Vallarta
Guadalajara
Leor
Irapua
JALISCO
Zar
ISLAS
REVILLAGIGEDO
Colima
More
MICHOACA
DE OCAMP
Manzanillo
COLIMA
Lazaro
Cardenas

Mexico

–··–··– International Boundary
–·– State (Estado) Boundary
★ National Capital
◉ State (Estado) Capital
——— Road
——— Railroad
——— Rivers

0   100   200   300 Kilometers
0   100   200   300 Miles

1. AGUASCALIENTES
2. DISTRITO FEDERAL
3. GUANAJUATO
4. HIDALGO
5. MEXICO
6. MORELOS
7. QUERETARO DE ARTEAGA
8. TLAXCALA

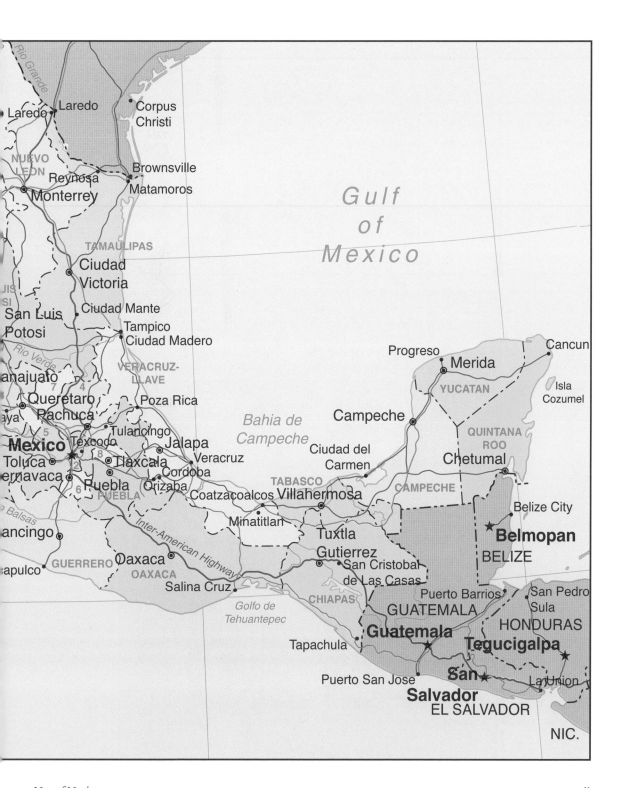

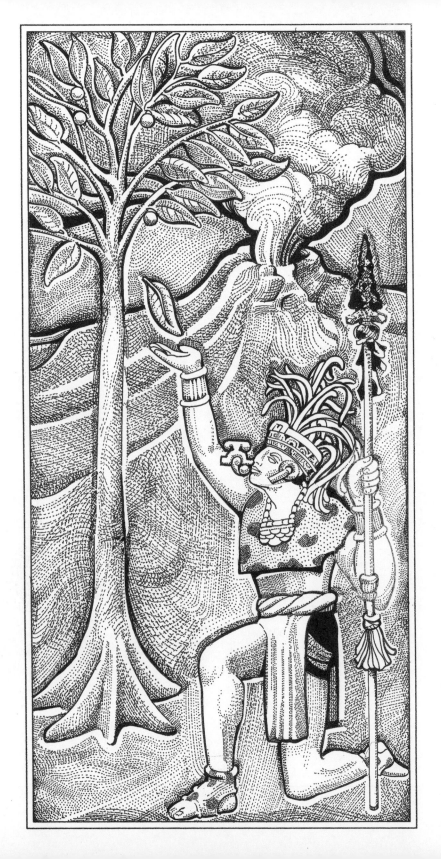

CHAPTER 1

Introduction to the Lands of the Book of Mormon

And I know that the record which I make is true; and I make it with mine own hand; and I make it according to my knowledge. (1 Nephi 1:3)

When we published the first edition of *Exploring the Lands of the Book of Mormon* in 1989, we included the following personal account by Joseph L. Allen, one of the authors of the second edition:

I can still hear the deep, mellow voice of my Grandfather Hancock singing the hymn, "May the Good Lord Bless and Keep You." That was in the year 1955. The occasion was my mission farewell to Argentina. I was surprised and excited when I learned five months later that my grandfather had been called to serve a two-and-a-half-year mission in Mexico. He was seventy years old.

I did not know at the time that one of the motivating factors for my grandfather's desire to serve a mission was a book written by Thomas S. Ferguson and Milton R. Hunter titled *Ancient America and the Book of Mormon.*[1]

1. Milton R. Hunter and Thomas Stuart Ferguson, *Ancient America and the Book of Mormon* (Oakland, CA: Kolob Book Company, 1950).

OPPOSITE: An artistic rendition portrays young Mormon in a physical and spiritual perspective. The jaguar symbols on his dress, his facial features, and the spear he holds represent his physical authority. The figure is shown in a kneeling position in front of the tree of life with quetzal feathers protruding from his headdress, all of which demonstrate his spiritual characteristics. (Drawing by Cliff Dunston.)

After I completed my mission, I experienced one of the greatest reunions of my life when I embraced my grandfather at the airport in Mexico City. On my way home in the company of four of my missionary companions, I had taken advantage of the opportunity to tour the ancient archaeological ruins in the countries of Bolivia, Peru, and Mexico.

As I reflected later, I realized that the events in my life at that time—my mission, my reunion with my grandfather, and my visit to the ancient ruins—were responsible for motivating me to pursue studies of the Book of Mormon and a career related to ancient Book of Mormon civilizations.

Before that time, I had never considered where or under what circumstances the Book of Mormon took place. I had gained a strong spiritual conviction of the truthfulness of the Book of Mormon in my early life, and so I assumed that all things relative to the history and geography of the Book of Mormon were already known. My assumption, however, was not correct. Though my testimony remained firm, I wanted to know more about the Book of Mormon.

I do not base my testimony of the Book of Mormon on my knowledge of archaeological sites. However, I consider the study of archaeological sites to be a very worthwhile endeavor. After all, the people whose names are written in the Book of Mormon are real people who lived somewhere. The Book of Mormon is not just a true doctrinal account written in a fictitious setting and is not just an allegory surrounded with doctrine.

Since the Book of Mormon's inception in 1830, we have approached its story in much the same way the early Christians approached the study of the Savior. That is, once the Christian church established its headquarters in Rome, the birth, baptism, and resurrection of Christ were interpreted in a European setting. We think we can say fairly that, in our own minds, we have done the same thing with the Book of Mormon by interpreting it in the context of surroundings common to us.

Satirically, Dr. Hugh Nibley at one time dealt with Book of Mormon geography by centering its geography on Antelope Island, which is located in the Great Salt Lake. Also satirically, we have always joked in our family about the fact that names like *Nephi*, *Manti*, *Lehi*, and *Bountiful*—cities in the state of Utah—must have been chosen because they indicate the geographic locations where the history of the Book of Mormon took place. We've joked especially about one family story associated with growing up in southern Utah and therefore knowing the exact location of one Book of Mormon place—the land of Desolation.

Although we may or may not be able to speak with complete authority about specific site locations in the Book of Mormon, we can analyze its history, culture, language, and geography in comparison with what we know about Mesoamerica. Such analyses give us the opportunity to study the Book of Mormon in great detail and can be a motivating

> The Book of Mormon is not just a true doctrinal account written in a fictitious setting and is not just an allegory surrounded with doctrine.

factor to study both its history and doctrine. Indeed, the more we know about the history, culture, language, and geography of the Book of Mormon, the more we know about the Book of Mormon. That knowledge can assist in reinforcing the deep spiritual messages contained within its pages.

THE BOOK OF MORMON

The Book of Mormon was translated into the English language and published in 1830. It was printed by E. B. Grandin of Manchester, New York. Money for the first five thousand copies was provided by Martin Harris, a local farmer, who mortgaged his farm to obtain the necessary funds to publish the book.

In the year 1982, the phrase "Another Testament of Jesus Christ" was added to the title of the Book of Mormon. The 1982 English edition of The Book of Mormon: Another Testament of Jesus Christ contains 531 printed pages. It has been published in approximately a hundred different languages. Its total circulation, from 1830 to 2008, is well over a hundred million copies. The average number of copies printed from 1830–1990 was 250,000 a year; and since 1990, the average has been in excess of four million copies a year.[2]

As stated by its adherents, "The Book of Mormon is a volume of holy scripture comparable to the Bible. It is a record of God's dealings with the ancient inhabitants of the Americas and contains, as does the Bible, the fulness of the everlasting gospel" (Introduction, Book of Mormon).

JOSEPH SMITH

The translator of the Book of Mormon was Joseph Smith Jr., who obtained an ancient civilization's records that had been deposited in a hill near his home in Palmyra, New York. The records were engraved on plates (thin sheets) of gold and were protected from exposure to the elements and other harm for over fourteen hundred years when Joseph Smith acquired them. The engravings on the plates were of an ancient language, and the plates' concealment through the centuries was accomplished by the use of a box made of stones that were cemented together. The box was buried in a small hill that today is called *Cumorah*.

The records were first shown to Joseph Smith in the year 1823 by a personage who identified himself as Moroni. Four years later, the actual records, or engravings, were entrusted to Joseph Smith, who at the time was almost twenty-two years old. Within another three years, and with an estimated time of sixty days of actual translation time, the Book of Mormon was published. Upon publication of the book, Joseph Smith proclaimed the Book of Mormon to be "the most correct of any book on earth" (Introduction, Book of Mormon).

Some forty days prior to the martyrdom of the Prophet Joseph Smith, Josiah Quincy, an author and a non-Mormon, stated, "It is by no means improbable that some future

The more we know about the history, culture, language, and geography of the Book of Mormon, the more we know about the Book of Mormon.

2. Information obtained from the Web site of The Church of Jesus Christ of Latter-day Saints, www.lds.org, April 29, 2003.

text-book, for the use of generations yet unborn, will contain a question something like this: What historical American of the nineteenth century has exerted the most powerful influence upon the destinies of his countrymen? And it is by no means impossible that the answer to that interrogatory may be thus written: *Joseph Smith, the Mormon Prophet.*[3] Upon Joseph's death, the following was written about him: "Joseph Smith, the Prophet and Seer of the Lord, has done more, save Jesus only, for the salvation of men in this world, than any other man that ever lived in it" (D&C 135:3).

3. Josiah Quincy, "Joseph Smith at Nauvoo," *Figures of the Past from the Leaves of Old Journals* (Boston: Roberts Brothers, 1883), 376.

FIGURE 1–1: "[Moroni] said there was a book deposited, written upon gold plates, giving an account of the former inhabitants of this continent, and the source from whence they spring. . . . Convenient to the village of Manchester, Ontario county, New York, stands a hill of considerable size, and the most elevated of any in the neighborhood. On the west side of this hill, not far from the top, under a stone of considerable size, lay the plates, deposited in a stone box" (Joseph Smith—History 1:34, 51). (Drawing by Cliff Dunston)

JOHN LLOYD STEPHENS

In the year 1841, barely eleven years after the Book of Mormon was published, Harper and Brothers published a book written by John Lloyd Stephens about his travels in Central America, Chiapas, and the Yucatan. An artist by the name of Frederick Catherwood accompanied Stephens and sketched, on paper, a variety of Maya[4] archaeological ruins, including the ruins of Copan in Honduras near the Guatemala border; the ruins of Quirigua in Guatemala; the ruins of Palenque in the state of Chiapas, Mexico, near the state of Tabasco, Mexico; and the ruins of Uxmal in the

4. In conventional usage, the word *Mayan* is used to refer to language and writing, and the word *Maya* is used to refer to all other aspects of the Maya people, including their archaeology. Throughout *Exploring the Lands of the Book of Mormon*, the word *Maya* is used in all instances so readers will not be confused with usage details.

FIGURE 1–2: "In 1839 Mr. [John Lloyd] Stephens and [I] made arrangements for a tour in Central America, with a view to the examination of the remains of ancient art said to exist in the dense forests of those tropical regions" (Frederick Catherwood, in *Incidents of Travel in Central America, Chiapas and Yucatan*, p. v). Shown here is a Catherwood drawing of an elaborately adorned post–Book of Mormon building in Uxmal, which is located in the land southward.

state of Yucatan, Mexico. Stephens's book became a best seller and is still on the market today, published in two volumes.[5]

Joseph Smith, then President of The Church of Jesus Christ of Latter-day Saints, was also editor of the *Times and Seasons,* a newspaper published by the Church. A statement that appeared in that newspaper reads, "It would not be a bad plan to compare Mr. Stephens' ruined cities with those in the Book of Mormon."[6]

Stephens traveled in the geographic area known today as Mesoamerica, the area where many Book of Mormon students feel that all the New World events recorded in the Book of Mormon took place.

MESOAMERICA

Mesoamerica is that area of land consisting of south and southeastern Mexico and the countries of Guatemala, El Salvador, Honduras, and Belize. The term *Mesoamerica* also refers to the time period before the conquest of Mexico or before the discovery of America by Columbus.

Therefore, *Mesoamerica* has direct reference to the great civilizations that flourished in Middle America during the pre-Columbian periods. The Mesoamerican cultures date from approximately 2600 BC to AD 1500.

The major civilizations of Mesoamerica that existed during the Book of Mormon time period include the lowland and highland Maya, the Olmec culture along the Gulf Coast of Mexico, the Zapotec culture core in the valley of Oaxaca, and the Teotihuacan culture core located in the valley of Mexico.

Fourteen Mexican states—Mexico, Puebla, Morelos, Guerrero, Michoacan, Hidalgo, Tlaxcala, Veracruz, Oaxaca, Tabasco, Chiapas, Campeche, Yucatan, and Quintana Roo—are all part of Mesoamerica. Oaxaca and Chiapas have the highest native populations of Mexico, and the Yucatan is still home to many Maya communities.

The twenty-two departments (states) of Guatemala, with Peten constituting the largest, form a sizable part of Mesoamerica. Historically, both the small country of Belize and the Mexican state of Chiapas were part of Guatemala.

The population of Mexico far outnumbers that of the other countries that now form part of ancient Mesoamerica. As of 2008, the entire country of Mexico has in excess of 110 million inhabitants. Guatemala has approximately twelve million inhabitants, with half of that number considered native to Guatemala. The natives live along the coast and in the mountains of Guatemala.

Most of Mesoamerica is an area that is almost completely surrounded by water. The topography is variable, consisting of dense jungles, high mountain regions, and tropical lowlands. The highest mountain peak is Mount Orizaba, stretching over eighteen thousand feet above sea level. The area in and around Villahermosa, Tabasco, measures several feet below sea level.

5. John Lloyd Stephens, *Incidents of Travel in Central America, Chiapas and Yucatan,* 2 vols. (New York: Dover Publications, 1969).

6. *Times and Seasons* 3:927.

"It would not be a bad plan to compare Mr. Stephens' ruined cities with those in the Book of Mormon."

—Joseph Smith

FIGURE 1–3: Four major Mesoamerican civilizations were in existence during the Book of Mormon time period.

The climate of Mesoamerica is also variable. Mexico City, with an elevation of seventy-four hundred feet, maintains a moderate temperature between sixty-five and eighty degrees Fahrenheit. Guatemala City, at forty-nine hundred feet elevation, is ideal year round and is often referred to as the "land of eternal spring." The jungle lowlands are hot and humid. The rainy season is generally from May to October.

NEPHITES

The Nephites were the record keepers of the Book of Mormon. The name *Nephites* is derived from a 600 BC prophet named Nephi who migrated with his family from Jerusalem. We are left to speculate as to who the Nephites really were in the complexity of the Mesoamerica picture. However, of noteworthy interest is the fact that in the sixteenth-century Spanish chronicles, reference is made to a people called Tultecas who were record keepers and who were considered to be wise men as well as men of science.[7] In all probability—for the most part—the "Nephites" consisted of people whom we know as the Maya and the Olmecs. Nephi states that the people who went with him to what became the land of Nephi were those who were willing to listen to

7. Bernardino de Sahagun, *Historia General de las Cosas de Nueva Espana: Florentine Codex*, ed. and trans. Arthur O. Anderson and Charles E. Dibble, 12 vols. (Santa Fe, NM: The School of American Research and the University of Utah, 1950), 10:167–97.

Exploring the Lands of the Book of Mormon

the warnings and revelations of God (see 2 Nephi 5:5–9), and Jacob comments that he would use the name "Nephites" in referring to those people who were friendly to Nephi (see Jacob 1:14).

The Nephites lived in several geographic and cultural areas from about 586 BC to AD 385. Mormon, who wrote or compiled the majority of the Book of Mormon, was a descendant of Nephi, as was Mormon's son, Moroni.

LAMANITES

The term *Lamanites* is used to describe a people who became followers of an original Book of Mormon figure by the name of Laman. The Lamanite civilization began about 586 BC. They became mortal enemies to the Nephites. Laman was the oldest brother of Nephi, but Laman lost his right to rule. He developed a following, and the hatred between the Lamanites and Nephites is a perpetual Book of Mormon theme. In essence, both the Nephites and the Lamanites were Maya—distinguished only by their allegiances and by where they lived.

FIGURE 1–4: The land of Nephi and the land of Zarahemla were located in the land southward (Maya territory). During various periods, the land southward was inhabited by the Nephites, Lamanites, and Mulekites.

The Lamanite culture continued after the close of the Book of Mormon, and that nation appears to be the predecessors of the same people who today are known as the Maya—suggesting that the largest portion of the Preclassic Maya (600 BC–AD 250) living south and east of the Isthmus of Tehuantepec may have been under the leadership of Lamanites. This observation further suggests that the people of the Classic Maya (AD 250–900) were also governed by the Lamanites or, as will be shown later, perhaps were under the control of a Mulekite hierarchy.

> The people of the Classic Maya (AD 250–900) were also governed by the Lamanites or, as will be shown later, perhaps were under the control of a Mulekite hierarchy.

MULEKITES

The first reference to a group of people we know as the Mulekites is in the book of Omni. The Mulekites came out of Jerusalem at the time of the Jewish captivity by the Babylonians in 586 BC. The book of 2 Kings in the Bible informs us that Zedekiah, a king of the Jews, witnessed the executions of his sons, who were heirs to the Jewish throne. The Babylonians then put out the eyes of Zedekiah, so the last events he witnessed were the executions of his sons: "And they slew the sons of Zedekiah before his eyes, and put out the eyes of Zedekiah, and bound him with fetters of brass, and carried him to Babylon" (2 Kings 25:7).

We first read about Mulek in the book of Mosiah, where we are told that Zarahemla was a descendant of Mulek. Mulek was a son of King Zedekiah (see Mosiah 25:2; Helaman 6:10, 21). Perhaps Mulek was a young baby or not yet born at the time of the assassination of his brothers when the Babylonians destroyed Jerusalem. Mulek and his party possibly were brought to the Americas by the seafaring Phoenicians.

The book of Helaman records that the Lord brought "Lehi into the land south" and "Mulek into the land north" (Helaman 6:10). In all probability, Mulekites lived on both sides of the narrow neck of land.

Between 200 BC and 180 BC, Mosiah, who lived in the land of Nephi, led a righteous group of Nephites from the land of Nephi to the land of Zarahemla—where Mosiah discovered the people of Zarahemla:

> Behold, I am Amaleki, the son of Abinadom. Behold, I will speak unto you somewhat concerning Mosiah, who was made king over the land of Zarahemla; for behold, he being warned of the Lord that he should flee out of the land of Nephi, and as many as would hearken unto the voice of the Lord should also depart out of the land with him, into the wilderness—
>
> And it came to pass that he did according as the Lord had commanded him. And they departed out of the land into the wilderness, as many as would hearken unto the voice of the Lord; and they were led by many preachings and prophesyings. And they were admonished continually by the word of God; and they were led by the power of his arm, through the wilderness until they came down into the land which is called the land of Zarahemla.

And they discovered a people, who were called the people of Zarahemla. Now, there was great rejoicing among the people of Zarahemla; and also Zarahemla did rejoice exceedingly, because the Lord had sent the people of Mosiah with the plates of brass which contained the record of the Jews.

Behold, it came to pass that Mosiah discovered that the people of Zarahemla came out from Jerusalem at the time that Zedekiah, king of Judah, was carried away captive into Babylon.

And they journeyed in the wilderness, and were brought by the hand of the Lord across the great waters, into the land where Mosiah discovered them; and they had dwelt there from that time forth.

And at the time that Mosiah discovered them, they had become exceedingly numerous. Nevertheless, they had had many wars and serious contentions, and had fallen by the sword from time to time; and their language had become corrupted; and they had brought no records with them; and they denied the being of their Creator; and Mosiah, nor the people of Mosiah, could understand them.

But it came to pass that Mosiah caused that they should be taught in his language. And it came to pass that after they were taught in the language of Mosiah, Zarahemla gave a genealogy of his fathers, according to his memory; and they are written, but not in these plates.

And it came to pass that the people of Zarahemla, and of Mosiah, did unite together; and Mosiah was appointed to be their king. (Omni 1:12–19)

Zarahemla was the leader of the Mulekites, and apparently the area where they lived was named either after him or one of his forebears with the same name, as this was the custom of the people (see Alma 6:7; see also Ixtlilxochitl:22[8]).

Zarahemla, who was apparently a descendant of the tribe of Judah, accepted the leadership of Mosiah as the king of Zarahemla's people. Mosiah was a descendant of the tribe of Joseph. As a result, in the New World, we see a partial fulfillment of Joseph's dream: "And Joseph dreamed a dream, and he told it his brethren: and they hated him yet the more. And he said unto them, Hear, I pray you, this dream which I have dreamed. For, behold, we were binding sheaves in the field, and, lo, my sheaf arose, and also stood upright; and, behold, your sheaves stood round about, and made obeisance to my sheaf. And his brethren said to him, Shalt thou indeed reign over us? or shalt thou indeed have dominion over us? And they hated him yet the more for his dreams, and for his words" (Genesis 37:5–8).

A literal fulfillment of Joseph's dream occurred some years later when his brothers went to Egypt in search of food and bowed down to him because of his role as the governor of Egypt. We live in a day when the tribe of Joseph, through Ephraim, has assumed the leadership role in preparing all things for the Second Coming of the Savior.

Zarahemla, who was apparently a descendant of the tribe of Judah, accepted the leadership of Mosiah as the king of Zarahemla's people. Mosiah was a descendant of the tribe of Joseph. As a result, in the New World, we see a partial fulfillment of Joseph's dream.

8. Throughout this text, references to Ixtlilxochitl's writings refer to chapter 11, "Fernando de Alva Ixtlilxochitl," and to the corresponding verse in Ixtlilxochitl's writings.

The event of Mosiah's uniting with the people of Zarahemla illustrates a partial fulfillment of Joseph's dream, as Joseph was told that his branches would "run over the wall . . . unto the utmost bound of the everlasting hills" (Genesis 49:22, 26).

Joseph's descendants, Lehi and Ishmael, came to the New World in fulfillment of prophecy; and his descendants, beginning with Mosiah, ruled over Judah (through Mulek) for the next four hundred years.

When Zarahemla recounted orally his people's history, he also recounted a portion of the history of the Jaredites. Zarahemla and his people had lived in the area of the Jaredites and had traveled into the south wilderness where Mosiah discovered them (Alma 22:31). Indeed, the Mulekites, or at least a branch of the Mulekites, may have lived among the Jaredites from the Mulekites' arrival in the New World in the sixth century BC up to the Jaredite destruction, estimated to be between 400 BC and 250 BC (see Omni 1:15–22; Alma 22:30–31).

JAREDITES

The mother race of the Book of Mormon cultures is called the Jaredites. We first read about the Jaredites in the book of Omni, the same place where we read about the people of Zarahemla: "And it came to pass in the days of Mosiah, there was a large stone brought unto him with engravings on it; and he did interpret the engravings by the gift and power of God. And they gave an account of one Coriantumr, and the slain of his people. And Coriantumr was discovered by the people of Zarahemla; and he dwelt with them for the space of nine moons. It also spake a few words concerning his fathers. And his first parents came out from the tower, at the time the Lord confounded the language of the people; and the severity of the Lord fell upon them according to his judgments, which are just; and their bones lay scattered in the land northward" (Omni 1:20–22).

Thus, during the days of King Mosiah, at the time he was living in the land of Zarahemla, a large stone was brought to him. The stone gave an account of the Jaredites and explained how their language had not been confounded at the Tower of Babel. They crossed the ocean and were led to the promised land.

About 121 BC, a Nephite by the name of Limhi, living in the land of Nephi, sent an expedition of forty-three men to try to locate the land of Zarahemla. They did not find Zarahemla. They did, however, find the remains of an ancient civilization we call the Jaredites. The Limhi expedition also discovered twenty-four gold plates (sheets of gold) with engravings and took the plates back to the land of Nephi (see Mosiah 8:7–11). Led by Ammon, a descendant of Zarahemla, Limhi and his people traveled to the land of Zarahemla. King Mosiah, the grandson of the Mosiah mentioned above, apparently translated the twenty-four gold plates (see Mosiah 22:11–14).

Over five hundred years later, Moroni, the son of Mormon, abridged the translation made by King Mosiah. That is the abridgement we have in the Book of Mormon today; it is called the book of Ether. It consists of thirty-one pages in the current English edition of the Book of Mormon.

The Jaredites developed a massive New World civilization dating from approximately 2600 BC to approximately 300 BC. (See chapter 3, "Looking at Dates," for a discussion on dating.) The Jaredites had a great influence on both the Mulekites and the Nephites. Many Mulekite names are of Jaredite origin, such as Coriantumr and Morianton. The Nephite Alma, the son of Alma, gave two of his sons Jaredite names—Shiblon and Corianton. Even today in Mesoamerica society, some Jaredite names, such as Shule (Xul), Com, and Kish, have survived the centuries, as they are names represented in the Maya cultures and in the stone engravings of Guatemala, Chiapas, and Yucatan.

The spoken language of the Jaredites was probably spoken by both Mulekites and Nephites. When Lehi's colony, as well as Mulek's colony, arrived in the promised land, the Jaredites significantly outnumbered them. Both the Nephites and the Mulekites lived simultaneously with the Jaredites for approximately three hundred years, after which the main part of the Jaredite kingdom fell (see Ether 14–15).

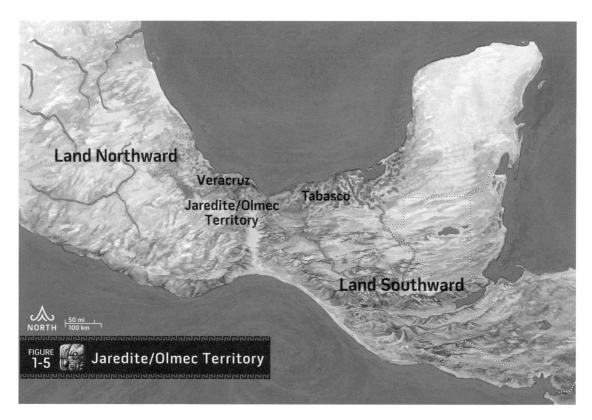

FIGURE 1–5: The ancient Olmec territory of Tabasco and Veracruz, Mexico, is the same area as the ancient Jaredite territory from 1500 BC to 300 BC.

MORMON (JAGUAR OF THE MOUNTAINS)

Mormon lived in the fourth century AD; and, according to what we surmise from the Book of Mormon, he lived in the land northward. He said his father carried him into the land southward, even to the land of Zarahemla, when Mormon was eleven years old (see Mormon 1:6). The land of Zarahemla was located in the land southward.

Mormon was sixteen years old when he was appointed head of a Nephite army. This was in the year AD 327–28. Mormon was, therefore, born in the year AD 311 or 312. The following chart shows his accomplishments.

From evidence that has surfaced in recent years, we can be comfortable in identifying Mormon as a Maya.

Event	Year	Age	Reference
Born	ca. AD 311	—	—
A sober child	AD 321	10	Mormon 1:2
Went to Zarahemla	AD 322	11	Mormon 1:6
Had a vision; saw Christ	AD 326	15	Mormon 1:15
Led Nephite army	AD 327–28	16	Mormon 2:2
Began writing Nephite history	ca. AD 335	24	Mormon 1:3; Mormon 2:17
Preached the gospel	ca. AD 360+	49	Mormon 3:2
Refused to lead army	AD 362	51	Mormon 3:16
Moved all the records	ca. AD 375	64	Mormon 4:23
Again led Nephite army	ca. AD 375+	64+	Mormon 5:1
Gave records to Moroni	ca. AD 385	74	Mormon 6:6
Hid records in Cumorah	ca. AD 385	74	Mormon 6:6
Final battle	AD 385	74	Mormon 6
Mormon writes	ca. AD 385+	74+	Mormon 7
Killed by Lamanites	ca. AD 385+	74+	Mormon 8:3

(Note: The abbreviation "ca." in front of the date refers to the Latin "circa" and means approximately.)

From evidence that has surfaced in recent years, we can be comfortable in identifying Mormon as a Maya. From information in the Book of Mormon and Mesoamerican archaeology and geography, we can ascertain that Mormon spent most of his life on the northward side of the Isthmus of Tehuantepec, in or near the present-day archaeological site of San Lorenzo, Veracruz, and close to the modern city of Minatitlan, Veracruz.

Mormon is a Maya name that may mean "jaguar of the mountains." The syllable *mor* in the Chorti Maya language means "hill" or "crest of the mountain," the same connotation given in the Book of Mormon; and the syllable *mon* is associated with wild or ferocious animals in the Book of Mormon. For example, Mormon was named after his father who was named after the waters of Mormon, which were located in a wilderness area that was "infested, by times or at seasons, by wild beasts" (Mosiah 18:4). The word *Tehuantepec* in the Nahuatl (Aztec) language carries with it the same meaning. *Tepec* means "hill or wilderness," and *tehuan* or *tecuani* means "wild beasts." These meanings are consistent with other names in the Nahuatl language, such as *coyotepec* (coyote hill) or *chapultepec* (grasshopper hill). The wilderness of Tchuantepec is located in the same area proposed as Hermounts in the Book of Mormon: "And it was that part of the wilderness which was infested by wild and ravenous beasts" (Alma 2:37). Because the majestic jaguar is the most savage of all wild animals, we take the liberty of referring to Mormon as "The Jaguar of the Mountains."

FIGURE 1–6: The most ferocious and most beautiful wild beast in Mesoamerica is the jaguar. The name *Mormon* is associated with mountains and wild beasts in both the Maya and the Nahuatl (Aztec) languages as well as in the Book of Mormon. Alma refers to the waters of Mormon as being near the forest of Mormon and as "having been infested, by times or at seasons, by wild beasts" (see Mosiah 18:4, 30).

Because the majestic jaguar is the most savage of all wild animals, we take the liberty of referring to Mormon as "The Jaguar of the Mountains."

MORONI (ANCIENT MOUNTAIN)

The last twenty-seven chapters of the Book of Mormon either were written by or were compiled by Moroni. These chapters are (1) Mormon 8–9; (2) the book of Ether, containing the abridgement of the record of the lineage of Jared; and (3) the book of Moroni.

As a name, *Moroni* in the Chorti Maya language means "ancient mountain." Like his father, Mormon, Moroni must have lived in the land northward, at least during the first part of his life. The final battle between the Nephites and Lamanites was fought about AD 385, during which time Moroni served as head of an army of ten thousand (see Mormon 6:12).

Moroni abridged the record of the ancient civilization that is referred to as the Jaredites. He states: "And now I, Moroni, proceed to give an account of those ancient inhabitants who were destroyed by the hand of the Lord upon the face of this *north country*" (Ether 1:1; emphasis added). "This *north country*" has reference to the area where the Jaredites lived and is the same area where Mormon, Moroni, and the struggling, wicked Nephites of the fourth century AD lived—until the Lamanites completely destroyed the Nephite nation. Both Mormon and Moroni lived during the early part of the Mesoamerica Classic Period.

The following chart represents a summary of Moroni's life:

Event	Year	Age	Reference
Born	ca. AD 350	—	—
Saw Christ	ca. AD 365	ca. 15	Ether 12:39
Served in Church leadership	ca. AD 375	ca. 25	Moroni 8:2
Led army of 10,000 in final battle	AD 385	ca. 35	Mormon 6:12
Abridged the record of lineage of Jared	AD 385–400	ca. 35–40	Ether 1:1
Would not deny Christ	AD 385–400	ca. 35–40	Moroni 1:3
Wandered for 21 years from homeland to New York	AD 400–21	ca. 40–61	Mormon 8:6; Moroni 10:1
Hid up records in hill in upstate New York	ca. AD 421	ca. 61	Moroni 10:2
Died	AD 421+	ca. 61+	—

As a resurrected being, Moroni entrusted the records to Joseph Smith on September 22, 1827 (see Joseph Smith—History 1:59).

By doing proficient and reputable research on Mesoamerica geography, native languages, ancient traditions, and local native customs, we may gain a deeper understanding of the people referred to in the Book of Mormon.

ARCHAEOLOGICAL EVIDENCE AND THE BOOK OF MORMON

Since the coming forth of the Book of Mormon in 1830, considerable dialogue about the book has taken place—both supporting and criticizing the publication. Critics of the Book of Mormon have devised all manner of evil to discredit its validity. Adherents, on the other hand, have done considerable research to prove that the Book of Mormon is a real history.

The burden is not on archaeology to prove either the historicity or the truthfulness of the Book of Mormon. Rather, by doing proficient and reputable research on Mesoamerica geography, native languages, ancient traditions, and local native customs, we may gain a deeper understanding of the people referred to in the Book of Mormon.

Archaeological discoveries no more prove the truthfulness of the Book of Mormon than does restoring the old homes of Nauvoo, Illinois, prove the truthfulness of Mormonism. In fact, the Book of Mormon is not a history book. It is no more a geographical or historical textbook of Mesoamerica than the Doctrine and Covenants is a geographical or historical textbook of America.

The truthfulness we seek from the Book of Mormon is spiritual, doctrinal proof that comes in two ways:

1. By adhering to the prescribed spiritual medication contained therein, "even to an experiment upon my words, and exercise a particle of faith" (Alma 32:27).

2. By seeking the confirmation from the same source that made the spiritual doctrine available in the first place: "If ye shall ask with a sincere heart, with real intent, having faith in Christ, he will manifest the truth of it unto you, by the power of the Holy Ghost" (Moroni 10:4).

In summary, the Book of Mormon is "a record of a fallen people" (D&C 20:9). Its intent is to convince "the Jew and Gentile that Jesus is the Christ" (Book of Mormon Title Page).

THE VALUE OF BOOK OF MORMON RESEARCH

If we submit (1) that the Book of Mormon is neither a geographical survey of Mesoamerica nor a historical analysis of such and (2) that whatever is discovered will neither prove nor disprove the Book of Mormon, we may then ask, "Of what value is Book of Mormon research?" The answer is simple. As previously stated, the more we understand about the culture, language, history, and geography of the Book of Mormon, the better we understand the Book of Mormon. Furthermore, the spiritual message of the Book of Mormon is enhanced as we understand the historical and geographical environment of the Book of Mormon.

From personal experiences, we know that our understanding and motivation for studying the Bible increases as we walk on the Mount of Olives and as we sail on the Sea of Galilee. Likewise, our hearts are touched and our thoughts are enlightened regarding the history of the restored gospel as we stand in the Sacred Grove and as we ponder at Carthage. These same kinds of experiences await us concerning the Book of Mormon when adequate research points us in a more secure direction.

Latter-day Saints have been promised that if they will study and ponder the Book of Mormon, their understanding of it will increase. The Church's thirteenth president, Ezra Taft Benson, states: "I bless you with increased understanding of the Book of Mormon. I promise you that from this moment forward, if we will daily sup from its pages and abide by its precepts, God will pour out upon each child of Zion and the Church a blessing hitherto unknown."[9]

A STATEMENT ON BOOK OF MORMON GEOGRAPHY

Most current literature supports the idea that the heartland of Book of Mormon culture is in the area called Mesoamerica. Justification for such stems from the following:

Language. The Book of Mormon was written during the period of time from approximately 600 BC to AD 421. During this thousand-year period, the only place where a written phonetic language has been discovered that is couched in the confines of a high civilization is in the areas located directly on both sides of the Isthmus of Tehuantepec in Mesoamerica.

Archaeology. The Book of Mormon speaks of many cities built over a long period of time. The Jaredite culture encompassed the time period of about 2600 BC to 300 BC.

Most current literature supports the idea that the heartland of Book of Mormon culture is in the area called Mesoamerica.

9. Ezra Taft Benson, "A Sacred Responsibility," *Ensign*, May 1986, 78.

The Lamanite-Nephite and Mulekite-Nephite time periods are recorded in the 600 BC to AD 400 time period. The Lamanite culture continued after AD 400. The only place where cultures and population centers meet this requirement is in Mesoamerica.

Tradition. Mesoamerica tradition makes reference to many cultural identifications, including the arrival of the first settlers from the great tower and accounts of the white god known as Quetzalcoatl. The oral and written traditions, along with the modern-day culture patterns emerging from Mesoamerica, mirror those gleaned from the Book of Mormon.

Geography. The geography of the Book of Mormon is unique. Geography of the Book of Mormon not only must include a study of mountains, lands, waters, trade routes, and so forth but also must include directions, distances, and cultural and language parallels. The Mesoamerica map matches in striking detail the criteria dictated by the Book of Mormon.

Any study of Book of Mormon geography must strictly adhere to two criteria:

1. We must take the Book of Mormon at face value. To alter *its* geographical directions, as some Book of Mormon literature suggests, or to demand unbelievable distances, as tradition outlines, is unacceptable.

2. We must be willing to accept existing maps at face value. To put water where none exists today, to create a make-believe narrow neck of land, or to alter the directions of the map confuses the issue and does nothing to solve the problem. By following both the Book of Mormon and the Mesoamerica map specifically, we find impressive geographical correlations.

Figure 1–7 illustrates the population centers that existed on the American continent during the time period when the history of the Book of Mormon took place. This time period is referred to as Preclassic and dates from approximately 2600 BC to AD 250.

Population centers are defined as civilizations whose cultures were advanced to the degree that temple mounds, pottery remnants, and other artifacts can accurately be identified and dated.

Note that an estimated 90 percent of the population centers in existence during the Book of Mormon time period are located in the area called Mesoamerica.[10]

> To put water where none exists today, to create a make-believe narrow neck of land, or to alter the directions of the map confuses the issue and does nothing to solve the problem.

FREQUENTLY ASKED QUESTIONS

Where appropriate in *Exploring the Lands of the Book of Mormon*, we will pose and then answer questions that tour members frequently ask during tours to the lands of Mesoamerica.

Question: How can you propose to create a reliable Book of Mormon map when "the face of the whole earth became deformed" at the death of Christ? (See 3 Nephi 8:17.)

10. Information obtained from Paul Gendrop, *Arte Prehispanico En Mesoamerica* (Mexico, DF: Editorial Trillas, 1979); Robert Silverberg, *Mound Builders of Ancient America* (Athens, OH: Ohio University Press, 1986); and Richard W. Keatinge, *Peruvian Prehistory: An Overview of Pre-Inca and Inca Society* (Cambridge: Cambridge University Press, 1988).

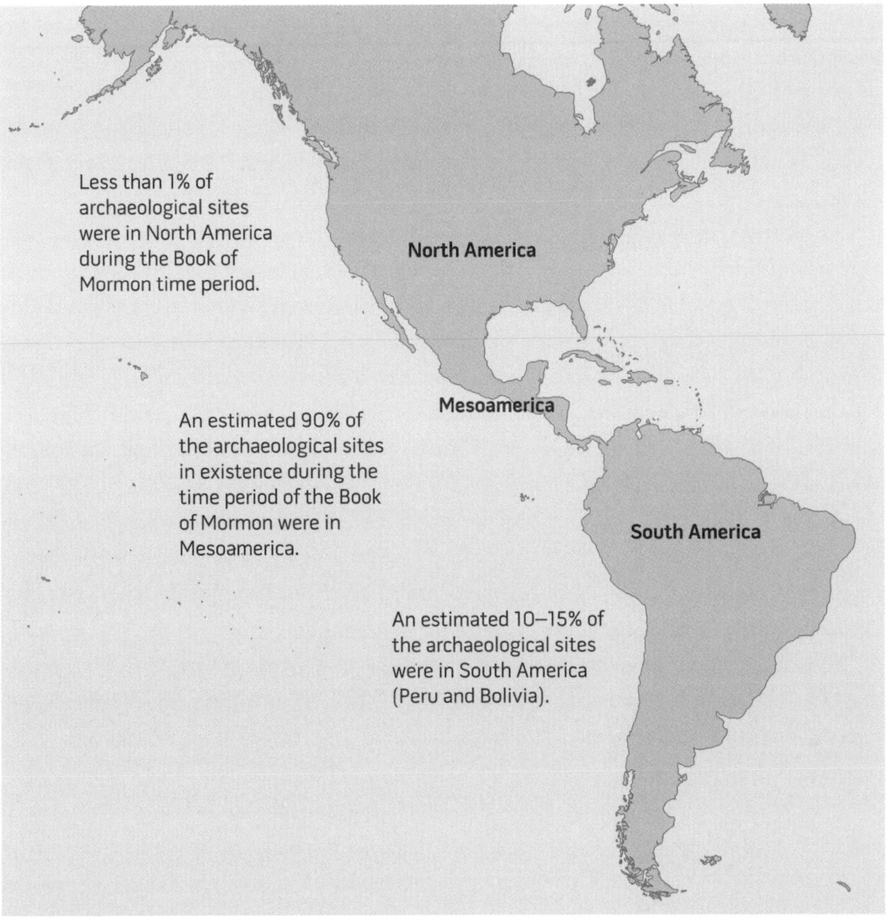

FIGURE 1–7: Preclassic
(Book of Mormon time
period) population centers
on the American continent.

Less than 1% of
archaeological sites
were in North America
during the Book of
Mormon time period.

North America

An estimated 90% of
the archaeological sites
in existence during the
time period of the Book
of Mormon were in
Mesoamerica.

Mesoamerica

South America

An estimated 10–15% of
the archaeological sites
were in South America
(Peru and Bolivia).

Archaeological sites that date back prior to the great destruction demonstrate evidence of destruction but do not demonstrate evidence of any geographical change.

Answer: As great as the destruction was, it did not alter geographical boundaries. The writers of the Book of Mormon used the same terms to describe the land after the destruction as they did before the destruction.

For example, Moroni, who abridged the predestruction Jaredite record, said that "the army of Coriantumr did pitch their tents by the hill Ramah; and it was that *same hill* where my father Mormon did hide up the records" (Ether 15:11; emphasis added).

The land southward, land northward, narrow neck of land, land of Nephi, and land of Zarahemla are other geographical locations mentioned both before and after the destruction. Furthermore, archaeological sites that date back prior to the great destruction demonstrate evidence of destruction but do not demonstrate evidence of any geographical change. Finally, the Book of Mormon itself makes it clear that the destruction did not distort the geography of the land: "And the earth did cleave together again, that it stood" (3 Nephi 10:10).

> Because some cities were covered with earth or water or otherwise preserved, we are enabled today, through archaeological research, to gather accurate information that dates to the time period of the Book of Mormon.

In reality, because some cities were covered with earth or water or otherwise preserved, we are enabled today, through archaeological research, to gather accurate information that dates to the time period of the Book of Mormon.

Question: We should not concern ourselves with Book of Mormon geographical locations because the Lord will reveal that information when He is ready. Is that not correct?

Answer: Yes, He has and will continue to reveal such information when He is ready. However, a better statement may be that He will reveal the additional information to us when *we* are ready. He has challenged us to study things out in our minds and ask if they are right (see D&C 9:8). We suspect that if we follow His counsel, we will learn many things about the Book of Mormon that we presently do not know.

Question: The above statements suggest a much more limited geographic area for the historical setting of the Book of Mormon than has been traditionally proposed. What is the justification for such a proposal?

Answer: The justification for this proposal is the essence of the second edition of this text, *Exploring the Lands of the Book of Mormon*. To understand the justification, you are encouraged to read *all* of this book and then judge for yourself whether a limited geographic area for the Book of Mormon has validity.

To place the limited geographic area in perspective at the outset, we propose that most of the events we read about in the Book of Mormon took place in the geographic area known as Mesoamerica.

GUIDELINES FOR BOOK OF MORMON RESEARCH

We published the first edition of *Exploring the Lands of the Book of Mormon* in 1989. During the process, those who were involved in its publication were constantly driven by the perception that we must be totally objective in presenting thoughts about the Book of Mormon's history, cultural traditions, language, and geography. However, because we have lived among the Mesoamerican peoples so much and traveled so extensively throughout Mesoamerica on scores and scores of occasions, we admit the tendency for personal feelings to enter into the picture.

Throughout the years since the first edition of *Exploring the Lands of the Book of Mormon*, we have tried to extinguish our admittedly biased feelings about Mesoamerica and the Book of Mormon by adhering to unwritten but nonetheless very evident guidelines for everything we say and do related to the history, cultural traditions, language, and geography of the Book of Mormon. We have felt so strongly about being objective and unbiased in our approach that we have put in writing our feelings about the need for total objectivity in everything we write for use in our tours of proposed Book of Mormon lands. Following are our guidelines for Book of Mormon research:

1. The Book of Mormon is indeed what it purports to be—that is, it is an ancient document written by ancient prophets and translated by a latter-day prophet to testify of Christ's divinity. Whatever else might be said about the translation process, the overriding statement that defines it is summed up in Joseph Smith's declaration that he translated the Book of Mormon "by the gift and power of God."

2. The power of the Book of Mormon to change lives comes to those who are willing to test its veracity by adhering to the spiritual formula provided within the text itself: remember how merciful the Lord is to us, ponder the words of the Book of Mormon, and ask God in the name of Christ if the things in the Book of Mormon are true—but ask with a sincere heart, with real intent, and with faith in Christ (see Moroni 10:3–5).

3. The objective, unbiased study of the history, cultural traditions, language, and geography of the Book of Mormon will increase any reader's understanding of the Book of Mormon.

4. The most important message of the Book of Mormon is its declared intent to convince readers that Jesus is the Christ. Knowing about the history, cultural traditions, language, and geography of the Book of Mormon is important because doing so legitimately supports the fundamental reason for the book's message about the Atonement.

5. The study of antiquities associated with the Book of Mormon can and should lead people to pursue a study of the text in a manner in which the Spirit will bear witness of the truths contained in the book.

6. The manner of writing of the Jews, as reflected in the Book of Mormon, is designed to utilize geography, topography, history, climate, and so forth as stepping stones to lead readers to the spiritual message of the Book of Mormon.

7. Standardized criteria that include the presence of language, archaeological evidence, cultural patterns, and a logical geographical model must be in place if readers are to test validly and reliably any proposed hypothesis on Book of Mormon geography and history.

8. Requiring two or more witnesses to verify historical and geographical hypotheses allows readers to test those hypotheses against the archaeological, cultural, and traditional history of the area in question. The absence of two or more witnesses should precipitate an acceptance of the possibility that the reader or researcher is standing on rather shaky ground.

9. Mesoamerica—and Mesoamerica only—fits the prescribed cultural, linguistic, archaeological, and traditional patterns required by the Book of Mormon itself. With that evidence in place, we can make geographical proposals with a high level of confidence.

10. Firsthand sources, by nature, are more reliable than secondhand or hearsay statements. Therefore, great pains should be taken to verify any quotation attributed to some particular authority, including the context and date in which the statement is purported to have been given.

11. Any legitimate study of Book of Mormon geography must pay strict attention to accurate maps, directions, distances, elevations, language and pottery trails, and cultural and historical patterns.

12. The destruction of the land at the time of Christ is not a detriment in any respect to the study of archaeology and the Book of Mormon. In fact, just the opposite is true. Discovering cities that were destroyed by earthquakes or that have been covered over with water can help determine the manner in which the people lived at the time of the destruction. Further, Mormon is the primary author of the Book of Mormon, and readers must keep in mind that he wrote his account over three hundred years after the great destruction. In the process, he identified the same landmarks that had existed prior to the visit of Christ to the Nephites. We can conclude, therefore, that the study of Book of Mormon geography and history is a legitimate endeavor.

13. The outcome is misleading, nonproductive, and even detrimental if we propose correlations in the Book of Mormon with events and buildings that do not fall into the time period and within a logical place setting as determined by internal statements in the Book of Mormon itself.

14. Any proposal about Book of Mormon geography should be written in such a manner that it can be tested scientifically by other scholars in the field.

15. Few things are more harmful in the field of academia than to present a bad argument to prove a worthy cause—that is, using faulty documentation, shoddy scholarship, or pure speculation in an attempt to support the Book of Mormon is counter productive.

16. Testimony bearing and the expression of feelings regarding geographical locations frustrate the principles of scholarly, scientific research and revelatory stewardship. We must always keep in mind that no definitive announcements regarding Book of Mormon locations have been made or accepted by The Church of Jesus Christ of Latter-day Saints. In the absence of an official proclamation by those in authority in the Church, no individual or group of individuals has the right to identify and pronounce Book of Mormon locations by revelation or inspiration.

17. The spirit of contention can be very detrimental to the study of Book of Mormon history and geography. Therefore, every attempt should be made to reach for truth in joint efforts as opposed to name calling or judgmental declarations of a person's character.

18. The lack of precise knowledge of Book of Mormon geography is not grounds to ignore—or diminish—the importance of the study of antiquities associated with the Book of Mormon, including studies and research in such things as language, history, culture, and geography.

19. All information pertaining to the time period and the area under consideration for Book of Mormon locations should be utilized, including the archaeological record, geology, astronomy, geography, literature, modern and ancient languages, customs, traditions, histories, and any other scientific means that can be used to arrive at an accurate picture of the ancient inhabitants who lived in the Americas during the time period of the Book of Mormon.

20. The outcomes of scientific investigations associated with archaeology and anthropology do and will continue to change. In that respect, the discovery of things that shed new light and understanding on the Book of Mormon does not undermine previous research or damage the good names of Church leaders, scholars, and lay members of the Church. In other words, as the sciences of medicine or archaeology or physics change, so does our ability to interpret the past in relation to the Book of Mormon change. Indeed, we can almost be assured that what we say or write today may be changed or updated tomorrow.

21. Arriving at the truth is far more important than seeking recognition for the discovery of such. All too commonly, researchers claim the right of discovery of things that someone else has already discovered and presented as the same or a similar conclusion. The value of a number of people arriving at the same conclusion independently of one another lends credibility to the accuracy of the discovery.

22. Whenever possible, readers and scholars of the Book of Mormon should be made aware of the abundant, ongoing information about the lands, lives, and happenings of the people who lived on the American continent during the time period of the Book of Mormon. Further, readers and scholars should seek the excitement of discovery that has existed in the lives of adherents and peaceful Church of Jesus Christ followers whose love for the Book of Mormon and its divine origins has played a supreme role in their everyday activities.

CHAPTER 2

And Then It Came to Pass

And now, behold, we have written this record according to our knowledge, in the characters which are called among us the reformed Egyptian, being handed down and altered by us, according to our manner of speech. (Mormon 9:32)

 had rented a car to drive from Merida, the capital city of the state of Yucatan, to Uxmal and then on to Chichen Itza. I didn't have any air conditioning in the car, so I had the window rolled down.

This experience was related by Joseph Allen in the 1989 edition of *Exploring the Lands of the Book of Mormon*.

As I was leaving the city, I stopped at a traffic light. A young man came over to me and asked in Spanish if I would give him and his wife and young child a lift. I said I'd be happy to. They got in the car, and he told me he was going to a town called Muna, which is located about fifteen minutes from Uxmal.

Although he and his wife were dressed in modern clothing, I knew they were of Maya descent; and I asked them if they spoke Maya. The young man's name was Chac

OPPOSITE: Shown is a portion of the Tablet of the Cross from Palenque. The glyphs are read in columns of two from left to right and top to bottom. These glyphs provide historical data associated with Pacal and his son, Chan Balaam. The glyph that has been interpreted as "and it came to pass" is found on the tablet on the lower left-hand corner of the section shown here. (Photo Courtesy of Blake Joseph Allen)

Zui, and he did all the talking. His wife, Nami, simply nodded in approval. Chac said that he spoke only Spanish because he had grown up in the city. However, he said that his mother understood both Maya and Spanish and that his grandmother, to whose place they were going, understood a little Spanish but spoke mostly Maya.

I remember thinking about how the Maya language has been spoken for over thirty-five hundred years; however, in this particular family, in just three generations, the family was beginning to lose the ability to speak the Maya language.[1]

1. The Mexican government continues to promote the study of the Maya language, as studies indicate that all the groups who speak Maya seem to have come originally from the same ancestral branch. The Yucatecan language, which is considered Maya, dates to 1600 BC.

The drive from Merida to Muna took only thirty-five minutes. During that time, we talked about how, in the sixteenth century, a priest by the name of Diego de Landa burned some of the Maya record books at the nearby town of Mani and about how scholars were still working to decipher the Maya hieroglyphs. (My drive from Merida occurred in 1979, which is the time that the Maya code was beginning to deciphered.)

As we approached the village of Muna, the women wearing their beautifully embroidered dresses were returning from the market where they had purchased the daily portions of food consisting of fruit, tortillas, and other items for the meals of the day.

Chac invited me to meet his grandmother, who lived in a thatch-covered home typical of all the homes in the village. Inside his grandmother's home, the hammocks were tied neatly against the wall, having served as beds for the family during the night. I observed that the architecture of the room was very similar to the rooms seen at the ninth century AD ruins of Uxmal in the area called the Quadrangle of the Nunnery.

The stove was belching forth smoke in a separate hut, and corn was stored in another small house located about ten feet from the kitchen. Other houses the size of Chac's grandmother's house were located close by and were the sleeping quarters of the extended family. All in all, three sons and their wives and fifteen grandchildren lived in the same complex.

Two pigs were tied not too far from the kitchen, and several chickens roamed throughout the yard. Orange trees and other fruit trees could also be seen in the yard.

Some of the women were sewing dresses and blouses to sell to tourists as well as at the local market. The men were in the field preparing their crops for the spring rains. The water for the homes was gathered in a cistern by the kitchen. (During the rainy season, the cistern fills up; but during the dry season, water is brought in to the homes from the central water well, called a *cenote*.)

I first thanked the family for their hospitality. And then, because they knew of my interest in the Maya language, we chatted a little about some Maya words. I asked the grandmother if she knew what the word *utchi* meant. Without hesitation, she said, "Hace tiempo algo pasó." Interpreted, that means, some time ago something happened—or, in other words, "and it came to pass."

AND IT CAME TO PASS

The clause "and it came to pass" occurs in the English translation of the Book of Mormon 1,381 times. It appears 202 times in 1 Nephi alone. The book of Alma records the highest number of "it came to pass" occurrences, 431. Only the book of Moroni fails to use the expression "and it came to pass."[2] Sometimes the clause is recorded as "now it came to pass" (Alma 62:37) or "for behold, it came to pass" (Alma 43:4) or "but behold, it came to pass" (Alma 53:16).

In addition, the future or prophetic clause such as "and it *shall* come to pass" (2 Nephi 29:13) is recorded another ninety-five times in the Book of Mormon. Only the small books of Jacob, Enos, and Omni do not use the prophetic clause "and it shall come to pass."

The clause "and it came to pass" is not unique to the Book of Mormon, as the Bible utilizes the same introductory wording. "And it came to pass," or one of its derivatives, occurs 526 times in the Old Testament and 87 times in the New Testament. This usage suggests that the clause "and it came to pass" is Hebrew in origin and correlates with Nephi's statement, "Yea, I make a record in the language of my father, which consists of the learning of the Jews and the language of the Egyptians" (1 Nephi 1:2). Moroni, who finished his father's record, writes:

> And now, behold, we have written this record according to our knowledge, in the characters which are called among us the reformed Egyptian, being handed down and altered by us, according to our manner of speech.
>
> And if our plates had been sufficiently large we should have written in Hebrew; but the Hebrew hath been altered by us also; and if we could have written in Hebrew, behold, ye would have had no imperfection in our record.
>
> But the Lord knoweth the things which we have written, and also that none other people knoweth our language; therefore he hath prepared means for the interpretation thereof. (Mormon 9:32–34)

The Maya people, who have lived for centuries in southeast Mexico and Guatemala, may have adopted the expression "and it came to pass." Discoveries in the translations

"AND THEN IT CAME TO PASS"

FIGURE 2–1: Artistic rendition by Cliff Dunston of a Maya hieroglyph from the Temple of the Inscriptions (tomb of Pacal) at Palenque, Chiapas. *Utchi* in the Yucatec Maya language is interpreted as "And then it came to pass." Its purpose in both the Maya language and in the Book of Mormon is to serve as either a date indicator or an event indicator.

2. Robert F. Smith presented a preliminary report to The Foundation for Ancient Research and Mormon Studies in which he outlined the number of times the clause "and it came to pass" appears in both the Bible and the Book of Mormon.

The Maya people, who have lived for centuries in southeast Mexico and Guatemala, may have adopted the expression "and it came to pass."

3. The late Linda Schele taught art at the University of Texas at Austin. She wrote her dissertation on the Maya verbs. She founded a yearly Maya symposium at the University of Texas and was one of the leading scholars and enthusiasts in the interpretation of the Maya hieroglyphs.

4. J. Eric Thompson (1898–1975, from England) was one of the most noteworthy personalities among the Maya investigators. His labeling and numbering of the glyphs are still used today for identification purposes. For example, "T126" in the literature refers to the glyph that Thompson numbered 126.

5. Robert J. Sharer, *The Ancient Maya*, 5th ed. (Stanford: Stanford University Press, 1994), 617.

6. Linda Schele, *Workbook in Maya Hieroglyphics* (Austin, TX: n.p., 1987), 26.

7. Schele, *Workbook in Maya Hieroglyphics*, 26.

8. Simon Martin and Nikolai Grube, *Chronicle of the Maya Kings and Queens: Deciphering the Dynasties of the Ancient Maya* (London: Thames and Hudson, 2000), 162.

of the glyphs of the seventh century AD Maya ruins of Palenque manifest the clauses "and then it came to pass" and "it had come to pass." In addition, another glyph has been interpreted as "and it shall come to pass."[3]

The noted Maya scholar Eric Thompson first observed and recorded two glyphs that followed a pattern of marking dates. He called the first one the Anterior Date Indicator (ADI) and the second the Posterior Date Indicator (PDI).[4] The Maya code became decipherable in the late 1970s and early 1980s as a result of its identification as both pictorial and phonetic in nature. As a result, the glyph under question can be broken into segments with each segment carrying its own meaning or own sound. In the illustration below, notice the three different parts, each with a different sound. These three added together form the Yucatec sound and meaning of *utchi*.

UT   CH   I

FIGURE 2–2: The breakdown of the Maya glyph *utchi*: "And then it came to pass." The Maya hieroglyphs are both pictorial (or logographic) and phonetic. Today, almost all specialists in Maya writing agree that the system was logosyllabic and that it displayed increased phoneticism over time.[5]

In 1985, a young Maya scholar, David Stuart, observed that the ADI and PDI functioned as a grammatical and literary feature in both colonial and modern Maya languages. He speculated correctly when he interpreted the sound of the glyph as "ut" in the Chol language and "utchi" in the Maya language, meaning "to happen, or to come to pass."[6]

Two years earlier, John Justeson and Will Norman found a consistency in an event indicator that appears as the word *"iwal,"* which means the action is ongoing at the time, such as "and" or "and then." Together, *ut-iwal* in the PDI in Maya glyphs reads "and then it came to pass" or "and now it came to pass."

Kathryn Josserand and Nicholas Hopkins discovered that the ADI has basically the same meaning. It reads *ut-ix,* "it had come to pass."[7]

A simple reading of the Maya glyphs located on the walls of the Temple of Inscriptions at Palenque gives the genealogy of the seventh-century king, who has been given the name of Pacal (K'inich Janaab Pacal I, meaning "great sun shield").[8] Pacal's tomb was discovered buried beneath the Temple of Inscriptions and was unearthed in 1952 by Alberto Ruz and his team of workers.

An additional interpretation of the inscriptions located on the temple panels appears to justify why Pacal should be king. The panel gives both his genealogy as well as significant events in his own life. The interpretation reads like a job resume.

FIGURE 2–3: Temple of the Inscriptions at Palenque, Chiapas, Mexico. Burial tomb of K'inich Janaab Pacal I (AD 603–683). This enormous pyramid/tomb was uncovered in 1952 by archaeologist Alberto Ruz. The structure at the top of the pyramid contains panels of Maya hieroglyphs depicting the genealogy of Pacal. The final completion of the tomb was accomplished by his son, Chan Balaam, around AD 690. (Photo courtesy of Phil Skousen)

Hence, a summarized version of the glyphs on the Temple of Inscriptions, with a loose interpretation to emphasize the clause "and it came to pass," might be as follows. The dates are representative of the dates on the Tomb of Pacal or that which earlier was called the Temple of Inscriptions:

And Pacal was born March 6, AD 603 (9.8.9.13.0 8 Ahau 13 Pop) and descended from great kings throughout the centuries, whose names are here recorded. *And it came to pass* that on the 29th of July, AD 615 (9.9.2.4.8 5 Lamat 1 Mol) Pacal was anointed to be king. *And it came to pass* that on the 25th of January, AD 633, he ascended to the throne. *And it came to pass* that on the 30th of August, AD 684, Pacal, the king, died.

The pattern of the Maya glyphs resembles certain grammatical and literary aspects of the Book of Mormon. Therefore, we can speculate that the record from which the Book of Mormon was translated manifested a clause, or glyph, similar to what is recorded in the Maya hieroglyphs. Furthermore, we now know, as already stated, that the lowland Maya of the sixth century AD did not invent writing in Mesoamerica. They simply adopted it from an earlier culture period that lived in the same area. The Maya writing system accelerated between the first and second centuries BC,[9] which corresponds to the same time period that Nephite writing was taught among the Lamanites (see Mosiah 24:1–6).

9. Schele, *Workbook in Maya Hieroglyphics*, 1.

In summary, the best translation that could be given by the Prophet Joseph Smith of the glyph under question, in correlation with the Maya language culture, is "and it came to pass" or "and now it came to pass." In the Spanish translation of the Book of Mormon, the term that is often used is *"y aconteció,"* meaning "and it happened." The English translation, taken directly from the gold plates, appears to give the best interpretation of the glyph, as it gives the connotation that the event is ongoing—"and it came to pass."

A WRITTEN LANGUAGE

The former noted Maya scholar Eric Thompson writes, "Middle America is the only part of the new world in which a system of embryonic writing developed."[10] This writing system was developed during the Preclassic Period (600 BC–AD 200)—a time period that correlates directly with the Book of Mormon time period.

10. J. Eric Thompson, *The Rise and Fall of Maya Civilization*, 2nd ed. (Norman, OK: University of Oklahoma Press, 1966), 189.

From 200 BC to AD 200, writing was used extensively throughout Mesoamerica—from the lowland areas of the Peten jungle to the highlands of Guatemala and Chiapas. A strong written language base has also been documented during the same time period in the Pacific lowlands at Izapa, where Stela 5, often called the Tree of Life Stone, was discovered. The use of a written language was first discovered at Monte Alban in Oaxaca, located west of the Isthmus of Tehuantepec.

"Middle America is the only part of the new world in which a system of embryonic writing developed."

—Eric Thompson

Sixty percent of the pages in the Book of Mormon encompass only 164 years of its history, a history that began with the reign of King Benjamin about 130 BC and that finished with Christ's ministry to the Nephites at AD 34. This 164-year period begins with page 145 and ends with page 464 in the 1981 edition of the Book of Mormon and includes the books of Mosiah, Alma, Helaman, and 3 Nephi. During this century-and-a-half time period, several significant events took place in the Book of Mormon, one of which was King Benjamin's sermon that was written and circulated among the people about 124 BC: "And it came to pass that he began to speak to his people from the tower; and they could not all hear his words because of the greatness of the multitude; therefore he caused that the words which he spake *should be written* and sent forth among those that were not under the sound of his voice, that they might also receive his words. And these are the words which he spake and caused to *be written*" (Mosiah 2:8–9; emphasis added).

Sometime between 145 BC and 121 BC, which falls precisely in the time period when "embryonic writing developed" in both the Maya lowlands and the Maya highlands, the Nephite written language was circulated throughout the region: "And now the name of the king of the Lamanites was Laman, being called after the name of his father; and therefore he was called king Laman. And he was king over a numerous people. And he appointed teachers of the brethren of Amulon in every land which was possessed by his people; and thus *the language of Nephi* began to be taught among all the people of the Lamanites. [And] they taught them that they should keep their record, *and . . . write one to another*" (Mosiah 24:3–4, 6; emphasis added).

Amulon was a Nephite—one of the priests of King Noah—and he was a contemporary of Alma, who baptized at the waters of Mormon. Amulon and some of the wicked priests of Noah married some Lamanite women and, subsequently, became part of the Lamanite culture.

Of interest here is the fact that the Nephite written language was used by the Lamanites at the same time as the archaeological records in Mesoamerica affirm that the Maya written language system was developed—a language that had been adopted from another culture. These events may suggest that the 125 BC "Lamanite Maya" people adopted their written language from the "Nephite Maya."

WRITTEN RECORDS

A very common type of record in Mesoamerica is called a codex. For the most part, codices consisted of written pages made from tree bark or from animal skins. The writing material was flattened and structured to fold in much the same way a map folds. The writing was accomplished in color with dye made from plants and animals.

From an incident that occurred during the missionary journey of Alma and Amulek about 80 BC, we learn that the Nephites also kept records on materials that would burn, as the people of the Nephite city, Ammonihah, burned the

> The Nephite written language was used by the Lamanites at the same time as the archaeological records in Mesoamerica affirm that the Maya written language system was developed—a language that had been adopted from another culture.

FIGURE 2–4: Page 9 of a Maya codex known as the Dresden Codex, discovered in Mexico but currently located in the state library of Dresden, Germany. This codex is written on a long sheet of paper that is folded like a map to make a book of thirty-nine pages, written on both sides. This manner of writing on paper, often made from tree bark, is reflected in the Book of Mormon and is reminiscent of the scripture in Alma 12:1 where Alma "unfolds" the scriptures beyond that which Amulek had done as Alma taught Zeezrom and the people of Ammonihah. The term "unfold" is used eight times in the Book of Mormon, whereas it is not used at all in the Old or New Testaments because scribes commonly created scrolls that would have been unrolled rather than unfolded. The reading was usually left to right, top to bottom. They were bound between decorated boards that, when completely opened, were quite long. For example, the Dresden Codex is about twelve feet long. (Photo courtesy of Blake Joseph Allen)

records and holy scriptures of the members of the church: "And they brought their wives and children together, and whosoever believed or had been taught to believe in the word of God they caused that they should be cast into the fire; and they also brought forth their *records which contained the holy scriptures,* and cast them into the fire also, that they might be burned and destroyed by fire" (Alma 14:8; emphasis added).

Histories and genealogies not only were written on codices but also were engraved on gold plates and stone monuments. The Book of Mormon was written on gold plates. Both archaeological evidence and the Book of Mormon affirm that significant dates and events were written on stone monuments (see Omni 1:20).

> Both archaeological evidence and the Book of Mormon affirm that significant dates and events were written on stone monuments.

LANGUAGE AT THE TIME OF THE CONQUEST

Because the time correlation and the language style of Mesoamerica and the Book of Mormon so closely parallel each other, we will examine the language base in existence at the time of the Spanish conquest in Mesoamerica. Although the sixteenth-century Maya were separated from the AD 200 Maya by thirteen hundred years, we still may expect to see language similarities.

The Aztecs, who lived in the Mexico City valley at the time of the Spanish conquest, spoke a language that is referred to as Nahuatl. In 1521, the Aztecs were the dominant culture north and west of the Isthmus of Tehuantepec at the time of the conquest. Most of the written documents dating from the sixteenth century are in the Nahuatl language. Even today, the best estimates suggest that four and a half million people, in and around Mexico City, still speak the Nahuatl language.

A student of the Spanish language soon learns that, in Mexico, a person will be exposed to an additional vocabulary consisting of Nahuatl names. For example, the largest park in Mexico City is called Chapultepec Park, which is a Nahuatl name meaning "grasshopper hill."

Although Guatemala is far from Mexico City, the Nahuatl language shows up in names of cities, such as Quetzaltenango, Chichicastenango, and Huehuetenango. These are Aztec, or Nahuatl, names of cities that are located in Maya territory. *Tenango* means "place of" or "near to." The quetzal is a beautiful bird native to Guatemala; hence, *Quetzal/tenango* means place of the quetzal.

The Spanish chronicles, written during the first two centuries of Spanish occupation, give a confused picture of the Maya people and lands. The Maya, whose history dates to 600 BC, were almost annihilated during the early Spanish occupation in the Yucatan, beginning in 1542.

Smallpox, a disease to which the natives had no resistance, was one of the main culprits that contributed to almost wholesale eradication of the Maya race. Smallpox epidemics, along with the conflict caused by the relocation of Maya people and the military hostility of the Spaniards, appear to have resulted in a population reduction of up to 90 percent of the Maya people in many areas. These conditions created the impossibility of getting an accurate picture of the language and the history of the Maya people. Hundreds of years elapsed before adequate studies could be made that would begin to piece together the complex and mysterious Maya language system.

Diego de Landa, a Spanish Catholic priest, is representative of a score of priests who migrated to Mesoamerica during the sixteenth century to assist in converting the natives to Christianity. Landa took up residency in the Yucatan. Conversion ("Christianization" or "civilizing the natives") was the objective of the Catholic Church and was brought about at all costs.

The written records, in the form of codices, appeared to the conquering priests to be works of the devil. Immediately, the priests began to destroy the records; consequently, the old written language was almost wiped out so the new Spanish language could be established.

In the Maya village of Mani, located between the ruins of Uxmal and Chichen Itza, Diego de Landa burned twenty-four Maya codices, or records, in one "marshmallow roast." This type of wanton destruction was either pursued by other priests or caused the Maya to destroy or to hide their own records.

> The written records, in the form of codices, appeared to the conquering priests to be works of the devil.

FIGURE 2–5: Bishop Diego de Landa's Maya alphabet. After burning many Maya records in the Yucatan, Diego de Landa, the first bishop of the Yucatan, ultimately enabled epigraphers to decipher the Maya code because he placed Spanish phonetic sounds of the hieroglyphs with illustrations of the glyphs in the Yucatec language.

Fortunately, some codices were preserved. At least three Maya codices and two Mixtec codices, the latter from the Oaxaca Valley, have been preserved. Ixtlilxochitl, a Catholic priest who wrote in the sixteenth century, stated that he obtained the information for his history from the written records available to him (see chapter 11, "Fernando de Alva Ixtlilxochitl").

Diego de Landa vindicated himself, at least in part, as he, with the aid of a Maya teacher, recorded the Maya alphabet. His work is partly responsible for breakthroughs in deciphering the codices of Mesoamerica.

However, the efforts of the early priests did not destroy the spoken language of the Maya, as it, or one of its many derivatives, is spoken today throughout the Maya territory. Spanish is the official language of the country; but in many villages, the native Maya language is still spoken in the homes. The table that follows illustrates language development in Mesoamerica during the Book of Mormon time period.[11]

11. Alberto Ruz, *The Mayas* (Mexico, DF: Salvat Mexicana de Ediciones, 1983).

Chronology of the Maya Languages

2600 BC	Mam
1800 BC	Huastec
1600 BC	Yucatecan
1400 BC	Lacandon
900 BC	Chontal
750 BC	Tzeltal
400 BC	Tojolabal
200 BC	Quiche
100 BC	Kekchi
AD 100	Kanjobal
AD 100	Aguacatec
AD 400	Chol

HEBREW LANGUAGE

Little evidence has surfaced to suggest that the Hebrew language constituted any real impact on Mesoamerica during the Book of Mormon time period.[12]

12. However, some preliminary studies suggest that the language of the Zapotecs, who live in the state of Oaxaca, Mexico, contains some Hebrew words. See John L. Sorenson, *An Ancient American Setting for the Book of Mormon* (Salt Lake City: Deseret Book and Foundation for Ancient Research and Mormon Studies, 1985), 80.

We should not be surprised too much, however, that a high percentage of the Hebrew language has not been found in Mesoamerica. First, the written language of the Nephites was what the Nephites referred to as "reformed Egyptian" (see 1 Nephi 1:2; Mormon 9:32). Second, the spoken language utilized by peoples in the Book of Mormon probably had a Jaredite base.

The Jaredite base language had its roots in the language of Adam—often referred to as Adamic—as the Jaredites' language was not confounded at the time of the Tower of Babel. As stated, the written language in Mesoamerica may well have followed the same pattern as the Book of Mormon—that is, reformed Egyptian. However, the actual

Exploring the Lands of the Book of Mormon

words spoken were what they (the Nephites and Lamanites) learned from the people who were already in Mesoamerica (descendants of the Jaredites; see Mosiah 8:12).

An added potential problem is evident because more than one language certainly was spoken during the Book of Mormon time period. For example, the 180 BC Mosiah-Nephite group, upon encountering the people of Zarahemla, discovered that the two groups spoke different languages, even though both groups had come out of Jerusalem. This difference in language suggests that the Nephites either spoke their original Jerusalem language or simply that their spoken dialect was different from that of the Mulekites—both of which, however, would have had a Jaredite base.

Perhaps we should be looking for more Egyptian language usage in Mesoamerica. But like Hebrew, archaeologists have failed to discover a strong Egyptian base in Mesoamerica. Again, this failure should not surprise us because Moroni, who finished his father's (Mormon's) record, writes: "And now, behold, we have written this record according to our knowledge, in the characters which are called among us the reformed Egyptian, being handed down and altered by us, according to our manner of speech" (Mormon 9:32).

Moroni continues by informing us that had the Nephites been able to write in Hebrew, no imperfections in the record would have resulted. He then writes, "But the Lord knoweth the things which we have written, and also that *none other people knoweth our language*" (Mormon 9:34; emphasis added).

In summary, the terminology and style of writing used by the later Lamanite Maya are probably patterned after the terminology and style of the early Nephite Maya.

LANGUAGE OF THE EGYPTIANS

In the beginning of his record, Nephi informs us that he wrote in the language of his father, which consisted of the "learning of the Jews and the language of the Egyptians" (1 Nephi 1:2).

We may ask why Nephi wrote in the Egyptian language when his familiar language was Hebrew. Even after a thousand years of Nephite records being passed from one generation to another, Moroni reports that his people could still write in Egyptian, or "reformed Egyptian," even though they understood how to write in Hebrew (see Mormon 9:32–34).

Several answers to this question are possible. First, the fact that the brass plates Nephi obtained from Laban were written in Egyptian (Mosiah 1:2–4), which was the original language introduced by Moses as he wrote the law on tablets of stone, may suggest that Egyptian was the sacred language in much the same way that Latin was the sacred biblical and liturgical language for many years in Catholicism. Second, we would do well to take Moroni at his word—that the size of the plates played a role in writing in Egyptian as opposed to Hebrew. Third, the Egyptians controlled Israel during the time

Little evidence has surfaced to suggest that the Hebrew language constituted any real impact on Mesoamerica during the Book of Mormon time period.

the sons of Lehi were growing up at Jerusalem. As a result of this Egyptian occupation, the official "king's language" at that time likely would have been Egyptian.

David Hadlock writes that "one of the common attacks on the Book of Mormon has been against the idea that a sacred record would have been written by the Jews in Egyptian rather than in Hebrew. . . . Evidence of the use of Egyptian scripts among the Israelites has been found in the Old World. Therefore, it would not be unreasonable to suppose that the American-Israelites utilized a similar writing system." According to the *Bible Archaeologist*, "In the royal administration of both Judah and Israel, hieratic (Egyptian) numerals were used, striking new evidence for the influence of Egyptian prototypes in the Israelite administration." William Hamblin notes that "scholars have also recently deciphered an Aramaic version of Psalm 20:2–6 that was written in demotic Egyptian characters. This is precisely what the Book of Mormon claims existed: a version of the Hebrew scriptures, but written using Egyptian characters."[13]

13. David Hadlock, "The Language of My Father," *Book of Mormon Archaeological Digest*, Winter 2003, 2.

THE LEARNING OF THE JEWS

The fact that the Book of Mormon writers wrote in Egyptian in no way diminishes the Hebrew influence in the writers' method and style of writing. Such thinking is also manifested in Hebrew names present in the Book of Mormon, such as Isaiah, Jeremiah, Enos, Jacob, and Joseph. Interestingly, Lehi gave a non-Hebrew name to his son Nephi while the family was living in Jerusalem, yet Lehi gave Hebrew names, Jacob and Joseph, to the younger sons who were born in the wilderness after the family had left Jerusalem.

Nephi writes that "there is none other people that understand the things which were spoken unto the Jews like unto them, save it be that they are taught after the manner of the things of the Jews" (2 Nephi 25:5).

The terms "learning of the Jews" and "after the manner of the Jews" have at least two implications. First, the usage has to do with the poetic style of writing known as chiasmus, or inverted parallelism, that is peculiar to the Jews. Second, the usage implies the reflection of a physical means to convey a spiritual message often called "types and shadows," which will be discussed later.

The Jewish style of writing is very important, as it not only lends beauty and emphasis to the language but also is designed to facilitate the memorization of the scriptures. To this day, many devout Jews excel in their ability to quote from memory long passages of scripture. In that respect, senior author Joseph Allen makes the following comments in his personal writing: "On one occasion, I was flying to Jerusalem on El Al, the Israeli airline. Waking up after a brief night's sleep, I began to make my way to the back of the plane only to see the aisles totally blocked by Orthodox Jews reciting their morning prayers and scriptures. It occurred to me that their ability to cite long passages of scripture is indeed remarkable. Their recitations of long texts are made easier by the manner in which the text is written."

> The Jewish style of writing is very important, as it not only lends beauty and emphasis to the language but also is designed to facilitate the memorization of the scriptures.

The Nephites, centered as they were in the Hebrew culture, were also great memorizers. For example, Moroni provides us with a thirty-king genealogy in the book of Ether and then informs us that he wrote it from memory (Ether 5:1). The ability of the original writer to write after the manner of the Jews aided the memorization process.

The style of writing called chiasmus, which is a unique manner of writing among the Jews and which is prevalent in both the Old and New Testaments, was discovered several years ago in the Book of Mormon. Dr. John Welch, who has long been associated with the Foundation for Ancient Research and Mormon Studies, discovered this method of Hebrewisms while serving a mission for the Church of Jesus Christ in Germany. The word "chiasmus" comes from the Greek letter *chi*, or χ, and is illustrated in such familiar passages as "the last shall be first and the first shall be last" and "wo unto them that call evil good and good evil."

The Greek Method

The ABC (English) Method

A. The **last** shall be
   B. **first,** and the
   B. **first** shall be
A. **last**

The Maya Method

A	B	B	A
The **last** shall be	**first,** and the	**first** shall be	**last**

FIGURE 2–6: Three formats for presenting a chiastic statement: the Greek (*chi* or X) method, the ABC (or English) method, and the Maya method. According to the *Oxford English Dictionary, chiasmus* is now often referred to as "inverted Hebrewism." Information about chiasmus was first published in the English language in 1871—or forty-one years after the publication of the Book of Mormon and almost three decades after the death of the Prophet Joseph Smith. Thus, Joseph Smith could have had no knowledge of this type of writing at the time of his translation of the Book of Mormon. Neither did Joseph Smith have any knowledge of the manner in which the ancient Maya formatted their glyphs. The three "methods" of illustrating/formatting a chiasmus are slightly different, as shown in the visual.

The discovery of this style of writing in the Book of Mormon is indeed monumental, as it is generally accepted that any document manifesting this style of writing that reflects a profound spiritual message is Hebrew in origin. In recent years, a number of books have been written on the subject. One in particular is called *The Book of Mormon Text Reformatted According to Parallelistic Patterns*.[14] This form of writing is not limited to small passages of text. The entire chapter of Alma 36 appears to be written in this style of writing with the focal, or most significant, point falling in the middle of the

14. Donald W. Parry, *The Book of Mormon Text Reformatted According to Parallelistic Patterns* (Provo, UT: Foundation for Ancient Research and Mormon Studies, 1992).

A. My son, give ear to my words (v.1)
  B. Keep the commandments and ye shall prosper (v. 1)
    C. Do as I have done (v.2)
      D. Delivered fathers out of bondage (v.2)
        E. He surely did deliver them (v.2)
          F. Trust in God (v.3)
            G. Supported in their trials (v.3)
              H. I know this of God (v.4)
                I. Born of God (v.5)
                  J. Destroy the church of God (v.6)
                    K. Lost the use of his limbs (v.10)
                      L. Fear of presence of God (v.14)
                        M. Pains of a damned soul (v.16)
                          N. Alma remembers one Jesus Christ (v. 17)
                            O. Christ will atone for sins of the world (v.17)
                        N. Alma calls upon Jesus Christ (v.18)
                      M. Joy as exceeding as was my pain (v.20)
                  L. Alma's soul longed to be with God (v.22)
                K. Regained the strength of his limbs (v.23)
              J. Desire to bring souls to God (v.24)
            I. Born of God (v.26)
          H. The knowledge which I have is of God (v.26)
        G. Supported under trials (v.27)
      F. Trust in him (v.27)
     E. He will deliver me (v.27)
    D. Delivered fathers out of bondage (v.28)
   C. Know as I do know (v.30)
  B. Keep the commandments and ye shall prosper (v.30)
A. This is according to his word (v.30)

FIGURE 2–7: Chiastic structure of Alma 36.

chiasmus. In the case of Alma 36, the important message is that Christ came to atone for the sins of the world (see Alma 36:17).

In figure 2–7, observe that beginning with (J), the statements are contrasting in nature. In the first (J), he sought to destroy the church of God; and in the second (J), he sought to bring souls unto God. In the first (K), he lost the use of his limbs; and in the second (K), he regained the use of his limbs.

Also, notice that several other Hebrew style parallelisms occur in Alma 36 within the chiastic structure. Verses 6 and 8 talk about the angel; verses 10 and 16 mention the length of three days; and so forth.

Some scholars have suggested that the entire text of 1 Nephi, as shown in figure 2–8, is written in this format. An example of this format dealing with a geographical statement is found in Helaman 6:10:

A. Now the land south was called Lehi
   B. and the land north was called Mulek
      C. which was after the son of Zedekiah [Lord]
      C. for the Lord did bring
   B. Mulek into the land north
A. and Lehi into the land south

THE NEPHITES AND THE MAYA LANGUAGE

A third language, the Maya, should also be a focus of our study regarding the Book of Mormon. Tracing of the language trail from the Old World to the promised land may help us in understanding the New World setting for the Book of Mormon. The discovery of chiasmus in Mesoamerica is perhaps indicative of an ancient link to the Hebrew culture.

Dr. Allen J. Christensen presented a revised translation for his dissertation from the University of Texas from an ancient Quiche Maya text called the *Popol Vuh* written about AD 1400 and discovered in the Guatemala mountain village of Chichicastenango. He studied under the late Dr. Linda Schele, one of the leading scholars in deciphering the Maya code. Christensen formatted the *Popol Vuh* in literary fashion in both the native Quiche Maya language and in English. The *Popol Vuh*, or "sacred book," contains, in rather fragmented form, elements of the creation and the flood as well as other historical details about the origin of the Guatemala Maya. Christensen refers to the original writing as "exquisite Hebrew style." A sample of this style of writing in the *Popol Vuh* is as follows:

The discovery of chiasmus in Mesoamerica is perhaps indicative of an ancient link to the Hebrew culture.

A. First there was created

    B. Earth

        C. Mountains, valleys

            D. Divided were its paths water,

                E. Made their way their branches

                E. Among mountains

            D. Merely divided existing waters

        C. Then were revealed great mountains

    B. Thus its creation earth this,

A. Then it was created by them.[15]

15. See Allen J. Christenson, ed. and trans., *Popol Vuh: The Mythic Sections—Tales of First Beginnings from the Ancient K'iche'—Maya* (Provo, UT: Foundation for Ancient Research and Mormon Studies, 2000).

We are now seeing this same style of writing manifest itself in the Maya Classic Period (AD 200–800) on the walls of various buildings throughout Mesoamerica. For example, the seventh century AD engravings on the walls of the Temple of the Cross at Palenque are written in typical Hebrew chiastic fashion; and Stela 5 at Izapa, engraved around 200 BC, demonstrates the same manner of writing (see figure 2–9).

TYPES AND SHADOWS

In talking to his son Helaman, Alma said, "And now, my son, I would that ye should understand that *these things are not without a shadow.* And now I say, *is there not a type in this thing*?" (Alma 37:43, 45; emphasis added). These words say much about language in the Book of Mormon.

Many members of the Church of Jesus Christ have had a difficult time understanding why so much is written in the Book of Mormon about wars, geography, and history when the purpose of the Book of Mormon is to "lead us to Christ." Why, when Mormon could not write a hundredth part of the things of his people (Words of Mormon 1:5; see also Alma 13:31; 3 Nephi 5:8; 26:6) would he dedicate so much time and space to history and geography?

Some Church members have said, "Geography is not important" and, as such, "Don't waste your time on unimportant things." Others have called that attitude hypocritical and have said, "If the study of history and geography is important in our understanding of the Bible and Church history, then it is also important to our understanding of the Book of Mormon."

After years of "wandering in the wilderness," we give our answer to the controversy as follows: Mormon put things such as history, geography, wars, climate, a monetary system, and cultural patterns—such as carrying burdens on their backs—to reinforce a spiritual or doctrinal principle and, simply put, to "lead us to Christ."

All readers of the Book of Mormon should be amazed at the ways in which Mormon and the other Book of Mormon writers utilize, in a masterful way, these historical, geographical, and cultural patterns to teach and drive home a powerful doctrinal message

> If the study of history and geography is important in our understanding of the Bible and Church history, then it is also important to our understanding of the Book of Mormon.

Ch. 1	A. Lehi's dream leads him to **prophesy warnings** to the Jews
Ch. 2	B. The **departure** from Jerusalem
Ch. 3–5	C. Nephi accomplishes great **feat**, obtains brass plates; **brothers confounded**
Ch. 7	D. **Ishmael** joins the group with his daughters
Ch. 8	E. **The tree of life**
Ch. 10	F. Lehi prophesies about the **Old World** and the **coming of Christ**
Ch. 11	G. **Nephi's vision of Christ**
Ch. 12–14	F. Nephi prophesies about the **New World** and the **coming of Christ**
Ch. 15	E. **The tree of life** (interpreted)
Ch. 16	D. Sons of Lehi marry the daughters of **Ishmael,** and **Ishmael** dies
Ch. 17	C. Nephi accomplishes a great **feat** by building a ship; **brothers confounded**
Ch. 18	B. The **departure** from the Old World
Ch. 19–22	A. Nephi **warns** the Jews and quotes the **prophecies** of Isaiah

A	B	E	G	E	B	A
Lehi	Journey	Lehi's dream	Prophecy of Christ	Nephi's dream	Journey	Isaiah

FIGURE 2–8: The entire book of 1 Nephi is written in chiastic form.

A. Sariah figure (supporting her prophet husband)
  B. Lehi figure (a prophet)
    C. Lemuel figure (back to the tree)
      D. The Tree of Life (Christ)
    C. Laman figure (back to the tree)
  B. Nephi figure (a prophet)
A. Sam figure (supporting his prophet brother)

FIGURE 2–9: Hebrew chiasmus as reflected on Stela 5 from Izapa, the Tree of Life Stone.

directly associated with teaching us about Christ and His Atonement. Therefore, we conclude that the more we understand about the archaeology, geography, language, and culture of the Book of Mormon and its doctrinal counterpart, the more we understand the nature of the Book of Mormon itself. The following example illustrates what we mean.

In Alma 46, we read about Moroni setting up a standard of liberty and the people making a covenant to obey the Lord. After a marvelous treatise on the concept of a

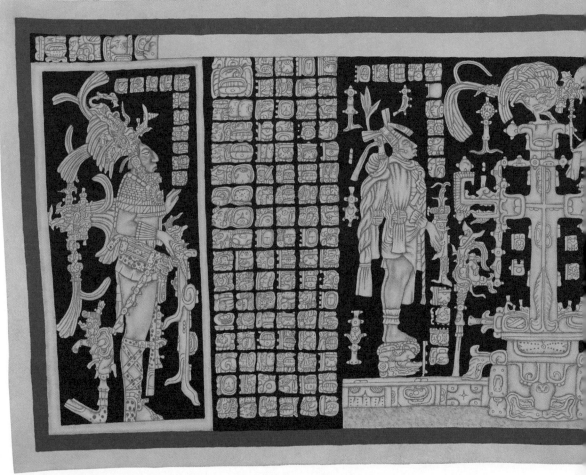

A   B   C   D

The manner in which the Hebrew writers take a physical situation to illustrate a spiritual point is called *dualism* or *types and shadows.*

covenant people, the last few verses end up sounding like a weather report. The manner in which the Hebrew writers take a physical situation to illustrate a spiritual point is called *dualism* or *types and shadows.* We are familiar with this concept, as it is manifested in the form of parables, allegories, or symbolism.

Alma 46: 39–41 is dissected as follows:

Verse 39:   A. Many people died, they believed in Christ, they rejoiced
Verse 40:   B. Many died because of fevers in the land
                    C. Plants and roots were prepared by the Lord
                    B. To overcome diseases as a result of the climate
Verse 41:   A. Many people died, they believed in Christ, they rejoiced

40

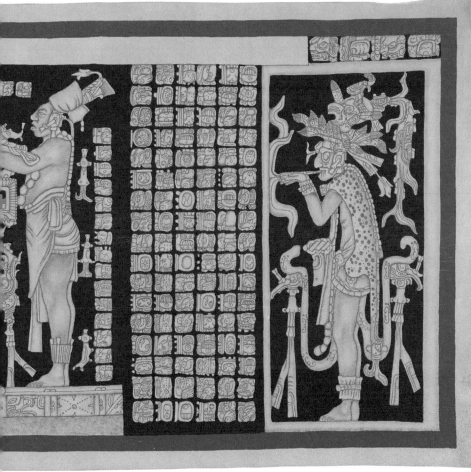

C   B   A

FIGURE 2–10: Reproduction of a panel located at the Temple of the Cross at Palenque, dating to the seventh century AD and written in chiastic format. Inverted Hebrew parallelism (or chiasmus) is manifested in a typical A-B-C-D-C-B-A format. Notice that the center panel of the mural is associated with Quetzalcoatl, similar to the way the central portion of 1 Nephi relates to Christ. The two panels labeled "C" show the father Pacal Na on the left and his son Chan Balaam on the right, much in the same way that Lehi and Nephi relate to each other in the analysis of the Tree of Life Stone. The two panels labeled "A" on the left and "A" on the right are important ancestral figures in the same way that Lehi, the father of Nephi, occupies the first position in 1 Nephi and that Isaiah, a favored prophet by Nephi, is quoted by Nephi in the final chapters. The "B" panels also show historical movements in both 1 Nephi and in the Temple of the Cross. That the Classic Maya would continue this style of writing after the close of the Book of Mormon is quite remarkable. (Photo Courtesy of Blake Joseph Allen)

Readers will observe that verses 39 and 41 are identical. This observation immediately informs us that this passage is written in chiasmus, or inverted Hebrewism. Verse 40 is also repetitive in the same style. However, the exciting thing about these three verses is that they are meant to be spiritual in nature as opposed to just telling us about the climate. The verses do tell us about the nature of the climate, which parallels the rainforest region of Peten, Guatemala, the area proposed where Moroni's standard of liberty was raised to the people. If Mormon had used the metaphor that many people froze to death in a snow bank, we would probably stay away from the hot and humid rainforest as a geographical setting for the Book of Mormon, but he did not. He talked about fevers, an illness that is common to this day in the department of Peten and in Belize.

Mormon obviously did not put that climate statement in the Book of Mormon to give us a "five o'clock weather report." Knowing that the intent of the Book of Mormon is to lead us to Christ, we must, therefore, translate the physical statement into a spiritual message. In this case, the translation of the spiritual message appears to be as follows:

Verse 39   A. We all die, but we rejoice because of our belief in Christ
Verse 40   B. We suffer physical death as a result of the fall of Adam
                    C. God gave His Only Begotten Son as an Atonement
                B. Jesus atones for sins of man as a result of the Fall of Adam
Verse 41   A. We all die, but we rejoice because of our belief in Christ

The Alma 46 account is not the only place, however, where the term "root and plant" refers to the Savior. For example, Isaiah prophesied that the Messiah would "grow up before him as a tender plant, and as a root out of a dry ground" (Isaiah 53:2). Abinadi quoted this same passage of scripture as he was preaching the gospel to Noah and his priests (Mosiah 14:2). When Nephi reported that he was taught in the learning of the Jews, he meant that he studied the law of Moses and that the writings of Isaiah were a primary part of his studies. By the same token, Mormon was trained in the same manner. He knew the prophecies of Isaiah about the Savior of the world, and, in a brilliant manner, he ties in the climate of Mesoamerica with the prophecy of Isaiah.

> Isaiah prophesied that the Messiah would "grow up before him as a tender plant, and as a root out of a dry ground" (Isaiah 53:2).

Alma referred to this style of writing as "types and shadows." Speaking to his son Helaman about the Liahona, he said, "I would that ye should understand that these things are not without a shadow; for as our fathers were slothful to give heed to this compass (now these things were temporal) they did not prosper; even so it is with things which are spiritual" (Alma 37:43). David Hadlock summarizes the concept of shadows as follows: "This relationship between the temporal and spiritual is the essence of the principle of 'shadows.' The temporal event casts a spiritual shadow. Just as physical objects when placed in light cast a visible shadow, physical objects and temporal events when placed in the light of Christ cast a spiritual shadow. . . . The Liahona casts a symbolic shadow, which shadow is the word of Christ. The Liahona and the word of Christ function in the same manner. Both guide the individual who gives heed to them."

The term "type" is also significant in our understanding of the Book of Mormon. A "type" is a prophecy; and, as a result, as Nephi instructed us, it is the Holy Spirit that teaches the deeper message. In the example of the Liahona, the temporal reality of arriving at the promised land of the Americas is symbolic of our literal entrance into the promised land of the celestial kingdom—if we but follow the words of Christ.[16] Finally, a similitude is also a type. Jacob compared Abraham's offering up his son Isaac as "a similitude of God and his Only Begotten Son" (Jacob 4:5).

16. Hadlock, "The Language of My Father," 5.

PROPER NAMES AND PLACES

As each year passes, we are learning more about the Maya language as it relates to proper names and phrases in the Book of Mormon. A few preliminary and elementary comparisons may give an idea of some of the possibilities for further and continued research in comparing the language of Mesoamerica and the Book of Mormon.

Xul/Shule. The name of a Jaredite king, *Shule* (see Ether 1:30–31), suggests an interesting comparison with the Maya place-name *Xul*, both of which are pronounced exactly the same way. The word *Xul/Shule* is one of the most common sounds in both highland Guatemala and the Yucatan. *Xul* is also the name of one of the Maya months. The "X," which in the Spanish sound of the Maya word is pronounced "sh," appears in such words as *Xelha, Xela,* and *Xultun.* The "sh" or "X" sound is also very common in Jaredite Book of Mormon names—such as Shiz, Shem, Shim, Shiblon, and so forth. In fact, *X-Balam,* a place-name in the Yucatan, may be the same word as the Book of Mormon name Shiblon. The latter part of the word, *Balam,* means tiger or jaguar.

Ha/Hah. The "ha" ending is common both in the Maya language and in proper names and cities in the Book of Mormon. For example, the names of Nephi(hah), Moroni(hah), and Ammoni(hah) all display the "ha" sound. Compare these names with Maya place-names, such as Xel(ha), Balam(ha), Altun(ha), Pulsi(ha), and so forth. Apparently, the "ha" ending performs the same function as the Hebrew word *beth* and the Aztec word *tenango*—that is, "house of," "near to," or "place of."

The "ha" ending in the Maya language of the Yucatan today means water. Hence, the word *Balam-ha* means the water or well of the jaguar. It also may refer to a person of that name. However, the cultural association with *ha/water* in the Yucatan and Peten has to do with the system of water supply. Because of the scarcity of water in the above-mentioned areas, each village is located in such a manner as to be near a well or cenote. The term *cenote* in the Maya language refers to a brook or bubbling up of water whose origin is an underground water or river system. One of the most famous wells or cenotes today is located at the Maya/Toltec ruins of Chichen Itza. Its reported purpose was, at one point, a place where young girls were sacrificed to the idol gods.

The *ha/water* concept manifests an interesting correlation with the "ha" ending of proper names in the Book of Mormon. The analogy in words such as "Nephihah" or "Moronihah" may mean "from the waters of Nephi" or "from the waters of Moroni," such as in the term, "from the loins of Judah."

As a mother gives birth to a baby, her water breaks. In Spanish, the term that is often used is "los fuentes se rompen," "the fountains burst."

Pahoran, Pacumeni, Paanchi. In a preliminary publication of the Chorti-Maya language with roots in the Peten region of Guatemala where the ruins of Tikal are located, the sounds of the proper names of three Nephite chief judges, who reigned in the middle of the first century BC, are recorded. In fact, of the ten proper names that start with the letter "P" in the Book of Mormon, five show up either as a proper name or

The reader is referred to the pronunciation guide at the beginning of the book. The pronunciation guide follows a Spanish or Latin concept of pronunciation applied to Maya and Nahuatl words.

as a cognate in the Chorti-Maya dictionary referred to above. They are *Paanchi, Pachus, Pacumeni, Pahoran,* and *Pekah*. Other proper names that start with the letter "P" are recognizable as Old World names such as *Palestina, Pharaoh,* and *Philistine*. The people who speak the Chorti-Maya language live in northern Honduras, having migrated from the Peten jungle region of Guatemala. We encourage readers to check the Internet under "Chorti-Maya" for more information and for the cognate meaning of the words above.

Shum. Some of our greatest experiences of traveling happen when we visit with the local people. On one occasion while traveling through the Guatemala highlands with a group of people, we stopped at the village of Nahuala and visited with a family. As we bid them farewell, Joe D. Jenkins, who speaks Spanish, asked their name. The man answered, "My name is Antonio Shum," which is written *Xum*. Interestingly, "shum" is a monetary measurement in the Book of Mormon (see Alma 11:5).

Moroni/Onihah. In the Chorti-Maya language, the cognate "oni" means ancient, and "mor' is associated with mountain or wilderness, thus suggesting the name for Moroni as "ancient wilderness." Moron is the name of the first capital city of the Jaredites (see Ether 7:5). Onihah is the name of one of the cities that appear to have been covered over by water at the waters of Mormon at the time of the great destruction and means "ancient waters"—that is, "oni" ancient and "ha" water (3 Nephi 9:7).

Cintepec/Shim. *Tepec*, the last part of the word *Cintepec*, means hill or mountain in the Nahuatl (Aztec) language. The front part of the word, *cin*, means corn. Hence, the word *Cintepec* means Corn Hill. The Hill Cintepec is located east of Lake Catemaco in the Tuxtla Mountains in the state of Veracruz, Mexico.

The location of Cintepec is close to the Hill Vigia, which is the leading candidate for the location where the last great battles, as discussed in the Book of Mormon, were fought.

"Shim" is the name of a hill in the Book of Mormon where Mormon received the records from Ammaron. Ammaron told Mormon that "when ye are about twenty and four years old . . . go to the land Antum, unto a hill which shall be called *Shim;* and there have I deposited unto the Lord all the sacred engravings concerning this people" (Mormon 1:3; emphasis added).

Shim in the Maya language also means corn. Therefore, Cintepec, the Tuxtla Mountains hill that is close to the Hill Vigia in the same area, may be the hill Shim mentioned in the Book of Mormon. Cintepec is the hill where the stone was quarried to construct the large Olmec stone heads discovered along the Gulf of Mexico. The Olmec culture dates to the Jaredite time period.

Co. A name that begins with "co" or "ko" is rather common and is also evident in the Maya language. The Book of Mormon names of (Co)hor, (Ko)rihor, (Co)rianton, and (Co)riantumr all begin with the "co" sound. Driving from Chichen Itza to Cancun in the Yucatan, a person travels through the town of Cocom, a word that not only manifests

> The location of Cintepec is close to the Hill Vigia, which is the leading candidate for the location where the last great battles, as discussed in the Book of Mormon, were fought.

the beginning sound of "co" but also the word "com," which is the name of a Jaredite king.

Lehi, Sariah, Nephi. In 1952, Dr. Wells Jakeman, then head of the Archaeology Department of Brigham Young University, published a report in which he proposed that the name of "Lehi" is recorded on a stone monument near the Mexico-Guatemala border in the state of Chiapas.[17]

Dr. Jakeman presents the hypothesis that Stela 5 at Izapa is a representation of the tree-of-life vision recorded in 1 Nephi 8 and 11. He suggests that the name "Lehi" is represented by a jawbone located near the figure of an older person, who is facing the tree in the sculptured monument. The comparison is arrived at by his comparing the jawbone with the biblical name of Lehi, which was probably named after the jawbone incident of Samson, when he slew a thousand Philistines with a jawbone (see Judges 15:15; also, see the Jakeman report).[18] Jakeman also proposed name correlations for Sariah and Nephi.

Laman Ayin. In the small country of Belize, which borders the Peten of Guatemala, are the remains of an archaeological site that carries the name of *Lamanai*. This Maya site dates to 100 BC, which is the Book of Mormon time period when a man by the name of *Lamoni* was the Lamanite king. It was also the time when the Nephites made a strong attempt, under the leadership of the military leader, Moroni, to drive the Lamanites out of the east wilderness. The Belize/Peten area is an excellent candidate for the east wilderness referred to in the Book of Mormon. The word *Laman* in the Maya language is associated with water, and *Ayin* is associated with crocodile; as a result, the popular translation of *Laman Ayin* is "submerged crocodile." New evidence has come to light to suggest that the name *Laman (Ayin)* is associated with a Lamanite king who was a contemporary of Mormon. His name is Yax Nuun Ayiin, who became the ruler at Tikal at AD 379, just six years prior to the final Cumorah battle. Furthermore, an artistic rendition by Dr. John Clark of the New World Archaeological Foundation shows a crocodile in the trunk of the tree of Stela 5 at Izapa. Although speculative in nature, the crocodile may suggest a name association of the person with his back to the tree as "Laman." (See chapter 8, "The Teotihuacan Culture," for more information on Yax Nuun Ayiin.)

Hermounts/Tehuantepec. Those things that Book of Mormon students look for in language correlations are names or places whose meanings are given in the Book of Mormon. A comparison can then be sought after with names of places or people that have trickled down through the centuries into modern terms.

One such possibility is the name "Hermounts" mentioned in Alma 2:37: "[The Lamanites] had reached the wilderness, which was called Hermounts; and it was that part of the wilderness which was infested by wild and ravenous beasts."

Because the term "Hermounts" is mentioned in reference to both "wilderness" and "wild and ravenous beasts," we can hypothesize that "mounts" equates to wilderness and "her" is equal to wild and ravenous beasts.

17. Wells Jakeman was appointed chairman of the Archaeology Department of Brigham Young University at the time the department was founded in 1946. Jakeman, with others, surveyed a stone with engravings located near Tapachula, Chiapas, Mexico, at a site called Izapa. He wrote a treatise on the Izapa stone, comparing the content of the engravings with Lehi's dream in the Book of Mormon.

18. See M. Wells Jakeman, "Unusual Tree-of-Life Sculpture from Ancient Central America," *University Archaeological Society Newsletter*, no. 4 (1953), 26–49; and M. Wells Jakeman, "The Complex Tree of Life Carving on Izapa Stela 5," *BYU Archaeology and Ethnohistory*, no. 4 (1958).

FIGURE 2–11: Map showing locations in Mesoamerica where Book of Mormon names have surfaced in the appropriate geographical locations either as a proper name or as a translation from another language. The Book of Mormon names manifest the same meanings as current geographical locations, such as Tehuantepec (wilderness of wild beasts/Hermounts); Hueyapan (large waters) Ripliancum; Xocalha (fish waters)/Sidon; Zactun (white limestone)/Sidom; and Cin (Ixim)/Shim. Some names are Maya names that describe a certain name or area, such as ancient waters/Onihah; jaguar-mountain (Moron, Mormon); and water basin/Mocum. Laman, Xul (Shule), Com, Kumen (Cunen), Pahoran, Pacumeni, Paanchi, Kish, and Lachoneus (Lacandone) are identifiable on the Mesoamerica map.

19. Personal communication with Joseph Allen, Provo, Utah, 1988.

Linguist Calvin Tolman[19] points out that the word *Tehuantepec* has the same meaning. Tehuantepec is an area consisting of mountains on the Chiapas side of the Isthmus of Tehuantepec by that same name; a city called Tehuantepec and a gulf called Tehuantepec are also found. All these are in the vicinity proposed as the narrow neck of land. *Tepec* in the Nahuatl (Aztec) language means hill, or mount, such as Chapultepec or Cintepec.

Tecuani, in Nahuatl, or *tehuan* (Spanish pronunciation) means wild beasts—hence,

20. Antonio Penafiel, *Nombres Geograficos de Mexico* (Mexico, DF: Litoimpresores, 1977), 54.

the meaning of Tehuantepec is "wilderness of wild beasts,"[20] the same meaning that the term *Hermounts* appears to have in the Book of Mormon and the same meaning that *Mormon* has in the Maya language.

Furthermore, the geographical location of Tehuantepec is in the same area proposed as the location of Hermounts in the Book of Mormon (see chapter 23, "Wilderness Areas").

Exploring the Lands of the Book of Mormon

Worth noting also is that both the Book of Mormon and the Spanish chronicles echo the fact that towns and cities were named after the people who settled them. That being the case, justification appears to exist for the comparison of place-names, which have retained their original names, with proper names of people and places in the Book of Mormon. Our challenge is to learn the meanings of the names in both the Book of Mormon language and comparative languages of Mesoamerica.

The following statements indicate that places were named after people:

From the Book of Mormon, we read: "Now it was the custom of the people of Nephi to call their lands, and their cities, and their villages, yea, even all their small villages, after the name of him who first possessed them; and thus it was with the land of Ammonihah" (Alma 8:7).

From the writings of the sixteenth-century Mexico author, Ixtlilxochitl, we read: "In each place where the Chichimecatl settled, whether it be a large city or a small village, it was their custom to name it according to the first king or leader who possessed the land. This same custom prevailed among the Tultecas. The general area was called Tollan. They named their large cities and their small villages after the first man or king who occupied it. . . . This custom was prevalent in naming other cities and villages throughout the land."[21]

Kumen/Cunen. A community in the frontiers of Mexico and Guatemala is named *Cunen.* In speaking about this name comparison, Harold B. Lee, former President of The Church of Jesus Christ of Latter-day Saints, says: "At the Guatemala conference President Elberto Moises Amado, president of the Central District, told an interesting experience. He had found in northern Guatemala a city by the name of Kumen. He wondered at the origin of this name since most of the names were of Spanish or Mesoamerican origin, but not so with the name Kumen. When he read the Book of Mormon, to his delight, he found that one of the twelve disciples called by the Master when he visited the Western Hemisphere was called Kumen. Undoubtedly, the city was named for that disciple who most likely had frequented this place."[22]

Kumenonhi/Mathoni/Mathonihah/Kumen/Shemnon. From a purely sound-alike perspective, five of the twelve Nephite disciples appear to have Maya names—that is, Kumenonhi, Mathoni, Mathonihah, Kumen, and Shemnon. Five are Old Testament/Hebrew names: Jonas, Jeremiah, Jonas, Zedekiah, and Isaiah. One, Nephi, is probably Egyptian; and one, Timothy, is probably Greek.

Lachoneus/Lacanha (Lacandone). In the year AD 15, the Gadianton robber leader wrote an epistle to Lachoneus, who was the governor of the land of Zarahemla. The events of the following eleven years resulted in Lachoneus gathering all the Nephites together to an area that had been chosen as their last place of defense against their enemies: "And the land which was appointed was the land of Zarahemla, and the land which was between the land Zarahemla and the land Bountiful, yea, to the line which was between the land Bountiful and the land Desolation" (3 Nephi 3:23).

21. Ixtlilxochitl:22; see chapter 11, "Fernando de Alva Ixtlilxochitl."

22. Harold B. Lee, "Mexico and Central America Area," *General Conference Report* (Salt Lake City: The Church of Jesus Christ of Latter-day Saints, 1972), 118.

From a purely sound-alike perspective, five of the twelve Nephite disciples appear to have Maya names.

The Nephites gathered provisions enough to last for seven years. Their intent was literally to starve the robbers to death. The robbers finally came to battle against the Nephites. Regarding that war, Mormon wrote that "there never was known so great a slaughter among all the people of Lehi since he left Jerusalem" (3 Nephi 4:11).

From the description of the location of the land identified above and from the general geographical statements presented in this text, *Exploring the Lands of the Book of Mormon*, we propose that this great battle took place in the general area of the Lacandone Mountains.

The valley and the area are called Lacanha. Today, Lacandone natives still live in the area. They dress in white robes, and the men wear their hair long. Some of the Lacandone natives are normally seen at the ruins of Palenque, where they sell their bows and arrows.

When we compare the name *Lacanha*, or *Lacandone*, with the Book of Mormon name of *Lachoneus*, the similarities are worth noting—at least suggesting the possibility that the name of the land was originally derived from the name of the great Nephite governor, Lachoneus. Therefore, Lacanha very likely could be the land where the Nephites gathered together to defend themselves against the Gadianton robbers.

> When we compare the name *Lacanha*, or *Lacandone*, with the Book of Mormon name of *Lachoneus*, the similarities are worth noting.

JAREDITE PROPER NAMES

An elementary proper name count of the genealogy list of Jaredite kings presents some rather interesting written and verbal comparisons with names in the Maya lowlands. Although not conclusive, the comparison suggests that further language name analyses may be advisable. The bolded names show Maya cognates.

Ether	To our knowledge, it has not yet been discovered as a Maya word.
Coriantor	The prefix "Co" in Yucatec Maya means "in the place of."
Moron	The Chorti-Maya dictionary shows "Mor" as hill or wilderness.
Ethem	To our knowledge, it has not yet been discovered as a Maya word.
Ahah	The last letter of the Maya alphabet is "Ahau," which means Lord.
Seth	To our knowledge, it has not yet been discovered as a Maya word.
Shiblon	Similar in spelling to the ancient Lamanite city, a derivative of *ix (sh) Balam (blon)*, which means first jaguar.
Com	The name of a major native tribe in the Yucatan. A village today named Cocom is located near Chichen Itza.
Coriantum	"Co" means in the place of. "Tum" may be "tun," which means stone.
Ammnigaddah	To our knowledge, it has not yet been discovered as a Maya word.
Aaron	To our knowledge, it has not yet been discovered as a Maya word.
Heth	May be "Het," a place in the Tuxtla Mountains of Veracruz.
Hearthom	To our knowledge, it has not yet been discovered as a Maya word.
Lib	The name "Lib" is common in Maya.

Kish	A name discovered on the Temple of the Cross at Palenque. According to Dr. Bruce Warren, Kish was a king who was born March 8, 993 BC, and was from San Lorenzo, Veracruz.[23]
Corom	See above. "Corum" is in the Chorti-Maya dictionary.
Kim	To our knowledge, it has not yet been discovered as a Maya word.
Morianton	See "Moron" and "Tum."
Riplakish	See "Kish."
Shez	To our knowledge, it has not yet been discovered as a Maya word.
Heth	Same as "Heth" above.
Com	Same as "Com" above.
Coriantum	Same as "Coriantum" above.
Emer	To our knowledge, it has not yet been discovered as a Maya word.
Omer	To our knowledge, it has not yet been discovered as a Maya word.
Shule	*Xul.*
Kib	A Maya calendar name.
Orihah	May be "Onihah," a name that means "ancient waters" in Chorti-Maya.
Jared	To our knowledge, it has not yet been discovered as a Maya word.

23. Bruce W. Warren, "Jaredite King Name Discovered," *Explorations in the Book of Mormon* (Orem, UT: Book of Mormon Tours, 1999), 9–13.

MAYA DAY NAMES AND THE HEBREW ALPHABET

With interest, we can note that three of the Maya day names appear to be of Hebrew origin. The following is a list of Maya day names compared with the names of the Hebrew alphabet:

Maya Day Names	Hebrew Alphabet
1. Imix	1. Alep
2. Ik	2. Bet
3. Akbal	3. Gimel
4. Kan	4. Dalet
5. Chicchan	5. He
6. Cimi	6. Waw
7. **Manik**	7. Zayen
8. **Lamat**	8. Het
9. **Muluc**	9. Tet
10. Oc	10. Yod
11. Chuen	11. **Kap**
12. Eb	12. **Lamed**
13. Ben	13. **Mem**
14. Ix	14. Nun
15. Men	15. Samek
16. Cib	16. Ayin

Notice that *Nun* and *Ayin* in the Hebrew alphabet are also used as Maya proper names in such instances as *Laman Ayin* and *Yax Nuun Ayiin* (see the index for references to these names).

17. Caban	17. Pe
18. Etznab	18. Sade
19. Cauac	19. Kap
20. Awau	20. Res
21. Sin	
22. Taw	

Notice the sequence of the Maya day names (numbers 7, 8, and 9): Manik, Lamat, Muluc.

Compare the above Maya day names with the Hebrew alphabet names (11, 12, and 13): Kap, Lamed, Mem.

David H. Kelley, emeritus Maya scholar with the University of Calgary, observed that both the sequence and the meaning of the three Maya glyphs and the three Hebrew letters of the alphabet are similar.[24]

24. David H. Kelley, *Deciphering the Maya Script* (Austin: University of Texas Press, 1976).

1. Both *Manik* (Maya) and *Kap* (Hebrew) are associated by a glyph or symbol of a hand. *Kaph* means hand in Hebrew. *Kah* means hand in Yucatec Maya.

2. The next sequence of the three sounds in Maya is *Lamat* and in Hebrew is *Lamed*. Obviously, they are very similar.

3. The third Maya day name, *Muluc*, and the Hebrew letter *Mem* both have the meaning of water.

SUMMARY

For many years following the initial publication of the Book of Mormon, the clause "and it came to pass" was used by critics to question the truthfulness of the Book of Mormon. Mark Twain quipped that if we took out the "it came to passes" in the Book of Mormon, we could reduce it to a pamphlet. Today, "and it came to pass" and its variants, along with other language usage in the Book of Mormon, are unique in suggesting interesting connections between present-day cultures and languages in proposed lands of the Book of Mormon and in the contents of the Book of Mormon itself. The following statements summarize what we can say today about language and culture associated with proposed lands of the Book of Mormon.

The only place in the New World where a written phonetic writing system was in use—at precisely the same time that the Book of Mormon was written—was in Mesoamerica.

1. The only place in the New World where a written phonetic writing system was in use—at precisely the same time that the Book of Mormon was written—was in Mesoamerica. No evidence exists that a written language was in use in any part of the American continent, in conjunction with a high civilization, other than in Mesoamerica during the time period in which the Book of Mormon was written. This fact lends support to present thinking that the events of the Book of Mormon occurred in the limited geographic area known as Mesoamerica—the proposed lands of the Book of Mormon.

2. The Classic Maya (AD 200–AD 900) adopted their written language from an earlier 600 BC–AD 200 culture. This adoption suggests that the Lamanite Maya adopted

their written language from the Nephite Maya—which is consistent with information we gather from the Book of Mormon. The time period and language structure of the Maya so closely parallel what we know from the Book of Mormon that we may conclude that the Classic Maya (AD 200) were "Lamanites" and that they adopted their language from the Preclassic (600 BC–AD 200) Nephite Maya.

3. Many records, or codices, of ancient Mesoamerica were destroyed by the early Spanish priests. Recent studies in Maya hieroglyphs are unlocking the meaning of the glyphs. These findings suggest interesting parallels with the Book of Mormon, such as the "and it came to pass" glyph discovered at the seventh century AD ruins of Palenque.

4. A Hebrew literary style called *chiasmus* has been discovered in the Book of Mormon. Preliminary indications suggest that the same type of literary style is present in Maya writing.

5. The name of a Jaredite king known as Kish (Ki'x), born March 8, 993 BC, is written in Maya on the walls of the Temple of the Cross at Palenque, which suggests parallel names of Book of Mormon people.

6. Few words of Hebrew origin have been discovered in the Mesoamerica languages—suggesting that the spoken language had a Jaredite base, although the style of writing was adopted from the Hebrew. Three of the Maya calendar day names appear to be Hebrew in origin.

7. We recommend further study comparing the languages of Mesoamerica with what we know about proper names, places, phrases, and style of writing in the Book of Mormon.

A major caution is in order. Just because a name "sounds like" a Book of Mormon name does not establish the relationship as a fact. Each name should be carefully analyzed not only as it sounds but also as to its meaning and the time and place of its origin. It should then pass through the hands of experts in the field of language comparisons and be subjected to review.

> Recent studies in Maya hieroglyphs are unlocking the meaning of the glyphs. These findings suggest interesting parallels with the Book of Mormon.

FREQUENTLY ASKED QUESTIONS

In most discussions about language and writing associated with proposed lands of the Book of Mormon, the following questions are typically asked. The answers support the current thinking that Mesoamerica is indeed the location of lands of the Book of Mormon.

Question: How do you account for the fact that both the Mulekites and the colony of Lehi came out of Jerusalem where people spoke Hebrew and yet very little evidence of the Hebrew language is found in the New World?

Answer: A twofold answer is offered.

1. Both the book of Ether and archaeology give us the answer. No date is given in the Book of Mormon for the downfall of the Jaredite nation. However, the Limhi expedition (121 BC) discovered bones that had not totally decayed (see Mosiah 8:8–11). In

addition, the archaeological record of the downfall of the Olmec nation (400–300 BC) supports the Jaredite dating. These events suggest that the Jaredite nation was still in existence at the time of the arrival of both Lehi and Mulek; the events also suggest that the native spoken language of Mesoamerica was the Olmec (Jaredite) language.

2. However, the written language kept by the Nephites was reformed Egyptian, which was taught and handed down from generation to generation among the Nephites.

Question: Is it possible that the record-keeping descendants of the Nephites both wrote and maintained the spoken language of the Jews?

Answer: Yes, it is possible. The question is, to what extent was Hebrew used as a spoken language? We do not have a credible answer to that question, but we can infer that the Nephites spoke a language that was understood by all "Lamanites"—not just those who were direct descendants of Laman and Lemuel (see Mosiah 8:12).

Question: This seems to imply that people were living in the Americas when Lehi landed. Is that true?

Answer: Yes, from the information available to us, we know that the Jaredites were still here. If the Jaredite nation did not fall until 400 BC–300 BC, then we know that Jaredites and Nephites and Mulekites were living in the same geographical areas for two to three hundred years.

This subject is, however, a rather delicate one, as Latter-day Saints have come to feel, traditionally, that every last man, woman, and child of the Jaredites was destroyed about 600 BC and that when Lehi arrived, the American continent had been swept clean and no other people were around. This picture is not accurate with what we have learned about the languages of Mesoamerica, with what archaeology teaches us, or with both internal and external dating of the Jaredite downfall. Archaeologically and linguistically, people were here when Lehi and Mulek arrived. Careful study of the Book of Mormon bears that out.

For example, within forty-five years after Lehi landed in the promised land, or fifty-five years from the time they left Jerusalem (see Jacob 1:1), the following had transpired:

1. Nephi separated from his brothers with *all* those who would listen to the warnings and revelations of God, and they went to a place they called "Nephi." Nephi taught them to be industrious and to build a temple, and he was made king and protector over his people. At this point, the Nephites had been in the promised land about twenty years (see 2 Nephi 5:5–28).

2. Nephi made *many* swords; and his people had wars and contentions with their brethren, whom they called the "Lamanites," within thirty years after they arrived in the promised land. At this point, even based upon a large family offspring, if the Nephite adults consisted only of Nephi, Sam, Zoram, Jacob, Joseph, and three sisters and their families, there could be only about twenty-four male Nephite soldiers over the age of fifteen.

NOTE TO THE READER: In this second edition of *Exploring the Lands of the Book of Mormon*, we have elected to label both Nephites and Lamanites as being affiiliated with the same culture, that which is referred to today as the Maya. Therefore, for clarification purposes, we will use the terms *Nephite Maya* and *Lamanite Maya* in our geographical discussions.

3. Fifty-five years from the time the Nephites left Jerusalem, or about forty-five years after they arrived in the promised land, Jacob was preaching to the Nephites in the temple at Nephi. He chastised the people for exhibiting too much pride, for having more than one wife, and for having concubines (see Jacob 1–2).

Again, if we consider that only Nephi, Sam, Zoram, Jacob, Joseph, and their sisters constituted the entire Nephite nation, Jacob, at the very most, would be chastising twenty to twenty-five couples over the age of twenty. That does not answer the question about where the additional women who served as concubines came from.

4. A somewhat casual comment about the continued existence of Jaredite people in the land southward after the last battle at the hill Ramah is found in one verse in the Book of Mormon. From the land of Nephi, King Limhi sent forty-three of his people to find the land of Zarahemla about 121 BC. This group failed to find Zarahemla but rather found evidence of the last battle of the Jaredites along with the twenty-four gold plates containing an account of the Jaredites.

King Limhi wanted the gold plates to be translated, but no one among his people could translate them. Later, after Ammon and his party from the land of Zarahemla located King Limhi and his subjects in the land of Nephi, Limhi said to Ammon: "Knowest thou of any one that can translate? For I am desirous that these records should be translated into our language; for, perhaps, they will give us a knowledge *of a remnant of the people who have been destroyed*, from whence these records came; or, perhaps, they will give us a knowledge of this very people who have been destroyed; and I am desirous to know the cause of their destruction" (Mosiah 8:12; emphasis added).

Buried in this verse is a hint that Jaredites were still living in the land southward long after the last Jaredite battle. "A remnant of the people who have been destroyed" suggests that some (a remnant) of the Jaredites were still living long after the battle at the hill Ramah and were known to Limhi and his people who were living in the land of Nephi about 121 BC.[25]

Apparently, either the Nephite nation consisted of more people than we read about (those who came to the New World with Lehi) or the Nephites and Lamanites associated themselves with the Jaredite line of people who had been in the promised land for two thousand years.

This line of reasoning is consistent with the Lord's dealings with His people. The Lord's covenant people have never been placed in an area of total isolation. The role of the covenant people has always been to "teach the gospel to the world."

࿓࿓࿓࿓࿓࿓࿓࿓࿓࿓࿓࿓࿓࿓࿓࿓࿓࿓࿓࿓࿓࿓࿓࿓࿓࿓࿓࿓

"A remnant of the people who have been destroyed" suggests that some (a remnant) of the Jaredites were still living long after the battle at the hill Ramah and were known to Limhi and his people who were living in the land of Nephi about 121 BC.

25. We thank Ted D. Stoddard, editor of *Exploring the Lands of the Book of Mormon*, for bringing this information to our attention. The precise wording, "a remnant of the people who have been destroyed," is important to our understanding the concept of the destruction of the Jaredites. This information from the Book of Mormon itself proves that Jaredites continued to live in Mesoamerica following the last great battle of the Jaredites at the hill Ramah.

CHAPTER 3

Looking at Dates

Even six hundred years from the time that my father left Jerusalem, a prophet would the Lord God raise up among the Jews—even a Messiah, or, in other words, a Savior of the world. (1 Nephi 10:4)

 During the spring and early summer of 1970, a father-son relationship developed between Joseph and Blake Allen, a relationship that was centered on Mesoamerica and the Book of Mormon and that would last a lifetime. Blake was only ten years old when he accompanied his father, Joseph, to Mexico City. At the time, Joseph was serving as director of the Institute of Religion at the University of Texas at El Paso and was completing work for his PhD in ancient and modern scriptures. His purpose in going to Mexico City was to conduct research at the National Museum of Anthropology in Mexico City. For his doctoral dissertation, he extracted and translated material written in Spanish about the white god Quetzalcoatl.

OPPOSITE: The panel of glyphs known as "Stela 31, Tikal" describes a historical event that dates to January 16, AD 378, seven years before the final Nephite-Lamanite battle at Cumorah. Several names are recorded on the Stela, including Yax Nuun Ayiin (First Crocodile), who was king over the region at the same time that Mormon wrote an epistle to the Lamanite king. Some evidence suggests that First Crocodile is associated with the name Laman. The photo is taken from a replica of Stela 31 located in the Teotihuacan Room of the National Museum of Anthropology in Mexico City. The original stela is located at a small museum at the archaeological zone of Tikal, Guatemala. (Photo courtesy of Richard Norman)

Regarding this occasion, Blake, later in life, commented that his experience as a young boy in wandering daily through that huge museum on pre-Columbian history—while his father was spending time in the archives—impacted his life and love for the ancient history of Mesoamerica in relation to the Book of Mormon. In speaking of this time period, Joseph recorded the following in the first edition of *Exploring the Lands of the Book of Mormon*:

> While I was conducting research, I took the opportunity to visit with the curator of that marvelous museum. On one occasion, I asked her if she would read the prophecies of Samuel the Lamanite as he foretold the signs of both the birth and the death of Christ (see Helaman 14). I also pointed out the precise dates of the fulfillment of those prophecies as recorded in the Book of Mormon (see 3 Nephi 8:5; 11:1–10). I then asked her if she saw any similarity between Christ and Quetzalcoatl. She subtly informed me that she was not of my faith. She then posed two questions that have remained a guideline for me from that time forth:
>
> 1. Did Quetzalcoatl and Christ live in the same area?
> 2. Did Quetzalcoatl and Christ live during the same time period?

The latter question is the one to which we will respond in this chapter, as it relates directly to our understanding of the historicity of the Book of Mormon. To develop a format for reliable Book of Mormon correlations with other cultures, we must be aware of the time periods in which the other cultures were in existence. Nevertheless, dates are very elusive and allow for a great degree of flexibility. For example, we are all aware of a 1492 date that is attached to the discovery of America by Columbus. We learn in school that in 1620, the first Pilgrims arrived at Plymouth Rock. The beginning date of the Spanish conquest is 1519. In Latter-day Saint history, the Church was organized on April 6, 1830.

The difference between 1492 and 1830 is 338 years, yet both dates reflect the beginning of a new culture in the Americas. We run into the same problem as we attempt to correlate Book of Mormon dates with secular dates of Mesoamerica, the latter being derived from the Spanish chronicles, archaeological radiocarbon dating, or calendar dating as recorded on stone monuments.

Many times, the dates are peculiar in nature, just as the 1830 date mentioned above is peculiar to Latter-day Saints. Other dates are universal—such as the flood and the coming of Christ. Still others are nationalistic—such as wars and local destructions.

Any serious student of Book of Mormon history should become acquainted with the accepted scientific dates of a particular people before attempting to make a correlation with any particular event in the Book of Mormon. Many tourists have stepped off a cruise ship in the Caribbean and, after visiting the Postclassic (AD 1200–1500) site of

Any serious student of Book of Mormon history should become acquainted with the accepted scientific dates of a particular people before attempting to make a correlation with any particular event in the Book of Mormon.

Tulum, have returned with the feeling they have just seen a Nephite city. Without our taking into consideration its location or the type of activities that took place there, the simple fact that Tulum did not exist as a city center until eight hundred years after the close of the Book of Mormon, regardless of its honeymoon setting, negates it as a potential candidate for its being a Nephite city based on what we see as we view its ruins.

A major key to understanding Book of Mormon geography and history is to understand the time period in which the events took place. On our tours, we always feel a measure of success in talking about Mesoamerica when a tour member asks, "What is the time period of this site, and when were these buildings built?"

With this introduction, we will proceed to present time charts that show some of the major archaeological sites with their respective occupation dates. Before doing that, however, we wish to plant in your mind the terms that are often used by Mesoamerica scholars. This terminology was originally assigned to the Maya but has now come to include all the Preclassic, Classic, and Postclassic cultures of Mesoamerica.

Most of the Book of Mormon history took place in the Preclassic Period, and yet most of the archaeological sites that have been restored fall in the Classic Period. The following table illustrates archaeological time zones in which the Book of Mormon history falls.

Early Preclassic	2600 BC–1500 BC	Early Jaredite time period
Middle Preclassic	1500 BC–600 BC	Middle Jaredite time period
Late Preclassic	600 BC–AD 250	Late Jaredite and Nephite time period

> A major key to understanding Book of Mormon geography and history is to understand the time period in which the events took place.

Early Classic	AD 250–AD 600	Nephite apostasy and post–Nephite time period
Late Classic	AD 600–AD 900	Post–Book of Mormon
Postclassic	AD 900–AD 1500	Post–Book of Mormon

Sometimes members of The Church of Jesus Christ of Latter-day Saints have a difficult time understanding that the Lamanite society actually increased in population and built more buildings after the downfall of the Nephite nation. Yet that is exactly what happened.

Sometimes members of The Church of Jesus Christ of Latter-day Saints have a difficult time understanding that the Lamanite society actually increased in population and built more buildings after the downfall of the Nephite nation. Yet that is exactly what happened. The latter part of the book of 4 Nephi puts it in perspective when it outlines the events that produced a massive building program. In Mesoamerica (or Maya) terminology, the events recorded in 4 Nephi 1:24–49, dating from AD 201 to AD 320, are actually outlining the Maya Classic Period. We call it the great Nephite apostasy period. (Coincidentally, it corresponds to the great apostasy time period of the Old World. In other words, Satan was simultaneously working to spread his influence and build his kingdom on both sides of the ocean.)

Take a few minutes to study the time charts in Figures 3–2, 3–3, and 3–4 that follow. You will notice that several of the Olmec sites fall in the Jaredite time period. You will also observe that some sites dating to the Nephite time period were already in existence when Lehi arrived at the New World and that some continued to exist after the close of the Nephite history. And you will note that a number of the most popular sites were not built until after the close of the Book of Mormon record.

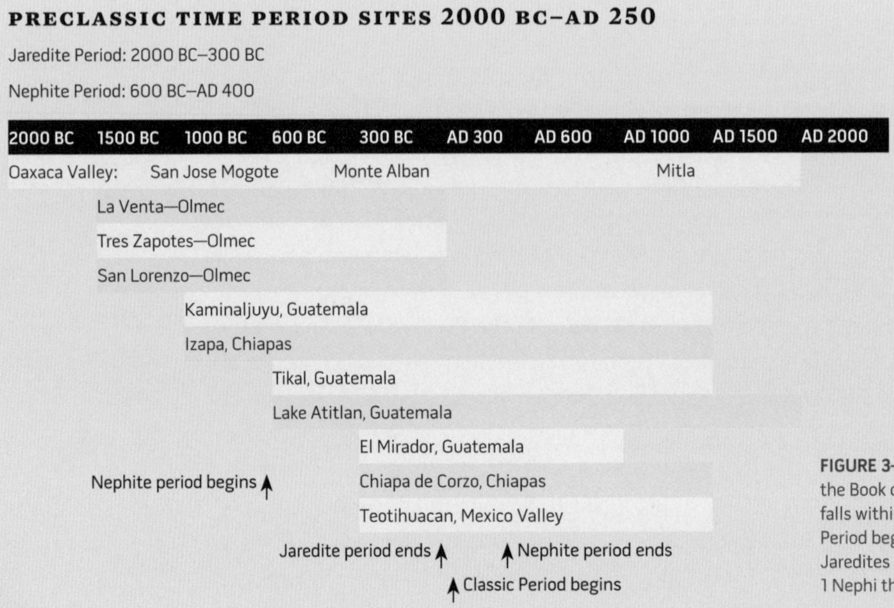
PRECLASSIC TIME PERIOD SITES 2000 BC–AD 250
Jaredite Period: 2000 BC–300 BC
Nephite Period: 600 BC–AD 400
2000 BC
1500 BC
1000 BC
600 BC
300 BC
AD 300
AD 600
AD 1000
AD 1500
AD 2000
Oaxaca Valley:
San Jose Mogote
Monte Alban
Mitla
La Venta—Olmec
Tres Zapotes—Olmec
San Lorenzo—Olmec
Kaminaljuyu, Guatemala
Izapa, Chiapas
Tikal, Guatemala
Lake Atitlan, Guatemala
El Mirador, Guatemala
Nephite period begins
Chiapa de Corzo, Chiapas
Teotihuacan, Mexico Valley
Jaredite period ends
Nephite period ends
Classic Period begins

FIGURE 3–2: The majority of the Book of Mormon record falls within the Preclassic Period beginning with the Jaredites and also including 1 Nephi through 3 Nephi.

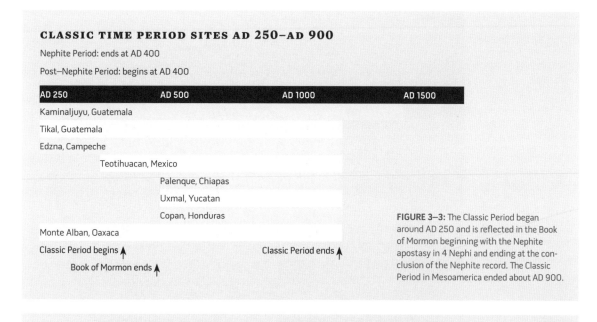

CLASSIC TIME PERIOD SITES AD 250–AD 900

Nephite Period: ends at AD 400

Post–Nephite Period: begins at AD 400

AD 250	AD 500	AD 1000	AD 1500

Kaminaljuyu, Guatemala

Tikal, Guatemala

Edzna, Campeche

Teotihuacan, Mexico

Palenque, Chiapas

Uxmal, Yucatan

Copan, Honduras

Monte Alban, Oaxaca

Classic Period begins ⬆

Book of Mormon ends ⬆

Classic Period ends ⬆

FIGURE 3–3: The Classic Period began around AD 250 and is reflected in the Book of Mormon beginning with the Nephite apostasy in 4 Nephi and ending at the conclusion of the Nephite record. The Classic Period in Mesoamerica ended about AD 900.

POSTCLASSIC TIME PERIOD SITES AD 900–AD 1500

Post–Book of Mormon

AD 900	AD 1200	AD 1500	AD 2000

Chichen Itza, Yucatan

Tulum, Quintana Roo

Mitla, Oaxaca

Tenochtitlan, Mexico

Tula, Hidalgo

FIGURE 3–4: The Postclassic Period occurred well after the close of the Book of Mormon and is signaled in Mesoamerica by a decline in building construction as well as the abandonment of many Maya cities. Some of the most popular and highly visited archeological sites fall within this time frame.

THE MESOAMERICAN DATING SYSTEM

We can appeal to the Mesoamerica calendar system to see if it can aid us in understanding more precisely some of the Book of Mormon dates. However, before we get into specific dating comparisons, we will outline some of the basic principles of the Mesoamerica calendar system.

Most people are familiar with the Aztec calendar stone, a massive stone weighing about twenty-five tons that was knocked down and covered up with debris during the 1519–1521 conquest of Mexico by the Spaniards. It remained hidden for over two hundred years. Since its discovery, it has played a significant role in the tradition and culture of Mexico. Today, this stone is situated in the Aztec Room of the National Museum of Anthropology in Mexico City.

The Aztecs, however, were latecomers. Their history did not even begin until about AD 1325 when, according to instructions by their prophet, Huitzilopochtli, they built their city on the spot where an eagle was standing on a cactus with a serpent in its mouth. The cactus was in the middle of a lake, and, as a result, Mexico City (Tenochtitlan) was literally built on a shallow lake bed.

The calendar used by the Aztecs was adopted from the Maya but lacked some of the finer details that were prevalent in the Maya calendar. For example, because the Maya calendar was actually based on two calendars, the religious (Totolamatl) and the secular (Haab), it was structured in such a way that every fifty-two years it began anew. The Aztec calendar lacked the structure to enable a continued calculation. Therefore, it became difficult to tell one fifty-two-year time period from another. That fifty-two-year cycle is called a calendar round, and its continued, completed cycle traditionally suggests the beginning of a new dawn. One of the cycle dates, as outlined in the Aztec calendar, fell on the year 1519 when Cortez entered into the Mexico valley and initiated the Spanish conquest. Some historians have suggested that it was a bad omen for Montezuma. The year 2012 is a significant date in the Maya calendar. The next fifty-two-year cycle falls in the year 2039. The last two have been 1935 and 1987.

Because the Aztec calendar was adopted from the Maya and because the Maya Preclassic Period correlates with the time period in which the Book of Mormon was written, an understanding of the Maya dating system may help us in understanding the Book of Mormon. In fact, it was the people of the Preclassic era, or Book of Mormon time period, who first introduced the concept of a calendar system. Mormon keeps us abreast of the time line, as he literally marked the calendar from year to year, such as "in the commencement of the twentieth year of the reign of the judges" (Alma 50:1) or "in the twenty and sixth year of the reign of the judges over the people of Nephi, behold, when the Lamanites awoke on the first morning of the first month, behold, they found Amalickiah was dead in his own tent" (Alma 52:1), or, using the birth of Christ as a base date, "in the thirty and fourth year, in the first month, on the fourth day of the month, there arose a great storm" (3 Nephi 8:5).

Just as the Nephites used an original base system correlated with the number of years from the time Lehi left Jerusalem and just as today we base our dating system on the birth of the Savior, the Maya used a base system that, when correlated with our calendar, dates to August 13, 3114 BC. We do not know to what event, if any, the 3114 BC date is attached. However, the date apparently is associated with some great event, such as the Flood or the Tower of Babel.

The counting system of the Maya is basically built on multiples of twenties, whereas our counting system is based on multiples of tens. The following chart illustrates the counting procedure.

Our System	Maya System	Comments
1 Day = (24 hours)	1 Kin = (24 hours) (day)	Kin = Sun
30 Days = 1 Month	20 Kin = 1 Uinal (month)	Uinal = Man
12 Months = 1 Year	18 Uinals = 1 Tun (year)	Tun = Stone
10 Years = 1 Decade	20 Tuns (years) = 1 Katun	20 Tuns (years)
100 Years = 1 Century	20 Katuns = 1 Baktun	400 Tuns (years)
1,000 years = 1 Millennium	20 Baktuns = 1 Pictun	8,000 Tuns (years)
	20 Pictuns = 1 Calabtun	160,000 Tuns (years)
	20 Calabtuns = 1 Kinchiltun	3,200,000 Years

The use of a "tun" marked the passing of each year. Mormon, who lived in the Early Classic Period, appears to have used this same pattern: "And thus did pass away the ninety and sixth year; and also the ninety and seventh year; and also the ninety and eighth year; and also the ninety and ninth year; And also an hundred years had passed away since the days of Mosiah, who was king over the people of the Nephites" (3 Nephi 2:4–5). The Book of Mormon language here almost reaches out and grabs us to remind us that Mormon is a Maya.

An understanding of the Maya dating system may help us in understanding the Book of Mormon. In fact, it was the people of the Preclassic era, or Book of Mormon time period, who first introduced the concept of a calendar system.

Year (Tun). Our year consists of 365 days, with a leap year of 366 days every four years. Our calendar has twelve months, with thirty or thirty-one days in each month, with the exception of February. The Maya year consisted of 360 days. There were eighteen months with twenty days in each month (18 x 20 = 360). The Maya subsequently added another month called *Uayeb*, which contained only five days. Hence, 18 x 20 + 5 = 365 days. We repeat, the word *tun* means *stone* in the Maya language. Every year a stone marker would be erected or engraved to reflect the passing of another year; hence, the word *tun* is used to represent one year. As mentioned above, we even get a hint of this type of yearly marking from Mormon's writings.

Month (Uinal). The name *uinal* comes from *uinic*, which means man and which may be associated with the twenty fingers and toes, as there are twenty days in each month. Regarding the Mesoamerica calendar system, Edmonson writes: "Perhaps the most remarkable of these features is its unity. Not only did it have a single origin, but despite its employment by nearly 100 ethnic groups speaking almost as many different languages, it has retained this unity over a period of 2,600 years. This is not just a matter of pattern similarity but of precise mathematical accuracy in the measurement of time and it is an astonishing civilizational achievement on a world scale."[1]

1. Munro Edmonson, *The Book of the Year: Middle American Calendrical Systems* (Salt Lake City: University of Utah Press, 1988), 5.

The names of the nineteen months in the Maya language are Pop, Uo, Zip, Zotz, Tzec, Xul, Yaxkin, Mol, Ch'en, Yax, Zac, Ceh, Mac, Kankin, Muan, Pax, Kayab, Kumku, and Uayeb. Figure 3–6 shows the Maya glyphs for these months.

FIGURE 3–6: Hieroglyphic drawings for the nineteen months of the Maya year.

Day (Kin). The word for *day* in the Maya language is *Kin*, which means Sun. The Classic Maya month consisted of twenty days, each with a different name. The twenty named days of the Aztec calendar, or the people of Anahuac, are (1) Alligator, (2) Wind, (3) House, (4) Iguana, (5) Serpent, (6) Death, (7) Deer, (8) Rabbit, (9) Water, (10) Dog, (11) Monkey, (12) Grass, (13) Cane, (14) Jaguar, (15) Eagle, (16) Buzzard, (17) Quake, (18) Flint, (19) Rain, and (20) Flower.[2] Figure 3–7 shows the Maya glyphs for these days.

2. See Edmonson, *The Book of the Year: Middle American Calendrical Systems*, 15, for more details.

Numerical Symbols. The numbering system of the Maya is quite similar to the Roman numerals, except the Maya ends with the number twenty, it being zero. The Maya utilized a system of bars and dots counting to twenty. With this method, they could utilize the above symbols at the beginning of a Baktun, Katun, Tun, and so forth. For example, figure 3–8 shows the Maya system of counting from one to nineteen, as well as their use of zero.

Exploring the Lands of the Book of Mormon

FIGURE 3–7: Hieroglyphic drawings for the twenty day names, or kins, in the Maya language.

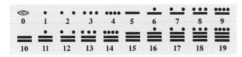

FIGURE 3–8: Maya hieroglyphic counting symbols.

Interestingly, a date was discovered in the 1960s by the New World Archaeological Foundation, an organization sponsored by The Church of Jesus Christ of Latter-day Saints, at the Maya site of Chiapa de Corzo in the Mexican state of Chiapas. It represents the oldest long count (Baktun, Katun, Tun, Uinal, Kin) date that had yet been discovered in Mesoamerica. That date corresponds to the early part of December 36 BC[3] and falls in the time period recorded in Helaman 4. It corresponds to the seventh Baktun and is transcribed in our numbering system as 7.16.3.2.13, which means 7 Baktun, 16 Katun, 3 Tun, 2 Uinal, and 13 Kin. By adding all these numbers together (that is, 1,008,000 days [7 Baktun], + 115,200 days [16 Katun], + 1,080 days [3 Tun], + 40 days [2 Uinal]) + 13 days [13 Kin], we arrive at 1,124,333 days. We will now compute the numbers as follows to arrive at the 36 BC date:

3. Michael D. Coe, *The Maya*, 4th ed. (London: Thames and Hudson, 1987), 50.

1,124,333 divided by 365.25 (number of days in year) = 3078.25 years.
Subtract 3078.25 from the Maya base year of 3114 BC = 35.74 or 36 BC.

FIGURE 3–9: This chart of Maya hieroglyphs, reproduced by artist Cliff Dunston, illustrates the finite detail of the Classic Period Maya scribes. These symbols were used to mark the passage of time by the Maya.

7 Baktun   1,008,000 days (7 x 144,000)

16 Katun   115,200 days (16 x 7200)

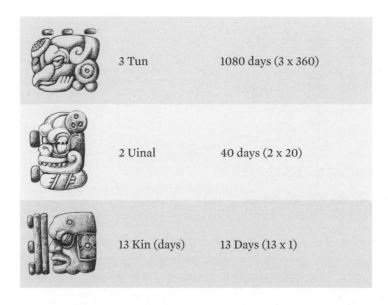

3 Tun	1080 days (3 x 360)	
2 Uinal	40 days (2 x 20)	
13 Kin (days)	13 Days (13 x 1)	

It was possible for the Maya to arrive at the precise date, which now can be associated with our calendar. The twenty day names and the eighteen month names were much like our weekdays. That is, they continued in rotation forever. It was necessary, therefore, to place numbers in front of each day name and each month day. For example, we call the first day of the week Sunday. We have fifty-two Sundays in each year—or 520 Sundays over a ten-year period. Without our month names (January, February, and so forth) accompanied with the dates 1, 2, 3 and the years 2006, 2007, and so forth, we would be lost as to the specific Sunday to which we are referring.

The Maya calendar, although extremely accurate, was not as functional as our calendar dating is today. It was necessary, therefore, to number both the day symbols and the month symbols and then to correlate them with the Baktuns, Katuns, and so forth described above.

You will see in the literature a date that reads 6 Ben and 16 Xul. This date means that on the sixth calendar rotation of the day Ben (Reed) with the sixteenth calendar rotation of the month Xul (pronounced Shule, which is the name of a Jaredite king), and in association with the above calculations, an event happened. For example, the date of 7.16.3.2.13–6 Ben 16 Xul corresponds, according to our calculations, with December 11, 36 BC.[4]

Sample Date Correlations. Some dates that have been discovered on the stela of Mesoamerica, as they correspond with our dates, are as follows.[5]

4. A number of books are available on the Maya dating system. Sylvanus Morley, the father archaeologist of Chichen Itza and the Yucatan, published a book in 1915 called *An Introduction to the Study of Maya Hieroglyphs*. Eric Thompson, the noted Maya scholar, wrote an introduction and a bibliography for the same book, which was republished in 1975. Today, a number of computer programs are sold to translate the Maya dates into our calendar dates.

5. See Edmunson, *The Book of the Year: Middle American Calendrical Systems*. Numerous other books are also available about deciphering of the Maya calendar system.

MAYA DATE		LOCATION	OUR DATE	EVENT
0.0.0.0.0	4 Ahau 8 Cumku	Base date	13 Aug 3114 BC	Perhaps the date of the Flood
6.3.10.9.0	2 Ahau 3 Ceh	Cuicuilco, Mexico	679 BC	A probable Olmec/Jaredite date
6.7.16.2.9	8 Muluc 7 Uo	Monte Alban, Oaxaca	594 BC	A possible Mulekite date
6.9.8.2.0	1 Ahau 3 Ceh	Monte Alban, Stela 13	563 BC	A possible Mulekite date
7.7.7.8.14	12 Ix 2 Uo	Monte Alban, Mound J	209 BC	A conquest date, perhaps Mosiah
7.10.10.8.2	8 Ik 0 Zotz	Kaminaljuyu, Altar 10	147 BC	Possible Noah/Limhi kingship transfer
BAKTUN 7				
7.16.3.2.13	6 Ben 16 Xul	Chiapa de Corzo	11 Dec 36 BC	Lamanites capture Zarahemla
7.16.6.16.18	6 Eznab 1 Uo	Stela C, Tres Zapotes	1 Sep 32 BC	Olmec date after destruction
7.19.15.7.12	12 Eb 0 Ceh	Abaj Takalik, Stela 2	AD 2 Mar 37	Time of Christ
BAKTUN 8				
8.12.14.8.15	13 Men 3 Zip	Tikal	AD 6 Jul 292	East wilderness Zarahemla
8.14.3.1.12	1 Eb 0 Yaxkin	Tikal	AD 15 Sep 320	East wilderness Zarahemla
8.14.10.13.15	8 Men 8 Kayab	---	AD 9 Apr 328	Mormon was about 17 years old
8.17.2.16.17	5 Kaban 10 Yaxk'in	Tikal, Stela 31	AD 12 Sep 379	Ascension of Yax Nuun Ayiin
BAKTUN 9				
9.0.0.0.0	8 Ahau 13 Ceh		AD 9 Dec 435	Post—Book of Mormon. Maya Classic
9.2.10.0.0	3 Ahau 8 Cumku		AD 21 Mar 485	Post—Book of Mormon. Maya Classic
9.3.0.0.0	2 Ahau 18 Muan		AD 28 Jan 495	Post—Book of Mormon. Maya Classic
9.12.6.5.8	3 Lamat 6 Zac		AD 14 Sep 678	Post—Book of Mormon. Maya Classic
BAKTUN 10				
10.0.5.0.0	13 Ahau 13 Uo		AD 15 Feb 835	Early Postclassic
10.3.0.0.0	1 Ahau 3 Yaxkin		AD 2 May 889	Early Postclassic
10.4.0.0.0	12 Ahau 3 Uo		AD 19 Jan 909	Early Postclassic
10.5.0.0.0	20 Ahau 8 Muan		AD 5 Oct 928	Early Postclassic
BAKTUN 11				
11.13.12.4.4	3 Kan 7 Zotz		AD 12 Oct 1492	Columbus discovered America
11.16.0.0.0	13 Ahau 8 Xul		AD 12 Nov 1539	Spanish occupation

We will now return to a discussion of some of the major dates in the Book of Mormon and analyze their correlations with dates in Mesoamerica.

3114 BC—THE GREAT FLOOD

In Genesis, we read, "And the flood was forty days upon the earth; and the waters increased, and bare up the ark, and it was lift up above the earth" (Genesis 7:17). Virtually every ancient culture records the tradition of a great flood. This is also true in Mesoamerica, as the Spanish chronicles speak freely of the event.

Ixtlilxochitl, a sixteenth-century writer in Mexico, states, "And it is recorded in the Tulteca history that this period or first world, as they called it, lasted for 1,716 years, after which time great lightning and storms from the heavens destroyed mankind, and everything in the earth was covered by water including the highest mountain called Caxtolmolictli, which is 15 cubits high."[6]

6. Ixtlilxochitl:4; see chapter 11, "Fernando de Alva Ixtlilxochitl."

Moroni wrote the following, which has a similar style to the writings of Ixtlilxochitl: "And as I suppose that the first part of this record, which speaks concerning the creation of the world, and also of Adam, and an account from that time even to the great tower, and whatsoever things transpired among the children of men until that time, is had among the Jews—Therefore I do not write those things which transpired from the days of Adam until that time" (Ether 1:3–4).

In the context of biblical history, scholars have a difficult time determining the actual date of the Flood. Ten generations are mentioned in the Bible from Adam to Noah, and ten generations are also mentioned in the Bible from Noah to Abraham. Further, the life span recorded in years prior to the Flood is much longer than those recorded after the Flood. The traditional flood date of 2350 BC appears much too late when compared with the total biblical history and the accounts of the Flood from other nations.

If we can assume that the Maya calendar base date of 3114 BC is not just a date in limbo but is actually tied into a significant event in history, we can then work with various options. Other than the Flood, the 3114 BC date could be associated with the date of the great tower, the arrival of the first settlers (Jaredites) to Mesoamerica, or even an earlier event. However, the 3114 BC date appears too early to be associated with either the tower or the arrival of the Jaredites in the New World.

For purposes of this chapter, we will place the 3114 BC date as representative of the Flood from both a Mesoamerica and a Book of Mormon perspective. It is difficult to reconcile the 2350 BC flood date, which scholars derive from the Bible, with archaeological reports or with Book of Mormon and Mesoamerican histories. In the future, perhaps this dilemma may be solved.

This placement of 3114 BC is in line with other cultures and their dating of the great deluge. For example, when we combine both Mesopotamian and Hindu views, a date of 3102 BC is established, a date very close to the 3114 BC Maya calendar base date.[7]

If we can assume that the Maya calendar base date of 3114 BC is not just a date in limbo but is actually tied into a significant event in history, we can then work with various options.

7. See SEHA Newsletter, March 1975, p. 3.

Exploring the Lands of the Book of Mormon

2600 BC—THE ARRIVAL OF THE JAREDITES/FIRST SETTLERS TO THE NEW WORLD

The date of the arrival of the Jaredites is based upon (1) the dating of the great tower (Tower of Babel) and (2) the archaeological and traditional evidence coming out of Mesoamerica in relationship to the first settlers.

From the information available to us in the writings of Ixtlilxochitl, we learn that 416 years elapsed from the time of the Flood until the confusion at Babel. The first settlers arrived in Mesoamerica 520 years later at a place along the Gulf of Mexico called Huehue Tlapallan.[8] This time period places the date of the arrival of the Jaredites at 2693 BC. Therefore, the date of 2600 BC is fairly consistent with both the early settlement patterns in Mesoamerica as well as with the Old World dating of the tower.

Traditional statements place the dating of the Jaredites at about 2200 BC. However, because no dates appear in the Book of Mormon regarding the arrival date of the Jaredites, we are left to choose between the archaeological dates of the Old World and the Spanish chronicles dates of the New World.

In this chapter, we use the date of 2600 BC as the date of the arrival of the Jaredites. This date causes the Tower of Babel dating to be prior to that. Ixtlilxochitl said that the first settlers, who came from the great tower at the time of the confusion of languages, wandered for 104 years before they settled at Huehue Tlapallan.[9]

The Bible, the Book of Mormon, and the Spanish chronicles all speak of the great tower. The Book of Mormon records the history of the people we call Jaredites as coming from the tower at the time of the confusion of tongues. The sixteenth-century writer Ixtlilxochitl is also definite in his account of the first settlers coming from the tower, preserving their language, and traveling great distances until they came to a good and fertile land. Mesoamerica archaeology affirms these events. (See chapter 5, "The Olmec [Jaredite] Culture.")

2600 BC–1500 BC—EARLY PRECLASSIC MESOAMERICAN SETTLEMENTS/EARLY JAREDITE PERIOD

If the Jaredites arrived in Mesoamerica around 2600 BC, then we can expect to see the beginnings of legitimate civilization centers around that time. Early settlement patterns along the Gulf of Mexico and in Oaxaca support that expectation. For example, the archaeological site of San Jose Mogote, located north of the city of Oaxaca, is an Early Preclassic settlement. Dr. Ignacio Bernal has proposed a relationship with the adobe bricks used in the construction and on display at the small museum at San Jose Mogote as having the same characteristics as "far-off Mesopotamia." In other words, the adobes seem to have the same architectural style as those discovered at the area of the Tower of Babel from whence the first settlers came.

8. Ixtlilxochitl:9; see chapter 11, "Fernando de Alva Ixtlilxochitl."

9. Ixtlilxochitl:9; see chapter 11, "Fernando de Alva Ixtlilxochitl."

The Bible, the Book of Mormon, and the Spanish chronicles all speak of the great tower.

1500 BC–600 BC—MIDDLE PRECLASSIC

10. Dating at National Museum of Anthropology, Mexico City.

The archaeological sites of San Lorenzo, La Venta, and Tres Zapotes in Veracruz, Mexico, tell the story of the Classic Period of the Olmecs. This period lasted roughly until 600 BC, when their civilization began to decline.[10]

By conducting a generation count in the book of Ether, we are justified in saying that events stated in Ether 10 correspond to the early part of the above date, probably in the 1300–1000 BC time period, the same time that Moses was leading the children of Israel out of Egypt and the time when the kingdom of Israel was established in ancient Mount Moriah, now present-day Jerusalem. Portions of Ether 10 state: "And they were exceedingly industrious. . . . And they did work in all manner of ore. . . . And they did have silks, and fine-twined linen. . . . And they did make all manner of tools. . . . And they did make all manner of weapons. . . . And never could be a people more blessed than were they" (Ether 10:22–28). In recent years, we have been able to become even more precise in some Jaredite dating. For example, the name of a Jaredite king named Kish, or Ki'x in the Maya language, has been discovered on the tablet of the Temple of the Cross at Palenque. The identifying glyph places the birth of Kish at March 8, 993 BC.[11]

11. To read an article about Kish, see Bruce W. Warren, "Jaredite King Name Discovered," *Explorations in the Book of Mormon* (Orem, UT: The Mesoamerica Project, 2000), 1:9–13.

600 BC–250 BC—JAREDITE AND OLMEC DESTRUCTION

No dates are given in the Book of Mormon pinpointing the destruction of the Jaredites. Mormon tradition places the date of the destruction fairly close to 600 BC. This dating probably comes about because of the scripture in Ether 11:21, which states that "the Lord God would send or bring forth another people to possess the land" (Ether 11:21).

However, we know that the Jaredites could not have been destroyed prior to 586 BC because that is when Jerusalem was destroyed and because Mulek did not come to America prior to that destruction.

The name of a Jaredite king named Kish, or Ki'x in the Maya language, has been discovered on the tablet of the Temple of the Cross at Palenque.

We are also inclined to move further away from the 586 BC date and closer to the 250 BC date for the following reasons:

1. The Mulekites first landed in the land northward, the place where the Jaredites lived (see Alma 22:30). A certain period of time was required for the people of Zarahemla, Zarahemla himself being a descendant of Mulek, to migrate to the land southward where Mosiah discovered them (see Omni 1:13–16).

2. Zarahemla's being a descendant of Mulek suggests that more than one generation had elapsed from the time of Mulek to Zarahemla (see Mosiah 25:2).

3. When Mosiah discovered the people of Zarahemla, they had become exceedingly numerous, they had fought many wars, and their language had become corrupt. We can expect that several generations had transpired for those events to occur (see Omni 1:17).

4. When the 121 BC Limhi expedition discovered the twenty-four gold plates that contained the history of the fallen Jaredites, they also reported that they saw ruins of buildings, *bones,* and *swords that had rusted* (see Mosiah 8:8–11). We know that the

Jaredites lived near the seashore and that their last battle was also near the seashore (see Ether 9:3). If the Jaredites were destroyed in a sea-level climate and if the Jaredite destruction was anywhere near 600 BC, certainly no evidence of bones or swords would have remained in 121 BC when the Limhi expedition discovered the Jaredite records.

The Mesoamerica records are a little more clear in terms of dating the last battle of the first settlers to Mesoamerica. We propose that the pre-Olmecs and the Olmecs of 2600 BC to 300 BC were the Jaredites (see chapter 5, "The Olmec [Jaredite] Culture"). If this is the case, then the destruction of the Olmecs (Jaredites), as determined by radiocarbon dating, is between 400 and 300 BC.[12] A publication written by Edmonson records an alternative date for Stela 13 at Monte Alban, a proposed captivity date, between 282 and 216 BC.[13] The date of the Jaredite destruction may be close to these dates.

Ixtlilxochitl records the destruction of the "giants" (Jaredites) at 240 BC. He was so precise in his dating of the destruction at the time of Christ, from which the 240 BC date is taken, that his dating lends credibility to the date of the destruction of the giants (Jaredites).[14]

In *Exploring the Lands of the Book of Mormon*, we will place the destruction of the Jaredites at 250 BC.

Besides the Jaredites, we know from the Book of Mormon that two other groups of people migrated to the New World—the Nephites and the Mulekites. From the Book of Mormon, the dates of these peoples and the lands of their inheritance are clearly identified. In any study of possible lands of the Book of Mormon, we must find comparable dates and locations of people who could have been the Nephites and Mulekites. In other words, to identify possible Nephite and Mulekite locations, we must understand the historical setting of the Book of Mormon.

12. See Michael D. Coe, *Mexico* (New York: Frederick A. Praeger Publishers, 1962), 90.

13. Edmonson, *The Book of the Year: Middle American Calendrical Systems*, 100–1, 117.

14. Ixtlilxochitl:18; see chapter 11, "Fernando de Alva Ixtlilxochitl."

Ixtlilxochitl records the destruction of the "giants" (Jaredites) at 240 BC.

NEPHITE DEPARTURE FROM JERUSALEM AND THE BIRTH OF CHRIST

In 1 Nephi 1:4, we are informed that Lehi lived in Jerusalem when Zedekiah was placed on the throne as king of Judah. In 1 Nephi 2:2, we read that Lehi was commanded by the Lord to take his family and depart into the wilderness.

We, therefore, assume that Lehi and his family left Jerusalem in the first year of the reign of King Zedekiah or shortly thereafter. Josiah, Judah's most righteous king, had ruled Judah for thirty-one years from 641–610 BC. Josiah had initiated a religious reform movement in the kingdom of Judah where Lehi lived with his family. Josiah was killed in a conflict with the Egyptian pharoah Necho, who was marching to join forces with Assyria after the Assyrian capital, Nineveh, had fallen to the Babylonians.[15]

From the death of Josiah, at 609 BC, until the first year of the reign of Mattaniah/Zedekiah, or Zedekiah III, at 597 BC, the kingdom of Judah was battered back and forth between Egypt and Babylon; and a heavy tax was imposed upon the people of Judah.

15. David Alexander and Pat Alexander, eds., *Eerdmans' Handbook to the Bible* (Grand Rapids, MI: William B. Eerdmans, 1974), 182–83; see also 2 Kings 23–24, 2 Chronicles 36, and Jeremiah 37–39.

Jehoahaz, the son of Josiah, became the king of Judah at the age of twenty-three upon the death of his father. Jehoahaz was an evil king who ruled only three months. He was taken captive by Pharoah Necho and died in Egypt.

ZEDEKIAH—A TITLE

We propose that the word *Zedekiah* became a title used by the Babylonians to designate the Jewish kings after Babylon gained control of Jerusalem a few years prior to Lehi's departure. We will refer to three Jewish kings of this time period as Zedekiah I, Zedekiah II, and Zedekiah III, with the following corresponding original names and dates:

Jewish King	Original Name	Began	Reference
Zedekiah I	Jehoiakim	609 BC	2 Kings 23:30–36
Zedekiah II	Jehoiachin	598 BC	2 Kings 34:1–6
Zedekiah III	Mattaniah	597 BC	2 Kings 24:12–18

Another son of Josiah, Jehoiakim/Zedekiah (Jeremiah 27:3), whom we will refer to as Zedekiah I, then began his rule in 609 BC at the age of twenty-five. He ruled for eleven years. He subjected the people first to the Egyptians and then to the Babylonians and then again to the Egyptians. This last act brought attacks from the Babylonians and repeated warnings from the prophet Jeremiah, a contemporary of the prophet Lehi. Zedekiah I began his reign as a puppet of Egypt and ended in servitude to the Babylonians.

Although this concept has not yet gained popularity among the Latter-day Saint scholarly community, we contend that it was Zedekiah I who began ruling at 609 BC (see 2 Kings 23:30–36), an event that Nephi was referring to when he wrote "the first year of the reign of Zedekiah, my father Lehi, having dwelt in Jerusalem in all his days" (1 Nephi 1:4). Nephi says further that "many prophets," including Lehi, prophesied to the people that they must repent or the great city of Jerusalem would be destroyed and that "many should be carried away captive into Babylon" (1 Nephi 1:4, 13). If Jehoiakim (Zedekiah I) is the king referred to by Nephi in 1 Nephi 1:4, then the footnote at the bottom of page one of the Book of Mormon should be 609 BC instead of 600 BC. The scripture refers to the first year of Zedekiah—*not* the departure of Lehi.

In a spirit of redundancy, if the above verses correspond to Zedekiah/Mattaniah, whom we refer to as Zedekiah III, there would be no need for Lehi or the other prophets to prophesy of the destruction of Jerusalem. By 597, the first year of Zedekiah III's reign, the first wave of destruction had already occurred (see 2 Kings 24:5–15).

Early in 597 BC, Jehoiachin, or Zedekiah II, the son of Zedekiah I, was placed on the throne and ruled for only three months, after which he also was removed from the throne by Nebuchadnezzar and taken captive to Babylon. Jehoiachin was eighteen

The word Zedekiah *became a title used by the Babylonians to designate the Jewish kings after Babylon gained control of Jerusalem.*

years old at the time. Along with the king and his mother and the treasury, "all the princes, and all the mighty men of valour" were deported to Babylon. Only the "poorest sort" remained at Jerusalem (2 Kings 24:14–15).

Lehi had left Jerusalem prior to the time that both Zedekiah II and Mattaniah, or Zedekiah III, ruled as kings of Jerusalem. Lehi left Jerusalem at 600 BC. Zedekiah II (Jehoiachin) and Zedekiah III (Mattaniah) did not become kings until 597 BC, three years after Lehi had left Jerusalem. With this type of turmoil going on at 597 BC in Jerusalem, we would expect Nephi to mention the turmoil in his account as opposed to mentioning Lehi's prophecies about it (1 Nephi 2:11). Laman and Lemuel, who were calling their father a "visionary man," desired to remain at Jerusalem and complained about leaving their gold and silver and precious things. However, if Laman and Lemuel had still been in Jerusalem at 597 BC when Zedekiah II and Zedekiah III were placed on the Jewish thrones, Laman and Lemuel would probably be grumbling in Babylon.

We believe there is enough evidence from the Old Testament, Babylonian records, Josephus, and the Book of Mormon to support the departure of Lehi at 600 BC instead of 597 BC as is traditionally supported. Furthermore, this thinking also validates the fact that Lehi's six-hundred-year prophecy of the birth of Christ (1 Nephi 10:4) was, in reality, six hundred years of 365.25 days per year.

THE BIRTH OF CHRIST

What about the date of the birth of Christ?

To extract six hundred years from the time Lehi left Jerusalem at 601/600 BC, we must place the birth of Christ at 1 BC/AD 1. Although many scholars have considered a 4 BC date a more accurate date for the birth of Christ, other scholars likewise feel comfortable with a 1 BC birth date. John Lefgren in his book *April Sixth* summarizes the birth of Christ as follows:

> In the search of the year of the death of Herod the Great and the pivotal point of Christ's birth, most scholars have identified the eclipse of the moon on the night of March 12–13, 4 BC (Julian calendar), as the eclipse referred to by Josephus. This, of course, implies that Christ was born no later than March 4 BC. Contrary to what some have assumed, the lunar eclipse of 4 BC is not conclusive evidence. W. E. Filmer has identified two other lunar eclipses visible from Jerusalem that could satisfy Josephus's account. One eclipse occurred on January 9, 1 BC (Julian calendar), and the other on December 29, 1 BC (Julian calendar). The second eclipse was visible when the moon rose over the eastern horizon of Jerusalem in the evening—a time when many people in Judea would have been awake to note the unusual phenomenon of a moon rising in eclipse. As early as the sixteenth century, Joseph Scaliger, the mastermind behind the Gregorian calendar reform

If Laman and Lemuel had still been in Jerusalem at 597 BC when Zedekiah II and Zedekiah III were placed on the Jewish thrones, Laman and Lemuel would probably be grumbling in Babylon.

16. John C. Lefgren, *April Sixth* (Salt Lake City: Deseret Book, 1980), 13.

17. John P. Pratt, "The Restoration of Priesthood Keys on Easter 1836; Part I: Dating the First Easter," *Ensign*, June 1985, 59–68.

and the Julian period used by astronomers, decisively maintained that the death of Herod the Great was connected with a 1 BC eclipse.[16]

John P. Pratt is also in agreement with Lefgren in placing the date of the birth of Christ at 1 BC.[17]

In summary, we propose the following. When Nebuchadnezzar changed the name of the 597 BC King Mattaniah to Zedekiah, the pattern had already been established when Nebuchadnezzar entered into Jerusalem in the year 605 BC. Further, the name *Zedekiah* apparently became a title, and Jehoiakim and Jehoiachin were also given the name or title of Zedekiah (see Jeremiah 27:3). After all, the Egyptians had changed Johoiakim's name from Eliakim eight years earlier when they were in control: "And the king of Egypt made Eliakim his brother king over Judah and Jerusalem, and turned his name to Jehoiakim. And Necho took Jehoahaz his brother, and carried him to Egypt" (2 Chronicles 36:4).

It may well be that Nebuchadnezzar created a kingship title called "Zedekiah" for all three of the Jewish kings who ruled while under the control of Babylon. This title may have been a political move to allow the Babylonians to control Judah peacefully.

The same pattern is followed for kingship rule in the New World. After the death of Nephi, who had been anointed king over his people, the succeeding kings were each called "Nephi." In other words, *Nephi* became a title: "Now Nephi began to be old, and he saw that he must soon die; wherefore, he anointed a man to be a king and a ruler over his people now, according to the reigns of the kings. . . . Wherefore, the people were desirous to retain in remembrance his name. And whoso should reign in his stead were called by the people, second Nephi, third Nephi, and so forth, according to the reigns of the kings; and thus they were called by the people, let them be of whatever name they would" (Jacob 1:9, 11).

Perhaps Nephi was setting up a kingdom in the New World patterned after what he saw in Jerusalem in the sixth century BC. A precedent had not been established in the New World, as Nephi was the people's first king. He left Jerusalem in 601/600 BC with his father. The tradition is not new, as in Egypt the ruler had been called *Pharoah*, a title that means "great house."

In summary, we prefer to date Lehi's departure from Jerusalem in the latter part of 601 or early part of 600 BC. This dating allows the proper time period to elapse (six hundred years) from Lehi's departure to the birth of Christ at 1 BC/AD 1, the meridian of time.

MULEKITE DEPARTURE AND ARRIVAL DATES

We often establish the departure date of the Mulekites from Jerusalem immediately following, or simultaneously with, the burning of Jerusalem at 586 BC. Some people speculate that Mulek was a young baby, or perhaps disguised as a daughter, which allowed him to escape the wrath of death instituted on each of the sons of Zedekiah/ Mattaniah by King Nebuchadnezzar. As stated earlier, it is possible that Mulek was not yet born. His mother may have been pregnant, or Mulek may have been born in captivity. Whatever the case, historical evidence supports the idea that Mulek was taken to the New World by his protectors and transported by the seafaring Phoenicians.

However, the Book of Mormon is silent on both the departure date from Jerusalem and the arrival date of the Mulekites to America. We first read about some of the descendants of the Mulekites, called the people of Zarahemla, in the book of Omni. The date of this encounter is probably between 200 BC and 180 BC when King Mosiah discovered the people of Zarahemla. Zarahemla reports to Mosiah that a Jaredite king by the name of Coriantumr had lived with Zarahemla's people for nine moons (see Omni 1:21).

Therefore, the two outside dates for the Mulekites are 586 BC (destruction of Jerusalem) and 180 BC (arrival of Mosiah at Zarahemla).

Bruce Warren, retired Brigham Young University archaeologist, pointed out to us that a Mesoamerica document date of 538 BC may be a possible date for the arrival of the Mulekites in Mesoamerica. This date suggests that Mulek may have been born after his father, Zedekiah III, was taken in bondage into Babylon. After all, Zedekiah III was only thirty-two years old when all his sons were killed by Nebuchadnezzar. This fact suggests that if Zedekiah III's oldest son was born when Zedekiah III was nineteen years old, all his sons, at that time, were under the age of thirteen. At any rate, as already stated, Mulek was either protected from death at the hand of Nebuchadnezzar at 586 BC or Mulek was born in captivity in Babylon.

If the latter is the case, then Mulek may not have left Jerusalem until after the Jews returned from Babylon. After serving many years in captivity, Zedekiah II (Jehoiachin), the grandson of Josiah, was released from the Babylonian prison and treated kindly by the new Babylonian king. Mulek was not in the rightful line to be king of Judah because he was a cousin to and not a son of Jehoiachin. It is also possible that Mulek was the son of Zedekiah II—thus putting him in the direct kingship line. Regardless, we are told that the Lord was the one who directed Mulek to the New World (see Helaman 6:10).

Mulek landed in the land northward, which was the area of the heartland of the Jaredites. Sometime later (the Book of Mormon record does not say what year), a group of the descendants of Mulek went into the wilderness in the land southward and settled in a place they called Zarahemla, which was located along the banks of the river Sidon.

A Mesoamerican document written in the Quiche Maya language called *The Title of the Lords of Totonicapan* appears to refer to the Mulekites, as the location of their initial settlement along the Gulf of Mexico is consistent with what we see in both the Book of Mormon and in the Mesoamerican archaeological record. If the Jaredites of the Book of Mormon are the same people as the Olmecs of Mesoamerica tradition, then the landing

Historical evidence supports the idea that Mulek was taken to the New World by his protectors and transported by the seafaring Phoenicians.

of the Mulekites was along the Gulf of Mexico. If that is the case, then the following from *The Title of the Lords of Totonicapan* may indeed be referring to the Mulekites. This document was written in AD 1554 and contains a brief history of the Quiche people and their legendary origins: "They came from where the sun rises, descendants of Israel, of the same language and the same customs."[18]

18. Adrian Recinos, trans., *Memorial de Solola Anales de Los Cakchiquele* (Guatemale: Direccion General de Antropologia y Historia, 1980), 170.

This document goes on to relate that the tribes tarried for a time on the shores of a lake, where they built houses; but that did not suit them, and they continued their journey. The wording of all the documents mentioned appears to localize these stages of the native peregrination in the regions of the Laguna de Terminos (Bay of Campeche, Mexico).

From there, compelled by the necessity of establishing themselves in a propitious spot and perhaps harried by their enemies, the tribes once more went up the Usumacinta and the Tabasco (Grijalva) Rivers and their tributaries and penetrated into the territory of present-day Chiapas, Mexico, and Peten, Guatemala. After a long journey, they found themselves in the hills and valleys of the interior, the land of Mam and the Volcano of Tacana, on the frontiers of Guatemala and Chiapas.[19]

19. Recinos, *Memorial de Solola Anales de Los Cakchiquele*, 39.

This conclusion is consistent with the Book of Mormon, wherein the people of Zarahemla went into the south wilderness and settled along the Sidon river. In the model presented in *Exploring the Lands of the Book of Mormon*, it is the area from the Bay of Campeche (Laguna de Terminos) through Tabasco and Chiapas, Mexico.

575 BC–121 BC—FORMATIVE PERIOD OF KAMINALJUYU AND LAND OF NEPHI

A short time (the date is not given) after the death of Lehi, Nephi was warned in a dream to separate from Laman and Lemuel. He wandered into the wilderness and built a temple in a place they called the land of Nephi. This same area was later called the land of Lehi-Nephi (see 2 Nephi 5).

Continued Nephite activity occurred in the land/city of Nephi for over 450 years. About 121 BC, Limhi and his people were led down to the land of Zarahemla. Alma, the prophet who was converted by Abinadi and who had also lived in the land of Nephi, migrated to Zarahemla around 121 BC.

The Formative Period of the excavated ruins of Kaminaljuyu, located in Guatemala City, corresponds with the same time period. Kaminaljuyu is proposed as the land/city of Nephi in this text, *Exploring the Lands of the Book of Mormon* (see chapter 28, "The Land of Nephi").

500 BC–100 BC—MAYA LATE PRECLASSIC; MONTE ALBAN PERIOD I; EARLY NEPHITE-MULEKITE PERIOD

This time period represents a great deal of activity in both the Book of Mormon and in Mesoamerica. Colonies of Mulekites probably lived on both sides of the narrow neck

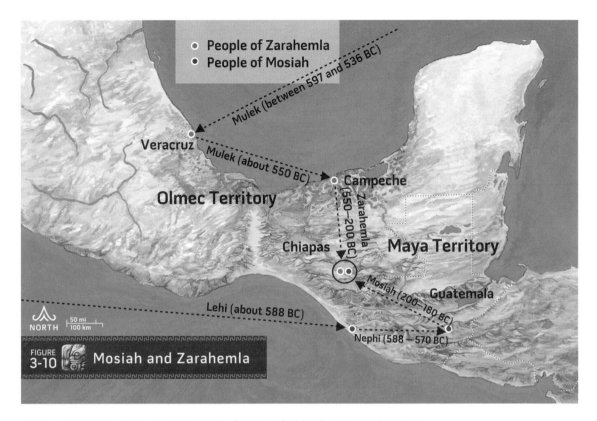

FIGURE 3–10: The proposed area settled by the people of Zarahemla (Mulekites) and the Mosiah-Nephites.

of land (Isthmus of Tehuantepec)—that is, in the land northward and in the land southward. The Nephites occupied territory in the land southward in both the land of Nephi and the land of Zarahemla. The latter was occupied jointly with the Mulekites.

In Mesoamerica, the archaeological ruins of Tikal date to 600 BC, and the Zapotec ruins in Monte Alban came into existence beginning at 500 BC. As we move closer toward the 100 BC date, other sites, such as Santa Rosa, San Bartolo, and El Mirador in the land southward and Teotihuacan in the land northward, came into existence (see chapter 4, "Archaeology in Mesoamerica").

300 BC–AD 200—MAYA LATE PRECLASSIC (NEPHITE-MULEKITE PERIOD)

Highly significant Book of Mormon events occurred during the time period of 300 BC to AD 200. From the perspective of proposed lands of the Book of Mormon, the Nephites discovered the Mulekites in the land of Zarahemla, and the two cultures merged into one. The Savior was crucified in Jerusalem and visited the Nephites in the New World.

This period begins in the Book of Mormon with the arrival of Mosiah I from the land of Nephi to the land of Zarahemla, where he discovered the people of Zarahemla. Zarahemla was a descendant of Mulek. Over 60 percent of the Book of Mormon covers this 380-year period.

Between approximately 200 and 180 BC, Mosiah led a group of Nephites from the land of Nephi to the land of Zarahemla. Benjamin, the son of Mosiah, became king about 159 BC. If Mosiah I became king at 200 BC, he would have been the king of the Nephite/Mulekite people for forty-one years.

The above Mosiah time period correlates precisely with the beginning of Monte Alban Period II, wherein archaeological evidence portrays a small group of people from Guatemala or Chiapas entering Monte Alban at 180 BC. The archaeological record states that this small group of would-be conquerors imposed a number of cultural traits on the inhabitants of Monte Alban Period I (see chapter 7, "The Zapotec [Mulekite-Nephite] Culture").

GREAT DESTRUCTION AND DEATH OF CHRIST—AD 30/AD 34

An ongoing debate has been taking place for many years over the year that Christ was born. The most commonly accepted dates are 4 BC and 1 BC. As mentioned earlier, the 4 BC date is associated with the death of Herod. However, some scholars point to a 1 BC date for the birth of Christ.[20]

By dating the birth of Christ at 4 BC, we then know that the great destruction occurred at AD 30. If we date the birth of Christ at 1 BC, then the great destruction occurred in AD 34. Christ was crucified in his thirty-fourth year. The date of the great destruction, according to the Book of Mormon calendar, was on the fourth day of the first month of that year (see 3 Nephi 8:5).

Ixtlilxochitl dates the destruction in the same year that Christ was crucified and says it was in the first few days of the year, the same date that is recorded in 3 Nephi 8:5.[21]

RESURRECTION OF CHRIST AND HIS APPEARANCE TO THE NEPHITES

The evidence suggests that both the Resurrection of Christ and the appearance of Christ to the Nephites fell on Passover. Christ resurrected three days after He was crucified. Pratt analyzed the dates of the death and resurrection of Christ and concluded that April 1, AD 33, (Friday) is the date that best represents the death of Christ and that April 3, AD 33, is the date of the Resurrection of Christ.[22]

The date of the appearance of Christ to the Nephites has been frequently debated. Because of Mormon's statement, we know that it was in the thirty-fourth year (AD 30–AD 33); but we are left to wonder if it was at the beginning or the end of the year. Mormon writes: "And it came to pass that in the *ending of the thirty and fourth* year, behold, I will show unto you that the people of Nephi who were spared, and also those who had been called Lamanites, who had been spared, did have great favors shown

20. Pratt, "The Restoration of Priesthood Keys on Easter 1836," 66.

21. Ixtlilxochitl:16; see chapter 11, "Fernando de Alva Ixtlilxochitl."

22. Pratt, "The Restoration of Priesthood Keys on Easter 1836," 67.

unto them, and great blessings poured out upon their heads, insomuch that *soon* after the ascension of Christ into heaven he did truly manifest himself unto them" (3 Nephi 10:18; emphasis added).

We suggest that when Mormon states "in the *ending* of the thirty and fourth year," he means that the Savior appeared to the Nephites toward the end of that year. Therefore, it appears that Christ resurrected the first part of the year in April at the time of the Passover and appeared to the Nephites in the last part of the year or the end of March, with both dates falling on the Passover—the same year.[23]

Without question, the appearance of Christ to the Nephites had an overwhelming effect on the people of Mesoamerica (see chapter 14, "The White God Quetzalcoatl").

AD 200–AD 350—EARLY CLASSIC MAYA (NEPHITE APOSTASY)

The period of time from AD 200 to AD 350 is extremely important in both Book of Mormon and Mesoamerica history. The year AD 201 marked the beginning of the great apostasy in the Book of Mormon. It also marked the beginning of the Maya Classic Period. In both cases, exactly the same things occurred:

1. A division of classes took place in which the priests distinguished themselves by wearing elaborate and costly apparel.

2. A massive building program took place wherein churches were built and adorned but in which their function was of no practical purpose.

3. The priests controlled the social, religious, and commercial activities of the people.

Excerpt accounts from 4 Nephi explain the above situation in the following words:

And now, in this two hundred and first year there began to be among them those who were lifted up in pride, such as the wearing of costly apparel. . . .

And they began to be divided into classes; and they began to build up churches unto themselves to get gain . . . and did administer that which was sacred unto him to whom it had been forbidden because of unworthiness. . . .

[The people] were led by many priests and false prophets to build up many churches. . . .

[And by AD 244] they did still continue to build up churches unto themselves, and adorn them with all manner of precious things. . . .

[And by AD 260] the people began again to build up the secret oaths and combinations. . . .

[And by AD 300] they lay up in store in abundance, and did traffic in all manner of traffic. (4 Nephi 1:24–49)

This same picture is painted in the archaeological records of Yucatan and Guatemala. One such example is the archaeological account of the ruins of Uxmal. Some excerpts

23. It was over the course of two of our calendar years but only one Nephite year from His death to his visit. See Bruce W. Warren, "1 Ben 6 Mak: Part Two," *Book of Mormon Archaeological Digest*, 2, no. 3 (1999), 1, 4–5, 13.

> The year AD 201 marked the beginning of the great apostasy in the Book of Mormon. It also marked the beginning of the Maya Classic Period. In both cases, exactly the same things occurred.

from the archaeological record are as follows: "Architecture was developed during this period and in particular a local architectonic style. The structures generally reflect a predominant use of massive stone to create an impressive exterior aspect with little concern for the practical use of interior spaces. . . . It is evident that a great part of the collective force was concentrated in building constructions which were not directly concerned with productivity."[24]

24. Alfredo Barrera Rubio, *Official Guide: Uxmal* (Mexico: Instituto Nacional de Antropologia e Historia, 1985), 32–33.

The beginning of this Maya Classic Period is AD 250, which coincides precisely with Book of Mormon dating. In Uxmal, as well as at other Early Classic (AD 250–AD 350) Maya sites, a complete dominance of a priestly hierarchy is illustrated—a hierarchy that had its beginnings in the first century BC. This is identical with the Book of Mormon time period when the king-men arose and claimed power (see Alma 61).

This priestcraft society was a strict minority that ruled Mesoamerica for the next seven hundred years (AD 200–AD 900), after which the great and massive structures that we now call the "ancient ruins" began to be abandoned.

FIGURE 3–11: The archaeological ruins of Uxmal, Yucatan, are indicative of many cities in Mesoamerica where a massive building program began as early as AD 200 and continued through the eighth century AD. (Photo courtesy of Sheryl Lee Wilson)

We conclude that the great mystical burden the wicked priestcraft society placed upon the masses could no longer be supported and, as a result, began to fall into ruins. (For additional information, see chapter 6, "The Maya [Lamanite-Nephite] Culture.")

AD 350–AD 900—CLASSIC MAYA; MONTE ALBAN PERIOD III; TEOTIHUACAN PERIOD IIB; NEPHITE DESTRUCTION

The year AD 350 in the Book of Mormon marked the beginning of the end. In a treaty with the Lamanites, as recorded in Mormon 2:28–29, the Nephites gave up all the land

Exploring the Lands of the Book of Mormon

southward to the Lamanites. The treaty also involved the robbers of Gadianton—a dictatorship that may have been in control of the Teotihuacan area: "And in the three hundred and fiftieth year we made a treaty with the Lamanites and the robbers of Gadianton, in which we did get the lands of our inheritance divided. And the Lamanites did give unto us the land northward, yea, even to the narrow passage which led into the land southward. And we did give unto the Lamanites all the land southward" (Mormon 2:28–29).

The date of AD 350 is one that marks the beginning of a decline in population in certain areas of Mesoamerica. Monte Alban Period III is a Zapotec site that manifested a culture change about AD 350.

In the year AD 360, Mormon called all Nephites who would respond to gather together in the land of Desolation to a city that was probably the city of Desolation, where Mormon lived.

In the year AD 385, the last battle was fought at Cumorah; and Moroni made his last entry in the Book of Mormon in the year AD 421.

Between AD 750 and AD 900, as mentioned above, many of the Mesoamerican sites were abandoned. Some of the sites that were abandoned are Monte Alban, Teotihuacan, Uxmal, Tikal, and Palenque.

Although a few archaeological sites depict a decline in civilization at AD 350, many other sites in Mesoamerica show a continued and dramatic growth over the next four hundred years. The overall picture of Mesoamerica and the Book of Mormon from AD 250 to AD 900 (Maya Classic Period) portrays civilizations on both sides of the Isthmus of Tehuantepec numbering in the millions. After the great AD 200 apostasy, the Nephites (members of the Church of Christ) were an extreme minority compared to the overall populace. The Nephites did, however, occupy a strategic land area localized around both sides of the Isthmus of Tehuantepec.

Because the archaeological record shows a high amount of trade activity between Mexico City (Teotihuacan) and Guatemala City (Kaminaljuyu), and including points in between (Oaxaca/Monte Alban), the wicked AD 350 Nephite culture was simply in the way of trade and commerce. The annihilation of the Nephites at AD 385 does not seem to show a major impact on the rest of Mesoamerica. From AD 350 to AD 900, a vast amount of building and commerce activity occurred in Mesoamerica. This activity is consistent with what we read in 4 Nephi at the beginning of the Nephite apostasy/Maya Classic Period at AD 250.

In summary, the Maya Classic Period was really the great apostasy in Mesoamerica. The people developed a massive building program and literally built gods unto themselves.

Human sacrifice began as early as AD 366 when the Lamanites sacrificed the women and children of the Nephites: "And [the Lamanites] did take many prisoners

The year AD 350 in the Book of Mormon marked the beginning of the end. In a treaty with the Lamanites, as recorded in Mormon 2:28–29, the Nephites gave up all the land southward to the Lamanites. The treaty also involved the robbers of Gadianton.

both women and children, and did offer them up as sacrifices unto their idol gods" (Mormon 4:14; see also Mormon 4:15, 21).

A few short years later (AD 385), Mormon lamented the destruction of the Nephites as he wrote: "O ye fair sons and daughters, ye fathers and mothers, ye husbands and wives, ye fair ones, how is it that ye could have fallen" (Mormon 6:19).

The sixth-century BC prophet Nephi prophesied the event almost a thousand years earlier when he stated, "I was overcome because of my afflictions, for I considered that mine afflictions were great above all, because of the destruction of my people, for I had beheld their fall" (1 Nephi 15:5).

AD 900–AD 1519—MAYA POSTCLASSIC (TOLTEC, AD 900–AD 1200; AZTEC, AD 1325–AD 1521)

The period of time from AD 900 to the beginning of the Spanish conquest in AD 1519 marked the darkest years of history in Mesoamerica prior to the conquest.

Nephi saw in vision that the Lamanites, whom we may call Maya Postclassic Period people, "dwindled in unbelief [and] became a dark, and loathsome, and a filthy people, full of idleness and all manner of abominations" (1 Nephi 12:23).

In Mesoamerica, these people became known as Postclassic Maya, Zapotec, Mixtec, Toltec, Aztec, and others.

AD 1521–AD 1821—CONQUEST OF MEXICO (THE SPANISH COLONIAL PERIOD)

The final battle between the conquering Spaniards and the Aztecs of Mexico City-Tenochtitlan was fought on August 13, AD 1521. The eighteen-year-old nephew of Montezuma, whose name was Cuauhtemoc, was captured on that date. Upon Cuauhtemoc's capture, Bernal Diaz reported him as saying, "I have surely done my duty in defence of my City, and I can do no more and I come by force and a prisoner into your presence and into your power, take that dagger that you have in your belt and kill me at once with it."[25]

Human sacrifice was brought to a close by the Spaniards. The bondage of the descendants of Lehi continued, however, for the next three hundred years. To this very day, the conquering Spaniards are not considered to be heroes in the country of Mexico. The Aztec warriors are the people's real heroes.

The three-hundred-year period from AD 1521 to AD 1821 is called the Spanish Colonial Period and is represented by Catholic domination. The Catholic inquisition was at its most severe in Mexico. The initial domination of the natives by the Catholic Church was by force; and gradually force was replaced by fear. It took the natives of Mexico a full three hundred years to throw off the Spaniard yoke. Ironically, a Catholic priest by the name of Miguel Hidalgo was the person who ignited the torch that began the independence of Mexico from Spain.

25. Bernal Diaz, *The Discovery and Conquest of Mexico—1517–1521*, trans. A. P. Maudslay (New York: The Noonday Press, 1972), 453

FIGURES 3–12: Obsidian knife and altar used in Aztec sacrificial ceremonies during the sixteenth century. (Knife photo courtesy of Mary O. Stoddard; altar photo courtesy of Merrill C. Oaks)

Nephi apparently saw both the conquest of Mexico and the subsequent domination by the Catholic Church, as he wrote: "For the praise of the world do they destroy the saints of God, and bring them down into captivity. . . . I beheld the wrath of God, that it was upon the seed of my brethren; and they were scattered before the Gentiles and were smitten" (1 Nephi 13:9, 14).

Interestingly, the year that Mexico gained its independence from Spain (1821) was one year after the date of the visitation of God the Father and Jesus Christ to Joseph Smith in 1820.

AD 1821–PRESENT: MODERN MEXICO PERIOD

Some of the major dates associated with the last two centuries of modern Mexico history include the following:

1845   Mexican-American War

1857   Separation of church and state

1862   French invasion of Mexico

1910–1914 Mexican Revolution

Mexico has not gone to war since the Mexican revolution; other Central American countries have not fared so well.

SUMMARY

Dates are important. A person's birth date is the most sacred date of his or her life. The ability for humans to mark time provides the welding link to the eternities. Anniversaries, graduations, and death dates are also important to humans.

We may reasonably assume that telestial dates are also important to the Lord. The birth, death, and resurrection dates are to be engraved on celestial scrolls.

In this chapter, we have proposed dates as they relate to the study of the Book of Mormon and Mesoamerica. Although some disagreement exists in relation to various dates and although we must allow for a margin of error of plus or minus fifty to one hundred years, we hope that further dialogue, study, and faith will develop better understanding.

By correlating the Book of Mormon with the accepted dating patterns of Mesoamerican scholars, we can gain a deeper appreciation of the historical setting of the Book of Mormon. Perhaps that will, in turn, draw us to a deeper understanding of its doctrinal message.

Dates in the Book of Mormon are precise, pervasive, and constantly associated with geographic locations. Dates, therefore, represent one clear marker that can help us understand and identify possible lands of the Book of Mormon.

At least some of the dated events in the Book of Mormon should have identifiable correlated dates and events in Mesoamerican history if the lands of the Book of Mormon are indeed found in Mesoamerica.

> Dates in the Book of Mormon are precise, pervasive, and constantly associated with geographic locations. Dates, therefore, represent one clear marker that can help us understand and identify possible lands of the Book of Mormon.

Exploring the Lands of the Book of Mormon

RADIOCARBON DATING

Throughout *Exploring the Lands of the Book of Mormon*, you'll see references to the technique of radiocarbon dating (also called carbon-14 dating) and its use by Mesoamerican archaeologists.

From the perspective of the credibility of the Book of Mormon, radiocarbon dating is clearly one of the most significant scientific discoveries of the twentieth century. Following World War II, a team of scientists led by Professor Willard F. Libby of the University of Chicago developed the radiocarbon method. Libby subsequently won the Nobel Prize in Chemistry in 1960 "for his method to use Carbon-14 for age determinations in archaeology, geology, geophysics, and other branches of science."

Other than the Book of Mormon account about the Jaredites, a unique, singular feature of the record is the pervasive use of dates by Mormon and other writers as they recorded events associated with their history. In general, the dates are very precise, enabling us to glance at the bottom of the page to see the BC and AD dates associated with the content of the page. When we examine Mormon's careful attention to the calendar, we can almost feel the process he went through of examining a year's worth of records from the Large Plates and then deciding what to include in his record.

But does the quite precise dating of Book of Mormon events correlate with dating from the archaeological and historical record of Mesoamerica?

Largely because of radiocarbon dating, today's Mesoamerican archaeological and historical reports enable us to compare events with the similar dates recorded in the Book of Mormon.

So what is "radiocarbon dating" that has brought about this revolution? From a simplistic viewpoint, right up to the moment of death, all living organisms maintain a content of carbon 14 in equilibrium with that available in the atmosphere. Radiocarbon dating then uses the amount of carbon 14 found in living creatures as a measuring stick. When an organism dies, the amount of carbon 14 available within it begins to decay at a half-life rate of 5,730 years (that is, 5,730 years elapse for one-half of the carbon 14 found in the organism that has decayed).

When scientists compare the amount of carbon 14 in a dead organism to available levels of carbon 14 in the atmosphere, they can estimate the date of the organism's death. The process, called radiocarbon dating, has altered the study of archaeology forever. Today, Mesoamerican archaeologists routinely apply the techniques of radiocarbon dating as they examine evidence from archaeological digs in the form of such things as charcoal, wood, seeds, bones, leather, mud and sediment, pollen, hair, pottery, wall paintings, textiles, fish remains, insect remains, antlers, and so forth in determining dates associated with a particular archaeological site.

Is radiocarbon dating foolproof and infallible? The answer: Definitely not. The process has many limitations, but it is continually being refined. The interesting, relevant point here is that radiocarbon dating is responsible, in general, for bringing the archaeological and historical dates for Mesoamerican sites into direct correlation with dates for Book of Mormon events. Though we don't advocate complete faith in radiocarbon-dating techniques, we suggest you keep that point in mind as you continue your reading of *Exploring the Lands of the Book of Mormon*.

CHAPTER 4

Archaeology in Mesoamerica

And they . . . discovered a land which was covered with bones of men, and of beasts, and was also covered with ruins of buildings of every kind, having discovered a land which had been peopled with a people who were as numerous as the hosts of Israel. (Mosiah 8:8)

n any study of the history of the Book of Mormon, we must be willing to let archaeological evidence assist in dictating where that history occurred. Placing events from the Book of Mormon in an area where little or no archaeological evidence exists or ignoring the scientific evidence of population centers whose time period dates to the time of the Book of Mormon is totally unproductive.

Accordingly, we have learned that a written language on the American continent was in use in the same general area where the vast majority of archaeological evidence exists. That area dates to the Book of Mormon; that area is Mesoamerica.

Archaeology is the scientific study of material remains of past human life and activity. These remains include such items as fossil relics, artifacts, and monuments. The science of archaeology as a discipline has become very exact and meaningful as interpretations of ancient civilizations have been brought to light.

> Placing events from the Book of Mormon in an area where little or no archaeological evidence exists is totally unproductive.

OPPOSITE: A panel of glyphs located at the archaeological zone of Monte Alban is examined by David Wilson. Although not yet interpreted, the glyphs at Monte Alban provide early evidence that a writing system existed in Mesoamerica over two thousand years ago. (Photo courtesy of Sheryl Lee Wilson)

The Mosiah 8:8 scripture at the first of this chapter expresses the archaeological evidence of a civilization that was ancient to the 121 BC Nephites. An expedition of forty-three men from the land of Nephi, in search of the land of Zarahemla, discovered the remains of the civilization we call Jaredites.

Archaeology enables us to examine both cultures—that is, the same Jaredite culture that the Nephites called "ancient" and also the culture that dates to the Nephite time period. Both the Jaredite and the Nephite cultures fall in the time period that archaeologists call Preclassic (2600 BC–AD 250).

An explorer and adventurer by the name of John Lloyd Stephens is often referred to as the "father of Mesoamerican archaeology." That title is bestowed upon him as a result of his AD 1840 travels throughout Mesoamerica in company with an artist named Frederick Catherwood. Two volumes of books describing their experiences, along with drawings of the ancient monuments and buildings, give credibility to their explorations. The books are still available for purchase today.[1]

1. John Lloyd Stephens, *Incidents of Travel in Central America, Chiapas and Yucatan*, 2 vols., illustrations by Frederick Catherwood, first published in 1841 (New York: Dover Publications, 1969).

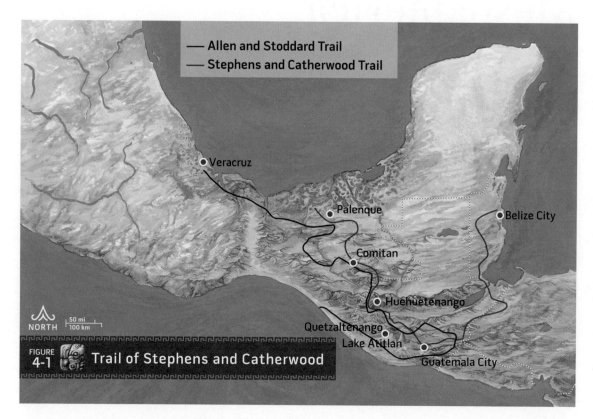

FIGURE 4–1: In 1982, Joseph Allen and Ted Stoddard, with other tour members, traced the trail of Stephens and Catherwood (1839–40). The parallel trail began in Guatemala City and continued on through Lake Atitlan, Almolonga (Quetzaltenango), Huehuetenango, the narrow strip of wilderness, and Comitan—ending in Palenque.

Exploring the Lands of the Book of Mormon

In 1982, along with the editor of *Exploring the Lands of the Book of Mormon*, Ted Stoddard, we structured a tour to trace, as closely as possible, the footsteps of Stephens and Catherwood. In retrospect, we probably should have called it the Allen and Stoddard expedition. We picked up the trail at Lake Atitlan and followed it along the highlands of Guatemala to Quetzaltenango. Lake Atitlan is proposed by some current writers on the subject of Book of Mormon geography as the waters of Mormon. Quetzaltenango and nearby Almolonga seem to fit the pattern for the valley of Alma and the land of Helam respectively.

Referring to Almolonga, Stephens reported the following:

> In the afternoon, in company with the corregidor, we rode to the warm springs of Almolonga. The road crosses a spur of the volcano, and descends precipitously into a deep valley, in which, about a league distant, stand the village and hot springs. There is a good bathing-house, at which we were not allowed to pay, being considered the guests of the city. Outside, in a beautiful natural reservoir, Indian men, women, and children were bathing together.
>
> We returned by another road, passing up a valley of extraordinary beauty, and the theme of conversation was the happiness the country might enjoy but for wars and revolutions. Beautiful as it was, all wished to leave it, and seek a land where life was safe—Mexico or El Norte.[2]

Archaeology enables us to examine the Jaredite and the Nephite cultures, which fall in the time period that archaeologists call Preclassic (2600 BC–AD 250).

2. Stephens, *Incidents of Travel in Central America*, 2:219.

FIGURE 4–2: Almolonga is an agriculture village close to the large city of Quetzaltenango. The natural hot water enters the valley from the surrounding volcanoes and provides irrigation year round to the valley and has earned it the title of the "garden village of Central America." The hot, pure water is also used for medicinal purposes. (Photo courtesy of Blake Joseph Allen)

Our group identified with Stephens's comments because Guatemala, at the time of our tour, was trying to recover from a hotly contested revolution through which the Communists were working to gain control of the government.

From Quetzaltenango, we traveled "northward" toward Mexico, stopping at Huehuetenango, an area that people refer to as a no-man's land. Our descent through the gap for another fifty miles placed us at the border crossing of La Mesilla, Guatemala, and Ciudad Cuauhtemoc, Mexico.

During this part of our journey, we were stopped several times and searched, and we had our passports examined by local deputized townspeople. In many cases, those who examined us were gun-carrying youngsters who did not exceed fourteen years of age. On one occasion, we were instructed to place our hands and arms extended against the sides of the bus as we were searched.

During the civil war that preceded our trip through Guatemala, the guerrillas took refuge in the surrounding mountains, thus making the area difficult for the government to control. We were detoured on several occasions, as bridges had been blown up by the guerrillas.

The terrain between Quetzaltenango and the Mexican border is rough and steep; and we discovered, as did Stephens and Catherwood, that the route we took was the most practical way to travel from Quetzaltenango, Guatemala, to Comitan, Mexico. The distance to the Mexican border is a little over a hundred miles. It is estimated that a native of Guatemala, carrying fifty pounds on his back supported by a strap over the forehead and traveling with his family, could travel about eight miles per day over these rugged mountains. This route may have been the trek that Alma's colony followed as they traveled from the valley of Alma to the land of Zarahemla: "And after they had been in the wilderness twelve days they arrived in the land of Zarahemla; and king Mosiah did also receive them with joy" (Mosiah 24:25).

As nearly as can be deduced, Stephens and Catherwood made the journey from Quetzaltenango to the Mexican border in twelve days. We accomplished the journey by bus in a day's travel time.

It is difficult to refrain from including more of Stephens's commentary as we reflect about our travels through the country 160 years after he wrote about it. One experience related by Stephens that was similar to our experience with the guerrillas occurred when his group reached the village of Todos Santos:

> We had again reached the tierras templadas, and in Europe or North America the beauty of this miserable unknown village would be a theme for poetry.
>
> As we rode through it, at the head of the street we were stopped by a drunken Indian, supported by two men hardly able to stand themselves, who, we thought, were taking him to prison; but, staggering before us, they blocked up the passage, and shouted "Passeporte!" . . . Not one of the three could read the passport,

Stephens and Catherwood made the journey from Quetzaltenango to the Mexican border in twelve days. We accomplished the journey by bus in a day's travel time.

and they sent for the secretary, a bare-headed Indian, habited in nothing but a ragged cotton shirt, who examined it very carefully, and read aloud the name of Rafael Carrera, which, I think, was all that he attempted to make out. We were neither sentimental, nor philosophical, nor moralizing travellers, but it gave us pangs to think that such a magnificent country was in the possession of such men.[3]

3. Stephens, *Incidents of Travel in Central America*, 2:235.

As our tour group arrived at the border and transferred to a Mexican bus, we were all impressed with the drastic change in terrain and climate. Again, we had the same feelings that Stephens expressed at this point in his travels: "Here we dismounted, slipped the bridles of our mules, and seated ourselves to wait for our Indians, looking down into the deep imbosomed valley, and back at the great range of Cordilleras, crowned by the Sierra Madre, seeming a barrier fit to separate worlds."[4]

4. Stephens, *Incidents of Travel in Central America*, 2:241.

This narrow mountain range, which reaches from the Atlantic Ocean on the Caribbean to the Pacific Ocean by the Gulf of Tehuantepec, seems to meet all the requirements necessary to be the narrow strip of wilderness in the Book of Mormon: "[The Land of Nephi] was divided from the land of Zarahemla by a narrow strip of wilderness, which ran from the sea east even to the sea west" (Alma 22:27). The narrow strip of wilderness is discussed in greater detail in chapter 24, "Wilderness Areas."

After that first trip, as detailed above, we determined not to travel that route with future Book of Mormon tours. However, after considering the probability that this trail probably was the route used by the ancient migrations between the land of Nephi and the land of Zarahemla, we continue to include this rugged and majestic leg in some of our tour journeys. In essence, it is like holding hands with the land of Nephi and the land of Zarahemla.

From our perspective, it is the geography associated with the culture and archaeology that increases our understanding of the historicity of the Book of Mormon.

In November of 2003, a similar incident as described above occurred on the Mexican side of the narrow strip of wilderness—or near the proposed site of Zarahemla—which drives home the cultural history. We were conducting fifty people through Guatemala to Chiapas, Mexico, via the massive narrow mountain range called the Cuchumatanes. Shortly after we crossed the border into Mexico, we were detained from crossing the Grijalva River bridge by the local people, one group of which is known as the "Zapatistas." With clubs in hands, several hundred people prohibited any vehicle from crossing the bridge because of grievances they had against the state government of Chiapas. After six hours of negotiation, we were allowed to pass. From a historical perspective, the culture patterns of the people who live in the mountains of Guatemala and Chiapas appear to have a familiar ring of conflict in the same area, as described in the Book of Mormon. An extreme account in the book of Mormon is the war between the Nephite

We continue to include this rugged and majestic leg in some of our tour journeys. In essence, it is like holding hands with the land of Nephi and the land of Zarahemla.

leader Lachoneus and the Gadianton robbers led by Giddianḥi in the first century BC (see 3 Nephi 3–4).

FIGURE 4–3: To the English-speaking world, John Lloyd Stephens and Frederick Catherwood brought to light the archaeological remains of an ancient civilization that has come to be called the Maya. Although Stephens was not aware of the exact dating of the ruins he described and Catherwood painted, their works have left an indelible impression on both Latter-day Saint and non-Latter-day Saint scholars. (Drawing by Frederick Catherwood)

5. See Beatriz de la Fuente, *Los Hombres de Piedra: Escultura Olmeca* (Mexico, DF: Universidad Nacional Autonoma de Mexico, 1977); Juan de Torquemada, *Monarchia Indiana*, vol. 1, as translated and condensed in Hubert Howe Bancroft, *Myths and Languages*, vol. 3 of *The Native Races* (San Francisco: A. L. Bancroft, 1883); Bernal Diaz, *The Discovery and Conquest of Mexico—1517–1521*, edited from the only exact copy of the original manuscript by Genaro Garcia, translated by A. P. Maudslay (New York: Noonday Press, 1972).

Catherwood made artistic drawings of the ruins of Copan, Quirigua, Huehuetenango, Palenque, and Uxmal. His meticulous drawings set the stage for continued studies in the archaeology of Mesoamerica.

For his information, Stephens relied heavily on sixteenth-century Spanish writers, primarily Fuente and Torquemada. Stephens also referenced the writer of *The Conquest of New Spain*, Bernal Diaz, who was a soldier in the army of Cortez.[5]

The works of Stephens aroused considerable interest in the ancient civilizations of Mesoamerica. People in the United States and Europe, including members of The Church of Jesus Christ of Latter-day Saints, wanted to know more. The headquarters of the Church were located in Nauvoo, Illinois, at the time that Stephens's books were published. Interestingly, John Lloyd Stephens and Joseph Smith were both born in the year 1805. Also, it is quite a coincidence that Stephens actually studied under Charles Anthon, the professor to whom Martin Harris showed a portion of the translated Book of Mormon writings.

In October 2004, Garth Norman presented a paper on the impact that Stephens's works and Catherwood's drawings had on the Prophet Joseph Smith and associate editor of the *Times and Seasons*, John Taylor. Norman writes:

Exploring the Lands of the Book of Mormon

October 1 is the anniversary of a little known event in early Church history that I believe, in consequence of significant research progress, now deserves recognition for identifying a region of major Book of Mormon lands and for initiating Book of Mormon archaeological historicity research. In a *Times and Seasons* editorial, October 1, 1842, the Prophet Joseph Smith after progressive study announced a discovery that the Book of Mormon "land southward" is located in Central America. . . . Joseph's discovery resulted from studying an exciting new book by explorer John Lloyd Stevens (*Incidents of Travel in Central America, Chiapas and Yucatan*, 1841) that for the first time was bringing major exposure to the outside world of magnificent ancient Maya ruins hidden in the jungles of Middle America. . . .

Stephens' explorations awakened keen interest, and are recognized today as the beginning of American archaeology. In a similar way, they can be recognized as the beginning of Book of Mormon archaeology. Shortly after Stephens' publications hit the book market in 1841, Joseph received them as a gift and commented in his personal Journal History about their importance to the Book of Mormon. On June 25, 1842, Joseph recorded that Stephens and Catherwood had succeeded in collecting in the interior of America "a large amount of relics of the Nephites, or the ancient inhabitants of America treated of in the Book of Mormon," which relics had recently landed in New York (*History of the Church* 5:44). While the relics were judged to be of the "Nephites," that was of course unknown, but illustrates Joseph's frame of reference at that early date.[6]

MAJOR ARCHAEOLOGICAL SITES IN MESOAMERICA

In the 160 plus years since Stephens's books garnered so much interest, archaeology techniques and methods have greatly improved, thereby increasing our knowledge of the Mesoamerican civilizations prior to the Spanish conquest in 1519. Among the major Mesoamerican archaeological excavations are several with which we will be concerned, as follows:

Teotihuacan. The ruins of Teotihuacan, located northeast of Mexico City and dating from 300 BC to AD 750, were initially restored in part for the centennial celebration of Mexico in 1910. New evidence has now surfaced indicating that Teotihuacan played a major role in the final downfall of the Nephite nation (see chapter 8, "The Teotihuacan Culture").

Chichen Itza and Uxmal. Sylvanus Morley, the father of archaeology of the Yucatan and a noted scholar, spent almost the entire decade of the 1930s among the Classic (AD 500–1200) ruins of Chichen Itza and Uxmal where he documented and restored some of the major sites.

6. V. Garth Norman, "Joseph Smith and the Beginning of Book of Mormon Archaeology: Did the Prophet Joseph Smith in 1842 Locate Book of Mormon Lands in Middle America?" *Meridian Magazine*, www.meridianmagazine.com/ideas (accessed March 12, 2007).

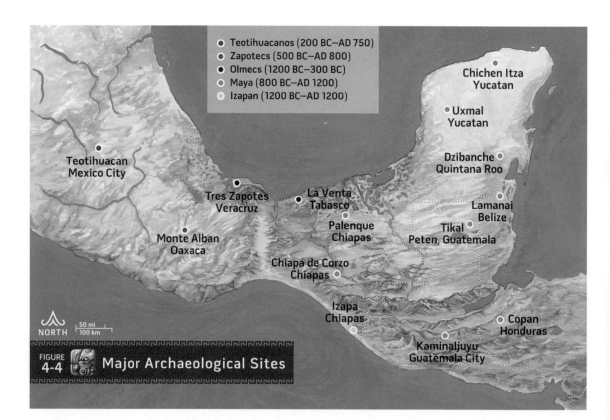

FIGURE 4–4: The above map is color coded to illustrate some of the major archaeological sites located in Mesoamerica, some of which date as early as 1200 BC, whereas others date as late as AD 1200.

Monte Alban and Mitla. The Zapotec ruins of Monte Alban in the state of Oaxaca, which date from 500 BC to AD 750, were restored by a Mexican archaeologist, Alfonso Caso. That writing existed in Mesoamerica during the Book of Mormon time period was first discovered at Monte Alban. Joseph Allen writes, "It was during my initial visit to Monte Alban in 1970 that I determined we could begin to do some serious and legitimate Book of Mormon correlations with Mesoamerica cultures." Mitla is a Postclassic Zapotec site that is also located in the Oaxaca valley.

Palenque. The Maya ruins of Palenque, which date from AD 300 to AD 800, have attracted the attention of many writers, linguists, and archaeologists. The most notable discovery was the uncovering of the tomb of Pacal in 1952 by the archaeologist Alberto Ruz. A monument was erected at Palenque in his honor for his work there. About half a century later, a tree was planted at Palenque in honor of another Maya scholar, Linda Schele. The following collage of pictures shows different archaeological sites with their designated time periods.

Teotihuacan	Chichen Itza	Uxmal	Palenque
Preclassic/Classic	Classic/Postclassic	Classic	Classic

Izapa. Dr. Wells Jakeman, an archaeologist from Brigham Young University, began investigating the Izapa culture in the late 1940s when he learned about Stela 5, which has been given the name of the Tree of Life Stone.

The Izapa culture is located along the Gulf of Tehuantepec in the state of Chiapas and dates from 1200 BC to AD 1200. The New World Archaeological Foundation (NWAF) conducted field work in the state of Chiapas from 1952 to 1988. V. Garth Norman, a Latter-day Saint archaeologist, worked with the NWAF for two seasons and conducted follow-up studies on the Tree of Life Stone and the Izapa culture.

Tikal. The Maya ruins of Tikal date from 600 BC to AD 750. These ruins are located in the Peten jungle of Guatemala and represent one of the most massive sites in Mesoamerica. Over three thousand separate structures, spread over ten square miles, have been analyzed at Tikal. The restoration work was accomplished by the University of Pennsylvania and the Guatemala government from 1956 to 1969. Edwin M. Shook, the great Maya enthusiast, was appointed the first field director in 1956.

Kaminaljuyu. One of the greatest of all archaeological sites in the New World is Kaminaljuyu. Swallowed up by modern-day Guatemala City, Kaminaljuyu reflects the Middle Preclassic Period, 1500 BC–600 BC. However, the majority of the mounds are Late Preclassic, 550 BC–150 BC. Identification and restoration work began as a result of a 1946 report on Kaminaljuyu from the Carnegie Institute of Washington, written by Alfred Kidder, Jesse Jennings, and Edwin Shook. Pennsylvania State University conducted field work at the site of Kaminaljuyu from 1968 to 1973.

El Mirador. El Mirador is located in northern Peten, Guatemala, and is only four miles from the Mexican state of Campeche. Perhaps the oldest Maya capital, this huge complex dates from 150 BC to AD 350, Late Preclassic time. El Mirador was abandoned at the beginning of the Classic Period. Mapping and investigation work were initiated by Bruce Dahlin and Ray Matheny in the early 1980s. And in March 2004, the newly elected president of Guatemala, Oscar Berger, expressed plans to restore El Mirador for

FIGURE 4–5: Four archaeological sites with their designated time periods. (Photos courtesy of Merrill C. Oaks and Sheryl Lee Wilson)

Izapa
Preclassic/Classic

Tikal
Preclassic/Classic

Kaminaljuyu
Preclassic/Classic

FIGURE 4–6:
Archaeological sites dating to the Preclassic and Classic Periods. (Photos Courtesy of George and Audrey DeLange, Nathan T. Allen, and Blake Joseph Allen)

future tourism. The pictures shown in figure 4–6 are images relating to the Preclassic and Classic Periods.

Cerros. The archaeological site of Cerros, located in northern Belize, dates to 50 BC and is an excellent candidate for the fortified city of Mulek. Dr. David Freidel conducted investigative work on the site during the latter part of the twentieth century and reported on his work in the book, *A Forest of Kings: The Untold Story of the Ancient Maya*, by Linda Schele and David Freidel. Two of the three constructed tombs were empty and, as Freidel speculated, were a probable result of the would-be occupiers of the tombs being killed in battle. The dating, location, and events that can now be interpreted show a correlation with the king-men in the Book of Mormon (see Alma 51; 60:15–18; 62:35). Two kings, Amalickiah and his brother Ammoron, were both killed on the battlefield by the Nephite warrior Teancum and would not be buried in tombs built for them. Teancum was exceedingly angry as he considered that Ammoron and Amalickiah his brother "had been the cause of this great and lasting war between them and the Lamanites, which had been the cause of so much war and bloodshed, yea, and so much famine" (Alma 62:35). Tubaloth, the son of Ammoron, did not have the power of his father and uncle. As Freidel notes, the experiment with kingship at Cerros, Belize, came to an end. For a more detailed account of these events, see chapter 24, "Wilderness Areas."

> Becan demonstrates the manner in which the fortified earthworks and trenches were built by Moroni in the east wilderness.

Becan. About a hundred miles inland in the southern Yucatan Peninsula, in the state of Campeche, lies the fortified city of Becan, a Maya word that means the "road of the serpent." Massive Preclassic defensive earthworks surround this Classic Period city. David Webster conducted research at Becan for his doctoral dissertation, in which we find intriguing information that archaeologically supports the Book of Mormon. A visit to this site is a favorite of our tour groups because, in vivid form, Becan demonstrates the manner in which the fortified earthworks and trenches were built by Moroni in the east wilderness (see Alma 49–55; see also chapter 24, "Wilderness Areas").

Dzibanche. In the Maya language, *Dzibanche* means "writing on wood," so named because of the engraved wooden lintels still visible on some of the major buildings at the site. This site, along with its close neighbors Kohunlich and Kinichna, formed a major megalopolis beginning in the Late Preclassic and Early Classic (100 BC to AD 400) Periods and continuing to about AD 800. Over two hundred buildings have been identified at these sites. The climate is mild, with a daily dew that enables the local farmers to grow crops year round. Today, the area around Dzibanche is very scarcely populated and has been open to the public for only a few years. It is located in the state of Quintana Roo, Mexico, in the southern Yucatan Peninsula just north of the small country of Belize and is in close proximity to other Book of Mormon time period sites—such as Cerros (probably Mulek; see Alma 51:26; 52:16–34), El Mirador in northern Peten, and the fortified city of Becan—and is patterned after the manner mentioned in Alma 49–50. Over the last few years, we have discovered that regardless of the number and magnitude of archaeological sites previously visited on any given tour, Dzibanche rises to the forefront. Evidence associated with time period, location, climate, and its relationship with the site of Cerros makes Dzibanche a viable candidate for the city of Bountiful that was highly fortified and that, as a result, would have been the place where the Savior visited the Nephites at the time of the Passover at the end of AD 34. See chapter 24, "Wilderness Areas," for more detail.

FIGURE 4–7: The two sites shown here, Becan and Dzibanche, date to Book of Mormon and post–Book of Mormon time periods. (Photos courtesy of Sheryl Lee Wilson)

Becan
Preclassic/Postclassic

Dzibanche
Preclassic/Postclassic

La Venta and Other Olmec Sites. Matthew Stirling led expeditions in 1939–1941 to Tabasco and Veracruz, Mexico, to uncover giant stone heads at La Venta. This culture has become known by the modern name of the Olmecs. It dates to the Middle Preclassic, 1200 BC to 600 BC.

The Olmec site of San Lorenzo was excavated by a Yale team, led by Michael Coe, from 1966 to 1969. This site is located along the Coatzacoalcos River.

Tres Zapotes, another Olmec site, is located at the base of the Hill Vigia in Veracruz. A stela fragment excavated there bears the date of 31 BC. Two large Olmec heads excavated there show much earlier occupation of the area.

Tula and Tenochtitlan. The Toltec ruins of Tula, Hidalgo, located north of Mexico City, date to the Postclassic Period, AD 900 to AD 1200. The Aztec ruins of Tenochtitlan, located in downtown Mexico City, date from AD 1325 to the Spanish conquest in AD 1519. The Mexican government conducted restoration work at the site in the early 1980s. Tenochtitlan was labeled the archaeological discovery of the century.

Serious excavation work was not conducted in Mesoamerica until the 1930s. After almost a century of study by Mesoamerican scholars, only 10 to 15 percent of the ruins existing in Mesoamerica have been excavated and analyzed satisfactorily.

Five major civilizations that existed in Mesoamerica during the Book of Mormon time period were the Olmec, Zapotec, Maya, Teotihuacan, and Izapa cultures. The Preclassic Kaminaljuyu culture, which coincides with the Book of Mormon time period, will be discussed as part of the larger Maya culture.

By developing an understanding of the archaeological data available on the cultures that flourished during the time period in which the Book of Mormon history occurred, we provide ourselves with a base from which we can begin to compare events and culture patterns that were indigenous to the Book of Mormon.

> By developing an understanding of the archaeological data, we can begin to compare events and culture patterns that were indigenous to the Book of Mormon.

THE OLMEC CULTURE CORE

The Olmecs and their predecessors, whose heartland was along the Gulf Coast of Mexico, date from 2500 BC to approximately 300 BC. The Olmec kingdom was massive and long, as it extended into El Salvador on the south to the state of Guerrero, Mexico, on the west. Oaxaca, Yucatan, and the Mexico valley all manifest patterns of Olmec-style culture. Recent studies also link the Hopewell culture of North America with the Olmec culture.

The Olmec culture parallels in striking detail with the Jaredites, to the extent that most Book of Mormon students who have studied Mesoamerica cultures have concluded that the Olmecs and the Jaredites were one and the same. They both came from the great tower; their languages were not confounded; their high cultures parallel each other; and the people in both instances were considered large in stature—all facts supported by the Book of Mormon, by archaeological evidence, and through ancient historical evidence. Furthermore, both the Olmec and the Jaredite cultures demonstrate a dramatic downfall because of a great civil war between 400 BC–200 BC.

THE MAYA CULTURE CORE

The largest and most enduring culture to exist in Mesoamerica during the same time period as the Book of Mormon was the Maya. The Maya occupied the area south and east of the Isthmus of Tehuantepec. Most native people living in that same area today trace their linguistic roots to the Maya. Even today, Maya and people of Maya descent still live in the Mexican areas of Chiapas and Yucatan as well as in the country of Guatemala.

The Maya history is very extensive and long. Their history, prior to the conquest, is usually divided into Preclassic, Classic, and Postclassic as follows:

Preclassic, 600 BC–AD 250 (Book of Mormon time period)

Classic, AD 250–AD 900 (late Book of Mormon time period and post–Book of Mormon)

Postclassic, AD 900–AD 1500 (post–Book of Mormon)

The Preclassic Maya developed over a period of eight hundred years, primarily as an agriculturally oriented society. However, once the Classic culture (AD 250–900) was developed, the priests controlled virtually everything, including the social life, religious activity, and commerce. For the most part, the massive buildings that are visible today are monuments to that minority ruling class.

Today's Maya territory probably was home to the 600 BC–200 BC Nephites, who lived in the land of Nephi, and the 200 BC to AD 350 Nephites, who lived in the land of Zarahemla. The Tree of Life Stone of the Izapa culture is located in Maya territory. Generally speaking, the Maya race represents an excellent candidate for the Lamanites and the Nephites in the Book of Mormon. We don't want readers to misunderstand us here. Because we now know that people were already living in the area where Lehi landed in the sixth century BC, it stands to reason that Nephi and Laman became "kings" over those people. Perhaps the situation is similar to the conquest of Mexico when a small group of conquerors became the ruling class over the Aztecs and Maya in the sixteenth century AD. Since the Spanish conquest, the leaders of Mexico, with the exception of Benito Juarez, have been of Spanish descent. Jacob wrote, "I shall call them Lamanites that seek to destroy the people of Nephi, and all those who are friendly

Generally speaking, the Maya race represents an excellent candidate for the Lamanites and the Nephites in the Book of Mormon.

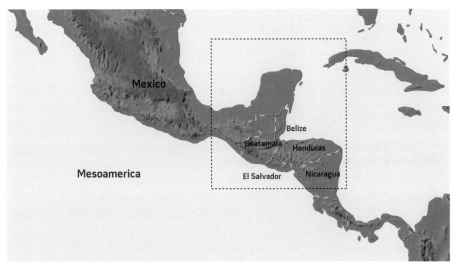

FIGURE 4–8: As shown in this map, the territory of the ancient Maya civilization is now broken down into six separate countries: southern Mexico, Belize, Guatemala, Honduras, El Salvador, and Nicaragua.

to Nephi I shall call Nephites, or the people of Nephi according to the reigns of the kings" (Jacob 1:14). Ironically, the ancient Maya territory is now occupied by six different countries.

THE ZAPOTEC CULTURE CORE

The Zapotecs lived in the Oaxaca valley. The ruins of Monte Alban, located on top of a mountain in the center of the valley, depict the Zapotec history. Monte Alban dates as follows:

Monte Alban Period I, 500 BC–100 BC (Mulekite time period)
Monte Alban Period II, 180 BC–AD 350 (Mosiah time period forward)
Monte Alban Period III, AD 350–AD 750 (post–Book of Mormon)

The valley of Oaxaca is located approximately three hundred miles southeast of Mexico City. Oaxaca is nestled in a valley with an elevation of about five thousand feet above sea level. It borders the Isthmus of Tehuantepec on the east. Its isolation has kept it relatively free from other cultures over the centuries. The city of Oaxaca, however, is a Spanish colonial city dating to the sixteenth century.

Monte means mount, and *Alban* is named after a white flower that grows on the mountain in the center of the valley of Oaxaca. Monte Alban is about a fifteen-minute drive from the city of Oaxaca. The original name of Monte Alban, however, according to Dr. Ignacio Bernal of the Mexican National Institute, may have been "Jaguar Hill."[7] This naming is consistent with the name of the ancient Jaredite capital of Moron: "Now the land of Moron, where the king dwelt, was near the land which is called Desolation by the Nephites" (Ether 7:6). As we pointed out in chapter 1, the name *Mormon*, like *Moron*, carries the meaning of "jaguar hill" or "jaguar mountain."

7. Ignacio Bernal, *El Valle de Oaxaca: Guia Official* (Mexico, DF: Instituto Nacional de Antropologia e Historia, 1992), 45.

The most prominent native tribe in the valley of Oaxaca is the Zapotec. They were, however, influenced by the Olmecs of the Gulf Coast. The Mixtec tribe developed a later culture in the Oaxaca valley. Many other native tribes who speak their own dialects live in the mountains of the state of Oaxaca.

Benito Juarez, a contemporary of Abraham Lincoln, is considered to be one of Mexico's finest presidents and was from the state of Oaxaca. Juarez was a full-blooded Zapotec.

THE TEOTIHUACAN CULTURE CORE

The Teotihuacan culture constitutes the fourth major civilization in Mesoamerica during the time period of the Book of Mormon. Many parts of the valley of Mexico were occupied during Book of Mormon times. However, the Teotihuacan culture is the most accessible. The general dating of Teotihuacan is as follows:

Teotihuacan Period I, 150 BC–AD 200 (Book of Mormon time period)

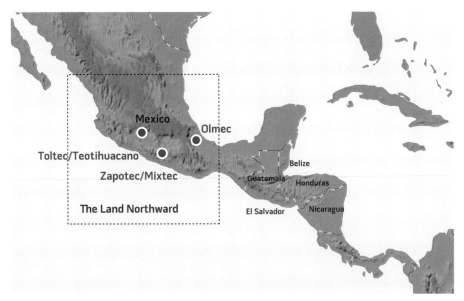

FIGURE 4–9: The area designated as the land northward is shown in this map. This area is the homeland of the Olmecs, Zapotecs, Mixtecs, Toltecs, Teotihuacanos, and Aztecs.

Teotihuacan Period II, AD 200–AD 700 (Book of Mormon time period and post–Book of Mormon)

Driving time to Teotihuacan from Mexico City is about forty-five minutes in a northeasterly direction. The ancient Teotihuacan culture was referred to by the later Aztec culture as "the place of the gods" or "the place where men became gods."

In the entrance of the Teotihuacan Room at the National Museum of Anthropology in Mexico City is the following statement on a wall plaque (the information for the plaque was obtained from the studies of a sixteenth-century scholar, Bernardino Sahagun):

> Before there was light
> Before there was day
> When it was still dark
> The gods met in council
> In Teotihuacan.

Teotihuacan seems to parallel the 50 BC migration cultures who went to the land northward. If Teotihuacan is the "land which was northward" in the Book of Mormon, then Teotihuacan played a major role in the final downfall of the Nephite nation.

If Teotihuacan is the "land which was northward" in the Book of Mormon, then Teotihuacan played a major role in the final downfall of the Nephite nation.

THE IZAPA CULTURE CORE

The Izapa culture is located within the larger Maya geographical boundaries. It is treated as a separate culture in *Exploring the Lands of the Book of Mormon* because of

The rapid decline in population in Izapa at AD 350 corresponds with the same time period in which the Nephites gave up all the land southward to the Lamanites.

its representation as a unique culture, both geographically and linguistically, during the time period of the Book of Mormon.

The Izapa culture core is also treated as a separate chapter because it was the Izapa culture that gave birth to Stela 5, commonly known as the Tree of Life Stone (see chapter 9, "The Izapa [Jaredite-Nephite-Lamanite] Culture").

The primary dating of the Izapa culture is strictly Book of Mormon time period, 300 BC to AD 350. The rapid decline in population in Izapa at AD 350 corresponds with the same time period in which the Nephites gave up all the land southward to the Lamanites. We propose that Izapa was located in the land southward.

Izapa may have been the city of Judea discussed in the Book of Mormon. Judea's strategic location near the Isthmus of Tehuantepec may have played a major role in the development of the Nephite/Mulekite society.

Chapters 5 through 9 give a more detailed account of the five major civilizations that were contemporary with the historical time periods of the Book of Mormon:

Olmec	2600 BC–300 BC*
Maya	Preclassic, 600 BC–AD 250*
	Classic, AD 250–AD 900
	Postclassic, AD 900–AD 1500
Zapotec	Period I, 500 BC–100 BC*
	Period II, 180 BC–AD 350*
	Period III, AD 350–AD 750
Teotihuacan	Period I, 150 BC–AD 200*
	Period II, AD 200–AD 350*
	Period III, AD 350–AD 600
	Period IV, AD 600–AD 900
Izapa	300 BC–AD 350*

*Equals Book of Mormon time period

FREQUENTLY ASKED QUESTION

A question that is commonly asked by students of the Book of Mormon when they become familiar with the Olmec, Maya, Zapotec, Teotihuacan, and Izapa cultures is the following: How are the divisions of the cultures brought about—that is, are the divisions determined by time period, by architectural style, by geographical location, or by linguistic separations?

The answer is that all four criteria play a major role when we determine boundary separations of major civilizations in Mesoamerica. We will summarize the four categories as follows:

1. Time Period Divisions

One of the main purposes of *Exploring the Lands of the Book of Mormon* is to deal specifically with those cultures that correspond in time period to the Book of Mormon (or the Preclassic Period). As a result, very little information about the Toltecs and the Aztecs is contained in *Exploring the Lands of the Book of Mormon*. Although they lived in the Mexico valley where the Teotihuacan culture developed, the time period of both the Toltecs, AD 900–AD 1200, and the Aztecs, AD 1325–AD 1519, are both very much post–Book of Mormon time. Therefore, the time-period separation is extremely important when we determine the boundaries of the ancient civilizations.

2. Architectural Style Divisions

Archaeologists and iconographers have determined boundary separations by the architectural style of the buildings, pottery styles, and artistic engravings on the monuments from an area. Furthermore, the extent of trade activity among the major civilizations can be determined during certain periods of time simply by an analysis of the potsherds. The semitrained eye can easily distinguish architectural styles between the Maya and the Olmec or between the Zapotec culture and the Teotihuacan culture.

3. Geographical Divisions

Natural boundaries played a major role in the divisions of the ancient cultures of Mesoamerica. The most common boundary lines consisted of mountains and bodies of water. The Isthmus of Tehuantepec has long been a natural dividing line. In the long

FIGURE 4–10: The pottery shown here is from the site of Cholula, Mexico, and is made from the fine clay of that region. During the time of the Aztecs, the emperors reportedly ate their food only on the fine plates from Cholula. (Photo courtesy of George and Andrey DeLange)

history of the Maya, including up to the present, the Maya never crossed to the west of the isthmus. The Book of Mormon probably honored that same idea, as it states that there was "a small neck of land between the land northward and the land southward" (Alma 22:32). Further, "And the Lamanites did give unto us the land northward, yea, even to the narrow passage which led into the land southward" (Mormon 2:29).

Today, the peaks of the mountains form the dividing lines between countries. The top of the volcanic mountain peak Tacana divides the state of Chiapas, Mexico, from the country of Guatemala. During the middle Nephite time period, 100 BC, the dividing line between the land of Nephi and the land of Zarahemla was a narrow strip of wilderness (see Alma 22:27). In all probability, this division consisted of a massive, narrow mountain range that today is called Los Cuchumatanes. It runs from the "east sea"—the Caribbean, Atlantic side, north of Lake Izabal—and extends in a westward direction through the Guatemalan cities of Coban and Huehuetenango until it connects with the "west sea"—the Gulf of Tehuantepec, Pacific side. There it merges with the Sierra Madres to form one mountain range that continues in a northwest direction—or, as

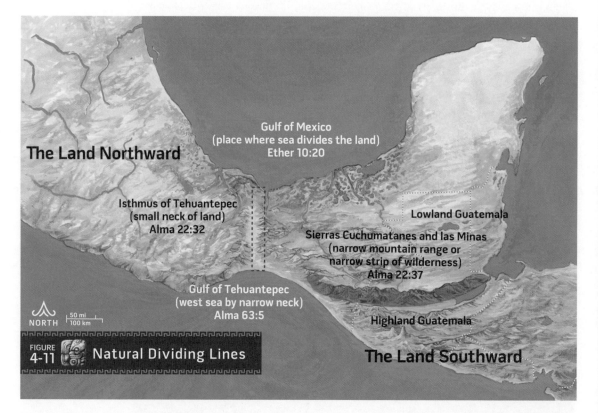

FIGURE 4–11: Like many other places in the world, the Mesoamerica dividing lines, both ancient and modern, were and are mountains, rivers, and trade routes. Observe that the Guatemala highlands are separated from the Guatemala lowlands by a narrow mountain range. The Maya culture was separated from the Mexico culture by an isthmus.

Exploring the Lands of the Book of Mormon

Alma 22:27 states, "round about on the borders of the seashore" until it reaches the area of Arriaga, Chiapas, Mexico, near the Gulf of Tehuantepec. In Mormon's words, "[The land of Nephi] was divided from the land of Zarahemla by a narrow strip of wilderness, which ran from the sea east even to the sea west" (Alma 22:27).

FIGURE 4–12: Model of the ruins of Cholula, Mexico, illustrating the manner in which one civilization was built on top of another. (Photo courtesy of George and Audrey DeLange)

4. Language Barriers

Language always plays a major role in the separation of peoples. Even today, the language barrier between English and Spanish is in some ways a larger separation between the United States and Mexico than is the Rio Grande.

Regarding the ancient Maya, Michael Coe writes: "There are few parts of the world where there is such a good 'fit' between language and culture: a line drawn around the Maya-speaking peoples would contain all those remains, and hieroglyphic texts, assigned to the ancient Maya civilization."[8]

8. Michael Coe, *Mexico* (New York: Frederick A. Praeger Publishers, 1962), 11.

Linguists have been developing a new discipline called glottochronology, which traces the history of peoples through their languages. A rather amazing fact is that after all the elapsed years, the hints of sounds and meanings that are emerging from Mesoamerica are similar to names of people and places in the Book of Mormon.

In summary, by utilizing all the tools available, including dating, architecture, geology/geography, and linguistics, we are able to determine the boundary lines of the ancient civilizations of Mesoamerica. By knowing the cultural boundaries of the Olmec, Maya, Zapotec, Teotihuacan, and Izapa cultures, we can then pursue comparative analyses with the Jaredite, Lamanite, Mulekite, and Nephite cultures as outlined in the Book of Mormon.

CHAPTER 5

The Olmec (Jaredite) Culture

And now I, Moroni, proceed to give an account of those ancient inhabitants who were destroyed by the hand of the Lord upon the face of this north country. (Ether 1:1)

At the entrance of the Olmec Museum at Jalapa, Veracruz, Mexico, the following words are written:

Mexicano detente:
This is the beginning of your history, your cradle and your altar.
Listen to the silent voice of Mexico's oldest culture,
Perhaps the mother civilization of our continent.
The Olmecs converted the rain into harvests,
The sun into the calendar, The rocks into scripture,
The cotton into clothing. Travels into commerce,
Mounds into thrones, Jaguars into religion, And men into gods.
(Augustin Acosta Lagunes, November 1986)

OPPOSITE: Several Olmec monuments from the archaeological zone of La Venta, Tabasco, have been transferred to the outdoor park in the city of Villahermosa. This intricately engraved monument shows a king with a scepter in his hand and with a massive headdress. The Olmec language, dating from 1500 to 300 BC, has not yet been interpreted. (Photo courtesy of Merrill C. Oaks)

The ancient inhabitants to whom Moroni referred and the oldest civilization of Mexico referred to above appear to be the same. The book of Ether speaks of a group of people who left the great tower at the time of the confusion of languages sometime during the third millennium BC. They were led to a promised land that today is called the Americas. From the Book of Mormon, we call these people Jaredites. They lived in an area that Moroni called "this north country."

A sixteenth-century Mesoamerican historian, Ixtlilxochitl, also wrote in his history of a group of people who came from the great tower. They were led to a good and fertile land that today is called Mexico. The early Spanish writers referred to these people as Quinametzin. They are also referred to as giants. They lived in an area in the northern parts of the land that, correlated with our maps today, is along the Gulf Coast of Mexico.[1]

1. Ixtlilxochitl:6, 8, 25, 26, 35; see chapter 11, "Fernando de Alva Ixtlilxochitl."

Because of the marked similarities between the account of Moroni and the account of Ixtlilxochitl, as will be seen later, we have reason to believe that the accounts of both the Book of Mormon and of the early Spanish writers refer to the same people.

In addition to the Book of Mormon and the writings of Ixtlilxochitl, a third witness corroborates the history of the first civilization in the Americas. The archaeological record of the people called the Olmecs provides us with a rather convincing parallel history of a group of people who settled along the "northern area," the area along the Gulf of Mexico.

> Because of the marked similarities between the account of Moroni and the account of Ixtlilxochitl, we have reason to believe that they refer to the same people.

Although both Moroni and Ixtlilxochitl wrote histories of an ancient civilization who came from the great tower and who settled in the north land, the archaeological record as it relates to people coming from the great tower is a bit sketchy.

We may, however, have an archaeological hint of the first settlers crossing the ocean from a monument discovered at the Olmec site of La Venta in the state of Tabasco, Mexico. The monument is now labeled Stela 27 and is located today at Parque La Venta, the outdoor museum in the city of Villahermosa, Tabasco (see figure 5–2).

Admittedly, the following account by Joseph Allen is speculative in nature. We include it, however, to illustrate the manner in which ideas can be conceived. We affirm that both physical evidence and spiritual enlightenment can blend together in formulating hypotheses—one by an archaeologist and another by a scriptorian in this instance:

> In the year 1980, as I was conducting a group of people through the museum at La Venta, one of the members in the group asked if a pamphlet was available describing the various monuments in the park. I asked the gentleman at the curio shop if such a pamphlet had been published. He informed me that he had a draft of a guide booklet that he was working on but that it was in Spanish. He said he would let me take it if I would return it.
>
> The gentleman further informed me that he was an archaeologist and that he had assisted in several projects in the area. As we parted, he asked me to pay

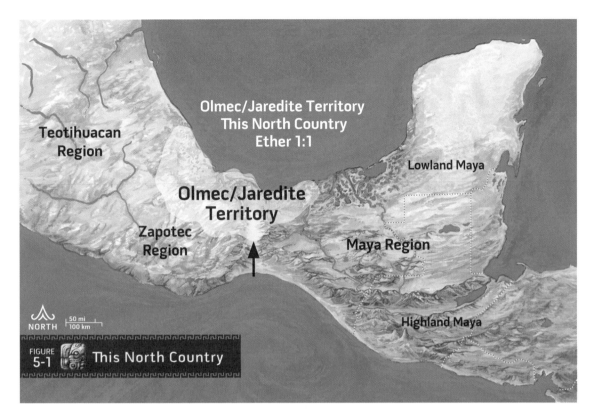

FIGURE 5–1: The land of the Olmecs (Jaredites), "this north country" (Ether 1:1). This map outlines the heartland of the high civilization called the Olmecs, who date from about 1500 BC to 300 BC. On the Mesoamerica map, this area is referred to as "north" because of the strong, seasonal, hurricane-type northern winds that blow from the Gulf of Mexico and touch land along the states of Veracruz and Tabasco. This is the same land that Alva de Ixtlilxochitl and Moroni, the son of Mormon, called "the northern parts of the land" or "this north country."

particular attention to what was then Stela 12, an engraved monument that may provide information regarding the crossing of the ocean by the original settlers to the New World.

The interest of the group was high as we proceeded through the park examining the several monuments, most of which date from 1200 to 600 BC, the Jaredite time period. As we arrived at Stela 12 (now Stela 27), we discovered that the resident archaeologist was detailed in his analysis.

He said that the lines flowing from the back of the individual's head represented sun rays—suggesting that the first settlers came from the west where the sun sets. He noted that the footprints suggest the people traveled great distances to arrive at their destination. And he pointed out that the sculpture's giant sea monster with jaws opened, together with the main character's warding off of the sea monster, suggests that the people crossed the ocean in their journeys.

Any allusions
in the Book
of Mormon to
engraved stone
monuments
should not
be viewed as
enigmatic
content in light
of ubiquitous
archaeological
discoveries of
Mesoamerican
stone
monuments
since the
publication
of the Book of
Mormon.

Needless to say, our interest was piqued by our experience at the monument. Jay Rawlings, an associate of mine, who unfortunately lost his life in an airplane accident a few months later, responded by saying, "As I flew from Mexico City this morning, I was reading an event in the book of Ether that may tie in with the sea monster carving on the stela." Jay then read the account of Jared and his brother's crossing of the great waters: "And thus they were driven forth; and *no monster of the sea could break them,* neither whale that could mar them; and they did have light continually, whether it was above the water or under the water. And thus they were driven forth, three hundred and forty and four days upon the water" (Ether 6:10–11; emphasis added).

The engraved stone monuments of La Venta are also reminiscent of the event recorded in the small book of Omni, in the Book of Mormon, which also mentions the Jaredites: "And it came to pass in the days of Mosiah, there was a large stone brought

FIGURE 5–2: The outdoor Parque de La Venta, which is located in the city of Villahermosa, Tabasco, consists of over thirty monuments that were transported from the ancient Olmec archaeological site of La Venta about sixty miles west of Villahermosa. One of the monuments is shown on the left and depicts a type of sea monster (shark) that is being detained by a bearded individual. The drawing on the right is an artist's illustration of the engraved monument. Other intriguing symbols are also present on the sculpture. (Photo courtesy of George and Audrey DeLange; drawing by Cliff Dunston)

Exploring the Lands of the Book of Mormon

unto him with *engravings* on it; and he did interpret the *engravings* by the gift and power of God. And they gave an account of one Coriantumr, and the slain of his people. And Coriantumr was discovered by the people of Zarahemla; and he dwelt with them for the space of nine moons. It also spake a few words concerning his fathers. And his first parents came out from the tower, at the time the Lord confounded the language of the people; and the severity of the Lord fell upon them according to his judgments, which are just; and their bones lay scattered in the land northward" (Omni 1:20–22; emphasis added).

Ixtlilxochitl also refers to the discovery of the bones of the first civilization in Mesoamerica.[2] "In this land called New Spain [Mexico], there were giants, as demonstrated by their bones that have been discovered in many areas."[3]

Although the interpretation of the monument under question may not be authenticated as referring to the Jaredite migration across the waters, when its interpretation is coupled with other similarities between the Jaredites in the Book of Mormon and the Quinametzin, of whom Ixtlilxochitl writes, it does suggest potential correlations. This conclusion is especially true when we consider other similarities between the Olmecs and the Jaredites. In many cases, these three witnesses, the Book of Mormon, the ancient Mexican history, and archaeological data, all appear to refer to the same people.

To make a more accurate assessment comparing the Olmec culture with the Jaredite culture, we will outline the archaeological record of the ancient Olmecs.

THE DISCOVERY OF THE OLMECS

The bombing of Pearl Harbor on December 7, 1941, rocked the world. Five months earlier, during the month of July 1941, an "intellectual bomb" was dropped at a round-table conference held in Mexico City, and this bomb literally rocked the world of archaeology.

The conference was sponsored by the Mexican Society of Anthropology. Two Mexican archaeologists, Alfonso Caso and Miguel Covarrubias, along with an American archaeologist, Matthew Stirling, calmly proclaimed that a culture that has become known as the Olmecs was the mother culture of Mexico. At this point, a majority of the Mesoamerican scholars opposed the concept of a culture predating the Maya.

A renowned Maya scholar, Eric Thompson, published a paper in that same month, July 1941, discrediting the ancient dating of the La Venta-Olmec people. Another scholar, Michael Coe, later wrote of this event as follows: "This was an enormously erudite paper that set out to prove several things at once. First, that all of the non-Maya inscriptions from the Olmec area, with their seemingly early dates, were in fact late. And second, that the archaeological Olmec were no earlier than AD 1200, contemporary with the Toltec of Mexico and Yucatan. Thompson's attack on the Olmec enthusiasts sounds like a minority view, but in actuality it was shared by most American

2. Ixtlilxochitl:25; see chapter 11, "Fernando de Alva Ixtlilxochitl."

3. See Ixtlilxochitl:25 in chapter 11, "Fernando de Alva Ixtlilxochitl."

In many cases, these three witnesses, the Book of Mormon, the ancient Mexican history, and archaeological data, all appear to refer to the same people.

archaeologists working in Mesoamerica at the time. It was Stirling who was very much in the minority party. The famous Mayanist Sylvanus G. Morley was also of Thompson's opinion. Indeed, the whole Maya field was up in arms—what civilization could possibly be more ancient than that of their beloved Maya?"[4]

4. Michael D. Coe, *America's First Civilization* (New York: American Heritage; Distributed by Van Nostrand, Princeton, New Jersey, 1968), 50.

The discovery and dating of the ancient Olmecs, reaching back to pre-Christian times during which most of the Book of Mormon history took place, perhaps should have caused a major stir among Latter-day Saints. Finally, a discovery had been made that scientifically vindicated the faith of Church members, which then totaled less than a million people. Certainly the Lord, in His own due time, had opened the earth to testify of a civilization that was contemporary with the Book of Mormon.

When we first started taking tours in 1970, almost none of the people who traveled with us had ever heard of the Olmecs. They readily admitted that prior to the tours, they had heard of the Maya and the Aztec, but they had never heard the word "Olmec." Today, however, the pendulum has shifted. The growing research since *Exploring the Lands of the Book of Mormon* was first published in 1989 has brought to light considerably more information about the mother culture of Mesoamerica that archaeologists call the Olmecs. And a growing number of members of the Church of Jesus Christ in Mexico have studied in the schools since their youth about the ancient Olmecs. The events leading up to the discovery of the Olmec culture and to its subsequent early dating are as follows:

1862. A report was printed in the *Bulletin of the Mexican Society of Geography and Statistics* in 1869 by J. M. Melgar. He recounted an experience he had in 1862 in the region of San Andres Tuxtla, Veracruz, of a colossal stone head that had been unearthed a few years earlier. San Andres is near the Hill Vigia, which today is labeled by some

FIGURE 5–3: Photo of an ancient Olmec mound located at the archaeological site of La Venta, Tabasco, near the Gulf of Mexico. This earthen pyramid dates to about 1000 BC and is proposed as the city of Lib (see Ether 10:20). (Photo courtesy of Sheryl Lee Wilson)

Latter-day Saint scholars as the site where the last Book of Mormon battles of the Jaredites and the Nephites/Lamanites were fought.

1905. More than forty years elapsed before additional commentary surfaced about giant stone heads in Veracruz, Mexico. A German archaeologist, Eduard Seler, visited the Tuxtla mountain range and examined the eight-foot-high, twenty-ton head that was constructed out of one piece of basalt. Although the rounded facial features bore no resemblance to the Maya, very little was reported on large stone heads for many years.

1925. Frans Blom was born in Denmark in 1893. The Mesoamerica cultures captured his interest when he worked as a young man for one of the foreign oil companies along the Gulf of Mexico. As an archaeologist and an explorer, he and another archaeologist by the name of Oliver La Farge traveled in the mosquito-infested swampland of the coastal areas of Veracruz and Tabasco. They then moved up the Tonala River, where they discovered La Venta.

La Venta is located in the state of Tabasco near the border of Veracruz. Today, an oiled road leads to the village of La Venta; and a park with a small but tastefully built museum has been constructed on the site. The museum was opened in January 1989. It was Blom and La Farge who, under very adverse conditions, saw multitudes of stone monuments patterned after the same style of the giant stone head at Tres Zapotes. Tres Zapotes is located in the Tuxtla mountain range some ninety miles from La Venta. Little did Blom and La Farge realize they had discovered the oldest New World civilization.[5]

We could note with considerable interest that the stone monuments viewed by Blom and La Farge in 1925 may be the same artifacts witnessed by the 121 BC expedition sent by the Nephite Limhi to find Zarahemla: "And they were lost in the wilderness for the space of many days. . . . [They] traveled in a land among many waters, having discovered a land which was covered with bones of men, and of beasts, and was also covered with ruins of buildings of every kind. . . . [And] they have brought back twenty-four plates which are filled with engravings, and they are of pure gold. . . . [And] they have brought breastplates, which are large" (Mosiah 8:8–10). Because La Venta is the first prominent point of contact with recognized Olmec sites when we travel from the east, we suggest a workable hypothesis that the monuments at La Venta may be the same ones as witnessed by the Limhi expedition.

1929. Marshall Savill, who was head of the Museum of the American Indians in New York City, proposed that the stone heads and other monuments from southern Veracruz

The stone monuments viewed by Blom and La Farge in 1925 may be the same artifacts witnessed by the 121 BC expedition sent by the Nephite Limhi to find Zarahemla.

5. Coe, *America's First Civilization*, 38–42.

FIGURE 5–4: These stone monuments from the Olmec culture were transferred from the city and archaeological site of La Venta, Tabasco, to the Parque de La Venta, the outdoor park in the city of Villahermosa, Tabasco. The ancient city of La Venta was destroyed by a civil war around 250 BC, more than a hundred years before the arrival of the Limhi expedition. This expedition very likely witnessed the same monuments that we see today more than two thousand years after the Limhi exploration party. (Photos courtesy of Sheryl Lee Wilson)

were indigenous to the area and that they reflected a new art style. He called the culture *Olmec,* which is derived from a Nahuatl/Aztec word meaning rubber—or simply meaning "the people from the lands where rubber is produced." "Olmec" is certainly not the name the people called themselves nor the name that other people called them.

1932. George C. Vaillant, curator at the American Museum of Natural History in New York City, worked as a field archaeologist in the Mexico City valley. In 1932, he submitted a report about a carved jade statuette that demonstrated the same characteristics as the Olmec stone monuments reported by his predecessors. He also used the term "Olmec," and so the term has remained to this day.

1938–43. At this point, Matthew W. Stirling appeared on the scene. He was an archaeologist working under the sponsorship of the National Geographic Society. He was born in 1896 and passed away in 1975, after a lifetime of exploration and archaeological work. The title of "discoverer of the Olmec civilization" has been bestowed upon him.[6]

Stirling first made the trip to the area of Tres Zapotes located at the base of the Cerro (Hill) Vigia in 1938. Tres Zapotes was formerly called *Hueyapan.* During the following two seasons, Stirling worked at the site of Tres Zapotes.

One of the great discoveries at the site of Tres Zapotes is a monument labeled Stela C. Mary Stirling, the wife of Matthew Stirling, who accompanied him on many of his expeditions, wrote about the occasion of this discovery as follows: "A hoped-for but quite unexpected find was that of Stela C. Matt rushed back to camp with the exciting news. Carved on the Stela in bars and dots were the numerals 15-6-16-18 with a terminal glyph 6 in front of a day sign."[7]

Initially, the date was thought to be August 24, AD 478. After more detailed analysis and the subsequent discovery of a broken fragment of the glyph, the date turned out to be 31 BC, much earlier than any Maya glyph to that date. Speaking of those circumstances, Mary Stirling said: "When Matt published the stela date as 7-16-6-16-18, 31 BC, the result was as expected. He was widely criticized, especially by the Mayanists, who claimed that the date was too early and not contemporary; but, when carbon-14 provided dates for Olmec sites, 31 BC was too late."[8]

Today, the dates indeed have proven to be much earlier than the 31 BC date. The accepted dates of the Olmec culture date from 1500 BC to 300 BC, which *falls precisely in the Jaredite time period.*

A list of reports published by Stirling on this excavation work is included in the bibliography of this text, *Exploring the Lands of the Book of Mormon.* Of the initial stone heads uncovered by Stirling, the numbers continue to increase, reaching thirty or more.

From 1940 to 1943, Stirling concentrated his efforts on the restoration of La Venta in the state of Tabasco. La Venta is also near the Gulf of Mexico, the Isthmus of Tehuantepec, and the wilderness of the state of Chiapas. The state of Chiapas appears

6. Michael D. Coe, *The Olmec and Their Neighbors: Essays in Memory of Matthew W. Stirling* (Washington, DC: Dumbarton Oaks Research Library and Collections, 1981), ix.

7. Coe, *The Olmec and Their Neighbors,* 6.

8. Coe, *The Olmec and Their Neighbors,* 6.

FIGURE 5–5: Shown here is the upper portion of a monument that bears the date of 31 BC and that was discovered by Matthew Stirling in 1941 near the town of Tres Zapotes, Veracruz—close to the Hill Vigia and the Papaloapan water basin, areas considered to be the hill Ramah and the waters of Ripliancum as spoken of in the book of Ether. The artifact is located in the small museum of Tres Zapotes. The bottom half of the monument is housed in the Gulf Coast Room of the National Museum of Anthropology in Mexico City. (Photo courtesy of George and Audrey DeLange)

to be the area referred to in the book of Ether as the land southward that was preserved as an area to hunt wild animals for food. This city may have originally been built by King Lib, the son of Kish. In Ether 10, we read: "And it came to pass that Kish passed away also, and Lib reigned in his stead. And it came to pass that Lib also did that which was good in the sight of the Lord. And in the days of Lib the poisonous serpents were destroyed. Wherefore they did go in to the land southward, to hunt food for the people of the land, for the land was covered with animals of the forest. And Lib also himself became a great hunter. And they built a great city by the narrow neck of land, by the place where the sea divides the land. And they did preserve the land southward for a wilderness, to get game. And the whole face of the land northward was covered with inhabitants" (Ether 10:18–21).

The pieces of the puzzle are intriguing, to say the least, and may even qualify as highly compelling. In fact, discoveries associated with the Olmecs, including dating, location, and cultural information, might be considered the most tangible and impressive evidence that points to an accurate setting for the Book of Mormon. In this instance, the evidence associated with dating, location, and cultural information is consistent with the dating, location, and historical analysis of La Venta in comparison with the city of Lib. The wording "the place where the sea divides the land" is the definition of a gulf. The wording "narrow neck of land" is the definition of an isthmus, and the area southward that was preserved as a place to hunt wild game is today called the wilderness of

Discoveries associated with the Olmecs, including dating, location, and cultural information, might be considered the most tangible and impressive evidence that points to an accurate setting for the Book of Mormon.

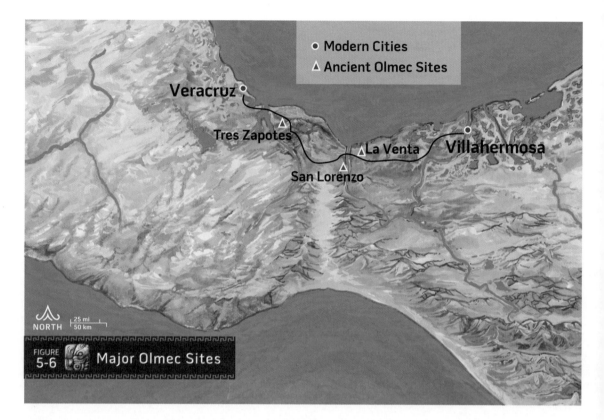

FIGURE 5–6: Three major Olmec sites from left to right are Tres Zapotes and San Lorenzo, Veracruz, and La Venta, Tabasco. Driving time from Villahermosa, Tabasco, to Veracruz, Veracruz, is about six hours. Today, Latter-day Saint temples are located in the cities of Veracruz, Villahermosa, and Tuxtla Gutierrez.

Tehuantepec, which means a wilderness of wild animals. To this day, that wilderness area located in the state of Chiapas is home to over 40 percent of the wild animals of the entire country of Mexico. Chiapas, however, is home to less then 4 percent of the country's human population.

1950s. During the decade of the 1950s, the idea to preserve the ancient Olmec artifacts from the archaeological site of La Venta was conceived by one of Tabasco's favorite sons, a poet by the name of Don Carlos Pellicer. Pellicer was also a student of the pre-Columbian era and was instrumental in re-creating a landscape similar to the flora and fauna that may have been in existence during Olmec times.[9]

The monuments were transferred from La Venta to Villahermosa, a distance of eighty miles—thus enabling both national and international tourists to examine first-hand the ancient Olmec monuments from La Venta.[10] At that time, no road had been built into La Venta; and the dirt road along the Gulf Coast was impassable by automobile during many months of the year because of the heavy rainfall.

9. Lorenzo Ochoa, *Olmecas y Mayas en Tabasco: Cinco Acercamientos* (Villahermosa: Gobierno Del Estado De Tabasco, 1985), 23–24.

10. Ochoa, *Olmecas y Mayas en Tabasco: Cinco Acercamientos*, 23–24.

1964–68. Not many miles from La Venta is San Lorenzo. It was here that Michael Coe, emeritus Yale professor, added his contribution to the understanding of the Olmec culture. Coe worked with the San Lorenzo site located along the mighty Coatzacoalcos River near the city of Minatitlan, Veracruz. San Lorenzo began about 1200 BC and continued to exist as a city center until the Olmec destruction about 300 BC. As a result of the deciphering of the Maya hieroglyphs and some investigative reporting by Bruce Warren, we can probably conclude that the Olmec site of San Lorenzo may have been the resident city of King Kish, a Jaredite king whose name, dates, and events correspond with what we now know about the kingship at San Lorenzo, Veracruz. This breakthrough is so significant that we have included its analysis by Dr. Warren as an appendage to this chapter. San Lorenzo may also have been the city of Desolation referred to by Mormon—the city where he had called for the Nephites to gather in the year AD 362: "And it came to pass that I did cause my people that they should gather themselves together at the land Desolation, to a city which was in the borders, by the narrow pass which led into the land southward" (Mormon 3:5).[11]

11. Naming the archaeological sites of San Lorenzo and La Venta as potential candidates for the cities of Kish and Lib respectively in the Book of Mormon is in no way an attempt on our part to suggest that Coe and other non-Latter-day Saint archaeologists agree with us. That work must be done by interested and dedicated students of the Book of Mormon.

FIGURE 5–7: These massive stone heads are representative of the rulers of the Olmecs—or the first settlers of Mesoamerica. Because of the dating of King Kish, we are now able to prepare a workable hypothesis of the Jaredite kings dating from 1250 BC to 250 BC, as shown in the chart that follows in "The Classic Period of the Olmecs" section. (Photos courtesy of Sheryl Lee Wilson)

1977. An excellent work written by Beatriz de la Fuente was published in Spanish titled *Los Hombres de Piedra* (Men of Stone). This 390-page book is complete with pictures of the monuments from the three Olmec sites of Tres Zapotes, La Venta, and San Lorenzo. She presents detailed measurements of eighteen giant stone heads.

THE OLMECS AND THE JAREDITES

1981. Several books and events that are associated with Latter-day Saint scholars and that support the thesis of *Exploring the Lands of the Book of Mormon* that the Jaredites and the Olmecs are one and the same people have surfaced beginning in 1981.

A book, *In Search of Cumorah,* was published in 1981. The author, David Palmer, now deceased, was a researcher, a chemist, and an avid student of Mesoamerican culture and the Book of Mormon. Regarding the Olmecs and the Jaredites, he states, "We will see that there is an excellent correlation between Jaredite history and the cultural history of the archaeological Olmecs."[12] Palmer also proposes that a hill called *Vigia*, which is located by the archaeological site of Tres Zapotes that Stirling excavated in 1939, is the same area where the last battles were fought, as recorded in the Book of Mormon. Palmer writes: "I will not prove definitively that it is the correct place. That could only be done absolutely by discovery of Mormon's record repository. However, there is strong archaeological evidence. Any other candidate would have to pass through the same strainer of criteria to which we will subject the Cerro Vigia."[13]

Palmer visited the site and examined the mounds, topography, and archaeology of the immediate area. With satellite pictures, he stated that he was fairly convinced Vigia was the hill Ramah/Cumorah as recorded in the Book of Mormon.

1982. Joseph Allen writes: "As a result of Palmer's book, and after having visited the area, I elected to write the Hill Vigia into our tour itinerary. The first Book of Mormon-oriented tour was taken to the area in 1982. I escorted Professor Eldin Ricks of Brigham Young University as well as other members of the tour group.

"The response of the group was positive. Since that time, we have taken hundreds of groups through the beautiful Tuxtla mountain region of Veracruz, Mexico, with the intent of investigating and analyzing the possibility of that area's being the heartland of the Jaredites and the land of Cumorah spoken of in the Book of Mormon. Since that first trip in 1982, many events have occurred. Some of our tour members have hiked up the Hill Vigia, and many others have ridden to the top of the hill in cattle trucks belonging

12. David A. Palmer, *In Search of Cumorah: New Evidences for the Book of Mormon from Ancient Mexico* (Bountiful, UT: Horizon Publishers, 1981), 18.

13. Palmer, *In Search of Cumorah*, 91.

"Any other candidate [for the hill Cumorah] would have to pass through the same strainer of criteria to which we will subject the Cerro Vigia."

—David Palmer

FIGURE 5–8: The Hill Vigia is located in the Tuxtla Mountains of Veracruz about one hour's drive southward of the city of Veracruz. The hill is about two thousand feet high and takes about two hours to hike to the top from the village of Santiago Tuxtla, Veracruz. The Hill Vigia is a candidate for the hill Ramah/Cumorah spoken of in the Book of Mormon. An Olmec head was discovered at the base of the Hill Vigia near the town of Tres Zapotes. (Photos courtesy of Keith Neeley)

Exploring the Lands of the Book of Mormon

to local residents in the nearby town of Santiago Tuxtla. Todd Allen, my son and a frequent tour director to Book of Mormon lands, has camped out overnight on top of the hill. In the late 1980s, some funds were donated by Ted Stoddard, Doug Christensen, Merrill Oaks, Greg Henderson, and me to sponsor a reconnaissance mission of three Latter-day Saint archaeologists to the Tuxtla area—Richard Hauck, Garth Norman, and Bruce Warren. They were accompanied by Merrill Oaks and Doug Christensen. That expedition, had it occurred fifty years earlier, would have been worthy of newspaper headlines."

Since 1982, many other people, including local Mexican members of The Church of Jesus Christ of Latter-day Saints, tour groups, and individuals have visited the Hill Vigia near Santiago Tuxtla, Veracruz, and the surrounding archaeological site of Tres Zapotes. The beautiful Lake Catemaco, the massive Papaloapan water basin, and the Hill Cintepec are also located in the same area. The two latter areas have been proposed as the waters of Ripliancum and the hill Shim, respectively.

Evidence now supports the Hill Vigia as the leading candidate for the hill Cumorah where the Nephites were defeated by the Lamanites. This hypothesis is strengthened because of the dramatic similarities between the Jaredites of the Book of Mormon and the Olmecs of Veracruz. Because the hill Ramah of the Jaredites and the hill Cumorah of the Nephites are the same hill, the hill Cumorah mentioned in Mormon 6 needs also to be in Veracruz. This reasoning simply suggests that Moroni carried only those few plates (see Moroni 6:6) that constitute our Book of Mormon, plus the sealed portion, to New York state where he buried them in a small hill near Palmyra, New York. (For a more detailed analysis on the location of the hills Ramah, Cumorah, and Shim, see chapter 27, "Hills and Valleys.")

1985. John Sorenson wrote a book about Mesoamerica and the Book of Mormon for the Latter-day Saint audience. At the time, Sorenson was serving as head of the Anthropology Department at Brigham Young University. He included in his book, *An Ancient American Setting for the Book of Mormon*, a comparison chart between the Olmec society of Mesoamerica and the Jaredites of the Book of Mormon, with a summary statement as follows: "That brief overview shows striking parallels between the archaeological picture (Olmec culture) on the one hand and what the Book of Mormon says (Jaredite culture) on the other. Enough parallels are visible that we can be optimistic about future, more detailed research results."[14]

Sorenson is credited with labeling the Hill Vigia as the most probable candidate where the last battles of the Jaredites and the Nephites/Lamanites were fought, as recorded in the books of Mormon and Ether.

1987–88. Two additional books were published by Latter-day Saint authors, each affirming the parallels between the Olmecs and the Jaredites.

Archaeologist Bruce Warren revised an early book written by Thomas S. Ferguson called *One Fold and One Shepherd*. Warren included additional material in the book. The

Evidence now supports the Hill Vigia as the leading candidate for the hill Cumorah where the Nephites were defeated by the Lamanites.

14. John L. Sorenson, *An Ancient American Setting for the Book of Mormon* (Salt Lake City: Deseret Book Company and Foundation for Ancient Research and Mormon Studies, 1985), 121–22.

book is called *The Messiah in Ancient America*. Although Warren writes very little about the Jaredite civilization, the setting of the book is in Mesoamerica, and Sorenson's map showing both the Jaredite culture and the hill Cumorah in the Gulf Coast region of Mexico are included in the book. Warren's book was updated in 2002.

Archaeologist Richard Hauck wrote his book, *Deciphering the Geography of the Book of Mormon,* in 1988. He writes: "The Olmec development bears a striking similarity to the history of the Jaredite people as abridged in the segment of the Book of Mormon known as the Book of Ether."[15]

15. F. Richard Hauck, *Deciphering the Geography of the Book of Mormon* (Salt Lake City: Deseret Book, 1988), 6.

1989. For two years, Mexican artists worked at the museum of La Venta making copies of all the monuments that had been moved to Villahermosa from the original site of La Venta. A new, small museum was opened in January 1989, utilizing some of the copies the artists had made. The museum is located at the archaeological site of La Venta in the town of La Venta, Tabasco. In addition, ongoing archaeological digs accompanied with continued investigative work by Dr. Rebecca Gonzalez, who resides at Villahermosa, Tabasco, have shed additional light on the ancient site of La Venta. Gonzalez and her crew uncovered an additional three massive Olmec heads located at the mound of La Venta. Many of the new findings are now on display at the small museum at the base of the La Venta mound. The museum was remodeled and reopened in 2002.

The unknown system of writing on the stone found in 2006 in Veracruz, Mexico, dates to about 1000 BC and is the earliest writing yet discovered in the New World.

1990–2000. During the last decade of the twentieth century, significant and ongoing investigations continued to reveal more about the ancient Olmec/Jaredite civilization. A massive hieroglyphic stone called the Mojarra stone was discovered in the Tuxtla mountain region, showing Maya text. On the wall panel of the Temple of the Cross at Palenque, the discovery of the name of Kish (Ki'x), which is discussed at the end of this chapter, shows a textual birth, ascension to the throne, and death date of a tenth century BC Jaredite king.

2006. Several archaeologists, including Stephen Houston of Brown University and formerly of Brigham Young University, reported the discovery of an engraved stone that was found in a gravel quarry in the heartland of the Olmecs in Veracruz, Mexico. The stone measures fourteen inches long, eight inches wide, and five inches thick and weighs twenty-six pounds. The researchers report that the writing on the stone links the Olmecs to literacy, documents a writing system, and reveals a new complexity to the Olmec civilization. The unknown system of writing on the stone dates to about 1000 BC and is the earliest writing yet discovered in the New World.[16]

16. Maria del Carmen Rodriguez Martinez, et al., "Did the Olmec Know How to Write," *Science*, 313, no. 5793 (September 15, 2006): 1537.

THE DATING OF THE OLMECS

Almost three-fourths of a century has passed since Matthew Stirling proposed that the Olmecs predated the Maya and that the Olmecs were the mother culture of Mesoamerica. With the advent of radiocarbon dating, most scientists generally agree with the dates of the Olmec.

Exploring the Lands of the Book of Mormon

As discussed in chapter 3, "Looking at Dates," we will use the following dating procedures for the Olmec culture:

2600 BC–1200 BC	Olmec Preclassic	(Maya Early Preclassic)
1200 BC–600 BC	Olmec Classic	(Maya Middle Preclassic)
600 BC–250 BC	Late Olmec	(Maya Late Preclassic)

A RECORD OF A DYNASTY

We may be inclined to say that if we have seen one Olmec head, we have seen them all. This statement, however, is not the case. Each sculpture is uniquely different. In Book of Mormon times, the amount of work required to carve out of basalt a detailed face and then to transport it down river from the Tuxtla Mountains to its resting place was probably an almost overwhelming task.

The archaeologists' examinations of the various monuments show that the monuments date to separate time periods, suggesting that the monuments represent a dynasty or a king lineage.

THE CLASSIC PERIOD OF THE OLMECS

The Classic Period of the Olmecs, as determined by the number and quality of monuments, encompasses the time from 1200 BC to 600 BC. This dating is consistent with the Classic Period of the Jaredites as described in Ether 10. This six-hundred-year period appears to embrace the kingships of Shiz to Com and occupies only one and a half pages in the book of Ether. By utilizing the date of ascension to the throne of King Kish at the age of twenty-six on Wednesday, March 5, 967 BC, as determined by the dates on the Temple of the Cross at Palenque, we can approximate the dates of the thirteen other kings mentioned in Ether 10. The reconstruction of the kingships in intervals of fifty years each is as shown below. By adding the last six Jaredite kings, plus Ether, a contemporary of Coriantumr, with intervals of fifty years, we arrive at an ending date for the Jaredites of 250 BC, which is almost identical to the date given by Ixtlilxochitl for the destruction of the "giants."

Shez	1250 BC
Riplakish	1200 BC
Morianton	1150 BC
Kim	1100 BC
Levi	1050 BC
Corom	1000 BC
Kish	**967 BC**
Lib	900 BC

> The Classic Period of the Olmecs encompasses the time from 1200 BC to 600 BC, which is consistent with the Classic Period of the Jaredites as described in the Book of Mormon.

Hearthom	850 BC
Heth	800 BC
Aaron	750 BC
Amnigaddah	700 BC
Coriantum	650 BC
Com	600 BC
Shiblom	550 BC
Seth	500 BC
Ahah	450 BC
Ethem	400 BC
Moron	350 BC
Coriantor	300 BC
Ether (Coriantumr)	250 BC

THE CLIMATE OF THE OLMEC HOMELAND

The climate along the Gulf of Mexico is hot and humid. Rain can occur at any time, as the weather does not follow strictly the prescribed pattern of the rest of Mesoamerica, although June to November produces the highest rainfall. The northers, or "nortes," consisting of strong winds blowing in from the Gulf Coast, can raise havoc at various times during the year.

The area is always lush and green because of the heavy rainfall, allowing the farmers to raise crops consisting of bananas, tobacco, pineapple, sugar cane, corn, beans, and all kinds of fruits and vegetables. The local home dwellers simply plant a post for their fences; and within a short period of time, the posts grow into trees.

The entire coastline is called "Mexico's golden lane," not only because of the area's agriculture productivity but also because the area is where the vast Mexican oil reserves are located.

THE VASTNESS OF THE OLMEC EMPIRE

The Olmec empire stretched as far west as Acapulco, Guerrero, and as far south as El Salvador. The state of Oaxaca, the archaeological zone of Izapa, and the coast of Guatemala all manifest strong Olmec influence.

THE DECLINE AND DESTRUCTION OF THE OLMECS

Apparently, a great internal destruction occurred in the Olmec area around 250 BC, although San Lorenzo may have fallen earlier. At La Venta, twenty-four of the forty monuments were intentionally mutilated.[17]

Regarding the monuments at San Lorenzo, Coe writes: "There is no evidence of an outside invasion. The amount of pent-up hatred and fury represented by this enormous act of destruction must have been awesome, indeed. These monuments [of both

> Local home dwellers in the heart of the Olmec homeland simply plant a post for their fences; and within a short period of time, the posts grow into trees.

17. William R. Coe, *Tikal: A Handbook of the Ancient Maya Ruins* (Philadelphia: The University Museum of the University of Pennsylvania, 1967, 3rd ed. 1970), 90–91.

Exploring the Lands of the Book of Mormon

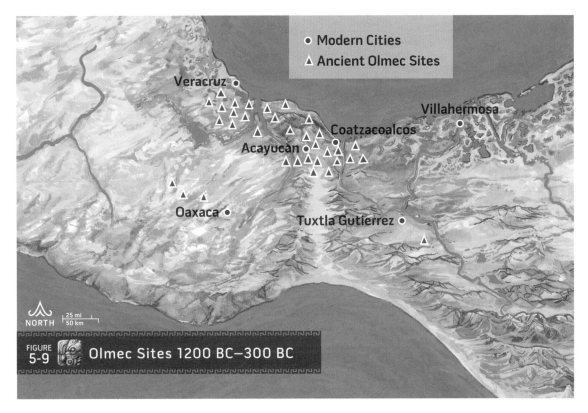

FIGURE 5–9: The above map is a representation of the many Olmec archaeological sites located along the Gulf Coast of Mexico in the states of Veracruz and Tabasco. Although the heartland of the Olmecs centered around the Gulf of Mexico beginning about 1500 BC and ending about 300 BC, other sites throughout Mesoamerica manifest Olmec influence both prior to and during the Gulf Coast era. For example, Oaxaca manifests Olmec-style evidence prior to 2000 BC, and Izapa developed Olmec art between 1000 and 800 BC.

FIGURE 5–10: These photos show defaced monuments as a result of a great civil war that occurred about 250 BC among the Olmecs/Jaredites. Images from both La Venta and San Lorenzo manifest severed heads, broken monuments, and defaced markings. (Photos courtesy of Sheryl Lee Wilson and Blake Joseph Allen)

La Venta and San Lorenzo] are very large, and basalt is a very hard stone. Wherever possible, heads were smashed from bodies, 'altars' were smashed to pieces, and strange, dimpled depressions and slots were cut into Colossal Heads."[18]

18. Coe, *America's First Civilization*, 86.

A REVIEW OF THE JAREDITE/OLMEC HISTORY

The Olmecs developed their central government along the Gulf Coast of Mexico. They reached their high culture from approximately 1200 BC to 600 BC. For the purpose of our discussion, we will correlate the Olmecs with the Jaredites in the Book of Mormon. Justification for our doing so is as follows:

Both the historical record and the Book of Mormon stipulate that the first settlers in Mesoamerica came from the Tower of Babel—a fact that cannot be dismissed as mere coincidence.

1. The Tower of Babel

The Jaredites came from the Tower of Babel when the languages were confounded. In the book of Ether, we read:

> And now I, Moroni, proceed to give an account of those ancient inhabitants who were destroyed by the hand of the Lord upon the face of this north country. . . .
>
> Jared came forth with his brother and their families, with some others and their families, from the great tower, at the time the Lord confounded the language of the people, and swore in his wrath that they should be scattered upon all the face of the earth; and according to the word of the Lord the people were scattered.
>
> And it came to pass that the brother of Jared did cry unto the Lord, and the Lord had compassion upon Jared; therefore he did not confound the language of Jared; and Jared and his brother were not confounded. (Ether 1:1, 33, 35)
>
> And thus they were driven forth, three hundred and forty and four days upon the water.
>
> And they did land upon the shore of the promised land. (Ether 6:11–12)

According to the historical record, the first settlers in Mesoamerica, whom archaeologists call Olmecs, also came from the great tower. A history of Mexico was written in 1568 by a Catholic priest, Fernando de Alva Ixtlilxochitl, of whom more is said in chapter 11, "Fernando de Alva Ixtlilxochitl." He wrote that after the flood, the people "built a Zaucalli very high and strong, which means 'The Very High Tower,' to protect themselves against a second destruction of the world. As time elapsed, their language became confounded, such that they did not understand one another; and they were scattered to all parts of the earth. The Tultecas, consisting of seven men and their wives, were able to understand each other; and they came to this land, having first crossed many lands and waters, living in caves and passing through great trials and tribulations. Upon their arrival here, they discovered that it was a very good and fertile land."[19]

19. Ixtlilxochitl:6–8; see chapter 11, "Fernando de Alva Ixtlilxochitl."

Thus, the Book of Mormon witnesses that the Jaredites came from the Tower of Babel, and the historical record witnesses that the Olmecs came from the Tower of Babel. Therefore, two witnesses—the Book of Mormon and Mesoamerican history—support our hypothesis that the Jaredites and the Olmecs are the same people.

2. A High Civilization

The Jaredites and the Olmecs both reached their high, or Classic Period, at the same time. The events that occurred in Ether 10 correspond with the 1200 BC–600 BC time period when the Olmecs built many cities and reached a high cultural period. We read in the book of Ether: "And they built a great city by the narrow neck of land, by the place where the sea divides the land. And they did preserve the land southward for a wilderness, to get game. And the whole face of the land northward was covered with inhabitants" (Ether 10:20–21).

The Olmecs built many cities in what we refer to as the "land northward" during this time period, as mentioned in the Book of Mormon. Figure 5-9 shows a map of archaeological sites in the area along the Gulf Coast of Mexico, illustrating the massive civilization that flourished in the area from 1500 BC to 300 BC.

The book of Ether describes the high period of the Jaredites:

> And they were exceedingly industrious, and they did buy and sell and traffic one with another, that they might get gain.
>
> And they did work in all manner of ore, and they did make gold, and silver, and iron, and brass, and all manner of metals; and they did dig it out of the earth; wherefore, they did cast up mighty heaps of earth to get ore, of gold, and of silver, and of iron, and of copper. And they did work all manner of fine work.
>
> And they did have silks, and fine-twined linen; and they did work all manner of cloth, that they might clothe themselves from their nakedness.
>
> And they did make all manner of tools to till the earth, both to plow and to sow, to reap and to hoe, and also to thrash.
>
> And they did make all manner of tools with which they did work their beasts.
>
> And they did make all manner of weapons of war. And they did work all manner of work of exceedingly curious workmanship.
>
> And never could be a people more blessed than were they, and more prospered by the hand of the Lord. And they were in a land that was choice above all lands, for the Lord had spoken it. (Ether 10:22–28)

The Olmec empire was vast and heavily populated. We emphasize that *their heartland was in the area that probably was considered the "land northward" by the Nephites.* The "land southward" was set aside as a place to hunt game. Even today, wild animals,

> The Olmec empire was vast and heavily populated, and their heartland is in the area that probably was considered the "land northward" by the Nephites.

including the jaguar, inhabit the area southeast of the Gulf Coast, which in our model is the land southward.

3. A Large People

The Book of Mormon, the Spanish chronicles, and archaeologists all bear witness that the first civilization's inhabitants of Mesoamerica were a large people. When Limhi's forty-three men tried on the rusted breastplates, they said the breastplates were large. The sixteenth-century Spanish writers recorded the Olmecs' history and called them giants. The archaeological record sculptured them as large people. Even today, Olmec "look-alikes" live along the Gulf Coast of Mexico. They are large people—not tall, just large.

Ixtlilxochitl called the people who lived along the Gulf Coast "giants" as he wrote: "In this land called New Spain there were *giants,* as demonstrated by their bones that have been discovered in many areas. The ancient Tulteca record keepers referred to the giants as Quinametzin; and as they had a record of the history of the Quinametzin, they learned that they had many wars and dissensions among themselves in this land that is now called New Spain. They were destroyed, and their civilization came to an end as a result of great calamities and as a punishment from the heavens for grave sins they had committed."[20]

The Limhi expedition discovered the remains of the Jaredite civilization about 121 BC, a civilization that had been destroyed an estimated 180–280 years earlier. With reference to the size of the Jaredites, Limhi says, "And behold, also, they have brought breastplates, which are *large*" (Mosiah 8:10; emphasis added). Speaking of the Jaredites, Moroni says, "And they were *large* and mighty men as to the strength of men" (Ether 15:26; emphasis added).

4. A Great Destruction

A great destruction was reported in both the Olmec and the Jaredite cultures many years prior to their final war.

The dates of the Ixtlilxochitl account are somewhat inconsistent, making it difficult to rely on them. However, the event that tells of a great hurricane that uprooted trees and buildings and that caused many of the animals to suffocate is consistent with both Mesoamerica history and Book of Mormon history. In fact, the Aztec calendar, whose replicas constitute a popular tourist purchase, depicts four major destructive periods of the world—periods that are also mentioned by Ixtlilxochitl. They are

Period I: Sun of Water (the earth was destroyed by a flood)
Period II: Sun of Air (the earth was destroyed by a hurricane)
Period III: Sun of Earth (the earth was destroyed by an earthquake)
Period IV: Sun of Fire (the earth will be destroyed by fire)

> The Book of Mormon, the Spanish chronicles, and archaeologists all bear witness that the first civilization's inhabitants of Mesoamerica were a large people.

20. Ixtlilxochitl:25; emphasis added. See chapter 11, "Fernando de Alva Ixtlilxochitl."

The destruction we are talking about took place in Period II—between the flood and the earthquake (3100 BC–AD 30). Using the Maya calendar base date (3114 BC) as the base date of the flood and using the first calculation of Ixtlilxochitl of the destruction by the hurricane (1,715 years from the flood), we arrive at the year of 1398 BC as the date for the great hurricane. Regarding this second destruction, Ixtlilxochitl writes:

> And 1,715 years after the flood, the people were destroyed by a very great hurricane that carried away trees, rocks, houses, and large buildings.[21] Many men and women escaped the storm by hiding in caves and other places where the great hurricane could not reach them.
>
> After a short period of time, they left the caves to see how much damage had taken place in the land. They discovered that it was populated and covered with monkeys that had been driven by the winds, as they had been in darkness all this time without being able to see the sun or the moon.
>
> From this event, the saying came about that men had turned into monkeys. This period became known as the second period, or the second world, called Ehecatonatiuh, which means sun of wind. After the destruction, men began again to rebuild and to multiply upon the face of the land.[22]

We read an almost-unnoticed account in the book of Ether about a great destruction that took place prior to the final great civil war that brought the Jaredite history to a close. This great destruction is recorded in Ether 11 as follows:

> And there came also in the days of Com many prophets, and prophesied of *the destruction* of that great people except they should repent, and turn unto the Lord, and forsake their murders and wickedness.
>
> And it came to pass that the brother of Shiblom caused that all the prophets who prophesied of *the destruction* of the people should be put to death;
>
> And there was great calamity in all the land, for they had testified that a great curse should come upon the land, and also upon the people, and that there should be a *great destruction* among them, such an one as never had been upon the face of the earth, and their bones should become as heaps of earth upon the face of the land except they should repent of their wickedness.
>
> And they hearkened not unto the voice of the Lord, because of their wicked combinations; wherefore, there began to be wars and contentions in all the land, and also many famines and pestilences, insomuch that there was a *great destruction,* such an one as never had been known upon the face of the earth; and all this came to pass in the days of Shiblom. (Ether 11:1, 5–7; emphasis added)

21. Today, hurricane winds are common to the coast of Veracruz, Mexico. They are called "nortes" or "northers." The great hurricane destruction referred to by Ixtlilxochitl correlates to 1399 BC and may be the same destruction referred to in the days of Shiblom in the book of Ether: "There was a great destruction, such an one as never had been known upon the face of the earth" (Ether 11:7).

22. Ixtlilxochitl:10–12; see chapter 11, "Fernando de Alva Ixtlilxochitl."

A correlation of the first settlers, whom the chroniclers call giants and the archaeologists call Olmecs, with the Book of Mormon Jaredites allows us to place their heartland along the Gulf Coast of Mexico in the states of Veracruz and Tabasco.

A correlation of the first settlers, whom the chroniclers call giants and the archaeologists call Olmecs, with the Book of Mormon Jaredites allows us to place their heartland along the Gulf Coast of Mexico in the states of Veracruz and Tabasco. Even today, at certain seasons of the year, tremendous winds blow inland from the Gulf of Mexico, causing great destruction. The local people call them *los nortes,* meaning the northern winds. A 175-mile-an-hour wind called Hurricane Gilbert ripped through that area in September 1988, and others just as devastating have continued into the twenty-first century.

5. A Civil War

Both the archaeological record and the Book of Mormon bear witness that the final war of the Olmecs/Jaredites was caused by internal strife and that it was indeed violent.

Both the Book of Mormon and archaeological records inform us that the great first civilization came to a close as a result of a civil war. According to the Book of Mormon, after years of Jaredite fighting, a last battle occurred as a result of internal conflicts:

> And it came to pass when Coriantumr had recovered of his wounds, he began to remember the words which Ether had spoken unto him.
>
> He saw that there had been slain by the sword already nearly two millions of his people, and he began to sorrow in his heart; yea, there had been slain two millions of mighty men, and also their wives and their children.
>
> And it came to pass that when they were all gathered together, every one to the army which he would, with their wives and their children—both men, women and children being armed with weapons of war, having shields, and breastplates, and head-plates, and being clothed after the manner of war—they did march forth one against another to battle; and they fought all that day, and conquered not. (Ether 15:1–2, 15)

Both archaeology and the Book of Mormon bear witness that this final war was caused by internal strife and that it was indeed violent. The book of Ether itself is a very violent record. A dynasty that lasted over two thousand years came to an end when Coriantumr cut off the head of his enemy, Shiz: "And it came to pass that when Coriantumr had leaned upon his sword, that he rested a little, he smote off the head of Shiz. And it came to pass that after he had smitten off the head of Shiz, that Shiz raised up on his hands and fell; and after that he had struggled for breath, he died" (Ether 15:30–31).

Ether had prophesied that Coriantumr and all his household would fall if they did not repent: "Otherwise they should be destroyed, and all his household save it were himself. And he should only live to see the fulfilling of the prophecies which had been spoken concerning another people receiving the land for their inheritance; and Coriantumr should receive a burial by them; and every soul should be destroyed save it were Coriantumr" (Ether 13:21).

Exploring the Lands of the Book of Mormon

That is exactly what happened. The lineage of Coriantumr, or all of his household, was destroyed. The kingdom fell.

The Olmec site of La Venta, which is located about fifteen miles inland from the Gulf of Mexico near the Coatzacoalcos River, was undoubtedly one of the most powerful and most holy places in the Olmec heartland. According to Michael Coe, the final destruction of the Olmecs was caused by internal strife and was violent: "La Venta was deliberately destroyed in ancient times. Its fall was certainly violent, as 24 out of 40 sculptured monuments were intentionally mutilated. This probably occurred in the beginning of Late Formative times, between 400 BC–300 BC."[23]

23. Coe, *Mexico*, 90.

For more proof than that found in the Book of Mormon and in archaeological records, we can again appeal to a third witness, Ixtlilxochitl, who wrote about the destruction of the first settlers, whom he called giants. Although his dating is inconsistent in this account, his description is adequate. He may be writing about the same Jaredite and Olmec destruction discussed above: "In this land called New Spain [Mexico], there were giants, as demonstrated by their bones that have been discovered in many areas. The ancient Tulteca record keepers called them Quinametzin. They became acquainted with them and had many wars and contentions with them, and in particular in all of the land that is now called New Spain. They [the Quinametzin] were destroyed, and their civilization came to an end as a result of great calamities and punishments from heaven for some grave sins that they had committed."[24]

24. Ixtlilxochitl:25; see chapter 11, "Fernando de Alva Ixtlilxochitl."

6. Ripliancum

The final comparison between the archaeological Olmecs and the Book of Mormon Jaredites is that prior to the final destruction, a great warm-up battle was fought between the army of Shiz and the army of Coriantumr:

> There had been slain two millions of mighty men, and also their wives and their children.
>
> And when Coriantumr saw that he was about to fall he fled again before the people of Shiz.
>
> And it came to pass that he came to the waters of Ripliancum, which, by interpretation, is large, or to exceed all; wherefore, when they came to these waters they pitched their tents; and Shiz also pitched his tents near unto them; and therefore on the morrow they did come to battle.
>
> And it came to pass that they fought an exceedingly sore battle, in which Coriantumr was wounded again, and he fainted with the loss of blood.
>
> And it came to pass that the armies of Coriantumr did press upon the armies of Shiz that they beat them, that they caused them to flee before them; and they did flee southward, and did pitch their tents in a place which was called Ogath.

The large body of water known as Ripliancum in the Book of Mormon is probably known today as the Papaloapan water basin that empties in the Gulf of Mexico by the city of Alvarado, Veracruz.

And it came to pass that the army of Coriantumr did pitch their tents by the hill Ramah; and it was that same hill where my father Mormon did hide up the records unto the Lord, which were sacred. (Ether 15:2, 7–11)

Thus, we see a geographical correlation when we compare the Olmec territory with what we read in Ether about a battle before the final battle. Shiz and his army had pursued Coriantumr and his army northward from Ramah/Cumorah to a large body of water called Ripliancum. The interpretation of Ripliancum is "large, or to exceed all."

There is such a body of water that is directionally correct and that seems to meet the distance requirement as outlined in the Book of Mormon from the Hill Vigia in Veracruz, Mexico. This massive area of water today is called the Papaloapan water basin that empties into the Gulf of Mexico by the city of Alvarado, Veracruz. It forms the natural barrier that the Jaredite record seems to require.

SUMMARY

We still have much to learn about the ancient Olmec race. However, the parallels that manifest themselves in detail with dating, parallel events, directions, distances, seashores, a narrow neck, waters, and mountains are indeed fascinating.

The Book of Mormon, as limited a history as it is, presents a very reliable guide in pointing us in the direction of proposing that the Jaredites were the same people as the so-called Olmecs of the Gulf Coast of Mexico. By studying the Olmec culture, we may uncover even greater knowledge of the ancient civilization of the Jaredites. And

FIGURE 5-11: The interpretation of the waters of Ripliancum in the Book of Mormon is "large, or to exceed all," which means the same as *Hueyapan,* the ancient name of the Papaloapan water basin in Veracruz. The syllable "hue" in the Nahuatl language means "large" and the syllable "pan" means "water." (Photo courtesy of Sheryl Lee Wilson)

Exploring the Lands of the Book of Mormon

the local history of Mesoamerica as reflected in both oral and written traditions adds a third witness to establishing the truth of the mother civilization of the Americas.

FREQUENTLY ASKED QUESTIONS

Over the years, tour members who have been on tours with us have asked the following typical questions about the Olmecs/Jaredites:

Question: If the Jaredites developed their heartland along the Gulf of Mexico where an abundance of rainfall occurs and where all kinds of things grow, including bananas and pineapple, why do the Nephites call the area the land of Desolation? Was any part of it desolate?

Answer: The Nephites called the land southward by the name of Bountiful, and they called the land northward by the name of Desolation (see Alma 22:31). The land northward was called Desolation because of the great destruction of the Jaredite nation and because the Nephites felt that a terrible curse was upon that land (see 3 Nephi 3:24). The land northward was not called Desolation because things would not grow there.

Mormon wrote the following: "And now no part of the land was desolate, save it were for timber; but because of the greatness of the destruction of the people who had before inhabited the land it was called desolate" (Helaman 3:6).

Question: If the Church has felt that the land northward was North America for all of these years, why are we now changing our orientation?

Answer: The early leaders and teachers of the Church are to be commended for proposing geographical locations with such a small amount of information at their disposal. As pointed out in this chapter, prior to 1941, virtually no information was available about a civilization whose time period correlated with the Jaredites.

We should be grateful that the Lord is indeed bringing forth additional light about the ancient cultures that were contemporary with the Book of Mormon time period. We then are able to propose more reliable correlations in terms of the geography and history of the Book of Mormon.

Question: Were not all the Jaredites killed at the last battle where Coriantumr cut off the head of Shiz?

Answer: Archaeology, Mexican history, and logic do not allow every last man, woman, and child to be killed in the last Jaredite battle.

When the Book of Mormon uses the term "all," the wording suggests that we consider *all* in the sense of "all they could" or "all his household," as in the following: "that they *might* get *all* who were upon the face of the land" (Ether 15:14; emphasis added) and "they should be destroyed, and *all his household*" (Ether 13:21; emphasis added).

Moreover, the Book of Mormon gives a hint that at least a "remnant" of the Jaredites survived the last great battle at the hill Ramah. Members of the Limhi expedition brought home to King Limhi the twenty-four gold plates containing a record of the

From a Church-history perspective, virtually no information was available prior to 1941 about a civilization whose time period correlated with the Jaredites.

Jaredites. King Limhi, speaking of the plates, asked Ammon, "Knowest thou of any one that can translate? For I am desirous that these records should be translated into our language; for, perhaps, they will give us a knowledge *of a remnant of the people who have been destroyed, from whence these records came;* or, perhaps, they will give us a knowledge of this very people who have been destroyed; and I am desirous to know the cause of their destruction" (Mosiah 8:12; emphasis added).

Question: I have read accounts that date the destruction of the Jaredites at about 600 BC—correlated with the arrival of the Nephites and the Mulekites. Why do you place the destruction at a later date of about 300 BC?

Answer: We believe that the 600 BC date is too early for the Jaredite destruction for the following reasons:

1. In Omni 1:17, we read that the Mulekites had become "exceedingly numerous," they had had "many wars," "their language had become corrupted," and they had lost the essence of their religion. Such historical events require a substantial number of years to transpire. Further, because Zarahemla knew both Coriantumr and Mosiah, a much later date than 600 BC for the Jaredite destruction seems reasonable.

2. The Limhi expedition discovered the Jaredite ruins about 121 BC, at which time they saw the bones of men and of beasts, breastplates, and swords (see Mosiah 8:8–11). These discoveries suggest that the time period from the destruction of the Jaredites to Limhi was not almost five hundred years (600 BC to 121 BC) but was a more believable scenario such as Ixtlilxochitl's destruction date of 236 BC—or a little over a hundred years for the decaying of the bones and swords.

3. Both archaeological and historical data support 300 BC, plus or minus fifty years, for the destruction of the first civilization.

4. Finally, from a logical perspective, Ether would not have prophesied that all of Coriantumr's household would perish, that Coriantumr would be buried by another people, and that this other people would receive the land for their inheritance if Coriantumr's people had been killed at 600 BC and if Mosiah were not that other kingdom leader. We can date the arrival of Mosiah among the Mulekites at about 200 BC, which would have to reflect only a short period after the demise of the Jaredite nation (see Ether 13:20–21).

Archaeology, Mexican history, and logic do not allow every last man, woman, and child to be killed in the last Jaredite battle.

UNIQUE OUTCOMES OF THE OLMEC CULTURE

Following are unique outcomes of the twentieth-century discovery of the Olmec culture:

The Book of Mormon reports an earlier culture than the Maya. From the outset of its publication in 1830, anti–Book of Mormon critics evidently lacked the intellectual expertise and knowledge to challenge the validity of the book based on its unstated but obvious claim that the mother culture of the Americas was a culture that predated the Maya by hundreds of years. With that claim now confirmed by twentieth-century archaeology and Mesoamerican historical records, if such critics of today were truly honest, they would apologize for their attacks and for their failure to study the book carefully enough to recognize the book's unstated but sensational claim that the Maya were not the mother culture of the New World.

The impact of the archaeological and historical discovery of the Olmec culture is highly significant. Aside from the testimony of the Spirit (see Moroni 10:4–5) that the Book of Mormon is what it claims to be, perhaps no other evidence supports its claim of validity as much as the twentieth-century archaeological and historical discovery of the Olmec culture. Amazingly, proponents of the book's claim to authenticity have done relatively little to capitalize on the impact of the Olmec culture for this purpose.

The Olmec history verifies the location of Jaredite, Nephite, and Lamanite lands. From a knowledgeable, logical perspective, readers of the Book of Mormon can safely assume that if they can identify the lands of the Jaredites, they can easily identify the lands of the Nephites, Lamanites, and Mulekites. Outcomes of the discovery and location of the Olmec/Jaredite culture should readily dispel such illogical, mistaken thinking that the hill Ramah/Cumorah, narrow neck of land, narrow strip of wilderness, land of Zarahemla, land of Nephi, and so forth are any place other than in Mesoamerica.

The Olmec history supports the continued existence of the Jaredites. The Olmec archaeological and historical evidence verifies that Jaredites/Olmecs continued to live in Mesoamerica following the last great civil war dated to circa 300 BC. The continued presence in Mesoamerica of Olmecs/Jaredites and their culture helps explain the reasonable outcomes associated with Nephite/Lamanite population demographics that careful scholars of the Book of Mormon have noticed—that is, other people were already living in Mesoamerica when Lehi arrived, and these people became part of the history of the Nephites, Lamanites, and Mulekites.

Jaredite dates are confirmed by archaeology and history. Approaching two centuries after the initial publication of the Book of Mormon in 1830, readers of the Book of Mormon are free to ponder whether Joseph Smith correctly identified—by luck and good fortune or by the gift and power of God as part of the translation process as he claimed—the event that marked the beginning date for the Jaredite/Olmec culture and the approximate date for the last great Jaredite battle. Without question, no source of any kind was available to Joseph in 1830 to coach him about the initial and terminal dates for the Jaredite/Olmec civilization—dates that have now been confirmed by the archaeological and historical records of Mesoamerica.

JAREDITE KING NAME DISCOVERED

By Bruce W. Warren

Many Latter-day Saints have been fascinated to learn about the strong correlations that exist between the Book of Mormon Jaredites and the ancient Olmec culture that lived along the Gulf Coast of Mexico. Some of the most striking parallels include the following:

- Both cultures enjoyed a high civilization during the same time period.
- Both collapsed in a violent internal struggle at about the same time.
- Both were said to have come from the great tower at the time the languages were confounded.
- Both were described as physically large.
- The regions occupied by both have matching geographical features. (Bruce W. Warren and David A. Palmer, "The Jaredite Saga," unpublished manuscript in possession of the authors)

What follows will focus on the discovery of yet another possible link between these two cultures: King Kish.

About 1000 BC, the Old Testament tells us that Saul's father was named Kish (1 Samuel 9:1). Interestingly, at about the same time in the Book of Mormon, a Jaredite king surfaces by that same name. From the Book of Mormon, scarcely more is mentioned about Kish than his name. We also know that he was the son of a righteous king named Corom and the father of a righteous king named Lib (Ether 1:18–19; 10:17–19). While the meager information we are given about his reign and genealogy could hardly classify as a biography,

FIGURE 5–12: This small monument, located at the archaeological site of San Lorenzo Tenochtitlan, Veracruz, shows the person's hands placed on the head of a serpent with feathers protruding from its head, thus identifying his name as U-Kish Kan, who was born on March 8, 993 BC. The monument's head has been severed from the body. (Photo courtesy of George and Audrey DeLange)

it does firmly establish Kish among the Jaredite monarchs.

Within the last twenty years a new technique has been developed to translate the Maya hieroglyphs. (Coe, *Breaking the Maya Code*, 260–69) It is a complex process that involves assigning sounds to as many of the glyphs as possible and then converting those sounds to the Maya language that is still spoken today by many of the natives. Prior to the development of this method of translation, little more than dates could be deciphered from the stone engravings. It is possible that among the many spectacular finds in the ruins, we have now identified the name of the Jaredite king, Kish, as well as his birthday, birthplace, and the day he ascended to the throne.

On the Tablet of the Cross at the Maya archaeological site of Palenque, there are engravings on a stone tablet which trace the genealogy of Kan Balaam, the son of King Pacal who is buried in the great tomb there. Among the names of Kan Balaam's royal ancestors, we find what may be the full name of King Kish, that is, U-Kish Kan. U-Kish Kan was an ancient king of the Olmec empire. (Warren and Palmer, "The Jaredite Saga")

"Kan" means serpent. One of the meanings of "Kish" is feathered. Now that the Maya code is being deciphered, the name of U-Kish Kan has been translated as "he of the feathered serpent." (Warren and Palmer, "The Jaredite Saga") This symbolic tie-in of U-Kish Kan with the feathered serpent suggests a relationship to Jesus Christ, or the white god of Mesoamerica, Quetzalcoatl, who is also known as "the Feathered Serpent." This, in combination with what the scriptures record about Moses lifting up the brazen serpent as a similitude of Christ (2 Nephi 25:20; Helaman 8:14; Alma 33:19; Numbers 21:6–9; John 3:14), may indicate that the serpent motif as a representation of Christ's condescension to earth was prominent in both Old and New World traditions.

U-Kish Kan was born on Wednesday, March 8, 993 BC. (Warren and Palmer, "The Jaredite Saga") In San Lorenzo Tenochtitlan in the state of Veracruz, Mexico, there is an engraved stone known as Monument 47. (Warren and Palmer, "The Jaredite Saga") It depicts a king who has a serpent around his waist and is holding the head of the serpent in his hands. The serpent has feathers on its head. This monument is Olmec in style and dates to the beginning of the first millennium BC. The monument's head is missing, but because of its dating and imagery, it seems reasonable that this could be a representation of Kan Balaam's ancestor, U-Kish Kan.

U-Kish Kan took the throne on Wednesday, March 25, 967 BC. Kish, an Olmec and a Maya name, is prominent throughout the Jaredite history and appears as a Nephite name root later in the Book of Mormon. KISH-kumen is one of several names that serve to manifest the Jaredite influence on the later Nephite culture. Other Nephite names, such as Shiblom and Coriantumr, descend wholly unchanged from the Jaredite culture. This same influence can be observed archaeologically from the Olmec culture to the Maya. (Warren and Palmer, "The Jaredite Saga")

The component "Kish" is also evident in the compound names of two other Jaredite kings, Ripla-KISH and A-KISH. To find the Jaredite name of Kish in the name of an Olmec king referred to in the Maya hieroglyphs is truly a remarkable discovery. Even if it isn't the same King Kish mentioned in the book of Ether, its very presence in the name of *any* Olmec king is not to be dismissed as mere coincidence.

CHAPTER 6

The Maya (Lamanite-Nephite) Culture

And also that the seed of this people may more fully believe his gospel, which shall go forth unto them from the Gentiles; for this people shall be scattered, and shall become a dark, a filthy, and a loathsome people. (Mormon 5:15)

THE LAMANITES AND NEPHITES

We believe that the 570 BC to AD 420 Lamanites and Nephites in the Book of Mormon were basically the same people as those whom archaeologists refer to as the Late Preclassic and Early Classic Maya who date to this same time period.

This assumption implies that both the Lamanites and the Nephites lived in the same general area and were both descendants of the people who today are called *Maya*. The defining differences between the Lamanites and the Nephites is to whom they paid their allegiance and where they lived. These statements do not mean that the descendants of the families of Lehi and Ishmael were Maya by blood. Rather, they suggest that their descendants became part of the larger Maya culture in the same way that the Spanish immigrants of the sixteenth century became part of the larger culture of Mexico.

OPPOSITE: Like Mormon, Pacal was a Maya. Kuk Balam (AD 391–431), the great ancestor of Pacal, was a contemporary of Moroni, the son of Mormon. Pacal was from the state of Chiapas. Moroni was probably from the bordering state of Veracruz.

An additional parallel between the Spanish and the Lehi colony is that the minority foreign immigrants culture provided leadership for the masses or native culture. For example, when the Nephites lived in the land of Nephi (ca. 570–200 BC), the people were designated as *Nephites* or *Lamanites* according to their preference, as stated by Jacob: "I shall call them Lamanites that seek to destroy the people of Nephi, and those who are friendly to Nephi, I shall call Nephites" (Jacob 1:14).

Once a branch of the Nephites under King Mosiah moved to Zarahemla (ca. 180 BC), the differences between the Nephites and Lamanites were not only according to allegiance but also according to territory. For almost 550 years (200 BC–AD 350), the Lamanites controlled the land of Nephi and the Nephites controlled the land of Zarahemla:

> For behold, he [Mosiah] being warned of the Lord that he should flee out of the land of Nephi, *and as many as would hearken unto the voice of the Lord* should also depart out of the land [Nephi] with him, into the wilderness. . . .
>
> And they were led by the power of his arm, through the wilderness until they came down into the land which is called the land of Zarahemla. (Omni 1:12–13; emphasis added)

The traditional belief that the basic difference between Nephites and Lamanites was skin color is not supported by either the Book of Mormon or Maya history. They were basically the same people. The "skin of blackness" attributed to the Lamanites after the Nephites left them in the "place of their fathers' first inheritance" is easily understood because that location was likely the hot, sun-drenched Soconusco region along the Pacific coast near Tapachula (see chapter 22, "Voyages of Lehi and Mulek"). That is, Mormon depicted the Lamanites as being naked except for a loincloth. The result was sun-drenched bodies with sun-darkened skin (2 Nephi 5:21; Alma 3:5).

In chapter 2, "And Then It Came to Pass," we introduced you to the concept of *dualism* in which an event has both physical and spiritual overtones or applications. The skin-color incident that occurred with the Lamanites after the Nephites moved to the land of Nephi is especially dualistic in nature. Physically, the "skin of blackness" that was caused by both genetic history and severe environmental exposure to the sun—long before Lehi ever arrived in the New World—resulted in a decadent lifestyle that caused the people who became known as Lamanites to be loathsome to those who became Nephites. More importantly, however, was the spiritual loathing that the Nephites reflected toward the Lamanites from that time on. The dualistic nature of this incident that originated in the "place of their fathers' first inheritance" is evident when we consult the index for the Book of Mormon under "physical darkness" and "spiritual darkness."

> The traditional belief that the basic difference between Nephites and Lamanites was skin color is not supported by either the Book of Mormon or Maya history. They were basically the same people.

Exploring the Lands of the Book of Mormon

We also know that during most of the Book of Mormon history, the Lamanites far outnumbered the Nephites, as in the 120 BC statement: "Now there were not so many of the children of Nephi, or so many of those who were descendants of Nephi, as there were of the people of Zarahemla, who was a descendant of Mulek, and those who came with him into the wilderness. And there were not so many of the people of Nephi and of the people of Zarahemla as there were of the *Lamanites;* yea, they were not half so numerous" (Mosiah 25:2–3; emphasis added).

After what appears to be a uniting of the cultures at the time of Christ—to the point that there were no more Lamanites "nor any manner of -ites"—by AD 244, those who rejected the gospel were again called Lamanites; and they "became exceedingly more numerous than were the people of God" (4 Nephi 1:40).

In the Latter-day Saint culture of today, the meaning of the term "Lamanite" has almost changed. People who are native to the Americas, who have accepted the gospel and have been baptized into The Church of Jesus Christ of Latter-day Saints, are called Lamanites. In some instances, Lamanite members of the Church are called "descendants of Lehi" or, according to the Book of Mormon term, "the remnant of Jacob." The term "Lamanite," as in "Lamanite nation" or "day of the Lamanite," can also refer to all Native Americans, not just to baptized members.

At any rate, no error is committed if we apply the name "Lamanite"—or "Nephite" for that matter—to what archaeologists refer to as the 600 BC to AD 400 Maya culture and also apply "Lamanite" to those whose civilization dates from 800 BC to AD 1542. Even today, Maya people, Maya villages, Maya traditions, and Maya languages exist.

Some readers may object to classifying the Lamanites and Nephites of the Book of Mormon time period as being the same people whom archaeologists call the Preclassic Maya. Nevertheless, the Maya world was the predominant culture—linguistically, archaeologically, and historically—on the American continent during the time period under question.

THE MAYA

The Maya culture literally maintained supreme control over their territory for twenty-three hundred years. That territory included what is now part of, or all of, seven countries: Mexico, Belize, Guatemala, El Salvador, and Honduras as well as the northern tips of Nicaragua and Costa Rica.

Phenomenally, during that long period of time, the Maya culture never extended beyond the Isthmus of Tehuantepec. Likewise, during the Aztec era, AD 1325 to AD 1521, the Aztecs did not encroach into Maya territory, although the two cultures did have significant trading and political relationships with each other.

Michael Coe writes about the territory of the Maya as follows: "There are few parts of the world where there is such a good 'fit' between language and culture: a line drawn

No error is committed if we apply the name "Lamanite"— or "Nephite" for that matter—to what archaeologists refer to as the 600 BC to AD 400 Maya culture.

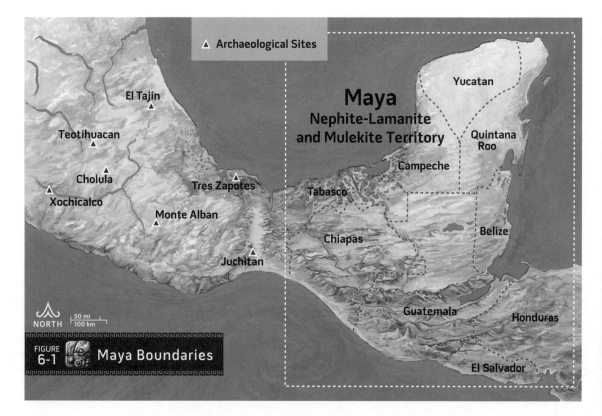

FIGURE 6–1: Maya boundary lines. For the major part of the thousand-year Nephite history, the Nephites, Lamanites, and Mulekites occupied the same territory and were basically the same people who today are called the ancient Maya. After the demise of the Nephite civilization in the fourth century AD, the Lamanites and Mulekites continued to live in the same area. We do not presently know at what point in time the term *Lamanite* was no longer used. When the Spaniards arrived, they called the natives according to their tribe name or the village in which they lived. For example, in the Yucatan, they were called the Com and Xui tribes, and the Lords of Totonicapan were named as a result of living in the village of Totonicapan.

1. Michael D. Coe, *The Maya*, 4th ed. (New York: Thames and Hudson, 1987), 11.

around the Maya-speaking peoples would contain all those remains, and hieroglyphic texts, assigned to the ancient Maya civilization."[1]

For every book or report written about the Olmec, fifty equivalent treatises have been written about the Maya. Most of the sites in Mesoamerica that are visited by tourists are Maya sites and, for the most part, are post–Book of Mormon, including the extant structures that tourists view. For example, of the ten most popular archaeological sites in Mesoamerica, seven are Maya. Of the seven Maya sites, all are considered to be Classic Maya sites—that is, late or post–Book of Mormon time period. Significantly, however, when archaeologists excavate to the interiors of many of the Classic structures, they often find ruins that date to the Book of Mormon time period.

MOST POPULAR ARCHAEOLOGICAL SITES

Some of the favorite archaeological sites visited by tourists are as follows:

Teotihuacan	Non-Maya	Book of Mormon and post–Book of Mormon
Monte Alban	Non-Maya	Book of Mormon and post–Book of Mormon
Mitla	Non-Maya	Post–Book of Mormon time period
Palenque	Maya	Late Book of Mormon and post–Book of Mormon
Uxmal	Maya	Late Book of Mormon and post–Book of Mormon
Chichen Itza	Maya/Toltec	Post–Book of Mormon time period
Tulum	Maya	Post–Book of Mormon time period
Coba	Maya	Post–Book of Mormon time period
Tikal	Maya	Book of Mormon and post–Book of Mormon
Copan	Maya	Late Book of Mormon and post–Book of Mormon
Kaminaljuyu	Maya	Book of Mormon and post–Book of Mormon
Laman Ayin	Maya	Book of Mormon and post–Book of Mormon
Cerros	Maya	Book of Mormon time period
Becan	Maya	Book of Mormon and post–Book of Mormon
Chiapa de Corzo	Maya	Book of Mormon time period

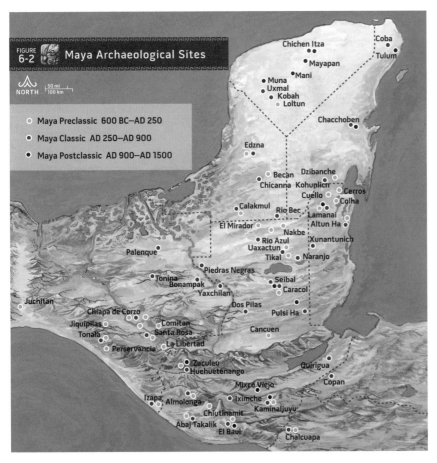

FIGURE 6–2: The archaeological history of the Maya is long, complex, and intriguing. Although the divisions where public architecture is dominant are labeled Preclassic, Classic, and Postclassic, a substantial amount of overlapping is evident. For example, a site like El Mirador existed only during the Preclassic Period. Tikal, on the other hand, endured through both Preclassic and Classic times. Tulum existed only during the Postclassic era. And Kaminaljuyu shows constant occupation and building programs encompassing all three periods. The sites illustrated on this map reflect this concept.

The ruins of Cholula, located in the state of Puebla, are non-Maya and include archaeological findings that pertain to both Book of Mormon and post–Book of Mormon time periods. The ruins of Tula, a Toltec site in the state of Hidalgo, are non-Maya and are post–Book of Mormon.

El Mirador is a Preclassic Maya site in Peten, Guatemala, that has received a lot of notoriety among members of the Church of Jesus Christ. The initial work was under the direction of Latter-day Saint archaeologist Ray Matheny. The site is a Preclassic Book of Mormon time period site that was not built upon by the Classic Maya.

As we look at the list of sites above, we should observe that they represent only a fraction of the Mesoamerican archaeological sites in existence, most of which correspond to the Maya culture.

WHAT ARE WE LOOKING FOR?

Over the years, Latter-day Saints have been frustrated in trying to correlate anything Maya with anything Book of Mormon. The result has usually been (1) to label *everything* Book of Mormon or (2) to ignore totally any archaeological site as being Book of Mormon related.

Both approaches are wrong. When John Lloyd Stephens reported his archaeological findings in 1841, he emphasized the ruins of Copan, Palenque, and Uxmal. All three are Maya ruins, and all three have proven to be post–Book of Mormon. This dating does not mean that Classic sites were not built upon Preclassic Book of Mormon time period cities.

FIGURE 6–3: This Postclassic building called the Governors Palace at Uxmal dates to about AD 800, four hundred years after the close of the Book of Mormon. However, earlier occupation at Uxmal demonstrates the same activity as outlined in 4 Nephi at AD 320 where wicked priests adorned their buildings and controlled the social, religious, and commercial lives of the people. (Photo courtesy of Sheryl Lee Wilson)

Exploring the Lands of the Book of Mormon

FIGURE 6–4: This AD 1000–1200 Toltec Temple of Kukulcan, one of the seven wonders of the world, is built over an AD 600 Maya temple, both of which are post–Book of Mormon. This temple is aligned with the spring equinox. When the shadows fall at that time, they give the appearance that the serpent on the stairway is moving. Upwards of fifteen thousand people gather at the square of the Temple of Kukulcan on March 21 of each year to witness this spectacular event. (Photo courtesy of Sheryl Lee Wilson)

In many cases, that is exactly what happened. Therefore, only the *visible* building structures of Copan, Palenque, and Uxmal are all post–Book of Mormon.

Nevertheless, early Church members expressed their enthusiasm about the possibility of the scientific world's proving the truthfulness of the Book of Mormon. When Stephens's book was published, early Church members felt that the ruins of Copan, Palenque, and Uxmal were Book of Mormon cities.[2]

That idea has persisted through the years. An interesting statistic would be to know how many Latter-day Saints have stood in front of the Temple of Kukulkan, a tenth century AD structure at Chichen Itza, and felt they were looking at a Book of Mormon temple.

The converse ideology is just as damaging. Because the Classic Maya, AD 300 to AD 800, do not fit into the Book of Mormon picture, no justification results in assuming the scientists are always wrong or in diminishing the importance of Book of Mormon research.

The latter concept implies that because the doctrine in the Book of Mormon is the most important aspect of the book, anything else that does not relate to doctrine is totally irrelevant. We would not want to tell Mormon to his face that he wasted space on gold plates telling us things that were not important. No matter how we look at it, the Book of Mormon is a spiritual account written in a geographical, cultural, and historical setting. In many instances, it is the understanding of that setting that carries us to the spiritual message of the Book of Mormon.

2. See *Times and Seasons* 3, no. 22 (September 15, 1842): 921–22.

A KEY TO UNDERSTANDING BOOK OF MORMON CULTURE

A better approach is to analyze, to the best of our abilities, the civilizations that existed during the time the Book of Mormon history was written. We then may develop a deeper understanding of the Book of Mormon and of the people whose lives graced the pages of the book.

The Maya region is the most practical place to begin a search. In the first place, as mentioned earlier, the area where written language evolved on the American continent during the time period in which the Book of Mormon was written was in Maya territory. Even the Inca of Peru, who developed an advanced civilization during post–Book of Mormon times, were totally illiterate.[3]

3. Coe, The Maya, 46.

Second, because of the number of populated centers that were in existence in the Maya territory during Book of Mormon times, we would have a difficult time transferring battle, city, and related geographic locations to a lesser-populated area. To do so would be to admit that the Book of Mormon peoples were an insignificant dot on the American continent, which is not the case.

Such questions as the following may be asked: Why have we not found more direct correlations between the Maya and the people of the Book of Mormon? Why have we not discovered the name "Nephi" in the ruins? Or, as we somewhat facetiously discuss related to this issue, why have archaeologists not found a tipped-over stela and raised it up to be greeted with the words "Welcome to Zarahemla"?

These questions have logical answers. However, we may want to reexamine our approach to asking questions. Instead of trying to predetermine how the Nephites fit into the history of the Americas, we might examine what was going on in the Americas during the time that specific and significant events in the Book of Mormon occurred. We could then let the culture teach us about the Book of Mormon. At that point, the Book of Mormon will lend exact detail to certain events.

An idea has surfaced in recent years that the Nephites were a small culture within a large culture, much like the Jewish community or the Latter-day Saints have been small cultures within large societies. Nevertheless, Jews, Gentiles, and Mormons all shop at Wal-Mart. Many of all three groups drive Ford cars and watch the news on Channel 5. The more we learn about the culture of the Maya, the more we can expect to learn about the cultures of the Lamanites and the Nephites.

This idea does not imply that the Nephites were an insignificant speck on the Mesoamerica map. On the contrary, it implies just what Mormon and Moroni stated. That is, the Lamanites far outnumbered the Nephites, and the records were kept primarily by the Nephites (see Mosiah 25:3; Helaman 3:15).

In a similar fashion, today we can say that the "Gentiles" in the United States far outnumber members of The Church of Jesus Christ of Latter-day Saints, although many of the people in the United States are Christians. And the Mormons are the genealogical record keepers of the world.

> Because of the number of populated centers that were in existence in the Maya territory during Book of Mormon times, we would have a difficult time transferring battle, city, and related geographic locations to a lesser-populated area.

Exploring the Lands of the Book of Mormon

FIGURE 6–5: Native dignitaries from the state of Chiapas. Anthropologists estimate that thirty-two or more dialects are spoken in Chiapas and Guatemala. The people shown here, who live in the mountains, are part of those called the Zapatistas today. (Photo courtesy of Merrill C. Oaks)

AMONG THE MAYA

Prior to 2000 BC, as far as we know, only one language has been discovered in Mesoamerica. Today, a uniformity of agreement exists that all groups who speak Maya came from the same ancestral branch.[4]

By 600 BC, that one language had evolved into six language groups. The groups with their corresponding chronological dating and locations are as follows:

Mam	2600 BC Maya Territory	Frontier Chiapas/Guatemala
Huastec	1800 BC non-Maya Territory	Northern Veracruz
Yucatecan	1600 BC Maya Territory	Yucatan Peninsula/Peten
Lacandon	1400 BC Maya Territory	Middle Usumacinta
Chontal	900 BC Maya Territory	Chiapas/Tabasco
Tzetal	750 BC Maya Territory	Highland Chiapas

By the same token, prior to 600 BC, several known settlements existed throughout the Maya territory. These include such sites as Kaminaljuyu (Guatemala City); Izapa (Tapachula, Mexico); El Baul (Pacific coast of Guatemala); Chiapa de Corzo (Chiapas depression); Cuello (Belize); Tikal (Guatemala), ; and Dzibilchaltun (Yucatan).

The above linguistic and archaeological picture suggests that, for their early development, the Maya were dependent upon the Olmec—that is, the Olmec culture formed a population base for the Maya civilization.

Between 600 BC and 300 BC, a type of fusion developed in Maya lands, as a number of the above-mentioned sites, as well as additional sites, manifested an increase in activity.

4. Alberto Ruz, *The Mayas* (Mexico, DF: Salvat Mexicana de Ediciones, 1983), 56–57; Coe, *The Maya*, 25.

The two most productive sites in Maya territory during the Late Preclassic, 600 BC to 300 BC, were Izapa and Kaminaljuyu. The north acropolis of Tikal was constructed around 600 BC. Altun Ha, located in Belize, dates to 500 BC. Uaxactun and other sites in the northern Peten are in the area where the Late Preclassic is defined the best.

Coe states, "The Middle Preclassic sees the establishment of Maya-speaking peasants everywhere; the flowering of Maya culture could only have taken place on this base."[5]

5. Coe, *The Maya*, 43.

Some minor evidence is surfacing showing a new language group entered the area of highland Guatemala and Honduras from 600 BC–300 BC. However, we know of no evidence to suggest that the Hebrew and Egyptian languages were introduced and spoken anywhere in the Americas between 600 BC and 300 BC.

FIGURE 6–6: This scene is located in section B of Izapa. What appears to be a dirt mound is an ancient pyramid dating to about 300 BC. The pillar-type monuments in front appear to have an astronomical orientation with the Orion belt. Although Izapa is located in Maya territory, the fact that it has Olmec-style monuments has caused archaeologists to label it a unique culture. The investigative work at Izapa was under the direction of the New World Archaeological Foundation. (Photo courtesy of George and Audrey DeLange)

Izapa is a very large site made up of eighty mounds. It was founded as a ceremonial site during Early Preclassic times—that is, prior to 600 BC—and continued until the Early Classic, about AD 350 (see chapter 9, "The Izapa [Jaredite-Nephite-Lamanite] Culture").

Kaminaljuyu is one of the greatest of all archaeological sites in the New World. The great majority of the mounds are definitely Preclassic. The cultural high point of Kaminaljuyu took place during 500 to 400 BC, Late Preclassic Period. The Middle Preclassic people of Kaminaljuyu are the forerunners of the Classic Maya. The elite of the valley of Kaminaljuyu (Guatemala City) were fully literate at this time period. Other Maya were just learning that writing even existed.[6]

6. Coe, *The Maya*, 40; see also chapter 26 in this text, "The Land of Nephi."

AMONG THE NEPHITES AND THE LAMANITES

The first significant Book of Mormon date that relates to the New World is given sometime after Nephi had departed from his brothers, Laman and Lemuel. Nephi and the

FIGURE 6–7: Kaminaljuyu, the valley of the dead, represents the ancient Maya antiquity at its best. In essence, it is the forerunner of the Maya of the lowlands. People were living in the area when Nephi arrived. During the early part of the Nephite history, Kaminaljuyu developed into a city/state. Irrigation was practiced, and writing was developed. (Photo courtesy of George and Audrey DeLange)

people who became known as Nephites built a temple, engaged in agriculture and metallurgy, constructed weapons of war, and developed a political and social structure. At this point, they had been in the New World only about twenty years, about 570 BC (see 2 Nephi 5:1–28).

After another twenty-five years had elapsed, the people who had taken upon themselves the name of Nephites had been engaged in wars and contentions with the Lamanites (see 2 Nephi 5:34). Nephi taught the Nephites the words of Isaiah because his people had not lived in Jerusalem and therefore knew not the manner of the Jews (see 2 Nephi 25:1, 6). He also instructed his people not to intermarry with the people who were called Lamanites. The name "Lamanite" was given to the people who tried to destroy the people of Nephi and undoubtedly included people other than the direct descendants of Laman and Lemuel and those who followed after them (see 2 Nephi 5:23; Jacob 1:14). Finally, Jacob went up into the temple, which was located in the land/city of Nephi, and talked to the people about pride. He chastised the men who had broken the law of chastity and who had taken concubines (see Jacob 2–4). The latter part dates to around 545 BC.

The headquarters for the Nephites were located in the city of Nephi for almost four hundred years—or until approximately 180 BC when Mosiah, a descendant of Nephi, led a branch of Nephites from the land of Nephi to the land of Zarahemla (see Omni 1:12–24).

During the time period under question, 600 BC–300 BC, the following major events transpired, as recorded in the Book of Mormon:

1. Nephi settled the land of Nephi (ca. 570 BC)
2. Nephi and his people built a temple (ca. 570 BC)
3. The Nephite/Lamanite wars began (ca. 565 BC)
4. Jacob taught in the temple (ca. 545 BC)
5. Enos went into the wilderness (ca. 500 BC)

> The name "Lamanite" was given to the people who tried to destroy the people of Nephi and undoubtedly included people other than the direct descendants of Laman and Lemuel and those who followed after them

The Nephites not only adopted the spoken language from the natives who already lived in highland Guatemala at the time of the Nephites' arrival but also adopted other traits from the natives, such as the reckoning of their monetary system.

6. Jarom began keeping the records (ca. 420 BC)

7. Omni began keeping the records (ca. 360 BC)

8. Amaron began keeping the records (ca. 315 BC)

THE NEPHITE/MAYA MARRIAGE

Clearly, the Nephites and Lamanites, during the 600 BC to 300 BC time period, adopted the spoken language of the people who already lived in the area of highland Guatemala. The spoken language of highland Guatemala was a derivative of the original language spoken by the early Olmec/Jaredite culture.

The written language, however, was preserved and handed down by Nephite royalty from generation to generation.

These conclusions are in agreement with both the archaeological record and with the Book of Mormon. King Benjamin taught his children the language of his fathers so the people could read the records that had been preserved (see Mosiah 1:2–4). And Moroni said that no other people could understand their written language: "But the Lord knoweth the things which we have *written*, and also that none other people knoweth our language; and because that none other people knoweth our language, therefore he hath prepared means for the *interpretation* thereof" (Mormon 9:34; emphasis added).

Obviously, both Benjamin and Moroni are referring to the written language. This reference is consistent with the archaeological account because even as of 2008, the written language that was in use in Kaminaljuyu between 600 BC and 300 BC has not been interpreted. As Michael Coe states, and as referred to above, the elite of the valley of Kaminaljuyu were very literate during this time period. The elite were probably the Nephite record keepers.

Interestingly, the Nephites not only adopted the spoken language from the natives who already lived in highland Guatemala at the time of the Nephites' arrival but also

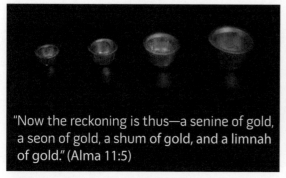

"Now the reckoning is thus—a senine of gold, a seon of gold, a shum of gold, and a limnah of gold." (Alma 11:5)

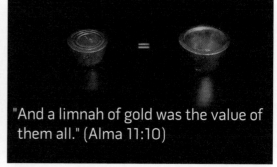

"And a limnah of gold was the value of them all." (Alma 11:10)

FIGURE 6–8: The mathematical ratios of the Nephite "monetary" system are illustrated in the "weights and measures" (known locally in Guatemala as "marcos") that are manufactured from lead, copper, and zinc in homes of the villagers of Chiantla, located a few miles from the city of Huehuetenango, Guatemala. The components of the devices precisely illustrate the weights-and-measures ratios for the senine, seon, shum, and limnah as described in Alma 11. The forerunners of these devices, which are used today by vendors in Guatemalan markets, predate the Spanish conquest and are similar in nature to those used in Saayin, Yemen, anciently (Photos courtesy of Merrill C. Oaks)

adopted other traits from the natives, such as the reckoning of their monetary system: "They did not reckon after the manner of the Jews who were at Jerusalem; neither did they measure after the manner of the Jews; but they altered their reckoning and their measure, according to the minds and the circumstances of the people, in every generation, until the reign of the judges, they having been established by king Mosiah" (Alma 11:4).

Both language and archaeology provide us with substantial justification to label the land of Nephi and the land of Kaminaljuyu to be one and the same. Today, the area is known as the land or department of Guatemala, with Guatemala City occupying the same real estate as the ruins of Kaminaljuyu.

In all of the Americas, Kaminaljuyu was the most prominent city center that had an appropriate written language base during Late Preclassic times, 600 BC to 300 BC.

Nephi was the most prominent city center with an appropriate written language base during early Nephite times, 600 BC to 300 BC.

Both accounts refer to a temple and ceremonial center built around 570 BC (see chapter 28, "The Land of Nephi").

300 BC–AD 250—MAYA LATE PRECLASSIC; NEPHITE/MULEKITE CLASSIC

Without question, the Late Preclassic Maya, 300 BC–AD 250, played a major role in the development of the Classic Maya, AD 250–AD 900. In reality, the Classic Maya did not invent anything. They only added to it. That includes language, architecture, warfare, and population: "The Classic Maya of the lowlands had a very elaborate calendar; writing; temple-pyramids and palaces of limestone masonry with vaulted rooms; architectural layouts emphasizing buildings arranged around plazas with rows of stone

Good evidence exists to indicate that the Preclassic Maya were influenced by outside cultures—implying that the native Mesoamericans of both the Middle and Late Preclassic Periods, 600 BC—AD 250, may have been subjected to trans-Pacific influences.

stelae lined up before some; polychrome pottery; and a very sophisticated art style expressed in bas-reliefs and in wall paintings. *These traits are now known to have been developed in the Late Preclassic (300 BC–AD 250) period.*"[7]

7. Coe, *The Maya*, 46–47; emphasis added.

Good evidence also exists to indicate that the Preclassic Maya were influenced by outside cultures—implying that the native Mesoamericans of both the Middle and Late Preclassic Periods, 600 BC–AD 250, may have been subjected to trans-Pacific influences.

Michael Coe of Yale University analyzes that issue in his book, *The Maya*. He points out the thinking of two scholars on the calendar systems, one a Mesoamerica scholar and the other a scholar on Chinese history.[8]

8. Coe, *The Maya*, 46.

Professor David Kelley of the University of Calgary has pointed out the similarity between the 260-day calendar that is so fundamental to Mesoamerica and that is also similar to eastern and southeastern Asian civilizations. He also observed in both cultures the similarity between the cardinal points of the universe in association with colors, plants, animals, and gods—cultures that are separated by thousands of miles of ocean. Kelley feels that the resemblance is far too close to be merely coincidental.[9]

9. Coe, *The Maya*, 46.

Joseph Needham agrees that the same complex formulas to predict lunar and solar eclipses were used by both Mesoamerica and Chinese astronomers. He wrote about the possibility that Asian intellectuals had contact with their Mesoamerican counterparts during Preclassic times.[10]

10. Coe, *The Maya*, 46.

Coe also recognizes Eastern influence. He states that we certainly have no evidence to believe that the entire Maya nation was just transplanted from the Old World. He suggests that the Maya may have been receptive to some important ideas originating from the eastern hemisphere during the Preclassic Period, 600 BC–AD 250.[11]

11. Coe, *The Maya*, 46.

A recent publication by Latter-day Saint writer Diane E. Wirth outlines the historical controversy that has existed among Maya scholars regarding internal growth versus outside influence: "Most laymen are unaware of the ongoing controversy between the archaeological establishment (isolationists) and the diffusionists which takes the form of verbal and written attacks on each other's research. In medieval times scientists were burned at the stake or imprisoned for their outlandish theories that were unacceptable to their peers. Today such things are often replaced with ostracism, and until traditional pre-Columbianists (isolationists) accept the challenge of new findings with their relevancy to this field of study, the heated debate will no doubt continue."[12]

12. Diane E. Wirth, *Parallels, Mesoamerican and Ancient Middle Eastern Traditions* (St. George, UT: Stonecliff Publishing, 2003), Introduction.

And from a historical perspective, Latter-day Saints can ill afford to smugly sit in their proverbial ivory towers and ignore scientific history on the subject. This smugness has traditionally surfaced in discussions that toss aside the scientifically established Bering Strait theory that has developed into our own brand of isolationism where we are unwilling to permit anybody to enter the borders of the promised land except those referred to in the Book of Mormon.

Righteous Jaredites flee to land
southward ca 1000 BC (Ether 9:31)

Coriantumr flees to land southward
(Zarahemla) ca 250 BC (Omni 1:21)

**Olmec Territory
1500 BC to 250 BC**

Villahermosa

Oaxaca

**Isthmus of Tehuantepec
Course of the Beasts**

Land of Zarahemla

Land Southward

NORTH 25 mi / 50 km

FIGURE
6–10 **Olmec Migrations**

FIGURE 6–10: Olmec influence in Maya territory. Mayanists have long discussed the relationship between the Olmecs and the Maya. Some Mayanists think they were one and the same people, whereas others suggest a distinct separation. The Book of Mormon helps us in this matter, as Jaredites migrated into the land southward on at least two occasions, one referred to in Ether 9:31–34 and the other at the end of the Jaredite record where Coriantumr was taken in by the Mulekites who lived in the land southward.

Perhaps a compromise can be reached by both parties—that is, between (1) the mainstream isolationists who close the door to transoceanic migrations and who hold fast to only internal growth as a result of one migration across the Bering land bridge thousands of years ago and (2) the diffusionists theory, which, as stated by Wirth, "is based on the concept of a mixing of indigenous cultures with small groups of foreigners who arrived as a result of early voyages to the Americas long before Columbus made the claim of being the first."[13]

Internal contact was ongoing in Mesoamerica during the Late Preclassic, 300 BC–AD 250. That is, highland Guatemala interacted with Chiapas and with lowland Guatemala. This interaction is best illustrated by the development of the calendar: "The 'Maya' calendar had reached what was pretty much its final form by the first century BC among peoples who were under powerful Olmec influence and who may not even have been Maya. From them, writing and the calendar were spread along the Pacific coast of

13. Wirth, *Parallels, Mesoamerican and Ancient Middle Eastern Traditions,* Introduction.

14. Coe, *The Maya*, 50.

Guatemala and into the Maya highlands, eventually reaching the developing states of the Peten forests."[14]

Some of the major population centers that developed during the Late Preclassic Period in the Maya territory, 300 BC–AD 250, are as follows:

Izapa (Pacific Coast). Although Izapa was founded as a ceremonial center during the Preclassic Period, 600 BC–300 BC, the majority of the construction and probably all the carved stones, including Stela 5, date to the Late Preclassic, beginning at 200 BC.

The spoken language was not Maya but was more related to the Mixe-Zoque on the opposite side of the Isthmus—in Oaxaca and Veracruz. Even the art work is ubiquitous, as the style of Izapa is found in Veracruz, Chiapas, and along both the Pacific coast and Guatemala highlands (see chapter 9, "The Izapa [Jaredite-Nephite-Lamanite] Culture").

Chiapa de Corzo (Chiapas Depression). Late Preclassic activity was very strong in the central depression in the state of Chiapas. The area was influenced by people who came from both the south and the north. An extension of the Kaminaljuyu and the Izapa cultures settled in the valley. Excavation work in the Chiapas area was conducted by the New World Archaeological Foundation beginning in 1960. The oldest discovered long count is inscribed on Stela 24 at Chiapa de Corzo and dates to 36 BC.

Between 600 BC and 400 BC, a group of people from the Olmec zone moved into Maya territory, migrating up the Grijalva and Usumacinta Rivers. During the Preclassic Period, beginning at 300 BC, a number of sites flourished in the region, including Tierra Blanca, Pomoca, Emiliana Zapata, and El Mirador.[15]

15. Lorenzo Ochoa and Marcia Castro, *Archaeological Guide of the Park—Museum of La Venta* (Villahermosa: Tabasco State Government, 1986).

The native document called *The Title of the Lords of Totonicapan* also speaks of a people who landed in Veracruz and settled along the Bay of Campeche. Subsequently, they migrated south up the Grijalva and Usumacinta Rivers and settled along the frontiers of Chiapas and Guatemala.

El Mirador (Southern Maya Lowlands-Northern Peten). El Mirador is a site located just four kilometers south of Campeche on the Campeche-Peten boundary and south of the Maya Classic site of Calakmul and north of Tikal. Although unexcavated, El Mirador's size is staggering. This massive site was constructed almost entirely during the Late Preclassic Period, 150 BC to AD 150, and the site became abandoned as a population center around AD 350. The rarity of El Mirador is that it was not occupied during the Classic Period. It features an eighteen-story building that is much larger than the largest structure at Tikal and taller than those of Egypt. Investigations and mappings were initiated in 1978 by Bruce Dahlin, who at that time was with the Catholic University of America. Beginning in 1979, Ray Matheny from Brigham Young University spent a number of seasons at El Mirador.

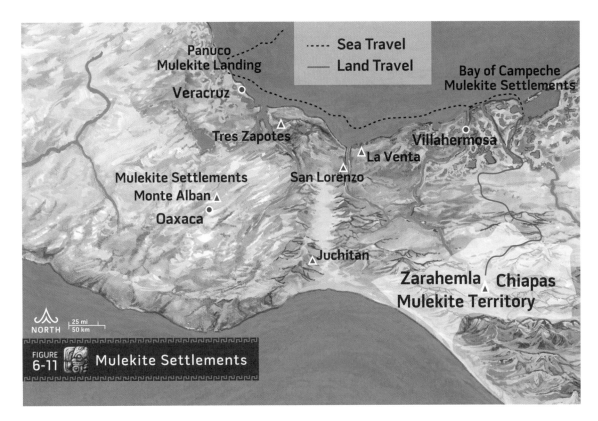

FIGURE 6–11: Proposed Mulekite migrations during the Preclassic Period. The above map illustrates the potential movements of the Mulekites to different areas of Mesoamerica—as determined by native documents, archaeological parallels, and statements from the Book of Mormon. For example, we know that the Mulekites landed among the Jaredites who lived in the land northward and that the Mulekites eventually migrated to the land of Zarahemla located in the land southward.

The National Geographic Society published a report on El Mirador in 1987. In this report, Matheny writes: "The uniqueness of El Mirador lies not only in its size but also in the fact that it was not torn down or substantially built over by Maya who lived here in the Classic period. . . . It was surprising to most Mayanists (Maya scholars) that so large a city, and one showing such superb engineering skills, could have been built during the second and first centuries BC; after all, the Preclassic Maya were not thought to have been capable of such achievement. Second, it was also believed that these early Maya were not capable of organizing a city-state type government." Beginning in the year 2004, plans were initiated to restore El Mirador for tourism purposes.

Uaxactun (Southern Maya Lowlands-Middle Peten). The Maya (Guatemala) highlands and the Pacific coast of Guatemala were not the only areas that were experiencing an extraordinary cultural effervescence in the Late Preclassic Period. The same Peten jungle that gave birth to El Mirador also gave birth to a multitude of city centers. This

> "The uniqueness of El Mirador lies not only in its size but also in the fact that it was not torn down or substantially built over by Maya who lived here in the Classic period."
> —Ray Matheny

building activity is especially true during the latter part of the Late Preclassic from about 100 BC to AD 250.

Uaxactun, a day's walking distance from Tikal, and El Mirador and a score of other cities began to glisten in the jungle sun with their white-limestone stuccoed buildings. It is during the last two decades of the twentieth century that scholars have begun to pay more attention to the Preclassic Period. Traditionally, scholars have been so engrossed with the Classic Maya Period that they have been blind to the equally remarkable fluorescence of Late Preclassic Maya culture.

Lamanai and Cerros (Belize). Representative of the Late Preclassic sites along the Caribbean that flourished beginning in the first century BC is a site called Cerros. This site was surveyed by David Freidel of Southern Methodist University.

Another site, with the peculiar name of Lamanai, was excavated by David Pendergast of the Royal Ontario Museum beginning in 1974.

Lamanai was built near the seacoast and has an ancient harbor located on the northern edge. *Lamoni* is the name of a Lamanite king who lived during the first century BC (see Alma 20). Also, during the first century BC, wars were fought between the Lamanites and the Nephites in the east wilderness, which appears to be located in the same area where the Maya ruins of Lamanai are located today. They date to the same time period (see Alma 50–52).

AD 250–AD 900—MAYA CLASSIC;
BEGINNING OF KINGS IN MAYA TERRITORY

The Classic Maya, AD 250–AD 900, were ruled over by a powerful, elite group of priests. These kingly priests gained power by their ability to interpret movements of the heavens. The beginning of this movement occurred in the first century BC, Late Preclassic Period: "During this period (AD 250–AD 900), the dominant group was a hereditary elite which emerged in the *last century before Christ*. Its authority extended throughout all aspects of social life, but in particular they were representatives or mediators between the community and the divine or supernatural forces."[16]

HISTORICAL HIGHLIGHTS IN THE BOOK OF MORMON DURING 300 BC–AD 250—MAYA LATE PRECLASSIC; NEPHITE/MULEKITE CLASSIC

The heart of Book of Mormon history transpired during the time period called Late Preclassic, 300 BC–AD 250. In the preceding discussion, we have seen the archaeological

FIGURE 6–12: Shown here is a National Geographic Society depiction of the preclassic site of El Mirador, which is located in the northern Peten jungle of Guatemala. The site is unique for at least two reasons. First, it is a Book of Mormon time period site that did not continue into the Classic Period. Second, the major temple is the tallest of all the pyramids of Mesoamerica, measuring four times larger than temple four of Tikal. (Used by permission: Terry W. Rutledge/National Geographic Image Collection)

16. Alfredo Barrera Rubio, *Official Guide: Uxmal,* trans. Helen Jones-Perrott de Mandri (Mexico, DF: Instituto Nacional de Antropologia e Historia, 1985), 33; emphasis added.

FIGURE 6–13: This picture taken at Lamanai is of the largest Preclassic building yet discovered in Belize. It dates to the Captain Moroni time period. The name of Laman Ayin appears to be associated with the title of Laman. Lamoni was a Lamanite king who was converted by the sons of Mosiah and who led his people to settle in Nephite territory near the east sea of the east wilderness. The Nephites could not hold the eastern seaboard cities, and they fell again into Lamanite hands. Although the above pyramid dates to that time period, the name is more likely tied in with the Lamanites as opposed to the Nephites. (Photo courtesy of Sheryl Lee Wilson)

record develop in a systematic pattern over the length and breadth of Maya territory during this five-hundred-year period. It is as if the buildings were constructed to comfortably wallpaper the sides of these ancient buildings with the pages of the Book of Mormon. The following sections will cover again the same time period, but this time we will list some of the historical highlights in the Book of Mormon to demonstrate how smoothly these highlights fit within the Maya time construct.

300 BC–200 BC MULEKITES IN MAYA TERRITORY

The Mulekites first landed in the area of the Jaredites—in the land northward. From there, a group of people who were descendants of Mulek, who were called the people of Zarahemla, traveled up into the south wilderness. The south wilderness was located in the land southward. The principal city of the Mulekites was Zarahemla, which was also located in the land southward and which was built along the banks of the Sidon river (see Alma 22:29–31; Mosiah 25:2).

By 300 BC, the beginning of the Maya Late Preclassic Period, a combination of Mulekite/Jaredite settlements was apparently well underway. These sites may have included Tikal, El Mirador, Chiapa de Corzo, and Izapa.

From the archaeological data, we observe the Olmec influence move into Maya territory. We also see another group of people—who were descendants of Abraham—move into the frontier of Chiapas and Guatemala from the Olmec zone of Veracruz and Tabasco. These dates and movements correspond with the above dates and internal movements of the Book of Mormon.

We conclude that the south wilderness in the Book of Mormon is the same general area where the 300 BC lowland and Chiapan Maya lived.

200 BC–AD 1: MOSIAH REIGNS OVER MULEKITES IN MAYA TERRITORY

About 180 BC, Mosiah led a righteous group of Nephites from the land of Nephi down to the land of Zarahemla. The Omni 1:12 scripture that reads "he being warned of the Lord that he should flee out of the land of Nephi" suggests that the flight may not have been under friendly conditions.

Mosiah, who was a descendant of Lehi, came in contact with Zarahemla, who was a descendant of Mulek. Mormon states that "the Lord did bring Mulek into the land north, and Lehi into the land south" (Helaman 6:10).

Nephi came from the south—from the land of Nephi. Zarahemla came from the north—from the land of Desolation. Or, in other words, Nephi came from Kaminaljuyu

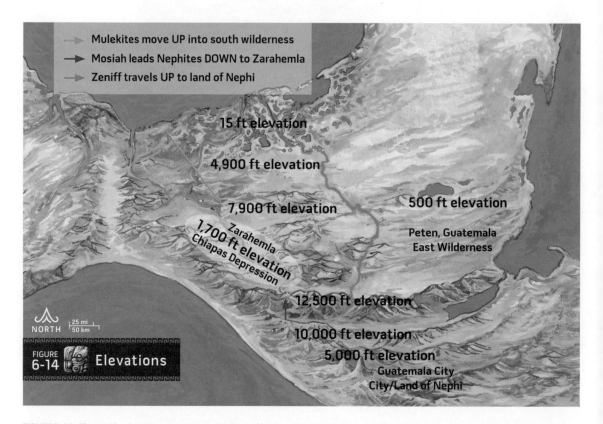

Mulekites move UP into south wilderness
Mosiah leads Nephites DOWN to Zarahemla
Zeniff travels UP to land of Nephi

15 ft elevation

4,900 ft elevation

7,900 ft elevation

500 ft elevation

Zarahemla
1,700 ft elevation
Chiapas Depression

Peten, Guatemala
East Wilderness

12,500 ft elevation

10,000 ft elevation

5,000 ft elevation
Guatemala City
City/Land of Nephi

NORTH

25 mi
50 km

FIGURE 6-14 Elevations

FIGURE 6–14: Observe the elevation statements in the Book of Mormon. The Mulekites traveled from the land northward (Veracruz) UP into the land southward, or Zarahemla (Alma 22:30–31 and Ether 9:30). Mosiah traveled from the land of Nephi DOWN to the land of Zarahemla (Omni 1:13). From Veracruz to Chiapas, the movement is UP. From Guatemala to the Chiapas depression, the movement is DOWN. Both the land of Nephi and the land of Zarahemla are in the land southward.

FIGURE 6–15: Although not conclusive, when the calendar trail is accompanied with the pottery trail and the architectural trail, the results are impressive. The following engraved monuments demonstrate sequential dates from Izapa, to Kaminaljuyu, to Chiapa de Corzo, to Tikal—or in the vernacular of the Book of Mormon, from Lehi's landing, to city of Nephi, to land of Zarahemla, to east wilderness of Zarahemla. The dates under consideration are as follows: Izapa, Stela 5, 200 BC; Altar 10, Kaminaljuyu, 147 BC; Stela 24, Chiapa de Corzo, 36 BC; Stela 31, Tikal, AD 378.

(Guatemala City), and Mulek came from the Gulf of Mexico by the Bay of Campeche. This movement corresponds with Late Preclassic movements in Maya territory.

THE CALENDAR

Mosiah taught the people of Zarahemla his language, which may have also included knowledge of the calendar. Zarahemla then gave a genealogy of his people, which was later written down. The people of Zarahemla had no records with them; their language had become corrupt; and they did not believe in God. Eventually, the two groups united, and Mosiah became the king (see Omni 1:17–19).

During the rest of the Maya Late Preclassic Period, 180 BC to AD 250, the Nephites represented the ruling class over the Mulekites.

The trail is not that difficult to follow, as we know the footsteps of the calendar in Mesoamerica. Assuming that the Nephites were the originators of the calendar system

FIGURE 6—16: An artististic rendition of Stela 5 of Izapa, which was engraved between 300 and 200 BC. The Nephites occupied the land of first inheritance intermittently from 570 BC to AD 350. These dates correspond to the time period when Mosiah left the land of Nephi and settled in the land of Zarahemla. Izapa appears to have been located in the land of Zarahemla for most of the Nephite history. (Courtesy of Cliff Dunston)

FIGURE 6—17: Altar 10 of Kaminaljuyu has the date of 147 BC engraved in three different languages. The Nephites occupied the land of Nephi intermittently from about 570 BC to 121 BC. These dates correspond with the date that the kingship was transferred from Noah to Limhi, both of whom lived in the land of Nephi under Lamanite control (see Mosiah 18–19). (Photo courtesy of George and Audrey DeLange)

Assuming that the Nephites were the originators of the calendar system in Mesoamerica and that they brought with them certain Asiatic characteristics of the calendar, we can track the Nephites through Mesoamerica.

in Mesoamerica and that they brought with them certain Asiatic characteristics of the calendar, we can track the Nephites through Mesoamerica.

Today, we can follow the Mormons from Ohio to Missouri to Illinois to Utah by simply looking at the calendar dates and the cultural and architectural patterns. If we tried to reconstruct the movements in reverse, it just would not fit.

The same is true in Mesoamerica. The Nephite trail follows a logical sequence. That trail appears to be as follows and as shown in figure 6–15.

As determined by the engraved dates on the stone, the calendar was initiated along the Pacific coast of Guatemala, the Nephite-Lamanite land of first inheritance. From there, the calendar moved into the highlands of Guatemala—or the land of Nephi. By 100 BC, Late Preclassic, the calendar moved to the borders of Guatemala and Chiapas—land of Zarahemla. Subsequently, we see the calendar in the Peten jungle—the east wilderness of the Book of Mormon. For example, Stela 5 at Izapa was engraved about 176 BC, Altar 10 at Kaminaljuyu dates to 147 BC, Stela 24 at Chiapa de Corzo dates to 36 BC, and Stela 31 at Tikal dates to AD 378.

THE WRITTEN LANGUAGE

The written language was also utilized extensively by the Nephites during the Late Preclassic Period, 300 BC to AD 250. King Benjamin had his address written down and circulated about 120 BC (see Mosiah 2:9). The Nephite people of Ammonihah burned the records of the members of the Church of Christ about 80 BC (see Alma 14:8). And Christ had the Nephite Christians write that which had been omitted at His coming (see 3 Nephi 23:11–13).

Exploring the Lands of the Book of Mormon

FIGURE 6–18: Stela 24, a wall panel at Chiapa de Corzo, bears the date of December 36 BC and is the oldest Maya long count date yet discovered. It corresponds with the date that the Nephites were driven out of the land of Zarahemla to the land Bountiful (see Helaman 4:4–6). (Photo courtesy of Phil Skousen)

Even the Lamanites got into the act during the Late Preclassic Period, as the Lamanite king appointed apostate Nephites to teach the Nephite written language among the Lamanites: "But they taught them that they should keep their record, and that they might *write* one to another" (Mosiah 24:6; emphasis added).

Inasmuch as the Classic Maya, AD 250–AD 900, adopted the written language from the Preclassic people living in Maya territory, 600 BC–AD 250, we can conclude that the Lamanites included the Classic Maya and that they adopted the language from the Nephites, who lived in the land southward during Preclassic times.

BUILDING OF CITIES

Perhaps nowhere is the comparison between the Preclassic Maya record and

FIGURE 6–19: Stela 31, Tikal. Although Tikal had existed for several centuries prior to the engraving of Stela 31, this monument corresponds to the last years of Nephite history. January AD 378 is a pivotal conquest date in both Maya and Nephite history. (Photo courtesy of Richard Norman)

the Classic Nephite (200 BC–AD 1) record more synonymously represented than in the building programs.

About 70 BC, Moroni ordered his armies into the east wilderness to drive the Lamanites back into their own lands, which were south of the east wilderness and south of the land of Zarahemla. The east wilderness was east of the land/city of Zarahemla (see Alma 50:1–10).

We read in Alma 50:13–15 the following: "And it came to pass that the Nephites began the foundation of a city, and they called the name of the city Moroni; and it was by the east sea; and it was on the south by the line of the possessions of the Lamanites. And they also began a foundation for a city between the city of Moroni and the city of Aaron, joining the borders of Aaron and Moroni; and they called the name of the city, or the land, Nephihah. And they also began in that same year to *build many cities on the north*, one in a particular manner which they called Lehi, which was in the north by the borders of the seashore" (Alma 50:13–15; emphasis added).

This massive building program undertaken by the first century BC Nephites in the east wilderness corresponds with the massive building program undertaken by the Preclassic Maya in the Peten jungle of Guatemala.

Both records also complement each other when they describe defensive cities in detail (see chapter 24, "Wilderness Areas").

The first century BC Nephites built along the east sea. The Late Preclassic Maya built along the shores of the Caribbean.

In the east wilderness, the first century BC Nephites built cities that they named Nephi*hah* and Moroni*hah*. The Late Preclassic Maya built cities in the Peten with names like Yax*ha* and Puls*iha*.

The Lamanites conquered the Nephites in the east wilderness in the first century BC, during which time the Lamanites had a king named Lamoni. The Late Preclassic Maya named one city Lamanai, which was built in the Late Preclassic Period in the country of Belize.

AN ELITE HIERARCHY ATTEMPTS TO ESTABLISH KINGS

About 65 BC, a serious attempt was made to reestablish kings in the Nephite/Mulekite territory. The Nephite people had not had a king for twenty-five years, as the sons of Mosiah refused the kingship from their father about 90 BC. From that time forth, the Nephites operated under a system of judges. The chief judge had always been a descendant of Nephi. Those who desired kings appear not to have been of Nephite descent but appear to have been descended from royalty: "And it came to pass that those who were desirous that Pahoran should be dethroned from the judgment-seat were called *king-men*, for they were desirous that the law should be altered in a manner to overthrow the free government and to establish a *king* over the land. Now those who were in favor of *kings* were those of high birth, and they sought to be *kings*, and they were supported

The massive building program undertaken by the first century BC Nephites in the east wilderness corresponds with the massive building program undertaken by the Preclassic Maya in the Peten jungle of Guatemala.

by those who sought power and authority over the people" (Alma 51:5, 8; emphasis added).

As we saw in the Maya record, the seeds were sown in the first century BC that subsequently resulted in the Classic, AD 250–AD 900, king-priest hierarchy in Mesoamerica. The date given by the Book of Mormon is about 65 BC, or during the first century BC. The inhabitants of Cerros, located in northern Belize, attempted to establish a kingship at the same time that the king-men and Amalickiah were determined to do the same in the east wilderness of Zarahemla.

AD 1–AD 250

The last two hundred years of the Maya Preclassic Period in the Book of Mormon fit nicely with what is known archaeologically about activities in Maya territory. This is the time period when many sites, including the sites discussed above (Tikal, El Mirador, Uaxactun, Lamanai, and Chiapa de Corzo) were flourishing. For the two hundred years following the birth of Christ, a definite growth was seen in Maya territory that set the stage for a seven-hundred-year history called the Classic Maya Period, AD 250–AD 900.

Lachoneus. Shortly after the birth of Christ and prior to His visit to the Nephites, a great cleansing process took place. Lachoneus, the chief judge of the Nephites, gathered the Nephites together in an area that was probably located in the mountains of Chiapas. This area, which was undoubtedly named after the chief judge, is called by the same name today, with just a minor spelling change. It is the area of the Lacandone Mountains. The Lacandone valley, the river of Lacanha, and an archaeological site called Lacantun also carry what appears to be the name of Lachoneus.

Speaking of this gathering and the subsequent war with the Gadianton robbers, Mormon writes: "And the land which was appointed was the land of Zarahemla, and the land which was between the land Zarahemla and the land Bountiful, yea, to the line which was between the land Bountiful and the land Desolation" (3 Nephi 3:23). Further, Mormon wrote about the defeat of the Gadianton robbers by saying that "terrible was the battle thereof, yea, great and terrible was the slaughter thereof, insomuch that there never was known so great a slaughter among all the people of Lehi since he left Jerusalem" (3 Nephi 4:11).

GREAT DESTRUCTION

At the time of the Crucifixion of Christ, the Book of Mormon records that a great and terrible destruction occurred in the New World (see 3 Nephi 8:5).

The land southward, which appears to be the same area as the Maya territory heretofore discussed, was the recipient of this great destruction. However, the destruction in the land southward was not as great as the destruction was in the land northward:

The inhabitants of Cerros, located in northern Belize, attempted to establish a kingship at the same time that the king-men and Amalickiah were determined to do the same in the east wilderness of Zarahemla.

"And there was a great and terrible destruction in the land southward. But behold, there was a more great and terrible destruction in the land northward" (3 Nephi 8:11–12).

In summary to this point, the area known as Maya territory, which is proposed as the land southward, is subject to frequent and massive earthquakes and hurricanes. The country of Guatemala alone reportedly has thirty-three volcanoes, many of them active. Everybody knows of the destructive storms that pour inland from the Caribbean near the Yucatan Peninsula and the countries of Belize, Honduras, and Guatemala.

COMING OF CHRIST TO THE AMERICAS

The highlight of the Book of Mormon is the coming of Christ to the Nephites:

> And it came to pass that while they were thus conversing one with another, they heard a voice as if it came out of heaven; and they cast their eyes round about,

FIGURE 6–20: The eruption of volcanoes is devastating. At Lake Atitlan, remnants of cities have been discovered under the water as a result of earthquakes and storms. Active volcanoes are still found in Guatemala today, one of which is called El Pacaya, south of Guatemala City, which has erupted twenty-three times since the Spanish conquest. (Photo courtesy of Cortney Boice)

> for they understood not the voice which they heard; and it was not a harsh voice, neither was it a loud voice; nevertheless, and notwithstanding it being a small voice it did pierce them that did hear to the center, insomuch that there was no part of their frame that it did not cause to quake; yea, it did pierce them to the very soul, and did cause their hearts to burn.
>
> And it came to pass that again they heard the voice, and they understood it not.

And again the third time they did hear the voice, and did open their ears to hear it; and their eyes were towards the sound thereof; and they did look steadfastly towards heaven, from whence the sound came.

And behold, the third time they did understand the voice which they heard; and it said unto them:

Behold my Beloved Son, in whom I am well pleased, in whom I have glorified my name—hear ye him. (3 Nephi 11:3–7)

Although the ancient histories of Mexico undoubtedly speak of the visit of Christ to Mesoamerica, the archaeological record is unclear. The task of knowing what to look for archaeologically that will indicate the visit of Christ to America is a difficult one (see chapter 14, "The White God Quetzalcoatl").

THE GOLDEN AGE OF THE NEPHITES

Clearly, the golden age of the Nephites is not the same as the Classic civilization of the Maya. The Nephite golden age dates from the coming of Christ, AD 34, to the year AD 200. The Classic age for the Maya began at AD 250.

The difference is in definition. The golden age of the Nephites had everytying to do with the spiritual nature of the people desiring to live the commandments of God. The Classic Period of the Maya is a physical declaration that is recognized by the size and number of their buildings.

Regarding the period from AD 34 to AD 200, Late Preclassic, Mormon writes: "And there were no envyings, nor strifes, nor tumults, nor whoredoms, nor lyings, nor murders, nor any manner of lasciviousness; and surely there could not be a happier people among all the people who had been created by the hand of God" (4 Nephi 1:16).

This scripture does not imply that the Nephites were idle or that they did not build buildings. During this time period, between AD 36 and AD 60, the city of Zarahemla was rebuilt: "Yea, even that great city Zarahemla did they cause to be built again" (4 Nephi 1:8). Architecturally, the Maya territory was gearing up for a great apostasy, an era wherein the massive building programs of the post–AD 200 period would literally cause pride to precede their fall.

AD 250–AD 350—NEPHITE APOSTASY; EARLY MAYA CLASSIC

The dates of the Maya Classic Period and the final Nephite apostasy are identical. The activity is the same in Maya territory as what we read in 4 Nephi. In the Book of Mormon, we are told that elaborate clothing distinguished one group from another. In Maya land, the priests began to wear elaborate clothing to set them above the common people.

> The golden age of the Nephites had everything to do with the spiritual nature of the people desiring to live the commandments of God. The Classic Period of the Maya is a physical declaration that is recognized by the size and number of their buildings.

The Book of Mormon informs us that many buildings were built to get gain. In Maya land, a massive building program took place wherein many of the buildings served no functional purpose.

The Book of Mormon tells us that the wicked priests exercised power and authority over the disciples of Christ and that the people trafficked in all manner of commerce. The Maya archaeological record states that the priests controlled the social, religious, and commercial activities of the people. A summation of these activities from both the Maya archaeological record and the Book of Mormon, during the 150-year time period known as Maya Early Classic, follows. A more detailed account of these activities is given in chapter 30, "The Maya Classic Period and the Nephite Apostasy."

From the book of 4 Nephi, we read the following:

AD 211. "And now, in this two hundred and first year there began to be among them those who were lifted up in pride, such as the wearing of costly apparel. . . . [And] they began to build up churches unto themselves to get gain" (vs. 24, 26).

AD 210. "And it came to pass that when two hundred and ten years had passed away there were many churches in the land; yea, there were many churches which professed to know the Christ, and yet they did deny the more parts of his gospel. . . . They did persecute the true church of Christ . . . . They did exercise power and authority over the disciples of Jesus. . . . They were led by many priests and false prophets to build up many churches" (vs. 27, 29, 30, 34).

AD 231. "They did wilfully rebel against the gospel of Christ" (v. 38).

AD 244. "And they did still continue to build up churches unto themselves, and adorn them with all manner of precious things. . . . [And] the wicked part of the people began again to build up the secret oaths" (vs. 41, 42).

AD 300. "And gold and silver did they lay up in store in abundance, and did traffic in all manner of traffic" (v. 46).

ca. AD 322. Regarding the land of Zarahemla, which is proposed to have been in Maya territory, we read from Mormon that "the whole face of the land had become covered with buildings" (Mormon 1:7).

AD 350. The clincher was in the year AD 350 when the Lamanites literally gained control over all the land to the narrow neck, which is proposed to be the Isthmus of Tehuantepec. This great Maya territory was not relinquished until the coming of the Spaniards in the sixteenth century. Mormon explains the division of the land northward and the land southward by saying, "And in the three hundred and fiftieth year we made a treaty with the Lamanites and the robbers of Gadianton, in which we did get the lands of our inheritance divided. And the Lamanites did give unto us the land northward, yea, even to the narrow passage which led into the land southward. And we did give unto the Lamanites all the land southward" (Mormon 2:28–29).

The story is almost as clear from an archaeological perspective as it is in the Book of Mormon. The apostate religious base developed into a highly political and economic base. The priestly caste turned into a powerful warrior-type society.[17] In other words, the church and the state became one.[18] From the archaeological record of Uxmal, we read the following: "This period runs from AD 200–AD 1000 . . . [during which] the high priests controlled . . . the social and economic life of the population. . . . The structures generally reflect a predominant use of massive stone to create an impressive exterior aspect with little concern for the practical use of interior spaces. . . . It is evident that a great part of the collective force was concentrated in building constructions which were not directly concerned with productivity."[19]

FIGURE 6–21: The Quadrangle of the Nunnery, located at Uxmal, represents Classic Maya, AD 250–AD 900, and is an example of the manner in which the buildings were adorned as described in 4 Nephi. As noted, the buildings were not directly related to productivity but were built mostly for their impressive exteriors. (Photo courtesy of Sheryl Lee Wilson)

17. Professor Michael Coe outlines the activities associated with the Maya Classic Period. He disregards the theory that the Maya priests ruled the people in Maya land during the Classic Period, AD 250 to AD 900. He falls into the error that priests represent "good guys." From both the Book of Mormon and from archaeology, the priestcraft movement of AD 250 clearly evolved into a powerful, war-oriented governmental society by AD 350. The rest of the Classic Period, as well as on through the Postclassic Period, illustrates this priest-government marriage. Coe writes: "The Classic period was a kind of Golden Age, not only for them [the Maya] but for the rest of the Mesoamerican peoples. Large populations, a flourishing economy, and widespread trade were typical of the Classic, but although it was once thought to have been a period of relative peace and tranquility in comparison with what followed, that notion has in the main been disproved. It is an equally unfounded assumption that the Classic peoples were ruled by priests. On the contrary,...the ancient Maya were just as warlike and had as thoroughly a secular a government as the supposedly more bloodthirsty states of the Post–Classic." (Coe, *The Maya*, 67)

18. That which happened in the Old World also happened in the Americas. For example, the Nicean Creed, written in AD 325, literally marked the beginning of a marriage between church and state in which the Catholic Church became the dominant force. By the same token, in Maya territory, a marriage between the church and government occurred at precisely the same time as in the Old World.

19. Rubio, *Official Guide: Uxmal*, 31–33.

The intellectual and artistic achievements during this period surpassed anything that had yet occurred on the American continent. The God of the Nephites was substituted for gods made by man, and the new gods were displayed on buildings and in artwork. The remains of these elaborate works, etched in stone, have endured for hundreds of years.

AD 350–AD 900—CLASSIC MAYA; NEPHITE DESTRUCTION

As stated previously, the great Maya heyday was well underway—buildings dotting the Maya map and most cities increasing in population. Yet, almost paradoxically, a few cities demonstrated just the reverse—that is, a decrease in population occurred.

Sites that fall into the second category include Izapa, Chiapa de Corzo, and El Mirador. Monte Alban, west of the Isthmus of Tehuantepec, also manifested a cultural change during this same period.

Apparently, the AD 350 treaty, through which the Lamanites gained control over the entire land southward, included "building permits" to construct magnificent buildings throughout Maya land. Often, these buildings were built on or over structures that could have previously been Nephite structures.

This period also highlights the Nephite activity during this same time period, as Mormon was in the process of calling all the Nephites together to the land of Desolation, or the land northward.

This activity by Mormon may explain why a decline in population occurred in a few selected sites, as mentioned above. Corresponding to the year AD 360, Mormon wrote the following: "And it came to pass that I did cause my people that they should gather themselves together at the land Desolation, to a city which was in the borders, by the narrow pass which led into the land southward" (Mormon 3:5).

Obviously, the AD 350 treaty, as outlined in Mormon 2:28–29, was not what the Nephites desired. For the next thirty-five years, from AD 350 to AD 385, the wars continued between the Lamanites and the Nephites. Many of the wars were fought in an attempt on the part of the Nephites to regain their lands located in the land southward.

From an archaeological point of view, it must have seemed necessary for the Lamanite/Maya nation to eliminate the haughty and proud Nephite minority to establish trade patterns with people living in the valley of Mexico. During AD 350 to AD 900, archaeology confirms that heavy trade traffic throughout all of Mesoamerica began shortly after the demise of the Nephite nation of AD 350–400. Information surfaced during the 1990s that outlines a direct link to Tikal and Teotihuacan at the same time the Nephites were destroyed. (See chapter 8, "The Teotihuacan Culture," for a treatise on this subject.)

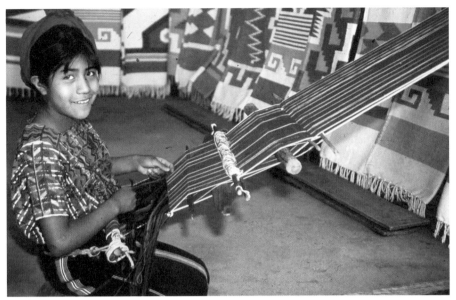

FIGURE 6–22: One-half of the people of Guatemala are considered native to the country. Many still maintain their native traditions of dress, dialect, and customs. Here a young Quiche Maya girl from Panajachel demonstrates the ancient method of weaving. (Photo courtesy of Merrill C. Oaks)

CULTURAL PATTERNS

Once we have determined that what archaeologists refer to as the Preclassic Maya were, in reality, the same people as the Lamanites, Nephites, and Mulekites in the Book of Mormon, new vistas will be opened for our understanding of the Book of Mormon.

We have strong reason to believe that many of the traits of the Classic and Postclassic Maya are the same as the Preclassic Maya. Hence, many of the traits of the Classic and Postclassic Maya may well be the same traits possessed by the Lamanites, Nephites, and Mulekites of the Book of Mormon.

For instance, if we want to see what type of cooking utensils the wife of Alma used around 70 BC, we might look at the style of pots that date to that time period in Maya country.

If we want to see what food she cooked in the pots, we can analyze what food is raised today that dates to the Preclassic times. The same is true of the clothes the Nephites and Lamanites wore and the style of houses they lived in.

We may learn many things about the Book of Mormon by following this procedure, such as the meaning of the following:

1. How they clapped their hands for joy (see Mosiah 18:11).
2. The manner of and use of their monetary system (see Alma 11:1–19).
3. How they carried burdens on their backs (see Mosiah 24:14).
4. How they built up their waste places (see Helaman 11:20).
5. What made up their flocks and herds (see Helaman 12:2).
6. The meaning of the term "wilderness" (see Mosiah 24:24).

From an archaeological point of view, it must have seemed necessary for the Lamanite/Maya nation to eliminate the haughty and proud Nephite minority to establish trade patterns with people living in the valley of Mexico.

7. How they planted and harvested corn (see Mosiah 9:9).

8. The manner of cloth the women worked (see Helaman 6:13).

9. The types of plants used for medicinal purposes (see Alma 46:40).

10. How they wrote letters (see 3 Nephi 3:2–10).

The above points are just a sampling of culture traits that leap out from the pages of the Book of Mormon as we become acquainted with the history, culture, climate, and topography of the territory of the ancient Maya. For a more detailed analysis of cultural comparisons, refer to chapter 16, "Customs and Traditions."

As we have escorted hundreds and hundreds of Latter-day Saints among the ruins of Mesoamerica, the most prevalent comments have been those reflecting their feelings comparing the culture patterns of Mesoamerica with those of the Book of Mormon. That has been our personal experience also. We firmly believe that Mesoamerica can teach us as much about the culture and geography of the Book of Mormon as the Book of Mormon teaches us about Mesoamerica.

FIGURE 6–23: A palace at Palenque. No other archaeological ruin has inspired the creativity of researchers over the years as much as Palenque has. Its sheer beauty, its magnificent setting, and its detailed artwork are an inspiration for epigraphers, archaeologists, and linguists. Frederick Catherwood prepared some of his most impressive drawings while at Palenque. A modern Palenque monument is dedicated to Alberto Ruz for his discovery of the tomb of Pacal, and a tree was planted at Palenque for the pioneer linguistic work of Linda Schele. (Photo courtesy of Sheryl Lee Wilson)

A FIRST VISIT TO PALENQUE

Following is Joseph L. Allen's account of his initial visit to Palenque, as found in the first edition of *Exploring the Lands of the Book of Mormon*:

I had waited a long time for the experience of visiting the Maya ruins of Palenque, located on the edge of the jungle in the state of Chiapas, Mexico.

In the year 1957, I gained my first exposure to archaeological sites located in the countries of Bolivia, Peru, and Mexico. I had returned many times to the Pyramid of the Sun and the Pyramid of the Moon just outside of Mexico City. I had also studied at the National Museum of Anthropology in Mexico City. I had visited the ruins of Uxmal and Chichen Itza in the Yucatan and was overwhelmed with their magnitude. And I felt a special spirit while visiting the ruins of Monte Alban in the state of Oaxaca, Mexico.

But my first visit to Palenque left an even greater lasting impression on my mind than did my visits to other sites. At that time, some members of the Church considered Palenque to be the city of Bountiful, not realizing that the primary dating corresponded to AD 600. This dating does not negate the concept that Maya Classic ruins were built on Preclassic Book of Mormon ruins. The "and it came to pass" glyph had not yet been interpreted at Palenque.

What occurred to me that day at Palenque changed my entire perspective about the geographical and cultural setting of the Book of Mormon. After that day, I could visualize the meaning of the term "wilderness" in the Book of Mormon. I could then understand how Alma could wander eight days in the wilderness, establish a community, and not be discovered for many years.

I could understand how the Lamanites could get lost in the wilderness in pursuit of the Nephites. Indeed, Spanish soldiers marched within a few miles of Palenque in the sixteenth century, not knowing it was even there.

I could understand how a party of Nephites from the land of Nephi could get lost and not find Zarahemla. I could see them passing through the swamplands and lagoons of the states of Tabasco and Campeche and wandering into the land northward. I could see them looking at the same Olmec ruins we see along the Gulf of Mexico.

At Palenque, I caught a glimpse of what a tower looked like in the Book of Mormon and the possible meaning of the term "temple." I could feel the control the Lamanite hierarchy held over the people for centuries following the closing of the Book of Mormon.

I felt I could understand Mormon's comment about the fevers that were prevalent during certain seasons of the year, as the day at Palenque was hot and humid. I could also identify with his statement about the Lord's providing an abundance of plants and roots with which to cure sickness (see Alma 46:40).

I felt the geographical significance of the land of many waters, the narrow passage, the river Sidon, and a flood of other cultural and geographical patterns.

I empathized with Mormon as I wandered through the ruins of Palenque and thought about his statement, "O ye fair ones, how could ye have departed from the ways of the Lord!" (Mormon 6:17). I marveled at the words of Nephi when

"Prior to my first visit to Palenque, I had never entertained the idea of studying the Book of Mormon from a geographical and cultural setting. My visit to Palenque changed my perspective because it helped me realize the value of understanding the pervasive geographical and cultural statements in the Book of Mormon."

—Joseph Allen

Palenque
contains
some of
the finest
architecture,
sculpture,
and bas-relief
carvings
the Maya
produced.

he said that "then shall they know and come to the knowledge of their forefathers" (1 Nephi 15:14).

I saw the day when the Lamanites would "blossom as the rose," as prophesied by the Prophet Joseph Smith (see D&C 49:24). I proclaimed to myself that day at Palenque, as I sat on the steps of the Temple of Inscriptions, "Surely that day is here."

Since that time, as we have conducted scores and scores of tours through the ruins at Palenque, we have felt the same impressions over and over. Although it is a medium-sized site that is much smaller than such huge sites as Tikal or Copan, Palenque contains some of the finest architecture, sculpture, and bas-relief carvings the Maya produced. It is a must-see site for all visitors to proposed Mesoamerican lands of the Book of Mormon.

FREQUENTLY ASKED QUESTIONS

One of the questions commonly asked by tour members deals with the last great battle of the Nephites and Lamanites at the hill Cumorah.

Question: The battle at Cumorah was devastating to the Nephite nation, as 230,000 Nephite soldiers were killed. And possibly that many or more of the Lamanites were killed. Why do we not see those statistical numbers showing up in the records of the Maya chronology?

Answer: At least three reasons stand out.

First, the archaeological data can show only that which transpired in the area researched. Maya territory was probably the same area that is called the land southward in the Book of Mormon. That area does indeed show a decline in population in some sites, as discussed earlier. The last battle was fought on the northern side of the narrow neck of land.

Second, the distance in time from AD 385, the last Nephite battle, is far removed from our day—or even the sixteenth century when the Spanish arrived. In Maya history, many wars had transpired over those twelve hundred years, many of which appear to be just as devastating in numbers as was the last Nephite-Lamanite war in the Book of Mormon.

This thinking is consistent with Moroni's statement when he wrote the following about the Lamanites in AD 400: "For behold, their wars are exceedingly fierce among themselves" (Moroni 1:2).

Finally, since the initial publication of *Exploring the Lands of the Book of Mormon* in 1989, almost twenty years ago, many changes have taken place and new information has come forward. The 1989 first edition of *Exploring the Lands* contains the following statement by Joseph L. Allen: "We should mention that the last chapter has not been written about the Maya. Further evidence will indeed continue to come forth. And I am not sure that the Lamanites were all that excited about talking about the Nephites. To the large Lamanite army, it is possible that the Nephite war may have been equivalent to just another internal revolution."

From Stela 31 at Tikal, we now have evidence suggesting that a combination of Lamanites (Maya) in the land southward together with a secret combination government in Teotihuacan (land northward) explains the political reasons for the downfall of the Nephite nation (see chapter 8, "The Teotihuacan Culture").

FIGURE 6–24: The ruins of Palenque are subject to heavy rainfall during much of the year, and that rainfall is responsible for the beautiful, lush, green foliage for most of the year at the site. Shown here are the remains of an ancient ball court that the grounds keepers keep neatly manicured at all times. (Photo courtesy of Sheryl Lee Wilson)

CHAPTER 7

The Zapotec (Mulekite-Nephite) Culture

Many of the Lamanites did go into the land northward; and also Nephi and Lehi went into the land northward. . . .

> *The land south was called Lehi,*
> *and the land north was called Mulek,*
> *which was after the son of Zedekiah;*
> *for the Lord did bring*
> *Mulek into the land north,*
> *and Lehi into the land south. (Helaman 6:6, 10)*

T he Zapotec ("people of the clouds") civilization had its beginnings in the valley of Oaxaca about 500 BC. As determined by culture patterns, language, and date correlations, the early Zapotecs may have been part of the Mulekite culture.

We believe that the Oaxaca valley played a vital role in the development of three major Book of Mormon civilizations: the Jaredites, the Mulekites, and the Nephites. The area may have been the land of Moron in the early Jaredite/Olmec history. As

OPPOSITE: This building at Mitla, Oaxaca, dates to the Postclassic Period and was still occupied at the time of the coming of the conquering Spaniards in the sixteenth century. Mitla became the capital of the Zapotec people after the downfall of Monte Alban in the seventh century AD. *Mitla* is a Zapotec word that means "burial place." The residents used their sophistication in design and construction to place hundreds of small, carved stones into the walls of the buildings so the stones could combine to create a serpent image. The Spaniards utilized the walls and the stones of Mitla to build their cathedrals and other buildings. In the foreground are leaves of the agave plant, commonly referred to in Mexico as maguey. (Photo courtesy of Sheryl Lee Wilson)

The Oaxaca valley may have been the land of Moron in the early Jaredite/ Olmec history. Certain sites, such as Monte Alban, give hints of their being under Nephite control beginning about 100 BC.

stated earlier, this concept is enhanced by the idea that the ancient name of *Monte Alban* has the same meaning as *Moron* or *Mormon* (jaguar hill). After the arrival of the Mulekites, the Oaxaca valley may have become one of the areas where a branch of their society made its home. Certain sites, such as Monte Alban, give hints of their being under Nephite control beginning about 100 BC.

The Oaxaca valley is located northwest of the Isthmus of Tehuantepec. If the Isthmus of Tehuantepec is synonymous with the narrow neck of land in the Book of Mormon, then the valley of Oaxaca was in the land northward.

The following table illustrates the time periods associated with the impressive archaeological center called Monte Alban in relationship to the Book of Mormon:

700 BC–500 BC	Olmec settlements	Jaredite history
500 BC–100 BC	Monte Alban Period I	Early Mulekite
100 BC–AD 350	Monte Alban Period II	Nephite/Mulekite
	Culture infusion	Mosiah to Mormon
AD 350–AD 750	Monte Alban Period III	Nephite destruction
	Decline of Monte Alban	Post–Book of Mormon

FIGURE 7–1: The city of Oaxaca is located three hundred miles southeast of Mexico City. With the exception of the state of Chiapas, the state of Oaxaca has the highest native population in Mexico. The two major cultures are called the Zapotec and the Mixtec. Here Doña Sofia from San Bartolo Coyotepec, Oaxaca, demonstrates the art of making black pottery from a clay that is indigenous to the area. (Photo courtesy of Merrill C. Oaks)

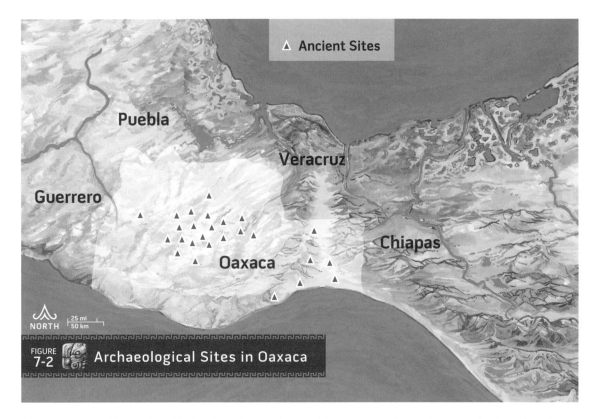

Archaeological Sites in Oaxaca

FIGURE 7-2

FIGURE 7–2: The city of Oaxaca is located in the valley of Oaxaca in the state of Oaxaca. The state of Oaxaca is surrounded on three sides by high, rugged mountains and on the south by the Pacific Ocean. It borders the states of Puebla, Guerrero, Veracruz, and Chiapas. Because of its location and history, the Zapotecs from this area are considered to be a different culture from either Mexico (the Toltecs and Aztecs) or the Maya. The Jaredite capital of Moron appears to have been located in the Oaxaca valley (see Ether 7:6).

FIGURE 7–3: A drawing of the archaeological site of Monte Alban located in the valley of Oaxaca. The drawing is on display in the Oaxaca room at the National Museum of Anthropology in Mexico City. Monte Alban dates from 500 BC to AD 700. (Photo courtesy of Merrill C. Oaks)

FIGURE 7–4: The archaeological site of San Jose Mogote is located about forty-five minutes north of the city of Oaxaca. It dates to the Jaredite time period. Archaeologist Ignacio Bernal proposed a comparison between some of the brick work at San Jose Mogote with that of ancient Mesopotamia, the area of origin of the Jaredites. (Photo courtesy of Sheryl Lee Wilson)

If you have not yet checked out thoroughly the "Pronunciation Guide" immediately preceding chapter 1, now is the time to do so. There you will learn that Oaxaca is pronounced wah HAH kah.

GETTING TO OAXACA

Some of our most memorable experiences in Mexico have centered around the train ride we used to take between the city of Oaxaca and Mexico City. The train took about thirteen hours and consisted of an overnight ride. In addition to first- and second-class seats, Pullman sleeping accommodations were available. The train would be delayed on occasion, and the mountainous terrain required the train to move rather slowly.

Comments from our tour members who traveled on the train ranged from "It was such a delightful experience; I felt like I was among the upper crust of society" to "It was the worst experience of my life."

The distance from Oaxaca to Mexico City is about three hundred miles. The trip by bus ranged from nine to ten hours but today is reduced to five hours because of the freeway; a trip by plane takes only forty-five minutes. The Zapotec ruins of Monte Alban are located on a mountain in the center of the Oaxaca valley.

On one of our train trips, a young college boy and a high-school girl were so fascinated with the ruins of Monte Alban that they decided they would return to the archaeological site of Monte Alban during the three hours that remained before the train left for Mexico City. The bus ride from the city center of Oaxaca to Monte Alban takes about twenty minutes.

As the time arrived for the group to transfer from the hotel to the train station, the mother of the girl expressed her concern about the young couple, as they had not yet returned. The tour director told the mother that he would stay behind and wait for half an hour, which should give the young couple plenty of time to return. Then, the director told the rest of the group to transfer to the station and to locate their compartments on the train.

The thirty minutes elapsed, and the young couple had not returned. The director later talked about the event as follows:

I thought that perhaps they had gone directly to the train station. I hired a taxi and hurried to the train station. Upon my arrival, the alarmed mother said, "No, they still haven't arrived!"

The time was now 5:40 p.m., and the train was scheduled to leave at 6:00 p.m. The conductor informed us that the train would definitely leave on time. I told the group, "Get on the train slowly and do what you can to hold it up. I'll make one more quick trip to the hotel and check one more time." As I was riding back to the hotel, I thought to myself, "How will I know if they make the train if I don't get back before it leaves?"

The last check at the hotel also proved futile; and the taxi driver, who by this time could drive the route blindfolded, did all that was required and then some to get back to the train station. I did not want to be without transportation, so I persuaded the driver to follow me to the train. The taxi stopped. I jumped out and made a run for the train—just as the whistle blew and the train left the station. Movie scenes flashed through my mind, but somehow I couldn't see myself trying to jump on the now fast-speeding train. Besides, I didn't know whether the two young people were on the train; and I still needed to pay the taxi fare.

Just as I ducked my head in despair, I heard the screeching of iron wheels. I looked up and saw sparks flying all over the place. The train came to an abrupt halt. I ran to the train car where the group was located and asked, "Did the kids make it?" One member of the group said, "Yes, they just barely arrived." I later found out that they were delayed because the buses had stopped running for the day from Monte Alban. They had to walk down the mountain. Luckily, they saw a police car patrolling the area at the foot of the mountain. The policeman brought them to the train station.

I handed the cab fare to the taxi driver, thanked him, and jumped on the train. We were all celebrating the return of everyone, and I turned and thanked the conductor for stopping the train. He said in a disgruntled voice, "I didn't stop the train. I don't know who did." Our group told me that the conductor was determined to leave on time.

At that moment, my nine-year-old son tugged on my shirttail and said, "Dad, can I talk to you for a minute in our room?" We went to the train compartment and Todd said, "Dad, I know why the train stopped. When everybody was worried, I came in here and knelt down and prayed to Heavenly Father and asked Him to let everybody get on the train. Heavenly Father stopped the train."

Sadly, the "El Oaxaqueño" train service from Mexico City to Oaxaca is no longer available. On our twenty-first century tours to lands of the Book of Mormon, however, we fly to most destinations and then use large, first-class buses that are among the finest in the world as we travel to site destinations.

Some of our lands of the Book of Mormon tour members consider Oaxaca to be the Ultimate Mexican destination. We try to spend a day at Monte Alban, the spectacular Zapotec ruins just outside of town. And we often spend another day exploring Oaxaca's huge mercado, one of the best and biggest in Mexico.

FIGURE 7–5: These photos are of the archaeological zone of Monte Alban, which is one of the cities in the Oaxaca valley and which is built on a hill. This center dates to the Olmec time period, and the archaeological evidence now shows that anciently it was called the Hill of the Jaguar, a title that correlates with the name of the ancient capital of the Jaredites, Moron. The Zapotec era began at 500 BC. However, these buildings date to the florescent time of Monte Alban from AD 400 to AD 700. Excavation work was initiated in the 1930s under the direction of Mexican archaeologist Alfonso Caso. (Photos courtesy of Sheryl Lee Wilson)

Years later, Todd Allen, the nine-year-old who today conducts tours to the lands of the Book of Mormon, sums up the experience by merely saying, "Yes, and afterward, my dad said that *now* is the time for us to kneel down and *thank* Heavenly Father for stopping the train."

For many years, Oaxaca has been a popular tourist center because of its Spanish colonial charm and its historic native population. The Zapotecs still hand weave many kinds of colorful articles made from wool.

The abundance of archaeological sites, which are in excess of two hundred, bears witness of ancient civilizations that graced this fascinating region of Mexico. The elevation is about five thousand feet above sea level, which provides a mild year-round climate. When water is available, farmers harvest a crop of hay every twenty days.

The archaeological ruins of Monte Alban, a city that was built on a hill and that dates back to Book of Mormon times, caused us to speculate whether the similarity of its being built on a hill could have a parallel with the cities in Israel, of which many were also built on hills. Jerusalem was built on a hill; Bethlehem was built on a hill; and Nazareth was built on a hill.

FIGURE 7–6: Between 200 and 100 BC (Mosiah time period), a small group of would-be conquerors entered the Oaxaca valley from Chiapas and Guatemala. However, the conquerors did not destroy those of the earlier (Mulekite) period. Little by little, the two groups merged.

Mosiah and Monte Alban

The Oaxaca valley may have been occupied by segments of the Mulekite/ Jewish society from the sixth to third centuries BC. The area may even have been home for the early Jaredite culture.

The Savior said: "A city that is set on a hill cannot be hid.... Let your light so shine before men, that they may see your good works, and glorify your Father which is in heaven" (Matthew 5:14, 16).

The Oaxaca valley may have been occupied by segments of the Mulekite/Jewish society from the sixth to third centuries BC. The area may even have been home for the early Jaredite culture. The location of the Oaxaca valley, which is northwest of the Isthmus of Tehuantepec, qualifies it as being in the land northward, a qualification requirement for both the Jaredites and the early Mulekites.

Nephite occupation after Mosiah left the land of Nephi may have extended into the Oaxaca valley; and, at the time of Mormon, Nephites must surely have lived in the Oaxaca valley.

A comparison of the small book of Omni and the official guide to Oaxaca, called *The Oaxaca Valley, Official Guide,* published by the National Institute of Anthropology and History of Mexico, presents some rather remarkable parallels.

The early excavation work in Monte Alban was accomplished under the able direction of a Mexican archaeologist, Alfonso Caso, and the major portion of the excavations was completed in the 1930s. The discovery of the magnificent Tomb 7 by Caso proclaimed the richness of culture among the ancient Zapotec people because of the tomb's cache of gold, turquoise, and jade. Maintenance and excavation work of the archaeological sites in the state of Oaxaca still continue today under the direction of the Mexican government.

MONTE ALBAN PERIOD I—500 BC–100 BC

The Oaxaca Valley report states, "As far [as] we have been able to ascertain and save for the uncertain evidence of the hearths, man first appeared in the Valley of Oaxaca during the period which has been entitled Monte Alban I and must probably be placed between 700 and 300 BC. This earliest culture, which had reached quite an advanced stage of development, has left us some important remains at Monte Alban, such as the Inner Building of the Dancers, the bas-reliefs with which it is adorned, the innermost structures of the Northern Platform and also some graves."[1]

A small museum was completed near the site of Monte Alban in 1987. The dating reflects the consensus of archaeologists accompanied by radiocarbon dating and pottery and glyph comparisons. The architectural styles identify both the dating and the culture of those who occupied the area. Evidence exists of a pre–Monte Alban Period I culture prior to 500 BC; however, the Zapotec development of Monte Alban Period I dates from 500 BC to 100 BC, which is strictly Mulekite time period.

The Book of Mormon has little to say about the Mulekites during this early time period of their existence in the New World. When Mosiah discovered them about 180 BC, "they had become exceedingly numerous. Nevertheless, they had had many wars and serious contentions, and had fallen by the sword from time to time; and their

1. *The Oaxaca Valley, Official Guide,* 5th ed. (Mexico, DF: Instituto Nacional de Antropologia e Historia, 1973), 5–6.

language had become corrupted; and they had brought no records with them; and they denied the being of their Creator; and Mosiah, nor the people of Mosiah, could understand them" (Omni 1:17).

If we are allowed to hypothesize that the archaeological Zapotec people of Monte Alban Period I are a branch of the Mulekites that date to that same time period (500 BC to 100 BC), we arrive at some interesting comparisons.

FIGURE 7–7: Writing was first discovered in Mesoamerica at Monte Alban. However, it is different from Maya writing and has not yet been interpreted. These engraved monuments are located in the archaeology zone of Monte Alban. (Photos courtesy of Sheryl Lee Wilson)

For example, a preliminary study was conducted by Peter Balk of the New World Archaeological Foundation through which he reported similarities of word comparisons between Hebrew and Zapotec. The study was conducted among the Zapotec people living in the town of Zaachila, which is located at the base of the hill where the ruins of Monte Alban are situated. Zaachila is also near the city of Oaxaca.[2]

An additional hint of Hebrew culture at Monte Alban is derived from a four-horned incense burner that is on display in the Oaxaca Valley Room of the National Museum of Anthropology in Mexico City. The urn dates to Monte Alban Period I, 500 BC to 100 BC, and is similar to the types of urns from Jerusalem dating to the same time period.

The archaeological handbook continues: "Although we do not know for certain who the inhabitants may have been during this first period, they were undoubtedly influenced by the so called 'Olmecs' of the Gulf Coast."[3]

You will recall that the Olmec culture is considered by Latter-day Saint Mesoamericanists to be the same civilization as the Jaredites (see chapter 5, "The Olmec [Jaredite] Culture"). We know from the Book of Mormon that the Mulekites

2. See *SEHA Newsletter* 112, February 1969.

3. *The Oaxaca Valley,* 1973, 6.

landed in Jaredite territory: "[Desolation was] so far northward that it came into the land which had been peopled and been destroyed, of whose bones we have spoken, which was discovered by the people of Zarahemla, it being the place of their first landing" (Alma 22:30).

Although the Book of Mormon does not tell us that the Mulekites were influenced by the Jaredites, simple reasoning suggests that if the Mulekites landed among the Jaredites, such influences would have occurred.

We do know from information contained in the Book of Mormon that the Mulekites, or at least branches of the Mulekites, migrated into the land southward to a place they called the land of Zarahemla: "And they [Mulekites] came from there [land northward] up into the south wilderness [land of Bountiful and Zarahemla]" (Alma 22:31).

We also know from information contained in the Book of Mormon that from what appears to be several generations after the arrival of Mulek, the people of Zarahemla, descendants of Mulek, gave refuge to the last Jaredite king by the name of Coriantumr: "And Coriantumr was discovered by the people of Zarahemla; and he dwelt with them for the space of nine moons" (Omni 1:21).

The archaeological data from Monte Alban illustrate Olmec/Jaredite influence in the following manner: "There are marked Olmec influences in all these manifestations. These influences came from Veracruz and Tabasco and extended widely throughout Mesoamerica. Period I is recognizable in Monte Alban in the inner structure of the Dancers building, in the lower levels of the north platform and in some tombs, and also in other valley sites such as Yagul."[4]

4. *The Oaxaca Valley*, 1985, 20–21.

The dancers referred to in the preceding quotation consist of several stone monuments engraved with figures of people. Because some of the figures appear to be represented in ballerina-type dancing positions, the group of monuments has been called *Los Danzantes,* or The Dancers.

Other students of the Zapotec culture have considered the monuments of the dancers to represent a type of medical school because many of the monuments illustrate the internal organs of individuals.

Julia Marcos, a student of the Zapotec culture, suggests that whoever the settlers were of Monte Alban Period I (500 BC–100 BC), their nudeness reflects some relationship to captivity. The custom of parading nude captive victims is both a sign of complete dominance as well as a sign of security for the oppressors—that is, nude captives have no place to hide weapons. The concept is universal in nature, even as recently as World War II when Hitler treated the Jews in like fashion.

Perhaps an earlier Jewish nation, the Mulekites of Mesoamerica, is simply telling the story of its captivity by the Babylonians. If so, they chose to do so by engraving on stone monuments; and the artists or engravers were of Olmec/Jaredite origin, which helps explain why the Zapotec/Mulekite people of Monte Alban Period I have their history depicted in facial characters of the original Olmec/Jaredite culture.

FIGURE 7–8: The so-called dancer monuments at Monte Alban date to period 1, around 500 BC. The drawings are Olmec in style and appear to represent a captivity scene. (Photos courtesy of Sheryl Lee Wilson)

Perhaps an earlier Jewish nation, the Mulekites of Mesoamerica, is simply telling the story of its captivity by the Babylonians.

We witness the same thing today. Much of our artistic understanding of the Book of Mormon is interpreted by Mormon artists from the United States. As a result, the sons of Helaman look more like Roman soldiers than they look like the native culture from which they came. Likewise, the history of the Savior, interpreted from European eyes, is substantially different from the reality of Jerusalem. And the conquest of Mexico, as seen through the artists' eyes of the Spaniards and the Mexicans, is vastly different from what actually happened.

Furthering the analogy, two of the dancer monuments depict figures who are crawling on their hands and knees. The figures appear to be blind. You will recall that the Mulekites were taken into captivity by the Babylonians and that Zedekiah, king of the Jews, had his eyes put out after the Babylonians had killed his sons, who were heirs to the throne.

The case in point here, however, is that the archaeological record of Monte Alban informs us that the Mulekite time period people, those called Zapotecs who lived at Monte Alban, which, according to the geographical picture, is in the land northward, were influenced by the Olmec/Jaredites of the Gulf Coast.

FIGURE 7–9: Olmec jade artifact from Monte Alban. Apparently, the Olmec society actually began in Oaxaca and did not move into the Gulf Coast region until about 2000 BC. This thinking is consistent with the book of Ether material that tells about Omer, the fifth king in succession who moved from the land of Moron (Oaxaca) to the Gulf of Mexico (Veracruz), near the hill Ramah (see Ether 9:3). (Photo courtesy of Blake Joseph Allen)

From the artifact shown in figure 7–9, you will observe the Olmec features from Monte Alban. You will also note that he is holding a baby jaguar—the ancient name associated with Monte Alban.

The Book of Mormon hints at a high degree of Jaredite influence among the Mulekite/Nephite culture. This influence is reflected in the names of people and places in the Book of Mormon. Many of the names appear to be neither Hebrew nor Egyptian but rather Jaredite/Olmec in origin (see chapter 2, "And Then It Came to Pass").

The writings of Ixtlilxochitl tell of a group of people called Ulmecas and Xicalancas who settled among the first settlers. The new settlers landed on the coast of Veracruz and migrated into the area of Puebla. Puebla borders the state of Oaxaca. The Ulmecas and Xicalancas were put under bondage by the first settlers, who were called giants or Quinametzin. Archaeologists call them Olmecs. The Book of Mormon calls them Jaredites. The Ulmecas and Xicalancas escaped by getting the first settlers drunk.

Much of the above has not been proven. However, the coincidences of the Monte Alban culture in comparison with fragments of the Book of Mormon are compelling.

Exploring the Lands of the Book of Mormon

MONTE ALBAN IIA—180 BC–AD 200

The 2000 edition of the archeological guide states the following: "Other people entered the Valley of Oaxaca towards 300 BC [the AD 2000 version places the date at AD 180]: they may perhaps have originated in Guatemala. At any rate, they brought with them a number of culture traits which mingled with those of the earlier period. This new culture has been entitled Monte Alban II. . . . The period lasted roughly until the beginnings of the Christian era, and the bearers of this culture only settled in a few places in the valleys. . . . This suggests that they were a small group of conquerors who imposed their power over the earlier inhabitants although these did not disappear: probably the two groups mingled in the course of time."[5]

The 1985 version of *The Oaxaca Valley,* authored by Dr. Ignacio Bernal of the National Institute of Anthropology and History, states: "The people of Period II, who may have come from Chiapas or Guatemala, inherited the above features [Monte Alban I features], but they also introduced a number of changes. The new ceremonial styles appear side by side with those already in common use. Period II is represented by relatively few, though important, sites, which suggests that the newly integrated settlers were a minority who in some way superimposed themselves on the inhabitants of the previous period. Little by little the two groups merged."[6]

The museum dating at Monte Alban places the beginning of Monte Alban II at 180 BC. As nearly as can be calculated from the Book of Mormon, this is the exact time period that Mosiah led a group of Nephites down from the land of Nephi, which is proposed in *Exploring the Lands of the Book of Mormon* to be highland Guatemala, to the land of Zarahemla, which is proposed in *Exploring the Lands of the Book of Mormon* to be the state of Chiapas, Mexico.

The discussion above suggests that the main branch of the Mulekites, whom the Book of Mormon calls the people of Zarahemla, possibly settled in the Chiapas area. The above comments also suggest that smaller branches of the Mulekites settled in a few places in the Oaxaca valley. Monte Alban may have been one of those settlements. If such is the case, then the influence of King Mosiah's reign would have extended into the Oaxaca valley—or into the land northward.

In the archaeological framework, the small group of conquerors who came from Guatemala and Chiapas may correspond with the small group of Nephites who came from the land of Nephi and the land of Zarahemla. We know that the Mosiah Nephites were small in number compared to the Mulekites: "Now there were not so many of the children of Nephi, or so many of those who were descendants of Nephi, as there were of the people of Zarahemla, who was a descendant of Mulek, and those who came with him into the wilderness" (Mosiah 25:2).

The archaeological record says that the newly integrated settlers (Monte Alban II) were a minority who imposed their power over the early inhabitants (Monte Alban

5. *The Oaxaca Valley,* 1973, 6.

6. Ignacio Bernal, *Guia Official: Teotihuacan* (Mexico, DF: Instituto Nacional de Antropologia e Historia, 1985), 22–23.

In the archaeological framework, the small group of conquerors who came from Guatemala and Chiapas may correspond with the small group of Nephites who came from the land of Nephi and the land of Zarahemla.

I). The archaeologists are surprised that the new group did not destroy the previous culture. Little by little, the two groups merged.

The answer to why the new settlers did not destroy the old settlers is clear from a Book of Mormon perspective. The small group of Mosiah Nephites, who superimposed themselves over the people of Zarahemla, did so by teaching the Mulekites the Nephite language, by teaching the Mulekites the Nephite religion, and by Mosiah's becoming king over the Mulekites:

> And at the time that Mosiah discovered them [the Mulekites], they had become exceedingly numerous. Nevertheless, they had had many wars and serious contentions, and had fallen by the sword from time to time; and their language had become corrupted; and they had brought no records with them; and they denied the being of their Creator; and Mosiah, nor the people of Mosiah, could understand them.
>
> But it came to pass that Mosiah caused that they *should be taught in his language.* And it came to pass that after they were taught in the language of Mosiah, Zarahemla gave a genealogy of his fathers, according to his memory; and they are written, but not in these plates.
>
> And it came to pass that the people of Zarahemla, and of Mosiah, *did unite together; and Mosiah was appointed to be their king.* (Omni 1:17–19; emphasis added)

FIGURE 7–10: Mound J at Monte Alban dates to the time of Christ and is labeled an observatory. The users of this facility would have observed both the signs given at the time of the birth of Christ and the signs given at His death. (Photo courtesy of Sheryl Lee Wilson)

Exploring the Lands of the Book of Mormon

A summary of the parallels between Monte Alban and the book of Omni follows:

1. The first culture of the Oaxaca valley dated to the Jaredite time period.

2. Monte Alban Period I dated to the Mulekite time period.

3. Monte Alban is located in the same area where the early Mulekites possibly lived.

4. A number of elements in the Monte Alban culture appear to be Jewish in origin.

5. The Zapotecs of Monte Alban were influenced by the Olmecs of the Gulf Coast in much the same manner in which the early Mulekites were apparently influenced by the late Jaredites.

6. A small group of conquerors came from Guatemala and Chiapas and superimposed their power over the inhabitants of Monte Alban I at the same time that Mosiah led a small group of Nephites to the land of Zarahemla and became king over both Nephites and Mulekites who lived in the area.

Coincidences or not, people were living in Monte Alban at the coming of Christ to the Nephites. Mound J at Monte Alban dates to the time of Christ. It is labeled by archaeologists to be an observatory. Regardless of who the scientists may have been during the early time period of this observatory (that is, whether they were Nephite or non-Nephite), they would have observed both the signs that were given at Christ's birth and the signs that were given at His death.

> The scientists at Monte Alban would have observed both the signs that were given at Christ's birth and the signs that were given at His death.

MONTE ALBAN IIB—AD 200–AD 350

In the latter part of Monte Alban Period II, we witness the greatest growth at Monte Alban. In parallel with the Maya culture, beginning at AD 200, a surge of building construction and population growth occurred at Monte Alban. Archaeologists estimate that by AD 350, more than thirty thousand people were dependent upon Monte Alban as their central government.

The Book of Mormon record reports the same type of activity as we see throughout Mesoamerica during this time period, including Monte Alban. Beginning with 4 Nephi 1:24, the following activities are recorded. These activities occurred about 167 years after Christ's visit to the Nephites:

AD 201	They began to be divided into classes and began wearing costly apparel.
	They began to build up churches unto themselves.
	They built up churches to get gain.
AD 210	Many churches were found in the land.
	They persecuted the true church.
	They denied the "more parts" of the gospel.
	They were led by many priests and false prophets.
	They built up many churches and did iniquity.

AD 231	A great division took place among the people.
	Those who rejected the gospel were called Lamanites.
AD 244	The more wicked part of the people waxed strong.
	The wicked were exceedingly more numerous than the people of God.
	They continued to build churches and to adorn them.
AD 260	Secret oaths were again established.
	The people of Nephi became proud, rich, and vain.
AD 300	Both Lamanites and Nephites were wicked.
	Gadianton robbers spread throughout the land.
	Trade was established throughout the land.
AD 320	The people still remained in wickedness.
	Ammaron hid up the records that were sacred.

> The origin of the serpent motif may be attributed to the coming of Christ to the Nephites.

And, from the book of Mormon, Mormon makes us aware of the following events:

ca. AD 321	Ammaron told Mormon that the records were hidden in the hill Shim.
ca. AD 334	Mormon took the records from the hill Shim and began to write a history of the people of Nephi.
ca. AD 346	The Nephites fought to defend their homes and families.

During the years between AD 200 and AD 350, the following activities are reported, as deduced from the archaeological record of Monte Alban:

1. The Christian Influence

By AD 200, the stepped-fret decoration, representing a serpent and called *xicalcoli-uhqui*, was a frequent motif and was to become very popular.[7] The origin of the serpent motif may be attributed to the coming of Christ to the Nephites (see chapter 14, "The White God Quetzalcoatl").

7. Bernal, *Guia Official: Teotihuacan*, 22.

2. A Massive Building Program

Beginning about AD 200, a change in architectural style appeared at Monte Alban. In contrast with the former structures that were built out of enormous stones, buildings of this era were constructed out of small, well-cut stones. Virtually all the buildings of Monte Alban postdate the AD 200 era. The buildings were decorated; and, as nearly as can be determined, many were painted red.[8]

8. Bernal, *Guia Official: Teotihuacan*, 24–26.

3. Control by Priests

Parallel with what we read in the Book of Mormon, the controlling factions during the AD 200–AD 350 period were the priests. Special places were apparently built where the dignitaries could observe the ball games, and the tombs of the priests became very important and spacious.[9]

9. Bernal, *Guia Official: Teotihuacan*, 28.

4. False Gods

The Book of Mormon speaks of much wickedness and departure from the true religion. At Monte Alban during this time period, that which is most noticeable is a vast increase in the number of gods that were worshiped by the people.[10]

10. Bernal, *Guia Official: Teotihuacan*, 27.

5. Trade Activity

Beginning at AD 300, as recorded in the Book of Mormon, the people grew rich in silver and gold and trafficked with one another. During this time period, trade activity at Monte Alban began from the north with Teotihuacan in the valley of Mexico, not from the south as before.[11]

11. Bernal, *Guia Official: Teotihuacan*, 23.

By AD 400, trade routes were established throughout Mesoamerica and continued until the coming of the Spaniards at the beginning of the sixteenth century.

Tomb 7 of Monte Alban revealed a cache of gold artifacts indicative of the availability of gold as mentioned in 4 Nephi.

MONTE ALBAN PERIOD III—(AD 350–AD 750)

By AD 350, Monte Alban appears to have reached its height in terms of population. Indeed, shortly after AD 350, a decline in population occurred at Monte Alban. This decline corresponds to the same time period that Mormon was calling the Nephites together to battle with the Lamanites. It also corresponds to the time period when the Nephites lost a major portion of their territory. Finally, it was the same time period when the Nephites were destroyed as a nation.

Shortly after AD 350, a decline in population occurred at Monte Alban. This decline corresponds to the same time period that Mormon was calling the Nephites together to battle with the Lamanites.

FIGURE 7–11: A common practice among Mesoamerican peoples was to bury costly items in the tombs of the elite. Tomb 7 at Monte Alban dates at AD 700 and manifests an array of elaborate items, including jade, gold, and alabaster. The cache from Tomb 7 is on display at the Regional Museum of Oaxaca near the Santo Domingo Church. The National Museum of Anthropology in Mexico City also displays some of the original items from the tombs at Oaxaca. (Photos courtesy of Sheryl Lee Wilson)

A summary of these scriptures, as recorded in the writings of Mormon, is as follows:

AD 350 A treaty was made with the Lamanites and the robbers of Gadianton through which the Nephites gave up all the land southward to the narrow passage that led into the land southward (see Mormon 2:28–29).

AD 360 Mormon began to gather his people into the land of Desolation (see Mormon 3:5–7).

AD 366 The Lamanites captured the city of Desolation. The Lamanites offered Nephite women and children as sacrifices to their idol gods (see Mormon 4:13–14).

AD 367 The Nephites drove the Lamanites out of the city of Desolation and the land of Desolation (see Mormon 4:15).

FIGURE 7–12: At the downfall of Monte Alban around AD 800, the Zapotecs moved their headquarters to Mitla. These post–Book of Mormon ruins show a sophistication of artwork because the individual stones are placed tightly into position to represent serpent movements. Mitla, so named because of burial tombs discovered on the site, was still under occupation at the time of the arrival of the Spaniards. Observe the Catholic cathedral that was built in the Mitla courtyard with the use of Mitla stones. (Photos courtesy of Sheryl Lee Wilson)

Exploring the Lands of the Book of Mormon

AD 375   The Lamanites defeated the Nephites at the city of Desolation in the land of Desolation (see Mormon 4:19).

AD 381   Mormon wrote an epistle to the Lamanite king and scheduled a battle to take place in four years at a hill called Cumorah (see Mormon 6:3–4).

AD 385   The Lamanites defeated the Nephites at the hill Cumorah (see Mormon 6:8–18).

At Monte Alban, the period from AD 350 to AD 750 is represented by continued building growth. However, the quality and style of both the buildings and the manufactured urns began to decline toward the end of Period III. Shortly before the end of Period III, the Great Plaza of Monte Alban was completed. Most of the visible buildings of Monte Alban date to Period III.[12]

12. Bernal, *Guia Official: Teotihuacan*, 29.

Moroni records the sad state of his condition and attaches to it the date of AD 400: "I am alone. My father hath been slain in battle, and all my kinsfolk, and I have not friends nor whither to go" (Mormon 8:5).

Moroni concluded his record by dating it to ca. AD 421 when he said that "more than four hundred and twenty years have passed away since the sign was given of the coming of Christ" (Moroni 10:1).

The Book of Mormon closed its historical doors early in the fourth century AD. However, the history in the Oaxaca valley continued right up to the time of the conquest of Mexico in the sixteenth century.

FIGURE 7–13: This mural is dedicated to Benito Juarez (1806–72), a Zapotec native from the mountains of Oaxaca who became governor of the state of Oaxaca and subsequently the president of the country of Mexico. He was a contemporary of Abraham Lincoln and Joseph Smith. In the year 1857, Benito enacted reform laws that brought about the separation of the church and the state. When Wilford Woodruff administered vicarious temple work for many leaders of the world in the St. George Temple, two Mexican names were on the list—Benito Juarez and his wife, Maria. (Photo courtesy of Merrill C. Oaks)

Monte Alban, the great city on the hill, lost its savor between AD 700–AD 750. Its decline allowed many other cities in the Oaxaca valley to develop. Some of these sites are Yagul, Dainzu, and Mitla.

Mitla, which contains one of the most ornate buildings in Mesoamerica, was still occupied at the coming of the Spaniards.

Today, several native tribes live in the state of Oaxaca, many of whom live in the mountains of Oaxaca. A Zapotec by the name of Benito Juarez, Oaxaca's favorite son, became president of the country of Mexico at the same time Abraham Lincoln was president of the United States. Juarez was a native of the small town of Guelatauo, located in the mountains near the city of Oaxaca.

BENITO JUAREZ

Benito Pablo Juarez was born in the year 1806, making him a contemporary of the Prophet Joseph Smith. When Juarez was about three years old, both of his parents died. His grandparents raised him until the age of about thirteen, when both of them passed away.

After herding sheep for his uncle for a time, he wandered into the big city of Oaxaca, the capital of the state of Oaxaca. His sister was serving as a maid for a wealthy Spaniard, who subsequently adopted Benito as his own son.

> Though small in stature but a giant in character, Benito Juarez, a full-blooded Zapotec from Oaxaca and a possible descendant of Father Lehi, cleared the way for his people to receive the Book of Mormon.

An extremely brilliant young man, Juarez obtained his schooling in the traditional Catholic society of the priesthood. He manifested a desire to practice law and graduated from the University of Oaxaca with a law degree.

Juarez practiced law from 1834–46 in Oaxaca and became a champion for justice. His integrity and concern for the poor became almost legendary.

In 1847, Juarez became the governor of Oaxaca and made Oaxaca a model province. A man with a keen sense of justice and discipline, he reportedly was so organized that the people could set their clocks according to his schedule for going to work.

Juarez developed a strong love for democracy and brought upon himself the ire of the establishment. He was exiled by the Mexican president Santa Ana in 1853 and spent some time in the United States.

He returned to Mexico as minister of justice in 1855, and in 1857 he drafted the reform laws that brought about the disenfranchisement of the Catholic Church. In other words, he brought about the separation of the church and the government. Juarez's work opened the door for missionary work by the Church of Jesus Christ in Mexico.

In reality, Benito Juarez's work meant the fulfillment of prophecy when Nephi wrote that "in the latter days, when our seed shall have dwindled in unbelief, yea, for the space of many years, and many generations after the Messiah shall be manifested in body unto the children of men, then shall the fulness of the gospel of the Messiah come unto the Gentiles, and from the Gentiles unto the remnant of our seed" (1 Nephi 15:13).

Though small in stature but a giant in character, Benito Juarez, a full-blooded Zapotec from Oaxaca and a possible descendant of Father Lehi, cleared the way for his people to receive the Book of Mormon by enacting laws that permitted the gospel to be preached in Mexico. Our personal feeling is that he was foreordained for that very purpose.

In 1861, Juarez was elected president of the country of Mexico, after having served as the provisional president for two years.

He was president of Mexico during the time period that France invaded Mexico and set up Maximillian as emperor. In 1866, Maximillian was executed; and the French were driven out of Mexico. Juarez was again elected president and died in office from a heart attack in 1872. He was sixty-six years old at the time of his death.

The predominant native tribe in Oaxaca today is the Zapotec people. A German writer by the name of Hans Helfritz observed the native characteristics of the Zapotecs as he wrote the following: "To this day there are still approximately 120,000 Indians living in the state of Oaxaca who speak the Zapotec language—descendants of the builders of the greatest sacred place of the Zapotecs [Monte Alban]. They are among the most intelligent people of Mexico. The superior character and intellectual capacity of these people was already noticed by the Spaniards when setting up a stronghold in Oaxaca, shortly after the conquest of Mexico."[13]

13. Hans Helfritz, *Mexican Cities of the Gods: An Archaeological Guide* (New York: Frederick A. Praeger, 1970), 71.

MUSEO NACIONA

CHAPTER 8

The Teotihuacan Culture

Before there was light
Before there was day
When there was still darkness
The gods met in council in Teotihuacan
(Bernardino de Sahagun)

ith reasonable certainty, we can now say that the early part of the Teotihuacan culture played a significant role in Nephite history from about 50 BC to AD 400. In the Nahuatl (Aztec) language, the word for "god" is *Teo*. The interpretation of *Teotihuacan* is "the pathway that leads to the city of the Gods." Teotihuacan is located in the valley of Mexico about forty-five minutes northeast of Mexico City. Today, a community by the same name is near the ancient ruins. Often, the ruins are simply referred to as "the pyramids." The Pyramid of the Sun and the Pyramid of the Moon are the most imposing structures at Teotihuacan.

The valley of Mexico where present-day Mexico City is located has been the homeland of many civilizations, including the AD 1325–1521 Aztecs. However, from 150 BC to AD 750, the ceremonial center of Teotihuacan flourished.

OPPOSITE: This representation of the rain god Tlaloc is located at the entrance of the National Museum of Anthropology in Mexico City. This original monument was transported from the archaeological zone of Teotihuacan. It is labeled a rain god and is associated with Quetzalcoatl, the god of wind, sun, rain, and earth. According to historical reports, a heavy rainfall occurred the day the monument was transported to its present location. (Photo courtesy of George and Audrey DeLange)

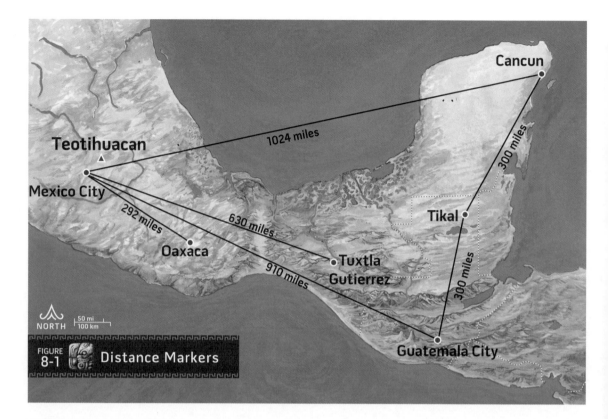

FIGURE 8–1: The distance from Mexico City to the ancient city of Teotihuacan is about thirty miles in a northeast direction, with travel time of about forty-five minutes. From Mexico City to Guatemala City, the distance is about nine hundred miles; and from Mexico City to Cancun, it is about one thousand miles. From both Cancun and Guatemala, the distance to Tikal is about three hundred miles. However, travel is calculated more in time rather than distance because of the variety of terrain—mountains, jungles, lowlands, and so forth. Observe that even though the direction from Mexico City to Cancun is northeast, because of the Isthmus of Tehuantepec, the entire area of Mexico from the isthmus to the east into and including the Yucatan Peninsula is referred to as being southeast of Mexico City.

The inhabitants of Teotihuacan were considered to be an ancient civilization by the thirteenth to sixteenth century AD Aztecs of Mexico City.

The people who occupied the Teotihuacan city center date from about 150 BC to AD 750, although people obviously were in the Mexico valley both preceding and following the Teotihuacan period. The inhabitants of Teotihuacan were considered to be an ancient civilization by the thirteenth to sixteenth century AD Aztecs of Mexico City.

About AD 1325, the civilization that we know as the Aztecs began to settle in and around the lakes in the valley. The early Teotihuacanos settled around the lakes—but not in the lakes. This area may be what is referred to in the Book of Mormon when a pre-Christian era migration of Nephites went to a land of large bodies of water and many rivers: "And they did travel to an exceedingly great distance, insomuch that they came to large bodies of water and many rivers" (Helaman 3:4).

Tradition reports that Teotihuacan was a religious center; as a result, "the place of the gods" and "pathway to the city of the gods" are considered by most Mesoamerican

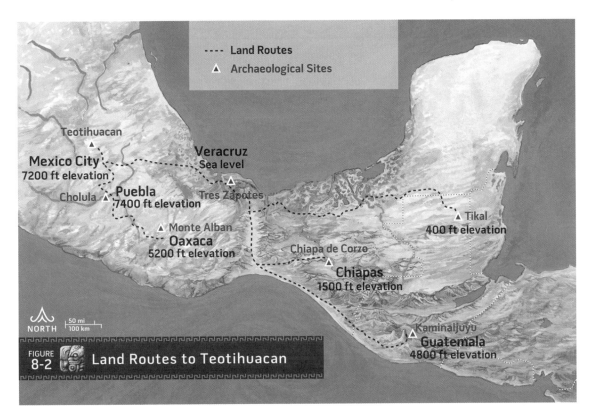

FIGURE 8–2: This map shows the travel routes from Chiapas and Oaxaca to the valley or altiplano of Mexico. Anciently, these same routes would have been used by the 55 BC Nephites who migrated into the "land which was northward" where large bodies of water were located (see Helaman 3:3–7).

scholars to be appropriate appellations. The plaque at the entrance of the Teotihuacan Room at the National Museum of Anthropology in Mexico City reads as follows:

> Before there was light
> Before there was day
> When there was still darkness
> The gods met in council in Teotihuacan

The climate of the Mexico valley is not as conducive to heavy vegetation growth as is the case in the majority of the Maya lands and along the Gulf of Mexico. As a result, the deterioration of the mounds at Teotihuacan has not been as great as in the other two mentioned areas. It is as if the pyramids have always been there.

Of all the Mesoamerican ruins, Teotihuacan was the first to be recognized as a tourist attraction. The Pyramid of the Sun was restored to highlight the one-hundredth

FIGURE 8–3: The pyramid of the Sun is the most imposing structure at Teotihuacan and was built during the second century BC. It is associated with the god Quetzalcoatl wherein legend tells of him traveling the course of the sun to gather bones together for the resurrection of mankind. (Photo courtesy of Merrill C. Oaks)

anniversary of Mexico's independence from Spain. The year of the celebration was 1910.

The sixteenth-century Catholic priests wrote about the traditional history of Teotihuacan. Foremost among them was the prolific scholar, Bernardino Sahagun. However, the first-known report about the pyramids in recent history is an account written by Ramon Almaraz in 1865. He provided descriptions and measurements of the Pyramid of the Sun and the Pyramid of the Moon.

Leopoldo Batres began excavation work at the pyramids in earnest. He undertook the restoration work of the Pyramid of the Sun and, as stated, prepared it for the commemoration of Mexico's centennial in 1910.

Under the direction of the Mexican government, restoration work at Teotihuacan has continued throughout the years; and the tourists who have visited the site number in the millions. Today, a small museum, along with many gift shops, is found in the area. Obsidian is indigenous to the area, and vendors are commonly heard to say, "Do you want to buy some of my junk?" or "Buy this for your second wife."

Both radiocarbon dating and the sophistication of the science of archaeology now provide for accurate dating patterns and population estimates. The following chart illustrates the chronology of Teotihuacan:

TEOTIHUACAN DATING AND JERUSALEM COMPARISON

Period	Dates	Population	Book of Mormon History	Jerusalem History
Teotihuacan I	150 BC–AD 200	25,000	Mosiah to 4 Nephi	Greek occupation
Teotihuacan II	AD 200–AD 350	50,000	4 Nephi to Mormon	Roman occupation
Teotihuacan III	AD 350–AD 600	200,000	Moroni and post-Nephite	Christian occupation
Teotihuacan IV	AD 600–AD 900	60,000	Post–Book of Mormon	Islamic Jerusalem

Of special interest is the fact that the Teotihuacan Period I falls in the time slot of the Roman occupation of Jerusalem, which began at 63 BC. This dating equates to the same period that king-men arose in the Book of Mormon (see Alma 51:5–8) with the intent to take over Zarahemla. The Temple of the Sun was built at Teotihuacan during Period I and correlates with the development of a secret society in the land northward led by a wicked man named Jacob at AD 29. This event may have been the beginning of a secret combination society at Teotihuacan. For additional information on what was happening at Jerusalem during Teotihuacan Period I, we refer you to the book, *Jerusalem: The Eternal City.*[1]

The maximum population of Jerusalem at any given time in the above time period did not exceed thirty thousand people. At AD 529, the estimated population at Teotihuacan was two hundred thousand people, and a massive building program developed during this time period throughout Mesoamerica. During this same time period in Jerusalem, an intensive building program was also underway as a result of the Byzantine occupation. During this period of growth at Jerusalem, twenty-four Catholic churches were built on the Mount of Olives alone.[2]

Observe that both Periods I and II fall within the Book of Mormon time period. Period III is consistent with the pattern throughout Mesoamerica when both a concentrated building program and an increase of population occurred. Rare exceptions are found to this rule, however, such as at Monte Alban in the Oaxaca valley.

TEOTIHUACAN PERIOD I (150 BC–AD 200)

A few years prior to the Christian era, the phase referred to as Teotihuacan Period I was initiated. During this 350-year time period, Teotihuacan expanded to occupy more than twelve square miles; and the population grew to an estimated twenty-five thousand to thirty thousand people. The increase in population of Teotihuacan during Period I was caused, in large part, by people who migrated to the Mexico valley and then settled in the city of Teotihuacan.

Archaeologists have determined that Teotihuacan was a city in the true sense of the word. People depended on each other for their livelihood. Although the main work during Period I was agricultural in nature, many other vocations were in evidence, including architects, painters, sculptors, businessmen, professionals, priests, and government officials.

Different social classes existed. The culture reflected both rich people and poor people. The climate, which provided a high seasonal rainfall during May through October, and the surrounding lakes assured Teotihuacan and other Mexico valley communities that they would have both fish for food and water for crops.

Crops consisted of corn, beans, fruits, and vegetables conducive to an elevation of seventy-two hundred to seventy-four hundred feet above sea level. Cactus, which grows in the area, has been utilized for centuries to produce a vegetable that looks and tastes

1. David B. Galbraith, D. Kelly Ogden, and Andrew C. Skinner, *Jerusalem: The Eternal City* (Salt Lake City: Deseret Book, 1996), 153.

2. Galbraith, Ogden, and Skinner, *Jerusalem: The Eternal City*, 264.

The increase in population of Teotihuacan during Period I was caused, in large part, by people who migrated to the Mexico valley and then settled in the city of Teotihuacan.

FIGURE 8–4: The Pyramid of the Moon was built during the second century AD. Recently, burial chambers have been discovered within the pyramid. The picture is taken from on top of the Pyramid of the Sun and shows the Avenue of the Dead in the foreground. (Photo courtesy of George and Audrey DeLange)

FIGURE 8–5A: City plan of Teotihuacan, showing the Pyramid of the Moon (Period II) and the Pyramid of the Sun (Period I). (Drawing by Cliff Dunston)

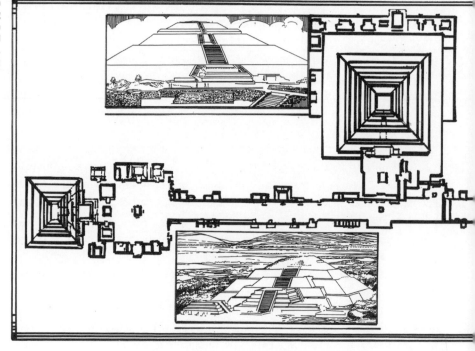

Exploring the Lands of the Book of Mormon

like string beans. It is still eaten today in the Mexico valley. A plant called the maguey plant had a variety of uses, the most popular being the extraction of a juice that is called pulque, which is still fermented to make a popular alcoholic drink.

An amazing amount of construction was undertaken during Period I of Teotihuacan. The main avenue, called the Avenue of the Dead, was laid out and was functional during this period. The Temple of the Sun was built during Period I virtually as it stands today. And the inner structure of the Temple of the Moon was also built during Period I. These buildings are contemporary with the great pyramid of Cholula, which is located on the other side of the two volcanic mountain peaks, Popocatepetl and Iztaccihuatl.

TEOTIHUACAN PERIOD II (AD 200–AD 350)

During the 150 years called Teotihuacan Period II, the population of the city doubled in size, reaching an estimated fifty thousand inhabitants. The pattern is the same as throughout Mesoamerica and became known as the Classic Period. This period corresponds with the period of apostasy in the Book of Mormon (see 4 Nephi 1:24–49—AD 201–321).

The Pyramid of the Moon was completed during this period, and many other buildings were built. The most sensational building that was constructed during Period

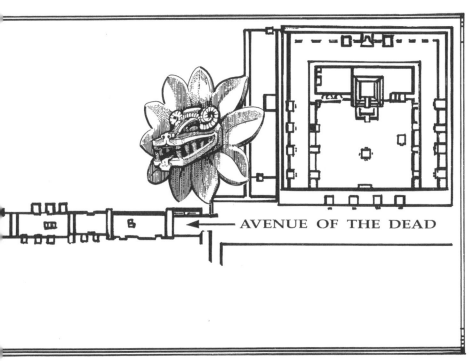

AVENUE OF THE DEAD

FIGURE 8–5B: City plan of Teotihuacan (continued), showing the Citadel of Quetzalcoatl (Period II). (Drawing by Cliff Dunston)

FIGURE 8–6: The picture on the left is of a replica of the Temple of Quetzalcoatl located in the National Museum of Anthropology in Mexico City. Built around the second century AD, the Temple of Quetzalcoatl on the right portrays the white god Quetzalcoatl in stone. The feathers around the neck represent the quetzal bird. The facial features with black obsidian stones for eyes represent Coatl (the serpent). (Photos courtesy of George and Audrey DeLange)

II is the Temple of Quetzalcoatl. This temple is considered to be one of the major architectural accomplishments of the Teotihuacanos.

Cement was utilized extensively in the construction of the buildings to hold lava rocks in place and to construct roadways and floors. Plaster covered the buildings, which were then painted in brilliant colors typical of the colors that are found in the simple home dwellings in Mexico today. Murals and frescos, which are also reminiscent of the manner in which the Mexican culture is portrayed today, graced the walls of the buildings of Teotihuacan during Period II.

Teotihuacan Period II was truly a fluorescent period. It is recognized for its elaborate buildings and art and its movement toward the people's worship of a pantheon of gods, foremost of which was the feathered-serpent god called Quetzalcoatl. Tlaloc, the rain god and a derivative of the god Quetzalcoatl, was also worshiped.

TEOTIHUACAN PERIOD III (AD 350–AD 600)

The advancement of Teotihuacan during Period III consisted of a continuation of Period II. The square of the Temple of the Moon was completed as well as the accompanying buildings, one of which is called the Palace of the Quetzal Butterfly. The walls on buildings of the latter were painted in very elaborate colors and detailed designs.

The population reached a high of about two hundred thousand inhabitants during this time period, which probably made Teotihuacan the largest city in the world during this 250-year time period. Today, Mexico City shares a similar fame—that is, greater Mexico City is among the largest cities in the world.

Migrations that had begun in the first century BC continued to be made into the Mexico valley during this period. It is interesting to note the foreign districts, which are typical of a metropolitan center. The most obvious foreign district in Teotihuacan was occupied by people from the Oaxaca valley. There is even a tomb patterned after the Monte Alban style.[3]

During the time period of Teotihuacan Period III, a great amount of trade activity took place throughout Mesoamerica. Trade goods from Teotihuacan, such as obsidian, began showing up in places like Oaxaca (Monte Alban), Guatemala City (Kaminaljuyu), and Peten (Tikal) early in the fourth century AD. And architectural features from Teotihuacan began showing up as well. A section of the city of Kaminaljuyu (Guatemala City) has been labeled "Little Teotihuacan." In Tikal, located in the Peten jungle of Guatemala, sections of the city were built after the Teotihuacan architectural style during Period III.

Also, during the beginning of Teotihuacan Period III, AD 350, a change in the political system took place. The same type of priestcraft society that began in AD 200 in Maya territory formed at the same time in Teotihuacan. However, whereas the Maya priest system continued throughout the Classic Period (AD 250 to AD 900) and until the conquest of Mexico in 1519, the Teotihuacan political system changed. The priest system declined, and the political system increased.

During Period III, the civil authorities of Teotihuacan, who became more militarily and economically oriented, began to enforce a more capitalistic system as opposed to the previous mystical and religious system. This new form of government was more interested in regional development than in building great temples to their gods. Such an interest does not mean that the priests lost their power. It only suggests that during Period III (AD 350–600), the priests did not have supreme control over the political and economic structure of the people of the Mexico valley as they did in Maya territory.

A type of humanism developed wherein a leadership combination evolved consisting of the priests and the wealthy merchants. This religious and civil combination became a magnificent epicenter, a type of civil mercantilism dedicated to human success as opposed to tall pyramids dedicated to gods.[4]

This type of government is what Moroni must have been referring to when he wrote the following: "And it came to pass that they formed a secret combination. . . . And they have caused the destruction of this people [Jaredites] of whom I am now speaking, and also the destruction of the people of Nephi" (Ether 8:18, 21).

The three most powerful groups that formed this combination beginning at AD 350 consisted of (1) merchants who traveled extensively throughout Mesoamerica, meeting with heads of states to promote trade and exact tribute, (2) a central military force adequate enough to enforce their activities, and (3) the priests who formed a type of merger with the previous two groups. The duty of the priests was to control the society through spiritual and supernatural interpretations. The priests were the educated class of the Teotihuacan culture.[5]

For all intents and purposes, Teotihuacan was administered by secret combinations from AD 350–600, Teotihuacan Period III. Information that began to surface in the

3. Ignacio Bernal, *Guia Official: Teotihuacan* (Mexico, DF: Instituto Nacional de Antropologia e Historia, 1985), 36.

This type of government is what Moroni must have been referring to when he wrote the following: "And it came to pass that they formed a secret combination. . . . And they have caused the destruction of this people [Jaredites] of whom I am now speaking, and also the destruction of the people of Nephi" (Ether 8:18, 21).

4. Bernal, *Guia Official: Teotihuacan*, 40–41.

5. Bernal, *Guia Official: Teotihuacan*, 44–46.

FIGURE 8–7: Yax Nuun Ayiin is depicted on Stela 31 at Tikal and shows his ascension to the throne of Tikal on September 12, 379 AD. His father, Spearthrower Owl, may have been from the secret combination dynasty of Jacob and was a dictator at Teotihuacan for sixty years. His name glyph is shown on the right. (Drawings by Cliff Dunston)

First Crocodile, or Yax Nuun Ayiin, has a name cognate similar to Laman Ayin, an ancient king of an archaeological site by that same name in the country of Belize.

6. See David Stuart, "The Arrival of Strangers': Teotihuacan and Tollan in Classic Maya History," in *Mesoamerica's Classic Heritage: From Teotihuacan to the Aztecs*, ed. David Carrasco, Linda Jones, and Scott Sessions (Boulder, CO: University of Colorado, 2000), 465–513.

As shown on page 49 in chapter 2, *Nun* and *Ayin* are Hebrew words found also in the Maya language.

1990s and that reached its pinnacle in the beginning of the new millennium relates directly to Stela 31 of Tikal. A dramatic breakthrough in fourth century AD history is reflected in a report by Dr. David Stuart, who outlined the thesis that the ruler, Sun Shield, a dictator who ruled Teotihuacan for sixty years and who was nicknamed Spearthrower Owl, sent a powerful military force to Tikal in Maya territory in the early part of the Teothihuacan III Period (AD 350–400). The reigning Tikal ruler at that time, who has been labeled Great Jaguar Paw, was killed on January 16, AD 378. Spearthrower Owl then placed his young son on the throne. This young son is referred to as Curl Snout, or Yax Nuun Ayiin, which is literally interpreted as "First Crocodile."

First Crocodile, or Yax Nuun Ayiin, has a name cognate similar to Laman Ayin, an ancient king of an archaeological site by that same name in the country of Belize. Yax Nuun Ayiin ascended to the throne at Tikal on September 12, AD 379, only six years prior to the war at Cumorah (AD 385). He ruled until AD 420.[6] We propose that it was this king, Yax Nuun Ayiin, to whom Mormon directed his epistle as recorded in Mormon 6:2: "And I, Mormon, wrote an epistle unto the king of the Lamanites, and desired of him that he would grant unto us that we might gather together our people unto the land of Cumorah, by a hill which was called Cumorah, and there we could give them battle."

TEOTIHUACAN PERIOD IV (AD 600–900)

Moroni warned, "And whatsoever nation shall uphold such secret combinations, to get power and gain, until they shall spread over the nation, behold, they shall be destroyed" (Ether 8:22).

That is precisely what happened at Teotihuacan during Period IV, AD 600 to AD 900. The population decreased from the estimated high of two hundred thousand down to sixty thousand inhabitants.

By AD 750, some of the buildings had already fallen into ruin; and by AD 900, Teotihuacan became abandoned as both a city center and a strong political force in Mesoamerica. Apparently, nearby Cholula had fallen captive to other invaders.

Exploring the Lands of the Book of Mormon

Cholula is a city located east of Mexico City and is home to the largest-based pyramid in the world. Although the ancient city of Cholula shared the same culture attributes as Teotihuacan, its political leadership was not the same. It may be compared to the Middle East countries throughout history—although the people are basically the same, the leadership and political boundaries change.

Ignacio Bernal believes that the principal reason for the decline of Teotihuacan was the excessive centralization of the major powers of the society—that is, the combination of the merchants, priests, and military. This combination, according to Bernal, brought about deep dissatisfaction of the people toward the government.[7]

7. Bernal, *Guia Official: Teotihuacan*, 54.

The so-called representative of the gods had evolved into a dictatorship who were a minority. The breakup of the society paved the way for the Toltecs to come on the scene. They then became the dominant military force in the Teotihuacan area (Mexico valley) for the next three hundred years—or from AD 900 to AD 1200.

In AD 1325, more than a hundred years after the downfall of the Toltec nation, the people we know as the Aztecs became the ruling force in the valley. Thus, we can well understand why the culture of Teotihuacan was considered to be an ancient civilization by the fourteenth-century Aztecs.

The gradual decay of Teotihuacan started a chain reaction throughout all of Mesoamerica. During the ninth century AD, other major centers whose governments deteriorated included Monte Alban, Tikal, Uxmal, and Chichen Itza. Chichen Itza was subsequently occupied by the Toltecs of the Mexico valley.

FIGURE 8–8: Two models, one of Teotihuacan and the other of Tenochtitlan (Mexico City), although close geographically, are five hundred years apart in time. The visitor often equates the two as contemporary sites. Teotihuacan fell around AD 800. Tenochtitlan did not begin until around AD 1300. (Photos courtesy of George and Audrey DeLange)

THE PYRAMIDS OF THE SUN AND MOON

For today's first-time visitor to Mexico City, a visit to the Teotihuacan pyramids is a must. The flavor of the vendors and the opportunity to climb to the top of both pyramids at Teotihuacan are highlights of a visit to Mexico. However, the first-time visitor will have difficulty separating the culture of the Aztecs in Mexico City (AD 1325–1521) from the culture of Teotihuacan (150 BC–AD 900).

The Pyramid of the Sun was virtually completed during Teotihuacan Period I (150 BC–AD 200). The inner structure of the Pyramid of the Moon was also completed during Period I, with the upper structure being completed later.

At the time of the building of the Pyramid of the Sun, we witness great activity in the Book of Mormon. The history recorded in the books of Mosiah, Alma, Helaman, 3 Nephi, and 4 Nephi all took place during Period I of Teotihuacan.

During this time period (55 BC), a large company of Nephites migrated into the "land which was northward"—that is, the land that was northward from the land of Zarahemla. If the land of Zarahemla was located in what today is Chiapas, Mexico, near the Isthmus of Tehuantepec, then perhaps this migration ended up in the Mexico valley. Mexico City is a land that is northward, and Teotihuacan manifested an increase in population during this time period as a result of migrations from the southern areas: "And it came to pass that in the thirty and seventh year of the reign of the judges, there was a large company of men, even to the amount of five thousand and four hundred men, with their wives and their children, departed out of the land of Zarahemla into the *land which was northward*. And it came to pass that Hagoth, he being an exceedingly curious man, therefore he went forth and built him an exceedingly large ship, on the borders of the land Bountiful, by the land Desolation, and launched it forth into the west sea, by the narrow neck which led into the land northward" (Alma 63:4–5; emphasis added).

During the first century BC, from both the archaeological data at Teotihuacan and from the Book of Mormon, the political climate was ripe for just such a migration. Mexico City is much cooler than the Chiapas depression where Zarahemla was probably located, and the Mexico valley with its mild climate and ample rainfall must have seemed an ideal place in which to settle. If some of the new settlers at Teotihuacan were Nephites, that fact would help explain some of the legends that have been handed down regarding the area.

For example, the idea behind the building of the Pyramids of the Sun and of the Moon reflects a Christian theme. The traditional history reports that the gods met in council at Teotihuacan before the earth was formed. They asked whom they should send down to bring about a new dawn. The account eventually was written down by a sixteenth-century Catholic priest, Bernardino Sahagun. Until recent years, this legend was portrayed in a light-and-sound production at Teotihuacan. The story has a familiar feeling when compared to the council in heaven as recorded in the Pearl of Great Price. We will quote first from the account in the Pearl of Great Price and follow that quotation with the legend reported by Sahagun:

> And the Lord said: Whom shall I send? And one answered like unto the Son of Man: Here am I, send me. And another answered and said: Here am I, send me. And the Lord said, I will send the first.

At the time of the building of the Pyramid of the Sun, we witness great activity in the Book of Mormon. The history recorded in the books of Mosiah, Alma, Helaman, 3 Nephi, and 4 Nephi all took place during Period I of Teotihuacan.

FIGURE 8–9: A sea route that carried people, supplies, and timber to the Mexico City area was developed beginning near the Gulf of Tehuantepec in the middle of the first century BC. These activities lasted for about eleven years.

And the second was angry, and kept not his first estate; and, at that day, many followed after him.

And then the Lord said: Let us go down. And they went down at the beginning, and they, that is the Gods, organized and formed the heavens and the earth. (Abraham 3:27–28; 4:1)

The mythological account associated with the Pyramids of the Sun and of the Moon has been passed down through the centuries as follows:

It is told that when yet [all] was darkness, when yet no sun had shone and no dawn had broken—it is said—the gods gathered themselves together and took counsel among themselves there at Teotihuacan. They spoke; they said among themselves:

"Come hither, O gods! Who will carry the burden? Who will take it upon himself to be the sun, to bring the dawn?"

The story of Teotihuacan has a familiar feeling when compared to the council in heaven as recorded in the Pearl of Great Price.

And upon this, one of them who was there spoke: Tecuciztecatl presented himself. He said: "O gods, I shall be the one."

And again the gods spoke: "[And] who else?"

Thereupon they looked around at one another. They pondered the matter. They said to one another: "How may this be? How may we decide?"

None dared; no one else came forward. Everyone was afraid; they [all] drew back.

And now present was one man, Nanahuatzin; he stood there listening among the others to that which was discussed. Then the gods called to this one. They said to him: "Thou shall be the one, O Nanahuatzin."

He then eagerly accepted the decision; he took it gladly. He said: "It is well, O gods; you have been good to me."[8]

8. Arthur O. Anderson and Charles E. Dibble, trans., *Historia General de las Cosas de Nueva Espana: Florentine Codex,* by Fray Bernardino de Sahagun, 12 vols. (Santa Fe, NM: The School of American Research and the University of Utah, 1950), 7:4–5.

The account, which is taken from the Florentine Codex and which was written by Sahagun, concludes by saying that Tecuciztecatl was afraid to jump into the fire to bring about the new dawn. On the other hand, Nanahuatzin did give his life by jumping into the fire. The great Pyramid of the Sun was dedicated in honor of Nanahuatzin.

This event relegated Tecuciztecatl to the role of a lesser god. Therefore, the gods took a rabbit and threw it into the moon to darken the moon. The Pyramid of the Moon was then built and dedicated to the lesser god.

THE TEMPLE OF QUETZALCOATL

The Temple of Quetzalcoatl was built during Teotihuacan Period II, AD 200–350. This time period corresponds with the beginning of the great apostasy in the Book of Mormon. The Temple of Quetzalcoatl, as previously stated, represents one of the major architectural accomplishments of the Teotihuacan history.

The Christian theme of the white god Quetzalcoatl is very prevalent in the temple at Teotihuacan, as represented by the engravings of the feathered-serpent motifs. Latter-day Saints are often confused as they try to associate the name or title of Quetzalcoatl with Christ. The confusion arises because the Aztec word *Quetzalcoatl* means feathered serpent. The quetzal is a beautiful bird that is native to Guatemala. The bird has long, green tail feathers. *Coatl* simply means serpent. (For more information, see chapter 14, "The White God Quetzalcoatl.") Apparently, however, the title or name of Quetzalcoatl came about as a result of the visit of the resurrected Christ to the Nephites.

9. For further information, see Joseph L. Allen, "A Comparative Study of Quetzalcoatl, the Feathered-Serpent God of Meso-America, with Jesus Christ, the God of the Nephites," (PhD dissertation, Department of Ancient Scripture, Brigham Young University, 1970).

From various accounts, we learn that Quetzalcoatl was born of a virgin. He came from the east. He was dressed in a long white robe. He taught his people the law of the fast, and he instructed them in baptism. He died, and three days later he was resurrected. He left from the area of Coatzacoalcos, Veracruz. He prophesied that his people would pass through much persecution but that he would return and they would become lords and heirs of the earth.[9]

Exploring the Lands of the Book of Mormon

FIGURE 8–10: The symbolism of the white god Quetzalcoatl is represented at Teotihuacan in both the image of a feathered serpent and the image of earthquake and rain as shown on the Temple of Quetzalcoatl. (Photos courtesy of George and Audrey DeLange)

Without going into great detail regarding the symbolism of Quetzalcoatl in association with the Savior, we will merely note that the name *Quetzalcoatl* became a title and that other priests or leaders took upon themselves the title or name of the deity. One such person is the tenth-century Toltec leader, Topiltzin Quetzalcoatl.

The stone-etched Teotihuacan sculptures of the serpents with collars of feathers etched around their necks and the accompanying rain god Tlaloc are representative of the powerful influence Quetzalcoatl had upon the people. Quetzalcoatl was also universal in nature—that is, his influence was felt throughout Mesoamerica.

We need to understand the concept of God as understood by the AD 200–350 residents of Teotihuacan. If we can deduce anything from the sculptures of Quetzalcoatl, it is that beginning at AD 200, the knowledge of the true nature of God was lost. By AD 350, the apostasy was well established. We learn this from Mormon's statement dated to AD 322: "But wickedness did prevail upon the face of the whole land, insomuch that the Lord did take away his beloved disciples, and the work of miracles and of healing did cease because of the iniquity of the people. And there were no gifts from the Lord, and the Holy Ghost did not come upon any, because of their wickedness and unbelief. . . . And it came to pass that there were sorceries, and witchcrafts, and magics; and the power of the evil one was wrought upon all the face of the land, even unto the fulfilling of all the words of Abinadi, and also Samuel the Lamanite" (Mormon 1:13–14, 19).

If we can deduce anything from the sculptures of Quetzalcoatl, it is that beginning at AD 200, the knowledge of the true nature of God was lost. By AD 350, the apostasy was well established.

With this type of environment at Teotihuacan in the third century AD, we can easily see why such a gruesome representation was made of Quetzalcoatl—or Christ. The people had lost the true concept of God. And that loss occurred at the same time the apostasy began in the Old World. Satan is also universal in nature. The Council of Nice was held in AD 325. During the course of this council in Italy, God was reduced to a being without body, parts, and passions. In Mexico, God was relegated to a silent stone serpent head with decorative feathers around its neck.

SUMMARY OF SCRIPTURES WITH POSSIBLE RELATIONSHIP TO TEOTIHUACAN

The following scriptures in the Book of Mormon are proposed as showing a possible relationship with the Mexico valley and the archaeological ruins of Teotihuacan:

Alma 63:4 (55 BC): "And it came to pass that in the thirty and seventh year of the reign of the judges, there was a large company of men, even to the amount of five thousand and four hundred men, with their wives and their children, departed out of the land of Zarahemla into the land which was northward."

As previously mentioned, the land which was northward is proposed as the valley of Mexico. The city of Teotihuacan may have been one of the cities to which the 55 BC Nephites migrated. This migration consisted of fifty-four hundred men with their wives and children. We cannot tell from the scripture whether the number of fifty-four hundred included the women and children or whether the number needs to be increased to include the women and children. At any rate, the time period is the same time that Teotihuacan was experiencing a high increase in growth as a result of migrations from the south. (See the discussion earlier in this chapter.)

Alma 63:5–6 (55 BC): "And it came to pass that Hagoth, he being an exceedingly curious man, therefore he went forth and built him an exceedingly large ship, on the borders of the land Bountiful, by the land Desolation, and launched it forth into the west sea, by the narrow neck which led into the land northward. And behold, there were many of the Nephites who did enter therein and did sail forth with much provisions, and also many women and children; and they took their course northward. And thus ended the thirty seventh year."

In this scripture, the area where Hagoth launched his ship is probably the Isthmus of Tehuantepec on the Pacific side—southeast of Acapulco about three hundred miles. Landing near Acapulco, the people would have then migrated inland to the Mexico valley and the surrounding areas (see chapter 19, "The Land Northward").

The route from Acapulco to Mexico City is much easier than either the route from Tehuantepec to Oaxaca to Mexico City or from Tehuantepec to Veracruz to Mexico City. At the time of the conquest of Mexico, native runners were still carrying fresh fish daily from Acapulco to the Aztec emperor Montezuma, who lived in Mexico City. The archaeological ruins of Xochicalco are located between Mexico City and Acapulco and for years during the Classic Period served as a way station on the trade route from Acapulco to Mexico City. This suggests that fish were carried in water tanks from way station to way station in much the same manner that relay stations were established to aid the movement of mail by the Pony Express of yesteryear.

According to Ixtlilxochitl, Tultecas who were exiled at the beginning of the fourth century AD embarked at Huatulco and sailed as far north as Guadalajara. Huatulco is near the Isthmus of Tehuantepec, located near the same area where we propose that Hagoth's ships were launched.

Alma 63:7–8 (54 BC): "And in the thirty and eighth year, this man [Hagoth] built other ships. And the first ship did also return, and many more people did enter into it; and they also took much provisions, and set out again to the land northward. And it came to pass that they were never heard of more. And we suppose that they were drowned in the depths of the sea. And it came to pass that one other ship also did sail forth; and whither she did go we know not. And it came to pass that in this year there were many people who went forth into the land northward. And thus ended the thirty and eighth year."

We are informed that two ships were lost. Mormon tradition suggests that at least one of these ships ended up in the Hawaiian Islands, thus accounting for the similarity in culture and traditions between the Polynesians and the people of Mesoamerica.

Communication apparently occurred between the Nephites in the land of Zarahemla and those who traveled by boat to the land which was northward, or to the land northward. The people knew which ships arrived and which ships did not arrive. They also seemed to know when provisions made it to the land northward.

Alma 63:10 (53 BC): "And it came to pass in the thirty and ninth year of the reign of the judges, Shiblon died also, and Corianton had gone forth to the land northward in a ship, to carry forth provisions unto the people who had gone forth into that land."

This scripture reaffirms that contact continued between the Nephites in the land of Zarahemla and the Nephites who went to the land northward by ship. The shipping distance from Tehuantepec to Acapulco is about three hundred miles. The distance is approximately 125 miles inland from Acapulco to Mexico City.

Helaman 3:3–4 (46 BC): "And it came to pass in the forty and sixth, yea, there was much contention and many dissensions; in the which there were an exceedingly great many who departed out of the land of Zarahemla, and went forth unto the land northward to inherit the land. And they did travel to an exceedingly great distance, insomuch that they came to large bodies of water and many rivers."

This period of time reflected great movements of people among the Nephites. The time period parallels the population growth that occurred in the Mexico valley, as illustrated at Teotihuacan, because of migrations from the south (see discussion earlier in this chapter). From a Book of Mormon perspective, the migrations occurred because of dissensions in the land of Zarahemla.

Mormon tradition suggests that at least one of Hagoth's ships ended up in the Hawaiian Islands, thus accounting for the similarity in culture and traditions between the Polynesians and the people of Mesoamerica.

"Bodies of water" and "many rivers" may refer to the lakes in the Mexico valley. Three shallow lakes remained on the valley floor at the time of the conquest of Mexico. According to tradition, one of the lakes was a salt-water lake. Mexico City was literally built on a lake. If people migrated inland to the Mexico valley, they most likely would have traveled the Veracruz route, which would have required them to cross many rivers, including the massive Papaloapan River system along the Gulf of Mexico.

The distance from Tuxtla Gutierrez, Chiapas, (proposed Zarahemla) to Mexico City (proposed land which was northward where large bodies of water were found) is about six hundred miles. Today, nine out of every ten buses travel the Veracruz route from Mexico City to Tuxtla Gutierrez. The trip is a long, difficult one. We would rather fly.

Helaman 3:7, 10–11 (46 BC): "And there being but little timber upon the face of the land, nevertheless the people who went forth became exceedingly expert in the working of cement; therefore they did build houses of cement, in the which they did dwell.... And it came to pass as timber was exceedingly scarce in the land northward, they did send forth much by the way of shipping. And thus they did enable the people in the land northward that they might build many cities, both of wood and of cement."

As mentioned earlier, the Book of Mormon account of the extensive use of cement occurred during the time period that the Pyramid of the Sun was built at Teotihuacan. Also, Teotihuacan's Avenue of the Dead, along with many buildings that were built of rock and cement, was constructed at Teotihuacan during the first century BC. Today's visitors to the Mexico valley, especially at Teotihuacan, cannot help but be curious about and impressed with the extensive use of cement in the construction of so many of the ancient structures. Nowhere else in Mesoamerica do we find such extensive use of cement for construction of buildings.

Even today, in the Mexico valley, most of the concrete buildings are constructed with cement. Lumber is very scarce. The type of lumber that is grown in the mountains around the valley of Mexico is not of the size and quality of that grown in the United States and Canada.

Helaman 3:12 (46 BC): "And it came to pass that there were many of the people of Ammon, who were Lamanites by birth, did also go forth into this land."

The Book of Mormon, as well as the archaeological record at Teotihuacan and other parts of the valley of Mexico, substantiates a rather large movement of people into the land northward (Mexico valley) during the first century BC.

3 Nephi 7:12 (AD 29): "Therefore, Jacob seeing that their enemies were more numerous than they, he being the king of the band, therefore he commanded his people that they should take their flight into the northernmost part of the land, and there build up unto themselves a kingdom, until they were joined by dissenters, (for he flattered them that there would be many dissenters) and they become sufficiently strong to contend with the tribes of the people; and they did so."

> Even today, in the Mexico valley, most of the concrete buildings are constructed with cement. Lumber is very scarce. The type of lumber that is grown in the mountains around the valley of Mexico is not of the size and quality of that grown in North America.

This migration may also have ended up in the Mexico valley. Jacob was appointed head of the secret combination society. This society is the one that had caused the regulations of the government to be destroyed. Teotihuacan was ruled by a religious and civil combination from AD 300 to AD 600. This combination may have been initiated by the wicked King Jacob in the first century AD.

3 Nephi 9:9 (AD 34): "And behold, that great city Jacobugath, which was inhabited by the people of king Jacob, have I caused to be burned with fire because of their sins and their wickedness, which was above all the wickedness of the whole earth, because of their secret murders and combinations; for it was they that did destroy the peace of my people and the government of the land."

The city of Jacobugath may have been located in the Mexico valley. We do not have enough evidence at this point to propose Jacobugath to be the city of Teotihuacan, but the pattern is similar to what we witness at Teotihuacan.

Mormon 2:28 (AD 350): "And the three hundred and forty and ninth year had passed away. And in the three hundred and fiftieth year we made a treaty with the Lamanites and the robbers of Gadianton, in which we did get the lands of our inheritance divided."

The AD 350 treaty was not just a treaty between the Nephites and the Lamanites. The robbers of Gadianton were included in the treaty. The governmental stronghold of the robbers of Gadianton possibly was at Teotihuacan in the valley of Mexico. Beginning at AD 350, the combination of government at Teotihuacan began to exercise control and to trade throughout Mesoamerica.

The Nephites who lived about the narrow neck of land may have simply been in the way of the trade activities between the Mexico City valley and Guatemala City area. In that respect, from a geographic perspective and as readers will see in chapter 23, "Things That Are Narrow," travelers who traveled between the land northward and the land southward had no choice but to go through the narrow neck of land. The extermination of the Nephites was well along by AD 350.

David Palmer writes the following: "Could an informal alliance have been struck between the two powerful cities [Kaminaljuyu/Guatemala City and Teotihuacan/Mexico City]? If so, the only thing preventing a consummation of that marriage would have been the presence of the hated 'Nephites' who controlled areas on both sides of the Isthmus."[10]

Palmer's proposal is not too far off. Apparently, the Gadianton robbers of the treaty were none other than descendants of the secret-combination people led by King Jacob, who entered the Mexico valley shortly after the birth of Christ (see 3 Nephi 7:9–13). Three hundred years later, this "Jacob" dynasty was still intact, as the person labeled Spearthrower Owl, who was discussed earlier in this chapter, may also have carried the title of "Jacob"—the first two letters of his five-letter name are JA _ _ _."[11]

The AD 350 treaty was not just a treaty between the Nephites and the Lamanites. The robbers of Gadianton were included in the treaty. The governmental stronghold of the robbers of Gadianton possibly was at Teotihuacan in the valley of Mexico.

10. David A. Palmer, *In Search of Cumorah: New Evidences for the Book of Mormon from Ancient Mexico* (Bountiful, UT: Horizon Publishers, 1981), 204.

11. Simon Martin and Nikolai Grube, *Chronicle of the Maya Kings and Queens: Deciphering the Dynasties of the Ancient Maya* (London: Thames and Hudson, 2000), 31.

Mormon 6:2: "And I, Mormon, wrote an epistle unto the king of the Lamanites, and desired of him that he would grant unto us that we might gather together our people unto the land of Cumorah, by a hill which was called Cumorah, and there we could give them battle."

From what we know about Stela 31 of Tikal, the Lamanite king to whom Mormon wrote his epistle may have been the young son of Spearthrower Owl from Teotihuacan. As mentioned previously, the name of the young son was Yax Nuun Ayiin, who became the king of Tikal on September 12, AD 379, and ruled until AD 420. Some preliminary indications show that the name of the Teotihuacan king was *Jacob* and that the title bestowed upon the young son who became the king of Tikal has an association with the name *Laman*. Time will tell if these suppositions are indeed the case.

SUMMARY

The ancient civilization of Teotihuacan, which began to fall into ruins by AD 750 and which was abandoned as a city center at AD 900, had its beginnings during the Book of Mormon time—about 150 BC.

From 55 BC to AD 29, the Book of Mormon records several migrations into the land which was northward, where large bodies of water were found. This was the same time period when Teotihuacan was experiencing a high growth rate; and, as a result, Teotihuacan may have been one of the cities where the migrating Nephites settled.

The Book of Mormon speaks about the people shipping provisions to the land northward. This shipping also may have been directed toward the valley of Mexico and its surrounding provinces.

The Book of Mormon speaks of the people in the land northward using cement to build houses because timber was scarce in the land. Teotihuacan manifests many buildings made of concrete that required cement, and timber indeed has always been scarce in the Mexico valley.

Secret combinations under the leadership of King Jacob fled into the land northward. Teotihuacan was subsequently ruled by a combination society.

The post–AD 200 activity of Teotihuacan certainly qualifies it to be called a wicked city. Jacobugath in the land northward was called a wicked city by the Lord.

The AD 350 treaty and the AD 385 destruction of the Nephites paved the way for the extended Mesoamerican trade activity that began at Teotihuacan in the early part of the fourth century AD. In fact, the activities described on Stela 31 of Tikal identify Teotihuacan as a dominating factor at the time of the final destruction of the Nephite nation.

> The activities described on Stela 31 of Tikal identify Teotihuacan as a dominating factor in the final destruction of the Nephite nation.

THE USE OF CEMENT IN MESOAMERICA

"The floors are of cement, as hard as the best seen in the remains of Roman baths and cisterns." Those are the words of John Lloyd Stephens as he describes "the Palace Palenque," a building in which he and Frederick Catherwood resided while exploring the ruins of Palenque a few years after the Book of Mormon was first published (see Stephens, *Incidents of Travel in Central America, Chiapas and Yucatan,* 2:313). Similar comments about the quality of construction involving cement are found in many archaeological reports about potential Book of Mormon sites in Mesoamerica.

However, upon its publication in 1830, anti-Mormon critics soon ridiculed Joseph Smith and the Book of Mormon because of the use of the word *cement* in the book of Helaman. Book of Mormon people could not be "exceedingly expert in the working of cement," reasoned the critics, because cement was a modern invention that was unknown in the New World in 46 BC (see Helaman 3:7). From the viewpoint of the critics, Terryl Givens puts the issue in perspective by labeling the inclusion of the word *cement* in the Book of Mormon as a candidate for a "historical blooper" by Joseph Smith (Givens, *By the Hand of Mormon,* 141). And the word *anachronistic* has been used to describe the situation. That is, the initial critics felt that Joseph Smith had made an unrecoverable error by chronologically placing the use of cement in an era when cement had not yet been invented.

However, any doubt about the validity of the word *cement* in the Book of Mormon—except by intentionally deceitful anti-Mormons—will evaporate for anyone who reads the archaeological reports about Teotihuacan. The same can be said

for anyone who personally examines the many structures at Teotihuacan and elsewhere that involved the use of cement for numerous construction purposes. Examining such structures at Teotihuacan is typically one of the highlights of our tours to the Mexico valley.

Today, knowledge about expert Mesoamerica cement technology during the Book of Mormon time period is a well-established archaeological fact. According to structural engineer David S. Hyman in his study about the use of cement in pre-Columbian Mesoamerica, "American technology in the manufacture of cement, its mixing and placement two thousand years ago, paralleled that of the Greeks and Romans during the same time period." Further, the earliest-known samples of such cement date to the first century AD when cement was a "fully developed product." Hyman notes that Mesoamerican cement work exhibits signs of great sophistication: "Technology and use in the manufacturing of calcareous cements in Middle America [were] equal to any in the world at the advent of the Christian Era." He explains that the workmanship of concrete floor slabs at Teotihuacan exceeds many twentieth-century building requirements. In summary, he asks, "Were these materials invented by an indigenous unnamed people far predating the occupation of Teotihuacan, or were they introduced by an exotic culture?" (See Hyman, *Pre-Columbian Cements: A Study of the Calcareous Cements in Prehispanic Mesoamerican Building Construction,* ii, 6–16.)

From the perspective of the use of cement at Teotihuacan, here is another instance in which the Book of Mormon record supports the archaeological and historical record of Mesoamerica.

CHAPTER 9

The Izapa (Jaredite-Nephite-Lamanite) Culture

And it came to pass that after we had sailed for the space of many days we did arrive at the promised land. (1 Nephi 18:23)

he archaeological ruins of Izapa may represent one of the most significant cultures in relation to the Book of Mormon. The famed Tree of Life Stone, labeled Stela 5, discovered there has been proposed to be representative of Lehi's dream as recorded in 1 Nephi 8.[1]

Strategically located along the Pacific coast by the Mexico and Guatemala border, Izapa may have been the area where Lehi first landed. It may also have been the Nephite city of Judea during the first century BC where Helaman led two thousand young warriors to battle:[2] "I, Helaman, did march at the head of these two thousand young men to the city of Judea, to assist Antipus, whom ye had appointed a leader over the people of that part of the land" (Alma 56:9).

1. M. Wells Jakeman, *The Complex "Tree-of-Life" Carving on Izapa Stela 5: A Reanalysis and Partial Interpretation* (Provo, UT: Department of Archaeology, Brigham Young University, 1958).

2. F. Richard Hauck, *Deciphering the Geography of the Book of Mormon* (Salt Lake City: Deseret Book, 1988), 8.

OPPOSITE: The ceiba tree is indigenous to Mesoamerica and is the national tree of Guatemala as well as the sacred tree of the Maya, who called it "the tree of life." Visitors to Mesoamerica will see this majestic tree not only in the sugarcane fields of Guatemala but also at the park entrances, such as at Tikal (shown here), the La Venta Museum in Villahermosa, Mexico, and the Panti Medicinal Trail in Belize. One such tree towers over the angel Moroni statue at the LDS temple in Villahermosa. The ceiba tree was the model for the famous Stela 5 monument at Izapa, which is also associated with the tree-of-life concept. (Photo courtesy of George and Audrey DeLange)

Izapa is located in the fertile Soconusco valley along the Pacific corridor that leads to the Isthmus of Tehuantepec. The New World Archaeological Foundation (NWAF) conducted field excavations at Izapa from 1961 to 1965. In its report published in 1982, the NWAF wrote: "Izapa is without doubt one of the largest ruins known on the Pacific coast of North or Central America, lying as it does within a very productive, well-populated region where communications are good."[3]

3. Gareth W. Lowe, Thomas A. Lee Jr., and Eduardo Martinez Espinosa, *Izapa: An Introduction to the Ruins and Monuments*, papers of the New World Archaeological Foundation, no. 31 (Provo, UT: NWAF, Brigham Young University, 1982), 1.

If, in reality, the area of Tapachula, Chiapas, where the Izapa ruins are located, was the land of first inheritance of Lehi and his colony, we then see a correlation with the concept of the Lord's placing His covenant people in a propitious spot. Just as the Lord placed the seed of Abraham in Israel, the crossroads of the Middle East, and just as He placed the Saints in these latter days in the crossroads of the West, so also does Izapa meet the criterion of being the crossroads of the Americas. In all three locations, anyone passing through the area would have the opportunity to become part of God's covenant people.

The road through Izapa represents the major trail of the ancient trade routes. From the Gulf of Mexico, travel was directly south through the Isthmus of Tehuantepec, the probable narrow neck of land in the Book of Mormon, and then along the Pacific coast and on through the area of Izapa.

FIGURE 9–1: The fertile Soconusco valley is located along the Pacific coast and is the area proposed by many Latter-day Saint scholars as the "land of first inheritance" where Lehi landed in the sixth century BC. The modern city of Tapachula and the ancient ruins of Izapa are located in this area. (Photo courtesy of Phil Skousen)

The people who lived in the Izapa area may well be representative of those people referred to in the allegory of Zenos: "And these will I place in the nethermost part of my vineyard, whithersoever I will, it mattereth not unto thee; and I do it that I may preserve unto myself the natural branches of the tree; and also, that I may lay up fruit thereof against the season, unto myself; for it grieveth me that I should lose this tree and the fruit thereof" (Jacob 5:13).

Exploring the Lands of the Book of Mormon

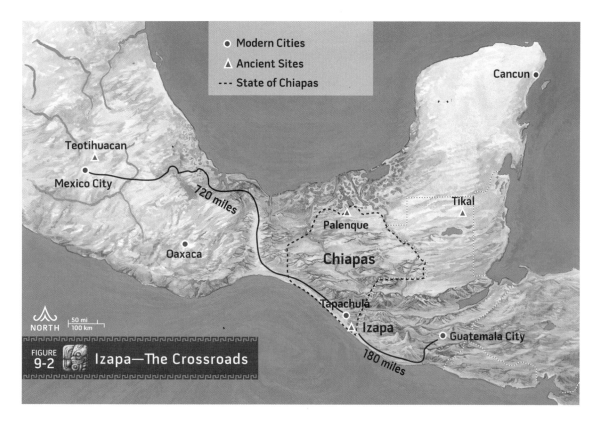

FIGURE 9–2: The above map shows the location of Izapa in relation to Mexico City and Guatemala City. The ruins of Izapa are located in the Mexican state of Chiapas, which originally was part of Guatemala. Driving time from Izapa to Guatemala City is about five hours. The state of Chiapas is outlined by the dotted line.

In Book of Mormon times, the terrain dictated that anyone traveling by land from north to south (from Mexico to Guatemala or even from North America to South America) *had* to pass through the Isthmus of Tehuantepec. Upon arriving on the Pacific side, the traveler could choose between two routes. The upper route took the traveler into the Chiapas depression and on into the Peten. The coastal route took the traveler through the heart of the Izapa country and on into Guatemala and El Salvador.

The road through Izapa represents the major trail of the ancient trade routes. From the Gulf of Mexico, travel was directly south through the Isthmus of Tehuantepec, the probable narrow neck of land in the Book of Mormon, and then along the Pacific coast and on through the area of Izapa.

When the Benjamin Cluff expedition crossed over the Isthmus of Tehuantepec (1901–3) and into the Mexican state of Chiapas where the Soconusco valley is located, they recorded their feelings as follows: "Geographically, we entered Central America and Tehuantepec, and, we think, entered the land of the Book of Mormon at the same place."[4]

4. Ernest L. Wilkinson and W. Cleon Skousen, *Brigham Young University: A School of Destiny* (Provo, UT: Brigham Young University Press, 1976), 158.

| Cocoa tree | Ripe cocoa pod | Dried cocoa beans |

FIGURE 9–3: The cocoa beans (cacao) shown here grow in abundance among the ruins of Izapa. Indigenous to Mesoamerica, cocoa beans were used as a form of bartering among the Maya. For example, one hundred grams of cocoa beans would buy a healthy rabbit. Chocolate, the hot drink derived from the cocoa beans, has often been referred to as the "drink of the gods." The word *chocolate* comes from the Aztec word *chocolatl* and means "warm liquid." (Photos courtesy of George and Audrey DeLange)

5. "Mr. Stephens' great developments of antiquities are made bare to the eyes of all the people by reading the history of the Nephites in the Book of Mormon. *They lived about the narrow neck of land, which now embraces Central America,* with all the cities that can be found. Read the destruction of cities at the crucifixion of Christ, pages 459–60. Who could have dreamed that twelve years would have developed such incontrovertible testimony to the Book of Mormon? Surely the Lord worketh and none can hinder" (*Times and Seasons* 3, no. 22, September 15, 1842, 915; emphasis added).

And it was this area that Joseph Smith referred to when he reported in the *Times and Seasons* that the Nephites lived about the narrow neck of land in Central America.[5]

Today, the valley in and around Tapachula is still the crossroads of the Americas and, as a result, plays the role of a traditional melting pot. German immigrants have cattle ranches. Chinese immigrants run coffee and cocoa plantations. Japanese immigrants are involved in the commercial activities of the area. Its near-sea-level elevation is ideal for the production of bananas, sorghum, cacao, and coffee. As in all of Mesoamerica, corn is the staple crop.

TRAVELING TO TAPACHULA (IZAPA)

The old saying, "You can't get there from here," applies to Tapachula to some degree. This saying is true in large part because of the border of Guatemala and Mexico. Prior to the advent of the train, walking was the best way to get to Tapachula. As roads were built, buses and automobiles began to move through the Isthmus of Tehuantepec and along the coast of Tapachula and on into Guatemala. However, a few hundred years ago, the state of Chiapas still belonged to the country of Guatemala. The border disputes have been everlasting, as this area was probably taken over by the Lamanite Maya in the AD 350 treaty with the Nephites: "And the Lamanites did give unto us the land northward, yea, even to the narrow passage which led into the land southward. And we did give unto the Lamanites all the land southward" (Mormon 2:29).

In the perspective of *Exploring the Lands of the Book of Mormon*, Izapa was in the land southward. In the ancient tradition of Maya geography, Izapa was in Maya territory. However, the culture of Izapa is quite different from the Maya culture. This difference suggests there was a remnant of the Jaredites living at Izapa when Lehi arrived (see Mosiah 8:12). It appears that following the 200 BC migration of Mosiah to

Exploring the Lands of the Book of Mormon

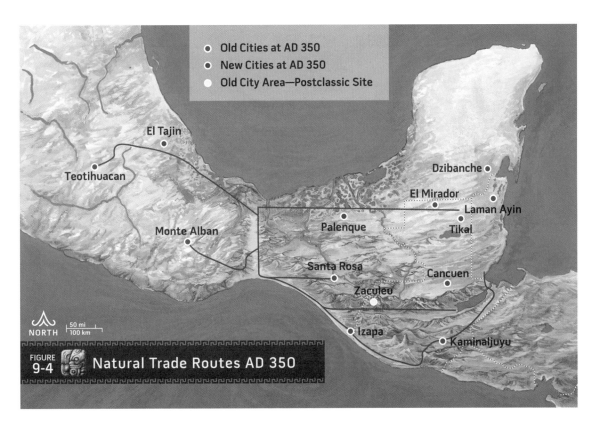

FIGURE 9—4: Izapa represents the crossroads for anyone traveling from Mexico to Guatemala or from North America to South America. Shortly after the AD 350 treaty, which is outlined in Mormon 2:28–29, the Maya developed an extensive trading system, as reflected here, utilizing natural trade routes.

the land of Zarahemla, Nephites lived in Izapa until approximately AD 350 when the Lamanites took total control of the area. If Izapa is indeed the place where Lehi landed shortly after 600 BC, then it becomes a viable candidate for the area where both Lehi and Sariah died and were buried. Some scholars have even suggested that Stela 5 at Izapa may have been a memorial to Lehi and Sariah.

In 1941, Matthew Stirling, whose work among the Olmecs is paramount, traveled with his wife to Izapa to analyze the Izapa culture. They traveled by train from Veracruz. He writes: "Permission from the Mexican authorities to clear and photograph the monuments [at Izapa] was readily granted. . . . Mrs. Stirling and I took the train at Piedras Negras [Veracruz] for the long trip, requiring two days and a night, to the extreme southwestern corner of Mexico."[6]

6. Lowe, Lee, and Espinoza, *Izapa: An Introduction to the Ruins and Monuments*, 1.

The distance from the Olmec site of Tres Zapotes, an Olmec archaeological site that lies at the base of a hill that has been proposed as the hill Ramah/Cumorah, to Tapachula is about four hundred miles. And the distance through the Isthmus of Tehuantepec, an area proposed as the narrow neck of land, is 150 miles. From the city of Veracruz to

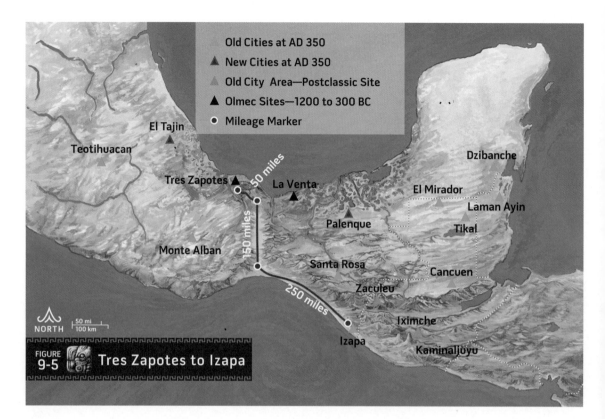

FIGURE 9–5: The distance through the Isthmus of Tehuantepec from the Gulf of Mexico to the Gulf of Tehuantepec is about 150 miles, and the distance from Tres Zapotes, Veracruz, to Tapachula, Chiapas (Izapa), is about four hundred miles. When climate and the terrain are taken into consideration, the journey by foot was an arduous one—especially during the rainy season. Traveling through the isthmus from the Pacific Ocean to the Gulf of Mexico or vice versa certainly would not have been "a day and a half's journey for a Nephite"—as some earlier literature suggests.

Tapachula (Izapa), the required travel time by bus takes about twelve hours. An alternative route to Izapa is from Oaxaca. However, because of the difficulty of terrain, for every one bus that travels from Mexico to Oaxaca to Tapachula, ten buses travel from Mexico to Veracruz to Tapachula.

Flying solves a lot of problems. The flight time from Mexico City to Tapachula takes one and a half hours; and from Oaxaca to Tapachula, the flying time is fifty-five minutes. From Tuxtla Gutierrez, Chiapas, to Tapachula requires only twenty-five minutes. And that's about it for flights into Tapachula. When the second edition of *Exploring the Lands of the Book of Mormon* was being planned, no flights were available from Guatemala or Central America to Tapachula. The Guatemala border is only about five miles from the Izapa ruins, and the driving time to Guatemala City is four and a half hours once a traveler crosses the border. What we are saying is that travelers have to want to go to Tapachula to get there. At least that is why we go there on our tours.

Exploring the Lands of the Book of Mormon

ESTABLISHING PEACE AMONG THE SEED OF JOSEPH

Following is a first-person, firsthand report by Joseph Allen of an incident that occurred near Tapachula in the year 2004:

It was 6:00 a.m. on January 6, 2004. The day ended up being the most traumatic day of my life in the travel business. Our capable and dependable bus driver, Filiberto Roca, with whom I had worked for many years, picked me up at the Marriott Hotel in Guatemala City to drive four hours in a twenty-six-passenger bus to meet with a group of thirty people whom Blake Joseph Allen, my son, had been traveling with in Guatemala. Upon our arrival at the Hotel Pension Bonifaz in Quetzaltenango, the plan was for all but twelve members of the group to continue on with Blake into the wilderness of Huehuetenango and then north into Mexico where they would spend another week. Richard and JoAn Berrett, long-time friends, were the directors of the group.

My job was to take the twelve members, mostly from two separate families, down southward to the Pacific coast Pan-American Highway and then west into Tapachula, Mexico, where we would visit the ruins of Izapa and Stela 5, often referred to as the Tree of Life Stone. We would then stay overnight and return to Guatemala City the next day. The group of twelve would fly home, and I was scheduled to pick up Wendell Jones and his group, some of whom had served missions in Guatemala, for another tour.

After visiting the village of Almolonga, the area proposed in *Exploring the Lands of the Book of Mormon* as the land of Helam, a land of pure water, we transferred the luggage of those who would be joining me to Filiberto's bus. Members of the group said their fond farewells, and Filiberto and I, along with the twelve tour members, made our way toward the Mexico border, a trip that would normally take two and a half hours. The first hour consisted of a drop in elevation from over seven thousand feet to about fifteen hundred feet, leaving lands where apples, potatoes, and all manner of vegetables are grown to places where pineapple, coconuts, coffee, cacao, and sugar cane are produced. Judge Maurice Richards and his wife Patricia; two of Maurice's sons, Brett Richards, an architect, and Reed Richards, an attorney, and their wives, Becky and Martha; their cousin, Dr. Edgar Allen, and his wife, Patricia; and attorney Val Morley and his wife, Jema, and his parents, Clair and Marcella Morley, constituted the small group of Latter-day Saints. The first hour and a half of the trip was pleasant and uneventful. I was impressed, however, with Brett Richards, a man who would be part of my life for only an hour and a half. He had a deep interest in and love for the Book of Mormon. He asked several insightful questions and commented on a number of things relative to our journey, as did other members of the group.

"After checking out of our hotel, we will visit the village of Almolonga. . . . We will then . . . cross the border into Mexico and visit the archaeological site of Izapa. While visiting Izapa, we will see Stela 5, the 'Tree of Life Stone.' This engraved stone dating back to 300 BC may depict Lehi's dream as recorded in 1 Nephi."

—Book of Mormon Tours, Day 7

As we traveled along the main highway leading to the Mexican border, I had just pointed out to the group a lone ceiba tree, which is commonly known as the "tree of life" and which is the image portrayed on Stela 5 at Izapa, when I noticed a small black pickup with three men in the back trying to crowd our twenty-six-passenger bus off the road.

Filiberto slowed down and stopped. Then, realizing that the men in the pickup were jumping off the pickup with guns in their hands and running toward the bus, he attempted to put the bus in reverse. That was to no avail, as one of the gunmen opened the driver's side door and shot Filiberto in the foot. Two more entered from the door on the right directly in front of where I was sitting. One helped the gunman, who had wounded Filiberto, wrestle Filiberto to the floor. A third attacked me as I attempted to lock the door and kicked me in the face several times. A fourth gunman positioned himself outside the bus as a backup. At this point, in a manner of courage and desire to help, Brett Richards stood up and moved forward to help Filiberto, who was lying on the floor. A shot rang out from the outside, and Brett fell back into the arms of his wife, proclaiming that he had been shot. As nearly as I have been able to calculate, all these events occurred in a matter of seconds.

In the next few minutes, the gunman who had shot Filiberto in the heel and who was a rather tall, slender man in his late twenties or early thirties sat in the driver's seat, turned the vehicle around, drove in the opposite direction for a few hundred yards, and then darted into the opposite side of a cornfield and into a secluded area of heavy brush, trees, and coffee plants. In the meantime, the gunmen on the bus kept shouting for us to close our eyes and shut up. At this moment, we were extremely concerned about Brett. He had been shot, and we of course were concerned that he would be able to live through it.

For the next twenty or thirty minutes, we were taken off the bus one at a time, physically robbed, tied up with our hands behind our backs, and instructed to lie face down on the ground. I didn't realize at the time that my senses were somewhat dulled because of the kicks I had received, but my sense is that virtually everyone in the group thought we would be killed. Separately, the gunmen had told both Filiberto and me that they were going to kill us. As I then considered what my last thoughts on this earth would be, my attention turned to my family. A little granddaughter would be born in a week, and I would not get to know her.

After they had robbed us and threatened us to stay on the ground for the next two hours, they left. Two of the sisters had not been tied up, so they untied the rest. The keys to the vehicle had been thrown out in the bushes, and we sensed that Brett had died. His wife had been allowed to stay with him on the bus.

Filiberto was in no condition to drive because of his injury, and my thoughts were to get help as soon as possible, hoping that Brett was still alive.

Within a hundred yards of the spot of the robbery was the highway where trucks and cars were passing constantly. Two men in a car stopped and picked me up. I was dazed, starry eyed, and in no way looked like a Guatemalan, and yet they picked me up. In Guatemala, police checkpoints are positioned along the highway every so often. Upon our arrival at the nearest checkpoint, two policemen were taking me back to the scene of the crime when I saw our bus coming toward us. The keys had been found, and Reed Richards was driving. We were taken to the hospital by the police. A short time after our arrival at the hospital, Brett was pronounced dead. During the course of all that had transpired during the preceding hour or hour and a half, I remember thinking that I had never seen more valiant women than I saw that day. There were deep tears of sorrow, but during the course of the ordeal, there was no screaming or great fear manifested.

Filiberto was attended to and the next day was transferred to a hospital in Guatemala City. He subsequently went through an operation, and although he required several months to recuperate, he continues to drive his bus through those beautiful mountains of Guatemala.

The robbery had taken place between 3:30 and 4:30 in the afternoon, and as members of the group began to call home and inform their families of the incident, darkness began to fall. Local mortuaries began posturing for the opportunity to take care of the deceased body. The director of the hospital gave me the name of a mortuary in Guatemala City that worked in foreign transfers. I passed that information on to the Richardses. The whisper came to call for the Church. I asked if anyone knew any Mormon bishops. One said he did, and within half an hour, the stake president of Retalhuleu arrived. I cannot express adequately the peace that came to my mind at that moment. From my perspective, this young, handsome descendant of Joseph of old, a Melchizedek priesthood holder and a presiding authority of the area, was sent by God. He immediately went to work. He called the area presidency and followed their every command. He contacted one of his bishops and transferred the group to his home where the bishop's wife and some Relief Society sisters prepared food, gave comfort, and provided access to long-distance telephone service to the states.

I had called home and informed my wife of what had happened. I now had the opportunity to talk with the area president, Spencer Jones, and his counselor, a Guatemalan Maya named Israel Perez. For the first time, I had to consider some other pressing questions. How do I contact my son Blake who was in Huehuetenango with the rest of the group to inform him of what had transpired and to counsel with him regarding several other tour groups that were sched-

> "It is proposed that we sustain the 134 Area Authorities, who are present with us today, as Seventies of The Church of Jesus Christ of Latter-day Saints to act in the office of Area Authority Seventies."
>
> —President Thomas S. Monson at the April 1997 General Conference; E. Israel Perez, mentioned in the robbery account, was one of the 134 sustained

uled to arrive during the next two and a half months—and one within two days? Should we advise them not to come? Should we close down the travel business? Should we discontinue taking lands of the Book of Mormon tours after thirty-four years? What is the practical thing to do? What does the Lord want us to do? The answer came from three sources: (1) the Lord's anointed; (2) the Book of Mormon; and (3) prayer and priesthood blessings.

I talked with President Perez for about an hour, explaining all that had transpired, and I asked for his counsel. We arrived at the conclusion that the robbery was a random act of violence and that we had taken the necessary safety precautions—a pattern I had established years ago. That is, we always traveled during daylight hours, we traveled on main roads, we traveled with reputable bus companies, we stayed in high-quality hotels, and we ate at safe restaurants. We have always been aware of the political activities in the areas where we travel, and we have always avoided those areas that are questionable. What had transpired that day was in line with all these guidelines. President Perez advised me not to let Satan win. Subsequently, my sons Blake and Todd and I were given priesthood blessings, in separate places, from different brethren, all stating the same thing.

As we transferred to a hotel where we could rest for a few hours, I took a few minutes to read and ponder the scripture that had been running through my mind since the robbery. This is a prophecy of Joseph of old, a thirty-five-hundred-year-old prophecy (2 Nephi 3:12; emphasis added):

> Wherefore, the fruit of thy loins shall write [the Book of Mormon]; and the fruit of the loins of Judah shall write [the Bible];
> and that which shall be written by the fruit of thy loins [the Book of Mormon] and also that which shall be written by the fruit of the loins of Judah [the Bible], shall grow together,
> unto the confounding of false doctrines and laying down of contentions,
> *and establishing peace among the fruit of thy loins,*
> and bringing them to a knowledge of their fathers in the latter days,
> and also to the knowledge of my covenants,
> saith the Lord.

The work of the gospel continues to grow in Guatemala. Within a few months of the publication of this book, *Exploring the Lands of the Book of Mormon*, a temple to the Most High will be built in Quetzaltenango—in the area where the events described above took place. Missionaries serve in the cities, towns, and villages in this area. *Peace will be established among the fruit of the loins of Joseph.*

In conclusion, I take this unique opportunity to thank many people for their support, encouragement, and kindnesses, including the following:

- The good and sympathetic people of Guatemala, both members and nonmembers.
- Those who work in the Guatemala tourism department; over half a million people a year visit this beautiful land.
- The Guatemala City Marriott Hotel workers.
- The American embassy personnel.
- The Guatemalan officials.
- The FBI investigators who were called in because the incident became international in scope. Much of what was stated in the press was not accurate. The national news media wanted my wife to respond, but she had a severe cold, which was a good excuse.
- Brent Hunsaker of ABC 4 News in Salt Lake City. He traveled with us for a few days on the tour following this event. From what I was able to ascertain, his reports were fair and accurate.
- Attorney Gordon Duval, who was my high priests group leader at the time.
- The members of our ward and stake and family and friends.
- The Richardses, the Morleys, and other members of the tour group.

My heart still goes out to the Brett Richards family. Two of the young men were arrested, convicted, and subsequently sentenced to life in prison, a prison that is in the same city where the new temple will be built. Several of us returned to Guatemala to testify during their trial.

One thing that did not help the robbers was a $2 bill found on one of them at the time of his arrest. Patricia Richards had a $2 bill taken from her at the time of the robbery. She explained to the court that there was a small tear in this bill that was taken from her. I suspect the robber was the only Guatemalan in the entire country who possessed a $2 bill. Filiberto identified one of the men; Sister Morley identified another; and I identified both of them. Nevertheless, my heart goes out to them and their families. A scripture that came to my mind at the time of the death of our nineteen-year-old-daughter several years ago is apropos here: "And then shall it come to pass, that the spirits of those who are righteous are received into a state of happiness, which is called paradise, a state of rest, a state of peace, where they shall rest from all their troubles and from all care, and sorrow" (Alma 40:12).

Occupation of the Izapa area began about 1500 BC. The period in which the majority of the monuments were engraved at Izapa falls between 300 BC and AD 250.

THE TIME PERIOD OF IZAPA

Because the ruins of Izapa fall within both Jaredite and Nephite time periods, we continue to visit that area on many of our tours. Occupation of the Izapa area began about 1500 BC. The period in which the majority of the monuments were engraved at Izapa falls between 300 BC and AD 250. Garth Norman calls Izapa the most important center on the Pacific coast from 600 BC to AD 400, serving both as a civil and a religious center.[7]

7. V. Garth Norman, *Izapa Sculpture*, part 2: text, papers of the New World Archaeological Foundation, no. 30 (Provo, UT: New World Archaeological Foundation, Brigham Young University, 1976), 1.

8. See Lowe, Lee, and Espinoza, *Izapa: An Introduction to the Ruins and Monuments*.

The following dating periods associated with the Izapa culture are set forth by the New World Archaeological Foundation, which conducted field work at Izapa from 1961–65.[8] As noted throughout *Exploring the Lands of the Book of Mormon*, the terms *Preclassic, Classic,* and *Postclassic* are terms identifiable with the overall culture in Mesoamerica. Preclassic is Book of Mormon time period. The Classic Period represents, Izapa excluded, a general period of growth and building in Mesoamerica. In Book of Mormon language, the Classic Period is equivalent to the religious apostate period described in 4 Nephi.

Early Preclassic	1500 BC–850 BC	Middle Jaredite Period
Middle Preclassic	850 BC–300 BC	Late Jaredite Period
		Early Nephite Period
		Early Mulekite Period
Late Preclassic	300 BC–AD 250	Middle Nephite/Mulekite
Early Classic	AD 250–AD 500	Late Nephite Period
Middle Classic	AD 500–AD 700	Post–Book of Mormon
Late Classic	AD 700–AD 900	Decline of Izapa
Early Postclassic	AD 900–AD 1200	Izapa abandoned

In Book of Mormon language, the Classic Period is equivalent to the religious apostate period described in 4 Nephi.

THE EARLY PRECLASSIC PERIOD (1500 BC TO 850 BC)

The first three hundred years of the Early Preclassic Period have been labeled the Ocos Phase, which represents the early beginnings of the formative period of Izapa. Two additional phases during the very early development of Izapa have been labeled (1) the Izapa-Cuadros Phase (1200 BC–1000 BC) and (2) the Izapa-Jocotal Phase (1000 BC–850 BC).

During the Izapa-Cuadros Phase, elements identifiable with the Olmec culture and the Mixe-Zoquean language were discovered by the archaeological team called The New World Archaeological Foundation, which is an affiliate of Brigham Young University.

The Olmec culture, which was centered along the Gulf of Mexico about three hundred miles northward from Izapa, was extremely well developed by 850 BC. Sites in the Oaxaca valley and in the Yucatan also date to this time period.

In the Book of Mormon during this time period, the Jaredite culture had become exceedingly industrious. The people worked in all manner of ore. They worked all manner of cloth to clothe themselves. They made all manner of agricultural tools. They made weapons of war and many things that they labeled "exceedingly curious workmanship" (see Ether 10:22–27).

The book of Ether states the following about this time period: "And never could be a people more blessed than were they, and more prospered by the hand of the Lord. And they were in a land that was choice above all lands, for the Lord had spoken it" (Ether 10:28).

Also, during the time period of 1500 BC–850 BC, the Jaredites preserved the land southward as a wilderness to get game. According to the geographical structure presented in *Exploring the Lands of the Book of Mormon*, Izapa is in the land southward.

SERPENTS AND FLOCKS

Finally, from 1500 BC to 850 BC, one of the most significant migrations to enter into the region of Izapa and extending southward along the Pacific coast was a remnant of Jaredites who fled from the Jaredite heartland as a result of a wicked government. Symbolically, Moroni compared the wicked secret combination government to poison serpents who "poisoned the hearts of the people." The flocks (those who believed the prophets) fled from the Gulf of Mexico (Jaredite/Olmec heartland) and traveled through the "course of the beasts" (the Isthmus of Tehuantepec, which carries the same meaning today) and settled along the Pacific coast. Thus, the Lord had prepared a people to accept the gospel that Nephi preached upon his arrival to the promised land, and this "remnant" of Jaredites (see Mosiah 8:12) would then form a large part of the Nephite kingdom beginning shortly after 600 BC.

Many Book of Mormon readers have assumed that no people were living in the area where Lehi and his colony anchored their ship about 588 BC in the promised land. This concept, however, is supported neither by archaeological information nor by Book of Mormon history.

The allegory of the serpents, the Jaredite secret combination government, and the flocks (God's righteous people) resulted in a remnant of the Jaredites migrating from the Gulf of Mexico to the Izapa region a few centuries prior to Lehi's claiming that land as his promised land. "And there came forth poisonous serpents also upon the face of the land, and did poison many people. And it came to pass that their flocks began to flee before the poisonous serpents, towards the land southward, which was called by the Nephites Zarahemla" (Ether 9:31).

Following the deaths of Lehi and Sariah, Nephi made it clear that it was not only family members who migrated with him to the place they called the land of Nephi but also other people as well: "And it came to pass that the Lord did warn me, that I, Nephi, should . . . flee into the wilderness, and all those who would go with me. . . . And all those

> Many Book of Mormon readers have assumed that no people were living in the area where Lehi and his colony anchored their ship about 588 BC in the promised land. This concept, however, is supported neither by archaeological information nor by Book of Mormon history.

The scenario we propose is that an Olmec/Jaredite remnant either followed Nephi, who became king of the Nephites, or became Lamanites as subjects of Laman.

who would go with me were those who believed in the warnings and the revelations of God" (2 Nephi 5:5–6).

All those who went with Nephi were probably, among others, none other than those Jaredite descendants who escaped the wrath of the poisonous serpent government and fled to Izapa and other sites along the Guatemala coast leading to the wilderness of Guatemala where Nephi built his city.

THE MIDDLE PRECLASSIC PERIOD (850 BC TO 300 BC)

The Middle Preclassic Period at Izapa represents a transitional period running from about 850 BC to 300 BC. This dating simply suggests that the structure of the society changed from a tribal-type society to a more sophisticated village-type society.

This transitional change may have come about as a result of immigration and expansion of a new people—and even quite suddenly as opposed to a gradual evolutionary development within the state of Chiapas.

The archaeological analysis becomes more complicated, as Izapa evidently was influenced from both directions—that is, from the Olmec area in the north and from the eastern areas of Chiapas and Guatemala: "Such intensive developments could only have been carried out by means of strong politico-religious force, either by concentrating an existing population or else by the outright immigration and expansion of a new people, or some combination of the two."[9]

9. Lowe, Lee, and Espinoza, *Izapa: An Introduction to the Ruins and Monuments*, 121.

From a Book of Mormon perspective, the new people are none other than the Nephite and Lamanite societies. The scenario proposed here is that this Olmec/ Jaredite remnant either followed Nephi, who became king of the Nephites, or became Lamanites as subjects of Laman, the brother of Nephi. Jacob wrote that those who were not Nephites were Lamanites (Jacob 1:14).

Interestingly, a new variety of maize, or corn, was introduced into the Chiapas area during this time period. During the early phase of Nephite-Lamanite history up to 450 BC, Izapa felt the impact of its first widespread, intensive occupation.

The archaeological record reports that during this phase called the Escalon Phase, 650 BC to 450 BC, large platforms and pyramids were first built throughout central and western Chiapas. Izapa played a central role in this expansion process.[10]

10. Lowe, Lee, and Espinoza, *Izapa: An Introduction to the Ruins and Monuments*, 127–29.

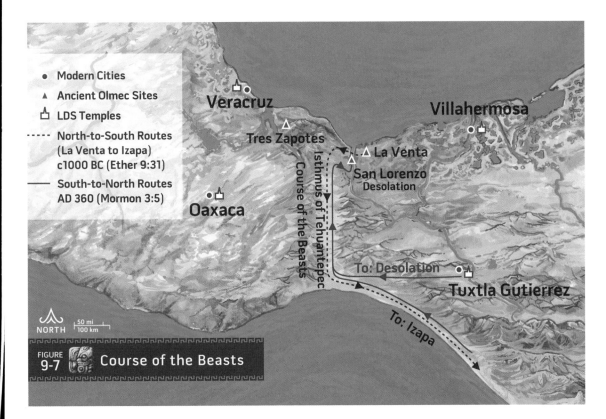

FIGURE 9–7: The Book of Mormon explains migrations through the isthmus in north-to-south and south-to-north directions. A remnant of Jaredites traveled north to south through the Isthmus of Tehuantepec (course of the beasts) about the eighth century BC, and the Nephites traveled from south to north into the land northward at AD 360.

Probably the most revealing thing that occurred during this time period is the development of a 260-day religious calendar of Mesoamerica, which had its roots at Izapa during the Escalon, or early Nephite, time period.[11] If Izapa is the same area that the Nephites called the land of first inheritance, then the Nephites probably were the inventors of the religious calendar. It can also be determined that the 365-day Mesoamerica calendar had its roots at Izapa.

11. Rafael Girard, *Los Mayas, Su Civilizacion: Su Historia Sus Vinculaciones Continentales* (Mexico: Talleres de B. Costa-Amic, 1966).

The final phase in the Middle Preclassic time frame is called the Frontera Phase, which extends from 450 BC to 300 BC. Izapa continued to develop during this 150-year period, and the evidence suggests that interaction occurred between the people living in Guatemala and El Salvador. During this time period in the Book of Mormon, the Nephites were well established in the land of Nephi, which we propose was located in the highlands of Guatemala. Also, this is the time period in which the Mulekites were migrating into the land southward: "And they [the Mulekites] journeyed in the wilderness, and were brought by the hand of the Lord across the great waters, into the land where Mosiah discovered them; and they had dwelt there from that time forth" (Omni 1:16).

The Mulekites, who were discovered by Mosiah, were living in the land southward at the time of their discovery. Izapa is located in the state of Chiapas and is considered to be part of the greater land of Zarahemla, which was in the land southward.

12. Lowe, Lee, and Espinoza, *Izapa: An Introduction to the Ruins and Monuments*, 129.

The most significant thing to transpire during the period from 450 BC to 300 BC, however, is the demise and fall of the Olmec culture at La Venta along the Gulf of Mexico: "It seems convenient, and historically correct, to think of the La Venta demise as ending the Middle Preclassic horizon all over the general Mixe-Zoque area."[12]

> The Mulekites, who were discovered by Mosiah, were living in the land southward at the time of their discovery. Izapa is located in the state of Chiapas and is considered to be part of the greater land of Zarahemla, which was in the land southward.

The destruction of the Olmecs at about 300 BC is discussed in some detail in chapter 5, "The Olmec (Jaredite) Culture," where we proposed that the Olmecs were the Jaredite civilization. The expansion of Izapa, following the destruction of the Jaredites, combined with the development of both the Nephites and Mulekites, provides the Book of Mormon student with some interesting possibilities. Those events certainly set the stage for the succeeding era at Izapa called the Late Preclassic Period.

THE LATE PRECLASSIC PERIOD (300 BC TO AD 250)

The Late Preclassic Period, like the preceding periods, is also divided into three separate phases. The first phase is called the Guillen Phase, which runs from 300 BC to 50 BC. These dates are purely Book of Mormon time period. The administrations of Mosiah I, Benjamin, Mosiah II, Alma, Moroni the military leader, Helaman I, and Helaman II all occurred during the Guillen Phase from 300 BC to 50 BC.

Julius Caesar and Mark Anthony conducted their military campaigns for the Roman empire during the latter part of the Guillen Phase in the first century BC. Their intent was to control the world. Three hundred years prior to the beginning of the Guillen Phase, the Lord told the prophet Lehi the following: "Inasmuch as those whom the Lord

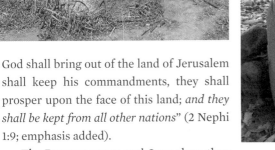

God shall bring out of the land of Jerusalem shall keep his commandments, they shall prosper upon the face of this land; *and they shall be kept from all other nations*" (2 Nephi 1:9; emphasis added).

The Romans conquered Jerusalem; they did not conquer Izapa. The Lord did not let them get close to the New World. In fact, the Lord kept the New World from *other nations* until He brought the Spaniards to the New World at the end of the fifteenth and the beginning of the sixteenth centuries.

At Izapa, almost all the stone monuments were carved and erected during this time period, 300 BC to 50 BC. The archaeological reports indicate that massive construction and sculptural activities during these two or three centuries can be described only as "phenomenal." The pyramid labeled Mound 60, which reached a height of more than sixty feet, equivalent to an eight-story building, was constructed during this phase. Stela 5, or the Tree of Life Stone, was also engraved during the time period from 300 BC to 50 BC.[13]

> At Izapa, almost all the stone monuments were carved and erected during this time period, 300 BC to 50 BC. The archaeological reports indicate that massive construction and sculptural activities during these two or three centuries can be described only as "phenomenal."

13. Lowe, Lee, and Espinoza, *Izapa: An Introduction to the Ruins and Monuments,* 129–35.

In the year AD 350, all of the land southward fell under the domain of the Lamanites. At AD 360, Mormon called all the Nephites who were living in the land southward to gather at the city of Desolation, which was in the land northward.

In summary, Izapa entered into an era of greatness during the period from 300 BC to 50 BC, whereas the Olmec sites of La Venta and San Lorenzo were relatively abandoned. In the year 121 BC, a group of Nephites, whom we call the Limhi expedition, traveled from the land of Nephi in search of the land of Zarahemla. We propose that their travels took them from Guatemala City to the Gulf of Mexico, as represented by the sites of La Venta and San Lorenzo (see Mosiah 8:8). This is the area in which the Olmecs (Jaredites) were destroyed.

Perhaps one of the reasons for the increase in population at Izapa during this time period was the abandonment of the above-mentioned Olmec, or Jaredite, sites. The great destruction in the land northward was apparent justification for the Nephites and Mulekites not wanting to live there. The land was cursed: "Now Lachoneus did cause that they should gather themselves together in the land southward, because of the great curse which was upon the land northward" (3 Nephi 3:24).

From 50 BC to the end of the Late Preclassic Period at AD 250, the growth of Izapa leveled off and eventually ceased. About a hundred years after the birth of Christ, the archaeological evidence suggests that heavy volcanic eruptions occurred in the area. The eruptions possibly may have been of an earlier date, which is required if they are to correlate with the destruction at the time of the death of Christ at AD 34.

FIGURE 9–9: These buildings date toward the end of the fluorescent period of Izapa and are located north of the highway that leads to Guatemala—about five miles from the border. Izapa is considered the area where both the 260-day religious calendar and the 365-day solar calendar were in use. (Photo courtesy of George and Audrey DeLange)

THE EARLY CLASSIC PERIOD (AD 250 TO AD 500)

Elements of non-Maya origin continued at Izapa during the Early Classic Period. During this period, Izapa appears to have been suffering from a slow death. These events are

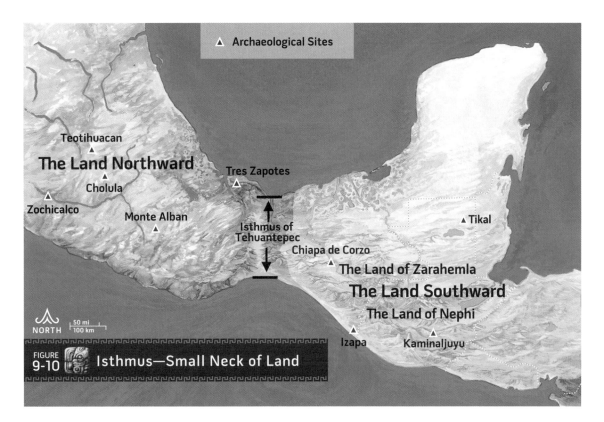

FIGURE 9–10: The Isthmus of Tehuantepec is the dividing line between the land northward and the land southward. The homeland of the Maya is on the southeast side of the isthmus, of which Izapa is a part. In the AD 350 treaty, the Nephites lost the land of Zarahemla. Both the land of Zarahemla and the land of Nephi were in the land southward.

contrary to what was going on in the rest of Mesoamerica, especially in Maya territory, the area in which Izapa is located.

Perhaps the Book of Mormon assists us in understanding what was going on at Izapa during this period. The apostasy began at AD 200; and, by AD 400, the Nephites had been destroyed. In the year AD 350, all of the land southward fell under the domain of the Lamanites. At AD 360, Mormon called all the Nephites who were living in the land southward to gather at the city of Desolation, which was in the land northward: "And it came to pass that I did cause my people that they should gather themselves together at the land Desolation, to a city which was in the borders, by the narrow pass which led into the land southward" (Mormon 3:5).

In all probability, Nephites who were living in Izapa during this time period migrated the three hundred miles from Tapachula (Izapa) to the area of Acayucan, Veracruz, the proposed area of the city of Desolation. This migration explains the decline in population during the Early Classic Period. It also helps to explain why Izapa was not considered a Maya (Lamanite) type city during this time period.

From AD 400 to the end of the Early Classic Period of Izapa, around AD 500, very little activity is reported. Those items that have been discovered and analyzed are typical of this time period throughout Mesoamerica.

THE MIDDLE CLASSIC PERIOD (AD 500 TO AD 700)

During the Middle Classic Period, most of Maya land and much of Mesoamerica, especially Teotihuacan, were in the middle of the greatest building and trade expansion in their history. Izapa maintained a status quo. However, some elements of Teotihuacan, along with boulder-type tombs, do show up on the scene at Izapa. The Pacific corridor is a normal—and the most accessible—trade route between Teotihuacan (Mexico City) and Kaminaljuyu (Guatemala City). Izapa may have been simply a border town or a resting station for travelers between the two major powers.

Indeed, this travel route may be what caused the AD 350 Nephites their greatest problem. The treaty, as recorded in Mormon 2:28–29, involved not only the Lamanites with the Nephites but also the Gadianton robbers. If the Gadianton robbers, as proposed in chapter 8, "The Teotihuacan Culture," formed the Teotihuacan government, then the Izapa Nephites were really "in the way"—especially if the wicked AD 350 Nephites were "money hungry" and demanded a toll for travelers to pass through their land. Perhaps the robbers and the Lamanites took the approach that they should remove the Nephites rather than pay the *mordida*, or pay a bribe. Mormon writes: "And in the three hundred and fiftieth year we made a treaty with the Lamanites and the *robbers of Gadianton*, in which we did get the lands of our inheritance divided. And the Lamanites did give unto us the land northward, yea, even to the narrow passage which led into the land southward. And we did give unto the Lamanites all the land southward" (Mormon 2:28–29; emphasis added).

THE LATE CLASSIC PERIOD (AD 700 TO AD 900)

The lack of new buildings being built at Izapa during the Late Classic Period is indicative of the limited activity that occurred during this period at Izapa. This is post–Book of Mormon time period.

THE EARLY POSTCLASSIC PERIOD (AD 900 TO AD 1200)

Apparently, light occupation or use of the ruined ceremonial centers occurred at Izapa during the Postclassic era. The candle had gone out at Izapa as well as in Mesoamerica in general. The prophet Nephi saw this day in vision as he wrote: "And it came to pass that I beheld, after they had dwindled in unbelief they became a dark, and loathsome, and a filthy people, full of idleness and all manner of abominations" (1 Nephi 12:23).

> If the Gadianton robbers formed the Teotihuacan government, then the Izapa Nephites were really "in the way"— especially if the wicked AD 350 Nephites were "money hungry" and demanded a toll for travelers to pass through their land.

THE ARCHAEOLOGICAL HISTORY OF IZAPA

The New World Archaeological Foundation conducted field work in the state of Chiapas from 1961 to 1988 and is recognized as a leading archaeological team in Mesoamerica. Investigative and reconstruction work was undertaken at the site of Izapa from 1961 to 1965. Gareth Lowe was the field director of the NWAF during the thirty-four years it had its headquarters in Chiapas (1954–88). Elder Howard W. Hunter served as chairman of the board of the NWAF from the time The Church of Jesus Christ of Latter-day Saints assumed sponsorship of the foundation beginning in 1961, a foundation initially started by Thomas Stuart Ferguson. Elder Hunter continued as the foundation chairman for thirty years, almost up to the time he was sustained as the Prophet and President of the Church.

Detailed reports on the findings of the foundation are available in the Harold B. Lee Library at Brigham Young University. A history of the NWAF is recorded in *The Messiah in Ancient America*, by Bruce Warren and Thomas Ferguson. While the second edition of *Exploring the Lands of the Book of Mormon* was being planned, Dr. John Clark from Brigham Young University was still serving as the director of the New World Archaeological Foundation.

Thomas A. Lee Jr., who worked with the NWAF, compiled a bibliography of the archaeological history of Izapa from 1935 to 1980. Some of the following information is taken from Lee's compilation and the publications of the Society for Early Historic Archaeology.

1935–40

In the year 1935, a Protestant minister by the name of Jose Coffin sent a letter to the director of Monumentos Prehispanicos in Mexico informing the director of some monuments located near Tapachula, Chiapas, Mexico. Coffin's brief letter was accompanied by photographs of three of the monuments from the area. A subsequent letter by Coffin resulted in a report by Ignacio Marquina in 1939.

Also, in a 1939 report by Carlos Culebro, crude drawings were presented of Stelas 2 and 5. Stela 5 was labeled a market scene by Culebro. Eleven years later, in 1950, Culebro presented a petition to classify Izapa as a national park.

1940–50

The visit to the site of Izapa in 1941 by Matthew and Mary Stirling gave credibility to the significance of the Izapa culture. Stirling wrote a report in 1943 in a Smithsonian Institute bulletin that included photographs taken by a *National Geographic Magazine* photographer. Forty-one Izapa monuments were described briefly in the bulletin, and most of them were illustrated by photographs. Stela 5 was one of the drawings illustrated in the report. Stirling proposed a possible early date for the Izapa culture. He

> The visit to the site of Izapa in 1941 by Matthew and Mary Stirling gave credibility to the significance of the Izapa culture. Forty-one Izapa monuments were described briefly by the Stirlings, and most of them were illustrated by photographs.

Wells
Jakeman and
Irene Briggs
arrived at the
conclusion
that Stela 5
is an actual
representation
of Lehi's tree-
of-life dream,
as recorded
in the Book of
Mormon.

also suggested an apparent relationship with the Izapa culture and the Olmec culture from the Gulf Coast region in the states of Tabasco and Veracruz, Mexico.

During the months of December 1943 and January 1944, Eulalia Guzman visited the site of Izapa and subsequently presented reports to the governor of the state of Chiapas. Her reports included a general description of the Izapa area, along with drawings of twenty-seven of the stone monuments.

Philip Drucker conducted limited field work at Izapa in 1947 and issued reports published by *National Geographic*, the INAH of Mexico City (Instituto Nacional de Antropologia e Historia), and Middle American Research at Tulane University. He reported on fourteen test pits that produced between three thousand and four thousand shards. Drucker's last report was submitted in 1948. In that same year, Rafael Girard proposed that the 260-day religious calendar was invented at Izapa.

One Maya scholar, J. Eric Thompson, conducted an archaeological reconnaissance near Escuintla, Guatemala, in 1948. Escuintla is about 125 miles southward from Izapa. In a report published by the Carnegie Institute in 1948, Thompson suggests a possible relationship between the areas of Escuintla and Izapa. It is the existence of the sites of La Blanca, Abak Takalik, El Baul, and La Democracia, all of which are located along Guatemala's Pacific coast, that lends credibility to the hypothesis that as Nephi migrated from Izapa to what became the city of Nephi (Kaminaljuyu/Guatemala City), a remnant of Olmecs joined with the new Nephite kingdom and became part of the new law-of-Moses religion.

1950–60

Following visits to the site of Izapa in 1950, Rafael Tapia Orellana wrote some articles about Izapa that were published in 1951 and 1952. Orellana interpreted the name of *Izapa* as meaning white river or cold river—associated with the Aztec language.

M. Wells Jakeman, an LDS archaeologist and head of the Archaeology Department at Brigham Young University, analyzed the 1943 drawings of Matthew Stirling and, with the aid of a student named Irene Briggs (Mrs. Hugh Woodford), made an exciting statement on the monument labeled Stela 5. Briggs wrote a thesis on the tree-of-life symbol, in association with the fair god of Mesoamerica. Jakeman and Briggs arrived at the conclusion that Stela 5 is an actual representation of Lehi's tree-of-life dream, as recorded in the Book of Mormon.

In 1953, Jakeman presented the first of four studies in the *Bulletin of the University Archaeology Society* at Brigham Young University. After two on-site expeditions and further study, including unsuccessful attempts to transfer Stela 5 to the National Museum of Mexico, researchers made a latex mold of the stone.

In 1958, under the direction of Dr. Ross T. Christensen, Carl Hugh Jones, and archaeological students Welby W. Ricks and Alfred L. Bush, a plaster cast was made to preserve the details of Stela 5. Two casts were made, one of which is located at the

Museum of Peoples and Cultures in Provo, Utah. The second is located at the residence of Omer Smith in Central, Arizona.

In 1958, Jakeman published a small booklet that contains his reanalysis of Stela 5. In the booklet, Jakeman scientifically justifies an earlier comparison of Stela 5 with Lehi's vision of the tree of life. More details on Stela 5 are presented in this chapter, based on the work of Jakeman, along with subsequent studies conducted by Garth Norman.[14]

14. See Jakeman, *The Complex "Tree-of-Life" Carving on Izapa Stela 5.*

Gareth Lowe, who served as director of the New World Archaeological Foundation from its inception, first visited the site of Izapa in 1956. He published a report in 1959 in which he analyzed ceramics that date to the Late Preclassic Period (350 BC to AD 250). As reported earlier, Lowe served as director of the NWAF for a third of a century.

1960–70

The decade of the sixties produced the most extensive investigative work at Izapa. This decade also marked the era in which a number of Latter-day Saint scholars became actively involved in the Izapa culture. The New World Archaeological Foundation was very active in Izapa during this decade.

Roman Pina Chan (1961, 1964, 1967). A Mexican archaeologist, Roman Pina Chan, served as director of the Prehispanic Monument Organization of Mexico. He visited Izapa in 1964. In 1967, he edited the *Archaeological Atlas of the Republic of Mexico* (*Atlas Arqueologico de la Republica Mexicana*). The atlas proposed that the art style of Izapa was derived from the Olmecs.

Michael Coe (1962, 1964, 1965). A popular book entitled *Mexico* was written by Michael Coe and published in 1962. Coe devoted two pages to the discussion of the Izapan civilization. Coe's book marked the first time that the term "Izapa" was used to denote the area as representative of separate cultures. He credited the Izapa culture, not necessarily Izapa, as the originators of the Maya long count as associated with the calendar. Coe also reported in the *American Antiquity Magazine* on the research that was being conducted by the New World Archaeological Foundation at Izapa. Coe suggests that the Izapa area was more closely related to the Mixe-Zoque language group of Oaxaca and the Gulf Coast than it was with the Maya. From a Book of Mormon perspective, this concept allows for the Jaredites, who appear to have initially settled at Oaxaca and subsequently moved to the Gulf Coast, as being the people referred to in the writings of Coe.

Ross Christensen (1962). Ross Christensen spent eight weeks in southern Mexico and was engaged in further analysis of the Izapa culture and specifically Stela 5. He concluded that Jakeman's original drawing/reproduction of Stela 5 had been remarkably faithful.

Gareth Lowe (1965, 1968). Parallel with the field work that was conducted under the supervision of Gareth Lowe, a number of articles and reports were written about the Chiapas area as well as about Izapa in particular.

The decade of the sixties produced the most extensive investigative work at Izapa. This decade also marked the era in which a number of Latter-day Saint scholars became actively involved in the Izapa culture.

In 1965, Lowe issued a report analyzing the function of the Izapa incense burner that dated from the Middle Preclassic to the Late Classic times (850 BC to AD 250).

Other archaeologists who worked on the Izapa project are Peter Balk, Bruce Warren, Susana Ekholm, and Thomas Lee Jr. Lee and Lowe presented a paper at the Society for American Archaeology meetings in Urbana, Illinois, in May 1968 wherein they outlined the reconstructed cultural history of Izapa.

Rafael Girard (1966). A book about the Maya written by Rafael Girard and published in 1966 included information on the Izapa zone. Izapa is in the area where the 260-day calendar was invented.

Wells Jakeman (1967). Wells Jakeman continued to be active as he presented a detailed rebuttal to some attacks that had been made about his interpretation of the Stela 5 carving as a depiction of Lehi's tree-of-life story in the Book of Mormon.

Ignacio Bernal (1969). Ignacio Bernal published a book called *The Olmec World*. Included in the book is a comparison of the Olmec art with the Izapan art style.

The most detailed work on the Izapa monuments, especially Stela 5, can be attributed to V. Garth Norman, a Latter-day Saint archaeologist and scholar.

1970–80

More detailed analyses emerged from the Izapa culture during the 1970s. The idea was proposed that both the 260-day religious calendar and the 365-day Mesoamerica calendar had their origins in the Izapa area. More than eighty monuments had been identified and analyzed. As a result, Izapa became a sort of art haven for the iconographers. A Latter-day Saint archaeologist, V. Garth Norman, published a detailed study on the Izapa culture.

Thomas Lee Jr. (1970, 1973, 1978). Thomas Lee Jr. was part of the New World Archaeological Foundation team during the 1970s and 1980s. On one of our tours, we visited with Lee at his home in San Cristobal de Las Casas, Chiapas. He had an extensive library on the publications and research of the NWAF that had been gathered over a thirty-year period. During the decade under discussion, Lee presented papers on the Izapa culture at conferences in Lima, Peru, and in Mexico City.

Jacinto Quirarte (1970, 1973, 1974, 1976, 1977). The large number of Izapa monuments proved to be fertile soil for iconographist Jacinto Quirarte. Several papers were presented by Quirarte involving the art and iconography of Izapa. Among these was a paper presented at the first roundtable to be held at Palenque in 1974. Quirarte used the drawings of Norman to illustrate his conclusions.

Tatiana Proskouriakoff (1971). A Maya scientist of Russian descent, Tatiana Proskouriakoff analyzed the role of the Izapa art style in relation to the Maya in a book that was published in 1971 called *Desarrollo Cultural de los Mayas*, edited by Evon Z. Vogt and Alberto Ruz.

V. Garth Norman (1973, 1976). The most detailed work on the Izapa monuments was accomplished by V. Garth Norman. A Latter-day Saint archaeologist, Norman spent two seasons at Izapa photographing and tracing the monuments. In 1973, Norman presented an analysis of thirty-three of the monuments. In 1976, Norman's analysis of the monuments was published by the New World Archaeological Foundation.

1980–89

During the 1980s, analyses of the Izapa culture continued, including the work of two individuals:

V. Garth Norman (1980, 1987). Garth Norman wrote his master's thesis on "Astronomical Orientations of Izapa Sculptures" in 1980. It was accepted by the Department of Anthropology of Brigham Young University. As a result of continued study, Norman is considered to be the foremost scholar on the Izapa monuments. He presented a detailed report on his findings at the 1987 Maya convention in Austin, Texas.

In reference to the archaeological site of Izapa, Norman writes: "For almost a thousand years from 600 BC, it [Izapa] seems to have been the largest and most important center on the Pacific Coast, undoubtedly serving both civil and religious functions."[15] Norman continues: "There is strong evidence that Izapa sculpture was primarily or entirely religious in origin and function."[16]

Gareth W. Lowe (1982). Under the editorship of Gareth W. Lowe, Thomas A. Lee Jr., and Eduardo Martinez Espinosa, the New World Archaeological Foundation published Paper No. 31 called "Izapa: An Introduction to the Ruins and Monuments."

Joseph L. Allen (1976). Joseph L. Allen first visited the site of Izapa in 1976 in the company of his wife and Webb Goodman and his wife. They reported that somewhat blindly, they stumbled through the pasture and jungle area where the Izapa monuments are located. Stela 5, which is known as the Tree of Life Stone, has attracted the most attention among Latter-day Saints. The stone stood upright in the corner of what obviously was an ancient city square. Although the monument was somewhat faded, the Allens and Goodmans could still make out the stone's carvings, which were quite clear in 1976.

For many years, we have made a practice of taking our tours to Izapa to see the Tree of Life Stone. Between Tapachula and the Guatemalan border lie the ruins of Izapa. As we enter the park where the ruins are located, one group of ruins is referred to as the "north group" on the north side of the road, and another section of the ruins is known as the "south group" on the south side of the road. By following a dirt road for about a mile through some cocoa trees and jungle-type vegetation, we come to a fork in the road. The right fork goes to the section labeled "Group A" where the Stela 5 and other monuments are located, and the left fork goes to another section of the Izapa pyramids called the "Lion Group." The dirt road leading south between Tapachula and the Guatemala border winds for about a mile. The fork in the road divides the lion group from the central group. Stela 5 is located in the central group.

15. Norman, *Izapa Sculpture*, 1.

16. Norman, *Izapa Sculpture*, 4.

"For almost a thousand years from 600 BC, [Izapa] seems to have been the largest and most important center on the Pacific Coast, undoubtedly serving both civil and religious functions."

—V. Garth Norman

FIGURE 9–11: Families continue to live in the archaeological zone of Izapa, and the Mexican government considers the ruins public domain. As a result, the small children grow up playing among the ancient ruins. (Photo courtesy of Phil Skousen)

Although not everyone agrees that a direct relationship is evident between Stela 5 and Lehi's dream, the fact remains that it exists and that it was engraved during the height of the Nephite history around 200 BC.

Bananas, cocoa beans, and corn are the main crops of the people who live in their cabin-type homes in the area. Brahma cows feed in the pasture where Stela 5 and a number of the other monuments are located. Some of our choicest experiences on our tours have taken place in the humid climate while we were standing by Stela 5, the tree-of-life monument.

Although not everyone agrees that a direct relationship is evident between Stela 5 and Lehi's dream, the fact remains that it exists and that it was engraved during the height of the Nephite history around 200 BC. It is evident that elements familiar to all readers of the Book of Mormon, such as a symbolic tree of life, filthy waters, and a rod leading up to the tree, are indeed reminiscent of that great tree-of-life account recorded in 1 Nephi. But the message is still spiritual. We know that—as Lehi desired and as faithful Latter-day Saints throughout the world today desire—our children can press forward by holding on to the iron rod that leads them to the tree of life, or Christ, and that they may partake of the fruit that is choicest above all others, the fruit of eternal life. The following comments suggest a possible correlation with Stela 5 at Izapa and the account of Lehi's dream in the Book of Mormon:

1. The location of the discovery of Stela 5 has been identified by a number of The Church of Jesus Christ of Latter-day Saint leaders and scholars as the place where Lehi landed and as a result would be the place where Lehi and Sariah died and were buried.

Hence, the location appears to be a suitable place for Lehi's descendants to construct a memorial to the first parents.

2. The date of the actual construction of the stone as an engraved monument or stela was about 200 BC, which falls in the Mosiah time period—a time when the process of engraving on stone was introduced in the Book of Mormon (Omni 1:20), thus allowing for Mosiah to culturally and historically commission a stone to be engraved in honor of the first parents.

3. The potential name glyphs for Sariah, Lehi, Nephi, and Sam, as proposed by M. Wells Jakeman, with a possible name correlation of Laman as a result of new evidence, cannot, in our opinion, be discarded as nonevidence.

4. The work of Garth Norman showing the presence of the biblical measurement of the cubit suggests some Old World contact.

5. The evidence that Stela 5 was written in classic Hebrew poetry style called chiasmus hints at a tie-in with the Old World and Izapa (see chapter 15, "Christ—The Tree of Life").

John E. Clark (1999). John E. Clark has served as the director of the New World Archaeological Foundation and as a board member for the Foundation for Ancient Research in Mormon Studies (FARMS). In 1999, he produced an updated drawing of Stela 5 in which his artist, Ayax Moreno, introduced some minor changes to Norman's original drawings.[17]

One contribution of the new drawing suggests the possibility of a crocodile forming part of the right side of the tree trunk. If this is true, we may then have a possible name glyph for Laman, the individual with his back to the tree.

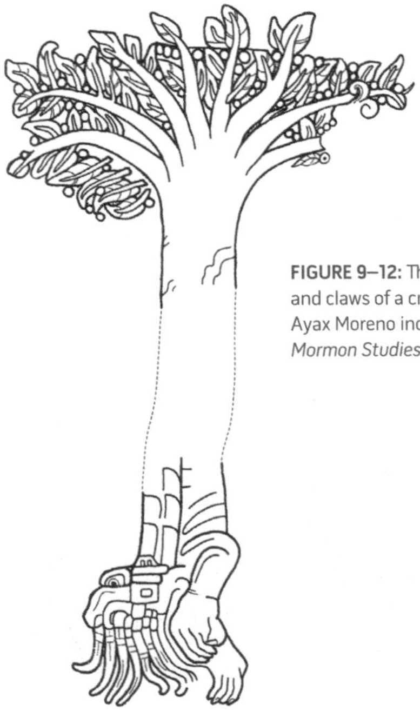

In the archaeological site called Laman Ayin, the name is associated with crocodile, and the young ruler of Tikal at the time of the Cumorah battle was named Yax Nuun Ayiin, or First Crocodile. Clark, however, rejects any correlation with the Stela 5 and Lehi's dream. He writes: "Any connection between the production of the new drawing and interpretation, LDS or non-LDS, of what the monument shows is purely incidental." Clark made an error in his scriptural analysis when he stated, "The period when the Izapa monuments were sculpted, 300 to 50 BC, is a dark time in terms of Nephite history and geography."[18] Although this is a difficult time for the people of Nephi, the darkest period

17. John E. Clark, "A New Artistic Rendering of Izapa Stela 5: A Step toward Improved Interpretation," *Journal of Book of Mormon Studies* 8, no. 1 (1999): 23–33. See also V. Garth Norman, "Tree of Life Stone Under Attack," *Book of Mormon Archaeological Digest* 2, no. 4 (1999): 1, 7–8, 13–14.

FIGURE 9–12: This drawing illustrates the face and claws of a crocodile that John Clark and Ayax Moreno included in the *Journal of Book of Mormon Studies*, Volume 8, Number 1, 1999.

18. Clark, "A New Artistic Rendering of Izapa Stela 5," 30.

of the Book of Mormon begins at AD 200 and continues to the close of the Book of Mormon. The time from 300 BC to 50 BC, when most of the monuments at Izapa were engraved, is the same as the fluorescent period of the Nephites and is the time when the books of Mosiah, Alma, and Helaman were written and the Nephites were led by great prophets such as Benjamin, Mosiah, the Almas, and the Helamans. And the geography of the Book of Mormon is explained in greater detail in those three books than in any other place in the Book of Mormon. Clark and his associates at FARMS have been seriously challenged by other Latter-day Saint scholars of Mesoamerican studies and archaeology for their artistic and literary conclusions.[19]

19. See Norman, "Tree of Life Stone Under Attack."

In Lehi's vision, he presents an analogy similar to the parable of the four soils given by the Savior (see Matthew 13) during His earthly ministry. A mist of darkness, or temptations of the world, causes some people to lose their way, while others hold fast to the iron rod. Many people go into forbidden paths and are lost. The people in the large and spacious building scoff at those who endeavor to live the gospel principles. Those who endure to the end do partake of the tree of life. That is, through the Atonement of Christ, these people may inherit eternal life.

Apparently, the literary analogy of the tree of life follows somewhat of a pattern of an Isaiah or Hebrew text. That is, the story is about Lehi and his family, but the real meaning has to do with our quest through life with the ultimate opportunity to partake of eternal life through Christ. Dr. S. Kent Brown, professor of religion at Brigham Young University and director of the Foundation for Ancient Research and Mormon Studies, has proposed some vivid imagery with Lehi's dream and the culture of the

FIGURE 9–13: This picture shows the tall buildings made out of mud in the city of Shibam, commonly referred to as the "Manhattan of the Desert." The twin cities of Shibam and Sayun are located about four hours' driving time almost straight east from the valley of Najem (Najom) on the modern highway that was built in 1999, just five months prior to the time that Joseph Allen led a pioneer Latter-day Saint group through Yemen. (Photo used by permission)

Exploring the Lands of the Book of Mormon

Middle East—more particularly the area along the Frankincense Trail from the Red Sea to Salalah, Oman, by the Arabian Sea. Such imagery includes the dark and dreary wilderness, as Lehi would have traveled by night through that vast, empty, desolate desert, traveling eastward through the country of Yemen, and the large and spacious building above the air is represented by the multistoried buildings at Shibam, Yemen (the so-called "Manhattan of the Desert").

In the words of Joseph Allen, "Having traveled through that area myself and having escorted the first Latter-day Saint group to attempt to follow the trail of Lehi from Jerusalem through Jordan and Yemen and terminating at Oman near the Arabian Sea, I have felt that same imagery—or, as Mormon puts it, 'types and shadows.' The historically valuable white fruit from the frankincense tree may well be symbolic of the fruit that was 'white above all that was white,' as worded by Lehi. In other words, the most precious of gifts anciently, including that which was taken to the Christ child, may well be a shadow of the greatest gift of all, eternal life."

> The historically valuable white fruit from the frankincense tree may well be symbolic of the fruit that was "white above all that was white."

FIGURE 9–14: The white resin, or fruit, of the frankincense tree from Salalah, Oman, may be the imagery used by Lehi to illustrate his words, "the fruit thereof was white" (1 Nephi 8:11). (Photo Courtesy of Mary O. Stoddard)

CHAPTER 10

Ancient Mesoamerican Documents

The language of the Nephites began to be taught among all the people of the Lamanites.
(Mosiah 24:4)

U p to this point in *Exploring the Lands of the Book of Mormon,* we have discussed two major reasons why the events recorded in the Book of Mormon were centered in the geographic area called Mesoamerica.

The first reason is associated with the written language. Scholars have determined that the only place on the American continent where a written language was in use during the time period in which the Book of Mormon history, coupled in the context of a high civilization, was in Mesoamerica. Indeed, the area in and around the Isthmus of Tehuantepec constituted the embryo for both the calendar system and the written language of the Americas. This fact alone virtually eliminates any other geographical area from being considered as "lands of the Book of Mormon."

OPPOSITE: Shown here are two Relief Society sisters from Patzicia, Chimaltenango, Guatemala, with their scriptures wrapped neatly in white linen. Three major documents have been discovered in this area of Mesoamerica. A fourth Mesoamerican document that is the most comprehensive and most detailed is the Book of Mormon, one of the books in the possession of the Relief Society sisters. (Photo courtesy of Merrill C. Oaks)

The Book of Mormon was made possible as a result of a written language. Place-names and phrases in the Book of Mormon in comparison with place-names and phrases in Mesoamerica are now surfacing as a result of continued study with the deciphering of the Maya code. Book of Mormon readers can look to the future with great assurance that additional understanding of the Book of Mormon will occur as more knowledge is gained through the study of ancient languages.

The second reason relates to the size and quality of population centers—as outlined in chapters 4 through 9 of *Exploring the Lands of the Book of Mormon*. Archaeologists have determined that the vast majority of discovered archaeological sites dating to the time period of the Book of Mormon are located in Mesoamerica.

> Archaeologists have determined that the vast majority of discovered archaeological sites dating to the time period of the Book of Mormon are located in Mesoamerica.

Everyone should be impressed with the vast amount of scholarly work that has been accomplished in the last half of the twentieth century and the beginning of the twenty-first century in piecing together the history of the ancient civilizations in Mesoamerica by means of archaeological research. In our opinion, to surrender the area of Mesoamerica as non–Book of Mormon territory would be as unsound as to ignore the fact that the earth is round. In addition, when we realize the extent of the internal consistencies in the Book of Mormon wherein much of its history took place between the city/land of Zarahemla and the city/land of Nephi, a distance estimated at 250 to 300 miles, we are almost forced to arrive at the conclusion that generalized pinpointing of Book of Mormon lands is not as difficult as it may first appear. In that respect, as we read the Book of Mormon, we should recognize that Mormon wrote as if he had a map of the lands of the Book of Mormon in front of him and that he expected us to relate to that map in helping us understand the content of his writing.

We will now discuss a third reason for centering the Book of Mormon in Mesoamerica. This third reason—the one that will be discussed in chapters 10 through 16—coincides with the traditional history of Mesoamerica in relation to the Book of Mormon.

The oral traditions, cultural patterns, and written history of Mesoamerica provide us with valuable insights in understanding the Book of Mormon. Indeed, the more we understand the language, history, and customs of Mesoamerica, the more we understand the Book of Mormon. We make a grave mistake in trying to piece together the historical puzzle of the Book of Mormon if we ignore the traditional history of Mesoamerica.

THE CODICES

Some of what we know about the ancient history of Mesoamerica was written in books called *codices*. Every pre–Spanish conquest priest had a codex. In fact, libraries of codices were typically found in the cities.

The vast majority of these native documents did not survive the conquest. In addition, many Maya priests, almost the only literate people among the Maya, were killed during the course of the conquest. The Spanish inquisition that resulted in the burning of the codices by the Catholic priests almost negated any possibility of retrieving a detailed history of the Maya.

Although remains of completely decayed codices have been discovered by archaeologists, only four Maya codices survived the conquest, though a significant number of fake Maya codices are also in existence today.[1] The following discussion gives a brief explanation of the four Maya codices plus a Mixtec codex called the Codex Nuttall.

The Dresden Codex

The Dresden Codex was discovered in 1739 when it was sold to the Royal Dresden Library at Vienna. It may have arrived at Vienna as a gift from Carlos V of Spain, who probably received it from the governor of the unconquered province of Yucatan in 1526.

The Dresden Codex was published in its entirety in volume three of Lord Kingsborough's *Antiquities of Mexico* (1831–48). The first facsimile was published in 1880 by Ernst Forstemann, director of the Dresden Library. During World War II, the codex was damaged by bombing. Today, the original Dresden Codex is located in the Saxon Regional Library of the German Democratic Republic.

Yurii Knorozov, a Russian scholar, conducted one of the most serious studies of the Dresden Codex. His work was translated by Sophie D. Coe from the Russian into English in 1982. (See figure 2–4, page 29, for a picture of the Dresden Codex.)

Unfolding the Scriptures. The concept of unfolding the scriptures is illustrated on these few pages of the Dresden Codex. The Dresden Codex consists of thirty-nine pages, enscribed on both sides (except for four pages that have been left blank), for a total of seventy-eight pages. Each page is 9 by 22 centimeters (3.5 by 8.7 inches) in size and is filled with beautiful writing. Ixtlilxochitl called the codices "painted books." The total length of the Dresden book is 3.56 meters, almost 12 feet. When it was folded together like a map and bound by two pieces of wood, it was about nine inches long. The Dresden Codex is divided into chapters, or themes, which include a ceremonial calendar, a table of solar and lunar eclipses, and tables for calculating the movement of the planets of Venus and Mars. It also speaks of a flood and outlines various predictions and prophecies.

The concept of unfolding the scriptures is also represented in the Book of Mormon on several occasions. When Alma and Amulek were preaching to the people of Ammonihah, Alma bore witness to or expanded upon on what Amulek had taught. Alma began to "explain things beyond, or to *unfold the scriptures* beyond that which Amulek had done" (Alma 11:1; emphasis added). In our culture, we say, "Open your scriptures." Joseph Smith at one time said that he and Oliver Cowdery "began to have the scriptures *laid open* to our understandings" (Joseph Smith—History 1:74; emphasis added). In the Jewish culture, they "unroll" the scriptures. In the Nephite/Maya culture, they

1. See Yurii Knorozov, *Maya Hieroglyphic Codices*, translated from Russian by Sophie D. Coe, publication no. 8 (Albany: Institute for Mesoamerican Studies, State University of New York at Albany, 1982).

> We make a grave mistake in trying to piece together the historical puzzle of the Book of Mormon if we ignore the traditional history of Mesoamerica.

"unfolded" the scriptures. The Nephites not only wrote on brass and gold plates but also on large stones (Omni 1:20) and on beautifully painted codices as shown in figure 10–1.

The Scribes. The Dresden Codex appears to have been written by eight different scribes. In Maya history, the scribes were as close to royalty without really being royalty as anyone could get. Often, the scribes were related to the ruler. Like the scribes in the Bible, the Maya scribes carried a lot of weight. Their primary objective during the Classic and Postclassic Periods was to propagandize the rulers so they would look good from a historical perspective. They wore a turban-style headdress that served as a holder of brushes with which to paint. The scribes were targets of the enemies of the city/state in which they served. Normally, only the elite and well educated could read and write, thus making it necessary for a reader to tell the common people what was contained in the books. Because the codices were typically made of tree bark or animal skins, they could be burned, as in the cases of Diego de Landa (see chapter 13, "Diego de Landa") and the people of Ammonihah: "They . . . brought forth their holy scriptures, and cast them into the fire . . . that they might be burned and destroyed by fire" (Alma 14:8).

The Paris Codex

One of the first students of the Maya writing was a French scholar by the name of Leon de Rosny. He is credited with finding the Paris Codex in the Paris Library in a basket of assorted papers in 1859. The manuscript was first published in 1872. The Paris Codex is incomplete and is in a very frayed condition. Today, the original is in the hands of the Mexican government.

The Madrid Codex

The Madrid Codex is presently located in the Museum of the Americas in Madrid, Spain. The Madrid Codex was found in two separate parts and, as a result, was initially considered to be two separate codices. The first part was referred to as the Cortez Codex, as apparently it was owned by the conqueror, Hernan Cortez. The second part was called the Troanus Codex.

Leon de Rosny published the Cortez Codex in 1892. Brasseur de Bourbourg published the Troanus Codex, named after the person he bought it from, in 1869. The two codices, which form the Madrid Codex when combined, consist of 112 pages, many of which are frayed and almost indistinguishable. The document was originally written by different Maya scribes.

The Grolier Codex

The Grolier Codex is an eleven-page codex that manifests heavy Mixtec influence. The Mixtecs lived in and around the Oaxaca valley.

The Grolier Codex is located in a private-society collection in New York City. The Grolier Codex was first published in 1973 by archaeologist Michael D. Coe.

The Nuttall Codex

The Nuttall Codex is a Mixtec codex. The Mixtec people lived in and around the Oaxaca valley. The original manuscript surfaced in the hands of an Englishman by the name of Lord Zouche. The first copy of the Nuttall Codex was made by Zelia Nuttall in 1902 and, as a result, carries the name of the Codex Nuttall. It was published by the Peabody Museum. In 1975, a complete color reproduction of the facsimile screenfold from the Peabody publication of the codex, in standard book format, was published by Dover. The 1975 edition includes commentary by Arthur G. Miller.

Shortly before his death in 1970, a renowned Mexican archaeologist, Alfonso Caso, translated the Codex Nuttall. The original manuscript includes history and genealogy of the Mixtecs dating from AD 838 to AD 1330.

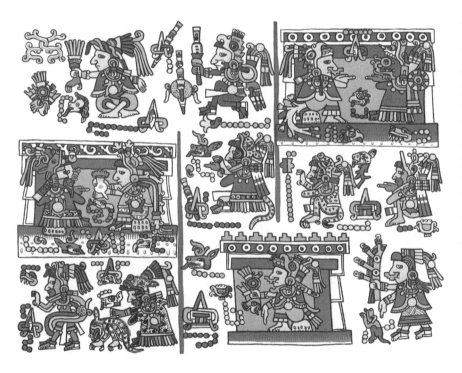

FIGURE 10–1: The Book of Mormon speaks of writing on gold plates. It also speaks of writing on material that could be circulated among the people and that also could be burned. The most common materials used for writing in Mesoamerica were tree bark or animal skins. The colors used by the scribes were elaborate and vibrant. This picture is from page 26 of the Postclassic Nuttall Codex of the Mixtec people of Oaxaca dating to the ninth and tenth centuries AD.

Translation of a page of the Nuttall Codex. The following discussion is a summary from the translation of figure 10-1 by archaeologist Alfonso Caso: This page is read by beginning at the right hand top and moving down and then moving up and then down between the red lines—like a snake. The first picture (upper right) shows a couple who were married in AD 992. The lord on the right is called 6 Crocodile with a surname of Sun of Rain. His wife is called 9 Eagle with a surname of Garland of Cacao Flowers. They had two sons named Bloody Tiger and Water Heron and a daughter named Jade Ornament.

Seated in another palace at the bottom of the page is a second wife of 7 Crocodile called Bluebird Jewel, whom he married in AD 1009, seventeen years after his first marriage. Two sons and one daughter are a result of this second marriage: 8 Dear, 9 Flower, and 9 Monkey. It is the daughter (left top) who is named 9 Monkey. Although she is older than 9 Flower, the fact that she is a girl causes her to be placed last.

The third palace houses 8 Deer, whose surname is Tiger Claw, with Lady Serpent of Flowers. They had two sons (bottom left). Tiger Claw or 8 Deer was considered a great conqueror. He wasn't married until after his fortieth birthday. Observe in the third palace that the wife, Lady Serpent of Flowers, is offering her husband, Tiger Claw, a bowl of chocolate, symbolic of the marriage ceremony. The names of the two sons of Tiger Claw are (count the dots), 4 Dog (tame coyote) and 4 Crocodile (serpent ball of fire).

THE NATIVE DOCUMENTS

Other books, which may or may not have been written originally in the native languages but which were written by the natives after the conquest—either from memory or from the ancient documents—fall into the category of native documents. Foremost among these documents is the *Popol Vuh*. Other native documents include *The Title of the Lords of Totonicapan, The Annals of the Cakchiquels,* and *The Books of Chilam Balam.*

It is indeed curious that from the above list, the first three originated in the highlands of Guatemala and that all three were found within fifty miles of each other. We propose this area to be the ancient land of Nephi where the waters of Mormon, land of Ishmael, and land of Helam were located and, as a result, to be the very area where writing was taught by the former Nephite priests of Noah to the Lamanites in the second century BC: "And he [King Laman] appointed teachers of the brethren of Amulon in every land which was possessed by his people; and thus the language of Nephi began to be taught among all the people of the Lamanites. And they were a people friendly one with another; nevertheless they knew not God. . . . But they taught them that they should keep their record, and that they might write one to another" (Mosiah 24:4–6).

Two things stand out in the above verses: (1) writing began to be circulated in the same area and at the same time as determined by both the Book of Mormon and scientific information and (2) the people were friendly with one another. Those who have traveled through the beautiful Guatemala highlands where over four million native Maya descendants live today probably would be willing to say that the one word that best describes them is "friendly."

> Those who have traveled through the beautiful Guatemala highlands where over four million native Maya descendants live today probably would be willing to say that the one word that best describes them is "friendly."

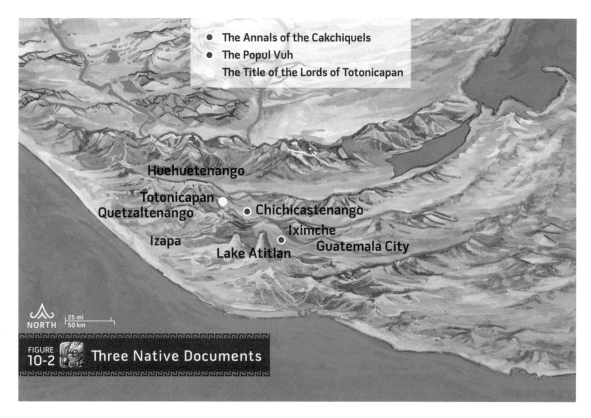

- The Annals of the Cakchiquels
- The Popol Vuh

The Title of the Lords of Totonicapan

Huehuetenango

Totonicapan
Quetzaltenango ○ ● Chichicastenango

Iximche
Izapa ○ Guatemala City
Lake Atitlan

NORTH
25 mi
50 km

FIGURE 10-2 Three Native Documents

FIGURE 10–2: Three major documents were discovered in an area in the highlands of Guatemala within a fifty-mile radius of each other. They are *The Title of the Lords of Totonicapan* from the village of Totonicapan, the *Popol Vuh* from Chichicastenango, and *The Annals of the Cakchiquels* from Iximche.

The Popol Vuh

The *Popol Vuh* is a Mesoamerican document that was written shortly after the Spanish conquest. The document was written by a Quiche native who had learned how to read and write Spanish. It has also been called the *Popol Buj, Book of the Council, Book of the Community,* the *Sacred Book,* or *National Book of the Quiche.*

The Quiche natives live in the country of Guatemala and are a branch of the Maya race. At the time of the Spanish conquest, the Quiche nation was the most powerful and cultured of all those who occupied the region of Central America. In 1524, Pedro de Alvarado, who was sent by Cortez, attacked the Quiche, caused them to surrender, and then burned their capital city, Utatlan. Some of the Quiche nobility moved from Utatlan to the neighboring town of Chichicastenango. The Spaniards named the place Santo Tomas Chichicastenango. Today, the town is a favorite place to visit among foreigners, especially on Sundays and Thursdays, which are the market days.

The *Popol Vuh* was apparently written by one or more of the nobles of the Quiches from oral traditions. It appears to have been written originally in the Quiche tongue through the use of Latin letters. It was discovered by Father Francisco Ximenez in the Santo Tomas Church at Chichicastenango early in the eighteenth century. Father Ximenez transcribed the record and translated it into Spanish. The original may have been returned to the Quiche people.

The *Popol Vuh* contains traditions of the Creation, the Flood, the origin of the Quiche nations, and the chronology of their kings down to the year 1550.

The *Popol Vuh* was first published in English in 1950. It was published from a Spanish version that was published in Spanish in 1947. The English version was published by Delia Goetz and Sylvanus Morley from the translation of Adrian Recinos and contains 158 pages.

In writing a seventy-two-page introduction, Recinos makes the following judgment about the *Popol Vuh:* "This manuscript is, without doubt, the most vigorous, literary, and significant effort achieved by the American Indian in the fields of mythology and history."[2]

Bancroft, in his history on the native races, was a little more conservative as he wrote: "Of all American people, the Quiches of Guatemala have left us the richest mythological legacy. Their description of the Creation as given in the *Popol Vuh*, which may be called the national book of the Quiches, is, in its rude strange eloquence and poetic originality, one of the rarest relics of aboriginal thought."[3]

The above statements deserve some consideration. However, when taken in the context of the overall picture, the *Popol Vuh* is a kindergarten text compared with the Book of Mormon. Nevertheless, as a historical document, it is invaluable.

Both the *Popol Vuh* and the Book of Mormon contain information on dogma, origins, history, and genealogy of the native Americans.

Both the *Popol Vuh* and the Book of Mormon were written originally by American natives and subsequently translated into English and Spanish languages.

However, the *Popol Vuh* contains only 158 pages of work compared to 531

2. Adrian Recinos, in Delia Goetz and Sylvanus G. Morley, trans. Adrian Recinos, *Popol Vuh* (Norman, OK: University of Oklahoma Press, 1950), in 1965 edition, 75.

3. Hubert H. Bancroft, *The Native Races: Myths and Languages* (San Francisco: A. L. Bancroft, 1883), 3:42.

FIGURE 10–3: The 2000 edition of the *Popol Vuh* has parallel columns in both English and Quiche Maya by Dr. Allen J. Christenson of Brigham Young University. Christenson pursued his studies as a doctoral candidate under the late Linda Schele of the University of Texas at Austin.

Exploring the Lands of the Book of Mormon

pages in the Book of Mormon. The *Popol Vuh* reads like a fragmented text. The Book of Mormon, on the other hand, develops a highly sophisticated doctrinal and historical narrative.

On a more positive note, the *Popol Vuh* was written in the same exquisite style of chiasmus as the Book of Mormon (see chapter 2, "And Then It Came to Pass").

Allen J. Christenson of Brigham Young University presented an updated translation of the *Popol Vuh* in the year 2000. He also edited the text into both a free translation and a literal translation, the latter in comparison with the format and style of the native language of the K'iche, or Quiche nation. The Christian accounts of the creation, first parents, and flood are prevalent in the *Popol Vuh*. Christensen makes it clear in his introduction that unlike the document called *The Title of the Lords of Totonicapan,* the *Popol Vuh* did not borrow any words, ideas, or concepts from the Spanish Bible: "The authors of the Popol Vuh apparently had no intention of showing their manuscript to the Spanish authorities. Quite the contrary, the text was kept jealously hidden from outsiders for over a century. It is unlikely that given the otherwise purely aboriginal nature of the Popol Vuh text, there would be any incentive for its authors to include intrusive material derived from Spanish missionaries. The preponderance of evidence thus suggests that the Popol Vuh reflects authentic Precolumbian concepts concerning the creation and the work of the primordial gods of the ancient K'iche'-Maya."**4**

The Title of the Lords of Totonicapan

The Title of the Lords of Totonicapan is a native document that also comes to us from the highlands of Guatemala. The same race of people who are responsible for the *Popol Vuh,* the Quiche (K'iche') natives of Guatemala, wrote *The Title of the Lords of Totonicapan.* It now appears that it was written prior to the year 1524 by the natives of the town of Totonicapan and translated in 1554 into the Quiche language using Latin letters. *The Title of the Lords of Totonicapan* was translated from the Quiche text into Spanish by Dionisio Jose Chonay. The English version was translated by Delia Goetz and was first published by the University of Oklahoma Press in 1953.

With new evidence that has come to light, we may have to change our attitude about the Totonicapan document. It, like the *Popol Vuh,* may indeed reflect a purely native document as opposed to being influenced by the literature in the Bible. This conclusion comes as a result of the work of Elder Ted E. Brewerton, General Authority Emeritus, and Israel Perez, a pure-blood Maya and a member of The Church of Jesus Christ of Latter-day Saints in Guatemala who has served in the area presidency of Guatemala. While serving as a mission president in Costa Rica in 1967, Elder Brewerton located a copy of the original text of *The Title of the Lords of Totonicapan* written in parallel columns in French and Spanish. Although it had been translated in 1834, it was not printed in the Spanish-French edition until 1885.

The *Popol Vuh* was written in the same exquisite style of chiasmus as the Book of Mormon.

4. Allen J. Christenson, trans. and ed., *Popol Vuh: The Mythic Sections, Tales of First Beginnings from the Ancient Ki'che'-Maya* (Provo, UT: Foundation for Ancient Research and Mormon Studies, Brigham Young University, 2000).

As stated above, the Totonicapan document was subsequently translated and printed in English by the University of Oklahoma from copies of the document that were reported as being available only in the museums in Europe. Elder Brewerton acknowledges that he was somewhat surprised to receive a copy of the original Spanish-French version of *The Title of the Lords of Totonicapan,* a copy he had purchased from the Transcom Bookstore in the Virgin Islands.

It appears that a high degree of excitement was generated at the village of Totonicapan when the mayor was apprised that Elder Brewerton had offered to provide them with a notarized copy of their own ancient history. Arrangements were made to hold a meeting at the National Theatre. Those in attendance were the mayor, the governor, the surrounding city mayors, and the public. Along with the notarized text of *The Title of the Lords of Totonicapan,* they were presented copies of the Book of Mormon in Spanish and in Quiche Maya. They were told that the Book of Mormon was a record of their people.[5] In essence, they were presented two native documents as a gift, *The Title of the Lords of Totonicapan* and The Book of Mormon: Another Testament of Jesus Christ.

5. Elder Ted E. Brewerton, conversation with Joseph Allen, October 18, 2003.

We will now take another look at the Totonicapan documents with the intent to show that they, along with the *Popol Vuh,* should be considered as being purely native as opposed to their containing borrowed concepts from the Spanish Bible about the Creation, Flood, Garden of Eden, and other Christian concepts. Elder Brewerton sent us information about some property deeds, or Guatemala land titles, as reported by Elder F. Burton Howard from the same area of Guatemala and dating previous to the Spanish conquest that may well reflect an association with the Totonicapan document and that would negate any biblical influence in the ancient text of *The Title of the Lords of Totonicapan.*

These land titles reported by Elder Howard were photographed by the Church microfilm crews on March 3, 1970. He writes: "The General Archives of Central America, including the initial parish registries and the land records of the Provincial Capital of Santiago de Guatemala, were photographed by LDS Church microfilm crews on March 3, 1970, and thereafter. Microfilm of these ancient records found in the General Archives of Central America as File No. 6062, Document No. 53957 during the 1970 microfilming of Guatemala records tell the story of the recording of one such claim."[6]

6. See F. Burton Howard, "Guatemala Land Titles and the Book of Mormon," unpublished report.

The land title reports that on August 18, 1659, a Spanish official by the name of Pedro de Cordoba presented a fifteen-page deed that was an original title inscription taken from a native chief by the Spanish conquerors in 1524 and written in the native K'iche' (Quiche) dialect. Elder Howard writes that "the law required the Notary to include a brief history of the title, showing the grantor's claim of right to the property. Such legal antecedents often revealed the ownership of land from its original acquisition up to the time of the new record."[7] The following statement then appears in the old land title: "We these principles declared that we claim title to this land because our parents and grandparents came here . . . [and] that we are descendants of Abraham, Isaac and

7. Howard, "Guatemala Land Titles and the Book of Mormon."

Jacob, as they were called, we are of Israel; that our parents and grandparents stayed in Canaan in this land where we are; that Abraham gave our Lord as a God to this people; that we likewise were in Babylon where all of the Indians with great effort made a large edifice, which remained unfinished, and the work did not progress."[8] *Thus, it appears that the original natives of Guatemala leaned upon both the Jaredite and the Lehi migrations to prove their land rights. In other words, God gave them this land.*

A number of other significant parallel accounts relating to the Jaredite and Nephite histories have surfaced in various writings, including the writings of Fernando de Alva de Ixtlilxochitl, Bernardino de Sahagun, and other sixteenth-century Spanish chroniclers.

The point here, however, is twofold: (1) the Book of Mormon does not stand alone as a native document of the Jaredites and Nephites, as the 1524 land title predates the publication of the Book of Mormon by 306 years, and (2) the 1524 land title document verifies the authenticity of *The Title of the Lords of Totonicapan* as a native document, as the document predates any known Spanish Catholic writings on the subject by thirty-three years. We are of the opinion that Father Domingo de Vico, who wrote about religious traditions of the Quiche people from the highlands of Guatemala in a Christian tract in 1553 and inserted some biblical traditions, wanted to show the parallel accounts between the two.[9]

To attempt to explain borrowing from the biblical text as a primary source for the ancient Quiche (Totonicapan) document is paramount to suggesting that the Jaredite record, as outlined in the Book of Mormon, was borrowed from the Bible. The Bible does not record anything about the Jaredites. The document of Totonicapan is about seventy-five pages in length and apparently was written without any Spanish (biblical) influence.

A significantly poignant historical event occurred when the Spanish conquerors confiscated the lands of the natives of Guatemala. At that point, many previous landowners went to the Spanish/Catholic priests seeking redress for their stolen lands. The priests, to their credit, sought compensation from the king of Spain. The authorization came from Spain, indicating that the lands could be returned to their original owners, providing they had documents to prove such was the case. The primary document that proved ownership was none other than the Totonicapan document, which indicated they were descendants of Abraham, Isaac, and Jacob, with the strong declaration: *God gave us this land.* This wording is reminiscent of the words of Lehi:

> But, said he, notwithstanding our afflictions, we have obtained a land of promise, a land which is choice above all other lands; a land which the Lord God hath covenanted with me should be a land for the inheritance of my seed. Yea, *the Lord hath covenanted this land unto me, and to my children forever,* and also all those who should be led out of other countries by the hand of the Lord.

8. Howard, "Guatemala Land Titles and the Book of Mormon"; see also *El Titulo de Totonicapan* (Mexico: Universidad Nacional Autonoma de Mexico, 1983).

9. Mark L. Grover, "El Titulo de Totonicapan," in A. Dean Larsen, ed., *A Gallimaufry of Acquisitions* (Provo, UT: Friends of the Brigham Young University Library, 1991).

The original natives of Guatemala leaned upon both the Jaredite and the Lehi migrations to prove their land rights. In other words, God gave them this land.

Wherefore, I, Lehi, prophesy according to the workings of the Spirit which is in me, that there shall none come into this land save they shall be brought by the hand of the Lord. (2 Nephi 1:5–6; emphasis added)

FIGURE 10–4: The highlands of Guatemala are among the most beautiful in the whole world. Maya natives grow corn, beans, squash, and barley on these mountain tops; the rains fall from May to November; and the climate is mild year round. The natives wrote in their documents that "God gave us this land." (Photo courtesy of Merrill C. Oaks)

The Annals of the Cakchiquels.

The Annals of the Cakchiquels is a document that was written by the Cakchiquel natives of Guatemala. The Cakchiquels are literally neighbors of the Quiche people who are associated with the *Popol Vuh*. *The Annals of the Cakchiquels* has also been referred to as the "Memoirs of Solola." The town and province (department) of Solola are the location of the beautiful Lake Atitlan. Lake Atitlan has been proposed to be the waters of Mormon in Book of Mormon geography. Although *The Annals of the Cakchiquels* contains some statements regarding their origin, the greatest value is that the document presents the native story of the Spanish conquest.

Brasseur de Bourbourg translated the Cakchiquel document into French around 1855. This translation was subsequently used for the Spanish translation. An American scholar, Dr. Daniel G. Brinton, acquired the original document in the Cakchiquel language along with de Bourbourg's translation. Brinton translated the works into English in 1885. He gave the originals to the library of the Museum of the University of Pennsylvania, where the document is today.[10]

Ted E. Brewerton also did some work with the Cakchiquel document. He reports: "We had the Cakchiquel text written in English and Spanish plus we discovered and

10. Information taken from Adrian Recinos and Delia Goetz, *The Annals of the Cakchiquels*, trans. from the Cakchiquel Maya (Norman, OK: University of Oklahoma Press, 1953).

microfilmed, in the western mountains of Guatemala, the original Cakchiquel text, which had been written in the Cakchiquel language after about the year 1560. We printed, after cleaning it up, the 89 pages and presented it to the leaders of the nation along with the Book of Mormon in Cakchiquel."

The Books of Chilam Balam. The early Spanish missionaries who arrived in the Yucatan in the sixteenth century learned the Maya language so they could teach Christianity to the natives. Further, the missionaries developed an alphabet based on the Latin alphabet.

Children of the leading Maya families were instructed and trained to become priests in a quasi-boarding-school arrangement. By the latter part of the century, these native priests, who had mastered the Spanish and Latin languages and yet retained their original tongue, attempted to record their ancient histories. Some of the documents were even written in a distorted type of ancient Maya hieroglyphic form.

These manuscripts have often been called *The Books of Chilam Balam,* named after a Maya prophet/priest named (Chilam) Balam, who lived during the Spanish conquest.[11]

THE SPANISH CHRONICLES

A third type of literature to surface about the ancient history and traditions of Mesoamerica includes the abundant amount of material written by the Spanish chroniclers. For the most part, the chroniclers consisted of the Catholic clergy who were either from Spain or who were of Spanish descent.

Some of the most famous of the sixteenth-century writers were Fernando de Alva Ixtlilxochitl, Bernardino de Sahagun, Diego de Landa, Juan de Torquemada, Diego Duran, San Bartolome de las Casas, and Bernal Diaz de Castillo. Chapters 11, 12, and 13 discuss the works of Ixtlilxochitl, Sahagun, and Landa in some detail. Castillo was a soldier in the army of Cortez. Diego Duran was a Basque from Spain. He arrived in New Spain (Mexico) as a Jew and then converted to Catholicism. His two texts show that his Spanish was clear enough but was not as elegant as that of Sahagun.

European historians, or Spanish chroniclers consisting primarily of friars or priests, migrated to the New World in the fifteenth and sixteenth centuries as ambassadors of Christianity. Most of the texts attributed to the Spanish chroniclers were written in sixteenth-century Spanish. Interestingly, as a reflection of his interest in the validity of the writings of the Spanish Chroniclers, Elder Ted E. Brewerton, formerly of the First Quorum of the Seventy and presently Emeritus General Authority of The Church of Jesus Christ of Latter-day Saints, has accumulated in his personal library many of the writings of the Spanish chroniclers.[12]

Joseph Allen writes, "I spent a considerable amount of time reading the writings of the sixteenth-century Spanish chroniclers in both Spanish and English in preparation for writing my doctoral dissertation, which was published in 1970. Twenty-four years later, my wife and I were called to serve a mission in northern Spain. Part of the mission

11. Information taken from Yurii Knorozov, *Maya Hieroglyphic Codices* (Albany, NY: Institute for Mesoamerican Studies, State University of New York at Albany, 1982).

12. Elder Brewerton lists the following native documents and Spanish chroniclers' texts among those listed in his "Recorders of Preconquest Ancient American History: Texts of Elder Ted E. Brewerton": *Popol Vuh* (1550); *Title of the Lords of Totonicapan* (1554); *Annals of the Cakchiquels* (1550s–1560s); Fernando de Alva Ixtlilxochitl (born 1578); Pedro Valasco Sulk'et (1592); *Codice Chimalpopoca, Anales de Cuauhtitlan 1570 y Leyenda de los Soles 1558; Annals of Cuauhtitlan* (1570); *Legend of the Suns* (1558); *Topiltzin Quetzalcoatl* (AD 843–895); *El Libro de los Libros de Chilam Balam* (1500s); *Recordacion Florida—Fuentes y Guzman* (born 1643); Bartolome de las Casas (born 1474); Toribio de Benavente o Motolinia (born 1482–1491); Bernal Diaz del Castillo (born 1492); Bernardino de Sahagun (born 1499); Diego de Landa (born 1524); Geronimo de Mendieta (born 1528); Diego Duran (born 1537); Juan de Torquemada (born 1557); Francisco L. de Gomara (born 1511); Lorenzo Boturini B. (born 1702); Mariano F. Veytia (born 1718); Hernan Cortes (born 1485); Friar Juan de Grijalva (born 1580); and *Coleccion de Documentos para la Historia de Mexico* (1857–1866).

boundaries included the hometowns of some of the Basque priests who had migrated to Mexico (New Spain) shortly after the Spanish conquest of Mexico in 1521. To pass through the villages in Spain where Sahagun, Torquemada, Duran, and Landa first lived was a pleasant experience for us."

Fernando de Alva Ixtlilxochitl (1578–1650). Ixtlilxochitl was born of both Spanish and Mexican royalty. He grew up in the native environment of Texcoco near Mexico City.

He wrote his works during the latter part of the sixteenth and the early part of the seventeenth centuries. He affirms that his source material consisted of the native painted records of the Mexicans. The first chapter of the works of Ixtlilxochitl occupies all of chapter 11, "Fernando de Alva Ixtlilxochitl," as written in Spanish by Chavero and translated into English by Joseph Allen.

Bernardino de Sahagun (1499–91). Sahagun also wrote during the sixteenth century. He spent a large part of his adult life in and around Mexico City. He utilized the services of his trilingual students to extract the oral history and traditions from the communities in the Mexico valley. Some of Sahagun's writings are included in chapter 12, "Bernardino de Sahagun"; the entire chapter is dedicated to him.

Diego de Landa (1524–79). Diego de Landa served the Catholic Church in the Yucatan, where he gained the information for his writings on the Maya people. He recorded their customs and was a part of the latter sixteenth-century movement to recreate the Maya alphabet. Some of Landa's works are included in chapter 13, "Diego de Landa." Speaking of Landa, Frans Blom, in his landmark historical account, *The Conquest of Yucatan,* says, "It is a strange turn of fate that he, Diego de Landa, who destroyed the greatest amount of the Maya books, and who had thousands of clay and stone images of Maya gods smashed and burned, became the one person who in his writings left us the most detailed and accurate information about the remarkable Maya people."[13]

Juan de Torquemada (1557–1664). Torquemada wrote a history of Mexico called *Monarquia Indiana.* He recorded the legends of the origins and migrations of the Mexican people. He also wrote about some of the legends of the white god, Quetzalcoatl. Chapter 14, "The White God Quetzalcoatl," analyzes the legends associated with Quetzalcoatl.

Diego Duran (1537–88). Duran was convinced that the native Mexicans were part of the lost tribes of Israel, as he observed many similarities between the religious customs of the Mexicans and the religious customs outlined in the Old Testament. A priest of Spanish descent, Duran spent most of his life in the Mexican states of Mexico, Puebla, and Morelos. His writings on the history, gods, and calendar rites remained in oblivion for many years. His contributions on the customs of the people of ancient Mexico, however, now classify him as one of the elite Spanish chroniclers of the sixteenth century.

San Bartolome de las Casas (1474–1566). Casas is considered to be the great champion of native rights. He was the first priest to be ordained in the Americas, being ordained in 1512 in Puerto Rico. He first set foot on Guatemalan soil in 1537. Casas published works extolling the virtues of the natives and proposing that conversion ought to be brought about by love instead of fear. The idea that the natives were mere animals was dispelled in the many excellent works of Casas.

Bernal Diaz del Castillo (1492–1584). A soldier in the army of Cortez, Bernal Diaz retired to Guatemala City, where he wrote his most informative book entitled *The Discovery and Conquest of New Spain*. This 478-page book is a classic, as it provides a firsthand Spanish account of the conquest of Mexico (1519–21). Reflecting on his feelings as he and the army of Cortez first saw the Aztec city of Tenochtitlan (Mexico City), Diaz wrote: "Gazing on such wonderful sights, we did not know what to say, or whether what appeared before us was real, for on the one side, on the land, there were great cities, and in the lake ever so many more, and the lake itself was crowded with canoes, and in the Causeway were many bridges at intervals, and in front of us stood the great City of Mexico."[14]

CUSTOMS OF THE PEOPLE

In addition to the native documents and the writings of the Catholic fathers and other Spanish writers, the customs of the natives who live in the high mountains of Guatemala and Chiapas or in the villages of the Yucatan are fascinating to observe.

Many of the customs that visitors still see today have changed very little from the customs as described by the sixteenth-century chroniclers. If customs are still

14. Bernal Diaz, *The Discovery and Conquest of Mexico, 1517–1521*, edited from the only exact copy of the original manuscript by Genaro Garcia; trans. A. P. Maudslay (New York: Noonday Press, 1972), 192.

FIGURE 10–5: The old customs, including types of food, manner of dress, and religious customs, still prevail among the native Maya of Guatemala and Chiapas. Shown here are native people dressed according to the style of the community of San Antonio, which is located on the borders of Lake Atitlan. (Photos courtesy of Merrill C. Oaks)

identifiable after 470 years, in spite of the massive changes in society that have taken place, then we can assume that, for the thousand to fifteen hundred years previous to the conquest, a relatively high degree of constancy remained. In that respect, in 1936, in introducing his chapter about the Maya titled "Daily Life," Frans Blom proceeds to look at how a "day passed for a Maya family at the time of the conquest, just as it had passed thousands of years earlier, and just as it passes today, four hundred years later."[15] Apparently, the old adage is true that the more things change, the more they remain the same.

15. Blom, *The Conquest of Yucatan*, 116.

SUMMARY

The purpose of this chapter has been to outline some of the historical traditions that have survived the centuries. These traditions include some of the writings of Ixtlilxochitl as well as a summary of some of the writings of Sahagun and Landa. Comments are made about the white god Quetzalcoatl. A brief summary is presented on the native documents of Mesoamerica. Finally, we took a look at some of the cultural patterns that may have been in existence during the time period of the Book of Mormon.

Exploring the Lands of the Book of Mormon

THE FATE OF ANCIENT MESOAMERICAN CODICES

In 1633, Bernardo de Lizana wrote: "[Bishop Diego de Landa] collected the books and the ancient writing and he commanded them burned.... They burned many historical books of the ancient Yucatan which told of its beginning and history, which were of much value if, in our writing, they had been translated because today there would be something original" (Lizana, *Historia de Yucatan,* part 2, 6:5; cited by Tozzer, *Landa's Relacion de las Cosas de Yucatan,* 78). In 1688, Diego Lopez Cogolludo wrote of the same incident: "With the suspicion of ... idolatry, they collected all the books and ancient writings which the Indians had and ... burned [them] publicly on the day of the auto and at the same time with these [were destroyed] the history of their antiquities" (Cogolludo, *Historia de Yucatan,* 1:6; cited by Tozzer, *Landa's Relacion de las Cosas de Yucatan,* 78).

Both Lizana and Cogolludo were writing about the Catholic Church's Inquisition in Mani (in the Yucatan) that ended with a ceremony called an auto de fe. During the July 12, 1562, ceremony, Bishop Diego de Landa burned a disputed number of Maya codices.

Mass destruction of the Maya codices that were extant in the sixteenth century occurred as a result of the Catholic Church's attempts to completely Christianize the Maya natives. In spite of extensive efforts to convert the Maya, the natives commonly reverted to preconquest worshiping activities—much to the dismay of the Catholic friars. Viewing the codices as one avenue of superstitions and lies of the devil, the friars systematically destroyed the books.

In 1590, in speaking about outcomes of the Spanish Inquisition and the Catholic thinking that Mesoamerican codices were inspired by Satan, Jose de Acosta said:

In the province of Yucatan ... there used to exist some books of leaves, bound or folded after a fashion, in which the learned [Maya] kept the distribution of their times. ... It appeared to a teacher of doctrine [Landa] that all this must be to make witchcraft and magic art; he contended that they should be burned and those books were burned.... The same has happened in other cases where our people, *thinking that all is superstition,* have lost many memories of ancient and hidden things which they might have used to no little advantage. This follows from a *stupid zeal,* when without knowing or even wishing to know the things of the [Yucatan], they say as in the sealed package, that *everything is sorcery* and that the peoples there are only a drunken lot and what can they know or understand. (Acosta, cited by Tozzer, *Landa's Relacion de las Cosas de Yucatan,* 78; emphasis added)

Thus, "flames devoured the precious Maya books," and "those flames of the auto da fe at Mani destroyed the cornerstone of the Maya civilization, reduced to ashes the scientific backbone of a highly civilized people and sounded the death-knell of independent Maya thought" (Blom, *The Conquest of Yucatan, 109*).

CHAPTER 11

Fernando de Alva Ixtlilxochitl
(ca. 1578–ca. 1650)

Of a truth I have the ancient histories in my hand, and I know the language of the natives, because I was raised with them, and I know all the old men and the principals of this land. . . . It has cost me hard study and work, always seeking the truth on everything I have written. (Ixtlilxochitl, 1600)

ᒷᒷᒷᒷᒷᒷᒷᒷᒷᒷᒷᒷᒷᒷᒷᒷᒷᒷᒷᒷᒷᒷᒷᒷᒷᒷᒷᒷᒷᒷᒷᒷᒷᒷ

The above statement was recorded about AD 1600 by a native-born scholar of Mexico named Fernando de Alva Ixtlilxochitl. He is considered by many to be the most prolific early writer on the history of Mexico. In a sense, he may be considered to be the Josephus of Mexico.

One biographer, Dr. Jose Maria Beristain y Souza, said that Ixtlilxochitl was one of the most distinguished students at the Colegio de Santa Cruz de Tlatelolco and that he was the most knowledgeable in the language, history, and antiquities of his people.[1] The author Clavijero called Ixtlilxochitl "the truly noble Indian concerning the antiquities of his nation."[2]

1. Jose Toribio Medina, *Biblioteca Hispano-Americana*, 1493–1810 microform (Santiago de Chile: J. T. Medina, 1898–1907), quoted in Alfredo Chavero, *Obras Historicas de Don Fernando de Alva Ixtlilxochitl*, Tomo I (Mexico, DF: Editora Nacional, 1965).

2. Francesco Saverio Clavijero, *Historia Antigua de Mexico* (Mexico, DF: Editorial Porrua, 1964), 37.

OPPOSITE: Fernando de Alva Ixtlilxochitl published his works approximately AD 1600. He wrote that the first settlers came from the great tower and that they landed on the Pacific side and eventually settled in the region of Veracruz. They were a large people—a description that is verified in the Book of Mormon and that is illustrated by the large sculptured Olmec head shown here. (Photo courtesy of Sheryl Lee Wilson)

Dr. Lara Pardo called Ixtlilxochitl a man of great talent and deep intellect and said that Ixtlilxochitl possessed a most excellent library containing the paintings and hiero-glyphic history of preconquest Mexico.[3]

3. Leduc-Lara Pardo, *Diccionario de Geografia e Historia y Biografias Mexicanas,* p. 492, as quoted in Chavero, *Obras Historicas de Don Fernando de Alva Ixtlilxochitl,* 1965.

Early writers placed the birth date of Alva Ixtlilxochitl somewhere near the year AD 1568. Edmundo O'Gorman, who published the writings of Ixtlilxochitl in 1975, with an update in 1985, determined that the date of Ixtlilxochitl's birth was in the year AD 1578. The place of birth was Texcoco, which is now a suburb of Mexico City.[4]

Ixtlilxochitl was born of royalty, being a descendant of both the last king of Texcoco and the next-to-the-last emperor of Mexico, Cuitlahuac. Ixtlilxochitl was also of Spanish descent, as his grandfather on his mother's side was the Spaniard Juan Grande.

4. Edmundo O'Gorman, *Fernando de Alva Ixtlilxochitl: Obras Historicas,* Tomo I Edicion, estudio introductoio y un apendice documental por Edmundo O'Gorman (Mexico, DF: Universidad Nacional Autonoma de Mexico, 1985), 17.

The writings on the history of Mexico, according to Ixtlilxochitl, consisted of many manuscripts that were first circulated in the year AD 1600. His works, *Sumaria Relacion de la Historia General,* were completed about AD 1625—more than two hundred years prior to the publication of the Book of Mormon. Traditionally, the date of the death of Ixtlilxochitl has been placed around 1648. O'Gorman's research indicates that Ixtlilxochitl died in 1650 at the age of seventy-two.[5]

5. O'Gorman, *Fernando de Alva Ixtlilxochitl,* 36.

We would have a goldmine of historical information if today we had access to the sources Ixtlilxochitl used in writing his history of Mexico. Perhaps at some point those histories will be discovered as archival holdings in Mexico or Spain. The best we can do for now is to conjecture about their content in support of the Book of Mormon, although such conjecturing has considerable substance because of Ixtlilxochitl's writings based on the ancient histories—a spiritual feast you are about to experience. Regarding the sources for his history of Mexico, Ixtlilxochitl's words at the beginning of this chapter are worth repeating: "Of a truth I have the ancient histories in my hand, and I know the language of the natives, because I was raised with them, and I know all of the old men and the principals of this land. . . . It has cost me hard study and work, always seeking the truth on everything I have written."[6]

6. Chavero, *Obras Historicas de Don Fernando de Alva Ixtlilxochitl,* 62.

Alfredo Chavero, a Mexican historian, wrote in the preface of his two volumes about Ixtlilxochitl as follows: "Ixtlilxochitl is the original chronista of the texcucanos [from Texcoco, a suburb of Mexico]. Few of our writers have enjoyed the fame and reputation that he has. Nevertheless, his numerous works are unknown."[7]

7. Chavero, *Obras Historicas de Don Fernando de Alva Ixtlilxochitl,* 5.

And that is certainly an understatement. To this very day, the works of Ixtlilxochitl are hardly known in the United States. Even Latter-day Saint writers who have a high interest in the history of the Book of Mormon have basically ignored the works of Alva Ixtlilxochitl.

We suspect that part of the reason for Latter-day Saints' lack of knowledge about Ixtlilxochitl is that his works have not been readily available in the English language. Milton R. Hunter and Thomas S. Ferguson, in their 1950 book, *Ancient America and the Book of Mormon,* did, however, publish segments of Ixtlilxochitl's works in English—segments that appeared to them to correlate with the Book of Mormon history.

Wells Jakeman and Thomas Ferguson acquired the services of a man named Arnulfo Rodriguez to translate segments of the 1892 publication of Alfredo Chavero.[8]

8. Milton R. Hunter and Thomas Stuart Ferguson, *Ancient America and the Book of Mormon* (Oakland, CA: Kolob Book Company, 1950), 14.

Although Ixtlilxochitl wrote in the 1600s, his work was not circulated widely until Lord Kingsborough of England published nine volumes of work entitled *Antiquities of Mexico.* Kingsborough included the writings of Ixtlilxochitl in Spanish, having obtained those writings from the National Library of Madrid.

Kingsborough's material on Ixtlilxochitl is similar to that of an early Mexican writer by the name of Boturini, who said that he copied his account of the writings of Alva from the handwriting of Alva Ixtlilxochitl. Lord Kingsborough's works were published between 1832–48, but because of the extensive cost, his *Antiquities of Mexico* was never widely circulated.

Under the mandate of Mexican president Porfirio Diaz, Alfredo Chavero edited and footnoted a compilation of Ixtlilxochitl by Jose Fernando Ramirez. This edition was published in 1892 to commemorate the four hundredth anniversary of the discovery of the New World by Columbus.

This same edition, consisting of two volumes of approximately five hundred pages each, was republished in 1965 with a preface by Lic. J. Ignacion Davila Garibi. Chavero called the books *Obras Historicas de Don Fernando de Alva Ixtlilxochitl.* The works of Ixtlilxochitl have been published as various editions in Spanish as follows:

Primera edicion: Kingsborough, *Antiquities of Mexico,* vol. 9, London, 1848

Segunda edicion: Chavero, *Secretaria de Fomento,* Mexico, 1891–92

Reediciones de la anterior: *Editora Nacional*, Mexico, 1952 y 1965

Tercera edicion: O'Gorman, *Instituto de Investigaciones Historicas,* Universidad Nacional Autonoma de Mexico, 1975

Cuarta edicion: O'Gorman, *Instituto de Investigaciones Historicas,* Universidad Nacional Autonoma de Mexico, 1985.

It is from Chavero's 1965 edition that we have translated into English the first section of Ixtlilxochitl's works called "The Summary Account" (*Sumaria Relacion*).

Ramirez and Chavero divided the works of Ixtlilxochitl into two main parts: (1) "Diverse Accounts" and (2) "The History of the Chichimeca."

The latter receives the most attention, as Ixtlilxochitl was a descendant of the Chichimeca people; and, as a result, he follows the Chichimeca trail right up through the conquest of Mexico.

The first part, "Diverse Accounts," deals with the origin of the first settlers, called Quinametzin, or giants. They came from the great tower. The first part also discusses a group of people called the Tulteca. They were wise men who worshiped a god they called Quetzalcoatl. A great dispersion among the Tultecas took place in the fourth century AD.

The "Diverse Accounts" section is the material that attracts the interest of students of the Book of Mormon, as a common trail appears in both accounts. Ixtlilxochitl called

We would have a goldmine of historical information if today we had access to the sources Ixtlilxochitl used in writing his history of Mexico. Perhaps at some point those histories will be discovered as archival holdings in Mexico or Spain.

this section *"Sumaria Relacion de todas las cosas que han sucedido en La Nueva Espana y de muchas cosas que los Toltecas alcanzaron."*

That's rather a long title patterned after the manner of the native Mexicans. It means "A summary account of all the things that happened in New Spain and many things that the Toltecs accomplished."

Chapter 1 ("Primera Relacion") of Chavero's works is only eleven pages, and that portion is what we have included in its entirety in this chapter of *Exploring the Lands of the Book of Mormon.* It covers the history of Mexico from the time of the great tower to about AD 439.

Chapter 2 ("Segunda Relacion") provides information about historical events that took place from AD 466 to AD 543. It also provides summary statements of the early history, typical of the way that Ixtlilxochitl wrote. For example, he writes, "The Tultecas were the third settlers of this land, counting the giants as the first, and the Ulmecas and Xicalancas as the second."[9]

9. Chavero, *Obras Historicas de Don Fernando de Alva Ixtlilxochitl,* 28.

Chapter 3 of Chavero consists of seven pages and covers the time period from AD 556 to AD 826.

Chapter 4 provides only one date, AD 880, but the chapter provides a summary of the nature and characteristics of the Tultecas. "The Tultecas were great architects, carpenters, and workers of arts such as pottery: They mined and smelted gold and silver, and worked precious stones."[10]

10. Chavero, *Obras Historicas de Don Fernando de Alva Ixtlilxochitl,* 40.

Chapter 5 (or "Quinta Relacion") is about thirty pages and provides information about the Tultecas up to the year AD 958. With the exception of a summary section at the end of volume one, the rest of the works of Ixtlilxochitl deal with the history of Mexico from AD 1000 to AD 1600. The majority of the history is centered in the sixteenth century.

Don Fernando de Alva Ixtlilxochitl indeed makes a significant contribution to our understanding of the preconquest civilizations of Mexico. His writings have been criticized, however, because they contain much repetition and because his chronology and dating often lack consistency. One writer says, "It would have been better if Alva Ixtlilxochitl had written less, and paid more detail and attention to the chronology."[11]

11. Garcia Icazbalceta, *Bibliography de Autores Mexicanos,* vol. 8, 271, as contained in Chavero, *Obras Historicas de Don Fernando de Alva Ixtlilxochitl,* in the "Prologo."

We could perhaps defend Ixtlilxochitl by noting that he was writing down only what he read in the different native records he was translating.

Some common elements with Ixtlilxochitl's writings and the Book of Mormon are the following:

1. They both speak of the first civilization coming from the great tower at the time of the confusion of tongues.

2. They both speak of a white god who was born of a virgin and who ascended to heaven after teaching his people.

3. They both record the date of a great destruction occurring in the first month of the thirty-fourth year—or at the death of Christ.

4. They both use the same terminology in describing the manner in which cities were named.

5. They both speak of three distinct civilizations that predate the coming of Christ.

6. They both record the destruction of the first civilization in the northern lands—or the land northward—that predates the coming of Christ.

7. They both speak of a nation whose principal area meant "land of abundance"—or "bountiful."

We give you below the translation by Joseph L. Allen of the words of Ixtlilxochitl in numbered "verses." We are confident that the translation is valid, and we invite you to join us in feeling the power of Ixtlilxochitl's words in uniquely supporting the words of the Book of Mormon.

INTRODUCTION

The Historical Works of Fernando de Alva Ixtlilxochitl. Edited and annotated by Alfredo Chavero and published as a second edition of the works of Jose Fernando Ramirez in 1892. The third edition was published in 1965 with a preface by Lic. J. Ignacio Davila Garibi. This treatise consists of volume 1, chapter 1, of Chavero, translated into English and arranged into verses by Joseph L. Allen. Notes and commentary with maps and pictures are also added by Allen.

SUMMARY ACCOUNT

1. A history of the events in New Spain including many things regarding the knowledge and accomplishments of the Tultecas from the creation of the world to its destruction, and up to the arrival of the third inhabitants called Chichimecas, and on up to the arrival of the Spanish, taken from the original history of New Spain.[12]

First Account

2. The creation of the world and things pertaining thereto, including the origin of man. The omniscience of God and what He has revealed to the Tultecas.

3. The Tultecas had a knowledge of the creation of the world by Tloque Nahuaque, including the planets, mountains, animals, and so forth. They also knew about how God created a man and a woman from whence all mankind descended and multiplied. They recorded many other events that are not included in this account, inasmuch as the same events are recorded by other nations in the world.[13]

4. The records indicate that the world was created in the year Ce Tecpatl, and the period of time from the creation to the flood is called Atonatiuh, which means the age of the sun of water because the world was destroyed by the flood. And it is recorded in the Tulteca history that this period or first world, as they called it, lasted for 1,716 years, after which time great lightning and storms from the heavens destroyed mankind, and

12. Following the conquest in AD 1521, Mexico was called New Spain. The name was entirely abandoned in the early part of the nineteenth century when Mexico gained her independence from Spain. New Spain also extended into Central America; and, as a result, portions of the history of Ixtlilxochitl may encompass all of Mesoamerica. The setting for his history, however, is the valley of Mexico. Ixtlilxochitl wrote that all of the natives of this land descended from two lineages, the Tultecas and the Chichimecas (Chavero, *Obras Historicas de Don Fernando de Alva Ixtlilxochitl*, 457).

13. Moroni wrote, "And as I suppose that the first part of this record, which speaks concerning the creation of the world, and also of Adam, and an account from that time even to the great tower, and whatsoever things transpired among the children of men until that time, is had among the Jews—Therefore I do not write those things which transpired from the days of Adam until that time" (Ether 1:3–4).

14. Genesis states that "fifteen cubits upward did the waters prevail; and the mountains were covered" (Genesis 7:20). Whether Ixtlilxochitl was quoting from the native records or was influenced by the biblical account is difficult to determine.

15. Aztec or Nahuatl words such as *Caxtolmolictli, Atonatiuh, Toptlipetlacalli,* and *Zacualli* are used extensively by Ixtlilxochitl. The word is normally followed by the interpretation or meaning of the word.

As time elapsed, their language became confounded, such that they did not understand one another; and they were scattered to all parts of the world.

everything in the earth was covered by water including the highest mountain called Caxtolmolictli, which is 15 cubits high.[14]

5. To this they recorded other events, such as how, after the flood, a few people who had escaped the destruction inside a Toptlipetlacalli, which interpreted means an enclosed ark, began again to multiply upon the earth.

6. After the earth began again to be populated, they built a Zacualli very high and strong, which means the very high tower, to protect themselves against a second destruction of the world.[15]

7. As time elapsed, their language became confounded, such that they did not understand one another; and they were scattered to all parts of the world.

8. The Tultecas, consisting of seven men and their wives, were able to understand one another, and they came to this land, having first crossed many lands and waters, living in caves and passing through great tribulations. Upon their arrival here, they discovered that it was a very good and fertile land.[16]

9. It has been reported that they wandered for 104 years in different parts of the land until they settled in Huehue Tlapallan, their homeland.[17] This was in the year Ce Tecpatl and 520 years had elapsed since the flood, which represent five periods of time.[18]

10. And 1,715 years after the flood, the people were destroyed by a very great hurricane that carried away trees, rocks, houses, and large buildings.[19] Many men and women escaped the storm by hiding in caves and other places where the great hurricane could not reach them.

11. After a short period of time, they left the caves to see how much damage had taken place in the land. They discovered that it was populated and covered with monkeys that had been driven by the winds, as they had been in darkness all this time without being able to see the sun or the moon.

16. It appears here that Ixtlilxochitl confuses the record-keeping Tultecas with the first civilization, whom he consistently calls Quinametzin or giants (see verses 16, 25, 32, and 37). The Quinametzin are probably the same people as the Jaredites in the Book of Mormon: "Which Jared came forth . . . from the great tower. . . . [And] the language of Jared . . . and his brother were not confounded. . . . And they

did land upon the shore of the promised land" (Ether 1:33, 35; 6:12).

17. Huehue Tlapallan is apparently the same place as Hueyapan, which is located in the Tuxtla Mountains of Veracruz, Mexico. Today, Huehue Tlapallan is the ancient Olmec site of Tres Zapotes, near the town of Santiago Tuxtla, Veracruz. Excavation on the site began in 1939 under the direction of Dr. Matthew

Stirling. The site dates to the Jaredite time period.

18. A period of time refers to the fifty-two-year calendar cycle. In this case, however, Ixtlilxochitl apparently is calling two calendar cycles a period of time. Hence, five periods of time equal 520 years. The 104 years that they wandered represents one period of time—or two fifty-two-year calendar cycles.

19. Today, hurricane winds are common to the coast of Veracruz, Mexico. They are called *nortes* or *northers.* The great hurricane destruction referred to by Ixtlilxochitl correlates to 1399 BC and may be the same destruction referred to in the days of Shiblom in the book of Ether: "There was a great destruction, such an one as never had been known upon the face of the earth" (Ether 11:7).

Exploring the Lands of the Book of Mormon

12. From this event, the saying came about that men had turned into monkeys. This period became known as the second period, or the second world, called Ehecatonatiuh, which means sun of wind. After the destruction, men began again to rebuild and to multiply upon the face of the land.

13. In the year 8 Tochtli,[20] which was 1,347 years after the second calamity and 4,779 years since the creation of the world, it is recorded in their history that the sun stood still one natural day without moving, and a myth evolved wherein a mosquito saw the sun suspended in the air in a pensive mood and said, "Lord of the world, why are you standing still and why are you in such deep thought? Why are you not doing the work you are supposed to do? Do you want to destroy the world as before?" And the mosquito said many other things to the sun, but the sun still did not move. The mosquito then stung the sun on the leg, and seeing that his leg had been stung, the sun began again to move along its course as before.

14. It had been 158 years since the great hurricane and 4,964 years since the creation of the world, when there occurred another destruction in this land.[21] The people who lived in this corner of the land, which they now call New Spain, were giants called Quinametzin. The destruction consisted of a great earthquake that swallowed up and killed the people when the high volcanic mountains erupted. All the people were destroyed and no one escaped; or if anyone did escape, it was those who were in the internal parts of the land. Many Tultecas, along with the Chichimecas, who were their neighbors, were killed. This was in the year Tecpatl, and they called this time period Tlacchitonatiuh, which means sun of the earth.

15. In the year Ce Tecpatl, which was 5,097 years since the creation of the world and 104 years after the total destruction of the giant Quinametzin, all of the land of this new age being at peace, a council was held of the leading scientific, astrological, and artistic scholars of the Tultecas in their capital city called Huehuetlapallan. Here they discussed many things, including the destruction and the calamities that had taken place, as well as the movements of the heavens since the creation of the world. They also discussed many other things; but because of the burning of the records, we do not know or understand any more than what is written here. Among other things, they added the leap year to the calendar to adjust it with the solar equinox; and they discussed many other interesting things as will be observed from their records and laws regarding the years, months, weeks, days, signs, and planets. These, along with other interesting things, were understood by them.

16. It had been 166 years since they had adjusted their calendar with the equinox and 270 years since the giants had been destroyed when the sun and the moon eclipsed and the earth quaked and rocks were broken into pieces and many other signs that had been given came to pass, although man was not destroyed. This was in the year Ce Calli, which, adjusted to our calendar, happened at the same time that Christ, our Lord, was crucified. And they say that this destruction occurred in the first few days of the year.[22]

20. Any time a number is in front of a name such as 8 Tochtli, the number refers to the day and the month and is correlated with a year. The date on which the sun stood still corresponds with 52 BC in the dates given by Ixtlilxochitl.

21. This destruction appears to be the same referred to in verse 16, which dates to the exact time the destruction occurred at the death of Christ (see 3 Nephi 8:5). The dating here, however, is inconsistent.

22. The Book of Mormon records the same date for the great destruction at the time of the crucifixion of Christ: "And it came to pass in the thirty and fourth year, in the first month, on the fourth day of the month, there arose a great storm, such an one as never had been known in all the land" (3 Nephi 8:5).

17. These, and many other things, from the creation of the world up to our time, were understood by the Tultecas. As I have heretofore stated, according to what appears in their histories and paintings, they made only an abridgement, primarily of their origins; I mean all of the things that are found in their paintings and histories are just an abridgement compared to the records that the first archbishop of Mexico ordered to be burned.[23]

18. It had been 305 years since the time of the eclipsing of the sun and the moon, 438 years since the time of the destruction of the large Quinametzin, and 5,486 years since the creation of the world, when Chalcatzin and Tlacamihtzin, chief leaders and descendants of the Tulteca royal lineage, following many years of quiet peace, commenced to desire the usurpation of the kingdom, desiring to overthrow the legitimate successor. This was the year 13 Acatl.

19. They were exiled, and there began to be wars, and they cast them out of the City of Tlachicalzincan, in the region of Hueytlapallan, their homeland. And they were cast out with their families and allies, their men as well as their women, and a great number were exiled. They left in the year following Ce Tecpatl, banished from all that land, as you will see in that which follows. And this transpired, according to our calculations, 449 years after the birth of our Christ the Lord.[24]

The Native Races

20. The ancestors of the natives of this land that is now called New Spain, according to the common and general opinion of everyone, as well as that which appears demonstrated in their paintings, came from the Occidental areas.

21. And all who are now called Tultecas, Aculhuas, and Mexicanas, as well as the other people in this land, boast and affirm that they are descendants of the Chichimecas. The reason, as it appears in their history, is that their first king, whose name was Chichimecatl, was the one who brought them to this new land where they settled. And it was he, as can be deduced, that came from the great Tartary, and was part of those who came from the division of Babylon. This account is described in great detail in their history, and it tells how he, their king, traveled with them crossing a large part of the world, arriving at this land, which they considered to be good, fertile, and abundant for human sustenance. As mentioned earlier, they populated the major part of the land, and more particularly that which falls along the northern part. And the Chichimecatl called the land by his own name.[25]

22. In each place where the Chichimecatl settled, whether it be a large city or a small village, it was their custom to name it according to the first king or leader who possessed the land. This same custom prevailed among the Tultecas. The general area was called the Land of Tollan, after the first king who was so named. Be that as it may, this custom was prevalent in naming other cities and villages throughout the land.[26]

23. It is difficult to determine the exact meaning of the last few lines of verse 17, as the wording is very awkward. Perhaps Ixtlilxochitl is referring to the statement recorded in verse 3, which indicates that he is working only with an abridgement of the history of Mexico. As to the burning of the records, Ixtlilxochitl must be referring to Bishop Zumarraga, who was the first archbishop of Mexico, meaning Mexico City. Diego De Landa, the bishop of the Yucatan, burned twenty-seven records or codices at the village of Muna. Also, many times the natives burned or hid their own records so the Spaniards could not profane the natives' sacred histories.

24. If the date of the exile of the Tultecas is 305 years from the AD 34 eclipse, then the above date would be AD 339 instead of AD 449. If we attempt to correlate the record-keeping Tultecas with the record-keeping Nephites, the AD 339 exile date is close to the exile of the Nephites from the land southward at AD 350 (see Mormon 2:28–29). The AD 449 date is closer to the AD 385 battle at Cumorah and the AD 421 closing date in the Book of Mormon.

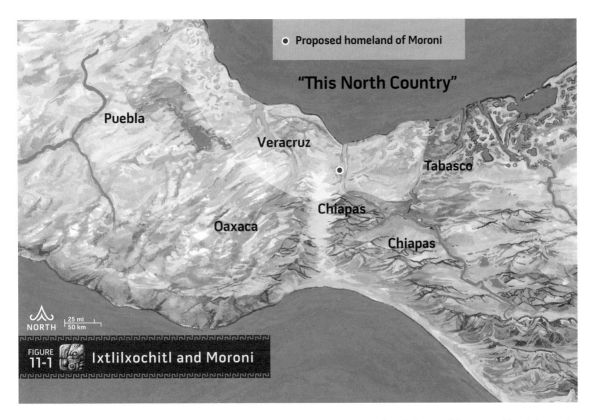

Proposed homeland of Moroni

"This North Country"

Puebla

Veracruz

Tabasco

Chiapas

Oaxaca

Chiapas

NORTH 25 mi / 50 km

FIGURE 11-1 Ixtlilxochitl and Moroni

FIGURE 11–1: This map shows the northern part of the land where, according to Ixtlilxochitl, the first inhabitants of the New World settled. Moroni wrote that the Jaredites lived "upon the face of this north country" (Ether 1:11). Because Mormon lived in the land northward by the narrow pass that led into the land southward, we can assume that his son Moroni grew up in that same area, which today is near the city of Minatitlan, Veracruz. Therefore, his statement that the Jaredites were destroyed *"upon the face of this north country"* is very descriptive.

25. Verse 21 is a repeat of verses 6–8, as it describes the first settlers who came from the great tower at the time of the confusion of the languages. The book of Ether records that the first king, Jared, and those who traveled with him traveled in "that quarter where there never had man been," and they traveled "many years" in the wilderness. They crossed the ocean in barges and landed "upon the shores of the promised land." Ixtlilxochitl calls it a good, fertile, and abundant land. (See Ether 2:5; 3:3; 6:8–12.)

The book of Ether does not tell which ocean the Jaredites crossed. However, from the above information, they apparently crossed from the Asiatic side, or the Pacific. Ixtlilxochitl said they came from the Tartary, which is the general area of China.

Ixtlilxochitl said that the first inhabitants settled primarily along the northern part, which is the northern coast of Veracruz. This is the same area that is the heartland of the ancient people archaeologists call the Olmecs. Moroni records the account of the "ancient inhabitants who were destroyed by the hand of the Lord upon the face of this north country" (Ether 1:1).

Ixtlilxochitl refers to the first king as *Chichimecatl*, whereas earlier he calls the first settlers *Quinametzin*. Ixtlilxochitl was a descendant of the Chichimecatls, who may have traced their ancestry to the Quinametzin. This practice was common during the Classic Maya era. The elitist person who is identified as Pacal, who was buried in the Temple of Inscriptions at Palenque, traced his lineage back to the first settlers, as determined by the glyphs on the temple. The Chichimecatl may be the same people whom the Book of Mormon calls Lamanites. Both Pacal and Ixtlilxochitl may have been more closely associated with the Lamanite/Chichimecatl lineage.

26. This same custom is mentioned by Mormon when he writes, "Now it was the custom of the people of Nephi to call their lands, and their cities, and their villages, yea, even all their small villages, after the name of him who first possessed them; and thus it was with the land of Ammonihah" (Alma 8:7).

Chapter 11: Fernando de Alva Ixtlilxochitl

27. Regarding the 180 BC Lamanites, Mormon writes, "They were a wild, and ferocious, and a blood-thirsty people, believing in the tradition of their fathers. . . . [And] . . . they were desirous to bring us [the Nephites] into bondage" (Mosiah 10:12; 9:12).

28. Apparently, Ixtlilxochitl traces his lineage, through the Chichimeca lineage, all the way back to the first settlers who came from the tower. The Book of Mormon may clear up this issue. Some of the 588–570 BC Lamanites, "the people who were now called Lamanites," (2 Nephi 5:14) were in all probability descendants from the Jaredite Tower of Babel people. Hence, the Chichimeca in Ixtlilxochitl's history may be the same as the Lamanites in Book of Mormon history, and yet many would have descended from the original Jaredite or Quinametzin king.

29. When Mosiah fled to the land of Zarahemla about 180 BC and encountered the people of Zarahemla, they informed him that they had "had many wars and serious contentions, and had fallen by the sword from time to time" (Omni 1:17). The Mulekites had landed in the land of the Jaredites approximately four hundred years prior to the uniting of the Nephites and the people of Zarahemla (see Alma 22:30; Omni 1:19). An expedition dating to 121 BC, sent out by Limhi in search of the land of Zarahemla, discovered the Jaredite ruins, including bones of men and breastplates that were large (see Mosiah 8:8). Verse 25 of Ixtlilxochitl may have reference to these accounts. This possibility suggests that the Quinametzin, who were large people, were the same people known in the Book of Mormon as the Jaredites.

23. Notwithstanding that some were called Tultecas, others Aculhuas, Tepanecas and Otomites, they all were proud to be of the lineage of the Chichimecas because they all descended from them. However, it is true that there were divisions among the Chichimecas themselves. And some were more civilized than others, such as the Tultecas. And others were more barbaric, such as the Otomites and others like them. Those who are pure Chichimecas, whose kings were direct descendants of the first king and founder Chichimecatl, were bloodthirsty men, warriors, and lovers of power, holding other nations in bondage.[27]

24. Although one nation was inclined to righteousness and another nation was full of mischief and idleness, being exceedingly haughty and proud and being warmongers, or although one nation was virtuous and another full of iniquity, both, as recorded in their history, came from the same lineage, the Chichimecas. And all are descended from the same forefathers; and as it has been said, they came from the Occidental areas.[28]

About the Giants

25. In this land called New Spain [Mexico], there were giants, as demonstrated by their bones that have been discovered in many areas. The ancient Tulteca record keepers called them Quinametzin. They became acquainted with them and had many wars and contentions with them and, in particular, in all of the land that is now called New Spain. They [the Quinametzin] were destroyed, and their civilization came to an end as a result of great calamities and punishments from heaven for some grave sins they had committed.[29]

26. It is the opinion of some of these ancient historians that these giants descended from the same Chichimecas mentioned earlier, and they say that in these northern lands where the ancient Chichimeca Empire was located that there are villages where

FIGURE 11–2: The archaeological culture of the Olmecs, the giants spoken of by Ixtlilxochitl, and the Jaredites of the Book of Mormon are all considered to be the same. Ixtlilxochitl records that they were destroyed by a civil war at about 250 BC. (Photos courtesy of Phil Skousen)

Exploring the Lands of the Book of Mormon

there are still men living who are over thirty hands tall. And it is of no wonder that even our own Spaniards have not yet entered into the interior of the lands but have only traveled along the coastal areas such as the lands of the Chicoranos and the Duharezasses, and they have found men in these parts who are eleven and twelve hands in height and have been told that there are others even taller.[30]

27. The greatest destruction that occurred among the Quinametzin was in the year and date that the natives call Ce Toxtli, signifying the date 1 Rabbit, 299 years after the birth of Jesus Christ, and with them ended the third age, which was called Ecatonatiuh because of the great winds and earthquakes. And almost everyone was destroyed.[31]

Brief Account

28. The Tultecas were the second civilization in this land after the destruction of the giants . . . and they had a knowledge of the creation of the world and of how the world had been destroyed by the flood; and many other things are recorded in their history and paintings. . . .

29. The word *Tulteca* means men of the arts and sciences because those of this nation were great artisans, as you can see today in many parts—and especially in the ruins of buildings, such as Teotihuacan, Tula, and Cholula.

Chichimeca History

30. The most serious authors and historians of the ancient pagans included Quetzalcoatl, who is considered to be the first. Some of the modern pagans include Nezahualcoyotzin, king of Texcuco, and the two infants of Mexico, Itzocatzin and Xiuhcozcatzin, sons of King Huitzilihuitzin. And there are many others I could mention if it were necessary.[32]

31. It is declared through their histories about the god Teotloquenahuaque, Tlachihualcipal Nemoanulhuicahua Tlaltipacque, which, according to the correct interpretation, means the universal god of all things, creator of them and in whose will lives all creatures, lord of the heaven and of the earth, and so forth. After having created all things, he created the first parents of men, from whence came forth all others; and the dwelling place and habitation that he gave them was the world.

32. It is said that the world had four ages. The first, which was from the beginning, was called Atonatiuh, which means son of water, signifying that the world was

30. Many scholars brush off the comment about giants as being native superstitions, saying that the large bones are remains of elephants. Too much consistency is evident, however, to ignore the idea of a large race of people. Although a discrepancy exists between thirty hands and eleven or twelve hands tall, the facts that the Book of Mormon Jaredites, the archaeological Olmecs, and the Quinametzin of Ixtlilxochitl are all large people and that they all lived in the land northward, the northern country or the northern lands, lend truth to the superstitions. The northern lands of both the Olmecs and Ixtlilxochitl are the area along the Gulf of Mexico in the state of Veracruz. This area appears to be the same area as the land northward in Jaredite history.

One hand is considered equivalent to 4 inches, in which cases the extremes of the above measurements are 4 feet to 10 feet. From an archaeological point of view, the Olmec were large people—but not necessarily tall people.

31. Four basic ages or periods of destruction are constantly referred to by Ixtlilxochitl and are also recorded by other early Mexican writers. The Aztec calendar stone also reflects four periods of destruction. The first period relates to the Flood and appears to date to 3114 BC. The second is the great hurricane, which has been dated to 1399 BC in this account, as outlined in verse 10. The third age correlates to the death of Christ in AD 34 and consisted of great earthquakes and storms. The fourth age usually refers to the time when the world will be destroyed by fire and is still in the future.

The date in verse 27 is difficult to reconcile and may reflect an error in transcribing. This destruction appears to be referring to the second period because of the context in which it is written.

32. The name "Quetzalcoatl" is prominent in the ancient histories of Mexico. The origin of the name dates back to the advent of Christ. Others were given the name of Quetzalcoatl, including a tenth century AD Toltec leader. The sixteenth-century Catholic priests made serious attempts to obliterate the name and power of Quetzalcoatl from the minds of the people. (See chapter 12, "Bernardino de Sahagun.")

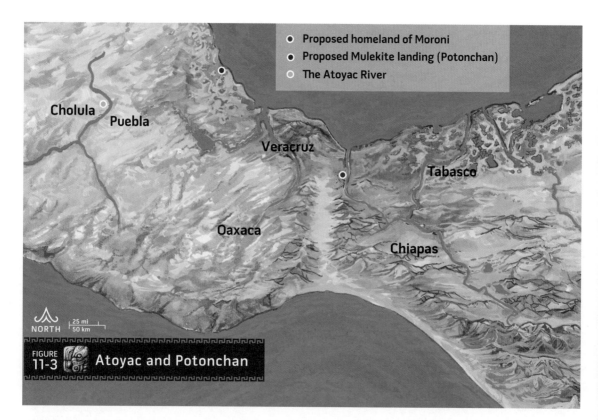

- Proposed homeland of Moroni
- Proposed Mulekite landing (Potonchan)
- The Atoyac River

Cholula
Puebla
Veracruz
Tabasco
Oaxaca
Chiapas

NORTH 25 mi / 50 km

FIGURE 11-3 Atoyac and Potonchan

FIGURE 11–3: We propose that Potonchan, also called Panuco, is the area where the Mulekites landed along the Gulf of Mexico. This is the same place where Cortez landed two thousand years later. The Jaredites, on the other hand, probably landed on the Pacific side, settled in the Oaxaca region, and subsequently migrated into the Veracruz region. The Atoyac River divides Puebla from Cholula, the latter being the area designated as the largest-based pyramid of the world.

33. Verse 33 apparently is the same destruction referred to in verses 10–12, in which case it is the second age or period of time instead of the third. The confusion may lie in the name of Ecatonatiuah, which is either transcribed wrong or which Ixtlilxochitl confuses with Ehecatonatiuh. Sometime after the great destruction at the time of Christ, as recorded in some of the traditions, the name of Ehecatl, which means wind, became part of the title of Quetzalcoatl—that is, Ehecatl Quetzalcoatl.

terminated by a flood. The second, called Tlachitonatiuh, means sun of earth because the world came to an end by great earthquakes in such a manner that almost all of mankind was destroyed. This age or time occurred during the time of the giants, who were called Quinametintzoculihicxime.

33. The third age, Ecatonatiuh, means sun of air because this period came to an end by winds that were so strong that they uprooted all of the buildings and trees and even broke the rocks in pieces; and the majority of mankind perished. And because those who escaped this calamity found a large number of monkeys that the wind must have brought from other parts, the survivors said man must have been changed into monkeys.[33]

34. Those who possessed this new world in this third age were the Ulmecas and Xicalancas; and according to what is found in their histories, they came in ships or boats from the east to the land of Potonchan, and from there they began to populate the land.[34]

Exploring the Lands of the Book of Mormon

35. On the banks of the Atoyac River, which is the one that passes between Puebla and Cholula, there were found some of the giants who had escaped the destruction and extermination of the second age. Taking advantage of their size and strength, they oppressed and enslaved their new neighbors.[35]

36. The principal leaders of the new settlers determined to liberate themselves, and the means they employed were to invite the old settlers to a very solemn feast. After the old settlers became full and intoxicated, they were killed and destroyed with their own weapons, with which feat the new settlers remained free and exempt from bondage, and this increased the domain and command of the Xicalancas and Ulmecas.[36]

34. Potonchan is near the present-day city of Veracruz, Mexico. It is the same place where the Spanish conquerors landed in the sixteenth century AD. Disagreement exists among Latter-day Saint writers as to whether the people who landed at Potonchan were the Jaredites or the Mulekites. Latter-day Saint writers commonly agree that the Mulekites came from the east across the Atlantic in the sixth century BC and landed among the Jaredites in the land northward, or the Gulf of Mexico (see Alma 22:30 and David A. Palmer, *In Search of Cumorah: New Evidences for the Book of Mormon from Ancient Mexico* [Bountiful, UT: Horizon Publishers, 1981], 60). The Mulekite time period correlates to the third age.

FIGURE 11–4: The ruins of Cholula (500 BC–AD 1521), located in the state of Puebla, Mexico. Considered to be the largest-based pyramid in the world, it shows several civilizations built on top of one another, the last being the Catholic church at the top of the pyramid. Ixtlilxochitl reported that Quetzalcoatl did not have a great deal of success at Cholula. This area is dotted with many Catholic churches and cathedrals. (Photo courtesy of George and Audrey DeLange)

35. Ixtlilxochitl's words here, "some of the giants who had escaped the destruction and extermination of the second age," are reminiscent of a somewhat obscure Book of Mormon verse in support of our contention that "all" the Jaredites did not die at the last battle at the hill Ramah. Limhi's 121 BC exploration party found the twenty-four gold plates left by the Jaredites, but initially no one could translate them. King Limhi said, "I am desirous that these records should be translated into our language; for, perhaps, they will give us a knowledge of a *remnant of the people who have been destroyed*, from whence these records came" (Mosiah 8:12; emphasis added). The inherent meaning of the word *remnant* suggests that some Jaredites survived the last battle at the hill Ramah.

36. The state of Puebla borders the state of Veracruz. This account suggests that the Mulekites liberated themselves from a branch of the Jaredites who had not been destroyed during the great hurricane destruction that Ixtlilxochitl calls period two or age of sun of air, dating from 1500 BC to 600 BC. This account is similar to a 121 BC Book of Mormon account wherein a branch of the Nephites escaped from Lamanite bondage after getting the Lamanite guards drunk (see Mosiah 22:3–13).

The largest-based pyramid in the world is Cholula (verse 35). It covers over forty acres of ground and dates to the Preclassic era (500 BC). It was destroyed at the time of Christ and has been rebuilt several times. A Catholic church sits peacefully on top of the pyramid today.

FIGURE 11–5: The Coatzacoalcos River divides the land northward and the land southward and empties into the Gulf of Mexico. The area appears to be the "place where the sea divides the land" as described in the book of Ether (Ether 10:20). (Photo courtesy of Sheryl Lee Wilson)

37. The Spanish translation at the beginning of verse 38 states: "*el primero que adoro y coloco la cruz.*" We have translated it as referring to Quetzalcoatl because that is consistent with the context of the verses preceding and following the statement. We have translated "coloco la cruz" as "placed in authority." Quetzalcoatl has been given many names, including the two above. The tree-of-life motif is associated with Christ and is prevalent throughout Mesoamerica. Quetzalcoatl is afforded the prominent position of all the gods of Mesoamerica. The original Quetzalcoatl is considered to be the same person as Jesus Christ. (See chapter 14, "The White God Quetzalcoatl.")

38. Coatzacoalco(s) has grown into a modern oil refinery city located in the state of Veracruz near the border of the state of Tabasco. The Coatzacoalcos River empties into the Gulf of Mexico at the top of the gulf by the city of Coatzacoalcos. The Aztec meaning of the word Coatzacoalcos is "the foundation of the religion of the feathered serpent." In most Mesoamerica geographical configurations, Coatzacoalcos is considered to be the northwest limits of the land Bountiful referred to in the Book of Mormon. The Savior appeared to the Nephites in the land Bountiful.

37. The people were living in a time of great prosperity when there arrived in this land a man whom they called Quetzalcoatl. Others called him Hueman because of his great virtues. He was considered just, saintly, and good, teaching them by deeds and words the road to virtue. He instructed them to refrain from vices and not to sin, and he gave them laws and sane doctrine. He told them to constrain their appetites and to be honest, and he instituted the law of the fast.

38. And [he was] the first to be worshiped and to be placed in authority, and for that reason [he] is called Quiauhtzteotlchicahualizteotl and Tonaceaquahuitl, which means god of the rains and of health and tree of sustenance or of life.[37]

39. After he [Quetzalcoatl] had preached the above mentioned to all the other Ulmeca and Xicalanca cities, and especially in the City of Cholula, where he spent a great deal of time, and seeing the small amount of fruit that resulted from his doctrine, he returned to the same place from whence he had come, which was to the east, disappearing at Coatzacoalco.[38]

40. And at the time of his farewell from these people, he told them of times to come. He said that in the year that would be called Ce Acatl, he would return and then his doctrine would be accepted, and his children would be lords and heirs of the earth. He also told them that they and their descendants would pass through great calamities and persecutions. He prophesied of many other things that would surely come to pass.

41. *Quetzalcoatl,* by literal interpretation, means serpent of the precious feathers, with an allegoric meaning of "man of exceeding great wisdom." And Huemac [Hueman], some say, was the name given to him because his hands were printed, or stamped, on

FIGURE 11–6: Tradition reports that the white god Quetzalcoatl departed from Coatzacoalcos, Veracruz, on a raft of serpents. It is difficult to tell if this account is referring to the Christ-Quetzalcoatl or Tolpiltzin-Quetzalcoatl, a tenth-century priest-warrior who carried the same name. The painting is by Diego Rivera and is located in the National Palace of Mexico. (Photo courtesy of George and Audrey DeLange)

39. Ixtlilxochitl's words here remind readers of the Book of Mormon account about Jesus's visit to the Nephites following His resurrection. The word "hands" is used pervasively throughout the Book of Mormon (197 times). However, in no place does it have such spiritual meaning as its use associated with the words of the resurrected Jesus: "Arise and come forth unto me, that ye may *thrust your hands into my side*, and also that ye may *feel the prints of the nails in my hands* and in my feet, that ye may know that I am the God of Israel, and the God of the whole earth, and have been slain for the sins of the world" (3 Nephi 11:14; emphasis added). Thereafter, according to the record, "And it came to pass that the multitude went forth, and *thrust their hands into his side, and did feel the prints of the nails in his hands* and in his feet; and this they did do, going forth one by one until they had all gone forth, and did see with their eyes and did *feel with their hands*, and did know of a surety and did bear record, that it was he, of whom it was written by the prophets, that should come" (3 Nephi 11:15; emphasis added).

a rock, like a very fine wax, as testimony that what he prophesied would come to pass. Others say that [Hueman] means "he with the great or powerful hand."**39**

42. A few days after he left, a great destruction and devastation took place, which is referred to as the third period of the world. At that time, the great building and tower

40. This destruction appears to be the same as those mentioned in verses 14 and 16. Verse 16 gives the same date as the date recorded in the Book of Mormon—that is, the first month of the thirty-fourth year (see 3 Nephi 8:5). Verse 42 says that the destruction took place a few days after Quetzalcoatl left. If this event is referring to Christ, it should read, "at the time of his death." Verse 43 records the destruction as occurring some years after the birth of Christ.

of Cholula, which was so famous and marvelous, was destroyed. It was like a second Tower of Babel that these people had built—with virtually the same idea in mind. It was destroyed by the wind.[40]

43. And later, those who escaped at the end of the third age, in place of the ruins, the people built a temple to Quetzalcoatl, whom they named the god of wind because the temple was destroyed by the wind. They understood that this calamity was sent by his hand. And they called it Ce Acatl, which was the name of the year of his coming. According to the history referred to, and from the records, the foregoing took place a few years after the birth of Christ our Lord.

44. After this age had passed, beginning at this time, entered the fourth age called Tletonatiuh, which means "sun of fire" because it is said that this fourth and last age will end by fire.

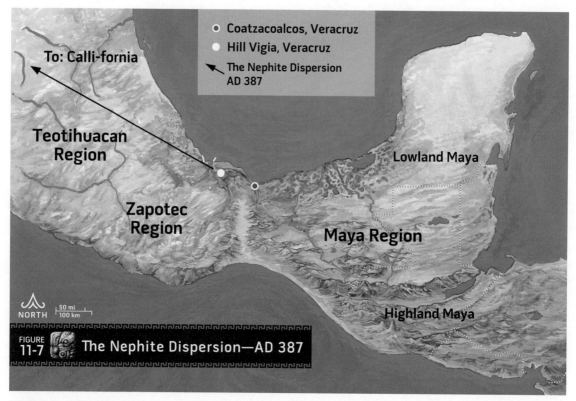

FIGURE 11–7: Map illustrating fourth century AD dispersion of the Tultecas. The fourth century AD Tultecas mentioned by Ixtlilxochitl may be the same people as the fourth century AD Nephites. They traveled along the Bay of Cortez and settled in California, a Nahuatl word that means "their homes by the sea."

45. Quetzalcoatl was a man of comely appearance and serious disposition. His countenance was white, and he wore a beard. His manner of dress consisted of a long, flowing robe.[41]

Historia Chichimeca

Banished from their homeland, the Tultecas embarked upon their journey along the coast. Traveling through the country, they arrived at their "Californias by the sea," which they called Hueytlapallan, which today is called Cortez, which name was given because of its reddish color. The date of their arrival was in the year Ce Tecpatl, which corresponds to AD 387.[42]

Following along the coast of Xalixco (Jalisco) and all along the south, leaving from the port of Huatulco[43] and traveling through diverse lands, they arrived at the province of Tochtepec, which is located along the north sea. And after walking and exploring, they settled in the Tolantzinco, living in the places where they had stopped.

The Tultecas were the third settlers of this land, counting the giants as the first, with the second being the Ulmecas and Xicalancas.[44]

41. This verse concludes the first chapter, or "Sumaria Relacion," as edited by Alfredo Chavero. The historical era covered in this first chapter was from the Flood, called the first age, and terminates with a great storm that occurred at the death of Christ, called the third age, or from approximately 3114 BC to AD 34. The second chapter of Chavero provides us with a beginning date of AD 466, with intermittent statements dating back to the third century AD.

42. The dispersion of the Tultecas at AD 387 correlates with the same time period in which the Nephites were dispersed from their homeland. The last Nephite battle was at AD 385. Moroni wrote the following statements between AD 385–400: "And now it came to pass that after the great and tremendous battle at Cumorah, behold, the Nephites who had escaped into the country southward were hunted by the Lamanites, until they were all destroyed. . . . And behold, the Lamanites have hunted my people, the Nephites, down from city to city and from place to place, even until they are no more" (Mormon 8:2, 7).

43. Huatulco is in southern Oaxaca. A new resort city is now located at Huatulco.

Xalisco is the same area as Jalisco in what is the state where Guadalajara is located.

These writings of Ixtlilxochitl hint at an AD 400 dispersion of the Nephites into northern Mexico and southern United States.

44. Chavero, *Obras Historicas de Don Fernando de Alva Ixtlilxochitl*, 28.

Banished from their homeland, the Tultecas embarked upon their journey along the coast. Traveling through the country, they arrived at their "Californias by the sea." The date of their arrival was in the year Ce Tecpatl, which corresponds to AD 387.

CHAPTER 12

Bernardino de Sahagun
(ca. 1499–1591)

"When we die, it is not true that we die; for still we live, we are resurrected. We still live; we awaken. Do thou likewise." (Sahagun, 1566)

꜖꜖꜖

T he sixteenth-century Catholic priest named Bernardino de Sahagun wrote a detailed, comprehensive analysis of the history, beliefs, and customs of the Mexican people. The traditions about which Sahagun wrote help us understand the culture of the Book of Mormon.

Every student of the Book of Mormon would do well to study the works of the Catholic priests who traveled with the conquering Spaniards to the New World. The priests played a major role in our understanding of the culture and traditions of the ancient inhabitants of Mesoamerica. They were five hundred years closer to the time that Moroni concluded his record than we are today. These writers have become known as the Spanish chroniclers. Many of them were of Basque descent, and they

OPPOSITE: The Spanish chroniclers of the sixteenth and seventeenth centuries were Catholic priests who wrote extensively concerning the ancient inhabitants of Mesoamerica. The work of the early priests was to Christianize the natives, and they did so by teaching, by fear, and by mysticism. A peasant by the name of Juan Diego (his Spanish or Christian name) is purported to have had a vision of the Virgin Mary. A shrine dedicated to this event is located at the Basilica in Mexico City. The picture shows him presenting his robe to Bishop Zumarraga. (Photo courtesy of George and Audrey DeLange)

The Book of
Mormon is
prophetically
very vocal
regarding the
conquest and
the Spanish
inquisition
in which
the Catholic
priests played
a major role.

came from the northern part of Spain. The Basque developed a tradition wherein they would not divide their lands among their children but deeded them only to the oldest son. Nevertheless, the other children could still claim the land as their family home. To this very day, many Basques spend their vacation time at the "family homestead."

Because the younger Basque sons did not have land ownership, they became miners, seafarers, court interpreters, and priests. The Basque are an independent and hardworking people. Many of them, including the women, are tall and have jet-black hair. Their native language is different than Spanish, and they consider themselves to be separate from the traditional Spanish population.

The Spanish priests were named according to the place in Spain from whence they came. One writer is named Juan de (from) Torquemada, another Diego de (from) Landa, and, as is the case in this chapter, Bernardino de (from) Sahagun. Sahagun is a small town in the north in the province of Leon, Spain.

The Book of Mormon is prophetically very vocal regarding the conquest and the Spanish inquisition in which the Catholic priests played a major role. Nephi wrote about the coming of Columbus, a man from Spain who would cross the Atlantic Ocean and who would be led by the Spirit unto the seed of Nephi's brethren who were in the promised land. Nephi saw in vision the workings of an abominable church that scattered and tortured the seed of his brethren (see 1 Nephi 13:5–14).

The task of Christianizing a pagan people—a people who had become "dark" and "filthy" and "loathsome"—was not an easy one. Mormon writes, "This people shall be scattered, and shall become a dark, a filthy, and a loathsome people, beyond the description of that which ever hath been amongst us" (Mormon 5:15).

Whatever the North Americans did to the native tribes in the United States, the Spaniards did a hundredfold more among the natives of Mesoamerica. In the first place, for every one North American native, a hundred or so Aztecs, Maya, and so forth lived in Mesoamerica at the time of the conquest. They were scattered, their villages were annihilated, and their women and children were murdered. They became "peons" to the Spanish-speaking Christians and remained so for over three hundred years until Mexico and Latin America gained their independence from Spain. One Basque, Simon Bolivar (1783–1830), became known as the great liberator of South America. Mexico gained her independence from Spain in 1821, the same year that Guatemala gained independence.

Whatever may be said about the conquest of Mexico, one thing stands above all others. As prophesied, the Catholic priests brought with them a book, and even though "many plain and precious things" had been taken away from the book, it became the basis for a new church, a new language, and a new culture in Mesoamerica. Large and ornate buildings were built in every village, and people began to crawl on their knees to pay homage to statues erected to represent Jesus Christ the Son of God and the Holy Virgin Mary.

FIGURE 12–1: This statue located near the Shrine of Guadalupe in Mexico City shows the people paying homage to the Virgin Mary. (Photo courtesy of George and Audrey DeLange)

The Catholic priests brought with them a book, and even though "many plain and precious things" had been taken away from the book, it became the basis for a new church, a new language, and a new culture in Mesoamerica.

Although many of the priests of the Catholic Church became corrupt over time and although the Catholic Church owned a large portion of the wealth in Mexico and Guatemala, these same priests and this same church also kept records—records of births, baptisms, marriages, and deaths. The following story illustrates this point.

Sylvia Rios was from San Diego, California. On one occasion, she and her two teenage children along with her mother went on a Book of Mormon tour to visit the ancient ruins of Mexico. Because her mother had grown up in Mexico City, they all expressed their excitement on being able to visit the Shrine of Guadalupe. Sylvia's mother explained that she would especially like to show Sylvia and her grandchildren the gravesite of her husband's grandfather, Chimalpopoca, who was buried in the hilltop cemetery where the Shrine of Guadalupe, or the Basilica, is located. This is sacred ground to the Catholic people because of a reported vision there of the Virgin Mary to the Aztec peasant Juan Diego shortly after the Spanish conquest.

As Sylvia, her mother, and her children arrived at the cemetery, they were disappointed that they could not find the gravesite of Sylvia's great-grandfather. Over fifty years had elapsed since her mother had visited the cemetery, but she knew the date of the death of Chimalpopoca because he had died on the same day that her husband, Sylvia's father, was born. The family knew that Chimalpopoca had not changed his Aztec name to a "Christian" name because he was a descendant of the last emperor of Mexico, Cuauhtemoc.

History reports that this eighteen-year-old Cuauhtemoc, when captured by the Spanish soldiers at the market place of Tlateloco (today called the Plaza of Three Cultures), said, "You would do me a great favor if you would take that dagger in your belt and kill me at once." Today, a sign on the grounds of the marketplace in front of the church reads, "This is the place of a new birth. It was not a glorious birth. Indeed it was a very painful birth. Nevertheless, it brought about what is known as the Mexico of today." Today, if travelers ask a person in Mexico City if he or she is Spanish or Aztec, the person will very likely say with pride, "Neither; I am a Mexican."

Although Sylvia and her family were disappointed in not being able to find the grave of Chimalpopoca, they were undaunted. They located a groundskeeper who let them look at the records for the location of the grave. They found it. They took pictures, and they were excited. But the story does not end here. As the family walked down the steps to return to their tour group, they passed a man carrying a large cross. They struck up a conversation with him and were surprised that he was taking the cross to put on the gravesite of none other than Chilmalpopoca. He explained to Sylvia that he was writing a genealogy of Chilmalpopoca, tracing him back to the emperor Cuauhtemoc. They exchanged detailed information, and when Sylvia returned to the bus, she reported to the group that she had just completed her genealogy back to the sixteenth century.

BERNARDINO DE SAHAGUN

Bernardino de Sahagun was without a doubt one of the outstanding scholars representative of the Spanish priests of the sixteenth century in the valley of Mexico. His method of collecting information from the natives was very unique and comprehensive. Sahagun developed a school of trilingual students. Besides their native Mexican language, Nahuatl (Aztec), they learned the biblical Latin as well as the Spanish language as required by law.

FIGURE 12–2: The robe of Juan Diego with its purported image of the Virgin Mary imprinted upon it has continually been on display near the hill of Tepeyac where the vision reportedly took place. The building shown here housed the robe for more than a hundred years. The vision is reported as having occurred on December 9, 1531. (Photos courtesy of George and Audrey DeLange)

Exploring the Lands of the Book of Mormon

After Fray Bernardino became a monk of the Order of St. Francis, he adopted the name of Sahagun in lieu of his family name of Ribeira—Sahagun being the name of the place where he grew up in Spain.

In 1529, Father Sahagun was one of nineteen Franciscan monks who set sail for New Spain (Mexico). Traveling with them were some Mexican natives who had been presented to the Spanish royal court by Cortez and who were being returned to Mexico. From these natives, Sahagun began his intensive study of the Aztec people and their language and customs.

From 1530 to 1536, he spent his time in the convent at Tlamanalco studying and dedicating himself to his faith. In 1536, he was appointed as a teacher of Latin at the College of Santa Cruz. He also spent his time preaching to and teaching the natives in both religion and languages—Spanish, Nahuatl, and Latin. From 1558 to 1566, Sahagun spent his time compiling and writing his *Historia General de las Cosas de Nueva Espana*.

Sahagun obtained his material through observation as well as by the unique method of assembling ten to twelve of the wisest old men of the communities along with his trilingual students and then having each group verify the other group's words as to the origin, history, and beliefs of the people. His account of the conquest of Mexico is from the Aztec point of view; and because of this orientation and other things in the record, his work was halted and almost destroyed by the Catholic Church—as had been the case with so many other records of the Aztecs. He was later forced to change parts of his accounts regarding the conquest. His writings are filled with notes and are well illustrated, with the art having been done by Aztec artists.

Sahagun died in 1591 when an epidemic of catarrh infested Mexico City. As a historian and scholar, he is considered the greatest authority on the Aztecs of the sixteenth century.[1]

The writings of Sahagun (sometimes referred to as the Florentine Codex) that are available to us today include twelve volumes of works that have been translated from the Nahuatl (Mexican) language into English. The translators of Sahagun's works are Arthur Anderson and Charles Dibble—the only two scholars at the time conversant enough with the Nahuatl language and with Mexican history to undertake the work.

The following are excerpts from Book 10 of the writings of Sahagun. They are included here to give a feeling of the traditions of the so-called Tultecas in ancient Mexican history. Some preliminary comparisons may suggest that the Tultecas in the Spanish chronicles were the Nephites in the Book of Mormon history. The evidence substantiates that the origin of the name or title "Quetzalcoatl" came about because of the advent of Christ to the Nephites.[2]

The word *Tula* also appears in Book 10 of Sahagun. Wells Jakeman associated the word *Tula* with Bountiful. *Tula* means "place of reeds" or "land of abundance."[3]

1. Fray Bernardino de Sahagun, *Historia General de las Cosas de Nueva Espana: Florentine Codex*, 12 vols, edited and translated to English by Arthur O. Anderson and Charles E. Dibble, 12 vols. (Santa Fe, NM: The School of American Research and the University of Utah, 1950), 1:1–17.

2. See Joseph L. Allen, "A Comparative Study of Quetzalcoatl, the Feathered-Serpent God of MesoAmerica, with Jesus Christ, the God of the Nephites," (unpublished PhD dissertation, Brigham Young University, 1970); and Bruce W. Warren and Thomas S. Ferguson, *The Messiah in Ancient America* (Provo, UT: Book of Mormon Research Foundation, 1987).

3. Joseph L. Allen, personal notes.

If the Tultecas, or Toltecas, of Sahagun are Nephites, if Quetzalcoatl is Christ, and if Tula is Bountiful, the following material makes for fascinating reading for the Book of Mormon student (italics added for emphasis):

Twenty-ninth chapter, which telleth of the various kinds of people, the people who dwelt everywhere here in the land; those who arrived, who came to settle, who came to cause the cities to be founded.

In this paragraph, here, the *Tolteca*[4] are mentioned, the first who settled here in the land; who [were] like the inhabitants of Babylon, wise, learned, experienced.

First, those named the *Tolteca*, so-called: these first came to live here in the land, called land of the Mexica, land of the Chichimeca. And for several four-hundreds of years [20 Katuns], they dwelt in the vicinity of Tollantzinco. Since they really lived there, they left many of their traces which they had fashioned. In that area they made what was their temple; its name was "house of beams." Today it stands; it exists, considering that it is indestructible, for it is of rock, of stone.

And these *Tolteca* were called Chichimeca.[5] There [was] no real word for their name. Their name is taken from—it comes from—their manner of life, their works. The *Tolteca* were wise. Their works were all good, all perfect, all wonderful, all marvelous; their houses beautiful, tiled in mosaics, smoothed, stuccoed, very marvelous.

Wherefore was it called a *Tolteca* house? It was built with consummate care, majestically designed; it was the place of worship of their priest, whose name was *Quetzalcoatl;* it was quite marvelous.

Very many were the marvelous houses which they made. The house of *Quetzalcoatl,* which was his place of worship, stood in the water; a large river passed by it; the river which passed by *Tula.* There stood that which was the bathing place of *Quetzalcoatl,* called "In the Waters of Green Stones" [Chalchiuapan]. Many houses stood within the earth where the *Tolteca* left many things buried.

And in this way were the *Tolteca* learned: they knew well, they understood well, that which pertained to herbs, to the nature of their essence; which ones were good, which esteemed, and which of them were just plants, which ones bad, evil, harmful, or really deadly.

They invented the art of medicine. The old men Oxomoco, Cipactonal, Tlaltetecui, Xochicaoaca, were Tolteca. They were the wise men who discovered, who knew of, medicine; who originated the medical art. . . .

And these *Tolteca* were very wise; they were thinkers, for they originated the year count,[6] the day count; they established the way in which the night, the day, would work; which day sign was good, favorable; and which was evil, the

4. Like Ixtlilxochitl, Sahagun labels the Tolteca, or Tulteca, as the first settlers of Mesoamerica. They may have been the record keepers who wrote about the first settlers like the Nephites wrote about the Jaredites.

5. In Ixtlilxochitl, *Tolteca* or *Tulteca* seems to be different than the Chichimeca. The Chichimeca were descendants of the first settlers. The Chichimeca may have been the same people the Book of Mormon calls Lamanites.

6. The year count refers to the calendar and the writing system. The writing system was invented or practiced from about 600 BC and was probably initiated by the Nephites, or the Preclassic Toltecas.

day sign of wild beasts. All their discoveries formed the book for interpreting dreams.

And so wise were they [that] they understood the stars which were in the heavens; they gave them names and understood their influence. And they understood well the movements of the heavens;[7] their orbits they learned from the stars. And they understood that there were many divisions of the heavens; they said there were *twelve divisions*. There existed, there dwelt, the true god and his consort. The name of the god of the heavens was Ome tecutli, and the name of his consort, the woman of the heavens, was Ome cihuatl; that is to say, they were lords, they were rulers, over the *twelve heavens*. It was said that there were we, the common people, created; thence came our souls. When babies were conceived, when they dropped [from heaven], *their souls came from there;* they entered into their [mothers'] wombs. Ome tecutli sent them.

These *Tolteca* were righteous. They were not deceivers. Their words [were] clear words. They addressed one as "the lord, my elder brother; the lord, my younger brother." They said: *"It is true; so is it; it is certain; yes; no."*[8]

Their food was that which is now used—maize, grains of maize. It was produced in abundance—green, blue, jade, turquoise [colored maize] with which to make purchases.

Their clothing was—indeed their privilege was—the blue knotted cape; their sandals were painted blue, light blue, sky blue. Also light blue were their sandal thongs.

They were tall; they were larger [than the people today]. Because they were very tall, they ran much and so were named *Tlanquacemilhuime*.[9]

They went about using the ground drum, the rattle stick. They were singers; they composed, originated, knew from memory, invented the wonderful songs which they composed.

They were devout. *Only one was their god;* they showed all attention to, they called upon, they prayed to one by the name of *Quetzalcoatl*. The name of one who was their minister, their priest, [was] also *Quetzalcoatl*. This one was very devout. That which the priest of Quetzalcoatl required of them, they did well. They did not err, for he said to them, he admonished them: "There is only one god; [he is] named *Quetzalcoatl*. He requireth nothing; you shall offer him, you shall sacrifice before him only serpents, only butterflies." All people obeyed the divine command of the priest. And they had very great faith in the *priest of Quetzalcoatl*[10] and were very obedient, very devout, and very reverent; for all obeyed, all had faith in *Quetzalcoatl* when he led them from *Tula*. He caused all to move, to depart, even though they were settled there, even though very marvelous were the temples, the palaces situated at *Tula*.

7. The Preclassic Period Nephites understood the movements of the heavens, as indicated by the following: "And thus, according to his word the earth goeth back, and it appeareth unto man that the sun standeth still; yea, and behold, this is so; for surely it is the earth that moveth and not the sun" (Helaman 12:15).

8. When the Savior appeared to the Nephites, He said, "Let your communication be Yea, yea; Nay, nay" (3 Nephi 12:37).

9. Interpreted means "to run all day without getting tired."

10. The sixteenth-century writers, including Sahagun, appeared to correlate the deity Quetzalcoatl (Christ) with the tenth-century priest Tolpiltzin Quetzalcoatl.

And as they had great faith in *Quetzalcoatl,* they made every effort to remove their women, their children, their sick. The old men, the old women departed; they moved. No one failed to obey; all moved when *Topiltzin Quetzalcoatl*[11] went to enter into the water at Tlapallan, where he went to disappear.

11. See previous note.

These *Tolteca,* as is said, were Nahua; they did not speak a barbarous tongue. However, their language they called Nonoalca. They said as they conversed: "My noble lord; my lord younger brother; my lord elder brother."

They were rich. By reason of their prudence they caused their goods to appear quickly. Thus it is now said of him who quickly gains goods that he is a son of Quetzalcoatl, that he is Quetzalcoatl's son.[12]

12. Sahagun 10:165–70.

THE SIXTEENTH-CENTURY SAHAGUN ABOUT QUETZALCOATL

Without question, the sixteenth-century writers, when referring to Quetzalcoatl, were thinking of Topiltzin Quetzalcoatl. Topiltzin Quetzalcoatl was born around 935 AD. He took upon himself the name of Quetzalcoatl, the deity. Quetzalcoatl the deity was probably associated with Christ, or rather Christ was probably given the name or title of Quetzalcoatl. (See chapter 14, "The White God Quetzalcoatl.")

The tenth-century Tolpiltzin Quetzalcoatl lived in Tula in the state of Hidalgo, north of Mexico City. This area was named *Tula* after the ancient Tula spoken of in the chronicles and should not be confused with the Tula that Sahagun is writing about. The name or title "Quetzalcoatl" surfaced at Tula, Hidalgo, causing modern scholars to think they had discovered the ancient Tula.

Following are more excerpts from the writings of Sahagun regarding the beliefs, customs, and history of the ancient Mexicans:

Quetzalcoatl

Quetzalcoatl—he was the wind, the guide and roadsweeper of the rain gods, of the masters of the water, of those who brought rain. And when the wind rose, when the dust rumbled, and it crackled and there was a great din, and it became dark and the wind blew in many directions, and it thundered; then it was said: "(Quetzalcoatl) is wrathful."[13]

13. This is typical of Catholic thought shortly after the conquest. To establish Christianity, the Catholic priests felt the need to destroy the ancient gods.

These, the ancients, worshipped an idol (called) Quetzalcoatl, who was ruler at Tula. And you named him Topiltzin.

He was a man. He was mortal, for he died; for his body corrupted. He is no god.[14]

14. It is apparent that Sahagun became frustrated with the constant reference in Mesoamerica tradition about Quetzalcoatl. His pen reflects his frustration.

And though a man of saintly life, who performed penances, he was not to be worshipped as a god. The things which he did (which were) like miracles, we know he did only through the command of the devil. He is a friend of devils. Therefore he must needs be accursed and abominated; for our Lord God hath caused him to be thrust into the land of the dead.

The ancients held that Quetzalcoatl went to Tlapallan; (that) yet he will return. He is still expected. This is not true; it is falsehood. For his body died; here on earth it became dust, it became filth. And his soul our Lord God damned and caused to be thrown into the land of the dead. In that place it is. It will forever suffer in the flames.[15]

One Wind. This One Wind, they said, was evil. At this time they made offerings to the one called Quetzalcoatl,[16] who was representative of the wind, the whirlwind.[17]

15. Sahagun, *Historia General de las Cosas de Nueva Espana*, 1:39–40.

16. Quetzalcoatl is called the Wind God. Wind God probably has reference to the great destruction at the time of Christ and perhaps in legend became associated with the coming of Christ.

17. Sahagun, *Historia General de las Cosas de Nueva Espana*, 4:101.

FIGURE 12–3: These large monuments located at the archaeological site of Tula, Hidalgo, about an hour's drive north of Mexico City, date to AD 900. They are referred to as the Toltecs. Because of the many symbols at Tula depicting the feathered-serpent god, it was initially speculated that this was the ancient Tula referred to in legend. However, it is more appropriately related to a tenth-century warrior named Tolpiltzin Quetzalcoatl. A mixture of folklore and history appear to be associated with Quetzalcoatl. (Photo courtesy of George and Audrey DeLange)

Council in Heaven[18]

18. This dialogue from Sahagun was portrayed in the light-and-sound production that was held for many years at the pyramids of Teotihuacan, near Mexico City.

It is told that when yet (all) was in darkness, when yet no sun had shone and no dawn had broken—it is said—the gods gathered themselves together and took counsel among themselves there at Teotihuacan. They spoke; they said among themselves:

"Come hither, O gods! Who will carry the burden? Who will take it upon himself to be the sun, to bring the dawn?"

And upon this, one of them who was there spoke: Tecuciztecatl presented himself. He said: "O gods, I shall be the one."

And again the gods spoke: "(and) who else?"

Thereupon they looked around at one another. They pondered the matter. They said to one another: "How may this be? How may we decide?"

None dared; no one else came forward. Everyone was afraid; they (all) drew back.

And now present was one man, Nanauatzin; he stood there listening among the others to that which was discussed. Then the gods called to this one. They said to him: "Thou shalt be the one, O Nanauatzin."

He then eagerly accepted the decision; he took it gladly. He said: "It is well, O gods; you have been good to me."

Then they began now to do penance. They fasted four days—both Tecuciztecatl (and Nanauatzin). And then, also, at this time, the fire was laid. Now it burned, there in the hearth. They named the hearth teotexcalli.

And this Tecuciztecatl: that with which he did penance was all costly. His fir branches (were) quetzal feathers, and his grass balls (were) of gold; his maguey spines (were) of green stone; the reddened, bloodied spines (were) of coral. And his incense was very good incense. And (as for) Nanauatzin, his fir branches were made only of green water rushes—green reeds bound in threes, all (making), together, nine bundles. And his grass balls (were) only dried pine needles. And his maguey spines were these same maguey spines. And the blood with which they were covered (was) his own blood. And (for) his incense, he used only the scabs from his sores, (which) he lifted up. For these two, for each one singly, a hill was made. There they remained, performing penances for four nights. They are now called pyramids—the pyramid of the sun and the pyramid of the moon.[19]

19. Sahagun, *Historia General de las Cosas de Nueva Espana*, 7:4–5.

Teachings

Thus they admonished them, that they might lead good lives; that they might not waste time nor live lazily.[20]

20. Sahagun, *Historia General de las Cosas de Nueva Espana*, 2:204.

Resurrection

When we die, it is not true that we die; for still we live, we are resurrected. We still live; we awaken. Do thou likewise.[21]

21. Sahagun, *Historia General de las Cosas de Nueva Espana*, 10:192.

They Ate the Flesh

Acatl Yiacapan Uei Calpulli; here they gathered together (the slaves) for the Tlalocs. And when they had assembled them all, then they here slew them.

And when they had slain them, then here they cut them in pieces, and cooked them; they put squash blossoms with their flesh.

Exploring the Lands of the Book of Mormon

And when they had cooked them, then the nobility, and all the important men ate (the stew); but not the common folk—only the leaders.[22]

Adultery

And in this way he would come to a bad end. Perchance he would commit adultery. Perhaps he would covet a woman. Perhaps he would covet another's woman. Perhaps he would eat another's food, lift his head from another's (bed). And the woman would be his companion in death; they would break and smash both their heads. Hence were adulterers called "broken heads" or "smashed heads."[23]

If a noblewoman was an adulteress, her head was crushed between two stones so that she died.[24]

If he had committed adultery, then he sentenced him to be stoned before the people, to die stoned.[25]

Fasting

They fasted for the deer, that they might hunt (them).[26]

Three Kingdoms

(This is) what the natives knew: the old ones and the chiefs. For all who died went to (one or another of) three places when they died.[27]

Family Relationships

(He is) married, has a spouse, (is) exempt from the priesthood, (is) a mature youth.

The good son-in-law (is) one who reveres, venerates, respects, esteems, loves (his parents-in-law).

The bad son-in-law (is) a fool. Covetous, he steals. He is given to pleasure; he lives in concubinage.[28]

One's father (is) the source of lineage, the beginning of lineage. (He is) the sincere one. One's father (is) diligent, solicitous, compassionate, sympathetic; a careful administrator (of his household). He rears, he teaches people; he rears, he teaches others. He advises, he admonishes one. He is exemplary; he leads a model life. He stores up for himself; he stores up for others. He is thrifty—he saves for the future, teaches thrift, looks to the future. He regulates, distributes with care, establishes order.[29]

One's grandfather (is) hardened, lean, white-haired, white-headed. He becomes impotent, childish.

The good grandfather (is) an adviser, an indoctrinator. He reprimands one, beats one with nettles, teaches one prudence, discretion.[30]

22. Sahagun, *Historia General de las Cosas de Nueva Espana*, 2:179. This is reminiscent of Mormon's description of the fourth-century AD Nephites: "And after they had done this thing, they did murder them in a most cruel manner, torturing their bodies even unto death; and after they have done this, they devour their flesh like unto wild beasts, because of the hardness of their hearts; and they do it for a token of bravery" (Moroni 9:10).

23. Sahagun, *Historia General de las Cosas de Nueva Espana*, 4:93.

24. Sahagun, *Historia General de las Cosas de Nueva Espana*, 4:6.

25. Sahagun, *Historia General de las Cosas de Nueva Espana*, 8:42.

26. Sahagun, *Historia General de las Cosas de Nueva Espana*, 2:124.

27. Sahagun, *Historia General de las Cosas de Nueva Espana*, 3:39.

28. Sahagun, *Historia General de las Cosas de Nueva Espana*, 10:8.

29. Sahagun, *Historia General de las Cosas de Nueva Espana*, 10:1.

30. Sahagun, *Historia General de las Cosas de Nueva Espana*, 10:4.

One's good son (is) obedient, humble, gracious, grateful, reverent. (He is) one who shows reverence, who obeys, humbles himself, is thankful, shows appreciation, resembles (father or mother) in body and character, (and) in way of life.[31]

31. Sahagun, *Historia General de las Cosas de Nueva Espana*, 10:2.

One's mother has children; she suckles them. Sincere, vigilant, agile, (she is) an energetic worker—diligent, watchful, solicitous, full of anxiety. She teaches people; she is attentive to them. She caresses, she serves others; she is apprehensive for their welfare; she is careful, thrifty—constantly at work.[32]

32. Sahagun, *Historia General de las Cosas de Nueva Espana*, 10:3.

One's daughter: the daughter (is) untouched, pure, a virgin. The good daughter (is) obedient, honest, intelligent, discreet, of good memory, modest, respectful, revered, well reared, well taught, well trained, well instructed, prudent, chaste, circumspect.[33]

33. Sahagun, *Historia General de las Cosas de Nueva Espana*, 10:3.

Talents of Women

And these women were good embroiderers, skilled in cotton work. And the men and women were beautiful, fair, tall, slender, firm. Their language was a barbarous tongue, although some spoke Otomi, some spoke Nahuatl, some spoke also the Huaxteca language. They were quite skilled in song; they were very able in the dance.[34]

34. Sahagun, *Historia General de las Cosas de Nueva Espana*, 10:184.

Sacrificed Those of Fair Skin

And then they hunted out men of fair hair and white faces; and they sacrificed them to the sun.[35]

35. Sahagun, *Historia General de las Cosas de Nueva Espana*, 7:36.

Deer[36]

And they removed each of the deer which bore men on their backs, called horses.[37]

36. Unaccustomed to horses, the Aztecs called them deer.

37. Sahagun, *Historia General de las Cosas de Nueva Espana*, 12:69.

SUMMARY

Almost five hundred years ago, the Spaniards conquered Mexico. The year was 1521, and the conquest was conducted under the name of Christianity. Beginning immediately after the conquest, Catholic priests arrived in Mexico to establish Christianity in the New World.

Bernardino de Sahagun is representative of these Spanish priests. His account of the origins, customs, and teachings of the sixteenth-century Mexicans may provide students of the Book of Mormon with insights into the culture of the people who lived in the same area where portions of the Book of Mormon history possibly occurred.

THE BOOK OF MORMON AND THE SPANISH CONQUEST

The Spanish conquest of Mexico and Central America should play a major role in our understanding of certain prophecies in the Book of Mormon. Let's call it "geography by prophecy." Twenty-one hundred years before the arrival of Columbus and Cortez to the land of promise, Nephi recorded the following as a result of a vision he had of the future of the seed of his brethren: "Behold, the wrath of God is upon the seed of my brethren. And I looked and beheld a man among the Gentiles. . . . And it came to pass that I beheld many multitudes of the Gentiles upon the land of promise; and I beheld the wrath of God, that it was upon the seed of my brethren; and they were scattered before the Gentiles and were smitten" (1 Nephi 13:11–14).

These verses speak of two events: (1) the discovery of America by Columbus and (2) the conquest of Mexico by Spain. These two events relate specifically to Mesoamerica because Columbus sailed under the flag of Spain in 1492 (v. 12) and Cortez sailed under the flag of Spain in 1519 (v. 14). One was a discoverer; the other was a conqueror. In both instances, observe that the wording "the wrath of God [was] upon the seed of [Nephi's] brethren" is used.

Without question, some of the content of these verses in this great prophecy speaks also of the Church of England (see verses 13, 15, 17, 18, and 19). These events include the Gentiles' coming out of captivity (AD 1620) and participating in the Revolutionary War (AD 1776). The key word here is "captivity." The Pilgrims left spiritual bondage in England and came to the United States. In other words, they went forth out of captivity (verses 13 and 16). The Spanish crown, on the other hand, conquered a people and put them in bondage for three hundred years (AD 1521–1821). The Aztecs, Zapotecs, and Maya (the seed of Nephi's brethren) were scattered before the Spanish conquerors (Gentiles) and were smitten. A case may be made that the same thing happened to the North American natives who lived north of the United States/Mexico border. However, the numbers and the activities were vastly different for at least two reasons:

1. For every one North American native who lived north of the border, a hundred or more lived in Mesoamerica. North American native villages north of the border were just that—villages. On the other hand, cities had developed in Mesoamerica. For example, Tenochtitlan was an Aztec city that today is called Mexico City. Estimations are that Tenochtitlan had between sixty thousand and two hundred thousand residents in the year 1519.

2. The Pilgrims crossed the Atlantic and came to America with their wives and children. The Spanish fleets crossed the Atlantic and came to Mesoamerica with single men and celibate Catholic priests. Unlike the English-speaking colonists of the United States, the majority of the Spanish colonists were single men who married natives or made concubines of them—and were even encouraged to do so by Queen Isabella in the earliest days of colonization.

The Spanish conquest was particularly devastating because hundreds of thousands of natives throughout Mexico and Guatemala were uprooted and displaced, tortured and killed, exposed to killer contagious diseases, subjected to extremely inhumane treatment, and forced to give up their religious beliefs and practices.

CHAPTER 13

Diego de Landa
(1524–1579)

"We found a great number of books and since they contained nothing but superstitions and falsehoods of the devil we burned them, which they took most grievously, and which gave them great pain." (Friar Diego de Landa, 1566)

The sixteenth-century Catholic Bishop Diego de Landa can be compared to Friar Bernardino de Sahagun in the sense that whereas Sahagun compiled the culture and oral traditions of the natives of the Mexico valley, Landa did the same in the Yucatan.

Of course, at the time, the Yucatan was not considered part of the Mexico culture. Mexico (the Mexico valley) was dominated by the Aztecs at the time of the Spanish conquest. The Yucatan was, and had been for centuries, considered as part of the great Maya culture. The Isthmus of Tehuantepec has been a natural dividing line throughout modern history. Not until 1840 did Yucatan become a legitimate part of the country of Mexico.

OPPOSITE: The conquest of Mexico by Spain in 1521 fulfilled prophecy and brought about a dramatic paradigm shift in the religion, culture, and language of the people. The National Cathedral of Mexico shown here was built on the site of the ancient Aztec capital city of Tenochtitlan, which today is the central square of Mexico City and is called the Zocalo. Immediately following the conquest, cathedrals began to be erected in every city and village. The first bishop of the Yucatan was Diego de Landa. The sole objective of the Catholic Church during this time was to Christianize the natives by any means possible. Spain was severely criticized by England, by France, and even by some of their own, such as the priest San Cristobal de las Casas, for the manner in which the natives were converted. (Photo courtesy of Phil Skousen)

Landa can also be compared to Bernal Diaz, the soldier in the army of Cortez who wrote a history of the conquest of Mexico. In his writings, *Relacion de las Cosas de Nueva Espana,* Landa included accounts of the conquest of the Yucatan. The Aztecs of Mexico City (Tenochtitlan) surrendered in the year 1521. The Maya of the Yucatan were not considered conquered until 1546.

Landa's *Relacion* "is intended for those who wish a general view of Maya life with emphasis on religion," and nearly every reputable writer who has written about the Maya has drawn extensively from Landa's material. The first edition was by Brasseur de Bourbourg and was published in Paris with a French translation in 1864. The first English edition was published in 1937. The importance of Landa's *Relacion* is per-haps indicated by the number of editions following the manuscript's discovery in the Biblioteca de la Academia de la Historia de Madrid.[1]

1. Diego de Landa, *Relacion de las Cosas de Yucatan,* ed. Alfred M. Tozzer, papers of the Peabody Museum of American Archaeology and Ethnology, Harvard University, vol. 18 (Cambridge: The Museum, 1941), vii–ix.

THE INQUISITION

In the eyes of history, Diego de Landa is considered to be both a benefactor and a scoun-drel. He has been labeled a scoundrel because he is considered the man responsible for burning the Maya codices, or records, at the village of Mani in the Yucatan in 1562. The natives were devastated at this action. Landa's contemporaries, though not devas-tated, were disappointed almost immediately, and they expressed dismay at the wanton destruction of records that contained the history, rituals, and customs of the people. The feelings of disgust and disdain for this act of Diego de Landa have not decreased in the hundreds of years that have passed.

> In the eyes of history, Diego de Landa is considered to be both a benefactor and a scoundrel.

We must remember, however, that during this period of time (the sixteenth cen-tury), the Catholic Inquisition, (*auto de fe*), was in full force. People could be flogged, branded, humiliated, ostracized from the community, put in prison, or even put to death for committing heresy or for violating the sacraments of the Catholic Church. The Maya of the Yucatan, for the most part, were forced to accept the covenants of the church.

The old Maya priests, who had represented a hierarchy of elite for more than a thousand years, yearned for the power they had lost under the new Spanish govern-ment. They began to encourage the natives to return secretly to their old religious ways but to continue to pay lip service to the so-called Christianity. When word leaked out in the area of Mani that virtually all members of the entire village had secretly returned to their old ways, the act of Landa in burning several dozen Maya codices apparently seemed justified in his mind.

THE MAYA ALPHABET

From a historical perspective, Landa redeemed himself to a degree because of his actions in writing a history of the traditions and culture of the Maya of the Yucatan. He was also one of a handful of Catholic priests who put forth the effort to learn the

Exploring the Lands of the Book of Mormon

language of the Maya. Landa wrote, to the best of his ability, the sounds and alphabet of the Maya language, as they related to Spanish. It is this alphabet that has proved to be invaluable in the present-day deciphering of the Maya hieroglyphs, and it is this contribution that has earned Landa the title associated with his being a great benefactor. See figure 2–5 in chapter 2 for a comparison of Classic Maya with Landa's alphabet.

In addition to identifying the Maya sounds with the Spanish language, Landa recorded the day and month signs of the Maya calendar.[2]

SIXTEENTH-CENTURY TRADITIONS IN THE YUCATAN

As to the history and traditions of the Maya of the Yucatan, Landa provides us with additional insights. His original *Relacion de las Cosas de Yucatan* was probably written in 1566. Just a note of caution, however. Some scholars have labeled him a great plagiarist, claiming that much of his material was taken from contemporary chroniclers.

Of great interest, nevertheless, is the process of comparing Landa's information about the religious, social, work-habit, and family customs with those among residents of current Maya villages. Landa reached back in history two hundred to three hundred years and observed that little difference existed between the AD 1200 Maya and the AD 1550 Maya. Now, almost five hundred years since the conquest, we observe a high degree of the same ethnic patterns among the small villages of the Yucatan Maya and the patterns we read about in Landa's writings.

2. Linda Schele, *Workbook in Maya Hieroglyphics* (Austin, TX: n.p., 1987), 5–6.

FIGURE 13–1: The manner of dress and the style of homes among the Maya have changed very little over the last fifteen hundred years. Still today, for their newly married children, a common practice for a Maya family is to build a home much like the one pictured here. Such homes consist of a dirt floor and doorways on opposite sides to help with ventilation. The family members sleep in hammocks that are hung along the wall during the day. (Photo courtesy of Sheryl Lee Wilson)

3. Landa, *Relacion de las Cosas de Yucatan*, 42–43.

Our travels throughout the Yucatan provide a time tunnel to the ancient customs of the Maya. From a Book of Mormon perspective, the sixteenth-century Maya were, in all probability, closely associated with the Lamanite culture of the Book of Mormon. What we observe in the extensive priestcraft society of the sixteenth-century Maya seems to parallel the beginnings of a hierarchy priestcraft society in the Book of Mormon at AD 200: "Nevertheless, the people did harden their hearts, for they were led by many priests and false prophets to build up many churches, and to do all manner of iniquity. And they did smite upon the people of Jesus; but the people of Jesus did not smite again. And thus they did dwindle in unbelief and wickedness, from year to year, even until two hundred and thirty years had passed away" (4 Nephi 1:34).

MAYA PROPHECY OF CONQUEST

Landa, as well as other sixteenth-century writers, recorded a prophecy of the Maya concerning the coming of the Spaniards. For example, historian Alfred Tozzer writes:

In the same way that the Mexican nation [meaning the Aztecs] had signs and prophecies of the coming of the Spaniards, and of the destruction of its power and its religion, so did the populations of Yucatan some years before the *Adelatado* Montejo conquered them; and in the mountains of Mani, which is in the province of Tutul Xiu, an Indian named Ah Cambal, (who held the) office (of) Chilan, (which means), "he who has the duty of giving the answers of the god (*demonio*)," announced to them publicly that they would soon be subjected by a foreign race, and that they would preach to them one God and the power of a tree, which in their language is called "*uahom che*," which means "a tree erected with great virtue against the evil spirit."[3]

We cannot determine where this man named Ah Cambal gained his knowledge to make such a prophecy—that is, whether it was gleaned from Maya written history or from his own insight. It was certainly available in written history, as the prophet Nephi proclaimed the same type of prophecy more than two thousand years earlier:

And I looked and beheld a man among the Gentiles, who was separated from the seed of my brethren by the many waters; and I beheld the Spirit of God, that it came down and wrought upon the man; and he went forth upon the many waters, even unto the seed of my brethren, who were in the promised land.

And it came to pass that I beheld the Spirit of God, that it wrought upon other Gentiles; and they went forth out of captivity, upon the many waters.

And it came to pass that I beheld many multitudes of the Gentiles upon the land of promise; and I beheld the wrath of God, that it was upon the seed of my brethren; and they were scattered before the Gentiles and were smitten. (1 Nephi 13:12–14)

Landa was intimately acquainted with a Cocom who had a book of his grandfather's that told of a conquering nation who would arrive on large deer (the natives called the horses of the Spaniards deer or cows): "He showed him a book which had belonged to his grandfather, a son of the Cocom who had been killed at Mayapan. In this was a painting of a deer, and his grandfather had told him that when large deer of this kind should come into that country (for this is what they call the cows), the worship of the gods would cease; and this was fulfilled since the Spaniards brought large cows with them."[4]

4. Landa, *Relacion de las Cosas de Yucatan*, 44, 46.

MAYA TRIBES IN THE YUCATAN

The Maya culture, at the time of the conquest, presents an interesting picture of tribes and their leaders that, historically, appear to have existed for centuries. About AD 29, Mormon records that the Nephite culture divided into tribes: "And every tribe did appoint a chief or a leader over them; and thus they became tribes and leaders of tribes. Now behold, there was no man among them save he had much family and many kindreds and friends; therefore their tribes became exceedingly great" (3 Nephi 7:3–4).

Landa wrote about two great tribes in the sixteenth century called the Cocoms and the Xius. It is of great interest to travel today through the small Maya villages. The road from Uxmal to Chichen Itza, via the towns of Mani and Sotuta, is very narrow, with low jungle growth closing in on both sides of the road. The distance between these two small villages is only about thirty miles. Perhaps travelers may see one or two motor vehicles in each town. Most of the transportation consists of the three-wheeled bicycle, which serves as the Maya taxi. The bicycle peddler provides a seat between the two hind wheels, where a woman may sit as she is transported from her home to market and other places of interest. The vehicle also has a large metal basket for the children to ride in.

Landa records that the Xius were the lords of Mani and the Cocoms were the natural lords of Sotuta. Alfred Tozzer, who wrote extensive notes in his publication of Landa, quotes another chronicler on this subject, as follows: "One province fought with another and the said province of Mani was always at war with that of Cotuta (Sotuta) with a lord of the ancient people of this land called Na Chi Cocom on account of the long standing enmity which the said Cocoms had against the Tutul Xius saying that the Cocoms were 'natural lords' and the Tutul Xius, foreigners."[5] The word *Cocom* means in "the place of the Com tribe." *Com* was the name of two Jaredite kings, one who lived about 600 BC and another who lived many centuries earlier.

5. Landa, *Relacion de las Cosas de Yucatan*, 56.

En route from Chichen Itza to Cancun, travelers pass a village named *Cocom*. So the reader does not get the idea that two small villages were all that belong to a tribe, we should point out that the division line between provinces apparently met at Sotuta and

Landa, as well as other sixteenth-century writers, recorded a prophecy of the Maya concerning the coming of the Spaniards.

Mani. In one war among the tribes some years prior to the conquest, 150,000 men died in battle.

Book of Mormon students have often wondered why the last Lamanite-Nephite battle does not show up extensively in Mesoamerican history, as 230,000 Nephite soldiers were killed. Logically, the sixteenth-century Maya people would have had no interest in recording a battle that occurred twelve hundred years earlier on the opposite side of the Isthmus of Tehuantepec—when they had battles of their own that killed hundreds of thousands of their own people and when such battles were occurring right up to the time of the Spanish conquest.

This conclusion is consistent with the AD 400 Book of Mormon historian, Moroni, who wrote, speaking of the Lamanites, "For behold, their wars are exceedingly fierce among themselves" (Moroni 1:2).

Reference was made to the Cocom in chapter 2, "And It Came to Pass." *Co* is a very common beginning of a proper name in the Book of Mormon, such as *Cohor* and

FIGURE 13–2: Map showing the villages of Chichen Itza, Sotuta, Mayapan, Mani, and Uxmal. Merida is the modern-day capital of the state of Yucatan. Several of the villages in the Yucatan were connected by roads called *zac be* (white road) because the roads were made of limestone. These roads ranged from broad intracity causeways and long, raised intercity roadways to small local pathways, and some of them can still be seen today.

Corianton. Com is the actual name of a Jaredite king. It is of further interest that the *Cocoms* were considered natural lords—that they were an aristocratic elite who traced their genealogy for centuries and who passed the high priest office from father to son.[6]

6. Landa, *Relacion de las Cosas de Yucatan*, 27.

BOOK OF MORMON AND *RELACION* PARALLELS

Serious readers of the Book of Mormon will find a treasure trove of intriguing parallels between incidents that are contained in the Book of Mormon and incidents found in Landa's *Relacion de las Cosas de Yucatan*. Here is a sampling of just a few of those parallels:

Human Sacrifice and Cannibalism

Much is said in the Book of Mormon about the depravity of its peoples at various times. Human sacrifice and cannibalism were two outcomes of such depravity.

Toward the end of the final Nephite era, the Nephites were especially grieved because the Lamanites captured Nephite women and children and sacrificed them: "[The Lamanites] did take many prisoners both women and children, and did offer them up as sacrifices unto their idol gods." Further, "in the three hundred and sixty and seventh year, the Nephites [were] angry because the Lamanites had sacrificed their women and their children, . . . [and] they did go against the Lamanites with exceedingly great anger" (Mormon 4:14–15).

During this same time period, Moroni talked about cannibalism among the people: "The Lamanites have many prisoners, [including] men, women, and children. And the husbands and fathers of those women and children they have slain; and they feed the women upon the flesh of their husbands, and the children upon the flesh of their fathers. . . . And notwithstanding this great abomination of the Lamanites, it doth not exceed that of our people in Moriantum. For behold, many of the daughters of the Lamanites have they taken prisoners; and after depriving them of that which was most dear and precious above all things, which is chastity and virtue—And after they had done this thing, they did murder them in a most cruel manner, torturing their bodies even unto death; and after they have done this, they devour their flesh like unto wild beasts, because of the hardness of their hearts" (Moroni 9:7–10).

In his *Relacion*, Landa tells the story about a group of Spaniards who were shipwrecked and ended up in a Yucatan province called *Maya*, "from which the language of Yucatan takes the name of *Maya than*, which means 'the language of Maya.' These wretched men then fell into the hands of a wicked *cacique*, who sacrificed Valdivia and four other companions to his idols, and gave their bodies to his people for a feast. He spared Aguilar and Guerrero and five or six others to fatten them."[7]

7. Landa, *Relacion de las Cosas de Yucatan*, 7–8.

Serious readers of the Book of Mormon will find a treasure trove of intriguing parallels between incidents that are contained in the Book of Mormon and incidents found in Landa's *Relacion de las Cosas de Yucatan.*

Origins of Mesoamerican Peoples

Much is said in *Exploring the Lands of the Book of Mormon* about the origins of the three primary groups mentioned in the Book of Mormon—the Jaredites, Nephites-Lamanites, and Mulekites. We might naturally think that the Spanish conquistadors would have heard accounts about the origins of the Mesoamerican groups they encountered and conquered.

Landa supports that thinking with an interesting paragraph in his *Relacion*: "Some of the old people of Yucatan say that they have heard from their ancestors that this land was occupied by a race of people, who came from the East and whom God had delivered by opening twelve paths through the sea. If this were true, it necessarily follows that all the inhabitants of the Indies are descendants of the Jews; since having once passed the Straits of Magellan, they must have extended over more than two thousand leagues of land which now Spain governs."[8]

8. Landa, *Relacion de las Cosas de Yucatan*, 16–17.

"Some of the old people of Yucatan say that they have heard from their ancestors that this land was occupied by a race of people, who came from the East and whom God had delivered by opening twelve paths through the sea."

—Diego de Landa

Infant Baptism

In the Book of Mormon, the doctrine of baptism was clearly understood by the early Nephites and was practiced throughout much of the Nephite history (see, for example, 2 Nephi 31; Alma 7; Moroni 6). At some point close to the final demise of the Nephites, the doctrine became polluted, resulting in the practice of infant baptism. Of this practice, Mormon said the following in an "epistle" to his son Moroni:

> There have been disputations among you concerning the baptism of your little children.
>
> And now, my son, I desire that ye should labor diligently, that this gross error should be removed from among you. . . .
>
> For immediately after I had learned these things of you I inquired of the Lord concerning the matter. And the word of the Lord came to me by the power of the Holy Ghost, saying:
>
> Listen to the words of Christ, your Redeemer, your Lord and your God. Behold, I came into the world not to call the righteous but sinners to repentance; the whole need no physician, but they that are sick; wherefore, little children are whole, for they are not capable of committing sin; wherefore the curse of Adam is taken from them in me, that it hath no power over them; and the law of circumcision is done away in me.
>
> And after this manner did the Holy Ghost manifest the word of God unto me; wherefore, my beloved son, I know that it is solemn mockery before God, that ye should baptize little children. (Moroni 8:5–9)

In his *Relacion*, Landa speaks of baptism in general among the Maya and of infant baptism in particular as follows: "Baptism is not found in any part of the Indies except in Yucatan, where it even exists under a name which means 'to be born anew or again'; which is the same as *renascor* in the Latin language, for in the language of Yucatan *sihil* means 'to be born anew or again,' and it is only used in compound words, and so *caput sihil* means 'to be born anew.' We have not been able to find its origin, more than that it is a custom that has *always existed*, and for which they had so much devotion that no one failed to receive it." Alfred Tozzer, the editor of Landa's *Relacion* as published in the eighth edition, comments as follows about Landa's statement that baptism was not found in the New World outside of the Yucatan: "This statement by Landa is obviously an error as Landa does not appear to have known of the customs in Mexico where the child, several days after birth, was baptized and purified by the invocation to the goddess Chalchiuhlicue, etc." [9]

FIGURE 13–3: Some Latter-day Saint guides have perpetuated the myth that the Maya baptized by immersion at a "baptismal font" at Chichen Itza. However, this structure is not a baptismal font but is a bath house that dates to AD 800. (Photo courtesy of Sheryl Lee Wilson)

9. Landa, *Relacion de las Cosas de Yucatan*, 102; emphasis added.

The polluted doctrine of infant baptism evidently continued from Moroni's time until and even after the Spanish conquest.

Death by Fire in a Furnace

In the Book of Mormon, we find references to furnaces into which people were thrown for the purpose of burning them to death (see, for example, 3 Nephi 28:21; 4 Nephi 1:32; Mormon 8:24). We may wonder how furnaces in Book of Mormon times could have been large enough to hold humans. Throughout Mesoamerica, archaeologists have found large kilns used for the making of pottery—large enough to cast human beings inside.

Landa writes about the "abominable sin of pederasty" (sodomy). He did not think this evil was practiced among the people of the Yucatan. However, in a footnote to Landa's words, Alfred Tozzer disputes Landa by quoting the *Relacion* of Chunchuchu, which says: "It is said of the lord of the Xius that in his time he had this sin punished by throwing those whom he found guilty of it into a burning furnace; and today this furnace may be seen in the ancient city of Mayapan which is seven leagues from this city (of Merida [in the Yucatan]) toward the southwest." [10]

10. Landa, *Relacion de las Cosas de Yucatan*, 124.

Mormon wrote about three things that are indigenous to Mesoamerica: (1) wild beasts, (2) poisonous serpents, and (3) fiery furnaces: "Even the fiery furnace could not harm them, neither wild beasts nor poisonous serpents" (Mormon 8:24).

The Cross

The Book of Mormon clearly alludes to the cross associated with the Crucifixion of Jesus. About 600 BC, Nephi said, "I . . . saw that [Jesus] was *lifted up upon the cross* and slain for the sins of the world" (1 Nephi 11:33; emphasis added). Years later, Jacob said, "We would to God that we could persuade all men not to rebel against God, to provoke him to anger, but that all men would believe in Christ, and view his death, and *suffer his cross* and bear the shame of the world" (Jacob 1:8; emphasis added). The word *cross* in these verses is a noun.

Interestingly, the word *cross* is used twice in the Book of Mormon as a verb in a verse that might refer to the cross of Jesus. About 75 BC, Alma counseled his son Corianton as follows: "Now my son, I would that ye should repent and forsake your sins, and go no more after the lusts of your eyes, but *cross yourself* in all these things; for except ye do this ye can in nowise inherit the kingdom of God. Oh, remember, and take it upon you, and *cross yourself* in these things" (Alma 39:9; emphasis added).

To "cross yourself" in all probability does not refer to making the sign of the cross as Catholics do in their worship but, in this verse, is used in a sense similar to that as defined by Noah Webster in 1828.[11] Thus, it simply means to follow Christ or to cross sin out of our lives. Members of The Church of Jesus Christ of Latter-day Saints do not make the "sign of the cross," wear crosses, or use crosses on their chapels or temples. Rather, we prefer to worship the resurrected Christ as opposed to the crucified Christ as symbolized by the sign of the cross or the emblem of the cross.

As Alfred Tozzer points out in a footnote in Landa's *Relacion*, "The Maltese cross is found among the Mayas." According to Diego de Landa, a native named Ah Cambal,

11. Noah Webster, *An American Dictionary of the English Language* (New York: S. Converse, 1828), s.v., "cross"; facsimile of first edition by the Foundation for American Christian Education.

FIGURE 13–4: The cross played a major role in the worship of the Maya. Whether the cross represented Christ is difficult to say. Nevertheless, this panel at Palenque shows a cross with the symbols of the quetzal bird on the top and the serpent monster (Coatl) on the bottom. The symbol of the cross appears in many places among the ruins, including the Temple of the Cross at Palenque.

perhaps the same person as Chilam Balam as identified in the *Relacion* of Merida, announced to the people prior to the conquest that "they would soon be subjected by a foreign race, and that they would preach to them one God and the power of a tree, which in their language is called '*uahom che*,' which means 'a tree erected with great virtue against the evil spirit.'" According to the *Relacion* of Merida, Chilam Balam "had that sign of the cross and others made of cut stone and placed in the courtyards of the temples where it could be seen by all, and he said that it was the great tree of the world. And many people went to see it as something new, and it would seem that they worshipped it from that time on. And afterwards when the Spaniards came and they knew that they brought the symbol of the holy cross *which was like that which their prophet Chilam Balam had drawn*, they believed what he had told them to be true and decided to receive the Spaniards peacefully and not make war on them but be their friends."[12]

12. Landa, *Relacion de las Cosas de Yucatan*, 42–43; emphasis added.

The Afterlife

The Book of Mormon is very clear and specific about life after death. In the words of Amulek, "If we do not improve our time while in this life, then cometh *the night of darkness* wherein there can be no labor performed" (Alma 34:33; emphasis added). He further says, "If ye have procrastinated the day of your repentance even until death, behold, ye have become subjected to the spirit of the devil, and he doth seal you his; ... and *the devil hath all power over you*; and this is the final state of the wicked" (Alma 34:35; emphasis added).

In speaking to his son Corianton, Alma said:

There must needs be a space betwixt the time of death and the time of the resurrection. . . .

And . . . what becometh of the souls of men from this time of death to the time appointed for the resurrection? . . .

There is a space between the time of death and the resurrection. And now, concerning this space of time, what becometh of the souls of men is the thing which I have inquired diligently of the Lord to know. . . .

Behold, it has been made known unto me by an angel, that the spirits of all men, as soon as they are departed from this mortal body, yea, the spirits of all men, whether they be good or evil, are taken home to that God who gave them life.

And then . . . the spirits of those who are righteous are *received into a state of happiness, which is called paradise*, a state of rest, a state of peace, where they shall rest from all their troubles and from all care, and sorrow.

And then . . . the spirits of the wicked, yea, who are evil— . . . these *shall be cast out into outer darkness*; there shall be weeping, and wailing, and gnashing of teeth. . . .

Prior to the spanish conquest, a Maya priest prophesied that they would soon be subjected by a foreign race and that they would preach to them one God and the power of a tree.

Now this is the state of the souls of the wicked, yea, *in darkness*, and a *state of awful, fearful looking for the fiery indignation of the wrath of God* upon them; thus they remain in this state, as well as the righteous in *paradise*, until the time of their resurrection. (Alma 40:6–14; emphasis added)

In his *Relacion*, Landa writes the following about the afterlife beliefs of the Maya:

This people has always believed in the immortality of the soul, more than many other nations, although they have not reached such a high state of civilization; for they believed that there was another and better life, which the soul enjoyed when it separated from the body. They said that *this future life was divided into a good and a bad life*—into *a painful one and one full of rest.* The bad and the painful one was for the vicious people, while the good and the delightful one was for those who had lived well according to their manner of living. The delights which they said they were to obtain, if they were good, were to go to a delightful place, where nothing would give them pain and where they would have an abundance of foods and drinks of great sweetness, and a tree which they call there *yaxche,* very cool and giving great shade, which is the ceiba, under the branches and the shadow of which they would rest and forever cease from labor. The penalties of a bad life, which they said that the bad would suffer, were to *go to a place lower than the other*, which they called *Metnal*, which means "hell," and be tormented in it by the devils and by great extremities of hunger, cold, fatigue and grief. They maintained that there was in this place a devil, the prince of all the devils, whom all obeyed, and they call him in their language Hunhau. And they said that these lives, bad and good, had no end for the soul has none. . . . They had no memory of the resurrection of the body and give no account from whom they learned of this heaven and hell of theirs.[13]

13. Landa, *Relacion de las Cosas de Yucatan*, 131–32; emphasis added.

SUMMARY

As can be seen, customs, beliefs, and traditions from the sixteenth century that probably reached back to Book of Mormon times jump out at readers from Landa's descriptions of Maya life. Further, the settlement of the Yucatan is consistent with what we glean from the Book of Mormon. The Lamanite-Nephite migrations always appear to come from the south. Mosiah led a righteous group of Nephites from the south about 180 BC. The Lamanites kept showing up on the "big screen" among the Nephites. Landa records: "The Indians say that numerous tribes with their chiefs came to Yucatan from the south, and it appears that they came from Chiapas, although the Indians have no more knowledge about it. But this author conjectures it because there are in Chiapas many remains of places which have been abandoned."[14] No dating is given by Landa, but the cultural patterns and movements express the culture patterns and movements

14. Landa, *Relacion de las Cosas de Yucatan*, 29–30.

in the Book of Mormon. The facts that they came from Chiapas and the Peten[15] and that the cities were abandoned reflect a possible Nephite movement.

15. Landa, *Relacion de las Cosas de Yucatan*, 22–30.

Yucatan may have been part of the state (or country) of Bountiful spoken of in the Book of Mormon. The land of Bountiful was north of the land of Zarahemla, and the land of Zarahemla was north of the land of Nephi. After the first century BC, Bountiful included the Peten and Belize regions of the Yucatan, which were north of the land of Nephi.

Landa probably wrote his original *Relacion* in 1566. He had supported a large number of natives during the famine of 1553. He was elected bishop of Yucatan on April 10, 1572. He had burned the books at Mani ten years earlier, in 1562. He died April 29, 1579. In reading his *Relacion*, knowledgeable Book of Mormon students will see a great many significant parallels between the content of *Relacion de las Cosas de Yucatan* and incidents in the Book of Mormon. The experience of reading Landa's *Relacion* and learning about the Yucatan Maya is a very rewarding one that we highly recommend.

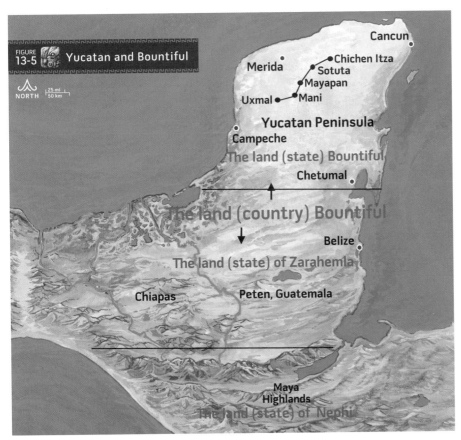

FIGURE 13-5: Yucatan and Bountiful

NORTH · 25 mi / 50 km

Cancun
Chichen Itza
Merida · Sotuta
Mayapan
Uxmal · Mani

Yucatan Peninsula
Campeche
The land (state) Bountiful
Chetumal

The land (country) Bountiful

Belize
The land (state) of Zarahemla

Chiapas · Peten, Guatemala

Maya Highlands
The land (state) of Nephi

FIGURE 13–5: This map shows the relationship of the proposed land of Zarahemla with the proposed land of Bountiful. Bountiful was north of Zarahemla. The country, or greater land Bountiful, was synonymous with the land southward: "The land on the southward was called Bountiful" (Alma 22:31).

CHAPTER 14

The White God Quetzalcoatl

All the glory of the godhead had the prophet Quetzalcoatl
All the honor of the people, sanctified his name and holy;
And their prayers they offered to him in the days of ancient Tula
(Sahagun, Florentine Codex)

irtually all sixteenth-century Spanish writers wrote about a white god called Quetzalcoatl. This tradition is strong and repetitive. Every school child in Mexico studies Quetzalcoatl and knows the importance of his role.

The symbol of the serpent has long been associated with deities of Mexico and Guatemala. In the Aztec language, the word *coatl* means serpent. The word *quetzal* comes from the quetzal bird, which has long, beautiful feathers. By placing the Aztec word *quetzal* in front of the word *coatl*, we have the word *Quetzalcoatl*. Quetzalcoatl, therefore, means "feathered serpent"—or quetzal bird serpent or serpent with precious feathers. Interestingly, the quetzal is the national bird of Guatemala, and it is also the name of the basic unit of currency of that country.

OPPOSITE: The artist Diego Rivera depicted the white god Quetzalcoatl floating on a raft in the image of a serpent after having taught the native people of Mexico. Tradition states that Quetzalcoatl was born of a virgin and that he taught baptism and the law of the fast and then left with a promise to return. Rivera's paintings are displayed at the National Palace in Mexico City. (Photo courtesy of George and Audrey DeLange)

FIGURE 14–1: The beautiful quetzal bird portrays a legendary mystique and romance unequaled in the lands of its nativity. The dense jungles and majestic mountains of Guatemala and Honduras are the natural habitat for this awe-inspiring bird. Its carmine red breast and bright yellow beak set off its long iridescent tail feathers, which are reminiscent of the Maya jade, Aztec gold, and Caribbean blue from whence it came. (Painting by Verl F. Morgan)

1. A. Labastille, "The Quetzal: Fabulous Bird of Maya Land," *National Geographic Magazine*, 135, no. 1 (January 1969), 141.

2. Constance Irwin, *Fair Gods and Stone Faces: Ancient Seafarers and the New World's Most Intriguing Riddle* (New York: St. Martin's Press, 1963), 33.

3. Ixtlilxochitl:45; see chapter 11, "Fernando de Alva Ixtlilxochitl."

4. Laurette Sejourne, *Burning Water: Thought and Religion in Ancient Mexico*, originally published in Spanish in 1957, translated to English by Laurette Sejourne and Irene Nicholson (London: Thames and Hudson, 1957), 25.

5. John Taylor, *The Mediation and Atonement* (Salt Lake City: Deseret News, 1882), 201.

The ancient inhabitants of the land that is called Mesoamerica by archaeologists literally paid reverence to the quetzal bird, as traditionally only persons of royal birth and individuals who were bestowed with a god-like status were permitted to wear the lustrous plumage of the quetzal on their headdresses.

The visit of Jesus Christ to the Americas was symbolized by the elegant quetzal bird. Just as Christ descended to the Nephites gathered at the temple in the land Bountiful, so is the descent of the quetzal. The white god Quetzalcoatl was so named to represent the splendor of the quetzal as described by one writer: "An ark of green fire in sun, an emerald meteor in mist, a cold viridian flame in rain moved the quetzal."[1]

Throughout pre-Columbian Mexican history, scores of individuals, both mythological and real, were given the name or title of *Quetzalcoatl*. In a similar fashion, this Mesoamerican custom continues today when almost countless parents give the deity name of *Jesus* to their offspring.

Attempts also have been made to attribute the name *Quetzalcoatl* to only one person. The following quotations are indicative of what is said about Quetzalcoatl:

In all of America's past no figure is more exciting, more tantalizing, or more frustrating than that of the Fair God Quetzalcoatl.[2]

Quetzalcoatl was a man of comely appearance and serious disposition. His countenance was white, and he wore a beard. His manner of dress consisted of a long, flowing robe.[3]

Just as our era began with Christ, so that of the Aztecs and their predecessors began—approximately at the same time—with Quetzalcoatl. His image, the plumed serpent, had for pre-Columbian people the same evocative force as has the Crucifix for Christianity.[4]

The story of the life of the Mexican divinity, Quetzalcoatl, closely resembles that of the Savior; so closely indeed, that we can come to no other conclusion than that Quetzalcoatl and Christ are the same being.[5]

We should, however, exercise caution as we correlate Jesus Christ with Quetzalcoatl because a tenth-century culture hero called Ce Acatl Topiltzin Quetzalcoatl took upon himself the title of the deity Quetzalcoatl. Nevertheless, the deity Quetzalcoatl apparently had its origin in the visit of Jesus Christ to the American continent.[6]

Similarities of Christ and Quetzalcoatl include the following:

1. Both Christ and Quetzalcoatl were recognized as creator of all things.[7]
2. Both Christ and Quetzalcoatl were born of virgins.[8]
3. Both Christ and Quetzalcoatl were described as being white or as wearing a white robe.[9]
4. Both Christ and Quetzalcoatl performed miracles.[10]
5. Both Christ and Quetzalcoatl taught the ordinance of baptism.[11]
6. Both Christ and Quetzalcoatl prophesied of future events.[12]
7. Both Christ and Quetzalcoatl were universal as opposed to just being recognized as local gods.[13]
8. A great destruction was associated with both Christ and Quetzalcoatl at exactly the same time period in history.[14]
9. The cross was a symbol to both Christ and Quetzalcoatl.[15]
10. Both Christ and Quetzalcoatl sent out disciples to preach their word.[16]
11. Both Christ and Quetzalcoatl promised they would come a second time.[17]
12. A new star was associated with both Christ and Quetzalcoatl.[18]
13. The children of both Christ and Quetzalcoatl will become lords and heirs of the earth.[19]

Question No. 1: If the parallels are so strong between Christ and Quetzalcoatl, why do some people question that they are one and the same?

Answer: From the time of Christ to the conquest of Mexico, many priests and royalty were given the name *Quetzalcoatl*. This practice suggests that Quetzalcoatl became a title in much the same way that Nephi became a title: "Wherefore, the people were

> "In all of America's past no figure is more exciting, more tantalizing, or more frustrating than that of the Fair God Quetzalcoatl."
>
> —Constance Irwin

6. See Joseph L. Allen, "A Comparative Study of Quetzalcoatl, the Feathered-Serpent God of Meso-America, with Jesus Christ, the God of the Nephites" (PhD dissertation, Department of Ancient Scripture, Brigham Young University, 1970).

7. Caesar A. Saenz, *Quetzalcoatl* (Mexico, DF: Instituto Nacional de Antropolgia o Historia, 1962), 19, 40; see also Mosiah 4:2.

8. Abel Gamiz, *Quetzalcoatl* (n.p.: Sociadad Folklorica de Mexico, 1941), 95; see also Alma 7:10.

9. Juan de Torquemada, *Monarchia Indiana,* 3 vols. (San Francisco: A. L. Bancroft, 1883), 3:47; see also 3 Nephi 11:8.

10. Sejourne, *Burning Water,* 136–37; see also 3 Nephi 26:15.

11. Irwin, *Fair Gods and Stone Faces,* 170; see also 3 Nephi 11:23.

12. See Ixtlilxochitl:40; see chapter 11, "Fernando de Alva Ixtlilxochitl."

13. Sejourne, *Burning Water;* see also 3 Nephi 16:1.

14. Ixtlilxochitl:40; see chapter 11, "Fernando de Alva Ixtlilxochitl"; also 3 Nephi 8:5.

15. Irwin, *Fair Gods and Stone Faces,* 165; see also 3 Nephi 27:14.

16. Diane E. Wirth, *A Challenge to the Critics: Scholarly Evidences of the Book of Mormon* (Bountiful, UT: Horizon Publishers, 1986), 55; see also 3 Nephi 12:1.

17. Fray Bernardino de Sahagun, *Historia General de las Cosas de Nueva Espano: Florentine Codex,* edited and translated to English by Arthur O. Anderson and Charles E. Dibble, 2 vols. (Santa Fe, NM: The School of American Research and the University of Utah, 1950), 1:40; see also 2 Nephi 6:14.

18. *Anales de Cauhtitlan y Leyenda de los Soles en Codice Chimalpopoca,* edited and translated by Primo F. Valazquez (Mexico, DF: Institute of Historic Investigations, National University, 1945; see also 3 Nephi 1:21.

19. Ixtlilxochitl:40; see chapter 11, "Fernando de Alva Ixtlilxochitl"; see also 4 Nephi 1:17.

desirous to retain in remembrance his name. And whoso should reign in his stead were called by the people, second Nephi, third Nephi, and so forth, according to the reigns of the kings; and thus they were called by the people, let them be of whatever name they would" (Jacob 1:11).

One such culture hero named Topiltzin Quetzalcoatl, born ca. AD 935, left a trail from the Mexico City area to the Yucatan. The great Temple of Kukulcan was dedicated to this Toltec Quetzalcoatl. *Kukulcan* is the Maya word for "feathered serpent."[20]

The priest Topiltzin Quetzalcoatl set about to establish a new golden age, a reincarnation of a utopia that existed centuries earlier under the reign of the deity Quetzalcoatl.[21]

Furthermore, many pagan attributes became associated with Quetzalcoatl over the years, either by another individual's being named Quetzalcoatl or by the people's entering into apostasy. Idol worship was introduced, as demonstrated in their art. A case in point is the Temple of Quetzalcoatl located by the pyramids of Teotihuacan. These stone serpents with feathers around their necks may have been originally associated with Christ. As time went by, they merely represented a distorted view of Christ.

Question No. 2: If the parallels are so strong between Christ and Quetzalcoatl, why would Christ be associated with the serpent? Is not the serpent a symbol for Satan?

Answer: In the Book of Mormon, the serpent is a symbol of Christ (see 1 Nephi 17:41; 2 Nephi 25:20; Alma 33:19–21; Helaman 8:14–15). However, the story of the serpents is in the Old Testament in the book of Numbers. The children of Israel were residing in the wilderness. Being plagued with poisonous serpents, Moses prayed to the Lord for his people. The Lord instructed Moses to make a bronze serpent and attach it to a pole. The Lord promised Moses that anyone who had been bitten by a poisonous serpent and who would look upon that brass serpent would live (see Numbers 21:6–9). Nephi, the son of Helaman in the Book of Mormon, provides an explanation of the meaning of the brazen serpent that Moses lifted up on a pole: "As he lifted up the brazen serpent in the wilderness, even so shall he be lifted up who should come. And as many as should look upon that serpent should live, even so as many as should look upon the Son of God with faith, having a contrite spirit, might live, even unto that life which is eternal" (Helaman 8:14–15).

John the Beloved portrayed the same type of symbolism as he wrote, "And as Moses lifted up the serpent in the wilderness, even so must the Son of Man be lifted up" (John 3:14).

CHRIST IN THE BOOK OF MORMON

The impact of Quetzalcoatl on the history of Mexico is overwhelming. Of the pantheon of gods celebrated by the ancient Mexicans, only Quetzalcoatl reached all cultures. An

20. Allen, "A Comparative Study of Quetzalcoatl, the Feathered-Serpent God of Meso-America, with Jesus Christ, the God of the Nephites," 86–94.

21. Enrique Florescano, "La Serpiente Emplumada, Tlaloc, y Quetzalcoatl," *Cuadernos Americanos* (March–April 1964): 164–66.

author by the name of Laurette Sejourne of the University of Mexico was so impressed with this concept that she wrote a book called *The Universality of Quetzalcoatl*.[22]

22. Laurette Sejourne, *El Universo de Quetzalcoatl* (Mexico: Fondo de Cultura Economica, 1962).

Although the concept of god became polluted throughout the centuries and although other people took upon themselves the name or symbolism of Quetzalcoatl, the Book of Mormon itself sets the stage for the beginning of the Mesoamerican legend of Quetzalcoatl:

> And it came to pass that while they were thus conversing one with another, they heard a voice as if it came out of heaven; and they cast their eyes round about, for they understood not the voice which they heard; and it was not a harsh voice, neither was it a loud voice; nevertheless, and notwithstanding it being a small voice it did pierce them that did hear to the center, insomuch that there was no part of their frame that it did not cause to quake; yea, it did pierce them to the very soul, and did cause their hearts to burn.
>
> And it came to pass that again they heard the voice, and they understood it not.
>
> And again the third time they did hear the voice, and did open their ears to hear it; and their eyes were towards the sound thereof; and they did look steadfastly towards heaven, from whence the sound came.
>
> And behold, the third time they did understand the voice which they heard; and it said unto them:
>
> Behold my Beloved Son, in whom I am well pleased, in whom I have glorified my name—hear ye him.
>
> And it came to pass, as they understood they cast their eyes up again towards heaven; and behold, they saw a Man descending out of heaven; and he was clothed in a white robe; and he came down and stood in the midst of them; and the eyes of the whole multitude were turned upon him, and they durst not open their mouths, even one to another, and wist not what it meant, for they thought it was an angel that had appeared unto them.
>
> And it came to pass that he stretched forth his hand and spake unto the people, saying:
>
> Behold, I am Jesus Christ, whom the prophets testified shall come into the world. (3 Nephi 11:3–10)

Every Book of Mormon prophet from Lehi to the coming of Christ prophesied of this singular, important event.

The impact of Quetzalcoatl on the history of Mexico is overwhelming. Of the pantheon of gods celebrated by the ancient Mexicans, only Quetzalcoatl reached all cultures.

QUETZALCOATL IN TRADITION

Not all statements about Quetzalcoatl refer to Christ. Excerpts from the following poem, "The Prophet," however, reflect the stature that the symbol of Quetzalcoatl played in the lives of the ancient Mesoamericans:

Just as a Mexican tradition today prescribes that children be named after great people, such as Jesus, Moses, or Quetzalcoatl, the title or name of Quetzalcoatl was adopted by other people.

All the glory of the godhead
Had the prophet Quetzalcoatl;
All the honor of the people.
Sanctified his name and holy;
And their prayers they offered to him
In the days of ancient Tula.
There in grandeur rose his temple;
Reared aloft its mighty ramparts,
Reaching upward to the heavens.
Wondrous stout and strong the walls were;
High the skyward-climbing stairway,
With its steps so long and narrow,
With its many steps so narrow
That there scarce was room for sitting,
Room for placing of the footsteps.
There he lies full-length extended;
Lies outstretched and ever mantled,
With his features closely covered.
Glory he of all the nations;
And his face is like unto a
Mighty echo-sounding fire-flame
That has just been fully muffled;
Pitilessly been extinguished.
See, his beard is very lengthy;
See, exceeding long his beard is;
Yellow as the straw his beard is!
Wondrous rich were all the Toltecs;
Masters they of wealth uncounted;
Every need was satisfied them;
Nothing lacked they in their households;
Hunger never dwelt among them;
And the small corn never used they
Save to heat their thermal baths with.
Quetzalcoatl offered penance
And with thorns his legs he punctured

Till the blood came oozing outward.
Ever bathed he in the night-time;
Bathed he in the Xippacoyan,
In the Bathing Place of Xipe.
And thus custom imitated
They the sacred fire expenders;
They the priests officiating
Kept the mode of Quetzalcoatl,
Master of their organization
And creator of their being;
Kept the usages of Tula,
Even as today we keep them;
Here in Mexico observe them.[23]

FIGURE 14–2: The tradition of the coming of the white god Quetzalcoatl has endured the centuries, and its symbolism has been transformed into an apostate stone image in much the same way that the image of the cross has overshadowed the reality of the resurrection. (Photo courtesy of George and Audrey DeLange)

23. John Hubert Cornyn, *The Song of Quetzalcoatl*, 2nd ed., translated from the Aztec (Yellow Springs, OH: Antioch Press, 1931), 78–85.

THE TENTH-CENTURY QUETZALCOATL

Just as a Mexican tradition today prescribes that children be named after great people, such as Jesus or Moses, the title or name of Quetzalcoatl was adopted by other people. Hence, "Quetzalcoatl," as stated earlier, became a title much in the same way that "Nephi" became a title after the death of Nephi, the son of Lehi (see Jacob 1:11). That apparent tradition has caused a great deal of confusion and even a great deal of misinformation.

So readers will not be confused, we give below a treatise about a tenth-century Mexico culture hero who took upon himself the title, or the name, of Quetzalcoatl. This Quetzalcoatl is the one who migrated from the Mexico valley to the Yucatan where he built the Temple of Kukulcan at Chichen Itza. *Kukulcan* is the Maya word for Quetzalcoatl. *Quetzalcoatl* is Aztec. Most written material about Quetzalcoatl today refers to the tenth-century Quetzalcoatl.

The material that follows is extrapolated from chapter 3 of "A Comparative Study of Quetzalcoatl, the Feathered-Serpent God of Meso-America, with Jesus Christ, the God of the Nephites."[24]

24. Allen, "A Comparative Study of Quetzalcoatl, the Feathered-Serpent God of Meso-America, with Jesus Christ, the God of the Nephites," 75–80.

For many years and among all the pre-Spanish themes, we find an overabundance of literature relative to the great Mesoamerican myth or legend of Quetzalcoatl. Nevertheless, in spite of the abundant amount of literature that has reference to this fascinating American myth or legend, the ancient figure of Quetzalcoatl continues to be developed in an inextricable mythological and legendary manner that creates a desire to know the real history. Perhaps the obscurity and confusion that are current today regarding the myth or legend of Quetzalcoatl can be attributed to the greatly exaggerated mythological subjectivity that is prevalent in a study of this type, and perhaps the problem lies with the myth or legend itself.

25. Florescano, "La Serpiente Emplumada, Tlaloc, y Quetzalcoatl," 121–122.

According to Enrique Florescano,[25] every person who has studied the Quetzalcoatl legend has elaborated on it and has inculcated his or her own personal myth. Apparently, all students of Quetzalcoatl work from the hypothesis that he was the great god of the Aztecs as well as of other ancient Mesoamerican tribes. Therefore, we need not be surprised that everyone has taken a little information from one source or another to develop a personal myth.

A number of reasons may suggest that any treatise on the personality of the feathered serpent would have subjective overtones. Paramount among these is the type of source material available for a study of this nature.

All that is known about Quetzalcoatl comes in the form of secondary sources. Further, all the written information about Quetzalcoatl that is available today has an origin in the sixteenth-century Spanish chronicles. The Spanish chroniclers were Spanish conquerors, Catholic missionaries, or natives like Ixtlilxochitl who used as source materials the Aztecs and Maya who were living at the time of the conquest. The natives, in turn, related those things they could remember from the oral and written traditions passed on to them from centuries back.

As a result, we can assume logically that the vast majority of material written in the sixteenth century has the probability of being biased. Perhaps it is biased from a Mesoamerican native point of view in an attempt to protect the religious beliefs, or perhaps it is biased on the part of the Spaniards in an attempt either to correlate the Mexican history with Christianity or to present the opposite point of view and to equate the history of the Mexicans with workings of the devil.

A second problem that occurs in an attempt to be objective in a study of Quetzalcoatl arises from the fact that, on many occasions, it is difficult, if not impossible, to determine whether the Spanish chroniclers were writing about human beings who were named Quetzalcoatl or if the chroniclers were indeed referring to the myths and legends that date back to the god Quetzalcoatl.

The major problem that arises in the study of Quetzalcoatl originates from the discussion of two distinct personalities, neither one having an apparent relationship with the other. On the one hand, Quetzalcoatl is seen as a human being existing in the tenth century who was filled with passions, fought with his people, and finally was exalted to the position of a god. The god Quetzalcoatl, on the other hand, seems to have a long life span with information about him beginning prior to the time of the Christian era and proceeding forward. The latter is considered in the annals as the Creator God of the earth and even of man himself.

26. Sejourne, *Burning Water*, 15–16.

Laurette Sejourne,[26] commenting on the extreme difficulty of separating the divine from the human in Quetzalcoatl, suggested that this outcome occurred because Quetzalcoatl jumps from one time period to another and from one city to another. In reality, his giant figure fills the scene during hundreds of years without any interruption. We must, therefore, consider Quetzalcoatl in all of his fabulous amplitude, accepting

> "In the firm relationship with the worship of the ancient supreme deity, Quetzalcoatl, it is known that among the Toltecs there was a priest by the name of Quetzalcoatl who sought to maintain the purity of the traditional worship."
>
> —Miguel Leon-Portilla

what he must have been—perhaps more profound than a personal king—to the extent that the Nahuatl nation declared him as their creator.

Pedro Armillas[27] proposed a solution to the problem in his writings. He said that in the Mexican myth and tradition, Quetzalcoatl presents distinct human and divine characteristics. We must, therefore, examine each separately to determine the age of the different individual concepts and to verify when and how they were integrated to constitute the complete figure of the sixteenth century.

Modern writers and archaeologists have amplified the Quetzalcoatl dilemma. Walter Krickburg[28] writes, "Quetzalcoatl . . . had . . . the function of a cultural hero character which resembled that of the Supreme Deity."

Michael Coe explains, "They [the Toltecs] were ruled by a great king who took on the title of the mighty Mesoamerican god Quetzalcoatl (Feathered Serpent), and the doings of this man have been forever mixed up with those more properly ascribed to the god."[29]

Miguel Leon-Portilla records, "In the firm relationship with the worship of the ancient supreme deity, Quetzalcoatl, it is known that among the Toltecs there was a priest by the name of Quetzalcoatl who sought to maintain the purity of the traditional worship."[30]

Jonathan Leonard also analyzed the Quetzalcoatl problem and the mistaken identity by modern historians: "As a youth, Topiltzin studied for the priesthood and eventually became a high priest of Quetzalcoatl, or the Feathered Serpent, the very ancient god of Teotihuacan and the patron of learning and civilized skills. When Topiltzin ascended the Toltec throne, he changed his own name to Quetzalcoatl. This was not an act of self-deification; high priests of the time were often called by the names of the gods they worshiped. But the change of name caused endless confusion. Both ancient Indian legend-makers and modern historians have often mistaken Topiltzin Quetzalcoatl, the man, for Quetzalcoatl, the god."[31]

In addition, Geoffrey Bushnell affirms the Quetzalcoatl problem as he writes: "The god who is most prominent in the art of Tula is the feathered serpent Quetzalcoatl. . . . Confusion has been caused by the adoption of the name by the ruler who founded the city . . . around whom many legends have gathered."[32]

The human characteristics are interwoven with the divine attributes of Quetzalcoatl to the extent that writers are forced to exclude one or the other or to create two or more Quetzalcoatls.

Daniel Brinton wrote at the close of the nineteenth century and interpreted Quetzalcoatl as follows: "This . . . national hero . . . was often identified with the supreme deity and the creator of the world. . . . He personally appeared among the ancestors of the nation, . . . taught them . . . [and] framed the laws which governed their social relations, and . . . he left them, not suffering death but disappearing in some way from their view. Hence it was nigh universally expected that at some time he would return."[33]

27. Pedro Armillas, "La Serpiente Emplumada," *Cuadernos Americanos* (February 1947): 163.

28. Walter Krickburg, *Las Antiquas Culturas Mexicanas,* translated from German by Sita Garst and Jasmin Reuter (Mexico, DF: Fondo de Cultura Economica, 1964), 135.

29. Michael D. Coe, *Mexico* (New York: F. A. Praeger, 1962), 13.

30. Miguel Leon-Portilla, *Quetzalcoatl* (Mexico, DF: Fondo de Cultura Economica, 1968), 36.

31. Jonathan Norton Leonard, *Ancient America* (New York: Time, 1967), 59.

32. Geoffrey H. S. Bushnell, *Ancient Arts of the Americas* (New York: F. A. Praeger, 1965), 53–54.

33. Daniel G. Brinton, *American Hero Myths* (Philadelphia: H. C. Watts, 1882), 27.

A single summary statement as recorded by Frederick Peterson is ample to synthesize the Quetzalcoatl problem: "History seems to become infused with legend, and confuses the individual Ce Acatl Topiltzin Quetzalcoatl with the deity Quetzalcoatl whom he served."[34]

34. Frederick A. Peterson, *Ancient Mexico: An Introduction to the Pre-Hispanic Cultures* (New York: Putnam, 1959), 68.

To add more confusion to the picture, we point out that the culture hero, about whom the above authors wrote, existed centuries earlier, stemming from the feathered-serpent motif or perhaps even adopting the feathered-serpent motif. The tenth-century culture hero has been labeled by several titles. These titles are Topiltzin, Ce Acatl, and Nacxipl; and some scholars have associated him with Ehecatl. All these names appear with the appendage of *Quetzalcoatl.*

Topiltzin, translated, means "Our Lord," and only Topiltzin Quetzalcoatl, of all of the gods of Mesoamerica, is called *Lord,* and there is even evidence to indicate that men swore by him.[35]

35. Lewis Spence, *The Gods of Mexico* (New York: Frederick A. Stokes, 1923), 127.

The Quetzalcoatl problem is intensified because Topiltzin Quetzalcoatl is attributed a virgin birth. He is depicted as wearing a long robe and of having the appearance of a white and bearded man. He also left Mexico with the promise he would return.

Ce Acatl is another name used to identify the tenth-century Mesoamerican culture hero; and the name is synonymous with *Topiltzin*—that is, both names appear to refer to the same individual. Ce Acatl is simply the day on which Topiltzin was born.[36]

36. Ancient kings or leaders rather commonly adjusted their birthdays to correlate with the birthday of a great previous leader. Thus, Topiltzin Quetzalcoatl not only may have adopted the name of Quetzalcoatl but also may have adopted his birthday—not the same year but the same month and day.

From almost all the accounts dealing with Quetzalcoatl, agreement is reached that Topiltzin Ce Acatl took upon himself the name of the deity whom he and his people worshiped.

CHRIST AND THE DEITY QUETZALCOATL

In exploring issues associated with Quetzalcoatl, Joseph Allen made the following analysis regarding Quetzalcoatl and the manner in which he approached the subject in the writing of his doctoral dissertation, "A Comparative Study of Quetzalcoatl, the Feathered Serpent God of Meso-America, with Jesus Christ, the God of the Nephites."[37] Chapter 5 of his dissertation details a comparison of the Mesoamerican legends ascribed to Quetzalcoatl with the Book of Mormon account of the appearance of Christ to the Nephites. Much of the content of that chapter follows, although it has been modified to fit the context of *Exploring the Lands of the Book of Mormon.*

37. Allen, "A Comparative Study of Quetzalcoatl, the Feathered-Serpent God of Meso-America, with Jesus Christ, the God of the Nephites."

In pursuing my investigation, I had to deal with the issue of parallel time periods between Mesoamerican legends of Quetzalcoatl and events in the Book of Mormon. To do so, I had to free myself from any preconceived opinions about the time periods in question. I then admitted that the tenth-century Ce Acatl Topiltzin Quetzalcoatl was neither the creator of life nor in any way the deity known as *Quetzalcoatl* who had been spoken of in the myths and legends of the ancient Mexicans. He was, as many archaeologists concur, a tenth-century culture hero. I concluded, therefore, that creative powers were ascribed to Topiltzin Quetzalcoatl because of the difficulty that sixteenth-century Mesoamerican natives had in differentiating between one century and another as they glanced back into history. That is, Topiltzin Quetzalcoatl was born near the middle of the tenth century. The Aztecs told the Spaniards their Quetzalcoatl legends, which occurred, if they dated back to Topiltzin, five hundred years before the time they were relating what had happened. I suggest the improbability of a person living in the sixteenth century in knowing whether a special event occurred five hundred years or fifteen hundred years previous to the time the Aztecs were relating their accounts.

Charles Hield, in writing for the *Saints' Herald,* a publication of the Community of Christ (formerly the Reorganized Church of Jesus Christ of Latter Day Saints), rebuked the criticism levied against the Book of Mormon and its claim that Jesus Christ had appeared on the American continent. He writes:

> For over a hundred years critics of the church have sought to discredit the Book of Mormon because of its claim that Christ appeared in America after his resurrection in Palestine. The critics said that the Mexican legendary god Quetzalcoatl—often equated as Christ—was none other than a very human Toltec king named Ce Acatl Topiltzin, who was born in AD 935, became king in AD 973, and was forced to leave Tula, his capital, his throne, and kingdom because of drunkenness and immorality in AD 987. How wrong the Latter Day Saints were, the critics said, to assert that Quetzalcoatl may well have been Christ! In recent years, however, several historians, scholars, archaeologists, and anthropologists are asserting that the man-king and the ancient god were *entirely different*. It is interesting to observe how truth gets a boost from the test of time.[38]

The point in fact is that the deity Quetzalcoatl is an ancient personage dating back to the time of Christ, and students of Mesoamerican history should be willing to "render unto Caesar that which is Caesar's"—or to permit those characteristics that are humanistic and date to the time period of the tenth century to remain with Topiltzin Quetzalcoatl and separate those godly characteristics that should be attributed to the deity Quetzalcoatl or to Quetzalcoatl, the God of Life. That this is entirely possible is adequately explained by Bartra: "The representation of Quetzalcoatl the great King and Priest of the Toltecs, is undoubtedly valid, having inter-wound and fused itself mythically with the pre-mortal Quetzalcoatl, God of life whose image of the feathered serpent, ciphering from a religious and cultural constellation that expanded over all of Meso-America for many centuries."[39]

"History seems to become infused with legend, and confuses the individual Ce Acatl Topiltzin Quetzalcoatl with the deity Quetzalcoatl whom he served."

—Frederick Peterson

38. Charles R. Hield, "The God Quetzalcoatl," *Saints' Herald,* March 1970, 53.

39. Agusti Bartra, *Quetzalcoatl* (Mexico, DF: Fondo de Culture Economica, 1960), 165.

FIGURE 14–3: The temple of Kukulcan at Chichen Itza in the Yucatan Peninsula of Mexico is dedicated to a tenth-century culture hero, Ce Acatl Topiltzin Quetzcalcoatl, who took upon himself the characteristics of the deity Quetzalcoatl. The word *Kukulcan* in the Maya language has the same meaning as *Quetzalcoatl* in the Nahuatl language: quetzal bird-serpent. The above pyramid, built in Toltec style and perhaps influenced by the architecture of southern Yucatan and Peten, dates between the tenth and twelfth centuries AD. This pyramid is labeled as one of the seven wonders of the world and, in all probability, has no relationship with the deity Quetzalcoatl, except in the minds of the natives. This pyramid covers a Maya pyramid that dates to the sixth to eighth centuries AD. (Photo courtesy of Sheryl Lee Wilson)

Saenz was also well aware of the fact that concepts relating to the god Quetzalcoatl were much older than the tenth century and had been developed over a great many years.[40]

Irwin talks of following a stream and trail of Quetzalcoatl, which has left behind pyramids and legends of bearded white gods; and then she affirms that Quetzalcoatl of Tula was not that original Quetzalcoatl.[41]

Even the Maya, as they spoke of their beloved Kukulcan, had a difficult time arranging his life in a proper time frame of reference. Landa presented the problem of not knowing whether to place Kukulcan before or after the invasion in the tenth century.

Roman Pina Chan, as quoted by Florescano, discovered a possible antecedent to the feathered-serpent symbol dating back to the Preclassic Period, ca. 600 BC.[42] Researchers have found evidence from La Venta and San Lorenzo that the serpent motif dates from the ninth century to the third century BC. King Kish, or U-Kish Kan, as deciphered from

40. Caesar A. Saenz, *Quetzalcoatl* (Mexico, DF: Instituto Nacional de Antropolgia o Historia, 1962), 46.

41. Irwin, *Fair Gods and Stone Faces*, 47.

42. Florescano, "La Serpiente Emplumada, Tlaloc, y Quetzalcoatl, 123.

Exploring the Lands of the Book of Mormon

Palenque, dates to 967 BC, and the serpent motif may be similar in nature to Moses, who placed the brazen serpent in the wilderness around 1200 BC.

Sejourne equates Quetzalcoatl and Jesus Christ in exactly the same time period: "Just as our era began with Christ, so that of the Aztecs and their predecessors began—approximately at the same time—with Quetzalcoatl."[43]

Having thus presumably disposed of the objection of parallel time periods between Quetzalcoatl and Jesus Christ, we will give a brief analysis of the space problem.

The Book of Mormon describes Christ as visiting the American continent during the first century AD. Although no consensus of opinion exists as to where specifically in the Americas Christ appeared, the problem is resolved in relation to the "White God" legends, including the myths surrounding the visits of Quetzalcoatl, because of visits to almost all parts of the Americas.[44]

From a logical point of view, no one should object to the pursuit of a comparative analysis of Quetzalcoatl and Jesus Christ. Only the areas in which there appears to be a direct parallel will be presented. The best quote or explanation will be used. Where possible and practical, we have used the sixteenth-century chronicles sources. Otherwise, the parallel quotations referring to Quetzalcoatl are from the works of Mesoamerican scholars. The accounts are given in parallel columns for the reader's comparison and examination. We propose that the references to Quetzalcoatl, as shown on the following pages, refer to the deity Quetzalcoatl rather than to the tenth-century culture hero.

FIGURE 14–4: This Olmec carving of a man within a serpent motif at the outdoor La Venta Museum in Villahermosa, Tabasco, dates between the twelfth and sixth centuries BC. The figure is seated encircled by the serpent, possibly indicating that the subject surrounded himself with the teachings or religion of the serpent deity. The individual is holding a container of copal, a religious incense. (Photo courtesy of Blake Joseph Allen)

43. Sejourne, Burning Water, 25.

44. Bancroft, Myths and Languages, 5:23; see also Saenz, Quetzalcoatl, 30–31.

CREATIVE POWERS OF JESUS CHRIST	CREATIVE POWERS OF QUETZALCOATL
"We believe in Jesus Christ, the Son of God, who created heaven and earth, and all things" (Mosiah 4:2).	"Quetzalcoatl had attributed to him the creation of man and of the world and of the arts and the calendar."[45]
"All men were created in the beginning after mine own image . . . [and] man have I created after the body of my spirit" (Ether 3:15–16).	"During the four eras previously destroyed, that earth was populated only by animals, and it was not until the advent of the Era of Quetzalcoatl that humanity was created."[46]
"Behold, I am Jesus Christ the Son of God. I created the heavens and the earth, and all things that in them are. I was with the Father from the beginning" (3 Nephi 9:15).	"Quetzalcoatl did not intervene only in the creation of the world, but he was also considered to be the creator of man."[47]

45. Saenz, *Quetzalcoatl,* 19.

46. Sejourne, *Burning Water,* 55.

47. Saenz, *Quetzalcoatl,* 40.

Both Quetzalcoatl and Jesus Christ are designated by the ancient Americans as being the creator of the world. Also, they were both given credit for having created man. Jesus Christ is attributed with having created the heavens and the earth and all things therein, whereas Quetzalcoatl was said to be the creator of the world, of agriculture, of the arts, and of the calendar.

BIRTH OF JESUS CHRIST	BIRTH OF QUETZALCOATL
"The virgin whom thou seest is the mother of the Son of God, after the manner of the flesh" (1 Nephi 11:18).	"From the bowels of the virgin, Chimalma, came forth Quetzalcoatl."[48]
"She being a virgin . . . shall be overshadowed and conceive by the power of the Holy Ghost" (Alma 7:10).	"The mother of Quetzalcoatl conceived by swallowing a jade stone."[49]
"This will I give unto you for a sign at the time of his coming; for behold, there shall be great lights in heaven, insomuch that in the night before he cometh there shall be no darkness, insomuch that it shall appear unto man as if it was day" (Helaman 14:3). "And behold, there shall a new star arise, such an one as ye never have beheld; and this also shall be a sign unto you" (Helaman 14:5). "And it came to pass also that a new star did appear, according to the word" (3 Nephi 1:21).	"The old people of the community, those who had had the most time to meditate and to learn, and to understand the things of life were admired by the younger people, and the young people asked them the following questions: "What is that star? "Where did it come from? "Why did it come?"[50]

48. Gamiz, *Quetzalcoatl,* 95.

49. *Codice Chimalpopoca,* 1945:7.

50. Gamiz, *Quetzalcoatl,* 94.

Although there are accounts of a virgin birth relative to both Quetzalcoatl and Jesus Christ, the manner of conception is entirely different. Jesus Christ was conceived by the power of the Holy Ghost, whereas Quetzalcoatl was conceived by his mother's swallowing a jade stone.

The appearance of a new star, signifying the birth of the Savior in Jerusalem, seemed to have a pronounced impact upon the Nephites. Likewise, the morning star is almost always associated with Quetzalcoatl. However, in regards to the latter, the reference is usually to the death of Quetzalcoatl and his becoming converted into the morning star.

TEACHINGS OF JESUS CHRIST	TEACHINGS OF QUETZALCOATL	
"[Jesus Christ] healed all their sick, and their lame, and opened the eyes of their blind and unstopped the ears of the deaf, and even had done all manner of cures among them, and raised a man from the dead, and had shown forth his power unto them" (3 Nephi 26:15).	"The Codex Borgie reminds us of his [Quetzalcoatl's] role as a performer of miracles."[51]	51. Sejourne, *Burning Water*, 136–37.
"While the angels were ministering unto the disciples, behold, Jesus came and stood in the midst and ministered unto them" (3 Nephi 19:15). "And now there cannot be written in this book even a hundredth part of the things which Jesus did truly teach unto the people" (3 Nephi 26:6).	"According to the many legends that surround his name, he [Quetzalcoatl] appeared in Mexico of a sudden and lingered long in several places, dispensing a vastness of information, for which he was called the bringer of knowledge."[52]	52. Irwin, *Fair Gods and Stone Faces*, 33.
"Love your enemies, bless them that curse you, do good to them that hate you, and pray for them who despitefully use you and persecute you" (3 Nephi 12:44).	"He forbade and prohibited, with much success, wars, robbery, and murder, and the other injuries which are done by men to each other."[53]	53. Torquemada, cited by Lord Kingsborough, *Antiquities of Mexico: Comprising Facsimiles of Ancient Mexican Paintings and Hieroglyphics*, 9 vols. (London: Henry G. Bohn, 1848), 6:258.
"Therefore, go ye unto your homes, and ponder upon the things which I have said, and ask of the Father, in my name, that ye may understand, and prepare your minds for the morrow, and I come unto you again" (3 Nephi 17:3).	"Quetzalcoatl taught men science, giving them the method to measure time and to study the revolutions of the stars. He taught them the calendar and invented the ceremonies and fixed the days for prayers and sacrifices."[54]	54. Alfonso Caso, *El Pueblo del Sol* (Mexico: Fondo de Cultura Economica, 1953), 39–40.
"Verily I say unto you, that whoso repenteth of his sins through your words and desireth to be baptized in my name, on this wise shall ye baptize them— Behold, ye shall go down and stand in the water, and in my name shall ye baptize them" (3 Nephi 11:23).	"The first four friars on Yucatan reported that before the advent of the Spaniards the Indians of Yucatan practiced such Christian rites as baptism, confession, and penance."[55]	55. Irwin, *Fair Gods and Stone Faces*, 170.

Continued on next page

TEACHINGS OF JESUS CHRIST	TEACHINGS OF QUETZALCOATL
"And they had all things common among them; therefore there were not rich and poor, bond and free, but they were all made free, and partakers of the heavenly gift" (4 Nephi 1:3).	"The priest Topiltzin Quetzalcoatl set about to establish a new golden age, a reincarnation of a utopia which existed centuries earlier under the reign of the deity Quetzalcoatl."[56]
"Therefore I would that ye should be perfect even as I, or your Father who is in heaven is perfect" (3 Nephi 12:48). "Therefore, all things whatsoever ye would that men should do to you, do ye even so to them, for this is the law and the prophets" (3 Nephi 14:12).	"Although bearing various names and appearing in different countries, American culture-heroes all present the same general characteristics. . . . They at once set about improving the people by instructing them in useful and ornamental arts, giving them laws, exhorting them to practice brotherly love and other Christian virtues."[57]
"And they also took of the firstlings of their flocks, that they might offer sacrifice and burnt offerings according to the law of Moses" (Mosiah 2:3)	"The recorded myths of the Quetzalcoatl cycle stress that he demanded sacrifice only of butterflies and snakes, not of humans."[58]

56. Florescano, "La Serpiente Emplumada, Tlaloc, y Quetzalcoatl," 164–65.

57. Bancroft, *Myths and Languages*, 5:23.

58. Coe, *Mexico*, 102.

The teachings of Quetzalcoatl and Jesus Christ have appearances of similarities. However, it would be very simple to compare similarities in teachings between Jesus Christ and many other great men, such as Buddha or Mohammed, and such a comparison would not even suggest that they were the same person.

It is interesting, however, to observe that the deity Quetzalcoatl reached heights in his teachings that no other Mesoamerican god obtained—with the exception of Jesus Christ. They both performed miracles, and they both appeared suddenly, taught the people, and left. A golden age followed both of their appearances. Jesus Christ required sacrifice of the firstlings of the flock, pointing to the time of His coming. The law of sacrifice was fulfilled in His coming, and when He visited the Nephites, He taught His followers to have a broken heart and a contrite spirit (see 3 Nephi 9:20–21). Quetzalcoatl demanded sacrifices only of snakes and butterflies and also required repentance.

Exploring the Lands of the Book of Mormon

THE UNIVERSALITY OF JESUS CHRIST	THE UNIVERSALITY OF QUETZALCOATL	
"I have other sheep which are not of this land, neither of the land of Jerusalem, neither in any parts of that land round about whither I have been to minister" (3 Nephi 16:1).	Sejourne has written a great deal regarding the universality of Quetzalcoatl. His appearance seems so prominent that she has written a book titled *El Universo de Quetzalcoatl* (*The Universality of Quetzalcoatl*).[59]	59. Sejourne, *El Universo de Quetzalcoatl*.
"I am Jesus Christ, whom the prophets testified shall come into the world" (3 Nephi 11:10).	"Quetzalcoatl was a mysterious figure throughout all Mexico and Yucatan."[60]	60. Victor W. Von Hagen, *The Ancient Sun Kingdoms of the Americas* (Cleveland: World Publishing, 1957), 51–52.
"They were taught that he would appear unto them after his resurrection" (Alma 16:20).	"Quetzalcoatl . . . taught by precept and example the paths of virtue in all the Nahua cities."	
"And now, because of the covenant which ye have made ye shall be called the children of Christ, his sons, and his daughters; for behold, this day he hath spiritually begotten you; for ye say that your hearts are changed through faith on his name; therefore, ye are born of him and have become his sons and his daughters" (Mosiah 5:7)	"Almost all of the historians of New Spain, during the sixteenth and seventeenth centuries, speak of Quetzalcoatl. Among others, Fray Bernardino de Sahagun described how Quetzalcoatl was tied intimately in the lives and customs of the Meso-American people."[61]	61. Saenz, *Quetzalcoatl*, 7.
"Behold, I am Jesus Christ the Son of God. I created the heavens and the earth, and all things that in them are" (3 Nephi 9:15).	"The universal distribution of the concept of the feathered-serpent, which extends from Arizona to Central America, and more or less from the southeastern part of the United States to the Mississippi Valley, and up into Canada, causes one to think that here is a concept of great antiquity."[62]	62. Saenz, *Quetzalcoatl*, 30–31.
"And now it came to pass that there were a great multitude gathered together, of the people of Nephi, round about the temple which was in the land Bountiful" (3 Nephi 11:1).	"Representations of Quetzalcoatl are not only found in Tula and Teotihuacan, but also in Texcoco, Cholula, Cempoala, and other parts, including Chichen Itza."[63]	63. Saenz, *Quetzalcoatl*, 16.

Perhaps the most outstanding similarity between Quetzalcoatl and Jesus Christ is represented in the universality of the two. Jesus Christ explained in simple terms that He was the God of the whole earth and that His mission was to visit all His people. By the same token, Quetzalcoatl figured prominently in the legends of almost all the Mesoamerican nations—and even in South America. This is more remarkable when we consider (1) that the ancient Mexicans worshiped a pantheon of gods and (2) for the most part, that each nation developed its individual and local gods. Quetzalcoatl, on the other hand, crossed both boundary and time lines to form part of the religious worship of the various nations of Mesoamerica. Therefore, we conclude that the universality of Quetzalcoatl and Jesus Christ in the Americas suggests a strong possibility that the origin of the two was one and the same.

	THE GREATNESS OF JESUS CHRIST	THE GREATNESS OF QUETZALCOATL
64. Spence, *The Gods of Mexico*, 127.	"All those who were true believers in Christ took upon them . . . the name of Christ" (Alma 46:15).	"Among all the gods only Quetzalcoatl was called Lord, and men swore by him."[64]
65. Edgar Lee Hewett, *Ancient Life in Mexico and Central America* (New York: Bobbs-Merrill, 1936), 31.	"I [Sherem, an anti-Christ] fear lest I have committed the unpardonable sin, for I have lied unto God; for I denied the Christ" (Jacob 7:19).	"All attempts to take Quetzalcoatl, plumed serpent deity . . . of his mythic world and make an ordinary astronomer or teacher of agriculture out of him have been . . . pathetic."[65]
66. Sejourne, 1954:5:159.	"Arise and come forth unto me, that ye may thrust your hands into my side, and also that ye may feel the prints of the nails in my hands and in my feet, that ye may know that I am the God of Israel, and the God of the whole earth, and have been slain for the sins of the world" (3 Nephi 11:14).	"One can be assured that the documents relative to the pre-Columbian history permits Quetzalcoatl, the man who was converted into a god, to rise above all others and to constitute the most prestigious figure of Meso-America. His essential role as the creator of the Nahua culture is not doubted by any of the historians of the sixteenth century, as they always specifically indicate that as our era began with Christ, the era of the Aztecs opened with Quetzalcoatl."[66]
67. Gamiz, *Quetzalcoatl*, 93.	"And whoso taketh upon him my name, and endureth to the end, the same shall be saved at the last day" (3 Nephi 27:6).	"He was called the beautiful serpent Quetzalcoatl. That was the name that gave hope to the hearts of everyone."[67]
68. Irwin, *Fair Gods and Stone Faces*, 55.	"And I, Nephi, did build a temple; and I did construct it after the manner of the temple of Solomon" (2 Nephi 5:16).	"In Cholula, according to legend, the people erected numerous temples in his honor."[68]

Both Quetzalcoatl and Jesus Christ have been labeled as the greatest figures in all American history. Apparently, the followers of each were required to take upon themselves the name of their god. Both were considered more than an ordinary human, and both are accredited with supernatural powers. Both Quetzalcoatl and Jesus Christ were responsible for initiating a new and greater era for the people living in the Americas. Apparently, the two were what gave hope to the ancient Americans; and in honor of Quetzalcoatl and Jesus Christ, temples were constructed.

A DESCRIPTION OF JESUS CHRIST	A DESCRIPTION OF QUETZALCOATL	
"They saw a Man descending out of heaven; and he was clothed in a white robe; [and] they thought it was an angel that had appeared unto them" (3 Nephi 11:8).	"Quetzalcoatl was a well-proportioned man, serious in nature, white and bearded. His manner of dress consisted of a long robe."[69]	69. Don Fernando de Alva Ixtlilxochitl, *Obras Historicas*, ed. Alfredo Chavero, 2 vols. (Mexico: Editors Nacional, 1965), 21.
"Jesus blessed them as they did pray unto him; and his countenance did smile upon them, and the light of his countenance did shine upon them, and behold they were as white as the countenance and also the garments of Jesus; and behold the whiteness thereof did exceed all the whiteness, yea, even there could be nothing upon earth so white as the whiteness thereof" (3 Nephi 19:25).	"They say of him that he was a white man, large of body, wide forehead, large eyes, long and black hair, large and round beard."[70]	70. Torquemada, *Monarchia Indiana*, 2:47, cited by Milton R. Hunter, *Christ in Ancient America: Archaeology and the Book of Mormon II* (Salt Lake City: Deseret News Press, 1959–68), 29–30. Fray Jean de Torquemada was a Franciscan friar, missionary, and historian in Mexico. He is most famous for his history, written in 1615, about the indigenous people. This history, entitled *Los Veinte y un Libros Rituales y Monarchia Indiana*, has never been published in English but was reprinted in 1969 as volumes 41–43 of the *Biblioteca Porrua*.
"Yea, why will he not show himself in this land as well as in the land of Jerusalem?" (Helaman 16:19).	"A stranger, a bearded white man dressed in a flowing robe, he is said to have come from afar and from the east."[71]	71. Irwin, *Fair Gods and Stone Faces*, 33.

In all the accounts describing Quetzalcoatl, he is portrayed as being white and dressed in a long robe. Other features are usually added, including a beard and long hair. In almost all the accounts, the color of his hair is black. The robe is usually described as white. However, on some occasions, a black robe is ascribed to him.

Jesus was born in Jerusalem and as a Jew could well have had long, black hair and a beard. The robe is also characteristic of the dress at the time of Jesus in Palestine. Because he was a Jew, white may not fit the color of the pigment of the skin of Jesus. The remarkable similarity, in a comparison of descriptions between Quetzalcoatl and Jesus Christ, does not seem to equate skin color. The scriptures in the Book of Mormon that allude to a description of the Savior speak of the whiteness of His robe and the whiteness of His countenance. In fact, this whiteness was so pronounced that he seemed to make an indelible impression on the scribes of the Book of Mormon.

The conclusion herein set forth is that the legends of Quetzalcoatl were handed down for more than fifteen hundred years, and the legend of the whiteness remained attached to the great god Quetzalcoatl. Therefore, the whiteness may or may not refer to the skin texture but could also apply to the robe and the countenance of the god. This comparison is significant because the great descriptive factor attributed to Jesus Christ, as He appeared to the Nephites, was the whiteness of His robe and of His countenance—so much so that when His countenance shown upon His disciples, they also became white. Likewise, the greatest identifying characteristic of Quetzalcoatl has been the mark of whiteness.

REFERENCES OF DEATH AND DESTRUCTION ASSOCIATED WITH JESUS CHRIST	REFERENCES OF DEATH AND DESTRUCTION ASSOCIATED WITH QUETZALCOATL
"I [Jesus Christ] did send down fire and destroy them, that their wickedness and abominations might be hid from before my face, that the blood of the prophets and the saints whom I sent among them might not cry unto me from the ground against them. And many great destructions have I caused to come upon this land, and upon this people" (3 Nephi 9:11–12).	"Quetzalcoatl—he was the wind, the guide and road-sweeper of the rain gods, of the masters of the water, of those who brought rain. And when the wind rose, when the dust rumbled, and it crackled and there was a great din, and it became dark and the wind blew in many directions, and it thundered; then it was said: '[Quetzalcoatl] is wrathful.'"[72]
"And there was also a great and terrible tempest; and there was terrible thunder, insomuch that it did shake the whole earth as if it was about to divide asunder. And there were exceedingly sharp lightnings, such as never had been known in all the land" (3 Nephi 8:6–7).	"It is said that a mountain, called Cacatepetl, burned. By night, it was evident from afar how it burned. The flames rose high. When the Toltecs saw it, they became very restless; they raised their hands to heaven; there was great anxiety. All cried out, all shouted together. No longer was there tranquility; no longer was there peace. And when they saw this omen of evil, they said: 'O Toltecs, now is all in truth going [from us]; already the power of the Toltecs goeth. Yea we are forsaken. What shall we do? Whither shall we go? O unhappy we! Let us take heart! Behold yet another act of sorcery. It is said that stones rained on the Toltecs.'"[73]
"And it came to pass in the thirty and fourth year, in the first month, on the fourth day of the month, there arose a great storm, such an one as never had been known in all the land" (3 Nephi 8:5).	"Two hundred and seventy years had passed since the giants had been destroyed, when the eclipse of the sun and the moon occurred. The earth shook, the rocks broke into pieces and many other things and signs came to pass. These things occurred during the time our Lord, Jesus Christ, reigned on the earth and they say it came about during the first days of the year."[74]
"The Holy Messiah, who layeth down his life according to the flesh, and taketh it again by the power of the Spirit, that he may bring to pass the resurrection of the dead, being the first that should rise" (2 Nephi 2:8).	"Clearly the White God was immortal, or he would not be a god. So when he died, the priests secretly laid him in a magnificent sarcophagus under pyramids, and told the people he had sailed across the sea but would one day return again, for so he had promised."[75]
"Behold, they will crucify him; and after he is laid in a sepulchre for the space of three days he shall rise from the dead, with healing in his wings; and all those who shall believe on his name shall be saved in the kingdom of God" (2 Nephi 25:13).	"They made a stone box. And when it was finished, there lay Quetzalcoatl. Four days only was he in the box. . . . They say that when he died, dawn did not appear for four days, because he had gone to dwell among the dead. . . . In eight days there appeared the great star called Quetzalcoatl. And they add that he was enthroned as lord."[76]
"And my Father sent me that I might be lifted up upon the cross" (3 Nephi 27:14).	"The cross, as other Spaniards later learned, was the symbol of Quetzalcoatl."[77]

72. Sahagun, *Historia General de las Cosas de Nueva Espano: Florentine Codex*, 1:3.

73. Sahagun, *Historia General de las Cosas de Nueva Espano: Florentine Codex*, 3:27.

74. Ixtlilxochitl, *Obras Historicas*, 1:4.

75. Pierre Honore, *In Quest of the White God*, translated from the German by Oliver Coburn and Ursula Lehrburger (London: Hutchinson and Co., 1963), 202.

76. *Anales de Cauhtitlan y Leyenda de los Soles en Codice Chimalpopoca*, 7.

77. Irwin, *Fair Gods and Stone Faces*, 165.

Among the Nephites, the great sign of the death of the Savior was a great and terrible destruction on the American continent.

Sahagun described destructions that occurred centuries earlier, as related to him by the Aztecs. Ixtlilxochitl was even more precise as he related events concerning a great destruction and placed the time during the advent of Christ on the earth.

The parallel appears to be extremely significant because the Book of Mormon labels the destruction as affecting the whole face of the land and because Ixtlilxochitl fixed the time period at the advent of the Savior, which agrees with the Book of Mormon time period. Ixtlilxochitl even indicated that the tempest occurred the first days of the year, paralleling the Book of Mormon, which says the great storm began on the fourth day of the first month of the thirty-fourth year after the signs of the star and a day, a night, and a day of lightness had been given.

The four days Quetzalcoatl spent in the grave may be contrasted with the three days Christ spent in the tomb. The visits to the land of the dead by both Quetzalcoatl and Jesus Christ seem to present significant parallels.

The cross motif in Mesoamerica is difficult to label as being derived from Christianity because it even predates Christ. However, there is enough evidence in the Book of Mormon that would allow the ancient inhabitants of America to know that the cross is a symbol of Christ, inasmuch as He was crucified on a cross.

THE SECOND COMING OF JESUS CHRIST	THE SECOND COMING OF QUETZALCOATL
"The Messiah will set himself again the second time to recover them; wherefore, he will manifest himself unto them in power and great glory" (2 Nephi 6:14).	"The people of Cholula always believed that he would return to govern them and to console them."[78]
"Yea, then will he remember the isles of the sea; yea, and all the people who are of the house of Israel, will I gather in, saith the Lord, according to the words of the prophet Zenos, from the four quarters of the earth" (1 Nephi 19:16).	"The ancients held that Quetzalcoatl went to Tlapallan; [that] yet he will return. He is still expected."[79]
"And then shall they know their Redeemer, who is Jesus Christ, the Son of God; and then shall they be gathered in from the four quarters of the earth unto their own lands, from whence they have been dispersed; yea, as the Lord liveth so shall it be" (3 Nephi 5:26).	"When the Spaniards came in 1519 Moctezuma thought it was either Quetzalcoatl or the sons of Quetzalcoatl returning. Moctezuma, not wanting to be disrespectful to the Spaniards, and thinking they were holy men, commanded his priests to take the soldiers to the Temple of Quetzalcoatl."[80]

The Book of Mormon is clear in its references to the second coming of Jesus Christ. Information is also clear that the ancient inhabitants of Mesoamerica expected the return of Quetzalcoatl. It is difficult to determine if the second coming of Quetzalcoatl had reference to the tenth-century culture hero or to the deity Quetzalcoatl or both. There is a possibility that the pre-Columbian people of Mesoamerica, for many years,

78. Torquemada, cited by Kingsborough, *Antiquities of Mexico: Comprising Facsimiles of Ancient Mexican Paintings and Hieroglyphics*, 6:262.

79. Sahagun, *Historia General de las Cosas de Nueva Espano: Florentine Codex*, 1:40.

80. Fray Diego Duran, *Historia de las Indias de Nueva Espana y Islas de la Tierra Firme*, La prepara y de a luz Angel Ma. Garibay K., 2 vols. (Mexico: Editoria Porrua, 1967), 2:511. Diego Duran was a Dominican friar who is best known for his work cited here. This publication was greatly criticized while he was alive because it helped the "heathens" maintain their culture.

Duran was fluent in Nahuatl, the Aztec language, and therefore had the ability to talk directly with the natives and also read the pictorial codices and the work done by previous friars. Because of his nature, he was able to gain the confidence of many of the natives who would not cooperate in sharing their histories with other Spaniards. His work, therefore, is unique because he documented many previously unknown legends.

handed down the myth that the deity Quetzalcoatl would return. Topiltzin Quetzalcoatl and his predicted return may have been issued in the form of a threat to return and gain possession of his land.

Conclusions

From our perspective, the following conclusions regarding the life of the culture hero Topiltzin Ce Acatl Quetzalcoatl seem appropriate:

Topiltzin translated into the English means "Our Lord." This name carries suggestive overtones of supreme deity.

Ce Acatl is the date given as the birth of Quetzalcoatl and corresponds to the Christian dating period of AD 935–947.

Topiltzin Ce Acatl has been described as having a virgin birth, of wearing a long robe, and of being white and bearded.

Topiltzin Ce Acatl is referred to as a Toltec king who reigned in Tula, Cholula, and other parts of Mesoamerica.

Topiltzin Ce Acatl is portrayed as having succumbed to adultery and of taking his own life.

Topiltzin Ce Acatl is referred to in other accounts as having left toward the east, with a promise to return some day to reconquer his domain.

Moctezuma (also commonly spelled *Montezuma*) is recorded as having expected the return of Topiltzin Ce Acatl and indeed thought he had returned when the Spaniards came in the year Ce Acatl (1519) and began the conquest.

A great deal of confusion still seems to exist among the scholars of Mesoamerica as they attempt to unravel the life of Topiltzin Ce Acatl from that of the deity Quetzalcoatl who existed centuries earlier and whose name Topiltzin Ce Acatl took upon himself.

An attempted correlation between Jesus Christ and Topiltzin Quetzalcoatl referred to above does not present itself as a serious problem for two reasons:

First, the tenth-century Quetzalcoatl apparently had no reference to the deity Quetzalcoatl (Christ); and second, we would expect the deity Quetzalcoatl to become paganized throughout the centuries, even as the characteristics of Jesus have been changed in Christianity.

During the period of more than one thousand years' time that elapsed between the close of the Nephite history (AD 421) and the discovery of America in 1492, no doubt the polluting of the true gospel continued to increase, resulting in corrupted, apostate, and untrue pagan practices. The worship of numerous gods, with religious beliefs and practices ranging from witchcraft to rather noble and true spiritual expressions, prevailed throughout the Americas. The peculiar thing is that such extremes in religious beliefs and practices could have existed side by side in the religious expressions of the same peoples. Enough perverted

FIGURE 14—5: An apostasy took place at almost identical time periods in both the Old World and the New World. In the Old World, men reduced God to a personage without body, parts, and passions. In the New World, men reduced God to a serpent motif associated with deity and then depicted the result as stone images on pyramids and other structures. Shown here is a ca. AD 1000 building at Chichen Itza with serpent heads protruding from the structure as a reflection of the New World apostasy. (Photo courtesy of Sheryl Lee Wilson)

truths remained, however, in clearly defined forms to make possible the identification of Quetzalcoatl and his religion as adulterated forms and counterfeits of Christ and the true gospel which he established in ancient America shortly following his resurrection.[81]

81. Hunter, *Christ in Ancient America,* 113.

CHAPTER 15

Christ—The Tree of Life

And the angel said unto me: Behold the Lamb of God, yea, even the Son of the Eternal Father! Knowest thou the meaning of the tree which thy father saw? (1 Nephi 11:21)

C hrist is *the* Tree of Life. Through that Tree, we receive life everlasting. And through that Tree, we are able to partake of the fruit that is white above all that is white—eternal life. Nephi concludes his analysis of the vision of Lehi, his father, about the tree of life and then writes, "I also beheld that the tree of life was a representation of the love of God" (1 Nephi 11:25). In other words, God so loved the world that He gave His Only Begotten Son as a ransom for our sins. Thus, Christ is *the* Tree of Life.

When *Exploring the Lands of the Book of Mormon* was first published in 1989, an analysis of Izapa Stela 5, often called the Tree of Life Stone, was included with the chapter labeled "The Izapa Culture." In the second edition of *Exploring the Lands,* however, because of the importance of the tree-of-life concept, we have elected to treat the

OPPOSITE: Izapa Stela 5, a fifteen-ton engraved stone monument that was originally discussed by Matthew Stirling in the *Scientific Review of the Smithsonian Institute* in 1943, has generated an enormous amount of interest. In 1952 and again in 1958, M. Wells Jakeman presented his thesis that this stela at Izapa, Chiapas, Mexico, has a direct relationship to the symbols mentioned in Lehi's dream of the tree of life as recorded in the book of 1 Nephi. Debate over the accuracy of this interpretation continues to this day. (Drawing courtesy of Cliff Dunston)

tree-of-life (Christ) concept and Stela 5 as separate chapters and to position the tree-of-life discussion in the middle of the book immediately following the chapter entitled "The White God Quetzalcoatl." Quetzalcoatl also manifests a strong similitude with Christ, as outlined in chapter 14.

Dr. Wells Jakeman, the first chairman of the Archaeology Department at Brigham Young University, was the first to propose a correlation with the engraved monument labeled Izapa Stela 5 and the tree-of-life dream of Lehi as recorded in 1 Nephi 11. Garth Norman is a Latter-day Saint archaeologist who has spent many years studying the Izapa civilization. His efforts have produced some interesting correlations with the Old World culture. For example, Norman discovered that the cubit was the principal form of measurement at Izapa. The cubit equals about eighteen inches and is the type of measurement used in ancient Israel. He also proposed an interpretation of the Tree of Life Stone not only as reflecting a representation of Lehi's dream but also as reflecting a spiritual representation of man's journey through life when viewers read the monument from right to left and observe a movement from the youngest to the oldest. Todd Allen, a student of Mesoamerican history and one who has escorted hundreds of people to Book of Mormon lands, pointed out the Hebrew style of chiasmus identifiable on Izapa Stela 5 (see chapter 2, "And Then It Came to Pass").

> Todd Allen, a student of Mesoamerican history and one who has escorted hundreds of people to Book of Mormon lands, pointed out the Hebrew style of chiasmus identifiable on Izapa Stela 5.

LEHI'S DREAM OF THE TREE OF LIFE

The initial work accomplished by Wells Jakeman and his associates resulted in the tree-of-life monument's becoming part of the Latter-day Saint educational literature. Further, the subsequent work by Norman has made it possible to analyze Stela 5 in conjunction with other monuments in the Izapa zone in more detail. Finally, the work accomplished by the New World Archaeological Foundation in regards to the Izapa site makes it possible to study the total environment.

The Book of Mormon account of the vision of Lehi and of the tree of life refers to the Atonement of Christ. Because of the possible relationship between the Book of Mormon story about the tree of life and the monument labeled Stela 5 at Izapa, we will first summarize the vision of Lehi and then present the suggested comparisons with the engravings on the monument.

From the time Lehi's people left Jerusalem until they arrived at the ocean front, which is probably the Indian Ocean near present-day Salalah, Oman, a total of eight years had elapsed (see 1 Nephi 17:4). A good portion of this time apparently took place in the valley of Lemuel. One of the most significant events was what we have come to know as "Lehi's vision of the tree of life." The vision, or dream, is recorded in 1 Nephi 8, 11, and 12. We are given the interpretation of the dream by Nephi, the son of Lehi. The basic elements of the vision, with their interpretations, are as follows:

1. A man dressed in a white robe told Lehi to follow him.
2. Lehi traveled through a dark and dreary waste.
3. Lehi prayed to the Lord for mercy.
4. Lehi saw a large and spacious field. We understand that this field represents the world.
5. Lehi saw a tree whose fruit was most desirable. Nephi informs us that this fruit symbolizes the love of God and most assuredly depicts the Atonement of Jesus Christ, which brings eternal life.
6. Lehi saw a river of water. Nephi instructs us that this river has reference to the depths of hell.
7. Lehi saw a rod of iron that extended along the bank of the river and that led to the tree. The rod of iron is indicative of the word of God. "Hold fast to the gospel" and associated precepts are those that allow a person to arrive at the tree of life—or to receive eternal life.
8. Lehi tells us of a narrow path that also led to the tree but that passed by a fountain, by the large and spacious field. Here, we understand that the narrow path represents adherence to the gospel principles; and the fountain of filthy waters and the field are worldly temptations, or the depths of hell.

Many years have elapsed since two events transpired: (1) the report by M. Wells Jakeman and his colleagues on a comparison of Christ and Lehi's vision with Izapa Stela 5—the Tree of Life Stone (1953) and (2) a comparative analysis of Quetzalcoatl, the Mesoamerican deity, with Christ as reported by Joseph Allen in a 1970 doctoral dissertation in connection with the content in the Book of Mormon.

Much has been written on the subjects of the White God Quetzalcoatl[1] and Izapa Stela 5, the Tree of Life Stone.[2] Regarding Quetzalcoatl, Diane Wirth writes:

Despite discrepancies among Quetzalcoatl myths in colonial sources and the fairly good mythology and symbolism in pre-Columbian inscriptions and iconography, we are left with several crucial points about Quetzalcoatl and the Maya Maize God that apply to Christ's premortal state, his mission on earth, and his role in the hereafter. Are there plausible links? Yes. Are there significant differences? Again, yes. This review should help us to see a complex picture of continuities and discontinuities between Quetzalcoatl and the Savior. Because parts of the picture are rather faint, there is a need for caution in our studies when we approach the intriguing and mysterious figures of Quetzalcoatl and the Maya Maize God and attempt to draw connections between them and the resurrected Jesus.[3]

"We are left with several crucial points about Quetzalcoatl and the Maya Maize God that apply to Christ's premortal state, his mission on earth, and his role in the hereafter."

—Diane Wirth

1. See, for example, Diane E. Wirth, "Quetzalcoatl, the Maya Maize God, and Jesus Christ," *Journal of Book of Mormon Studies*, 11, no. 1 (2002): 4–15.

2. See, for example, Stewart W. Brewer, "The History of an Idea: The Scene on Stela 5 from Izapa, Mexico, as a Representation of Lehi's Vision of the Tree of Life, *Journal of Book of Mormon Studies*, 8, no. 1 (1999): 13–21.

3. Wirth, "Quetzalcoatl, the Maya Maize God, and Jesus Christ," 15.

Stewart Brewer, who wrote a detailed analysis of the history of Stela 5 covering the time period from Jakeman's 1953 drawing to Clark's 1999 drawing, as referred to in chapter 9, "The Izapa (Jaredite-Nephite-Lamanite) Culture," concludes:

> It may be expected that the new Moreno drawing of Stela 5 (the first in over twenty years) will change our views of what the art of Izapa represents. Clark's pictorial presentation and brief analysis of Stela 5 marks the beginning of a new stage in the study of this renowned piece of ancient art, not a completion of research on it. The process of study that Jakeman began with his first interpretation of the stela 46 years ago is still far from played out, either for Latter-day Saints in general, or for scholars. In light of the Moreno-Clark project, it remains to be seen whether Latter-day Saints will embrace or neglect new evidence as it becomes available and whether they will rethink their past loyalties in the light of new findings.[4]

4. Brewer, "The History of an Idea," 20.

CONCLUSIONS

As the authors of the second edition of *Exploring the Lands of the Book of Mormon*, we present the following conclusions about the White God Quetzalcoatl and the iconography of the motif of the Tree of Life Stone:

> In the absence of tree-of-life symbols or white-god metaphors in Mesoamerica, the Book of Mormon still bears witness of Christ as a *tree of life* and of Christ as a *white god.*

1. In the absence of tree-of-life symbols or white-god metaphors in Mesoamerica, the Book of Mormon still bears witness of Christ as *a tree of life* (1 Nephi 11:25) and of Christ as *a white god* (see 3 Nephi 19:25–30).

2. Regardless of which drawing of Stela 5 is used or which legend is quoted about Quetzalcoatl, a definite and fixed pattern emerges to illustrate similarities of all writers and researchers. For example, all artists would agree that the central figure of Stela 5 is a tree-of-life motif, and all would agree that the deity Quetzalcoatl was associated with whiteness.

3. All serious students of Mesoamerican studies and the Book of Mormon would agree that the time periods in which the concept of the deity Quetzalcoatl surfaced and in which the engravings on Stela 5 were engraved fall in the Book of Mormon time period.

4. All students of Mesoamerican thought would agree that there is something tangible or intangible or something detailed or vague about Mesoamerican tree-of-life symbolism and Quetzalcoatl (quetzal bird-serpent) symbolism. If that were not the case, we would not see so much discussion on the subjects.

Having drawn those conclusions, we have adapted the symbolisms of Izapa Stela 5, the Tree of Life Stone, with the Book of Mormon theme of Lehi's vision and Nephi's interpretation of the vision of Christ, who is *the* Tree of Life, and have taken into consideration new evidence that has come forth since the initial publication of *Exploring the Lands of the Book of Mormon* in 1989. The discussion that follows reflects our thinking at this point.

STELA 5 AT IZAPA

Of the more than eighty carved monuments at Izapa, the monument labeled Stela 5 is the most famous. The early proposed identification by Jakeman in 1951 as being associated with Lehi's dream caused a great deal of interest among Latter-day Saints. The fact that the initial analysis by Jakeman corresponded with the same time period in which Alberto Ruz uncovered the tomb of Pacal at Palenque, in 1952, gave emphasis to the tree-of-life concept. The lid of the Palenque tomb had engraved on it a tree-of-life motif. Ruz accepted an invitation to speak to Latter-day Saints at the Mormon Tabernacle, and he spoke to an attentive audience.

To this day, Stela 5 of Izapa is considered by many to be one of the most significant Mesoamerican discoveries in relationship to the Book of Mormon. Some Latter-day Saint Mesoamericanists, however, do not endorse the comparison of Lehi's dream and Stela 5 of Izapa. Justification for such a viewpoint comes from what is considered a lack of convincing evidence—*or a lack of accurate artistic renditions of the stela.*

Brewer (see above) invites readers to reevaluate their thinking with new evidence that has come forth: "It remains to be seen whether Latter-day Saints will embrace or neglect new evidence as it becomes available and whether they will rethink their past loyalties in the light of new findings."[5] The new findings Brewer is referring to are associated with the 1999 artistic rendition of Stela 5 by John Clark and Ayax Moreno.

The irony of the situation is that somehow the 1999 drawings by Clark and Moreno are supposed to be superior to Norman's photography and drawings twenty-six years earlier and far superior to Jakeman's drawings and latex extractions almost fifty years earlier. Such thinking probably lacks substance because of the deterioration of Stela 5 between 1952 and 1999.

Without question, considerable deterioration of Stela 5 has occurred over the last sixty years as a result of the stela's exposure to the elements. A picture taken in 1955 is much more revealing than a picture taken today, regardless of whether we put floodlights on the monument as did Clark and

> Of the more than eighty carved monuments at Izapa, the monument labeled Stela 5 is the most famous.

5. Brewer, "The History of an Idea," 20.

FIGURE 15–1: The massive lid that covered the sarcophagus of a seventh century AD Maya priest, K'inich Janaab' Pacal I of Palenque, uncoverd by Alberto Ruz and his associates in 1952, presents a detailed depiction of the Maya tree-of-life concept. The carving has the appearance of a tree of life sprouting from the heart of the king, which is reminiscent of Alma's discourse on planting the seed of faith in our hearts and nurturing it to become a tree (see Alma 32). (Photo courtesy of George and Audrey DeLange)

FIGURE 15–2: Observe the similarities among three major renditions of Izapa Stela 5: Jakeman in 1952, Dunston 1989, and Clark and Moreno in 1999. All three distinctly show a fruit-laden tree as the central theme. All three show six human figures in identical positions at the base of the tree. All three outline water symbols. And all three illustrate symbols related to the deity Quetzalcoatl. If you study each drawing carefully, you will also note some differences among the three renditions.

In the final analysis, it really doesn't matter much whose drawings are endorsed—the central and most prominent motif is the tree itself.

Moreno or throw water on it in an effort to highlight its features as others have apparently done.

In the final analysis, it really doesn't matter much whose drawings are endorsed—that is, Jakeman, Norman, Clark, or the artistic rendition in *Exploring the Lands of the Book of Mormon;* the major elements are still there. In other words, the central and most prominent motif is the tree itself. We see fruit on the tree in all the drawings. We see six figures along the base of the tree in all the drawings, two of which have their backs to the tree. And we see represented on the stone the concepts relating to water, fish, angels, serpents, and birds.

Nevertheless, other objections that would negate Stela 5 at Izapa as representing a Book of Mormon theme must be stated. Some of these objections include the statements that Stela 5 is merely representative of a *Popol Vuh* theme, that the name glyphs proposed by Jakeman are inaccurate, that the second century BC Nephites would not have remembered or known about Lehi's dream, or that Izapa does not figure into Book of Mormon geography.

John Clark writes: "In any case, the period when the Izapa monuments were sculpted, 300 to 50 BC, is a dark time in terms of Nephite history and geography. Little is said in the Nephite record that can be connected to Izapa even by inference."

Clark continues: "I had always considered the tree of life narrative in the Book of Mormon to be masterful, linking themes that subsequently appeared in Nephite preaching about Christ and the atonement. I now think this is wrong. To Latter-day Saints, that may seem plausible because the Lehi story appears in the front of the book we now have. Yet we recall that the record (the small plates of Nephi) was not a public document. Most of the later prophets give no hint of being informed of its content, while most of the kings may have been no better informed because they relied on their royal record."

Clark adds: "Is there any evidence that any of the later prophets preached about, or even referred to, Lehi's dream? No. Even Nephi spoke of it only as the catalyst for obtaining his own vision of the prophetic future (see 1 Nephi 11:1–9). The older siblings in Lehi's family might have remembered most or much of the dream because they heard it directly from Lehi's lips (see 1 Nephi 8:2, 'he spake unto us'). Yet centuries later Alma's teaching about the tree of life goes down a different road; he talks about the tree in the Garden of Eden rather than the one seen by Lehi (see Alma 12:22–23; 42:2–5)."

Regarding Lehi's vision, Clark concludes: "Perhaps those accounts were considered too sacred for common reference by religious teachers, just as modern apostles typically refrain from talking directly about personal experiences with the Lord. So it seems quite possible that the Nephites generally, let alone the Lamanites, did not know enough about Lehi's vision to have responded to it even if it had been represented for them on a stone."[6]

Alan Miner offers the following rebuttal to Clark's conclusion in the above paragraph:

6. See John E. Clark, "A New Artistic Rendering of Izapa Stela 5: A Step toward Improved Interpretation," *Journal of Book of Mormon Studies* 8, no. 1 (1999): 23–33.

As for Clark's claim that there is no evidence "that any of the later prophets preached about, or even referred to Lehi's dream," a simple word search summary by Clark would have easily provided the reader with a number of examples of subsequent preachings concerning elements contained in the dream. . . . Perhaps the most striking evidence that the Nephites had a knowledge of Lehi's dream is found in the fact that Alma's description of the fruit of the Tree of Life is virtually identical to that given to Lehi. Lehi described it as "sweet, above all that I ever before tasted . . . [and] white, to exceed all the whiteness that I had ever seen" (1 Nephi 8:11). Alma, preaching to the expelled Zoramites, said that the fruit was "sweet above all that is sweet, and . . . white above all that is white" (Alma 32:42).[7]

7. Alan Miner, "Did the Nephites Know of Lehi's Dream?" *Book of Mormon Archaeological Digest* 2, no. 4 (1999): 6.

Diane Wirth, author and Mesoamerican scholar, challenged the work of the artist Moreno in the Clark drawing. She writes: "One must understand Mesoamerican art and epigraphy in order to pick out the subtleties of lines that could possibly represent one object or another. . . . Some portions of the new drawing of Stela 5 may be useful . . . [and] other areas of the stela may have incorporated lines that are not part of the original rendering. . . . One could . . . pick apart the various interpretations presented by Clark. . . . In time, and with a broader range of scholars studying Izapan art, perhaps we will be able to ascertain more precisely the meaning and significance of Stela 5, and not throw the baby out with the bath water, writing off previously held opinions that there is a connection of this stela with Lehi's vision of the Tree of Life."[8]

8. Diane E. Wirth, "A Review by Diane E. Wirth," *Book of Mormon Archaeological Digest* 2, no. 4 (1999): 5, 10–11.

V. Garth Norman, archaeologist and scholar of Izpan art and culture, has spent almost half a century studying Izapa Stela 5. He responds to the work of Clark and Moreno as follows: "The stated goal of the Clark drawing project has been to employ methods and skills to achieve the most complete and accurate reconstruction of this extremely weathered monument possible. Since this goal was accomplished by the NWAF Izapa Sculpture project . . . and has been successfully time tested for nearly twenty-five years, the alleged need for a new, more accurate drawing is unclear."[9]

9. V. Garth Norman, "Tree of Life Stone Under Attack: New FARMS Drawing Creating Temporary Confusion," *Book of Mormon Archaeological Digest* 2, no. 4 (1999): 7.

10. Norman, "Tree of Life Stone Under Attack: New FARMS Drawing Creating Temporary Confusion," 13.

Norman summarizes his analysis of the Moreno-Clark project as follows: "I cannot accept the Moreno-Clark drawing on faith, as Clark seems to expect. Until he completes his homework, he should not be foisting untested drawings like this on the public, especially with no photographic and research documentation to confirm the superior accuracy of his new work against prior work."[10]

From what has been written, both pro and con, on the subject of the tree-of-life concept and from our own personal studies and experiences, we have arrived at the following conclusions:

> The Nephites would have remembered the concept of the tree of life as taught by Lehi and Nephi. It was written down. Christ, who is *the* Tree of Life, is the paramount concept of the Book of Mormon.

1. The Nephites would have remembered the concept of the tree of life as taught by Lehi and Nephi. It was written down. Christ, who is *the* Tree of Life, is the paramount concept of the Book of Mormon.

2. The idea that the time period in which Stela 5 of Izapa was engraved (300 to 50 BC) was a dark period of the Nephite history is simply not true. Almost half of the history contained in the Book of Mormon pertains to this time period. The 250 years from 300 BC to 50 BC cover 228 pages of the 531 total pages in the Book of Mormon (Omni to Helaman). And these pages record the lives and teachings of such great men as Mosiah I, Benjamin, Mosiah II, Abinadi, Alma, Alma the younger, Amulek, and the sons of Mosiah as well as the activities of Moroni, Lehi, Teancum, and the sons of Helaman.

This time period includes the Book of Mormon geography content related to the migrations of Mosiah, Zeniff, Alma, Limhi, Limhi's expedition, the missionary journeys of the sons of Mosiah and of Alma, and the establishment and annexation of the east wilderness and the wars fought from the west sea to the east sea—and much more.

3. Although the name glyphs may present some challenges as representing the names of Sariah, Lehi, Nephi, and so forth, the concepts of names dating to the Olmec Preclassic Period and continuing through the Maya Classic Period have identifying characteristics somewhere near the body or included in the headdress of an individual. The names of U-Kish Kan, an Olmec king displayed on a monument at San Lorenzo, and of Yax Nuun Ayiin taken from Stela 31 of Tikal are examples already covered in *Exploring the Lands of the Book of Mormon*.

4. To state that Lehi's dream cannot be associated with Stela 5 of Izapa because it and other monuments at Izapa are associated with the *Popol Vuh* is not logical. Even though the *Popol Vuh* is a fifteenth century AD document and Stela 5 is a second century BC monument, we cannot logically suggest that they could *not* have come from the "same source."

5. As to Izapa's not being associated with any geographic setting in the Book of Mormon, we invite readers to read *Exploring the Lands of the Book of Mormon* in its

entirety and then make their own judgment as to the geographic possibility of Izapa's relationship with Nephi's history.

If indeed Stela 5 is an artist's rendition of Lehi's dream, it then could be compared in importance to the paintings of Michelangelo of the Last Supper of Christ or of a modern Latter-day Saint artist's conception of the Sacred Grove experience.

Wells Jakeman, who conducted the initial study, writes the following: "This inclusion of apparently actual persons in the scene discussing the symbolic tree suggests, of course, that this divergent Izapa representation of the tree of life was an attempt on the part of the ancient artists of Izapa to portray some actual event featuring that holy tree. If so, the interesting question which now arises is that of the identity of these six persons shown participating in this event thus commemorated."[11]

Bruce Warren and Thomas Ferguson make the following summary statement: "The Book of Mormon also gives the meaning and interpretation of the symbols carved on the stone. The river represents the barrier of evil between people and happiness. The rod of iron represents the word of God, which, if followed, leads one to the tree of eternal life and happiness. The tree represents the love of God—and if one loves God he will keep His commandments, and this leads to the fruits of the tree—happiness and eternal life. *It is an entire philosophy of life set out succinctly on 15 tons of stone.*"[12]

Stela 5 of Izapa appears to present both a story of a family in association with a tree of life and a personal philosophy as we journey through this life. Of course, that is exactly what the vision and the interpretation of the vision of Lehi are about. Therefore, both Stela 5 and Lehi's vision may be an Isaiah-type text—that is, both may represent the story and the depth of the meaning as they relate to the story of Lehi and our individual quest for eternal life.

A correlation with Stela 5 and Lehi's dream is further enhanced by two recent observations: (1) the true Hebrew chiastic structure and (2) the white fruit in Lehi's dream.

A true chiastic structure requires the outside figures to bear witness of the central figure. A case in point is found in Alma 46:39–41. The two outside verses specifically mention Christ, and the central portion of the chiasmus symbolically refers to Christ as "plants and roots," the same terminology used by Isaiah in reference to Christ (Isaiah 53:2; Mosiah 14:2). In the Izapa Stela 5 structure, the artist framed the entire motif with a two-headed serpent. In Mesoamerican art, the serpent represents deity, such as the white god Quetzalcoatl (quetzal bird-serpent). The central portion of the entire Izapa

11. M. Wells Jakeman, *The Complex "Tree-of-Life" Carving on Izapa Stela 5: A Reanalysis and Partial Interpretation* (Provo, UT: Department of Archaeology, Brigham Young University, 1958), 11.

12. Bruce W. Warren and Thomas S. Ferguson, *The Messiah in Ancient America* (Provo, UT: Book of Mormon Research Foundation, 1987), 74; emphasis added.

FIGURE 15–3: A 2007 painting of Stela 5, the Tree of Life Stone, by Guatemalan artist Erick Bustamante shows some of the detail that is difficult to see in photographs.

Stela 5 structure is the ceiba tree, or the tree of life, also symbolically associated with Christ.

The ceiba tree is the national tree of Guatemala, and throughout Mesoamerica, it is actually referred to as "the tree of life." Once a year a white, cotton-like substance grows on the ceiba tree, perhaps representing the white fruit Lehi saw in vision.

An analogy of the Tree of Life Stone (Izapa Stela 5) is presented below.

FIGURE 15–4: The tree as depicted in Stela 5 of Izapa. (Drawing by Cliff Dunston)

13. V. Garth Norman, *Izapa Sculpture*, part 2: text, papers of the New World Archaeological Foundation, no. 30 (Provo, UT: New World Archaeological Foundation, Brigham Young University, 1976), 166.

The Tree of Life

Dominating Stela 5 is a fruit-laden tree situated in the center of the carved design, with its roots in a base of "ground" panel and its upper branches extending into a sky panel.[13]

As mentioned, the tree in Stela 5 has an appearance of the great free-standing ceiba tree that is common to the area in which the stone is located. The tree that bears fruit above all that is white is also the central theme of the vision.

The tree of life, simply stated, represents Jesus Christ, the Savior of the world. He is *the* Tree of Life. By partaking of the fruit of the tree, we may have eternal life, which is made possible through the Atonement of Christ.

FIGURE 15–5: The two cherubims that guard the tree of life. (Drawing by Cliff Dunston)

Angels

Angels, or cherubims, play a major role in both the vision of Lehi and the tree-of-life carving. They guard the tree of life at Izapa. In the Book of Mormon, an angel leads Lehi to the tree of life, and an angel gives Nephi the interpretation.

The two cherubims (or deities or angels) are the same size. The bird-like face masks appear to be of a purely symbolic nature. The large stature of the cherubims and the fact that all other figures make contact directly or indirectly with these deities suggest that a person must go through them to partake of the fruit of the tree.

FIGURE 15–6: The legendary ancestor representing Lehi and his name glyph as indicated by the jawbone. (Drawing by Cliff Dunston)

Lehi

The story element of both Stela 5 and Lehi's vision relates to the experience of Lehi. On the monument, Lehi may be represented by the figure of the old man. In this representation, Lehi represents the legendary ancestor spoken of in Mesoamerican history. He is leaning forward with his hand in a gesturing or teaching position. He is sitting on a cushion similar to the altars that rest in front of many of the stone monuments in the area where Stela 5 is located.

A jawbone located immediately behind his head was proposed by Jakeman to be a glyph representing Lehi's name. The valley of Lehi where Samson slew a thousand

Philistines with a jawbone may be the symbol for Lehi in the Book of Mormon and the legendary ancestor.

Nephi

Jakeman proposed that figure 15–7 represents the prophet Nephi, the son of Lehi. The Nephi figure is the same size as the Lehi figure and is gesturing in an authoritative manner in much the same way as the Lehi figure. The Nephi figure has an instrument in his left hand, which may be a stylus or a chisel. He has the appearance of writing on records. His headdress, consisting of grain, represents a young grain god whose Egyptian name is known as Nepri or Nepi.[14]

FIGURE 15–7: Nephi, the son of Lehi, as represented by the large figure with a stylus in his hand. (Drawing by Cliff Dunston)

14. Jakeman, The Complex "Tree-of-Life" Carving on Izapa Stela 5, 45.

The fringed parasol or umbrella that is held over the Nephi figure is both a Maya as well as an Old World symbol that represents royalty. The headdress appears to identify the Nephi figure as a high priest of God. The inverted question-mark symbol near his mouth suggests that he is speaking. Contact of the speaking glyph with Angel "B" suggests that the Nephi figure speaks in behalf of God.

The small skull head that rests on the forehead of the Nephi figure has what appears to be a piece of the fruit from the tree in its mouth, perhaps suggesting that the Nephi figure is willing to partake of the fruit of the tree or is willing to follow the commandments of God. As a result, after death, as represented by the skull, the Nephi figure can lay claim to eternal life through the Atonement of Christ.

Sam

Sam, the older brother of Nephi, expressed a willingness to keep the commandments of God. When Lehi blessed Sam, Sam was blessed jointly with Nephi: "[Lehi] spake unto Sam, saying: Blessed art thou, and thy seed; for thou shalt inherit the land like unto thy brother Nephi. And thy seed shall be numbered with his seed; and thou shalt be even like unto thy brother, and thy seed like unto his seed; and thou shalt be blessed in all thy days" (2 Nephi 4:11).

FIGURE 15–8: Sam, the son of Lehi and the brother of Nephi, as represented by the figure holding the parasol. (Drawing by Cliff Dunston)

The highlighted portion of figure 15–8 possibly represents Sam. His height and seated position qualify him to be more than just an attendant to the Nephi figure. The parasol rests over both the Nephi figure and the Sam figure. This positioning suggests more of a supportive role as opposed to a servant role by the Sam figure.

The facial features of the Sam figure on Stela 5 have been eroded, which causes that detail to be indecipherable. However, contact with the Sam figure with what Norman identified as the serpent's body aligns Sam with Quetzalcoatl (feathered serpent) or Christ (see chapter 14, "The White God Quetzalcoatl"). As a result, the stone text of

Stela 5 may illustrate that Sam is willing to partake of the fruit of the tree of life. Sam expressed that willingness to follow Nephi into the wilderness as they separated from their brethren, Laman and Lemuel: "I, Nephi did take my family . . . and also Sam, mine elder brother and his family" (2 Nephi 5:6).

Additional symbolism is associated with the Sam figure in terms of the resurrection and eternal life. Norman discovered that the engravings on Stela 5 not only depict the story of Lehi's family but also outline the responsibility of mankind in pursuit of eternal life through the Atonement of Christ.

The back of the Sam figure is close to what appears to be flowing water. As the rains descend in the jungle area of Izapa, the evaporation process begins immediately toward heaven. This process may symbolically relate to our birth and the subsequent ascension of the spirit after death to the spirit world and to the god who gave us life.

FIGURE 15–9: Old female figure may represent Sariah. (Drawing by Cliff Dunston)

Sariah

The highlighted figure in figure 15–9 appears to be a woman associated with the Lehi figure. The female features are indicated by what appears to be a head covering flowing over the shoulders and the kneeling position, both of which are typical of the native women of Guatemala today. This head covering suggests that the figure may represent Sariah, the wife of Lehi and the mother of Laman, Lemuel, Sam, and Nephi. The Sariah figure has bent shoulders similar to the Lehi figure. The bent shoulders suggest that she is an old person who is associated with the Lehi figure as either an attendant or a wife.

The horned headdress is rare in Mesoamerica. The presence of feathers suggests royalty associated with deity, such as a priestess. The eye contact of the Sariah figure looking toward the angel or the tree may manifest the willingness on her part to partake of the fruit of the tree. The feathers between the horns are symbols of death and, as such, suggest the concept of life springing out of death or the resurrection. In Hebrew, the name *Sara,* or *Sariah,* means princess. The headdress of the Sariah figure justifies the requirement.

The dualism of the Nephi figure in relation to the Sariah figure also bears mentioning. Whereas the Nephi figure has birth symbols associated with it, the Sariah figure has death symbols associated with it—the latter being represented by the bent back and old age plus the figure's elevated position in an upward motion.

The resurrection symbols, as mentioned, are also present in the Sariah figure. Hence, the text of Stela 5 may represent our journey through life.

Finally, the ring-tailed fish in the right hand of the Sariah figure has apparently been sacrificed with the instrument in the left hand. Two fish are also present at the very top of the sculpture as well as above the Lemuel figure near angel "A." The two fish above the Lemuel figure have what appear to be pieces of fruit in their mouths. The fruit may suggest Lehi's desire for his family to partake of the fruit. The fruit may also represent death. The resurrection is represented by the same two fish, at the top of the panel, who are now returning to earth.

Laman

Seated in front of the Nephi figure are two figures. The figure with his back to the trunk of the tree is proposed as Laman for the sake of discussion. Of all the figures on the right-hand side of the tree, the Laman figure is the only figure with his back to the tree. Clark and Moreno's drawing shows a crocodile near the Laman figure, which, in reality, may be associated with his name.

FIGURE 15–10: Figure with back to the tree facing the Nephi figure may represent Laman. (Drawing by Cliff Dunston)

The small figure between the Nephi figure and the Laman figure may be either a child figure or a figure representing a type of ancestral connection. The death bundle may suggest the latter. If it is an ancestral figure, it may relate to the birthright. Laman was the oldest son of Lehi and was therefore entitled to the leadership role as a result of birth. Laman lost his birthright, as indicated in the incident when an angel appeared and told Laman and Lemuel that the Lord had chosen Nephi to be the ruler: "Know ye not that the Lord has chosen him [Nephi] to be a ruler over you, and this because of your iniquities?" (1 Nephi 3:29).

The dualism of the Stela 5 text shows up again here, as the symbols of birth, death, and resurrection are present.

Lemuel

The highlighted figure in figure 15–11 is seated in much the same position in relation to the tree as is the Laman figure. With their backs to the tree, this positioning may suggest Laman's and Lemuel's refusal to partake of the fruit of the tree: "And it came to pass that I saw them [Laman and Lemuel], but they would not come unto me and partake of the fruit" (1 Nephi 8:18).

FIGURE 15–11: Figure with back to the tree facing the Lehi figure may represent Lemuel. (Drawing by Cliff Dunston)

Both the Nephi figure and the Lehi figure are shown partaking of the fruit, whereas both the Laman and Lemuel figures are not partaking of the fruit.

The authoritative manner in which the Lehi figure is offering a sacrifice and in which he appears to be instructing the Lemuel figure brings to mind the following statement of Lehi: "And as I partook of the fruit thereof it filled my soul with exceedingly great joy; wherefore, I began to be desirous that my family should partake of it also; for I knew that it was desirable above all other fruit" (1 Nephi 8:12).

The pointed cap worn by both the Lehi figure and the Lemuel figure is reminiscent of a Yucatan custom wherein a pointed cap was part of a priest's ornamental dress.[15]

The smoke rising from the incense burner flows in such a way that it blinds the eyes of the Lemuel figure. Lemuel was blind as to the gospel.

15. Alfred M. Tozzer, ed. of trans., *Landa's Relacion de las Cosas de Yucatan*, papers of the Peabody Museum of American Archaeology and Ethnology, Harvard University, vol. 18 (Cambridge: The Museum, 1941), 153.

Again, the dualism in an Isaiah-text concept is spelled out in its association with the Lemuel figure. The smallness in size of both the Lemuel and the Laman figures and their relative position at the base of the tree may suggest the beginning stages of our journey through life.

FIGURE 15–12: Figure showing extension of lines from the pyramids. (Drawing by Cliff Dunston)

Rod of Iron

The ground panel is indeed intriguing. The incised lines may represent a rod of iron or pathways that lead to the tree of life.

The six triangles or pyramids are even more intriguing. As shown in figure 15–12, Norman discovered that by extending the lines of the pyramids, six extend to ears of different individuals. Two lead to the eyes of the Sariah figure and the ancestral figure. And two lines extend to the top of the stone or to the sky panel.

The parable of the tree of life parallels the parable of the four soils. The Savior said: "Behold a sower went forth to sow; And when he sowed, some seeds fell by the *way side,* and the fowls came and devoured them up: Some fell upon *stony places,* where they had not much earth: and forthwith they sprung up, because they had no deepness of earth: And when the sun was up, they were scorched; and because they had no root, they withered away. And some fell among *thorns;* and the thorns sprung up, and choked them: But other fell into *good ground,* and brought forth fruit, some an hundredfold, some sixtyfold, some thirtyfold" (Matthew 13:4–8; emphasis added).

The Savior then said, "Who hath ears to hear, let him hear" (Matthew 13:9). This concept may also be represented in the Stela 5 monument.

The Savior emphasized the following point when asked why He spoke in parables: "Therefore speak I to them in parables: because they *seeing see* not; and *hearing* they *hear* not, neither do they understand" (Matthew 13:13; emphasis added).

We will now summarize the parallels between the parable of the four soils with the different people represented in Lehi's dream and the fifteen-ton stone monument at Izapa, Stela 5.

FOUR SOILS	TREE OF LIFE
1. Some fell by the wayside.	1. Some did not partake of the fruit.
2. Some fell in stony places.	2. Some got lost in forbidden paths.
3. Some fell among thorns.	3. Some partook of the fruit and then were ashamed.
4. Some fell in good ground.	4. Some held on to the iron rod and partook of the fruit.

As stated above, we observe that when the lines are extended from the pyramids, six of them point to the ears, perhaps suggesting the concept of "who hath ears let him hear." Two of the lines extend to the eyes, which may suggest the Savior's statement, "and seeing they see not."

As the picture puzzle is unraveled in more detail, we will see that, in reality, four groups of people are moving toward the tree in the Izapa monument, Stela 5, just as four groups of people are mentioned in the parable of the four soils and just as four groups of people are found in the dream of Lehi.

FIGURE 15–13: The heavy line leading along the base panel to the bottom of the tree may represent the rod of iron. (Drawing by Cliff Dunston)

Filthy Waters

The water panel located at the base of Stela 5 was proposed by Jakeman to represent the fountain of filthy waters in Lehi's dream: "And the angel spake unto me, saying: Behold the fountain of filthy water which thy father saw; yea, even the river of which he spake; and the depths thereof are the depths of hell" (1 Nephi 12:16).

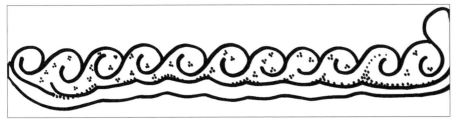

FIGURE 15–14: The swirls along the base panel may represent the filthy waters. (Drawing by Cliff Dunston)

The water panel in Stela 5 has the appearance of waves as well as the appearance of a flowing river. The rainfall patterns on the right-hand side of the panel behind the back of the Sam figure also suggest the appearance of dangerous floodwaters entering into the panel.

The Izapa ruins are located about fifteen miles inland from the Pacific Ocean. The rainfall in the Izapa area is very abundant during the months of May through October. A person can be easily destroyed in the depths of the ocean or by sudden and heavy and dirty floodwaters. The symbolic representation of being swallowed up in the depths of hell is totally appropriate.

FIGURE 15–15: The twelve roots of the tree may represent the twelve tribes of Israel. (Drawing by Cliff Dunston)

The Twelve Tribes

Twelve roots that extend into the ground are evident on the tree. Christ is *the* Tree of Life, and the roots may be representative of the twelve Nephite disciples, the twelve Apostles of Christ, or the twelve tribes of Israel. Some count thirteen tree roots. Thirteen is a common number in Mesoamerica art and history. For example, 4×13=52, the number of cycles in the Maya calendar.

Inasmuch as Nephi's interpretation of the dream of Lehi is centered around the coming of Christ and His subsequent Atonement, the twelve roots may represent the twelve Apostles of Christ.

On the other hand, because the Lehi story is a dispersion story of the house of Israel, the twelve roots may indicate the twelve tribes of Israel. The manner in which the roots are separated from each other suggests the separation of the tribes of Israel. Three prominent roots on the left portion of the tree may even suggest the portion of three tribes that traveled to Mesoamerica—that is, Lehi, the tribe of Manasseh; Ishmael, the tribe of Ephraim; and Mulek, the tribe of Judah.

In line with the dualism theme of Stela 5, the twelve roots may represent both the twelve Apostles and the twelve tribes of Israel. The twelve tribes would represent the historical part of the text, and the twelve Apostles would represent the spiritual part of the text. When Nephi received the interpretation of his father's dream, the twelve Apostles of Christ, the twelve tribes of Israel, and the twelve Nephite disciples were all part of it: "And the angel spake unto me, saying: Behold the twelve disciples of the Lamb, who are chosen to administer unto thy seed. And he said unto me: Thou rememberest the *twelve apostles* of the Lamb? They are they who shall judge the twelve tribes of Israel; wherefore, the twelve ministers of thy seed shall be judged of them; for ye are of the house of Israel. And these *twelve ministers* whom thou beholdest shall judge thy seed" (1 Nephi 12:8–10; emphasis added).

The number eight, which is represented by the top branches of the tree, is very common in Mesoamerica literature. It almost always has to do with the migration of eight tribal leaders from the main twelve or thirteen root branches.[16]

16. See Norman, *Izapa Sculpture,* 210–11.

Blind Person

On the left side of the tree with his hands touching the tree and his back almost touching the back of the Lemuel figure is a figure that has a hood over his head. The hood probably indicates that the person has lost his way. Norman writes: "The hooded head covering . . . I have related to a journey in pursuit of the life giving (but unseen?) tree."[17]

FIGURE 15–16: The figure with a hood over its head touching the tree may represent those people who are blinded to the truth. The smoke rising up in front of the Lemuel figure may also represent being blinded and wandering off the path that leads to the tree. Norman and Clark present a different artistic rendition of this figure. (Drawing by Cliff Dunston)

17. Norman, *Izapa Sculpture*, 214.

The dream of Lehi speaks of the eyes of people being blinded by the temptations of the devil: "And the mists of darkness are the temptations of the devil, which *blindeth the eyes,* and hardeneth the hearts of the children of men, and leadeth them away into broad roads, that they perish and are lost" (1 Nephi 12:17; emphasis added).

The blind figure in Stela 5 seems to represent that group of people who, like the seed that is sown in stony places, do not take root in the gospel plan. The temptations of Satan are too strong for them, and their eyes are blinded to the principles of the gospel. The blind person touched the tree but did not partake of the fruit of the tree.

The Ashamed Person

About midway up the tree, with its back to the tree and facing the angel on the left side of the tree, is a person wearing a skull cap with a chin strap. The person is holding a piece of fruit from the tree.

FIGURE 15–17: The figure with his back to the tree above the blinded figure may represent those who partake of the fruit and then are ashamed. (Drawing by Cliff Dunston)

This figure may represent those people whom Lehi saw in his dream who partook of the fruit and then fell away because they were ashamed. This is a group that is represented by the Savior's parable of the seed that fell in sandy soil but whose roots were not deep enough to produce fruit: "And after they had partaken of the fruit of the tree they did cast their eyes about as if they were ashamed. And after they had tasted of the fruit they were ashamed, because of those that were scoffing at them; and they fell away into forbidden paths and were lost" (1 Nephi 8:25, 28).

Symbols of Eternal Life

The story engraved on Stela 5 at Izapa is no more than a story and meaningless symbols—unless we can arrive at the point where we understand the mighty realities behind the symbols.

FIGURE 15–18: The serpent, the fish, and the humming birds are symbols of Christ, resurrection, and eternal life. (Drawing by Cliff Dunston)

The circumstantial evidence of the mighty realities behind the symbols on Stela 5 is that Jesus is the Christ and that, in our journey through life, we may inherit eternal life by adhering to the teachings and the ordinances of the gospel of Jesus Christ. That is the message of the tree of life as recorded in the early chapters of 1 Nephi.

Perhaps the real debate regarding Stela 5 is not if it can be determined intellectually to be an authentic sculpture associated with the vision of Lehi but rather if it can be determined spiritually to have gospel truths represented in its symbolic engravings.

We gain a deeper appreciation and understanding of Lehi's dream by becoming acquainted with a 300 BC analysis of what seems to be an account of that dream engraved on stone.

Symbols of Christ and eternal life seem to be adequately spelled out in symbols on the stone. The serpent, the fish, and the humming birds are all associated with Christ and eternal symbols of our birth, death, and resurrection. The inverted "U" glyph at the top of the panel may even represent the celestial kingdom.

Two fish are shown in the stone, with pieces of fruit in their mouths, signifying that if we partake of the fruit of the tree of life, we will ascend into heaven. Two fish are also present at the top of the panel with their faces returning to earth, which may symbolize our resurrection.

Two humming birds have their beaks attached to the nostrils of the two-headed serpent. If the serpent is representative of Christ, then the two humming birds represent the gaining of eternal life through the nostrils of the serpent. It is strange, but very interesting, that some species of humming birds attach their beaks to a tree during the winter months and literally die, according to their appearances. When spring arrives, life is restored to the humming birds, and they are reborn, or resurrected.

SUMMARY

In this treatise, we have touched only lightly upon the symbolism associated with gospel principles and the Tree of Life Stone called Stela 5, which is located near Tapachula, Mexico. Although disagreement exists among scholars as to the interpretation of Izapa Stela 5, the fact that it is a large stone with engravings merits a comparison with what we read in the Book of Mormon, both from a historical perspective and as a method of writing on large stones (see Omni 1:20).

Two of the most significant breakthroughs in recent years are the linguistic and mathematical correlations with the Hebrew culture. First, linguistically, the chiastic manner in which Stela 5 is written, as proposed by Todd Allen, lends credibility to its being a Jewish text. Second, mathematically, the Hebrew measurement of the cubit, as discovered by V. Garth Norman, enhances the stone as having a Jewish origin.

Norman also concluded that the history recorded on the stone itself is patterned after a type and a shadow, a theme common to the Book of Mormon. In other words, from a point of view of both Lehi and the artist of Izapa, Stela 5 presents a physical story of a family and lets the story apply to our own experience as we travel through life's journey. In other words, the account of Lehi's vision of the tree of life, along with Nephi's interpretation of his father's dream, is literally a vision about the advent of Christ, or the Messiah. Christ is *the* Tree of Life. Nephi writes: "I also beheld that the

> Perhaps the real debate regarding Stela 5 is not if it can be determined intellectually to be an authentic sculpture associated with the vision of Lehi but rather if it can be determined spiritually to have gospel truths represented in its symbolic engravings.

tree of life was a representation of the love of God" (1 Nephi 11:26). God so loved the world that he sent his Only Begotten Son. And that fruit which was "white to exceed all whiteness" is eternal life, the greatest of all gifts (1 Nephi 8:11; D&C 14:7). As readers will see, therefore, the tree-of-life story is not just a historical account of a family; rather, it is a prophecy of the mission of Jesus Christ. As a result, its impact has worldwide consequences.

CHAPTER 16

Customs and
Traditions

Now it was the custom of the people of Nephi to call their lands, and their cities, and their villages, yea, even all their small villages after the name of him who first possessed them; and thus it was with the land of Ammonihah. (Alma 8:7)

hether walking down the streets of the Old City of Jerusalem or visiting the village of San Juan Chamula in Chiapas, Mexico, travelers can easily be left with the feeling that things have not changed very much over the last two thousand years. If we read the accounts of the customs and traditions of Mesoamerica by Diego de Landa or Bernardino de Sahagun, written in the sixteenth century, we soon come to a similar realization that many customs and traditions in Mesoamerica are the same after several hundred years.

Clothing, houses, food, and family customs appear to have changed very little over the years among many native people in Mesoamerica. A case in point is some

OPPOSITE: In addition to language and archaeology, another criterion for legitimate Book of Mormon research should include a comparative study of timeless traditions of the area under consideration for Book of Mormon lands. In turn, these traditions may help us understand more about the Book of Mormon. This picture shows a young girl at Almolonga, Guatemala, measuring out corn using a balance scale. The one-pound weight is called a "marcos." See illustrations in this chapter for the monetary breakdown comparing these marcos with the weights and measures referred to in Alma 11. (Photo courtesy of Cortney Boice)

Virtually all
customs and
traditions
mentioned
in the Book
of Mormon
have been
discovered
as having
existed in
Mesoamerica
during the
time period
required by
the Book of
Mormon.

investigative work that began at the end of the 1990s on an old town site called Ceren in El Salvador. The old village had been destroyed by an earthquake around AD 500. Much of the work consisted in uncovering homes where the people had lived. The result: it's as if time had stood still. Archaeologists determined that the early inhabitants' manner of living was similar to present-day living situations, including the traditional three-stone fire hearth, food consisting of beans and tortillas, and the ever-present chickens in the yard. Such findings are exciting, as the excavated portions are only a hundred years removed from the close of the Book of Mormon.

Interestingly, when the Book of Mormon was published in 1830, very little was known about Mesoamerica. People often criticized the Book of Mormon on the grounds that many things mentioned in it (such as the use of cement) did not exist during the time required by the Book of Mormon. At the middle of the eighteenth century, only about 20 percent of so-called external evidences relating to the Book of Mormon had been discovered in Mesoamerica. That figure has now reversed because virtually all customs and traditions mentioned in the Book of Mormon have been discovered as having existed in Mesoamerica during the time period required by the Book of Mormon.

The following discussion represents a sampling of interesting comparisons between the customs and traditions in the Book of Mormon with Mesoamerican customs and traditions. The list is not intended to be exhaustive; it simply serves as a "liahona" to point to the need for continued and more detailed research—both in the Book of Mormon and in Mesoamerica.[1]

1. Bruce Warren has prepared a lengthy list of religious and cultural traits that are common to Mesoamerica and the Near East. He says, "If there were Israelites in Mesoamerica centuries before Christ was born, they should have left things behind." See his list in Blaine M. Yorgason, Bruce W. Warren, and Harold Brown, *New Evidences of Christ in Ancient America* (Provo, UT: Stratford Books, 1999), 283–99.

ASTRONOMY

Alma said to the antichrist, Korihor, "Even the earth, and all things that are upon the face of it, yea, and its motion, yea, and also *all the planets which move in their regular form* do witness that there is a Supreme Creator" (Alma 30:44; emphasis added).

Nephi, the son of Helaman, said, "And thus, according to his word the earth goeth back, and it appeareth unto man that the sun standeth still; yea, and behold, this is so; *for surely it is the earth that moveth and not the sun*" (Helaman 12:15; emphasis added).

These BC prophets understood things pertaining to the movements in the heavens. The Spanish writers recorded that the ancient Tultecas of Mesoamerica were men of science who understood things pertaining to astronomy. (See comments by Ixtlilxochitl in chapter 11, "Fernando de Alva Ixtlilxochitl," and by Sahagun in chapter 12, "Bernardino de Sahagun.")

The Classic Maya (AD 250–AD 900) went to great lengths to erect observatories to understand better the movements of the planets. The Maya observatory at Chichen Itza, the Toltec temple at Chichen Itza, the Maya temple of Tulum, and Mound J at Monte Alban are positioned in relationship to the sun. During the spring and fall equinoxes, the shadows slowly descend down the temple steps at Chichen Itza—finally settling upon the head of the serpent and thus giving the impression that the serpent is moving.

CEMENT

About 45 BC, a large group of Nephites migrated to the "land which was northward"—the place proposed in *Exploring the Lands of the Book of Mormon* as being in the Mexico City valley. Speaking of this group of Nephites, Mormon said, "And there being but little timber upon the face of the land, nevertheless the people who went forth became exceedingly expert in the working of cement; therefore they did build houses of cement, in the which they did dwell" (Helaman 3:7).

Teotihuacan, located in what is considered to be the "land which was northward" (Alma 63:4), was in existence during the

FIGURE 16–1: This eighth century AD building at Chichen Itza has been labeled an observatory. Even after the close of the Book of Mormon, the Maya priests continued to be great observers or astronomers, which enabled them to predict movements in the heavens. Much of their stone-engraved work reflects their knowledge of the planets and the stars. Their belief in a life hereafter is a constant theme among the ancient inhabitants of Mesoamerica as well as in the Book of Mormon. (Photo courtesy of Sheryl Lee Wilson)

FIGURE 16–2: This picture shows concrete floors made with cement in the courtyard of the Postclassic site of Mitla, Oaxaca. In several instances, newly poured concrete of today is not as durable as the fifteen-hundred-year-old concrete of the Zapotecs. In the Mexico valley today, most of the dwellings are still constructed with concrete that is made with cement. The large stone pillars shown here are not "poured cement" but are carved from the nearby mountains. (Photo courtesy of Sheryl Lee Wilson)

time period referred to above (150–45 BC). Teotihuacan has a city center that literally is built of aggregate and cement to produce concrete for construction. Construction by this process is found extensively throughout Mesoamerica. Mitla, a Zapotec site in the state of Oaxaca, although built during a later time period (AD 1300–1500), is an outstanding accomplishment in the workings of concrete made possible by the hardening component of cement.

In fact, until recently, when steel started to play a major role in construction in the Mexico City valley, most modern buildings were built with aggregate and cement. Timber is scarce and is very expensive. As a result, the extensive government home-building projects that have sprung up along the highway from Mexico City to the pyramids of Teotihuacan are built almost exclusively of aggregate and cement. One of the keys to understanding the Book of Mormon is to pay attention to the area where a particular trait or custom mentioned in the Book of Mormon is located. Almost always, the customs tie in with the geography.

> One of the keys to understanding the Book of Mormon is to pay attention to the area where a particular trait or custom mentioned in the Book of Mormon is located. Almost always, the customs tie in with the geography.

CLIMATE

Only a few scriptures in the Book of Mormon give any hint about the climate. About 70 BC, Mormon said that some of the people died with fevers, "which at *some seasons* of the year were very frequent in the land." Mormon then informs us that the excellent qualities of plants and roots helped cope with the diseases that the people were subjected to because of "the *nature of the climate*" (Alma 46:40; emphasis added).

The lowland jungle area of Guatemala is proposed as the general area of Zarahemla's east wilderness, and this area certainly meets such climatic descriptions as given above. Mormon often uses the concept of dualism to teach a spiritual principle. For example, in the above scripture, he makes reference to the quality of roots and plants. They are a type and shadow, or a representation of Christ, such as in the prophecy quoted by Abinadi, "For he shall grow up before him as a tender plant, and as a root out of dry ground" (Mosiah 14:2).

On another occasion, Nephi, the son of Helaman, was shown to plead with the Lord not to let the people be destroyed by the sword but to send a famine that would cause the people to be stirred up in remembrance of the Lord. When the people repented, Nephi asked the Lord to "send forth *rain* upon the face of the earth, that she may bring forth her fruit, and her grain in *the season of grain*" (Helaman 11:13; emphasis added).

The people of Mesoamerica absolutely depend on the rainy season for production of their crops. Those familiar with the seasons of Mesoamerica well know that, as opposed to winter, summer, spring, and fall, the seasons in Mesoamerica are measured in terms of the "rainy season" (May–October) or the "dry season" (October–May). A deeper understanding of the Book of Mormon is realized as we understand the climatic conditions of Mesoamerica.

CLOTHES

Both elaborate clothing and scanty clothing are mentioned in the Book of Mormon. Five years before the birth of Christ, Samuel the Lamanite warned the people that the day would come when they would accept false prophets, when the people would give their substance to the false prophets, and when the people would clothe the false prophets in *costly apparel* (see Helaman 13:28). Two hundred one years after the coming of Christ, the prophecy was fulfilled literally, as there were "those who were lifted up in pride, such as the wearing of costly apparel" (4 Nephi 1:24).

Today, in the mountains of the state of Chiapas, Mexico, and in highland Guatemala, where over five million native people live, the manner of dress consists of beautiful, embroidered, colorful material. Each village is distinguished by its own particular style and color of dress. One set of clothing today, called *huipiles,* is traditionally associated with rank and status.

In the lowlands, along the coast of Guatemala, and in the Yucatan, the style of dress is less elaborate and, in many cases, is scanty. Traditionally, the Maya of Peten, Guatemala, dressed in simple loincloths—a practice that coincides with Mormon's description of the Lamanites: "Now the heads of the Lamanites were shorn; and they were naked, save it were skin which was girded about their loins, and also their armor, which was girded about them, and their bows, and their arrows, and their stones, and their slings, and so forth" (Alma 3:5).

A deeper understanding of the Book of Mormon is realized as we understand the climatic conditions of Mesoamerica.

FIGURE 16–3: The beautiful colors of Guatemala are demonstrated in the huipiles worn by the native Maya in their many embroidered creations. The traditions of distinctive, beautifully colored, embroidered clothing still identify the women according to the village in which they reside. This picture shows vendors at Santiago Atitlan, Guatemala. (Photo courtesy of Merrill C. Oaks)

CORN (GRAINS)

From a casual reading of the Book of Mormon, we know that the most staple food product during the middle Nephite time period was corn. Corn, or maize, is native to Mesoamerica. That corn existed for thousands of years in Mesoamerica is well documented. It apparently was a staple food product at the time Zeniff was living in the land of Nephi: "And we began to till the ground, yea, even with all manner of seeds, with seeds of corn, and of wheat, and of barley, and with neas, and with sheum, and with seeds of all manner of fruits; and we did begin to multiply and prosper in the land" (Mosiah 9:9).

In the southern Yucatan Peninsula near the archaeological zone of Dzibanche, corn can be grown year round, as the dew from heaven falls daily. In Guatemala and Chiapas, the beauty of the golden season (October–November) is overwhelming when the corn stocks, which reach heights of ten feet, wave in the cool mountain breezes. Although the corn stalks do not produce a heavy yield of ears, the production is, nevertheless, adequate to provide food for the year—if the rainy season has been normal. The corn is made into tortillas and is used as a base for beans, fowl, fish, and other foods. The blue tortilla, made from the colored kernels of corn, is common in Chiapas. Corn tortillas with refried beans are served during every meal of every day among the natives of Guatemala and Chiapas, Mexico. On our tours today, if we go into the local fast-food chicken place, Pollo Campero, in a town like Chimaltenango, which is located west of Guatemala City, we see the local people bringing their own tortillas with them to eat along with the chicken. They don't get very excited about the KFC type of biscuits.

We may even call this aspect of Mesoamerican culture "geography by agriculture." It is like Hansel and Gretel, who left a trail of bread crumbs. In a similar way in Mesoamerica, we can follow the people by the food they ate in the past in comparison with what they eat today. A simple case in point is that corn, a primary product in the land of Nephi (see Mosiah 9:9), was prevalent in the same place and at the same time period where the land of Nephi is proposed to be located (Guatemala City area). The concept of food and geography can be driven home by our pointing out that corn did not enter the eastern part of the United States until after the close of the Book of Mormon.

This observation simply means that the geography of the Book of Mormon, from an agricultural point of view, did *not* take place in New York. Archaeologists have been able to determine the dates when corn became a

> Corn did not enter the eastern part of the United States until after the close of the Book of Mormon. This observation simply means that the geography of the Book of Mormon, from an agricultural point of view, did *not* take place in New York.

FIGURE 16–4: Corn has been the staple product for over three millennia in Mesoamerica. Further, the concept of a maize god is pronounced in the Mesoamerica tradition. A variety of different colors of corn, as shown in this visual, is used for tortillas that carry with them the color of the corn. Corn is a major agricultural product in the Book of Mormon, but corn did not reach the United States until between AD 400 and AD 500, the time of the final Nephite dispersion. (Photo from USDA Agricultural Research Center, courtesy of Keith Weller)

Figure 16–5. Agricultural crops in the highlands of Guatemala and Chiapas revolve around the rainy season, which lasts from May through October. At the village of Almolonga, Guatemala, hot, natural mineral waters spring forth from the nearby volcanic mountains, enabling crops, such as the large bundles of lettuce and carrots shown here, to be raised year round. (Photo courtesy of Cortney Boice)

part of the diet by examining the remains of the people and the way their teeth have been ground down. Perhaps some readers may think that this is a minor point in determining Book of Mormon geography, but that's not true. The native people of New York were not tilling corn in 100 BC when Zeniff mentions it. In other words, from a scientific perspective, the Nephites did not live in New York.

Barley and wheat are also mentioned in the Book of Mormon, and they are produced in the highlands of Guatemala. The farmers farm the steep, high mountain ridges, leaving very little ground to waste.

Another item mentioned in the Zeniff account is neas. In all probability, this word should be *beans*. By examining the handwriting of Oliver Cowdery in the original manuscripts that are now available to us, we can see how an error in typesetting could be made from the word "beans" to "neas." In Mesoamerica, of course, beans, like corn, are a staple product—and have been for centuries.[2] No reason exists to suggest that a dramatic change in the diet of the native people of Mesoamerica has occurred over the last three thousand years.

DEFENSIVE EARTHWORKS

The question has often been asked as to why Mormon included so much content about military conquests in his abridgement decisions. That is a question directly related to customs and traditions. We can possibly understand his decisions partially by realizing that he was, by virtue of the leadership role he assumed, a military person. But if we assume that everything in the Book of Mormon is there "by inspiration" and "for

2. See Royal Skousen, ed., *The Original Manuscript of the Book of Mormon* (Provo, UT: Foundation for Ancient Research and Mormon Studies, 2001); and Royal Skousen, *The Printer's Manuscript of the Book of Mormon*, 2 parts (Provo, UT: Foundation for Ancient Research and Mormon Studies, 2002).

a purpose," we should realize the importance of understanding the consequences of reading about the military conquests throughout the book.

In that respect, one of the most significant military undertakings contained in the Book of Mormon is found in Alma 49–50 where Mormon tells us about Moroni's construction of defensive earthworks in the east wilderness. Why did Mormon include this content in the book? Perhaps the answer is found in relatively recent archaeological findings associated with defensive earthworks.

That is, David Webster wrote his doctoral dissertation about the defensive earthworks at Becan. Prior to this time, most so-called "Mesoamerican authorities" stated emphatically that the Maya had always been a peace-loving people. One of Webster's conclusions, however, is that "the 'peaceful Maya' theory has become so untenable that it seems permissible to assume that warfare may have played an essential role in Maya civilization from very early times."[3] Certainly that statement is supported by the warfare content of the Book of Mormon.

3. David L. Webster, *Defensive Earthworks at Becan, Campeche, Mexico: Implications for Maya Warfare*, Publication 41 (New Orleans: Middle American Research Institute, 1976), 108.

Archaeologists have discovered and analyzed the defensive earthworks in Mesoamerica within the lifetimes of all members of the Church of Jesus Christ who are presently forty or so years old. Indeed, an exhilarating experience happens when we contemplate that fact and then read such statements as the following by Webster: "Perhaps the most knotty problem is how to explain the uniqueness of the fortifications themselves.... There remains the possibility that the fortifications at Becan were the brainchild of some local innovator; the basic pattern is simple enough, as its widespread occurrence suggests."[4] According to Mormon, that "local innovator" was the 72 BC military leader named Moroni (see Alma 49–50). We will discuss the unique consequences of defensive earthworks in detail in chapter 24, "Wilderness Areas."

4. Webster, *Defensive Earthworks at Becan*, 108.

Again, notice the dualistic nature of this section. Just like Becan was surrounded by a serpent-like defensive earthwork to protect the people from their enemies, so should we take upon ourselves the name of Christ, that "serpent" Moses spoke about, as a defense against Satan, our greatest enemy.

> Just like Becan was surrounded by a serpent-like defensive earthwork to protect the people from their enemies, so should we take upon ourselves the name of Christ, that "serpent" Moses spoke about, as a defense against Satan, our greatest enemy.

DIRECTIONS

The Maya lived and breathed by the sun. They were dedicated to the cardinal directions and even associated them with colors. East was associated with the color red, as the sun rises in the east. West was associated with the color black, or night. North was white, and south was yellow.

The Mesoamerica map works well as we pay attention to the directions therein. Such terms as "southward," "northward," "sea east," "sea west," and "west sea, south" (Alma 22:21–22; Ether 9:31; Moroni 2:29; Alma 53:8) are all Book of Mormon terms that adequately relate to the Mesoamerica map. Understanding the cardinal directions as they apply to the Mesoamerica map is a key to understanding the customs and traditions of peoples of the Book of Mormon.

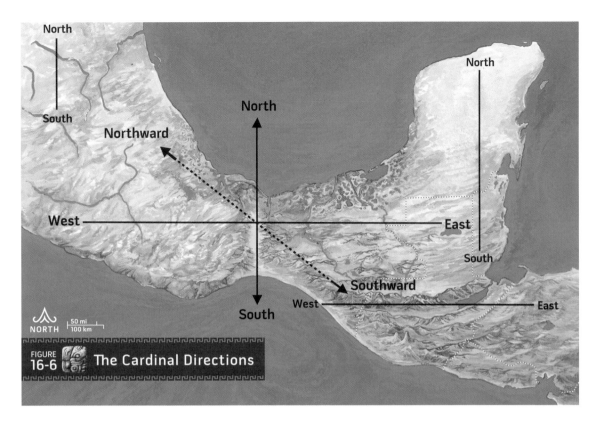

FIGURE 16–6: No tangible evidence suggests that any other configuration than the cardinal directions was used by either Maya or Book of Mormon writers.

We will read additional unique information about directions in chapter 23, "Things That Are Narrow," and chapter 24, "Wilderness Areas."

We must adhere to two cardinal rules when discussing cardinal directions: (1) do not alter the Mesoamerica map, and (2) do not alter the directions given in the Book of Mormon. We should also remember that when Mormon and the Maya speak of directions, east is where we were born and west is where it becomes dark when we die (see Alma 34:33–34).

FOOD

We would need countless pages or even books to discuss adequately the food in Mexico and Guatemala. In addition to the staple products of corn and beans, the major diet of the Mexicans consists of fruit, fish, and chicken.

Food experts point out that many food products, such as corn, cocoa, tomatoes, potatoes, beans, and a variety of fruits, are "gifts" to the world from Mesoamerica. The American consumer has fallen in love with much of the Mexico style of cooking.

> We must adhere to two cardinal rules when discussing cardinal directions: (1) do not alter the Mesoamerica map, and (2) do not alter the directions given in the Book of Mormon.

However, some of the cooking methods via the fast-food outlets have Americanized the food. On one occasion, when our young family had spent the summer in Mexico, the time arrived when everyone was eager to return home. Todd, who was ten years old at the time said, "I can hardly wait to get home so I can go to Taco Bell to get some real Mexican food."

The manner in which the food is prepared by the native populations of Mexico and Guatemala may give us hints as to the type of food and the manner in which the food may have been prepared in Book of Mormon times.

Also, the experience of walking through the museums in Mexico and Guatemala to observe the pottery that dates to the time period of the Book of Mormon is very interesting. Perhaps such experiences can even provide us with a glimpse of the types of "pots and pans" that the wives of Alma, Helaman, or Mormon used for cooking purposes.

HORSES

The term "horse" is used twenty-four times in the Book of Mormon. The last time it is used dates to AD 29 (see 3 Nephi 6). When the Spaniards arrived in the year 1519, they did not discover horses in either Mexico or Guatemala. The natives were surprised to see the Spaniards riding horses. The natives referred to the horses as "deer."

> When the Spaniards arrived in the year 1519, they did not discover horses in either Mexico or Guatemala. The natives were surprised to see the Spaniards riding horses. The natives referred to the horses as "deer."

The horse of the Spaniards became an extremely successful instrument in the conquest of Mexico. Reportedly, the natives considered the horse and rider to be of the same mind.

A great deal of speculation still exists among students of the Book of Mormon as to what happened to the horses. Some students suggest that the horses became extinct because of famine or that the horses may have been used as food for human consumption. Others suggest that the term "horse" may have reference to a four-legged animal that may not necessarily have been like the horse we know today. Still others propose that only the elite used horses and that their horses were more like a small draft animal that pulled the chariots.

Interestingly, three horse bones that were discovered in a cave in Loltun, Yucatan, and that date to Book of Mormon times are occasionally put on display at the Maya Room of the National Museum of Anthropology in Mexico City. On one occasion, we had a veterinarian with us who was able to determine that the bones were from a mare and that the horse was relatively small in size.[5] As we think about customs and traditions associated with the "horse" question in the Book of Mormon, we may be wise to simply withhold judgment until further information becomes available.

5. Joseph L. Allen, "Horses," *The Book of Mormon Archaeological Digest*, 2, no. 6 (2000): 1.

HOUSES (FAMILY LIFE)

The present-day typical houses of Chiapas, Veracruz, Tabasco, Campeche, and the Yucatan are all built with thatched roofs. They consist of simple one-room homes with additional small buildings for cooking and storage and living quarters for the extended families.

The Maya homes in the villages of the Yucatan closely parallel the Classic Period (AD 200–AD 900) room in the Quadrangle of the Nunnery at the ruins of Uxmal. This historical fact suggests that very few changes in Mesoamerican home styles have occurred over the centuries.

FIGURE 16–7: The people of Guatemala are a friendly people and are also loving parents. Mothers commonly carry their small children on their backs, as shown in this picture. The setting for the picture is the marketplace at Almolonga, a land of pure water. (Photo courtesy of Cortney Boice)

THEY CLAPPED THEIR HANDS FOR JOY

The following anecdote was reported by Joseph Allen:

On one of our tours, my wife and I were walking through the marketplace at Chichicastenango, Guatemala. Our group was shopping when a native Quiche woman came up to us and said, "May I be your guide to take you through the church?"

The church is the place where the native document, the *Popol Vuh,* was discovered, so we were eager to take the tour. On the tour, our guide not only explained about things in the church but also took us through the little museum.

We joked a little with her, and she got so excited that several times she said something and then laughed and laughed. I asked my wife, "Do you see what she's doing? Do you remember reading in Mosiah, when Alma baptized at the waters of Mormon, that all the people clapped their hands for joy?"

"And now when the people had heard these words, *they clapped their hands for joy,* and exclaimed: This is the desire of our hearts" (Mosiah 18:11; emphasis added).

"Look at what she's doing every time she laughs."

We smiled and agreed. "That's right. She swings her hands together so they meet about eye level. She then gives a little jump and laughs."

I then recalled that I had seen this behavior hundreds of times in Mesoamerica. One lady named Dona Sofia at the black pottery shop in Oaxaca does the very same thing. Her behavior reminds me of the Book of Mormon Lamanite queen who was converted. Upon her conversion, she "cried with a loud voice, saying: O blessed Jesus, who has saved me from an awful hell! O blessed God, have mercy on this people! And when she had said this, she *clasped* [clapped] her hands, being filled with joy" (Alma 19:29–30; emphasis added).

In all probability in the above verse, the word *clasped* should be *clapped,* as in Mosiah 18:11. The word *clapped* is used later in the following manner: "And it came to pass that when Alma had said these words, he *clapped* his hands upon all them who were with him. And behold, as he *clapped* his hands upon them, they were filled with the Holy Spirit" (Alma 31:36; emphasis added). Being filled with joy and filled with the Holy Spirit are probably synonymous.

From the work of Royal Skousen,[6] we can deduce that the word *clasped* as recorded in Alma 19:30 should indeed be *clapped.* His analysis documents the fact that both the original manuscript and the printer's manuscript of the Book of Mormon show the word *clapped* rather than *clasped* in Alma 19:30.[7]

Perhaps the typesetter simply made an error in setting the type for the word, or perhaps he read the handwritten text as *clasped.* This word was used by Joseph Smith's mother when she wrote her history of her son: "In this moment of distraction, my husband and myself *clasped* our hands, fell upon our knees by the bedside, and poured out our grief to God, in prayer and supplication, beseeching him to spare our child yet a little longer."[8]

Joseph Smith probably translated the word correctly as *clapped,* reinforcing a custom that is still prevalent today in Mesoamerican culture. The typesetter in 1829 may have read the one passage as *clasped* because that word was common in his culture.

LIQUOR

Both the Book of Mormon and Ixtlilxochitl speak of getting guards drunk and then escaping. King Noah, a Nephite king who lived in the land of Nephi about 130 BC, kept vineyards; and he became a wine-bibber (see Mosiah 11:15). The Nephite soldiers provided wine in its strength to Lamanite guards (see Alma 55:10–13).

6. See Royal Skousen, "Towards a Critical Edition of the Book of Mormon," *BYU Studies,* 30, no. 1 (Winter 1990): 42–69; and Royal Skousen, *Analysis of Textual Variants of the Book of Mormon* (Provo, UT: Foundation for Ancient Research and Mormon Studies, Brigham Young University, 2004).

7. Skousen, *The Original Manuscript of the Book of Mormon,* 235; Skousen, *The Printer's Manuscript of the Book of Mormon,* 491.

8. Lucy Mack Smith, *The History of Joseph Smith by His Mother* (American Fork, UT: Covenant Communications, 2004), 57.

If the wine given by the Nephite soldiers was the same as wine made today in Mesoamerica, then the wine was probably made from the maguey plant or from other similar plants. The maguey plant is a relative to the century plant and has a large center with the appearance of a giant pineapple. The unfermented pulque juice is processed into tequila or mescal.

MEDICINE

The Tultecas were the inventors of medicine in Mesoamerica. The Book of Mormon makes reference to the use of herbs for medicinal purposes: "And there were some who died with fevers, which at some seasons of the year were very frequent in the land—but not so much so with fevers, because of the excellent qualities of the many plants and roots which God had prepared to remove the cause of diseases, to which men were subject by the nature of the climate" (Alma 46:40).

Herbs and roots of many varieties are used today in Mesoamerica for the treatment of illnesses, and many of our modern medicines that are used worldwide are being discovered in the tropical rainforests of Mesoamerica.

METAL (IRON)

The Book of Mormon refers to metals on many occasions. Some evidence exists of metal use during pre-Columbian times in Mesoamerica. Small metal weapons are displayed at the Olmec museum of Santiago, Tuxtla. This museum contains artifacts from the site of Tres Zapotes dating to 800 BC. And the Oaxaca room of the National Museum of Anthropology in Mexico City has several metal objects, including iron, on display.

MONEY

The native Mesoamericans traded with cocoa beans, quetzal feathers, and copper figures, and they used a weights-and-measures system that is still utilized today. These weights consist of four small cups, each weighing various amounts, and a small, solid weight. The cups nestle inside one another much like the measuring cups we use in our American kitchens. The small, solid cap fits inside the smallest cup.

> The native Mesoamericans traded with cocoa beans, quetzal feathers, and copper figures, and they used a weights-and-measures system that is still utilized today.

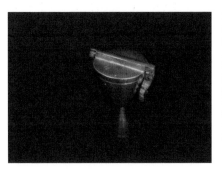

FIGURE 16–8: The "weights and measures" that are used by the native people of Guatemala and El Salvador to measure their produce consist of four small cups inside a one-half-pound container and are made of zinc, iron, and copper. (Photo courtesy of Merrill C. Oaks)

You will observe in both the chapter heading of Alma 11 as well as in the index of the Book of Mormon that the terms "coinage" and "coins" are used. However, the term *coin* was not used in the original Book of Mormon text. In fact, the Mesoamerican society did not use coins in the manner in which we use them today or in the manner in which the Romans used them. The "monetary" exchange system is outlined in Alma 11:4 and is consistent with the Mesoamerican concept of weights and measures: "Now these are the names of their different pieces of their gold and of their silver, according to their value. And the names are given by the Nephites, for they did not reckon after the manner of the Jews who were at Jerusalem; neither did they measure after the manner of the Jews."

The following discussion represents an analysis of the "weights and measures" shown below compared with the Book of Mormon's description of "weights and measures" as found in Alma 11. This discussion is not presented as conclusive evidence but rather as an exercise to compare the two systems.

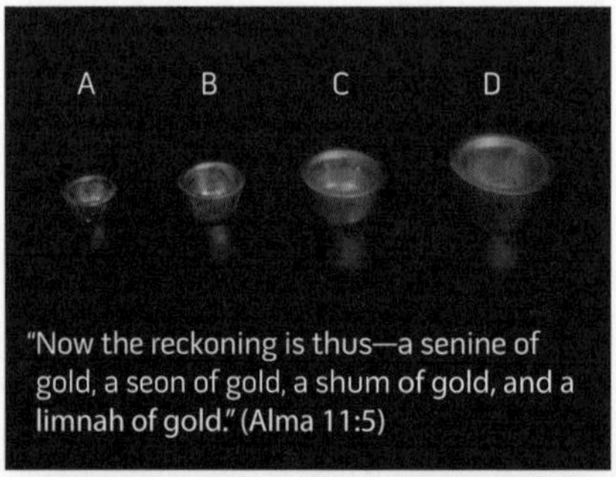

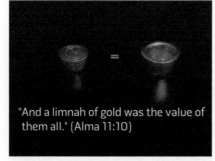

Figure 16–9: The four cups both weigh and measure proportionally: 1/8, 1/4, 1/2, and one. (Photo courtesy of Merrill C. Oaks)

A   B   C   D

"Now the reckoning is thus—a senine of gold, a seon of gold, a shum of gold, and a limnah of gold." (Alma 11:5)

Figure 16–10. The four cups combined are equal to the total weight or volume of the container. (Photo courtesy of Merrill C. Oaks)

"And a limnah of gold was the value of them all." (Alma 11:10)

The measurements of the sets of weights used today follow the same pattern as described in the Book of Mormon:

A	B	C	D
A senine of gold	A seon of gold	A shum of gold	A limnah of gold

(A) Now the reckoning is thus—a senine of gold, a seon of gold, a shum of gold, and a limnah of gold. (Alma 11:5)

(B) Now the amount of a seon of gold was twice the value of a senine. (Alma 11:8)

(C) And a shum of gold was twice the value of a seon. (Alma 11:9)

(D) And a limnah of gold was the value of them all. (Alma 11:10)

The above is just a preliminary statement on the type of exchange system used by the Nephites. Nevertheless, Mesoamerica does have a system of weights and measures that appears to predate the Spanish conquest and that is still used today. And the calibrations are the same. The natives do not today, however, use the "weights and measures" to measure. They use them only to weigh their produce. The monetary system as explained in Alma 11 appears to be a type and shadow of the spiritual concepts of justice and mercy (see Alma 11–12). Amulek wrote: "And thus mercy can satisfy the demands of justice, and encircles them in the arms of safety, while he that exercises no faith unto repentance is exposed to the whole law of the demands of justice; therefore

The monetary system as explained in Alma 11 appears to be a type and shadow of the spiritual concepts of justice and mercy.

only unto him that has faith unto repentance is brought about the great and eternal plan of redemption" (Alma 34:16).

SERPENTS

The serpent motif is very strong in both the Book of Mormon and in Mesoamerica. Quetzalcoatl, the feathered serpent, is a representation of Christ. An abundance of serpent motifs is found in Mesoamerica. (See chapter 14, "The White God Quetzalcoatl," for further discussion.)

STONE BOXES

Moroni buried the gold plates in a stone box in New York. That stone box, however, was not exactly like the typical stone boxes in Mesoamerica. Joseph Smith said the plates were buried in a stone box. He said: "The box in which they lay was formed by laying stones together in some kind of cement. In the bottom of the box were laid two stones crossways of the box, and on these stones lay the plates and the other things with them" (Joseph Smith—History 1:52).

The fact that the New York stone box in which Joseph Smith found the gold plates is not exactly like the stone boxes discovered in Mesoamerica suggests that Moroni had to manufacture a stone box similar to those from Mesoamerica with which he was familiar. If he did not carry tools with him from Mexico to New York, he would have used his knowledge of cement and his basic concept of a box to create a safe and secure storage place for the gold plates. They were preserved for over fourteen hundred years.

Figure 16–11: The serpent motif is prevalent throughout Mesoamerican art. Shown here is a serpent head carved in stone and located at the entrance of the ball court at Chichen Itza. Notice the ring in the background of the ball court. (Photo courtesy of Sheryl Lee Wilson)

Figure 16–12: Traditionally, black obsidian was traded throughout ancient Mesoamerica. Among other things, it was formulated to make weapons of war. Its fine, sharp edges were attached to a piece of wood to create a heavy club or cutting instrument. During the Spanish conquest, such an obsidian device reportedly was used to literally cut off the head of a horse. (Photo courtesy of Merrill C. Oaks)

WEAPONS (CIMETERS AND THICK CLOTHING)

We read a lot about weapons in the Book of Mormon, including the sword, the axe, the spear, and the cimeter. Moroni's army also used thick clothing to protect themselves from the weapons of the Lamanites.

In Mesoamerica, a person is exposed to a variety of stones used for weapons. In the museum at Chichen Itza, visitors can see the thick-clothing concept illustrated. The thick clothing that the Maya used consisted of small patches of cloth sown together with pockets of sand inside, thus making a type of arrow-proof jackets.

Although all scholars do not agree, some have suggested that the heavy club with obsidian insets used by pre-Spanish Guatemalan warriors, called *maccuahuitl*, was the cimeter referred to in the Book of Mormon. The maccuahuitl was a formidable weapon, as it is said to have been lethal enough to cut off a horse's head.

CONCLUSION

In conclusion, we have presented only a few of the cultural and external components mentioned in the Book of Mormon. We feel that the closer we get to the culture of the Book of Mormon, the more we understand the Book of Mormon. In many instances, Mesoamerica teaches us more about the Book of Mormon culture than the Book of Mormon teaches us about the Mesoamerican culture. The primary reason, however, for understanding the culture, history, and geography of the Book of Mormon is to help us understand the types and shadows associated with the Book of Mormon. Money, climate, weapons of war, clothing, defensive earthworks, clapping of hands, writing letters, and so forth are all items that carry a dual meaning—one physical and the other spiritual.

CUSTOMS OF THE NEPHITE MAYA AND THE LAMANITE MAYA

Mormon was a Nephite Maya. That is, according to him, about a hundred years after Christ's visit to Mesoamerica, there were no "-ites" among the people (see 4 Nephi 1:17). About a hundred years later, or near the beginning of the Maya Classic Period, "there began to be Lamanites again in the land" (4 Nephi 1:20). Based on (1) the geographic area in which the Nephites and Lamanites lived and (2) the Maya historical record, we can thereafter think of the Nephites and the Lamanites as the Nephite Maya and the Lamanite Maya. Mormon lived at the end of the Nephite Maya Classic Period.

Therefore, if we want to understand the daily-life customs of the Book of Mormon people whom Mormon writes about, we can examine the historical record of the Maya for assistance in doing so. For example, we can consult the Maya historical record for insights about such questions as What foods did the people eat? How did they prepare these foods? How did the people plant their food crops? What specific roles did men and women assume in the planting of crops? and What did the people do between the time of planting and harvesting of crops?

In his 1936 treatise about the Maya, *The Conquest of Yucatan*, Frans Blom uses the Maya historical record to answer these and many other questions about the customs of the Maya—and hence the customs of the Nephites and Lamanites. He invites readers to "see how [a] day passed for a Maya family at the time of the conquest, just as it had passed thousands of years earlier, and just as it passes today, four hundred years later" (p. 116). In other words, according to Blom, "As it was—so it is" (p. 122). This is the invitation we extend to readers of *Exploring the Lands of the Book of Mormon*: Examine the historical record of the Maya to gain significant insights about the customs of Book of Mormon peoples.

Following are a few insights from Blom about some of the daily-life customs of the Maya (for our purposes, the Nephite Maya and the Lamanite Maya):

- "Early each morning, while it is still dark and before the stars have paled, the women rise to their daily task of grinding maize [corn] into a fine dough of which they make the corn cakes called *tortillas*.... The women move their bodies forward and backward in a rhythmic wave to the accompaniment of pressing the stone rolling-pin against the surface of the grinding-stone. Chunk—chunk—chunk—chunk. . . . Hour after hour one hears the monotonous sound" (pp. 117–18).
- "At about dawn the men arise and prepare themselves for their day's work. . . . When dressed, they go to the kitchen hut for their morning meal of corn cakes and some boiled meat, beans or dried meat, or maybe meat flavored with native herbs. . . . [Then] the men depart for the fields, . . . and in their pouches . . . they carry a ball of corn dough, . . . which makes their noon meal" (p. 118).
- "While the men till the soil, the women are busy looking after the children, weaving, making the clay household goods, or doing other household work" (p. 119).
- "Maize was and is as important to the [Maya] of [Mesoamerica] as rice to the Chinese" (p. 118).

CHAPTER 17

A Review of Literature on Book of Mormon Geography

It would not be a bad plan to compare Mr. Stephens' ruined cities with those in the Book of Mormon. Light cleaves to light and facts are supported by facts. The truth injures no one.[1] *(Joseph Smith)*

1. *Times and Seasons,* 3:927.

ᒋᒪ

Since the publication of the Book of Mormon in 1830, many attempts have been made, and continue to be made, to place the Book of Mormon in a geographical setting. Some theories have been presented in dogmatic fashion, and others prescribe a tentative caution. The frustration has even caused many in The Church of Jesus Christ of Latter-day Saints to ignore completely anything that has the appearance of Book of Mormon geography.

Joseph Allen addresses the issue as follows:

My own personal battle has followed the circuit from embracing Book of Mormon external evidences to ignoring any geographical model—followed by an attempt to take a deeper look at geography and the Book of Mormon. I

OPPOSITE: Enthusiasm about the geography of the Book of Mormon began only eleven years after its publication as a result of the drawings of Frederick Catherwood. During the first visit to Mesoamerica by John Lloyd Stephens and Catherwood, they visited well-known archaeological sites of today, including Copan, Quirigua, Tonina, and Palenque. On a subsequent visit, they visited the Yucatan ruins of Uxmal, Kabah, Labna, Chichen Itza, Izamal, and Tulum. This drawing by Catherwood shows the Maya arch from the Classic Maya ruins of Uxmal.

subsequently came to the conclusion that the geography should be studied in conjunction with archaeological evidence, language associations, and cultural and traditional patterns.

My initial study caused me to place a great deal of emphasis in Peru with the Inca and the Chavin peoples—while at the same time holding steadfastly to the concept that the last battles were fought in upstate New York. I was aware of certain legends, traditions, and cultures that existed in Mesoamerica, but I never felt that in my lifetime I would propose or endorse a particular geographical area in regards to the Book of Mormon, much less attempt to identify site names on an existing map with those in the Book of Mormon.

Even after conducting research for my dissertation at the National Museum of Anthropology in Mexico City, I still felt reluctant to express the possibility that Book of Mormon history was limited to Mesoamerica. Under Dr. Wells Jakeman, my studies in drawing a Book of Mormon map and in studying Maya hieroglyphs convinced me of the importance of historical geography. Nevertheless, I was still hesitant to approach the study of the Book of Mormon from a historical, geographical point of view.

I suspect the change in my life has been taking place gradually as I have escorted hundreds of Latter-day Saints on tours from New York to Mexico to Peru. After years of research, study, and travel throughout the Americas, I have come to the conclusion that understanding the possible cultures in which the Book of Mormon emerged has great value. Indeed, I felt that I would even be untrue to my personal convictions if I did not "search out of the best books and learn even by study and by faith." I am convinced that the more we know about the history, culture, and geography of the Book of Mormon, the better we understand the Book of Mormon.

Much of my learning has taken place in the presence of Book of Mormon teachers as they have served as directors on the tours we have conducted. I have gained insights one step at a time from many Latter-day Saints who have traveled with us and who have asked countless questions and proposed a variety of solutions.

I subsequently eliminated Peru as the heartland of the Book of Mormon, as the archaeological evidence there is minimal and the linguistics evidence is nil when compared to Mesoamerica. Nor does the Peruvian archaeological time period correspond substantially with the Book of Mormon. Although Peru was my first love, I came to understand that the ruins of Machu Pichu and other Inca sites are post–Book of Mormon. Peru shows evidence of minor cultures in existence during Book of Mormon time—but certainly not to the extent that the Book of Mormon seems to require and not to the extent of civilizations already discovered and documented in Mesoamerica.

My impression is that most students of Book of Mormon geography look first at the map and second at the culture patterns of a given area. My approach has been just the reverse. I have seriously attempted first to understand the traditional history, the archaeological history, and the linguistic history of an area before attempting to establish a Book of Mormon geographical picture.

Only when I satisfied myself that Mesoamerica—and only Mesoamerica—fits the prescribed cultural, linguistic, archaeological, and traditional patterns required by the Book of Mormon did I then feel comfortable in attempting to propose a geographical picture in relation to the Book of Mormon.

From that time forth, I have always tried to be true to the two- or three-witness criteria. This statement simply means that if we make a Book of Mormon geographical hypothesis, we ought to test that hypothesis against the archaeological, cultural, and traditional history of the area. In the absence of these two or three witnesses, I feel that we stand on rather shaky ground. Furthermore, being true to the Book of Mormon text is imperative. That is, sites in relation to each other, directions in relation to each other, and distances in relation to each other must be scholastically reliable according to the text itself—the Book of Mormon.

> "I have seriously attempted first to understand the traditional history, the archaeological history, and the linguistic history of an area before attempting to establish a Book of Mormon geographical picture."
>
> —Joseph L. Allen

In chapters 18 through 30, we have included key Book of Mormon references, in addition to logic and documentation, that cause us to draw the conclusions that follow. Readers are encouraged to test these geographical hypotheses with the information presented, with additional available information, or with any forthcoming information. Indeed, much of what we say today will perhaps change tomorrow. We need to be cautious about quoting outdated material when more recent research is available. We would be appalled if we sent our students to school where they studied out of a 1940 physics textbook. Yet we continue to quote geographic and cultural statistics about the Book of Mormon from old sources.

Any study of Book of Mormon geography must strictly adhere to criteria that do not alter the Book of Mormon text, the proposed map that is based on internal content in the Book of Mormon, or established scientific dating systems. The locations of lands, oceans, rivers, mountain ranges, and boundaries in relationship to distances and relative positions in the Book of Mormon must match.

HISTORY OF BOOK OF MORMON GEOGRAPHY

We present below a short chronological history of people and events that have impacted thinking associated with Book of Mormon geography. If readers are to understand our conclusions today about geography—based on our personal travels throughout and constant testing of proposed locations in Mesoamerica hundreds of times—we feel they should first be knowledgeable about significant historical aspects of Book of Mormon geography.

1830–47. Eleven years after the Book of Mormon was published, a two-volume book entitled *Incidents of Travel in Central America, Chiapas and Yucatan* was written by John Lloyd Stephens. Accompanied by an artist named Frederick Catherwood, Stephens visited some of the known ancient ruins in Mesoamerica. His book not only caused a great deal of interest among the public at large but also caught the attention of members of the Church of Jesus Christ at Nauvoo. The Church publication, *Times and Seasons,* commented on different occasions about Stephens's work. In fact, in several issues beginning in 1842, entire sections of Stephens's book were published in the *Times and Seasons.*

Until Stephens's book appeared, we can be quite sure that little thought was given by Church members to identifying Mesoamerica as the setting for the Book of Mormon. That was probably the situation because the Church leaders and members were so immersed in other activities: moving from New York to Ohio, moving from Ohio to Missouri, moving from Missouri to Nauvoo, overseeing missionary activities in England where additional copies of the Book of Mormon were being printed, colonizing, defending their lives, and preaching the gospel. Stephens was born in the same year that Joseph Smith was born. As a result of Stephens's explorations and writings, he is now known as the "father of Mesoamerican archaeology." The work of Stephens must have been like a breath of fresh air to members of the Church at Nauvoo. Indeed, Stephens may be one of those people whom the Lord prepared to further His work in the last days. An example of Stephens's writings that were printed in the *Times and Seasons* and that pertain to the ancient ruins of the Copan area is the following:

> As at Copan, it was my business to prepare the different objects for Mr. Catherwood to draw. Many of the stones had to be scrubbed and cleaned; and as it was our object to have the utmost possible accuracy in the drawings, in many places scaffolds were to be erected on which to set up the camera lucida. Pawling relieved me from a great part of this labour. That the reader may know the character of the objects we had to interest us, I proceed to give a description of the building in which we lived, called the palace.
>
> A front view of this building is given in the engraving. It does not, however, purport to be given with the same accuracy as the other drawings, the front being in a more ruined condition. It stands on an artificial elevation of an oblong form, forty feet high, three hundred and ten feet in front and rear, and two hundred and sixty feet on each side. This elevation was formerly faced with stone, which has been thrown down by the growth of trees, and its form is hardly distinguishable.

The work of Stephens must have been like a breath of fresh air to members of the Church at Nauvoo. Indeed, Stephens may be one of those people whom the Lord prepared to further His work in the last days.

Exploring the Lands of the Book of Mormon

FIGURE 17–1: The Maya ruins of Copan, Honduras, date to the Classic Period (post–Book of Mormon). In the year 1839, John Lloyd Stephens purchased the land upon which the ruins are located for a mere $50 and had plans to transport the artifacts to the United States. Today the land and artifacts are owned by the Honduran government. (Photo courtesy of Nathan T. Allen)

The building stands with its face to the east, and measures two hundred and twenty eight feet front by one hundred and eighty feet deep. Its height is not more than twenty-five feet, and all around it had a broad projecting cornice of stone. The front contained fourteen doorways, about nine feet wide each, and the intervening piers are between six and seven feet wide. On the left (in approaching the palace) eight of the piers have fallen down, as has also the corner on the right, and the terrace underneath is cumbered with the ruins. But six piers remain entire, and the rest of the front is open.[2]

Joseph Smith was the editor of the *Times and Seasons,* and John Taylor and Wilford Woodruff, who both later became Presidents of the Church, were assistant editors. As best we can tell, they were responsible for saying the following: "Facts are stubborn things. From an extract from Stephens' 'Incidents of Travel in Central America,' it will be seen that the proof of the Nephites and Lamanites dwelling on this continent, according to the account of the Book of Mormon, is developing itself in a more satisfactory way than even the most sanguine believer in that revelation, could have anticipated. It certainly affords us a gratification that the world of mankind does not enjoy, to give publicity to such important development of the remains and ruins of those mighty people."[3]

Whoever the initial authors of the article in the *Times and Seasons* were, they said, referring to the Nephites, that they lived about the narrow neck of land, which now embraces Central America, and then added the following comments: "We can not but

2. "Truth Will Prevail," *Times and Seasons,* 3, no. 22, September 15, 1842; content taken from John Lloyd Stephens, *Incidents of Travel in Central America, Chiapas and Yucatan,* 2 vols., illustrations by Frederick Catherwood (New York: Dover Publications, 1969; first published in 1841), 309–10.

3. *Times and Seasons,* 3:921–22.

think the Lord has a hand in bringing to pass his strange act, and proving the Book of Mormon true in the eyes of all the people. . . . The world will prove Joseph Smith a true prophet by circumstantial evidence."[4]

4. *Times and Seasons,* 3:922.

The article, under the auspices of Joseph Smith, the editor, then quotes a portion of Stephens's work where he is quoting a sixteenth-century Spanish writer by the name of Fuentes, telling about the Tultecas from whence the Quiche and Cakchiquel natives of Guatemala descended.

Earlier in the same publication, the Church periodical reported that "Mr. Stephens' great developments of antiquities are made bare to the eyes of all people by reading the history of the Nephites in the Book of Mormon. . . . Who could have dreamed that twelve years would have developed such incontrovertible testimony to the Book of Mormon? Surely the Lord worketh and none can hinder."[5]

5. *Times and Seasons,* 3:915.

Probably the most-often-quoted statement from the *Times and Seasons* by those students who feel that the Book of Mormon history took place in Mesoamerica is the following, which is attributed to Joseph Smith: "It will not be a bad plan to compare Mr. Stephens' ruined cities with those in the Book of Mormon. Light cleaves to light and facts are supported by facts. The truth injures no one."[6]

6. *Times and Seasons,* 3: 927

1847–1900. From the time the Saints arrived in the Salt Lake Valley in 1847 until the late 1800s, very little additional information emerged from Mexico and Central America regarding their ancient civilizations. Latter-day Saints who had a desire to know about the geographical setting of the Book of Mormon studied it in earnest and compared its geographical references with a map of the entire geographic area of North and South America.

The thinking that was representative of that era is summarized by Orson Pratt when he outlined the historical setting of the Book of Mormon. His geographical philosophy became a part of the general Latter-day Saint thinking for the next hundred years. He gave several talks on the subject commencing in 1868.

Pratt's basic geographical premise was that all of North America was the land northward and all of South America was the land southward. The Isthmus of Panama was designated as the narrow neck of land. He proposed that Lehi landed near Valparaiso, Chile. Excerpts from a talk he delivered in 1872 follow:

[The Book of Mormon] contains . . . a compilation of sacred books, books delivered by divine inspiration in ancient times to prophets, revelators and inspired men who dwelt upon this continent, both in North and South America. . . . They were brought forth from the land of Jerusalem in the first year of Zedekiah, King of Judah, six hundred years before the birth of our Lord and Savior. By revelation from the Lord they traveled southwest from the city of Jerusalem, and after reaching the Red Sea they continued along its eastern borders and

> "Mr. Stephens' great developments of antiquities are made bare to the eyes of all people by reading the history of the Nephites in the Book of Mormon. . . . Who could have dreamed that twelve years would have developed such incontrovertible testimony to the Book of Mormon?"
>
> —Joseph Smith

afterwards bent their course eastward, arriving at the Indian Ocean. There they were commanded by the Almighty to build a vessel. . . . On board this vessel they embarked, and were guided by the Almighty across the great Indian Ocean. Passing among the islands, how far south of Japan I do not know, they came round our globe, crossing not only the Indian Ocean, but what we term the great Pacific Ocean, landing on the western coast of what is now called South America. As near as we can judge from the description of the country contained in this record *the first landing place was in Chili,* [*sic*] not far from where the city of Valparaiso now stands.

Being so severely persecuted by the Lamanites, the Nephites were commanded of the Lord to depart from their midst, that is to leave the first place of colonization in the country which the Spanish now call Chili [*sic*]. They came northward from their first landing place traveling, according to the record, as near as I can judge, *some two thousand miles.* The Lamanites remained in possession of the country on the South. The Nephites formed a colony not far from the *head waters of the River Amazon.* . . .

Forty-five years before the coming of Christ there was a vast colony came out of South America, and it is said in the Book of Mormon that they went an exceeding great distance, until they came to large bodies of water and to many rivers and fountains, and when we come to read more fully the description of the country it answers to *the great Mississippi Valley.* There they formed a colony. We know that to be the region of country from the fact that these plates were taken from a hill in the interior of the State of New York, being the descendants of those same colonists that settled in the valley of the Mississippi. . . . The valley of the Mississippi does not mean a small valley like these valleys here in the Rocky Mountains, but it means a vast area of territory some fifteen hundred thousand square miles in extent, enough to accommodate several hundred millions of inhabitants, almost a world of itself. There the Nephites became a great and powerful people. In process of time they spread forth on the right and on the left, and *the whole face of the North American continent was covered by cities,* towns and villages and population. . . .

The great and last battle, in which several hundred thousand Nephites perished was on *the Hill Cumorah, the same hill from which the plates were taken by Joseph Smith.* . . . Mormon, one of the prophets of the Nephites, who had the records in his possession, being commanded of the Lord, hid up the records in the Hill Cumorah before the battles commenced. I mean all the records except an abridgement. . . . This abridgment, reserved and not hid up by Mormon, he gave to his son Moroni. . . . Moroni tells us, as a prophet of God, that he was commanded of the Lord to hide up these records in the Hill Cumorah, not in the

"It will not be a bad plan to compare Mr. Stephens' ruined cities with those in the Book of Mormon. Light cleaves to light and facts are supported by facts. The truth injures no one."

–Joseph Smith

7. Orson Pratt, "Nephite America—The Day of God's Power—The Shepherd of Israel," *Journal of Discourses* (London: Latter-day Saints' Book Depot, 1854–86), 14:324–31; emphasis added.

same place where the other records had been hidden by his father Mormon, but in another place.[7]

Primarily as a result of Pratt's philosophy, some footnotes in the 1879 edition of the Book of Mormon included geographical descriptions. Changes in the 1920 edition included the deletion of the geographical statements in the footnotes along with the addition of dates in the footnotes and chapter headings.

FIGURE 17–2: Orson Pratt conceived the idea that Nephite territory embraced all of North and South America. He proposed South America to be the land southward and North America to be the land northward. For Pratt, the Isthmus of Panama was the small neck of land spoken of in the Book of Mormon. He proposed the landing of Lehi in Chile and the destruction of the Jaredites and Nephites in New York. (Pratt's Map, 1876)

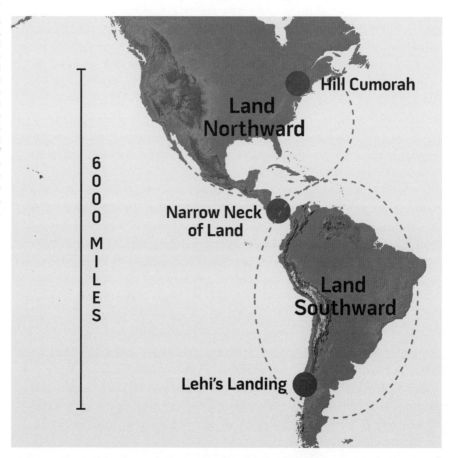

Below we paraphrase the following geographical statements that were written in the footnotes of the 1879 edition of the Book of Mormon:

1. The landing of Lehi was believed to be on the coast of Chile, South America (1 Nephi 2:20).

2. The land of Zarahemla was supposed to have been north of the headwaters of the River Magdalena, its northern boundary being a few days' journey south of the Isthmus of Panama (Omni 1:13).

3. The river Sidon was supposed to be the River Magdalena in Colombia (Alma 2:15).

4. The Caribbean Sea was considered to be the "depths of the sea" where the bones of the Lamanites and the Amlicites ended up after their bodies were thrown into the river Sidon (Alma 3:3).

5. The area south of the land of Desolation was considered to be South America (Alma 46:17).

6. The land on the north was considered to be North America (Alma 46:17).

7. The land northward where the Jaredites were destroyed was considered to be North America (Alma 46:22).

8. The land which was northward was considered to be North America (Alma 50:22).

9. All references in the 1879 edition of the Book of Mormon to the term "land north-ward" were considered to be in North America (Alma 51:30, Alma 52:2, Alma 52:9, Alma 63:4, Helaman 3:8, Helaman 3:9, Helaman 3:10, Helaman 6:6, Helaman 7:1, Mormon 2:20, and so forth).

10. All references in the 1879 edition to the term "land southward" were considered to be South America (Helaman 3:8, Helaman 5:16, Mormon 1:6, Ether 9:31, and so forth).

11. The following statement was made in reference to 3 Nephi 10:9 where the conclusion of the destruction at the death of Christ is recorded: "Making an allowance for the 7 1/2 hours for the difference of longitude between Jerusalem and the Land Bountiful, *south of the Isthmus,* the three days of darkness must have commenced and ended at 7 hours and 30 minutes in the morning, the beginning of darkness being the time in Bountiful when Jesus expired" (emphasis added).

12. The Lord brought Mulek into North America and Lehi into South America (Helaman 6:10).

13. The hill Cumorah named in the Book of Mormon was considered to be in Manchester, Ontario County, New York (Mormon 6:1).

14. The Jaredites were brought to a land that was choice above all other lands. The 1879 footnotes state that "The Lord brought them upon the western coast of North America—and probably south of the Gulf of California" (Ether 1:42, Ether 6:12).

15. When Omer arrived at a place called Ablom, which was by the seashore, the 1879 Book of Mormon footnote states that Ablom was "probably on the shore of the New England States" (Ether 9:3).

16. When prophets foretold a Jaredite destruction wherein "their bones should become as heaps of earth," the footnote in the 1879 edition states that the verse referred to "the ancient mounds of North America" (Ether 11:6).

17. The waters of Ripliancum were considered to be Lake Ontario (Ether 15:8).

"The Book of Mormon shows so many striking similarities to the Mesoamerican setting that it seems to me impossible for rational people willing to examine the data to maintain that the book is a mere romance or speculative history written in the third decade of the nineteenth century in New York State."

—John L. Sorenson, *An Ancient American Setting for the Book of Mormon*, 354

George Reynolds shared the same philosophy as Pratt when Reynolds wrote a book in 1888 called *The Story of the Book of Mormon*. Reynolds became a member of the Quorum of the Seventy in 1890. We point out that in the late 1800s when Pratt and Reynolds wrote their feelings on Book of Mormon geography, the event occurred fifty years prior to legitimate archaeology in Mesoamerica. Further, another fifty years would elapse before the Maya code would be deciphered.

B. H. Roberts, a great champion of the Book of Mormon and a contemporary of George Reynolds, disagreed with both Pratt and Reynolds. Roberts studied the intercontinental movements of the Nephites during the period of time from 600 BC to 46 BC and concluded that the Nephites were confined to a relatively small area. He refers to the 55 BC migration of the Nephites into the "land which was northward" and makes the following statement:

> Here it will be proper to dispel what I regard as a misapprehension of *the extent of Nephite occupancy of the north continent,* at this period of Nephite history. From the fact that in the foregoing quotation it is said that the Nephites removing from Zarahemla traveled "to an exceeding great distance, insomuch that they came to large bodies of water, and many rivers," some have supposed that the Nephites at this time extended their colonization movements as far north as the great lakes in the eastern part of North America; and from the fact that it is also said that "they began to cover the face of the whole earth, from the sea south, to the sea north, from the sea west, to the sea east," it has been supposed that these expressions meant to convey the idea that the Nephites at this time had extended their settlements over both continents; and that "from the sea south to the sea north" meant from the sea at the southern extremity of South America (south of Cape Horn), to the Arctic Ocean, north of North America. *There is no evidence,* however, in the Book of Mormon *that warrants such a conclusion* as to the extent of Nephite occupancy of the western hemisphere in 46 BC. Allowance for hyperbole must be made in the expression, "They began to cover the face of the whole earth," since the facts set forth in the whole history of the Nephites in the Book of Mormon are against the reasonableness of such an

Roberts concluded that the Nephites did not travel the breadth and length of the American continent as his contemporaries believed but rather occupied a very small part of the continent.

FIGURE 17–3:
Archaeologist Bruce W. Warren worked nine seasons with the New World Archaeological Foundation in Chiapas, Mexico, beginning in the late 1950s. He taught at Brigham Young University until his retirement. He is recognized as a world scholar on ancient Mesoamerican pottery.

expression if taken literally. From the landing of Lehi's colony early in the sixth century BC, to the date corresponding to the year 55 BC, when the first considerable migration into the north land took place, Nephite occupancy of the promised land was confined to portions of the west and the extreme north part of what is now the south continent of America; and as compared with the rest of South America, as now known to us, the extent of country occupied was but *a very small part of the continent.* . . .

I conclude, therefore, that this migration of Nephites at this time extended no further northward than southern parts of Mexico, say about the twenty-second degree north latitude; in other words, the Nephites were occupying the old seat of Jaredite empire and civilization, and the land of Moron which the Nephites called "desolate."[8]

8. B. H. Roberts, *New Witnesses for God,* 3 vols. (Salt Lake City: Deseret News, 1909), 199–200; emphasis added.

9. Lord Kingsborough, *Antiquities of Mexico: Comprising Facsimiles of Ancient Mexican Paintings and Hieroglyphics,* 9 vols. (London: Henry G. Bohn, 1848).

Roberts, through his writings, introduced members of the Church of Jesus Christ to the sixteenth-century Spanish chronicles, including some of the writings of Ixtlilxochitl. He derived his information from Lord Kingsborough's *Antiquities of Mexico.*[9]

However, the school of thought as reflected in the writings of Orson Pratt and George Reynolds seemed acceptable to most Church members and became virtually a "Mormon tradition." When we began escorting tours to Mexico and Guatemala beginning in 1970, the general thinking of almost all Latter-day Saints who traveled with us was that Panama was the narrow neck of land.

Though most Church members were convinced that Pratt and Reynolds were correct, a few more theories emerged that proposed contrasting geographical settings for the Book of Mormon. This type of environment prompted George Q. Cannon, a member of the First Presidency of the Church in 1890, to make the following statement:

There is a tendency, strongly manifested at the present time among some of the brethren, to study the geography of the Book of Mormon. We have heard of numerous lectures, illustrated by suggestive maps, being delivered on this subject during the present winter, generally under the auspices of the Improvement Societies and Sunday Schools. . . .

We have been led to these thoughts from the fact that the brethren who lecture on the lands of the Nephites or the geography of the Book of Mormon are not united in their conclusions. . . .

The Book of Mormon is not a geographical primer. It was not written to teach geographical truths. What is told us of the situation of the various lands or cities of the ancient Jaredites, Nephites and Lamanites is usually simply an incidental remark connected with the doctrinal or historical portions of the work. . . .

It must be remembered that geography as a science, like chronology and other branches of education, was not understood nor taught after the manner or by the methods of the moderns. . . .

The First Presidency have often been asked to prepare some suggestive map illustrative of Nephite geography, but have never consented to do so. Nor are we acquainted with any of the Twelve Apostles who would undertake such a task. The reason is, that without further information they are not prepared even to suggest. . . .

We have strong objections to the introduction of maps and their circulation among our people which profess to give the location of the Nephite cities and settlements.[10]

10. George Q. Cannon, "Editorial Thoughts—The Book of Mormon Geography," *The Juvenile Instructor* 25, no. 1 (January 1, 1890): 18–19.

This attitude has developed a tendency among some Latter-day Saints to ignore any study of Book of Mormon history and geography. However, Cannon concluded by supporting the idea of studying geography in relation to the time period of the Book of Mormon as follows: "Of course there can be no harm result from the study of the geography of this continent at the time it was settled by the Nephites, drawing all the information possible from the record which has been translated for our benefit."[11]

11. Cannon, "Editorial Thoughts—The Book of Mormon Geography," 19.

1900–50. Benjamin Cluff was born in 1858. In the year 1901, Cluff, president of Brigham Young Academy, the forerunner of Brigham Young University, requested and received permission from the First Presidency of the Church to form a "Zarahemla Expedition." The expedition's intent was to locate the land of Zarahemla. Cluff felt that a discovery of this nature would be advantageous to the educational institution of the Church. The general feeling of the organizers of the expedition was that the heartland of the Book of Mormon was in Central and South America. When the expedition arrived at the Isthmus of Tehuantepec, they recorded the following: "Geographically we entered Central America and Tehuantepec, and, we think, entered the land of the Book of Mormon at the same place. Many of our brethren . . . think that Hagoth had his ship yards on the gulf of Tehuantepec. . . . One thing is certain. . . . There are remains of many cities . . . that must be very ancient. . . . Over the country we now travel lived many a happy Nephite family."[12]

FIGURE 17–4: Blake Joseph Allen, born in 1960, was first introduced to Mesoamerica at the age of ten when he accompanied his father to the National Museum of Anthropology in Mexico City. He is coauthor of the second edition of *Exploring the Lands of the Book of Mormon*. He has conducted over one hundred tours to Mesoamerica.

12. Benjamin Cluff Jr. to George H. Brimhall, February 24, 1901, Cluff Presidential Papers, quoted in Ernest L. Wilkinson and W. Cleon Skousen, *Brigham Young University: A School of Destiny* (Provo, UT: Brigham Young University Press, 1976), 158.

A man by the name of Paul Henning accompanied Cluff on the expedition. Henning was a well-educated German scientist who also spoke Spanish. (He remained in Guatemala after the two-year expedition came to an end and wrote many articles and conducted a great deal of research about Mesoamerica.)

The Cluff expedition initially headed for Colombia, as they felt that the Magdalena River was the best candidate for the river Sidon. The expedition never reached Colombia because of a revolution in the country. However, regarding the accomplishments of the 1901 expedition, Cluff noted that the expedition accomplished the following:

1. Opened to members of the Church a knowledge of the countries where the ancient Nephites and Lamanites lived.

2. Probably furnished some evidence to support the theory of Anthony W. Ivins and other Book of Mormon authorities that the narrow neck of land spoken of in the Book of Mormon is the Isthmus of Tehuantepec.

3. Promoted an increased interest in the ruins of Central and South America and to stimulate scholars to do all they can to date the construction of those ruins.[13]

13. Wilkinson and Skousen, *Brigham Young University: A School of Destiny*, 161.

Despite the expedition's findings, most members of the Church remained firm in their belief that the history of the Book of Mormon covered a large amount of ground from South America to North America.

In 1916, Joel Ricks authored some works with maps called "Helps to the Study of the Book of Mormon." His work represented one of the first attempts at placing Book of Mormon cities on a map.

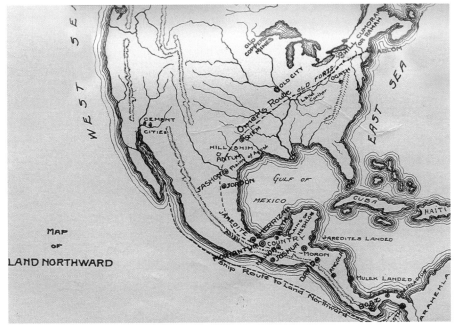

FIGURE 17–5: Joel Ricks proposed the country of Colombia as the land of Zarahemla, Panama as the land of Desolation, and Texas as the location for the hill Shim. His map was also published in 1940. (Ricks, 1916)

In 1919, Lewis E. Hills, a member of the Reorganized Church of Jesus Christ of Latter Day Saints (now the Community of Christ), proposed maps with a Mesoamerican setting. He labeled Veracruz, Mexico, as the place where both the Jaredites and the Mulekites landed; and he labeled El Salvador as the landing site of the Nephites.

During the 1930s and 1940s, serious excavation work was accomplished among the ancient sites in Mesoamerica. The Pyramid of the Sun at Teotihuacan had already been restored in time for the 1910 Mexican celebration of Mexico's one hundredth anniversary of its independence. In the 1930s, Chichen Itza, under the direction of Sylvanus Morley, and Monte Alban, supervised by Alfonso Caso, were studied; and great restoration programs were in effect.

These restoration projects caused schisms among Church members—a majority were in agreement with Pratt and Reynolds versus those who were not. Furthermore, members who did not agree with the traditional theory proposed by Pratt and Reynolds did not necessarily agree with each other. Rumors circulated in those days that the only consistent statements about Book of Mormon geography were that (1) no consensus of agreement existed and (2) the history of the Nephites took place where the person who wrote on the subject served his mission. The divisions of thought are summarized below.

Traditional statement. The history of the Book of Mormon took place in both North America and South America. South America was the land southward, and North America was the land northward. The narrow neck of land was the Isthmus of Panama, and the last battles recorded in the Book of Mormon were fought in upstate New York at the Hill Cumorah.

Doctrinal approach. The geographical information in the Book of Mormon is extremely limited; therefore, attempts to correlate any geographical setting with an existing map are futile. Furthermore, because the doctrine is that which is important, studying geography of the Book of Mormon should be avoided.

Limited geographical theory. The relative distances in the Book of Mormon were much shorter than traditionally assumed and could be figured out by a reader's looking only at the Book of Mormon record without reference to any existing map.

One writer, J. Niles Washburn, developed just such a map and religiously refrained from correlating it with an existing map.[14] The experience of analyzing his map taken totally from the Book of Mormon is an interesting one. We escorted Washburn on a tour to Mexico when he was eighty years old. We were delighted with his enthusiasm and his knowledge of the internal structure of the Book of Mormon.

Washburn's internal geographical approach seemed to be acceptable in authorized Church literature, as evidenced by an article that appeared in 1938 in the Church's publication, *The Improvement Era*. Lynn C. Layton is the author of the article, and he included a rather limited drawing of Book of Mormon lands. The editorial comment to Layton's article states: "Many individual members of the Church, in private capacity,

14. J. Niles Washburn, *Book of Mormon Lands and Times* (Bountiful, UT: Horizon Publishers, 1974), 81.

Exploring the Lands of the Book of Mormon

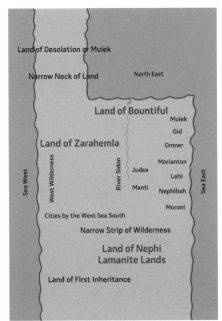

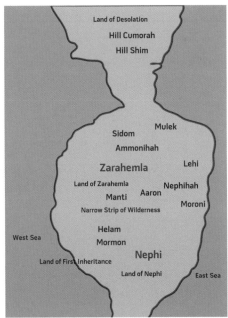

FIGURE 17–6: Lynn Layton's Book of Mormon internal geography map. No attempt was made to place any cities or landmarks in the land northward. The hill Cumorah is left off the map. (Layton, 1938)

FIGURE 17–7: J. Niles Washburn's Book of Mormon geography map made no attempt to place it on an existing map. This drawing is an adaptation of that map. (Washburn, 1939)

have expressed their views and their theories concerning Book of Mormon geography. Here is another view—representing merely the personal beliefs of one student of the subject and not necessarily representing the views of the Church or its members generally. But this presentation is unique in that it does not attempt to place the scene of action on the present-day map, but merely indicated the relative positions of one place with respect to another, as inferred from a study of the text itself."[15]

Over the last seventy years, some readers have continued to promote an internal, nongeneric map of the Book of Mormon with no attempt to place Book of Mormon locations on an existing map. Although this approach may sound noble, it does nothing to solve Book of Mormon geographical issues. By putting Book of Mormon geography on a blank sheet of paper, analysts end up without any rivers to follow or mountains to climb. In essence, they lose the valuable lay of the land to help them understand the geography of the Book of Mormon.

In 1946, another important event took place that set a significant tone for the study of the history and geography of the Book of Mormon. Elder John A. Widtsoe, a member of the Quorum of the Twelve Apostles of the Church, organized the Department of Archaeology at Brigham Young University. Dr. Wells Jakeman, then a recent recipient of a PhD in ancient history from the University of California, Berkeley, was appointed

15. See Lynn C. Layton, "An 'Ideal' Book of Mormon Geography," *The Improvement Era* 41 (July 1938), 394–95, 439.

Land of Desolation
Mexico Valley
Teotihuacan
Hill Ramah-Cumorah ??

Lowland Maya

Land of Bountiful
Palenque

Narrow Neck of Land

Tikal

River Sidon
Usumacinta

Land of Zarahemla

NORTH
50 mi
100 km

Izapa

Highland Maya

FIGURE 17-8 M. Wells Jakeman Map 1965

FIGURE 17–8: Wells Jakeman's Book of Mormon geographical map. This theory became known as the Limited Tehuantepec Theory. Jakeman was a strong proponent of the theory that the history of the Book of Mormon took place in Mesoamerica.

as the chairman of the newly formed Archaeology Department. Jakeman, considered by many to be the "father of Book of Mormon historical geography," pursued the limited geographical approach and further proposed that the history of the Book of Mormon took place in the area called Mesoamerica. This proposal became known as the "Limited Tehuantepec Theory."

However, before he became chairman of the BYU Archaeology Department and during his years at Berkeley, Jakeman became acquainted with Thomas Stuart Ferguson, a Latter-day Saint law student at the same university. Together, they founded the Itzan Society, an organization that focused on the study of archaeology and the Book of Mormon. The Itzan Society endured from 1938 to 1944.

Thomas Ferguson made twenty-five trips to Mexico beginning in 1946 and ending in 1983. Like Jakeman, Ferguson favored the Mesoamerica or "Limited Tehuantepec Theory"—which maintains that virtually all the New World history recorded in the Book of Mormon occurred in Mexico and Central America. Ferguson wrote a seventy-eight-page booklet, *Cumorah—Where?* in 1947.

1950–2000. Jakeman continued as chairman of the Brigham Young University Archaeology Department until 1960. He was responsible for the identification and analysis of the Tree of Life Stone, as discussed in chapter 9, "The Izapa (Jaredite-Nephite-Lamanite) Culture," and chapter 15, "Christ—The Tree of Life." The enthusiasm about the Tree of Life Stone that was generated in the early 1950s was fueled by the excavation of a tomb in Palenque. A tree-of-life motif was sculptured on the lid of the tomb uncovered at the ruins of Palenque in the state of Chiapas, Mexico, by Alberto Ruz in 1952. An organization called the Society for Early Historic Archaeology was formed at Brigham Young University, with Wells Jakeman as chairman.

Thomas Ferguson continued to be a driving force in Mesoamerican archaeology and the Book of Mormon. In 1950, he and Milton R. Hunter, a member of the Quorum of the Seventy, wrote a book, *Ancient America and the Book of Mormon,* in which they made a serious attempt to correlate the writings of the Spanish chronicles with the cultures of the Book of Mormon—including the first time that portions of the writings of Ixtlilxochitl had been recorded in English. In 1958, Ferguson wrote *One Fold and One Shepherd.*

Ferguson's untiring efforts in Book of Mormon and Mesoamerican research led to the establishment of the New World Archaeological Foundation (NWAF) in 1952, which received financial support from the Church beginning in 1955. From 1961 to the time of the publication of this second edition of *Exploring the Lands of the Book of Mormon,* the organization became known as BYU-NWAF. In 1988, the headquarters were moved from Chiapas, Mexico, to the campus of Brigham Young University, leaving only a field office in San Cristobal de las Casas, Chiapas. Following the death of Ferguson in 1983, a tribute was made in his honor at meetings of the Society for Early Historic Archaeology held at Brigham Young University. In summarizing his comments during this tribute, Fred W. Nelson Jr. said, "Thomas Ferguson has either directly or indirectly influenced thousands of people's thinking on archaeology. . . . Many of us are the benefactors of his foresight and vision, his incredible drive and energy, and his ability to see a need and to organize a solution and see it through to fruition. . . . [His] legacy as being instrumental in the founding of the Archaeology Department at Brigham Young University . . . and as founder of the New World Archaeological Foundation stands as a shining example to us all."[16]

Archaeologist Gareth Lowe served as the field director of NWAF during most of the years from 1960–88. Howard W. Hunter, a member of the Quorum of the Twelve Apostles, served as chairman of the

> By putting Book of Mormon geography on a blank sheet of paper, analysts end up without any rivers to follow or mountains to climb. In essence, they lose the valuable lay of the land to help them understand the geography of the Book of Mormon.

FIGURE 17–9: Thomas Stuart Ferguson (1915–1983) and his wife, Ester.

16. Fred W. Nelson Jr., "Thomas Stuart Ferguson 1915–1983," Paper presented at the thirty-second annual symposium of the Society for Early Historic Archaeology, October 22, 1983, 16–17.

organization during that same period. Thomas Ferguson served as secretary until his death in 1983. Archaeologists Bruce Warren, Garth Norman, Tom Lee, and Pierre Agrinier, along with scores of students and workers, made the NWAF the leader in Mesoamerican archaeology during these many years. Emphasis was placed on archaeological research without inference to the Book of Mormon.[17] At the time of the writing of the second edition of *Exploring the Lands of the Book of Mormon,* John E. Clark continues as the director of the NWAF.

17. For a more detailed analysis of the NWAF, see Warren and Ferguson, *The Messiah in Ancient America,* 247–84.

From 1950 to 2000, the most prominent schools of thought regarding Book of Mormon geography were as follows:

1. Mesoamerica: More than 85 percent of the literature that surfaced from 1950 to 2000 endorsed Mesoamerica as the land of the Book of Mormon.

2. Peru and New York: A limited number of writings aggressively pursued either Peru or New York as the place where the Book of Mormon history occurred.

3. Nongeography: As the twentieth century came to a close, many teachers and members of the Church retained either a noncommittal attitude about or a negative commitment toward Book of Mormon historical geography.

As a result of the vast amount of information that came out of Mesoamerica during the last twenty-five years of the twentieth century, most Book of Mormon scholars now emphatically state that virtually all legitimate information leads to a Mesoamerican setting for the Book of Mormon, including the location for the final demise of both the Jaredite and the Nephite nations.

Attorney Jack West and author Dewey Farnsworth demonstrated early interest in Book of Mormon historical evidence. West took several trips to various parts of South and Central America, including Peru and the Yucatan. He circulated a series of slides that became known as the Jack West slides. Farnsworth published *Book of Mormon Evidences in Ancient America* in 1953.

Elder Milton R. Hunter of the Quorum of the Seventy, who was a staunch advocate of history, became intensely interested in archaeology and the Book of Mormon. He wrote the book *Christ in Ancient America,* which was published in 1959.

Dr. Paul Cheesman, professor of Religion at Brigham Young University, wrote several books, including (1) *Early America and the Book of Mormon—A Photographic Essay of Ancient America,* 1972; (2) *World of the Book of Mormon,* 1978, 1984; (3) *Book of Mormon Lands—A Photographic Essay,* 1978; and (4) *Pathways to the Past—A Guide to the Ruins of Mesoamerica,* 1984.

Cheesman, a distinguished gentleman, refrained from labeling any geographical land mass with the Book of Mormon. His efforts were concentrated in researching external evidences of the Book of Mormon, such as stone boxes and gold plates.

Dr. Sidney Sperry and Dr. Hugh Nibley were prolific writers during this era, but their works were not centered on Mesoamerica. Sperry, however, wrote the following about the so-called Two-Cumorah Theory:

As a result of the vast amount of information that came out of Mesoamerica during the last twenty-five years of the twentieth century, most Book of Mormon scholars now emphatically state that virtually all legitimate information leads to a Mesoamerican setting for the Book of Mormon.

Exploring the Lands of the Book of Mormon

It may be well to observe that when King Limhi's men found a land covered with bones of men and beasts, ruins of buildings and remains of weapons of war, they had happened upon the last battlefields and ruined remains of Jaredite civilization. That this is the case is made more certain by the fact that they found the twenty-four plates of Ether which were expressly hidden by that Jaredite prophet in such a way that the men of Limhi found them. Now, if the last battlefield of the Jaredites was around the Hill Ramah-Cumorah in New York—it would be necessary to assume that Limhi's men traveled about six thousand miles altogether in their attempts to find the land of Zarahemla, a distance completely unreasonable to assume when we consider that the elder Alma brought his group of Zeniff's people to the land of Zarahemla in twelve days. And if Alma's group had taken twenty days, to make up for any difference in position as compared with Limhi's people, they would only have traveled about four hundred miles (at the rate of twenty miles per day) to come to Zarahemla. *In view of these facts, isn't it reasonable to assume that the Hill Cumorah (Ramah to the Jaredites), around which the last great battles of the Nephites and Jaredites took place, was in Middle America,* somewhere in the conservative range of 400 to 500 miles from Zarahemla?[18]

18. Sidney B. Sperry, *Book of Mormon Compendium* (Salt Lake City: Bookcraft, 1968), 198–99.

During the 1980s, a surge of literature surfaced that served to break up the old schools of thought. Today, although some writers still ignore any discussion about Book of Mormon geography or continue to believe North and South America to be the geographic location of Book of Mormon history, most writers highly favor a Book of Mormon setting in Mesoamerica. This development has come about as a result of intensive studies in both Mesoamerica and the Book of Mormon. The knowledge that has come forth and that continues to come forth is indeed quite marvelous. Consider, if you will, some of the reasons why our knowledge has dramatically increased:

1. The ease with which the common person can travel and view the sites firsthand and the ease with which we can test the geographical landmarks and distances within the Book of Mormon are exciting developments.

2. The comprehensive and continued excavation and archaeological work that is taking place is impressive. The El Mirador site in northern Guatemala,[19] where archaeological work was initiated by Ray Matheny, archaeologist at Brigham Young University, and which is now continued under the auspices of the Guatemalan government, along with other sites in Guatemala, continues to receive considerable attention. In 1989, Vanderbilt University began excavation work at two new sites south of Tikal, Guatemala, and investigative work continues throughout Mesoamerica that reveals activity during the Preclassic Period, such as Cerros and Corozal located in Belize and

19. See Ray T. Matheny, "An Early Maya Metropolis Uncovered, El Mirador," *National Geographic,* 172, no. 3 (September 1987): 316–39.

San Bartolo located in the Peten of Guatemala. The same is true with respect to other parts of Mesoamerica.

3. The dating methods of the sites have become refined and verified by many different scholars. The reliability of the radiocarbon dating procedure lends great credibility to the time period of the ancient ruins and artifacts.

4. The deciphering of the Maya hieroglyphs represents a major breakthrough in our understanding of Mesoamerica and the Book of Mormon.

5. A deeper understanding of the literature and of the political structure of the Book of Mormon in relationship with Hebrew and Mesoamerican patterns sheds new light on the Book of Mormon.

Literature that came forth in the 1980s includes the following:

David Palmer, *In Search of Cumorah*
John Sorenson, *An Ancient American Setting for the Book of Mormon*
Bruce Warren and Thomas Ferguson, *TheMessiah in Ancient America*
Richard Hauck, *Deciphering the Geography of the Book of Mormon*
Joseph L. Allen, *Exploring the Lands of the Book of Mormon*

Dr. John Sorenson, who literally opened the door for further research, presented the Book of Mormon in relation to Mesoamerican archaeological sites. His detailed analysis culminated a lifetime of work as an anthropologist and a Mesoamerican scholar. His work set the stage for additional study on the subject. Sorenson served as chairman of the Department of Anthropology at Brigham Young University from 1978 until 1986. He retired in 1986 but continues to work with the Foundation for Ancient Research and Mormon Studies (FARMS).

Figure 17–10 is a general map by Sorenson. Notice that he, along with Palmer, rotates the Mesoamerica map sixty-five degrees to a position he calls "Nephite north." In this map, Lehi landed near El Salvador. Kaminaljuyu (Guatemala City) is the city/land of Nephi. The Chiapas depression (state of Chiapas, Mexico) is the land of Zarahemla. The River Grijalva is labeled the river Sidon, whereas Jakeman preferred the Usumacinta River. Sorenson, like Palmer, labels the Hill Vigia in Veracruz, Mexico, as a possible candidate for the hill Cumorah. Sorenson's rotated-compass concept became shrouded in controversy, and today the majority of Book of Mormon academic scholars who deal with geography reject the rotated-compass theory as a viable alternative for understanding the geography of the Book of Mormon. Sorenson designed his hourglass-shaped map strictly from an internal perspective and then forced it to fit in the physical setting of Mesoamerica. This tilted, internal map is still used as a model in some literature today.

The Foundation for Ancient Research and Mormon Studies (FARMS) was organized in 1979 by John W. Welch with the objective of serving as a catalyst for Book of

"I have now come to a point where what I know seems worth sharing with others. Specifically, I have developed a picture or model of how Book of Mormon events took place. This model is *plausible*. That means that the setting described could reasonably have been as I represent it."

—John L. Sorenson, *An Ancient American Setting for the Book of Mormon*, xix–xx

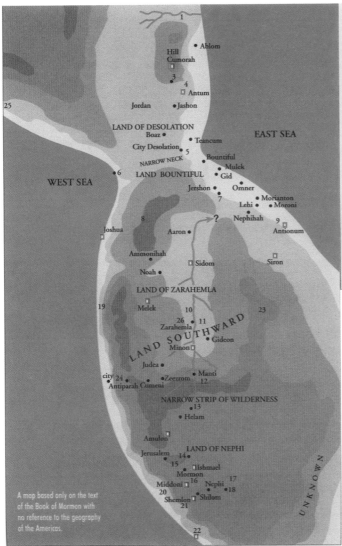

Key to Numbers
1. Waters of Ripliancum
2. Limit of Nephite retreat
3. Shiz's death; plates left
4. Hill Shim
5. Narrow passage
6. Hagoth's ships
7. Moroni's camp
8. Refuge between the land of Bountiful and the land of Zarahemla (see 3 Nephi 3)
9. Hill Onidah
10. Hill Manti
11. Hill Amnihu
12. Hill Riplah
13. Valley of Alma
14. Missionary dispersal point
15. Waters of Mormon
16. Hill north of Shilom
17. Mount Antipas
18. Place Onidah
19. Wilderness west of the land of Zarahemla
20. Wilderness west of the land of Nephi
21. Lamanite king's land
22. Land of first inheritance
23. Wilderness (see Alma 43:22)
24. Mountain pass
25. Hagoth's destination (?)
26. Wilderness of Hermounts

▫ Land: no city mentioned
River tributaries illustrative only

FIGURE 17–10: Sorenson's map of Mesoamerica and the Book of Mormon.[20] Sorenson pursued the hourglass concept and then superimposed it on a Mesoamerican map, thereby proposing a shift in Nephite directions from the standard cardinal directions, rotating the map and calling the result by the name of "Nephite north." This theory has received an abundant amount of negative criticism, as there is no evidence from either the Book of Mormon or Maya culture that hints at a directional shift. (Sorenson, 1985)

20. John L. Sorenson, *An Ancient American Setting for the Book of Mormon* (Salt Lake City: Deseret Book and Foundation for Ancient Research and Mormon Studies, 1985), 37.

Mormon research. FARMS has now become part of Brigham Young University. As of 2008, Kent Brown was serving as its director.

Our approach, which will be followed in *Exploring the Lands of the Book of Mormon*, has the objective of analyzing each geographical statement in the Book of Mormon in relation to the geographical and historical structure of Mesoamerica. In that sense, *Exploring the Lands of the Book of Mormon* becomes a test tube for evaluating the information available to us in both the Book of Mormon and in Mesoamerica.

The evaluation is really not as difficult as it appears on the surface. For example, the distance requirement between the city/land of Nephi and the city/land of Zarahemla

Exploring the Lands of the Book of Mormon becomes a test tube for evaluating the information available to us in both the Book of Mormon and in Mesoamerica.

is less than thirty days. This distance represents about two hundred to three hundred miles at the rate of eight to ten miles per day, which is the calculated distance that a Maya or a Guatemalan native can travel today with sixty pounds on his back. A large part of the Book of Mormon history occurred between the land of Nephi and the land of Zarahemla, so regardless of where the geography of the Book of Mormon is placed, the book's events can occupy only the distances as outlined in the Book of Mormon.

We have attempted to locate Book of Mormon lands, waters, mountains, and boundaries with the natural boundaries and geological structures that exist today in Mesoamerica. Although a great and terrible destruction indeed occurred at the time of Christ, that event did not alter significantly the geologic structure, geographical landmarks, or traditional travel routes of Mesoamerica.

Book of Mormon readers should recognize the importance of realizing that the language and cultural patterns existent today in Mesoamerica help a great deal in our understanding of the Book of Mormon.

You will observe that our geographical analysis of the Book of Mormon does not rotate the compass directions as some writers in the last century proposed.

Nevertheless, now may be the right time for Book of Mormon readers to begin looking for areas of agreement by Book of Mormon historical-geographers as opposed to areas of disagreement. For example, many dedicated Church members and qualified scholars of Book of Mormon history and geography agree on the following:

Areas of Agreement

1. General Book of Mormon lands	Mesoamerica
2. Land northward	Area northwest of Tehuantepec
3. Land southward	Area southeast of Tehuantepec
4. East sea	Atlantic Ocean (Caribbean)
5. West sea	Pacific Ocean (Gulf of Tehuantepec)
6. Lehi's landing	Tapachula (Izapa) Mexico
7. Land of Nephi	Guatemala highlands
8. Land of Zarahemla	Chiapas, Peten, Belize
9. Waters of Mormon	Lake Atitlan
10. Narrow strip of wilderness	Cuchumatanes mountain range
11. Narrow neck of land	Isthmus of Tehuantepec
12. Hill Ramah/Cumorah	Hill Vigia, Veracruz, Mexico

The Book of Mormon provides adequate detailed information to draw some geographical conclusions. Indeed, Mormon seemed to write as if we would have a map in front of us as we read his abridgement in the Book of Mormon.

We learn a great deal about the city locations in relation to each other because of the wars, missionary journeys, and miscellaneous travels of people in the Book of Mormon.

Place where the sea divides the land

Hill Cumorah
Hill Shim
Waters of Ripliancum
Land among many waters
The Narrow Neck of Land
Sea East
Sidon River
NORTH
50 mi
100 km
Sea West
The Narrow Strip of Wilderness
Waters of Mormon
FIGURE 17–11
Natural Landmarks

FIGURE 17–11: Most Latter-day Saint students of Book of Mormon geography agree that most of the history recorded in the Book of Mormon took place in Mesoamerica. Significant natural landmarks such as a narrow strip of wilderness, a narrow neck of land, the hills Shim and Ramah\Cumorah, along with identifiable bodies of water, account for much of the agreement.

For example, from the missionary journeys of the sons of Mosiah, we learn about the Lamanite cities of Middoni, Ani-Anti, Ishmael, Jerusalem, and Midian.

From Alma's missionary journeys in the land of Zarahemla, we learn about such Nephite cities as Gideon, Melek, Aaron, Ammonihah, and Sidom.

From the Nephite-Lamanite wars, during the military leader Moroni's time, we learn about the eastern cities of Moroni, Lehi, Nephihah, Aaron, Gid, Omner, Mulek, Bountiful, Morianton, and Moronihah. These cities, plus many other walled cities, were built by the Nephites and were probably located in what is now the Peten jungle area of Guatemala, along the coast in the country of Belize, and some perhaps extending into the Yucatan Peninsula.

We learn about Judea, Zeezrom, Antiparah, and Cumeni from the sons of Helaman and their war campaign.

The cities of Zarahemla and Manti, both near the river Sidon, are mentioned many times.

> The language and cultural patterns existent today in Mesoamerica help a great deal in our understanding of the Book of Mormon.

The Lamanite cities and lands in the land of Nephi are given to us by Nephi, the first Book of Mormon prophet; by Alma, who baptized in the waters of Mormon; and by the sons of Mosiah, who spent fourteen years among the Lamanites in the land of Nephi. These cities and lands include Nephi, Helam, Midian, Shimnilom, Shilom, Amulon, Lemuel, Middoni, Jerusalem, Shemlon, Ishmael, and the village of Ani-Anti.

The following cities are mentioned as having been destroyed or damaged by the great destruction at the time of Christ: Josh, Onihah, Mocum, Gad, Kishkumen, Gadiomnah, Gimgimno, Gilgal, Gadiandi, Laman, Jerusalem, Zarahemla, Moroni, Moronihah, Jacob, and Jacobugath.

We can tell a lot about where the cities were located by the language names they carry. The last two cities mentioned above, Jacob and Jacobugath, were probably

FIGURE 17–12: As of the year 2008, the publication year of the second edition of *Exploring the Lands of the Book of Mormon*, a few proponents of the Great Lakes and the Peruvian theories for Book of Mormon geography can still be found. For the most part, however, among Latter-day Saint scholars, the Mesoamerica model has considerably more credibility than either New York or Peru. The lack of acceptable credibility for New York or Peru especially results from the absence of (1) a written language associated with a high civilization, (2) logical and legitimate geographical configurations that match the geographical statements in the Book of Mormon, (3) radiocarbon-based dates and historical data that coincide with Book of Mormon dates and information, and (4) name correlations with the names of people and places in the Book of Mormon.

located in the "land which was northward"—perhaps in the area of the valley of Mexico City. The wicked Jacob fled into the land northward.

Jaredite names continued throughout the generations. Nevertheless, the book of Ether records those landmarks that were used in the land northward during Jaredite times. These include such names as Nehor, Moron, Heth, Ablom, Corihor, hill Shim, hill Ramah, plains of Heshlon, plains of Agosh, valley of Shurr, and the valley of Gilgal. We are also told that many mighty cities were built and that a great city, probably Lib, was built by the narrow neck of land by the place where the sea divides the land (see Ether 10:20).

We learn the names of some Nephite-occupied cities after the AD 350 treaty with the Lamanites. These cities were located in the land northward near the narrow neck of land. Perhaps a couple of these cities extended south, near to the Gulf of Tehuantepec. Most, however, were probably on the Gulf of Mexico side in the present-day states of Veracruz and Tabasco. These include the cities of Desolation, Boaz, Teancum, Shem, Jashon, Joshua, Angola, and David, all of which were probably in the land Desolation (land northward).

Three things that have helped to solidify geography studies during the last thirty years are the following:

1. A great amount of scholarly evidence has been produced out of Mesoamerica.

2. Most Book of Mormon students who have studied the archaeological and geographical structure of the Americas agree that Mesoamerica is the location of the lands of the Book of Mormon.

3. When we identify potential lands/cities of the Book of Mormon by working with the internal map of the book and then by matching the clues given by its writers to the geography and topography of Mesoamerica, we discover that Mesoamerica indeed "fits" the "map" that Mormon gives us in the Book of Mormon.

However, even Book of Mormon/Mesoamerican scholars continue to have differing opinions about the internal geography of the Book of Mormon. These differing views are healthy, as the process provides us the opportunity to test the theories against each other and allows for more intense research. Many of the answers will come through the study of languages. By prayerful study and research, we may still identify additional Mesoamerican culture records that relate to the Book of Mormon. On the other hand, as pointed out above, a great deal of similarity or agreement is found among writers who write about the geography of the Book of Mormon in connection with key places such as the narrow neck of land, the landing site of Lehi, the land of Nephi, the narrow strip of wilderness, and the location and history of the ancient Jaredites.

REVIEW SUMMARY

The evolution of Book of Mormon mapmaking has followed an interesting course since the Book of Mormon was published in 1830. Within twelve years after the publication of Stephens's book, *Incidents of Travel in Central America, Chiapas and Yucatan,*

A great deal of similarity or agreement is found among writers who write about the geography of the Book of Mormon in connection with key places such as the narrow neck of land, the landing site of Lehi, the land of Nephi, the narrow strip of wilderness, and the location and history of the ancient Jaredites.

the reports of Stephens and Catherwood caused some early members of the Church of Jesus Christ to proclaim Mesoamerica as the location of the "lands of the Book of Mormon." However, that proclamation did not seem to preclude—in the minds of many Church members—that all lands of North and South America were also the "lands of the Book of Mormon." No doubt seemed to exist in the minds of nineteenth-century Latter-day Saints that the last battles recorded in the Book of Mormon were fought in any place other than New York state. The map of the American continent seemed ideal for a land northward (North America), a land southward (South America), and a narrow neck of land (Isthmus of Panama).

As the Church moved into the twentieth century, some intense readers of the Book of Mormon began to feel that the apparent distances were far too great for the Book of Mormon people to roam freely from Chile to New York. The proposal that took root in the 1940s, suggesting that Book of Mormon internal statements required the hill Ramah/Cumorah to be near the narrow neck of land, was shrouded in controversy.

A substitute approach ensued in which geography maps of the Book of Mormon were devoid of any suggestive locations. These were called "internal geography maps."

Since the 1980s, and with additional knowledge coming out of Mesoamerica and with some students devoting their lives to the study of cultural patterns of both Mesoamerica and the Book of Mormon, a new surge of Book of Mormon maps has appeared. For the most part, these maps are centered in Mesoamerica, with differences being within their geographical boundaries.

Some of the best information and some of the worst on the subject of Book of Mormon history and geography have surfaced during the 1990s and the first part of the twenty-first century. One outstanding endeavor, which is made possible in our modern era, has come forth as a result of the efforts of Dr. Alan Miner. He has an ongoing project wherein he has researched and recorded comments that have been made about Book of Mormon history and geography since the coming forth of the Book of Mormon. Two major trends may be deduced from this research: (1) until the Latter-day Saint population becomes more educated on the ancient history of Mesoamerica and the criteria for legitimate scientific study, shoddy and folklore-type material will continue to come forth, and (2) the position of the Church Educational System under the direction of the Church leadership continues to remain neutral on the subject. Church leaders have not made any definitive statements regarding the geography of the Book of Mormon, and in many instances, traditional statements remain the norm.

Another thing that is driving Book of Mormon geography in this new millennium is travel and tourism. The moment we put the name "Book of Mormon" on a tour, the implication is that we are taking people to places where the Book of Mormon history took place—and that is indeed the intent. The problem is the lack of any scholarly control over whatever may be said. A case in point is that at least six different sites are currently being espoused in tour itineraries as the city of Bountiful where the Savior

Until the Latter-day Saint population becomes more educated on the ancient history of Mesoamerica and the criteria for legitimate scientific study, shoddy and folklore-type material will continue to come forth.

Exploring the Lands of the Book of Mormon

appeared to the Nephites. In each case, a testimony meeting may be held, hymns may be sung, and the feeling of "I walked today where Jesus walked" is strong.

QUESTION

One question is always asked on our tours: What do the Brethren say about Book of Mormon geography? The short answer is "Not much." However, a sampling of what some of the Brethren have said is as follows:

Elder John A. Widtsoe expressed the feeling of future study when he said, "Out of diligent, prayerful study, we may be led to a better understanding of times and places in the history of the people who move across the pages of the divinely given Book of Mormon."[21]

While speaking to the faculty of Brigham Young University, President Spencer W. Kimball said: "The Lamanite-Nephite culture means much to the people of the Church, and properly so. Here at B.Y.U., should we not have the greatest collection of artifacts, records, writings, concerning them in the world? Through revelation we have received much knowledge concerning these peoples. Should not B.Y.U. then be pre-eminent in the field of culture?"[22]

In a personal letter to Joseph Allen regarding the first edition of *Exploring the Lands of the Book of Mormon*, President Howard W. Hunter wrote the following on July 6, 1989:

Dear Brother Allen,

Thank you for sending me a copy of Chapter 11 of the manuscript of your book, *Exploring the Lands of the Book of Mormon*. [This chapter became chapter 9, "The Izapa Culture," in the published version.]

I have found it to be most interesting. The approach you have used and the comparison of your research with the Book of Mormon has never been attempted to my knowledge by anyone else, although the sources have often been used for comparison.

I have spent several evenings on the subject matter of Chapter 11. This information that you have compiled will add greatly to the literature concerning the Book of Mormon.

I have thanked Dale Tingey for bringing this excerpt to me and I have told him of the great use that will be made of this monumental endeavor. I thank you for your thoughtfulness in sending this to me and I wish you the very best in its ultimate publication. I look forward to the completion of your work.

Sincerely,

Howard W. Hunter

21. Milton R. Hunter and Thomas Stuart Ferguson, *Ancient America and the Book of Mormon* (Oakland, CA: Kolob Book Company, 1950), 146.

22. Spencer W. Kimball, paper presented to the faculty of Brigham Young University, Provo, UT, September 12, 1967.

On November 10, 1985, Ezra Taft Benson was set apart as Prophet, Seer, and Revelator and President of The Church of Jesus Christ of Latter-day Saints. In his first general conference address as President, in April 1986, he vividly proclaimed the importance of the Book of Mormon with strong words that continue to the present:

> Unless we read the Book of Mormon and give heed to its teachings, the Lord has stated in Section 84 of the Doctrine and Covenants that the whole Church is under condemnation: "And this condemnation resteth upon the children of Zion, even all." (D&C 84:56) The Lord continues: "And they shall remain under this condemnation until they repent and remember the new covenant, even the Book of Mormon and the former commandments which I have given them, not only to say, but to do according to that which I have written." (D&C 84:57)
>
> Now we not only need to say more about the Book of Mormon, but we need to do more with it. . . .
>
> The Prophet Joseph said that "The Book of Mormon was the most correct of any book on earth, and the keystone of our religion, and a man would get nearer to God by abiding by its precepts, than any other book." (Book of Mormon, Introduction) The Book of Mormon has not been, nor is it yet, the center of our personal study, family teaching, preaching, and missionary work. Of this we must repent.[23]
>
> I bless you with increased *understanding* of the Book of Mormon. I promise you that from this moment forward, if we will daily sup from its pages and abide by its precepts, God will pour out upon each child of Zion and the Church a blessing hitherto unknown—and we will plead to the Lord that He will begin to lift the condemnation—the scourge and judgment. Of this I bear solemn witness.[24]

23. Ezra Taft Benson, "Cleansing the Inner Vessel," *Ensign*, May 1986, 5.

24. Ezra Taft Benson, "A Sacred Responsibility," *Ensign*, May 1986, 78.

The time between President Benson's statement above to the writing of the second edition of *Exploring the Lands of the Book of Mormon* is twenty-one years. The year 2005 was a phenomenal year in the Church in one respect because so many members diligently read the Book of Mormon. That is, about halfway through the year, President Gordon B. Hinckley challenged members to read the entire Book of Mormon by the end of the year. The result was almost a Book of Mormon revolution as young and old alike rose to the challenge. People were seen reading the Book of Mormon on buses, in hallways of buildings, on park benches during lunch hours, and on temple grounds throughout the world.

For example, one young man turned down a New Year's Eve party so he could finish reading the Book of Mormon, and a little three-year-old announced to everyone as her family visited her grandparents during the Christmas holidays, "We can't stay long because we have to go home and finish reading the Book of Mormon."

What these developments mean is that the Church now has a generation of young members who are in fulfillment of the blessing of President Benson—that is, because of obedience as members of the Church in reading and studying the Book of Mormon, testimonies have increased and greater understanding has and will continue to come forth about this marvelous work and a wonder, Another Testament of Christ.

MY FAVORITE STORIES

By Jessica Allen,
(2004, age 13)

I love stories.
I always have.
My favorite story
Came from the dust,
Written for my day.

The Book of Mormon,
Another Testament of
Christ.

Nephi, struggling to
Retrieve the brass plates.
Always brave.
Always faithful.

Abinadi, calling
King Noah to repentance.
Refusing
to deny the Christ.

Ammon, protecting
King Lamoni's sheep,
Being protected
by a Higher King.

Helaman, leading 2,000
Boys into battle.
"They did not doubt
their mothers knew it."

The Brother of Jared,
Seeing the finger of the
Lord.
Leading His people
To a Promised Land.

Moroni, encouraging us to
Know for ourselves.
Read, ponder, pray.

Men of God.
All of them.
Standing up for what
They know is right.

I love the Book of
Mormon.
I always have.
This ancient record is
My favorite story.

The Church now has a generation of young members who are in fulfillment of the blessing of President Benson—that is, because of obedience as members of the Church in reading and studying the Book of Mormon, testimonies have increased and greater understanding has and will continue to come forth about this marvelous work and a wonder, Another Testament of Christ.

Desolation
(Represents Eternal Damnation)

Bountiful
(Represents Eternal Life)

Zarahemla
(The land of the Nephites—represents good)

Nephi
(The land of the Lamanites—represents evil)

NORTH

25 mi
50 km

CHAPTER 18

Geography and the Plan of Salvation

My soul delighteth in proving unto my people the truth of the coming of Christ; for, for this end hath the law of Moses been given; and all things which have been of God from the beginning of the world, unto man, are the typifying of him. (2 Nephi 11:4)

၎၎၎၎၎၎၎၎၎၎၎၎၎၎၎၎၎၎၎၎၎၎၎၎၎၎၎၎

By nature, study of Book of Mormon geography requires that any proposed map must adhere to both the internal consistency of the Book of Mormon text and to the geographical and topographical structure of the area to which the comparison is made. In addition, the proposed locations must be consistent with the archaeological, linguistic, and historical information in the proposed area. In those respects, Mesoamerica serves as the geographical setting for the Book of Mormon model discussed in this chapter.

Now that we have discussed the evolvement of Book of Mormon mapmaking, we will analyze some of the key geographical statements in the Book of Mormon to see

OPPOSITE: Upwards of 25 percent of the information recorded in the Book of Mormon is written in relation to geography. We believe that Mormon included geographical statements to use as a springboard to illustrate spiritual messages. This process is called "types and shadows," and the following scripture emphasizes this concept: "The land of Nephi [representing evil] was divided from the land of Zarahemla [representing good] by a narrow strip of wilderness, which ran from the sea east even to the sea west [from where we are born to where we die]" (Alma 22:27). This map shows the narrow strip of wilderness that divided the land of Nephi from the land of Zarahemla or, symbolically speaking, the narrow way that divides good from evil.

By nature, study of Book of Mormon geography requires that any proposed map must adhere to both the internal consistency of the Book of Mormon text and to the geographical and topographical structure of the area to which the comparison is made.

how they fit on a map of Mesoamerica. As you will observe, numerous similarities exist between the "internal maps" referred to in chapter 17, "A Review of Literature on Book of Mormon Geography," and the Mesoamerica model we will now present.

We estimate that about a fourth of the content of the Book of Mormon is directly related to geographical statements. Therefore, as we begin this chapter, we ask readers to ponder an answer to the following question: Why did Mormon include so many geographical references in his abridgement? Our answer is twofold. First, Mormon communicates with us as if he had a map in front of him and as if he expects us to refer to this same map as an aid in understanding what he is saying. Second, we will introduce in this chapter the concept of types and shadows and present an interpretation of the manner in which Mormon utilizes geography to develop a spiritual or doctrinal principle.

Two chapters from Alma provide us with a fair overall picture of Book of Mormon geography. Alma 22 and Alma 50 outline the geographical framework for the following exercise. Alma 22:27–34 describes the Lamanite-Nephite boundaries in the first century BC from a Lamanite perspective. The occasion is the missionary journeys of the sons of Mosiah. Aaron, one of the sons of Mosiah, taught the gospel to the Lamanite king, who was king over all the land of the Lamanites and who lived in the land of Nephi. The Lamanite king sent to his people a proclamation that provided a license for the sons of Mosiah to preach the gospel among the king's people.

Mormon adds his commentary to this geographical account. For the most part, however, he appears to have taken his information from the accounts of the four sons: Ammon, Aaron, Omner, and Himni. We can assume that the portion of the actual proclamation of the Lamanite king was included in the accounts, although we are given several of Mormon's editorial comments in the process. The important concept here, however, as will be explained, is that Mormon uses these geographical statements to teach spiritual principles. In that respect, Nephi writes, "My soul delighteth in proving unto my people the truth of the coming of Christ. . . . All things which have been given of God from the beginning of the world . . . *are the typifying of him*" (2 Nephi 11:4; emphasis added).

GEOGRAPHICAL STATEMENTS IN ALMA 22:27–34

We invite you to picture the scene that is taking place preceding, during, and following the eight verses of Alma 22:27–34. That is, preceding verse 27, Mormon is abridging from the large plates and is telling the story of the missionary activities of the sons of Mosiah among the Lamanites in the land of Nephi. As he begins verse 27, Mormon tells us about a proclamation that the Lamanite king sent out to all his people to direct them not to harm Ammon, Aaron, Omner, Himni, and "their brethren" during their missionary activities "in any part of" the Lamanite lands.

At this point in the large plates, Mormon probably encountered a description of the areas throughout which the proclamation was sent from the perspective of the Lamanite king. Mormon then took upon himself the task of telling readers about the lands under the control of the Nephites and Lamanites as of the first century BC—intermingled with his editorial comments about Nephite/Lamanite geography in the fourth century AD.

Following his geographical summary, Mormon then says in verse 35, "And now I . . . return again to the account of Ammon and Aaron, Omner and Himni, and their brethren."

We will now analyze the eight verses in Alma 22 as we experiment with a Mesoamerica map.

> An important concept is that Mormon uses geographical statements to teach spiritual principles.

Alma 22:27 (see figure 18–1)

And it came to pass that the [Lamanite] king sent a proclamation throughout all the land, amongst all his people who were in *all his land,* who were in *all the*

FIGURE 18–1: Alma 22:27—The Lamanite king who lived in the land of Nephi sent a proclamation to all his people (the Lamanites) who lived in the regions round about, which extended from the sea on the east to the sea on the west. If the land of Nephi was located in the Guatemala highlands and Honduras, then the Atlantic Ocean was the sea east, and the Pacific Ocean was the sea west.

regions round about, which was bordering even to the *sea,* on the *east and on the west* . . . (emphasis added)

We will label the Lamanite land ("all his land" and "all the regions round about") to be the highlands of Guatemala; we will label the two seas to be the Atlantic Ocean and the Pacific Ocean.

Alma 22:27 (continued; see figure 18–2)

. . . and which was divided from the *land of Zarahemla* by a *narrow strip of wilderness,* which ran from the *sea east* even to the *sea west* and round about on the borders of the *seashore,* and the borders of the *wilderness* which was on the *north* by the *land of Zarahemla,* through the borders of *Manti,* by the *head of the river Sidon,* running from the *east towards the west*—and thus were the Lamanites and Nephites divided. (emphasis added)

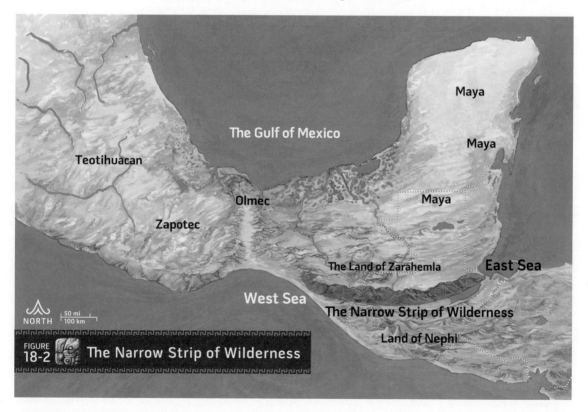

FIGURE 18–2: Alma 22:27 (continued)—The land of Nephi was divided from the land of Zarahemla by a narrow strip of wilderness—or a narrow mountain range—that ran from the sea east to the sea west "and round about on the borders of the seashore." The Cuchumatanes mountain range divides the highlands of Guatemala from Chiapas and the Peten. It runs from the east to the west and continues "round about" along the Sierra Madres and along the seashore toward the Isthmus of Tehuantepec. Manti was in the land of Zarahemla bordering the land of Nephi. The river Sidon had its beginnings in the mountains of the land of Nephi.

Exploring the Lands of the Book of Mormon

By placing the land of Nephi in the highlands of Guatemala, we can then place the land of Zarahemla in the state of Chiapas, Mexico, and in the northern lowlands of Guatemala (the department of Peten, including the small country of Belize, which was originally part of Guatemala). Chiapas belonged to Guatemala prior to its annexation to Mexico in the nineteenth century. The most significant geographical landmark associated with Mesoamerica and the Book of Mormon is a narrow mountain range ("narrow strip of wilderness") that divides the highlands from the lowlands—or that divides the land of Nephi from the land of Zarahemla (see chapter 23, "Things That Are Narrow").

References to the sea east and the sea west above are consistent with the first part of the scripture in association with the Atlantic and the Pacific Oceans.

We propose that the Lamanites occupied all the area on both the Atlantic and the Pacific sides of the Guatemala highlands, which also included Honduras on the Atlantic side and El Salvador on the Pacific side. The Lamanite area also included a portion of Mexico's Pacific coast from Tapachula to Tonala—or, as the record states, "round about on the borders of the seashore." You will note from the verses that follow that a portion of the Lamanite lands was west of Zarahemla.

We are informed that the northern borders of the Lamanites are in the mountains ("wilderness") and that they connect with the borders of the land of Zarahemla. We are also given the name of a land called "Manti," which is located in the land of Zarahemla.

Alma 22:28 (see figure 18–3)

Now, the more idle part of the Lamanites lived in the *wilderness*, and dwelt in tents; and they were spread through the *wilderness* on the *west*, in the *land of Nephi*; yea, and also on the *west* of the *land of Zarahemla*, in the *borders* by the *seashore*, and on the *west* in the *land of Nephi*, in the place of their *fathers' first inheritance*, and thus bordering along by the *seashore*. (emphasis added)

The statement that the "more idle part of the Lamanites lived in the wilderness" parallels very closely today with the fact that of all the people who currently live in Guatemala (over ten million according to the 2000 census), almost one-half live in the mountains of Guatemala and are truly indigenous people (see chapter 24, "Wilderness Areas").

We are told in the above reference that these "idle" Lamanites lived in the mountains ("wilderness")—located west (in) the land of Nephi and west (of) the land of Zarahemla by the ("borders of the seashore") and west (in) the land of Nephi also by the ("seashore") by the place of their fathers' (Lehi, Laman, and Lemuel's) "first inheritance."

The most significant geographical landmark associated with Mesoamerica and the Book of Mormon is a narrow mountain range ("narrow strip of wilderness") that divides the highlands from the lowlands—or that divides the land of Nephi from the land of Zarahemla.

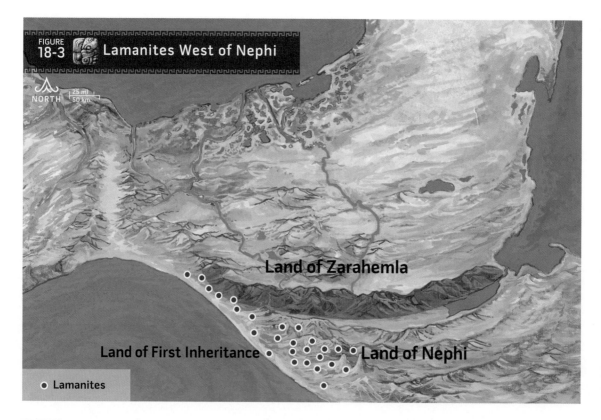

FIGURE 18–3: Alma 22:28—Lamanites lived west of the city of Nephi. They also lived west of the land of Zarahemla along the seashore. And they lived on the west by the seashore in the place of their fathers' first inheritance—or where Lehi landed (proposed area of Izapa).

Alma 22:29 (see figure 18–4)

And also there were many Lamanites on the *east by the seashore,* whither the Nephites had driven them. And thus the Nephites were *nearly surrounded* by the Lamanites. (emphasis added)

The Nephites would have driven the Lamanites from Chiapas and the Peten rainforest to the Caribbean, or Atlantic Ocean, which is east by the seashore, to the area of the small country of Belize. Interestingly, even to this day, border disputes occur between Belize and Guatemala. Guatemala still claims that the country of Belize belongs to Guatemala. This geographical configuration would cause the Nephites to be "nearly surrounded" by the Lamanites.

Alma 22:29 (continued; see figure 18–5)

. . . nevertheless, the Nephites had taken possession of all the *northern* parts of the land bordering on the *wilderness,* at the *head of the river Sidon,* from the *east*

Exploring the Lands of the Book of Mormon

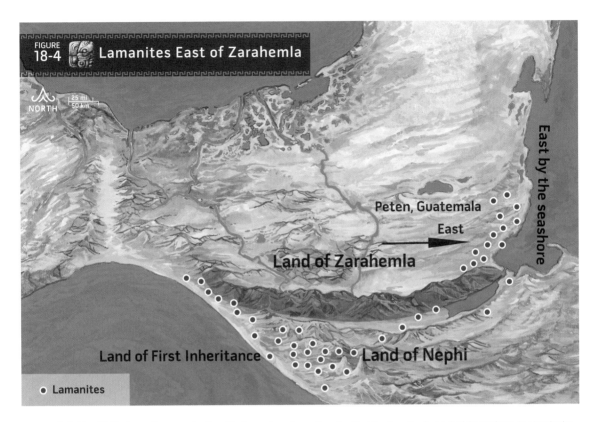

FIGURE 18–4: Alma 22:29—Lamanites were also found by the east seashore where the Nephites from Zarahemla had driven them. As a result, the Nephites were almost surrounded by the Lamanites.

to the *west,* round about on the *wilderness* side; on the *north,* even until they came to the land which they called *Bountiful.* (emphasis added)

This statement is repetitive, as it refers to the northern border of the Lamanites—implying that the Nephites occupied the mountains ("wilderness"), which run from the east to the west.

Today, the boundary lines are the same. The mountain peaks divide one country from another. The volcanic peak of Tacana divides the state of Chiapas, Mexico, from Guatemala. Likewise, Honduras and El Salvador are separated from Guatemala by mountain peaks or mountain ranges.

The verse is also repetitive because it appears to be describing the narrow strip of wilderness referred to earlier. This section is likely an insert by Mormon, as he tells us that the Nephite land of Zarahemla was bordered on the south side by the land of Nephi and on the north side by the land (state) of Bountiful. We learn more about the relationship of the land of Zarahemla to the land of Bountiful in Alma 50. Because of the

FIGURE 18–5: Alma 22:29 (continued)—Zarahemla was north of Nephi, and Bountiful was north of Zarahemla. Today, the area is referred to as the Maya highlands (land of Nephi), the southern Maya lowlands (land of Zarahemla), and the northern Maya lowlands (land of Bountiful).

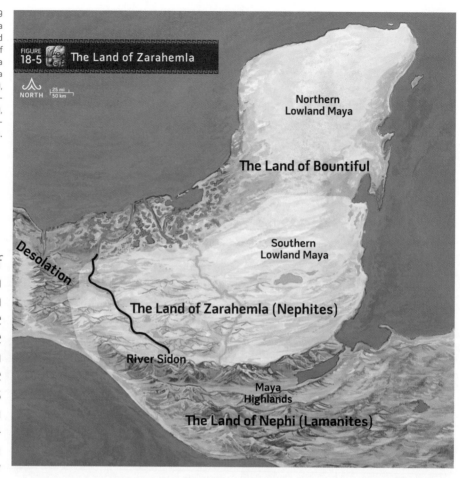

FIGURE 18-5 · The Land of Zarahemla

NORTH 25 mi / 50 km

Northern Lowland Maya

The Land of Bountiful

Southern Lowland Maya

Desolation

The Land of Zarahemla (Nephites)

River Sidon

Maya Highlands

The Land of Nephi (Lamanites)

Because of the repetition in Alma 22:29, we arrive at the conclusion that the eight verses in Alma 22:27–34 are written in a Hebrew parallelistic style of writing.

repetition in Alma 22:29, we arrive at the conclusion that the eight verses under consideration are written in a Hebrew parallelistic style of writing, as we will show later in this chapter.

Alma 22:30 (see figure 18–6)

And it [*Bountiful*] bordered upon the land which they [the first century BC Nephites] called *Desolation*, it [*Bountiful*] being so far *northward* that it came into the land which had been peopled and been destroyed, of whose bones we have spoken [see Mosiah 8:8–11], which was discovered by the people of Zarahemla, it [land northward/Desolation] being the place of their [Mulekites'] first landing. (emphasis added)

Alma 22:30 is a rather difficult scripture to assess, as it deals with the land Bountiful/land southward, the land Desolation/land northward, and the landing site of the

FIGURE 18–6: Alma 22:30—The west boundary of Bountiful bordered upon Desolation's east boundary. *Bountiful* is synonymous with the land southward in the same way that *Desolation* is synonymous with the land northward (see Alma 22:31). Zarahemla was also in the land southward and may have been considered part of the greater land of Bountiful, such as in the scripture "the land southward which was called by the Nephites Zarahemla" (Ether 9:31). The land southward was the location the Jaredites preserved as an area to hunt wild animals (Ether 10:21). Today, 40 percent of the wild animals of the entire republic of Mexico are found in the state of Chiapas, the area proposed as the land of Zarahemla in the land southward.

Mulekites. This scripture also appears to be Mormon's commentary on the geography in the fourth century AD as opposed to the actual proclamation of the Lamanite king who lived in the first century BC.

For the exercise in this chapter, we will simply position the land Bountiful north of Zarahemla and bordering the land of Desolation in the land northward, with the land northward designated as the landing site of the Mulekites. We will go into more detail in other chapters.

Alma 22:31 (see figure 18–7)

And they [the Mulekites] came from there [the land northward/Desolation] up into the *south wilderness*. Thus the *land on the northward was called Desolation*, and the *land on the southward was called Bountiful*, it [Bountiful] being the *wil-*

derness which is filled with all manner of wild animals of every kind, a part of which had come from the *land northward* for food. (emphasis added)

We again seem to be given geographical information directly from Mormon. The south wilderness from the proposed landing site of the Mulekites must be the Chiapas mountains (Bountiful wilderness), which even today is an area of wild animals (see chapter 19, "The Land Northward," and chapter 20, "The Land Southward").

We must understand the location and perspective of the individuals involved in the events and the writing of Alma 22. To the Lamanite king who lived in the land of Nephi/ Guatemala, the northern wilderness, or narrow strip of wilderness by the headwaters of the river Sidon, is located where the Mexico-Guatemala border is located today. To the AD 350 Mormon, who lived in the area of Desolation/Gulf of Mexico, the south wilderness (Bountiful) is "up" in the Chiapas mountains. Mormon's "south wilderness"

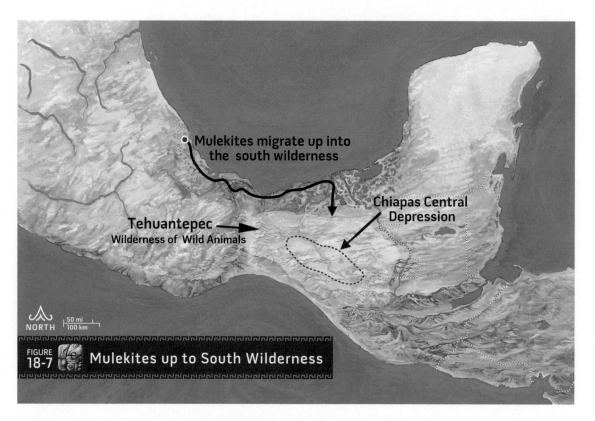

FIGURE 18–7: Alma 22:31—The Mulekites landed in the land northward and subsequently migrated to the land southward—or the land of Zarahemla—which was part of the wilderness that was filled with all manner of wild animals.

and the Lamanite king's "north wilderness" are two separate mountain ranges that form almost a U-shape around the Chiapas depression.

For the most part, this verse simply reaffirms the relative positions of the land southward/Bountiful with the land northward/Desolation.

Alma 22:32 (see figure 18–8)

And now, it was only the distance of a day and a half's journey for a Nephite, on the *line Bountiful* and the *land Desolation, from the east* to the *west sea.* (emphasis added)

This verse represents the central point of the chiastic structure of this section on geography. It is also one of the most controversial geographical statements in the Book of Mormon because it is so often misread by readers. For the exercise in this chapter, we will render the following interpretation: "It was only the distance of a day and a half's

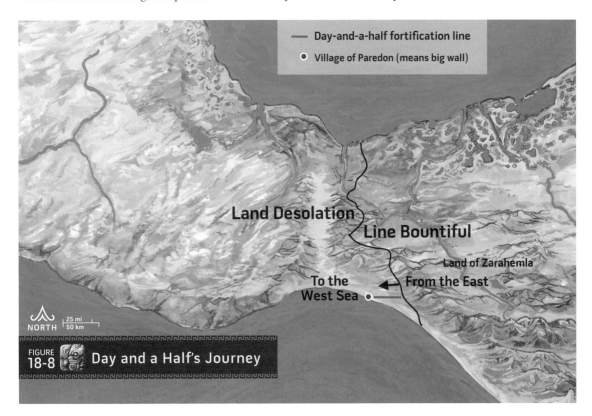

FIGURE 18–8: Alma 22:32—The defensive line that is the length of a day and a half's journey (about twelve miles) in the Nephite measuring system runs from Desolation's east boundary to the Pacific Ocean—or the west sea. The purpose of the twelve-mile defensive line was to keep the Lamanites from getting into Zarahemla and from going into the land northward (see Alma 22:33). Today, the twelve-mile line runs from the archaeological ruins of Tonala to the town of Paredon, which is located on the seacoast. *Paredon* means "big wall," and remnants of the wall can still be detected. The twelve-mile line runs from the mountains to the ocean.

journey for a Nephite from the [boundary] line [of] Bountiful and [Desolation] to the west sea."

Since the initial publication of the Book of Mormon in 1830, many of its readers have routinely wanted a Nephite to cross from ocean to ocean in a day and a half. This verse *does not* say that. It does not say from the *east sea* to the *west sea*. It says "from the *east* to the *west sea*." It simply states that the east orientation is the dividing line between Bountiful and Desolation. The west orientation is the west sea, which we believe is the Pacific Ocean by the Gulf of Tehuantepec. According to our model, the day-and-a-half marker begins near the archaeological site of Tonala (candidate for the city of Melek) on the east and ends at the ocean fishing village of Paredon on the west. The distance is twelve miles, which is consistent with Maya travel distance of eight miles a day—or twelve miles in a day and a half. "For a Nephite," from our perspective, is simply Mormon's way of saying that in the Nephite measuring system, a day-and-a-half's travel time is equal to about twelve miles.

Also of interest is the name of the village located on the ocean's front (west sea). It is *Paredon*. *Pared* is a Spanish word that means "wall," and *Paredon* means a "big wall." The local people tell of an ancient wall that was built beginning at the ocean, by the cemetery, and that extended directly east toward the mountain twelve miles away. This historical fact is very important because to this very day, an immigration checkpoint is located in the same area near Tonala. This is a crucial landmark because the high, rugged mountains on the east and the Gulf of Tehuantepec on the west provide a natural defensive area to inhibit or prohibit people from entering into the central depression of Chiapas or to travel through the Isthmus of Tehuantepec into areas of Mexico that are west (and "northward") of the isthmus.

> Whether guards were posted or whether a wall was built along the defensive line, the results would be the same. The motive was to keep the Lamanites from traveling into the land of Zarahemla or into the land northward.

Whether guards were posted or whether a wall was built along the defensive line, the results would be the same. The motive was to keep the Lamanites from traveling into the land of Zarahemla or into the land northward. Prior to the military checkpoint, a Lamanite army had entered into the city of Ammonihah unimpeded and had destroyed the city: "The [Lamanites] took their armies and went over into the borders of the land of Zarahemla, and fell upon the people who were in the land of Ammonihah and destroyed them" (Alma 25:2; see also Alma 10:23; 16:9).

Ammonihah was located three days' travel time (twenty-four miles) north of Mulek (Tonala), which would place it, according to our calculations, north of the city of Arriaga near the archaeological mound of El Mirador (not to be confused with El Mirador in northern Peten; see Alma 8:3–6).

The above concept is extremely important because it not only provides us with location, distance, direction, and a name correlation but also provides us with the motive for this being the area of the fortification line, which is a distance of a day and a half's journey for a Nephite defender. The purpose of the fortification wall or line was to keep the Lamanites from coming along the coast from Guatemala toward Mexico—or from the land of Nephi to the land of Zarahemla: *"Thus the Nephites in their wisdom, with their guards and their armies, had hemmed in the Lamanites on the south, that thereby they should have no more possession on the north, that they might not overrun the land northward"* (Alma 22:33; emphasis added).

As mentioned above, prior to the time the Nephites built the day-and-a-half fortification barrier, the city of Ammonihah was vulnerable to an attack from the Lamanites. You will remember that seven years after the sons of Mosiah went up to the land of Nephi to preach the gospel to the Lamanites, Alma resigned his political position as chief judge and began to preach the gospel among the Nephites. He started in the city of Zarahemla and then went "over upon the east of the river Sidon, into the valley of Gideon" (Alma 6:7). He returned to Zarahemla for a time and then went to the west mountains to Melek. From there, he traveled north three days to the land of Ammonihah (see Alma 8:6–9).

His missionary companion, Amulek, made it clear to the people of Ammonihah that their city had been spared only because of the prayers of the righteous. He proclaimed, *"If ye will cast out the righteous from among you then will not the Lord stay his hand; but in his fierce anger he will come out against you; then ye shall be smitten by famine, and by pestilence, and by the sword; and the time is soon at hand except ye repent"* (Alma 10:23; emphasis added).

Now here is the poetic justice. The converts of the sons of Mosiah, who had buried both their sins and their weapons of war, were being persecuted and killed in the land of Nephi during the same time that the Nephite Christians who were taught by Alma and Amulek were being tortured and burned in the land of Ammonihah. Hence, the Lamanites in the land of Nephi determined that their anger was greater against the Nephites in the land of Zarahemla than against the people of Anti-Nephi-Lehi. Therefore, the Lamanites *"took their armies and went over into the borders of the land of Zarahemla, and fell upon the people who were in the land of Ammonihah and destroyed them"* (Alma 25:2; emphasis added).

Although it is true that wicked people destroy righteous people, it is also true that wicked people destroy wicked people. Most of the Lamanites of this time period never gave up their hatred toward the Nephites, and although the military leader Moroni developed a massive defensive program, the Lamanites continued to attack the Nephites in the land of Zarahemla.

But again, as stated in Alma 22:33, the Nephites were wise to keep the Lamanites from going in the back door of Zarahemla and to keep them from going into the land northward via the narrow pass through the Isthmus of Tehuantepec, not far from Paredon, "the big wall."

> Although it is true that wicked people destroy righteous people, it is also true that wicked people destroy wicked people.

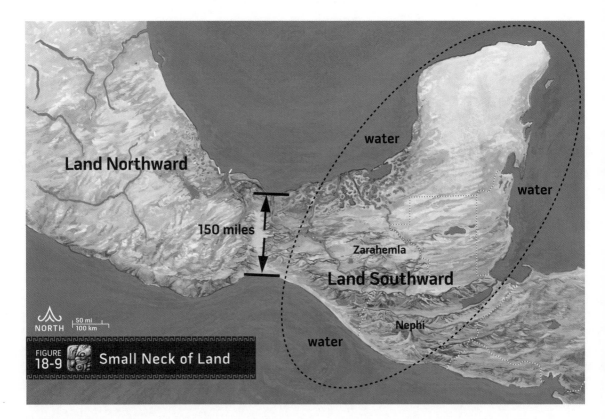

FIGURE 18–9: Alma 22:32 (continued)—A small neck of land divided the land northward from the land southward. Today, the small neck of land is called the Isthmus of Tehuantepec, which, in the Nahuatl language, means "the wilderness of wild animals." The distance from the Gulf of Tehuantepec on the south to the Gulf of Mexico on the north is about 150 miles. The land of Nephi and the Land of Zarahemla, therefore, were nearly surrounded by water.

Alma 22:32 (continued; see figure 18–9)

. . . and thus the *land of Nephi* and the *land of Zarahemla* were nearly surrounded by water, there being a *small neck of land* between the *land northward* and the *land southward.* (emphasis added)

The Isthmus of Tehuantepec ("small neck of land") is a natural dividing line between Mexico and Yucatan-Central America ("between the land northward and the land southward"). The land southward is the same geographical area that constituted the Maya boundaries from the Classic Period (AD 350) to the Spanish conquest (AD 1521). Both the land of Nephi and the land of Zarahemla were in the land southward and, as such, *were nearly surrounded by water.*

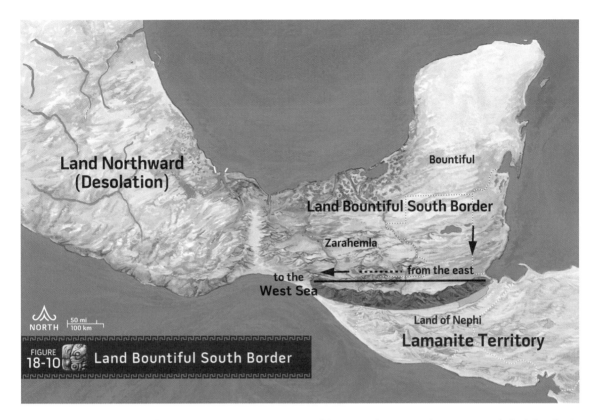

FIGURE 18–10: Alma 22:33—In the first century BC, the Nephites were successful in keeping the Lamanites from coming into the land of Zarahemla as well as into the land northward. The terms *Bountiful* and *Zarahemla* are used interchangeably in the Book of Mormon. The land of Zarahemla was probably part of the land of Bountiful.

Alma 22:33 (see figure 18–10)

And it came to pass that the Nephites had inhabited the *land Bountiful,* even from the *east* unto the *west sea,* and thus the Nephites in their wisdom, with their guards and their armies, had hemmed in the Lamanites on the *south,* that thereby they should have no more possession on the *north,* that they might not overrun the *land northward.* (emphasis added)

In Mormon's mind, the land of Zarahemla and the land of Bountiful/land southward were apparently in the same specific area. The land of Zarahemla was probably included in the larger land of Bountiful (similar to the way Chiapas is included in the country of Mexico today). By using the above guidelines, we can place Nephite territory during the first century BC as running from the Peten jungle (on the east) to the Gulf of Tehuantepec (by the west sea). You will remember that Lamanites were also living in the borders of the *east sea* (see Alma 22:29).

As explained above, the Nephites could hem off the Lamanites along the Pacific coast (west sea), thus preventing them from traveling through the Isthmus of Tehuantepec (narrow pass) into the Gulf of Mexico/Veracruz area (land northward).

GEOGRAPHICAL STATEMENTS IN ALMA 50:7–15

To fully complete the geographical picture of the Mesoamerica map, we will analyze several verses from Alma 50. Alma chapters 46–62 cover a period of sixteen years and are usually referred to as the "war years" in the Book of Mormon. From 73 BC to 57 BC, the same time period that population centers were being developed in the Peten, Guatemala, "many Nephite cities" were built in the east wilderness.

We are exposed to a great deal of geography in Alma 46–62 as we follow the chief commander of the Nephites, Moroni, through his war-campaign trail. Much of the fighting occurred in an area called the east wilderness, where the Nephites defined

FIGURE 18–11: Alma 50:7–10—The Nephite-Lamanite boundary line appears to be the same line that today divides the highlands of Guatemala from Chiapas, the department of Peten, Guatemala, and Belize. Nephites went into the east wilderness in the first century BC and, in essence, homesteaded the land under the protection of Moroni and his armies. This is the same time that growth occurred in several sites in the Peten and in Belize.

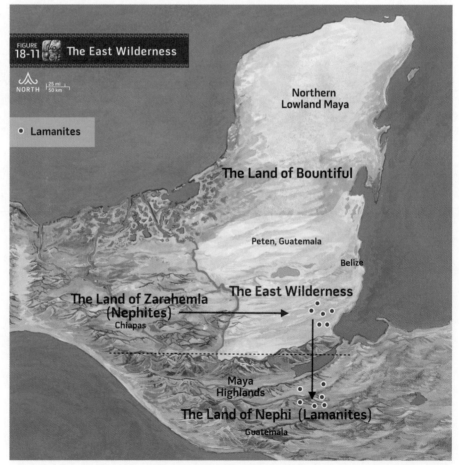

their boundaries by building cities and by driving out the Lamanites. In this exercise, we will discuss only nine verses in Alma 50, beginning with verse 7.

Alma 50:7 (see figure 18–11)
And it came to pass that Moroni caused that his armies should go forth into the *east wilderness;* yea and they went forth and drove all the Lamanites who were in the *east wilderness* into their [the Lamanites'] *own lands,* which were *south* of the *land of Zarahemla.* (emphasis added)

The Peten jungle of Guatemala is an excellent candidate for the east wilderness—not only because it is directly east of almost everybody's Zarahemla but also because both the language development and population centers date to the precise time period required.

The Nephites drove the Lamanites to the land of Nephi, which is south of the land of Zarahemla's east wilderness.

Alma 50:8 (see figure 18–11)
And the land of Nephi did run in a straight course from the *east sea* to the *west.* (emphasis added)

Because we are dealing with the east wilderness area, we are justified in stating that Mormon used the east sea as the initial point, moving along the mountains of highland Guatemala toward the west.

Alma 50:9 (see figure 18–11)
And it came to pass that when Moroni had driven all the Lamanites out of the *east wilderness,* which was *north* of the lands of their [Lamanites'] own posses-sions, he caused that the inhabitants who were in the *land of Zarahemla* and in the *land round about* should go forth into the *east wilderness,* even to the *borders by the seashore,* and possess the land. (emphasis added)

Moroni's strategy appears to be an amazing homestead act, as it caused people to go into the Peten jungle (east wilderness) to build cities. This is the same area where many cities were built in the first century BC, as evidenced by archaeological documentation (see chapter 24, "Wilderness Areas," for more details).

The inhabitants in the land of Zarahemla (Chiapas) and in the land round about apparently settled all the way to the seashore along the coast of Belize. Again, we are told that the east wilderness (Peten-Belize) is north of the land of Nephi (highland Guatemala).

The Peten jungle of Guatemala is an excellent candidate for the east wilderness—not only because it is directly east of almost everybody's Zarahemla but also because both the language development and population centers date to the precise time period required.

Moroni's strategy appears to be an amazing homestead act, as it caused people to go into the Peten jungle (east wilderness) to build cities. This is the same area where many cities were built in the first century BC, as evidenced by archaeological documentation.

Alma 50:10 (see figure 18–11)

And he [Moroni] also placed armies on the *south,* in the *borders* of their possessions, and caused them to erect fortifications [see chapter 24, "Wilderness Areas"] that they might secure their armies and their people from the hands of their enemies. (emphasis added)

The map in figure 18–11, consistent with all other references about the same area, places Nephite armies along the Nephites' south border. This area is located where the highlands of Guatemala and the lowlands of Guatemala meet.

Alma 50:11 (see figure 18–12)

And thus he [Moroni] cut off all the strongholds of the Lamanites in the *east wilderness,* yea, and also on the *west,* fortifying the line between the Nephites and the Lamanites, between the *land of Zarahemla* and the *land of Nephi,* from the *west sea,* running by the head of the *river Sidon.* (emphasis added)

Whereas Alma 50:10 deals with building defenses along the borders by the *east sea* (Atlantic side), this reference moves us over to the *west sea* (Pacific side). The northern boundary point is the head of the river Sidon. By standing on top of the highest mountain between the Atlantic and the Pacific, a person can almost feel that he or she is holding hands with both oceans—oceans that we label the "east sea" and the "west sea" (see chapter 26, "Bodies of Water," for more details).

We can see from the previous two references that the boundary between the land of Nephi and the land of Zarahemla is very well defined. It was very difficult to defend, but it is very well defined. The narrow strip of wilderness (Cuchumatane Mountains) probably represents the most visible internal landmark in the Book of Mormon; and the sea east-sea west (Atlantic-Pacific) language probably represents the ocean boundaries required in the Book of Mormon.

When we add to these natural land and water boundaries the east wilderness (Peten-Belize jungle) where massive population centers were built during the time required by the Book of Mormon, a high degree of confidence in Book of Mormon geography develops.

Alma 50:11 (continued; see figure 18–12)

. . . the Nephites possessing all the *land northward,* yea, even all the land which was northward of the *land Bountiful,* according to their pleasure. (emphasis added; see also figure 18–7)

This statement appears to be another insert by Mormon, who points out again that the land northward was *northward* of the land Bountiful. The land (state) of Bountiful

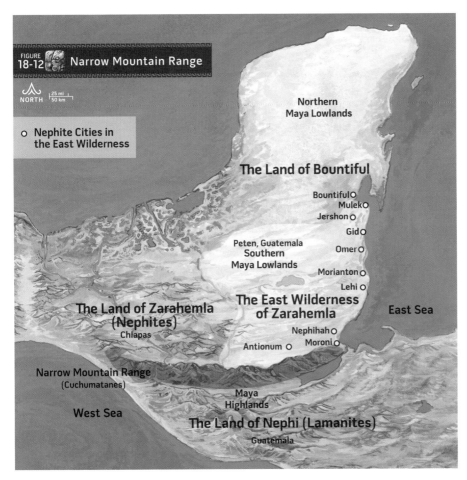

FIGURE 18–12: Alma 50:11–15—One of the most significant geographical landmarks in the Book of Mormon is the Cuchumatanes mountain range that divides the Maya highlands from the Maya lowlands—or the land of Nephi where the Lamanites lived from the land of Zarahemla where the Nephites lived. These mountains extend from the sea east to the sea west. The city of Moroni was by the east sea and on the south by the possessions of the Lamanites. The city of Lehi was north by the borders of the seashore.

was north of the land of Zarahemla. The land northward is northward of the narrow neck (Isthmus of Tehuantepec)—hence, it is northward of both the state of Bountiful (Yucatan-Campeche) as well as the country of Bountiful (land southward).

Alma 50:13 (see figure 18–12)

And it came to pass that the Nephites began the foundation of a city, and they called the name of the city *Moroni;* and it was by the *east sea;* and it was on the *south* by the line of the possessions of the Lamanites. (emphasis added)

These descriptions are excellent in pinpointing the location of the city of Moroni. In fact, we have no need for additional description. The city of Moroni, like many other cities that were built in the first century BC (Preclassic Period), was built as a defensive city. Remember that the city of Moroni sank into the sea at the time of the great destruction at the death of Christ (see 3 Nephi 8:9).

Alma 50:14 (see figure 18–12)

And they also began a foundation for a city between the *city of Moroni* and the *city of Aaron,* joining the borders of *Aaron* and *Moroni;* and they called the name of the *city, or the land, Nephihah.* (emphasis added)

The "many cities" requirement describes very appropriately the "many archaeological ruins" that have been discovered in the Peten-Belize (east wilderness) area.

The only other place in the Book of Mormon where we read about a city called Aaron is in relation to Alma's missionary journey in the land of Zarahemla. Alma left the city of Ammonihah and was going toward the city of Aaron (see Alma 8:13–14).

Some students of the Book of Mormon have suggested that two different cities were named Aaron, and perhaps that is the case. Even the index of the Book of Mormon suggests that possibly two different cities were named Aaron.

We can assume that one of the cities of Aaron (if there *were* two) was between the city of Ammonihah and the city of Zarahemla.

The other city of Aaron is associated with the city of Moroni, which was located on the east sea, whereas the city of Ammonihah was located near the west sea. We read in Alma 50:13 that the city of Moroni "was by the east sea; and was south by the line of the possessions of the Lamanites." And in the following verse, Alma 50:14, we read that the city of Nephihah, a new city, was located between the city of Moroni and the city of Aaron. We know that the city of Moroni is close to the city of Nephihah because of what we read in Alma 51:24: "and those who fled out of the city of Moroni came to the city of Nephihah." This wording suggests that the city of Moroni was east of Nephihah and that the closest neighbor on the west, the wilderness side, was the city of Aaron. We have not proposed precise archaeological sites for the city of Aaron or the city of Nephihah.

Alma 50:15 (see figure 18–12)

And they also began in that same year to build *many cities* on the *north,* one in a particular manner which they called *Lehi,* which was in the *north* by the *borders of the seashore.* (emphasis added)

The "many cities" requirement describes very appropriately the "many archaeological ruins" that have been discovered in the Peten-Belize (east wilderness) area. The city of Lehi was apparently north of the city of Moroni along the Caribbean seacoast (Belize). As of the beginning of the twenty-first century, only 10 to 15 percent of these "many cities" have been archaeologically investigated.

The foregoing exercise will give you an idea of the type of geographical analysis that is possible as we analyze geographical statements in the Book of Mormon in relation to a Mesoamerican setting. Witnessing the geographical consistency within the pages of the Book of Mormon is truly fascinating. To paint a valid picture, however, we must be sure that all geographical statements interconnect. We must also establish a geographical

FIGURE 18-13: This map of the Maya territory shows a sampling of archaeological sites dating to the Preclassic, Classic, and Postclassic Periods. Notice that the general occupational movement was from the south to the north—or from the highlands of Guatemala to northern Yucatan. This movement is consistent with the Book of Mormon occupational movements from Nephi to Zarahemla to Bountiful.

We must look at comparisons other than geography before we draw geographical conclusions. For that reason, in *Exploring the Lands of the Book of Mormon*, we have preceded this chapter's geographical discussion with chapters on the languages, traditions, and archaeology of Mesoamerica.

point of reference as to who is doing the writing or the talking. Furthermore, we cannot change directions either within the Book of Mormon text or within the Mesoamerica map.

Most importantly, we must look at comparisons other than geography before we draw geographical conclusions. For that reason, we have preceded this chapter's geographical discussion with chapters on the languages, traditions, and archaeology of Mesoamerica.

The next several chapters consist of a detailed analysis of geographically related scriptures in the Book of Mormon in connection with the languages, cultures, archaeology, and geography of Mesoamerica.

Other writers may still desire to place Book of Mormon geography in a location other than Mesoamerica. However, by so doing, we create some *extreme* inconsistencies. We are left with a heavily populated Mesoamerica culture that dates contemporarily with the Book of Mormon, and at the same time, in any other part of the Americas, we find an absence of language, cultures, and archaeological sites that correlate strongly with the Book of Mormon.

We cannot have it both ways. That is, we cannot place the heartland of the Book of Mormon in Mesoamerica and at the same time place Book of Mormon sites in North America and in South America. The Book of Mormon does not allow us that degree of latitude. Furthermore, we cannot place Book of Mormon history in North America and/or in South America. The Mesoamerica culture does not allow our doing so.

GEOGRAPHY AND THE PLAN OF SALVATION

This chapter would not be complete if we did not respond to the following question: Because Mormon could write only one hundredth of what took place among the Book of Mormon peoples, why does he waste valuable space talking about geography?

We contend that Mormon uses geography to teach a spiritual message. This thinking suggests that Mormon uses geography as a type and shadow to emphasize the plan of salvation, which, by the way, is the central theme of the so-called geography section of the Book of Mormon (Alma 22:27–34).

This thinking is highlighted in the account of the acceptance of the gospel by the old Lamanite king who was taught the gospel by Aaron: "O God, Aaron hath told me that there is a God; and if there is a God, and if thou art God, wilt thou make thyself known unto me, and I will give away all my sins to know thee, and that I may be raised from the dead, and be saved at the last day" (Alma 22:18).

If the verses in Alma 22:27–34, which are written in Hebrew-style parallelism, are not placed in the text by Mormon to emphasize a spiritual concept, then they are out of context with the stated purpose of the Book of Mormon and theme of Alma 22. But when we translate this section into a spiritual format, it is both beautiful and powerful.

We maintain that the eight verses in Alma 22:27–34 are written in the Hebrew parallelistic style of writing and that they together form a literary masterpiece. The overall passage appears to have been written in a chiasmic format, and chiasmic structures are also found within the overall passage. For example, verses 29–31 repeat the following:

> Bountiful
> > Desolation
> > Desolation
> Bountiful

For this exercise, we will extract the chiasmus of the entire text in general to illustrate the spiritual message Mormon emphasizes. The text follows a pattern of Mesoamerica-type couplets in which two words or phrases are side by side as repetitive statements or as contrasting statements. The central theme of the chiasmus deals

Mormon uses geography as a type and shadow to emphasize the plan of salvation, which, by the way, is the central theme of the so-called geography section of the Book of Mormon.

Exploring the Lands of the Book of Mormon

with the distance for a Nephite from the east boundary line of Desolation to the west sea with a dualistic concept of man's journey through this life.

We will first introduce the chiasmic structure of these eight verses and then follow with a more detailed account as outlined in Alma 22:27–34.

A. The land of Nephi
   B. Sea on the east and on the west
      C. A narrow strip of wilderness
         D. Surrounded by Lamanites
            E. The land Bountiful and the land Desolation
               F. A day and a half's journey
            E. The line Bountiful and the land Desolation
         D. Surrounded by water
      C. A small neck of land
   B. The east unto the west sea
A. The land of Nephi

And it came to pass that the [Lamanite] king sent a proclamation throughout all the land,

A. **amongst all his people [land of Nephi]** who were in all his land, who were in all the regions round about, which was bordering even to

   B. **the sea, on the east and on the west**, and which was divided from the land of Zarahemla by

      C. **a narrow strip of wilderness**, which ran from the sea east even to the sea west, and round about on the borders of the seashore, and the borders of the wilderness which was on the north by the land of Zarahemla, through the borders of Manti, by the head of the river Sidon, running from the east towards the west—and thus were the Lamanites and Nephites divided. Now, the more idle part of the Lamanites lived in the wilderness and dwelt in tents; and they were spread through the wilderness on the west, in the land of Nephi; yea, and also on the west of the land of Zarahemla, in the borders by the seashore, and on the west in the land of Nephi, in the place of their fathers' first inheritance, and thus bordering along by the seashore. And also there were many Lamanites on the east by the seashore, whither the Nephites had driven them. And thus the Nephites were

         D. **nearly surrounded by the Lamanites**; nevertheless the Nephites had taken possession of all the northern parts of the land bordering on the wilderness, at the head of the river Sidon, from the east to the

An interesting outcome results when we remember that most of the punctuation in the Book of Mormon was inserted by the typesetter rather than by Joseph Smith or Oliver Cowdery.

Consider the clarification of the geographic statement in Alma 22: 32 when we punctuate it with parenthetical punctuation: "It was only the distance of a day and a half's journey for a Nephite (on the line Bountiful and the land Desolation from the east) to the west sea."

west, round about on the wilderness side; on the north, even until they came to the land which they called

E. **Bountiful**. And it bordered upon the land which they called **Desolation**, it being so far northward that it came into the land which had been peopled and been destroyed, of whose bones we have spoken, which was discovered by the people of Zarahemla, it being the place of their [the Mulekites'] first landing. And they [the Mulekites]) came from there up into the south wilderness. Thus the land on the northward was called Desolation, and the land on the southward was called Bountiful, it being the wilderness which is filled with all manner of wild animals of every kind, a part of which had come from the land northward for food

F. **AND NOW, IT WAS ONLY THE DISTANCE OF A DAY AND A HALF'S JOURNEY FOR A NEPHITE,** on the

E. **line Bountiful and the land Desolation**, from the east [of the line] to the west sea; and thus the land of Nephi and the land of Zarahemla were

D. **nearly surrounded by water**, there being a

C. **small neck of land** between the land northward and the land southward. And it came to pass that the Nephites had inhabited the land Bountiful [land southward], even from

B. **the east unto the west sea**, and thus the Nephites in their wisdom, with their guards and their armies, had hemmed in the Lamanites on the south, that thereby they should have no more possession on the north, that they might not overrun the land northward. Therefore, the Lamanites could have no more possession

A. **only in the land of Nephi**, and the wilderness round about. Now this was wisdom in the Nephites.

The central part of the chiasmus is that it was a distance of a day and a half's journey (estimated at twelve miles) from Desolation's east boundary (Tonala, Chiapas) to the west sea (Gulf of Tehuantepec near the village of Paredon, Chiapas). (See chapter 23, "Things That Are Narrow.")

By translating these eight verses of Alma chapter 22 into a spiritual message, which we believe Mormon intended, we come up with a marvelous study of how geography is utilized as a type and shadow of the plan of salvation.

The following chart illustrates the couplets, or parallelistic structures, and their symbolic counterparts as outlined in Alma 22:27–34:

Alma 22:27	Sea east	Sea west	The rising of the sun in the east represents birth. The going down of the sun represents death.
Alma 22:27, 32	Narrow strip of wilderness	Narrow neck of land	The narrow path divides good from evil and eternal life from death and hell.
Alma 22:27	Nephites	Lamanites	Nephites represent good. Lamanites represent evil.
Alma 22:28, 32	Land of Zarahemla	Land of Nephi	Land of Zarahemla represents good. Land of Nephi represents evil.
Alma 22:29, 32	Surrounded by Lamanites	Surrounded by water	We are surrounded by the world (Lamanites). Through baptism and Christ, we are surrounded by the Living Water.
Alma 22:29–32	Bountiful	Desolation	Bountiful represents eternal life. Desolation represents eternal damnation.
Alma 22:31–32	Land southward	Land northward	Synonymous with Bountiful and Desolation

Aaron preached the creation, the fall, and the redemption to the old Lamanite king, who was the father of Lamoni, and to his brother, Anti-Nephi-Lehi. In Alma 22:18, the king says, "I will give away all my sins to know thee, and [to know] that I . . . [will be] saved at the last day." If the old Lamanite king could repent and be saved after all he had done, we, too, can also repent and be saved.

Does it seem likely that Mormon would interrupt such a spiritual and doctrinal treatise to talk about geography if it were not for the purpose of driving home the message of repentance and the redemption of Christ?

In the context of Mormon's writing, we understand that the land of Nephi, which was taken over by the Lamanites, represented evil and that the land of Zarahemla, the new promised land to the 200 BC Nephites, represented good. When the two Nephite colonies of Limhi and Alma returned to Zarahemla, they were received by King Mosiah with open arms. These events may be likened unto us when we return repentant to God, who will receive us with open arms. Our desire is to go to the land of Bountiful, which represents paradise or eternal life, as opposed to going to the land of Desolation, which represents death and hell. You will notice that even the animals left the land northward (land of Desolation) to get food that was available in the land southward (land of Bountiful). Both Zarahemla and Nephi (good versus evil) and Bountiful and Desolation (eternal life versus eternal damnation) are separated by "that which is narrow"—that is, Nephi was separated from Zarahemla by a narrow strip of wilderness, and Bountiful was separated from Desolation by a narrow (small) neck of land.

This analysis is reminiscent of the scripture where we are told that "whosoever will may lay hold upon the word of God, which is quick and powerful, which shall divide

By translating these eight verses of Alma chapter 22 into a spiritual message, which we believe the writer intended, we come up with a marvelous study of how geography is utilized as a type and shadow of the plan of salvation.

asunder all the cunning and the snares and the wiles of the devil, and lead the man of Christ in a *strait and narrow course across that everlasting gulf of misery* which is prepared to engulf the wicked" (Helaman 3:29; emphasis added).

The climax of this geography allegory is that it is only a day and a half's journey for a Nephite (those who are striving to keep the commandments) from the time we are born in the east as represented by the rising of the sun to where we die in the west—or in this case in a "watery grave" in the west sea. The Maya directions are oriented toward the east as opposed to our north orientation, and the east is associated with a new dawn or a new birth. The color for east in Maya terminology is red (the sun or birth), and for west it is black (the night or death).

Amulek, the missionary companion of Alma, drove home this point when he said: "For behold, this life is the time for men to prepare to meet God; yea, behold *the day of this life is the day* for men to perform their labors. And now, as I said unto you before, as ye have had so many witnesses, therefore, I beseech of you that ye *do not procrastinate the day* [or day and a half in this case] of your repentance until the end; for after *this day of life,* which is given us to prepare for eternity, behold, if we do not improve our time while in this life, then cometh the night of darkness wherein there can be no labor performed" (Alma 34:32–33; emphasis added).

The Book of Mormon is another testament of Christ. Its purpose is to bear witness of Christ. The Nephite writers were skilled in the art of dualism—or types and shadows. Here, in only eight verses in Alma 22, Mormon utilizes geography in such a manner as to teach the plan of salvation.

Abinadi reinforced this concept when he told the priests of King Noah, "If ye teach the law of Moses, also teach that it is a shadow of those things which are to come. Teach them that the redemption cometh through Christ the Lord, who is the very Eternal Father" (Mosiah 16:14–15).

We believe that when we talk about the Book of Mormon, it is of the utmost importance to incorporate the concept of types and shadows associated with the history and geography that it defines. In other words, we believe that geography and history lead us to the spiritual and doctrinal messages of the Book of Mormon. Therefore, we echo the words of Abinadi. When we teach the history and geography of the Book of Mormon, we have determined to teach that it is a shadow of the redemption of Christ. Hence, we have labeled this chapter "Geography and the Plan of Salvation."

DUALISM IN THE LIVES OF THE NEPHITE MAYA

Jacob introduces readers to the concept of dualism when he says, "It must needs be, that *there is an opposition in all things.* If not so, . . . righteousness could not be brought to pass, neither wickedness, neither holiness nor misery, neither good nor bad" (2 Nephi 2:11; emphasis added). Further, Jacob alludes to the extent that dualism dominated the thinking of the Nephites when he says, "And if ye shall say there is no law, ye shall also say there is no sin. If ye shall say there is no sin, ye shall also say there is no righteousness. And if there be no righteousness there be no happiness. And if there be no righteousness nor happiness there be no punishment nor misery. And if these things are not there is no God. And if there is no God we are not, neither the earth; for there could have been no creation of things, neither to act nor to be acted upon; wherefore, all things must have vanished away" (2 Nephi 2:13).

Jacob's reasoning mirrors the philosophy of dualism found among Mesoamerican peoples, especially the Maya. As Michael Coe, the renowned Maya archaeologist, says, "A distinctly macabre streak appears in the art of the inhabitants of Tlatilco [1200 BC]. . . . Let it be noted here that dualism, the unity of basically opposed principles such as life and death, *constitutes the very basis* of the later religions of Mexico, no matter how great their complexity. Here we see the origin of the concept" (Coe, *Mexico*, 61; emphasis added).

Whether the concept of dualism among the Nephites originated at Tlatilco is subject to debate. If it did, then Lehi's posterity adopted it from the Jaredite remnant they associated with soon after their arrival in the New World (see Mosiah 8:12). In any event, according to the Mesoamerica

historical record as well as the Book of Mormon record, dualism thinking was a dominant force in the daily lives of both the Nephite Maya and the Lamanite Maya.

An interesting dimension of reading the Book of Mormon is to look intentionally for examples of dualism. They are noticeably pervasive in many chapters. From the words of Jacob, here is a sampling of the religious/spiritual dualism from the Nephite Maya perspective:

good	evil	2 Nephi 2:5
happiness which is affixed	punishment which is affixed	2 Nephi 2:10
righteousness	wickedness	2 Nephi 2:11
holiness	misery	2 Nephi 2:11
good	bad	2 Nephi 2:11
life	death	2 Nephi 2:11
corruption	incorruption	2 Nephi 2:11
happiness	misery	2 Nephi 2:11
sense	insensibility	2 Nephi 2:11
righteousness	sin	2 Nephi 2:12
righteousness/ happiness	punishment/ misery	2 Nephi 2:13
tree of life	forbidden fruit	2 Nephi 2:15
sweet	bitter	2 Nephi 2:15
joy	misery	2 Nephi 2:23
doing good	sinning	2 Nephi 2:23
good	evil	2 Nephi 2:26
liberty and eternal life	captivity and death	2 Nephi 2:27

El Tajin

Tula

MEXICO

Teotihuacan

Tenochtitlan

Calixtlanhuaca

Tizatlan

Malinalco

Cholula

Zochicalco

Zempoala

VERACRUZ

Chalcatzingo

Tres Zapotes

Cerro de les Mesas

Tatocapan

Ahualulco

Napiloa

Agaltepec

Comalcalco

Monte Flor

La Venta

San Mig

Yacunudahui

San Jose Mogote

Rio Chiquito

Tuzantepetl

Mone Negro

Yagul

San Lorenzo

Monte Alban

Lambityeco

Potrero Nuevo

Dainzu

Mitla

Los Cerritos

OAXACA

Piedra Parada

Cerro Grande

Guiengola

San Francisco

Arriba

○	Toltec/Aztec
●	Olmec/Huastec
○	Zapotec/Mixtec

NORTH

25 mi
50 km

CHAPTER 19

The Land Northward

The land on the northward was called Desolation. (Alma 22:31)

꒒꒒꒒꒒꒒꒒꒒꒒꒒꒒꒒꒒꒒꒒꒒꒒꒒꒒꒒꒒꒒꒒꒒꒒꒒꒒꒒꒒꒒

S everal Book of Mormon historical events are associated with the land generally referred to as the "land northward" (see, for example, Alma 22:30–31; Mormon 2:28–29; Mormon 3:5; and Ether 7:6). That is the name given to the area that was the heartland of the ancient Jaredites. The Mulekites landed in the land northward. The Nephites lived in the land northward during a portion of their thousand-year history. The last battles recorded in the Book of Mormon were fought in the land northward. The Nephites called the land northward "Desolation." And the land northward was separated from the land southward by a narrow neck of land.

NATURE OF THE LAND NORTHWARD

By the sheer number of references, one of the most dominant geographical locations in the Book of Mormon is the land northward. It played a central role in the lives of all the

OPPOSITE: We propose that the land northward was separated from the land southward by the Isthmus of Tehuantepec. The land northward is also referred to as the land of Desolation. The first Jaredite capital, called the city of Moron, was located in the land northward. The hills Ramah (Cumorah) and Shim were located in the land northward, and the wicked cities of Jacob and Jacobugath were located in the land northward.

The Nephites may have been left with only a small portion of the land northward, as they probably were left to claim the land along the Gulf Coast of Mexico, which lies north and west of the Coatzacoalcos River and which today constitutes the states of Tabasco and Veracruz, Mexico.

New World people mentioned in the Book of Mormon—that is, the Jaredites, Mulekites, Nephites, and Lamanites. This chapter explores, in a comprehensive approach, the primary references to the land northward, along with references to other geographical locations associated with the word "north."

The Nephites clearly related to the cardinal directions in naming the sites and locations throughout the Book of Mormon. That is, the Nephites distinctively understood and used the cardinal directions of east, west, north, and south. That fact seems evident when we think about the suffix "ward" in "land northward." The "land northward," as this chapter will forcefully point out, was not due north—hence, "northward" is very appropriate as a means of using the cardinal directions to name this geographic area.

In the AD 350 treaty with the Lamanites, the Nephites were left with the land northward: "And the three hundred and forty and ninth year had passed away. And in the three hundred and fiftieth year we made a treaty with the Lamanites and the robbers of Gadianton, in which we did get the lands of our inheritance divided. And the Lamanites did give unto us *the land northward*, yea, even to the narrow passage which led into the land southward. And we did give unto the Lamanites all the land southward" (Mormon 2:28–29; emphasis added).

In reality, the Nephites may have been left with only a small portion of the land northward, as they probably were left to claim the land along the Gulf Coast of Mexico, which lies north and west of the Coatzacoalcos River and which today constitutes the states of Tabasco and Veracruz, Mexico. For centuries previously, this area was inhabited by the Olmecs—or the Jaredites—who are now considered to be the mother civilization of the Americas. At the time of the AD 350 land-division treaty, the Jaredite civilization had been destroyed for more than six hundred years; and their buildings were left in ruins. The Jaredite lands were the logical place for the Nephites to claim. From a Book of Mormon perspective, the area is referred to as "Desolation." The term "Desolation" comes from Jaredite ruins that predated the Nephite occupation of the area. Speaking of the land northward, the historian Mormon says, "And now no part of the land was desolate, save it were for timber; but because of the greatness of the destruction of the people who had before inhabited the land it was called desolate" (Helaman 3:6).

Ten years after the AD 350 treaty, or in the year AD 360, the Lamanites were determined to annihilate the people called Nephites. The Lamanite king, whose name was Yax Nuun Ayiin,[1] sent an epistle to the historian-prophet military leader, Mormon, warning him of the event. Mormon wrote, "And it came to pass that I did cause my people that they should gather themselves together at the land Desolation, to a city which was in the borders, by the narrow pass which led into the land southward" (Mormon 3:5).

The greater land northward was located north and west (northward) of the Isthmus of Tehuantepec and virtually covered not only the states of Veracruz and Tabasco but also the states of Mexico that are now known as Oaxaca, Puebla, and Guerrero.

1. Simon Martin and Nikolai Grube, *Chronicle of the Maya Kings and Queens: Deciphering the Dynasties of the Ancient Maya* (London: Thames and Hudson, 2000), 32. See also various Internet sites, using "Yax Nuun Ayiin."

Exploring the Lands of the Book of Mormon

FIGURE 19–1: The Book of Mormon distinguishes between the "land northward" (Veracruz) where the Olmecs (Jaredites) lived and the "land which was northward" (Alma 50:29; Alma 63:4) or "the northernmost part of the land" (3 Nephi 7:12) where Jacob established a secret combination society in the first century BC (Mexico).

Furthermore, the land northward probably extended into what is now known as the Mexico City valley, where Mexico City is located. As such, we are justified in identifying the Mexico City valley as "the northernmost part of the land." "Therefore, Jacob seeing that their enemies were more numerous than they, he being the king of the band, therefore he commanded his people that they should take their flight into *the northernmost part of the land,* and there build up unto themselves a kingdom, until they were joined by dissenters, (for he flattered them that there would be many dissenters) and they become sufficiently strong to contend with the tribes of the people; and they did so" (3 Nephi 7:12; emphasis added).

In this model, the land northward is bordered by two oceans—the Gulf Coast of Mexico, which is part of the Atlantic Ocean that reaches from there to the east coast of Mexico, and the Pacific Ocean, which runs along the borders of present-day Salina Cruz, Acapulco, and Zihuatenejo on the west coast of Mexico.

Justification for placing the land northward in that area is as follows:

1. The ancient Jaredite culture lived in the land northward, which was very heavily populated. Therefore, evidence must support a heavily populated area during Jaredite times: "And they built a great city by the narrow neck of land, by the place where the sea divides the land. And they did preserve the land southward for a wilderness, to get game. And the *whole face of the land northward was covered with inhabitants*" (Ether 10:20–21; emphasis added).

The Gulf Coast of Mexico, which primarily consists of the states of Veracruz and Tabasco today, was very heavily populated during Jaredite times. Referring to this area, archaeologist Michael Coe says: "The most ancient Mexican civilization is that called 'Olmec.' For many years, archaeologists had known about small jade sculptures and other objects in a distinct and powerful style that emphasized human infants with snarling, jaguar-like features. Most of these could be traced to the sweltering Gulf Coast plain, the region of southern Veracruz and neighboring Tabasco, just west of the Maya area."[2]

2. Michael D. Coe, *Mexico* (New York: Frederick A. Praeger Publishers, 1962), 83.

2. The land northward must show evidence that a high culture with the presence of a written language existed during the Middle Preclassic Period (1500 BC–600 BC). That high culture is evidenced in many statements associated with the Jaredites. For example: "And they were exceedingly industrious, and they did buy and sell and traffic one with another, that they might get gain. . . . And they did make all manner of weapons of war. And they did work all manner of work of exceedingly curious workmanship" (Ether 10:22, 27).

During the years of 1938–41, Matthew Stirling excavated a number of the large Olmec heads located along the coast of Veracruz. These Olmec heads, along with other monuments such as those discovered and excavated by Michael Coe at the site of San Lorenzo, are evidence of the fact that the early settlers, the Jaredite-Olmec culture, worked all manner of work of "curious workmanship"—and they had a written language.

3. The Book of Mormon reports that the ancient inhabitants who lived in the land northward came from the great tower when the languages were confounded. They arrived in present-day Mexico, which they labeled a "promised land." Both tradition and archaeology support this thesis: "Which Jared came forth with his brother and their families, with some others and their families, from the great tower, at the time the Lord confounded the language of the people, and swore in his wrath that they should be scattered upon all the face of the earth; and according to the word of the Lord the people were scattered" (Ether 1:33).

The history of Ixtlilxochitl states the following:

> Everything in the earth was covered by water including the highest mountain called Caxtolmolictli, which is 15 cubits high.
>
> To this they recorded other events, such as how, after the flood, a few people who had escaped the destruction inside a Toptlipetlacalli, which interpreted means an enclosed ark, began again to multiply upon the earth.

The ancient Jaredite culture lived in the land northward, which was very heavily populated. Therefore, evidence must support a heavily populated area during Jaredite times.

Exploring the Lands of the Book of Mormon

FIGURE 19–2: See chapter 5, "The Olmec (Jaredite) Culture," for a discussion on the ancient Olmecs in comparison with the Jaredites. Large Olmec monuments carved out of basalt stone from the Tuxtla Mountains of Veracruz, like the one shown here, demonstrate a high sophistication of workmanship dating to the middle Jaredite time period. Notice the massive jaguar headdress. (Photo courtesy of Sheryl Lee Wilson)

After the earth began again to be populated, they built a Zacualli very high and strong, which means the *very high tower,* to protect themselves against a second destruction of the world.

As time elapsed, their language became confounded, such that they did not understand one another; and they were scattered to all parts of the world.

The Tultecas, consisting of seven men and their wives, *were able to understand one another,* and they came to this land, having first crossed many lands and waters, living in caves and passing through great tribulations. Upon their arrival here, *they discovered that it was a very good and fertile* land.[3]

A stela, or stone monument, taken from the site of La Venta and now situated in the outdoor La Venta Museum in Villahermosa contains inscriptions that perhaps depict that first voyage. It is a sculpture showing people traveling a great distance—from the west. They traveled in the ocean and were protected against a shark or a "sea monster," which is reminiscent of Moroni's statement in the book of Ether: "And thus they were driven forth; and no monster of the sea could break them, neither whale that could mar them; and they did have light continually, whether it was above the water or under the water" (Ether 6:10).

4. The Book of Mormon reports that the Jaredites destroyed themselves in a great civil war in the land northward—sometime between 600 and 121 BC. Archaeological evidence, as well as tradition, also supports this report, demonstrating the destruction to be around 300 BC. Moroni tells us the following:

3. Ixtlilxochitl:4–8; emphasis added. See chapter 11, "Fernando de Alva Ixtlilxochitl."

Wherefore, they were for the space of four years gathering together the people, that they might get all who were upon the face of the land, and that they might receive all the strength which it was possible that they could receive.

The Book of Mormon land northward requires a land southward suitable to hunt wild animals.

And it came to pass that when they were all gathered together, every one to the army which he would, with their wives and their children—both men, women and children being armed with weapons of war, having shields, and breastplates, and head-plates, and being clothed after the manner of war—they did march forth one against another to battle; and they fought all that day, and conquered not. . . .

And it came to pass that when they had all fallen by the sword, save it were Coriantumr and Shiz, behold Shiz had fainted with the loss of blood.

And it came to pass that when Coriantumr had leaned upon his sword, that he rested a little, he smote off the head of Shiz.

And it came to pass that after he had smitten off the head of Shiz, that Shiz raised up on his hands and fell; and after that he had struggled for breath, he died.

And it came to pass that Coriantumr fell to the earth, and became as if he had no life. (Ether 15:14–15, 29–32)

Speaking of the ancient ruins of La Venta, Coe says: "La Venta was deliberately destroyed in ancient times. Its fall was certainly violent, as 24 out of 40 sculptured monuments were intentionally mutilated. This probably occurred in the beginning of Late Formative times, around 400–300 BC."[4]

4. Coe, *Mexico*, 90.

5. The Book of Mormon land northward requires a land southward suitable to hunt wild animals. The area south and east of the Isthmus of Tehuantepec is a wilderness area consisting of the state of Chiapas, Mexico, and its neighbors. Even today, this area is a natural habitat for wild animals, including deer, ocelot, wild boars, wild cows, jaguars, birds, serpents, and smaller animals of various types.

6. The land northward in the Jaredite record requires such landmarks as the waters of Ripliancum, the land of Moron, and an eastern seaboard. The geographical and topographical configurations of the area proposed as the land northward fit all of these requirements.

The Oaxaca valley is a suitable candidate for the land of Moron in Jaredite times. The great Papaloapan water basin, flowing down from the Puebla and Veracruz Mountains and emptying into the Gulf of Mexico, is very suitable for the distance required as well as for its position in relation to the last battle for the waters of Ripliancum.

Toward the end of the Jaredite civilization, the army of Shiz was pursuing the army of Coriantumr: "And it came to pass that he came to the waters of Ripliancum, which, by interpretation, is large, or to exceed all; wherefore, when they came to these waters they pitched their tents; and Shiz also pitched his tents near unto them; and therefore on the morrow they did come to battle" (Ether 15:8).

The fact that the Gulf Coast of Mexico forms a northeastern seaboard, moving from Oaxaca, justifies the geographical requirement of the land of Moron and the northeastern seaboard.

7. The land northward, during the Nephite time period, requires a land called Desolation, where there were ruins of buildings and a lack of timber. The area in discussion supports that thesis:

> La Venta was undoubtedly the most powerful and holy place in the Olmec heartland, sacred because of its very inaccessibility, but other great Olmec centres
>
> also flourished in the Middle Formative [Period]. About 100 miles north-west of La Venta lies Tres Zapotes, in a setting of low hills above the swampy basin formed by the Papaloapan and San Juan Rivers. It comprises about 50 earthen mounds stretched out along the bank of a stream for two miles. . . .
>
> About midway between Tres Zapotes and La Venta is the San Lorenzo group, comprising three sites, San Lorenzo, Rio Chiquito, and Potrero Nuevo. All are located on a ridge of high land near the flat bottoms of the Coatzacoalcos River, and are, like most Olmec sites, complexes of earthen mounds enclosing courts.[5]

FIGURE 19–3: Southward from the site of La Venta, Tabasco, shown here, are the mountains and forests of the state of Chiapas where many wild animals exist today. During the days of King Lib about 1000 BC, he being a great hunter, the land southward was established as a place to hunt wild animals. "They did preserve the land southward for a wilderness, to get game" (Ether 10:21). (Photo courtesy of Sheryl Lee Wilson)

5. Coe, *Mexico*, 91.

8. The land northward requires that a narrow, or small, neck of land separate the land northward from the land southward: "And now, it was only the distance of a day and a half's journey for a Nephite, on the line Bountiful and the land Desolation, from the east to the west sea; and thus the land of Nephi and the land of Zarahemla were nearly surrounded by water, there being *a small neck of land* between the land northward and the land southward" (Alma 22:32; italics added).

The Isthmus of Tehuantepec, located in southeastern Mexico, meets the requirement for the narrow neck of land (see chapter 23, "Things That Are Narrow").

9. The land northward must provide a means, during Nephite times, for the people to flee from the hands of the Lamanites from the land southward. The Isthmus of Tehuantepec separates the state of Oaxaca from the state of Chiapas. The pass through the mountains extending through the southeastern portion of the state of Oaxaca to the state of Veracruz appears to be the only legitimate route that meets this requirement. The land northward meets this criterion, as the road moves northward along the Pacific

corridor and then runs directly north between two mountain ranges to connect with the Gulf of Mexico on the Atlantic side. Thus, a group of people living in the area designated as Zarahemla on the proposed map would be able to escape from the Lamanites coming up from the south. Mormon says, "Therefore the Lamanites could have no more possessions only in the land of Nephi, and the wilderness round about. Now this was wisdom in the Nephites—as the Lamanites were an enemy to them, they would not suffer their afflictions on every hand, and also that they might have a country whither they might flee, according to their desires" (Alma 22:34).

10. The land northward must have an area of lakes suitable for a large migration of people to extend themselves. The land in question meets that requirement. The Mexico City area was once a land of large lakes. The ruins of Teotihuacan give ample evidence that people lived in the area during Nephite Book of Mormon times. The Book of Mormon contains three accounts where people moved or attempted to move to the "land which was northward."

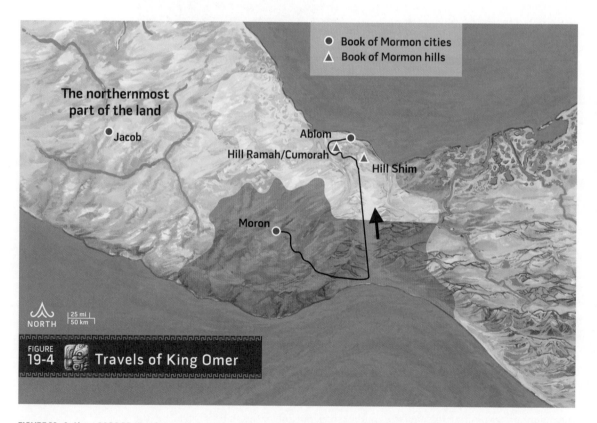

FIGURE 19–4: About 2000 BC, King Omer was warned in a dream to depart out of the land of Moron. In the course of his travels, he passed by both the hill Shim and the hill Ramah (Cumorah) and settled in a place called Ablom, which was east by the seashore (see Ether 9:3). The distance from Oaxaca to Veracruz is about 250 miles through the isthmus. Even with today's travel by bus, travel time is seven hours—from Oaxaca (Moron) to Lerdo (Ablom).

Exploring the Lands of the Book of Mormon

Account 1 (68 BC)

Morianton put it into their hearts that they should flee to the land which was northward, which was covered with large bodies of water, and take possession of the *land which was northward*. (Alma 50:29; emphasis added)

Account 2 (55 BC)

And it came to pass that in the thirty and seventh year of the reign of the judges, there was a large company of men, even to the amount of five thousand and four hundred men, with their wives and their children, departed out of the land of Zarahemla into *the land which was northward*. . . .

And it came to pass in the thirty and ninth year of the reign of the judges, [53 BC] Shiblon died also, and Corianton had gone forth to *the land northward* in a ship, to carry forth provisions unto the people who had gone forth into that land. (Alma 63:4, 10; emphasis added; see also Helaman 3:3–12)

Account 3 (AD 29)

[Jacob] commanded his people that they should take their flight into the *northernmost part of the land,* and there build up unto themselves a kingdom. (3 Nephi 7:12; emphasis added)

SCRIPTURAL OVERVIEW

Book of Mormon passages that refer to the "land northward," "the land north," and the "land which was northward," with associated maps and commentary, are as follows:

The first time we are exposed to the term "the land northward" is in the most detailed geography chapter in the Book of Mormon, Alma 22:27–35.

These nine verses describe the Lamanite-Nephite boundaries in the first century BC, from a Lamanite perspective, with intermittent comments from Mormon. Alma 22 mentions the term "land northward" three times and the term "Desolation" two times. "Far northward" and "possessions in the north" are each mentioned once.

Verse 31 states: "Thus the land on the northward was called *Desolation*" (emphasis added).

Verse 32 states: "There being a small neck of land between the *land northward* and the land southward" (emphasis added).

And verse 33 adds: "That they might not overrun the *land northward*" (emphasis added).

On the Mesoamerica map, the land northward encompasses the Preclassic population centers of the Mexico valley, the Oaxaca valley, the Pacific coast of Mexico, and the Gulf Coast of Mexico. The Gulf of Tehuantepec forms the southeastern border.

The first time we are exposed to the term "the land northward" is in the most detailed geography chapter in the Book of Mormon, Alma 22:27–35. These nine verses describe the Lamanite-Nephite boundaries in the first century BC, from a Lamanite perspective, with intermittent comments from Mormon.

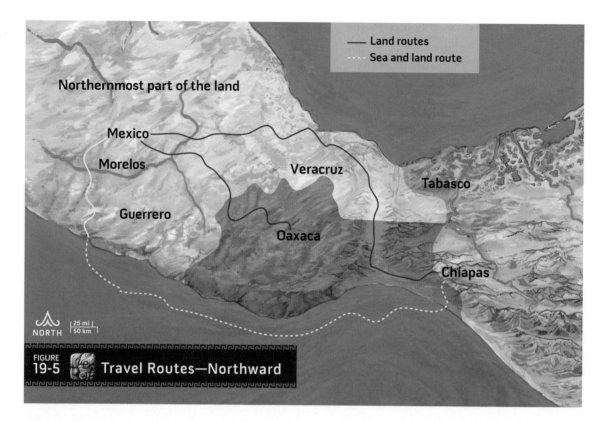

FIGURE 19–5: This map shows travel routes from Chiapas (land of Zarahemla) to Mexico City (northernmost part of the land). The Veracruz route involves crossing over the Papaloapan water basin. The Oaxaca route is extremely difficult traveling through high and rugged mountain ranges. The Guerrero route involves traveling a good portion of the distance by boat (dotted line). The distance from Chiapas to Mexico is over six hundred miles.

THE LAND DESOLATION

Clearly, the first century BC Nephites also called the land northward "Desolation," as stated in Alma 22:31: "the land *on the northward* was called Desolation" (emphasis added).

Earlier in the same chapter, verse 30, we are given a geographical reference for the land Desolation that is a little difficult to interpret. The verse refers to a land, or state, that was north of the possessions of the Nephites and that bordered the land Desolation: "And it [presumably Bountiful] bordered upon the land which they [the first century BC Nephites], called Desolation, it [presumably Desolation] being so far northward that it [presumably Desolation] came into the land which had been peopled and been destroyed, of whose bones we have spoken, which was discovered by the people of Zarahemla, it [presumably Desolation] being the place of their [Mulekites'] first landing" (Alma 22:30).

In summary, *Desolation* is either synonymous with the land northward or at least refers to the section along the Gulf Coast that was occupied by the 1500 to 300 BC Jaredites (Olmecs).

THE LIMHI EXPEDITION

About 121 BC, the Limhi expedition discovered the bones of people and the ruins of the buildings of these people who are referred to in Alma 22:30 above:

> And they were lost in the wilderness for the space of many days, yet they were diligent, and found not the land of Zarahemla but returned to this land, having traveled in a land among many waters, having discovered a land which was covered with bones of men, and of beasts, and was also covered with ruins of buildings of every kind, having discovered a land which had been peopled with a people who were as numerous as the hosts of Israel.
>
> And for a testimony that the things that they had said are true they have brought twenty-four plates which are filled with engravings, and they are of pure gold.
>
> And behold, also, they have brought breastplates, which are large, and they are of brass and of copper, and are perfectly sound.
>
> And again, they have brought swords, the hilts thereof have perished, and the blades thereof were cankered with rust; and there is no one in the land that is able to interpret the language or the engravings that are on the plates. Therefore I said unto thee: Canst thou translate? (Mosiah 8:8–11)

MULEKITES LANDED IN THE LAND NORTHWARD

From Alma 22:30, we also learn that the Mulekites landed in the land northward/ Desolation. Helaman 6:10 affirms that "the Lord did bring Mulek into the *land north*" (emphasis added). We must also remember that the name "Desolation" is a term used by the first century BC Nephites to denote a land that was northward of the narrow neck and that was inhabited by an ancient civilization whose cities had become uninhabited. "Desolation" in the Book of Mormon does not mean a desolate area: "And now no part of the land was desolate, save it were for timber; but because of the greatness of the destruction of the people who had before inhabited the land it was called desolate" (Helaman 3:6).

Indeed, the area proposed as the first century BC Nephite Desolation is a land that today is full of banana plantations, pineapple fields, tobacco plantations, and mango groves. That is, the fertile Gulf Coast of Mexico is proposed as the land of Desolation. The area includes the Mexico states of Veracruz and Tabasco.

Desolation is either synonymous with the land northward or at least refers to the section along the Gulf Coast that was occupied by the 1500 to 300 BC Jaredites (Olmecs).

SUMMARY OF ADDITIONAL SCRIPTURES

Additional scriptures that refer to the land northward, the land Desolation, the land north, north, land which was northward, northerly, and northward are those that follow.

Alma 46:17 (73 BC)—The Land Desolation

And it came to pass that when he [Moroni] had poured out his soul to God, he named all the land which was south of the *land Desolation,* yea, and in fine, all the land, both on the north and on the south—A chosen land, and the land of liberty. (emphasis added)

As shown, Moroni, the chief military commander of the first century BC Nephites, proclaimed the land described in verse 17 above as the Nephites' "chosen land, and the land of liberty" (Alma 46:17).

This scripture is consistent with the decision to make the land northward and the land Desolation synonymous with each other to the extent that the land northward/ Desolation constituted the western boundary for the first century BC Nephites. The words in verse 17, "all the land, both on the north and on the south—A chosen land, and the land of liberty," may mean one of the following:

1. A general, nongeographical statement,

2. The land northward/Desolation's being designated as part of the chosen land, or

3. The immediate land area in the land of Zarahemla where chief commander Moroni fought for the next sixteen years (see Alma 46–62; ca. 73 BC–57 BC).

If the third definition is the case, Moroni was probably labeling, as a land of liberty, all the Nephite territory from the "narrow strip of wilderness" to the "narrow neck of land." This area includes the present-day Mexican states of Chiapas, Quintana Roo, Yucatan, and Campeche and also includes Peten, Guatemala, and the small country of Belize. This option appears to be the most viable because the scripture implies that the land of Zarahemla was south of Desolation, which is the case (see figure 19–6). This act of declaration by Moroni added the entire east wilderness to the land of Zarahemla, both "on the north and on the south."

Alma 46:22—The Land Northward

Now this was the covenant which they made, and they cast their garments at the feet of Moroni, saying: We covenant with our God, that we shall be destroyed, even as our brethren in the land northward, if we shall fall into transgression; yea, he may cast us at the feet of our enemies, even as we have cast our garments at thy feet to be trodden under foot, if we shall fall into transgression.

> The land of Zarahemla was south of Desolation. Moroni's "land of liberty" declaration added the entire east wilderness to the land of Zarahemla, both "on the north and on the south."

The northernmost part of the land

The Land Northward

Land of Moron

Land of Desolation

Land of Zarahemla

Moroni and his army

Nothern Maya Lowlands

Land on the North

Land on the South

Southern Maya Lowlands

NORTH
50 mi
100 km

FIGURE 19-6 Land Northward vs. "on the north"

FIGURE 19–6: Mormon distinguishes between the land on the north and the land northward. "All the land, both on the north and on the south" (the land that was south of the land of Desolation) appears to refer to the Maya northern lowlands and the Maya southern lowlands, as shown on the map. This area was declared to be a land of liberty by the military leader, Moroni (see Alma 46:17).

This verse seems to justify further the position that Moroni was declaring Nephite territory (Yucatan, Peten, and so forth) as a land of liberty. The content of the verse correlates with Mormon's comments about the land northward in Alma 22:34 and Mormon 2:28–29. In the former, we are told about the wisdom of the Nephites in having an escape route into the land northward. The latter talks about the AD 350 treaty (440 years after the first statement) in which the Nephites did indeed have to move into the land northward. All three of the above scriptures seem to be referring to the same land mass:

> Therefore the Lamanites could have no more possessions only in the land of Nephi, and the wilderness round about. Now this was wisdom in the Nephites—as the Lamanites were an enemy to them, they would not suffer their afflictions on every hand, and also that they might have a country whither they might flee, according to their desires. (Alma 22:34)

And the three hundred and forty and ninth year had passed away. And in the three hundred and fiftieth year we made a treaty with the Lamanites and the robbers of Gadianton, in which we did get the lands of our inheritance divided.

And the Lamanites did give unto us the land northward, yea, even to the narrow passage which led into the land southward. And we did give unto the Lamanites all the land southward. (Mormon 2:28–29)

Alma 50:9—North

And it came to pass that when Moroni had driven all the Lamanites out of the east wilderness, which was *north* of the lands of their own [Lamanites'] possessions, he caused that the inhabitants who were in the land of Zarahemla and in

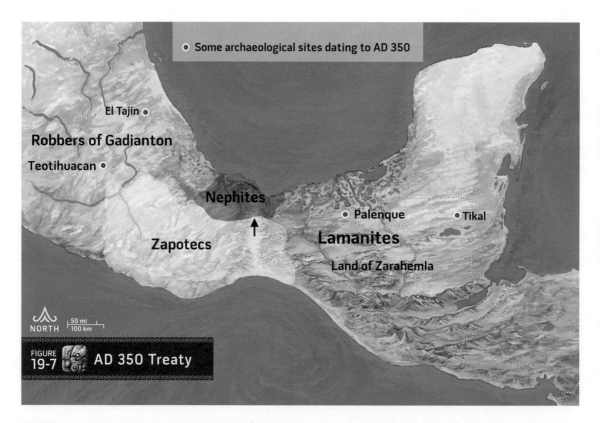

FIGURE 19–7: "The Lamanites did give unto us the land northward, yea, even to the narrow passage, which led into the land southward" (Mormon 2:29). In the AD 350 treaty, the Nephites lost control of the land of Zarahemla and were given the ancient Jaredite land of Desolation. We have no indication that the Nephites were given the greater land northward, or Teotihuacan, because that area was controlled by secret combinations (see chapter 8, "The Teotihuacan Culture").

Exploring the Lands of the Book of Mormon

the land round about should go forth into the east wilderness, even to the borders by the seashore, and possess the land. (emphasis added)

In this scripture, the term "north" is used. This wording in itself suggests that the scripture is not referring to the area northward just discussed. When we read Alma 50:9 in its proper context, we realize that this "north" is referring to a section of land that is *north* of the Lamanite lands (land of Nephi) and *east* of Zarahemla, thus causing the area referred to above actually to be in the land southward.

Alma 50:11—Land Northward

. . . the Nephites possessing all the *land northward,* yea, even all the land which was northward of the land Bountiful, according to their pleasure. (emphasis added)

Like the references in Alma 22, "land northward" in Alma 50:11 appears to refer to the land northward of the Isthmus of Tehuantepec on the Gulf Coast. Conveniently, the Nephites claimed the area along the Gulf Coast as their territory, as apparently it had not been reoccupied since the great Jaredite (Olmec) destruction two hundred years earlier. A good possibility also exists that sites like Monte Alban in the state of Oaxaca (land northward) were controlled by the first century BC Nephites. The archaeological evidence at Monte Alban shows that a minority civilization gained control during this time period, quite possibly the Nephite-Mulekite fusion (see chapter 7, "The Zapotec [Mulekite-Nephite] Culture").

Apparently, the Nephites had access to the limited land northward, which may have included both the states of Veracruz and Oaxaca.

Alma 50:31—Land Northward

And it came to pass that she [Morianton's maidservant] fled, and came over to the camp of Moroni, and told Moroni all things concerning the matter, and also concerning their intentions to flee into the *land northward.* (emphasis added)

Morianton's intention was to flee into the land northward. Because Morianton was near the land of Lehi, which was near the east sea (Caribbean) in northern Belize, Morianton would have had to travel from the present-day city of Chetumal to Palenque to Tabasco and then to Veracruz. He may also have had the intention of moving on into the Mexico valley.

Alma 50:33–34—Land Northward

Therefore Moroni sent an army, with their camp, to head the people of Morianton, to stop their flight into the *land northward.*

A good possibility exists that sites like Monte Alban in the state of Oaxaca (land northward) were controlled by the first century BC Nephites. The archaeological evidence at Monte Alban shows that a minority civilization gained control during this time period.

And it came to pass that they did not head them until they had come to the borders of the land Desolation; and there they did head them, by the narrow pass which led by the sea into the *land northward,* yea, by the sea, on the west and on the east. (emphasis added)

Alma 51:30; Alma 52:2—Land Northward

And it came to pass that he headed Amalickiah also, as he was marching forth with his numerous army that he might take possession of the land Bountiful, and also the *land northward.* (Alma 51:30; emphasis added)

And now, when the Lamanites saw this they were affrighted; and they abandoned their design in marching into the *land northward,* and retreated with all their army into the city of Mulek, and sought protection in their fortifications. (Alma 52:2; emphasis added)

Amalickiah's intention seemed to be to take possession of the land (state) of Bountiful and also the "land northward." The Lamanites' desire to want to move into Tabasco and Veracruz and the Mexico valley areas at this early date (64 BC) may seem a little inconsistent. However, the ambitious Amalickiah may have been determined to be the ruler of all of Mesoamerica, which then justifies the above thinking.

Another interpretation may be that the "land northward" in this instance is the Yucatan, although this supposition is doubtful because the Yucatan was probably part of the land (state) of Bountiful and because the scripture says "the land Bountiful, and also the land northward."

Alma 52:9—Land Northward

And he [Moroni] also sent orders unto him [Teancum] that he should fortify the land Bountiful, and secure the narrow pass which led into the *land northward,* lest the Lamanites should obtain that point and should have power to harass them on every side. (emphasis added)

Let's review the circumstances. Moroni sent orders to Teancum, who had been leading the military campaign in the east wilderness (Peten) and in the land (state) of Bountiful (Yucatan/Quintana Roo and Campeche). He told Teancum to maintain that quarter of the land: "And Moroni also sent unto him, desiring him that he would be faithful in maintaining that quarter of the land, and that he would seek every opportunity to scourge the Lamanites in that quarter, as much as was in his power, that perhaps he might take again by stratagem or some other way those cities which had been taken out of their hands; and that he also would fortify and strengthen the cities round about, which had not fallen into the hands of the Lamanites" (Alma 52:10).

Some readers may disagree with this analysis on the grounds that the area of Quintana Roo-Yucatan-Campeche-Tabasco is too large of an area to control. We must remember, however, that that is exactly what happened historically in Mesoamerica. The Maya nation extended all the way from the Isthmus of Tehuantepec (narrow neck) to the Yucatan to the Peten and into Central America.

Moroni was fortifying the area along the west sea (Pacific Ocean-Gulf of Tehuantepec). As mentioned on other occasions, the Nephites needed to prevent the Lamanites from going through the narrow pass (Isthmus of Tehuantepec) into the land northward (Veracruz-Mexico). Apparently, Moroni was instructing Teancum to fortify the land Bountiful (Yucatan-Campeche-Tabasco), which would automatically "secure the narrow pass which led into the land northward." By preventing the Lamanites from capturing the city Bountiful (in the Yucatan) and other cities in the land (state) of Bountiful and by Moroni's fortifying the pass in the southwest, the Nephites ensured the security of the narrow pass.[6]

Some readers may disagree with this analysis on the grounds that the area of Quintana Roo-Yucatan-Campeche-Tabasco is too large of an area to control. We must remember, however, that that is exactly what happened historically in Mesoamerica. The Maya nation extended all the way from the Isthmus of Tehuantepec (narrow neck) to the Yucatan to the Peten and into Central America.

Alma 56:22—Northward

And it came to pass that we kept spies out round about, to watch the movements of the Lamanites, that they might not pass us by night nor by day to make an attack upon our other cities which were on the *northward*. (emphasis added)

In this instance, Helaman was relating the battles of his young warriors to Moroni. Helaman had arrived in Judea, which was possibly in the area of present-day Tapachula, Chiapas, Mexico. The ancient ruins of Izapa are near Tapachula. Helaman and the Nephite captains were fighting in the western sector.

Alma 63:4–7; 9–10—Land Which Was Northward-Land Northward

And it came to pass that in the thirty and seventh year of the reign of the judges, there was a large company of men, even to the amount of five thousand and four hundred men, with their wives and their children, departed out of the land of Zarahemla into the *land which was northward.*

And it came to pass that Hagoth, he being an exceedingly curious man, therefore he went forth and built him an exceedingly large ship, on the borders of the land Bountiful, by the land Desolation, and launched it forth into the west sea, *by the narrow neck which led into the land northward.*

And behold, there were many of the Nephites who did enter therein and did sail forth with much provisions, and also many women and children; and they took their course northward. And thus ended the thirty and seventh year.

And in the thirty and eighth year, this man built other ships. And the first ship did also return, and many more people did enter into it; and they also took

6. The parentheses are the authors' and are to be considered as proposals.

By preventing the Lamanites from capturing the city Bountiful (in the Yucatan) and other cities in the land (state) of Bountiful and by Moroni's fortifying the pass in the southwest, the Nephites ensured the security of the narrow pass.

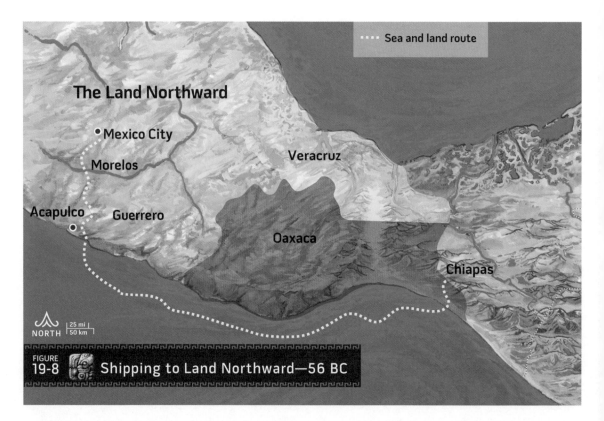

FIGURE 19–8: "The first ship did also return, and many people did enter into it; and they took much provisions, and set out again to the land northward" (Alma 63:7). The shipping lane from Chiapas to Guerrero and then inland to Mexico's altiplano cut out considerable land travel, as opposed to going the longer route through Veracruz. Today, the travel time by bus from Tehuantepec to Mexico through Veracruz is ten hours. From Acapulco, Guerrero, to Mexico is three hours.

much provisions, and set out again to the *land northward*. (Alma 63:4–7; emphasis added)

And it came to pass that in this year there were many people who went forth *into the land northward*. And thus ended the thirty and eighth year.

And it came to pass in the thirty and ninth year of the reign of the judges, Shiblon died also, and Corianton had gone forth *to the land northward* in a ship, to carry forth provisions unto the people who had gone forth into that land. (Alma 63:9–10; emphasis added)

These verses give an account of a man named Hagoth, who launched a ship in the west sea by the borders of the land Bountiful (in the land southward) and Desolation (land northward). About 50 BC, a large group of people had migrated into the "land which was northward" (Mexico valley and west coast). Provisions were taken by boat to the Nephite colonists in the land northward. Some ships never returned. Corianton, the son of Alma, had gone into the "land which was northward."

From our perspective, the west sea is the Gulf of Tehuantepec. The "land which was northward" in this instance is the Mexico valley and the west coast of Mexico.

Helaman 6:9–10, 12—Land North-North

They did have an exceeding plenty of gold, and of silver, and of all manner of precious metals, both in the land south and in the *land north*.

Now the land south was called Lehi, and the *land north* was called Mulek, which was after the son of Zedekiah; for the Lord did bring Mulek into the *land north,* and Lehi into the land south. . . .

They did raise grain in abundance, both in the *north* and in the south; and they did flourish exceedingly, both in the *north* and in the south. (emphasis added)

On this occasion, the Book of Mormon terminology changes from "land northward-land southward" to "land north-land south."

We can interpret these "lands" in the perspective of Mesoamerica in at least two ways. We will try to explain the two alternatives as clearly as possible.

Option 1. To be consistent with the overall context of the Book of Mormon, we can assume that the "land north" in the scriptures above is synonymous with the term "land northward" that is used throughout the Book of Mormon text.

If the Gulf of Mexico is in the Jaredite heartland, then we can assume that Mulek landed off the shores of Veracruz, Mexico. Alma 22:30 says that the area in which the remains of the Jaredites were found is the same area where the Mulekites first landed. If this is the case, then the land north where the Lord brought Mulek is in the land northward.

This option also suggests that Mulekites were living in the areas of Veracruz-Oaxaca-Mexico (land north-northward) during the time period of 26 BC. The archaeological record supports strong settlements in the land northward (Veracruz-Oaxaca-Puebla-Mexico) during this Preclassic Period. Sites such as Monte Alban, Teotihuacan, and Cholula were all active city centers prior to the coming of Christ (see Helaman 6:9–10, 12).

Option 2. A second approach to understanding the Helaman 6 scriptures that make reference to the "land north" is to consider it to be representative of lowland Maya. In this case, then, the land south is southern lowland Maya.

If we follow this analogy, we maintain a consistency in the overall directions in the Book of Mormon. That is, the land northward is a different area than the land north referred to in Helaman 6 (see figure 19–6).

If the Gulf of Mexico is in the Jaredite heartland, then we can assume that Mulek landed off the shores of Veracruz, Mexico.

An abundance of Preclassic archaeological sites is found in the Peten and in Yucatan to satisfy the population requirements of this area as the land north.

From the Book of Mormon, we know that sometime after the Mulekites landed in the land northward (Desolation), they (or at least a certain colony of the Mulekites) journeyed into the land southward to Zarahemla. Nevertheless, Zarahemla is still north of the land of Lehi-Nephi. Hence, the Lord brought Lehi into the land south (Guatemala) and Mulek into the land north (Peten-Chiapas-Yucatan).

A sixteenth-century document called *The Title of the Lords of Totonicapan* speaks of a colony of Jews who settled around the Lake of Campeche and subsequently migrated up both the Usumacinta and Tabasco (Grijalva) Rivers where they established city centers. One of these two rivers was probably the river Sidon in the Book of Mormon. For the reasons given in chapter 26, "Bodies of Water," we firmly believe that the Grijalva—not the Usumacinta—is the Book of Mormon's river Sidon.

If the Maya lowlands (Peten, Chiapas, Belize, Yucatan, Quintana Roo, Campeche, and Tabasco) is the general area where the Mulekites lived, then this area would most likely be referred to as the place where "the Lord brought Mulek into the land north."

This thinking also explains why the city of Mulek mentioned in Alma 51–53 would be located on the coast of the Yucatan Peninsula or in Belize.

Helaman 7:1–3—Land Northward

Behold, now it came to pass in the sixty and ninth year of the reign of the judges [about 23 BC] over the people of the Nephites, that Nephi, the son of Helaman, returned to the land of Zarahemla from the *land northward*.

For he had been forth among the people who were in the *land northward*, and did preach the word of God unto them, and did prophesy many things unto them;

And they did reject all his words. (emphasis added)

Consistent with the Book of Mormon text, the land northward mentioned in these verses was probably where the present-day Mexican states of Veracruz, Oaxaca, Puebla, and Mexico are located.

Ixtlilxochitl makes an interesting statement that is reminiscent of the lack of success that Nephi, the son of Helaman, had in the land northward. Ixtlilxochitl states that the white god Quetzalcoatl taught his doctrine in Cholula (near Puebla/land northward), where Quetzalcoatl had very little success.[7]

3 Nephi 3:24—Land Northward

Now Lachoneus did cause that they should gather themselves together in the land southward, because of the great curse which was upon the *land northward*. (emphasis added)

A sixteenth-century document called *The Title of the Lords of Totonicapan* speaks of a colony of Jews who settled around the Lake of Campeche and subsequently migrated up both the Usumacinta and Tabasco (Grijalva) Rivers where they established city centers.

7. See Ixtlilxochitl:39; see chapter 11, "Fernando de Alva Ixtlilxochitl."

About eighteen years after the birth of Christ, the Nephites were severely persecuted by the Gadianton robbers. The leader of the Gadianton robbers was a man named Giddianhi. He wrote an epistle to Lachoneus demanding that Lachoneus surrender and give up the Nephite cities, lands, and possessions.

Lachoneus, a just man and the chief judge of the Nephites, sent a proclamation to his people admonishing them to gather together in one body to defend themselves against the robbers. The Nephites prepared themselves in such a manner that they had seven years of provisions; and they abandoned their cities and gathered in one body (see 3 Nephi 4:4). The land to which they gathered was between the land Bountiful (southward) and the land of Zarahemla. The most probable and natural area for this gathering is up in the mountains, likely the Chiapas Mountains near Ocosingo or San Cristobal.

FIGURE 19–9: "The Land which was appointed was the land of Zarahemla, and the land Bountiful, yea, to the line which was between the land Bountiful and the land Desolation" (3 Nephi 3:23). Lachoneus, the Nephites' chief judge, called his people together to defend themselves against the robbers of Gadianton. The location he chose appears to be in the same area that is called the Lacandone Mountains, the area where the Zapatistas seek refuge today.

And it came to pass that they did come *up* to battle; and it was in the sixth month; and behold, great and terrible was the day that they did come *up* to battle; and they were girded about after the manner of robbers; and they had a lamb-skin about their loins, and they were dyed in blood, and their heads were shorn, and they had headplates upon them; and great and terrible was the appearance of the armies of Giddianhi, because of their armor, and because of their being dyed in blood. (3 Nephi 4:7; emphasis added)

Further justification for this location of the Nephites under Lachoneus is that today, places close to the proposed area have names very similar to the word "Lachoneous."

Further justification for this location of the Nephites under Lachoneus is that today, places close to the proposed area have names very similar to the word "Lachoneus." The Lacandone Mountains, the valley of Lacanha, and the Lacanha River are all located in the proposed area where Lachoneus gathered the Nephites. The Lacandones still live in the area today.

The scripture under discussion at this point, however, is the one that says the Nephites gathered in the land southward because of the great curse that was upon the land northward.

The land northward is the same land northward used throughout the Book of Mormon text. However, the referent for "the great curse that was upon the land northward" is not clear. The year AD 18 may be too distantly removed (three hundred to four hundred years) for the Jaredite last battle curse still to be upon the land northward. If that is the curse, the scripture may be referring only to the Gulf Coast of Mexico, as archaeological evidence indicates strong settlements in Oaxaca, Puebla, and Mexico during this time period. Apparently, Nephites were living in both the land southward and the land northward at this time. The concept of the "curse" is still prevalent among many native tribes today. If a person gets killed while working on the construction or repair of a home, the home is abandoned because of the perceived curse that is upon it.

3 Nephi 4:1—Land North

And [the Gadianton robbers] began to take possession of the lands, both which were in the land south and which were in the *land north,* and began to take possession of all the lands which had been deserted by the Nephites, and the cities which had been left desolate. (emphasis added)

This scripture lends credibility to option two discussed in reference to Helaman 6:9–10, 12 in which the land north is designated as the northern lowland Maya area—and as a result is a separate geographical location from the land northward. See figure 19-6.

The Nephites had vacated their cities and gathered together to a place in the land southward near the border of the land of Desolation (land northward).

The Gadianton robbers were established in the land southward. Obviously, there-fore, the Nephite cities that the robbers were occupying at this time were in the land southward. If this is the case, then the land north referred to above is the Yucatan. Thus, we are consistent with the overall text in differentiating the land northward (Veracruz-Oaxaca-Mexico) from the land north (Yucatan-Campeche-Tabasco).

3 Nephi 4:23—Land Northward

Zemnarihah did give command unto his people that they should withdraw themselves from the siege, and march into the furthermost parts of the *land northward*. (emphasis added)

Zemnarihah, in a rather desperate move, elected to take his army into the further-most parts of the land northward. This area is probably Teotihuacan in the Mexico valley or perhaps even farther toward the northwest coast of Mexico by present-day Morelia and Guadalajara.

You will recall that the intention of a previous Lamanite leader named Amalickiah was to conquer or to occupy the land northward: "And it came to pass that he [Teancum] headed Amalickiah also, as he was marching forth with his numerous army that he might take possession of the land Bountiful, and also the *land northward*" (Alma 51:30).

Also, the Nephites were determined to maintain an escape route into the land northward: "And it came to pass that the Nephites had inhabited the land Bountiful, even from the east unto the west sea, and thus the Nephites in their wisdom, with their guards and their armies, had hemmed in the Lamanites on the south, that thereby they should have no more possession on the north, that they might not overrun the *land northward*" (Alma 22:33; emphasis added).

Ultimately, we see that the Gadianton robbers did gain control of the land north-ward. Mormon tells us that the Gadianton robbers, or their secret combinations, proved to be the cause of the entire destruction of the Nephites: "And they have caused the destruction of this people of whom I am now speaking, and also the destruction of the people of Nephi" (Ether 8:21). (See also Mormon 2:28 and 3 Nephi 7:12–14.)

3 Nephi 6:2—Land Northward-North

They did return to their own lands and their possessions, both on the *north* and on the south, both on the *land northward* and on the land southward. (emphasis added)

Mormon tells us in 3 Nephi 6:2 that the Nephites returned to their lands located "on the north and on the south, both on the land northward and on the land southward."

> The Gadianton robbers eventually gained control of the land northward, and Mormon says that they, or their secret combinations, proved to be the cause of the entire destruction of the Nephites.

This wording has the sound of Hebrew parallelism because Mormon repeats "northward" for "north" and "southward" for "south." With this interpretation, the terms are synonymous.

A second interpretation is that this verse is a figurative statement, simply stating that the Nephites returned to their homes on the north and on the south. They merely went home.

A third interpretation is to consider each of the statements as a specific geographical area. The Nephites were living both in the land northward and the land southward during this time period (see the story of Hagoth and the story of the missionary journey of Nephi, the son of Helaman, to the land northward). North and south—that is, the Maya northern lowlands and the Maya southern lowlands—were also considered Nephite territory during the time period under question.

> Ixtlilxochitl agrees with both the Book of Mormon dating and the Mixtec calendar date, as he said that the great destruction occurred in the first few days of the year in which Christ was crucified.

3 Nephi 7:12—Northernmost

Therefore, Jacob seeing that their enemies were more numerous than they, he being the king of the band, therefore he commanded his people that they should take their flight into the *northernmost* part of the land, and there build up unto themselves a kingdom. (emphasis added)

The outcome that the Lamanite king Amalickiah desired and that the robber leader Zemnarihah tried to bring about was accomplished by Jacob, the secret-combination leader.

Jacob was a wicked king who spoke against the prophets who testified of Christ. The regulations of the government were destroyed, and the Nephites broke into tribes. However, the tribes combined their efforts against Jacob and the Gadianton robbers. Jacob then motivated a group of dissenters to follow him to the land northward (*northernmost* part of the land) with the idea that they would develop enough strength to battle against the Nephite tribes.

This event occurred about thirty years after the birth of Christ. We propose that the land where Jacob and his dissenters fled is in the valley of Mexico (Mexico City) and perhaps is represented by the ruins of Teotihuacan. This is the same area where some 50 BC Nephites migrated as they went into the land northward.

The great and wicked city of Jacobugath was inhabited by the people of King Jacob and was destroyed by fire four years later—at the time of the destruction associated with the Crucifixion of Christ (see 3 Nephi 9:9).

3 Nephi 8:12—The Land Northward

But behold, there was a more great and terrible destruction in *the land northward;* for behold, the whole face of the land was changed, because of the tempest and the whirlwinds, and the thunderings and the lightnings, and the exceedingly great quaking of the whole earth. (emphasis added)

This great destruction occurred when Christ was crucified, and it began on the fourth day of the first month (see 3 Nephi 8:5). The Mixtec culture of Oaxaca began its new year on April 3. Christ was crucified on the evening of April 6. This correlation places the storm's arising on the fourth day of the year in the Mixtec calendar. Ixtlilxochitl agrees with both the Book of Mormon dating and the Mixtec calendar date, as he said that the great destruction occurred in the first few days of the year in which Christ was crucified.[8]

8. Ixtlilxochitl:16; see chapter 11, "Fernando de Alva Ixtlilxochitl."

Although we are not certain as to the cities destroyed that were located in the land northward, we can eliminate several cities that we know were in the land southward, such as Zarahemla, Moroni, Moronihah, and Jerusalem.

Sixteen cities, as mentioned in 3 Nephi 9, were destroyed, as follows:

City	Destruction Process	Location
Zarahemla	Burned	Land southward
Moroni	Sank into the sea	Land southward
Moronihah	Covered with earth	Land southward
Gilgal	Sank; inhabitants buried	?
Onihah	Covered by water	Probably land southward
Mocum	Covered by water	Probably land southward
Jerusalem	Covered by water	Land southward
Gadiandi	Covered with earth	?
Gadiomnah	Covered with earth	?
Jacob	Covered with earth	Probably land northward
Gimgimno	Covered with earth	?
Jacobugath	Burned	Probably land northward
Laman	Burned	Probably land southward
Josh	Burned	?
Gad	Burned	?
Kishkumen	Burned	Probably land southward

Of the sixteen cities mentioned, we can only guess that the city of Jacob and the city of Jacobugath were located in the land northward. Possibly some of the other cities mentioned above were also in the land northward. Very likely, other land northward cities, in addition to those mentioned above, were destroyed at the time of the great destruction when Christ was crucified. Mormon's statement that "there was a more great and terrible destruction in the land northward" seems to justify this statement.

An elementary knowledge of earthquake, volcano, and hurricane activities in the regions of Mesoamerica is adequate to provide us with a mental picture of the events recorded in 3 Nephi.

Within recent years, some of the major destructive activities in Mesoamerica include the following:

1943   Pericutin, Mexico, volcanic explosion turned a cornfield into a mountain.

1976   Massive earthquake in Guatemala/land southward. Guatemala has over thirty-three volcanic mountains. El Pacaya and others are consistently active.

1982   Earthquake in state of Oaxaca/land northward.

1983   Volcanic eruption in El Chichonal in the state of Chiapas/land southward.

1985   Destructive earthquake in Mexico City/land northward.

1988   Destruction by Hurricane Gilbert/land southward and land northward.

1994   Volcanic activity reported about Popocatepetl (Smoking Mountain)

1999   Hurricane Mitch killed some ten thousand people in the region, mostly in mudslides.

2000   Destructive hurricane activity in Belize and Honduras/land southward.

2005   Destructive volcanic mudslide at Panabaj, near Lake Atitlan, that buried a thousand people.

Beginning in February of 1943, the city of Pericutin, state of Michoacan, west of Mexico City, was covered over by volcanic eruptions. By 1952, the only visible evidence

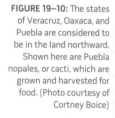

FIGURE 19–10: The states of Veracruz, Oaxaca, and Puebla are considered to be in the land northward. Shown here are Puebla nopales, or cacti, which are grown and harvested for food. (Photo courtesy of Cortney Boice)

Exploring the Lands of the Book of Mormon

remaining of the community was the steeple of the Catholic church. This event is reminiscent of what appeared to happen to the cities of Moronihah, Gadiandi, Gadiomnah, Jacob, and Gimgimno: "And behold, the city of Gadiandi, and the city of Gadiomnah, and the city of Jacob, and the city of Gimgimno, all these have I caused to be sunk, and made hills and valleys in the places thereof; and the inhabitants thereof have I buried up in the depths of the earth, to hide their wickedness and abominations from before my face, that the blood of the prophets and the saints should not come up any more unto me against them" (3 Nephi 9:8).

We can speculate that either the city of Jacob or the city of Jacobugath—or both—were in the land northward for the following reasons:

1. King Jacob's activity four or five years prior to the destruction occurred when he went into the northernmost part of the land to build up a kingdom (see 3 Nephi 7:12).

2. The Nephite custom was to name the land after the person who settled it (see Alma 8:7 and Ixtlilxochitl:22).

The archaeological ruins of Teotihuacan appear to fit the criteria as being in the "northernmost part of the land" and is a fair candidate for the city of Jacobugath referred to in 3 Nephi 9:9. The city of Jacobugath was burned.

The archaeological ruins of Cuicuilco, located near the University of Mexico in Mexico City, were covered by a lava flow dating to 34 AD.

The largest-based pyramid in the world, located at Cholula in the state of Puebla, was also destroyed at the time of the great destruction at the death of Christ. The ancient Mexicans attributed the destruction of the Cholula pyramids to Quetzalcoatl. This event probably caused Quetzalcoatl to become associated with the wind god.

Regarding the destruction of the ruins of Cholula, Ixtlilxochitl said that "a great destruction and devastation took place, which is referred to as the third period of the world. At that time, the great building and tower of Cholula, which was so famous and marvelous, was destroyed. It was like a second tower of Babel that these people had built, with virtually the same idea in mind. It was destroyed by the wind."[9]

The pyramid was subsequently rebuilt and dedicated to Quetzalcoatl. Ixtlilxochitl says that "in place of the ruins, the people built a temple to Quetzalcoatl, whom they named the god of wind, because it was destroyed by the wind. They understood that this calamity was sent by his hand. And they called it Ce Acatl, which was the name of the year of his coming."[10]

In referring to the destruction, Ixtlilxochitl provides us with two or three destruction dates. In some places, he reports that the destruction took place (1) a few days after Quetzalcoatl left, (2) a few years after the death of Christ, and (3) the first few days of the year in which Christ was crucified. The latter, as mentioned earlier, correlates with both the Mixtec calendar and the Book of Mormon: "And it came to pass in the thirty and fourth year, in the first month, on the fourth day of the month, there arose a great storm, such an one as never had been known in all the land" (3 Nephi 8:5).

The largest-based pyramid in the world, located at Cholula in the state of Puebla, was also destroyed at the time of the great destruction at the death of Christ. The ancient Mexicans attributed the destruction of the Cholula pyramids to Quetzalcoatl.

9. Ixtlilxochitl:42; see chapter 11, "Fernando de Alva Ixtlilxochitl."

10. Ixtlilxochitl:43; see chapter 11, "Fernando de Alva Ixtlilxochitl."

We get a hint that one of the symbols on the Aztec calendar stone is also referring to the great destruction at the time of Christ's death. The symbol is the square that is called the "Sun of Earth," which is a representation of the time when a great destruction occurred because of heavy earthquakes in the land. The other three squares are representative of the earth's being destroyed by water, by wind, and by fire.

3 Nephi 20:13—The North

And then shall the remnants, which shall be scattered abroad upon the face of the earth, be gathered in from the east and from the west, and from the south and from *the north*. (emphasis added)

This statement is not a specific geographical statement but rather a prophecy that the remnants will be gathered in from different parts of the earth.

Mormon 2:3—North Countries

The Lamanites did come upon us with exceedingly great power, insomuch that they did frighten my armies; therefore they would not fight, and they began to retreat towards the *north countries*. (emphasis added)

A careful study of Mormon's individual record, which he also called the book of Mormon and which comprises only twenty pages, provides us with a historical overview of Nephite-Lamanite interaction from AD 311 to AD 385.

This time period is considered Early Classic; and from a Book of Mormon perspective, Mormon outlines movements and activities centered on both sides of the narrow neck of land. His record culminates with the final Lamanite-Nephite battle at Cumorah in AD 385 when the Nephite nation was destroyed.

> Mormon lived in the land northward—close to the narrow neck of land.

We are almost certain that Mormon lived in the land northward—close to the narrow neck of land—because of the following:

1. When he was eleven years old, he was taken by his father to the land of Zarahemla in the land southward (see Mormon 1:6).

2. In AD 350, the Nephites gave up to the Lamanites, by treaty, all of the land southward. The Lamanites gave the Nephites the land northward, starting at the narrow pass that led into the land southward (see Mormon 2:28–29).

3. In the year AD 360, Mormon called all of the Nephites to the land of Desolation (land northward) to a city called Desolation. This city was in the borders, by the narrow pass that led into the land southward (see Mormon 3:5, 7). In all probability, Mormon lived in the city of Desolation.

4. Moroni, the son of Mormon, wrote about the Jaredites who lived upon the face of this north country (see Ether 1:1).

We can, therefore, assume that when Mormon states in Mormon 2:3 that the Nephites began to retreat from the Lamanites toward the north countries, the Nephites were retreating into the land northward—just on the other side of the narrow neck (the Isthmus of Tehuantepec). The north countries, therefore, are the Gulf of Mexico coastal regions, near the Isthmus of Tehuantepec and beyond.

The above conclusion is further warranted because even after the Nephites retreated toward the north countries, they were still battling the Lamanites on both sides of the narrow neck of land (the Isthmus of Tehuantepec; see Mormon 2:28–29).

Mormon 2:20—Northward

And it came to pass that in this year [AD 345] the people of Nephi again were hunted and driven. And it came to pass that we were driven forth until we had come *northward* to the land which was called Shem. (emphasis added)

We are not told exactly where the land of Shem is; but three verses later (Mormon 2:23), we are told that Mormon told his people to defend their houses and their homes boldly against the Lamanites. Also, nine verses later (Mormon 2:29), we learn that in a treaty, the Lamanites gave the Nephites the land northward to the narrow passage.

Because we see in the next chapter, Mormon 3, that fighting was still occurring around the narrow passage that led into the land southward (Mormon 3:5), the "northward" in Mormon 2:20 cannot be very far northward from the narrow neck (the Isthmus of Tehuantepec). The distance from the hill Shim to the top of the narrow neck (Isthmus of Tehuantepec) is about fifty miles.

Mormon 2:29—Land Northward

And the Lamanites did give unto us the *land northward,* yea, even to the narrow passage which led into the land southward. (emphasis added)

This scripture has been referred to several times in *Exploring the Lands of the Book of Mormon.* In the AD 350 land-division treaty, the Nephites gave up the land southward, which included the land of Zarahemla and the greater portion of the land Bountiful. The Nephites were given the land northward, which included the land Desolation. The treaty, however, lasted only thirty-five years, as the Nephites were destroyed in AD 385.

Mormon 3:5, 7—Land Desolation/City of Desolation

And it came to pass that I did cause my people that they should gather themselves together at the *land Desolation,* to a city which was in the borders, by the narrow pass which led into the land southward. . . .

> The land Desolation was in the land northward. The city of Desolation was in the land Desolation and was located by the narrow pass that led into the land southward.

The Lamanites did come down to the *city of Desolation* to battle against us. (emphasis added)

The land Desolation was in the land northward. The city of Desolation was in the land Desolation and was located by the narrow pass that led into the land southward. As a point of reference, the city of Desolation was probably located where the present-day city of Acayucan in the state of Veracruz is located. Acayucan is near the Olmec ruins of San Lorenzo.

The road connecting the Gulf of Tehuantepec on the Pacific side and the Gulf of Mexico on the Atlantic side is an ancient trade route—or the trail of wild animals, the same meaning as expressed in Ether 9:34.

As you drive from Juchitan, Oaxaca, north through the Isthmus of Tehuantepec, a distance of about 110 miles, you will arrive at Acayucan. At the southern base of the Isthmus of Tehuantepec, where the road turns straight north, the distance is about fifty miles to the borders of the states of Veracruz and Oaxaca. This road connecting the Gulf of Tehuantepec on the Pacific side and the Gulf of Mexico on the Atlantic side is an ancient trade route—or the trail of wild animals, the same meaning as expressed in Ether 9:34. It is the most passable route from Central America to the northern part of Mexico.

To cross into northern Mexico from the Tabasco-Campeche north side is very difficult because of the many river drainages and countless lagoons in that area. To travel directly east to west from Central America to northern Mexico is also very difficult because of the rugged mountain ranges separating the narrow passage that goes between the two mountain ranges.

The railroad tracks go the same south-north route from Juchitan to Acayucan. Acayucan is about twenty-eight miles from the Gulf of Mexico on the eastward side and seventy-two miles from the Oaxaca Mountains on the westward side. Farther up along the northwestward side of the Sierra Villa Altas (Oaxaca Mountains), travelers run into the impassable Papaloapan water basin. Thus, the most practical way to get from the city Desolation (Acayucan), in the land northward, to Juchitan, toward the land southward, is through the narrow pass that leads into the state of Oaxaca and into Chiapas and Guatemala.

Even today, most of the traffic from northern Mexico to Guatemala and Central America travels through the narrow pass from Acayucan to Juchitan.

Mormon 4:1, 2, 3, 8, 13, 19—Land of Desolation/City Desolation

[In AD 363] the Nephites did go up with their armies to battle against the Lamanites, out of the *land of Desolation*. (Mormon 4:1; emphasis added)

The armies of the Nephites were driven back again to the *land of Desolation*. And while they were yet weary, a fresh army of the Lamanites did come upon them; and they had a sore battle, insomuch that the Lamanites did take possession of the *city Desolation*. (Mormon 4:2; emphasis added)

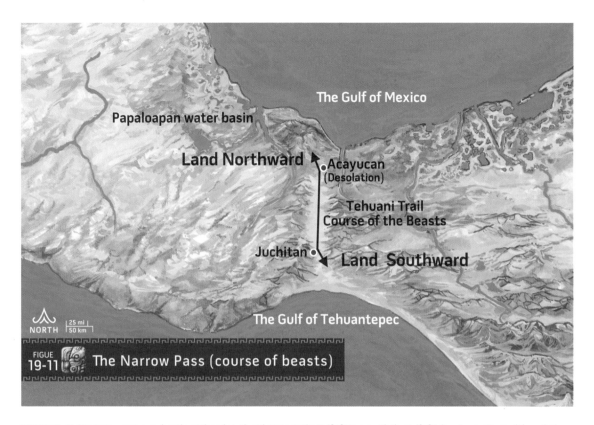

FIGURE 19–11: The narrow pass runs directly north and south and connects the Gulf of Mexico with the Gulf of Tehuantepec. The road through the narrow pass is an ancient trade route that is also called "the course of the beasts." The narrow pass runs through the Isthmus of Tehuantepec—or the small neck of land. The narrow pass leads into the land northward and the land southward, as shown by the arrows.

The city Teancum lay in the borders by the seashore; and it was also near the *city Desolation.* (Mormon 4:3; emphasis added)

[The Nephites] took possession again of the *city Desolation.* (Mormon 4:8; emphasis added)

The Lamanites did take possession of the *city Desolation.* (Mormon 4:13; emphasis added)

[In AD 375] the Lamanites did come down against the *city Desolation;* and there was an exceedingly sore battle fought in the *land Desolation,* in the which they did beat the Nephites. (Mormon 4:19; emphasis added)

In Mormon 4, we read about the city Desolation's changing back and forth between Nephite and Lamanite occupations.

In AD 375, the battles were still being fought around the narrow neck of land by the city Desolation. Again, we need to remind ourselves that the city Desolation was in the land of Desolation and that the land of Desolation was in the land northward. Ten years later (AD 385), the Nephites were destroyed at Cumorah. Cumorah was near the hill Shim (see Ether 9:3), which appears to be fairly close to the city Desolation (see Mormon 1:3; 2:17; 2:23; 2:29; and 3:5, 7). The city Desolation was by the narrow pass that led into the land southward.

SUMMARY OF BOOK OF ETHER REFERENCES

The verses in the book of Ether (the Jaredite record) that make reference to the land northward, north country, north countries, northward, and land Desolation are as follows:

Ether 1:1—North Country

And now I, Moroni, proceed to give an account of those ancient inhabitants who were destroyed by the hand of the Lord upon the face of *this north country*. (emphasis added)

"This north country" appears to establish the area in which Moroni, the son of Mormon, lived. In AD 360, Mormon was gathering all the Nephites, those who would come, to the city Desolation in the land Desolation (see Mormon 3:5, 7). Both the city Desolation and the land Desolation were in the land northward—or in "this north country," as Moroni describes it.

The area most assuredly is, as discussed previously, the area northwest of the Isthmus of Tehuantepec, with the heartland located along the Gulf of Mexico in the state of Veracruz. This is the area that archaeologists identify as the heartland of the ancient Olmec culture (see chapter 5, "The Olmec [Jaredite] Culture").

Placing "this north country" along the Gulf of Mexico is also consistent with the writings of Ixtlilxochitl wherein he refers to the first settlers who came from the tower of Babel as follows: "They populated the major part of the land, and more particularly that which falls along the *northern part*."[11] And again: "They say that in these *northern lands,* where the ancient Chichimeca Empire was located. . . ."[12] The land that Ixtlilxochitl is referring to is along the Gulf of Mexico.

Ether 1:42; 2:1—Valley Which Is Northward

Thou [brother of Jared] shalt go at the head of them down into the *valley which is northward*. And there will I meet thee, and I will go before thee into a land which is choice above all the lands of the earth. (Ether 1:42; emphasis added)

And it came to pass that Jared and his brother, and their families, and also the friends of Jared and his brother and their families, went down into the *valley which was northward*. (Ether 2:1; emphasis added)

11. See Ixtlilxochitl:21; emphasis added. See chapter 11, "Fernando de Alva Ixtlilxochitl."

12. See Ixtlilxochitl:26; emphasis added. See chapter 11, "Fernando de Alva Ixtlilxochitl."

Exploring the Lands of the Book of Mormon

Both of the above references discuss an area located in the Old World before the Jaredites crossed the ocean to the promised land. As such, these references have no connection with the Mesoamerica map.

Ether 7:6—Desolation

Now the land of Moron, where the king dwelt, was near the land which is called *Desolation* by the Nephites. (emphasis added)

Obviously, Moroni is familiar with at least a portion of the geography of the Jaredites. From Ether 10:21, we can assume that the land of Moron was in the land northward: "And they did preserve the land southward for a wilderness, to get game. And the whole face of *the land northward* was covered with inhabitants" (Ether 10:21; emphasis added).

John Sorenson proposes the land of Moron to be in the Oaxaca valley. The state of Oaxaca borders the state of Veracruz. Archaeological evidence justifies Sorenson's position, as the archaeological site of San Jose Mogote in the Oaxaca valley dates to the Jaredite time period.[13] Also, the inhabitants of Monte Alban Period I (500 BC–100 BC) were influenced by the Olmecs of the Gulf Coast.[14]

Readers will recall that the Mulekites had direct contact with the Jaredites, as the Mulekites landed in the midst of the Jaredite lands (see Alma 22:30). The last surviving Jaredite king lived among the Mulekites for nine moons (see Omni 1:21).

The above analysis suggests that a branch of the Mulekites may have lived in the Oaxaca valley, which may have been the Jaredite land of Moron.

Ether 9:35—North Countries

[The Lord] did send rain upon the face of the earth; . . . and there began to be fruit in *the north countries,* and in all the countries round about. (emphasis added)

The above scripture appears to be both a general figurative statement as well as a geographical statement.

If the term "the north countries" has reference to the states of Tabasco and Veracruz along the northern part of the Gulf of Mexico, then both the statements about "the rain" and "the fruit" fit.

The banana belt of Mexico is in the state of Tabasco along the Gulf of Mexico. The pineapple belt of Mexico is in the state of Veracruz along the Gulf of Mexico. Landowners in the Tuxtla Mountains of Veracruz merely have to cut a small tree to use as a fence post and then watch as, within a short time, the post begins to sprout new leaves. Everything depends on the rains along the Gulf of Mexico.

13. John L. Sorenson, *An Ancient American Setting for the Book of Mormon* (Salt Lake City: Deseret Book and Foundation for Ancient Research and Mormon Studies, 1985), 15.

14. *The Oaxaca Valley: Official Guide,* 5th ed. in English (Mexico, DF: Instituto Nacional de Antropologia e Historia, 1973), 6.

The place where the sea divides the land is probably where the mighty Coatzacoalcos River empties into the Gulf of Mexico, and it is literally a place where the sea divides the land.

Although these comments are in no way conclusive evidence that the area referred to is along the Gulf of Mexico, they nevertheless agree with the circumstances mentioned.

Ether 10:20–21—Land Northward

And they [the Jaredites] built a great city by the narrow neck of land, by the place where the sea divides the land.

And they [the Jaredites] did preserve the land southward for a wilderness, to get game. And the whole face of the *land northward* was covered with inhabitants. (emphasis added)

This scripture is a classic statement in the Book of Mormon. It not only gives us the geographical location of a city that was probably called Lib but also provides us with a statement about population, topography, direction, and the use of the land.

By placing the land northward along the Gulf of Mexico where both archaeology and tradition dictate, we can make the following conclusions:

15. Sorenson, *An Ancient American Setting for the Book of Mormon*, 117.

16. F. Richard Hauck, *Deciphering the Geography of the Book of Mormon* (Salt Lake City: Deseret Book, 1988), 104.

1. A great city was built where the ancient Olmec sites of La Venta or San Lorenzo are located. John Sorenson favors the Olmec site of San Lorenzo as the city of Lib.[15] Richard Hauck places the city of Lib on the Isthmus of Tehuantepec (Pacific side).[16] We agree with Sorenson because of the Olmec sites in the northern area. Both San Lorenzo and La Venta were in existence around 1200 BC, the time period when the city of Lib was built—as best as we can deduce from the book of Ether. However, the site of La Venta near Coatzacoalcos may be an even better candidate for the city of Lib.

2. The place where the sea divides the land is probably where the mighty Coatzacoalcos River empties into the Gulf of Mexico, and it is literally a place where the sea divides the land. The eleventh edition of *Merriam-Webster's Collegiate Dictionary* defines a *gulf* as "a part of an ocean or sea extending into the land." Today, large tankers transport oil from the refineries of Minatitlan to the ocean entrance at Coatzacoalcos, a distance inland of about twenty-two miles.

3. We have proposed on several occasions that the land southward is located on the southeast side of the Isthmus of Tehuantepec. The Chiapas Mountains area is just such an area as outlined in the above scriptural reference. It is an area that could be preserved as a place to get game. You will recall that the term "Hermounts" in the Book of Mormon means a wilderness of "wild and ravenous beasts" (see Alma 2:37). *Tehuantepec* is an Aztec, or Nahuatl, word that also means "a wilderness of wild and ravenous beasts." Hermounts was located west and north of Zarahemla. The mountains of Tehuantepec are located west and north of the Chiapas depression. Both Hermounts in the Book of Mormon and Tehuantepec on the Mesoamerica map are located in the land southward.

Exploring the Lands of the Book of Mormon

As to the animals in the forests or wilderness of the Chiapas Mountains (land south-ward), we can get a glimpse of these animals as we visit the zoo in Tuxtla Gutierrez in the state of Chiapas. This zoo includes animals indigenous to the state of Chiapas. If we contemplate that some of the animals in the Tuxtla Gutierrez Zoo are descendants of the "game" mentioned in Ether 10:21, we may then get a feel for some Book of Mormon animals.

Some of the most impressive Tuxtla Gutierrez Zoo animals that probably served as food are the deer, the wild boar, the tapir, the jaguar, the fox, the coyote, muskrat-sized animals of various sizes, more serpents than anyone would want to see in a lifetime, and all manner of birds. Also, the turtle, the crocodile, and other water animals are found in the Tuxtla Gutierrez Zoo.

4. Ether 10:21 states that the whole face of the land northward was covered with inhabitants. This statement is heavily supported by both archaeology and tradition. Moroni wrote that "the whole face of the land northward was covered with inhabitants" (Ether 10:21).

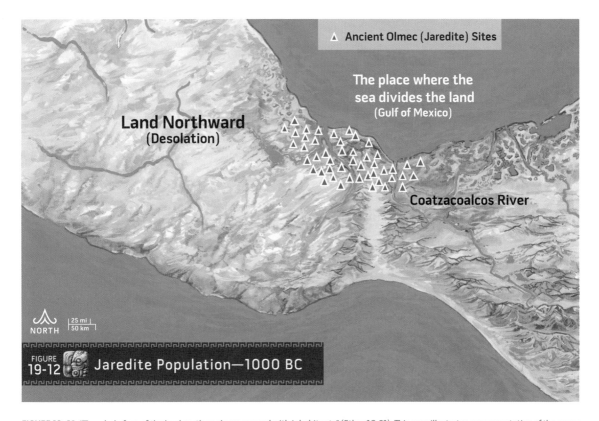

FIGURE 19–12: "The whole face of the land northward was covered with inhabitants" (Ether 10:21). This map illustrates a representation of the many archaeological sites that have been identified along the Gulf of Mexico, the area proposed as the heartland of the Jaredites from 2000 BC to 300 BC. Three major sites are La Venta, San Lorenzo Tenochtitlan, and Tres Zapotes.

Ether 13:11—North Countries

They are they who were scattered and gathered in from the four quarters of the earth, and from the *north countries*. (emphasis added)

This scripture refers to the gathering of the lost tribes from the north. As a result, the scripture is not relevant to our study of Book of Mormon/Mesoamerica geography.

SUMMARY

The geographical position and archaeological data of the states of Tabasco and Veracruz establish a very convincing argument for their being the land northward (Desolation).

The land northward is a major geographical land area referred to many times in the Book of Mormon. The land of Desolation, the heartland of the ancient Jaredites, was located in the land northward. A narrow neck of land, or isthmus, separated the land northward from the land southward.

About 45 BC, many people migrated from the land southward to the land northward to a place that had large bodies of water.

The geographical position and archaeological data of the states of Tabasco and Veracruz establish a very convincing argument for their being the land northward (Desolation). Information regarding the first settlers of Mexico, as derived from sixteenth-century Spanish writers, provides additional testimony that the Gulf Coast of Mexico (Tabasco and Veracruz) was indeed the land northward in the Book of Mormon.

The Isthmus of Tehuantepec, with a narrow passage running through the two mountain ranges separating northern Mexico from Chiapas, Guatemala, and Yucatan, is an excellent candidate for the narrow neck of land. The narrow passage between the mountain ranges is the natural travel route between the proposed land southward and the proposed land northward.

The area of the greater land northward in the Mexico City valley provides both geographical and archaeological credibility for it to qualify for the "land which was northward" with "large bodies of water." This area is where we propose that many Nephites migrated during the first century BC. Archaeological data of Teotihuacan show migrations from the south entered into Teotihuacan in the first century BC.

A great and terrible destruction occurred in the land northward at the time of the Crucifixion of Christ. Both the Spanish chronicles and archaeological evidence bear witness to this destruction. The ruins of Cholula near Puebla and the ruins of Cuicuilco in the state of Mexico also bear testimony of such destruction.

Many land northward Jaredite landmarks are mentioned in the Book of Mormon. Some Nephite cities located in the land northward are also mentioned.

During the fourth century AD, the Nephite cities or lands of Desolation, Teancum, Boaz, and Cumorah are mentioned. The city of Desolation was near the narrow neck of land. The present-day city of Acayucan near the Olmec ruins of San Lorenzo appears to be in the proper geographical area to be the city of Desolation.

The city of Desolation was near the narrow neck of land and was also near the seacoast. The hill Shim appears to be close to the hill Ramah/Cumorah.

The leading candidate for the hill Ramah/Cumorah, where both the last Jaredite and Nephite battles were fought, is a hill called Vigia, which is located in the Tuxtla Mountains of Veracruz, Mexico.

The hill Shim, the hill Cumorah, and the waters of Ripliancum are all located in the land northward—all of which are near the narrow neck of land that leads into the land southward.

The large Papaloapan water basin that empties into the Gulf of Mexico, near the city of Alvarado, Veracruz, is an impressive candidate for the waters of Ripliancum in the Book of Mormon.

The Olmec archaeological sites of Tres Zapotes by the Hill Vigia, La Venta at the top of the Isthmus of Tehuantepec, and San Lorenzo near Acayucan are all located in the area proposed as the land northward (Desolation).

Monte Alban and San Jose Mogote are located in the Oaxaca valley in what is considered to be part of the land northward.

Teotihuacan in the Mexico valley and Cholula in the state of Puebla are considered to be in the greater land northward in our model.

FREQUENTLY ASKED QUESTION

Question: Does the land northward extend into the United States?

Answer: From a Book of Mormon geographical frame of reference, the land northward probably did not extend as far north as the United States. The most likely northern boundary line for the land northward is from Mazatlan on the west to Tampico on the east. This line was perhaps determined by the ability to survive and is referred to as the "green belt" of Mexico.

The northern states of Mexico are much like southern Texas, New Mexico, and Arizona—where survival has traditionally been very difficult. This statement does not mean that settlements during the Book of Mormon time period did not extend into the United States. For example, the Hopewell and Adena people, who settled in Ohio and Florida, date to the Book of Mormon time period; and current theories support the idea that they were an extension of the Mesoamerica culture. So although remnants of the Mesoamerica/Book of Mormon culture may be found in the United States, the geographical heartland would be in Mesoamerica. In addition, the New World geographical statements we read in the Book of Mormon are clearly associated with Mesoamerica rather than with North America.

> The leading candidate for the hill Ramah/Cumorah, where both the last Jaredite and Nephite battles were fought, is a hill called Vigia, which is located in the Tuxtla Mountains of Veracruz, Mexico.

Preclassic 600 BC–AD 250
Classic AD 250–AD 900
Postclassic AD 900–AD 1500

Note: Two or three contiguous dots show
that the site existed in more than one
period

Coba
Tulum
Chichen Itza
Mayapan
Mani
Muna
Uxmal
Kobah
Loltun
Chacchoben
Edzna
Becan
Dzibanche
Chicanna
Kohunlich
Cuello
Cerros
Calakmul
Rio Bec
Lamanai
El Mirador
Nakbe
Altun Ha
Rio Azul
San Bartolo
Palenque
Uaxactun
Xunantunich
El Peru
Tikal
Naranjo
Piedras Negras
Tonina
Seibal
Bonampak
Caracol
Yaxchilan
Dos Pilas
Pulsiha
Juchitan
Chiapa de Corzo
Jiquipilas
Comitan
Cancuen
Tonala
Santa Rosa
La Libertad
Perservancia
Quirigua
Zaculeu
Huehuetenango
Copan
Mixco Viejo
Izapa
Almolonga
Iximche
Chiutinamit
Kaminaljuyu
Abaj Takalik
El Baul
Chalcuapa

NORTH

25 mi
50 km

CHAPTER 20

The Land Southward

I [Mormon], being eleven years old, was carried by my father into the land southward.
(Mormon 1:6)

ᒧᒧᒧᒧᒧᒧᒧᒧᒧᒧᒧᒧᒧᒧᒧᒧᒧᒧᒧᒧᒧᒧᒧᒧᒧᒧᒧᒧᒧᒧᒧᒧᒧᒧᒧᒧᒧᒧ

D uring the Jaredite (Olmec Classic) time period (1200 BC–600 BC), the land southward was preserved as a wilderness to get game (see Ether 10:21).

If the land northward is, in reality, the area described in chapter 19, "The Land Northward," then logic establishes the general boundaries for the land southward. Therefore, we propose that the land southward described in the Book of Mormon is located south and east (southward) of the Isthmus of Tehuantepec. The area includes what are now the Mexican states of Chiapas, part of Tabasco, Campeche, Yucatan, and Quintana Roo; the countries of Guatemala, El Salvador, Honduras, and Belize; and the northern tip of the countries of Nicaragua and Costa Rica. This area represents about four hundred thousand square miles of rugged mountains, dense jungles, lush

OPPOSITE: Most of the Nephite and Lamanite history that is recorded in the Book of Mormon took place in the land southward. Both the land of Nephi and the land of Zarahemla were located in the land southward—that is, southward of the Isthmus of Tehuantepec (narrow neck of land). The Nephites controlled the land of Nephi for four hundred years and the land of Zarahemla for an additional 550 years. The land southward is synonymous with the greater land Bountiful. This map represents some of the many cities that existed both during and after the history recorded in the Book of Mormon in the area designated as the land southward.

valleys, and humid coastlines along sandy beaches. It is comparable in size to the land northward discussed in chapter 19. This theory suggests that, as opposed to covering all of South America as tradition outlines, the land southward is limited to the above-described area.

This vast, rugged mountain land, which is offset by dense jungles, is almost completely surrounded by water (see Alma 22:32; 2 Nephi 10:20). If we are correct in our assessment of the land southward, then Mesoamerica was home for Jaredite descendants as well as for the Mulekite, Nephite, and Lamanite peoples who followed later.

Those referred to as "Lamanites" and "Nephites" in the Book of Mormon, who correlate well with the Maya, spread throughout all of the land southward. After the Lamanite Maya destroyed the Nephite Maya nation around AD 385, the Lamanite Maya built a massive empire. At the close of the Book of Mormon, the Lamanite Maya culture entered into a seven-hundred-year Classic Period. They developed a pagan civilization that was based on serpent cults, astronomy, and mathematics. Their culture

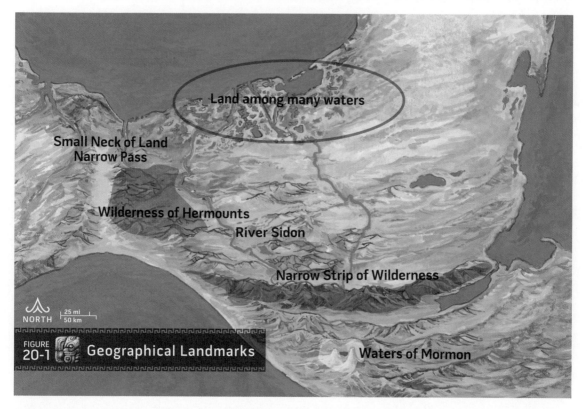

FIGURE 20–1: Natural geographical landmarks that coincide with geographical statements in the Book of Mormon and that are located in the land southward are shown in this map. The waters of Mormon (Lake Atitlan) is in the land of Nephi; the Sidon river (Grijalva) is located in the land of Zarahemla. The narrow strip of wilderness (Cuchumatanes mountain range) divides the land of Nephi from the land of Zarahemla, and the narrow neck of land (Isthmus of Tehuantepec) divides the land northward from the land southward. The wilderness of Hermounts (Tehuantepec) and the land among many waters (lagoons of Tabasco and Campeche) are also shown on the map.

flourished through the ninth century AD, when many of their city centers began to be abandoned.

The land southward was separated from the land northward by a small neck of land, probably the Isthmus of Tehuantepec, which consists of a narrow passage of land that runs north and south between two mountain ranges and connects the Gulf of Tehuantepec on the south with the Gulf of Mexico on the north. Undoubtedly, at the top of the Isthmus of Tehuantepec, near the Gulf of Mexico, the Jaredites built a great city during the days of King Lib. They preserved the land southward as a wilderness in which to hunt game: "And they built a great city by the narrow neck of land, by the place where the sea divides the land. And they did preserve the *land southward* for a wilderness, to get game. And the whole face of the land northward was covered with inhabitants" (Ether 10:20–21; emphasis added).

The southeast coast of the land southward is probably where Lehi's colony landed. This location may have been close to Tapachula, Mexico, where the ancient ruins of Izapa are located. The land of Nephi, the land of Zarahemla, the waters of Mormon, the river Sidon, and the narrow strip of wilderness are all in the land southward.

When Lehi's colony arrived in the promised land, they called it the land of first inheritance. In the land of first inheritance, the climate was such that seeds planted by the people grew in abundance. Members of Lehi's group were probably greeted by the scantily clothed, sun-baked, dark-skinned natives living along the coast. These natives were probably part of the great Jaredite nation.

Most likely, Laman and Lemuel, in their traditional jealousy of Nephi, assumed the leadership of these natives. Thus began the great Lamanite Maya culture.

Nephi, on the other hand, taught the gospel of Jesus Christ to those same natives who would listen. After being warned by the Lord, Nephi departed into the wilderness to a place his followers called Nephi. With him, he took the brass plates of Laban, from which he had taught the people. Eventually, his followers made him their king:

> And it came to pass that the Lord did warn me, that I, Nephi, should depart from them and flee into the wilderness, and all those *who would go with me.*
>
> Wherefore, it came to pass that I, Nephi, did take my family, and also Zoram and his family, and Sam, mine elder brother and his family, and Jacob and Joseph, my younger brethren, and also my sisters, and *all those who would go with me.* And *all those who would go with me* were those who believed in the warnings and the revelations of God; wherefore, they did hearken unto my words.
>
> And we did take our tents and whatsoever things were possible for us, and did journey in the wilderness for the space of many days. And after we had journeyed for the space of many days we did pitch our tents.
>
> And *my people* would that we should call the name of the place Nephi; wherefore, we did call it Nephi.

The land southward was separated from the land northward by a small neck of land, probably the Isthmus of Tehuantepec, which consists of a narrow passage of land that runs north and south between two mountain ranges and connects the Gulf of Tehuantepec on the south with the Gulf of Mexico on the north.

And *all those who were with me* did take upon them to call themselves the people of Nephi. (2 Nephi 5:5–9; emphasis added)

Today, the most representative site for the city of Nephi is the archaeological ruins of Kaminaljuyu, located in the mountainous, modern-day Guatemala City area. These ruins demonstrate evidence of a highly developed religious center between 550 BC–100 BC.

The beautiful, mountainous land surrounding Guatemala City represents the land of Nephi, located in the land southward. Eventually, the Lamanites occupied this land. By approximately 180 BC, when Mosiah led a righteous group of Nephites from the land of Nephi down to Zarahemla, the entire land of Nephi was controlled by the Lamanites.

From this perspective, the land of Zarahemla is separated from the land of Nephi by a high, narrow mountain range that extends from the Atlantic Ocean on the east to the

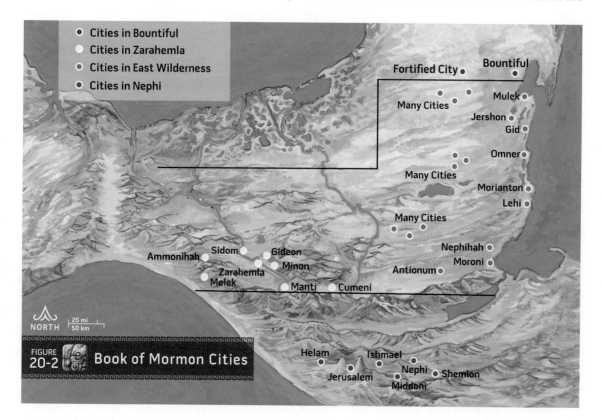

FIGURE 20–2: Over 80 percent of the history recorded in the Book of Mormon took place in the land southward. This map shows possible locations of selected cities in the land of Nephi, the land of Zarahemla, the east wilderness of Zarahemla, and the land Bountiful. They are determined by both the Book of Mormon and Mesoamerican archaeological, historical, and geographical information, as outlined in the second edition of *Exploring the Lands of the Book of Mormon.*

Pacific Ocean on the west. The Book of Mormon term for the narrow mountain range is "narrow strip of wilderness"—not to be confused with "narrow neck of land." Both the land of Zarahemla and the land of Nephi are located in the land southward.

The best probable candidate for the land of Zarahemla is a lowland central depression area located in the modern-day state of Chiapas, Mexico. The state of Chiapas borders the country of Guatemala. With the passage of time, the middle Usumacinta valley, including the Peten wilderness, and Belize were probably annexed to Zarahemla.

The movement from the land of Nephi to the land of Zarahemla was *down,* even though the directional route was in a north or northwest line. That is, Mosiah led his righteous group of Nephites *down* from the mountains of Nephi (probably Guatemala) to the valley of Zarahemla (probably Chiapas):

> Behold, I am Amaleki, the son of Abinadom. Behold, I will speak unto you somewhat concerning Mosiah, who was made king over the land of Zarahemla; for behold, he being warned of the Lord that he should flee out of the land of Nephi, and as many as would hearken unto the voice of the Lord should also depart out of the land with him, into the wilderness—
>
> And it came to pass that he did according as the Lord had commanded him. And they departed out of the land into the wilderness, as many as would hearken unto the voice of the Lord; and they were led by many preachings and prophesyings. And they were admonished continually by the word of God; and they were led by the power of his arm, through the wilderness until they came *down into the land* which is called the land of Zarahemla. (Omni 1:12–13; emphasis added)

Mosiah was made king over the Mulekites, whom he had discovered living in the land of Zarahemla, which is in the land southward. Some time later, a man named Zeniff led a group of people back *up* to the land of Nephi (Guatemala).

The Nephite King Noah was a son of Zeniff. Noah lived a fairly peaceful life among the Lamanites in the land of Nephi (Guatemala), but his corruption brought about his downfall. One of his priests, Alma, was converted by the prophet Abinadi. Alma fled to a place he called the waters of Mormon, also located in the land southward. This area may have been what is known today as Lake Atitlan, a three-hour drive by bus through the mountains from Guatemala City.

During Limhi's time, about 121 BC (Limhi being a son of Noah), an expedition was sent from Nephi (probably Guatemala) to try to locate Zarahemla (probably Chiapas). Most likely, the expedition mistakenly dropped down over the northeastern side of the mountain range leading into the Zarahemla (Chiapas) area. They then traveled northwest (or northward), following the Usumacinta River leading to the Gulf of Mexico. From there, they may have wandered through the swampy Villahermosa wetlands, fording rivers and bodies of water en route. They subsequently ended up in the area

The land of Zarahemla is separated from the land of Nephi by a high, narrow mountain range that extends from the Atlantic Ocean on the east to the Pacific Ocean on the west.

The ancient city of La Venta in Tabasco, close to the Veracruz border, would have revealed the results of the devastating Jaredite civil war.

1. V. Garth Norman, *Izapa Sculpture,* Part 2: Text, Papers of the New World Archaeological Foundation, no. 30 (Provo, UT: New World Archaeological Foundation, 1976).

where the Jaredites were destroyed. The ancient city of La Venta in Tabasco, close to the Veracruz border, would have revealed the results of the devastating Jaredite civil war.

"And they were lost in the wilderness for the space of many days, yet they were diligent, and found not the land of Zarahemla but returned to this land, having traveled in a land among many waters, having discovered a land which was covered with bones of men, and of beasts, and was also covered with ruins of buildings of every kind, having discovered a land which had been peopled with a people who were as numerous as the hosts of Israel." (Mosiah 8:8)

Additional events that occurred in the land southward are the following:

1. About 30 BC, Lamanite prophets came *down* to Zarahemla from the land of Nephi. Their plan was to exhort the Nephites to repentance (see Helaman 6:4). In 6 BC, Samuel the Lamanite traveled to Zarahemla to preach repentance and to prophesy the Nephite destruction (see Helaman 13–15).

2. Upon the death of Christ, a great and terrible destruction took place in the land southward (see 3 Nephi 8:12).

3. In the year AD 350, the Nephites made a land-division treaty with the Lamanites and the Gadianton robbers in which the Nephites gave all of the land southward to the Lamanites: "And the Lamanites did give unto us the land northward, yea, even to the narrow passage which led into the land southward. And we did give unto the Lamanites all the land southward" (Mormon 2:29).

4. Izapa Stela 5 was discovered in the state of Chiapas near the Guatemala border. This stone has engravings that have been correlated with Lehi's dream in the Book of Mormon.[1]

5. The east wilderness in the Book of Mormon is the designated area where the military commander Moroni caused many cities to be built from 72 BC–65 BC. The Peten jungle of Guatemala and the small country of Belize seem to fit the geographical and cultural structure to be the east wilderness.

6. Bountiful, in addition to being the general area of the land southward, appears also to have been a land or state much like the land of Nephi and the land of Zarahemla. From this perspective, the land (state) of Bountiful was probably located in the lowland Mexican states of Yucatan, Quintana Roo, Campeche, and part of Tabasco.

Ether 9:31–32—Land Southward

And there came forth poisonous serpents also upon the face of the land, and did poison many people. And it came to pass that their [Jaredites'] flocks began to flee before the poisonous serpents, towards the *land southward,* which was called by the Nephites Zarahemla.

And it came to pass that there were many of them which did perish by the way; nevertheless, there were some which fled into the *land southward.* (emphasis added)

During the Jaredite time period, the land southward was not extensively inhabited. This land consisted of high, rugged mountains and low, dense jungles—both of which are very difficult land types to conquer and to eke out a living.

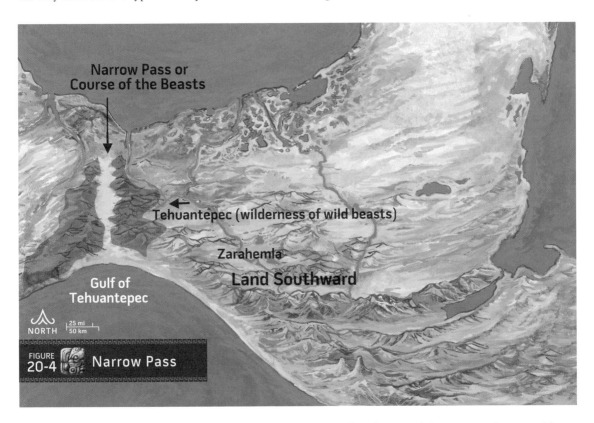

FIGURE 20–4: "And it came to pass that the people did follow the course of the beasts" (see Ether 9:31–34). The narrow pass that runs north from the Gulf of Tehuantepec to the Gulf of Mexico literally means "course of the beasts." The syllables *Tehuani* in the word *Tehuantepec* mean wild beasts. Thus, the narrow pass runs through the Isthmus of Tehuantepec—or the small neck of land. The narrow pass leads into the land southward, as indicated by the arrow.

The area that was called *Zarahemla* may well have been the rugged, jungle-type mountains that now constitute the beautiful but wilderness-type land mass of the state of Chiapas.

The land of Zarahemla subsequently may even have included the Peten jungle of Guatemala and Belize. These areas were developed by a heavily populated culture after the close of the Jaredite period. However, during the Jaredite period, as indicated in Ether 9:31–32, the land southward was virtually uninhabited.

A careful reading of these and subsequent verses suggests the dualism imagery that can be associated with this occasion and time period. That is, the Jaredite flocks (a righteous remnant of people) were pursued by wild serpents (secret combinations or governments) as the people fled from the land northward toward the land southward, probably in search of peace and liberty: "And there came forth poisonous serpents . . . and [they] did poison many *people* . . . [and] many of them . . . did perish by the way; nevertheless, there were some which fled into the land southward. . . . And it came to pass that the *people* did follow the course of the beasts" (Ether 9:31–34; emphasis added).

> The "course of the beasts" where the flocks (people) would have traveled is the trail or road through the Isthmus of Tehuantepec, and this route still carries the same meaning today.

The "course of the beasts" where the flocks (people) would have traveled is the trail or road through the Isthmus of Tehuantepec, and this route still carries the same meaning today. That is, the path of the Tehuani through the isthmus has the same meaning as "the course of the wild beasts." Further, the word *Tehuantepec* means "wilderness of wild beasts." Some of the descendants of these Jaredite people may have gone with Nephi to establish the city of Nephi and may be associated with the "remnant" of the Jaredites alluded to by King Limhi (Mosiah 8:12; see the discussion about this verse

FIGURE 20–5: The powerful jaguar is the most feared of all animals in Mesoamerica and is indigenous to the area designated as the land southward. The mountains of Chiapas, which we propose are located in the land of Zarahemla, are home to many species of the cat family. Mormon's name appears to be associated with the ferocious jaguar. Forty percent of the wild animals of Mexico are native to the state of Chiapas. (Photo courtesy of Courtney Boice; photo taken at the outdoor La Venta Museum)

Exploring the Lands of the Book of Mormon

in chapter 2, "And Then It Came to Pass"; see also chapter 9, "The Izapa [Jaredite-Nephite-Lamanite] Culture").

The Book of Mormon account is consistent with the archaeological record, as the area proposed as the land southward shows a much smaller population during the Jaredite time period—unlike the heavily populated land northward. The reference to Zarahemla's being the land southward apparently has reference to a portion of the land southward's being called Zarahemla—like Chiapas is a state in Mexico today.

The similitude of comparing a wicked "secret combination" government to poisonous serpents "which did poison many people" (Ether 9:31) is consistent with the concept of dualism—or the manner of writing of the Jews—and correlates with the culture and environment of the area under consideration. Today, serpents are still in great abundance in the area proposed as both the land northward and the land southward. One entire building at the zoo in Tuxtla Gutierrez, Chiapas, is dedicated to snakes. Tuxtla Gutierrez is located in the area that is proposed in *Exploring the Lands of the Book of Mormon* as the land southward.

Ether 10:21—Land Southward

And they did preserve the *land southward* for a wilderness, to get game. And the whole face of the land northward was covered with inhabitants. (emphasis added)

Consistent with this scripture, the land southward (Chiapas) during the Jaredite time period was sparsely inhabited. In fact, it became a hunting ground for the inhabitants in the land northward to search out wild animals for food.

The area designated as the land southward in *Exploring the Lands of the Book of Mormon* fits that description in an exciting manner. We can only assume that many of the kinds of animals that were hunted three thousand years ago by the Jaredites are still in existence today. If that is the case, the Jaredites hunted such animals as the deer, the wild boar, and a number of species of the jaguar family.[2] To this very day, over 40 percent of the wild animals of the entire country of Mexico have their habitat in the state of Chiapas. Only 4 percent of the people population of Mexico reside in Chiapas.

Helaman 4:8—Land Southward

And thus those dissenters of the Nephites, with the help of a numerous army of the Lamanites, had obtained all the possession of the Nephites which was in the *land southward*. And all this was done in the fifty and eighth and ninth years of the reign of the judges [about 34 BC]. (emphasis added)

The similitude of comparing a wicked "secret combination" government to poisonous serpents "which did poison many people" (Ether 9:31) is consistent with the concept of dualism—or the manner of writing of the Jews—and correlates with the culture and environment of the area under consideration.

2. A sixteenth-century writer, Sahagun, described the manner in which the natives hunted the beautiful and lightning-fast jaguar. If the hunter shot an arrow, the jaguar oftentimes fended it off with his paw and then devoured the hunter. The problem was solved by making a slit in one side of a leaf and placing it carefully on an arrow. As the arrow was in flight toward the targeted jaguar, the leaf fell off the arrow, thus distracting the jaguar and allowing the arrow to hit its target.

The archaeological record of Mesoamerica manifests a large number of Middle Preclassic sites (250 BC–AD 50). All cities were either Maya or Maya related during the time period in question.

The above scripture also implies that Nephites were living in the land northward during this time period. In the model we propose, the archaeological site of Monte Alban is located in the land northward, a site that was probably inhabited by Nephites from 180 BC–AD 360.

Over 40 percent of the wild animals of the entire country of Mexico have their habitat in the state of Chiapas. Only 4 percent of the people population of Mexico reside in Chiapas.

Alma 22:30–32—Land Southward-Bountiful

And it [Bountiful] bordered upon the land which they called Desolation, it being so far northward that it came into the land which had been peopled and been destroyed, of whose bones we have spoken, which was discovered by the people of Zarahemla, it [land northward] being the place of their [Mulekites'] first landing.

And they [Mulekites] came from there up into the *south wilderness*. Thus the land on the northward was called Desolation, and the land on *the southward* was called Bountiful, it being the wilderness which is filled with all manner of wild animals of every kind, a part of which had come from the land northward for food.

And now, it was only the distance of a day and a half's journey for a Nephite, on the line Bountiful and the land Desolation, from the east to the west sea; and thus the land of Nephi and the land of Zarahemla were nearly surrounded by water, there being a small neck of land between the land northward and the *land southward*. (emphasis added)

The term "land southward" was first used by the Nephites between 90 and 77 BC in relationship to the mission of the sons of Mosiah among the Lamanites in the land of Nephi. "Land southward" and "land northward" may have been Jaredite terminology, as the Nephites seemed to associate both Zarahemla and Bountiful with the land southward.

In verses 30–32, the term "Bountiful" appears to be synonymous with the land southward. This association is consistent with the Spanish chronicles, which state that the second settlers from the time of the giants called the general area Tollan (Tula). *Tula* means place of reeds or land of abundance (Bountiful).

This rationale suggests that Bountiful in the Book of Mormon not only was a city and a state but also served as an umbrella place-name over the entire land southward and thereby functioned as a country. For example, the land of Nephi, the land of Zarahemla, and the land of Bountiful were all lands or states within the country, or general area, of Bountiful.

This thinking is consistent with Mexico culture today. The state of Veracruz, the state of Oaxaca, and the state of Mexico are all states within the country of Mexico. And the principal city of each of these states bears the same name as the state, just as the city of Nephi, the city of Zarahemla, and the city of Bountiful carried the names of the larger land areas.

This explanation helps solve a major geographical issue in the Book of Mormon. Some writers have attempted to solve the problem by (1) rotating the map and creating a new direction called the "Nephite north"[3] or (2) creating two lands of Bountiful equal in land mass.[4] Bountiful in the Book of Mormon makes boundary contact with both the east sea and the west sea. Allowing Bountiful to function as a city, state, and country is fundamental to understanding both Book of Mormon and Mexican cultures.

Almost all references about Bountiful in the Book of Mormon appear to refer to the state of Bountiful or to the city of Bountiful—as opposed to the country of Bountiful. The exceptions occur where the scriptures seem to be talking about the large general area, as is the case in Alma 22:30–32 or in cases where the scriptures are talking about "Bountifulites," much in the same way that the term "Mexican" is used today.

The limited city and land of Bountiful, however, are totally separate from the city and land of Zarahemla. The limited land Bountiful was probably the northern lowlands and, as such, included the Mexican states of Tabasco, Campeche, Yucatan, and Quintana Roo (Cancun). The land of Zarahemla probably encompassed the southern lowlands, including the state of Chiapas, Mexico, the department of Peten, Guatemala, and the small country of Belize.

3. John L. Sorenson, *An Ancient American Setting for the Book of Mormon* (Salt Lake City: Deseret Book and Foundation for Ancient Research and Mormon Studies, 1985).

4. F. Richard Hauck, *Deciphering the Geography of the Book of Mormon* (Salt Lake City: Deseret Book, 1988).

Helaman 6:10—Land South

Now the *land south* was called Lehi, and the land north was called Mulek, which was after the son of Zedekiah; for the Lord did bring Mulek into the land north, and Lehi into the *land south*. (emphasis added)

The terms "land north" and "land south" in the above scripture are probably different from the terms "land northward" and "land southward" referred to throughout the Book of Mormon and illustrated in chapters 19 and 20 of *Exploring the Lands of the Book of Mormon*.

In this situation, both of the terms "land north" and "land south" are probably located in the land southward. Although the people of Zarahemla (Mulekites) landed among the Jaredites in the land northward (Alma 22:31) in the sixth century BC, the people of Zarahemla migrated into the land southward where they made their homeland. They were subsequently discovered by Mosiah around 200 BC (see Omni 1:12–17).

In this context, the term "land north" referred to in Helaman 6:10 is the land of Zarahemla, which today includes Chiapas; Peten, Guatemala; Belize; and perhaps part of the Yucatan Peninsula. The term "land south" refers to the land of Nephi (Guatemala

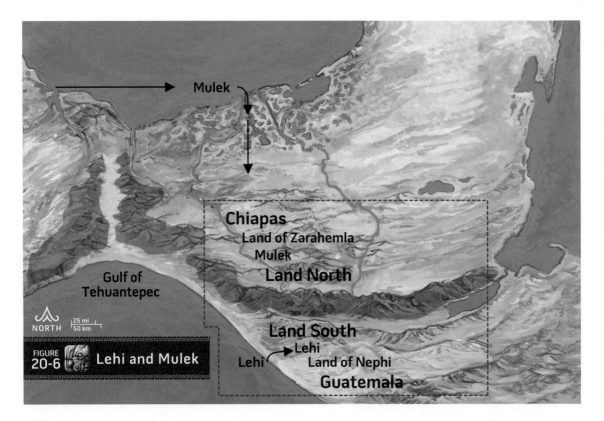

FIGURE 20–6: The Lord brought Mulek into the land north (Zarahemla-Chiapas) and Lehi into the land south (Nephi-Guatemala). The land of Zarahemla where the Lord brought Mulek is north of the land where the Lord brought Lehi. Hence, the Lord brought Mulek into the land north and Lehi into the land south (see Helaman 6:10). Both Zarahemla (land north) and Nephi (land south) are located in the greater land southward. Gold, silver, and jade would have been mined in the mountains between the land of Nephi the land of Zarahemla—or between the land on the north and the land on the south.

highlands), which was established by Nephi in the sixth century BC (see 2 Nephi 5:5–8). Therefore, the terms "land north" and "land south" do not appear to be specific geographical statements as much as directional statements, indicating that the Lord brought Mulek into the northern part of the land southward and Lehi into the southern part of the land southward. Both Zarahemla (the land of the Mulekites) and Nephi (the land of Nephi) were in the land southward.

Note that the following information involves the same scriptures in the chapter 19 discussion about the land northward.

Helaman 3:8—Land Southward

And it came to pass that they did multiply and spread, and did go forth from the *land southward* to the land northward, and did spread insomuch that they began

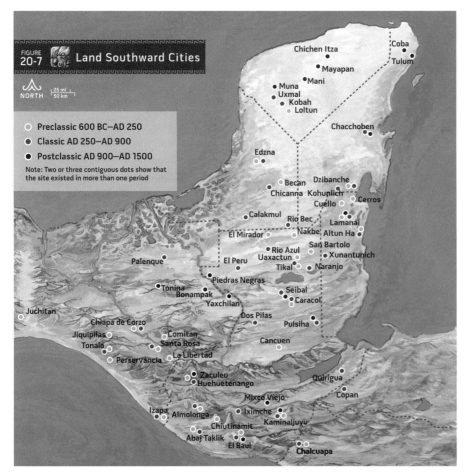

FIGURE 20–7: As shown in this map, many cities existed in the land southward (Maya territory) during the Book of Mormon time period. Also, many cities existed prior to the arrival of Lehi to the promised land, including Tikal, Izapa, and Kaminaljuyu. And many cities were built after the close of the Book of Mormon, including Yaxchilan, Chichen Itza, and Tulum.

to cover the face of the whole earth, from the sea south to the sea north, from the sea west to the sea east. (emphasis added)

Helaman 11:20—The Southward

And thus it did come to pass that the people of Nephi began to prosper again in the land, and began to build up their waste places, and began to multiply and spread, even until they did cover the whole face of the land, both on the northward and on *the southward,* from the sea west to the sea east. (emphasis added)

This general geographical picture accurately describes the Mesoamerica map. It not only gives us a northward-southward direction but also gives us the general coastlines.

If we lived near the Isthmus of Tehuantepec today—where Mormon probably lived— we might say, "They did cover the whole face of the land, both in the land northward and in the land southward, from the Atlantic to the Pacific."

Again, this statement appears to be a more general one, as opposed to a specific geographical statement, and means just what the scripture states: "They spread all over the land." This interpretation fits the geographical picture of Mesoamerica during this time period (about 15 BC). For example, this is the same time that the Maya site of El Mirador was flourishing in northern Guatemala.

Alma 63:5—Bountiful

And it came to pass that Hagoth, he being an exceedingly curious man, therefore he went forth and built him an exceedingly large ship, on the borders of the land *Bountiful,* by the land Desolation, and launched it forth into the west sea, by the narrow neck which led into the land northward. (emphasis added)

In this scripture, the land Bountiful appears to be synonymous with the land southward as used in other scriptures. For example, the narrow pass always leads into the land northward or the land southward. In this case, the identification points are "the land Bountiful," "by the land Desolation," "west sea," "narrow pass," and "land northward."

The border of the greater (country) Bountiful borders Desolation, like the land northward borders the land southward. The Isthmus of Tehuantepec, a narrow pass, is the dividing line between the two larger land masses—land northward (Desolation) and land southward (Bountiful). The west sea, although south of the probable ship-launching area, is still the Pacific Ocean.

3 Nephi 3:24—Land Southward

And there were a great many thousand people who were called Nephites, who did gather themselves together in this land. Now Lachoneus did cause that they should gather themselves together in the *land southward,* because of the great curse which was upon the land northward. (emphasis added)

5. This scripture also lends credibility to a limited geographical area. If the traditional (North America-South America) geographic picture were to be pursued, 3 Nephi 3:24 would require Lachoneus to call Nephites who were living in North America to travel five thousand miles to South America to gather together and to withstand the Gadianton robbers for seven years in the land southward. They would run out of food before they even arrived at the place Lachoneus chose.

During this time period (AD 18), the headquarters of the Nephite record keepers were still in the city of Zarahemla. The threat of the Gadianton robbers was so intense that the Nephite chief judge, Lachoneus, structured a welfare program patterned after the program of Joseph of Egypt. That is, the Nephites laid up provisions for seven years. They gathered themselves into one body in the land southward. The leaders called the Nephites (we could refer to them as "church members") together from both the land northward and the land southward—or from both sides of the isthmus (or narrow neck).[5]

The area Lachoneus and the Nephites chose was a part of the land of Zarahemla between the center land of Zarahemla bordering on Desolation and Bountiful:

And it came to pass in the forty and ninth year of the reign of the judges, there was continual peace established in the land, all save it were the secret combinations which Gadianton the robber had established in the more settled parts of the land, which at that time were not known unto those who were at the head of government; therefore they were not destroyed out of the land. (Helaman 3:23)

And the land which was appointed was the land of Zarahemla, and the land which was between the land Zarahemla and the land Bountiful, yea, to the line which was between the land Bountiful and the land Desolation. (3 Nephi 3:23)

A probable location of this seven-year fortified area appears to be in the mountains, as the robbers had to go "up" to battle against the Nephites (see 3 Nephi 4:4). The general area that seems to fit this description, from a cultural, geographical, and distance perspective, is the mountains of the state of Chiapas between Palenque and San Cristobal de las Casas.

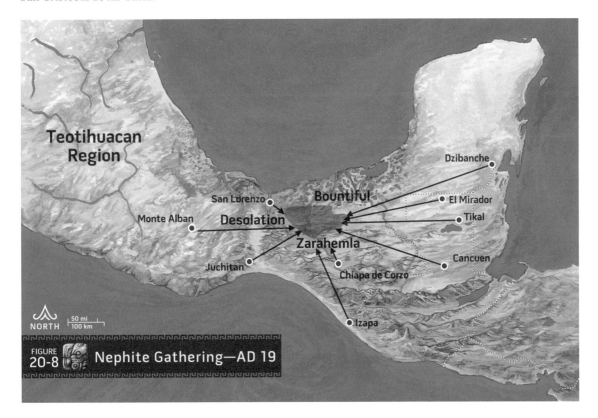

FIGURE 20–8: "The land which was appointed was the land of Zarahemla . . . and the land Bountiful, yea, to the line which was between the land Bountiful and the land Desolation" (3 Nephi 3:23). Lachoneus, the chief judge of the Nephites, called his people to defend themselves against the robbers. As shown in this map, the location chosen is in the same mountains where the native people today (guerillas) hide out from the government of Mexico. Even though Mexico's military forces take tanks into the Chiapas Mountains to combat the guerillas, these heavy, armored vehicles are of little value in the steep, rugged mountain terrain.

3 Nephi 4:1—Lands on the South

[The Gadianton robbers] began to take possession of the lands, both which were in the land south and which were in the land north, and began to take possession of all the lands which had been deserted by the Nephites, and the cities which had been left desolate.

Once the Nephites had gathered together, the robbers began to inhabit the cities and lands left "desolate" by the Nephites. These cities were probably located in Chiapas and perhaps even in the Guatemala Peten and the Mexico Yucatan areas. This lowland jungle environment requires a tremendous amount of physical labor just to survive. Apparently, the robbers were not of a disposition to work that hard—so they robbed to sustain their existence.

As suggested, "land south" and "land north" in this scripture are probably the Peten and the Yucatan. At any rate, they do not appear to refer to the "land northward" or to the "land southward."

3 Nephi 6:2—Land Southward-On the South

And it came to pass that they had not eaten up all their provisions; therefore they did take with them all that they had not devoured, of all their grain of every kind, and their gold, and their silver, and all their precious things, and they did return to their own lands and their possessions, both on the north and *on the south,* both on the land northward and on the *land southward.* (emphasis added)

In this scripture, all four terms are used—that is, "land north," "land south," "land northward," and "land southward." The term "south" may be synonymous with the land southward.

However, when taken in the context of the previous scripture (3 Nephi 4:1), all four terms may mean different geographical areas. The land southward and the land northward have already been defined. The land north and the land south, when reported in conjunction with the Nephites' returning to their lands, may have reference to the Peten (land south) and Yucatan (land north), as proposed previously (see figure 19–6 in chapter 19, "The Land Northward").

3 Nephi 8:11—Land Southward

And there was a great and terrible destruction in the *land southward.* (emphasis added)

The great destruction recorded in the Book of Mormon at the Crucifixion of Christ is also recorded in the Spanish chronicles, and the dates are identical.

> The great destruction recorded in the Book of Mormon at the Crucifixion of Christ is also recorded in the Spanish chronicles, and the dates are identical.

Ixtlilxochitl said that "the sun and the moon eclipsed and the earth quaked and rocks were broken into pieces and many other signs that had been given came to pass, although man was not destroyed. This was in the year Ce Calli, which, adjusted to our calendar, happened at the same time that Christ, our Lord, was crucified. And they say that this destruction occurred in the first few days of the year."[6]

6. See Ixtlilxochitl:16 in chapter 11, "Fernando de Alva Ixtlilxochitl."

In 3 Nephi 8:5, we learn that the destruction began on the fourth day of the thirty-fourth year. It is common knowledge—and well documented—that the area referred to as the land southward is extremely sensitive to earthquakes and volcanoes.

The capital city of the country of Guatemala has been moved three times because of destructive earthquake activity. In 1976, a devastating earthquake shook Guatemala, which is in the area we call the land southward. Ninety percent of the town of Patzicia (population 13,000 at the time) was destroyed in the earthquake of 1976.

Rarely a year goes by without some type of earthquake and volcanic activity in the "land southward" area. Thirty-three volcanic mountains are found in the country of Guatemala, a country about half the size of the state of Utah in the United States.

A volcanic mountain by the name of Tacana divides the countries of Mexico and Guatemala today near Tapachula, Chiapas, Mexico. These volcanic mountains are beautiful to behold, but they wreak death and turmoil when they erupt. The relatively recent volcanic eruptions of El Chichonal in the Mexican state of Chiapas reminded residents of the continual geological danger in the area.

CITIES ASSOCIATED WITH THE AD 34 DESTRUCTION

The land southward cities that are mentioned as being destroyed or damaged during the great AD 34 earthquake are Zarahemla, Moroni, Moronihah, and Jerusalem. Laman, Gad, Kishkumen, Josh, Onihah, and Mocum may also have been in the land southward. They were burned, covered over with debris, or otherwise damaged in the AD 34 earthquake.

Zarahemla

Behold, that great city Zarahemla have I burned with fire, and the inhabitants thereof. (3 Nephi 9:3)

The city/land of Zarahemla is mentioned more often than any other city or land in the Book of Mormon. John Sorenson, in his book, *An Ancient American Setting for the Book of Mormon,* proposes that the archaeological site of Santa Rosa in the upper Grijalva valley in the state of Chiapas, Mexico, was the ancient city of Zarahemla.[7] Some writers consider sites located in the middle Usumacinta valley, along the banks of the Usumacinta River, as Zarahemla. One such site is the Maya site of Yaxchilan. However, this site is post–Book of Mormon and does not satisfy the time period required to be Zarahemla.

7. Sorenson, *An Ancient American Setting for the Book of Mormon,* 152.

For a more detailed discussion of the city/land of Zarahemla, see chapter 29, "The Land of Zarahemla."

On the Mesoamerica map, the city of Moroni probably was near the borders of the countries of Belize and Guatemala. No archaeological site is representative of the city of Moroni, as it sank into the east sea during the AD 34 destruction.

Moroni

That great city Moroni have I caused to be sunk in the depths of the sea. (3 Nephi 9:4)

In Alma 50:13, we learn that the city of Moroni was by the east sea, on the south by the borders of the Lamanites. This directional location of the city of Moroni makes it very identifiable if we establish highland Guatemala as the land of Nephi (Lamanite territory). On the Mesoamerica map, the city of Moroni probably was near the borders of the countries of Belize and Guatemala. No archaeological site is representative of the city of Moroni, as it sank into the east sea during the AD 34 destruction. The city of Moroni was located in the land southward.

Moronihah

That great city Moronihah have I covered with earth. (3 Nephi 9:5; see also 3 Nephi 8:10, 25)

The city of Moronihah was probably named after Moronihah, the son of the military leader Moroni (see Alma 8:7). It was probably built in the first century BC, during which time many Nephite cities were built in the east wilderness (Alma 50:15), including the city of Moroni mentioned above.

No geographical guidelines are found in the Book of Mormon to help us establish the location of the city of Moronihah. However, by making the assumption that the city was named after the son of the military leader Moroni, we might speculate that the city of Moronihah was in Chiapas, Peten, or the Yucatan—all of which are located in the land southward.

Jerusalem

The city of Jerusalem and the inhabitants thereof; and waters have I caused to come up in the stead thereof. (3 Nephi 9:7)

The first time the New World city of Jerusalem is mentioned is about 90 BC in relation to the missionary journeys of the sons of Mosiah. The city was built in Lamanite territory by Lamanites and Nephite dissenters. Amulon, who was a colleague of Alma in the Nephite King Noah's court, appears to have been the driving force behind the building of the city. The city of Jerusalem was also by the borders of Mormon, which was by the waters of Mormon (see Alma 21:1; see also Mosiah 18:4, 5, 8). The land of Mormon was located in the greater land of Nephi. All the above places were located in the land southward.

Upon entering the borders of the Lamanites, the sons of Mosiah separated themselves and went to different sections of the land. Aaron, one of the sons of Mosiah, went to the city of Jerusalem. From Jerusalem, lying in a northwest direction, is Lake Atitlan. Beautiful and serene, this lake has been proposed by many Book of Mormon scholars as the waters of Mormon. Assuming that Lake Atitlan is the waters of Mormon and knowing that the city of Jerusalem was near the forest of Mormon, we can deduce that a preliminary candidate for the city of Jerusalem is the town of Santiago Atitlan in Solola, Guatemala. Because the city of Jerusalem was covered with water by the destruction at the time of the Crucifixion of Christ, the city must meet the following requirements:

1. Be located near the borders of the Lamanites and near the borders of the land of Mormon.

2. Be an inland lake not too far removed from the city of Nephi.

3. Have evidence of settlements dating to 100 BC.

4. Reflect geological evidence of water covering the area. The volcanic peak of San Pedro demonstrates just such a blowout, indicating the possibility of water's covering an inland city.

All four requirements are met with the site of Santiago Atitlan.

Onihah

The city of Onihah was also covered by water at the time of the great destruction (see 3 Nephi 9:7). Although no other geographical description is given, because of the city's suffix ending, "hah," we might assume that Onihah has both a prefix "oni" from Moroni, meaning ancient, and a suffix "ha," meaning water. Because it is mentioned as being covered by water, it, like Jerusalem, may have been another city by the waters of Mormon in the land southward.

Mocum

The city of Mocum was also covered by water at the time of the destruction (see 3 Nephi 9:7). The name has a familiar ring when associated with the Maya word "cum," meaning a water gourd. It, like Jerusalem and Onihah, was probably another city that was covered by the waters of Mormon. In recent years, underwater archaeology has revealed artifacts at Lake Atitlan dating to the time of Christ.

Gadiandi and Gadiomnah

The city of Gadiandi and the city of Gadiomnah were covered with earth at the destruction (see 3 Nephi 9:8). No additional information is given. The prefix of "Gad" may suggest a Gadianton robber affiliation, but this deduction is not certain. Besides, the Gadianton robbers seemed to sprout up in both the land northward and in the land southward. The locations of these two cities are very uncertain.

The name *Mocum* has a familiar ring when associated with the Maya word *cum*, meaning a water gourd. Mocum was probably another city that was covered by the waters of Mormon during the great AD 34 destruction. In recent years, underwater archaeology has revealed artifacts at Lake Atitlan dating to the time of Christ.

Gimgimno

The city of Gimgimno was also covered with earth (see 3 Nephi 9:8). This city may have been located in the land northward because Gimgimno is mentioned in the same statement with the city of Jacob, which possibly was in the land northward. Gimgimno's location is a toss-up between the land northward and the land southward.

Laman

The city of Laman was burned by fire (see 3 Nephi 9:10). This city was probably located in the land southward and was most likely located in the land of Nephi. The city of Laman was probably named after Laman, the son of Lehi. An ancient Maya site named Lamanai is located in the country of Belize. Lamanai is in the area we have labeled as the east wilderness. The city of Laman might also have a connection with Lamoni, who was a Lamanite king and a contemporary of the sons of Mosiah and of Moroni in the books of Mosiah and Alma.

Josh

The city of Josh was also destroyed by fire. We have no indication as to its location (see 3 Nephi 9:10).

Gad

The city of Gad was destroyed by fire (see 3 Nephi 9:10). If Gad is named after Gadianton, it was probably located along the Guatemala (land of Nephi) and Chiapas (land of Zarahemla) frontiers in the land southward.

Kishkumen

The city of Kishkumen was also destroyed by fire (see 3 Nephi 9:10). This city was probably named after the robber Kishkumen and, like the city of Gad, may have been located along the Chiapas and Guatemala borders. Even today, the mountains near Huehuetenango, Guatemala, are the refuge of the guerrillas who hide in these mountains and who engage in guerrilla warfare.

> Even today, the mountains near Huehuetenango, Guatemala, are the refuge of the guerrillas who hide in these mountains and who engage in guerrilla warfare.

ADDITIONAL LAND SOUTHWARD SCRIPTURES

We will now return to our general discussion of scriptures that pertain to the land southward.

Mormon 1:6—Land Southward

And it came to pass that I, being eleven years old, was carried by my father into the *land southward*, even to the land of Zarahemla. (emphasis added)

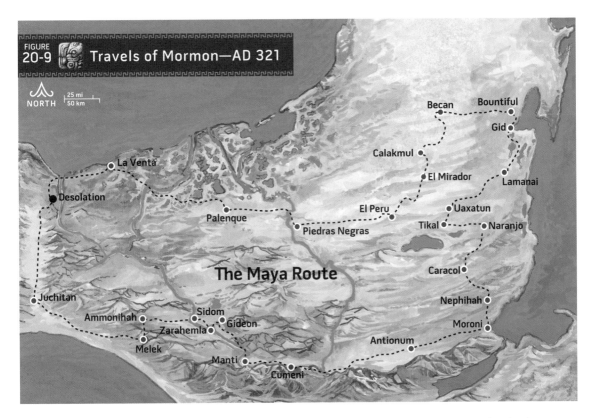

FIGURE 20–9: Mormon wrote, "I, being eleven years old, was carried by my father into the land southward, even to the land of Zarahemla. The whole face of the land had become covered with buildings" (Mormon 1:6–7). We can only speculate about the places he may have visited. However, because this is the beginning of the Maya Classic Period when many cities were beginning to be built, we can assume that he visited not only the city of Zarahemla but also the regions of Peten, Belize, and southern Yucatan. This map projects Mormon's travels from the city of Desolation (where he lived in the land northward) into the land southward, following a possible Maya route in the early fourth century.

This statement represents a date of approximately AD 322, well into the Maya Classic Period. Beginning at AD 200, a massive pyramid-building program began in the area called the land southward. Major archaeological sites dating to this period include Tikal, El Mirador, Kaminaljuyu, Uxmal, Bonampak, Uaxactun, Coba, Becan, Copan, Dzibanche, Kohunlich, Lamanai, and many others. The land southward was heavily populated, and the priests (or hierarchy) controlled the social, religious, and commercial activities of the people. Mormon says, "The whole face of the land had become covered with buildings, and the people were as numerous almost, as it were the sand of the sea" (Mormon 1:7).

Mormon was eleven years old when his father took him to the land of Zarahemla, which was in the land southward. Mormon's statement suggests, and is substantiated by other references, that Mormon lived in the land northward—or on the northward side of the narrow neck of land (Isthmus of Tehuantepec).

Mormon 2:29—Land Southward

And the Lamanites did give unto us the land northward, yea, even to the narrow passage which led into the *land southward*. And we did give unto the Lamanites all the *land southward*. (emphasis added)

In a treaty that became effective at AD 350, the Nephites lost control of everything southward of the narrow neck of land. The area described as the land southward fits both the geographical and archaeological detail with the area located south and east of the Isthmus of Tehuantepec during this time period. On the one hand, great buildings continued to be built to honor the priestly rulers, whereas some sites declined in population.

El Mirador, a magnificent site in northern Guatemala near the Mexican state of Campeche, appears to have been totally abandoned at this time. This archaeological finding is consistent with the Book of Mormon account, which states that by AD 360, the people had gathered together at the land Desolation (see Mormon 3:5).

Mormon 3:5—Land Southward

And it came to pass that I did cause my people that they should gather themselves together at the land Desolation, to a city which was in the borders, by the narrow pass which led into the *land southward*. (emphasis added)

The AD 350 treaty apparently was not a friendly treaty, as we read in the Book of Mormon that the Nephites continued to go to battle against the Lamanites. Ten years after the treaty (AD 360), the people were gathered at the land Desolation. The land Desolation was in the land northward near the narrow pass that led into the land southward.

Mormon 8:2—Country Southward

And now it came to pass that after the great and tremendous battle at Cumorah, behold, the Nephites who had escaped into the *country southward* were hunted by the Lamanites, until they were all destroyed. (emphasis added)

Most Latter-day Saint Mesoamericanists today propose that the last Nephite-Lamanite battle at AD 385 was fought at a hill called Vigia, about ninety miles north of the Gulf of Tehuantepec. This location is consistent with internal geographical statements in the Book of Mormon, especially the Book of Mormon requirement that the hill Ramah/Cumorah be near the narrow neck of land (see chapter 27, "Hills and Valleys").

Logically, the defeated Nephites probably wanted to return to their homelands in the land southward from where they had been called some fifteen years earlier to

In a treaty that became effective at AD 350, the Nephites lost control of everything southward of the narrow neck of land. The area described as the land southward fits both the geographical and archaeological detail with the area located south and east of the Isthmus of Tehuantepec during this time period.

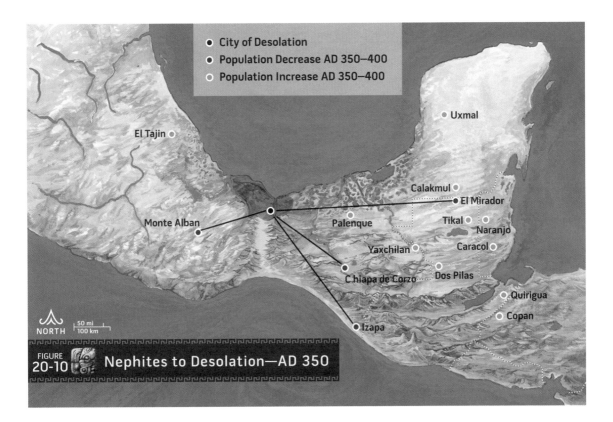

FIGURE 20–10: At the close of the Book of Mormon, a population explosion occurred, and many new cities were under construction. These developments correlate with the beginning of the Maya Classic Period. Some of the old Nephite cities decreased in population following the AD 350 treaty (see Mormon 2:28–29) and the call of Mormon for the Nephites to gather into the land Desolation at AD 362. Some major archaeological sites that declined in population at this time were Izapa, Chiapa de Corzo, and El Mirador.

reoccupy the cities they had abandoned. Once the Nephite nation fell, the dissenters were either killed by the Lamanites, were integrated into the Lamanite culture by submitting to Lamanite government, or became part of a Nephite diaspora. Under those circumstances, they and their descendants may still have occupied space in the land southward.

As we think about the location of the hill Cumorah as described in the Book of Mormon itself, we should consider the following points:

1. Mormon charged the Nephites to fight for their homes (see Mormon 2:23, AD 346).

2. The Nephites gathered their people to the city of Desolation located by the narrow pass that led into the land southward (see Mormon 3:5, AD 360).

3. After the great battle at Cumorah, many Nephites escaped into the land southward (see Mormon 8:2, AD 385).

These statements indicate that Cumorah was not too far from the narrow neck of land—certainly not the two to three thousand miles required if the Book of Mormon Cumorah were the New York Cumorah.

FIGURE 20–11: Chiapas, Mexico, the area designated as the land of Zarahemla, is located in the land southward and is home to the largest native population of Mexico. Shown here is a beautiful native girl from the state of Chiapas, Mexico. (Photo courtesy of Cortney Boice)

The geographical configuration of the land southward fits the Mesoamerican map with its mountain ranges, oceans, rivers, narrow neck, valleys, and other necessary criteria.

SUMMARY

Based on the above discussion about the land southward, we can say the following:

1. Archaeological evidence satisfies the requirement that people were living in the area designated as the land southward during the time period in question.

2. Written language on the American continent was given birth in the area proposed as the land southward.

3. The archaeological ruins explored by John Lloyd Stephens in 1839–40, which were proposed as possible Book of Mormon sites by Joseph Smith as recorded in the *Times and Seasons,* are in the area proposed as the land southward.

4. The geographical configuration of the land southward fits the Mesoamerican map with its mountain ranges, oceans, rivers, narrow neck, valleys, and other necessary criteria.

5. Although limited information is given in the Book of Mormon, the distances between places seem to satisfy the travel time required in the journeys of the Book of Mormon people throughout the land southward.

6. Most Latter-day Saint scholars today who have studied the area of Mesoamerica and the Book of Mormon tend to agree that the area discussed in this chapter is the land southward.

7. The area proposed as the land southward is the same area that the great Maya nation developed during the Book of Mormon time period and continued to dominate up to the Spanish conquest.

8. The land southward is probably separated from the land northward by the Isthmus of Tehuantepec.

9. The land southward is where Lehi's colony first landed and where the land of Nephi, waters of Mormon, land of Zarahemla, and land of Bountiful were located.

FREQUENTLY ASKED QUESTIONS

Question: Didn't Joseph Smith say that Zarahemla was in the area proposed as the land southward, thus giving credibility to the above-stated thesis?

Answer: The *Times and Seasons* (January 15, 1842) reports that the cities described by John Lloyd Stephens are representative of the cities in the Book of Mormon.

In another issue of the *Times and Seasons,* an article appeared with the title "Zarahemla." And because the Prophet Joseph Smith was the editor, the article does have great credibility. A portion of the text is as follows:

> It is certainly a good thing for the excellency and veracity, of the divine authenticity of the Book of Mormon, that the ruins of Zarahemla have been found where the Nephites left them: and that a large stone with engraving upon it, as Mosiah said; and a large round stone, with the sides sculptured in hieroglyphics, as Mr. Stephens has published, is also among the left remembrances of the, (to him) lost and unknown. We are not going to declare positively that *the ruins of Quirigua are those of Zarahemla,* but when the land and the stones, and the books tell the story so plain, we are of the opinion, that it would require more proof than the Jews could bring to prove the disciples stole the body of Jesus from the tomb, to prove that the ruins of the city in question are not one of those referred to in the Book of Mormon.

The ruins of Quirigua are located in Guatemala near the Honduras border in the area proposed as the land southward in *Exploring the Lands of the Book of Mormon.* No question exists but what the nineteenth-century Latter-day Saint writers felt that the ruined cities in Mesoamerica reported and illustrated by Stephens and Catherwood were Book of Mormon cities. On October 1, 1843, John Taylor, who was editor of the *Times and Seasons,* wrote the following: "The 'Book of Mormon' unfolds their history [meaning the history of the people whose ruins were reported by Stephens and Catherwood]; and published [in the Book of Mormon] as it was, years before these discoveries were

No question exists but what the nineteenth-century Latter-day Saint writers felt that the ruined cities in Mesoamerica reported and illustrated by Stephens and Catherwood were Book of Mormon cities.

made, and giving as it does, accounts of a people, and of cities that bear a striking resemblance to those mentioned by Mr. Stephens, both in regard to *magnificence* and *location*, it affords the most indubitable testimony of the historical truth of that book."[8]

8. John Taylor, *Times and Seasons*, October 1, 1843.

If the early brethren considered the Isthmus of Tehuantepec to be the narrow neck of land, then the archaeological ruins described by Stephens are in the land southward. On the other hand, if the Isthmus of Panama were viewed as the narrow neck of land, then Stephens's ruined cities would be in the land northward. Among other places, Catherwood's illustrated buildings and monuments from the sites of Quirigua, Guatemala; Palenque, Chiapas; and Uxmal, Yucatan, would not have been in Nephite territory.

From the time of Stephens's publication in 1841 to the present, additional information and research have dated the just-listed ruins to a Maya Classic time period as follows:

Quirigua   ca. AD 300–AD 900
Palenque   ca. AD 300–AD 900
Uxmal   ca. AD 200–AD 900

This dating does not preclude the fact that earlier populations existed in the above areas. It simply implies that the visible monuments drawn by Catherwood were, for the most part, post–Book of Mormon.

Question: Is Peru then eliminated as part of the land southward?

Answer: Yes. Peru is eliminated as being part of the internal geographical picture of the Book of Mormon that included the land southward. The Inca civilization did not even begin until after the close of the Book of Mormon. This dating does not mean, however, that small settlements extending from Mesoamerica did not reach Peru during Book of Mormon times. Neither does it preclude the possibility that other people lived in the area—people who were not related to the Book of Mormon. Certainly, missionary activity may have taken place among the pre-Inca and the Chavin people of Peru. Peru reflects distinct and impressive traditional records about a white god; and oral traditions demonstrate a feeling of Jewish-Christian ethics. These facts, however, do not qualify Peru to be the geographical backdrop of the Book of Mormon. See chapter 21, "Voyage of the Jaredites," and chapter 22, "Voyages of Lehi and Mulek" for further information.

Peru is eliminated as being part of the internal geographical picture of the Book of Mormon that included the land southward. The Inca civilization did not even begin until after the close of the Book of Mormon.

COMMENTS ABOUT JOHN LLOYD STEPHENS'S
LAND SOUTHWARD EXPLORATIONS

In 1842 and 1843, the Church's newspaper, the *Times and Seasons*, published several quotations from John Lloyd Stephens's books, *Incidents of Travel in Central America, Chiapas and Yucatan* and *Incidents of Travel in Central America*. Stephens's explorations took place in the area we designate as the land southward. The following *Times and Seasons* quotations of Joseph Smith and John Taylor are associated with Stephens's explorations in the land southward. Such quotations negate totally the possibility that the land southward is in Peru or anywhere else in South America.

- The stupendous ruins, the elegant sculpture, and the magnificence of the ruins of [Guatemala], and other cities, . . . show that a great and mighty people—men of great minds, clear intellect, bright genius, and comprehensive designs inhabited this continent. Their ruins speak of their greatness; the Book of [Mormon] unfolds their history. (*Times and Seasons* 3, no. 18, 860)
- Mr. Stephens' great developments of antiquities are made bare to the eyes of all the people by reading the history of the Nephites in the Book of Mormon. They lived about the narrow neck of land, which now embraces Central America, with all the cities that can be found. . . . Who could have dreamed that twelve years would have developed such incontrovertible testimony to the Book of Mormon? (*Times and Seasons* 3, no. 22, 915)
- From an extract from "Stephens' Incidents of Travel in Central America," it will be seen

that the proof of the Nephites and Lamanites dwelling on this continent . . . is developing itself in a more satisfactory way than the most sanguine believer in that revelation, could have anticipated. It certainly affords us a gratification that the world of mankind does not enjoy, to give publicity to such important developments of the remains and ruins of those mighty people. (*Times and Seasons* 3, no. 22, 921–22)

- It is certainly a good thing for the excellency and veracity, of the divine authenticity of the Book of Mormon, that the ruins of Zarahemla have been found where the Nephites left them. . . . We are not going to declare positively that the ruins of Quirigua are those of Zarahemla, but . . . we are of the opinion, that it would require more proof than the Jews could bring to prove the disciples stole the body of Jesus from the tomb, to prove that the ruins of the city in question, are not one of those referred to in the Book of Mormon. (*Times and Seasons* 3, no. 23, 927)
- It will not be a bad plan to compare Mr. Stephens' ruined cities with those in the Book of Mormon: light cleaves to light, and facts are supported by facts. The truth injures no one. (*Times and Seasons* 3, no. 23, 927)
- This is a work [*Incidents of Travel in Central America*] that ought to be in the hands of every Latter Day Saint; corroborating, as it does the history of the Book of Mormon. There is no stronger circumstantial evidence of the authenticity of the latter book. (*Times and Seasons* 4, no. 22, 346)

CHAPTER 21

Voyage of the Jaredites

I will bless thee and thy seed, and raise up unto me of thy seed, and of the seed of thy brother, and they who shall go with thee, a great nation. And there shall be none greater than the nation which I will raise up unto me of thy seed, upon all the face of the earth. (Ether 1:43)

The Book of Mormon speaks of three groups of people who migrated from the Old World to the promised land. Moroni, the son of Mormon, refers to the first group of people as "the ancient inhabitants who were destroyed by the hand of the Lord upon the face of this north country." We simply call them *Jaredites*. The name "Jaredite" is taken from the first king mentioned in the book of Ether, whose name was Jared. The Jaredites traveled to the promised land at the time of the confusion of the languages as recorded in Genesis.

The second group of people is subsequently divided into two subgroups in the Book of Mormon. They are called Lamanites and Nephites. Laman (Lamanites) and Nephi (Nephites) were brothers. Their father's name was Lehi. Lehi led his family and another

OPPOSITE: "[The Jaredites] were driven forth; and no monster of the sea could break them.... They were driven forth, three hundred and forty and four days upon the water. And they did land upon the shore of the promised land" (Ether 6:10–12). This Olmec monument located at the outdoor La Venta Park Museum was engraved between 1200 and 600 BC—during the Jaredite time period. It suggests a sea voyage, as a man is defending himself against what appears to be a shark or, as stated in Ether, a sea monster. (Photos courtesy of Sheryl Lee Wilson)

It is rather paradoxical that the Jaredites lived in what today are the two richest oil-producing areas in the world. Their history began at the great tower of Babel near the Persian Gulf and then came to an end at Veracruz and Tabasco along the Gulf of Mexico.

1. John L. Sorenson, *An Ancient American Setting for the Book of Mormon* (Salt Lake City: Deseret Book and Foundation for Ancient Research and Mormon Studies, 1985), xvi-xvii.

man's family by the name of Ishmael out of Jerusalem in the year 600 BC. About twelve years later, they arrived in the promised land.

The third group of people referred to in the Book of Mormon was called the people of Zarahemla. Zarahemla was a descendant of Mulek (see Mosiah 25:2). Mulek was a son of King Zedekiah III, who ruled in the sixth century BC in Jerusalem (see Helaman 8:21). Since the publication of the Book of Mormon, Latter-day Saints have called this third group "Mulekites."

In this chapter, we will discuss the voyage of the Jaredites, and in chapter 22, we will discuss the voyages of Lehi and Mulek.

The places of landing in the New World of these three groups have long been of interest to students of the Book of Mormon. Many readers have speculated—and still continue to speculate—where each group landed. Other students of the Book of Mormon prefer not to speculate about the landings.

John Sorenson, in his book, *An Ancient American Setting for the Book of Mormon*, writes of the dilemma as follows: "The task of establishing a realistic setting for the Book of Mormon is a big, challenging one. Research by Latter-day Saints and others over the past [sixty] years has made it possible for us to know a good deal of concrete detail about the Jerusalem from which Lehi led his family; in our mind's eye we can now follow his party through a line of campsites down the Red Sea side of the Arabian peninsula and across to a specific 'bountiful land' on the Hadhramaut coast. But the minute the party climb into Nephi's ship and launch their journey into the Indian Ocean, we lose that sense of concreteness. Landed in the New World, they are just vaguely 'somewhere.'"[1]

Although minute detail may be lacking as to where the three migrating groups of people landed, by utilizing both internal and external sources, we may hypothesize a general area for the landing sites of the Jaredites, Lehites, and Mulekites. In other words, we may be able to reduce the "vaguely somewhere" to a more limited space to capture a more realistic picture of the Book of Mormon story.

THE VOYAGE OF THE JAREDITES

The Jaredites migrated to the New World from the Tower of Babel about 2800 BC. They journeyed a great distance and then crossed the ocean in 344 days. They developed a mighty nation in an area the Nephites called the land northward—Desolation.

As previously discussed, the heartland of the Classic Period of the Jaredite civilization (1500 BC–600 BC) manifests definitive evidence to have been along the Gulf of Mexico. That area probably continued to function as the headquarters for the Jaredites until their destruction around 250 BC. The area also may have been the central location of the early Jaredites beginning with the fifth king from Jared, a man named Omer (see Ether 9:3).

These deductions, however, do not specifically localize the landing spot of the Jaredites. Moroni, the fourth-century AD Book of Mormon writer, gives us an account of the ancient inhabitants "who were destroyed by the hand of the Lord upon the face of *this north country*" (see Ether 1:1; emphasis added).

Ixtlilxochitl, who wrote in the sixteenth century, also tells us that the first settlers, who came from the Tower of Babel, "populated the major part of the land, and more particularly the *northern part*."[2]

2. Ixtlilxochitl:21; emphasis added; see chapter 11, "Fernando de Alva Ixtlilxochitl."

The "north country" in Moroni's writing and the "northern part" in Ixtlilxochitl's history are, in all probability, the Gulf of Mexico area that today is called the "Faja de Oro," or golden lane, because of its fertile environment and the abundance of oil that has been discovered there. This is the same area where archaeology bears testimony of the most ancient civilization of Mesoamerica and the most populous and advanced civilization of the New World—the Olmecs. It is rather paradoxical that the Jaredites lived in what today are the two richest oil-producing areas in the world. Their history began at the great tower of Babel near the Persian Gulf and then came to an end at Veracruz and Tabasco along the Gulf of Mexico.

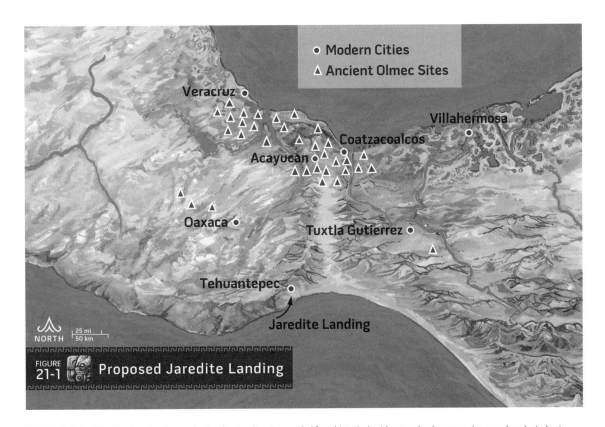

FIGURE 21–1: Justification for a Pacific crossing by the Jaredites is provided from historical evidence, calendar comparisons, archaeological evidence, and information from the Book of Mormon. We propose that the Jaredite landing was near the Gulf of Tehuantepec by the present-day state of Oaxaca, Mexico.

Just because the Jaredites lived near the Gulf of Mexico does not suggest an Atlantic Ocean voyage. We see at least five reasons why the Jaredites in their eight barges crossed the Pacific as opposed to the Atlantic Ocean:

1. The distance of travel time for the Jaredites consisted of 344 days (Ether 6:11). Historically, the travel time by ship from the Old World to the New World via the Atlantic route required only thirty days.

2. The historian Alva de Ixtlilxochitl wrote that the first settlers came from the land of the tartars (Asia), which would require a Pacific crossing.

3. The parallel structures of the Maya calendar with the Chinese calendars suggest a positive correlation for Pacific commerce in ancient times.

4. Many Olmec monuments manifest oriental facial features, suggesting a relationship with Mesoamerica and the East in the time of the Jaredites.

5. The Jaredite capital of Moron where the king dwelt bordered on the land that the Nephites called Desolation (Ether 7:5–6), suggesting that the Jaredites landed and

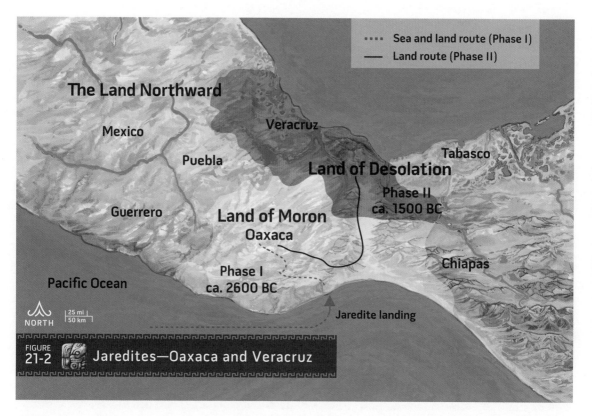

FIGURE 21–2: Three witnesses—the archaeology of the Olmecs, the writings of Ixtlilxochitl, and the book of Ether—all bear witness that the heartland of the Jaredites from about 1500 BC to 250 BC was in the north, which today is the area along the Gulf of Mexico and which includes the states of Veracruz and Tabasco, Mexico. Evidence also supports the thesis that the Jaredites crossed the Pacific Ocean and initially settled in the Oaxaca valley.

Exploring the Lands of the Book of Mormon

settled initially in Oaxaca and then several generations later migrated to the Atlantic side (Gulf of Mexico).

As stated above, just because the heartland of the Jaredite culture was located along the Gulf of Mexico does not justify placing the Jaredite landings along the Atlantic side of Mesoamerica. The Olmecs did not begin to flourish along the Gulf Coast of Mexico until between 2000 and 1500 BC, which is consistent with the book of Ether where we are informed that several generations had passed from the time the Jaredites arrived at the promised land until they settled along the seashore (see Ether 9:3).

The above statement does not imply that the Jaredites landed initially in some place in the New World other than in Mesoamerica. It simply means they landed on the Pacific side—probably near the Gulf of Tehuantepec where the present-day state of Oaxaca is located, and from there they extended up into the Oaxaca valley where their capital city, Moron, was built.

FIGURE 21–3: Several Olmec monuments manifest oriental features, such as the one shown here from the museum in Xalapa. Calendar correlations have also demonstrated a relationship with China and Mesoamerica. This relationship suggests a plausible Pacific crossing for the Jaredites. (Photo courtesy of Sheryl Lee Wilson)

When the Jaredites settled the Gulf Coast of Mexico several centuries later, they still maintained their occupation of the Oaxaca region. By that time, they had also spread to other regions of Mesoamerica, including the altiplano of Mexico, the state of Guerrero, the Yucatan Peninsula, the Peten region, Izapa, Kaminaljuyu, and El Salvador. By 800 BC, their influence had reached into the southeastern part of the United States and perhaps into the southeastern part of Mesoamerica. The Jaredites, whose downfall as a nation occurred around 250 BC, became the foundation for the Nephite, Lamanite, and Mulekite cultures—and perhaps even other cultures.

The Jaredites (Olmecs) were not the only people who occupied the landscape of the Americas, nor were they the only people who existed in Mesoamerica. They were, however, the mother civilization and the most prominent early culture dating from 2600 BC to dominate the region and ultimately fulfill the promise given to the brother of Jared: "And there shall be none greater than the nation which I will raise up unto me of thy seed, upon all the face of the earth" (Ether 1:43). The ancient Olmec culture, whose origins began in Oaxaca at 2600 BC and flourished beginning at 1500 BC along the Gulf of Mexico until about 250 BC, fulfills those requirements as outlined in chapter 5, "The Olmec (Jaredite) Culture."

The Jaredites (Olmecs) were not the only people who occupied the landscape of the Americas, nor were they the only people who existed in Mesoamerica. They were, however, the mother civilization and the most prominent early culture.

To land the Jaredites at some position in the New World other than Mesoamerica distorts the geography of the Book of Mormon and negates any relationship between the Olmecs and the Jaredites. From time to time, reports surface that attack the Mesoamerica setting as the place where the Jaredites landed and lived out their lives.

PERU AND NEW YORK

We recognize that members of The Church of Jesus Christ of Latter-day Saints who present either a New York or a Peru scenario for Book of Mormon lands do so with a sincerity of purpose. Nevertheless, the Book of Mormon does not allow for the Jaredite city of Lib, the city of Zarahemla, the city of Nephi, the narrow neck of land, or the narrow strip of wilderness to be in more than one place. Further, we cannot legitimately place the Jaredite hill Ramah (which is the same hill as Cumorah) in both Peru and in Mesoamerica, in both New York and in Mesoamerica, or in Peru, New York, Chile, and Mesoamerica. The Book of Mormon does not describe two or three or four hill Cumorahs. Clearly, it identifies only one.

Therefore, the suggestion or proposal to identify some place other than the lands of the Olmecs as being synonymous with the lands of the Jaredites indicates (1) a lack of knowledge of the historical and geographical analysis of Mesoamerica, (2) a lack of understanding of the content of the Book of Mormon itself, or (3) merely a subjective hypothesis to meet some personalized criteria for Book for Mormon lands. In fact, all three options are possible in some instances.

For example, at the time of the final writing of the second edition of *Exploring the Lands of the Book of Mormon,* a report was issued that claimed to have "evidence" that the Jaredites landed in Peru and that Peru was the Jaredite land of promise.[3]

The author, George Potter, who has lived in Saudi Arabia for several years and who has been active in researching the ancient trails of Lehi and Jared, writes the following: "Those who teach that the Olmecs and the Jaredites are the same people and that Mesoamerica is an unconditional setting for the Jaredites are teaching nonsense. Such teaching places the adherents of these hypotheses in a weak position."

The reader will need to determine if the information presented in *Exploring the Lands of the Book of Mormon* is "nonsense" or if the information presents a "weak position." However, any analysis needs to consider the Jaredites in relation to both the Nephites and the Mulekites, as they are all closely linked together. Any analysis needs to present historical evidence of the magnitude of the Book of Mormon. Any analysis needs to demonstrate the evidence of writing during both Jaredite and Nephite time periods. Any analysis needs to include population centers to match the numbers recorded in the Book of Mormon. And any analysis needs to present hypotheses that can be tested regarding name correlations, relative distances, natural landmarks, and marked elevation statements.

3. George Potter, "Did the Jaredites Land in Peru?" The Nephi Project, Bear River City, Utah, www.nephiproject.com, April 1, 2007.

Just because metal working, gold, llamas, and traditions of a white god are available in Peru does not change the information that is in Mesoamerica. And just because tradition places the hill Cumorah in New York does not alter the geographical information in Mesoamerica.

Although it is true that the Chavin of Peru date to the Jaredite time period and although it is also true that some of the ancient mounds discovered in the United States date to the Nephite time period, the limited areas and populations in both places do not negate the Olmecs as being the "mother nation" of the Americas.

We do not intend to enter into a border dispute with Peru and New York. Just because the geography of the Book of Mormon centers in Mesoamerica does not reflect negatively on any other places in the New World any more than the geography of Utah reflects negatively on members of the LDS Church who live in other parts of the world today.

Our thesis remains the same as outlined in chapter 1, "Introduction to the Lands of the Book of Mormon," which is that Mesoamerica is the setting for *all* New World events recorded in the Book of Mormon. We support this thesis with the following comments:

1. A written language. The four hundred AD Incas did *not* have a written language. No evidence exists to suggest that the ancient Chavin of Peru or the natives of New York wrote their histories. On the other hand, the Olmecs did have a written language. For example, in the year 2006, an inscribed stone slab was discovered in the ancient Olmec land of Veracruz. This Olmec artifact is described by archaeologists who have examined it as tantalizing, authentic, worthy of a new era of focus on the Olmec civilization, and an exciting discovery of great significance.[4] Its location is from the same area of and dates to the same time period as King Kish, who has already been discussed in this text and whose ruling date and ascension to the throne are recorded on the Temple of the Cross at Palenque.

2. Population centers. Although the evidence supports a few ancient cities in Peru dating to the Jaredite time period, the numbers are minimal in comparison with the hundreds of cities in Mesoamerica dating to the same time period. Very little evidence has surfaced in the New York region to date artifacts to the Jaredite time period. About two hundred years after the events recorded in Ether 10, Kish became king. According to the genealogy on the Temple of the Cross at Palenque, the date of the ascension to the throne by Kish was in the year 967 BC. In other words, the Mexico Gulf Coast dates of 1200 BC to 600 BC manifest a massive building program during the same time as recorded in the book of Ether. Therefore, instead of a few cities covering a limited area along the Pacific coast of Peru, the Gulf Coast region of Mexico located along the Atlantic manifests hundreds of cities with a network extending hundreds of miles.

3. Historical evidence. The history of the white god Viracocha, which is prevalent in Peruvian legends and which is intriguing, does not establish geographical boundaries.

Just because the geography of the Book of Mormon centers in Mesoamerica does not reflect negatively on any other places in the New World any more than the geography of Utah reflects negatively on members of the LDS Church who live in other parts of the world today.

4. Maria del Carmen Rodriguez Martinez, et al., "Did the Olmec Know How to Write?" *Science*, 313, no. 5793 (September 15, 2006): 1537.

In other words, legends about a white god may be similar among the Incas, the Hopis, or the Aztecs, but they do not always tell us how these legends came about or where the people lived when the events took place. Information can be carried by migrations, by missionaries, or by other means to various parts of the world. Just because the story of the First Vision is taught in Australia does not justify placing the Sacred Grove in Sydney.

4. Geographical landmarks. Peru *does not* meet the standard of geographical criteria to become the Jaredite lands referred to in the Book of Mormon. In fact, we have to stretch our imagination to call that area a "civilization" because of its lack of a bona fide written language. The same is true of New York state.

Today, we can travel from one end of the Chavin zone in Peru to the other end in a few hours. In Mesoamerica, however, seven hours of travel time by bus are required from Oaxaca to Tres Zapotes, and another three hours are required to travel from Tres Zapotes to La Venta and San Lorenzo. By itself, the relative geographic size and location of Peru tell us that Peru is not the land of the Jaredites. If Peru were to be considered as the land northward where the Jaredites lived, that means that both the land of Zarahemla and the land of Nephi would have to be south of Peru. That geographic orientation would negate any Book of Mormon relationship with Mesoamerica—the area where there was a written language, an area where large population centers existed, and an area where archaeological, geographical, and historical evidence provides minute detail to the information contained in the Book of Mormon.

Finally, the above discussion does not take into account several other significant geographical criteria as found in the Book of Mormon. That is, neither Peru nor New York satisfies the Book of Mormon criteria for such geographic requirements as a narrow mountain range that runs from the east sea to the west sea, an isthmus that separates a land "northward" from a land "southward," a narrow pass that runs through two mountain ranges associated with that isthmus, a hill Ramah/Cumorah that is located near the narrow pass, and a land of Nephi that is "up" in elevation in relation to Jaredite lands but yet is within a relatively short distance from the ancient Jaredite ruins. But then again, those aspects of geography are the essence of this book, *Exploring the Lands of the Book of Mormon*. In reality, the lands teach us as much about the Book of Mormon as the Book of Mormon teaches us about the lands. No evidence is available to suggest that the geography of New York or Peru teaches us anything substantial about Book of Mormon geography.

As stated earlier, we have no reason to believe that good members of the Church of Jesus Christ who write on the subject of Book of Mormon historical geography have any other motive than to promote the Book of Mormon as a true and sacred record. However, until members of the Church require standardized criteria, we will continue to see vast differences of opinion. If we cannot agree that the areas under investigation as the lands of the Book of Mormon need to fit prescribed archaeological, linguistic,

> In reality, the lands teach us as much about the Book of Mormon as the Book of Mormon teaches us about the lands. No evidence is available to suggest that the geography of New York or Peru teaches us anything substantial about Book of Mormon geography.

historical, and geographical criteria, then New York and Peru will continue to be presented as *possible* areas where the Book of Mormon history occurred. The result then becomes fodder for the anti–Book of Mormon writers. *With all the evidence that has come forth in just the last thirty years of the twentieth century and continuing into the twenty-first century, we should be surprised that there are still proponents of a Peruvian theory or a New York theory for lands of the Book of Mormon.*

We will now return to the voyage of the Jaredites.

TOWER OF BABEL

Perhaps if we can determine where the Jaredites launched their eight barges, we may gain additional evidence as to which side of the American continent they landed. The Bible, the Book of Mormon, and the sixteenth-century Mexican writers all refer to a great tower.

The biblical account of the great tower is as follows:

And the whole earth was of one language, and of one speech.

And it came to pass, as they journeyed from the east, that they found a plain in the land of Shinar; and they dwelt there.

And they said one to another, Go to, let us make brick, and burn them throughly. And they had brick for stone, and slime had they for morter.

And they said, Go to, let us build us a city and a tower, whose top may reach unto heaven; and let us make us a name, lest we be scattered abroad upon the face of the whole earth.

And the Lord came down to see the city and the tower, which the children of men builded.

And the Lord said, Behold, the people is one, and they have all one language; and this they begin to do: and now nothing will be restrained from them, which they have imagined to do.

Go to, let us go down, and there confound their language, that they may not understand one another's speech.

So the Lord scattered them abroad from thence upon the face of all the earth: and they left off to build the city.

Therefore is the name of it called Babel; because the Lord did there confound the language of all the earth: and from thence did the Lord scatter them abroad upon the face of all the earth. (Genesis 11:1–9)

Shinar is the name given to the place where the great tower was built. Shinar was located in the valley of the Tigris and Euphrates Rivers. This location is in the same area where the ancient city of Ur was located—the birthplace of Abraham of old. Shinar

> If we cannot agree that the areas under investigation as the lands of the Book of Mormon need to fit prescribed archaeological, linguistic, historical, and geographical criteria, then New York and Peru will continue to be presented as *possible* areas where the Book of Mormon history occurred.

5. Ironically, the Jaredites lived in the Persian Gulf area and subsequently settled in the Gulf of Mexico, the two richest oil-producing areas in the world today.

6. David Alexander and Pat Alexander, eds., *Eerdmans' Handbook to the Bible* (Grand Rapids, MI: William B. Eerdmans, 1974), 135.

was in the area of ancient Babylon, about sixty miles south of where the present-day city of Baghdad, in the country of Iraq, is located.[5]

The Tower of Babel was probably a multistoried temple tower, or ziggurat, similar to those developed in Babylonia in the early third millennium BC.[6]

The Book of Mormon refers to the Tower of Babel as "the great tower" or just "the tower" in describing what apparently is the same event mentioned in the Bible. Moroni wrote in the book of Ether as follows: "Jared came forth with his brother and their families, with some others and their families, from *the great tower,* at the time the Lord confounded the language of the people, and swore in his wrath that they should be scattered upon all the face of the earth; and according to the word of the Lord the people were scattered" (Ether 1:33; emphasis added; see also Ether 1:3, 5; Omni 1:22; Mosiah 28:17; and Helaman 6:28).

7. Ixtlilxochitl:6, 21; see chapter 11, "Fernando de Alva Ixtlilxochitl."

Ixtlilxochitl referred to the tower as both "the very high tower" and the "tower of Babel."[7] He reported that after the Flood, "the earth began again to be populated, [and] they built a Zacualli, very high and strong, which means '*the very high tower,*' to protect them against a second destruction of the world. As time elapsed, their language became confounded, such that they did not understand one another; and they were scattered to all parts of the world."[8]

8. Ixtlilxochitl:6–7; emphasis added; see chapter 11, "Fernando de Alva Ixtlilxochitl."

Without any question, the Bible, the Book of Mormon, and Ixtlilxochitl are all talking about the same event. Independently, none of the accounts provides us with a definitive clue as to where the Jaredites launched their boats in the Old World or where they landed in the New World. However, by adding archaeological, historical, and geographical evidence to the mix, we are at least able to present a workable hypothesis, which is that the Jaredites traveled from Babel to the Arabian Sea, crossed through both the Indian and Pacific Oceans, and landed near the Gulf of Tehuantepec. They established their initial homeland in the Oaxaca valley. Several generations later, a segment of their society migrated to the neighboring state of Veracruz where they built a massive empire, lived out their lives, and witnessed their kingdom fall (see chapter 5, "The Olmec [Jaredite] Culture").

THE BOOK OF ETHER

The Lord wanted us to have the information contained in the book of Ether to serve as another witness of the Nephite record that Jesus is the Christ. We can reason that He caused Limhi's expedition to get lost and discover the records of the Jaredites—"twenty-four plates which are filled with engravings, and they are of pure gold" (Mosiah 8:8–9). The expedition members then carried the plates from Veracruz to the land of Nephi (Guatemala). The Lord then caused Limhi to take them to Zarahemla (Chiapas) where Mosiah could translate them (see Mosiah 8:11–18).

By the time Mormon was ten years old, these same records had been carried from Zarahemla (Chiapas) to Bountiful (southern Yucatan) and then to the hill Shim in the

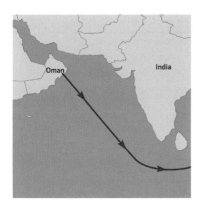

Tuxtla Mountains of Veracruz, virtually the same area where the Limhi expedition had discovered them five hundred years earlier (Mormon 1:1–2). And then at AD 400, Moroni wrote and wandered as he carried these same twenty-four gold plates (the sealed portion) along with the "few records" (the Book of Mormon) from Veracruz to New York (see Mormon 8:4; Moroni 1:1–4; Moroni 9:23–24; Mormon 6:6; Joseph Smith—History 1:33–35, 50–54, 59; Introduction to the Book of Mormon). The Lord really does want us to have those records.

THE SEALED PORTION

It is Moroni's account of the Jaredites that we have today. As of the publication date for the second edition of *Exploring the Lands of the Book of Mormon,* we obviously do not have the things that Moroni sealed up. Joseph Smith was told to "touch them not" (Ether 5:1). They were yet to be translated. They tell the "things" from the beginning to the end of the world. The keys were given to John the Revelator (Ether 4:16), and those sealed records will yet come forth in our day because "the day cometh that the words of the book which were sealed shall be read upon the house tops; and they shall be read by the power of Christ; and the things shall be revealed unto the children of men which ever have been among the children of men, and which ever will be even unto the end of the earth" (2 Nephi 27:11).

In other words, from our perspective, the record written on the twenty-four plates of gold will be read via satellite (upon the house tops) by those in authority (the First Presidency and the Quorum of the Twelve Apostles). Moroni carried the records of the Jaredites that his father had given him (see Moroni 9:23–24) along with "those few records" (our Book of Mormon) that his father had given him earlier (see Mormon 6:6) to New York and buried them in a "hill" near Palmyra. Moroni informed Joseph Smith in the following words that he was not to translate the sealed portion or the record of the Jaredites: "And now, I Moroni, have written the words which were commanded me, according to my memory; and I have told you [Joseph Smith] the things which I have

FIGURE 21–4: When we pursue the hypothesis that the Jaredites launched their barges in the Arabian Sea, we then realize they would have crossed the Indian Ocean to Malaysia and then continued on to the New World, following the Pacific route where the water currents would have taken them into the Gulf of Tehuantepec.

From our perspective, the record written on the twenty-four plates of gold will be read via satellite (upon the house tops) by those in authority (the First Presidency and the Quorum of the Twelve Apostles).

sealed up; therefore, touch them not in order that ye may translate; for that thing is forbidden you, except by and by it shall be wisdom in God" (Ether 5:1).

MORIANCUMER

The brother of Jared, whom we have come to know as Mahonri Moriancumer, was "a large and mighty man," a description that seems to follow the Jaredites for centuries and a description that may have both physical and spiritual connotations. Jared, the tribal leader, asked his brother to "cry again unto the Lord" and ask Him to turn away His anger from their friends and not confound their language (Ether 1:36). Moroni then simply writes that "the Lord had compassion upon their friends and their families also, and they were not confounded" (Ether 1:39).

This scripture apparently is not just talking about the verbal language that was not confounded but also is talking about the language of the Spirit as well. In other words, the people were living in a time of great apostasy. They were confused and confounded if they thought the way to get to God was to build a high tower. Like Moses, Lehi, Mosiah, and Brigham Young, who were all driven out of their lands, the Jaredites were driven out of their land as they listened to the Lord who would lead them to a land of promise. By having faith in God, they were not confounded by false doctrine. The wonderful and unmistakably clear language of the Spirit causes people to listen to the warnings and prophesies of God (see Omni 1:13; 2 Nephi 3:12).

TYPES AND SHADOWS

Because the book of Ether is a spiritual account couched in a historical context and written in Hebrew parallelism, we must, of necessity, sort out the actual travels of the Jaredites. For example, as we read the book of Ether, we must take into consideration that the content is both historical and prophetic in nature. It is a classic account that not only gives the reader a historical overview but also defines the doctrine of Christ in a manner that leaves an indelible impression. It is a Mesoamerican document with Semitic roots from both a Nephite and a Jaredite perspective. The entire book of Ether is written in chiastic style and is structured in a spiritual format of types and shadows.

The spiritual message is more important than the physical story, so the physical story is secondary in nature. However, it is this physical story that bears witness of the reality of God's dealings with His covenant people and the blessings and consequences of abiding by or rejecting that covenant. Just as Jared and his brother, their families, and their friends and their families traveled through the wilderness and through the depths of the ocean and had light from sixteen stones as they were directed toward the promised land, so can we with our families and relatives and their families and our friends and their families have the light of the Holy Ghost to guide us through this wilderness where because of faith in the Atonement of Christ, no monster of the sea (Satan) can harm or mar us as we journey toward the promised land (eternal life).

> Because the book of Ether is a spiritual account couched in a historical context and written in Hebrew parallelism, we must, of necessity, sort out the actual travels of the Jaredites.

A CHOICE LAND (ETHER 1:38, 42; 2:4, 7, 9, 10; 6:5, 8, 11, 12)

The promised land, or the land that was choice above all other lands, described by Moroni is the Americas. From the abundance of available archaeological, historical, linguistic, and geographical evidence, we can determine that, specifically for the Jaredites, it is the area called *Mesoamerica* today. The Prophet Joseph Smith labeled the entire American continent a promised land, or a Zion, because the gospel of Jesus Christ was restored upon this land. In reality, Zion, or the concept of a choice land, may be any place where the political environment allows for a stake of the Church to be established and a temple to be built. Escalante, Utah, is the "land choice above all other lands" for some, and Prince Edward Island is the "promised land" for others.

But the issue is not where God's covenant people live today, nor is the address of the ancient Jaredite civilization a cause for bragging rights. The fulfillment of the scriptures from a geographical point of view is equivalent to searching out one's roots from a genealogical point of view. The land establishes the legality of a remnant of Jacob, and genealogy establishes the legal rights to become heirs to all the blessings in the kingdom of God. Whether our roots come through Ephraim, Manasseh, Judah, or some other member of the house of Israel (Jacob) or whether they come from Mexico, Peru, the United States, England, Japan, or Africa, we must realize the importance of understanding that the covenants of God, rather than the land, are what is truly important.

Nevertheless, the land is extremely important in helping us identify who we are and where we came from and in helping us "bind the hearts of the children to their fathers." The land choice above all other lands for the Jaredites was Mesoamerica. It was their promised land. Furthermore, Mesoamerica was the promised land for the Nephites because both the Jaredites and the Nephites occupied the same real estate. A truly great historical parallel account is reflected in the Lehi migration and the Jaredite migration. The Jaredite record written by Moroni not only is a second witness of Christ but also is a second witness of God's dealings with His children.

Both Jared and Lehi left their homelands when the people were in a state of apostasy.

Both Jared and Lehi wandered and traveled in the vast Arabian Desert.

Both Jared and Lehi arrived at the place called Bountiful (Irreantum).

Both groups built ships in the same place to sail to the promised land.

Both groups were led by the Spirit—the Jaredites by sixteen stones and the Nephites by the Liahona.

Both groups landed in the same area along or near the shores of the Gulf of Tehuantepec.

Both groups were destroyed near the same Ramah/Cumorah hill (Veracruz, Mexico).

> The land establishes the legality of a remnant of Jacob, and genealogy establishes the legal rights to become heirs to all the blessings in the kingdom of God. We must realize the importance of understanding that the covenants of God, rather than the land, are what is truly important.

THE VALLEY OF NIMROD (ETHER 1:33, 42; 2:1–3)

The history of God's dealings with His children on His earth has always consisted of the concept of scattering and gathering. And the history is often couched in relation to a migration. The same is true with the Jaredites.

The Lord confounded the language of the people, which means the people were in a state of great apostasy. The Lord "swore in his wrath that they should be scattered upon all the face of the earth; and according to the word of the Lord the people were scattered" (Ether 1:33).

Jared and those who went with him were to be gathered to a place where they could worship God according to the dictates of their conscience. The wicked Babylon was the point of this scattering, and Mesoamerica was the point of their gathering—where the Lord said He would go with them and make them a great nation if they would serve him. He said there would be no greater nation upon the face of the earth than the nation He would raise up unto Himself (Ether 1:43).

The gathering process takes time. In our day, it has taken two hundred years to gather the tribe of Joseph—a gathering that is not yet over, a gathering that began with the restoration of the gospel with migrations from New York to Ohio, from Ohio to Missouri, from Missouri to Nauvoo, from Nauvoo to the Salt Lake Valley, and from England and many parts of the world to Utah. From there, the gathering of God's people has taken place throughout the world wherever a stake of Zion is organized.

The first leg of the Jaredite gathering took them from Babylon northward to Nimrod. They followed the same route that later became known as the "road of the patriarchs," the trail from Ur to Haran to Egypt. This is the route Abraham used as he fled from the wickedness of Ur several generations after the departure of the Jaredites. The distance is about two hundred miles from the headwaters of the Euphrates. After having followed the River Euphrates from Babel to Nimrod, near the ancient city of Mari, and before moving into Turkey or Israel or Egypt, the Jaredites would have had to make a decision. Do they continue north into Haran where many people lived, or do they go south? Traditional Latter-day Saint history takes the Jaredites to Turkey where they then turned west overland through China. This concept was reflected in the 1989 edition of *Exploring the Lands of the Book of Mormon*. A better alternative has now surfaced.

THAT QUARTER WHERE NO MAN HAD BEEN (ETHER 2:5, 6, 7, 13; 3:3)

Once travelers arrive at the valley of Nimrod, they normally would never consider going south into the treacherous, inhospitable sand desert. However, the Lord said, "Go at the head of them down into the valley which is northward [of Babel]. And there I will meet thee, and I will go before thee into a land which is choice above all the lands of the earth" (Ether 1:42). "And . . . the Lord commanded them that they should go forth into the wilderness, yea, *into that quarter where there never had man been*. And it came

> The gathering process takes time. In our day, it has taken two hundred years to gather the tribe of Joseph—a gathering that is not yet over.

to pass that the Lord did go before them, and did talk with them as he stood in a cloud, and gave them directions whither they should travel" (Ether 2:5; emphasis added). The Lord did not tell them to keep going north from Nimrod. He said, in essence, "I will meet you there, and I will guide you through the wilderness."

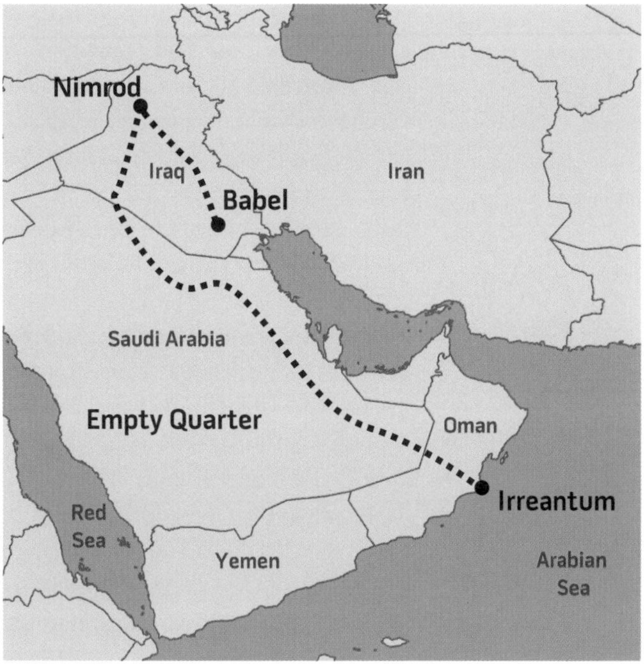

That is the same thing the Lord tells us through Adam: "Therefore I, the Lord God, will send him forth from the Garden of Eden, to till the ground from whence he was taken" (Moses 4:29). Speaking of tilling the ground, the Lord says, "Thorns and thistles shall it bring forth" (Moses 4:24). But the Lord made a coat of skins for Adam and Eve and gave them the Holy Ghost. In the case of Jared and Moses, He led them in a cloud, which is the same thing. And He gave a Liahona to Lehi, which is also the same thing. As we are born into this earth—or driven from God's presence—we travel through this desert of life, and the Holy Ghost gives us directions and leads us to a place choice above all others—that of eternal life.

George Potter suggests that the Jaredites traveled south from the valley of Nimrod through that vast empty quarter to southern Oman. He writes that the Book of Mormon states specifically that "the Lord commanded them that they should go forth into the wilderness, yea, into *that quarter where there never had man been*" (Ether 2:5; emphasis added). Potter then states the following:

> This clue is meaningless to most westerners, but for someone living in the Near East, where the Jaredites started their saga, it is a clear reference to southern Arabia. To an Arab, crossing the quarter *where no man has ever been* is as descriptive as telling an American that the Utah pioneers crossed the *Rocky Mountains*. Arab mythology holds that God created the world—two quarters were where people lived, one quarter was the sea, and one quarter was the desert where no man ever lived. To this day, the great sand desert of southern Arabia is called the Ar Rub Khali, or *Empty Quarter*. Larger than the state of Utah, the Empty Quarter of Arabia is the largest sand desert in the world, and no one has ever found evidence that man has ever dwelt in this vast area.[9]

FIGURE 21–5: We propose that both the Jaredites and the Nephites set sail from the same place—a place called Bountiful by the Nephites. It was by the sea in a place called Irreantum. Irreantum is a Jaredite word that means "many waters" (1 Nephi 17:5). The cognate *antum* from *Irreantum* is found in the Jaredite words of *Antum*, which is close to the hill Shim, and *Coriantum*, a Jaredite king. The map shows the migratory route of the Jaredites from Babel (Iraq) to Irreantum (Oman).

9. George Potter, "An Alternative Model for the Jaredite Trail," The Nephi Project, Bear River City, Utah, www.nephiproject.com, December 6, 2007.

If Jared and his colony went south through the wilderness and headed toward Salalah, Oman (Bountiful-Irreantum), they would have arrived at the same place where Nephi launched his ship over two thousand years later to travel to the promised land. We are not told how many years the Jaredites were in that empty quarter, but apparently they were there for a long time. Ether's words are "for these many years we have been in the wilderness" (Ether 3:3). Moses was in the wilderness desert of Sinai for forty years, Lehi was there for eight years, and our journey in this wilderness of life may be either a short time or a hundred plus years.

JAREDITE BARGES (ETHER 2:6, 16, 17, 18, 19, 20; 6:2, 4)

The Lord brought Jared's colony forth even to the great sea that divided the lands. They dwelt in tents upon the seashore for the space of four years. The brother of Jared made the barges as God directed him—after the manner of barges they had built earlier. This means they either crossed some big water earlier or they had learned how to make barges while they were still in Babel. The fact that they had prepared vessels to carry fish as they lived in the wilderness suggests that they probably knew how to fish. That also means they could have built fishing barges in southern Iraq before they ever left for the valley of Nimrod. At any rate, they built eight barges and then asked the Lord to touch sixteen stones so they could have light as they crossed the ocean. Likewise, we need the light of Christ and the Holy Ghost to guide us through the raging oceans of our lives. As Moroni writes, Christ is "the light, and the life, and the truth of the world" (Ether 4:12).

The Book of Mormon and the Spanish chronicles inform us that the Jaredites traveled great distances over both land and water. Ixtlilxochitl, in writing about the people who came from the Tower of Babel, says that "they came to this land [Mexico], having first crossed many lands and waters, living in caves and passing through great tribulations."[10] The caves were probably in the Arabian Desert, and the many waters are the Indian and Pacific Oceans.

10. Ixtlilxochitl:8; see chapter 11, "Fernando de Alva Ixtlilxochitl."

NO MONSTER COULD MAR THEM (ETHER 2:19, 22, 25; 3:1, 3, 4, 6, 14, 22; 6:2, 5, 10, 11)

The colony needed eight vessels to transport its people, provisions, and animals to the New World. Furious winds drove them across the ocean to the promised land.

And it came to pass that they were many times buried in the depths of the sea, because of the mountain waves which broke upon them, and also the great and terrible tempests which were caused by the fierceness of the wind.

And it came to pass that when they were buried in the deep there was no water that could hurt them, their vessels being tight like unto a dish, and also they were tight like unto the ark of Noah; therefore when they were encom-

Exploring the Lands of the Book of Mormon

passed about by many waters they did cry unto the Lord, and he did bring them forth again upon the top of the waters.

And it came to pass that the wind did never cease to blow towards the promised land while they were upon the waters; and thus they were driven forth before the wind.

And they did sing praises unto the Lord; yea, the brother of Jared did sing praises unto the Lord, and he did thank and praise the Lord all the day long; and when the night came, they did not cease to praise the Lord.

And thus they were driven forth; and *no monster of the sea could break them,* neither whale that could mar them; and they did have light continually, whether it was above the water or under the water.

And thus they were driven forth, three hundred and forty and four days upon the water.

And they did land upon the shore of the promised land. (Ether 6:6–12).

FIGURE 21–6: Shown here is a portion of the restored ruins at San Jose Mogote, Oaxaca, Mexico. These ruins date to the Jaredite time period. Oaxaca is proposed to be the land of Moron in the second edition of *Exploring the Lands of the Book of Mormon.* According to Ignacio Bernal, a style of brick has been discovered at San Jose Mogote that parallels bricks of far-off Mesopotamia. (Photo courtesy of Sheryl Lee Wilson)

CHAPTER 22

Voyages of Lehi and Mulek

There shall none come into this land save they shall be brought by the hand of the Lord. Wherefore this land is consecrated unto him whom he shall bring. (2 Nephi 1:6–7)

꧃꧃꧃꧃꧃꧃꧃꧃꧃꧃꧃꧃꧃꧃꧃꧃꧃꧃꧃꧃꧃꧃꧃꧃꧃꧃꧃꧃꧃꧃

THE VOYAGE OF LEHI'S COLONY

Lehi and his family and Ishmael and his family probably left Jerusalem at the time of the Passover in the first month of the year 600 BC. They traveled in a southeasterly direction along the Red Sea. Upon their arrival in the New World, they called it a promised land.

The Book of Mormon time period from Lehi to Moroni is a thousand years. The fourth son of Lehi was a prophet named Nephi. Moroni was the son of Mormon, and Mormon was a descendant of Nephi. The fabulous history of this family is one of the greatest epics of all time. The members of this genealogical family literally were the historical record keepers of the Americas (see Helaman 3:15).

OPPOSITE: Both Lehi and Mulek came out of a Jewish environment dating to the sixth century BC. Mulek was from the tribe of Judah, and Lehi was from the tribe of Joseph. Lehi brought records with him that contained the law of Moses. Mulek brought no records with him. As noted in Helaman 6:10, the Lord brought Lehi into the land south and Mulek into the land north. Lehi left knowing that in six hundred years, the Messiah would be born in the very city that Lehi was leaving. Shown is a picture of the Garden Tomb, a candidate for the burial place of Jesus. (Photo courtesy of Boyd Hoglund)

As nearly as can be determined, the people who became known as the Nephites introduced both the calendar and the written language to the New World. This family, descendants of Abraham, is the family that fulfilled the role of the covenant people as they developed a high civilization around the narrow neck of land.

The Lord made the following solemn promise to the Nephites, the covenant people of the Americas:

> Wherefore, this land is consecrated unto him whom he shall bring. And if it so be that they shall serve him according to the commandments which he hath given, it shall be a land of liberty unto them; wherefore, they shall never be brought down into captivity; if so, it shall be because of iniquity; for if iniquity shall abound cursed shall be the land for their sakes, but unto the righteous it shall be blessed forever.
>
> And behold, it is wisdom that this land should be kept as yet from the knowledge of *other nations*; for behold, *many nations* would overrun the land, that there would be no place for an inheritance.
>
> Wherefore, I, Lehi, have obtained a promise, that inasmuch as those whom the Lord God shall bring out of the land of Jerusalem shall keep his commandments, they shall prosper upon the face of this land; and they shall be kept from all *other nations*, that they may possess this land unto themselves. And if it so be that they shall keep his commandments they shall be blessed upon the face of this land, and there shall be none to molest them, nor to take away the land of their inheritance; and they shall dwell safely forever. (2 Nephi 1:7–9; emphasis added)

From the arrival of the Nephites shortly after 600 BC until the year AD 1519, knowledge about America was kept from other nations.

Scriptures and Comments. In this section, we present material in an attempt to follow Lehi from Jerusalem to the promised land. The Book of Mormon itself assists us greatly in this endeavor.

1 Nephi 2:4–6, 8: Lehi Leaves Jerusalem and Arrives at the Valley of Lemuel

[Lehi] departed into the wilderness. . . .

And he came down by the borders near the shore of the Red Sea; and he traveled in the wilderness in the borders which are nearer the Red Sea; and he did travel in the wilderness with his family, which consisted of my mother, Sariah, and my elder brothers, who were Laman, Lemuel, and Sam.

And it came to pass that when he had traveled three days in the wilderness, he pitched his tent in a valley by the side of a river of water.

And it came to pass that he called the name of the river, Laman, and it emp-tied into the Red Sea; and the valley was in the borders near the mouth thereof.

We learn the following as ascertained from the above verses as well as from other references in 1 Nephi:

1. Lehi left from the city of Jerusalem with his colony and traveled in the wilderness (see also 1 Nephi 3:2).

2. They traveled down in elevation from Jerusalem until they arrived at the borders by the Red Sea (see also 1 Nephi 3:9).

3. After arriving at the borders near the Red Sea, they traveled another three days until they arrived at a valley they called Lemuel (see also 1 Nephi 2:10).

4. They pitched their tents in a valley that Lehi called Lemuel, which was located by a river that emptied into the Red Sea. Lehi called the river Laman after his oldest son (see also 1 Nephi 2:9).

From Jerusalem to the Red Sea. The first leg of the journey took the Lehi col-ony from Jerusalem to the Red Sea, and "the valley was in the borders near the mouth thereof" (1 Nephi 2:8).

We are not told how long they took to travel from Jerusalem to the "borders" by the Red Sea. The distance is about two hundred miles. In 1986, a group of students from Brigham Young University left Jerusalem, under the direction of Dr. Kelly Ogden, and intermittently covered the distance in sixty-five hours.[1]

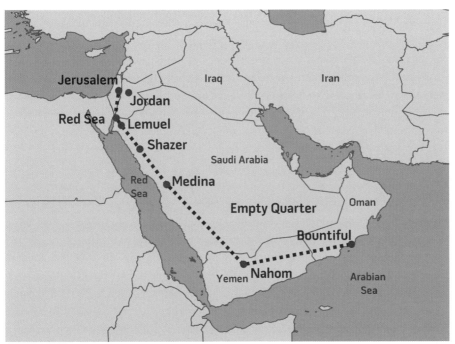

1. *Church News,* January 2, 1988, 11.

FIGURE 22–1: Lehi and his followers left Jerusalem and probably crossed the Jordan River where they picked up the Frankincense Trail. They traveled south to the Red Sea. After eight years of living in the same area where Moses spent forty years, Lehi was told by the Lord that Lehi would be led to a promised land. A Liahona, or compass, was provided for him to help in his travels. The colony continued along the Frankincense Trail through Saudi Arabia into Yemen. At the valley of Marib in the region known as Nahem (Nahom), they traveled east to the coun-try of Oman in the region of Dophar (Ophir), which means Bountiful.

The "borders" near the Red Sea may be the territorial borders between Egypt and the Babylonian empire.

Lehi's colony traveled another three days in the wilderness before pitching their tents at the valley they called Lemuel. If the colony traveled fifteen miles a day, they required nearly two weeks to get to the borders. Another three days' travel time constitutes almost seventeen days to travel from Jerusalem to the valley of Lemuel. If we add to that time the additional time that might be required because of the adverse weather conditions of extreme cold or extreme heat and the slow movement caused by provisions, we may expect the journey to take at least two and perhaps three weeks.

The report of the BYU students states: "The 60 students who left Jerusalem to begin the trek on a blustery, early spring morning walked 30 miles in two days. They camped overnight but couldn't sleep because of the cold. Groups walking during the summer months traveled at night to avoid daytime temperatures soaring well above 100 degrees. Even beginning at 2 a.m., Dr. Ogden reported it 'was an oven.'"[2]

2. *Church News*, January 2, 1988, 11.

That the first leg of the journey (Jerusalem to the valley of Lemuel) was arduous is also implied in the Book of Mormon account when the sons of Lehi (Laman, Lemuel, Sam, and Nephi) returned to Jerusalem, once to get the biblical record contained on the plates of brass and a second time to bring Ishmael and his family to the valley of Lemuel. Sariah suspected—or at least worried—that her sons had perished in the wilderness as they went for the plates of brass (see 1 Nephi 5:2).

In the year 2000, the senior author of *Exploring the Lands of the Book of Mormon* led a pioneer group of twenty-five people following the old Frankincense Trail from Jordan to the Red Sea and from Yemen to Oman. (The term "frank" is French for "pure"; therefore, it was the trail where pure incense was transported, sometimes simply called the Incense Trail or Spice Trail.)

Knowing the great lengths that the Jewish King Jehohiakin (Zedekiah I) took to send troops all the way to Egypt to bring the prophet Urijah back to Jerusalem and then execute him indicates the need for Lehi and his family to get out of Jewish territory as quickly as possible. Just as the lives of Urijah and Jeremiah were in danger, so was Lehi's life in danger—"and they also sought his life that they might take it away" (1 Nephi 1:20). The objective was to get out of Jewish territory as quickly as possible.

> From a practical point of view, we can assume that the journey of Lehi and his family and the two subsequent journeys of the sons of Lehi would avoid any route that would cause them to spend much time on the Israeli side of the Jordan River.

Therefore, from a practical point of view, we can assume that the journey of Lehi and his family and the two subsequent journeys of the sons of Lehi would avoid any route that would cause them to spend much time on the Israeli side of the Jordan River. Some people have promoted the hypothesis that a cave located south of Jerusalem in the valley of Lehi may have been the cave where the sons of Lehi hid from the pursuit of Laban. However, this thinking has been seriously challenged on various occasions—such as the statement by Dr. Jeffrey Chadwick found in the margin on page 517. The lands of inheritance of the sons of Joseph, Ephraim, and Manasseh were north of Jerusalem in the area of Galilee. Their travels would have taken them down from Jerusalem in a northern direction to obtain their precious items that would be confiscated by Laban. Furthermore, they would have had no difficulty in finding caves to hide in between Jerusalem and Jordan. After all, the caves where the Dead Sea scrolls were discovered lie between Jerusalem and Jordan.

The initial work of attempting to follow the trail of Lehi was accomplished by Lynn and Hope Hilton with subsequent work and travels by Warren Aston. In recent years, George Potter and his associates and Kent Brown and a team from Brigham Young University have pursued the trail of Lehi. In addition to our own travels along the Frankincense Trail, we will reference others who have worked in the area, including the Hiltons.[3] We believe that the first two hundred miles of the trip would have been along the Jordanian side of the river, a journey that would have taken them from Jerusalem to the Red Sea. Both Jerusalem and the Red Sea are obviously identifiable today.

3. Kent P. Jackson, ed., *Studies in the Scripture, Volume 7: 1 Nephi to Alma 29* (Salt Lake City: Deseret Book, 1987).

From the Red Sea to the Valley of Lemuel. The travel time of three days from the Red Sea to the valley of Lemuel creates an interesting crossroads decision if we are to trace the travels of Lehi and his colony. Most writers on the subject seem to favor the Wadi El Atal by the Gulf of Aqaba as the valley of Lemuel. This route takes the colony along the eastern side of the Red Sea in a southeast direction. The most current work on the subject has been reported by George Potter. He writes:

Finding a river of running water in the ancient land of Midian was not what Craig Thorsted and I had in mind on that day in May 1995. In fact, he and I were searching for one of the Arabian candidates for Mount Sinai when our journey became one of unexpected discovery.

We had come to the oasis town of al-Bad to explore the Wells of Jethro, the priest of Midian. To obtain authorization to enter that area, we stopped at the mayor's office. The mayor sent one of his supervisors to show us the sites and explain their history. The supervisor was justly proud of the city's history and appealed to the Qur'an to relate the stories of Moses, Jethro, and the town of al-Bad. Complimenting me on my knowledge of the Qur'an, he said that if we were really interested in Moses, we should visit the Waters of Musa (Moses) near Maqna. Maqna is a small, isolated village that lies 20 miles west of al-Bad on the Gulf of Aqaba. . . . (It wasn't until my fourth trip to the area, 3 1/2 years later, that I finally discovered that the Waters of Moses we had heard about in al-Bad were actually located at Maqna itself. By a turn of events, the captain had directed us to the wrong spot farther north along the coast. Some may say that it was by pure luck that we came, not to the traditional Waters of Moses but to another source that we might easily never have seen. I see the experience as providential. By "mistake," we had intentionally stumbled upon the river Laman in the valley of Lemuel.) . . .

"I've done quite a bit of research on the area known in Arabic as *Beit Lei* . . . and affirm that it has nothing to do with Lehi or the Book of Mormon. The name does not refer to 'Lehi' or the 'house of Lehi' at all. And the good folk who spend their time there are pursuing a fantasy."

—Dr. Jeffrey R. Chadwick, Associate Professor of Church History and Jerusalem Center Professor of Near Eastern Studies, Brigham Young University, February 2008

I have escorted over a dozen people into the valley. Several others have made their own way there based on my directions. Are we witnesses of the river Laman in the valley of Lemuel? In my view, the characteristics of the site are compelling evidence that this is so. In the four years since the discovery, I have surveyed the entire Arabian shoreline of the Gulf of Aqaba and the valleys that open onto it. With the exception of the springs at Maqna, which are not in a valley, I have found only rocky valleys almost entirely devoid of vegetation and with no flowing water. Although I have not conducted a thorough survey of the entire region, I have so far found no other place within three-days' walk of the tip of Aqaba that is as inviting as these Waters of Moses.[4]

4. George D. Potter, "A New Candidate in Arabia for the 'Valley of Lemuel,'" *Journal of Book of Mormon Studies,* 8, no. 1 (1999), 54–63.

The valley of Lemuel played an important role in the early pages of the Book of Mormon. The first sixteen chapters, including the marriages of the children and the vision of Nephi, took place while the colony lived in the valley of Lemuel. Eight years elapsed from the time Lehi's people left Jerusalem initially until they arrived at Bountiful where they launched their ship (see 1 Nephi 17:4). A large amount of that time appears to have been spent at the valley of Lemuel: "Now, all these things were said and done as my father dwelt in a tent in the valley which he called Lemuel" (1 Nephi 16:6).

From the Valley of Lemuel to Shazer. The river of Laman must also have been important to Lehi. It is mentioned a number of times in the early pages of the Book of

FIGURE 22–2: Traveling almost east from Nahom, Lehi and his party traveled through the empty desert known as "Rub Al Kahli." The desert tradition is to travel at night because of the immense heat of the day and also to avoid robbers. Nephi reported that this desert area caused them to suffer the most. On our tour of the area, we traveled in an air-conditioned bus for four straight hours through the first part of the empty quarter. (Photo courtesy of Boyd Hoglund)

Mormon. Nephi mentions specifically that they crossed the river as they pursued the journey that would eventually take them to Bountiful: "And it came to pass that we did take our tents and depart into the wilderness, across the *river Laman*" (1 Nephi 16:12; emphasis added).

A Near Eastern tradition is to give temporary and personal names to places. Apparently, Lehi assumed that right. For example: "And it came to pass that we traveled for the space of four days, nearly a south-southeast direction, and we did pitch our tents again; and we did call the name of the place Shazer" (1 Nephi 16:13). In all probability, however, they called the name of the place Shazer because it was already named Shazer.

Four days' journey in a south-southeast direction carried Lehi's colony to Shazer. The distance traveled probably ranged from sixty to a hundred miles. The Hiltons proposed the place called Al Azian to be Shazer.

This leg of their journey took them downstream to the shores of the Red Sea, where they continued down the Tihama. If we accept the seventy-two miles from Aqaba to Al-Beba as the three-day journey into the wilderness (twenty-four miles per day), then a four-day journey would cover about ninety-six miles. This calculation would bring the colony approximately to Wadi Al Azlan, along an important and large oasis on the Red Sea coastal plain, which may have been the locale of Shazer. The area is a stretch of sterile sand with gently rising mountains on the east and the Red Sea on the west. "The route . . . is the ancient coastal frankincense trail."[5]

5. Hilton and Hilton, *In Search of Lehi's Trail*, 77.

The Liahona. Prior to departing the valley of Lemuel, someone who was inspired of God made a "compass" and left it at the tent door of Lehi. A tent is an elaborate type of housing in the desert, and the comment that Lehi dwelt in a tent is not trivial in any sense of the word. It is also very Arabic to leave an object at the tent door without disturbing the people inside. The compass was called the Liahona.

In using any compass, users must have faith that it will direct them in the direction they want to go; otherwise, they will stop using the compass. The same was true with Lehi and his followers. Alma compared the Liahona to Christ when he wrote: "I would that ye should understand that these things are not without a shadow; for as our fathers were slothful to give heed to this compass (now these things were temporal) they did not prosper; even so it is with things spiritual. . . . And now I say, is there not a type in this thing? For just as surely as the director did bring our fathers, by following its course, to the promised land, shall the words of Christ, if we follow their course, carry us beyond this vale of sorrow into a far better land of promise" (Alma 37:43, 45).

From Shazer to Jeddah
And we did go forth again in the wilderness, following the same direction, keeping in the most fertile parts of the wilderness, which were in the borders near the Red Sea.

Prior to departing the valley of Lemuel, someone who was inspired of God made a "compass" and left it at the tent door of Lehi.

And it came to pass that we did travel for the space of many days. . . . And after we had traveled for the space of many days, we did pitch our tents for the space of a time. (1 Nephi 16:14–17)

Lehi's party pursued their course along the more fertile parts of the wilderness in a south-southeast direction along the borders of the Red Sea.

No specific time is given for this leg of the journey, except that they traveled for the "space of many days." This new campsite constituted the area where Nephi broke his steel bow.

The Hiltons propose the ancient port of Jeddah as the place where Nephi broke his bow. Jeddah is located between the two holy cities of Medina and Mecca.

From Jeddah to Nahom

And it came to pass that we did again take our journey, traveling nearly the same course as in the beginning; and after we had traveled for the space of many days we did pitch our tents again, that we might tarry for the space of a time.

And it came to pass that Ishmael died, and was buried in the place which was called Nahom. (1 Nephi 16:33–34)

Thus, the course is the same as before; the distance is "the space of many days." And Ishmael was buried at a place called Nahom.

Some readers propose that the name of Nahom was given to the place in the same manner that Lehi named the valley of Lemuel and the river of Laman. However, the area predated Lehi as a burial area and, as such, was already called Nahom prior to the death of Ishmael. In Hebrew, the word *Nahom* is derived from the consonants NHM, meaning "to be sorry or to console oneself" or, more literally, "a place of sorrow." The daughters of Ishmael mourned exceedingly there because of the loss of their father and because of their afflictions in the wilderness. The name of the place where Ishmael was buried is equivalent to a massive burial ground that existed prior to the arrival of Lehi and that still exists today. Traditionally, the tomb marker of each patriarch was placed on the top of a small, rolling hill with those of his ancestors and then proceeding in a straight line below. Regarding the daughters of Ishmael, we may see a play on words as "they lamented at the valley of lamentations [Nahom]."

As travelers move along the route from Sana'a, Yemen, to the Nahom valley (in Yemen, it is pronounced Nehem) and then to the town of Marib, the evidence is indeed compelling that it is the same trail Lehi followed twenty-six hundred years ago.

From Nahom, Yemen, to Dophar, Oman

And it came to pass that we did again take our journey in the wilderness; and we did travel *nearly eastward* from that time forth. And we did travel and wade

> The name of the place where Ishmael was buried is equivalent to a massive burial ground that existed prior to the arrival of Lehi and that still exists today.

through much affliction in the wilderness; and our women did bear children in the wilderness.

. . . we did live upon raw meat in the wilderness . . . and they [the women] began to bear their journeyings without murmurings.

And we did sojourn for the space of many years, yea, even eight years in the wilderness.

And we did come to the land which we called Bountiful, because of its much fruit and also wild honey; and all these things were prepared of the Lord that we might not perish. And we beheld the sea, which we called Irreantum, which, being interpreted, is many waters.

And it came to pass that we did pitch our tents by the seashore; and notwithstanding we had suffered many afflictions and much difficulty, yea, even so much that we cannot write them all, we were exceedingly rejoiced when we came to the seashore; and we called the place Bountiful, because of its much fruit. (1 Nephi 17:1–2, 4–6; emphasis added)

The "nearly eastward" direction would take the colony from Nahom to the twin cities of Shibam and Sayun, then on to the border of Oman, and then eventually on to Bountiful.

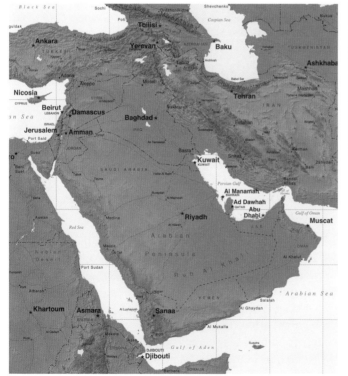

FIGURE 22–3: The distance from Sana'a, the capital city of Yemen, to Marib, the valley of Nehem (Nahom), is about one hour, excluding time spent at the military checkpoints. The ancient name of NHM (Nahom) is recorded in stone. Interpreted, it means "place of mourning." This is the area where Ishmael died. (Photo courtesy of Boyd Hoglund)

FIGURE 22–4: This modern map of the Arabian Peninsula shows the area where Lehi and his family traveled in the sixth century BC. Once they arrived at Oman, they discovered that the area was indeed a fertile area where both wild honey and fresh fruit were available. Today, signs are posted in English announcing "Wild honey for sale."

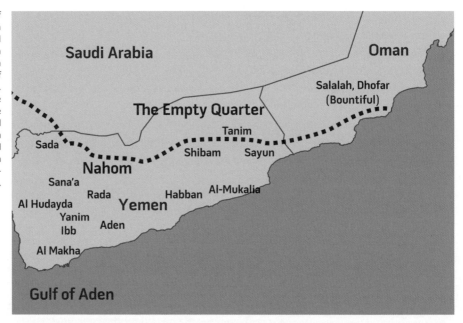

FIGURE 22–5: This map of Yemen shows the direction Lehi and his party would have traveled from Nahom to Shibam and from Shibam to the border of Oman (Dhofar-Bountiful). This area is a portion of the great empty quarter where Nephi reported that "we did travel nearly eastward from that time forth. And we did travel and wade through much affliction in the wilderness" (1 Nephi 17:1).

The culture patterns of this area in correlation with the hints in the Book of Mormon are impressive. Spicy, raw, partially dried meat is still consumed in the area today. The Arabs call it *"bastern,"* which literally means raw meat. The distance from Al Kunfidah (Nahom) to Salalah, the probable site of Bountiful by the sea, is about eight hundred miles. The distance and the geological and weather conditions certainly justify Nephi's statement that "we did travel and wade through much affliction."

The Hiltons summarized the efforts of their journeys in search of Lehi's trail by stating: "On the coast of Salalah, we believe that we found the end of Lehi's trail from Jerusalem to Bountiful. We discovered no contradictions, no absurdities in the record Nephi had left behind him. Nothing that we discovered in the volumes on geography and history contradicted that ancient prophet [Nephi]."[6]

6. Hilton and Hilton, *In Search of Lehi's Trail,* 115.

Today the region is called Dhofar, which is a derivative of the biblical word Ophir, meaning gold or abundance (see 1 Kings 9:28). It was the place of Job and was named after one of Job's so-called friends, Zophar (see Job 2:11, 11:1, 20:1). Tradition indicates that Job was buried in the province of Zophar (Dhofar) in southern Oman near the city of Salalah. A visit to his proposed burial place is recommended.

Joseph Allen writes:

In the year 1999, when our pioneer group of twenty-five traveled from Sana'a to Marib to Shibam, we found we could easily identify with Nephi's writings. We traveled in October. Only five months earlier, a highway had been completed from Marib (valley of Nahom) to Shibam, the "Manhattan of the desert." Prior

Exploring the Lands of the Book of Mormon

to May 1999, the travel along this 250-mile stretch of empty desert land was by camel or four-wheel-drive vehicles. Our bus made the trip in a little over four hours. It was the first time that most of the local people at the twin cities of Shibam and Sayun had seen a bus. It is the trip through the country of Yemen and time spent in southern Oman that made an impact on our lives. Some of those highlights include the following:

1. The affection for and the value of the camel in transporting goods and people through that empty quarter of desert where food and water are scarce and hardships and danger are prevalent even today. It is in this context that Nephi wrote, "We did travel and wade through much affliction in the wilderness" (1 Nephi 17:1).

2. The historical presence of the old Incense Trail or Spice Road. Remains of the palaces of the Queen of Sheba served as a reminder that this trail was where she passed—with a very great train, with camels that bore spices, and with very much gold and precious stones that she gave to King Solomon three hundred years prior to the time of Lehi (see 2 Kings 10:2). It is also the trail that the wise men from the east would have followed six hundred years after Lehi passed through as they carried gifts of gold, frankincense, and myrrh to give to the Christ child (Matthew 2:11).

3. The historical evidence of an ancient reservoir dating to 800 BC, the manner of farming, and the customs and traditions of the people were gentle reminders that people were living in the area when Lehi passed through and that some things have not changed much over the last twenty-six hundred years.

4. The images portrayed by Nephi in explaining the vision of his father about a tree that gave life as a result of the presence of fountains of living water (an oasis in the desert). This tree was a tree whose fruit was white to exceed all and was desirable to make one happy (white fruit from the frankincense tree). The pride of the world, as represented by people who would have mocked them from their buildings raised like skyscrapers in the desert, were vivid testimony of the types and shadows that Nephi used to explain the principles of the Fall, Atonement, and eternal life.

5. The accuracy of names, distances, and directions combined to serve as landmarks of the ancient Lehi trail. In addition to Jerusalem and the Red Sea, the names of Nahom and Bountiful (Dophar) stood out. After crossing through the desert, we saw shops selling fresh fruit and signs announcing wild honey for sale, both of which were reminiscent of Nephi's words, "We did come to a land which we called Bountiful, because of its much fruit and also wild honey" (1 Nephi 17:5).

"Our bus made the trip in a little over four hours. It was the first time that most of the local people at the twin cities of Shibam and Sayun had seen a bus."

—Joseph Allen

FIGURE 22–6: Nephi wrote that his father saw "a great and spacious building, and it stood as it were in the air." Traveling at night, Lehi perhaps had seen a lamp in one of the upper rooms of one of the tall mud buildings that existed in his day, such as those shown in this picture. In his vision, Lehi said that the great and spacious building was full of people who were mocking and pointing their fingers at those who were partaking of the fruit of the tree. The great and spacious building is but one of several vivid images from Lehi's tree-of-life vision. (Photo courtesy of Boyd Hoglund)

With preliminary work by the Hiltons and the Astons and recent work by Potter and his associates and Kent Brown and his associates and after having personally traveled the route from Amman to the Red Sea and from Nahom (Nehem) to Oman, we are convinced that the Frankincense Trail is the trail followed by Lehi and his colony in the sixth century BC.

Nephi poetically wrote:
We did sojourn for the space of many years,
Even eight years in the wilderness.
We did come to the land we called Bountiful, because of its much fruit and wild honey;
We beheld the sea, which we called Irreantum,
Which, being interpreted, is many waters.

We did pitch out tents by the seashore;
When we came to the seashore;
We called the place Bountiful, because of its much fruit (see 1 Nephi 17:4–6).

Regarding the specific place where Nephi launched his ship, Aston proposes an ocean inlet called Wadi Sayq. Potter and Wellington convincingly present ten reasons why nearby Khor Rori is the most likely candidate where Nephi launched his ship.[7]

7. Richard Wellington and George Potter, "Lehi's Trail from the Valley of Lemuel to Nephi's Harbor," The Nephi Project, Bear River, Utah, www.nephiproject.com.

Exploring the Lands of the Book of Mormon

As Book of Mormon readers travel through the region following the old Frankincense Trail from Jordan to Aqaba and from Nahom (Nehem) eastward and then travel through southern Oman, which is called Dophar (Bountiful), where Lehi set sail toward the promised land, they will realize that their intellectual and spiritual journey, just like Lehi's physical journey, is just beginning.

Building a Ship. Nephi wrote that the Lord showed him from time to time the manner in which he should work the timbers of the ship (1 Nephi 18:1). We would be in error in assuming that no people were living along the Arabian coast when Lehi arrived or that no one knew how to build ships around 600 BC. The career of being a sailor at that time period was prestigious in nature. These conclusions, however, do not negate the fact that the Lord's hand was evident in the building of Nephi's ship, a ship whose "workmanship was exceedingly fine" (1 Nephi 18:4).

> And it came to pass that on the morrow, after we had prepared all things, much fruits and meat from the wilderness, and honey in abundance, and provisions according to that which the Lord had commanded us, we did go down into the ship, with all our loading and our seeds, and whatsoever thing we had brought with us, every one according to his age; wherefore, we did all go down into the ship, with our wives and our children. . . .
>
> And it came to pass after we had all gone down into the ship, and had taken with us our provisions and things which had been commanded us, we did put forth into the sea and were driven forth before the wind towards the promised land. (1 Nephi 18:6, 8)

Anciently, many hands were required to move a caravan through a desert and move a ship across the ocean. More than likely, "Lehi's people" who were involved in these accounts consisted of more than just the family members mentioned by Nephi.

From Bountiful (Dophar) to the Promised Land (Izapa). As to where Lehi landed in the New World, we can appeal to both archaeological and traditional data for assistance.

> And it came to pass that I, Nephi, did guide the ship, that we sailed again towards the promised land.
>
> And it came to pass that after we had sailed for the space of many days we did arrive at the promised land; and we went forth upon the land, and did pitch our tents; and we did call it the promised land. (1 Nephi 18:22–23)

The Jaredite record informs us that the Jaredites took 344 days to cross the ocean. Nephi wrote that his group landed in the promised land after they had sailed for "the space of many days."

We would be in error in assuming that no people were living along the Arabian coast when Lehi arrived or that no one knew how to build ships around 600 BC.

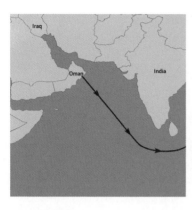  

FIGURE 22–7: We propose that the voyage of Lehi paralleled the voyage of the Jaredites, who had crossed the ocean more than two thousand years earlier. That is, both groups sailed the Pacific Ocean to arrive at their promised land. The Jaredites would have landed on the west side of the narrow neck of land (Isthmus of Tehuantepec), and Lehi would have landed on the east side near the present-day port of Tapachula, Chiapas, Mexico. Justification for this landing site for Lehi is explained in the text.

Trips from the Arabian Peninsula to China dating from the sixth century AD traditionally took four months of straight sailing time. Ships had to sail around the tip of India and through the Straits of Malacca into the South China Sea. If a ship were blown off course, it would end up in the Pacific and eventually "fall off the edge of the earth."

Lehi's ship was directed by a "compass" called the Liahona. According to Nephi, the Liahona consisted of a round ball of "curious workmanship" with two spindles that pointed the way Lehi's group was to travel. It worked according to their faith (see 1 Nephi 16:16; 1 Nephi 18:12, 21).

The above comments suggest that Lehi's voyage probably took a year to a year and a half to complete. This time period does not take into consideration any time consumed while they stopped for provisions along the way. The record of Nephi taken from the small plates of Nephi does not fill us in on the details.

Nephi mentions that they sailed for the "space of many days" (1 Nephi 18:9). When Lehi's group was driven by the wind toward the promised land, they would have sailed from Arabia through the Straits of Malacca and up the coast toward Hong Kong. Laman and Lemuel, the brothers of Nephi, became rude and bound Nephi. The Liahona stopped working. Not until after four days of being blown off course did Laman and Lemuel loosen Nephi's bonds. Nephi's ship perhaps suffered the same fate that vessels used to suffer in this area. Once blown into the Pacific, ships were never heard of again. This time, however, the shipload of emigrants was being led to a promised land.

Where on the American continent did Lehi's colony land? Several statements from Latter-day Saint history give us potential answers. The most common is that they landed in South America by Chile or Peru. This landing site leaves a lot of latitude, as the extreme distance from the southern border of Chile to the northern border of Peru is almost four thousand miles.

One of the most common traditional statements about the landing site of Lehi's colony is that he landed near the Isthmus of Darien, which is now called the Isthmus of Panama.

FIGURE 22–8: We propose that the shore off the Soconusco valley in southern Chiapas, Mexico, is the place of Lehi's landing—or the place of their first inheritance. The seeds they brought with them grew "exceedingly." In the forests, they found animals of every kind, both domesticated and wild. Gold, silver, and copper were discovered in the mountains. They were blessed in abundance, and they called their new home the promised land (see 1 Nephi 23–25). (Photo courtesy of Phil Skousen)

However, in recent years, the coast of either El Salvador or Mexico has received considerable attention as the place where Lehi landed.

The matter is not as complicated as it may seem. If we can assume that the place of Lehi's first inheritance is the same place where Lehi landed, then the Book of Mormon itself solves the puzzle. The location is mentioned in Mormon's narrative of the missionary endeavors of the sons of Mosiah. According to Mormon, the place of Lehi's first inheritance was along the seashore west in the land of Nephi: "Now, the more idle part of the Lamanites lived in the wilderness, and dwelt in tents; and they were spread through the wilderness on the west, in the land of Nephi; yea, and also on the west of the land of Zarahemla, in the borders by the seashore, and on the west in the land of Nephi, *in the place of their fathers' first inheritance*, and thus bordering along by the seashore" (Alma 22:28; emphasis added). This description places Lehi's landing near the present-day ruins of Izapa, in southern Mexico by the Guatemala border along the Pacific coast.

Alma 22:28 simply says that by 80 BC (five hundred years after Lehi landed), the Lamanites occupied the territory along the seashore west of the land of Nephi. This area is what was called the "place of their fathers' first inheritance."

Apparently, not very many years passed from the time that the colony of Lehi first landed until Nephi, being warned in a dream, left the coastline (the place of their first inheritance) and traveled inland into the mountains:

> And it came to pass that the Lord did warn me, that I, Nephi, should depart from them and flee into the wilderness, and all those who would go with me.
>
> Wherefore, it came to pass that I, Nephi, did take my family, and also Zoram and his family, and Sam, mine elder brother and his family, and Jacob and Joseph, my younger brethren, and also my sisters, and all those who would go with me.

> The question of where Lehi's party landed is not as complicated as it may seem. If we can assume that the place of Lehi's first inheritance is the same place where Lehi landed, then the Book of Mormon itself solves the puzzle.

And all those who would go with me were those who believed in the warnings and the revelations of God; wherefore, they did hearken unto my words.

And we did take our tents and whatsoever things were possible for us, and did journey in the wilderness for the space of many days. And after we had journeyed for the space of many days we did pitch our tents.

And my people would that we should call the name of the place Nephi; wherefore, we did call it Nephi. (2 Nephi 5:5–8)

Nephi again gives us the term of "the space of many days" as the travel time from the place of their first inheritance to the place of Nephi.

These "many days" to the place of Nephi, however, were not so far distant from the place of their fathers' first inheritance that the Nephites did not keep in contact with the Lamanites. After the death of Nephi, Jacob, the brother of Nephi, spoke to the people who were now called Nephites (see Jacob 1:14), saying, "Behold, ye have done greater iniquities than the Lamanites, our brethren" (Jacob 2:35). And again he said that "except ye repent they [the Lamanites] shall possess the land of your inheritance [land of Nephi]" (Jacob 3:4).

That is exactly what happened. Around 200 to 180 BC, Mosiah, a Nephite, had to flee out of the land of Nephi; and from that time forth, the land of Nephi was ruled by the Lamanites (see Omni 1:12).

About a hundred years after Mosiah fled out of the land of Nephi, the sons of Mosiah, as Nephite missionaries, went to the land of Nephi to preach the gospel to the Lamanites. From this event, we learn that "the place of their fathers' first inheritance" was along the seacoast west of the land of Nephi.

The only other place in the Book of Mormon where we read about "the place of their fathers' first inheritance" in reference to the place where Lehi landed is in Mosiah 10:13: "And again, . . . they were wronged while in the land of their first inheritance, after they had crossed the sea, and all this because that Nephi was more faithful in keeping the commandments of the Lord—therefore he was favored of the Lord, for the Lord heard his prayers and answered them, and he took the lead of their journey in the wilderness."

The ruins of Izapa on the Mexico-Guatemala border are also proposed by Richard Hauck in *Deciphering the Geography of the Book of Mormon* as "the place of their fathers' first inheritance."[8] Hauck further proposes that the city name in the Book of Mormon used to identify "the place of their fathers' first inheritance" was *Judea*. We read about Judea in Alma 56, in reference to Helaman's warriors.

The Izapa ruins, where the Tree of Life Stone is located, are certainly tangible evidence of a Jewish background community. In addition to the Izapa Stela 5 stone, which some researchers feel portrays the dream of Lehi (see chapter 9, "The Izapa [Jaredite-Nephite-Lamanite] Culture," and chapter 15, "Christ—The Tree of Life"),

8. F. Richard Hauck, *Deciphering the Geography of the Book of Mormon* (Salt Lake City: Deseret Book, 1988), 8.

Exploring the Lands of the Book of Mormon

other indications of Jewish influence include such things as the cubit as a unit of measurement and the manifestation of doctrinal concepts of a messiah and eternal life.

The Quiche Maya, who reside around beautiful Lake Atitlan in the Guatemala highlands, record accounts of their origins in their history. The *Popol Vuh*, a native American document discovered in a Catholic church at Chichicastenango, expresses the tradition of the Quiche Maya as moving from a southward coastal direction into the highlands.

Another native document, *The Title of the Lords of Totonicapan*, speaks of a Jewish people's coming from the Gulf of Mexico.

These documents agree with the movements of the Book of Mormon peoples. The Nephites came from the south (Guatemala), and the Mulekites came from the north (Campeche, Mexico), as pointed out by Helaman, who says that "the Lord did bring Mulek into the land north, and Lehi into the land south" (Helaman 6:10).

In addition, the distance from the coast of the Guatemala-Mexico border to Guatemala City is about 130 miles. Therefore, Nephi's traveling through the rugged

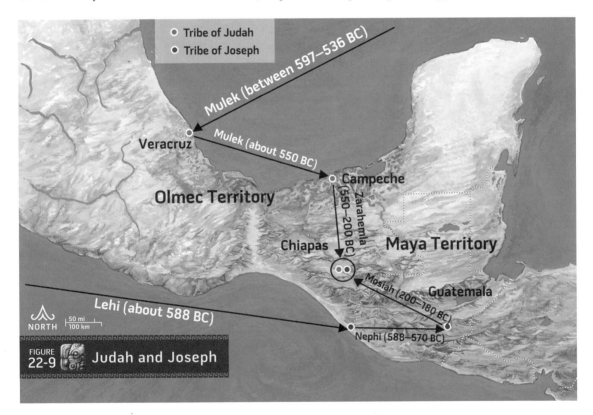

FIGURE 22–9: We propose that Mulek landed on the Atlantic side by the Gulf of Mexico and that Lehi landed on the Pacific side by the Gulf of Tehuantepec. Mulek migrated into the land southward (Chiapas), which is north of where Nephi established a kingdom (Guatemala). Four hundred years would elapse (600 BC to 200 BC) before the descendants of Mulek from the tribe of Judah would become part of the kingdom of Nephi, who were descendants of the tribe of Joseph.

mountains of Guatemala and making about eight miles a day must have required about sixteen days, which makes Izapa a likely candidate for the land of first inheritance.

The question is often asked, "If Lehi landed along the coast of Guatemala or Mexico, how do you account for the statement of the Prophet Joseph Smith that the Nephites landed in Chile or Peru?" This question apparently refers to a statement that was in the handwriting of Frederick G. Williams, a counselor to the Prophet Joseph Smith during the Kirtland era.

A piece of paper with that information written on it was in the possession of the grand-son of Frederick G. Williams, and its contents were reported in the book *A Compendium of the Gospel*, by Franklin D. Richards and James A. Little. The book was published in 1886. The statement was written on the same sheet of paper as a handwritten account of Doctrine and Covenants 7. Both Doctrine and Covenants 7 and the statement about the landing site of Lehi were in the handwriting of Frederick G. Williams. The statement is as follows: "The initial landing site of Lehi's colony, sometime after 600 B.C.,

9. Franklin D. Richards and James A. Little, *A Compendium of the Doctrines of the Gospel* (Salt Lake City: F. D. Richards and J. A. Little, 1886), 298.

was in South America in Peru or Chile, thirty degrees south latitude."[9]

Apparently, some people assumed that the geography statement regarding the landing site of Lehi was a revelation because it was written on the same sheet of paper as the revelation about John, which is now recorded in Doctrine and Covenants 7.

Without additional information, the above conclusion does not seem justified. B. H. Roberts, who was a member of the First Council of the Seventy, writes: "Now, if no more evidence can be found to establish this passage in Richards and Little's compendium

FIGURE 22–10: As nearly as can be determined from the Book of Mormon, Lehi landed on the Pacific coast near the archaeological zone of Izapa and the Guatemala border. The ruins of Izapa are close to the city of Tapachula, Chiapas, Mexico. This area is in the fertile Soconusco valley. The trees shown here produce the desirable cacao (cocoa) beans. (Photo courtesy of George and Audrey DeLange)

Exploring the Lands of the Book of Mormon

as a revelation to Joseph the Seer, than the fact that it is found in the handwriting of Frederick G. Williams, and on the same sheet of paper with the body of revelation about John, the beloved disciple, the evidence of its being a revelation to Joseph the Seer, rests on a very unsatisfactory basis."[10]

10. B. H. Roberts, *New Witnesses for God*, 3 vols. (Salt Lake City: Deseret News, 1909), 3:501–2.

Justification for identifying the landing site of Lehi along the Pacific coast in the Soconusco valley is as follows:

1. If the ruins of Kaminaljuyu (Guatemala City) are the remains of the ancient city-state of Nephi, then Izapa meets the directional and location requirements to be where Lehi landed "on the west in the land of Nephi, in the place of their fathers' first inheritance, and thus bordering along by the seashore" (Alma 22:28).

2. If the Maya religious calendar had its origin at Izapa, then the calendar is possibly Nephite in origin. The Maya calendar may, however, be identifiable with the Mosiah time period (200 BC) as opposed to the Nephi time period (600 BC). This statement, however, does not forfeit the right of Izapa's being the place of Lehi's landing.

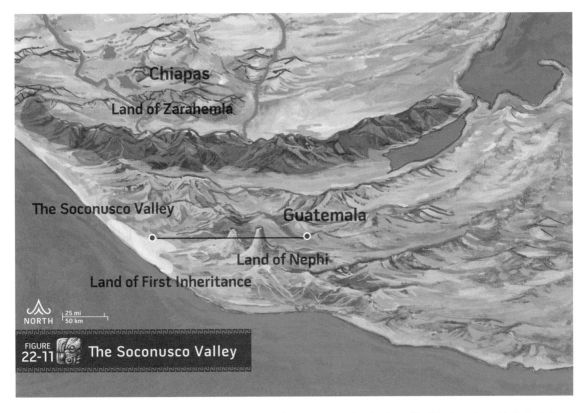

FIGURE 22–11: The Soconusco valley is west in Guatemala-Chiapas in the same manner that the place of first inheritance is west in the land of Nephi (see Alma 22:28). This is an extremely fertile area in which many products, including coffee, bananas, pineapple, and cacao, are grown.

3. If the Cuchumatane mountain range is the narrow strip of wilderness that is spoken of in Alma 22 and that divided the land of Nephi from the land of Zarahemla, then Izapa is in the proper location to have been occupied by both Lamanites and Nephites at different periods throughout the thousand-year Nephite history. Just like today, the Soconusco valley, where Izapa is located, is part of the state of Chiapas, Mexico, as opposed to being part of the country of Guatemala. However, according to the text, in 600 BC, the statement that "the place of their first inheritance" (site of Lehi's landing) was west *in* the land of Nephi (see figure 22–11).

THE VOYAGE OF MULEK

Joseph of Egypt was hated by his brothers "for his dreams, and for his words" (see Genesis 37:8). Joseph said to his brothers: "Hear, I pray you, this dream which I have dreamed: For, behold, we were binding sheaves in the field, and lo, my sheaf arose, and also stood upright; and, behold, your sheaves stood round about, and made obeisance to my sheaf. And his brethren said to him, Shalt thou indeed reign over us? or shalt thou indeed have dominion over us?" (Genesis 37:6–8).

We see a temporal fulfillment of this dream in Genesis 43, where the brothers of Joseph did indeed bow down to Joseph, the great governor of Egypt, as the famine drove the sons of Jacob to Egypt in search of grain.

Latter-day Saints live in a day when the climax of that vision is taking place. Ephraim and Manasseh, sons of Joseph, are preparing the way for their brothers, the lost tribes (descendants of the brothers of Joseph) to return.

An intermediate fulfillment also comes to fruition in the Book of Mormon. In Genesis 49:22, Jacob blessed Joseph and told him that he was a fruitful bough and that his branches would run over the wall.

More than a thousand years after this blessing was given, around six hundred years before the birth of Christ, Lehi and Ishmael, descendants of Ephraim and Manasseh, the sons of Joseph, crossed over the ocean in fulfillment of the Genesis 49 prophecy.

Four hundred years after the arrival of Lehi in the promised land, or about two hundred years before Christ was born, a portion of the tribe of Joseph, represented by Mosiah, went down from the land of Nephi to the land of Zarahemla, where they discovered a portion of the tribe of Judah, represented by the people of Zarahemla. Through this event, the dream of Joseph of Egypt reached a partial fulfillment in the New World; and for the next four hundred years, Joseph (the Nephites) ruled over his brother, Judah (the Mulekites).

The first place in the Book of Mormon where we are made aware of another culture that came to the New World from the Old World (other than the Nephites and the Lamanites) is in the small book of Omni.

> When Mosiah's group went from the land of Nephi to the Land of Zarahemla, the dream of Joseph of Egypt reached a partial fulfillment in the New World; and for the next four hundred years, Joseph (the Nephites) ruled over his brother, Judah (the Mulekites).

The book of Omni discussion between Mosiah and Zarahemla about a man by the name of Coriantumr, who had lived with the people of Zarahemla for nine moons, also gives us our first introduction to the people we call Jaredites.

From the Book of Mormon, we learn the following about a group of people whom we have come to call Mulekites:

1. They received Mosiah with open arms because the Lord had sent him to them with the brass plates that contained a record of the Jews, whereas the Mulekites had brought no records with them. This event took place about 200–180 BC (see Omni 1:14, 17).

2. The people of Zarahemla, or their forefathers, came out of Jerusalem at the time that Zedekiah, king of the Jews, was taken captive into Babylon. Zarahemla gave Mosiah a genealogy of his people from memory. Jerusalem was taken into captivity in 586 BC (see Omni 1:15, 18; see also 2 Kings 25:1–2).

3. Mulek was a son of Zedekiah III, who was the king of the Jews at the time of the Babylonian captivity (see Helaman 8:21).

4. The Lord brought Mulek into the land north and Lehi into the land south (see Helaman 6:10).

5. The Mulekites landed in the land northward in the area where the Jaredites lived (see Alma 22:30).

6. The forefathers of the people of Zarahemla journeyed in the wilderness and crossed the great waters, and subsequently a colony of Mulekites migrated to an area they called the land of Zarahemla (see Omni 1:16; see also Alma 22:30–31).

7. By the time Mosiah discovered the people of Zarahemla, they had become exceedingly numerous and had experienced many wars and serious contentions (see Omni 1:17).

8. The Mulekites far outnumbered the Nephites (see Mosiah 25:2).

9. The Mulekites' language had become corrupt, and the people of Mosiah could not understand the Mulekites (see Omni 1:17, 18).

10. The Mulekites denied the being of their creator (see Omni 1:17).

In Ezekiel 17, we read about a prophecy of Judah and his captivity and subsequent release from Babylon. We will paraphrase the writings of Ezekiel as follows: "Thus saith the Lord, Judah has despised my oath and broken my covenant. And I will spread my net upon him and he shall be taken in my snare and I will bring him to Babylon. They that remain shall be scattered toward all winds. Thus saith the Lord God, I will crop off a tender twig from the highest branch and plant it upon a mountain and it shall bring forth boughs and shall bear fruit.

"He took also of the seed of the land and planted it in a fruitful field. He placed it by great waters. And it grew and became a spreading vine of low stature whose branches turned toward him. There was also another great eagle with great wings and many feathers; and, behold, this vine did bend her roots toward him and shot forth her

The Lord brought Mulek into the land north and Lehi into the land south (see Helaman 6:10). The Mulekites landed in the land northward in the area where the Jaredites lived.

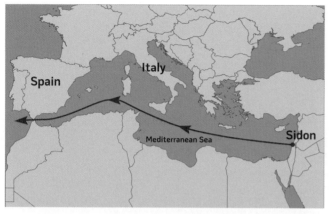

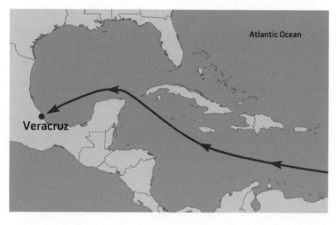

FIGURE 22–12: Some scholars suggest that the Mulekites departed from the Red Sea. Although this route is possible because the returning Jewish captives may have traveled from Iraq to southern Jordan, leaving from the port of Aqaba, the Mulekites more likely sailed from the port of Sidon, traveling though Syria to get to the Mediterranean port. The first leg of the journey would parallel the voyage of Paul in the first century from Caesarea to Rome.

branches toward him, that he might water it by the furrows of her plantation. It was planted in a good soil by great waters, that it might bring forth branches, and that it might bear fruit, that it might be a goodly vine" (Ezekiel 17:18–24; 17:1–10).

If Mulek is the tender twig and Lehi is the great eagle, then we can see through prophecy that which took place historically in the New World. Once Mulek was let out of captivity by Babylon, he found his way to a land by the great waters, where God directed him. About 200 BC, the Lord led Mosiah, from the tribe of Joseph, to the land of Zarahemla where he became king over the branches of Mulek (Judah), and they both bowed toward God.

The Book of Mormon is primarily a record of the lineage of Nephi; and, as a result, we learn about the Mulekites only from their association with the Nephites. We have limited help from the Old Testament, as it deals with the father of Mulek, who was either Zedekiah II or Zedekiah III, kings of Judah at the time of the Babylonian captivity. *Zedekiah* was also the name or title of the king at the time Lehi left Jerusalem. Therefore, we are not sure when Mulek and his party left Jerusalem, nor do we know what route they took to get to the promised land.

We have a little more help once the Mulekites arrive in the promised land. The Book of Mormon, along with native Mesoamerican documents and archaeological data, provides us with a few rays of insight to the Mulekite-Jewish society.

The Jaredites and the Nephites probably sailed the Pacific to get to America, whereas the Mulekites arrived at the promised land through the Atlantic seaway. The Mulekites probably departed somewhere off the Mediterranean Sea, perhaps near the port of Sidon. The most probable place for the landing of Mulek's party is off the shores of Veracruz, Mexico.

Scriptures and Commentary. Scriptures from the Book of Mormon about the landing site of the Mulekites, with commentary from native Mesoamerica records and archaeological data, are as follows:

Helaman 8:21—Mulek, a Son of Zedekiah

And now will you dispute that Jerusalem was destroyed? Will ye say that the sons of Zedekiah were not slain, all except it were Mulek? Yea, and do ye not behold that the seed of Zedekiah are with us, and they were driven out of the land of Jerusalem?

Zedekiah III, whose Hebrew name was Mattaniah, was placed on the Jewish throne by Nebuchadnezzar, king of the Babylonians, as a puppet king. He began his reign in the year 597 BC. Zedekiah/Mattaniah, forsaking the counsel of the prophets, among whom was the prophet Jeremiah, rebelled against the Babylonians; and Jerusalem was burned. A terrible famine in the land also occurred at the same time.

Lehi and Ishmael, descendants of Joseph of old, listened to the counsel of the prophets and fled Jerusalem. In the land of promise, Zedekiah/Mattaniah's own descendants, the tribe of Judah, were ruled over by the descendants of the prophet Lehi, the tribe of Joseph.

The Bible does not tell us about Mulek, but it does inform us about the death of the other sons of King Zedekiah III: "And they slew the sons of Zedekiah before his eyes, and put out the eyes of Zedekiah, and bound him with fetters of brass, and carried him to Babylon" (2 Kings 25:7).

Zedekiah/Mattaniah, or Zedekiah III (see chapter 3, "Looking at Dates"), was twenty-one years old when he was placed on the throne of Judah by Nebuchadnezzar. Eleven years later, when Jerusalem was destroyed, Zedekiah/Mattaniah was only thirty-two years old. His age suggests that all of his sons, would-be heirs to the Jewish throne but killed by the Babylonians, were under fourteen years of age. This reasoning is based on the assumption that Zedekiah III's oldest son was born when Zedekiah III was eighteen years old.

The question has always been raised as to how Mulek escaped the onslaught when all the sons of Zedekiah III were killed. At least four answers to this question are possible, none of which is conclusive:

1. Some Book of Mormon readers suggest that Mulek was only a baby and that those who were charged with his care carried him away from Jerusalem and saw to it that he was brought to the New World.

2. Other readers propose that perhaps Mulek was disguised as a daughter and was taken into Egypt prior to coming to the promised land.

3. A further possibility is that the mother of Mulek may have been pregnant at the time and that she was one who escaped the wrath of the Babylonians. This proposal would explain, as do the above two proposals, the reason for this group's not having any records with them. They had no time to collect records, as they were fleeing. If Mulek's mother were pregnant, probably her major concern was the protection of her unborn

> The Book of Mormon is primarily a record of the lineage of Nephi; and, as a result, we learn about the Mulekites only from their association with the Nephites.

child; and, as such, she likely played the role of other great women in history who were inspired by the Lord and knew that their children had very significant missions to fill.

4. A fourth proposal reflects the possibility that Mulek was not born at the time his older brothers were killed. This proposal suggests that Zedekiah III (Mattaniah) had children while in captivity among the Babylonians. Fifty years later, when the Jews were released from Babylon, would then be the time that Mulek, now a young man, was led by the Lord to the "land north." This proposal is in line with the commentary of archaeologist Bruce Warren, who identifies the date of the Mulekites' arrival to Mesoamerica at about 536 BC, which, according to Warren, matches a significant date inscribed in the Nuttall Codex from Mesoamerica.

Of considerable interest here, and as previously mentioned, is the existence of a group of so-called "dancer" monuments at the archaeological site of Monte Alban, located near the city of Oaxaca in the state of Oaxaca, Mexico.

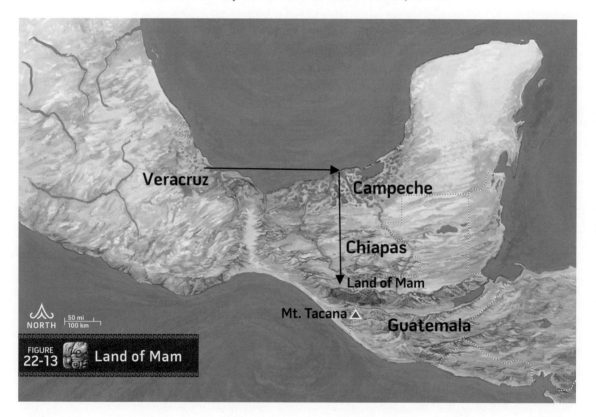

FIGURE 22–13: This map shows the movements of the Mulekites from Veracruz to Campeche to the borders of Chiapas and Guatemala. The highlands of western Guatemala are known as the land of Mam, and the language of the Maya who live there is of a very ancient origin. The last king of the Jaredites, Coriantumr, was either exiled to or simply sought refuge among the people of Zarahemla. The mountain regions of Chiapas and Guatemala present remarkable natural boundaries. The volcanic mountain of Tacana divides Mexico from Guatemala.

These monuments date to Monte Alban Period I, whose early dating corresponds to the middle of the fifth century BC. Monte Alban may have been a Jewish-Mulekite community. If this is the case, then the figures at Monte Alban may be depicting the Babylonian captivity. (See figure 22–14.)

Alma 22:30—The Mulekites Landed in the Land Northward

And it [Bountiful] bordered upon the land which they called Desolation, it [Bountiful or Desolation] being so far northward that it came into the land which had been peopled and been destroyed, of whose bones we have spoken, which was discovered by the people of Zarahemla, it [Desolation] being the place of their first landing.

The place where the people had been destroyed was called "the land Desolation" by the Nephites—not because it was geologically desolate but because it had become uninhabited as a result of the great Jaredite civil war (see Helaman 3:5–6).

From the archaeological records and the dates of native documents, as well as from hints in the Book of Mormon, we can conclude that the Jaredite nation did not fall for approximately 250–300 years after the Mulekites arrived. This conclusion suggests that the Mulekites and the Jaredites lived together simultaneously for this length of time. It also explains why, if the dancer monuments are depicting the Babylonian captivity, the figures are Olmec (Jaredite) in style.

Thus, if the Olmecs were in reality the Jaredites, then the Jaredites would have their established headquarters along the Gulf of Mexico. We could then conclude that the initial landing site of the Mulekites was by Veracruz, or perhaps as far north as Tampico, Mexico—in either case, near Jaredite headquarters.

The sixteenth-century Catholic writer, Sahagun, records the following regarding the landing of a particular group of people: "Countless years ago the first settlers[11] arrived in these parts of New Spain [Mexico], which is almost another world, and they came in ships by sea approaching this northern port; and because they disembarked there it was called Panutla, or Panoayan, 'place where they arrived who came by sea' now corruptly called Pantlan [Panuco]."[12]

Panuco is near the present-day city of Tampico, Mexico. The account continues by explaining that the settlers traveled along the Gulf Coast of Mexico and eventually settled in the areas of Campeche and Chiapas on the southeast side of the Isthmus.[13]

Sahagun, in talking about the same people in his first book, indicates that the settlers came from the sea north.[14] The sea north to the sixteenth-century writers was the Gulf of Mexico, which is part of the Atlantic Ocean.

Another Spanish writer by the name of Juan de Torquemada writes the following, as recorded in a 1723 edition of his works: "Some years after the origin and beginning of Tulla,[15] there came from the northern part of Mexico [Veracruz] a certain people that

11. This statement, referring to the first settlers, causes some students of the Book of Mormon to favor an Atlantic Jaredite crossing. However, Ixtlilxochitl, in referring to the same people, calls them the third settlers (see Ixtlilxochitl:34 in chapter 11, "Fernando de Alva Ixtlilxochitl"). The reasons for bringing the Jaredites along the Pacific as opposed to the Atlantic are outlined in chapter 21, "The Voyage of the Jaredites."

12. Bernardino de Sahagun, *Historia General de las Cosas de Nueva Espana: Florentine Codex*, 12 vols., edited and translated to English by Arthur O. Anderson and Charles E. Dibble (Santa Fe, NM: The School of American Research and the University of Utah, 1950), Book Nine.

13. Sahagun, *Historia General de las Cosas de Nueva Espana*, Book Nine.

14. Sahagun, *Historia General de las Cosas de Nueva Espana*, Book One.

15. Probably Tula. The word *Tula* is associated with a land of abundance or a bountiful land—or the land Bountiful.

landed in the vicinity of Panuco. . . . Concerning this nation, it is not known where they originated because there is no data on the subject, other than that given above which says they landed at Panuco."[16]

16. Sahagun, *Historia General de las Cosas de Nueva Espana*, 1:254–55.

Ixtlilxochitl states: "Those who possessed this new world in the third period were the 'Ulmecas and Xicalancas,' and according to their history they came in ships or boats from the eastern hemisphere to the land of Potonchan."[17]

17. See Ixtlilxochitl:34 in chapter 11, "Fernando de Alva Ixtlilxochitl."

Ixtlilxochitl, Sahagun, and Torquemada are all evidently talking about the same people. With their information, as well as the archaeological data suggesting that the Olmecs (Jaredites) were established along the Gulf Coast of Mexico, we can deduce that Panuco is an excellent landing location for the Mulekites. The location appears more feasible as we pursue the trail of the Mulekites from their initial landing site to a secondary location and ultimately to the place they called Zarahemla.

Mulek may not have left for the Americas until after the return of the Jews out of captivity in 536 BC. The ships on which the Mulekites traveled were apparently manned by Phoenicians who were from the ancient port of Sidon, which is located north of Jerusalem in Lebanon. *Sidon* is the name that was given by the descendants of Mulek to the major river that ran through Zarahemla; it means "fish waters."

The Paraiba Stone. The concept of an Atlantic crossing for Mulek is further enhanced by the studies of the late Hebrew scholar, Dr. Cyrus Gordon. He reports a discovery of some writings in Hebrew on a stone discovered in Paraiba, Brazil, referred to as the Paraiba stone. Gordon reports the stone's translation, which tells about ten ships of Jews leaving the port of Sidon after the return of the Jews from the Babylonian captivity. According to Gordon, one ship, the one that landed in Brazil, got off track. The other nine ships, as reported by the Spanish chroniclers, may have been the fleet of ships that arrived at Panuco—ships that carried the descendants of Abraham and Jacob. Following is a summation critique written in 1979 by Frank Moore Cross, professor emeritus from Harvard Divinity School. Cross challenged Gordon's conclusions and labeled the Paraiba stone a forgery.

> The Paraiba inscription is said to be a Phoenician inscription carved in stone and found in northeastern Brazil in 1872. After raising a minor stir in the 1870's, the Paraiba inscription was almost forgotten—until another copy of the inscription was publicized in the 1960's by Professor Cyrus Gordon, then of Brandeis University and now at New York University. Based on this newly found copy, Gordon, in 1968, published an article declaring the inscription to be authentic. In a three-column headline, the *New York Times* declared "Phoenicia Linked to America."
>
> The contents of the inscription are remarkable—although a skeptic might suggest that it is precisely what we should expect from a Phoenician inscription found in Brazil!

> Mulek may not have left for the Americas until after the return of the Jews out of captivity in 536 BC. The ships on which the Mulekites traveled were apparently manned by Phoenicians who were from the ancient port of Sidon, which is located north of Jerusalem in Lebanon.

The text recites the story of ten Phoenician ships manned by Sidonians that sailed from Ezion-Geber, down the Red Sea, around the southern tip of Africa, and then headed north, presumably with the intention of sailing through the strait of Gibraltar, into the Mediterranean Sea and then to Phoenicia on the eastern coast of the Mediterranean. Off the coast of Africa, however, one of the ships was separated by a storm and was eventually cast "on this distant shore." On board were twelve men and three women. . . .

Professor Gordon, in his analysis of the inscription, tells us only that "The script is Sidonian, close to the Eshmunazar inscription (N.B. the *shin*) of the early fifth century BC. However, the *zayin* and *yod* are more archaic and suggest a sixth-century [BC] date." This is the sum total of his paleographic analysis. In response to my detailed paleographical analogies, Gordon has stated only that different scholars vary in their dating and that I present an excessively precise picture.[18]

18. For further details, see Frank Moore Cross, "The Phoenician Inscription from Brazil: A Nineteenth-Century Forgery," *Orientalia*, 37 (1968): 437–60; C. H. Gordon, "The Authenticity of the Phoenician Text from Parahyba," *Orientalia*, 37 (1968): 75–80. The comments in the text are from Frank Moore Cross, "Phoenicians in Brazil?" *Biblical Archaeological Review* 5, no. 1 (January/February 1979): 36–43.

The route of the ships described on the Paraiba stone supposedly indicates a Red Sea departure and may represent as much a possibility as a departure from the port of Sidon. At any rate, the Phoencians or Sidonians appear to be the navigators of the ships Mulek and his people traveled on, as they were the seafarers of the sixth century BC.

In Gordon's favor is the arrival of ships at Veracruz, Mexico, carrying descendants of Abraham and Jacob as reported by the sixteenth century Spanish priests of Mesoamerica. Neither the writer of the Paraiba stone nor Professor Gordon would have had any knowledge of the landing place of the other nine ships.

Helaman 6:10—The Mulekites Were Brought into the Land North

Now the land south was called Lehi, and the land north was called Mulek, which was after the son of Zedekiah; for the Lord did bring Mulek into the land north, and Lehi into the land south.

This scripture was discussed in both chapter 19, "The Land Northward," and chapter 20, "The Land Southward." Nevertheless, it is significant here as well because it states that the Lord brought Mulek to the land north (see figure 22–9).

The "land north" in this instance is probably not referring to the initial landing site proposed above but rather to the site of the second landing or settlement of at least a portion of the Mulekites. This second place is undoubtedly the area of the Bay of Terminos (Campeche) located in the state of Campeche, Mexico, east of the Isthmus of Tehuantepec.

From this second settlement location, the Mulekites, or a branch of the Mulekites, moved again, in typical Jewish fashion, to escape their enemies. This time they moved up the Grijalva and Usumacinta Rivers to the frontiers of Guatemala where they established their settlements, including the great city of Zarahemla.

Therefore, in reference to Helaman 6:10, the "land north" may well mean the land north of the land of Nephi, and the "land south" may mean the land south of the land of Zarahemla. In other words, the Yucatan-Campeche-Chiapas area where the Mulekites lived is in the land north; and highland Guatemala, where the Nephites lived for the first four hundred years in Mesoamerica, is called the land south. Hence, "the Lord did bring Mulek into the land north, and Lehi into the land south."

Further justification for the above hypothesis, as reported from native documents and the archaeological data, is as follows.

Archaeological data. The archaeological data from the area in and around the states of Tabasco and Chiapas, Mexico, depict a small group of settlers who moved out of the area north of the isthmus (Tabasco-Veracruz) to the shores of the Bay of Campeche, which was previously called Bay of Terminos. Not considered to be of great importance, as compared to the overall culture, the beginning of this small group, which dates from 600 BC to 400 BC, demonstrates a pattern of internal differentiation.[19]

The Title of the Lords of Totonicapan. This native Quiche Maya document describes a group of people who were descendants of Abraham and Jacob and who crossed the ocean and settled in the area of the Bay of Campeche mentioned above. They were an agriculture-based people who lived in houses made of sticks. They had things in common.[20]

The Annals of the Cakchiquels. This native Mesoamerican document, which is similar to *The Title of the Lords of Totonicapan*, describes what is apparently the same group of people. It states that this Guatemala tribe (1) came from the north (Tampico), (2) arrived at the Gulf of Mexico (Veracruz and Tabasco), and (3) lived many years in the region of the lagoons of Terminos (Campeche), located between Tabasco and Yucatan.[21]

This area is the same area that later is called the "land among many waters" by the Limhi expedition (see Mosiah 8:8–11): "And they were lost in the wilderness for the space of many days, yet they were diligent, and found not the land of Zarahemla but returned to this land, having traveled in a land among many waters" (Mosiah 8:8).

Alma 22:31—The Mulekites Moved up into the South Wilderness

And they [the Mulekites] came from there [the place of their first landing] up into the south wilderness. Thus the land on the northward was called Desolation, and the land on the southward was called Bountiful, it being the wilderness which is filled with all manner of wild animals of every kind, a part of which had come from the land northward for food.

19. Lorenzo Ochoa and Marcia Castro, *Archeological Guide of the Park—Museum of La Venta* (Villahermosa: Tabasco State Government, 1986).

20. P. Dionisio Jose Chonay, trans. Adrian Recinos, Introduction and Notes, *Titulo de Los Senores de Totonicapan* (Guatemala: Direccion General de Antropologia e Historia, 1980).

21. Adrian Recinos and Delia Goetz, *The Annals of the Cakchiquels*, translated from the Cakchiquel Maya (Norman, OK: University of Oklahoma Press, 1953).

As we follow the trail of the Mulekites from the northern part of the Gulf of Mexico across to the Bay of Campeche, we again gain considerable assistance from both archaeological and traditional history that correlates with the Mulekites' third move in the Book of Mormon.

The above scripture informs us that the Mulekites, or at least a portion of the Mulekites, traveled up into the south wilderness. The area directly south of Tabasco and Campeche is the Chiapas mountains.

On our tours, we customarily take a boat ride on the Grijalva River in the area of the central depression of the state of Chiapas. We board the boat at the town of Chiapa de Corzo. We then boat for about an hour and fifteen minutes to the Chicuasen Dam. This majestic canyon-land gorge cuts through the high mountain walls. The river continues through the rough, awe-inspiring wilderness and finally snakes lazily through the lowlands of the Gulf of Mexico. It runs through the middle of the city of Villahermosa and then meets up with the Usumacinta River before emptying into the Atlantic Ocean via the Gulf of Mexico.

Once we leave the boat, we usually ascend up into the mountains to eight thousand feet elevation and end up at the picturesque town of San Cristobal de las Casas. The next day, the trip continues from San Cristobal to Ocosingo, past the beautiful, blue waterfalls (Aguas Azules) and then on to the Maya ruins of Palenque.

This is the area that probably constitutes the south wilderness through which the Mulekites traveled. Their journey ended in the land of Zarahemla where they settled, grew in strength and number, and began to influence other cultures.

The archaeological record states that "toward 600–400 BC some groups from the metropolitan Olmeca zone began moving out and settled in the basin of the Middle Usumacinta; their influence was then felt more clearly, to the extent that local cultures were transformed."[22]

Some of the archaeological sites that were occupied or transformed during this time period include Tierra Blanca, Pomoca, Emiliano Zapata, and El Mirador. These sites are just a few of those that begin to depict this transformation.

The native document, *The Title of the Lords of Totonicapan*, also confirms the above movement, as it describes how these descendants of Abraham and Jacob, "compelled by the necessity of establishing themselves in a propitious spot and harried perhaps by their enemies, the tribes once more went up the Usumacinta and Tabasco [Grijalva] rivers and their tributaries and penetrated into the territory of present Guatemala. After a long journey they found themselves in the hills and the valleys of the interior, the land of Mam and the Volcano of Tacana, on the frontiers of Guatemala and Chiapas. Then they dispersed into the interior of the country, occupying all the places which are referred to in the manuscript under their ancient names."[23]

The archaeological record states that "toward 600–400 BC some groups from the metropolitan Olmeca zone began moving out and settled in the basin of the Middle Usumacinta; their influence was then felt more clearly, to the extent that local cultures were transformed."

22. Ochoa and Castro, *Archeological Guide of the Park—Museum of La Venta*, 18.

23. Adrian Recinos, trans., Introduction and Notes, *Memorial de Solola Anales de Los Cakchiquele* (Guatemala: Direccion General de Antropologia y Historia, 1980), 39.

FIGURE 22–14: Several stone monuments at Monte Alban date to about 500 BC and reflect people who are suffering, who are naked, and who appear to be in bondage. Some scholars propose that these monuments may be a historical presentation of the Jewish captivity in the sixth century BC. A branch of the Jewish Mulekites may have migrated to the Oaxaca valley where they wrote their history in art form—in stone. (For more information, see chapter 7, "The Zapotec [Mulekite-Nephite] Culture"; photo courtesy of Sheryl Lee Wilson)

FIGURE 22–15: Our arrival at the seashore near Salalah, Dhofar, Oman, caused us to contemplate about Nephi's building a ship twenty-six hundred years earlier at or near this location. "Dhofar" is interpreted as land of abundance—or Bountiful. (Photo courtesy of Boyd Hoglund)

The regions that are referred to by both the archaeological account and *The Title of the Lords of Totonicapan* are precisely the same regions that are proposed to be the land of Zarahemla in the Book of Mormon.

Omni 1:15–16—Mosiah Discovered the Mulekites

Behold, it came to pass that Mosiah discovered that the people of Zarahemla [Mulekites] came out from Jerusalem at the time that Zedekiah, king of Judah, was carried away captive into Babylon.

And they [the Mulekites] journeyed in the wilderness, and were brought by the hand of the Lord across the great waters, into the land where Mosiah discovered them; and they had dwelt there from that time forth.

The puzzle fits together as we witness the potential settlement of the Mulekites along the Usumacinta and Grijalva Rivers—having traveled into the south wilderness after landing in the land northward.

The stage is set for Mosiah to come down from the Guatemala highlands (land of Nephi) to Zarahemla, where he discovered the people of Zarahemla. Zarahemla was a descendant of Mulek. Mosiah, who was of the tribe of Joseph and a descendant of Nephi, became king over the land of Zarahemla. The people of Zarahemla were descendants of Zedekiah/Mattaniah; and, as a result, Zarahemla was of the tribe of Judah. As mentioned earlier, Joseph ruled Judah for the next four hundred years.

Mosiah 25:2—Mulekites Were More Numerous Than the Nephites

Now there were not so many of the children of Nephi, or so many of those who were descendants of Nephi, as there were of the people of Zarahemla, who was a descendant of Mulek, and those who came with him into the wilderness.

We learn from this verse that there were many more Mulekites than Nephites. This information is consistent with the Spanish chronicle accounts, which tell us that several ships arrived in the north—ships whose passengers we conclude to be Mulekites. As far as we know, the Nephites came over in only one ship. We should also remember that only a righteous branch of the Nephites followed Mosiah when he fled out of the land of Nephi.

The above scripture also seems to imply that not all of the Mulekites followed Zarahemla into the wilderness of the Peten and Chiapas. This thinking substantiates the conclusion that Monte Alban, located on the west side of the Isthmus, was also a Jewish community.

Mosiah 25:4—Mulekites and Nephites Were in Separate Bodies

And now all the people of Nephi were assembled together, and also all the people of Zarahemla, and they were gathered together in two bodies.

Although Mosiah was the king of both the Nephites (tribe of Joseph) and the Mulekites (tribe of Judah), the two groups still maintained their identities. The separate

Not all of the Mulekites followed Zarahemla into the wilderness of the Peten and Chiapas.

Beginning in the first century BC, a group of the elite in Mesoamerica began to rally for control. By AD 200, their influence was much stronger; and during the strength of the Maya Classic Period, which extended to the tenth century AD, the elite hierarchy ruled totally in Mesoamerica.

24. Alfredo Barrera Rubio, *Official Guide: Uxmal*, trans. Helen Jones-Perrott de Mandri (Mexico: Instituto Nacional de Antropologia e Historia, 1985), 33.

identities had far-reaching effects, as we see later in the Book of Mormon history when a group of king-men arose, claiming their right to rule: "And it came to pass that those who were desirous that Pahoran should be dethroned from the judgment-seat were called king-men, for they were desirous that the law should be altered in a manner to overthrow the free government and to establish a king over the land.... Now those who were in favor of kings were those of high birth, and they sought to be kings; and they were supported by those who sought power and authority over the people" (Alma 51:5, 8).

This movement took place about 67 BC and ultimately caused the Nephite-Mulekite nation to divide into tribes: "And every tribe did appoint a chief or a leader over them; and thus they became tribes and leaders of tribes. Now behold, there was no man among them save he had much family and many kindreds and friends; therefore their tribes became exceeding great" (3 Nephi 7:3–4).

The archaeological record of Mesoamerica is identical in describing the activity mentioned in the above passages of scripture. Beginning in the first century BC, a group of the elite in Mesoamerica began to rally for control. By AD 200, their influence was much stronger; and during the strength of the Maya Classic Period, which extended to the tenth century AD, the elite hierarchy ruled totally in Mesoamerica. In analyzing the archaeological history of the Maya ruins of Uxmal, located about forty miles south of the city of Merida, Yucatan, Alfredo Barrera Rubio says: "During this period the dominant group was a hereditary elite which emerged in the last century before Christ. Its authority extended throughout all aspects of social life, but in particular they were representatives or mediators between the community and the divine or supernatural forces, utilizing magical/religious means. The group controlled the knowledge of the times, much of which, in order to maintain a relationship with the direct production of the people, determined social behavior."[24]

As we balance the history and culture recorded in the Book of Mormon with the archaeological and traditional records of Mesoamerica, we can perhaps perceive that the Mulekites, or at least the hierarchy elite among the Mulekites, were not always satisfied being ruled over by the tribe of Joseph. The 67 BC and AD 30 attempts to establish kings may have been Mulekite (tribe of Judah) attempts to gain the glory of the olden days in Jerusalem. They may even have succeeded in part, as the Maya Classic Period shows just such a hierarchy.

SUMMARY

If the Classic Maya priests were descendants of the Mulekite king-men, then there is more archaeological and traditional data that refer to the Mulekites than data that refer to the Jaredites or Nephites. The Book of Mormon, however, provides less information on the Mulekites than it does on the other two groups. Nevertheless, when we examine the consistency of archaeology, tradition, Book of Mormon, and the geological and geographical structure of the areas around the Isthmus of Tehuantepec, a very believable case can be presented for the Mulekite migrations and history.

The Mulekites probably landed along the northern part of the Gulf of Mexico; and then at least a portion of them settled for many years around the Bay of Campeche. From there, they settled many communities along the middle Usumacinta and Grijalva valleys. Between 200–180 BC, Mosiah traveled down from highland Guatemala to Chiapas, Mexico, where he discovered the people of Zarahemla.

Mormon gives emphasis to the migrations of Lehi and Mulek by writing a summary statement in chiastic form. Notice that the center portion is associated with the Savior because *Zedekiah* means "my Lord is righteous."

> A. Now the land south was called Lehi,
>> B. and the land north was called Mulek,
>>> C. which was after the son of *Zedekiah*;
>>> C. for the *Lord* did bring
>> B. Mulek into the land north,
> A. and Lehi into the land south. (Helaman 6:10; emphasis added)

If the Classic Maya priests were descendants of the Mulekite king-men, then there is more archaeological and traditional data that refer to the Mulekites than data that refer to the Jaredites or Nephites.

Gulf of Mexico

Land Northward

Isthmus of
Tehuantepec

Wilderness
of Tehuantepec

Land Southward

Gulf of Tehuantepec

NORTH

25 mi
50 km

CHAPTER 23

Things That Are Narrow

O then, my beloved brethren, repent ye, and enter in at the strait gate, and continue in the way which is narrow, until ye shall obtain eternal life. (Jacob 6:11)

he two most significant geographical landmarks associated with the Book of Mormon are (1) a narrow neck of land and (2) a narrow strip of wilderness. A narrow neck of land, also referred to as a small neck of land, divided the land southward from the land northward, and a narrow strip of wilderness divided the land of Nephi from the land of Zarahemla. From the limited information we have in the Book of Mormon, the term "narrow strip of wilderness" is apparently synonymous with a narrow mountain range; the term "small neck of land" seems to fit the requirement of an isthmus; and the terms "narrow pass" and "narrow passage" suggest a narrow path or narrow road that runs through the isthmus.[1]

1. The following scriptures refer to the narrow neck of land/narrow pass: (1) Alma 22:32: "a small neck of land between the land northward and the land southward"; (2) Alma 50:34: "they did head them, by the narrow pass which led by the sea into the land northward, yea, by the sea, on the west and on the east"; (3) Alma 52:9: "secure the narrow pass which led into the land northward"; (4) Alma 63:5: "and launched it forth into the west sea, by the narrow neck which led into the land northward"; (5) Mormon 2:29: "Lamanites did give unto us the land northward, yea, even to the narrow passage which led into the land southward"; and (6) Ether 10:20: "And they built a great city by the narrow neck of land, by the place where the sea divides the land."

OPPOSITE: This map outlines the narrow pass. The Isthmus of Tehuantepec plays a pivotal role in our understanding of Book of Mormon geography and history. Its geographical and historical prominence does not result merely from the manner in which it divides two large land masses—as stipulated in the concept of a small neck of land that divided the land northward from the land southward. Rather, the isthmus is important because of the manner in which the narrow passage directs travelers in a south to north direction between the western mountains of Oaxaca and the eastern mountains of Tehuantepec.

The small neck of land (isthmus) divided the land northward from the land southward, and the narrow strip of wilderness divided the land of Nephi from the land of Zarahemla, both of which were located in the land southward. We will first discuss the location of the narrow neck of land followed by an analysis of the narrow strip of wilderness.

THE NARROW NECK OF LAND

Through the years, considerable confusion has arisen among readers of the Book of Mormon as they have tried to decipher the exact relationships among the terms "narrow neck of land," "narrow neck," "narrow pass," and "narrow passage."

The terms are inextricably related and are used in connection with two land masses more so than with two oceans or seas. The *Merriam-Webster's Collegiate Dictionary*, eleventh edition, defines "isthmus" as "a narrow strip of land connecting two larger land areas." Most students of the Book of Mormon tend to agree that an isthmus is involved with the narrow neck of land.

Some early members of the Church designated the Isthmus of Panama (Darien) as the small neck of land referred to in Alma 22:32: "The land of Nephi and the land of Zarahemla were nearly surrounded by water, there being a small neck of land between the land northward and the land southward."

However, for reasons already discussed in previous chapters, almost all current students of historical geography of the Book of Mormon have concluded that the Isthmus of Tehuantepec is the narrow neck of land referred to in the Book of Mormon.

Understanding that the narrow pass runs through the isthmus in a north-south direction and also runs between two mountain ranges—as opposed to running between two oceans or seas—solves a major geographical issue in the Book of Mormon. We propose that the narrow pass is the old trade route that runs along the Pacific side by the Gulf of Tehuantepec and then goes directly north for about 125 miles and parallels the Gulf Coast of Mexico on the Atlantic side. The road either goes on into the Mexico City valley or takes the traveler northward all along the Gulf Coast toward the United States border. In other words, the term "narrow pass" refers to the width of the pass between two mountain ranges rather than to the length or distance of the pass from ocean to ocean.

Placing the narrow pass within the narrow neck between two mountain ranges is very significant. This placement solves many directional problems that have been associated with Book of Mormon geography—and may even be the most important key to understanding the geography of the Book of Mormon.

The reasons for placing the narrow neck of land/narrow pass in the above-described area, with the narrow pass running north and south between the two mountain ranges, are as follows:

Placing the narrow pass within the narrow neck between two mountain ranges is very significant. This placement solves many directional problems that have been associated with Book of Mormon geography.

Exploring the Lands of the Book of Mormon

FIGURE 23–1: The narrow mountain range looking south from the Chiapas, or Zarahemla, side. From many statements in the Book of Mormon, readers can easily determine that although the land of Nephi was south of the land of Zarahemla, Nephi was up in elevation. (Photo courtesy of Cortney Boice)

1. The Book of Mormon requires that the narrow neck of land/narrow pass must divide the land southward from the land northward: "And now, it was only the distance of a day and half's journey for a Nephite, on the line Bountiful and the land Desolation, from the east to the west sea; and thus the land of Nephi and the land of Zarahemla were nearly surrounded by water, there being a small *neck of land* between the land northward and the land southward" (Alma 22:32; emphasis added).

Assume today that we were to drive north through the narrow neck of land/narrow pass from the city of Tehuantepec toward Acayucan, Veracruz. We would notice that the flat plains along Tehuantepec suddenly devolve into a very narrow passageway for a distance of several miles. We would be hemmed in by mountains on either side. We would find this route to be a natural dividing line between the land northward on the one hand and the land southward on the other.

The Lamanites and Nephites must have thought that the narrow neck of land/narrow pass was a natural dividing line as well. About 350 years after the birth of Christ, the Lamanites had successfully overpowered the Nephites and had driven them out of the land of Zarahemla, which was southward of the narrow neck of land. Thus, the Nephites were forced to move into the land northward. Mormon states: "And the Lamanites did give unto us the land northward, yea, even to the narrow passage which led into the land southward. And we did give unto the Lamanites all the land southward" (Mormon 2:29).

This land southward, divided by the narrow passage, subsequently became the country that was occupied by the massive Maya (Lamanite) nation. It is the area that is proposed in *Exploring the Lands of the Book of Mormon* as Lamanite Maya and Nephite Maya territory during the time period of the Book of Mormon (see chapter 4, "Archaeology in Mesoamerica").

The land northward probably included the Mexican states of Oaxaca, Veracruz, Puebla, Tlaxcala, Guerrero, Morelos, and Mexico.

2. The narrow neck of land/narrow pass must be situated so it provides an escape route into the land northward. Mormon indicates that the Nephites, in their wisdom, protected the narrow neck of land/narrow pass to hem the Lamanites in on the south. This strategy prevented the Lamanites from having any possession in the land northward and also prevented them from overrunning the land northward. Mormon further notes that this plan provided the Nephites, according to their desire, with a country into which they might flee from the Lamanites (see Alma 22:33–34).

The narrow neck of land/narrow pass is a natural passage route. On the southwestern side of the Isthmus of Tehuantepec lie the rugged Oaxaca Mountains. These mountains are a natural barrier for any realistic type of movement through the area. On the southeastern side of the isthmus are the mountains of Tehuantepec that form a barrier to movement just like the Oaxaca Mountains on the southwestern side. The only possibility for going north and south in this area is through the narrow pass because the mountains on the west and on the east are, essentially, impenetrable.

FIGURE 23–2: Archaeologists carved this narrow tunnel through the great pyramid of Cholula, Puebla, Mexico. Cholula is located on the northward side of the Isthmus of Tehuantepec—or the narrow neck of land. (Photo courtesy of Cortney Boice)

In addition, on the northeastern side of the isthmus are extensive swampy waters as well as numerous river tributaries—all feeding into the Gulf of Mexico. Prior to the construction of modern bridges and highways to accommodate trains and automobiles in this area, these barriers made east-west passage across the top of the isthmus extremely difficult, especially during the rainy season.

These geographic features dovetail precisely with what we read in the Book of Mormon about the narrow neck of land and the narrow pass through the narrow neck. That is, in Book of Mormon times, the only feasible way to travel between the land northward and the land southward was through the narrow pass in the narrow neck of land. From the perspective of what we read in the Book of Mormon, the geographic features associated with the Isthmus of Tehuantepec fulfill precisely the geographic needs of the narrow neck of land and the narrow pass.

MORIANTON AND TEANCUM AND THE NARROW PASS

The statement in the Book of Mormon referring to Morianton, a Nephite dissenter who was trying to take possession of the land which was northward (the land that was covered with large bodies of water), in all probability is referring to both the overabundance of rivers and lagoons along both the Campeche and Veracruz sides of the Gulf of Mexico as well as the Mexico City valley. He was detained by Teancum at a certain point near the narrow pass that led into the land northward: "And it came to pass that they did not head them until they had come to the borders of the land Desolation; and there they did head them, by the narrow pass which led by the sea into the land northward, yea, by the sea, on the west and on the east" (Alma 50:34). Mormon provides us with three orientation statements or three defining points: (1) "the borders of the land Desolation"; (2) "the narrow pass which led . . . into the land northward"; and (3) "by the sea, on the west and on the east."

From statements in the Book of Mormon and from archaeological evidence, we can be quite definitive as to the location of the land of Desolation. We can also propose with a high degree of confidence the location of the narrow pass that led into the land northward.

Although the following comments are different from what was written in the 1989 edition of *Exploring the Lands of the Book of Mormon*, it is more likely that item three above, "by the sea, on the west and on the east," is referring to the Gulf of Mexico. Mormon lived in this area when he was abridging the Book of Mormon. The modern city of Coatzacoalcos appears to be close to where Mormon called the Nephites together in the fourth century AD: "I did cause my people that they should gather themselves together at the land Desolation, to a city which was in the borders, by the narrow pass which led into the land southward" (Mormon 3:5).

As shown in figure 23–3, this area is located where the water divides the land northward from the land southward. Therefore, on the Tabasco/Campeche side (land

The geographic features associated with the Isthmus of Tehuantepec fulfill precisely the geographic needs of the narrow neck of land and the narrow pass.

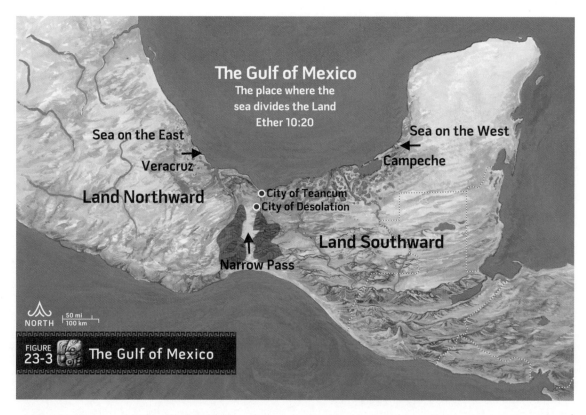

The Gulf of Mexico
The place where the
sea divides the Land
Ether 10:20

Sea on the East

Veracruz

Sea on the West

Campeche

Land Northward

City of Teancum
City of Desolation

Land Southward

Narrow Pass

NORTH   50 mi / 100 km

FIGURE
23-3   The Gulf of Mexico

FIGURE 23–3: "They did not head them until they had come to the borders of the land Desolation; and there they did head them, by the narrow pass which led by the sea into the land northward, yea, by the sea, on the west and on the east" (Alma 50:34). We define the word "gulf" as a place where the sea divides two land masses. In that respect, as shown in this map, the Gulf of Mexico divides the state of Veracruz from the state of Campeche. From Veracruz, the sea is on the east. From Campeche, the sea is on the west. Moroni refers to the same area as "the place where the sea divides the land" (Ether 10:20).

southward), the sea is on the west; and from the Veracruz side (land northward), the sea is on the east. In other words, the references here appear to be talking about a gulf, which in this case would be referring to the Gulf of Mexico. Moroni gives credibility to this concept when he describes the same area where a great city was built "by the narrow neck of land, by the place where the sea divides the land" (Ether 10:20).

Teancum, a Nephite military leader, did not head off Morianton and his people until they had come to the borders of the land of Desolation. A result of this first century BC battle between Teancum and Morianton may be what caused the Nephites to name a city in that region in honor of this great Nephite warrior, Teancum. In AD 363, the Nephites were defeated by the Lamanites at the city of Desolation, and the Nephite inhabitants fled to the city of Teancum. Mormon writes, "Now the city Teancum lay in the borders of the seashore; and it was also near the city Desolation" (Mormon 4:3).

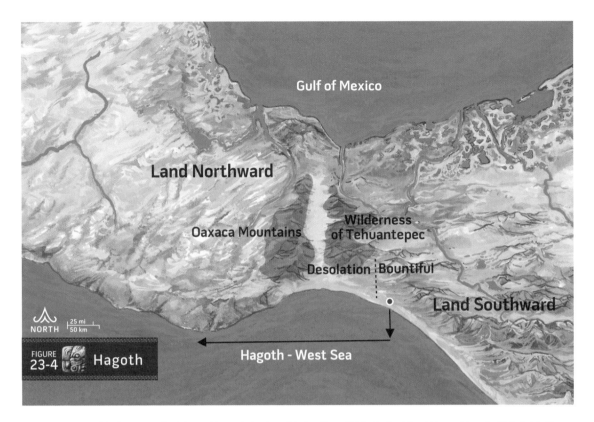

FIGURE 23–4: Hagoth built "an exceedingly large ship, on the borders of the land Bountiful, by the land Desolation, and launched it forth into the west sea, by the narrow neck which led into the land northward" (Alma 63:5). He later built and launched other ships in this area. When we travel through this area with our tours, we are very much aware of the logging trucks and sawmills that are engaged in the harvesting of timber.

HAGOTH AND THE NARROW NECK

Hagoth launched his ship into the west sea by the narrow neck that led into the land northward: "And it came to pass that Hagoth, he being an exceedingly curious man, therefore he went forth and built him an exceedingly large ship, on the borders of the land Bountiful, by the land Desolation, and launched it forth into the west sea, by the narrow neck which led into the land northward" (Alma 63:5).

In all probability, this scripture refers to the Gulf of Tehuantepec located on the southern tip of the narrow neck of land/narrow pass that leads up from the Gulf of Tehuantepec to the Gulf of Mexico.

The verse refers to the west sea because the Gulf of Tehuantepec is part of the Pacific Ocean, which fits the criterion for its being the west sea. For a discussion about the boundary lines of the land of Bountiful and the land of Desolation, see chapter 20, "The Land Southward." The above scripture states that Hagoth was an exceedingly curious man from the land of Bountiful (land southward), which bordered the eastern boundary of the land of Desolation. Mormon is simply telling us that Hagoth launched his ship in the Gulf of Tehuantepec on the Pacific Ocean at the bottom of the narrow neck of land/narrow pass.

THE JAREDITES AND THE NARROW NECK

"And the whole face of the land northward was covered with inhabitants."

The Book of Mormon requires that an area must exist on the northern part of the Isthmus of Tehuantepec, or the Gulf of Mexico side, for the construction of cities. This is the area where the Jaredites built a great city by the narrow neck of land, by the place where the sea divides the land: "And they built a great city by the narrow neck of land, by the place where the sea divides the land. And they did preserve the land southward for a wilderness, to get game. And the whole face of the land northward was covered with inhabitants" (Ether 10:20–21).

The "great city," built somewhere around 1000 BC, is probably the site of La Venta at the northern part of the isthmus, near the ancient Olmec ruins of San Lorenzo and a hundred miles from the site of Tres Zapotes, which is located on the northwestern side of the Gulf of Mexico at the base of the Hill Vigia near Santiago Tuxtla, Veracruz. This conclusion coincides with the fact that, from an archaeological point of view, the entire land northward was inhabited by the Olmec people during the Jaredite time period (see chapter 9, "The Izapa [Jaredite-Nephite-Lamanite] Culture").

CLEARING UP THE CONFUSION

As mentioned earlier in the chapter, readers often become confused by internal language associated with "narrow neck of land" and "narrow pass." Some of the confusion about the narrow neck of land/narrow pass seems to come from a casual reading—or perhaps misreading—of Alma 22:32. Readers assume that a Nephite required only a day and a half to travel from the sea east (Atlantic Ocean) to the sea west (Pacific Ocean) or from the Gulf of Tehuantepec to the Gulf of Mexico. *The Book of Mormon does not say that.* It says that, in a day and a half, a Nephite could travel from the borderline (western border) of the land Bountiful and the eastern border of the land Desolation to the sea west (Pacific Ocean). Or, as Ludlow says:

> Some students of the Book of Mormon interpret this verse to mean that the entire narrow neck of land separating the land northward from the land southward could be traversed by a Nephite in a day and a half. However, a careful reading of this verse does not necessarily justify this conclusion. The historian's statement concerning a line "from the east to the west sea" does not necessarily mean the same as though he had said that the line existed from the *east sea* to the *west sea*. The statement may mean that it was a day and a half's journey for a Nephite *from the east of the line to the west sea.*
>
> In Helaman 4:7 the author mentions this same area again: "And there they did fortify against the Lamanites, from the west sea, even unto the east; it being

a day's journey for a Nephite, on the line which they had fortified." Again, note that the word "sea" does not follow the word "east." Also, a Nephite can now travel this distance in only one day's journey, and it is quite clear the distance being covered is "the line which they had fortified" and not necessarily the distance between two seas.[2]

2. Daniel H. Ludlow, *A Companion to Your Study of the Book of Mormon* (Salt Lake City: Deseret Book, 1976), 209.

The ease with which this confusion can arise is suggested by the Spanish translation of the Book of Mormon. Even though the English version says "from the east to the west sea," the translator of the Spanish edition mistakenly translated the wording as "from the east sea to the sea on the west" ("desde el mar del este al de oeste"). In other words, the translator mistakenly saw this distance as extending from sea to sea. In a like manner, some Book of Mormon scholars incorrectly read or interpret the language in this verse.

SPIRITUAL IMPORTANCE OF THE NARROW NECK OF LAND

Thus far in this chapter. we have discussed the geographical significance of the narrow neck of land/narrow pass. Yet this same area has a spiritual significance as well. The Lord sent three groups of people to this area, which is divided by the narrow neck of land. This land route is the only one that people could travel on to go all the way from North America to South America—or vice versa. The area serves the same purpose as the great land bridge in ancient Israel, where the movement was from Egypt to Syria. By necessity, travelers had to travel through Israel, where they came in contact with God's covenant people, thus providing travelers the opportunity of hearing about God's covenants with the house of Israel.

The same parallel is evident in Mesoamerica. The evidence suggests that the Nephite/Mulekite people settled on both sides of the Isthmus of Tehuantepec, or narrow neck of land. This thesis simply implies that people who traveled through that area might have had the opportunity to be influenced by God's covenant people, as was the case in ancient Israel.

It may well be that Mormon is also using the geographical statement of a narrow neck of land as a type to illustrate a spiritual connotation. That is, just as a narrow neck or a narrow pass separated the land of Bountiful from the land of Desolation, so does a narrow line divide us from good (Bountiful) and evil (Desolation). Mormon used both terms—a narrow course and a gulf—to teach a spiritual message: "a strait and narrow course across that everlasting gulf of misery which is prepared to engulf the wicked" (Helaman 3:29).

"The historian's statement concerning a line 'from the east to the west sea' does not necessarily mean the same as though he had said that the line existed from *the east sea* to the *west sea*."

—Daniel H. Ludlow

Without question, the most reliable and significant geological statement regarding Book of Mormon geography is a narrow mountain range that runs from the east to the west and touches two oceans.

THE NARROW STRIP OF WILDERNESS

Without question, the most reliable and significant geological statement regarding Book of Mormon geography is a narrow mountain range that runs from the east to the west and touches two oceans.

The Book of Mormon says that the Lamanites were divided on their north from the Nephite land of Zarahemla "by a *narrow strip of wilderness, which ran from the sea east even to the sea west*" (Alma 22:27; emphasis added).

We solve a problem in Book of Mormon geography in the New World when we designate the term "wilderness" as "mountainous region" instead of "desert." Therefore, when Mormon refers to a narrow strip of wilderness, he is talking about a narrow mountain range. We know this because the land of Nephi was literally *up* in elevation from the land of Zarahemla and because the headwaters of the river Sidon were *on* the borders of Nephi and Zarahemla. In other words, all references regarding the dividing line of Nephi and Zarahemla have to do with rugged mountains and not with sandy deserts.

A natural boundary for the 90 BC Lamanites and Nephites may well be the high mountain range that runs from the Pacific Ocean to the Atlantic Ocean north of Guatemala City. This narrow mountain range, or narrow strip of wilderness, provides a massive boundary line separating highland Guatemala from lowland Guatemala and from the central depression of Chiapas, Mexico. This mountainous region today is called the Sierras Cuchumatanes, a part of the great Sierra Madre mountain range.

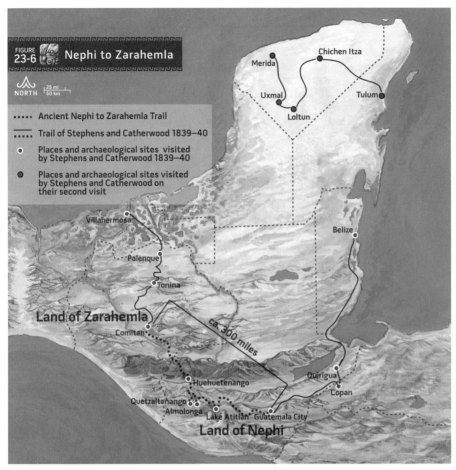

FIGURE 23–6: This map shows the travels of John Lloyd Stephens and Frederick Catherwood from Copan to Palenque, the trip that we have duplicated on dozens of occasions as we have escorted tour members through this beautiful, rugged country and introduced our tour groups to the friendly people who are native to Guatemala and Mexico. The trail also appears to be the ancient migratory trail of the Nephites (Guatemala City to Comitan) from the land of Nephi to the land of Zarahemla in the second and first centuries BC.

The only place in the New World where a narrow mountain range runs in an east-west direction and touches two oceans, both Book of Mormon requirements, is the Cuchumatanes Mountains.

The only place in the New World where a narrow mountain range runs in an east-west direction and touches two oceans—both Book of Mormon requirements—is the Cuchumatanes Mountains. For example, although the Uinta Mountains in Utah run in an east-west direction, they do not touch two oceans.

The following example gives further understanding to the hypothesis that the narrow mountain range extending from the Atlantic Ocean (sea east) east of Guatemala to the Pacific Ocean (sea west) by Salina Cruz, Mexico, is a natural dividing line.

Explorer John Lloyd Stephens traveled this mountain range in the 1830s. Stephens refers to the Sierra Madre mountain range as a "vast wilderness of mountains."[3] He continues by saying: "At half past two we reached the top of the Sierra Madre, the dividing line of the waters. . . . The ridge of the mountain was a long level table about half a mile wide, with rugged sides rising on the right to a terrific peak."[4]

After their journey from Guatemala into Mexico, Stephens and his party looked back at the Sierra Madre mountain range, and Stephens said they found themselves "looking

3. John Lloyd Stephens, *Incidents of Travel in Central America, Chiapas and Yucatan*, 2 vols., illustrations by Frederick Catherwood, first published in 1841 (New York: Dover Publications, 1969), 2:226.

4. Stephens, *Incidents of Travel in Central America, Chiapas and Yucatan*, 2:232–33.

5. Stephens, *Incidents of Travel in Central America, Chiapas and Yucatan,* 2:241; emphasis added.

down into the deep imbosomed valley, and back at the great range of Cordilleras, crowned by the Sierra Madre, *seeming a barrier fit to separate worlds.*"[5]

Several years ago, we made the intentional decision to follow the trail of Stephens and Catherwood that opened up a legitimate trail between the land of Nephi and the land of Zarahemla.

We repeat, the narrow strip of wilderness is undoubtedly the most prominent physical feature associated with Book of Mormon geography. We have arrived at this conclusion by analyzing satellite and topographical maps, traveling through those mountains on dozens and dozens of occasions, and comparing the distances, directions, elevations, customs, and other significant criteria to what we read in the Book of Mormon.

In his 1841 book, in talking about the Sierra Madre mountain range that he and his party were traversing, John Lloyd Stephens said they were "looking . . . back at the great range of Cordilleras, crowned by the Sierra Madre, seeming a barrier fit to separate worlds."

Tour members who travel with us through this mountain range are inevitably left with an indelible impression about the simplistic and yet highly significant role of this narrow strip of wilderness. Indeed, they *feel* the acute meaning behind John Lloyd Stephens's statement that they are experiencing "a barrier fit to separate worlds." That is, the experience feels like we are holding hands with the land of Nephi and the land of Zarahemla.

If we are accurate in this assessment, then we have found the ancient Nephite trail over which ten Book of Mormon migrations took place. In the process, we have solidified the entire Book of Mormon geographical puzzle. The movement is always "down" to Zarahemla and "up" to Nephi. The major Nephite migrations are summarized as follows:

1. MOSIAH, 200 BC–180 BC (FROM NEPHI TO ZARAHEMLA)

"They were led by the power of his arm, through the wilderness until they came down into the land which is called the land of Zarahemla" (Omni 1:13). In a modern vernacular, Mosiah and his followers left Guatemala City (land of Nephi) about 180 BC and traveled in a northward direction through the wilderness of Huehuetenango, passing over the rugged, narrow Cuchumatanes mountain range until they came down to the central depression of Chiapas (Zarahemla). This was a political migration, as Mosiah *fled* from the land of Nephi. The proposed route is the same that is used today when refugees from Guatemala flee into Mexico. The distance from Guatemala City to Comitan, Chiapas, is less then three hundred miles.

2. NEPHITE ARMY, 200 BC–180 BC (FROM ZARAHEMLA TO NEPHI)

Amalaki writes, "And now I would speak somewhat concerning a certain number who went up into the wilderness to return to the land of Nephi; for there was a large number who were desirous to possess the land of their inheritance" (Omni 1:27). He continues: "Wherefore, they went up into the wilderness. And their leader being a strong and mighty man, and a stiffnecked man, wherefore he caused a contention among them; and

FIGURE 23–7: A relief map illustrates the extended height of several mountain ranges—the most prominent known as the Cuchumatanes and the Sierra de las Minas—that move in an east-to-west direction, giving the impression that the view is that of a continuous mountain. We propose that people migrating from the land of Nephi (Guatemala) to the land of Zarahemla (Chiapas) would have crossed this designated narrow mountain range. (Photo courtesy of Merrill C. Oaks)

they were all slain, save fifty, in the wilderness, and they returned again to the land of Zarahemla" (Omni 1:28). This same event is mentioned again in Mosiah 9:1–2 where we learn that an army was raised to go back *up* to the land of Nephi (Guatemala) to recapture the city of Nephi. The Nephite army from Zarahemla never reached the city/land of Nephi. The wilderness battle probably took place in the region of the narrow strip of wilderness (Cuchumatanes) in what today is the department of Huehuetenango.

Similar militaristic events have occurred in our time in that same area. Interestingly, however, among the fifty thousand inhabitants of the city of Huehuetenango, four stakes of the Church have been organized, involving 15 to 20 percent of the city's population.

3. ZENIFF, 200 BC–180 BC (FROM ZARAHEMLA TO NEPHI)

Zeniff, who was one of the survivors of the above-mentioned battle, stated that he was overzealous to inherit the land of his fathers. Therefore, he collected as many as were desirous to go *up* to possess the land (Mosiah 9:3–8). The migration trail would have taken them *up into* the wilderness of Huehuetenango, over the narrow strip of wilderness (Cuchumatanes), and on to the city/land of Nephi (Kaminaljuyu, Guatemala). Zeniff made a treaty with the Lamanite king and was permitted to reoccupy the cities and rebuild the walls of Lehi-Nephi and Shilom.

The walls had apparently been knocked down in the Lamanite-Nephite confrontation that caused Mosiah to flee out of the land. In Mosiah 7:1, 2, 4, 21 and 9:6, 8, the name of Lehi-Nephi is used instead of just Nephi. Some scholars have suggested that two separate cities are involved here—one Lehi-Nephi and the other Nephi. However, because the city of Nephi is mentioned in Mosiah 7:6, 9:15 and again in Mosiah 21:1, we can assume that the names Lehi-Nephi and Nephi are used interchangeably in referring to the same city. This outcome is further justified when we consider that the temple, the center of Nephite worship, was in the city of Nephi, the most important city the Nephites would want to reinhabit. Perhaps the Lamanite king required a name change when he made the treaty with Zeniff.

4. LIMHI EXPEDITION LEAVES, ABOUT 121 BC (FROM NEPHI TO ZARAHEMLA)

Limhi, the grandson of Zeniff, was under severe bondage to the Lamanites and decided to appeal to the Nephites in the land of Zarahemla to help deliver Limhi and his people from bondage. He sent forty-three of his people on an expedition to find Zarahemla so he could deliver them from bondage. Although the distance from Nephi to Zarahemla does not exceed three hundred miles, the nature of the terrain and the lack of communication presented a formidable obstacle to the expedition. Anyone who has traveled in the mountains of Guatemala knows the ease with which a person can get lost.

The expedition would have had to exercise supreme caution as to whom they talked to and would have had to travel almost incognito for fear of capture by the Lamanites. Their directions could have guided them to the town of Todos Santos, Huehuetenango, on top of the Cuchumatanes (narrow strip of wilderness) with instructions to follow

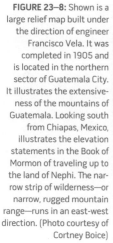

FIGURE 23–8: Shown is a large relief map built under the direction of engineer Francisco Vela. It was completed in 1905 and is located in the northern sector of Guatemala City. It illustrates the extensiveness of the mountains of Guatemala. Looking south from Chiapas, Mexico, illustrates the elevation statements in the Book of Mormon of traveling up to the land of Nephi. The narrow strip of wilderness—or narrow, rugged mountain range—runs in an east-west direction. (Photo courtesy of Cortney Boice)

Exploring the Lands of the Book of Mormon

the river. If they followed the Usumacinta River, they would not have found Zarahemla. Nevertheless, as the scripture states, they would have traveled in a land among many waters and subsequently discovered some ruins of the ancient Jaredites.

5. LIMHI EXPEDITION RETURNS, ABOUT 122 BC (FROM ZARAHEMLA TO NEPHI)

The Limhi expedition never found Zarahemla, and they returned by the same route—crossing the narrow strip of wilderness to get to the land of Nephi and then reporting the results of their expedition to Limhi, their king. The total travel time would have been approximately three to four months, and they would have traveled a distance of about eight hundred miles—about four hundred each way. They returned with large breastplates and twenty-four gold records. They had to walk through mosquito-infested marshes, ford muddy rivers, climb rugged mountains, search constantly for food, and suffer from both cold and heat. But because of their efforts, we have the record of the Jaredites.

6. AMMON EXPEDITION, ABOUT 124 BC (FROM ZARAHEMLA TO NEPHI)

While Limhi was trying to contact the Nephites at Zarahemla, some of the Nephites in Zarahemla were anxious to found out about the Nephites who had lived in the land of Nephi for the past three generations (Mosiah-Benjamin-Mosiah). A strong man named Ammon, along with sixteen men, left Zarahemla to go up to the land of Lehi-Nephi (Nephi). They wandered forty days, much of which would have been in the wilderness of Huehuetenango, as they crossed over the Cuchumatanes (narrow strip of wilderness). Today, we make the trip by traveling through and not over the Cuchumatanes, crossing several bridges en route. Anciently, travelers would have proceeded over the mountains in the same manner in which Stephens did as reported in his 1841 book, *Incidents of Travel in Central America, Chiapas and Yucatan.*

7. LIMHI AND HIS PEOPLE, ABOUT 124 BC (FROM NEPHI TO ZARAHEMLA)

Interestingly, Ammon (not to be confused with Ammon, the son of Mosiah) was a strong and mighty man and a descendant of Zarahemla (Mosiah 7:3). Although speculative in nature, Ammon may have had some Jaredite blood running through his veins, which would explain his large stature. When he was given permission by King Limhi to speak to the people, Ammon was asked to tell about the "last words of King Benjamin." Limhi showed Ammon the twenty-four gold plates that the Limhi expedition had discovered and expressed hope that Ammon could translate them because they might give information about a remnant of the people who had been destroyed. Moroni uses the same terminology in describing the brother of Jared—that is, he was a "large and mighty

The Limhi expedition had to walk through mosquito-infested marshes, ford muddy rivers, climb rugged mountains, search constantly for food, and suffer from both cold and heat. But because of their efforts, we have the record of the Jaredites.

man." To this very day, descendants of the large Olmecs who live in Chiapas can be readily distinguished from the descendants of the smaller Maya.

At any rate, after three generations of living under the rule of the Lamanites in the land of Nephi (Zeniff-Noah-Limhi), Limhi and his people, after getting the Lamanite guards drunk, were led by Ammon and his deliverers to the land of Zarahemla where they joined with Mosiah's people and became his subjects. Mosiah received them with joy; and he also received their records and the records that had been found by the people of Limhi (Mosiah 22:13).

8. ALMA AND HIS PEOPLE, ABOUT 145 BC (FROM NEPHI TO ZARAHEMLA)

Limhi told Ammon about the mourning of the people of Limhi over the death of Abinadi and about the departure of Alma and the people who went with him after Alma had formed a church of God (Mosiah 22:30). Abinadi may have been the son of Abinadom and the brother of Amaleki, as suggested by Amaleki's writing of the return of Zeniff from Zarahemla to Nephi: "And I, Amaleki, had a brother, who also went with them" (Omni 1:30). Alma, a priest of Limhi's father, Noah, had previously listened to the words of Abinadi. We can follow the trail of Alma from the city of Nephi, then to the waters of Mormon, and finally to the land of Helam where they lived for about twenty-five years.

We then pick up their trail again as they traveled from Helam to the valley of Alma and from the valley of Alma to the land of Zarahemla where Mosiah received them with joy (Mosiah 24:25). Like Limhi's people, they had experienced heavy burdens placed upon their shoulders and their backs (Mosiah 21:3; 24:14); and, like Limhi's people, the escape from bondage was a result of the Lamanite guards becoming incapacitated—in one instance by getting them drunk and in the other by God's causing a deep sleep to come over them, all reflecting principles of works and faith. (For a more detailed account of Alma's journeys involving distances, directions, elevations, and so forth, see chapter 24, "Wilderness Areas.")

9. THE SONS OF MOSIAH, 90 BC (FROM ZARAHEMLA TO NEPHI)

"They departed out of the land of Zarahemla
> and took their swords,
> and their spears,
> and their bows,
> and their arrows,
> and their slings;

and this they did that they might provide food for themselves while in the wilderness. And thus they departed into the wilderness with their numbers which they had

FIGURE 23–9: The Postclassic ruins of Zaculeu are located on the Guatemala side of the Cuchumatanes Mountains. Observe the narrow strip of wilderness in the background to the north. This area was one of the last to be conquered by the Spaniards, as it is difficult to get to. Although the ruins are labeled Postclassic, people have lived in the area for thousands of years. The Mam language, which is the native language of this region, reportedly dates to 2600 BC. (Photo courtesy of Courtney Boice)

selected, to go up to the land of Nephi, to preach the word of God unto the Lamanites" (Alma 17:7–8).

The consistency with which the terms "up to Nephi" and "down to Zarahemla" are used in all of the migration statements is a testimony of Joseph Smith's work as a translator. The fact that the land of Nephi is southeast of the land of Zarahemla suggests that the term "up to Nephi" is an elevation statement as opposed to a directional statement. If it were a directional statement, our culture would dictate that the term would be just the reverse as to what it is in the Book of Mormon in relation to both the land of Nephi and the land of Zarahemla.

Understanding the lay of the land is imperative. Once a reliable geographical thesis is established, Mesoamerica then assumes the role of teaching us about Book of Mormon geography. We need only to stand on the Chiapas (Zarahemla) side of the narrow strip of wilderness (Cuchumatanes) to realize that even though the direction is south, the sons of Mosiah would use the exact terminology that Mormon used as an author and that Joseph Smith used as a translator: *they departed into the wilderness . . . to go up to the land of Nephi.*

10. THE SONS OF MOSIAH, 76 BC (FROM NEPHI TO ZARAHEMLA)

After preaching the gospel among the Lamanites for fourteen years, because of the great destruction caused by the unbelievers against the believers, the Nephite missionaries were directed by the Lord to escort the converted Lamanites to the land of Zarahemla. The Lamanite king, whose name was Anti-Nephi-Lehi, who himself had been converted and whose name the converted Lamanites had taken upon themselves, suggested to Alma that if they were to go to the land of Zarahemla, the Nephites would destroy them. Anti-Nephi-Lehi, who was also the brother of Lamoni, told Ammon that if they did go, they would be willing to be slaves to the Nephites. Ammon informed Anti-Nephi-Lehi that his father, Mosiah, had established antislavery laws. The paraphrased dialogue between Ammon and Anti-Nephi-Lehi is as follows (see Alma 27:2–14):

Ammon: "Let us gather together this people of the Lord and let us *go down* to the land of Zarahemla."

Anti-Nephi-Lehi: "If we *go down*, the Nephites will destroy us because of the many murders and sins we have committed against them."

Ammon: "I will go and inquire of the Lord, and if He says that you should *go down* unto your brethren, will you go?"

Anti-Nephi-Lehi: "If the Lord saith such unto us, we will *go down* unto our brethren and will be their slaves."

Ammon: "It is against the law of our brethren that there should be any slaves; therefore, let us *go down* and rely upon the mercies of our brethren."

"They gathered together all . . . the people of the Lord, and did gather together all their flocks and herds, and departed out of the land [of Nephi], and came *into the wilderness which divided the land of Nephi from the land of Zarahemla* and came *over* near the borders of the land [of Zarahemla]" (Alma 27:14).

That wilderness is the same narrow strip of wilderness that all the above-mentioned migrations would have traveled through and over to *go down* to the land of Zarahemla and vice versa. Mormon's use of such "geographical prepositional pointers" as *up, down, over,* and *into* is consistent, reliable, and valid. We simply cannot legitimately make up Book of Mormon geography in an attempt to prove our own thinking about directions and geography. That is, if we require standardized criteria involving the presence of a written language, the presence of population centers dating to the right time period, the presence of an adequate pottery trail, the presence of extant terrain that "just happens to be in the right place," along with the presence of supporting historical and cultural data, the geography of the Book of Mormon will take care of itself.

The critical key to our understanding of Book of Mormon geography is the presence of a rugged, narrow mountain range that moves in an east-west direction and that makes contacts with two seas. We note here that prior to modern times, the only way to travel from Guatemala (Nephi) to Zarahemla (Chiapas) was either by the coastal route or the mountainous route, the latter being the route under consideration for the above-mentioned migrations.

The above migrations are merely a sampling of migrations that have transpired from Guatemala City to Chiapas, Mexico, over the last five millennia. Today, this mountainous

Mormon's use of such "geographical prepositional pointers" as up, down, over, over upon, and into is consistent, reliable, and valid.

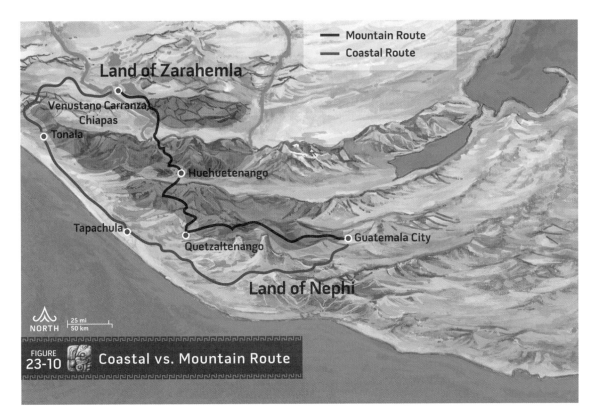

FIGURE 23–10: Prior to modern times, travelers could choose from only two routes to get from Guatemala to Chiapas or vice versa—the coastal route or the mountain route. The coastal route is less strenuous, but it is much longer. Both routes figure into Book of Mormon geography. However, if we read the Book of Mormon carefully, we will see that most, if not all, of the Nephite migrations followed the mountain route—the same route that Stephens and Catherwood followed in 1839. The distance from Guatemala to the upper Grijalva valley of Chiapas via the mountain route is about three hundred miles.

route is a branch of the Pan-American Highway that wends itself through the beautiful mountains and dense, rugged wilderness of the highlands of Guatemala.

Through it all, Mormon paints a beautiful picture on a broad canvas as he illustrates our journey through this wilderness of life, traveling through both joy and sorrow, carrying heavy burdens that are made light though the comforter, getting lost in the wilderness, being exposed to the principles of faith (Alma) and works (Limhi) as we escape from evil (Lamanites—land of Nephi) for good or for eternal life (land of Zarahemla), and subsequently being received by the King of Kings, even Christ, with open arms, as Limhi and Alma were received with open arms by King Mosiah. Also, like Mosiah, Limhi, and Alma, we will have the opportunity to present our records of that which has transpired in our lives as we cross over that narrow strip of wilderness.

CHAPTER 24

Wilderness Areas

Let us go up upon the mountains and into the wilderness. (3 Nephi 3:20)

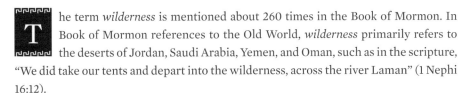

The term *wilderness* is mentioned about 260 times in the Book of Mormon. In Book of Mormon references to the Old World, *wilderness* primarily refers to the deserts of Jordan, Saudi Arabia, Yemen, and Oman, such as in the scripture, "We did take our tents and depart into the wilderness, across the river Laman" (1 Nephi 16:12).

For New World purposes in the Book of Mormon, the term *wilderness* refers to mountain lands or forests as well as dense jungles. From a definition perspective, the term *wilderness* implies uninhabited areas—at least uninhabited during certain time periods. The geographical terrain of Mesoamerica and the directions that are given in

OPPOSITE: The word *wilderness* may refer to a desert, a jungle, a mountainous region, or any place that is considered inhospitable, uninhabited, or even sparsely inhabited. Synonyms include "wild," "rough country," "backcountry," "wastelands," and so forth. Mesoamerica consists of rugged mountain wildernesses, lowland rainforest wildernesses, and desert coastal wildernesses. Most often when referring to New World geography, the Book of Mormon uses the word *wilderness* in connection with mountainous, forested land and lowland jungle areas. Shown here is a heron perched on the tip of a tree in the wilderness rainforest of Peten, Guatemala. (Photo courtesy of Merrill C. Oaks)

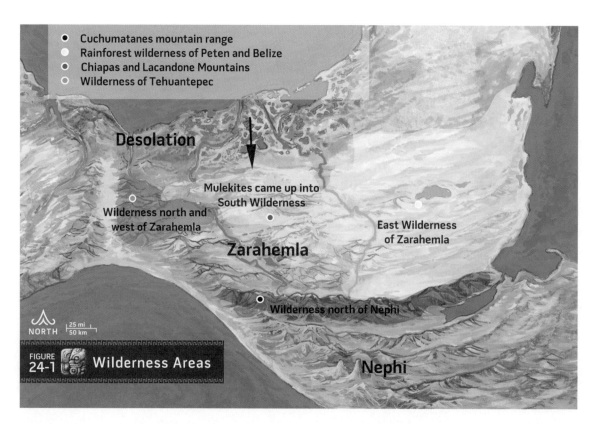

- Cuchumatanes mountain range
- Rainforest wilderness of Peten and Belize
- Chiapas and Lacandone Mountains
- Wilderness of Tehuantepec

Desolation

Mulekites came up into
South Wilderness

Wilderness north and
west of Zarahemla

East Wilderness
of Zarahemla

Zarahemla

Wilderness north of Nephi

NORTH · 25 mi / 50 km

FIGURE 24-1 — Wilderness Areas

Nephi

FIGURE 24–1: This map illustrates some of the major "wilderness" designations used by Mormon. To understand Book of Mormon references to the word *wilderness*, we must determine who is writing, the point of origin of his writing, and the time period involved. For example, the Nephites' east wilderness is east of Zarahemla (Chiapas), and the Jaredites' south wilderness is south of the Gulf of Mexico.

the Book of Mormon in relationship to wilderness areas provide some very interesting, convincing parallels.

Throughout the years, we have observed with more than casual interest the reactions of people who have traveled with us through the mountainous (wilderness) regions of Guatemala and Chiapas. We have routinely taken ten to fifteen trips a year through these beautiful, wild, majestic mountains. Approximately four million people live in the mountains or highlands of Guatemala today. We hear people on our tours say such things as "I can now see how an army could get lost in pursuit of Limhi's or Alma's colony," "No wonder the expedition of Limhi couldn't find Zarahemla," or "How could people travel through this wilderness country?"

We have observed again and again that traveling through the geographical locations of the various wilderness areas mentioned in the Book of Mormon, when accompanied with intense analysis and exposure to language, customs, and archaeology, is like the experience of viewing the Discovery Channel on television or like following the footsteps of the ancient Nephite missionaries and the ferocious Lamanite warriors.

In this chapter, we will discuss the major New World areas that are labeled "wilderness" in the Book of Mormon. The areas of highland and lowland Guatemala, the Mexican state of Chiapas, and the small country of Belize seem to meet—in convincing fashion—all necessary criteria for New World Book of Mormon comments about "wilderness." The nine wilderness areas that are discussed in this chapter are as follows:

1. The wilderness that Nephi went into when he separated from his brothers.
2. The wilderness that Mosiah went into as he fled from the land of Nephi and traveled to Zarahemla.
3. The occasion when the Limhi expedition wandered in the wilderness in search of Zarahemla.
4. The experiences of Ammon and sixteen strong men who wandered in the wilderness for forty days in search of the land of Nephi.
5. The eight days of travel time by Alma and his group when they traveled in the wilderness from the waters of Mormon to the land of Helam and then twelve days of travel time from the valley of Alma to the land of Zarahemla.
6. The occasion when the Lamanites fled to the wilderness of Hermounts.
7. The south wilderness in which the Mulekites settled.
8. The north wilderness—or the wilderness that was on the north by Zarahemla.
9. The wilderness of Lachoneus.

A tenth wilderness area, called the east wilderness because of its importance in Nephite, Mulekite, and Lamanite history, will be discussed separately in chapter 25, "The East Wilderness."

In an attempt to locate the various wilderness areas mentioned in the Book of Mormon, we emphasize pointedly that we must determine who was writing, where he was living at the time he was writing, and the time period involved.

For example, the east wilderness is east of Zarahemla; and the wilderness of Hermounts is north and west of Zarahemla. However, the so-called north wilderness, as described by the Lamanite king, is north of the land of Nephi. That description really makes the north wilderness south of the land of Zarahemla.

Likewise, the south wilderness is an area referred to when the Mulekites traveled in a north-to-south direction to settle in the land of Zarahemla. That means the south wilderness is really north of the land of Zarahemla.

We can deduce these geographical outcomes if we carefully analyze the directional and topographical pointers that Mormon gives us in his abridgement. In doing so, we cannot help but be impressed with the consistency of Mormon's directional pointers. With those thoughts in mind, we will look at nine of ten New World wilderness areas that are alluded to at various points in the Book of Mormon.

In an attempt to locate the various wilderness areas mentioned in the Book of Mormon, we must determine who was writing, where he was living at the time he was writing, and the time period involved.

1. THE WILDERNESS WHERE NEPHI TRAVELED TO GET TO THE LAND OF NEPHI

And it came to pass that the Lord did warn me, that I, Nephi, should depart from them and flee into the wilderness, and all those who would go with me. . . .

And we did take our tents and whatsoever things were possible for us, and did journey in the wilderness for the space of many days. And after we had journeyed for the space of many days we did pitch our tents.

And my people would that we should call the name of the place Nephi; wherefore, we did call it Nephi. (2 Nephi 5:5, 7–8)

When Lehi and his family arrived at the promised land, they journeyed in the wilderness where they found beasts of the forests, including Book of Mormon domesticated animals that are referred to *in the translation* as the horse, the cow, the ox, the ass, and the goat. They also discovered that the wilderness contained gold, silver, and copper (see 1 Nephi 18:25; 19:1).

Apparently, they called the place where they first set foot and established their initial settlement as the "place of their fathers' first inheritance." We know they settled initially by the seashore because of a statement in Alma 22 that describes the Lamanite boundaries. That is, the Lamanite territory extended along the seashore, "west of the land of Zarahemla, in the borders by the *seashore*, and on the west in the land of Nephi, in the *place of their fathers' first inheritance*, and thus bordering along by the *seashore*" (Alma 22:28; emphasis added).

> Most students of the Book of Mormon agree that Lehi landed on the Pacific coast.

Most students of the Book of Mormon agree that Lehi landed on the Pacific coast (see chapter 22, "Voyages of Lehi and Mulek"). The ruins of Izapa, located along the Pacific coastline, are the proposed candidate for the area where Lehi's colony first settled (see chapter 9, "The Izapa [Jaredite-Nephite-Lamanite] Culture" and chapter 15, "Christ—The Tree of Life"). We further propose that the city of Nephi was probably located on the site of the ancient ruins of Kaminaljuyu in Guatemala City (see chapter 28, "The Land of Nephi").

As we pursue this logic, we can assume that Nephi wandered many days east from Izapa until he arrived at Kaminaljuyu/Guatemala City. On the Mesoamerican map, Kaminaljuyu/Guatemala City is east of Izapa/Tapachula.

The distance between the two sites is approximately 130 miles. The question arises as to which route Nephi took—the mountain route through Quetzaltenango or the coastal route through Esquintla. The coastal route seems more likely, especially when we take into consideration that the coastal villages of La Blanca, Abaj Takalik, and El Baul showed a decline in population at the same general time period that Nephi traveled from the "place of their fathers' first inheritance" to the city of Nephi.

We propose that Kaminaljuyu, an archaeological site located where Guatemala City is today, was the city/state of Nephi. Among other reasons for this hypothesis are the

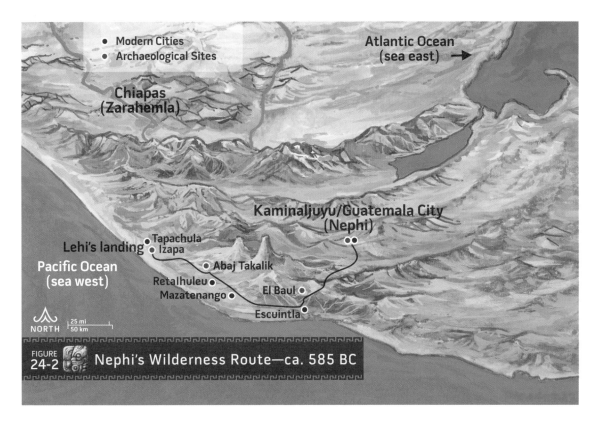

FIGURE 24–2: Nephi said, "We . . . did journey in the wilderness for the space of many days" (2 Nephi 5:7). This map illustrates the journey of Nephi and those who went with him along the coastal route from the land of first inheritance where Lehi landed (Izapa) to the city/land of Nephi (Kaminaljuyu, Guatemala).

facts that (1) Kaminaljuyu is located in the mountains and (2) Kaminaljuyu shows an increase in population during the early Nephite time period—both requirements for the city of Nephi. The possibility also exists that people from the intermediate villages also became followers of Nephi. If Nephi and his followers traveled at a rate of eight miles per day, they arrived at the place they named Nephi in about sixteen days. However, when we consider the terrain and travel through unknown territory and any exploration that took place en route, we conclude that the journey probably took longer. The statement of "many days" is very applicable to the proposed journey of Nephi into the wilderness.

2. THE WILDERNESS IN WHICH MOSIAH TRAVELED AS HE FLED FROM THE LAND OF NEPHI TO THE LAND OF ZARAHEMLA

Behold, I will speak unto you somewhat concerning Mosiah, who was made king over the land of Zarahemla; for behold, he being warned of the Lord that he should flee out of the land of Nephi, and as many as would hearken unto the voice of the Lord should also depart out of the land with him, into the wilderness—

. . . And they departed out of the land into the wilderness, . . . and they were led by the power of his [God's] arm, through the wilderness until they came *down* into the land which is called the land of Zarahemla. (Omni 1:12–13; emphasis added)

Clearly, Mosiah and his followers had to flee out of the land of Nephi. The above verses do not tell us how long they took to travel from the land of Nephi to the land of Zarahemla. That information is obtained from the journey of Alma when he led his colony to Zarahemla. We do learn, however, that Zarahemla is *down* in elevation from the land of Nephi, which is consistent throughout the Book of Mormon text.

The land of Zarahemla was north of the land of Nephi, as explained in Alma 22 where the Lamanite borders or land of Nephi borders are outlined. The Lamanite (land of Nephi) northern border was the same as the Nephite (land of Zarahemla) southern border: "[The land of Nephi] was divided from the land of Zarahemla by a narrow strip of wilderness, which ran from the sea east even to the sea west, and round about on the borders of the seashore, and the borders of the wilderness which was on the north by the land of Zarahemla" (Alma 22:27).

The narrow strip of wilderness mentioned in the above verse is undoubtedly the narrow mountain range that divides highland Guatemala from lowland Guatemala and Chiapas (see chapter 23, "Things That Are Narrow").

The distance between the city/land of Nephi and the city/land of Zarahemla is estimated at approximately three hundred miles and is covered in more detail in item number five of this chapter.

The distance from Kaminaljuyu/Guatemala City to Santa Rosa/Chiapas is approximately three hundred miles (see chapter 29, "The Land of Zarahemla"). Using travel routes that have been employed throughout the history of the area, we can easily chart the proposed course of Mosiah and his followers from the land of Nephi through the wilderness to the land of Zarahemla. The wilderness journey from Guatemala City to the border of Mexico presents a very vivid picture of what the wilderness was like that Mosiah may have traveled. This same wilderness route is the proposed trail for at least ten migrations that are mentioned in the Book of Mormon and that have been discussed in previous chapters. This route is the same one traveled by Stephens and Catherwood in 1839–40 and probably parallels the same route that a branch of the Pan-American Highway traverses today through these areas.

As we travel on our tours in four hours' time from the high point of ten thousand feet elevation near the Quetzaltenango and Totonicapan (in Guatemala) lookout to about twenty-three hundred feet elevation at the Mexico border, the distinct impression of traveling *down* to Zarahemla is *engraved* in our minds. The elevation in the

> Using travel routes that have been employed throughout the history of the area, we can easily chart the proposed course of Mosiah and his followers from the land of Nephi through the wilderness to the land of Zarahemla.

Chiapas depression bottoms out at fifteen hundred feet elevation. Guatemala City/ Kaminaljuyu/Nephi is about forty-eight hundred feet elevation.

Worth repeating here is information about the Monte Alban archaeological data that record the migration of a small group of people into the Oaxaca valley. This group came from Guatemala and Chiapas. They imposed a number of cultural traits on the existing culture in the Oaxaca valley. The date was 180 BC, which is the same time period that Mosiah traveled from the land of Nephi to the land of Zarahemla. This correlation suggests that Mulekites may have been living in the Oaxaca valley and were subsequently under the kingship influence of Mosiah (see chapter 7, "The Zapotec [Mulekite-Nephite] Culture").

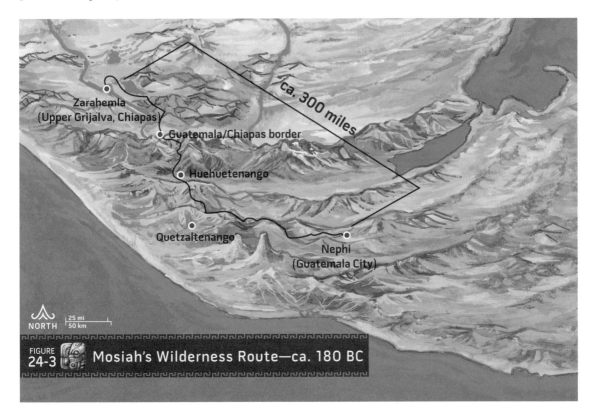

FIGURE 24–3: This map illustrates the proposed route of Mosiah and his followers in the second century BC from the city/land of Nephi to the city/ land of Zarahemla. From a modern geographical perspective, the journey would take a traveler from Guatemala City to the central depression of Chiapas, a distance of about three hundred miles. "They were led by the power of his arm, through the wilderness until they came down into the land which is called the land of Zarahemla" (Omni 1:13). Observe that "the borders of the wilderness which was on the north [of the land of Nephi] by the land of Zarahemla" (Alma 22:27) is the same wilderness as the narrow strip of wilderness discussed in chapter 23, "Things That Are Narrow." This border wilderness is located in what today is the department of Huehuetenango, Guatemala. It borders the southeastern part of the central depression of Chiapas, Mexico.

3. THE LIMHI EXPEDITION TRAVELS IN THE WILDERNESS

And they were lost in the wilderness for the space of many days, yet they were diligent, and found not the land of Zarahemla but returned to this land, [land of Nephi] having traveled in a land among many waters, having discovered a land which was covered with bones of men, and of beasts, and was also covered with ruins of buildings of every kind, having discovered a land which had been peopled with a people who were as numerous as the hosts of Israel. (Mosiah 8:8)

After Mosiah journeyed into the wilderness and traveled from the land of Nephi to the land of Zarahemla about 180 BC, Zeniff and some Nephites returned to the land of Nephi—even though it was under Lamanite control. We can readily understand their desire to return when we experience the climate differences between Guatemala City and the Chiapas valley. The cool, fresh, mountain air of Guatemala City is much more desirable than the hot, humid air of the Chiapas valley. Zeniff and those who went with him lived among the Lamanites in the land of Nephi for three generations.

Limhi, who was the grandson of Zeniff, lived in the land of Nephi around 121 BC. Limhi sent an expedition of forty-three men to locate the land of Zarahemla. We may wonder why Zarahemla was so difficult to find if it was only three hundred miles away from Nephi.

However, we merely need to travel through the proposed area of the Limhi expedition to learn about this Book of Mormon lesson in geography. When John Lloyd Stephens traveled through the same area where we travel today on our tours, which is the route that we propose to connect Nephi with Zarahemla, he followed an interesting pattern. He hired natives from village number one to escort his group to village number two. To get to village number three, Stephens had to hire natives from village number two because the natives in village number one did not know how to get to village number three. The situation is a direct reflection of the meaning of the word "wilderness" in connection with the area.

In all probability, the Limhi expedition, while traveling through the wilderness, headed down the wrong river. They may have followed the Usumacinta River until they arrived at a "land among many waters" (lagoons of Campeche and Tabasco; see Mosiah 8:8) and then would have continued on to the Gulf of Mexico where they discovered the ancient ruins of the Jaredites, which they initially thought were the ruins of Zarahemla (see Mosiah 21:26). The Grijalva River, the preferred candidate for the Book of Mormon river Sidon, is fifty to seventy-five miles west of the Usumacinta. At any rate, the journey would have been an arduous one. The scripture states that the Limhi expedition was lost in the wilderness for "the space of many days."

Traditional Book of Mormon geography from the nineteenth and twentieth centuries ludicrously requires the Limhi expedition to travel from Peru to New York, a seven-thousand-mile, one-way journey. The Mesoamerica picture meets the Limhi

In all probability, the Limhi expedition, while traveling through the wilderness, headed down the wrong river. They may have followed the Usumacinta River until they arrived at a "land among many waters" (lagoons of Campeche and Tabasco) and then would have continued on to the Gulf of Mexico where they discovered the ancient ruins of the Jaredites.

Exploring the Lands of the Book of Mormon

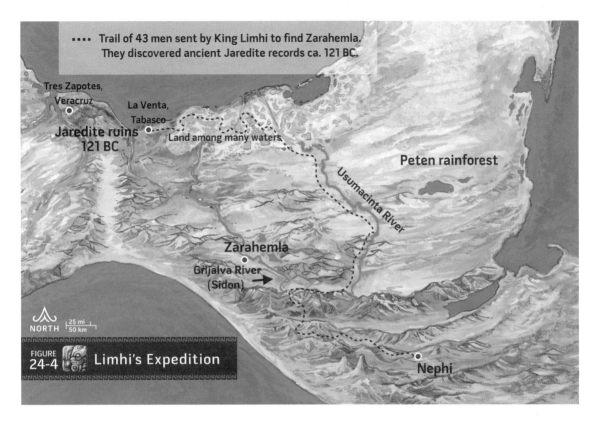

FIGURE 24–4: King Limhi said, "I caused that forty and three of my people should take a journey into the wilderness, that thereby they might find the land of Zarahemla" (Mosiah 8:7). They probably followed the wrong river. Instead of taking them to Zarahemla, the Usumacinta River would have taken them to a "land among many waters" (lagoons of Tabasco and Campeche) until they discovered the ancient Jaredite ruins (Olmec) and the twenty-four gold plates as reported in Mosiah 8:7–12. They then returned to the land of Nephi without locating the land of Zarahemla. The round-trip distance traveled would have been more than eight hundred miles. Because no cities existed along the Usumacinta River in the first century BC, the expedition would have continued its journey to the Gulf of Mexico, having bypassed the land of Zarahemla.

expedition requirement in a much more palatable fashion. (For further discussion on the Limhi expedition, see chapter 26, "Bodies of Water.") Our knowledge of the geography and topography of the area helps us chart the proposed journey of the Limhi expedition into the wilderness from the land of Nephi in their attempt to locate the land of Zarahemla.

4. SIXTEEN STRONG MEN ARE LED BY AMMON INTO THE WILDERNESS TO FIND THE LAND OF NEPHI

And it came to pass that king Mosiah granted that sixteen of their strong men might go *up* to the land of Lehi-Nephi, to inquire concerning their brethren [Nephite people of Limhi].

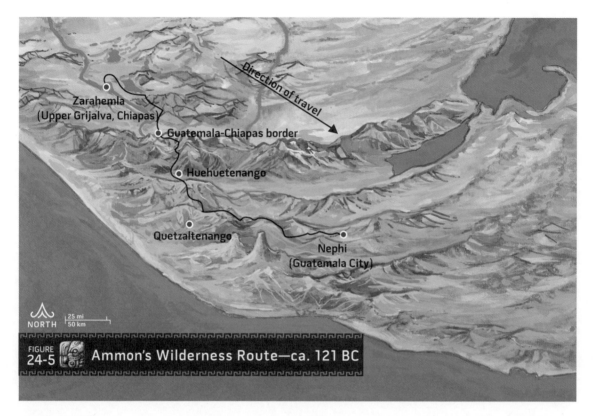

FIGURE 24-5

NORTH
25 mi
50 km

Ammon's Wilderness Route—ca. 121 BC

Zarahemla
(Upper Grijalva, Chiapas)

Direction of travel

Guatemala-Chiapas border

Huehuetenango

Quetzaltenango

Nephi
(Guatemala City)

FIGURE 24–5: "They knew not the course they should travel in the wilderness to go up to the land of Lehi-Nephi; therefore they wandered many days in the wilderness, even forty days" (Mosiah 7:4). Mosiah sent sixteen strong men to find the people of Limhi who were living under bondage to the Lamanites. The fact that Ammon and his men required only forty days of travel time through a rugged wilderness and then got lost suggests that the distance between Zarahemla and Nephi is not extensive from a distance perspective.

And it came to pass that on the morrow they started to go *up*, having with them one Ammon, he being a strong and mighty man, and a descendant of Zarahemla; and he was also their leader.

And now they knew not the course they should travel in the wilderness to go *up* to the land of Lehi-Nephi; therefore they wandered many days in the wilderness, even forty days did they wander. (Mosiah 7:2–4; emphasis added)

We should note with interest that these sixteen men knew the direction to the land of Nephi (Lehi-Nephi), and they also knew that it was *up* in the mountains. However, they still did not know exactly where the land of Nephi was located. They wandered forty days before they arrived at a location where they could *see* the land of Nephi down in a valley.

Normally, the time required to travel from Nephi to Zarahemla was less than thirty days. However, Ammon and his men took forty days.

Exploring the Lands of the Book of Mormon

Perhaps a side note is in order here. If you have has not yet determined that the Book of Mormon lands are limited to a small geographical area, consider the following. A major portion of Book of Mormon history occurred between the two land areas of Nephi and Zarahemla. Traveling through any terrain from South America to North America would require great effort. A distance of eight to twelve miles a day seems adequate to travel in a Book of Mormon day, especially when travelers had to take care of their food and shelter requirements along the way.

Whether we calculate the distance of Limhi's expedition, the distance of Ammon's travels, or the distance of Alma's journey, we are limited to a few hundred miles—not thousands of miles required by the extended-geography approach that designates South America as the land southward and North America as the land northward.

Without question, we know that the elevation was *up* from Zarahemla to Nephi, even though Nephi was southward of Zarahemla. In that respect, Book of Mormon readers have to be impressed with the geographical consistency of Mormon's writings (and the consistency of Joseph Smith's translation work). Even after Ammon's group traveled *up* from Zarahemla, they arrived at a hill that was north of Shilom, a city that was near the city of Nephi. They then went *down* to Nephi. Guatemala City/Kaminaljuyu fits that requirement. It is located in a beautiful valley located in the highlands of Guatemala.

In our geographical model, the journey of the sixteen men with Ammon as their leader would have taken them from the state of Chiapas in Mexico to Guatemala City. As travelers move southward toward Guatemala from Chiapas, they observe that a massive, narrow mountain range runs from the west to the east—or from the Pacific to the Atlantic.

5. ALMA'S SOJOURN IN THE WILDERNESS

From the journeys of Alma, we gain some of our most significant information about the distance from Nephi to Zarahemla and points in between. Just as the Latter-day Saints were driven from Ohio to Missouri to Nauvoo to Utah, the Book of Mormon Saints under the leadership of Alma journeyed from Nephi to the waters of Mormon and then to the land of Helam and finally to the land of Zarahemla. We first pick up Alma's story in Mosiah 17 when he was a priest in King Noah's court in the land of Nephi. Alma was converted by the teachings of the prophet Abinadi: "But there was one among them whose name was Alma, he also being a descendant of Nephi. And he was a young man, and he believed the words which Abinadi had spoken" (Mosiah 17:2).

Alma believed the words of Abinadi and pleaded with the king to spare Abinadi's life: "But the king was more wroth, and caused that Alma should be cast out from among them, and sent his servants after him that they might slay him" (Alma 17:3).

Whether we calculate the distance of Limhi's expedition, the distance of Ammon's travels, or the distance of Alma's journey, we are limited to a few hundred miles.

FIGURE 24–6: Ancient ruins in the wilderness of Palenque. (Photo courtesy of Cortney Boice)

Alma fled from King Noah, repented of his sins, and began to teach the words of Abinadi privately among the people. As many as believed went forth to a place called Mormon: "And it came to pass that as many as did believe him did go forth to a place which was called Mormon, having received its name from the king, being in the borders of the land having been infested, by times or at seasons, by wild beasts" (Mosiah 18:4).

In addition to being called the waters of Mormon, the area was also called "the place of Mormon" and "the forest of Mormon." It was in the borders by the land of Nephi (see also chapter 26, "Bodies of Water").

The distance from the city of Nephi to the waters of Mormon is not given. It has to be close enough for contact between Alma and his converts, yet it has to be far enough away so Alma could stay out of the reach of the king. It also has to meet the requirement that it is in the *borders* of the land of Nephi.

The leading candidate today for the waters of Mormon is the beautiful Lake Atitlan, which is located about eighty miles by road or about forty miles as the crow flies west of Guatemala City. This Book of Mormon journey from Guatemala City/city of Nephi to Lake Atitlan probably took an estimated eight to ten days with women, children, and flocks. It would take less time traveling if a person were alone. Today, the natives of Guatemala say they can cover the distance in four days—eating along the way and stopping only briefly to sleep.

After a short stay at the waters of Mormon, where Alma taught his people, baptized them, and organized the Church of Christ, the people had to depart into the wilderness: "And it came to pass that Alma and the people of the Lord were apprised of the coming of the king's army; therefore they took their tents and their families and departed into the wilderness. And they were in number about four hundred and fifty souls" (Mosiah 18:34–35).

Five chapters later, we are told more about this particular journey of Alma:

> Now Alma, having been warned of the Lord that the armies of king Noah would come upon them, and having made it known to his people, therefore they gathered together their flocks, and took of their grain, and departed into the wilderness before the armies of king Noah.

> The leading candidate today for the waters of Mormon is the beautiful Lake Atitlan, which is located about eighty miles by road or about forty miles as the crow flies west of Guatemala City.

Exploring the Lands of the Book of Mormon

And the Lord did strengthen them, that the people of king Noah could not overtake them to destroy them.

And they fled *eight days' journey into the wilderness.*

And they came to a land, yea, even a very beautiful and pleasant land, a land of pure water. . . .

And it came to pass that they began to prosper exceedingly in the land; and they called the land Helam. (Mosiah 23:1–4, 19; emphasis added)

As we travel through the highlands of Guatemala on our tours, we vicariously follow the trail of Alma from Guatemala City/Nephi to Lake Atitlan/waters of Mormon and on to the land of Helam. When we began to follow this geographic model, we soon

FIGURE 24–7: The map and the figures below illustrate the route and distances of Alma and the early Christians from the city of Nephi to the land of Zarahemla. They stopped at the waters of Mormon, the land of Helam, and the valley of Alma. They lived about twenty-four years in the land of Helam. The total travel time from Nephi to Zarahemla is thirty-one days—or approximately 250 miles. Another five days, or about forty miles, would be required to arrive at Comitan, Chiapas, Mexico. A comparison of modern names with Book of Mormon names and the conversions of miles to days are as follows: Guatemala City to Lake Atitlan, 80 miles (city of Nephi to waters of Mormon, 10 days); Lake Atitlan to Almolonga, 65 miles (waters of Mormon to land of Helam, 8 days); Almolonga to San Francisco Valley, 8 miles (Helam to the valley of Alma, 1 day); San Franciso Valley to Chiapas, Mexico, 96 miles (valley of Alma to the land of Zarahemla, 12 days). Total travel time from Nephi to Zarahemla, 249 miles (or 31 days).

realized that Almolonga is an excellent candidate for the land of Helam for the following reasons:

1. Fleeing from King Noah, Alma would have moved away from Nephi, which would be in a northward direction. Because this wilderness region follows the ridge of the mountain instead of the valley floor, only one basic mountain route is available to travel from Guatemala City (land of Nephi) to Chiapas, Mexico (land of Zarahemla).

2. The distance from Lake Atitlan to Almolonga is about sixty-five miles—a walking distance for Alma and his people of about eight days, the same time as reported in Mosiah 23:34.

3. Almolonga is a very pleasant land and a land of pure water—both of which are key characteristics of the land of Helam (see Mosiah 23:4, 19).

> The route that Alma took with his followers is probably the same route that Stephens took in the nineteenth century and that we take today on our tours through that beautiful and awesome country.

Although it is not stipulated in Alma's journey, we estimate that an additional six days—or about fifty miles—are required to travel from the Guatemala-Mexico border to the upper Grijalva (city of Zarahemla). If we take into consideration any backtracking and then add the time from the border of Zarahemla to the city of Zarahemla, we then estimate the number of days required to travel from the city of Nephi to the city of Zarahemla to be thirty-four days—or about three hundred miles.

The travel time from the waters of Mormon to the land of Helam was eight days. The scripture states that Alma's group took their flocks and carried their grain. We can assume that Alma and his party carried their grain in the same manner in which the natives carry their grain today. A strap about two inches wide is placed on the forehead and is attached to the load, which is carried on the back. Men, women, and children all carry the burdens. Carrying such burdens would certainly lengthen travel time. This method of carrying grain, wood, and all manner of things is also reminiscent of another statement made about Alma's group wherein their burdens were made light upon their shoulders and upon their backs (see Mosiah 24:14).

The distance from Lake Atitlan to Almolonga is about sixty-five miles. It is a beautiful community that is called the horticulture capital of Central America. The natural hot springs that flow from the mountains make the valley green throughout the year, which is certainly in keeping with Alma's statement that the land of Helam was "a very beautiful and pleasant land, a land of pure water" (see Mosiah 23:4).

Alma and his followers lived in the land of Nephi (including the waters of Mormon and the land of Helam) for twenty-four years. From his comments, we know that the land of Helam was a delightful place. As noted, he called Helam a very "pleasant land, a land of pure water."

When John Lloyd Stephens visited Almolonga in 1840, he expressed the same feelings when he said that his exploration party wanted to stay in Guatemala. However, because of the revolution, as Stephens notes, he went north to Mexico to avoid revolutionary conditions. The route that Alma took with his followers is probably the same

route that Stephens took in the nineteenth century and that we take today on our tours through that beautiful and awesome country.

The land between Lake Atitlan and Almolonga certainly meets the requirements for a wilderness. Today, the natives of Guatemala farm on the sides and on the tops of the mountains. In the summer, the mountains are a spectacular green. In the autumn, the mountains look like gold with the ripened wheat, barley, and corn blowing in the cool breezes. As the year moves along, the picture we see is that of a giant, hand-embroidered, patchwork quilt as it manifests a variety of colors.

The distance from the city of Nephi to the waters of Mormon is estimated to be about ten days—or eighty to ninety miles. The distance from the waters of Mormon to the land of Helam is eight days, which is estimated to be about sixty-five miles. Therefore, the distance from the city of Nephi to the land of Helam is estimated to be about 150 miles, or approximately eighteen days' travel time at the rate of eight miles per day. Eventually, Alma and his followers were discovered in the land Helam by Amulon and his brethren. Alma and his people were placed in bondage to the Lamanites, but the Lord delivered them. Alma and his people departed into the wilderness. After traveling one day, they stopped in the valley of Alma to give thanks. "And it came to pass that they departed out of the valley [of Alma], and took their journey into the wilderness. And after they had been in the wilderness *twelve days* they arrived in the land of Zarahemla; and king Mosiah did also receive them with joy" (Mosiah 24:24–25; emphasis added).

Almolonga is within five miles of Quetzaltenango, the capital city of the department of Quetzaltenango—or, as the natives call it in their native tongue, Xelaju. Near

It is no coincidence that the wilderness areas in the right location correspond with those mentioned in the Book of Mormon.

Quetzaltenango are four crossroads (cuatro caminos). The eastern route takes travelers to Totonicapan, the western route goes to Quetzaltenango, the southern route leads to Guatemala City, and the northern route is the road to Huehuetenango and on to the Mexican border. The road to Mexico leads to a no-man's land. It is the wilderness that leads to the division of Guatemala and Mexico, and it is sometimes referred to as the "division of the waters." This is the wilderness that we propose to be the division line between the lands of Nephi and Zarahemla.

The present-day mileage-marker signs at the four crossroads indicate that Huehuetenango is forty-eight miles away and that the border of Mexico is another forty-eight miles, making a total of ninety-six miles—the exact distance projected by Alma and his followers from the valley of Alma to the borders of Zarahemla. That is, twelve days of travel at eight miles a day is ninety-six miles. From the border of Ciudad Cuauhtemoc, Mexico, to the upper Grijalva River, the area proposed as the city of Zarahemla, the distance is about another fifty miles.

The wilderness that Mosiah, Zeniff, Ammon, Limhi, the sons of Mosiah, the first-century BC Nephi and Lehi, and others who traveled from Nephi to Zarahemla and Zarahemla to Nephi is proposed to be that hundred-mile area from the crossroads of Quetzaltenango/Totonicapan to the border of La Mesilla/Ciudad Cuauhtemoc.

Today, the route is part of the Pan-American Highway. But the area is still a wilderness journey. The most ancient of all native tribes, the Mam tribe, whose language dates to 2600 BC, lives in the rugged and, in many instances, somewhat barren wilderness. The area is the mountainous region where the guerrillas seek refuge during revolutionary conflict. The area may be the same location that served as the hideout for the Gadianton robbers in ancient Book of Mormon times. It is the same area where Rigoberta Menchu Tun lived, whose biography earned her a Nobel peace prize in 1992.

> Not only the direction but also the meaning of the word *Hermounts* establishes the validity of the proposed location of the wilderness of Hermounts.

6. THE WILDERNESS OF HERMOUNTS (WEST WILDERNESS)

The wilderness of Hermounts is north and west of Zarahemla. We read about this wilderness in an account where the Nephites drove the Lamanites into the wilderness that was west and north of Zarahemla: "And they fled before the Nephites towards the wilderness which was west and north, away beyond the borders of the land; and the Nephites did pursue them with their might, and did slay them. Yea, they were met on every hand, and slain and driven, until they were scattered on the west, and on the north, until they had reached the wilderness, which was called *Hermounts*; and it was that part of the wilderness which was infested by wild and ravenous beasts" (Alma 2:36–37; emphasis added).

On the Mesoamerica map, the wilderness of Hermounts is placed west and north of the proposed land of Zarahemla. This wilderness—or mountainous region—forms the eastern border of the Isthmus of Tehuantepec.

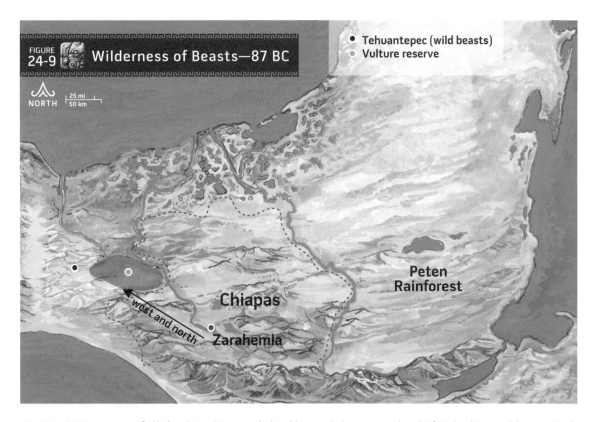

FIGURE 24–9: "[The Lamanites] fled before the Nephites towards the wilderness which was west and north [of Zarahemla] . . . until they . . . reached the wilderness [that] was called Hermounts" (Alma 2:36–37). This map illustrates the proposed location of the wilderness of Hermounts, which is the same as the wilderness of Tehuantepec. It is also in the wilderness where a vulture preserve is located today (see Alma 2:38).

As discussed earlier, not only the direction but also the meaning of the word *Hermounts* establishes the validity of the proposed location of the wilderness of Hermounts. We understand from the above scripture that Hermounts is associated with "wild and ravenous beasts." The word *Tehuantepec* is an Aztec, or Nahuatl, word that also means "wilderness of wild and ravenous beasts." The word *tepec* refers to mount or mountain or wilderness. The word *tecuani* means "wild tiger or ferocious beast" (see a Nahuatl dictionary).

Mormon, whose name has the same meaning in the Maya language as *Tehuantepec* does in the Nahuatl language, reports that "many died . . . of their wounds, and were devoured by those beasts and also the vultures of the air; and their bones have been found, and have been heaped up on the earth" (Alma 2:38). Vultures are plentiful in this region today—so much so that the Mexican government has established a bird refuge dedicated to the vultures in the mountains of Tehuantepec. A city close to Tuxtla Gutierrez, the capital of Chiapas, is called Ocozocoautla, which means "land of the vultures."

On one of our tours, Francois Radzik, who is from Switzerland and is author of the book *Alles über Josef* (*All about Joseph*), proposed a correlation with the above scripture and the coming forth of both the Bible and the Book of Mormon. That is, Mormon apparently talks about the wilderness of Hermounts (Tehuantepec) because he is emphasizing a prophecy recorded in the standard works. In this prophecy, people will be gathered from the four corners of the earth as a result of the ancient religious histories contained in the Bible and the Book of Mormon; and, like vultures or birds of the air, they will feast upon the words of Christ—or the writings of the ancient prophets. Here are some of the associated scriptures:

Deuteronomy 28:25–26

The Lord shall cause thee to be smitten before thine enemies: thou shalt go out one way against them, and flee seven ways before them: and shalt be removed into all the kingdoms of the earth. And thy carcase shall be meat *unto all fowls of the air, and unto the beasts of the earth*, and no man shall fray them away.

1 Samuel 17:44, 46

And the Philistine said to David, Come to me, and I will give thy flesh *unto the fowls of the air, and to the beasts of the field.* . . . This day will the Lord deliver thee into mine hand; and I will smite thee, and take thine head from thee; and I will give the carcases of the host of the Philistines this day *unto the fowls of the air, and to the wild beasts of the earth*; that all the earth may know that there is a God in Israel.

Jeremiah 19:7

And I will make void the counsel of Judah and Jerusalem in this place; and I will cause them to fall by the sword before their enemies, and by the hand of them that seek their lives: and their carcases will I give to be meat for *the fowls of the heaven, and for the beasts of the earth.*

Matthew 24:28, 34

For wheresoever the carcase is, *there will the eagles be gathered together.* . . . Verily I say unto you, This generation shall not pass, till all these things be fulfilled.

Joseph Smith—Matthew 1:27

And now I show you a parable. Behold, wheresoever the carcass is, *there will the eagles be gathered together;* so likewise shall mine elect be gathered from the four quarters of the earth.

Mormon apparently talks about the wilderness of Hermounts (Tehuantepec) because he is emphasizing a prophecy recorded in the standard works.

Alma 2:38

And it came to pass that many died in the wilderness of their wounds, and were devoured *by those beasts and also the vultures of the air*; and their bones have been found, and have been heaped up on the earth.

Mosiah 12:2

Yea, wo be unto this generation! And the Lord said unto me: Stretch forth thy hand and prophesy, saying: Thus sayeth the Lord, it shall come to pass that this generation, because of their iniquities, shall be brought into bondage, and shall be smitten on the cheeks; yea, and shall be driven by men, and shall be slain; and *the vultures of the air, and the dogs, yea, and the wild beasts,* shall devour their flesh.

Alma 16:10–11

In one day it was left desolate; and the carcases were *mangled by dogs and wild beasts* of the wilderness. Nevertheless, after many days their dead bodies were heaped up upon the face of the earth.

Scattering of Israel (A Concept of Dualism)

We can be assured that the above scriptures are of great value. Joseph Smith referred to them as parables, and Abinadi called them prophecies. With the exception of Alma 2:38 and Mosiah 12:2, all the above quotations use the word *carcase* or *carcass*. In Alma 2:38, in lieu of *carcass*, we read that their bones were found and heaped up on the earth. In Mosiah 12:2, instead of the word *carcass*, we read that they will be driven and slain. The prophecy of Abinadi appears to have a temporal fulfillment as well.

The combined words of *carcass, smitten, driven, bondage, death, flee,* and *removed* are used synonymously to represent the scattering of the children of Israel or, in the case of 1 Samuel, to illustrate that God will also be with Israel.

If the above scriptures reflect a similitude or a type and shadow of the scattered Israel, then the outcome emphasizes the historical fact that the children of Israel have been scattered, driven, killed, and persecuted and that their carcasses have been heaped up on the earth. The important thing to remember, however, is that these people whose bones lie dormant are the same people who gave us the Bible: "Thou fool, thou shall say: A Bible, we have got a Bible, and we need no more Bible. Have ye obtained a Bible save it were by the Jews?" (2 Nephi 29:6).

And these carcasses also belong to those who gave us the Book of Mormon: "And it shall be as if the fruit of thy loins had cried from the dust; for I know their faith. And they shall cry from the dust; yea, even repentance unto their brethren" (2 Nephi 3:19–20).

> If the above scriptures reflect a similitude or a type and shadow of the scattered Israel, then the outcome emphasized the historical fact that the children of Israel have been scattered, driven, killed, and persecuted and that their carcasses have been heaped up on the earth.

Gathering of Israel (A Concept of Dualism)

The phrases that are also common to the above scriptures are *fowls of the air*, *vultures of the air*, and *eagles gathered together* along with the earthly terms of *beasts*, *wild beasts*, and *dogs*. Because it is birds of the air that devour the carcasses (the histories contained in the Bible and Book of Mormon), then we are the vultures or eagles or fowls of the air. For example, Parley P. Pratt, upon receiving a copy of the Book of Mormon, stated that he did not want to eat or sleep until he had finished reading, or devouring, it. Vreni Lechmann, after visiting the National Museum of Anthropology in Mexico City, stated, "We were like vultures in the museum, devouring all we could in the short time we had."

Millions of people have symbolically represented those fowls of the air as they have "devoured" the sacred records that have come forth from the dust and that were written by those whose carcasses lie heaped up on the earth. And, as a result of the missionary work in these latter days, the Book of Mormon has been and is being carried throughout the earth. Further, as written by Joseph Smith in his revision of Matthew 24, "Mine elect shall be gathered from the four corners of the earth." The eagles (those who accept Christ and are baptized) will be gathered together.

The prophetic intent of the words "beasts," "wild beasts," and "dogs," which are earthly creatures, may be terms associated with Satan, whose goal is to destroy God's covenant people.

7. THE SOUTH WILDERNESS OR WILDERNESS IN THE LAND SOUTHWARD

The only place in the Book of Mormon where the term "south wilderness" is used is in Alma 22 where Mormon informs us that the Mulekites landed in the place where the Jaredites were destroyed and that the Mulekites traveled from there into the south wilderness:

> And it [Bountiful] bordered upon the land which they called Desolation, it being so far northward that it came into the land which had been peopled and been destroyed, of whose bones we have spoken, which was discovered by the people of Zarahemla, it being the *place of their first landing*.
>
> And they [people of Zarahemla, or Mulekites] came from there up into the south wilderness. Thus the land on the northward was called Desolation, and the land on the southward was called Bountiful, it being the wilderness which is filled with all manner of wild animals of every kind, a part of which had come from the land northward for food. (Alma 22:30–31; emphasis added)

Apparently, Mormon is making an editorial comment in a section that describes the Lamanite boundaries. As nearly as we can tell from the Book of Mormon, Mormon lived in the land northward. His father "carried" him to the land southward when Mormon was eleven years old. Also, Mormon apparently lived in the city of Desolation, which was near the narrow passage that led into the land southward (see Mormon 1:6; 2:28–29; 3:5, 7).

Therefore, from the perspective of Mormon's writing about the south wilderness, the south wilderness clearly is in the land southward as opposed to the land northward. The south wilderness is southward of the Mulekite landing site and southward of where the Jaredites were destroyed.

The area is undoubtedly the same location referred to by the Jaredites in Ether 10: "And it came to pass that Lib also did that which was good in the sight of the Lord. And in the days of Lib the poisonous serpents were destroyed. Wherefore they did go into the land southward, to hunt food for the people of the land, for the land was covered with animals of the forest. And Lib also himself became a great hunter. And they did preserve the land southward for a wilderness to get game" (Ether 10:19, 21). Today, this

"Lib . . . became a great hunter. And they did preserve the land southward for a wilderness to get game" (Ether 10:21).

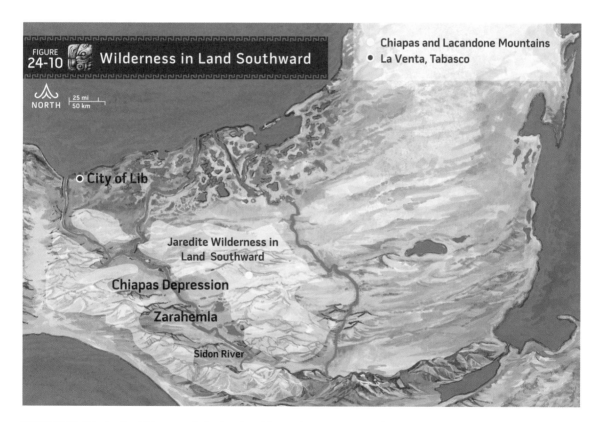

FIGURE 24–10: "[The Jaredites] did preserve the land southward for a wilderness, to get game" (Ether 10:21). The proposed location of the wilderness located southward of the Gulf of Mexico, Olmec/Jaredite territory, consists of the mountains of Tehuantepec, the mountains of Chiapas, and the Lacandone mountains. It is one of nature's climatic ironies where the mountains on the east side of the isthmus receive moisture in the dry season from the Gulf of Mexico, thus providing food for the abundance of wild animals that live in the mountains.

FIGURE 24–11: Wild turkey in the wilderness of Peten, Guatemala. (Photo courtesy of Merrill C. Oaks)

area is the state of Chiapas. It is still a massive, mountainous region of wild animals. Chiapas has only about 4 percent of the human population of the entire country of Mexico, yet it is home to over 40 percent of Mexico's animal population.

The wilderness in the land southward is also where the Mulekites settled or traveled through to get to Zarahemla. And it is probably the same area where Lachoneus, the Nephite chief judge, gathered the Nephites shortly before the coming of Christ to starve out the Gadianton robbers: "And the land which was appointed was the land of Zarahemla, and the land which was between the land Zarahemla and the land Bountiful, yea, to the line which was between the land Bountiful and the land Desolation. And there were a great many thousand people who were called Nephites, who did gather themselves together in this land. Now Lachoneus did cause that they should gather themselves together in the *land southward*, because of the great curse which was upon the land northward" (3 Nephi 3:23–24; emphasis added).

Today, a hundred thousand Chamula natives live in the mountains of Chiapas in the area that we propose as the south wilderness in the Book of Mormon. It is also the traditional area where wild animals are found. The land is southward from Veracruz and south from Campeche. The south wilderness is not south of Zarahemla, or Chiapas, but is part of Zarahemla/Chiapas. The south wilderness probably also included the wilderness of Hermounts described above.

8. THE WILDERNESS THAT WAS ON THE WEST OF ZARAHEMLA

Although the word "wilderness" occurs about 260 times in the Book of Mormon, for the most part, only directions are given, such as when Alma preached the gospel in the land of Melek: "[Alma] took his journey over into the land of Melek, on the west of the river Sidon, on the west by the borders of the wilderness" (Alma 8:3).

This wilderness is not called the "west wilderness," even though it is west of Zarahemla. After preaching the gospel in Melek, Alma traveled three days' journey (an estimated twenty-four miles) north to the land of Ammonihah. For the next several chapters, we read about the experiences of Alma and Amulek in the city of Ammonihah. (For a more detailed discussion of Alma's missionary journey, see chapter 29, "The Land of Zarahemla.")

The land of Melek is also where the converted Lamanites (people of Ammon) moved after they left the land of Jershon (see Alma 35:13). This wilderness constitutes

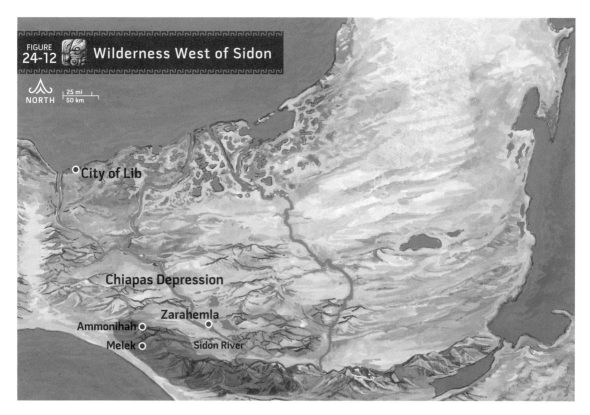

FIGURE 24–12: Alma took his journey over into the land of Melek, on the west of the river Sidon, on the west by the borders of the wilderness (see Alma 8:3). This wilderness was on the west sea, south (Alma 53:8). It is also the area where the sons of Helaman fought to support the people who were in the borders of the land on the south by the west sea (see Alma 53:22).

the Lamanite-Nephite western border. It is the area the sons of Helaman defended, which was on the borders south by the west sea (Alma 53:22).

9. THE WILDERNESS OF LACHONEUS

About halfway between the birth of Christ and His appearance to the Nephites, Lachoneus, the chief judge of the Nephites, received a threatening and arrogant letter from the governor of the secret society of Gadianton in which Lachoneus was invited to unite with the Gadianton robbers and become acquainted with their secret works. In the letter, Lachoneus was told that "if you will not do this, I swear unto you with an oath, that on the morrow month I will command that my armies shall come down against you, and they shall not stay their hand and shall spare not, but shall slay you, and shall let fall the sword upon you even until ye shall become extinct" (3 Nephi 3:8).

This is a marvelous story of intrigue, geographical and historical accuracy, and dynamic spiritual dualism. (You may want to take a few minutes here to read chapters 2 through 6 of 3 Nephi before continuing.)

Lachoneus did not respond to the letter; instead, he and his great chief captain, Gidgiddoni, gathered both Nephites and the Lamanites who had united with the Nephites (see 3 Nephi 2:14) into one place and eventually established themselves in a defensive posture in the center of the land. They marched forth by the "thousands and tens of thousands" (3 Nephi 3:22) to prepare themselves for what became, at that time, the greatest "slaughter among all the people of Lehi since he left Jerusalem" (3 Nephi 4:11). In other words, this was a major historical event in Nephite history.

The Nephites from both the land northward and the land southward, as well as some Lamanites, gathered supplies to last for seven years (see 3 Nephi 4:4; 6:2). They followed Lachoneus and Gidgiddoni up into the mountains and the wilderness. "And the land which was appointed was the land of Zarahemla, and the land which was between the land of Zarahemla and the land Bountiful, yea, to the line which was between the land Bountiful and the land Desolation" (3 Nephi 3:23).

Time and again with compass, altimeter, and Book of Mormon in hand, we have traveled through the proposed area where the above events took place. After years and years of on-site and in-text analysis, we are now prepared to say unequivocally that virtually everything we read in this section is historically, geographically, and culturally accurate. We read about the origin of the secret society of Gadianton in the book of Helaman; and from our reading, we know that much of what we read about this band occurred over a short period of time—that is, from about thirty years before the birth of Christ to the death of Christ at AD 34, thus covering a period of about sixty-four years.

Furthermore, most of the activity of the Gadianton band took place in the mountains between the land of Zarahemla and the land of Nephi—or, as nearly as we can determine, the headquarters of the robbers for the most part were in what today is the department of Huehuetenango, Guatemala. Even the Lamanites who lived south of this area had serious problems with the Gadianton robbers (see Helaman 6:37). We see here something that goes beyond mere coincidence. That is, even during our time period, this area is the hideout for guerillas who have the same reputation that the Gadianton robbers had.

You will observe that the Nephites told the Nephite chief captain Gidgiddoni that they should "go *up upon* the mountains and *in* the wilderness" (3 Nephi 3:20; emphasis added). But Gidgiddoni responded, "The Lord forbid; for if we should go up against them the Lord would deliver us into their hands; therefore we will prepare ourselves in the center of our lands" (3 Nephi 3:21). Later, Gidgiddoni commanded his armies that they should pursue the Gadianton band only to the borders of the wilderness. Even modern historical events prove that robbers can hunker down in these Cuchumatane Mountains and never be found.

On the other side of the central depression of Chiapas—that is, on the north side of the Sumidero Canyon—is an area called the Chiapas and Lacandone Mountains, and the descriptions in terms of direction, location, and tradition are just as accurate as

> "The land which was appointed was the land of Zarahemla, and the land which was between the land of Zarahemla and the land Bountiful, yea, to the line which was between the land Bountiful and the land Desolation" (3 Nephi 3:23).

FIGURE 24–13: Waterfalls in the wilderness of Chiapas. (Photo courtesy of Merrill C. Oaks)

those discussed above. It is the general area where the Lacandone natives live today. We are not prepared to say that the Lacandone Mountains were named after Lachoneus, but the location is the same today where the Zapatistas, or *Marcos* as they are called, located themselves several years ago to avoid the tanks and modern military equipment of the Mexican government. It is the area between San Cristobal de las Casas and Palenque. The largest town is called Ocosingo, which is not very far from the beautiful Blue Water Falls.

Notice the location where Lachoneus gathered the Nephites and some Lamanites together. It is "the land of Zarahemla, and the land which was between the land of Zarahemla and the land Bountiful, yea, to the line which was between the land Bountiful and the land of Desolation" (3 Nephi 3:23). Observe how Mormon describes locations. They are fairly easy to identify because of his descriptions. Today, this area is called the Black Forest, and it is in Chiapas (Zarahemla) and between Chiapas and Tabasco (the western edge of the land Bountiful), all the way to the line of Veracruz (land of Desolation).

Lachoneus—Types and Shadows

We will now discuss the spiritual implications of this wilderness story. Frankly, it reads a lot like an Isaiah text in which the spiritual message is couched in a historical setting. Mormon describes the Gadianton band as being "girded about after the manner of robbers; and they had a lamb-skin about their loins, and they were dyed in blood" (3 Nephi

> We see here something that goes beyond mere coincidence. That is, even during our time period, this area is the hideout for guerillas who have the same reputation that the Gadianton robbers had.

FIGURE 24–14: Iguana in the Yucatan wilderness. (Photo courtesy of Sheryl Lee Wilson)

Just as Lachoneus and Gidgiddoni were great prophets who gathered the people together in the center of their lands to defend themselves against the secret combinations, so do the great prophets in these latter days gather the remnant of Jacob from all parts of the earth.

4:7). This description strikes us as a great sacrilege. Christ is the Lamb of God, and He gave His blood to save mankind.

Mormon used this account to quote the following prophecy: "As surely as the Lord liveth, will he gather in from the four quarters of the earth all the remnant of the seed of Jacob, who are scattered abroad upon all the face of the earth. . . . And then shall they know their Redeemer, who is Jesus Christ, the Son of God; and then shall they be gathered in from the four quarters of the earth unto their own lands, from whence they have been dispersed; yea, as the Lord liveth so shall it be. Amen" (3 Nephi 5:24–26).

Just as Lachoneus and Gidgiddoni were great prophets (see 3 Nephi 3:18–19) who gathered the people together in the center of their lands to defend themselves against the secret combinations, so do the great prophets in these latter days gather the remnant of Jacob from all parts of the earth to the stakes of Zion to protect them against the buffeting of Satan in anticipation of the Second Coming of our Redeemer, even Jesus Christ.

Limhi and Alma—Types and Shadows

The travels of Limhi and Alma are parallel accounts and are also couched in the concept of types and shadows. Mormon probably placed them in the same area in the Book of Mormon to teach a lesson on the plan of salvation. Figure 24–15 shows a summary of the geography history of Alma and Limhi. Enrique Romero of the Chihuahua Stake originally introduced the idea that the plan of salvation is reflected symbolically in the travels of Alma and Limhi.

THE EAST WILDERNESS (72 BC–57 BC, FIFTEEN YEARS—THE WAR YEARS)

The east wilderness is the most prominent wilderness area spoken of in the Book of Mormon. In fact, the Book of Mormon contains more content about the east wilderness, or the wilderness east of Zarahemla, than about any other wilderness area mentioned in the Book of Mormon. Thus, a major portion of content that Mormon selected for his abridgement takes place in the wilderness east of Zarahemla.

Because the east wilderness became a part of the land of Zarahemla in the first century BC, we will discuss it in chapter 25, "The East Wilderness."

THE ACCOUNT	THE DUALISM
The people of Limhi and the people of Alma were in bondage to the Lamanites. Heavy burdens were placed upon their backs.	The people of Limhi and the people of Alma lived in the land of Nephi (Lamanite territory), which represents the world. Heavy burdens are placed upon us because we are subject to the Fall.
The Nephites were governed by Noah and his wicked priests, who taught false doctrine.	We live in a world where Satan and his followers teach false doctrine.
Alma listened to the words of the prophet Abinadi and fled into the wilderness.	We have living prophets today who guide us through the wilderness of life.
Alma organized the Church of Christ and baptized at the waters of Mormon. He led his people to a land of pure water.	Through the power of the priesthood, the Church is organized. The land of pure waters represents Zion where the pure in heart dwell.
Burdens were made light, and a deep sleep came upon the Lamanites. "None could deliver [the Nephites] except it were the Lord their God" (Mosiah 24:21).	Through Christ, our burdens are made light. Sin is overcome through His Atonement. It is only through Christ that we are saved.
Alma gave thanks at the valley of Alma. Alma and Limhi escaped from bondage and were led through the wilderness until they arrived at Zarahemla where King Mosiah received them with open arms.	God's children worship Him. He guides them through the wilderness of life, and when they die, He receives them with open arms.

FIGURE 24–15: This chart depicts dualism involved in the allegory of Limhi and Alma (Mosiah 21:3–14; 23:6–14; 24:13–25). From the perspective of types and shadows, the allegory proposes that the plan of salvation is reflected symbolically in the travels of Alma and Limhi.

FIGURE 24–16: Ruins in the Tikal wilderness. (Photo courtesy of Merrill C. Oaks)

CHAPTER 25

The East Wilderness

And it came to pass that Moroni caused that his armies should go forth into the east wilderness; yea, and they went forth and drove all the Lamanites who were in the east wilderness into their own lands, which were south of the land of Zarahemla. (Alma 50:7)

 n 1965, I was enrolled in a Brigham Young University class on Book of Mormon geography under the direction of Dr. Wells Jakeman, who was the first chair of the BYU Archaeology Department. I can still remember his statement: "A great key to understanding the Maya nation would be uncovered if we could determine why they settled in the jungle lowlands of Guatemala."

This experience was related by Joseph Allen in the 1989 edition of *Exploring the Lands of the Book of Mormon.*

The Peten jungle on the Guatemala panhandle is truly a hot, humid rainforest from May to October. Throughout the entire year, it is a dense jungle filled with all manner of wildlife, including snakes, monkeys, jaguars, ocelots, and beautiful birds.

The independent country of Belize, which borders Guatemala on the west and the Caribbean on the east, also forms part of the vast Maya heartland. This area was heavily

OPPOSITE: The archaeological ruins of Laman Ayin are located in Belize, which we propose to be part of the east wilderness. This rainforest became part of the land of Zarahemla at the time of its annexation by the Nephites in the year 72 BC. At the time when many Nephites went into the east wilderness, numerous villages and cities were already in existence in the east wilderness. (Photo courtesy of Sheryl Lee Wilson)

populated beginning at 150 BC and continuing to the conquest of Mexico in the sixteenth century. The area is literally dotted with ruins of ancient buildings, including Tikal, El Mirador, Bonampak, Uaxactun, Rio Negro, Lamanai, and Altun Ha.

The Book of Mormon provides us with a very adequate solution as to why the people settled the area in question. Alma 22 helps us to understand that boundaries had been established at that time between the Lamanites and the Nephites. Basically, it appears that the highlands of Guatemala were considered Lamanite territory; and the lowlands of Guatemala, of which until recent years both the state of Chiapas in Mexico and the small country of Belize were a part, belonged to the Nephites.

If the land of Zarahemla was located in the central depression of the state of Chiapas, then the east wilderness was what is now called the Peten jungle of Guatemala and the current country of Belize. They are directly east of Chiapas. Belize borders what would be the eastern seashore in this same directional analysis. The dating of the archaeological sites in the area is testimony that people inhabited the area at the required 72 BC time period. Defensive earthworks also bear witness to the culture patterns in existence in the east wilderness at the time Moroni was fighting the Lamanites (see the map in figure 25–1).

THE PETEN RAINFOREST

We propose that the Peten jungle was settled so the Nephites could establish adequate and legitimate boundaries. The Nephites were almost completely surrounded by the Lamanites (see Alma 22:29, 34), and the threat of total enclosure by the Lamanites was a major concern for the Nephites, who lived in the isolated land of Zarahemla. In essence, Moroni initiated a homestead act in the first century BC to get the Nephites to move into the east wilderness of the Peten jungle and Belize.

Even today, these boundary lines are difficult to defend. The country of Guatemala has long maintained that Belize is, in reality, part of Guatemala. In fact, the Mexican state of Chiapas was part of Guatemala until it was annexed by Mexico in the nineteenth century.

The Book of Mormon scripture that justifies the settlement of the east wilderness as a "homestead act" is as follows:

> And it came to pass that Moroni caused that his armies should go forth into the *east wilderness*; yea, and they went forth and drove all the Lamanites who were in the *east wilderness* into their own lands, which were south of the land of Zarahemla.
>
> And the land of Nephi did run in a straight course from the east sea to the west.
>
> And it came to pass that when Moroni had driven all the Lamanites out of the *east wilderness*, which was north of the lands of their own possessions, *he*

> If the land of Zarahemla was located in the central depression of the state of Chiapas, then the east wilderness was what is now called the Peten jungle of Guatemala and the current country of Belize.

caused *that the inhabitants* who were in the land of Zarahemla and in the land round about should go forth into the *east wilderness*, even to the borders by the *seashore*, and possess the land. (Alma 50:7–9; emphasis added)

This military movement evidently was literally an annexation of the east wilderness area by the Nephite government, which had its headquarters in Zarahemla (Chiapas). In other words, this annexed area became Zarahemla's "east wilderness." This annexation means that the Peten and Belize rainforests constituted the east wilderness of Zarahemla. Therefore, if the central depression of Chiapas is the land of Zarahemla and if the areas of Peten and Belize became part of Zarahemla in the first century BC, then *all directional statements are accurate in every detail in reference to both the land of Zarahemla and the land of Nephi* as proposed in various chapters of *Exploring the Lands of the Book of Mormon.*

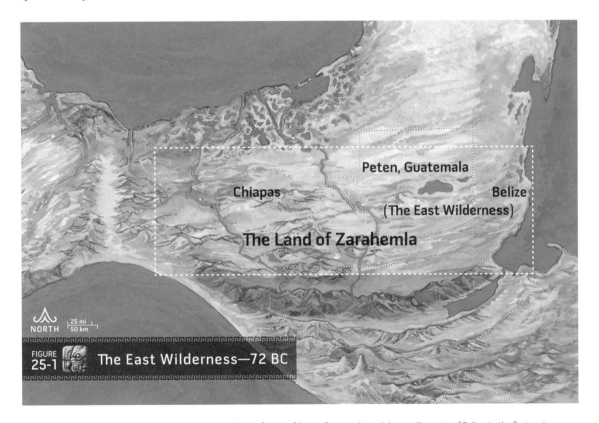

FIGURE 25–1: The area outlined in this map represents the rainforests of Peten, Guatemala, and the small country of Belize. In the first century BC when this area was annexed by Zarahemla, it became known in the Book of Mormon as the "east wilderness," meaning the east wilderness of Zarahemla. Many Maya villages were already inhabited in the region, including El Mirador, Tikal, San Bartolo, and Lamanai. The inhabitants who owed allegiance to the Lamanites were driven out of the east wilderness.

In clarifying some statements from the above account, we might say that the land of Nephi ran in a straight course from the sea east to the west. As a reflection of that statement, the mountain range that separates the highlands of Guatemala from the lowlands of Guatemala runs in a straight course from the east sea (Atlantic Ocean) to the west. After the Nephites had driven all the Lamanites out of the east wilderness (the Peten and Belize) south into their (the Lamanites') own land—that is, the highlands of Guatemala—the Nephites went forth into the east wilderness, or the Peten, to occupy it. They went as far as the borders of the seashore (Belize) to possess the land.

DEFENSIVE EARTHWORKS

Moroni built fortifications along the Nephites' south line to keep the Lamanites in their own lands. Because we are talking about the east wilderness and because it is situated in what today is the Peten jungle of Guatemala and the country of Belize, we would expect to see parallel historical and cultural patterns in that area. One such cultural pattern is the building of defensive earthworks. Below are selected paragraphs in one archaeological report published in 1967 by archaeologists Dennis E. Puleston and Donald W. Callender Jr.[1] We have juxtaposed content from this report alongside selected verses from Alma 49–50 so you can easily compare the two accounts. The language of the archaeological report is similar to the language in other archaeological reports about defensive earthworks in Mesoamerica.

1. Dennis E. Puleston and Donald W. Callender Jr., "Defensive Earthworks at Tikal," *Expedition* 9, no. 3 (Spring 1967): 40–48; emphasis added.

For access and potential discussion purposes, we have included the verse numbers from Alma 49–50 and have numbered the archaeological report's paragraphs. For emphasis purposes in both accounts, we have taken certain liberties in capitalizing and italicizing the material.

Puleston and Callender	**Alma 49**
1. For the weeks, months, and even years one spends carrying out fairly routine work there is always the possibility of stumbling onto something important that is *totally unexpected*. The discovery of what appears to be a 9 1/2 km. long defensive earthworks 4.5 km. north of the Great Plaza of Tikal is an example of just such a chance.	1. And now it came to pass in the eleventh month of the nineteenth year, on the tenth day of the month, the armies of the Lamanites were seen approaching towards the land of Ammonihah.
2. The earthworks lie directly between Tikal and the nearest large site, Uaxactun. These two sites are about five hours apart in terms of	2. And behold, the city [Ammonihah] had been rebuilt, and Moroni had stationed an army by the borders of the city, and they had *cast up dirt round about* to shield them from the arrows and the stones of the Lamanites; for behold, they fought with stones and with arrows.

walking distance; the earthworks are one hour's walk north of Tikal. *Frankly, a DEFENSIVE BARRIER of this magnitude, or for that matter of any magnitude, was not one of the things we expected to find in the process of a project to explore and map the outlying areas of Tikal. . . .*

3. The Tikal earthworks were discovered in the process of the systematic mapping of the remains of house platforms and other structures along the 1/2 km.-wide, 12-km.-long strip which extends north from Tikal's center. The *TRENCH* is the most prominent feature of the *EARTHWORKS*, but when it was first discovered it appeared to be nothing more than a natural arroyo or ravine. As we followed it, however, it soon became evident that it was not a natural formation. *First, it had a continuous raised embankment along the south side, and second, it passed up and down over hills, following a fairly straight line. . . .*

4. Compass bearings were taken every 40 to 50 meters and distances were paced off as accurately as possible, revealing finally that over their known length *the earthworks extended for a total of 9 1/2 km.* At both the east and west ends the earthworks disappeared into large swamps through which they may or may not have continued. . . .

5. With the realization that this new feature was not natural, but was something constructed with great effort by the Maya themselves, we

3. Behold, I [Mormon] said that the city of Ammonihah had been rebuilt. I say unto you, yea, that it was in part rebuilt; and because the Lamanites had destroyed it once because of the iniquity of the people, they supposed that it would again become an easy prey for them.

4. But behold, how great was their disappointment; for behold, the Nephites had dug up a *RIDGE OF EARTH ROUND ABOUT THEM*, which was so *high* that the Lamanites could not cast their stones and their arrows at them that they might take effect, neither could they come upon them save it was by their *PLACE OF ENTRANCE. . . .*

7. And being thus prepared they supposed that they should easily overpower and subject their brethren to the yoke of bondage, or slay and massacre them according to their pleasure.

8. But behold, to their [the Lamanites'] uttermost astonishment, [the Nephites] were prepared for them, in a manner *which never had been known* among the children of Lehi. Now they were prepared for the Lamanites, to battle after the manner of the instructions of Moroni.

12. Therefore they [the Lamanites] retreated into the wilderness, and took their camp and marched towards the land of Noah, supposing that to be the next best place for them to come against the Nephites.

13. For they knew not that Moroni had fortified, or had built *forts of security*, for every city *in all the land round*

"A defensive barrier of this magnitude, or for that matter of any magnitude, was not one of the things we expected to find."

—Puleston and Callender

were left with the question of *why? What was the function of this great trench and embankment* situated so far from the center of Tikal? At first we considered the possibility that it might have served as a canal in a water distribution system of some kind. However, this intriguing idea had to be rejected on the basis of two factors, both of which preclude the possibility that the trench could have held water: first, the extremely porous nature of limestone bedrock; and second, *the way in which the trench goes up and down the sides of large hills without changing its depth.*

6. On the other hand, its potential as a *BARRIER to human movement* was obvious. . . . Though we did not know its depth before we began excavation, the *FOUR-METER WIDTH OF THE TRENCH posed an obstacle few Maya could have crossed by jumping.* To have tried to do so would have been additionally difficult. . . . Over almost its entire length outsiders would have had to run uphill to approach the trench, and . . . they would have had to jump upwards, as well as across the trench, to get onto the embankment which abutted the south lip. . . .

7. It should be remembered that this embankment must have been considerably steeper and higher a thousand years ago than it is today. . . . That *THE TRENCH WAS IMPASSABLE is suggested by the fact that at four or five widely separated points along its length we found what*

about; therefore, they marched forward to the land of Noah with a firm determination; yea, their chief captains came forward and took an oath that they would destroy the people of that city.

14. But behold, to their astonishment, the city of Noah, which had hitherto been a weak place, had now, by the means of Moroni, become strong, yea even to exceed the strength of the city Ammonihah.

18. Now behold, the Lamanites could not get into their [the Nephites'] *forts of security* by any other way save by THE ENTRANCE, because of the *HIGHNESS OF THE BANK which had been thrown up*, and the *DEPTH OF THE DITCH which had been dug round about*, save it were by *THE ENTRANCE.*

19. And thus were the Nephites prepared to destroy all such as should attempt to climb up to enter the fort by any other way, by casting over stones and arrows at them.

20. Thus they were prepared, yea, a body of their strongest men, with their swords and their slings, to smite down all who should attempt to come into their place of security by *the place of entrance*; and thus were they prepared to defend themselves against the Lamanites.

21. And it came to pass that the captains of the Lamanites brought up their armies before *the place of entrance*, and began to contend with the Nephites, to get into their *place of security*; but behold, they were driven

"What was the function of this great trench and embankment situated so far from the center of Tikal?"

—Puleston and Callender

Exploring the Lands of the Book of Mormon

appeared to be CAUSEWAYS across it. At each of these there was an equivalent *GAP in the embankment.* If the earthworks were not a barrier to human passage these "*GATES*" would have little reason to exist. . . .

8. Several days' work in the trench revealed that *it had been cut into limestone bedrock to a DEPTH OF THREE METERS* and that in its original state the walls of the trench had been nearly vertical. Clearly, anyone who might have fallen into it would have had some difficulty getting out. . . .

9. *The limited exploration of most lowland Maya sites makes it impossible to say that defensive earthworks of this nature are unique to Tikal or even rare.* The trench we have described above is crossed at one of its more impressive points by the well-traveled trail between Uaxactun and Tikal. Many well-known archaeologists have crossed it without recognizing it for what it was, probably with some discomfort as their mules slid down or scrambled up the steep south edge. *Who is to say that similar earthworks do not exist elsewhere?* . . .

10. Here is one of those rare instances when hazy shadows of something approaching history begin to emerge.

back from time to time, insomuch that they were slain with an immense slaughter.

22. Now when they found that they could not obtain power over the Nephites *BY THE PASS,* they began to dig down their *BANKS OF EARTH* that they might obtain a pass to their armies, that they might have an equal chance to fight; but behold, in these attempts they were swept off by the stones and arrows which were thrown at them; and instead of filling up their *DITCHES* by pulling down the *BANKS OF EARTH,* they were filled up in a measure with their dead and wounded bodies. . . .

Alma 50

1. And now it came to pass that Moroni did not stop making preparations for war, or to defend his people against the Lamanites; for he caused that his armies should commence in the commencement of the twentieth year of the reign of the judges, that they should commence in digging up heaps of earth round about *ALL* the cities, throughout all the land which was possessed by the Nephites.

2. And upon the top of these *ridges of earth* he caused that there should be *timbers,* yea, *works of timbers built up to the height of a man,* round about the cities.

> "Who is to say that similar earthworks do not exist elsewhere?"
>
> —Puleston and Callender

Since the report of Puleston and Callender, archaeologists have discovered that defensive earthworks surrounded the entire complex of Tikal. Also, similar defensive earthworks have been found at other archaeological sites in the same geographical area as Tikal, including Becan, Coba, Cerros, Lamanai, and El Mirador, to name a few. During

FIGURE 25—2: Classic Period building at Becan, Campeche, Mexico. The Maya ruins of Becan were surrounded by defensive earthworks dating to the Preclassic Period. (Photo courtesy of Sheryl Lee Wilson)

the 1989 season at a place called Punta de Chiminov, archaeologist Arthur DeMarest of Vanderbilt University reported the discovery of a highly fortified city. The report in the *Los Angeles Times* states, "It's as if [the Maya] . . . were spending 75% of [their] budget on defense."[2]

2. *Los Angeles Times,* August 14, 1989, p. 3.

As you can see, the descriptions are remarkably similar between archaeological accounts of defensive earthworks and those recorded in the Book of Mormon. Most of the Mesoamerican defensive earthworks are also in the same area proposed as the east wilderness in the Book of Mormon.

Mormon informs us that the military leader Moroni constructed these fortifications round about every city in the land. The plan backfired to a degree, however, as within three years the Lamanites took control of some of the cities by the seashore, and they were then protected within the walls of the newly fortified cities.

In this fifteen-year war, cities changed ownership back and forth between the Nephites and the Lamanites. Apparently, most of the battles of Moroni took place in the Peten and Belize jungles. Possibly they even occurred farther north into the Yucatan. Helaman and his warriors and their allies appear to have been defending the land south and west of Zarahemla. At any rate, Moroni continued to fortify cities by using the defensive measures mentioned above.

THE CITY BOUNTIFUL AND THE CITY OF MULEK

One particular city that was extensively fortified was the city Bountiful. The city Bountiful was near the city Mulek, and Mulek was located in the east wilderness of Zarahemla. Bountiful was located in the land Bountiful, which was north of the land

FIGURE 25–3: Model showing defensive earthworks at Becan, Campeche, Mexico. (Photo courtesy of Sheryl Lee Wilson)

of Zarahemla. Mulek was on the eastern seashore and was north of Moroni, Lehi, Morianton, Omner, and Gid—all of which were on the east borders by the seashore (Alma 51:26). Mulek was south of the city Bountiful (see Alma 52:22–27).

In Alma 52, we learn that by 64 BC, the Lamanites had captured almost all of the eastern seaboard cities. Moroni, with his companions, Teancum and Lehi, was successful in regaining the city of Mulek by working a decoy. Again, you will notice the extreme consistency of the Book of Mormon in terms of directions. Teancum took a small number of men and marched down *near the seashore*; and during the night, Moroni and his army marched in the wilderness on the west of the city of Mulek. When the Lamanites saw the small army of Teancum, they began to chase them down by the *seashore, northward.*

Teancum, with his small army, circled back—moving toward the city of Bountiful, which was inland. Lehi had been left to guard the city of Bountiful. Therefore, when Teancum arrived with his small army while being pursued by the Lamanites under the leadership of a man named Jacob, Lehi with his fresh army began to engage the Lamanites.

Meanwhile, Moroni had split his army. He sent part of them in to recapture the city of Mulek, which they easily did in the absence of the Lamanite army. With the rest of

FIGURE 25—4: The city of
Bountiful was northward
and inland from the city of
Mulek. Mulek was on the
eastern seashore and was
within a day's march of
Bountiful. The Preclassic
and Classic Maya ruins of
Dzibanche are proposed to
be the city of Bountiful, and
the archaeological site of
Cerros, Belize, is proposed
to be the city of Mulek.

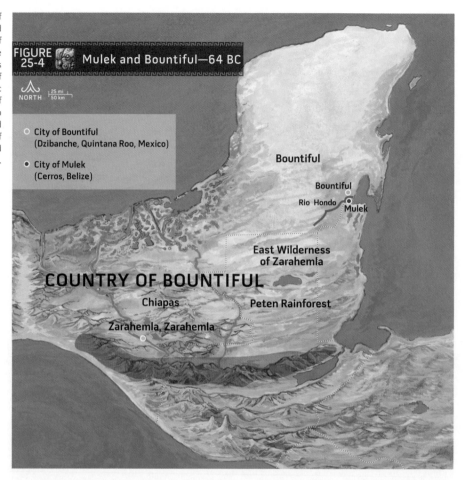

FIGURE 25-4 — Mulek and Bountiful—64 BC

NORTH | 25 mi / 50 km

○ City of Bountiful
(Dzibanche, Quintana Roo, Mexico)

● City of Mulek
(Cerros, Belize)

Bountiful

Bountiful
Rio Hondo
Mulek

East Wilderness
of Zarahemla

COUNTRY OF BOUNTIFUL

Chiapas   Peten Rainforest

Zarahemla, Zarahemla

The archaeological site of Cerros existed primarily during the Preclassic phase around 50 BC.

his soldiers, Moroni followed Jacob and the Lamanites as they pursued Teancum and his small army of Nephites. All three armies were moving toward the city of Bountiful.

The Nephites defeated the Lamanites and killed and captured many. The Lamanites who would not surrender their weapons of war were taken prisoners. After they had buried the dead, Teancum was put in charge of the Lamanite prisoners. The Nephites used the Lamanite prisoners as a labor gang to dig a ditch all around the city of Bountiful: "And he caused that they should build a breastwork of timbers upon the inner bank of the ditch; and they cast up dirt out of the ditch against the breastwork of timbers; and thus they did cause the Lamanites to labor until they had encircled the city of Bountiful round about with a strong wall of timbers and earth, to an exceeding height. And this city became an exceeding stronghold ever after" (Alma 53:4–5).

During the time that Moroni served as the military leader of the Nephites, a major expansion program occurred in the east wilderness. This expansion correlates with the first century, or Late Preclassic Period, where a great deal of activity occurred in the

Peten of Guatemala. Mormon writes that beginning at 72 BC, "they also began in that same year to build many cities on the north" (Alma 50:15).

Dzibanche is located in the Mexican state of Quintana Roo, and the area manifests a "bountiful-type climate," as the clouds from the Bay of Campeche and the Caribbean near Chetumal collide to provide a daily mist or dew like manna from heaven, making it possible to raise crops year round. The archaeological site of Cerros existed primarily during the Preclassic phase around 50 BC. Three tombs with their historical accounts make it possible to present the hypothesis that they were associated with Amalickiah, Ammoron, and Tubaloth of the same time period. If Cerros is Mulek, then Dzibanche is a good candidate for the city of Bountiful.

The following discussion represents an analysis of the archaeological zones of Cerros, Belize, and Dzibanche, Quintana Roo, Mexico, as primary candidates for the city of Mulek and the city of Bountiful.

THE ARCHAEOLOGICAL SITE OF CERROS AND THE CITY OF MULEK

In Alma 53:6, we read that after the Lamanites obtained control of the city of Mulek, it became one of the "strongest holds" of the Lamanites "in the land of Nephi." However, Mulek was *not* in the land of Nephi; it was in the land of Zarahemla—or rather in Zarahemla's east wilderness. When we utilize the research of Royal Skousen and read the original manuscript written by Oliver Cowdery, we see that Alma 53:6 should read as follows: "Mulek became one of the strongest holds of the Lamanites in *the land of the Nephites*." The land of the Nephites encompassed Zarahemla and the east wilderness of Zarahemla as well as the land Bountiful, which was north of Jershon.

We should understand the geographic location of the city of Mulek because *its location provides us with an identifying marker for the city Bountiful where the Savior appeared to the Nephites.* Further, Mulek shows evidence of being the same place as an archaeological site named Cerros (hills or pyramids). Cerros is located across the Bay of Corozal in *northern* Belize in the area we have identified as the east wilderness of Zarahemla. Cerros is just a few miles south of the Mexican border and is close to the archaeological sites of Kohunlich and Dzibanche, *candidates for the city of Bountiful.*

Non-LDS Maya scholar David Freidel conducted investigative work at Cerros. Freidel and the late Linda Schele describe their findings in chapter three, "Cerros: The Coming of Kings," of *A Forest of Kings: The Untold Story of the Ancient Maya.* Speaking of kingship, they describe it as a "social invention" that arose in Cerros about 50 BC (plus or minus fifty years). They elaborate, "It would be misleading for us to say that they invented this new institution whole-cloth from their own experience, because kings had been around in Mesoamerica for a long time—at least a thousand years."[3]

> We should understand the geographic location of the city of Mulek because *its location provides us with an identifying marker for the city Bountiful where the Savior appeared to the Nephites.*

3. Linda Schele and David Freidel, *A Forest of Kings: The Untold Story of the Ancient Maya* (New York: William Morrow, 1990), 97.

Book of Mormon kingship in the first century BC

Beginning with the Jaredites, kingship is a recurring issue throughout the Book of Mormon as well. In Alma 46, about 73 BC, the idea is introduced and discussed anew when a man by the name of Amalickiah is characterized simply as "desirous to be a king." He became extremely influential but was forced to flee with just a few of his followers into Lamanite territory when Moroni and his army—for the sake of national stability—came against them.

As for what motivated the rise of kingship in Cerros, Schele and Freidel speculate: "Cerros is too wealthy a prize to exist for long without a king, and too important a link in the trade network to pretend obscurity. The people of the community also need a resolution to their own ambiguous feelings toward the wealthy and powerful among them."[4] This information might help to explain why only six years after Amalickiah was chased out of the country, a group attempting to establish a kingship appeared again.

4. Schele and Freidel, *A Forest of Kings*, 103.

Amalickiahites were king-men

> The king who planned to bury himself in the summit of the eastward-facing acropolis never occupied his sepulcher—it was left open and empty.

Fortunately, the voice of the people came out against the "king-men," which enabled Pahoran to retain the judgment seat, but it "was a critical time for such contentions to be among the people of Nephi" (Alma 51:9). In the midst of this internal strife, the Lamanite army, led by Amalickiah, came crashing down on the unprepared Nephites. Because the king-men were so glad about Amalickiah's attack, at least some of them likely were actually the same people previously identified as Amalickiahites.

Although Moroni eventually managed to force the king-men to arms and temporarily put them down, he was not successful in preventing a kingship from being established in his country. Amalickiah had taken advantage of the Nephites' moment of weakness and was now in control of the cities "on the east borders by the seashore." In spite of Moroni's efforts, the east wilderness ended up with a king.

Effects of kingship

Schele and Freidel write: "The people of Cerros did decide consciously to embrace kingship as an institution and the consequences of that decision were profound for all. In the space of two generations, this small fishing village transformed itself into a mighty acropolis. Every living soul in Cerros participated in that transformation. . . . Around 50 BC, the community of Cerros began the revolutionary program of 'urban renewal' which buried their village completely under broad plastered plazas and massive temples."[5]

5. Schele and Freidel, *A Forest of Kings*, 103.

Schele and Freidel give a lengthy explanation of the construction process and the building of a major temple patterned after the ancient pyramids of the Olmecs. The details of the buildings have been preserved over two thousand years and provide us with a glimpse of this grand attempt to develop a royal lineage complete with symbols and power associated with a king. Great attention is given to coordinate the temple with the movements of the sun and the stars.

A charismatic king

Regarding the king, Schele and Freidel say, "The beauty and complexity of this building is concrete testimony to the charismatic power of the Cerros king, a ruler strong enough to attract and retain the services of skilled artisans literate in the complex theology and imagery of the new religion."[6] If this new king were Amalickiah, the description of him is certainly appropriate.

6. Schele and Freidel, *A Forest of Kings*, 120.

Further evidence adds to the hypothesis that Cerros was among the east wilderness cities taken over by Amalickiah. Schele and Freidel continue: "By this time in the history of Cerros, the first king had died and been replaced by a successor. We know this because of a special political message placed in the second temple. Below the summit where the new king stood for public rituals, he buried a set of royal jewels, including the jades of a royal headband and the chest pectoral of a king. . . . We believe these jewels were valued because they were the very ones used by the first king of Cerros. . . . The second king buried them in his own temple to invoke this power and to link himself with the former king, who was presumably his ancestor."[7]

7. Schele and Freidel, *A Forest of Kings*, 120–21.

Burial tombs were not used

Shortly after Amalickiah commenced his conquest of the east wilderness cities, he was killed by Teancum. Rather than pass the throne in the traditional manner from father to son (as Schele and Freidel presume happened at Cerros), the dead king was succeeded by his brother Ammoron (see Alma 51:37, 52:3).

During Ammoron's reign, the Nephite king-men reorganized, overthrew Pahoran, took over Zarahemla, appointed a king over themselves, and even made an alliance with Ammoron, the new Lamanite king. Moroni subsequently marched to Pahoran's rescue and put down the king-men.

The brief duration of kingship at Cerros was apparently enough to prompt Schele and Freidel to conclude: "In the long run, however, the pressures from within and without upon this newborn kingdom were evidently more than it could withstand. The king who planned to bury himself in the summit of the eastward-facing acropolis never occupied his sepulcher—it was left open and empty. Why this happened we do not know. One possibility is that this unfortunate king may have died far from home, taken captive in battle. Regardless of what the true story may have been, his successor ultimately failed to fulfill the promise inherent in the Maya vision of kingship."[8] Seven years after the death of Amalickiah, his brother Ammoron was also killed by Teancum (see Alma 62:35–36). Both Amalickiah and his brother Ammoron were killed *on the battlefield*, thus making it impossible for them to be buried in their royal tombs back home.

8. Schele and Freidel, *A Forest of Kings*, 126–27.

9. Schele and Freidel, *A Forest of Kings*, 127.

"The failed attempt to bury a king at the summit of the eastward-facing acropolis marked the beginning of the end of the experiment with kingship at Cerros."[9] The day following Ammoron's death, Moroni finally drove the Lamanites out of Nephite territory. Ammoron's son, Tubaloth, apparently became the next king of the Lamanites. Following tradition, he made a couple of attempts to take possession of Nephite cities but was consistently defeated by Moroni's son, Moronihah, who simply turned the Lamanites back to their own lands.

Kingship put down

One last quote from Schele and Freidel will suffice: "The heir to that ruler did manage to rally the people temporarily and to launch the construction of another temple along the designs of the first and second ones, . . . but its construction work was shoddy and no offerings were deposited in the building's summit. Shortly after this final effort, the Maya of Cerros gave up their brief embrace of kingship and systematically released the power from the sacred mountains [pyramids] which they had lifted up from their own earth. The kings were gone."[10] Or, as Mormon would say, the kings were "put down."

10. Schele and Freidel, *A Forest of Kings*, 127.

We, therefore, conclude that the archaeological site of Cerros located in northern Belize may have been the city of Mulek (see Alma 52:16–40) in the Book of Mormon for the following reasons:

CERROS	MULEK
1. Cerros is located on the eastern shores of the Caribbean in Belize.	1. Mulek was located on the east borders by the seashore in Zarahemla's east wilderness (Alma 51:26).
2. Cerros is located within fifteen to twenty miles southeast from the major archaeological sites of Kohunlich and Dzibanche in another country, the southern Yucatan Peninsula of Mexico.	2. Mulek was located within a day's march from another land and city called Bountiful.
3. Kingship was put down at Cerros after two royal tombs (pyramids) had been built. The third king did not have the power to rally the people. The kings were not buried in the tombs. Schele and Freidel speculate that this may have been because they were killed in battle, far from home.	3. King-men were put down by Moroni. Two kings, namely Amalickiah and Ammoron, were killed in battle and so probably would not have been buried at home. The third king, Tubaloth, apparently never had the power to rally the people (Helaman 1:16–33).
4. Cerros became a royal city in the first century BC.	4. The city name of Mulek implies a royal title dating back to Zedekiah, a Jewish king. Amalickiah, Ammoron, Tubaloth, and Jacob (a king-man defender of the city of Mulek) were all descendants of Zoram, a Jew (Alma 54:23, 52:33).
5. The dating of these events in Cerros is the middle of the first century BC.	5. The dating of these events in Mulek stretches from about 73 BC to 51 BC (Alma 46–Helaman 1).

Shortly after this final effort, the Maya of Cerros gave up their brief embrace of kingship and systematically released the power from the sacred mountains [pyramids] which they had lifted up from their own earth. The kings were gone. Or, as Mormon would say, the kings were "put down."

Exploring the Lands of the Book of Mormon

DZIBANCHE AND THE CITY OF BOUNTIFUL

By locating the city of Mulek, we can then determine the location of the city Bountiful. The city of Mulek and the city Bountiful were in close proximity to each other, as outlined in Alma 52:18–24. Mulek was located along the east seashore, and it became a part of the land of Zarahemla during the first century BC Nephite expansion (see Alma 50:7–8; 51:26; 52:22).

Because the city of Mulek was close to the city Bountiful, we can also determine that Mulek was located north of other eastern seaboard cities such as Moroni, Gid, Omner, Lehi, and Morianton. Hence, Bountiful and Mulek were neighbors, even though they were located in different lands. The city of Mulek was located in the land of Zarahemla's east wilderness, and the city of Bountiful was located in the land of Bountiful. Today, that situation is comparable to Corozal, Belize, located near Chetumal, Quintana Roo, Mexico. They are close, but they are in two separate countries.

If the archaeological site of Cerros located in northern Belize is the city of Mulek, as proposed in the previous section, then Dzibanche is an excellent candidate for the city Bountiful. After regaining the city of Mulek in the year 65 BC, the Nephites caused the Lamanite prisoners to fortify the city Bountiful. Mormon makes a correction in the text when he states, "Moroni caused that they [the Lamanite prisoners] should commence laboring in digging a ditch round about the land, *or the city*, Bountiful" (emphasis added). Mormon tells us that it is the city Bountiful and not the land Bountiful that had defensive earthworks surrounding it. Of course, the land Bountiful would have been too large for such an undertaking. The city of Bountiful became an "exceeding stronghold" from that time forth (Alma 53:3–5).

Many archaeological sites have been proposed over the last half century as the city Bountiful where the Savior appeared. Although many places have been proposed as the city Bountiful, unless they meet the established criteria outlined above, then by logic they need to be ruled out as candidates for such. For example, the 300 BC to AD 350 site of El Mirador may generate a feeling of the makeup of a Bountiful-type city. However, El Mirador is too far inland to be considered as a likely candidate for the city Bountiful. The same is true with the archaeological site of Becan. Even though it is a fortified city, it is too far inland to be considered seriously as a candidate for the city of Bountiful. Although other places have been proposed, the most likely candidate for the city of Bountiful is Dzibanche or Kohunlich. Because they are neighbors, they may be considered to be part of the same cosmopolitan city of Bountiful.

Joseph Allen writes:
I first visited Dzibanche in February of 1997 with a group of about forty people. The site had just been opened for visitors. We were encouraged by people in Chetumal to be sure we visited Dzibanche. In my early writings, I had proposed that general area as the location of the city of Bountiful because of its locative

By locating the city of Mulek, we can then determine the location of the city Bountiful. The city of Mulek and the city Bountiful were in close proximity to each other.

Not until "the ending of the thirty and fourth year" did the resurrected Christ truly manifest Himself unto the Nephites. His appearance to the Nephites was apparently almost a full year after the great destruction that occurred at the time of the Crucifixion.

description in the Book of Mormon and its approximation to the archaeological site of Cerros in northern Belize.

As we entered the site of Dzibanche on that delightful February day, several things for which I was unprepared caught my attention:

First, we saw newly planted green stalks of corn growing alongside golden eight-foot stalks ready to harvest. And intermediate sizes of corn were growing in different fields. The farmer instinct in me caused me to begin looking for irrigation water, a sprinkling system, or some other source of water. Not until later did we discover that the crops were watered by a gentle dew each morning, which provided the means for crops to grow year round.

Second, I was overwhelmed with the large number and immense size of the buildings. As we entered the city, we could still see the remains of the fortified earthworks embankment that had been constructed centuries earlier to protect the city. To get into what are several large plazas, visitors must ascend the remains of an ancient dirt embankment that surrounds the "city of wood." Of course, the timber palisades on top of the embankment are gone, but the dirt ditch with a high inner embankment still remains. Like its neighbors Becan, Cerros, Calakmul, and Tikal, defensive earthworks can still be detected at Dzibanche.

Third, the most impressive thing to me about the site of Dzibanche was its multitude of peaceful groves located among the ruins where we had adequate room to walk between the towering trees. This situation is different from Tikal, which has dense, tall jungle growth, and from northern Yucatan, which has thick scrub brush.

I have always empathized with the people who were present when the Savior visited them in the New World, as I pictured them spending several hours in the sauna-like climate of the Yucatan. But that is not the case at Dzibanche. A fresh, cool breeze seems to circulate perpetually among the tall, stately trees. Even in March, probably the month when the Savior visited the Nephites and the month that is one of the hottest of the year throughout Mesoamerica, the pleasantness of the site corresponds with the feelings of the words describing the visit of Christ to His other sheep: "Behold, I am Jesus Christ, whom the prophets testified shall come into the world. And behold, I am the light and the life of the world; and I have drunk out of that bitter cup which the Father hath given me, and have glorified the Father in taking upon me the sins of the world, in the which I have suffered the will of the Father in all things from the beginning" (3 Nephi 11:10–11; see also 3 Nephi 15:21–24).

The Savior's appearance at Bountiful at the time of the Passover. The resurrected Christ spoke to the Nephites saying, "Marvel not that I said unto you that old things had passed away, and that all things had become new. Behold, I say unto you that the law was fulfilled that was given unto Moses. Behold, I am he that gave the law, and I am he who covenanted with my people Israel; therefore, the law in me is fulfilled, for I have come to fulfill the law; therefore it hath an end" (3 Nephi 15:3–5).

Christ literally fulfilled the purpose of the Passover. What would be more fitting than for Him to appear on the very date the Passover occurred in the time of Moses as well as on the very date the Savior was born and was subsequently resurrected?

Although we are told that the destruction signifying His death began on the fourth day of the thirty-fourth year and lasted for only three days, 3 Nephi 10:18–19 indicates that it was not until "the ending of the thirty and fourth year" that Christ truly manifested Himself unto them. His appearance to the Nephites was apparently almost a full year after the great destruction that occurred at the time of the Crucifixion.

The first day of the Nephite thirty-fifth year would have been March 29, AD 34, on our Gregorian calendar, so the ending of the thirty-fourth year would almost certainly have been in AD 34 as well. That would give us the year of His appearance as AD 34.[11]

We emphasize the great significance of the Savior's appearance at Bountiful on the Passover. The Passover was initiated at the time of Moses to prophesy about the coming of the Messiah. His death and resurrection at Jerusalem fell at the time of the Passover,

11. Bruce W. Warren, "1 Ben 6 Mak: Part Two," *The Book of Mormon Archaeological Digest* 2, no. 3 (1999): 4–5.

FIGURE 25–5: Ruins of Tikal, Peten, Guatemala. Picture Tikal as a lowland jungle area roughly equivalent in size to Provo, Utah. The entire area of Tikal was surrounded by massive defensive earthworks as described earlier in this chapter in one archaeological report and in the Book of Mormon. Such defensive earthworks—unknown by modern archaeologists until the latter half of the twentieth century—provide intriguing archaeological support for the Book of Mormon. (Photo courtesy of Merrill C. Oaks)

FIGURE 25–6: Maya ruins
of Kohunlich, Quintana
Roo, Mexico. Kohunlich is
a neighbor to Dzibanche,
our candidate for the city of
Bountiful. (Photo courtesy
of Sheryl Lee Wilson)

and now we have come to understand that His appearance to the Nephites probably occurred at the time of the Passover almost one year after His death.

The faithful Nephites were gathered together at the temple in Bountiful and were discussing the fulfillment of the prophecies, particularly those that referred to the death of the Savior, which meant He would soon come to visit them (see 3 Nephi 11:2).

Dr. Bruce Warren states the following: "We believe that Christ appeared to the Nephites in Bountiful on the sixth day of Passover, 6 Ahau 3 Mak, Sunday, March 26, AD 34, which was the Passover Sabbath of His resurrection."[12]

12. Blaine M. Yorgason,
Bruce W. Warren, and
Harold Brown, New
Evidences of Christ in
Ancient America (Provo,
UT: Stratford Books, 1999),
169.

The movement of the Church's headquarters from Zarahemla to Bountiful. We may ask the question as to why the Savior appeared at Bountiful rather than in Zarahemla. Three temple sites are mentioned in the Book of Mormon: (1) the temple at the land/city of Nephi; (2) the temple at the land/city of Zarahemla; and (3) the temple at the land/city of Bountiful.

The Nephites lost control of the land of Nephi about 200 BC when Mosiah was driven out of the land (Omni 1:12). Zeniff made a successful attempt to regain the rights to the temple at the city of Nephi, a development that lasted for three generations—or until about 121 BC (see Mosiah 9:3, 8 and Mosiah 22:10, 15). No more mention is made of Nephite control of the temple at the city of Nephi after the 121 BC date.

The temple at Zarahemla gains its status in the Book of Mormon from the discourse of King Benjamin (Mosiah 2–5). This event dates to about 124 BC. The temple at Bountiful is not mentioned until the appearance of the Savior at AD 34. The walls around the city Bountiful were built in 64 BC, about ninety-eight years before the appearance of the Savior. These facts suggest that the temple at Bountiful was built sometime between 64 BC and AD 34.

FIGURE 25–7: This Tikal marker provides information about the AD 378 "entrada" of Teotihuacanos to Tikal. Interestingly, with the passing of each decade, radiocarbon dating and historical dating reflect intriguing date correlations between ancient Mesoamerican sites and the Book of Mormon. (Photo courtesy of Cortney Boice)

The fact that the Savior appeared to the Nephites at Bountiful rather than at Zarahemla (or at least the record is silent concerning any appearance at Zarahemla) suggests that the Church had moved its headquarters from Zarahemla to Bountiful sometime before the visit of Christ.

Dr. Mark Cutler, who traveled with us on a lands of the Book of Mormon tour, proposed in a presentation to the travel group that a shift in Church headquarters from Zarahemla to Bountiful apparently took place between 38 and 30 BC (see Helaman 1–5).

> In the fifty and sixth year of the reign of the judges [36 BC], there were dissenters who went up from the Nephites unto the Lamanites; and they succeeded with those others in stirring them up to anger against the Nephites. . . .
>
> They did come down against the Nephites to battle, and . . . they succeeded in obtaining possession of the land of Zarahemla; yea, and also all the lands, even unto the land which was near the land Bountiful.
>
> *And the Nephites and the armies of Moronihah were driven even into the land of Bountiful.* (Helaman 4:4–6; emphasis added)

During the restoration work of Chiapa de Corzo, Chiapas, in the 1960s, investigators for the New World Archaeological Foundation discovered stone pieces that, when combined, yielded the engraved date of 36 BC, the same year mentioned above when a civil war was declared by Nephite dissenters and Lamanites from the land of Nephi against the government. A year later, the Nephite believers were driven into the Bountiful area. Within a few years, the Lamanites had gained total control of Zarahemla, and at 30 BC, Nephi gave up the judgment seat (see Helaman 5:4).

FIGURE 25–8: This map illustrates the moving of Nephite headquarters from the city/land of Zarahemla to the city/land of Bountiful in about 36 BC (Helaman 4:4–7). The Savior appeared to the Nephites at Bountiful in AD 34: "A great multitude gathered together, of the people of Nephi, round about the temple which was in the land Bountiful" (3 Nephi 11:1).

This shift in headquarters from Zarahemla to Bountiful helps us understand why the twelve disciples chosen by Christ would have been living near Dzibanche (Bountiful) and why Lehi and Nephi began their preaching in that same area shortly before the visit of Christ to the Nephites: "They went forth to teach the word of God among all the people of Nephi, beginning at the city of Bountiful" (Helaman 5:14).

Geographical consistency. The Book of Mormon seems to maintain internal consistency in relation to larger lands overlapping smaller lands. For example, the land of Zarahemla appears to be a land surrounding the city of Zarahemla. Also, other lands seem to fall under a larger land of Zarahemla. The lands of Mulek, Sidom, Manti, Moroni, and Nephihah are just a few of the lands that seem to fall under the larger umbrella of the land of Zarahemla.

The same conclusion can be proposed in reference to the land of Bountiful. In reality, the land of Bountiful may even be one step larger. For example, the city of Bountiful, as discussed above, was near the city of Mulek, which was near the east coast—or the

Atlantic seaboard. The land Bountiful surrounded the city Bountiful—constituting the role of a state today. And the country Bountiful covered the entire area, as stated in Alma 22:31: "The land on the southward was called Bountiful."

This type of geography is consistent with several city and state names today in Mexico. For example, Oaxaca is a city in the state of Oaxaca, Puebla is a city in the state of Puebla, Veracruz is a city in the state of Veracruz, and Mexico City is a city in the state of Mexico. All these are also located within a larger land called the country of Mexico.

In conclusion, the Maya archaeological site of Dzibanche is hereby proposed as the city of Bountiful mentioned in the Book of Mormon for the following reasons:

1. The immense size of Dzibanche, along with its neighbor Kohunlich, meets a large population requirement.
2. The early dating is consistent with the El Mirador Preclassic Period.
3. The structure of the walls around the city of Dzibanche meets the defensive earthworks requirement.
4. The distance requirement from the seacoast to Dzibanche meets that stipulation.
5. The relationship of Dzibanche to Cerros appears to be the same as the relationship between Bountiful and Mulek.
6. The climatic conditions of Dzibanche suggest a satisfactory name correlation with the name *Bountiful*.

CITIES OF MORONI AND NEPHIHAH

And it came to pass that the Nephites began the foundation of a great city, and they called the name of the city *Moroni*; and it was by the *east sea*; and it was on the south by the line of the possessions of the Lamanites. (Alma 50:13; emphasis added)

The directions given by Mormon are clear. The city of Moroni was near the east sea—or the Caribbean (Atlantic Ocean). "South by the line of the possessions of the Lamanites" is also clear. And the next verse gives us information about the city of Nephihah: "And they also began the foundation for a city between the *city of Moroni* and the city of Aaron, joining the borders of Aaron and Moroni; and they called the name of the city, or land, Nephihah" (Alma 50:14; emphasis added).

Thus, the city/land of Nephihah, which was in the east wilderness, is placed in the Peten jungle in proximity to the city of Moroni.

The city of Moroni was the southernmost city on the east coast nearest Lamanite territory. The following scripture reaffirms the location of the city/land of Moroni, as it was located in the borders by the seashore: "The Lamanites had come into the *land of Moroni, which was in the borders by the seashore*" (Alma 51:22; emphasis added).

> The directions given by Mormon are clear. The city of Moroni was near the east sea—or the Caribbean (Atlantic Ocean).

FIGURE 25–9: The city of Moroni was "by the east sea; and it was on the south by the line of the possessions of the Lamanites" (Alma 50:13). The city of Nephihah was close to the city of Moroni (see Alma 62:25–30). The lands (departments or municipalities) of Zarahemla, Manti, Nephihah, Moroni, and Lehi were all part of the greater land of Zarahemla. This map illustrates the 61 BC march of Moroni and Pahoran from Zarahemla to Nephihah (Alma 62:14).

The Nephites had fortified the strategically located city of Moroni but were able to hold it for only five years (72 BC–67 BC), after which the Lamanites captured it. A few years later, the Lamanites still had possession of the city of Moroni. They fled there to escape the armies of the military leader Moroni: "Now when Moroni saw that they were fleeing before him, he did cause that his men should march forth against them, and slew many, and surrounded many others, and took them prisoners; and the remainder of them fled into the *land of Moroni*, which was *in the borders of the seashore*" (Alma 62:25; emphasis added). Soon, all the armies of the Lamanites were gathered together in the land of Moroni:

> And it came to pass that Moroni and his army did pursue them from city to city, until they were met by Lehi and Teancum; and the Lamanites fled from Lehi and Teancum, even down upon the *borders by the seashore*, until they came to the *land of Moroni*.

And the armies of the Lamanites were all gathered together, insomuch that they were all in one body in the *land of Moroni*. Now Ammoron, the king of the Lamanites was also with them.

And it came to pass that Moroni and Lehi and Teancum did encamp with their armies round about in the borders of the *land of Moroni*, insomuch that the Lamanites were encircled about in the borders *by the wilderness on the south*, and in the borders *by the wilderness on the east*. (Alma 62:32–34; emphasis added)

Moroni and his armies had recaptured a number of cities that the Lamanites had taken, including the city of Nephihah. From there, he met up with Lehi and Teancum, two of his military leaders. They marched toward the city of Moroni. Although we do not know the distance from the city of Nephihah to the city of Moroni, it may have been as much as fifty miles, as determined from the statement that "the Nephites and the Lamanites also were weary because of the *greatness of the march*" (Alma 62:35; emphasis added).

The hot, humid climate of the Peten jungle must have made marching difficult through the area. As a side note, we can assume that the heavy fighting took place during the dry season (November to May) or perhaps after the crops were harvested and prior to planting, which would be from December to February.

Teancum lost his life when he went into the city of Moroni by night and killed the Lamanite king, Ammoron. The last military battle of Moroni consisted of retaking the city of Moroni. The long war that had lasted for a good part of fifteen years was concluded at the end of 60 BC (see Alma 62:39).

The following two scriptural references indicate that the city of Moroni sank into the sea at the time of the great destruction that occurred when Christ was crucified. The location of the city is again consistent, as it is placed close to the ocean:

And the *city of Moroni* did sink into the depths of the sea, and the inhabitants thereof were drowned. (3 Nephi 8:9; emphasis added)

And behold, *the great city Moroni* have I caused to be sunk in the depths of the sea, and the inhabitants thereof to be drowned. (3 Nephi 9:4; emphasis added)

Some Mesoamerica Book of Mormon maps place the cities of Moroni and Nephihah near the Gulf of Mexico area. However, that location cannot be seriously entertained for the following reasons:

1. The city of Moroni was east of Zarahemla, not northwest. It was also on the south by the borders of the Lamanites who lived in the land of Nephi (highland Guatemala).

> Moroni and his armies had recaptured a number of cities that the Lamanites had taken, including the city of Nephihah.

2. The archaeological evidence pertaining to the Nephites is extremely strong in the Belize/Honduras area as compared to the Gulf of Mexico area during the same time period. The Gulf of Mexico is Olmec territory.

3. The purpose of the city of Moroni was to fortify the Nephite lands in the east wilderness. If the city of Moroni were near the Gulf of Mexico, the entire land of Zarahemla would be vulnerable. Further, the Nephites would have no need to try to stop the Lamanites from going into the land northward because the Lamanites would already be there.

> "John Sorenson erroneously placed Nephihah and Moroni along the Gulf of Mexico on his rotated map, thus distorting the accurate geographical location of these two cities."
>
> —Joseph Allen

The city of Nephihah was near the city of Moroni. Mormon writes, "And they also began a foundation for a city between the city of Moroni and the city of Aaron, joining the borders of Aaron and Moroni; and they called the name of *the city, or the land, Nephihah*" (Alma 50:14; emphasis added).

The city of Nephihah, as discussed earlier, was in the east wilderness. From the evidence in the Book of Mormon, as well as from the archaeological sites that have been identified in the Peten area, the city/land of Nephihah was probably in the Peten jungle of Guatemala. We place the city/land of Nephihah by the Peten/Belize boundary (near the city of Moroni). Many archaeological sites are located in the area of Belize, including the sites of Altun Ha and Pusilha, both of which manifest the same Maya word ending as Nephi(*hah*). Potential sites in the area where we propose that Nephihah was located are Caracol, Aguateca, and Seibal. You will note that on the map in figure 25–9, we have used Book of Mormon cities, placing them where the internal geography dictates. We have also included archaeological sites that date to the same time period under question.

We will not go into detail regarding all the scripture references to the city/land of Nephihah. A few scriptures relating to the subject, however, are worth mentioning.

The first reference consists of the Lamanites capturing the east wilderness cities that the Nephites had fortified. The question arises as to whether the city of Nephihah was captured by the Lamanites. The Nephites who were at the city of Moroni when it was captured by the Lamanites fled to the city of Nephihah:

> But it came to pass that Amalickiah would not suffer the Lamanites to go against the *city of Nephihah* to battle, but kept them down by the seashore, leaving men in every city to maintain and defend it.
>
> And thus he [Amalickiah] went on, taking possession of *many cities, the city of Nephihah*, and the city of Lehi, and the city of Omner, and the city of Gid, and the city of Mulek, all of which were on the east borders by the seashore. (Alma 51:25–26; emphasis added)

Exploring the Lands of the Book of Mormon

That's the reason the country of Belize exists today. A Chiapas government or a Guatemala government simply could not control its geographic area. The Maya Mountains divide Belize from the Peten jungle, and the Sierra de las Minas divide Guatemala from Belize. The Spanish offered the English pirates that section of land if they would quit pirating their ships, and the English wanted to profit from the special type of lumber in Belize (British Honduras). The Maya fled into the Peten and Guatemala, and the English brought in people of African descent to work the land. English became and still is the official language of the small, independent country of Belize.

To Moroni's great sorrow, the Lamanites captured the city of Nephihah (see Alma 59:11). However, within a year, by stratagem, the Nephites were able to recapture the city of Nephihah (see Alma 62:18–26). The recapture of the city of Nephihah is explained below.

> And it came to pass that Moroni and Pahoran, leaving a large body of men in the land of Zarahemla, took their march with a large body of men towards the land of Nephihah, being determined to overthrow the Lamanites in that city. (Alma 62:14)

En route from Zarahemla to Nephihah (see figure 25–9), Moroni and Pahoran encountered a large body of Lamanites. They killed many, but about four thousand covenanted to join the converted Lamanites, who by this time were called the people of Ammon (see Alma 62:15–17).

> When they [Moroni and Pahoran) had sent them [the surviving Lamanites] away they pursued their march towards *the land of Nephihah*. And it came to pass that when they had come to *the city of Nephihah*, they did pitch their tents in *the plains of Nephihah*, which is near *the city of Nephihah*. (Alma 62:18; emphasis added)
>
> And it came to pass that they [Moroni's soldiers] were all let down into the city [Nephihah] by night, by the means of their strong cords and their ladders; thus when the morning came they [the Nephite soldiers] were all within the walls of the city. . . . Thus had Moroni and Pahoran obtained the possession of the city of Nephihah without the loss of one soul. (Alma 62:23, 26)

The flat jungle land of the Peten meets the requirement of "the plains of Nephihah" as opposed to its being in a mountainous region.

Another description explains the importance of the location of the city of Nephihah. This has to do with the war that was being waged on the southwestern part of the land of Zarahemla. Nephite armies had been strategically placed to stop the Lamanites from

"To understand the geography of the Book of Mormon, we must adhere to the cardinal directions. Both the Book of Mormon and the Mesoamerica map demand such."

—Joseph Allen

going into Zarahemla or into the land northward. Two thousand sons of the converted Lamanites were called the "sons of Helaman" because Helaman was their military leader. In an epistle to Moroni, Helaman describes the valor and success of his small army in conjunction with the Nephite army of Antipus, who was fighting in the same area.

The "sons of Helaman" and the other Nephite armies who were defending the cities or lands of Manti, Zeezrom, Cumeni, Antiparah, and Judea had the Lamanites hemmed in to the point they impeded their march to the city of Zarahemla or to the city of Nephihah. Regarding the Lamanites, Helaman writes, "Neither durst they march down against the city of Zarahemla, neither durst they cross the head of Sidon, *over to the city of Nephihah*" (Alma 56:25; emphasis added).

This statement is included in an epistle that Helaman sent to Moroni recounting the state of the war with the Lamanites on the southwestern borders of the Nephites. The head of the river Sidon, the city of Zarahemla, and the city of Nephihah are all mentioned (see figure 25–9).

> The manner in which Mormon utilizes this war story to illustrate the battles we fight in this life is indeed revelatory.

The manner in which Mormon utilizes this war story to illustrate the battles we fight in this life is indeed revelatory (see the story about Chris Munson in chapter 29, "The Land of Zarahemla").

THE CITIES OF LEHI AND MORIANTON

And they also began in that same year [72 BC] to build many cities on the north, one in particular they called *Lehi*, which was in the north by the *borders of the seashore*. (Alma 50:15; emphasis added)

The city of Lehi was north of the city of Moroni. It was also on the borders of the east sea (see Alma 50:13–14). Just how far north the city of Lehi was located we are not told. However, it was apparently still in the east wilderness section (Peten-Belize). Therefore, we would not expect it to be as far north as the land (state) of Bountiful (Quintana Roo, Mexico). It may be somewhere near the Maya sites of Pusilha or Caracol—or perhaps as far north as Lamanai.

The Lamanites captured the city of Lehi. It was recaptured by the Nephites and again recaptured by the Lamanites, in whose control it remained for almost the duration of Book of Mormon history.

Lamoni was a Lamanite king during the same time period under question. Logically, the Lamanites, upon capturing the cities along the Caribbean, would have given one of them the name of a Lamanite king (Lamanai/Lamoni), making the Preclassic site of Lamanai one of the Book of Mormon cities referred to in the Book of Mormon.

The city of Morianton is a city located along the borders of the east sea and is mentioned in relationship to the city of Nephi. A serious contention arose between the land of Lehi and the land of Morianton in the year 68 BC (see figure 25–11):

FIGURE 25–10: The ruins of Lamanai are located in a beautiful setting about a forty-five-minute boat ride up the New River of Belize. It is southwest of the city of Orange Walk. Travelers also reach Lamanai by a dirt road that passes by a Mennonite community. The name *Laman Ayin* is associated with both water and crocodile and is a Book of Mormon name that has survived the centuries. The building here dates to the Book of Mormon time period. (Photo courtesy of Sheryl Lee Wilson)

And it came to pass that in the commencement of the twenty and fourth year of the reign of the judges [68 BC], there would also have been peace among the people of Nephi had it not been for a contention which took place among them concerning the land of Lehi, and the *land of Morianton*, which joined upon the borders of Lehi; both of which were *on the borders by the seashore*. (Alma 50:25; emphasis added)

This contention resulted in an attempt on the part of Morianton to go to the "land which was northward," where large bodies of water were located, probably the Mexico valley.

The location of the city of Morianton is rather clear, as it is near the city of Lehi and near the borders of the east sea (see also Alma 51:26).

Moroni's army did not stop the flight of Morianton until Morianton arrived at the narrow pass by the land of Desolation: "Therefore Moroni sent an army, with their camp, to head the people of Morianton, to stop their flight into the land northward. And it came to pass that they did not head them until they had come to the borders of the land Desolation; and there they did head them, by the narrow pass which led by the sea into the land northward, yea, by the sea, on the west and on the east" (Alma 50:33–34).

Morianton was met at the narrow pass by Teancum, who had been sent by Moroni. Apparently, Morianton and his followers moved through the states of Yucatan, Campeche, and Tabasco before Teancum caught them. A battle took place during which Morianton was killed, and his people were then taken back to Moroni. Following

The most likely place for the two armies to meet is in the area between Acayucan and Coatzacoalcos, Veracruz. This battle between Morianton and Teancum may have been the reason that a Nephite city located in that same area was named after Teancum.

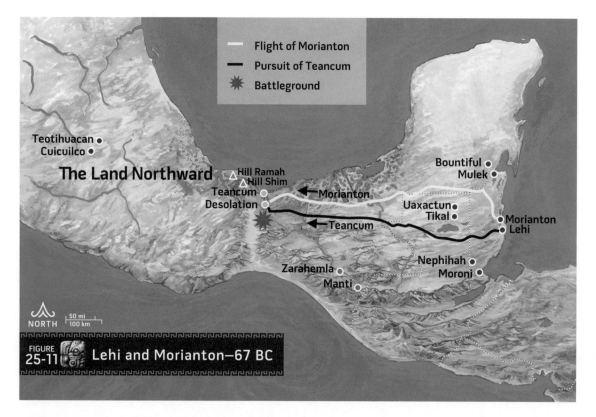

FIGURE 25–11: As illustrated on this map, the battle between the armies of Morianton and Teancum would have taken place near the hill Shim and the hill Ramah/Cumorah where four hundred years later the Nephite Maya would fall under the hands of the Lamanite Maya. The battle took place where there is a sea on the west and a sea on the east—or, in other words, where there is a gulf.

a covenant of peace, a land agreement was reached between the people of Lehi and Morianton.

The most likely place for the two armies to meet is in the area between Acayucan and Coatzacoalcos, Veracruz. This battle between Morianton and Teancum may have been the reason that a Nephite city located in that same area was named after Teancum: "Now the city Teancum lay in the borders by the seashore; and it was also near the city Desolation" (Mormon 4:3).

CITIES OF OMNER AND GID

And thus he [Amalickiah] went on, taking possession of many cities, the city of Nephihah, and the city of Lehi, and the city of Morianton, and the *city of Omner*, and the *city of Gid*, and the city of Mulek, all of which were on the *east borders by the seashore*. (Alma 51:26; emphasis added)

FIGURE 25–12: Model of Tikal, Peten, Guatemala. (Photo courtesy of Merrill C. Oaks)

The cities of Nephihah, Moroni, Mulek, Bountiful, Lehi, and Morianton have already been discussed. The placement of the cities of Omner and Gid must be along the Caribbean close to both the city of Mulek and the city of Bountiful. As mentioned previously, the area along the coast of Belize is a practical area for these eastern cities.

Alma 51:26 is the only reference to the city of Omner. However, the city of Gid is mentioned six more times. Abbreviated, the references are as follows:

Now the Nephites were guarded in *the city of Gid*. (Alma 55:7; 63 BC; emphasis added)

And Moroni had prepared his men with weapons of war; and he went to the *city Gid*, while the Lamanites were in a deep sleep and drunken, and cast in weapons of war unto the prisoners insomuch that they were all armed. (Alma 55:16; emphasis added)

And it came to pass that he [Moroni] did cause the Lamanites, whom he had taken prisoners, that they should commence a labor in strengthening the fortifications round about the *city Gid*. (Alma 55:25; emphasis added)

And it came to pass that when he had fortified the *city Gid*, according to his desires, he caused that his prisoners should be taken to the city Bountiful; and he also guarded that city with an exceedingly strong force. (Alma 55: 26; emphasis added)

Lehi and Nephi, the sons of Helaman, taught the gospel in the city Bountiful and in nearby cities beginning about 30 BC: "And from thenceforth [city Bountiful] to the city of Gid; and from the city of Gid to the city of Mulek."

The land of Jershon was south of the land Bountiful and was also east by the sea. The Nephites placed armies between the land of Jershon and the land of Nephi to protect the converts because they had taken an oath not to fight.

Lehi and Nephi, the sons of Helaman, taught the gospel in the city Bountiful and in nearby cities beginning about 30 BC: "And from thenceforth [city Bountiful] to the *city of Gid*; and from *the city of Gid* to the city of Mulek" (Helaman 5:15; emphasis added).

The above scriptures about the city of Gid provide both war and missionary work perspectives. Clearly, the city of Gid was rather close to the city of Bountiful and the city of Mulek, which have already been discussed in this chapter.

JERSHON AND ANTIONUM

And it came to pass that the voice of the people came, saying: Behold we will give up the *land of Jershon*, which is on the east by the sea, which joins the land Bountiful, which is on the south of the land Bountiful; and this land Jershon is the land which we will give unto our brethren for an inheritance. (Alma 27:22; emphasis added)

The converted Lamanites who migrated with Ammon and the other sons of Mosiah were given the land of Jershon as an inheritance. Because the Nephites gave the land of Jershon as a place of inheritance for the converted Lamanites (now called the people of Ammon) to live, the Nephites must have had control of the east wilderness because that is where the land of Jershon was located. Therefore, it must be considered as the wilderness east of Zarahemla—or Zarahemla's east wilderness. The land of Jershon was south of the land Bountiful and was also east by the sea. The Nephites placed armies between the land of Jershon and the land of Nephi to protect the converts because they had taken an oath not to fight.

In a scripture about the land of Antionum and the land of Jershon, we learn that the land of Jershon was also near an area that was full of Lamanites: "Now the Zoramites had gathered themselves together in a land which they called Antionum, which was east of the land of Zarahemla, which lay nearly bordering the seashore, which was south of the land of Jershon, which also bordered upon the wilderness south, which wilderness was full of the Lamanites" (Alma 31:3).

The statement about Jershon's joining the land Bountiful may suggest that it was close to the Mexican border and close to the archaeological sites of Kohunlich and Dzibanche (candidates for the city of Bountiful; see figure 25–4).

SUMMARY

The east wilderness of Zarahemla is the stage for many historical events in the Book of Mormon, such as the occasions when Moroni took his armies into the east wilderness, Alma took missionaries to preach the gospel into the east wilderness among the Zoramites, and Ammon took his people to the land of Jershon, which was located in the east wilderness. A long list of Book of Mormon people lived or passed through Zarahemla's east wilderness.

Although Book of Mormon scholars have designated several locations as the city/land Bountiful where the Savior appeared to the Nephites, the facts that the city of Bountiful was in the land or territory of Bountiful and that it was close (less than a day's march) to the city of Mulek, which was in the land or territory of the land of Zarahemla and which was on the east seashore, require Bountiful to be nearby.

We propose that the most viable location for the city/land Bountiful where the temple was located and where the Savior appeared is nearby the megalopolis centers of Dzibanche, Kinichna, and Kohunlich. Furthermore, the sites of Tikal, El Mirador, Tulum, Palenque, Izapa, and so forth that have been proposed sporadically as candidates for the city Bountiful fail to meet the distance and directional and historical criteria that are required. In other words, if we have found Mulek, we can identify Bountiful. And if we cannot locate a candidate for the city of Mulek that passes the test, the city of Bountiful becomes more difficult to identify.

FIGURE 25–13: Trees growing from an unexcavated mound at Tikal. (Photo courtesy of Merrill C. Oaks)

CHAPTER 26
Bodies of Water

And thus the land of Nephi and the land of Zarahemla were nearly surrounded by water. (Alma 22:32)

꧁꧁꧁꧁꧁꧁꧁꧁꧁꧁꧁꧁꧁꧁꧁꧁꧁꧁꧁꧁꧁꧁꧁꧁꧁꧁꧁꧁꧁꧁꧁꧁꧁꧁

A ny study of the geography of the Book of Mormon must necessarily include a discussion about Book of Mormon bodies of water. The bodies of water not only must exist but also must be in the same relative position and description as dictated internally by the Book of Mormon. That is, a river must be a river, and a lake must be a lake. Of vital importance also is the stipulation that the bodies of water interrelate with each other as well as with the other geographical features mentioned in the Book of Mormon. For example, the "land of many waters" must be situated in such a position that the 121 BC Limhi expedition would be unable to avoid the area en route from the land of Nephi in search of the land of Zarahemla, and the "large or to

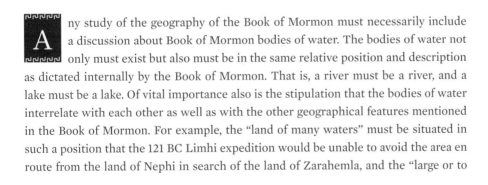

OPPOSITE: The Misol-Ha Waterfall near Palenque, Chiapas, Mexico, is representative of the abundance of water found in many areas in the Mesoamerica region. Several bodies of water are mentioned in the Book of Mormon, and they are discussed in this chapter. (Photo courtesy of Merrill C. Oaks)

exceed all" waters of Ripliancum must be in Jaredite territory close to the hill Ramah (Cumorah).

The principal bodies of water that deal with the internal geography of the Book of Mormon are the following:

1. The east sea and the west sea
2. The waters of Mormon
3. The waters of Sebus
4. A land of pure water
5. The river Sidon
6. The land of many waters
7. The place where the sea divides the land
8. The waters of Ripliancum
9. The land northward, which contained large bodies of water

You will get an initial overall perspective of the Mesoamerica locations we propose for these bodies of water when you reach figure 26–3.

1. THE EAST SEA AND THE WEST SEA

> The bodies of water not only must exist but also must be in the same relative position and description as dictated internally by the Book of Mormon.

The east sea is mentioned several times in conjunction with the west sea, such as in the proclamation by the Lamanite king when he indicated that the land of Nephi was separated from the land of Zarahemla by the narrow strip of wilderness that ran from the sea east even to the sea west (see Alma 22:27).

Most students who have attempted to relate Book of Mormon geography to a twenty-first-century map of Mesoamerica agree that the sea west is the Pacific Ocean. However, each "west sea" statement in the Book of Mormon must be analyzed in relation to this hypothesis. We must try to understand where any Book of Mormon person was living or standing at the time a statement about a west sea was made and under what circumstances the statement was made. Even today, a person may be standing along a certain coastline and, by looking in the correct cardinal direction, he or she could see the Pacific Ocean. For example, a person may be standing on the shores of the Gulf of Tehuantepec and look directly south into the Pacific Ocean (west sea). During the sixteenth century, some mapmakers who had a Central America orientation saw the Pacific Ocean (Gulf of Tehuantepec) as the south sea and the Atlantic Ocean (Gulf of Mexico) as the north Sea.

For the most part, however, the consistency of both Book of Mormon descriptions of the west sea and modern maps permits us to acknowledge that the sea that is west of the American continent, the Pacific Ocean, is the west sea in the Book of Mormon.

The initial east sea-west sea orientation in the Book of Mormon is given from a land of Nephi (Guatemala City) orientation. This orientation places the west sea in a

FIGURE 26–1: The concept that the land of Nephi and the land of Zarahemla were nearly surrounded by water (see Alma 22:32) is illustrated on a map of the western hemisphere. In *Exploring the Lands of the Book of Mormon*, we designate the Pacific Ocean as the west sea and the Atlantic Ocean as the east sea.

westerly direction (Pacific Ocean) and the east sea in an easterly direction (Atlantic Ocean).

Scriptures that refer to the west sea in the Book of Mormon, together with appropriate commentary, are as follows:

Alma 22:27—Sea East to Sea West

And it came to pass that the king sent a proclamation throughout all the land, amongst all his people who were in all his land, who were in all the regions round about, which was bordering even to the sea, on the east and on the west, and which was divided from the land of Zarahemla by a narrow strip of wilderness, which ran from the *sea east even to the sea west*, and round about on the borders of the seashore, and on the borders of the wilderness which was on the north by the land of Zarahemla. (emphasis added)

This scripture is the first time that the sea west is mentioned in the Book of Mormon. It is part of Mormon's abridgement of the large plates of Nephi and relates to the Preclassic Maya and Classic Nephite historical period of 90 BC–72 BC. The circumstances revolve around the missionary experiences of the sons of Mosiah in the land of Nephi. After the sons of Mosiah had a somewhat shaky period in their young lives, they dedicated themselves to preaching the gospel of Christ among the Lamanites.

The sons of Mosiah eventually gained the confidence of the Lamanite king who was king over all the Lamanite territory that was called the land of Nephi. Aaron, one of the sons of Mosiah, preached the gospel to the king; and the king and his household were converted. Subsequently, the king sent a proclamation throughout all the land of Nephi, forbidding the people to harm the sons of Mosiah and, for missionary purposes, giving the sons of Mosiah access to the Lamanites' houses, temples, and sanctuaries.

We propose that the highlands of Guatemala are the land of Nephi. From the perspective of the Guatemala highlands, the sea west is directly west of Guatemala, running along the west coasts of El Salvador, Guatemala, and southern Mexico. Therefore, the sea west is the Pacific Ocean.

Alma 22:32—From the East to the West Sea

And now, it was only the distance of a day and a half's journey for a Nephite, on the line Bountiful and the land Desolation, *from the east to the west sea*; and thus the land of Nephi and the land of Zarahemla were nearly surrounded by water, there being a small neck of land between the land northward and the land southward. (emphasis added)

As pointed out in chapter 23, "Things That Are Narrow," this scripture is one of the most misquoted geographical statements in the Book of Mormon. Many Book of Mormon readers interpret this statement as reading "from the east sea to the west sea." However, the scripture does not say that. It says "from the *east* to the west sea." Mormon is very consistent in both his terminology and his geographical statements. If he had meant the east sea, he would have said the east sea. And if the Prophet Joseph Smith had read "east sea" in the translation process, he would have put *east sea* in the text.

This point may seem a minor one; but from a west sea-east sea geographical perspective, the distinction makes a major difference in our overall understanding of Book of Mormon geography. Changing the wording in the Book of Mormon from "east" to "east sea" has caused some writers in the past literally to rotate the Mesoamerica map and to inaccurately label the Gulf of Mexico as the "east sea."[1] That type of reasoning not only violates the inherent direction implied in the designated name "sea east" but also distorts other geographical landmarks in the Book of Mormon where the sea east is involved.

1. See, for example, John L. Sorenson, *An Ancient American Setting for the Book of Mormon* (Salt Lake City: Deseret Book and Foundation for Ancient Research and Mormon Studies, 1985), and David A. Palmer, *In Search of Cumorah: New Evidences for the Book of Mormon from Ancient Mexico* (Bountiful, UT: Horizon Publishers, 1981).

A greater problem, however, is the distance a Nephite would have to travel from the so-called sea east to the sea west. Wherever we place the sea east—that is, whether we place it along the Gulf of Mexico or in the Caribbean—the distance between the two seas is too great for a Nephite to travel in a day and a half, regardless of his physical condition. The highway distance from the Gulf of Tehuantepec (sea west) to the Gulf of Mexico (designated by some writers in the past to be the sea east) is about 150 miles. It is four times that far to the Caribbean. This subject is also discussed in chapter 18, "Geography and the Plan of Salvation."

Alma 22:33—From the East unto the West Sea

And it came to pass that the Nephites had inhabited the land Bountiful, even from *the east unto the west sea*, and thus the Nephites in their wisdom, with their guards and their armies, had hemmed in the Lamanites on the south, that thereby they should have no more possession on the north, that they might not overrun the land northward. (emphasis added)

This reference immediately follows Alma 22:32 and is similar to it. In fact, Alma 22:33 solidifies the *west sea* statement. To keep the Lamanites from moving into the land northward, the Nephites had to fortify the area along the west sea (Gulf of Tehuantepec on the Pacific Ocean).

Like the previous scripture, the east sea does not figure in this discussion. The Nephites inhabited the land Bountiful (land southward) from the east (not *east sea*) to the west sea. Recall that the Nephites called the land southward "Bountiful" (see Alma 22:31).

Alma 50:11—From the West Sea

And thus he cut off all the strongholds of the Lamanites in the east wilderness, yea, and also on the west, fortifying the line between the Nephites and the Lamanites, between the land of Zarahemla and the land of Nephi, from *the west sea*, running by the head of the river Sidon—the Nephites possessing all the land northward, yea, even all the land which was northward of the land Bountiful, according to their pleasure. (emphasis added)

Moroni, the chief commander of the Nephites, fortified the lands of the Nephites. He cut off the Lamanites on the west by fortifying the line between the Nephites and Lamanites all the way from the west sea over to the headwaters of the river Sidon. The Nephites possessed all of the land north of this fortified line. This event took place about 72 BC.

Changing the wording in the Book of Mormon from "east" to "east sea" has caused some writers in the past literally to rotate the Mesoamerica map and to inaccurately label the Gulf of Mexico as the "east sea."

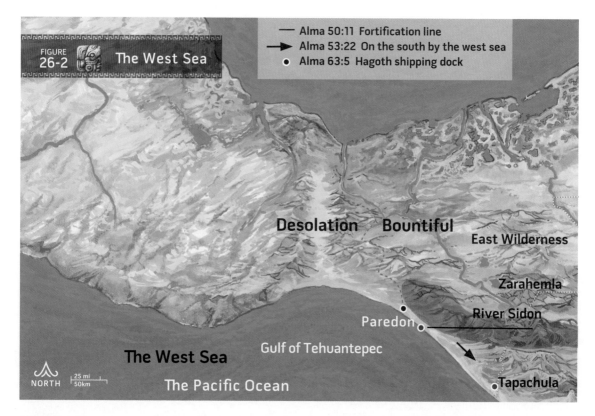

FIGURE 26–2: This map illustrates the proposed fortification line from the west sea to the headwaters of the river Sidon (Grijalva River). The Nephites designed this fortification line to stop the Lamanites from going along the Pacific coast and moving into Zarahemla or entering into Oaxaca or Veracruz. This is also the area where the sons of Helaman fought along the "west sea, south." And Hagoth launched his ships in the west sea by the narrow pass that led into the land northward. The red dotted line between Desolation and Bountiful is the boundary line.

Alma 52:11–12—Borders of the Land by the West Sea

The east wilderness was located east of the city of Zarahemla and was probably in the area of present-day Peten and Belize.

And he also said unto him, I would come unto you, but behold, the Lamanites are upon us in the *borders of the land by the west sea*; and behold, I go against them, therefore I cannot come unto you.

Now, the king (Ammoron) had departed out of the land of Zarahemla, and had made known unto the queen concerning the death of his brother, and had gathered together a large number of men, and had marched forth against the Nephites *on the borders by the west sea.* (emphasis added)

About 66 BC, Teancum, a great Nephite warrior, killed the Lamanite king, whose name was Amalickiah, in a Lamanite-Nephite war that was fought in the east wilderness (see Alma 51:33–34). The east wilderness was located east of the city of Zarahemla and was probably in the area of present-day Peten and Belize. The brother of Amalickiah, whose name was Ammoron, became the king of the Lamanites after the death of his

Exploring the Lands of the Book of Mormon

brother. Both Amalickiah and Ammoron were former Nephites. A year after the death of Amalickiah, his brother, Ammoron, devised a plan to weaken the armies of the Nephites in the east wilderness. Ammoron did this by sending an army of Lamanites to march against the Nephites on the borders by the west sea.

We propose that the area near the west sea where Ammoron sent a large army was in the areas between present-day Tapachula and Paredon, Mexico. The border of Mexico and Guatemala is located near Tapachula. The Izapa ruins, which date to the time period under discussion, are close to Tapachula (see figure 26–2).

Alma 53:8—West Sea, South

And now it came to pass that the armies of the Lamanites, on the *west sea, south*, while in the absence of Moroni on account of some intrigue amongst the Nephites, which caused dissensions amongst them, had gained some ground over the Nephites, yea, insomuch that they had obtained possession of a number of their cities in that part of the land. (emphasis added; see figure 26–2).

The geographical description "west sea, south" is an intriguing and a very descriptive directional statement. The location that is described is probably the same as the preceding scripture—near Tapachula, Mexico—and, as a result, is close to the archaeological sites of Izapa and Tonala. This directional statement fits nicely on the Mesoamerica map.

Alma 63:5—Hagoth Launched Ship into West Sea

And it came to pass that Hagoth, he being an exceedingly curious man, therefore he went forth and built him an exceedingly large ship, on the borders of the land Bountiful, by the land Desolation, and launched it forth into the west sea, by the narrow neck which led into the land northward. (See figure 26–2.)

The place along the Pacific Ocean where Hagoth launched his ships is by the narrow neck—or by the Isthmus of Tehuantepec.

This scripture is comparable to Alma 22:32 because it utilizes the boundaries of the land Bountiful (land southward) and the land of Desolation (land northward) to establish the east-west point of where Hagoth launched his ships. The west sea is the Pacific Ocean. The place along the Pacific Ocean where Hagoth launched his ships is by the narrow neck—or by the Isthmus of Tehuantepec. During this period of time, many people migrated by ship into the land northward. The land northward in this scenario may have been the west coast of Mexico where present-day Acapulco and Puerto Vallarta are located.

The area is very suitable for shipbuilding. Even today as we travel from Salina Cruz by the Gulf of Tehuantepec through the narrow pass to Acayucan, numerous logging trucks and sawmills are in evidence.

Alma 50:34—By the Sea, on the West and on the East

And it came to pass that they did not head them until they had come to the borders of the land Desolation; and there they did head them, by the narrow pass which led by the sea into the land northward, yea, by the sea, *on the west and on the east*. (emphasis added)

The above scripture is not a sea west statement. As discussed earlier, this verse seems to be referring to the Gulf of Mexico and also appears to be the same area labeled "the place where the sea divides the land" (Ether 10:20).

Helaman 3:8—From the Sea South to the Sea North, from the Sea West to the Sea East

And it came to pass that they did multiply and spread, and did go forth from the land southward to the land northward, and did spread insomuch that they began to cover the face of the whole earth, *from the sea south to the sea north, from the sea west to the sea east*. (emphasis added)

Helaman 3:8 presents an interesting situation. This scripture has caused some Book of Mormon students to place a sea north and a sea south on an internal geographical map.

Perhaps this scripture should be read as more of a generalized statement as opposed to a specific geographical statement. We get a small clue in this respect when Mormon states that the people "began to cover the face of the whole earth." The term "whole earth" sounds rather all-encompassing; however, in typical Hebrew writing, "all" means a "localized all."

If this scripture is a generalized statement, then it means that people began to settle all over the land; and the terms "sea south," "sea north," "sea west," and "sea east" simply mean that people spread out all over the land. A Mesoamerica map does not pose a directional problem, as bodies of water are found on the north, south, east, and west. It is just more likely that the two seas in the Book of Mormon called "sea south" and "sea north" provide general directions. This is the only scriptural reference that refers to these two seas. On the other hand, both *sea east* and *sea west* are used extensively as specific geographical locations throughout the Book of Mormon.

Helaman 11:20—Sea West to Sea East

And thus it did come to pass that the people of Nephi began to prosper again in the land, and began to build up their waste places, and began to multiply and spread, even until they did cover the whole face of the land, both on the northward and on the southward, from the *sea west to the sea east*. (emphasis added)

> The term "whole earth" sounds rather all-encompassing; however, in typical Hebrew writing, "all" means a "localized all."

This scripture is similar in context to the previous one. People who lived just prior to the coming of Christ began to populate throughout the land. The terms "sea south" and "sea north" are left out of this statement, and it, too, appears to be a general geographical statement in nature.

Alma 27:22—On the East by the Sea

And it came to pass that the voice of the people came, saying: Behold, we will give up the land of Jershon, which is *on the east by the sea*, which joins the land Bountiful, which is on the south of the land Bountiful; and this land Jershon is the land which we will give unto our brethren for an inheritance. (emphasis added)

The land of Jershon was a place that was given by the Nephites to the Lamanite converts of Ammon. Ammon was one of the sons of Mosiah who spent fourteen years among the Lamanites in the land of Nephi. While living in the land of Nephi among the Lamanites, the converted Lamanites were called the people of Anti-Nephi-Lehi, after the Lamanite king whose name was Anti-Nephi-Lehi.

The land of Jershon was located in such a position so as to protect the people of Ammon from Lamanites who might come into the land of Zarahemla. The sea referred to in this scripture is undoubtedly the east sea. Alma 27:23 indicates that the Nephites placed an army between the land of Jershon and the land of Nephi. The land of Jershon was just south of the border of the land Bountiful and was north of the land of Nephi. Therefore, Mormon gives us a north, south, and east direction to spell out where the land of Jershon was located.

A projection on today's map places the land of Nephi in highland Guatemala. The Nephites placed their armies north of that and along the Caribbean by Belize. The converted Lamanites moved to the land of Jershon, which was north of both the land of Nephi and the Nephite army and yet south of the land (state) of Bountiful.

Alma 50:8—From the East Sea to the West

And the land of Nephi did run in a straight course from the east sea *to the west*. (emphasis added)

This statement is consistent with statements about the west sea coming from the opposite direction. The dividing boundary line of the Lamanites who lived in the land of Nephi was at a point probably near the Honduras-Belize-Guatemala border following the mountain range toward the Pacific Ocean.

> The converted Lamanites were called the people of Anti-Nephi-Lehi, after the Lamanite king whose name was Anti-Nephi-Lehi.

Alma 50:13—It Was by the East Sea

And it came to pass that the Nephites began the foundation of a city, and they called the name of the city Moroni; and *it was by the east sea*; and it was on the south by the line of the possessions of the Lamanites. (emphasis added)

This verse gives an excellent description for the location of the city of Moroni and also confirms the position of the east sea. When we take into consideration the preceding scripture, Alma 50:8, the northern boundary of the land of Nephi ran in a straight course from the sea east to the west. In this scripture, the Nephites built a city called Moroni in the southern boundaries of the Nephites by the line of the possessions of the Lamanites. The city of Moroni was built by the east sea. The city of Moroni sank into the sea at the time of the great earthquake 105 years after the city was first built.

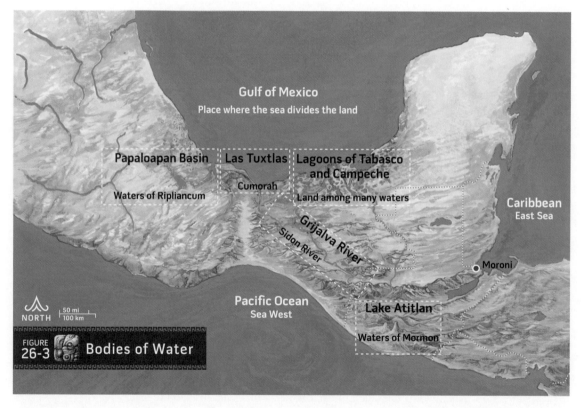

FIGURE 26–3: Basic Book of Mormon geography consists of an east sea, a west sea, a narrow strip of wilderness, the land of Nephi, and the land of Zarahemla. However, the finite testing of all geographical statements in relation to each other either proves or disproves any hypothesis on the subject of Book of Mormon historical geography. This map illustrates areas where bodies of water are mentioned in relationship to lands, rivers, cities, hills, and so forth—all in relation to the Mesoamerica map.

Exploring the Lands of the Book of Mormon

Alma 52:13—On the Borders by the East Sea

And thus he [Ammoron] was endeavoring to harass the Nephites, and to draw away a part of their forces to that part of the land, while he had commanded those whom he had left to possess the cities which he had taken, that they should also harass the Nephites *on the borders by the east sea*, and should take possession of their lands as much as it was in their power, according to the power of their armies. (emphasis added)

This scripture was discussed in the section on the west sea. Moroni had initiated a military campaign to drive the Lamanites out of the east wilderness (Peten, Guatemala, and Belize). The Nephites built many cities and fortified them with the intent to keep the Lamanites in their own lands (highland Guatemala).

The Lamanites captured some Nephite cities in the east wilderness; and, in return, the Nephites recaptured some of the same cities. The Lamanites countered by sending an army along the west sea with the intent of weakening the armies in the east wilderness and of retaking all the cities along the east sea.

In the big picture, the east sea is located along the Caribbean Sea, which forms the eastern borders for the country of Belize and the state of Quintana Roo, Mexico.

2. THE WATERS OF MORMON

The Book of Mormon refers to the waters of Mormon in eight scriptural references. All the references relate to the activities that took place in or near the waters of Mormon as opposed to descriptions about a specific geographical location. Six of those references are as follows:

1. "Behold, here are the *waters of Mormon*" (Mosiah 18:8; emphasis added).
2. "They were baptized in the *waters of Mormon*" (Mosiah 18:16; emphasis added).
3. "And now it came to pass that all this was done in Mormon, yea, *by the waters of Mormon, in the forest that was near the waters of Mormon; yea, the place of Mormon, the waters of Mormon, the forest of Mormon*, how beautiful are they to the eyes of them who there came to the knowledge of their Redeemer; yea, and how blessed are they, for they shall sing to his praise forever" (Mosiah 18:30; emphasis added).
4. "Therefore, Alma did go forth into the water and did baptize them; yea, he did baptize them after the manner he did his brethren in the *waters of Mormon*; yea, and as many as he did baptize did belong to the church of God; and this because of their belief on the words of Alma" (Mosiah 25:18; emphasis added).
5. "Blessed art thou, Alma, and blessed are they who were baptized in the *waters of Mormon*. Thou art blessed because of thy exceeding faith in the words alone of my servant Abinadi" (Mosiah 26:15; emphasis added).
6. "He did baptize his brethren in the *waters of Mormon*" (Alma 5:3; emphasis added).

> In the big picture, the east sea is located along the Caribbean Sea, which forms the eastern borders for the country of Belize and the state of Quintana Roo, Mexico.

Noah, who was a Nephite king living in Lamanite territory, was a son of Zeniff and the father of Limhi. Alma, who in approximately 148 BC organized the Church of Christ at the waters of Mormon, or the land of Mormon, had been a priest in the court of the Nephite King Noah in the land of Nephi.

The prophet Abinadi suffered death by fire at the hands of King Noah. Alma began to preach in private to the Nephites in the land of Nephi. Subsequently, Alma and his followers went forth to the place they called the waters of Mormon, which was in the forest in the land of Mormon:

> And it came to pass that as many as did believe him did go forth to a place which was called Mormon, having received its name from the king, being in the borders of the land having been infested, by times or at seasons, by wild beasts.
>
> Now, there was in Mormon a fountain of pure water, and Alma resorted thither, there being near the water a thicket of small trees, where he did hide himself in the daytime from the searches of the king. . . .
>
> And it came to pass that he said unto them: Behold, here are the waters of Mormon. (Mosiah 18:4–5, 8)

The distance from Kaminaljuyu, proposed city of Nephi, to Lake Atitlan, proposed waters of Mormon, is about eighty miles.

We are not told just how far the waters of Mormon, or the land of Mormon, is from the city of Lehi-Nephi and the city of Shilom. Because the waters of Mormon was located on the borders of the greater land of Nephi and because the land of Ishmael was between the city of Nephi and the land of Mormon, we can deduce that the distance between the city of Nephi and the land of Mormon was substantial. In addition, because the land of Mormon was located near a forest of wild beasts, from whence it gets its name, we can deduce that the distance was considerable. The distance from Kaminaljuyu, proposed city of Nephi, to Lake Atitlan, proposed waters of Mormon, is about eighty miles:

> And these things were done *in the borders of the land, that they might not come to the knowledge of the king.*
>
> But behold, it came to pass that the king, having discovered a movement among the people, sent his servants to watch them. Therefore on the day that they were assembling themselves together to hear the word of the Lord they were discovered unto the king. (Mosiah 18:31–32; emphasis added)

Lake Atitlan and the Waters of Mormon

We propose that these events took place at Lake Atitlan, which is located in one of the world's most beautiful settings. Flanked by three volcanoes, it is nestled picturesquely in the valley of a massive geological crater. Lake Atitlan is a freshwater lake, and several villages surround it. Spanish and the Cakchiquel and Quiche-Maya languages, along

FIGURE 26–4: Lake Atitlan shown here is located in Solola, Guatemala. Lake Atitlan is located about eighty miles west of Guatemala City and is a popular area for visitors. The lake is situated about five thousand feet above sea level with a depth of a thousand feet. We propose that Lake Atitlan is the location of the waters of Mormon and the forest of Mormon. (Photo courtesy of Chad Clark)

with other dialects, are spoken in the area of the lake. Several features qualify Lake Atitlan as a viable candidate for the waters of Mormon, including the following: (1) its distance from Guatemala City (city of Nephi) is not excessive, (2) it is located on the "borders of the land," (3) underwater archaeology has revealed Preclassic Period pottery (200 BC to AD 200) close to the shores of the lake, and (4) the distance and direction to Almolonga (land of pure water) agree with Book of Mormon statements.

If Lake Atitlan is the waters of Mormon and if the city of Lehi-Nephi (Nephi; see Mosiah 9:6–8, 14–15) is in the area of Guatemala City, then approximately ten days of travel time were required for Alma and his converts to travel to the land of Mormon.

Lake Atitlan also meets the requirement stipulated in Mosiah 18:5: "There was in Mormon a fountain of pure water, and Alma resorted thither, there being near the water a thicket of small trees, where he did hide himself in the daytime from the searches of the king." Both fountains of natural water and thickets of trees are identifiable at Panajachel, a city by the lake. And the jacuzzi at Hotel del Lago facing the lake comes from natural hot springs—or a fountain of pure water.

We receive additional help about both the land of Mormon and the waters of Mormon from the account of the missionary efforts of the sons of Mosiah, about 90 BC. Having traveled up from the land of Zarahemla in a southward direction, they arrived at the borders of the Lamanites. The brothers and their missionary companions separated themselves to preach in different sections of the country. Aaron, one of the sons of Mosiah, went to a land called Jerusalem, which bordered the land of Mormon: "Now when Ammon and his brethren separated themselves in the borders of the land of the Lamanites, behold Aaron took his journey towards the land which was called by the Lamanites, Jerusalem, calling it after the land of their fathers' nativity; and it was away joining the *borders of Mormon*. Now the Lamanites and the Amalekites and the people of Amulon had built a great city, which was called Jerusalem" (Alma 21:1–2; emphasis added).

The city of Jerusalem was covered with water at the time of the Crucifixion of Christ—or, as the scripture states, "waters have I caused to come up in the stead thereof" (see 3 Nephi 9:7). That language is distinctively different from the words Mormon used in describing the destruction of the city of Moroni: "That great city Moroni have I caused to be sunk in the depths of the sea." Thus, waters "came up" to cover the city of Jerusalem, whereas Moroni "sank into" the sea. This distinction helps us understand that Jerusalem's demise probably came about as a result of volcanic and hurricane activities.

Knowing that Jerusalem bordered the land of Mormon or the waters of Mormon, we can assume that Jerusalem was located near Lake Atitlan. According to Bruce Warren and Thomas Ferguson, "During a period of low water in the 1930s, ruins were detected in the water [Lake Atitlan], and Samuel Lothrop, then with Harvard, was able to recover some ceramics which had the same style and pattern as the Miraflores ceramics from nearby Kaminaljuyu and dated from about the time of Christ, as did the ash layer immediately beneath the Ilopango volcano in El Salvador. It is reasonable to hypothesize that this city in the lake was Preclassic, was occupied near the time of Christ, and was

FIGURE 26–5: As reflected in this picture, Lake Atitlan is a highland lake surrounded by forests and volcanoes. (Photo courtesy of Cortney Boice)

covered subsequently by the lake waters. There are, interestingly, several volcanoes in the mountains surrounding the lake."[2] From our discussions with the local natives, we know they are aware of this ancient underwater city and have given it the name of Chiutinamit, which means "city by the lake," with an implied meaning that it is covered over by mud and water.

FIGURE 26–6: View of Lake Atitlan with volcanoes in the background. (Photo courtesy of Phil Skousen)

2. Bruce W. Warren and Thomas S. Ferguson, *The Messiah in Ancient America* (Provo, UT: Book of Mormon Research Foundation, 1987), 44.

During the first decade of the twenty-first century, as a result of underwater archaeology, artifacts dating to the time of Christ have been discovered in other areas of the lake. The pottery style is called Miraflores, which is the same style as pottery that has been discovered at Kaminaljuyu dating to the Preclassic Period.

This is an important discovery because the Nephite time period from King Noah to the time of the destruction at the death of Christ falls in this period. Furthermore, it shows that the same people who lived at Kaminaljuyu are related to some of the people who were living at Lake Atitlan during this time period.

In addition to artifacts that were originally discovered at the place called Chiutinamit, artifacts from at least two other places around the lake have been excavated. These artifacts correlate with information contained in the Book of Mormon. Not only was Jerusalem destroyed at the time of Christ but also two other cities were covered over by water—Mocum and Onihah, both of which are Maya words (see 3 Nephi 9:7).

Questions: In Alma 17:13–19, we read that when the sons of Mosiah and the missionaries who were with them arrived in the borders of the land of the Lamanites, they separated themselves one from another. Ammon went to the land of Ishmael. We then read in Alma 21:1–2 that Aaron took his journey "towards the land which was called . . . Jerusalem," which "was away joining the borders of Mormon." First, do we know where the place is that the Nephite missionaries were blessed and then separated themselves one from another? Second, is the land of Jerusalem a separate land from the land of Mormon?

Answers: As to where the missionaries were blessed and then separated themselves from one another, we receive some help from the movement of the people who followed Alma from the city/land of Nephi to the land or waters of Mormon. Mormon was *in the borders of the land* of Nephi—the same description as provided by Ammon and Aaron—and Mormon was infested "by times or at seasons, by wild beasts" (Mosiah 18:4). The word *Mormon* is associated with both wilderness and wild beasts (see chapter 1, "An Introduction to the Lands of the Book of Mormon"). Alma uses the terms "waters of Mormon," "place of Mormon," "forest of Mormon," "the forest that was near the waters of Mormon," and simply "Mormon" (see Mosiah 18:30). In 3 Nephi 5:12, the

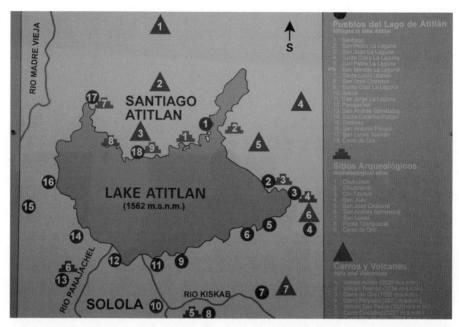

FIGURE 26–7: Several villages are located around Lake Atitlan, as shown in the map. (Photo courtesy of Merrill C. Oaks)

If Lake Atitlan is the waters of Mormon, then the place of separation of the missionaries (borders of the land) would be near the area that today is called Los Encuentros (where the roads meet).

term "land of Mormon" is used. In Mosiah 18:31, the term *"in the borders of the land"* is used again.

If Lake Atitlan is the waters of Mormon, then the place of separation of the missionaries (borders of the land) would be near the area that today is called Los Encuentros (where the roads meet). At these crossroads, north leads to Chichicastenango, east leads to Guatemala City, west leads to Quetzaltenango, and the fourth road leads down (south) to Lake Atitlan, which is located in the department of Solola.

Alma's people would have arrived at this same spot, having traveled in an east-to-west direction from the city/state of Nephi to the borders of the land of Nephi. The sons of Mosiah would have arrived at the same place, Los Encuentros, by traveling in a southeast direction from Zarahemla. Both Alma and his followers and Aaron and the missionaries who went with him would have dropped down to the lake, a distance of about twelve miles. The lake is visible from the main highway as we travel on our tours from Guatemala City to Los Encuentros.

We can test the hypothesis as to whether the land of Mormon, where the waters of Mormon is located, is the same as the department of Solola where Lake Atitlan is located by using the criteria established in chapter 1—that is, the criteria of archaeology, language, customs, and geography. However, before doing that, we will respond to the second question.

Land of Jerusalem and Land of Mormon

Is the land of Jerusalem a separate land from the land of Mormon? Answer: Yes. The lake appears to be literally a dividing line between the place where Alma took his followers and the land the Lamanites called "Jerusalem, calling it after the land of their fathers' nativity; and it was away joining the borders of Mormon" (Alma 21:1–2).

Eighteen villages are located near and around Lake Atitlan (see figure 26–7), including Santiago Atitlan, which is "away" on the other side, or south side, of the lake and which manifests a different language than that spoken on the north side of the lake where Panajachel and Solola are located. The spoken language at Santiago Atitlan is called Tzutuhil. The statement that Aaron took his journey toward the land of Jerusalem, which "was away joining the borders of Mormon," is equivalent to saying that we crossed Lake Atitlan to go to Santiago Atitlan, which was away (on the other side of the lake), bordering Lake Atitlan.

We will now apply the criteria of archaeology, language, customs, and geography in helping us relate to the words of the Book of Mormon about the waters of Mormon and the land of Mormon.

Archaeological Evidence

Although the Tzutuhil people who live at Santiago Atitlan today did not migrate into the area until after the close of the Book of Mormon, archaeological evidence shows that people lived there during the time periods of Alma and the sons of Mosiah. Figure 26–8 shows pottery that was retrieved from the water on the Santiago Atitlan side of the lake from villages that have been covered over with volcanic mudslides and water. To understand what is going on, we *must* note the difference in terminology used by Mormon when he refers to the cities that were destroyed at the time of Christ. Jerusalem, Mocum, and Onihah had waters "come up in the stead thereof" (3 Nephi 9:7). That language is different from the wording used by Mormon in describing the city of Moroni when it "did sink into the depths of the sea" (3 Nephi 8:9).

The facts that Jerusalem, Mocum, and Onihah are mentioned in the same verse and were destroyed by water coming "up in the stead thereof" may suggest that all three cities were lake cities located in the land of Nephi—or Lamanite territory. All the rest of the destroyed cities mentioned in 3 Nephi 9:1–9 are north of the narrow strip of wilderness. For example, Gilgal is a Jaredite city in the land northward (Ether 13:27), and Moroni was in the east wilderness of Zarahemla, by the seashore, "on the south by the line of the possessions of the Lamanites" (Alma 50:13).

We propose that the three lake cities, as a result of the massive volcanic and hurricane activities, did not sink. They were covered over with water and debris. From what we can learn from both land and underwater archaeology, the terrible mudslides from the overlooking volcanoes at Lake Atitlan would have covered the cities with both water and mud. This same thing happened on October 5, 2005, in a village called

> The facts that Jerusalem, Mocum, and Onihah are mentioned in the same verse and were destroyed by water coming "up in the stead thereof" may suggest that all three cities were lake cities located around Lake Atitlan.

FIGURE 26–8: Pottery dating to the Alma and sons of Mosiah period has been discovered under the lake near Santiago Atitlan. (Photo courtesy of Merrill C. Oaks)

Right two ceramics date in range of 200 BC to AD 200

FIGURE 26–9: Picture of a preclassic artifact taken from Lake Atitlan. (Photo courtesy of Merrill C. Oaks)

Período Preclásico Tardío (600 a.C.-300 d.C.)

Panabaj near Santiago Atitlan. The mudslide from the rain-soaked volcano near Santiago Atitlan covered homes and took the lives of fourteen hundred people who were buried in a vast river of congealed mud up to forty feet deep. The devastating rains associated with Hurricane Stan prompted the statement that "there were no children left . . . [and] there were no people left." One seventy-two-year-old man said, "I lost all of my children. . . . I lost all of their children." Some of our friends lost family members in that devastating mudslide.

The force and amount of earthen matter that would have entered into the lake at the time of Christ would have caused both mud and water to cover portions of the cities. Waves would have reached upwards of fifty feet high and would have landed with a thunderous water explosion over the cities. Artifacts have been discovered dating from 200 BC to AD 200 at sites proposed to be the cities of Jerusalem, Mocum, and Onihah (see figure 26–9).

We make a mistake if we assume these cities sank into the lake. Lake Atitlan is a crater lake several thousand feet deep. Things that have fallen into the center of the lake or people who have drowned near the center of the lake have never been recovered, including soldiers whose barge overturned and missionaries whose boat capsized.

Language

Mormon. The Book of Mormon defines the land of Mormon as a place where it was infested "by times or at seasons by wild beasts." The forest, or wilderness, surrounding Lake Atitlan is in a land in which wild beasts migrate down near the lake for food and water during the dry season. It is also a wilderness area where dissidents to the central government of Guatemala can hide out.

Jerusalem. King Noah named the place Mormon, which means wilderness of wild beasts (see Mosiah 18:1, 4). This naming suggests that both Alma and the other ex-priests of Noah knew where the lake was located. Alma sought it as a place to hide out, and the wicked priests built a city named Jerusalem where they could continue practicing their style of the law of Moses. Although we know of no name correlation with the word *Jerusalem*, by locating the ex-priests of Noah at the lake, we see a reasonable opportunity for it to be located on the borders of the waters of Mormon because that is an area that was familiar to them.

Mocum and Onihah. *Mocum* and *Ohihah* are Maya names associated with water. *Cum* from *Mocum* is a squash gourd and is used to denote a water basin or water container. *Oni-hah* means "ancient waters" in the Chorti-Maya language. The Maya names of the archaeological sites where artifacts have been retrieved from the lake near Santiago Atitlan dating to the Late Preclassic (200 BC–AD 200) are Chiutinamit, Chukumuk, and Cerro de Oro.

Chiutinamit means "village by the lake" in the Tzutuhil language. *Chukumuk* means "village beneath the hill" in the same language. And *Cerro de Oro* is Spanish for "hill of gold." Artifacts have also been retrieved from the lake dating to the Classic and Postclassic Periods.

Customs and History

The people in and around Lake Atitlan speak several different dialects. They dress in native attire and exhibit many of the ancient customs, such as "clapping their hands for joy," "carrying burdens on their backs," and using weights and measures that are equivalent to those described in the Book of Mormon. Lake Atitlan is located within a few miles of the areas where the *Popol Vuh*, *The Title of the Lords of Totonicapan*, and *The Annals of the Cakchiquels* were written. (See chapter 10, "Ancient Mesoamerican Documents," for further information about these ancient documents.)

Geography

If Kaminaljuyu is the city/state of Nephi and if Almolonga is the land of Helam, then Lake Atitlan is the waters of Mormon. The distance, directions, language, and cultural comparisons match. (See chapter 24, "Wilderness Areas," and chapter 28, "The Land of Nephi," for additional support for this geographical reasoning.) Some have suggested that Mormons get carried away with the beauty of Lake Atitlan and, for that reason, want to identify it with the waters of Mormon. Although objective evidence supports the hypothesis that Lake Atitlan is a likely candidate for the waters of Mormon, the beauty of it is not a detriment. After all, Alma is the one who related to the waters of

> The people in and around Lake Atitlan speak several different dialects. They dress in native attire and exhibit many of the ancient customs, such as "clapping their hands for joy."

FIGURE 26–10: Young Maya girls from the highlands of Guatemala sell their goods. Note their colorful native attire. (Photo courtesy of Merrill C. Oaks)

> As we observe the beauty of Lake Atitlan, a natural conclusion we can draw is that the area is precisely the kind of place that the riotous-living King Noah would favor as a resort for himself and his priests.

Mormon by saying, "How beautiful are they to the eyes of them who there came to the knowledge of their Redeemer" (Mosiah 18:30).

As we observe the beauty of Lake Atitlan, a natural conclusion we can draw is that the area is precisely the kind of place that the riotous-living King Noah would favor as a resort for himself and his priests. After all, King Noah named the place "Mormon" (see Mosiah 18:4). The area was on the borders of Lamanite territory much in the same manner that Galilee was on the borders of Jerusalem at the time of Christ. Although the Romans controlled the area politically, the Jews could move rather freely in areas they claimed as their own.

Finally, Alma was a priest in King Noah's court. He would have had opportunity to scout the area to find that special "thicket" where he could hide from the searches of the king (see Mosiah 18:5).

3. THE WATERS OF SEBUS

We read about the waters of Sebus in connection with the missionary activities of Ammon, the leader of the missionary journey undertaken by the sons of Mosiah. Therefore, we know that the waters of Sebus are in the land of Nephi.

After setting apart the missionaries for their different assignments, Ammon went to the land of Ishmael, which was in the greater land of Nephi: "And Ammon went to the land of Ishmael, the land being called after the sons of Ishmael, who also became Lamanites" (Alma 17:19).

While in the land of Ishmael, Ammon engaged in the service of the Lamanite king over that land. Ammon was assigned to watch over the king's flocks near the waters of Sebus, where he defended the other servants and flocks against plunderers. Because of

Exploring the Lands of the Book of Mormon

the heroic efforts of Ammon at the waters of Sebus, he was able to preach the gospel to the Lamanite King Lamoni (see Alma 18):

> [Ammon] was with the Lamanitish servants going forth with their flocks to the place of water, which was called the *water of Sebus*. (Alma 17:26; emphasis added)
>
> Therefore, they did as Ammon commanded them, and he went forth and stood to contend with those who stood by the *waters of Sebus*; and they were in number not a few. (Alma 17:34; emphasis added)
>
> Now it was the practice of these Lamanites to stand by the *waters of Sebus* to scatter the flocks of the people, that thereby they might drive away many that were scattered unto their own land, it being a practice of plunder among them. (Alma 18:7; emphasis added)
>
> And others rebuked them, saying: The king hath brought this evil upon his house, because he slew his servants who had had their flocks scattered at the *waters of Sebus*.
>
> And they were also rebuked by those men who had stood at the *waters of Sebus* and scattered the flocks which belonged to the king, for they were angry with Ammon because of the number which he had slain of their brethren at the *waters of Sebus*, while defending the flocks of the king. (Alma 19:20–21; emphasis added)

The department of Chimaltenango, the area we propose as the land of Ishmael, has a town that may suggest the location for the waters of Sebus. The town is near the village of Patzicia where the headquarters of a stake of the Church are located, and the stake embraces the nearby villages. Members are mostly descendants of the Cakchiquel Maya.

After Lamoni, the Lamanite king over the land of Ishmael, was converted through the efforts of Ammon, Lamoni traveled with Ammon toward a place called Middoni, where Ammon's fellow missionaries were in jail. En route to Middoni, Lamoni and Ammon met the king over all the Lamanite lands. The Lamanite king, who was the father of Lamoni, was very upset to see his son with a Nephite. Furthermore, the father was upset that his son, Lamoni, had not attended a great feast in the city of Nephi (see Alma 20).

This account suggests that Middoni, which was down in elevation from Ishmael, may have been located where the city of Antigua, Guatemala, is today and that the distance between the land (state) of Nephi and the land of Ishmael, where the waters of Sebus is located, was not very great. Patzicia (Ishmael) is thirty-eight miles from Guatemala City.

Middoni, which was down in elevation from Ishmael, may have been located where the city of Antigua, Guatemala, is today.

We may wonder why the waters of Sebus is even mentioned and what spiritual message (types and shadows) is associated with Ammon's cutting off the arms of the robbers. In regards to water, even though the rainfall is heavy and occurs on a daily basis for six months out of the year in the highlands of Guatemala, when the dry season comes beginning in November and ending in May, water is at a premium.

The story of Ammon's cutting off the arms of the robbers may suggest a concept of dualism. For Ammon to save the flocks (followers of Christ) from the robbers (Satan) and to have the story associated with the waters of Sebus (living waters, or Christ) probably is Mormon's intent for reporting this account.

The story of King Lamoni also represents a concept of dualism if it is meant to emphasize the resurrection of Christ. Just as King Lamoni was raised from his sleep on the third day, so would Christ rise from the dead on the third day. Following two days and two nights without any signs of life, Lamoni was presumed by some of his subjects to be deceased. But the queen, whose faith was great, said that he did not stink to her and that they should not bury him because on the morrow (the third day) he would rise again.

Prior to that event, the servants of King Lamoni had carried the severed arms to the king, and the scripture says that "they were not a few" (Alma 17:38). One Mesoamerican tradition has a parallel in the later Aztec culture where the greatest warriors were those who severed the arms of their enemies, thus causing them to be incapable of fighting any more. The Lamanite King Lamoni did not dare even to speak to this great hero, Ammon, but considered the possibility that Ammon was the "great spirit."

4. A LAND OF PURE WATER

The land of pure water is mentioned in the Book of Mormon in conjunction with the land of Helam. Alma and his followers left the waters of Mormon and traveled eight days' journey until they came to a land of pure water: "And they fled eight days' journey into the wilderness. And they came to a land, yea, even a very beautiful and pleasant land, a *land of pure water*" (Mosiah 23:3–4; emphasis added).

This statement is made just after Alma had left the waters of Mormon, one of the most beautiful spots on earth, and yet he describes the land of Helam as a very beautiful and pleasant land. His description should make readers want to go there. The land of Helam may be the area called Almolonga today, which is about five miles from the city of Quetzaltenango.

We cannot describe adequately the beauty of this area of Guatemala. Driving along the highway on our tours from Lake Atitlan to Quetzaltenango, which the locals call Xela, or Xelaju, the old Maya name, we reach a summit of ten thousand feet above sea level after about two hours' driving time. A first glimpse of Quetzaltenango (or Xela) on the left (Pacific side) and of Totonicapan on the right (northern side) is a sight almost beyond description. The document, *The Title of the Lords of Totonicapan*,

came from that city. In December 2006, the Church of Jesus Christ announced that another temple will be built in Guatemala, this one at Quetzaltenango, near the valley of Almolonga—a very beautiful and pleasant land, a land of pure water.

The distance, direction, name correlation, heavy burdens, and pure water all combine to make Almolonga an exciting candidate for the land of Helam.

The distance from Lake Atitlan (waters of Mormon) to the land of Helam (Almolonga) is sixty-four miles, the same as stipulated in the Book of Mormon—that is, eight days' travel time at eight miles a day equals sixty-four miles.

On their backs, young men in this area carry bundles of agricultural products weighing up to two hundred pounds. They place a strap traditionally made of leather on their foreheads to help support the heavy cargoes they carry up into the trucks. Mormon may have used this imagery of heavy burdens borne by Alma's people to illustrate a principle of the Atonement where Christ relieves the burdens that are placed upon His children.

As mentioned previously, the pure, hot water that comes out of the volcanic mountains surrounding Almolonga has labeled this village as the horticulture capital of Central America. The beautiful produce that consists of large carrots, radishes, onions, and so forth is raised year around. Every day is market day, and women in their colorful costumes with baskets of produce on their heads are lined up in rows at the market place to sell crops from the field to the brokers.

John Lloyd Stephens, who visited Almolonga in the year 1839, describes the village in the following words:

In the afternoon, in company with the corregidor, we rode to the warm springs of Almolonga. The road crosses a spur of the volcano, and descends precipitously into a deep valley, in which, about a league distant, stand the village and hot springs. There is a good bathing-house, at which we were not allowed to pay, being considered guests of the city. Outside, in a beautiful natural reservoir Indian men, women and children were bathing together.

We returned by another road, passing up a valley of extraordinary beauty, and the theme of conversation was the happiness the country might enjoy but for wars and revolutions. Beautiful as it was, all wished to leave it, and seek a land where life was safe—Mexico or El Norte.[3]

3. John Lloyd Stephens,
*Incidents of Travel in
Central America, Chiapas
and Yucatan*, 2 vols.,
illustrations by Frederick
Catherwood, first published
in 1842 (New York: Dover
Publications, 1969), 2:219.

Alma and the members of the Church must have felt the same way as they left the beautiful land of Helam, where they were under bondage, and traveled through the valley of Alma and then left it to seek a land where life was safe—north and then toward the land of Zarahemla.

5. THE RIVER SIDON

The most prominent river in the Book of Mormon is the river Sidon. The city of Zarahemla was built along its banks.

The river Sidon is mentioned in connection with military movements at the river, baptisms in the river, and bodies floating to the sea in the river. Further, the headwaters of the river served as a point of reference for the north-south boundary line of the Nephites and Lamanites. That is, the headwaters of the river Sidon are in the top of the Cuchumatane Mountains (narrow strip of wilderness). From the headwaters, the river flowed downhill toward Zarahemla. Even today, the headwaters area serves as a dividing line between countries.

Traditionally, the two leading candidates for the river Sidon in Mesoamerica have been the Usumacinta River, which forms the border between Peten, Guatemala, and Chiapas, Mexico, and the Grijalva River, which originates in the mountains of Guatemala and runs through the big Chiapas valley in Mexico. These two rivers represent the fourth and fifth longest rivers in Mexico.

However, because of a lack of population centers along the Usumacinta during the Preclassic Period (Mosiah to 4 Nephi time period—130 BC to AD 200), we disqualify it as a serious candidate for the river Sidon. Further, the distance and terrain differentials of the Usumacinta, the location of the day and a half's journey, the obvious distance to the narrow neck of land (Isthmus of Tehuantepec), and the location of the wilderness of Hermounts (mountains of Tehuantepec) are other reasons for our rejecting the Usumacinta River as a viable candidate for the river Sidon that runs through the land of Zarahemla.

FIGURE 26–13: The Grijalva River as it enters into the Sumidero Canyon near Chiapa de Corzo, Chiapas, Mexico. Because of the Grijalva's origins, route, and numerous archaeological sites that date to the Book of Mormon time period, we propose the Grijalva to be the river Sidon. (Photo courtesy of Cortney Boice)

The name *Sidon* was undoubtedly a name given by the Mulekites, as the port of Lebanon, which is south of Beirut, is also called Sidon, which in Hebrew means "fishery" or "fish waters," the same name used today in the upper Grijalva valley. These waters are called *Xocal Ha* in the Maya language, which means "fish waters," the same as *Sidon* in Hebrew. One town on the upper Grijalva is called *Xocaltenango*, a combination of two words, one in Maya and the other in Nahuatl, which means "place of the fish." Some archaeological evidence hints at the possibility that the ancient Nephites/Mulekites called all the water "fish waters," or "waters of Sidon," as many tributaries flow into the Grijalva.

The terms "Sidon," "river Sidon," and "waters of Sidon" are used thirty-seven times in the Book of Mormon. We will quote only those river Sidon scriptures that suggest a geographical location.

> The terms "Sidon," "river Sidon," and "waters of Sidon" are used thirty-seven times in the Book of Mormon.

Alma 2:15—The River Sidon Ran by the Land of Zarahemla

And it came to pass that the Amlicites came upon the hill Amnihu, which was east of the river Sidon, which ran by the land of Zarahemla, and there they began to make war with the Nephites.

The sons of Mosiah declined the kingship offered by their father and chose to go on a mission among the Lamanites. Alma, the son of Alma who baptized at the waters of Mormon, became the first chief judge of the people of Zarahemla.

During the eight years that Alma was chief judge, both internal and external conflicts occurred. A Nephite by the name of Amlici desired to be king. In the subsequent revolution, 19,304 Nephites were killed. Amlici united with a numerous host of Lamanites. In the course of this devastating war, the crops of the fields were destroyed. The number of dead on both sides was so great that they were not numbered. Finally, Alma killed Amlici. The Lamanites returned in battle, and Alma was wounded. These battles all took place during the fifth year of Alma's judgeship in approximately 87 BC (see Alma 1–3).

The river Sidon played a major role in the battles alluded to above. It is mentioned nine times alone in Alma 2–3. As a result, we learn several things about the river, including the following:

1. The river Sidon ran by the land of Zarahemla (see Alma 2:15).
2. The hill Amnihu was east of the river Sidon (see Alma 2:15).
3. Alma drove the Amlicites east of the river Sidon over to the valley of Gideon (see Alma 2:17–20; see also chapter 27, "Hills and Valleys").
4. Upon discovering that the Amlicites had united with the Lamanites in the Nephite land of Minon, which was above the city of Zarahemla, Alma and his army retreated back to the city of Zarahemla. As they were crossing the river from the east to the west, they encountered the Amlicites and the Lamanites (see Alma 2:24–27).
5. Alma and his army drove back the armies of the Amlicites and Lamanites toward the west. Alma had his men clear off the west bank of the river by throwing the bodies of the Lamanites who had been destroyed into the river (see Alma 2:31–34; 3:3).
6. The Lamanites fled west and north away from the river Sidon and were slain by the Nephites and driven to the wilderness of Hermounts (see Alma 2:35–37; see also chapter 24, "Wilderness Areas").

> Compelling evidence identifies the River Grijalva that runs through the Chiapas valley as the river Sidon.

Compelling evidence identifies the River Grijalva that runs through the Chiapas valley as the river Sidon. Plotting the possible movements of the Nephite and Amlicite/Lamanite armies as described in the above scriptures is relatively easy because the movements are associated with the river Sidon, the land and city of Zarahemla, the hill Amnihu, the land of Minon, the "course" of the land of Nephi, and the wilderness that was west and north of Zarahemla called the wilderness of Hermounts.

Alma 4:4—Alma Baptizes in the Waters of Sidon

And they began to establish the church more fully; yea, and many were baptized in the *waters of Sidon* and were joined to the church of God; yea, they were baptized by the hand of Alma, who had been consecrated the high priest over the people of the church, by the hand of his father Alma. (emphasis added)

Alma 4:4–5 indicates that the Church of Christ began to be established more fully and that in the seventh year, thirty-five hundred people were baptized into the Church. They were baptized in the waters of Sidon. Two years later, after eight years of government service, Alma gave up the judgeship to devote his entire time to preaching the gospel. Prior to that time, Alma had played a dual role of both prophet and chief judge (see Alma 4:20).

The city of Zarahemla may have been located at the top of the large valley called the Chiapas depression. The Grijalva River (Sidon) snakes its way through the valley and may be as wide as 150 feet in certain areas. During the dry season, the river is rather shallow, which certainly qualifies it for the Book of Mormon statements that require the people to cross the river back and forth. During the rainy season (May–October), the river is much deeper. Today, four dams and associated reservoirs have been built along the river. The ruins of Santa Rosa, considered to be the leading candidate for the city of Zarahemla by those who have studied in the area, are immersed under one of the reservoirs.

On our tours, we board motor boats at the city of Chiapa de Corzo, which is located in the lower Chiapas valley. The river bends at Chiapa de Corzo and changes from its westward direction until it runs almost directly north through sheer canyon walls. At

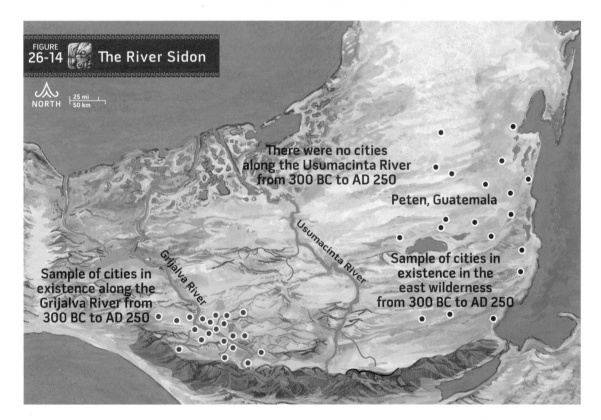

FIGURE 26-14

The River Sidon

NORTH 25 mi / 50 km

There were no cities along the Usumacinta River from 300 BC to AD 250

Peten, Guatemala

Grijalva River

Usumacinta River

Sample of cities in existence along the Grijalva River from 300 BC to AD 250

Sample of cities in existence in the east wilderness from 300 BC to AD 250

FIGURE 26–14: Maps located in the Museum of Archaeology in Tuxtla Gutierrez, Chiapas, reflect the many cities located along the Grijalva River from 300 BC to AD 250 as well as the absence of any major cities along the Usumacinta River during the same time period. "Permanent" cities were not built along the Usumacinta River until after AD 250.

one point, the distance is over three thousand feet from the water to the top of the cliffs. This boat ride takes an hour and fifteen minutes to the Chicuasen Dam. Before entering the canyon, the river along the valley floor is calm and meets the requirement for baptizing in its waters. When we first started taking tours down the Grijalva, the boats had no life preservers, so we took our own and left them at the hotel for the next tour. Subsequently, the boat owners bought our life preservers, and today all boats carry life preservers on board.

Alma 6:7—East of the River Sidon

And now it came to pass that when Alma had made these regulations he departed from them, yea, from the church which was in the city of Zarahemla, and went over upon the *east of the river Sidon*. (emphasis added)

The ruins of Santa Rosa, considered to be the leading candidate for the city of Zarahemla by those who have studied in the area, are immersed under one of the reservoirs of the Grijalva River.

This scripture describes the valley of Gideon, as this valley was located "over upon" the east. The valley of Gideon may have been located in the area between present-day Comitan and San Cristobal de las Casas in the state of Chiapas, Mexico. The *over upon* description is a great way to describe the area. Because of the manner in which the Grijalva River enters into the upper Chiapas depression, everything east is "over upon."

Alma 8:3—The land of Melek Was West of the River Sidon

And it came to pass in the commencement of the tenth year of the reign of the judges over the people of Nephi, that Alma departed from thence and took his journey over into the land of Melek, on the *west of the river Sidon*, on the west by the borders of the wilderness. (emphasis added)

After Alma surrendered his position as chief judge of the land (country) of Zarahemla, he went throughout the land preaching the gospel and setting the Church of Christ in order. He began in the city of Zarahemla, where he lived. He then went to the land of Gideon and returned again to the city of Zarahemla.

At the beginning of the tenth year of the reign of the judges, about 82 BC, Alma continued his missionary labors in the land of Melek. The land of Melek was located west of the river Sidon and was also located on the west by the borders of the wilderness. Again, if we pursue the Chiapas depression as the land of Zarahemla, then Melek is located along the mountain range west of the archaeological site of Santa Rosa. Melek may have been in the Rio Pando Valley where the ruins of Tonala are located. Tonala is located southwest of present-day Tuxtla Gutierrez in the mountains. It is north of present-day Tapachula, where the ancient ruins of Izapa are located. (For additional information, see chapter 24, "Wilderness Areas," and chapter 29, "The Land of Zarahemla.")

Alma 16:6–7—East Side of the River Sidon

The Lamanites will cross the river Sidon in the south wilderness, away up beyond the borders of the land of Manti. And behold there shall ye meet them, on the *east of the river Sidon*, and there the Lord will deliver unto thee thy brethren who have been taken captive by the Lamanites.

And it came to pass that Zoram and his sons crossed over the *river Sidon*, with their armies, and marched away beyond the borders of Manti into the south wilderness, which was on the east side of the river Sidon. (emphasis added)

The prophet Alma told the Nephite military leader Zoram that the Lamanites would cross the river Sidon on the east side in the south wilderness beyond the borders of the land Manti.

We learn from other sources that the land of Manti is located near the headwaters of the river Sidon. The south wilderness, which was south of the land of Zarahemla, in this instance consists of the mountains that divided the land of Nephi from the land of Zarahemla. The south wilderness here appears to be the mountains where the highlands of Guatemala begin. This south wilderness is not to be confused with the "south wilderness" that the Jaredites preserved as a place to get game (see Ether 10:21), although it may still be considered as an extension of the Jaredite south wilderness. Nor is it to be confused with the south wilderness that the Mulekites moved into (see Alma 22:31), although it may also be considered an extension of the mountain ranges south of the Gulf of Mexico and the Bay of Campeche. The point we make here is that the Lamanites crossed the river Sidon up in the mountains south of Zarahemla. They ended up on the east side of the river Sidon.

> The land of Manti is located near the headwaters of the river Sidon.

Alma 22:27, 29—The Head of the River Sidon

[The land of Nephi] was divided from the land of Zarahemla by a narrow strip of wilderness, which ran from the sea east even to the sea west, and round about on the borders of the seashore, and the borders of the wilderness which was on the north by the land of Zarahemla, through the borders of Manti, by the *head of the river Sidon.* . . .

The Nephites had taken possession of all the northern parts of the land bordering on the wilderness, *at the head of the river Sidon* (emphasis added).

These two verses inform us that

1. The Lamanite northern border and the Nephite southern border are where the river Sidon begins—that is, the dividing line between the land of Nephi and the land of Zarahemla is the top of the narrow strip of wilderness. John Lloyd Stephens called it the dividing line of the waters.

2. The land of Manti appears to extend to the top of the mountain where the river Sidon begins. On the other hand, the city of Manti appears to be located at the base of the mountain.

3. The Nephites had taken possession of the northern parts of the wilderness at the head of the river Sidon from the east to the west.

In our model, the northern border of the land of Nephi is the Sierra de las Minas and the Cuchumatanes mountain ranges, which separate highland Guatemala from Chiapas and lowland Guatemala. If such is the case, this mountain range constitutes the southern border of the land of Zarahemla.

We have conducted many of our tours down through this massive mountain range. About one and a half hours are required to travel from Quetzaltenango to Huehuetenango and another two hours to reach the Guatemala-Mexico border. Although we constantly see the high mountains ahead of us in a northern direction, the road cuts down through the mountains. In three and a half hours, we drop from ninety-eight hundred feet elevation to thirty-two hundred feet elevation. By the time we reach Tuxtla Gutierrez in the Chiapas depression, our altimeter places us at only fifteen hundred feet above sea level.

This area from Quetzaltenango to Huehuetenango and then to the Mexico border is much less fertile than the lush, beautiful lands to the south behind us. In these mountains, the guerrillas who battle against the government take refuge. The Mam natives, whose language registers to be the oldest of Mesoamerica, live in these mountains between Guatemala and Mexico. The language structure dates to 2600 BC.[4] The terrace farms give new meaning to the term "agriculture," as the mountains appear to be too steep to climb, let alone to farm.

4. Alberto Ruz, *The Mayas* (Mexico, DF: Salvat Mexicana de Ediciones, 1983), 56.

As we continue to travel northward from Huehuetenango, where the Postclassic Maya ruins of Zaculeu are located, we observe that we are following a river. This is the beginning of the Grijalva River that runs through the Chiapas valley in Mexico. We cross the border at La Mesilla on the Guatemala side and Ciudad Cuauhtemoc on the Mexico side. About ten miles from the border at the last customs stop, we cross the river. The ruins of La Libertad, a candidate for the city of Manti, are in this area.

As we look behind, we see the area that may be referred to above where the Nephites occupied from the "east to the west." The land structure has changed; the elevation has changed; the mountain range seems impenetrable; and Guatemala seems a world away behind us. We travel in a northwestward direction as we circle the mountain range that flanks the Chiapas depression. The River Grijalva parallels us a considerable distance to our left as it drops down into the big Chiapas valley. The river runs from the "east towards the west."

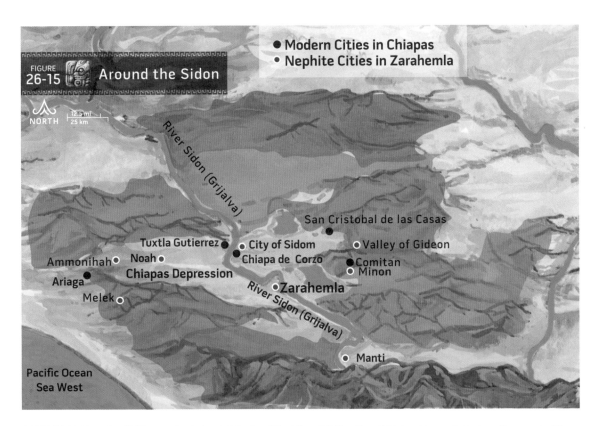

FIGURE 26–15: The valley of Gideon was located east of the river Sidon (Alma 6:7). The cities of Melek and Ammonihah, where Alma preached the gospel, were located west of the river Sidon (Alma 8:3). In a war that took place about 80 BC, Mormon uses the terms "south wilderness" (wilderness south of Zarahemla), "beyond the borders of the land of Manti," and "east of the river Sidon" (Alma 16:6–7).

Although the evidence is not absolutely conclusive, when accompanied with the archaeological history in the area, the geography is most impressive, especially for the following reasons:

1. A narrow strip of wilderness, or mountain range, separates highland Guatemala (land of Nephi) from lowland Guatemala and Chiapas, Mexico (land of Zarahemla). The state of Chiapas used to be part of Guatemala.
2. The distance from the valley of Quetzaltenango in Guatemala to the Mexican border is about a hundred miles. Today, as noted previously, the natives of Guatemala and the Yucatan carry loads in excess of a hundred pounds on their backs supported by leather bands about their foreheads and average eight miles per day in their walking.[5] That calculates to twelve days of walking time that are required to travel the above distance. This proposed journey is the one that took Alma and his group the same amount of time to accomplish—twelve days. The people were driving their flocks before them. They were also fleeing from the Lamanites.

5. See Ruz, *The Mayas*, 78–79.

3. The headwaters of the Grijalva (Sidon) River come out of the mountains, flow past the archaeological site of La Libertad (Manti), and travel from the east toward the west through the Chiapas valley (land of Zarahemla). The land is also associated appropriately for the wilderness directions in the Book of Mormon as well as the valley of Gideon and the land of Minon.

Alma 43:22—Head of the River Sidon

[The Lamanites] took their journey round about in the wilderness, away *by the head of the river Sidon*, that they might come into the land of Manti and take possession of the land; for they did not suppose that the armies of Moroni would know whither they had gone. (emphasis added)

Alma 43 and 44 are chapters of war and intrigue. In the year 74 BC, the Lamanites came against the Nephites in battle. The war began in the east wilderness, east of the land of Zarahemla near the lands of Jershon and Antionum. Antionum was not too far from the seashore and was also close to the Lamanite borders. Antionum was south of the land of Jershon. The land of Antionum was possessed by the Zoramites, and the land of Jershon was possessed by the Lamanite converts of Ammon. Following the same boundary-line patterns that exist today, we discern that the land of Manti was close to the headwaters of the river Sidon. All four of these areas—that is, the land of Jershon, the land of Antionum, the land of Manti, and the river Sidon—figure in the war between the Nephites and the Zoramites/Lamanites. The wilderness referred to in this section is south of the land of Zarahemla and is probably the narrow strip of wilderness that divided the land of Nephi from the land of Zarahemla.

The Nephites gathered their army at the land of Jershon, and the Lamanites gathered their army at the land of Antionum. Moroni was the chief military leader over the Nephites. When the Lamanites/Zoramites discovered that Moroni had prepared his soldiers with armor and thick clothing, the Lamanites/Zoramites dared not come to battle against the Nephites. As a point of interest, the Maya did indeed wear thick clothing as body armor. They sewed pockets of sand or grain in their vests to provide the necessary thickness so the arrows could not penetrate.

The Lamanites decided to take their journey back into the mountains and moved toward the head of the river Sidon with the intent of capturing the land of Manti. They assumed that the Nephites would be weak in that area and that Moroni would not know where they had gone. The approximate distance from the base of the Maya Mountains (land of Antionum and land of Jershon area) to the headwaters of the Grijalva River (river Sidon) by the city of Todos Santos Cuchumatane, Guatemala, is about 150 miles. An army could cover the distance in ten to fourteen days.

As we look behind, we see the area that may be referred to above where the Nephites occupied from the "east to the west." The land structure has changed; the elevation has changed; the mountain range seems impenetrable; and Guatemala seems a world away behind us.

Exploring the Lands of the Book of Mormon

Upon gathering the necessary information, Moroni left a part of his army at Jershon to guard that area; and he marched the rest of his army over into the land of Manti, gathering recruits as he traveled the estimated distance of 150 miles.

When Moroni arrived at the land of Manti, he concealed an army on the west side of the river Sidon near the place where the Nephites suspected the Lamanites would cross. He also concealed armies in the west valley, west of the river, and stationed army platoons all along the borders of the land of Manti (see Alma 43:26–32).

In addition, on the east of the river Sidon, Moroni placed a military leader by the name of Lehi, together with an army (see Alma 43:40 and also Alma 49:16). He positioned them on the south and east of the hill Riplah. When the Lamanites passed by on the north of the hill Riplah, Lehi pursued them. Just as the Lamanites began to cross the border, they discovered that they were being followed by Lehi and his men. The Lamanites turned and gave battle. As the Lamanites saw they were losing ground, they crossed over from the east of the river Sidon to the west of the river Sidon. Here they encountered Moroni and his army.

Although the Lamanites were much more numerous than the Nephites, the Nephites under Moroni's command drove the Lamanites toward the land of Manti. Zerahemna, the leader of the Lamanites, was captured and scalped. The Lamanites were defeated, as they were surrounded by two of Moroni's armies on both ends of the valley, west of the river Sidon, and by Lehi's army, which was positioned on the east of the river Sidon (see Alma 43:41–54; Alma 44).

The terrain with the river, valleys, hills, and mountains in relation to each other presents a rather convincing argument as to this area's being the possible location of this 74 BC battle. It also does nothing to detract from the idea that the Grijalva River is the river Sidon referred to in the Book of Mormon. It is this area and the wilderness south of Chiapas that provided the hiding places for the Gadianton robbers and, in our day, for the antigovernment factions of Guatemala. We have traveled through this proposed battle area on many occasions. On one occasion, we were detained five hours by the same people—if we are correct in our assessments—of the lineage of those who fought in the 74 BC battle. They carried big clubs.

The Maya did indeed wear thick clothing as body armor. They sewed pockets of sand or grain in their vests to provide the necessary thickness so the arrows could not penetrate.

Alma 44:22—Bodies of the Dead Were Cast into the Waters of Sidon

And it came to pass that they did cast their dead into the *waters of Sidon*, and they have gone forth and are buried in the depths of the sea. (emphasis added)

Both the Usumacinta River and the Grijalva River empty into the Gulf of Mexico about thirty miles north of Villahermosa, Tabasco. The Grijalva River, also called the Chiapas or Tabasco River, actually divides the city of Villahermosa. Today, two temples of the Church are located where the Grijalva River flows—one at Tuxtla Gutierrez, Chiapas, and another at Villahermosa, Tabasco.

Alma 50:11—By the Head of the River Sidon

And thus he cut off all the strongholds of the Lamanites in the east wilderness, yea, and also on the west, fortifying the line between the Nephites and the Lamanites, between the land of Zarahemla and the land of Nephi, from the west sea, running by the head of the *river Sidon*—the Nephites possessing all the land northward, yea, even all the land which was northward of the land Bountiful, according to their pleasure. (emphasis added)

This reference is consistent with all other geographical statements about the river Sidon. The landmarks in this verse include the east wilderness and the boundary line between the Lamanites in the land of Nephi and the Nephites in the land of Zarahemla.

The verse also specifies the relationship between the west sea and the river Sidon and reaffirms the position of the land northward. The land Bountiful in this instance probably refers to the land southward; as a result, Mormon is talking about the greater land Bountiful (see Alma 22:31).

Alma 56:25—The Head of the Sidon

Neither durst they march down against the city of Zarahemla; neither durst they cross *the head of Sidon*, over to the city of Nephihah. (emphasis added)

This scripture is important not only because it defines the river Sidon but also because it allows the river Sidon to pinpoint the general location of the land/city of Nephihah. The Lamanites did not dare to pass by Helaman in that area. Neither dared they march down against the city of Zarahemla. Finally, they did not dare to cross the head of the Sidon over to the city of Nephihah. That leaves only one place for the location of the city of Nephihah—in the east wilderness. Placing Nephihah in the east wilderness is consistent with what we read about the foundation of the city of Nephihah in Alma 50:14. Nephihah was built in the east wilderness.

Mormon 1:10—Waters of Sidon

And it came to pass that the war began to be among them in the borders of Zarahemla, by the *waters of Sidon*. (emphasis added)

This verse represents the final statement about the river Sidon in the Book of Mormon. The verse dates to AD 322 when Mormon's father took him to the land of Zarahemla when Mormon was eleven years old. By AD 350, the Lamanites gained control of the entire land southward (see Mormon 2:28–29). Zarahemla was in the land southward. The river Sidon ran through the Zarahemla valley.

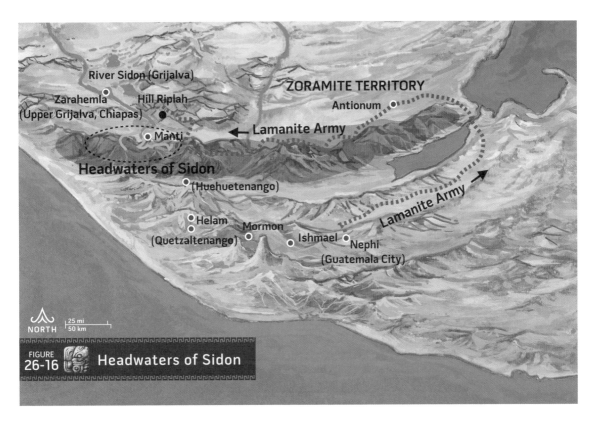

FIGURE 26–16: The land of Manti was located near the headwaters of the river Sidon (Alma 43:22). The terms "Sidon," "river Sidon," and "waters of Sidon" are mentioned thirty-seven times in the Book of Mormon. "Sidon" is mentioned fourteen times in Alma 43 in reference to a Nephite battle with the Zoramites in 74 BC. You may want to read Alma 43–44 as you study this map.

The Usumacinta River is not the river Sidon. The Usumacinta river was an early proposal by M. Wells Jakemen as a possible candidate for the river Sidon. Other readers of the Book of Mormon still maintain that tradition today. And some tour directors take tours along the Usumacinta River under the guise that the city of Zarahemla was located along its banks. They do so, however, without authorization of archaeological evidence dating from the fifth to second centuries BC, a strict requirement for any candidate to be the city of Zarahemla. Although over fifty sites located in the Chiapas valley along the Grijalva River dating from 500 BC to AD 250 have been documented, no sites of any consequence dating to that time period have been documented along the Usumacinta River.

The two most prominent sites along the Usumacinta are Piedras Negras and Yaxchilan, both of which are Maya Classic sites that were not founded until after AD 250—or toward the end of the history recorded in the Book of Mormon. They are located about twenty-five miles from each other, and they are about a hundred miles west of Tikal. They are approachable from Palenque when travelers drive to the Usumacinta

Today, two temples of the Church are located where the Grijalva River flows— one at Tuxtla Gutierrez, Chiapas, and another at Villahermosa, Tabasco.

River and take a launch upstream. They follow the same political and developmental pattern as the Classic ruins of Palenque, Calakmul, and Copan. A brief analysis of these two sites follows.

Piedras Negras is not a Book of Mormon city. Excavation work was initiated at Piedras Negras from 1931 to 1939 by the University Museum, University of Pennsylvania. That is more than twenty years prior to the investigative work conducted by the New World Archaeological Foundation at Santa Rosa, which is discussed in chapter 29, "The Land of Zarahemla." Beginning in 1997, the site of Piedras Negras became part of a combined Guatemalan and American project led by Hector Escobedo and Stephen Houston, the latter formerly on the faculty of Brigham Young University but not a member of the Church of Jesus Christ.

Like Palenque and Copan, Piedras Negras may have been settled as a small village beginning at AD 250 to AD 300; however, the first ruler, who is simply labeled Ruler A, appears to have ascended to the throne around AD 460, which is 82 years after Spearthrower Owl of Teotihuacan sent his young son Yax Nuun Ayiin to overthrow Tikal and set up a dynasty there and 110 years from the time the Nephites had been exiled from the land of Zarahemla and the land southward. Piedras Negras is the largest site along the Usumacinta River. In its three-hundred-year post–Book of Mormon history, Piedras Negras was fraught with many wars. Its collapse also appears to be military in nature, coming directly from its neighbor to the south, Yaxchilan. After the fall of Piedras Negras in the eighth century AD, evidence shows that the Usumacinta continued as a major trade route for another century.[6]

Thus, we see that the site of Piedras Negras did not begin until at least six hundred years after the founding of Santa Rosa, which is located in the Chiapas valley. That is, Piedras Negras did not even have a ruler until after the close of the Book of Mormon. *Piedras Negras is not a Book of Mormon city!*

No Nephite ever lived at Yaxchilan. Like its neighbor Piedras Negras, Yaxchilan is a Maya Classic Period site whose dynasty began on July 23, AD 359, more than five hundred years after Mosiah traveled from Nephi to Zarahemla and became king over the land of Zarahemla. Yaxchilan did not exist as a structured city with a ruler until nine years after the Nephites were exiled from the land of Zarahemla. In other words, *no Nephite ever lived at Yaxchilan.*

Yaxchilan is situated in a horseshoe bend of the Usumacinta River, and although its dynasty describes an origin in the fourth century AD, most of what is seen today is the result of two eighth-century rulers who dominated its landscape.

Just as no serious scholar of historical geography of the Book of Mormon today would consider Palenque, Uxmal, or El Tajin to be a Book of Mormon city, likewise, no reputable student of Mesoamerican history and geography would label Yaxchilan or Piedras Negras a Nephite site. Therefore, *we must disqualify the Usumacinta River* as a candidate for the river Sidon.[7]

6. See Simon Martin and Nikolai Grube, *Chronicle of the Maya Kings and Queens: Deciphering the Dynasties of the Ancient Maya* (London: Thames and Hudson, 2000), 138–54.

7. See Martin and Grube, *Chronicle of the Maya Kings and Queens,* 116–37.

We need only to look at the maps in the Museum of Archaeology at Tuxtla Gutierrez—maps that were designed by the New World Archaeological Foundation—to get the picture of the many cities or towns that were located along the Grijalva during the Preclassic Period in comparison with the Usumacinta, where there were none.

The above comments do not mean that the Usumacinta did not play a role in Nephite history. The 121 BC expedition of Limhi probably followed the Usumacinta River until they came to the land among many waters and subsequently entered into Jaredite/Olmec territory by La Venta, Tabasco. Had they followed the Grijalva River, they would have run into thousands of people and hundreds of towns and cities. And they would have spoken the same language as the Mosiah-Nephites and would have been familiar with the kind of pottery being used by the Mosiah-Nephites in Chiapas, as it is the same kind that was being used at Kaminaljuyu in Guatemala during the same time period.

Not only the presence of cities and pottery but also the name correlations of places like Chiapa de Corzo and the wilderness of Hermounts qualify the Grijalva River to be the river Sidon. Further, the distances and directional and geographical lay of the land regarding the land of Manti, the valley of Gideon, and the day and a half's fortification line that was intended to stop the Lamanites from going into the land northward support Grijalva as the river Sidon. Finally, the relationship of the Grijalva River with Izapa, the Isthmus of Tehuantepec, the land southward hunting grounds of the Jaredites, and the migratory route through the narrow strip of wilderness solidify the Grijalva—not the Usumacinta—as the river Sidon.

Some readers may think that the issue is not a major one because the distances between the Grijalva and Usumacinta Rivers are not that great. However, before readers arrive at that conclusion, we suggest that they fly over the wilderness from Comitan, Chiapas, to Yaxchilan, Chiapas. That area consists of massive canyons, thick forestation, and at least seven major river tributaries that drain into the Usumacinta basin. In other words, no direct relationship exists between the Usumacinta River and the west sea (Pacific Ocean), a Book of Mormon requirement.

In connection with the historical documentation of 200 BC to AD 200, the ancient document called *The Title of the Lords of Totonicapan* (see chapter 10, "Ancient Mesoamerican Documents") mentions that descendants of Abraham and Jacob went up the Grijalva and Usumacinta Rivers and settled along the frontiers of Chiapas and Guatemala. Although the Usumacinta River is mentioned, nothing in the document suggests that anyone settled along the Usumacinta—a fact that is verified by the lack of archaeological evidence.

Latter-day Saint Mesoamericanist V. Garth Norman continues to embrace the Usumacinta River as the river Sidon. His justification for doing so appears to rest on his proposed location for the city of Manti. Norman writes: "Moroni's fortification ruins, which we have dated to this time period for Manti, have been found in the Coban area of Alta Verapaz, Guatemala on the east side of the headwaters of the Usumacinta/Sidon.

Piedras Negras did not even have a ruler until after the close of the Book of Mormon. Piedras Negras was not a Book of Mormon city!

This location is precisely as Mormon described in Alma 22:27, where a mountain spur extends north from the Narrow Strip of Wilderness mountain range and runs 'round about . . . the borders of the wilderness (Cuchumatanes mountains), which was on the north by the land of Zarahemla (south wilderness), through the borders of Manti by the head of the River Sidon.'"[8]

8. V. Garth Norman, *Book of Mormon—Mesoamerican Geography: History Study Map* (American Fork, UT: ARCON with Ancient America Foundation, 2008), 7–8.

"It is the land that dictates the locations of Zarahemla.The Grijalva River runs through the land of Zarahemla. The land is primary; the river is secondary."

—Joseph Allen

Even if the Grijalva River, our proposed river Sidon, did not exist, we see at least two obvious reasons why we have to challenge the Usumacinta/Sidon scenario. We have already discussed the first reason—that is, population centers dating to the Late Preclassic Period (200 BC to AD 200), *of the magnitude and location required by the Book of Mormon,* have never been discovered along the Usumacinta River. For example, at 83 BC on the banks of the river Sidon, nineteen thousand soldiers were killed in a battle to gain control of the city of Zarahemla (see Alma 2:19). If they had been fighting on both sides of the Usumacinta, they would have been fighting to get control of a city that did not exist at that time!

We are not suggesting an entire absence of settlements along the Usumacinta in the first century BC. Small Preclassic settlements existed, as determined by pottery fragments that have been documented at Yaxchilan, Piedras Negras, El Cayo, Fideo, Macabilero, El Kinel, La Tecnica, and Zancudero, all of which were located in close proximity to each other. At Zancudero, large defensive walls have been discovered that are apparently patterned after those at Becan and that date to the time period of Becan. Although Zancudero is not located specifically along the Usumacinta River, it is nearby. However, before we could even consider the Usumacinta as the river running through Zarahemla, we would have to look at two archaeological outcomes connected with the Usumacinta: (1) a wide pattern of abandonment of sites occurred in this region about AD 250 and (2) the sites were very sparsely populated.[9]

9. See Charles Golden and Andrew Scherer, "Border Problems: Recent Archaeological Research along the Usumacinta River," *The PARI Journal* 7, no. 2 (Fall 2006): 7–13.

In connection with our first reason for challenging the Usumacinta/Sidon proposal, we should recall that young Mormon visited Zarahemla at AD 322, seventy-two years after La Tecnica and Zancudero were abandoned. On that occasion, a war broke out in the borders of Zarahemla by the waters of Sidon. Thirty thousand Nephite soldiers were recruited to fight against the Lamanites (Mormon 1:6–11). Therefore, we ask the following question: If no cities existed along the Usumacinta with a *continual* occupation from 500 BC to AD 322, why did the Nephites need thirty thousand soldiers for this battle? Further, at AD 331, a battle ensued that entailed forty-four thousand Lamanites and forty-two thousand Nephites. They were fighting somewhere—but they were *not* fighting in an attempt to capture the towns located in the Yaxchilan district of the Usumacinta River because, according to recent archaeological testing, *those sites had already been abandoned.*

The second reason the Usumacinta River is not a legitimate candidate for the river Sidon is its geographical location. Alma 22:27 goes on to say that the land of Nephi "was divided from the land of Zarahemla by a narrow strip of wilderness, which ran from the *sea east even to the sea west, and round about on the borders of the seashore*, and the borders of the wilderness which was on the north by the land of Zarahemla." In other words, the narrow strip of wilderness (narrow mountain range) runs from the Atlantic to the Pacific and then "round about the borders of the wilderness." Thus, the narrow strip of wilderness does not stop at the borders of the Usumacinta River, as Norman suggests in his model for Usumacinta/Sidon.

6. THE LAND OF MANY WATERS

The term "many waters" is used in a number of occasions in the Book of Mormon. It is also used as a term to identify different geographical areas. Most often, the term is used (1) to designate the Atlantic or Pacific Oceans, such as in the statement, "I looked and beheld *many waters*; and they divided the Gentiles from the seed of my brethren" (1 Nephi 13:10; emphasis added) or (2) to describe the Jaredites' crossing of the ocean in barges when "they were encompassed about by *many waters*" (Ether 6:7; emphasis added).

The term is also used to designate a specific ocean, such as in the statement of Nephi when he and his family arrived at the seashore prior to setting sail toward the New World: "And we beheld the sea, which we called Irreantum, which, being interpreted is *many waters*" (1 Nephi 17:5; emphasis added).

Two separate and distinct geographical locations wherein the term "many waters" is used will now be discussed. Both are very important to an understanding of Book of Mormon geography. And any proposed Book of Mormon map must take into account these two geographical locations in relation to distances and topography as outlined in both the Book of Mormon and the proposed geological and geographical map.

We propose that the first "land among many waters" is the area in which the Limhi expedition passed through in search of Zarahemla and that the second "land of many waters, rivers, and fountains" is the area where Mormon chose to have the last decisive battle with the Lamanites. That battle was in the land of Cumorah, and it was in the area of the hill Cumorah. These locations will now be discussed in that order.

Mosiah 8: 7–8—Land among Many Waters

And the king [Limhi] said unto him [Ammon]: Being grieved for the afflictions of my people, I caused that forty and three of my people should take a journey into the wilderness, that thereby they might find the land of Zarahemla, that we might appeal unto our brethren to deliver us out of bondage.

And they were lost in the wilderness for the space of many days, yet they were diligent, and found not the land of Zarahemla but returned to this land, having traveled in a *land among many waters*, having discovered a land which was covered with bones of men, and of beasts, and was also covered with ruins of buildings of every kind, having discovered a land which had been peopled with a people who were as numerous as the hosts of Israel. (emphasis added)

> The term "many waters" is used in a number of occasions in the Book of Mormon. It is also used as a term to identify different geographical areas.

FIGURE 26–17: The 121 BC Limhi expedition did not find Zarahemla. The headwaters of the Usumacinta and the Grijalva both originate in the mountains of Guatemala in close proximity to each other. Selecting the wrong river in 121 BC would have been an easy mistake to make. We propose that the Limhi expedition followed the Usumacinta River, which would have carried them to the massive lagoon systems of Campeche and Tabasco. They called the area "a land among many waters," which indeed it is (see Mosiah 8:8). (Photo courtesy of Merrill C. Oaks)

Any candidate for a "land among many waters" must be located in such a manner that the people involved in the Limhi expedition would bypass the land of Zarahemla and travel through "many waters," never finding Zarahemla.

Traditional Book of Mormon history proposes that the forty-three people sent by Limhi traveled from Peru to New York, a distance of nearly six thousand miles one way, and then returned with twenty-four gold plates that contained the history of the Jaredites.

Both the land of Nephi and the land of Zarahemla are southward of the narrow neck of land. Even if we allow the land of Nephi and the land of Zarahemla to be in Central America (or two thousand miles northward from Peru), the distance to New York, where Book of Mormon readers have traditionally assumed that the Jaredites were destroyed, is about four thousand miles one way that the Limhi expedition would have had to travel.

From Central America, they would need to cross steep mountains, dense jungles, dry deserts, and many rivers. The total travel time would require at least two years, not just thirty days, the calculated distance from Nephi to Zarahemla, plus another thirty days to arrive into the Jaredite-Olmec territory. We should remember that the Book of Mormon record gives us no indication that Limhi was ignorant of the distance between Nephi and Zarahemla. Limhi and his people simply did not know the route. The distance, as pointed out earlier, is estimated at two hundred to three hundred miles. Limhi's grandfather, Zeniff, had traveled the route from Nephi to Zarahemla and from Zarahemla to Nephi. The Zeniff-Noah-Limhi Nephites had lived in the land of Nephi only about sixty years. Oral history probably dictated the general direction and approximate time of travel to the land of Zarahemla. Only the trail to get there would have been lost.

In chapter 5, "The Olmec (Jaredite) Culture," We proposed that the Jaredites lived in the area along the Gulf Coast of Mexico. If such is the case, then that is the area where the twenty-four gold plates that contained the history of the Jaredites were found.

Therefore, we logically should survey the Mesoamerica map to determine if a "land among many waters" that fits the prescribed Book of Mormon requirements actually exists between the proposed land of Nephi and the proposed land of Desolation, where the twenty-four gold plates were found. Any candidate for a "land among many waters" must be located in such a manner that the people involved in the Limhi expedition would bypass the land of Zarahemla and travel through "many waters," never finding Zarahemla.

Such a place does exist. An area that qualifies itself in distance, location, direction, and size is the area where the massive water pools, lagoons, and river systems drain from the Chiapas Mountains into the Gulf of Mexico in the states of Tabasco and Campeche.

The average rainfall in the area between Villahermosa, Tabasco, and Ciudad Carmen, Campeche, is among the highest in the world and is comparable to the rainfall on the island of Laie, Hawaii. This Mesoamerican sea-level area, characterized by the many river systems and the high rainfall, has lagoons of stagnant water—producing massive swamplands and making travel through the area very difficult. It wasn't until the middle of the twentieth century that bridges were built across the rivers, thus allowing motorized vehicles to travel from Tabasco to the Yucatan.

In all probability, in searching for Zarahemla, the Limhi expedition dropped down from the highlands of Guatemala and located the wrong river. They probably followed the Usumacinta River instead of the Grijalva River.

If they followed the Usumacinta River route, the Limhi expedition ended up right in the middle of the great lagoon systems described above. Their diligence would then take them across the top of the Gulf of Mexico to the ancient Olmec site of La

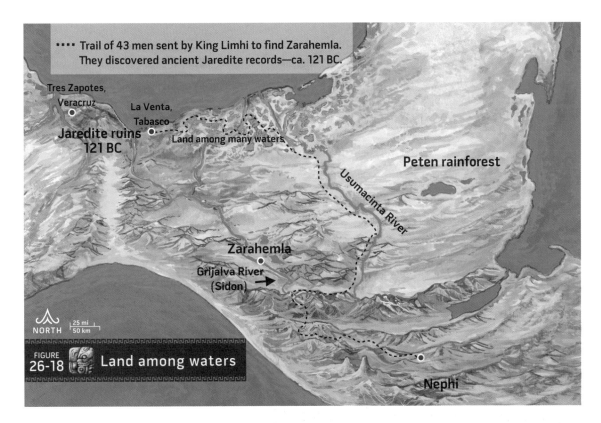

FIGURE 26–18: In search of Zarahemla, the forty-three men in the Limhi expedition appear to have followed the wrong river, a route that took them to a "land among many waters" (Mosiah 8:8). From there, they continued until they found some of the ancient ruins of the Jaredites, along with twenty-four engraved gold plates. The same areas that we propose as the Limhi route and that contain the ancient Jaredite ruins can be visited today. They give vivid testimonies of the consistency and impact of natural barriers, the existence of bodies of water that "just happen" to be in the right places, and archaeological evidence that supports the geography and history reflected in the Book of Mormon.

Venta. They would have completely missed the land of Zarahemla. The distance from Guatemala/Nephi to La Venta/Desolation is about five hundred miles.

Mormon 6:2, 4—Land of Many Waters, Rivers, and Fountains

The second land of many waters is a "land of many waters, rivers, and fountains" located in the land of Cumorah. A hill called Cumorah is also in the area of the *land of many waters, rivers, and fountains*. In fact, the definition of *Cumorah* is probably just that—a land of many waters, rivers, and fountains. *Cum* in Maya means gourd and is associated with water, like a water gourd. *Ha* or *ah* means water in the Maya language, suggesting "many waters, rivers, and fountains," and *mor* means mountains, lands, hills, or wilderness.

> And I, Mormon, wrote an epistle unto the king of the Lamanites, and desired of him that he would grant unto us that we might gather together our people unto the land of Cumorah, by a hill which was called Cumorah, and there we could give them battle. . . .
>
> And it came to pass that we did march forth to the land of Cumorah, and we did pitch our tents around about the hill Cumorah; and it was in a *land of many waters, rivers, and fountains*; and here we had hope to gain advantage over the Lamanites. (emphasis added)

From what is explained in the Book of Mormon, the distance between the narrow neck of land and the land of Cumorah clearly is not very great. This short distance is additionally reinforced by a statement Mormon makes wherein he tells us that the Nephites were fighting for their land: "And it came to pass that I did speak unto my people, and did urge them with great energy, that they should stand boldly before the Lamanites and fight for their wives, and their children, and *their houses, and their homes*" (Mormon 2:23; emphasis added).

This area is northward of the Isthmus of Tehuantepec and is about 175 miles northward from the lagoons of Tabasco and Chiapas—or the "land among many waters." The Tuxtla Mountains are in the state of Veracruz, Mexico, where water is found in abundance. The local people claim the water to be the purest in the entire country of Mexico.

FIGURE 26–19: Lake Catemaco is located in Veracruz, Mexico, in the Tuxtla Mountains and is the area proposed as the land of Cumorah, "a land of many waters, rivers, and fountains" (Mormon 6:4). (Photo courtesy of Cortney Boice)

The Tuxtla Mountains are in an area where a number of lakes are found. On many occasions, we spend the evening with our tour groups at La Finca Hotel, which is located on the shores of the beautiful Lake Catemaco. Natural hot springs emerge from the lake.

Also, many rivers are located in and around the area of the Tuxtla Mountains. Rainfall can take place year round, and the scenery is reminiscent of the Hawaiian Islands. Sugar cane, rice, and pineapple are among the major crops that are grown in the area. The area is so fertile that if a farmer cuts down a tree and uses it to build a fence, within a few years, it has grown into a tree again.

Springs of water not only bubble up in the lakes but also are seen to surface out of the side of a hill or to seep up from the ground. Members of our tour groups often state that they cannot imagine a more delightful area than the Tuxtla Mountains areas of Veracruz, Mexico. (For additional information on the Tuxtla area, see chapter 27, "Hills and Valleys.")

The area of the "land among many waters" is so fertile that if a farmer cuts down a tree and uses it to build a fence, within a few years, it has grown into a tree again.

7. THE PLACE WHERE THE SEA DIVIDES THE LAND

A Book of Mormon place that constitutes a significant geographical landmark and that involves water is an area associated with the Jaredites. The heartland of the Jaredites was in the land northward. The land southward was preserved for hunting grounds. A gulf and an isthmus apparently divided the two larger land masses: "And they built a great city by the narrow neck of land, by the *place where the sea divides the land*. And they did preserve the land southward for a wilderness, to get game. And the whole face of the land northward was covered with inhabitants" (Ether 10:20–21; emphasis added).

This scripture represents what appears to be one of the most obvious geographical locations in the Book of Mormon. A gulf is literally a place where the sea divides the land. When we add to this the great Coatzacoalcos River that serves as a dividing

line between the two land masses, we have a natural dividing line that has endured for thousands of years.

The Coatzacoalcos River probably constituted the northernmost borders of the land Bountiful in Book of Mormon times. The latter part of the Aztec word *titlan* from *Minatitlan* means "land of abundance"—or bountiful. Ixtlilxochitl said that the white god Quetzalcoatl took leave of his people at Coatzacoalcos. The word "Coatzacoalcos" means "the place of the establishment of the serpent religion." Christ is associated with the serpent in the Book of Mormon (see Helaman 8:13–15).

> Mormon, who compiled the Nephite history during the middle of the fourth century AD, lived in the land northward, probably in the city of Desolation, which was in the land of Desolation.

Mormon, who compiled the Nephite history during the middle of the fourth century AD, lived in the land northward, probably in the city of Desolation, which was in the land of Desolation. The city of Desolation was by the narrow pass that led into the land southward. Around AD 360, Mormon called all the Nephites to gather at the city of Desolation: "And it came to pass that I did cause my people that they should gather themselves together at the land Desolation, to a city which was in the borders, by the narrow pass which led into the land southward. . . . And it came to pass that in the three hundred and sixty and first year the Lamanites did come down to the city of Desolation to battle against us" (Mormon 3:5, 7).

The activities described in the above two scriptures apparently took place close to the same area as the "place where the sea divides the land." The Lamanites probably came down from Chiapas to Veracruz to battle the Nephites on the western side of the Coatzacoalcos River. We propose that the city of Desolation was in the area of Acayucan, Mexico. The ancient Olmec site of San Lorenzo is also nearby.

The city of Teancum was also probably located near the Gulf of Mexico. In an AD 363 battle where the Lamanites defeated the Nephites, the Nephites fled to the city of Teancum, which was by the seashore as well as close to the city of Desolation: "And the remainder did flee and join the inhabitants of the city Teancum. Now the city Teancum lay in the borders by the seashore; and it was also near the city Desolation" (Mormon 4:3).

8. THE WATERS OF RIPLIANCUM

Geography provides us with another body of water located in the right area with a parallel name correlation and with precise directional and distance references. The book of Ether calls this body of water "the waters of Ripliancum": "And it came to pass that he [Coriantumr] came to the *waters of Ripliancum*, which, by interpretation, is large, or to exceed all; wherefore, when they came to these waters they pitched their tents; and

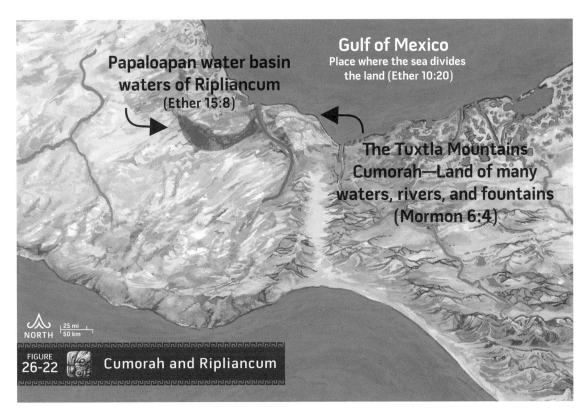

FIGURE 26–22: The land of Cumorah and the waters of Ripliancum are located in the land northward in the territory of the ancient Jaredites. The Gulf of Mexico (or "the place where the sea divides the land"; see Ether 10:20), the Coatzacoalcos River, and the Papaloapan water basin serve as water borders to the Tuxtla Mountains, or the land of Cumorah.

Shiz also pitched his tents near unto them; and therefore on the morrow they did come to battle" (Ether 15:8; emphasis added).

This is a battle that was fought four years prior to the great war of total Jaredite destruction near Ramah/Cumorah. Coriantumr defeated Shiz in this battle and drove him back southward to a place called Ogath. Coriantumr then camped by the hill Ramah, which is the same hill, the hill Cumorah, where the Nephites were later destroyed: "And it came to pass that the army of Coriantumr did pitch their tents by the hill Ramah; and it was that *same hill* where my father Mormon did hide up the records unto the Lord, which were sacred" (Ether 15:11; emphasis added).

Mormon hid up all the records in the hill Cumorah, with the exception of his abridged history that he gave to his son Moroni: "I [Mormon] made this record out of the plates of Nephi, and hid up in *the hill Cumorah* all the records which had been entrusted to me by the hand of the Lord, *save it were these few plates*, which I gave to my son Moroni" (Mormon 6:6; emphasis added).

> Mormon hid up all the records in the hill Cumorah, with the exception of his abridged history that he gave to his son Moroni.

In looking for a place that meets the qualifications of the waters of Ripliancum, we must consider the following:

1. The army of Shiz pursued the army of Coriantumr in a northward direction until they were hemmed in by a vast amount of water that they called *Ripliancum*.
2. Coriantumr drove Shiz back in a southward direction to a place called Ogath. Coriantumr camped at the hill Ramah, which is the same hill where Mormon hid up all the records except the portion that we have now, which we call the Book of Mormon, plus the sealed portion that Joseph Smith did not translate.
3. The hill Ramah where Coriantumr camped is the same hill as the Nephite hill Cumorah where the Lamanites defeated the Nephites in AD 385. It is also in the same general area where the Jaredite nation fell four years after the Coriantumr-Shiz battle described above.

The distance from the waters of Ripliancum to the hill Ramah is not given. However, the distance cannot be so great that the army could not march to it after their battle. But it must be far enough for the armies to be separated from each other.

The old name of *Tres Zapotes* is *Hueyapan*, which has the same meaning as Ripliancum in the Book of Mormon—exceedingly large waters (see Ether 15:8).

On our tours, we travel from the Tuxtla Mountains area toward the Gulf of Mexico for about thirty minutes when we begin to see a large water drainage system off to the left (westward). We soon realize that it is not the ocean because the Gulf of Mexico is off to our right. As we come in contact with the toll bridge, we notice a big bridge that crosses over a waterway to the Mexican city of Alvarado. To the right is the Gulf of Mexico. To the left is the massive Papaloapan water basin that drains from the mountains of Oaxaca and Veracruz. It just happens to be there.

The distance from the Papaloapan water basin (proposed waters of Ripliancum) to Hill Vigia (proposed hill Ramah) is fifteen to twenty miles of walking distance. The direction from Papaloapan/Ripliancum to Vigia/Ramah is southward, which is the direction required in the text. The archaeological site of Tres Zapotes is located at the base of the Hill Vigia/Ramah. And since the 1989 edition of *Exploring the Lands of the Book of Mormon*, we have learned that the old name of *Tres Zapotes* is *Hueyapan*, which has the same meaning as *Ripliancum* in the Book of Mormon—exceedingly large waters (see Ether 15:8).

9. LARGE BODIES OF WATER

In chapter 8, "The Teotihuacan Culture," and in chapter 19, "The Land Northward," the Mexico valley was proposed as the "land which was northward" in the Book of Mormon. The area is also the place where "large bodies of water" were found: "Therefore, Morianton put it into their hearts that they should flee to the *land which was northward*, which was covered with *large bodies of water*, and take possession of the *land which was northward*" (Alma 50:29; emphasis added).

The most probable candidate for the area described in Alma 50:29 is the area in and around Mexico City. Mexico city is located seventy-two hundred feet above sea level in a valley that once consisted of three large lakes. And Tenochtitlan (Mexico City) was literally built on a lake. (See chapter 8, "The Teotihuacan Culture," and chapter 19, "The Land Northward," for more details.)

FIGURE 26–23: A panoramic view of Lake Atitlan. Mormon made a spiritual comparison with the waters of Mormon when he wrote, "how beautiful are they to the eyes of them who there came to the knowledge of their Redeemer" (Mosiah 18:30). (Photo courtesy of Phil Skousen)

SUMMARY

In this chapter, we have discussed twelve major Book of Mormon bodies of water and their correlated geographic landmarks: (1) west sea (Pacific Ocean), (2) east sea (Atlantic Ocean), (3) waters of Mormon (Atitlan), (4) waters of Sebus (Chimaltenango), (5) Helam, land of pure water (Almolonga), (6) Sidon river (Grijalva), (7) a river (Usumacinta) that the Limhi expedition followed in search of Zarahemla, (8) land among many waters (lagoons of Campeche and Tabasco) encountered by the Limhi expedition, (9) a gulf (Gulf of Mexico)—the place where the sea divides the land, (10) Cumorah (Tuxtla Mountains)—land among many waters, rivers, and fountains; (11) Ripliancum (Papaloapan water basin)—waters to exceed all, and (12) a land (Mexico valley) that was northward where there were "large bodies of water and many rivers."

An apparently obvious conclusion is that mere coincidence did not place these Book of Mormon bodies of water in Mesoamerican geographic areas that just happen to be where they are supposed to be. We should be impressed that the archaeological, topological, linguistic, and practical-distances evidences associated with bodies of water in the land area where the Book of Mormon took place coincide very closely with what we read in the Book of Mormon. We can conclude further that our discussion about bodies of water is designed to be a continuation of serious geography study in establishing the historicity of the Book of Mormon.

Coincidence did not place bodies of water that relate to the geographical structure of the Book of Mormon in areas where appropriate archaeological, topological, and linguistic evidences are found.

CHAPTER 27

Hills and Valleys

Yea, and in the valley of Alma they poured out their thanks to God because he had been merciful unto them, and eased their burdens, and delivered them out of bondage. (Mosiah 24:21)

 n this chapter, we will present an overview of major Book of Mormon events associated with hills and valleys. Our understanding of the Book of Mormon increases as we geographically analyze the events that occurred in locations such as the valley of Alma and the hill Cumorah.

VALLEYS

Six valleys that have names attached to them are mentioned in the Book of Mormon, as follows:

1. Valley of Lemuel—by the Red Sea (1 Nephi 2:14)
2. Valley of Alma—in the land of Nephi (Mosiah 24:20)

OPPOSITE: The geography of the Book of Mormon is consistent throughout its pages. Hills, mountains, and valleys play a major role in our understanding the history of the Book of Mormon. Mountains separate the land of Nephi from the land of Zarahemla. Shown here is a picture from the Chiapas (Zarahemla) side looking south into the highlands of Guatemala—or the land of Nephi. (Photo courtesy of Cortney Boice)

Our
understanding
of the Book
of Mormon
increases
as we
geographically
analyze the
events that
occurred in
locations such
as the valley of
Alma and the
hill Cumorah.

3. Valley of Gideon—in the land of Zarahemla (Alma 2:26)

4. Valley of Nimrod—Jaredite valley in the Old World (Ether 2:1)

5. Valley of Corihor—Jaredite valley in the land northward (Ether 14:28)

6. Valley of Shurr—Jaredite valley in the land northward (Ether 14:28)

1. The Valley of Lemuel

The valley of Lemuel was located near the Red Sea by Egypt. Speaking to his son Lemuel, Lehi said: "O that thou mightest be like unto this valley, firm and steadfast, and immovable in keeping the commandments of the Lord!" (1 Nephi 2:10).

Valley of Lemuel was the name given to the valley by Lehi. The area constituted the first major campsite for the 600 BC Lehi colony, and the valley is in northern Saudi Arabia not too far from the Red Sea port of Aqaba, an arm of the Red Sea. The valley of Lemuel is located in the same area where Moses camped with the children of Israel for forty years.

2. The Valley of Alma

Just as Joseph Smith was an instrument in the hands of the Lord in restoring His Church in these latter days, so was Alma an instrument in the Lord's hand in restoring the Church of Christ among the Nephites in the second century BC. Alma had been a priest of the Nephite King Noah in the city of Nephi. Alma listened to the words of the prophet Abinadi; preached in private; set forth the covenant of baptism; and then, in the waters of Mormon, baptized those who were converted. He established the Church of Christ about 147 years prior to the birth of the Savior (see Mosiah 18:7).

While in the land of Mormon, Alma ordained priests and instituted laws for the government of the Church of Christ. After a short period of time, King Noah discovered Alma and his followers at the waters of Mormon. Numbering 450 people, Alma and his followers were apprised of the coming of the king's army, so Alma's people took their tents and their families and departed into the wilderness (see Mosiah 18:34–35).

After traveling eight days in the wilderness, they arrived at a very beautiful and pleasant land, a land of pure water (see Mosiah 23:3–5). They called the place the land of Helam; and, as was their custom, they named the city and the land after the person who first possessed it (see Alma 8:7). Helam was the first who was baptized by Alma at the waters of Mormon. Alma and members of the Church of Christ lived in the land of Helam for twenty-five years. Some readers have suggested that Helam was the father of Alma because of the above events and because *Helam*, such as in the name *Helaman*, became a family name. Alma named his oldest son Helaman.

While they were living in the land of Helam, Alma and his followers were discovered by the Lamanite army who had pursued Limhi and his people as they escaped from the land of Nephi and went to the land of Zarahemla. The Lamanites placed Alma and members of the Church of Christ under bondage and placed Amulon, a Nephite and former colleague of Alma, as master over them.

About the year 120 BC, the Lord caused a deep sleep to come over the Lamanite guards, and Alma and his group departed from the land of Helam. After traveling for one day, they arrived at a place they called the valley of Alma:

> And Alma and his people departed into the wilderness; and when they had traveled all day they pitched their tents in a valley, and they called *the valley Alma*, because he led their way in the wilderness.
>
> Yea, and in the *valley of Alma* they poured out their thanks to God because he had been merciful unto them, and eased their burdens, and had delivered them out of bondage; for they were in bondage, and none could deliver them except it were the Lord their God. (Mosiah 24:20–21; emphasis added)

The concept of the Lord's easing the burdens placed upon their backs and delivering them from bondage is dualistic in nature. Just as the Lord eased the burdens from the shoulders and the backs of those prayerful and faithful Nephites, so does He lift the burdens of all His children who come unto Him—burdens caused by sickness, death, sorrow, and suffering. The ultimate burdens that Christ lifts from our shoulders and our backs are the bondage of death through the Resurrection and the bondage of sin through repentance.

Mormon makes it clear that his intent in putting the stories of both Alma and Limhi, parallel accounts, in the Book of Mormon was to teach us about the Atonement of Christ. Mormon writes that "they were in bondage, and none could deliver them except it were the Lord their God" (Mosiah 24:21). We are in bondage, and no one except Christ, the Redeemer, can deliver us from the bondage of death and hell.

The Lord caused a deep sleep to come upon the Lamanites, thus allowing Alma and his people to escape and then travel through the wilderness. When they arrived in the land of Zarahemla, King Mosiah (a vicarious representative of God) received them with open arms. He previously had received Limhi and his people with open arms. Limhi and his followers had administered wine to the Lamanite soldiers, which caused them to fall into a deep sleep.

The valley by the village of San Francisco el Alto, Guatemala, and close to the "cuatro caminos" crossroads is a viable candidate for the valley of Alma. After twelve more days of travel time, Alma and his followers arrived in the land of Zarahemla (see Mosiah 24:25). Their travels would have taken them through Huehuetenango and the Cuchumatane wilderness, where they arrived at the border of Mexico near present-day Ciudad Cuauhtemoc, Chiapas. The distance is ninety-six miles, which, if divided by the suggested travel time per day of eight miles, is the same as outlined in the Book of Mormon. Twelve days times eight miles a day equals ninety-six miles.

Just as the Lord eased the burdens from the shoulders and the backs of those prayerful and faithful Nephites, so does He lift the burdens of all His children who come unto Him.

This is the same route that John Lloyd Stephens took in 1839, which took him the same amount of time as it took Alma and his followers. Today, the distance can be covered by bus in four hours. Nevertheless, it represents a vicarious experience of traveling from the valley of the shadow of death (valley of Alma) to paradise (the land of Zarahemla).

The city of Huehuetenango is about halfway between San Francisco el Alto and the border town of La Mesilla. As of the year 2008, four stakes of the Church have been organized at Huehuetenango, a city with a population of about fifty thousand, thus making it a very high Mormon to non-Mormon ratio.

3. The Valley of Gideon

We virtually have a parallel account of Alma's journey in the Book of Mormon as we trace the footsteps of the people of Limhi from the land/city of Nephi to the valley of Gideon in the land of Zarahemla.

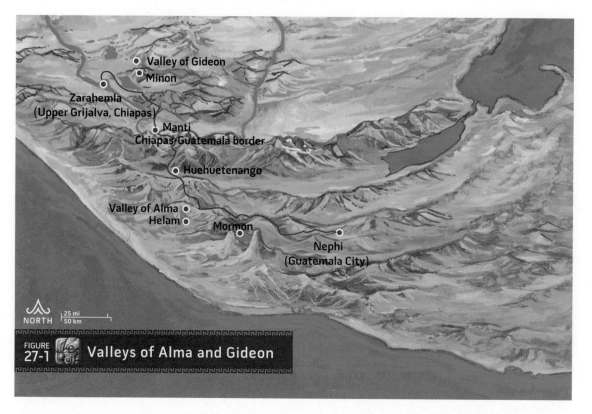

FIGURE 27-1: Valleys of Alma and Gideon

FIGURE 27-1: The valley of Alma was located in the land of Nephi, and the valley of Gideon was located in the land of Zarahemla, east of the river Sidon. The valley of Gideon is a neighbor to the city of Minon, which is projected to be at, or near, the present-day Ciudad Real Comitan, Chiapas. The valley of Gideon and the town of Minon were higher in elevation than the city of Zarahemla, as they were "above" Zarahemla. The valley of Alma was only a day's travel from the land of Helam, the "land of pure water."

Both the journey of Alma and his colony and of Limhi and his colony appear to have taken place about the same time period, around 120 BC.

Both Limhi and Alma were well acquainted with the Nephite King Noah, who lived in the land of Nephi. Alma had been a priest in the court of the wicked king. Limhi was the son of the same wicked king.

Alma escaped to Zarahemla when the Lord caused a deep sleep to come over the guards. Limhi's people escaped when they were able to get the Lamanite guards drunk. The man who suggested that Limhi get the guards drunk was named Gideon—the person after whom the valley of Gideon was named. The valley of Gideon is in the land of Zarahemla. We can easily plot the suggested route of Limhi, Gideon, and the Nephites who had been living in the land of Nephi for three generations. Obviously, the proposed route of Limhi and Gideon is similar to the route proposed for Alma and should not be confused with the journey of the Limhi expedition that went in search of Zarahemla but did not find it. This mountain route is the *only* way to travel once travelers leave the crossroads—by Quetzaltenango—and travel to the Guatemala-Mexico frontier at the headwaters of the River Grijalva. As outlined in chapter 26, "Bodies of Water," the River Grijalva is the river Sidon.

The distance from Guatemala City (land of Nephi) to the Mexican border near Ciudad Cuauhtemoc is about 250 miles. Traveling the distance in thirty days, the estimated travel time from Nephi to Zarahemla, constitutes an average distance of about eight miles per day.

The candidate for the valley of Gideon is a beautiful valley along the Chiapas Mountains ridge northwest of Ciudad Cuauhtemoc not far beyond the present-day city of Comitan in the state of Chiapas, Mexico.

The identifying scriptures for the valley of Gideon are as follows:

Alma 17:1
And it came to pass that as Alma was journeying from the land of Gideon southward, away to the land of Manti, behold to his astonishment, he met with the sons of Mosiah journeying towards the land of Zarahemla.

The border of Guatemala near Ciudad Cuauhtemoc, which is likely where the land of Manti is located, is southward from Comitan, which is close to the area we propose to be the valley of Gideon. The sons of Mosiah would have to travel toward Comitan prior to dropping down into the upper Grijalva valley of Zarahemla. To do otherwise would be almost prohibitive because of the terrain.

Alma 2:20
When Alma could pursue the Amlicites no longer he caused that his people should pitch their tents in the valley of Gideon.

The ancient Nephite migratory route from the land of Nephi to the land of Zarahemla can still be followed today and parallels the travels of John Lloyd Stephens in 1839.

The candidate for the valley of Gideon is a beautiful valley along the Chiapas Mountains ridge northwest of Ciudad Cuauhtemoc.

Alma had sent spies to monitor the movements of the Amlicites. The spies returned in haste and reported, "Behold, we followed the camp of the Amlicites, and to our great astonishment, *the land of Minon, above the city of Zarahemla, in the course of the land of Nephi,* we saw a numerous host of the Lamanites; and behold, the Amlicites have joined them" (Alma 2:24; emphasis added).

We can determine that the land of Minon is not too far from the valley of Gideon and is in the course of the land of Nephi—the same route Alma was taking when he met the sons of Mosiah after their fourteen-year mission among the Lamanites. We should also note that both Minon and Gideon appear to be higher in elevation than the city of Zarahemla. That statement describes the topography very well in relation to Comitan and the upper Grijalva valley, as Comitan is like a large shelf above the Grijalva valley.

Alma 2:26–27

And it came to pass that the people of Nephi took their tents, and departed out of *the valley of Gideon* towards their city, which was *the city of Zarahemla.*

And behold, as they were crossing *the river Sidon,* the Lamanites and the Amlicites, being as numerous almost, as it were, as the sands of the sea, came upon them to destroy them." (emphasis added)

Now we see the river Sidon put into the mix. Originating in the mountains of Guatemala from a southeasterly direction, it (the Grijalva River) runs though the entire Chiapas depression, an area about twenty-five miles wide and over a hundred miles long. The river runs in a northwestern direction until it reaches the Sumidero Canyon in the lower Grijalva where it turns north and winds its way to the Gulf of Mexico, dividing the city of Villahermosa, Tabasco. The wording in the above scripture suggests that the city of Zarahemla is on the westward side of the river, as was the case of the archaeological ruins of Santa Rosa, a likely candidate for the city of Zarahemla, before the ruins were covered over by water as a result of the construction of the Angostura Dam.

Alma 6:7

After eight years serving as chief judge, Alma resigned his position and dedicated his time to preaching the gospel. After teaching in the city of Zarahemla, he "went over upon the east of the river Sidon into the valley of Gideon." Again, the same terminology is used in relation to Zarahemla and the land of Gideon. Minon and Gideon were *above the city of Zarahemla,* and Gideon was *over upon the east of the river Sidon.*

4. Valley of Nimrod

Nimrod was the valley where the early Jaredites went in the Old World as they left the Tower of Babel. It was here where the Lord came down and talked with the brother of Jared (see Ether 2:1, 4).

5. Valleys of Corihor and Shurr

The valleys of Corihor and Shurr are located in Jaredite territory in the New World and are mentioned in relationship with the war between Shiz and Coriantumr, which took place between 400 BC and 250 BC. The following scriptures written by Moroni record the events that took place in these two valleys:

> **Ether 14:26–28**
>
> And it came to pass that Shiz did pursue Coriantumr *eastward, even to the borders by the seashore*, and there he gave battle unto Shiz for the space of three days.
>
> And so terrible was the destruction among the armies of Shiz that the people began to be frightened, and began to flee before the armies of Coriantumr; and they fled to the land of Corihor, and swept off the inhabitants before them, all them that would not join them.
>
> And they pitched their tents in the *valley of Corihor*; and Coriantumr pitched his tents in the *valley of Shurr*. Now the valley of Shurr was near the hill Comner. (emphasis added)

This terrible destruction led up to the final demise of the Jaredite kingdom, which involved the same two military leaders as mentioned here, Shiz and Coriantumr, culminating in the death of over two million people (see Ether 15:2). These valleys may have been located somewhere in the Tuxtla Mountains of Veracruz and close to the Gulf of Mexico. And the cities that were destroyed may have been La Venta, San Lorenzo, and others between La Venta and Tres Zapotes.

We have enough evidence to determine that the battle between Shiz and Coriantumr took place near the archaeological site of Tres Zapotes, which is located at the base of the Hill Vigia (Ramah-Cumorah) by the Papaloapan water basin (anciently called Hueyapan)—which we can now identify as the waters of Ripliancum referred to by Moroni (see Ether 15:8–11).

HILLS

Ten different hills are mentioned in the Book of Mormon. The two most famous hills are the hill Shim and the hill Cumorah. The hill Cumorah was called Ramah during the time of the Jaredites.

We have enough evidence to determine that the battle between Shiz and Coriantumr took place near the archaeological site of Tres Zapotes, which is located at the base of the Hill Vigia by the Papaloapan water basin.

The term "mount" is also used in the Book of Mormon, although only three specific geographical names are used with "mount." They are (1) the mount that was called Antipus (see Alma 47:7–10); (2) a wilderness with the word "mounts" as part of its title, Hermounts, which means a wilderness of wild and ravenous beasts (see Alma 2:37); and (3) a mount in the Old World, Mount Shelem, where the brother of Jared acquired the stones to provide light in the boats as the Jaredites crossed the ocean (see Ether 3:1).

The terms "mountain" and "mountains" are used several times in the Book of Mormon. For the most part, however, they are used in figurative or poetic terms such as the following:

> How beautiful upon the *mountains* are the feet of him that bringeth good tidings; that publisheth peace. (Mosiah 12:21; emphasis added)
>
> I was caught away in the Spirit of the Lord, yea, into an exceedingly high *mountain*. (1 Nephi 11:1; emphasis added)
>
> The *mountain* of the Lord's house shall be established in the top of the *mountains*. (2 Nephi 12:2; emphasis added)

When the term "mountain(s)" is used in the Book of Mormon as a geographical description, it is utilized as a general term. Two such instances are in relation to the Gadianton robbers and the great destruction at the time of Christ. For example:

> The Gadianton robbers, who dwelt upon the *mountains*. (3 Nephi 1:27; emphasis added)
>
> In the place of the city [Moronihah] there became a great *mountain*. (3 Nephi 8:10; emphasis added)

The term "forest" is also used as a general term in such instances as when Alma baptized at the waters of Mormon. He also called the area "the forest of Mormon": "And now it came to pass that all this was done in Mormon, yea, by the waters of Mormon, in the forest that was near the waters of Mormon; yea, the place of Mormon, the waters of Mormon, *the forest of Mormon*, how beautiful are they to the eyes of them who there came to the knowledge of their Redeemer; yea, and how blessed are they, for they shall sing to his praise forever" (Mosiah 18:30; emphasis added).

On several occasions, the term "forest" is also used in association with wild beasts or animals. For example, "for the land [land southward] was covered with animals of the *forest*" (Ether 10:19; emphasis added).

Enos wrote: "I went to hunt beasts in the *forests*" (Enos 1:3; emphasis added).

The Nephite King Limhi gathered his people together to give battle to the Lamanites: "[They] laid wait for them in the fields and in the *forests*" (Mosiah 20:8; emphasis added).

The most commonly used term in the Book of Mormon comparable to the terms "hills," "mountains," and "forest" is the term "wilderness."

The most commonly used term in the Book of Mormon comparable to the terms "hills," "mountains," and "forest" is the term "wilderness" (see chapter 24, "Wilderness Areas"). In many instances, the term "wilderness" is synonymous with the term "mountain":

They would retreat back into the *mountains, and into the wilderness.* (Helaman 11:25; emphasis added)

And they were again obliged to return out of the *wilderness and out of the mountains* unto their own lands, because of the exceeding greatness of the numbers of those robbers who infested the mountains and the wilderness. (Helaman 11:31; emphasis added)

From the perspective of Mesoamerica, the best term that could possibly be used to point out a specific site is the term "hill." The terms "mountains" or "wilderness" are, for the most part, general terms. And because almost everything in Mesoamerica is either mountainous or a jungle, the inappropriateness of referring to hill Shim or hill Cumorah as the mountain Shim or the mountain Cumorah is evident. This conclusion is true, in spite of the fact that the candidates for these two hills in Mesoamerica are of considerable size.

Simply stated, if you lived in the mountains where more than five million natives live in the highlands of Guatemala and Chiapas, you would not say, "I'm going over to that mountain." You are already on the mountain. You would say, however, "I am going over to that hill." "That hill" is just another rambling peak in the tops of the mountains or a specific hill in a certain mountainous or wilderness region. Such a reference would be true of a hill located in the Tuxtla mountain range of Veracruz or a hill rising above the jungle floor of the Peten.

As mentioned, the two most prominent hills in Book of Mormon history are hill Shim and hill Cumorah (hill Ramah to the Jaredites). They are both located on the northward side of the narrow neck of land. They appear to be in the same general vicinity of each other, and they play a major role in both the Jaredite and the Nephite histories. We will first present an analysis of the hill Shim followed by a discussion about the hill Cumorah.

> The two most prominent hills in Book of Mormon history are hill Shim and hill Cumorah. The hill Cumorah is the same hill that the Jaredites called Ramah.

The Hill Shim

Mormon, Jaguar of the Mountains, was a descendant of Nephi, the son of Lehi. Nephite records had been kept for over nine hundred years when Mormon received the charge to make an abridged record concerning his people. This charge was given to him by the record-keeping Ammaron when Mormon was ten years old (see Mormon 1:1–4). The time was approximately AD 321. The records were hidden in a hill that was called Shim. From sources in the Book of Mormon, we know that Mormon lived in the land northward near the narrow passage that led into the land southward (see Mormon 1:6; 3:5, 7). The hill Shim was also in the land northward and was apparently close to where Mormon lived:

> Ammaron said unto me: I perceive that thou art a sober child, and art quick to observe;
>
> Therefore, when ye are about twenty and four years old I would that ye should remember the things that ye have observed concerning this people; and when ye are of that age go to the land Antum, *unto a hill which shall be called Shim;* and there have I deposited unto the Lord all the sacred engravings concerning this people.
>
> And behold, ye shall take the plates of Nephi unto yourself, *and the remainder shall ye leave in the place where they are;* and ye shall engrave on the plates of Nephi all the things that ye have observed concerning this people. (Mormon 1:2–4; emphasis added)

The Tuxtla Mountains in southern Veracruz, Mexico, provide the most likely spot for the location of the hill Shim.

Mormon was instructed to go to a hill called Shim that was near his home and take the plates of Nephi and make a record of his people: "And behold, I had gone according to the word of Ammaron, and taken the plates of Nephi, and did make a record according to the words of Ammaron" (Mormon 2:17).

Joseph Smith was instructed by Moroni nearly fifteen hundred years later to go to a hill near his home in Manchester, New York, take the records that Mormon had engraved on gold plates, and translate them. "On the twenty-second day of September, one thousand eight hundred and twenty-seven, having gone as usual at the end of another year to the place where they were deposited, the same heavenly messenger delivered them up to me" (Joseph Smith—History 1:59).

Mormon, Jaguar of the Mountains, was about twenty-four years old when he took the plates of Nephi from the hill Shim to engrave on them a history of his people (about AD 325). Joseph Smith, the great American Prophet, was twenty-four years old when he finished translating the record that Mormon prepared (AD 1830).

The hill Shim, which is near the city of Desolation where Mormon received his records, and the hill in New York, which Latter-day Saints have come to call Cumorah, are two separate hills. They are located in two vastly different areas. The hill Shim is located near the narrow neck of land. The Latter-day Saint Hill Cumorah is located in the state of New York. If the narrow neck of land is the Isthmus of Tehuantepec, as we propose, then the hill Shim is nearby and most logically is located in the state of Veracruz, Mexico.

Mormon, who lived to see the downfall of his people, lived a very full and productive life. He was a prophet who, at the age of fifteen, was visited of the Lord (see Mormon 1:15). He was a military leader of the Nephites, beginning at the age of sixteen (see Mormon 2:1). And at the age of twenty-four, he began to write a history of his people from records he obtained from the Nephite "library" located in the hill Shim (see Mormon 1:17).

The Tuxtla Mountains in southern Veracruz, Mexico, provide the most likely spot for the location of the hill Shim. A number of volcanic mountains are found in the area. Today, one hill in the area north of the narrow pass that runs through the Isthmus of Tehuantepec is called Cintepec. It is located in the Tuxtla Mountains of Veracruz and is the same hill where the basalt rock that was used to carve the giant Olmec heads was quarried. The heads were then shipped down the river to La Venta in the state of Tabasco. The word "Cintepec," with the ending *tepec*, denotes "mount" or "hill." In the Nahuatl language, the beginning of the word, *cin*, means "corn." Hence, the place where the giant stone heads were quarried was called "corn hill."

Therefore, we conclude that the hill Shim, as recorded in Mormon 1:2, is the same hill that today is called *Cintepec*, which literally means "corn hill." It is located about twenty-five miles north of Acayucan, Veracruz, close to the area we propose where Mormon lived. During Mormon's time, the place where Mormon lived was called the city of Desolation (see Mormon 4:8). The city of Desolation was called that name by the Nephites because of the great Jaredite destruction (see Helaman 3:5). We propose that the city of Desolation where Mormon probably lived is the same place as the Jaredite/Olmec ruins of San Lorenzo Tenochtitlan. These ruins may have been where the ancient

"Hill Shim" means "Corn Hill" and has the same meaning as "Hill Cintepec," which is located in the Tuxtla Mountains of Veracruz, Mexico.

FIGURE 27–2: Shown is the Hill Cintepec, which we propose as the most logical candidate for the Book of Mormon hill Shim. Mormon was told that when he reached twenty-four years of age, he was to go to the hill Shim where he would have access to records that had been kept by the Nephites for nine hundred years previously. Some of these records (the brass plates of Laban) had been carried from Jerusalem through the desert to the Arabian Sea and then across the ocean to the land of first inheritance. From there, all the records, as they accumulated, were carried to the land of Nephi by Nephi, from Nephi to Zarahemla by Mosiah, and from Zarahemla to Bountiful just prior to the visit of Christ. We are not told who took them to the hill Shim or when they were taken there. The hill Shim was in Jaredite territory. (Photo courtesy of Sheryl Lee Wilson)

King Kish lived, as determined by a monument discovered there and by the writings on the Temple of the Sun at Palenque (see chapter 5, "The Olmec [Jaredite] Culture").

Cintepec, or the hill Shim, is within a fifteen-minute drive south of beautiful Lake Catemaco, which is located in a land of many rivers, lakes, and springs. To our knowledge, no one has ever proposed a hill Shim in the New York area where Joseph Smith retrieved the plates from Moroni in the year 1827. In the absence of anyone's locating a viable candidate for the hill Shim in the New York area, we have no legitimate geographical reason to suggest that the hill Cumorah is in New York.

The Hill Cumorah (Hill Ramah)

Many members of the Church are not aware that the hill Ramah of the Jaredites is the same hill as the hill Cumorah of the Nephites (see Ether 15:11). Scientific and scriptural analyses have been presented beginning in the 1940s proposing the hypothesis that the Hill Cumorah in New York is not the hill Cumorah of the Book of Mormon.

> If the Olmecs are the same people as the Jaredites, then the Book of Mormon hill Cumorah is in Veracruz, Mexico.

The hypothesis is stated as follows: If the Olmecs, who had their headquarters along the Gulf of Mexico, are the same people as the Jaredites in the Book of Mormon, then the hill Cumorah referred to in the Book of Mormon is in Veracruz, Mexico, and not in upstate New York. That hypothesis is based on Book of Mormon givens that the hill Ramah was located in Jaredite territory and that the Jaredite hill Ramah is the same hill as the Nephite hill Cumorah.

Nevertheless, the issue is still a sensitive one. Traditional history of the Church affirms that the hill in New York is, indeed, the hill Cumorah referred to in the Book of Mormon. In the year 1868, Orson Pratt, an Apostle of the Church, presented an overview of Book of Mormon geography that is recorded in the *Journal of Discourses* (vol. 14:324–31) wherein he states that "the great and last battle, in which several hundred thousand Nephites perished was on the hill Cumorah, the same hill from which the plates were taken by Joseph Smith."

Very few members of the Church ever lived in Palmyra where the Prophet Joseph Smith received the gold plates because, within just a few years, the Church moved its headquarters from New York to Ohio and subsequently to Missouri, Illinois, and Utah. Nevertheless, tradition dictated that the "hill of considerable size" (Joseph Smith—History 1:51), where the Prophet retrieved the plates and which was located near the Smith home in Ontario County, New York, was the actual hill where the final Nephite-Lamanite battle was fought (see Mormon 6:6).

A careful reading of Mormon 6:6 has caused adherents of a Mexico hill Cumorah to reinforce their position by illustrating that Mormon "hid up in the hill Cumorah all the records" that the Lord entrusted to him except "these few plates" that he gave to his son, Moroni (Mormon 6:6). The "few plates," they say, are the plates (our Book of Mormon) that Moroni carried from Mexico to New York. In his own words, he writes,

"I will write and hide up the records in the earth; and whither I go it mattereth not" (Mormon 8:4).

Fifteen years later, at about AD 400, Moroni wrote that he had made an end of abridging the book of Ether and had not yet left the lands of the Lamanites. He wrote that he would wander "whithersoever" for the safety of his life (Moroni 1:3). It is during that time of wandering from AD 400 to his last entry in AD 421 that adherents of the Mexico hill Cumorah say he would have wandered from Veracruz, Mexico, to upstate New York.

This concept, which became known as the "two-Cumorah theory," proposed the existence of two separate hill Cumorahs—one in Mesoamerica where the last battles were fought and another in upstate New York where Joseph Smith was directed to the plates left there by Moroni. However, that thinking is not a totally accurate assessment because the Book of Mormon speaks of *only one* hill Cumorah—and it is the same hill that the Jaredites called Ramah (see Ether 15:11). As far as we know, no valid information has come forth between 1823 when Moroni first appeared to Joseph Smith to the present time to suggest that Joseph Smith ever stated that the hill in New York is *the* hill Cumorah/Ramah where the last battles of the Nephites/Lamanites and Jaredites took place.

Further, as far as we know, when Moroni appeared to Joseph Smith yearly over a four-year period, Moroni never referred to the New York hill as the hill Ramah or hill Cumorah. In writing about the hill at a later time, Joseph simply says, "Convenient to the village of Manchester, Ontario county, New York, stands a hill of considerable size, and the most elevated of any in the neighborhood" (Joseph Smith—History 1:51). This statement does not mean that at some point Joseph or other members of the Church did not feel that the hill where the plates were retrieved is not the hill Cumorah referred to in Mormon 6:6. A case in point is a letter written by Joseph Smith to the Church dated September 6, 1842, which is now section 128 of the Doctrine and Covenants. Joseph uses what might be considered poetic, figurative language in this letter when he writes, "And again, what do we hear? Glad tidings from Cumorah! Moroni, an angel from heaven, declaring the fulfillment of the prophets—the book to be revealed" (D&C 128:20). If current members of the Church view this statement as a revelation on Book of Mormon geography, then they would probably not want to entertain the idea that the hills Ramah and Cumorah are in Mexico. On the other hand, if Joseph's words are considered a generalized statement about events that occurred during the restoration process and leading up to the section 128 central theme of baptism for the dead, then Joseph's words should not be viewed in connection with Book of Mormon geographical issues.

A hill in Mesoamerica that has received the most attention over the last thirty years as a candidate for the hill Ramah/Cumorah is the Hill Vigia located near the Papaloapan water basin about ninety miles southeast of the city of Veracruz.

No valid information has come forth between 1823 when Moroni first appeared to Joseph Smith to the present time to suggest that Joseph Smith ever stated that the hill in New York is the hill Cumorah/Ramah where the last battles of the Nephites/Lamanites and Jaredites took place.

Following is a brief review of the development of a hypothesis to that effect.

In 1947, a seventy-six-page booklet entitled *Cumorah—Where?* was written by Thomas S. Ferguson.[1] Ferguson put in writing what some students of the Book of Mormon were discussing in regard to the hill Cumorah. The conclusion of the booklet was that the last battles in the Book of Mormon probably took place somewhere in Mexico.

David Palmer wrote a book in 1981 called *In Search of Cumorah: New Evidences for the Book of Mormon from Ancient Mexico* in which he writes: "The impact of placing Mormon's Cumorah in the State of New York is to grossly distort the geography of the Book of Mormon. Doing this makes it impossible to reconcile the internal geography of the Book of Mormon with actual maps. Without a valid geography of the Book of Mormon there cannot be any serious studies of the correlation between the geography and the Book of Mormon."[2]

Four years later, in 1985, John Sorenson, an anthropologist at Brigham Young University, published his book, *An Ancient American Setting for the Book of Mormon.* Sorenson is credited with being the person who originally labeled a hill called Vigia located in the Tuxtla Mountains of Veracruz, Mexico, as the Nephite hill Cumorah.[3]

Other books and articles were written on the subject, expressing agreement on the Nephite Cumorah/Vigia concept. One such book was written in 1988 by Richard Hauck, a Latter-day Saint archaeologist, who titled his book *Deciphering the Geography of the Book of Mormon.* In 2007, John L. Lund, author of *Mesoamerica and the Book of Mormon: Is This the Place?* wrote: "There were two Cumorahs: one in Mesoamerica where the final battles of the Jaredites and Nephites took place, and another Cumorah near Palmyra, New York where Moroni traveled after the last great battle of the Nephites."[4]

Following the publication of David Palmer's book in 1981, we began routing our tours through Veracruz where the Hill Vigia is located. In addition to surveying the hill and analyzing the surrounding archaeological data, we take the opportunity to visit the site of La Venta and the Coatzacoalcos River area en route to the Hill Vigia.

The Hill Vigia is a rather freestanding hill, and with the exception of some volcanic mountains in the area, Vigia is the most prominent. The community of Santiago Tuxtla rests peacefully at the base of the Hill Vigia, and the ancient archaeological Olmec site of Tres Zapotes flanks the opposite side of the hill. Families live on the hillside of Vigia, and cows and other animals graze in its pastures. Springs of water spout up at different places on the hill. The Hill Vigia is considerably larger than the hill in Palmyra, New York. The local people from the town of Santiago Tuxtla require about two hours to walk to the top of the Hill Vigia. Our tour members require between three and four hours, so we usually go to the top in the back of a cattle truck. From the top of the hill, on a clear day, visitors can observe the plains to the south and the rolling hills that extend to the Gulf of Mexico to the north.

1. Thomas S. Ferguson, *Cumorah—Where?* (Independence, MO: Press of Zion's Printing and Publishing Co., 1947).

2. David A. Palmer, *In Search of Cumorah: New Evidences for the Book of Mormon from Ancient Mexico* (Bountiful, UT: Horizon Publishers, 1981), 18.

3. John L. Sorenson, *An Ancient American Setting for the Book of Mormon* (Salt Lake City and Provo, UT: Deseret Book and Foundation for Ancient Research and Mormon Studies, 1996), 349.

4. John L. Lund, *Mesoamerica and the Book of Mormon: Is This the Place?* (n.p.: The Communications Company, 2007), 136.

"The impact of placing Mormon's Cumorah in the State of New York is to grossly distort the geography of the Book of Mormon."

—David Palmer

FIGURE 27–3: The defining statement regarding Book of Mormon geography is in relation to the location of the hill Cumorah where the last great Nephite-Lamanite battle took place in AD 385. This battle occurred during the early part of the Maya Preclassic Period when a major revolution was taking place in Mesoamerica. Shown here is the Hill Vigia, which is located in the Tuxtla Mountains of Veracruz, a hill that presently is the most logical candidate for the Book of Mormon hill Cumorah. Therefore, we designate the Hill Vigia as the focal point of the AD 385 battle in which 230,000 Nephites were killed. (Photo courtesy of Merrill C. Oaks)

Proposing the Hill Vigia to be the same hill as the hill Cumorah of the Book of Mormon, Palmer writes: "After examination of satellite pictures, visits to the hill and the ancient mounds which surround it, and analysis of the topography and archaeology of the immediate area, I have become fairly convinced it is the correct spot."[5]

Palmer then proceeds to outline the qualifications necessary for the hill Cumorah preceded by the following statement: "At the present time it does not appear that there is any alternative site which has archaeological support to the degree that the Cerro Vigia does."[6]

Reasons for Labeling the Hill Vigia to Be the Hill Cumorah

A careful reading of the Book of Mormon will pinpoint several requirements for the hill Cumorah, all of which are met by the Hill Vigia and the surrounding area.[7] The hill Cumorah must be

1. Near an eastern seacoast. The eastern side of the Gulf of Mexico constitutes an eastern seacoast and is in close proximity to the Hill Vigia.
2. Near both the hill Shim and the narrow neck of land. The Hill Vigia is about sixty miles from the top of the pass that runs through the Isthmus of Tehuantepec.
3. Situated so it overlooks a coastal plain, possibly near other mountains and valleys. The Hill Vigia meets those requirements.

5. Palmer, *In Search of Cumorah*, 91.

6. Palmer, *In Search of Cumorah*, 91.

7. See Palmer, *In Search of Cumorah*, 96–101. In addition to Palmer's analysis, we have made several editorial comments on the requirements outlined in the text.

4. Located a distance of a one-day journey from a large body of water called the waters of Ripliancum. The Papaloapan water basin that empties into the Gulf of Mexico is about eighteen miles from the base of the Hill Vigia.

5. Located in a land of many waters and rivers. The Hill Vigia is located in a land of beautiful lakes and picturesque rivers.

6. Located in a land where "fountains" are found. The Hill Vigia is located in a land of pure water where streams of underground water spring forth.

7. Located in an area where an abundance of water is available to provide sustenance for men, women, and children and a military advantage. The Tuxtla Mountains area, where the Hill Vigia is located, meets that requirement.

8. Located in an area wherein Nephites escaping to the south countries could escape without being captured by the Lamanites. A secluded route between the coast and the Tuxtla Mountains meets this requirement.

9. Large enough for Mormon to view hundreds of thousands of bodies. The Hill Vigia is about twenty-four hundred feet high and fulfills that requirement.

10. A significant landmark because two nations perished on the spot and because sacred records were hidden there.

11. Freestanding so people could camp around it. It must also be situated in such a manner that it could serve as a protection for the women and children. The Hill Vigia meets those requirements.

12. Located in a temperate climate because of the absence of any reference to snow or cold in the Book of Mormon. The Tuxtla Mountains area is the "Hawaii of Mexico."

13. Located in an area that is subject to volcanoes and earthquakes, a requirement for the land northward. Mesoamerica is a land of volcanic activity and earthquake eruptions. The San Martin Volcano last erupted in 1793.

> The words *Ramah* and *Vigia* have the same meaning—that of a lookout hill, or a hill overlooking a designated area.

Although the above list is compelling, the primary reasons that the hill Cumorah is in the area of the Tuxtla Mountains are the facts that it is the same hill as the hill Ramah of the Jaredites and that it is close to the hill Shim, a hill identified by both the Jaredites and the Nephites. This reasoning simply means that if the Jaredites and the Olmecs are the same people, as defined in *Exploring the Lands of the Book of Mormon*, then the hill Cumorah is in the area of Veracruz because that is where the hill Ramah is located. The words *Ramah* and *Vigia* have the same meaning—that of a lookout hill, or a hill overlooking a designated area.

We took our first tour group to Mexico in 1970. Since 1982, we have conducted thousands of Latter-day Saints to the Hill Vigia and to Santiago Tuxtla where the Hill Vigia is located. The process of observing the responses of the people has been extremely interesting. Many tour members, prior to their trip, had never heard of the idea that the hill Cumorah/Ramah was in Mexico. Others have struggled with the idea and have concluded that the traditional Latter-day Saint Cumorah in New York must still be the site of the last battles. The majority of the people, however, have concluded that, with the information in the Book of Mormon accompanied with geographical and archaeological evidence of the Hill Vigia, Mexico is the more likely candidate for the place where the last battles were fought as recorded in the Book of Mormon.

If both the Nephites and Jaredites fought great battles on and around the Hill Vigia, then historically, it is a virtual graveyard. To this very day, it is considered a witches' headquarters where conventions associated with that thinking are held on an annual basis. Ironically, much of a recent movie called *Apocalypse* was filmed in this same area.

MORONI WANDERED FOR TWENTY YEARS

Mormon took all the records from the hill Shim and hid them in the hill Cumorah—with the exception of the few plates that he gave to his son, Moroni. Those few plates that he gave to his son Moroni are what constitute our present-day Book of Mormon: "I [Mormon] made this record out of the plates of Nephi, and hid up in the hill Cumorah all the records which had been entrusted to me by the hand of the Lord, save it were these few plates which I gave unto my son, Moroni" (Mormon 6:6).

After the great battle at Cumorah, AD 385, Moroni writes:

I, Moroni, do finish the record of my father.

After the great and tremendous battle at Cumorah, behold, the Nephites who had escaped into the country southward were hunted by the Lamanites, until they were all destroyed.

And my father also was killed by them, and I even remain alone to write the sad tale of the destruction of my people. . . . And whether they will slay me, I know not.

Therefore I will write and hide up the records in the earth; and *whither I go* it mattereth not. . . .

My father hath been slain in battle, and all my kinsfolk, and I have not friends *nor whither to go.* . . .

Behold, four hundred years have passed away since the coming of our Lord and Savior. (Mormon 8:2–6; emphasis added)

And then, on his own plates, after having written an account of the ancient Jaredites, he writes:

I have not as yet perished; and I make not myself known to the Lamanites lest they should destroy me. . . .

> If both the Nephites and Jaredites fought great battles on and around the Hill Vigia, then historically, it is a virtual graveyard.

For behold their wars are fierce among themselves; and because of their hatred they put to death every Nephite that will not deny the Christ.

And I, Moroni, will not deny the Christ; wherefore, I wander *withersoever* I can for the safety of mine own life. (Moroni 1:1–3; emphasis added)

From the above statements, we can see that Moroni apparently was doing what he could to stay out of the reach of the Lamanites. His statement about the wars being exceedingly fierce among the Lamanites is totally accurate, as will be explained shortly in connection with writings on Stela 31 of Tikal. Moroni had only those records that his father, Mormon, had entrusted to him. The rest of the plates, referred to in the Book of Mormon as "all of the plates," remained in the hill Cumorah (Ramah). Moroni finished his father's record and abridged the Jaredite record on the same plates. The plates were not quite full, so he wrote a book he called after himself, the book of Moroni. However, by this time, fifteen years had elapsed from the time of the great battle at the Nephite Cumorah/Jaredite Ramah.

Moroni must have wandered "whithersoever" for the next twenty years—or until AD 421, at which time he deposited the records in a hill near Palmyra, New York, where, fourteen hundred years later, as "an angel from on high," he revealed to a young boy named Joseph Smith the place where he had deposited the ancient records.

> Moroni would have wanted to safeguard the records in a stone box. Having a knowledge of cement, he would have built the box in the manner in which Joseph Smith described it.

Certainly the possibility appears to be much more logical for Moroni to wander alone for twenty years with an armful of plates (records) than for the entire Nephite nation to travel with its women and children and "all" the records to an unknown land, a land associated with heat, cold, and snow. The trip from Mexico (an area that *has* a narrow neck of land) to New York (an area that *does not have* a legitimate narrow neck of land) is about twenty-seven hundred miles. Traveling that distance would be not only an unwise military decision on the part of Mormon but also suicide for the entire Nephite nation. Furthermore, the Lamanites would have had no need to pursue the Nephites for at least two reasons:

1. The Lamanites wanted the Nephites out of the land. That would have been accomplished without a battle.
2. The Lamanites would not have needed to pursue the Nephites because the Nephites probably would not have survived the trek in such a short period of time.

Another point of interest is that the stone box in which the Prophet Joseph Smith found the gold plates is similar to—but not exactly like—the stone boxes found in Mesoamerica. The stone boxes in Mexico consist of one piece with the center carved out.

However, Joseph Smith described the stone box in which the gold plates were found as follows: "The box in which they lay was formed by laying stones together in some kind of cement. In the bottom of the box were laid two stones crossways of the box, and on these stones lay the plates and the other things with them" (Joseph Smith—History 1:52).

Moroni did not have a stone box from Mesoamerica with him, nor would he have had the tools with which to carve the stone box. He also would have had a difficult task finding the type of volcanic stone that is used in Mesoamerica for stone boxes. However, coming from the Mesoamerica environment, Moroni would have wanted to safeguard the records in a stone box. Having a knowledge of cement, he would have built the box in the manner in which Joseph Smith described it.

Knowledge of gospel principles and legends about Christ stemming from North American natives may also have been a result of Moroni's wanderings and teachings. In any event, the guiding hand of the Lord played a major role in Moroni's depositing the Book of Mormon record in upstate New York.

In addition to Moroni, other Nephites possibly were exiled or fled out of the land. We will refer to these potential events as the Nephite diaspora. The justification for this possibility is as follows.

First, Moroni states that the Lamanites put to death all those who would not deny Christ. Then he adds, "I, Moroni will not deny the Christ, wherefore; I wander whithersoever I can for the safety of my life" (Moroni 1:3). Certainly other God-fearing families may have survived—just like there have also been Jews who have been committed to their religion and who have left or been exiled. In 1492, the Jews and the Moors were expelled from Spain. But not all Jews were exiled—only those who would not deny their religion were exiled.

Second, although some scholars have questioned the accuracy of the dates, we read in the writings of sixteenth-century Alva de Ixtlilxochitl that "Banished from their homeland, the Tultecas embarked upon their journey along the coast. Traveling through the country, they arrived at their Californias by the sea. . . . The date of their arrival was AD 387" (see chapter 11, "Fernando de Alva Ixtlilxochitl").

Third, corn first appeared in upstate New York between AD 400 and AD 500. Although not conclusive evidence, this fact does explain a possibility as to how corn could arrive in upstate New York at the same time the gold plates with the ancient history arrived there. Corn, like the ancient Nephite and Jaredite history, originated from Mesoamerican soil.

Some readers have asked why Moroni stated that some Nephites escaped into the land southward. Why did they not go north? The answer is that the powerful Teotihuacan culture in combination with the new El Tajin culture would not have allowed that to happen. At the conclusion of this chapter, we will show evidence to that effect from a treatise that was originally called "Mormon's Epistle to Yax Nuun Ayiin."

> Corn first appeared in upstate New York between AD 400 and AD 500. This fact suggests that someone from Mesoamerica carried the seeds to New York after the close of the Book of Mormon record.

THE BOOK OF MORMON REQUIRES THE HILL CUMORAH TO BE NEAR THE NARROW NECK OF LAND

A careful reading of the Book of Mormon shows that the hill Cumorah/Ramah *must* be located near the narrow neck of land. That fact alone excludes the New York Cumorah from serious consideration as the hill Cumorah/Ramah. The internal historical information that pinpoints the proximity of the hill Cumorah/Ramah to the narrow neck of land follows.

1. A treaty was made in AD 350 involving the land around the narrow neck

In the year AD 350, a treaty was made between the Lamanites and the Nephites wherein the Lamanites took control of all the land southward. The Lamanites gave the Nephites the land northward to the narrow passage that led into the land southward: "And the three hundred and forty and ninth year had passed away. And in the three hundred and fiftieth year we made a treaty with the Lamanites and the robbers of Gadianton, in

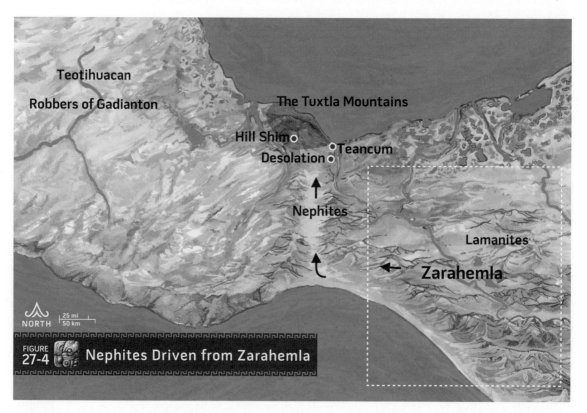

FIGURE 27–4: Nephites Driven from Zarahemla

FIGURE 27–4: Mormon, Jaguar of the Mountains, was already living in the land northward when the AD 350 treaty was signed to set up the last battle at the hill Cumorah. Near this time, the Nephites lost control of their cities in the land southward. Thirty-five years after the treaty was signed, the Nephites were destroyed in the land northward—near the "narrow passage which led into the land southward" (Mormon 2:29).

which we did get the lands of our inheritance divided. And the Lamanites did give unto us the land northward, yea, even to the *narrow passage* which led into the land southward. And we did give unto the Lamanites all the land southward" (Mormon 2:28–29; emphasis added).

2. In the year AD 360, Mormon gathered his people together near the narrow neck of land

Specifically, Mormon gathered his people together at the land of Desolation, to the city of Desolation, which was by the narrow pass that led into the land southward:

> And I did cry unto this people, but it was in vain; and they did not realize that it was the Lord that had spared them, and granted unto them a chance for repentance. And behold they did harden their hearts against the Lord their God.
>
> And it came to pass that after this tenth year had passed away, making, in the whole, three hundred and sixty years from the coming of Christ, the king of the Lamanites sent an epistle unto me, which gave unto me to know that they were preparing to come again to battle against us.
>
> And it came to pass that I did cause my people that they should gather themselves together at the *land Desolation*, to a *city which was in the borders*, by the narrow pass which *led into the land southward*.
>
> And there we did place our armies, that we might stop the armies of the Lamanites, that they might not get possession of any of our lands; therefore we did fortify against them with all our force. (Mormon 3:3–6; emphasis added)

In the year AD 350, a treaty was made between the Lamanites and the Nephites wherein the Lamanites took control of all the land southward.

The city of Desolation was near the city of Teancum, which was near the seashore: "And the remainder did flee and join the inhabitants of the city Teancum. Now the *city Teancum* lay in the *borders by the seashore* and it was also near the *city Desolation*" (Mormon 4:3; emphasis added).

3. In the year AD 375, the Lamanites defeated the Nephites at the city of Desolation, which was near the narrow neck of land

"And it came to pass that the Lamanites did come down against the *city Desolation*; and there was an exceedingly sore battle fought in the land Desolation, in which they did beat the Nephites" (Mormon 4:19; emphasis added).

The city of Desolation is identified in figure 27–4.

4. The hill Shim is near both the narrow neck of land and the hill Cumorah

In that same year (AD 375), Mormon went to the hill Shim, took all the records, and transferred them to the hill Cumorah because the Lamanites were about to overthrow the land:

And now I, Mormon, seeing that the Lamanites were about to overthrow the land, therefore I did go to the hill *Shim*, and did take up all the records which Ammaron had hid up unto the Lord. (Mormon 4:23; emphasis added)

And it came to pass that when we had gathered in all our people in one to the land of *Cumorah*, behold I, Mormon, began to be old; and knowing it to be the last struggle of my people, and having been commanded of the Lord that I should not suffer the records which had been handed down by our fathers, which were sacred, to fall into the hands of the Lamanites, (for the Lamanites would destroy them) therefore I made this record out of the plates of Nephi, and hid up in the hill *Cumorah* all the records which had been entrusted to me by the hand of the Lord, save it were these few plates which I gave unto my son Moroni. (Mormon 6:6; emphasis added)

Prior to that (about AD 345), Mormon had taken the plates of Nephi from the hill Shim and made a record of the history of the Nephites:

And now, the city of Jashon was near the land where Ammaron had deposited the records unto the Lord, that they might not be destroyed. And behold I had gone according to the word of Ammaron, and taken the plates of Nephi, and did make a record according to the words of Ammaron.

And upon the plates of Nephi I did make a full account of all the wickedness and abominations; but upon these plates I did forbear to make a full account of their wickedness and abominations, for behold, a continual scene of wickedness and abominations has been before mine eyes ever since I have been sufficient to behold the ways of man. (Mormon 2:17–18)

The hill Shim was near the hill Cumorah, as indicated in the book of Ether where Omer passed by the hill Shim and came over by the place where the Nephites were destroyed (hill Cumorah) and from there went eastward to the seashore: "And the Lord warned Omer in a dream that he should depart out of the land; wherefore Omer departed out of the land with his family, and traveled many days, and came over and passed by the *hill of Shim*, and came over by *the place where the Nephites were destroyed*, and from thence eastward, and came to a place which was called Ablom, by the seashore, and there he pitched his tent, and also his sons and his daughters, and all his household, save it were Jared and his family" (Ether 9:3; emphasis added).

5. *The Nephites were defending their lands, which were near the narrow neck*
During the Lamanite-Nephite wars under Mormon's leadership, the Nephites were encouraged to stand boldly before the Lamanites and to fight for their wives, their children, their houses, and their homes: "And it came to pass that I did speak unto

Exploring the Lands of the Book of Mormon

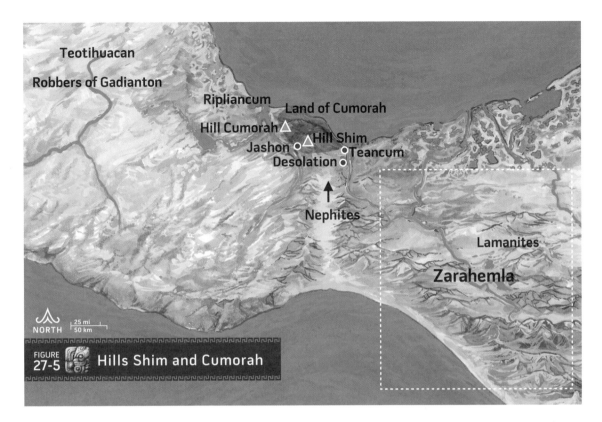

FIGURE 27–5: The hill Shim and the hill Ramah, both Jaredite-named hills, played a major role in Nephite history. The ancient Nephite records were originally deposited in the hill Shim. They were subsequently moved to the hill Ramah. The Nephites called the hill Ramah by the name of the hill Cumorah. From internal Book of Mormon statements, we know clearly and conclusively that both the hill Shim and the hill Ramah/Cumorah were near the narrow neck of land.

my people, and did urge them with great energy, that they would stand boldly before the Lamanites and fight for their wives, and their children, and *their houses*, and *their homes*" (Mormon 2:23; emphasis added).

In summary, the Book of Mormon clearly requires the hill Cumorah to be near the narrow neck of land for the following reasons:

1. The narrow neck of land separated the land southward from the land northward.
2. The city of Desolation was in the land northward and was near the narrow pass that led into the land southward.
3. The hill Shim was close to the city of Desolation.
4. The hill Cumorah was close to the hill Shim.
5. Therefore, the narrow neck of land was close to the hill Cumorah.

> The Book of Mormon clearly requires the hill Cumorah to be near the narrow neck of land.

Remember that the Nephites were fighting to defend their lands. If the narrow neck of land is the Isthmus of Tehuantepec, then the hill Cumorah is in Veracruz, Mexico. The most probable candidate for the hill Cumorah (Ramah) is the Hill Vigia, and the most probable candidate for the hill Shim is the nearby hill with that same name today.

As Mesoamerican archaeological discoveries continue, we often see instances in which we can "marry" an account in the Book of Mormon with an archaeological account.

MORMON'S HILL CUMORAH WAR EPISTLE TO THE KING OF THE LAMANITES

The eighty-year period from AD 320 to AD 400 was a very dramatic time, as reported by both the Book of Mormon and the archaeological history of Mesoamerica. As Mesoamerican archaeological discoveries continue, we often see instances in which we can "marry" an account in the Book of Mormon with an archaeological account. Such is the case with the name of the Lamanite king to whom Mormon wrote prior to the great battle at the hill Cumorah.

About AD 384, Mormon wrote the following: "And I, Mormon, wrote an epistle unto the king of the Lamanites, and desired of him that he would grant unto us that we might gather together our people unto the land called Cumorah, by a hill which was called Cumorah, and there we could give them battle. And it came to pass that the king of the Lamanites did grant unto me the thing which I desired" (Mormon 6:2–3).

The Lamanite king's name in the Maya language is Yax Nuun Ayiin (also referred to as "Yax Nun Ayin" or "Yax Ayin"), but because the engravings of Stela 31 at Tikal show this same figure with a curled nose, he has been nicknamed "Curl Snout" or "Curl Nose." A more literal translation may be "First Crocodile."

However, before we present the Tikal story, we will review some of the most important Book of Mormon events that transpired during the Early Classic Period and that led up to the last great battle at the hill Cumorah. What follows is an adaptation of an article that originally appeared in *The Book of Mormon Archaeological Digest*.[8] Although some of the content is duplicated elsewhere in *Exploring the Lands of the Book of Mormon*, the background material is important as you learn about Yax Nuun Ayiin. The archaeological information that follows is rather routinely discussed among Mesoamerican archaeologists and can be perused in greater depth on various Internet sites.

8. Joseph L. Allen, "Mormon's Epistle to Yax Ayin," *Book of Mormon Archaeological Digest* 3, no. 2 (June 2001): 1–5.

Book of Mormon: AD 320

When Mormon was ten years old, Ammaron realized that Mormon was a sober child who was quick to observe and that he should go to the hill Shim when he was twenty-four years old and write a history of the people (see Mormon 1:2–3). Ammaron was the record keeper of the Nephites at AD 320, and he gave Mormon, at the age of ten, the charge to prepare a condensed history. At that time, all the records that had been kept by the Nephites from the time of Nephi the son of Lehi to Ammaron had been placed in the hill Shim.

Shim is a Maya word that means "corn." As stated above, a hill today that is called by the same name in the Aztec (Nahuatl) language is Cintepec, which is located in the Tuxtla Mountains of Veracruz close to the Isthmus of Tehuantepec. Tehuantepec is considered by most current Latter-day Saint scholars to be the narrow neck of land. Mormon lived near the narrow neck of land in the city of Desolation (see Mormon 3:5–7).

The city of Desolation was in the land northward and appears to have been the ancient Olmec city of San Lorenzo, near present-day Acayucan, Veracruz. It was also near the seashore.

Book of Mormon: AD 321

When Mormon was eleven years old, his father took him to the land of Zarahemla. Mormon mentions the great number of buildings dotting the land and the numerous inhabitants living there. During this same year, a war began between the Nephites and the Lamanites (see Mormon 1:8). By AD 321, the land of Zarahemla extended from the Pacific Ocean on the west all the way to the Atlantic Ocean on the east and probably included the areas known today as Chiapas, Peten, Belize, and southern Yucatan.

Many archaeological sites that are known to us today were in existence at AD 321, including Tikal, El Mirador, Becan, Lamanai, Chiapa de Corzo, Kaminaljuyu, Izapa, and far-away Teotihuacan in the Mexico valley.

Book of Mormon: AD 325

Mormon informs us that when he was fifteen years old, he was visited of the Lord (see Mormon 1:15). The time was one of great wickedness. The Gadianton robbers were among the Lamanites, and sorceries, witchcrafts, and magic arts were found throughout the land (see Mormon 1:18–19).

These activities were consistent with what was going on in Mesoamerica during the early part of the fourth century. The Gadianton robbers, who were among the Lamanites, may have been from the Mexico valley region of Teotihuacan. We will later see a connection between Tikal and Teotihuacan.

Book of Mormon: AD 326

When Mormon was sixteen years old, war broke out again, and he was appointed leader of the Nephite armies (see Mormon 2:1–2). Although sixteen seems a very young age for a person to be in charge of an army, such delegations were a fairly common practice at that time period. Even as late as AD 1521 when the Spaniards conquered Mexico, the emperor of the Aztecs, the nephew of the deceased Montezuma, was only eighteen years old.

When Mormon was eleven years old, his father took him to the land of Zarahemla. Mormon mentions the great number of buildings dotting the land and the numerous inhabitants living there.

Between the years AD 326 and 330, Mormon reports that the people were involved in one complete revolution throughout all the face of the land. The Lamanite army numbered forty-four thousand, and the Nephite army numbered forty-two thousand. A man by the name of Aaron was the Lamanite king (see Mormon 2:8–9). We will show later that a complete revolution was indeed taking place throughout Mesoamerica during the above-mentioned years.

Mormon was in a precarious position. We know from the local history that foreigners from the west (Mexico City area) were encroaching into the Maya region. Mormon lived near the narrow neck of land, which meant that he had problems on both sides of the isthmus—one on the Zarahemla side (Chiapas and Peten) and the other on the Mexico side (Teotihuacan).

> Mormon lived near the narrow neck of land, which meant that he had problems on both sides of the isthmus.

Book of Mormon: AD 344

Ten years prior to AD 344, Mormon retrieved the records from the hill Shim to abridge the history of his people (see Mormon 2:17). The wars that had begun at AD 326 continued all the way up to AD 350. We could easily be amazed that with all the military problems with which Mormon was involved, he was still able to write the history of his people.

Traditional Maya warfare took place during the inactive part of the agricultural season during the months of January and February. However, in the Tuxtla Mountains region where Mormon lived, rain falls even during the months of the dry season. Nevertheless, if we were to make an "educated guess," we could assume that Mormon probably wrote during the rainy season and that the fighting took place during the dry months.

Book of Mormon: AD 350

The wars continued from year to year. Some early writings about the Book of Mormon report that the Nephites were driven farther and farther north. This thinking is *not* true. The Nephites had lived in the land of Zarahemla for about five hundred years. Mormon urged his people to fight for their wives, their children, and their houses and homes (see Mormon 2:23).

However, AD 350 was indeed a crucial time, as the Nephites lost control of the land of Zarahemla when they signed a treaty with the Lamanites and the Gadianton robbers. The Lamanites gave the Nephites the land northward to the narrow passage that led into the land southward, and the Nephites gave the Lamanites the land southward (see Mormon 2:28–29).

The fact that the Gadianton robbers are mentioned in this treaty may provide a hint that the powerful city-state of Teotihuacan from the Mexico valley was also involved. Shortly after the treaty, we begin to see trade activity between Mexico and Tikal (Guatemala). Interestingly, the Maya never violated this treaty. Even up to the time of the Spanish conquest, the Maya stayed on the eastward side (land southward) of the Isthmus of Tehuantepec.

Book of Mormon: AD 360

Ten years after the treaty, Mormon received an epistle from the Lamanite king informing Mormon that the Lamanites were coming to battle Mormon and his people (see Mormon 3:4). This Lamanite king is not Yax Nuun Ayiin referred to above. We will elaborate on this shortly.

We might ask the question as to why the Lamanites would come to battle against the Nephites when the Nephites had already given up the land of Zarahemla (Chiapas and Peten). The answer may be that the Nephites, who were now in a very wicked state, became a thorn in the side of Teotihuacan and Tikal. That is, at AD 362, Mormon was calling the Nephites to gather to the land of Desolation. The Nephites, who now lived in the region of Veracruz, Mexico, controlled the narrow pass that led into the land southward and therefore probably created problems in trading between Tikal and Teotihuacan. The wicked Nephites probably charged high tariffs for anyone to traffic through their territory by the narrow neck of land. From an economic and political point of view, that could not be tolerated by the Lamanites and the Gadianton robbers.

> From an economical and political point of view, the wicked fourth century AD Nephites were in the middle of any trafficking between Teotihuacan and the land southward.

Book of Mormon: AD 378

By AD 378, things had become so bad that the Nephites were beginning to look like a fallen nation. They had actually defeated the Lamanites in three separate battles, but by AD 378, they were in a weakened state and had lost the city of Desolation (see Mormon 4:2), although they did regain control of the city of Desolation for a time. They were able to maintain their other cities (see Mormon 5:4).

Mormon realized the great danger his people were in, and he went to the hill Shim and took all the records and transferred them to the nearby hill Cumorah, which was known as the hill Ramah to the Jaredites (see Mormon 4:23; 6:6; Ether 9:3; 15:11).

On occasion, readers of the Book of Mormon have suggested that the history of the Book of Mormon peoples took place in Mesoamerica but that the Cumorah battle between the Lamanites and the Nephites was fought in upstate New York. However, the New York battle location is *not* consistent with what we read in the Book of Mormon. From the above discussion, note that the Nephites continued to fight for their "houses and their homes" that were around the narrow neck of land. Nothing in these chapters in the Book of Mormon indicates an extensive migration from Mesoamerica to New York. Neither is such a migration consistent from the archaeological history. It defies logic that the Nephites would travel twenty-seven hundred miles, the distance from Veracruz to upstate New York, and then invite the Lamanites to travel the same distance to fight them. Mexico City and Guatemala wanted the Nephites out of the way of the Isthmus of Tehuantepec (narrow neck of land).

Book of Mormon: AD 385

As stated earlier, Mormon wrote an epistle to the Lamanite king and proposed that the two groups go to battle with each other at the land of Cumorah. Mormon hid all the records in the hill Cumorah except "these few plates" (our current Book of Mormon), which he gave to his son Moroni (see Mormon 6:2, 6).

After the great and tremendous battle at Cumorah where the Nephite nation was destroyed, Moroni wrote that he would "write and hide up the records [our Book of Mormon] in the earth; and whither I go it mattereth not" (Mormon 8:4).

Any commentary in relation to the great battle at Cumorah should take into consideration the number of people involved. Because Cumorah and Ramah are the same hill, we should also consider the number of people involved in the Jaredite wars, although we have a difficult time determining exact figures because population centers change, definitions change, and other conditions increase or reduce populations. For example, in some areas of Mesoamerica, up to 90 percent of the Maya reportedly were killed in certain areas at the time of the Spanish conquest in the sixteenth century because of war, famine, and disease. New York and Peru also suffered from the same type of activities.

We also have a difficult time accurately determining populations during the time of the Book of Mormon. Two million people were killed in Jaredite wars around 300 BC, and that was just the preliminary battles and included only the soldiers (see Ether 15:2). On occasion, upwards of eighty thousand soldiers fought in wars between the Nephites and the Lamanites (see Mormon 2:9), and in the AD 385 war, 230,000 Nephite soldiers were killed (see Mormon 6:10–14). The number of Lamanites killed is not recorded.

Members of the Church of Jesus Christ in 2008 numbered over 1.5 million in the ancient Mesoamerica (Mexico and Central America) territory, whereas fewer than a hundred thousand members lived in Bolivia and Peru and many fewer than that in upstate New York.

The bottom line, however, is rather simple. If we can estimate that twenty million or more people are required to satisfy the total numbers requirement in the Book of Mormon in the battles at Ramah (Cumorah), then the New York statistics would not satisfy that number. In other words, skeptics of the stance that Ramah/Cumorah is in Mesoamerica cannot possibly prove that the last Nephite and Jaredite wars were fought in upstate New York because the area simply did not contain enough people. Basically, for every one Native American living on the northern side of the Rio Grande today, a hundred live on the opposite side.

That which follows are excerpts from a letter written by a member of the Church who, upon his retirement, did archaeological investigations around the New York Cumorah area. He had not heard of the concept that the hill Cumorah referred to in the Book of Mormon was located in Veracruz, Mexico, at the time he wrote the letter.[9]

> Nothing in the Book of Mormon indicates an extensive migration from Mesoamerica to New York. Neither is such a migration consistent from the archaeological history.

9. See *Book of Mormon Archaeological Digest* 3, no. 1 (2001): 5.

To: Book of Mormon Archaeological Digest

From: Langdon Smith, New Haven, Vermont, 2001

Working with the state archaeologists I get to see things the average person does not see. Awhile ago I saw the state site map for the state of New York. With my interest in history and pre-historic times, I looked around Palmyra. South of Syracuse on the east below this area there are several campsite areas as well as below Rochester to the west, but up around the Palmyra area it is several miles to the closest listed sites. Wherever there are early American sites, collectors will find them. Plowed fields are the best places to look and there are plowed fields in the Palmyra area. . . .

On my own or as I work with professionals I find early sites. At this time I have found 298 new early American campsites. I have reported these and obtained site numbers from the state historic preservation office. . . . So I do have experience in searching out and finding sites. . . .

I have read the stories written by Mr. Bean and also Mrs. Samson as they lived in the Hill Cumorah area. Stories which state how they, when plowing in the area, would pick up arrowheads by the basketful and then sell them to the tourists. . . .

Having this interest in artifacts, out I drove to the Cumorah area. . . .

I searched the field on the east, then went to the farm north of the Hill and asked to look through their fields. They stated that I was the first one that they knew of to go out looking for arrowheads there. . . . I did not find one single piece of evidence of any kind. There were not any arrowheads, nor were there any pieces of broken flints that would have been left over from the making points—the waste. . . .

Chips are always left. Why pick them up? They are waste. There are about 75-85% waste in making artifacts. Langdon Smith.

> "The Book of Mormon is true. Nevertheless, there aren't any artifacts of the kind spoken of in the Book of Mormon around that hill near Palmyra. The battle must have been fought at some other hill."
> —Langdon Smith

In his letter, Smith refers to a man who lived in the Palmyra region who was a collector of artifacts. The man was not a member of the Church, but he had read the Book of Mormon. According to Smith, the elderly man, whose name is J. Golden Fisher, stated, "There just aren't any artifacts of the kind spoken of in the book [Book of Mormon] around that hill." Smith concludes by expressing his faith that the Church is true and that the Book of Mormon is a second witness of Christ. He then says, "But the battle, well, it must have been fought at some other hill."

Book of Mormon: AD 400

Moroni reported the death of his father, Mormon. Moroni still had not left the area around the narrow neck of land (Isthmus of Tehuantepec). He wrote that the wars

FIGURE 27–6: Pictured is the North Acropolis at Tikal. The history recorded on Stela 31 at Tikal outlines events that parallel the Book of Mormon and that date to the end of the fourth century and beginning of the fifth century AD. Stela 31, which was discovered inside the North Acropolis of Tikal, reveals the name of the Lamanite king at Tikal when Mormon wrote his epistle requesting that the final battle take place at Cumorah (Mormon 6:2). (Photo courtesy of Merrill C. Oaks)

10. David Stuart, "'The Arrival of Strangers': Teotihuacan and Tollan in Classic Maya History," PARI Online Publications, Newsletter 25, July 1998, www.mesoweb.com/ pari/publications/news (accessed April 13, 2007).

11. Linda Schele and David Freidel, *A Forest of Kings: The Untold Story of the Ancient Maya* (New York: William Morrow and Company, 1990).

12. Simon Martin and Nikolai Grube, *Chronicle of the Maya Kings and Queens: Deciphering the Dynasties of the Ancient Maya* (London: Thames and Hudson, 2000).

13. Guy Gugliotta, "Maya Rise and Fall," *National Geographic Magazine* 212, no. 2 (August 2007): 68–109.

among the Lamanites were "exceedingly fierce" and that they "put to death every Nephite that will not deny the Christ" (Moroni 1:2).

As mentioned previously, in 1492, when the Jews were cast out of Spain, only the Jews who would not deny their religion were exiled from Spain. Moroni said that he would "not deny the Christ"; therefore, he would "wander whithersoever" for the safety of his life. He wrote what is called the book of Moroni, with his last entry at AD 421. He and possibly other Nephites who would "not deny the Christ" traveled a great distance to what we now know as the northeastern part of the United States. There he buried "these few plates" that his father, Mormon, had given him. He also had the Jaredite records, which we know as the "sealed portion."

MESOAMERICA: AD 320–426

Much of the information that follows is based on a paper presented at Princeton University by Dr. David Stuart of the Peabody Museum at Harvard University, now of the University of Texas at Austin.[10] Additional commentaries in relation to the Book of Mormon are taken from *The Book of Mormon Archaeological Digest*, from a book about Mesoamerica by Linda Schele and David Freidel, *A Forest of Kings: The Untold Story of the Ancient Maya*, primarily chapter 4, "A War of Conquest: Tikal against Uaxactun,"[11] from *Chronicle of the Maya Kings and Queens: Deciphering the Dynasties of the Ancient Maya* by Simon Martin and Nikolai Grube,[12] and from a 2007 article by Guy Gugliotta, "Maya Rise and Fall," published in the August 2007 issue of *National Geographic Magazine*.[13]

Both Teotihuacan and Tikal played a major role in the political structure of Mesoamerica from AD 320 to AD 400 and beyond. The oldest long count date at Tikal is AD 292. Dates reflecting AD 317 and AD 320 closely follow. All three of these dates fall within the 4 Nephi apostate time period. Because of the great building activity in Mesoamerica, the above dates fall in the Maya Early Classic Period.

Jaguar Paw: AD 317–AD 378

Stela 31 at Tikal records the name of one ruler called "Jaguar Paw," who was among the earliest documented rulers of the Early Classic Period associated with the long count date 8.14.0.0.0 (AD 317). Jaguar Paw was a contemporary of Mormon. That is, Mormon was born about AD 310 and was killed sometime after the AD 385 battle at Cumorah.

The AD 317 date of Jaguar Paw may have been the date of his birth or perhaps the date of his ascension to the throne. He either died or was killed on January 16, AD 378.

Aaron, a Lamanite King

As nearly as can be determined, Jaguar Paw was a Lamanite Maya king. *Balaam* is the Maya word for jaguar. There does not appear to be a connection between Balaam (Jaguar Paw) and another Lamanite king named Aaron who, in AD 336, led an army against Mormon (see Mormon 2:9).

Although both Aaron and Jaguar Paw are contemporaries, we do not have enough evidence to link the two. From an epistle written by Mormon to his son Moroni, we can speculate that Aaron had been killed prior to the battle at Cumorah (see Moroni 9:17). Mormon wrote that he feared lest the Lamanites might destroy the Nephites (see Moroni 9:3). He would have had no need to write this epistle after the Cumorah battle because by then the Lamanites had destroyed the Nephites.

For the sake of this discussion, we can assume that Aaron was a king of the Lamanites as stated in Mormon 2:9—in the same manner that Lamoni, who was converted by Ammon, the son of Mosiah, was a king. We should remember that Lamoni's father was the king over the whole Lamanite land and that other kings ruled over other parts of the land.

By the same token, Jaguar Paw, a contemporary of both Mormon and Aaron, appears to have been more than just a local king over Tikal. We will see that when his successor, Yax Nuun Ayiin (also referred to as Curl Snout or First Crocodile), became the king over Tikal, he ruled the whole Peten region. Shortly after the Nephite destruction, the cities of Calakmul in southern Yucatan and Copan in Honduras entered the scene, along with Tikal and Palenque, as major players in a cooperative kingship relationship.

Kaminaljuyu, Chiapas, Izapa, and El Mirador were relegated to minor positions. The plot thickens as we see a major change in Lamanite kingship on January 16, AD 378. But first we will look at the famous AD 350 treaty.

Both Teotihuacan and Tikal played a major role in the political structure of Mesoamerica from AD 320 to AD 400 and beyond.

We believe
that
Spearthrower
Owl was the
leader of the
Gadianton
robber
government.
He had his
headquarters
in
Teotihuacan.

AD 350 Treaty Signers

Who were the signers of the treaty referred to in Mormon 2:28–29 in which the Nephites lost the land of Zarahemla? Three parties were involved in the treaty: (1) the Nephites, (2) the Lamanites, and (3) the robbers of Gadianton.

Mormon never mentions the name of the Nephite chief judge while Mormon was the military leader. Perhaps Mormon, who at the age of forty was a participant on the Nephite side, was a signer of the treaty. Included among the possibilities for Lamanite signers of the treaty are Jaguar Paw and Aaron. Because Aaron apparently was "a" king of the Lamanites and because Jaguar Paw was strategically located in the Peten area, Jaguar Paw may have been the Lamanite signer. However, we cannot discount the role of Kaminaljuyu, the ancient city of Nephi, in this monumental treaty. Not only do we see trade activity among Tikal, Kaminaljuyu, and Teotihuacan during this time period but also we begin to see buildings in both Kaminaljuyu and Tikal that are patterned after the buildings at Teotihuacan.

FIGURE 27–7: Artist drawing of Spearthrower Owl. Spearthrower Owl from Teotihuacan ruled from AD 374–439. He is also known as Spearthrower Shield. There is a possible relationship with the name Jacob. (Drawing by Cliff Dunston from Tikal Stela 31)

Spearthrower Owl: Ruled AD 374 to AD 439 (Also Known as Spearthrower Shield)

Spearthrower Owl, probably of the King Jacob dynasty, ruled Mexico (Teotihuacan) for over sixty years. He was a ruthless dictator (see chapter 7, "The Teotihuacan Culture"). He was probably not the person who signed the AD 350 treaty (see Mormon 2:28–29) in behalf of the Gadianton government. The signer may, however, have been the predecessor of this powerful new character whom the historical records refer to as Atlatl Cauac (Spearthrower Owl).

We do not have the birth date of Spearthrower Owl; however, Dr. David Stuart establishes the case that Spearthrower Owl was the king in Teotihuacan for over six decades, AD 374 to AD 439. Spearthrower Owl comes on the scene at the height of the last Nephite-Lamanite wars. He began his rule eleven years before the Cumorah battle and continued to rule after the death of Mormon and the exile of Moroni and the Nephites who would not deny Christ.

We need to keep our eye on Spearthrower Owl, as his personality seems to be akin to the famous Amalickiah of the Book of Mormon, who became king over the Lamanites through deception and treachery. We believe that Spearthrower Owl was the leader of the Gadianton robber government and that he had his headquarters in Teotihuacan. We will see that he introduced a type of international warfare, the likes of which had never been known among the Maya. Although his name glyph appears on Stela 31 at Tikal, we have no evidence that suggests he ever lived there.

Spearthrower Owl is the father of Yax Nuun Ayiin, whom we propose to be the Lamanite king to whom Mormon wrote his epistle recorded in Mormon 6:4. As we reported in chapter 5, "The Teotihuacan Culture," Spearthrower Owl plausibly is Jacob,

FIGURE 27–8: The Nephites were surrounded by the Lamanites. Mormon wrote that the forthcoming battle would be the last struggle of his people (see Mormon 6:6). Teotihuacan, with its vassal-ally El Tajin, had the Nephites hemmed in on the north. Tikal, with its vassal-ally Palenque, was positioned to march via the narrow neck of land and destroy the Nephites, who were stationed around the hill Cumorah.

taken from the "secret combination" dynasty of King Jacob, who fled the region of Tikal just a few years prior to the appearance of Christ to the Nephites (see 3 Nephi 7:12–13).[14] If this is the case, then he would be related to the longstanding "king-men," antagonists to the Nephites, dating to the middle of the first century BC and later surfacing at AD 200. This possibility also suggests a tie-in with Teotihuacan and the Tikal region with the Mulekites. Our position is that the Mulekites, descendants of the tribe of Judah, may have been the Maya priests who began to control the ancient Nephite territory at the beginning of the Maya Classic Period (AD 200 to AD 320). (See 4 Nephi 1:24–49; see also chapter 30, "The Maya Classic Period and the Nephite Apostasy.")

14. Martin and Grube, *Chronicle of the Maya Kings and Queens*, 31.

Before we continue with our discussion about Spearthrower Owl, however, we will introduce another figure.

Siyaj K'ak' (Fire Is Born; Also Known as Smoking Frog) AD 378

The year AD 378 was a pivotal point in Mesoamerica history. Siyaj K'ak' played a major role in the great revolutionary movement of the last part of the fourth century AD. The

original common name of this figure, as deciphered from Tikal Stela 31, was Smoking Frog. This same individual has been identified on monuments at El Peru and Uaxactun, cities in the Peten. His Maya name is Siyaj K'ak'. A better translation for his name might be "Fire Is Born" as opposed to "Smoking Frog." From the information on the glyphs, we know he was a foreigner from Teotihuacan and, as such, an intruder to the Peten region. Although he was not the king of Teotihuacan, nevertheless, he played a dominant role in the conquering of the Peten region in the fourth century AD. In one sense, he can be compared to the military leader Moroni, who served as the military leader under King Pahoran in the first century BC in the same area. Siyaj K'ak' (Fire Is Born) was the military leader of Spearthrower Owl, the king or ruler of Teotihuacan.

Martin and Grube echo this same theme as they write, "Siyaj K'ak' [Fire Is Born], the practical agent of the *entrada* mission, seems more like a general sent to further Teotihuacan's ambitions among its Maya neighbors."[15]

15. Martin and Grube, *Chronicle of the Maya Kings and Queens*, 31.

Regarding Siyaj K'ak', *National Geographic Magazine* follows the same theme:

The stranger arrived as the dry season began to harden the jungle paths, allowing armies to pass. Flanked by his warriors, he marched into the Maya city of Waka [El Peru, located about fifty miles west of Tikal], past temples and markets and across broad plazas. Its citizens must have gaped, impressed not just by the show of force but also by the men's extravagant feather headdresses, javelins, and mirrored shields—the regalia of a distant imperial city.

Ancient inscriptions give the date as January 8, 378, and the stranger's name as Fire Is Born. He arrived in Waka, in present-day Peten, Guatemala, as an envoy from a great power in the highlands of Mexico [Teotihuacan]. In the coming decades, his name would appear on monuments all across the territory of the Maya, the jungle civilization of Mesoamerica. And in his wake, the Maya reached an apogee that lasted five centuries.[16]

16. Gugliotta, "Maya Rise and Fall," 74.

Within a week after arriving at El Peru, Sayaj K'ak' (Fire Is Born) arrived at Tikal with his military escort and the young son of Spearthrower, soon to be the new king of Tikal. The date was January 16, AD 378.

Schele and Freidel propose that because of the important date of January 16, AD 378, inscribed on glyphs at both Tikal and Uaxactun, the date must represent Tikal's victory over Uaxactun when Jaguar Paw was killed in battle. They suggest that the next king came from Kaminaljuyu.

Stuart disagrees. He presents evidence that the new king was from Mexico (Teotihuacan). This is exciting information. It suggests that the wars from AD 360 to

AD 385, as recorded in the Book of Mormon, were not only between the Nephites and the Lamanites but also included the Gadianton robber government of Teotihuacan and its ally, El Tajin. They had now infiltrated the ranks of the Lamanite Maya, and like the wicked Zoramite named Amalickiah in the first century BC, they would do anything to gain control over all the land (see Alma 46–48).

In all probability, the wicked Nephites, seeing the Lamanites and the Gadianton robbers fighting in the Peten jungle, thought they could slip back into Chiapas and regain control of the land of their inheritance, Zarahemla. But this was not to be the case. Almost unnoticed by the people, the military leader Siyaj K'ak' (Fire Is Born) appears to have moved into Tikal, killed the Maya King Jaguar Paw, and placed the young Teotihuacan son of Spearthrower Owl on the throne.

Stuart writes, "There is no choice but to conclude that Siyaj K'ak' is a foreigner and may well be the instigator of the Teotihuacan presence in the region of Tikal. If allowed to speculate, I would go so far as to view him as the leader of a military force that overthrew Tikal's dynasty in 378, killing its ruler Jaguar Paw and installing a new ruler, Nun Yax Ayin, in his place."[17]

This viewpoint is consistent with Book of Mormon history. On several occasions, as already mentioned, we see instances of both a chief judge and a military leader—such as Pahoran and Moroni or Lachoneus and Gidgiddoni.

Yax Nuun Ayiin (Curl Snout; Also Known as First Crocodile)

Yax Nuun Ayiin became the king of Tikal, as well as of the Maya world, at AD 379 and ruled until approximately AD 404. He is not the son of the Lamanite Maya ruler Jaguar Paw, nor is he the son of Siyaj K'ak' (Fire Is Born). He is the son of the Teotihuacan king, Spearthrower Owl-Shield (dynasty of Jacob). Although Yax Nuun Ayiin was from Teotihuacan, he became king over the Lamanites at Tikal at AD 379, just six years before the Cumorah battle. *He appears to be the king to whom Mormon wrote his epistle as recorded in Mormon 6:2.*

Yax in the Maya language means *first* or *green*. *Ayiin* means crocodile. Several small jade alligator heads, along with a skeleton of a crocodile body with a jade crocodile head, were found in the tomb of Yax Nuun Ayiin. For this reason, the meaning of his name is First Crocodile.

His tomb, which is located in the north acropolis at Tikal, also contained remains of three turtles, two pygmy owls, and several other birds. Other items related to bloodletting and Teotihuacan-style vessels, the latter of which would indicate a Teotihuacan connection, were also found in his tomb.[18]

Yax Nuun Ayiin died around AD 404, four years after Moroni wrote that he was getting out of Lamanite territory (see Moroni 1:1–2). As mentioned above, the word *Ayiin*

As shown on page 49 in chapter 2, *Nun* and *Ayin* are letters in the Hebrew alphabet. These words are also used as proper names in the Maya language.

17. Stuart, "The Arrival of Strangers," 7.

FIGURE 27–10: Artistic rendition of Yax Nuun Ayiin (Curl Snout). Also known as First Crocodile, he was the young son of Spearthrower Shield and was placed on the throne of Tikal on September 12, AD 379. He was probably the king Mormon wrote to at AD 384 (see Mormon 6:2). First Crocodile, as nearly as can be determined, died at AD 404. (Drawing by Cliff Dunston from Tikal Stela 31)

18. See *Maya Lowland Centers: Tikal*, p. 2; www.athenapub.com/tikal.

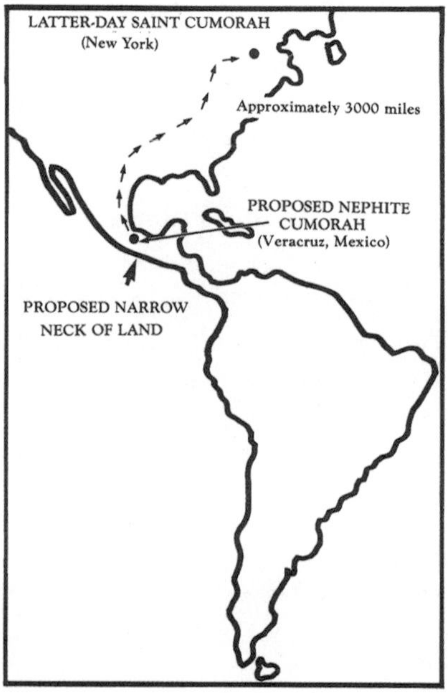

FIGURE 27–11: Map of Moroni's travels. Mormon buried all the records in the hill Cumorah except the few records (our Book of Mormon) that he gave to his son Moroni. About AD 400, Moroni left the land of his fathers and traveled to upstate New York where he deposited the records in a hill that today we call Cumorah.

Stela 31 at Tikal is probably the most important text in helping us understand the archaeological details of the demise of the Nephite nation.

19. Stuart, "The Arrival of Strangers," 11.

is associated with *crocodile*. For example, at the archaeological site of Lamanai in northern Belize, that name is recorded as "Laman Ayin." In 1 Nephi 2:8–9, *Laman* is the name given to a river. The word *Laman* in Maya is also associated with water because the words *Laman Ayin* mean *submerged crocodile*. Whether a name correlation is possible with the two kings, Yax Nuun Ayiin and Laman Ayin, is difficult to ascertain.

Stuart proposes that Yax Nuun Ayiin was a young boy at the time the military leader Siyaj K'ak' placed him on the throne at Tikal. Yax Nuun Ayiin's portrait glyph states that he was a "katun" lord, which would make him less than twenty years old. The facts that his father, Spearthrower Owl, did not begin to rule in Teotihuacan until AD 374 and died sixty-five years later suggest that Yax Nuun Ayiin was only a young boy at AD 379 when he began to rule. His rule ended at AD 404, many years prior to the death of his father.

The great Maya scholar, Tatiana Proskouriakoff, reported over three decades ago that Tikal Stela 31 is the single most important text for studying early Tikal history. We not only agree with her statement but also are prepared to state the probability that Stela 31 at Tikal is the most important text in helping us understand the archaeological details of the demise of the Nephite nation.

Regarding the placement of the foreigner Yax Nuun Ayiin on the throne of Tikal at AD 379, Stuart writes: "I view this as the single most important political or military episode of the early Classic Maya history, when Teotihuacan established itself as a dominant force in the politics and elite culture of the central Peten."[19]

And indeed it was. For 550 years, the Nephites had been able to hold their own with the Lamanites. Both groups lived in the land southward—meaning southward of the Isthmus of Tehuantepec. But once we add the powerful Teotihuacanos to the equation, two things happen: (1) the Lamanites lost control of their kingdom and (2) the Nephites were no match for the bloodthirsty combined kingdom of Guatemala and Mexico, especially under the bloodthirsty leadership of Spearthrower Owl and his military leader, Siyaj K'ak'. This new dynasty at Tikal began an anniversary date of January 16, AD 378, that lasted unbroken for almost two hundred years.

FIGURE 27–12: The Temple of Inscriptions (Tomb of Pacal Na) shown here was not built until two hundred years after the close of the Book of Mormon. Nevertheless, Palenque was strong enough at the time of the Cumorah battle to form an alliance with Tikal and Teotihuacan, which resulted in the downfall of the Nephite nation. (Photo courtesy of Sheryl Lee Wilson)

Siyaj Chan K'awiil (Stormy Sky or Sky Born)

We conclude this portion of the Mesoamerica history in the fourth century AD with the introduction of Siyaj Chan K'awiil (Stormy Sky), the son of Yax Nuun Ayiin. Yax Nuun Ayiin (First Crocodile) died in the year AD 404. Siyaj Chan K'awiil began to reign at Tikal on November 26, AD 411, and died February 3, AD 456. The son of Yax Nuun Ayiin apparently took upon himself the name of the military leader, Siyaj, and, at the same time, a Maya name, Chan. From information recorded on Tikal Stela 31, we are able to determine that the father of Siyaj Chan K'awiil (Stormy Sky) was a Teotihuacano and his mother was a Maya.

FIGURE 27–13: Volcanoes have played a major role in Mesoamerica in the destruction of many people throughout history. At the time of Christ, the whole face of the land was changed by volcanic upheaval. Over thirty volcanoes are found in the country of Guatemala, such as the San Pedro Volcano shown here overlooking Lake Atitlan. (Photo courtesy of Cortney Boice)

We assume that the marriage of his parents, Yax Nuun Ayiin and Lady K'inich Son, united the kingdom—a kingdom that endured for thirty-nine generations and included both Copan to the south and Calakmul to the north.

Of course, the Book of Mormon is silent during the reign of Stormy Sky and successive rulers in Mesoamerica.

Kaminaljuyu, Tikal, Palenque, El Tajin, and Teotihuacan

Kaminaljuyu, Tikal, Palenque, El Tajin, and Teotihuacan all appear to have played a role in the demise of the Nephite Maya nation. The first influence has to do with the change of Lamanite headquarters from Kaminaljuyu to Tikal.

Architecture characteristics have been discovered at both Kaminaljuyu and Tikal that are similar to the architecture of Teotihuacan. Archaeologists have suggested that warrior merchants from Teotihuacan conquered Kaminaljuyu and established a Maya outpost in imitation of their homeland in the Mexico valley.[20] Subsequently, Teotihuacan architecture showed up at Tikal dating to the middle of the fourth century.

20. Stuart, "The Arrival of Strangers," 1.

From a Book of Mormon perspective, the transfer of the Lamanite kingdom from Kaminaljuyu to the Peten region makes a lot of sense. The results of the AD 350 treaty, wherein the Lamanites gained control of both the Peten and Chiapas regions, would have required a strong presence in Tikal. It would allow the Lamanite Maya there to have total control of the Maya lowlands, including Palenque. Palenque became a major player near the end of the Book of Mormon and continued in that role for another four hundred years after the close of the Book of Mormon. There now appears to be a family relationship with the leaders of Palenque and the new AD 378 leaders of Tikal. Palenque was in a strategic position to help destroy the nation at Cumorah.

El Tajin, on the other hand, is located northward of the Hill Vigia (site of Cumorah). The people there had just recently become strong allies with Teotihuacan. This alliance simply means that at AD 385, the Nephites were excluded from an escape route to the north. They were literally surrounded.

> Along with Teotihuacan and Tikal, Palenque and El Tajin also became major players in the destruction of the Nephites. All four city-states endured another four hundred years.

FREQUENTLY ASKED QUESTIONS

Question: Is it possible for Mesoamerica to be the land of the Book of Mormon and for the last battles to have taken place in New York?

Answer: No. If the hill Cumorah where the last battles took place is in New York, then the narrow neck of land needs to be in the United States. If the narrow neck of land is in the United States, then the land of Zarahemla and the land of Nephi have to be in the United States. If the Jaredites, Nephites, and Lamanites lived in the United States, then a massive parallel civilization was going on in Mesoamerica during the same time the Book of Mormon people were living in the United States. The Lord told the brother of Jared, "I will bless thee and thy seed, and raise up unto me of thy seed . . . a great nation. And there shall be no greater than the nation which I will raise up unto me of thy seed, upon all the face of the earth" (Ether 1:43). The greatest pre-Columbian nation that existed in all the Americas is the Olmec civilization that we have already discussed.

The problem is that virtually no evidence exists today to support the thinking that massive civilizations lived in the New York area during the time the Book of Mormon history took place. Neither a written language nor any other required archaeological evidences have been found in the New York area dating from 600 BC to AD 400 detailing the historicity of the Book of Mormon—evidences that do exist in Mesoamerica, as outlined throughout *Exploring the Lands of the Book of Mormon*.

Question: Does that mean that the United States is not the promised land?

Answer: No. Just because the history of the Nephites and the Jaredites did not take place in New York in no way demeans the importance or the sacredness of the hill where Joseph received the plates. In the wisdom of the Lord, the only place in the world where the gospel could be restored and where the gold plates could have been translated and published in the early 1800s was the free land of the United States of America.

The Smith family suffered successive years of crop failure, which resulted in their moving near to Palmyra, New York, which was near the hill where Moroni had deposited the sacred records some fourteen hundred years earlier. Joseph Smith, who had been raised up for that very purpose, translated that sacred record by the gift and power of God.

This work had been prophesied by prophets of old, including Nephi, the son of Lehi, who prophesied that the Book of Mormon would come to the descendants of Lehi by way of the free land of the United States of America—or, in other words, by way of the Gentiles. Nephi said that "many generations after the Messiah shall be manifested in body unto the children of men, then shall the fulness of the gospel of the Messiah come unto the Gentiles, and from the Gentiles unto the remnant of our seed" (1 Nephi 15:13).

Question: Were there not wagon loads of records discovered in the New York hill?

Answer: A talk given by Brigham Young after the Saints arrived in the Salt Lake Valley has been used as an argument on occasion to suggest that the hill Cumorah was in New York. The feeling has been that the New York hill opened up and that some of the leaders went inside where they saw wagonloads of records and the sword of Laban. On a follow-up visit, the men saw that the sword of Laban had been unsheathed. Many Latter-day Saints assumed the last battles had been fought around New York because the hill "opened up."

The statement of Brigham Young was printed in mainstream Latter-day Saint literature. However, a statement about the same experience, given by Heber C. Kimball, was not included in the literature. Perhaps the issue can be clarified with the following statements.

First, Brigham Young said that Oliver Cowdery and others went "into the hill." Second, Heber C. Kimball said that the incident was a "*vision*" that the brethren had of the hill.

In summary, this traditional account is not a geographical statement. It is a statement of a *vision*. Nephi, who had a vision of the history of the house of Israel, as recorded in 1 Nephi, was carried to an exceedingly high mountain *in spirit*. He never left his bed physically. The statements of Brigham Young and Heber C. Kimball are as follows:

Virtually no evidence exists today to support the thinking that massive civilizations lived in the New York area during the time the Book of Mormon history took place.

Brigham Young

Oliver Cowdery went with the prophet Joseph when he deposited these plates. Joseph did not translate all of the plates; there was a portion of them sealed, which you can learn from the book of Doctrine and Covenants. When Joseph got the plates, the angel instructed him to carry them back to the hill Cumorah, which he did. Oliver says that when Joseph and Oliver went there, the hill opened, and they walked into a cave, in which there was a large and spacious room. He says he did not think, at the time, whether they had the light of the sun or artificial light; but that it was just as light as day. They laid the plates on a table; it was a large table that stood in the room. Under this table there was a pile of plates as much as two feet high, and there were altogether in this room more plates than probably many wagon loads; they were piled up in the corners and along the walls. The first time they went there the sword of Laban hung upon the wall; but when they went again it had been taken down and laid upon the table across the gold plates; it was unsheathed, and on it was written these words: "This sword will never be sheathed again until the kingdoms of this world become the kingdom of our God and his Christ." I tell you this as coming not only from Oliver Cowdery, but others who were familiar with it, and who understood it just as well as we understand coming to this meeting, enjoying the day, and by and by we separate and go away, forgetting most of what is said, but remembering some things. So is it with other circumstances in life. I relate this to you, and I want you to understand it. I take this liberty of referring to those things so that they will not be forgotten and lost. Carlos Smith was a young man of as much veracity as any young man we had, and he was a witness to these things. Samuel Smith saw some things, Hyrum saw a good many things, but Joseph was the leader.[21]

21. Brigham Young, *Journal of Discourses* (London and Liverpool: Latter-day Saints' Book Depot, 1854–86), 19:38.

Heber C. Kimball

Brother Mills mentioned in his song, that crossing the Plains with hand-carts was one of the greatest events that ever transpired in this Church. I will admit that it is an important event, successfully testing another method for gathering Israel, but its importance is small in comparison with the visitation of the angel of God to the Prophet Joseph, and with the reception of the sacred records from the hand of Moroni at the hill Cumorah.

How does it compare with the *vision* that Joseph and others had, when they went into a cave in the hill Cumorah, and saw more records than ten men could carry? There were books piled upon tables, book upon book. Those records this people will yet have, if they accept of the Book of Mormon and observe its precepts, and keep the commandments.[22]

22. Heber C. Kimball, *Journal of Discourses*, 4:105; emphasis added.

Question: What about the Mound Builders of the eastern part of the United States? Could they not be part of the Book of Mormon people?

Answer: They could well be part of the Book of Mormon people. But a large enough cultural base does not exist from either the Hopewell or the Adena people of the Ohio Basin to form part of the heartland geographical base of the Book of Mormon.

In the first place, Ohio is not New York. We cannot claim to have a strong Book of Mormon culture in New York where none has been discovered. Nor can we legitimately say that Ohio is close enough to New York to qualify it as part of the Book of Mormon lands.

The Hopewell and the Adena of Ohio both appear to have a Mesoamerica origin that ties in with the Olmec and the Maya Preclassic Periods. Indeed, the dating of the Mound Builders follows the same pattern as Mesoamerica—the dating ranges from 800 BC to AD 900 for the Adena and 600 BC to AD 1500 for the Hopewell. Early dates go back to 1000 BC. Consistent with Mesoamerica dating, the Hopewell manifest radiocarbon dates of a cultural climax between 100 BC and AD 200—strictly Preclassic Mesoamerica and middle Book of Mormon time period.

Robert Silverberg, in his book, *Mound Builders of Ancient America*, writes: "The Mexican site most frequently discussed as a point of origin for the Ohio Valley mound-building concepts is La Venta, on an island covering two square miles, about a dozen miles inland from the Gulf of Mexico in a swamp near the Tonala River."[23]

You will recall that La Venta is designated as the heartland of the Olmec culture in Mesoamerica.

The above comments suggest that the Book of Mormon society may have reached into North America; however, the geographical heartland must still be in Mesoamerica. That situation is similar to the headquarters of The Church of Jesus Christ of Latter-day Saints being located in Utah but with branches of the Church reaching both into Canada and Mexico.

Question: What about the Zelph Story?

Answer: One of the most common points used in an attempt to "prove" that the last battles were fought in New York is the account of some human remains that were discovered in Illinois as a result of a march of 205 brethren of the Church, called Zion's Camp, in the year 1834.

As a result of several of the brethren who traveled on the "Zion's march" recording the incident of Zelph in their journals, two official and separate accounts of the incident have been recorded in the *History of the Church*. Both accounts speak of a vision that opened up to the Prophet Joseph Smith wherein he identified the bones from the grave to be that of a white Lamanite by the name of Zelph. One account identified Zelph with fighting that occurred in the Lamanite-Nephite battle at Cumorah, and the other account deleted any reference to the hill Cumorah or to the last Lamanite-Nephite battle.[24]

"Those who try to support a particular historical or geographical point of view about the Book of Mormon by citing the Zelph story are on inconclusive grounds."
—Kenneth Godfrey

23. Robert Silverberg, *Mound Builders of Ancient America: The Archaeology of a Myth* (Athens, OH: Ohio University Press, 1968).

24. See Joseph Smith, *History of the Church of Jesus Christ of Latter-day Saints*, 2nd ed. rev. (Salt Lake City: Deseret Book, 1976), 2:79–80.

Dr. Kenneth Godfrey analyzed several of the journal accounts of the Zelph story. Each account varies somewhat in detail. Godfrey concludes: "Most sources agree that Zelph was a white Lamanite who fought under a leader named Onandagus (variously spelled). Beyond that, what Joseph said to his men is not entirely clear, judging by the variations in the available sources. Therefore, those who try to support a particular historical or geographical point of view about the Book of Mormon by citing the Zelph story are on inconclusive grounds."[25]

25. Kenneth A. Godfrey, "The Zelph Story," paper no. GOD-89 (Provo, UT: Foundation for Ancient Research and Mormon Studies, 1989), 23.

Question: Doesn't a statement in the Doctrine and Covenants about the borders of the Lamanites define the United States as Book of Mormon lands?

Answer: We read in the Doctrine and Covenants section 32, directed to Parley P. Pratt, the following: "And that which I have appointed unto him is that he shall go with my servants, Oliver Cowdery and Peter Whitmer, Jun., into the *wilderness among the Lamanites*" (D&C 32:2; emphasis added).

Certainly, no one has any argument about the Native Americans of the United States being considered "Lamanites" (we cannot, however, label them "Lamanite Maya"). Nor should anyone debate against the western part of the United States being labeled "Lamanite territory." In 1830, the western portion of the United States belonged to Mexico. Missouri and points west must be considered the borders of the Lamanites.

These conclusions do not, however, pinpoint New York as the place of the great Cumorah struggle. Today, the gospel continues to be taught to all nations, including all Native Americans. However, preaching the gospel to God's children throughout the world does not necessarily define geography. Missionaries bear witness of the First Vision in England, but that does not mean that is where the Sacred Grove is located.

Therefore, we conclude that if we have found the Jaredites, we have found the Nephites. If the Olmecs and the Jaredites are the same people, then the hill Cumorah is in Veracruz, Mexico, because the hill Ramah was located where the Jaredites lived. Because the hill Ramah and the hill Cumorah are the same hill, then again we must say that the hill Cumorah is in Veracruz. Therefore, if we have found the Jaredites, we have found the Nephites.

STATEMENTS ABOUT THE HILL CUMORAH

Most adult members of the Church of Jesus Christ have been taught that the last battles of the Nephites and the Jaredites took place around the Hill Cumorah in New York. Since the middle of the twentieth century, however, some Book of Mormon scholars and others have disputed this stance. For example:

David A. Palmer: "Each summer since 1937, the Church has staged the Cumorah Pageant at [the site of the western New York Hill Cumorah]. Entitled *America's Witness for Christ*, [the pageant] depicts important events from Book of Mormon history. This annual pageant has reinforced the common assumption that Moroni buried the plates of Mormon in the same hill where his father had buried the other plates, thus equating this New York hill with the Book of Mormon Cumorah. Because the New York site does not readily fit the Book of Mormon description of Book of Mormon geography, some Latter-day Saints have looked for other possible explanations and locations, including Mesoamerica." (In Ludlow, *Encyclopedia of Mormonism*, 1:346–47)

Angel Abrea: "I have been asked to respond to your earlier letter to President Gordon B. Hinckley regarding a Hill Cumorah Pageant advertisement. You expressed concern that the ad was misleading because it stated, 'The Hill Cumorah, where a great battle was fought in ancient America....' We appreciate your concern and have directed those responsible for the pageant to remove the phrase from the advertisements for all future products of the Hill Cumorah Pageant." (LDS Church Missionary Department letter to Al Shumate, February 12, 1990, copy in authors' possession)

David A. Palmer: "There are two hills called Cumorah. The one in the state of New York was where Moroni buried the plates later given to Joseph Smith. The original hill Cumorah is in Mexico. It was the place where Mormon buried the Nephite library and where the Nephites were destroyed." (Palmer, *In Search of Cumorah*, 26)

Rex C. Reeve Jr.: "Just when [the] New York hill was first called Cumorah is difficult to determine, but by 1835 the name Cumorah seemed to be well-known, at least among Church members. Joseph Smith referred to the hill but only used the name Cumorah once in his personal writings: 'Glad tidings from Cumorah!' (D&C 128:20). The U.S. Geological Survey of 1898 called the hill 'Mormon Hill.' In 1952, however, the name was officially changed to Hill Cumorah." (In Largey, *Book of Mormon Reference Companion,* 224)

Jeff Lindsay: "The idea that the Hill Cumorah/Ramah described in the Book of Mormon is in New York simply doesn't fit the text, though many early Mormons made that assumption. Joseph never said that the hill where he found the plates was the Hill Cumorah of the Nephites—though it's an easy thing for people to assume, at least initially." ("Nice Photo of a Prime Candidate for the Real Hill Cumorah," www.mormanity.blogspot.com, accessed March 15, 2008)

John E. Clark: "Archaeologically speaking, [the Hill Cumorah] is a clean hill. No artifacts, no walls, no trenches, no arrowheads. The area immediately surrounding the hill is similarly clean. Pre-Columbian people did not settle or build here. This is not the place of Mormon's last stand. We must look elsewhere for that hill." (Clark, "Archaeology and Cumorah Questions," 151)

CHAPTER 28

The Land of Nephi

And my people would that we should call the name of the place Nephi; wherefore, we did call it Nephi. (2 Nephi 5:8)

ᕮᕮᕮᕮᕮᕮᕮᕮᕮᕮᕮᕮᕮᕮᕮᕮᕮᕮᕮᕮᕮᕮᕮᕮᕮᕮᕮᕮ

Even though the city of Nephi was originally named after the great Mesoamerican prophet Nephi, the son of Lehi, it eventually fell under the control of the people who became known as Lamanites. In approximately 200 BC, Mosiah led a righteous group of Nephites from the mountains of the land of Nephi down to the lowlands of the land of Zarahemla. From that time forth, the land of Nephi was governed by Lamanites. It remained under their dominion throughout the rest of Book of Mormon history.

We learn about other Lamanite cities in the land of Nephi from the accounts of Zeniff, Noah, and Limhi—three generations of Nephites who left Zarahemla and returned to Nephi to live under Lamanite government. The migration of Alma and the

OPPOSITE: Altar 10, Kaminaljuyu, 147 BC, see pages 725–29. The ruins of Kaminaljuyu, Guatemala, are proposed in *Exploring the Lands of the Book of Mormon* to be the ancient city of Nephi that was occupied by the Nephites from the sixth to the second centuries BC. About 200 BC, it fell into the hands of the Lamanites. Altar 10 at Kaminaljuyu manifests the date of 147 BC and correlates to the time period that the Nephite King Noah died, resulting in the transfer of his crown to his son Limhi. The picture shows a copy that is located in the National Museum of Archaeology in Guatemala City. (Photo courtesy of Cortney Boice)

missionary activities of the sons of Mosiah give us additional information about those cities in the land of Nephi. And we glean further information about them at the time of the Crucifixion of Christ. The land of Nephi is sometimes referred to as the land of Lehi-Nephi (see Mosiah 7:1–4).

Book of Mormon cities and smaller lands that fall under the umbrella of the land of Nephi are the following:

The city of Nephi (Lehi-Nephi)
The city of Ishmael
The city of Middoni
The city of Jerusalem
The city of Shilom
The city of Shemlon
The land of Mormon
The city/land of Helam
The city/land of Amulon

THE CITY OF NEPHI

The ruins of Kaminaljuyu, located where Guatemala City now stands, have been proposed as the location for the city of Nephi.

Few places in the world can equal the absolute virgin beauty of the country of Guatemala. It is bordered by Mexico on the north and west. The three countries of Belize, Honduras, and El Salvador constitute its eastern and southern borders. Both the Atlantic and Pacific Oceans form the coastlines of Guatemala.

The word *Guatemala* means "land of many trees." The entire country covers about forty thousand square miles and is smaller than the state of Utah. However, because two-thirds of the country is mountainous and volcanic, travel has presented a major problem over the centuries.

Guatemala City gracefully sits on a plateau surrounded by mountains. With an elevation of forty-eight hundred feet above sea level, this capital city of Guatemala presents a year-round, ideal, spring-like climate. Guatemala City has been affectionately called the "city of eternal spring." Approximately three million people live in the city, and another nine million live in other parts of the country. About one-half of the total population of the country of Guatemala live in the mountains or along the coast and are considered native to Guatemala. By the year 2025, the country of Guatemala is projected to have a population of about twenty-five million.

Buried beneath the city of Guatemala are some very extensive and old archaeological ruins. A portion of these ruins has been preserved as a national park and today consists basically of dirt mounds. Pennsylvania State University has, however, carried on excavation work in the area over the past thirty years. The ruins are called Kaminaljuyu.

The ruins of Kaminaljuyu, located where Guatemala City now stands, have been proposed as the location for the city of Nephi and the land of Nephi spoken of in the

Book of Mormon. In fact, the only city or land that is mentioned more often than the city or land of Nephi in the Book of Mormon is the city or land of Zarahemla. Dr. John Sorenson, who proposes that Kaminaljuyu was anciently the city of Nephi, presents the following arguments in his book, *An Ancient American Setting for the Book of Mormon*:

> Two strong reasons stand out why the Valley of Guatemala should be considered the original land of Nephi. The first is that the site of Kaminaljuyu was for many centuries the dominant culture center for all highland Guatemala, the most important spot for several hundred miles around. The great size (at least a mile square) and impressive constructions of Kaminaljuyu underline its key importance and that of the valley. The land of Nephi is portrayed in the Book of Mormon as dominant among its neighbors to the same degree. A second big reason for considering Nephi to have been here is that customs, details of terrain, and the dating of the archaeological remains correlate closely with what is reported in the Book of Mormon.[1]

1. John L. Sorenson, *An Ancient American Setting for the Book of Mormon* (Salt Lake City: Deseret Book and Foundation for Ancient Research and Mormon Studies, 1985), 141.

In reality, Kaminaljuyu *is* Guatemala City. However, to state that the archaeological ruins of Kaminaljuyu could be the city or land of Nephi, we must be aware of the time period we are most concerned with, analyze what was taking place in Kaminaljuyu at that time, and make certain all is consistent with what we read in the Book of Mormon. The following discussion provides a rather detailed analysis of the ruins of Kaminaljuyu in relation to the land/city of Nephi.

The prophet Nephi, after being warned in a dream, left the land of first inheritance sometime between ten and thirty years from the time that Lehi's party left Jerusalem (see 2 Nephi 5:5–28).

By adjusting our calendar with the date Nephi left Jerusalem, we can see that Nephi and his followers probably arrived in the location that later became the land/city of Nephi between 587 and 567 BC. The median date places the arrival at 578 BC. Eight generations elapsed from the time of Nephi to Mosiah—namely, Jacob, Enos, Jarom, Omni, Amaron, his brother Chemish, Abinadom, and Amaleki, who entrusted the records to Benjamin, the son of Mosiah.

When Omni gave the records to his son, Amaron, 282 years had passed away from the

FIGURE 28–1: Corn was a major product dating from the Preclassic Period and continues to be the same today among the native people of Guatemala. In some places, once the cornstalks have grown to a healthy state, beans are planted; and the cornstalks literally serve as beanpoles. According to dates in the Book of Mormon, corn existed at least prior to the second century BC—or seven hundred years before corn's existence in the northeastern part of the United States. In other words, "No corn, no Nephites." (Photo courtesy of Sheryl Lee Wilson)

2. Joseph W. Michaels and
William T. Sanders, eds.,
*The Pennsylvania State
University Kaminaljuyu
Project, 1969–1970
Season: Mound Excavations*
(University Park, PA:
Pennsylvania State
University, 1973), 8.

time Lehi's people left Jerusalem, making the date approximately 315 BC. When King Benjamin conferred the kingdom upon Mosiah in about 121 BC, 476 years had passed from the time of Lehi's departure. We have, therefore, a total of about 457 years, from 578 BC to 121 BC, where a substantial amount of Nephite activity was going on in the land of Nephi. In addition to the names above, we can add to the list of Nephites who lived in the land of Nephi at one time or another the following: Zeniff, Noah, Limhi, Abinadi, and Alma. The missionary sons of Mosiah went up to the land of Nephi even later than the 121 BC date.

At any rate, if we are to attempt a correlation with Kaminaljuyu and the land of Nephi, we need to look closely at what was going on in Kaminaljuyu between 578 and 121 BC, which might give us a clue about Nephite culture. The above time period falls into what is called the Late Formative Period of Kaminaljuyu. The Late Formative Period is listed at 500 BC to 200 BC with an estimated standard error of plus or minus a hundred years.

The following chart shows the Pennsylvania State University Kaminaljuyu Project culture sequence.[2]

Modern Period	AD 1800–1971
Colonial Period	AD 1500–1800
Late Postclassic Period	AD 1200–1500
Early Postclassic Period	AD 1000–1200
Late Classic Period	AD 700–1000
Middle Classic Period	AD 400–700
Early Classic Period	AD 200–400
Late Terminal Formative Period	AD 1–200
Early Terminal Formative Period	200–1 BC
Late Formative Period (Nephite)	500–200 BC
Middle Formative Period	1000–500 BC
Early Formative Period	2500–1000 BC
Archaic Period	8000–2500 BC

3. Alfred V. Kidder, Jesse
D. Jennings, and Edwin
M. Shook, *Excavations at
Kaminaljuyu, Guatemala*
(Washington, DC: Carnegie
Institute of Washington,
1946), 3.

In 1946, a report was published by the Carnegie Institute of Washington entitled *Excavations at Kaminaljuyu, Guatemala*.[3] In reference to the discovery of these vast archaeological ruins, Kidder, Jennings, and Shook write:

Archaeological digging is a good deal like deep sea fishing off the New England coast: you never know whether you are going to pull up a cod or a sculpin—often you get nothing at all. But once in a great while you hook a big halibut and then you are in for a long, tough struggle. That is about what happened to us at the ruins of Kaminaljuyu in the outskirts of Guatemala City.

FIGURE 28–2: Artistic rendition of the ancient city of Kaminaljuyu, Guatemala. This was an important city in the Guatemala highlands area during the first six hundred years of Nephite history. As both the Book of Mormon and the archaeological data of Kaminaljuyu affirm, kings ruled over the land during that time period. Corn and beans were the primary agricultural products, and worship centered around building complexes that constituted part of the culture of the early people at the city of Nephi and the ruins of Kaminaljuyu. (Photo courtesy of Merrill C. Oaks)

Early in 1936 Licenciado J. Antonio Villacorta C., Minister of Public Education of Guatemala, asked us to investigate a mound on the Finca La Esperanza, a part of Kaminaljuyu, in which a wall had become exposed. Oliver G. Rickertson and I went out and looked it over and decided we could do the job in three weeks or so at a cost of about a hundred and fifty dollars.

At the end of those weeks I was cabling Washington for a special extra appropriation. We had our halibut.[4]

From 1968 to 1973, the Department of Anthropology at Pennsylvania State University conducted field work at the site of Kaminaljuyu.

Today, a section of Kaminaljuyu, now surrounded by the ever-growing Guatemala City, is fenced off as a national monument. Several dirt mounds are visible along with minor displays and some serious excavation works that date to the Late Formative (Nephite) Period.

For our purposes, however, an impressive mound excavation that dates early in the Late Formative Period attracts our attention. The mound is referred to as B-V-6.

Sometime between 600–400 BC, according to the archaeologists who worked the site, the area around mound B-V-6 was transformed into a ceremonial center.[5]

Construction of the mound appears to have involved a single continuous effort rather than a succession of discrete episodes over several years. We believe that even with a modest labor force construction of the mound could have been completed within the agriculturally inactive period of a single year.[6]

The construction of B-V-6 demonstrates a great deal of sophistication in planning, workmanship, and knowledge of the problems of structural stresses involved in the erection of large conical mounds.[7]

4. Kidder, Jennings, and Shook, *Excavations at Kaminaljuyu, Guatemala,* Introduction.

5. Michaels and Sanders, *The Pennsylvania State University Kaminaljuyu Project,* 82.

6. Michaels and Sanders, *The Pennsylvania State University Kaminaljuyu Project,* 87.

7. Michaels and Sanders, *The Pennsylvania State University Kaminaljuyu Project,* 87.

FIGURE 28–3: This picture shows a segment of a major building that has been retored at Kaminaljuyu. The upper portion of the building dates to AD 400 and shows architecture similar to that of Teotihuacan. The lower portion of the building dates to the formative period from 500 BC to 200 BC. The archaeological analysis depicts it as an ancient temple where burned offerings were used in religious ceremonies. (Photo courtesy of Merrill C. Oaks)

FIGURE 28–4: In addition to corn and beans, many other agricultural products are harvested in the cool Guatemala highlands that are five thousand to seven thousand feet in elevation. About 200 BC, Zeniff, who lived in the land of Nephi, wrote of several types of seeds, including "seeds of corn, and of wheat, and of barley, and with neas [probably beans], and with sheum [probably squash], and with seeds of all manner of fruit" (Mosiah 9:9). (Photo courtesy of Blake Joseph Allen)

The people who occupied the Kaminaljuyu area during the Late Formative Period were agriculturally oriented. Irrigation was developed in the sixth century BC, which allowed for crops to grow year round

8. Michaels and Sanders, *The Pennsylvania State University Kaminaljuyu Project*, 241.

9. Michaels and Sanders, *The Pennsylvania State University Kaminaljuyu Project*, 82.

Other mounds of the Late Formative Period (Nephite 578–121 BC) also show remarkable construction patterns. These mounds fall in the time period of 555 BC to 321 BC—strictly Nephi, Jacob, Enos, Jarom, and Omni time periods.

Actually, five chronological phases have emerged from the excavation; the first three fall in with the Late Formative Period (500 BC–200 BC). Furthermore, on the basis of the data from the settlement pattern test trenches, the initial occupation likely occurred only shortly before mound construction began and would therefore date to the Late Formative Period. This dating corresponds with the 555 BC date. Jacob went "up into" the temple to preach to the Nephites within ten to twenty years of this date (see Jacob 2:2).

At its completion, the surface of what are called Mounds B-V-3 through B-V-6 capped a flat area of about twenty meters in length and several meters in width. These mounds appear to demonstrate a ceremonial complex consisting of steep temple centers.[8]

Additional evidence suggests that the people who occupied the area during the Late Formative Period were agriculturally oriented. Irrigation was developed in the sixth century BC, which allowed for crops to grow year round. Evidence also exists to indicate that special-purpose buildings were built in which certain things were burned—perhaps related to a type of ceremony.[9]

As a summary here, the archaeological report states the following: "It therefore appears that the Late Formative mound complex in Finca El Mirador (Kaminaljuyu) served principally if not exclusively as a center for public religious ceremony and ritual.

Exploring the Lands of the Book of Mormon

And that the five principal mounds represent platforms upon which dramatic spectacles could be performed and witnessed by large numbers of people located in the flat, open, plaza-like area bordered on the west by four-mound alignment."[10]

10. Michaels and Sanders, *The Pennsylvania State University Kaminaljuyu Project*, 241.

Some interesting parallels seem evident between what we read in the Book of Mormon and what we know about Kaminaljuyu as a possibility for its being the city/land of Nephi:

1. The dating of the Late Formative Period, when a significant amount of building occurred at Kaminaljuyu, coincides precisely with the Nephi to Mosiah time period.
2. The location of Kaminaljuyu in relationship with the Isthmus of Tehuantepec and other significant and possible sites correlating with Book of Mormon culture is impressive.
3. The climate, agriculture base, and mountainous regions all parallel nicely with limited statements in the Book of Mormon. For example, irrigation began at Kaminaljuyu about 600 BC.
4. Temple mounds showing a high degree of workmanship with an apparent function of ceremonial and ritual use, including burned areas involving animal sacrifice, remind us of Nephi and his temple: "And I, Nephi, did build a temple; and I did construct it after the manner of the temple of Solomon save it were not built of so many precious things; for they were not to be found upon the land, wherefore, it could not be built like unto Solomon's temple. But the manner of the construction

Temple mounds at Kaminaljuyu show a high degree of workmanship with an apparent function of ceremonial and ritual use, including burned areas involving animal sacrifice.

FIGURE 28–5: A trip through the highlands of Guatemala is like traveling through time on television's Discovery Channel. The variety of colors, the high volcanic mountains, beautiful Lake Atitlan, humble homes, and friendly people tell the story of an ancient culture referred to in the Book of Mormon as simply "a remnant of Jacob." (Photo courtesy of Cortney Boice)

was like unto the temple of Solomon; and the workmanship thereof was exceedingly fine" (2 Nephi 5:16). This temple was built somewhere around 578 BC, during the Kaminaljuyu Late Formative Period.

5. The discovery of Altar 10 (sometimes referred to as Stela 10) with the date of 147 BC has been proposed as a transfer of kingship from King Noah to his son Limhi. Because the information contained on Altar 10 at Kaminaljuyu is such an important discovery, we are inserting the information from chapter 7, "Monumental Evidence: Stela 10 and the City of Nephi," of *Explorations in the Book of Mormon*.[11] The information is based on research by Dr. Bruce Warren, an LDS archaeologist who is now retired from Brigham Young University, and concerns Altar 10 that was discovered among the Kaminaljuyu ruins in 1959. Although little can presently be translated from the inscriptions on the monument, following is a list of what we *do* know about the monument. The letters in the list correlate with the the letters in figuire 28–6

11. See Joseph Willard, "Monumental Evidence: Will Stela 10 Confirm Kaminaljuyu as the City of Nephi?" *Book of Mormon Archaeological Digest* 1, no. 1 (Spring 1998): 5.

A. Three different calendars on the stone all record the year date of 147 BC

Three different calendars (the local Kaminaljuyu, the Teotihuacan, and the Olmec) are used on Altar 10 to register the year date of 147 BC. The threefold repetition of the date manifests the extreme significance of the event described in the monument's inscription.

B. The dominant figures on the stone are marked by apostasy

The human figure in the upper left has a crown-like symbol over his eye. This symbol indicates adherence to the notion of "divine kingship"—or the apostate belief that the king possessed certain godlike attributes or abilities.[12]

12. Linda Schele and David Freidel, *A Forest of Kings: The Untold Story of the Ancient Maya* (New York: William Morrow and Company, 1990), 115.

13. Michael D. Coe, *The Maya*, 4th ed. (New York: Thames and Hudson, 1987), 59.

Michael D. Coe, a renowned scholar of Mesoamerican archaeology, has labeled the bearded figure on the right as one of "several Izapan gods."[13] We should remember that Izapa is considered to be the land of first inheritance of the Nephites and the Lamanites. Therefore, any Nephite claiming kingship rights would make it a point of showing a genealogical relationship with Lehi and Nephi. Perhaps the figures of the "Izapan gods" are simply glyphs identifying King Noah's relationship with royalty.

C. The orientation of the crown is significant

As stated above, the crown-like symbol indicates a belief in divine kingship. This symbol would normally appear as a right-side-up crown. The fact that it is upside down communicates that the divine kingship figure it is placed on is, ironically, dead.[14] "And they were angry with the king [Noah] and caused that he should suffer, even death by fire" (Mosiah 19:20).

14. Willard, "Monumental Evidence," 5.

D. The stone bears another human figure, a time count of three hundred days, and a "captivity" glyph

Adjacent to the lower inscription is another human figure. Presumably, the inscription records information about him and about the significant event taking place, but archaeologists have so far been able to translate only two of the symbols from it. The first is a time count of three hundred days, and the second is a glyph meaning "captivity."

FIGURE 28–6: This artistic drawing of the figures on Altar 10, shown on page 718 of this chapter, brings into sharp relief the information on the altar. The alphabetic letters on the drawing refer to the letters in the list on page 726 of the chapter as follows. (A) Dates: All three dates on Altar 10 of Kaminaljuyu fall in the year 147 BC and correlate to the Noah/Limhi time period (see Mosiah 10–19; Maya = 7.10.10.8.2 = 147 BC; see Edmonson, *The Book of the Year: Middle American Calendrical Systems*, 25). (B) Wicked kings and priests in both the ancient Maya and Nephite cultures laid heavy taxes on their people and purported to have divine or supernatural abilities. (C) The king with the upside-down crown over the eyelid indicates that the king is dead, which may be representative of the death of King Noah. (D) Three hundred days after the death of the king, a new king was installed. Dr. Bruce Warren proposes this figure to be Limhi, the son of wicked King Noah (see Mosiah 19:26).

At first glance, we recognize the seeming impossibility of drawing any satisfactory conclusions from such scanty facts, but Dr. Bruce Warren offers the following intriguing analysis as a possible interpretation and Book of Mormon correlation of the preceding details:

1. November 8 is the date of the harvest festival (A)

The significance of the date can best be appreciated when we understand that November 8 is recognized by the Maya natives at Lake Atitlan even today as the time of the "harvest festival." This annual day of celebration commemorates the New Year and the day when kings officially ascended to the throne.[15]

Interestingly, the northern tribe of Ephraim celebrated its harvest date at about the same time.[16] The monument likely represents the ascension of a new king to the throne in 147 BC. If a Book of Mormon correlation can be made with Altar 10, the connection of this date with the ascension of a king is probably the key to discovering it. The period between 148 and 147 BC corresponds with Abinadi's preaching to the wicked King Noah in the land of Nephi, their subsequent deaths, and eventually Limhi's ascension as the new king (see Mosiah 11–19).

2. King Noah was an apostate idolater (B)

In a Book of Mormon interpretation, the figure in the upper left of the engraving would naturally be the former king, or King Noah. A belief in the self-exalting doctrine of "divine kingship" would certainly be consistent with the man whose response to Abinadi's doomsday prophecies was, "Who is Abinadi, that I and my people should be judged of him, or *who is the Lord*, that shall bring upon *my* people such great affliction?" (Mosiah 11:27; emphasis added).

Among the multitude of sins of which the abusive leader was guilty, we are told specifically that through the monstrous tax he laid on his people, he and his priests "were supported in their laziness, and in their idolatry" (Mosiah 11:6). His iniquity corrupted the people until they too "became idolatrous, because they were deceived by the vain and flattering words of the king and priests" (Mosiah 11:7).

3. King Noah was dead when Limhi took the throne (C)

From the Book of Mormon, we know that the custom associated with an aging king was to choose and appoint a successor to the throne before the king's death (see Mosiah 1:9; 10:22; 28:10). Although this custom may have been the case, Altar 10 seems to indicate that at the time of the official appointment of the new king, the old one was already dead.

These are precisely the circumstances surrounding King Limhi's ascension to the throne (Mosiah 19:26). In accordance with common practice, Zeniff, king of the Nephites in the land of Nephi, had "conferred the kingdom upon Noah, one of his sons" (Mosiah 11:1). Although we have every reason to believe that Noah intended to continue this tradition with one of his own sons someday, he was never given the opportunity to select his successor. His tyranny eventually turned his own men against him and led to his premature death by fire (Mosiah 19:19–20). This event, in turn, necessitated

15. Allen Christenson, "Maya Harvest Festivals and the Book of Mormon," *Review of Books on the Book of Mormon*, vol. 3, ed. Daniel C. Peterson (Provo, UT: Foundation for Ancient Research and Mormon Studies, 1991), 2–31.

16. *Westminster Dictionary of the Bible* (Philadelphia: Westminster Press, 1944), 646.

Altar 10 seems to indicate that at the time of the official appointment of the new king, the old one was already dead.

the breach of custom by which the voice of the people appointed Limhi their next king (Mosiah 19:26).

4. King Limhi became the king while his people were in captivity to the Lamanites (D)

Three hundred days' differential from the death of the first king to the ascension to the throne of the second king is also significant. This time period is possibly indicative of the time during which Limhi had acted as the unofficial king, awaiting the new year's date of November 8 to formalize his title and position. During this same period, Limhi and his people were in bondage to the Lamanites, which explains the presence of the "captivity" glyph adjacent to the Limhi figure (Mosiah 19:28; 7:15).

Although we still have much to learn about Altar 10, everything that has been translated thus far can be paralleled with the Book of Mormon account of King Noah and King Limhi. Because of the monument's location and dating, we expect that as epigraphers translate more of the inscriptions, Altar 10 may provide us with some valuable assistance in positively identifying Kaminaljuyu as the city of Nephi.

Further, although we do not have enough evidence either to prove or to disprove the ruins of Kaminaljuyu as being the city or land of Nephi, the fact that such archaeological evidence exists during the right time period and in a proper general vicinity seems to warrant justification in placing Kaminaljuyu as that early Nephite city.

Some people are disappointed as they look at the dirt mounds that are proposed as the city of Nephi where Nephi built a temple of fine workmanship and where Noah built a magnificent palace. We need to be aware of at least two things when visiting the ancient archaeological sites:

1. The more recent the site, the less the amount of deterioration that has taken place. Therefore, an AD 900 post–Book of Mormon site is much better preserved than a 550 BC Nephi time period temple.
2. The architecture of the Maya Classic Period (AD 250–AD 900), whose aim was to build elaborate buildings as monuments to false gods or as burial tombs for wicked and powerful rulers, demonstrates a much more classical style than a Book of Mormon culture whose aim was to build functional buildings as places of worship.

If reason and study allow us to propose Kaminaljuyu as the most likely site for the city of Nephi in the Book of Mormon, we can begin to develop a most impressive model of the geography of the Book of Mormon. We are also allowed the luxury of placing the Book of Mormon in a historical and cultural context that literally brings that sacred, ancient record to life.

Although we still have much to learn about Altar 10, everything that has been translated thus far can be paralleled with the Book of Mormon account of King Noah and King Limhi.

FIGURE 28–7: Guatemala is divided into geographic areas called departments. The northern lowland rainforest of Peten is the largest department. The city of Guatemala is located in the department of Guatemala and is one of twenty-two departments in the country. The small country of Belize has long been disputed as belonging to Guatemala, and the state of Chiapas, Mexico, was formerly part of Guatemala. The ownership of these same areas was disputed anciently. Chiapas, Peten, and Belize are proposed in *Exploring the Lands of the Book of Mormon* as belonging to the land of Zarahemla. The highlands and coastal areas of Guatemala, Honduras, and El Salvador are proposed as the land of Nephi.

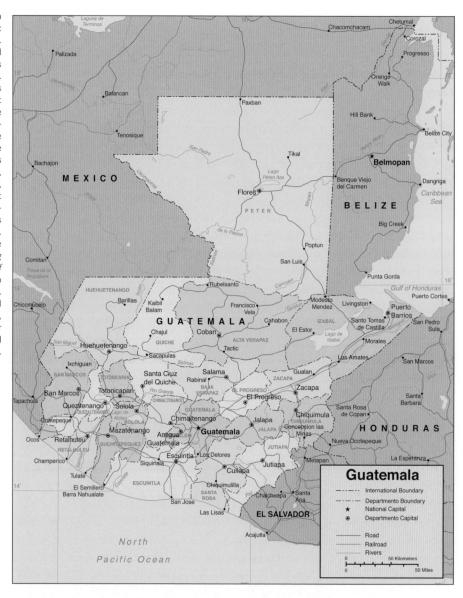

OTHER CITIES AND LANDS IN THE LAND OF NEPHI

As discussed earlier, the land of Nephi not only fulfilled the role of a city and a state but also served the purpose of a country. The structure appears to have been the same as is in existence today. Guatemala City is the major city located in the department of Guatemala. (A department is like a state or a province; a department is about the size of a county in Utah.) The country is also called *Guatemala* (land of trees). In addition to the department of Guatemala, the other departments, such as Peten, Solola, and Quetzaltenango, all fall under the bigger country umbrella of Guatemala.

During the Nephite time period (Maya Preclassic), lands or departments, such as the land of Ishmael, the land of Middoni, and the land of Mormon, fell under the country umbrella of Nephi. In summary:

Guatemala = the principal city.
Guatemala = the department or state surrounding the city.
Guatemala = the country over all other departments or states, of which Guatemala
       is one.
Nephi = the principal city in Lamanite territory after 200 BC.
Nephi = the land, department, or state surrounding the city.
Nephi = the country over all other states or departments in Lamanite territory.

(The land of Zarahemla, the land of Bountiful, and the land of Desolation appear also to fulfill the same role as the greater land of Nephi—that is, of a city, state, and country.)

We will now discuss some of the major cities and lands in the land (country) of Nephi.

Lehi-Nephi

And now it came to pass that after king Mosiah had had continual peace for the space of three years, he was desirous to know concerning the people who went *up to dwell in the land of Lehi-Nephi, or in the city of Lehi-Nephi*; for the people had heard nothing from them from the time they left the land of Zarahemla. (Mosiah 7:1; emphasis added)

The King Mosiah spoken of in this verse is the grandson of the Mosiah who left the land of Nephi about sixty years previously. This event is the first time in the Book of Mormon where the term "Lehi-Nephi" is used. The city of Lehi-Nephi was located in the greater land, or country, of Nephi. This location is evident from the statement of Zeniff, who returned from the land of Zarahemla to the land of Nephi to occupy it again:

I, Zeniff, having been taught in all the language of the Nephites, and having had a knowledge of the land of *Nephi*, or of the land of our fathers' first inheritance. (Mosiah 9:1; emphasis added)

And I went in unto the [Lamanite] king, and he covenanted with me that I might possess the *land of Lehi-Nephi, and the land of Shilom.* . . .

In essence, King Noah is like King Herod of the New Testament. Both Noah and Herod ruled over a people who were in bondage to another power—Herod to the Romans and Noah to the Lamanites. Both kings were wicked, and both feigned allegiance to the law of Moses.

And we began to build buildings, and to repair the walls . . . of the *city of Lehi-Nephi, and the city of Shilom.* (Mosiah 9:6, 8; emphasis added)

The city of Lehi-Nephi is mentioned only seven times in the Book of Mormon, and all seven instances refer to a city that was either the same as the old city of Nephi or that was within the confines of the greater city of Nephi. Perhaps the returning Nephites wanted to distinguish their city from the major city of Nephi, which by this time was a Lamanite city. In reality, the city of Lehi-Nephi was probably a suburb of the greater city of Nephi. As such, it would be considered to be part of the ancient ruins of Kaminaljuyu.

The fact that Zeniff had to rebuild the walls of the cities suggests that the cities were abandoned and that the departure of Mosiah from the land of Nephi had not been a pleasant one. The scripture in Omni states that Mosiah had to "flee out of the land of Nephi" (see Omni 1:12).

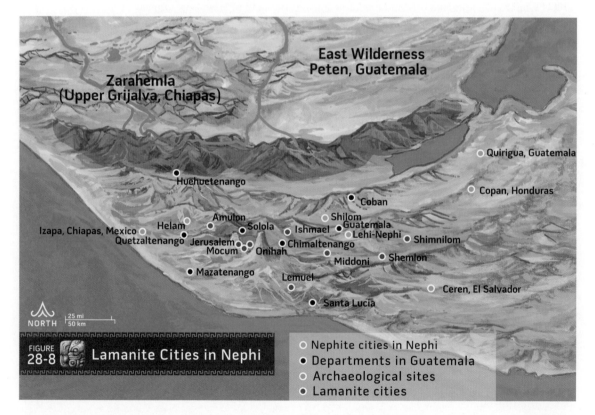

FIGURE 28–8: The Nephite cities of Lehi-Nephi (Nephi) and Shilom were under the political control of the Lamanites during the first and second centuries BC. Shemlon, Shimnilom, Lemuel, Middoni, and Ishmael were Lamanite cities that are mentioned in the Book of Mormon and that were located in the same general area of Lehi-Nephi and Shilom. Several Preclassic sites are identifiable in the departments of Guatemala, Esquintla, and Chimaltenango.

Exploring the Lands of the Book of Mormon

FIGURE 28–9: Crops are gathered on a daily basis and taken to market at Almolonga, Guatemala (proposed land of Helam) where they are brokered, sorted, and trucked to places throughout Guatemala and Central America. In many locations, natural springs from the volcanic mountains provide water for year-round irrigation. About five million natives live in the ancient land of Nephi. (Photo courtesy of Cortney Boice)

Shilom

And Ammon took three of his brethren, and their names were Amaleki, Helem, and Hem, and they went *down* into the *land of Nephi*.

And behold, they met the king of the people who were in the *land of Nephi*, and in the *land of Shilom*. (Mosiah 7:6–7; emphasis added)

Zeniff returned to occupy the smaller lands (departments) of Lehi-Nephi and Shilom about 180 BC. They both fell under the country, or greater land, umbrella of Nephi.

Ammon came up from the land of Zarahemla about 121 BC and helped Limhi, the grandson of Zeniff, to get back down to the land of Zarahemla.

You will observe that all the references in the Book of Mormon speak of "going *up* to Nephi" and "*down* to Zarahemla"; nevertheless, Mosiah 7:6 states that they "went *down* to the land of Nephi." The potential problem is easily solved when we take into consideration the terrain around Guatemala City. The department of Guatemala and the city of Guatemala are situated in a large valley: "And when they [Ammon and sixteen men] had wandered forty days they came to a hill which is north of the *land of Shilom*, and there they pitched their tents. . . . And they went *down into the land of Nephi*" (Mosiah 7:5–6; emphasis added).

Leaving the city of Guatemala on our tours, we travel in a direction west toward Antigua, Lake Atitlan, Chichicastenango, and Quetzaltenango. After we pull up out of the valley, we can look back and see the city and department of Guatemala below. If we

> The fact that Zeniff had to rebuild the walls of the cities suggests that the cities were abandoned and that the departure of Mosiah from the land of Nephi had not been a pleasant one.

were to place ourselves in Ammon's shoes after he camped out on top of the ridge, we would turn around and then go *down* to the land of Shilom and the land of Nephi.

Shemlon

Another city/land that was probably located in the large Guatemala valley is the Lamanite city/land of Shemlon. The city/land of Shemlon may have extended south into the Amatitlan valley.

Today, travelers can travel in and around the larger city of Jerusalem in the country of Israel and can observe both Jewish and Arabic cities in the suburbs. The same situation appears to be true with the cities located in the land of Nephi. That is, both Lamanite and Nephite cities were located in the same general area.

Six Book of Mormon scriptures relate to the city/land of Shemlon. A couple of these scriptures make reference to a high tower that the Nephite King Noah used to overlook the valley and see the land of Shemlon:

> And it came to pass that he [King Noah while living in Lehi-Nephi] built a tower near the temple; yea, a very high tower, even so high that he could stand upon the top thereof and overlook the land of Shilom and also the *land of Shemlon, which was possessed by the Lamanites*; and he could even look over all the land round about. (Mosiah 11:12; emphasis added)

The Nephites, who were living in the land of Nephi under the reign of the Nephite King Noah, rebelled against the wickedness of their king. At length, Gideon, a strong man and an enemy to the king, pursued Noah to the top of the tower in an effort to kill him:

FIGURE 28–10: Writing, archaeology, geography, agriculture, and customs all play roles in helping us understand the people whose lives are highlighted in the Book of Mormon. The concept of people carrying heavy burdens on their backs is highlighted with a bumper crop of carrots that are irrigated with natural mineral water and harvested daily from the rich volcanic soil. (Photo courtesy of Cortney Boice)

Exploring the Lands of the Book of Mormon

And it came to pass that he fought with the king; and when the king saw that he was about to overpower him, he fled and ran and got upon *the tower which was near the temple*.

And Gideon pursued after him and was about to get upon the tower to slay the king, and the king cast his eyes round about towards *the land of Shemlon*, and behold, the army of the Lamanites were within the borders of the land. (Mosiah 19:5–6; emphasis added)

Other scriptures that refer to the city/land of Shemlon are Mosiah 10:7; 20:1; 24:1; and Alma 23:12.

Cities of Shimnilom and Lemuel

The Lamanite cities of Shimnilom and Lemuel were also in Lamanite territory in the land of Nephi. They are mentioned in the Book of Mormon in reference to the missionary activities of the sons of Mosiah among the Lamanites in the first century BC. Neither directions nor geographical locations are given in the Book of Mormon regarding the cities of Shimnilom and Lemuel. In *Exploring the Lands of the Book of Mormon*, these two cities are tentatively placed south of Guatemala City around the Preclassic archaeological sites of El Baul and Monte Alto. Aaron and his brethren went from city to city and established churches in the land of the Lamanites (see Alma 23:4).

The Lamanite cities of Shimnilom and Lemuel were also in Lamanite territory in the land of Nephi.

FIGURE 28–11: Crops are grown among the trees on the mountaintops of Guatemala. Crops primarily consist of corn, beans, squash, wheat, and barley—the same as mentioned in Mosiah 9:9. During the first few weeks in July, the rains stop, enabling the farmers to plant a second crop. The natives refer to this break in the weather as the "canicula." (Photo courtesy of Merrill C. Oaks)

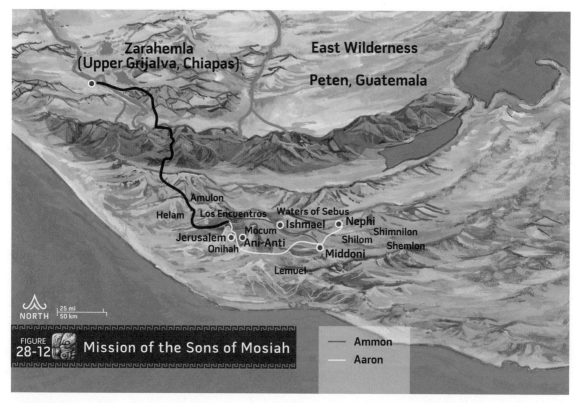

FIGURE 28–12: During the latter part of the first century BC, the sons of Mosiah led a group of missionaries from the land of Zarahemla to the land of Nephi. One of the sons, Aaron, traveled to the waters of Mormon and the villages surrounding the waters. He subsequently taught at Middoni and the city of Nephi. Another son, Ammon, spent considerable time in the land of Ishmael, which we propose to be in the department of Chimaltenango.

Now these are they who were converted unto the Lord.

The people of the Lamanites who were in the land of Ishmael.

And also the people of the Lamanites who were in the land of Middoni.

And also of the people of the Lamanites who were in the city of Nephi.

And also of the people of the Lamanites who were in the land of Shilom, and who were in the land of Shemlon, and in the *city of Lemuel, and in the city of Shimnilom.* (Alma 23:8–12; emphasis added)

The word *shim* in Shimnilom is a Book of Mormon name (see Mormon 1:3). It means corn in the Maya language. An archaeological site near Patzicia in the department of Chimaltenango is named X'imche (Iximche) and is pronounced "Sheem-chay," which means "corn tree," "corn among the trees," or "corn as tall as trees."

Jerusalem, Ani-Anti, Mocum, and Onihah

The sons of Mosiah with their numbers would have journeyed "many days in the wilderness" (see Alma 17:9) after leaving the central depression of Chiapas, Mexico, crossing over the rugged Cuchumatane Mountains, and dropping down into Huehuetenango. They would have continued their journey through the sparsely inhabited region, finally arriving at a place that is called today "Los Encuentros" ("where the roads meet"). From there, they would have taken their several journeys throughout the land after having been blessed and set apart (Alma 17:18).

> Now when Ammon and his brethren separated themselves in the borders of the land of the Lamanites, behold Aaron took his journey towards the land which was called by the Lamanites, *Jerusalem*, calling it after the land of their fathers' nativity; and it was away *joining the borders of Mormon*.
>
> Now the Lamanites and the Amalekites and the people of Amulon had built a great city, which was called *Jerusalem*. (Alma 21:1–2; emphasis added)

Before we continue with Aaron's mission, we will fast forward about a hundred years to the destruction at the time of Christ.

As determined in Alma 21:1–2, Aaron took his journey into the land of Jerusalem, which joined the borders of the land of Mormon. Thus, the site of the waters of Mormon was in the land of Mormon. Today, the area is associated with Lake Atitlan, which is located in the Guatemalan department of Solola (see chapter 26, "Bodies of Water,"

The word *shim* in Shimnilom is a Book of Mormon name (Mormon 1:3). It means corn in the Maya language.

FIGURE 28–13: The Kaminaljuyu Museum in Guatemala City shows a white style of pottery dating to the Mosiah through Alma time period. By analyzing pottery, we can follow the trail of the Nephites from Kaminaljuyu to Lake Atitlan and then to the upper Chiapas valley. (Photo courtesy of Blake Joseph Allen)

for further information). Jerusalem bordered the land of Mormon, and because waters came upon the city of Jerusalem at the time of the great destruction at the time of Christ, it may have been located on the far side of Lake Atitlan: "and the city of Jerusalem and the inhabitants thereof; and waters have I caused to come up in the stead thereof" (3 Nephi 9:7).

The town of Santiago Atitlan is located on the southern side of the banks of the beautiful, freshwater Lake Atitlan. A breach in the lake is obvious to the visitor. This is the area that is proposed as one of three cities mentioned in the Book of Mormon where the Lord caused "waters to come up in the stead thereof" (3 Nephi 9:7). The cities are Jerusalem, Onihah, and Mocum.

The local people from the village of Santiago Atitlan are well aware of the ancient city that was covered over by mud and water, and today it is called *Chiutinamit*, which means "a city by the water's edge." It was buried anciently as a result of both the massive mudslides sloshing down from the high San Pedro Volcano, one of three that overlook the lake, and by the giant waves from the bathtub-like lake that would have completely covered over the city of Jerusalem. The words Mormon uses, "waters in the stead thereof," are highly significant because that is what would have happened.

In the year 2005, after a serious season of heavy rainfall, another village in the same area was covered over as result of a heavy mudslide. The village did not border the lake; nevertheless, a thousand people were buried beneath the mud. There is some indication that Chiutinamit was destroyed at a later date during the Postclassic era. This does not, however, rule out the destruction during the time of Christ.

FIGURE 28–14: The Miraflores style of pottery of Kaminaljuyu has been discovered at Lake Atitlan. Pottery dating to the time periods of Alma, the sons of Mosiah, and the great destruction at the time of Christ has been recovered from the lake as a result of underwater archaeology. Places where pottery has been retrieved are Chiutinamit, Chukumuk, and Cerro de Oro, all of which are located near the Tzutuhil city of Santiago Atitlan. The piece of pottery shown here is on display at the Hotel Posada de Don Rodrigo at Panajachel, Solola. (Photo courtesy of Merrill C. Oaks)

In addition to the destruction of Chiutinamit, two other villages located near Santiago have been covered over with both mud and water. They are Chukumuk and Cerro de Oro. The former means "pueblo under the mountain" in the Tzutuhil language, and the latter means "hill of gold" in the Spanish language. Pottery dating to the Preclassic Period (200 BC to AD 200) has been discovered at all three sites—Chiutinamit, Chukumuk, and Cerro de Oro (see figure 28–14; see also chapter 26, "Bodies of Water").

Speaking of Onihah, Mocum, and Jerusalem, Jesus says: "The city of Onihah and the inhabitants thereof, and the city of Mocum and the inhabitants thereof, and the city of Jerusalem and the inhabitants thereof; and waters have I caused to come up in the stead thereof, to hide their wickedness and abominations from before my face, that the blood of the prophets and the saints shall not come up any more unto me against them" (3 Nephi 9:7).

The cities of Onihah and Mocum may have been neighbors to Ani-Anti and Jerusalem, places mentioned where Aaron preached the gospel. Both *Mocum* and *Onihah* are Maya words. In the Maya language, the syllable *cum* in Mocum is associated with a water basin. Lake Atitlan is a large, cone-shaped water basin whose depth has not yet been determined; hence, the name *Mocum* may literally mean "the place on the shores of the water basin." *Onihah* is derived from *oni*, meaning ancient, and *ha*, meaning water. Hence, the name means the village by the "ancient waters."

As we have stated, in recent years, underwater explorations on the far side of Lake Atitlan have revealed pottery dating to both the Late Preclassic Period (time of Christ) and the Classic Period, patterned after the Late Preclassic pottery of Kaminaljuyu. This important information ties the lake cities in with the Nephites during the time of King Noah, who named the lake, to the waters of Mormon, to Aaron's mission journey, to the city of Jerusalem and other cities surrounding the lake, and to the great destruction at the time of Christ.

We will now return to the missionary journey of Aaron and his companions to the land of Mormon. Lake Atitlan is flanked by three large volcanoes that today are called San Pedro, Santiago Atitlan, and San Lucas Toliman. In addition to Chiutinamit, Chukumuk, and Cerro de Oro, several other archaeological sites have been located near the water's edge.

Jerusalem was a Lamanite-Israelite-type city. Aaron, who preached at Jerusalem, followed the pattern of the Apostle Paul when Paul preached among the Gentiles. Aaron went into the synagogues to preach. Also, like Paul, when Aaron opened the scriptures concerning the coming of Christ and the resurrection of the dead, most of the people would not listen.

Aaron left Jerusalem and may have preached the gospel to the other villages around the lake. Today, several villages border Lake Atitlan, including San Marcos, San Antonio, Santa Caterina, San Lucas, and Panajachel.

Underwater explorations on the far side of Lake Atitlan have revealed pottery dating to the Late Preclassic Period.

One of the villages that Aaron preached to was called Ani-Anti: "Therefore, when he [Aaron] saw that they [people of Jerusalem] would not hear his words, he departed out of their synagogue, and came over to a *village* which was called *Ani-Anti,* and there he found Muloki preaching the word unto them" (Alma 21:11; emphasis added).

Cities/Lands of Ishmael and Middoni

When Aaron went to Jerusalem to preach to the Lamanites, Ammon, another son of Mosiah and the leader of the group, went to the land of Ishmael: "And Ammon went to the *land of Ishmael,* the land being called after the sons of Ishmael, who also became Lamanites" (Alma 17:19; emphasis added).

The experiences of Ammon with the Lamanite king over the land (department) of Ishmael represent one of the greatest conversions recorded in the Book of Mormon. The name of the Lamanite king was Lamoni. After his conversion, King Lamoni volunteered to go with Ammon to the land of Middoni to get Ammon's brothers out of prison. King Lamoni, in typical Mexican tradition, told Ammon that he (Lamoni) could help

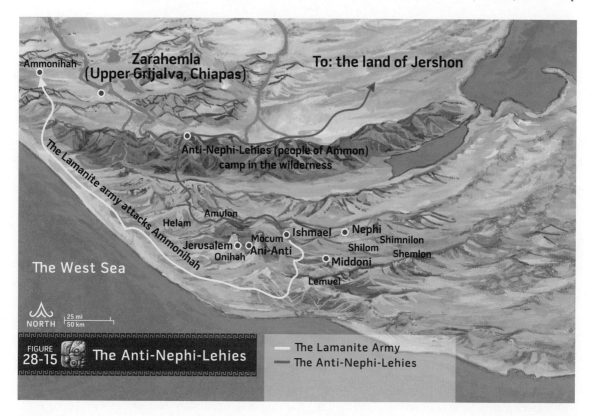

FIGURE 28–15: The cities of Jerusalem, Onihah, Mocum, Amulon, and Helam are all part of the greater land of Nephi. The first three mentioned cities bordered the waters of Mormon. Helam and Amulon appear to be located in the same general area in the department of Quetzaltenango.

get the brothers free because he was a friend to the king of the land of Middoni: "Now Lamoni said unto Ammon: . . . I will go with thee to the *land of Middoni*; for the king of the *land of Middoni*, whose name is Antiomno, is a *friend* unto me; therefore I go to the *land of Middoni*, that I may *flatter* the king of the land, and he will cast thy brethren out of prison" (Alma 20:4; emphasis added).

The two cities/lands of Ishmael and Middoni are mentioned in conjunction with each other, which causes us to think that they were in somewhat the same area. From the information that follows, we may also assume that Ishmael and Middoni were between the land of Mormon (Lake Atitlan) or the land of Jerusalem and the land (department) of Nephi/Guatemala City.

Some of the towns between Lake Atitlan and Guatemala City today are Patzun, Patzicia, Chimaltenango, Sumpango, and Antigua.

The land of Ishmael may have been what is now the department of Chimaltenango, which includes the communities of Patzicia, Patzun, and Sumpango.[17] These towns are located in a picturesque valley where a degree of level crop farming is possible.

17. Bruce W. Warren and Thomas S. Ferguson, *The Messiah in Ancient America* (Provo, UT: Book of Mormon Research Foundation, 1987), 44.

During the 1976 earthquake, this area was hit extremely hard. The estimations of damage note that 90 percent of the town of Patzicia was destroyed. Many people were killed. Pablo Choc, who was the branch president at the time the earthquake hit, lost his wife and three of his children in the earthquake. The area is the same location where a young missionary, Elder Randall Ellsworth, sustained severe injuries in the 1976 earthquake.

As Lamoni and Ammon were traveling to Middoni to free the brothers of Ammon, they met the father of Lamoni, who was king over all the land. The geography fits. On our tours, when we travel from Patzun, Patzicia, or Chimaltenango, we move in the direction of Guatemala City/Nephi. At a given point, we turn south and drop down to the quaint and ancient capital of Guatemala called Antigua.

The meeting of the Lamanite king over all the land with his son Lamoni, who was accompanying Ammon, manifests some interesting native traditions. Lamoni's father said to his son, "Why did ye not come to the feast on the great day when I made a feast unto my sons, and unto my people?" (Alma 20:9).

The people are very forgiving in Mexico and Guatemala. But if you are a family member, you must not consider staying away from a party to which you are invited.

Because Lamoni did not go to the "party," his father called Ammon a few negative words, such as "Nephite" and "one of the children of a liar." When things finally got straightened out, Ammon and Lamoni continued to Middoni, where they were able to get the brothers of Ammon out of prison (see Alma 20:13–30).

Antigua is probably the best we can do at this point in designating a potential location of the city/land of Middoni. Antigua was the capital of Guatemala after the Spanish conquest. However, earthquakes caused the capital of Guatemala to be moved to present-day Guatemala City. Antigua is down in elevation from the Chimaltenango

> The land of Ishmael may have been what is now the department of Chimaltenango.

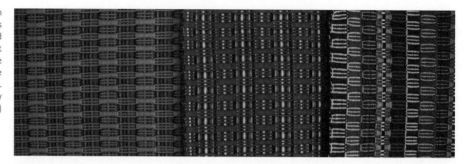

area. Middoni was down in elevation from the Ishmael area, as in the following statement: "And he [Lamoni] said unto Ammon: Come, I will go with thee *down* to the land of Middoni, and there I will plead with the king that he will cast thy brethren out of prison" (Alma 20:7; emphasis added).

We receive the same information from a later statement when the Lamanite king over all the land inquired about Ammon, "I desire to know the cause why he has not *come up* out of *Middoni* with thee" (Alma 22:3; emphasis added).

Land of Amulon

Barley, wheat, and corn are among the crops grown in the high mountainous regions of the area of Totonicapan.

Shortly after the death of the Nephite King Noah, his wicked priests kidnapped some Lamanite women. Their chief leader was a man by the name of Amulon. Consistent with Mesoamerica tradition, the group named the place they settled Amulon. They were subsequently discovered by Lamanite soldiers, who were in search of Limhi and his people who had escaped to the land of Zarahemla: "Now the armies of the Lamanites, which had followed after the people of king Limhi, had been lost in the wilderness for many days. And behold, they had found those priests of king Noah, in a place which they called *Amulon*; and they had begun to possess the *land of Amulon* and had begun to till the ground" (Mosiah 23:30–31; emphasis added).

The movement of Limhi and his people from the land (department or state) of Nephi to the land of Zarahemla probably took them through many of the areas already discussed. As they reached the borders of the Lamanites at the four crossroads, Limhi probably continued on through the wilderness to the Mexican/Zarahemla border by way of Huehuetenango.

A logical assumption is that the priests of Noah who were discovered by the Lamanite armies were in the area of the crossroads, possibly the area of Totonicapan. Barley, wheat, and corn are among the crops grown in the high mountainous regions of the area. The native document, *The Title of the Lords of Totonicapan*, was discovered there.

Subsequently, Amulon gained favor with the Lamanites. When Alma was discovered in the land of Helam, Amulon, a former colleague of Alma in King Noah's court, was granted his request to be taskmaster over Alma and his people. The proposed land of Helam (Almolonga in the Quetzaltenango valley) and Totonicapan, the proposed land of Amulon, are across the mountain from each other. If you stop at a lookout prior to dropping down into the Quetzaltenango valley, you will see Quetzaltenango on the west and Totonicapan on the northeast.

Land of Mormon, Valley of Alma, Land of Helam

The land of Mormon, valley of Alma, and land of Helam were discussed in chapters 24 and 26, "Wilderness Areas" and "Bodies of Water." Therefore, they will not be discussed in this section.

FIGURE 28–17: The word *Mormon* is associated with both forests and wild beasts. This wilderness region bordering Lake Atitlan is still home to the wild jaguar and is a place antigovernment factions have used as a place of refuge. (Photo courtesy of Cortney Boice)

CONCLUSION

We cannot help but be fascinated when we realize that the present-day lay of the land in Guatemala dictates the travel routes and the settlement routes both presently and anciently. That is, the movements within the Book of Mormon, when placed in the areas discussed above, present a believable geographical picture. Linguistic studies show continued occupation of the areas since Book of Mormon times, which is also confirmed by archaeological data.

When we add the information inscribed on Altar 10 at Kaminaljuyu, which dates to 147 BC, to the already significant information from Kaminaljuyu, Lake Atitlan, and Almolonga, we can comfortably arrive at the conclusion that indeed the land of Guatemala was the ancient land of Nephi.

This designation is further reinforced when we add the fact that the three major Mesoamerican documents, *Annals of the Cakchiquels*, *Popol Vuh,* and *The Title of the Lords of Totonicapan,* which predate the Spanish conquest, came out of a radius of thirty miles in the highlands of Guatemala that we are proposing as the land of Ishmael, land of Mormon, and land of Helam. The latter two documents have in them biblical and Book of Mormon themes, such as the creation, the flood, and the emigration of people from the world of Mesopotamia who were descendants of Abraham, Isaac, and Jacob. And the manner of writing that has been discovered by Allen Christenson in the *Popol Vuh* is in exquisite chiastic format—the same as is contained in numerous instances in the Book of Mormon. The results obviously show a literate people who lived in the area prior to the coming of the Spaniards.

> The movements within the Book of Mormon, when placed in the areas discussed, present a believable geographical picture.

The Land of Zarahemla

And they were admonished continually by the word of God; and they were led by the power of his arm, through the wilderness until they came down into the land which is called the land of Zarahemla. (Omni 1:13)

T **HE BOOK OF OMNI**

The book of Omni introduces us to the most prominent land in the Book of Mormon and the city that is mentioned the most often—Zarahemla. The land of Zarahemla was named after a Mulekite leader by the same name who had migrated from the land northward into the land southward.

We learn about the cities in the land of Zarahemla from Alma's missionary activities, the war campaigns of Helaman and Moroni, and the several migrations that took place between Zarahemla and Nephi. In addition to the city of Zarahemla, other Nephite cities in the land of Zarahemla were Manti, Minon, Gideon, Melek, Ammonihah, Sidom, Noah, Aaron, Antiparah, Zeezrom, Judea, and Cumeni.

OPPOSITE: A Maya long count date of December 36 BC discovered at Chiapa de Corzo is shown here superimposed over the archaeological site of Chiapa de Corzo, Chiapas, Mexico. The Maya name of this site is Zactun, which has the same meaning as Sidom in Alma 15:1–3. The 36 BC date corresponds to the time period in which the Lamanites gained control of Zarahemla and the Nephites moved their headquarters to the land Bountiful. (Site photo courtesy of Cortney Boice; inset photo courtesy of Blake Joseph Allen)

The small book of Omni makes a major contribution to our understanding of the history and chronology of the Book of Mormon. Omni consists of only three pages (thirty verses) and is written by five writers—namely, Omni, Amaron, Chemish, Abinadom, and Amaleki. It covers the period of time from approximately 361 BC to 130 BC. The book of Omni is the last book included in the small plates of Nephi.

The last writer of the small plates, and of the book of Omni, is Amaleki. In twelve verses (Omni 1:12–23), he brings together the three groups of the Book of Mormon—the Nephites, Mulekites, and Jaredites.

If Kaminaljuyu/ Guatemala and the surrounding area is the land of Nephi and if the Isthmus of Tehuantepec is the narrow neck of land, then the land of Zarahemla has to fit somewhere in between.

About 180 BC, Mosiah was called by the Lord to depart out of the land. Mosiah's people were led by the Lord into the wilderness. They traveled in the wilderness until they came *down* into the land of Zarahemla. There they discovered a people called the people of Zarahemla—hence the name of the place. We are not sure just how long Zarahemla had lived there. We do know that his people had traveled from the land northward *up* into the south wilderness where Mosiah discovered them (see Alma 22:31).

We also know that Zarahemla's people were excited to see Mosiah. They recognized that the Lord had brought Mosiah to them with the plates of brass that contained the record of the Jews. The people of Zarahemla were Jews who came out of Jerusalem about the same time that Mosiah's forefather, Lehi, had come out of Jerusalem. We call the people of Zarahemla "Mulekites" because they were followers of Mulek, the son of King Zedekiah. Mulek had traveled to the New World with a large number of people (see Mosiah 25:2).

When Mosiah discovered the people of Zarahemla, or the Mulekites, about 180 BC, they had become numerous and had had wars and contentions. Their flight from Jerusalem four hundred years earlier was swift; and, as a result, they had brought no records with them. For four hundred years, their Hebrew traditions in the New World were probably transmitted orally from generation to generation. When Mosiah found the Mulekites, their language had become corrupted; they had no records; and they denied the being of their creator.

Mosiah taught the Mulekites his language; he recorded their history as told from memory; he taught them the gospel; and he was appointed to be their king.

Also, during the days of King Mosiah, the people of Zarahemla brought to Mosiah a large stone with engravings upon it. The engravings were interpreted by King Mosiah by the gift and power of God (see Omni 1:20). It gave an account of Coriantumr and the slain of his people. It told how more than two thousand years before either Lehi or Mulek arrived in Mesoamerica, a group of people were led by the Lord from the great tower to the promised land (see Ether 1:33).

These people have become known as Jaredites because their leader who brought them from the tower was a man named Jared. Jared was their king, and his brother was their prophet. After more than two thousand years of lineage history, we come to the

Exploring the Lands of the Book of Mormon

last king of the Jaredites, whose name was Coriantumr. The Jaredite kingdom came to a close when Coriantumr leaned upon his sword and smote off the head of Shiz: "And it came to pass that when Coriantumr had leaned upon his sword, that he rested a little, he smote off the head of Shiz" (Ether 15:30).

After the downfall of his nation, Coriantumr was cared for by the people of Zarahemla for the space of "nine moons" (see Omni 1:21).

The book of Omni bridges the gap of civilizations. The Nephites, Mulekites, and Jaredites are somewhat "brought together" at this point in the Book of Mormon.

SUMMARY OF PROPOSED LOCATIONS

If Kaminaljuyu/Guatemala and the surrounding area is the land of Nephi and *if* the Isthmus of Tehuantepec is the narrow neck of land, *then* the land of Zarahemla has to fit somewhere in between. *Because* Zarahemla is always *down in elevation from the land of Nephi* (see, for example, Omni 1:13; Alma 27:5, 7–8; Alma 51:11–12) and *because*

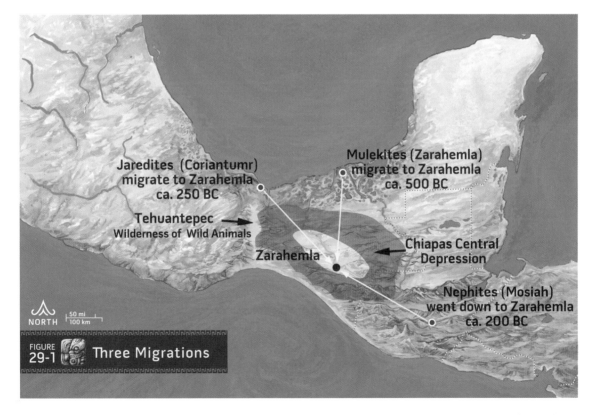

FIGURE 29–1: Three Book of Mormon cultures converge at Zarahemla (Chiapas) in the third and second centuries BC. The Mulekites (people of Zarahemla) had settled along the Chiapas-Guatemala frontier. Coriantumr was cared for after being exiled from the land of Desolation (land northward), and Mosiah led a group of Nephites from the land of Nephi to the land of Zarahemla. Mosiah became king over the people of Zarahemla and the old Jaredite territory (see Ether 13:21).

Chapter 29: The Land of Zarahemla

the wilderness that is north of the land of Nephi is by the land of Zarahemla, *then* Zarahemla is located in a northward direction from Nephi (see Alma 22:27) and *then* we will be looking for a land that is lower in elevation in a northward direction and that is located between Guatemala and the Isthmus of Tehuantepec. We will also be looking for a major river to call *Sidon*, which runs through Zarahemla (see Alma 2).

And we need to have an east wilderness—that is, an east wilderness that is east of Zarahemla and north of Nephi (see Alma 50). We will want population centers to appear in the land of Zarahemla beginning at the Mosiah time period between the second and first centuries BC. We will expect to see many cities built in the east wilderness and north of the land of Nephi (Alma 50:7, 14; Alma 51:26). We will also anticipate that many of the cities will be walled or defensive cities because of Moroni's activities in the first century BC. We will expect to see a cultural impetus about 180 BC and a cultural decline about AD 350. Finally, we will expect to see some culture patterns, such as weapons of war and a written language.

With these many and varied requirements in mind, we will look at the map. In doing so, we will place Zarahemla in the Chiapas depression, or Chiapas valley. We will call the Grijalva River the river Sidon, and we will call the Peten jungle of Guatemala the east wilderness. We will place the city of Moroni, which sank into the sea during the great AD 34 destruction, off the coast of Belize, and we will put Nephihah somewhere between Belize and Chiapas in the Peten jungle of Guatemala.

> We believe that after Moroni annexed the Peten and Belize regions in the first century BC, they became part of the greater land of Zarahemla.

LAND OF ZARAHEMLA

We have already stated our reasons for identifying Kaminaljuyu as the land of Nephi. Several strong reasons exist to place Zarahemla in the Chiapas valley, and we will reinforce those reasons later in this chapter. We believe that after Moroni annexed the Peten and Belize regions in the first century BC, they became part of the greater land of Zarahemla. The reasons we favor Zarahemla as being located in the Chiapas depression are as follows:

1. It fits the directional and distance requirements for Mosiah to lead a group of people from Nephi/Kaminaljuyu.
2. It fits the directional requirements for the people of Zarahemla to come up into the south wilderness.
3. It allows for an east wilderness in the Peten of Guatemala with its archaeological ruins and fortified cities.
4. It allows the Isthmus of Tehuantepec to play its proper role in Book of Mormon geography as the narrow neck of land.
5. It permits the Limhi expedition to bypass Zarahemla and wander through the state of Tabasco—in the area proposed as the "land of many waters"—to get into the land northward.

6. It is in an adequate location for Alma and Limhi to return to Zarahemla through an ancient trail that passed over the "narrow strip of wilderness," or a narrow mountain range.

7. It is in the proper general area for language development. That is, from 600 BC–AD 200, we witness a written language in use that was adopted by the later Classic Maya culture.

8. Ample archaeological population centers are found in the Chiapas valley during the 180 BC–AD 350 time period when much of the Nephite history in the land of Zarahemla occurred.

9. The archaeological ruins of Santa Rosa located in the upper Grijalva valley present compelling evidence as the city of Zarahemla.

10. Finally, a manifested decline in population occurred in the area around AD 350, the time period when the Nephites were forced to leave the land southward. Zarahemla was in the land southward.

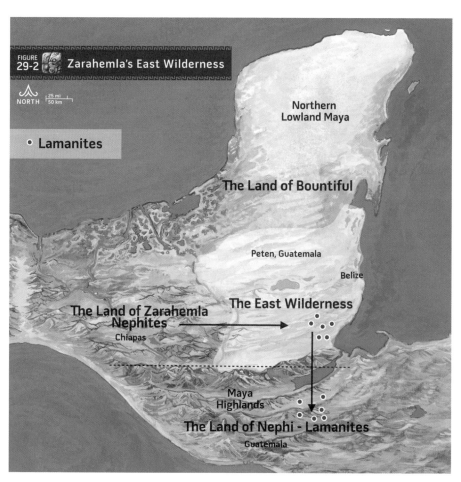

FIGURE 29-2: The Lamanite king outlined his boundaries as recorded in Alma 22:27–33. In the year 72 BC, Moroni led his armies into the east wilderness and claimed that land as Nephite territory by driving the Lamanites into the land of Nephi (Alma 50:7–12). This "homestead act" caused many Nephites to move into the east wilderness where they built many cities. In essence, Zarahemla annexed the east wilderness, as from this time forth in Nephite history, the east wilderness is part of the land of Zarahemla. The Nephites also laid claim to the land Bountiful, which was north of Zarahemla. Earlier, under the leadership of King Mosiah, the Nephites acquired the ancient land of Desolation.

We will demonstrate that archaeological sites have been found whose dating and culture patterns coincide precisely with Mosiah's and with the people of Zarahemla's dating and culture patterns. A large portion of the Book of Mormon (Omni to Mormon) presents us with theological statements and events, couched in geography that took place between what we call Nephi (Kaminaljuyu) to Zarahemla (Chiapas).

MOSIAH AND THE PEOPLE OF ZARAHEMLA

We have established the following data—or facts—in relationship to Mosiah and the people of Zarahemla:

> Archaeological sites have been found whose dating and culture patterns coincide precisely with Mosiah's and with the people of Zarahemla's dating and culture patterns.

1. The people of Zarahemla, whom we have come to know as Mulekites, came out of Jerusalem sometime after 586 BC, either at the time Jerusalem was destroyed by the Babylonians or fifty years later after their return from captivity. Zarahemla's people probably landed off the coast of Veracruz, Mexico, and eventually migrated to Chiapas, Mexico, where Mosiah discovered them around 180 BC. In all probability, other Mulekite settlements were established on both sides of the Isthmus of Tehuantepec.

2. The Jaredites saw their government fall sometime between 400 BC–200 BC. Their last surviving king, a man by the name of Coriantumr, was nurtured by the Mulekites for about "nine months" prior to his death. These Jaredites had come from the Old World between 3000 BC–2500 BC at the time the Lord confounded the languages of the people. The Jaredites had established a mighty nation, with its heartland located in all probability along the Gulf Coast of Mexico in the state of present-day Veracruz, Mexico.

3. Mosiah, who was a descendant of Nephi, came from the land of Nephi (Kaminaljuyu) down to the land of Zarahemla (Chiapas) about 200 BC. His forefathers, dating back to Nephi, lived in Nephi (Kaminaljuyu) since the time Nephi had settled there between 586 BC–577 BC. Nephi came across the ocean with his father Lehi and his brothers about 586 BC. Lehi was a descendant of Joseph, the son of the biblical Jacob. When Mosiah arrived in Zarahemla (Chiapas), he became king over the people of Zarahemla and the Nephites who had come with him. He taught the people of Zarahemla his language and the gospel.

MONTE ALBAN AND THE LAND OF ZARAHEMLA

Although Monte Alban is located on the west of the Isthmus of Tehuantepec, in the state of Oaxaca, some very impressive time period and cultural correlations result when we compare the Monte Alban culture with the events described in the book of Omni (see chapter 7, "The Zapotec [Mulekite-Nephite] Culture").

We propose that Monte Alban Period I (500 BC–100 BC) was a city inhabited by the Mulekites and that Zarahemla, which was located east of the Isthmus of Tehuantepec, was not the only Mulekite city in Mesoamerica. A four-horned incense burner of Hebrew fashion, dating to Monte Alban Period I, was discovered at Monte Alban. Also, the first written language of Mesoamerica was discovered at Monte Alban. The famous dancers at Monte Alban also date to Monte Alban Period I.

The inhabitants of Monte Alban Period I were undoubtedly influenced by the Olmecs/Jaredites of the Gulf Coast. Indeed, Coriantumr, the last surviving king of the Jaredites, certainly must have made an impact on the Nephites. The story of Coriantumr also suggests that the Mulekites lived simultaneously with the Jaredites—before the Jaredite nation fell.

We further propose that Monte Alban was part of the greater Nephite society from 180 BC forward. At least we know that as early as 55 BC, Nephites lived in the land northward (see Alma 63:4). The following statement, which dates to AD 29, is recorded in 3 Nephi: "And it came to pass that they had not eaten up all their provisions; therefore they did take with them all that they had not devoured, of all their grain of every kind, and their gold, and their silver, and all their precious things, and they did return to their own lands and their possessions, both on the north and on the south, both on the land northward and on the land southward" (3 Nephi 6:2).

This time period is labeled Monte Alban Period II and falls in the dates of 180 BC–AD 350. The archaeological record of Monte Alban tells us that "other people entered the valley of Oaxaca about 180 BC. They may have perhaps originated in Guatemala or Chiapas."[1] At any rate, they brought with them a number of culture traits that they imposed on the existing civilization. You will recall that when Mosiah's people arrived in Zarahemla, they pursued a course that was acceptable to the people of Zarahemla of teaching them the gospel and of teaching them the Nephite language. Mosiah was even made king over both the Nephite newcomers and the established Mulekites. The archaeological record states that "probably the two groups merged in the course of time."[2]

One of the highlights of Monte Alban Period II (180 BC–AD 350) was the coming of Christ. Mound J of Monte Alban is labeled an observatory and dates back to the time of Christ. We are certainly safe in assuming that whoever the scientists were who occupied the observatory, they probably recorded both the astrological events that occurred at the birth of Christ and the catastrophic events that occurred at the time of His death. In respect to those events, let us consider the following:

> And it came to pass that there was no darkness in all that night, but it was as light as though it was mid-day. And it came to pass that the sun did rise in the morning again, according to its proper order; and they knew that it was the day that the Lord should be born, because of the sign which had been given. (3 Nephi 1:19)

Some very impressive time period and cultural correlations result when we compare the Monte Alban culture with the events described in the book of Omni.

1. Ignacio Bernal, *Official Guide: Oaxaca Valley*, translated by Helen Jones-Perrott de Mandri (Mexico, DF: Instituto Nacional de Antropoligia e Historia, 1985), 22.

2. Bernal, *Official Guide: Oaxaca Valley*, 23.

FIGURE 29–3: The Grijalva River, proposed river Sidon, runs through the Chiapas valley, a portion of which is shown here. This valley is also referred to as the Chiapas depression. Notice the mountains of Guatemala in the background. The country of Israel could be placed inside the Chiapas depression, the area proposed in *Exploring the Lands of the Book of Mormon* as the land of Zarahemla. (Photo courtesy of Cortney Boice)

And it came to pass in the thirty and fourth year, in the first month, on the fourth day of the month, there arose a great storm, such an one as never had been known in all the land. (3 Nephi 8:5)

Both Santa Rosa and Chiapa de Corzo manifested a rapid decline around AD 350.

The ending of Monte Alban Period II is dated at AD 350. This is the precise time that the Nephite period was coming to a close. Mormon 2:28–29 tells us of the treaty wherein the Nephites gave up, to the Lamanites, the land southward all the way to the narrow pass that led into the land northward: "And the three hundred and forty and ninth year had passed away. And in the three hundred and fiftieth year we made a treaty with the Lamanites and the robbers of Gadianton, in which we did get the lands of our inheritance divided. And the Lamanites did give unto us the land northward, yea, even to the narrow passage which led into the land southward. And we did give unto the Lamanites all the land southward" (Mormon 2:28–29).

The date of the Nephite-Lamanite treaty is the same date as the archaeological dating at Monte Alban when a culture change began to occur—AD 350. Mormon also informs us that this is the time period when he called all the Nephites together at the land Desolation, to a city that was in the borders, by the narrow pass that led into the land southward: "And it came to pass that I did cause my people that they should gather themselves together at the land Desolation, to a city which was in the borders, by the narrow pass which led into the land southward" (Mormon 3:5).

Both Santa Rosa and Chiapa de Corzo manifested a rapid decline around AD 350. Of interest also is the evidence of trade among Oaxaca, Kaminaljuyu, and Teotihuacan of the Mexico valley around AD 400. This trading activity may account for the Lamanites' and Gadianton robbers' desire to exterminate their enemies; they wanted the Nephites "out of the way."

Apparently, the old squeeze play was put into effect by the robbers of Gadianton, who may have been the administrators of the land northward in the valley of Mexico, and by the Lamanites, who controlled all of the land southward. The Nephites were probably in the way of commercial and cultural interchange between the two larger nations with headquarters in what are now Guatemala City and Mexico City.

Monte Alban Period III is placed from AD 350–AD 750. This is post–Nephite time period. By AD 750–AD 800, Monte Alban was abandoned as a center for administrative and commercial activity.

In summary, the dating of Monte Alban is the following:

Pre–Monte Alban: Jaredite time period
Monte Alban Period I: 500 BC–100 BC, Mulekite time period
Monte Alban Period II: 100 BC–AD 350, Nephite (Mosiah) time
Monte Alban Period III: AD 350–AD 750, post–Book of Mormon

The archaeological record of Monte Alban states the following:

As far as we have been able to ascertain, . . . man first appeared in the valley of Oaxaca during the period which has been entitled Monte Alban I and must probably be placed between 700 and 300 B.C. . . . [Note: Recent datings place Monte Alban I beginning about 500 BC.]

Although we do not know for certain who the inhabitants may have been during this first period, they were undoubtedly influenced by the so-called "Olmecs" of the Gulf Coast.

Other people entered the valley of Oaxaca toward 300 BC: they may perhaps have originated in Guatemala. [Note: Current data place the infusion of this culture at 180 BC and indicate that they came from Chiapas or Guatemala.] At any rate, they brought with them a number of culture traits which mingled with those of the earlier period.

This new culture has been entitled Monte Alban II. . . . The period lasted roughly until the beginnings of the Christian era, and the bearers of this culture only settled in a few places in the valleys. . . . This suggests that they were a small group of conquerors who imposed their power over the earlier inhabitants although these did not disappear: probably the two groups mingled in the course of time.[3]

> The Nephites were probably in the way of commercial and cultural interchange between the two larger nations with headquarters in what are now Guatemala City and Mexico City.

3. *The Oaxaca Valley: Official Guide*, 5th ed. in English (Mexico, DF: Instituto Nacional de Antropologia e Historia, 1973), 5–6.

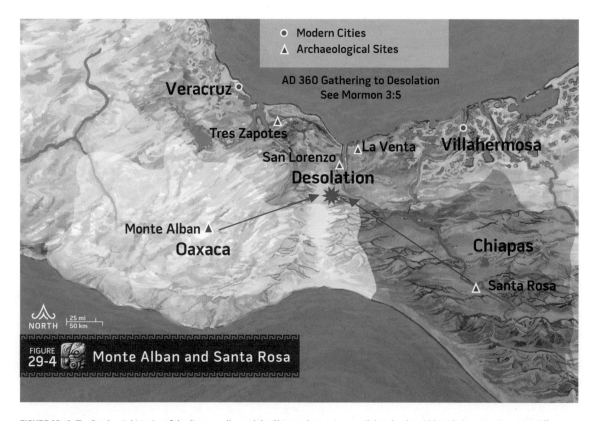

FIGURE 29–4: The Preclassic histories of the Oaxaca valley and the Chiapas depression parallel each other. Although their peoples spoke different languages and were considered different cultures, several migratory periods are held in common. For example, both manifest early Olmec influence, both show evidence of a non–Olmec culture dating to 500 BC, both were influenced from political migrations from Guatemala between 200 and 100 BC, and both decreased in population between AD 350 to AD 400. Oaxaca appears to have been the ancient land of Moron, and Chiapas was probably the ancient land of Zarahemla.

The 1985 updated version of the "official guide" of the Oaxaca valley states the following:

> Period II is represented by relatively few, though important sites, which suggests that the newly integrated settlers were a minority who in some way superimposed themselves on the inhabitants of the previous period. Little by little the two groups merged.[4] [Note: New dating places this infusion at 180 BC.]
>
> Whoever the first inhabitants were, they were influenced by the so-called Olmecs. . . . Other people entered the valley of Oaxaca about 180 BC. These came from Guatemala or Chiapas.[5]

4. Bernal, *Official Guide: Oaxaca Valley*, 23.

5. Bernal, *Official Guide: Oaxaca Valley*, 22–23.

MIGRATIONS BETWEEN ZARAHEMLA AND NEPHI

The books of Omni and Mosiah cover a ninety-year period of time from 180 BC to 90 BC. They record the events of three generations of Jewish Nephites who lived simultaneously in the land of Nephi and in the land of Zarahemla.

The Nephite kings who presided in the land of Zarahemla during this time period were Mosiah, Benjamin, and Mosiah.

The Nephite leaders and kings who lived in the land of Nephi, which by this time in history was Lamanite territory, were Zeniff, Noah, and Limhi.

During this time period, we witness a number of migrations between the land of Zarahemla and the land of Nephi. They are as follows:

Zeniff wanted to return to the land of Nephi. He did so with a group of people. With the permission of the Lamanite king, Zeniff's people were permitted to reside in the land of Lehi-Nephi and the land of Shilom (see Mosiah 9).

Sometime around 121 BC, Limhi, the grandson of Zeniff and the son of Noah, desired to return to Zarahemla along with his followers. They were unsuccessful in finding Zarahemla, so they returned to the land of Nephi. After the return of Limhi's forty-three men, around 121 BC, a Mulekite by the name of Ammon was sent by King Mosiah to go up to the land of Nephi to inquire about the status of the Israelites/Nephites who lived there. Limhi, who worked under the advice of Gideon, caused the Lamanite guards to get drunk and followed Ammon back down to the land of Zarahemla.

Alma, who had been a priest under the reign of Noah, the father of Limhi, was converted by the prophet Abinadi. Alma led a group of believers to the land of Mormon and from there to a place they called Helam. Several years later, they were led by the Lord to the land of Zarahemla.

All the above events are recorded in the book of Mosiah and include migrations from the land of Zarahemla to the land of Nephi and from the land of Nephi to the land of Zarahemla. A brief synopsis follows. A more detailed account, with cultural and geographical implications, is included in chapter 24, "Wilderness Areas."

ZENIFF'S MIGRATION FROM ZARAHEMLA TO NEPHI

Mosiah and his followers were forced out of the land of Nephi—perhaps in somewhat the same way as the Latter-day Saints were forced out of Nauvoo. Or Mosiah's people may have left because of persecution or taxation by the Lamanites. The account says merely that they "fled" out of the land of Nephi (see Mosiah 11:13 and Omni 1:12).

Shortly after Mosiah and his followers arrived at Zarahemla, Zeniff was sent out to spy on the Lamanite armies. He saw that which was good among the Lamanites and proposed to his fellow Nephites in the wilderness that they try to go among the Lamanites in peace. A terrible internal strife occurred; many were killed; and Zeniff and the survivors returned to Zarahemla to relate the sad tale to the wives and children (see Mosiah 9:1–3).

> Mosiah and his followers were forced out of the land of Nephi—perhaps in somewhat the same way as the Latter-day Saints were forced out of Nauvoo.

Zeniff was very persistent; and, as he says, he was overzealous to inherit the land of Nephi—which was the land of first inheritance. In spite of famine and "sore afflictions," they were successful in returning to the land of Nephi. Zeniff made a covenant with the Lamanite king to possess the land of Lehi-Nephi and the land of Shilom. The motive of the Lamanite king, of course, was eventually to place these returning Nephites under bondage (see Mosiah 9:3–13).

> The total travel time from the city of Nephi to the city of Zarahemla was approximately thirty days.

The travel distance from the land of Nephi to the land of Zarahemla was approximately thirty days (250 miles). We arrive at that number of days by combining the eight days that Alma and his people took to go from the land of Mormon to the land of Helam and the twelve days they took to go from the land of Helam to the land of Zarahemla, plus the estimated time from the land of Nephi to the waters of Mormon. The record does not say what the distance was from the land (state) of Nephi to the land of Mormon. We could estimate it took eight to ten days to go that distance, which would make the total travel time from the city of Nephi to the city of Zarahemla approximately thirty days.

Ammon and sixteen strong men, in search of the land of Nephi, took forty days to get from Zarahemla to Nephi. However, they wandered many days in the wilderness—not knowing exactly where the land of Nephi was located.

By placing the land (state) of Nephi where Guatemala City is today and by placing the land (state) of Zarahemla where the central depression of the Mexican state of Chiapas is today, we are presented with some interesting and rather convincing parallel statements.

The high, dense, rugged mountains of Guatemala do not cause us to wonder how people could easily get lost. The term "wilderness" is certainly very adequate to describe this wild, beautiful, mountainous region. The lower elevation of the Chiapas depression, with its tropical-type heat, is adequate to suggest why Zeniff and his friends were desirous to return to the spring-like climate in the mountainous setting of Guatemala.

The "ups" and "downs" are consistent in the Book of Mormon and are dramatically spelled out on the trip from Guatemala to Chiapas where travelers drop from almost ten thousand feet elevation to twenty-two hundred feet elevation in four hours of bus travel. This is the route through which we propose the migratory interchange occurred between the land of Nephi and the land of Zarahemla. Today, the trip would be like traveling from Guatemala City to Lake Atitlan, then to Quetzaltenango, then to Huehuetenango, and then to the border of Mexico. From here, the trip requires an hour and fifteen minutes for the bus ride to Comitan, Chiapas. The valley of Zarahemla may have been off to the northwest in the central depression area of the state of Chiapas.

Archaeological data and population centers that date to the time in question (180 BC–90 BC) justify the above conclusions.

THE RUINS OF SANTA ROSA (CITY OF ZARAHEMLA)

Although other sites have been proposed and although some inherent problems may still exist with Santa Rosa's being the most likely candidate for the city of Zarahemla, the evidence far exceeds that for any other candidate we have studied as a likely representative of that multicultural capital city. And since the original publication of *Exploring the Lands of the Book of Mormon* in 1989 until the date of this second edition, 2008, no other candidate has surfaced with higher credentials as the city of Zarahemla than the ancient archaeological site of Santa Rosa. The site is located in the upper Grijalva valley and was investigated during the 1958–59 seasons by the highly reputable New World Archaeological Foundation prior to the site's being covered with water as a result of the Angostura Dam. Underwater archaeology could also reveal more information at Santa Rosa in the same manner that information has been obtained by divers at Lake Atitlan.

Below are some general statements about Santa Rosa as a candidate for the city of Zarahemla. They will be followed by an abstract analysis of the investigative results at the site of Santa Rosa.

General Statements

1. Santa Rosa is in the proper direction and manifests the same elevation relationship to Guatemala as the city of Zarahemla does to the land of Nephi.
2. Santa Rosa is situated along the banks of the Grijalva River and is in close proximity to many other neighboring archaeological sites dating to the time period in which Zarahemla and its neighboring sites flourished.
3. The discovery of the Miraflores style and workmanship of pottery originating from Lake Atitlan and Kaminaljuyu in Guatemala dating from the second century BC at Santa Rosa verifies an emigration relationship from the city of Nephi and the waters of Mormon to the city of Zarahemla.
4. Evidence manifesting distinct culture districts within the city of Santa Rosa itself was discovered dating between 500 BC and 100 BC and demonstrating it to be a multicultural city in the same manner that the city of Zarahemla was home to three distinct cultures: the Mulekites, the Jaredites, and the Nephites.

The "ups" and "downs" are consistent in the Book of Mormon and are dramatically spelled out on the trip from Guatemala to Chiapas

It was during the 1940s and 1950s when Wells Jakeman and Thomas Stuart Ferguson, the latter a tireless worker and organizer, were breaking ground for a limited geographical concept of Book of Mormon lands that Chiapas came on the scene. The investigations of Santa Rosa in 1958–59 were under the auspices of the newly formed New World Archaeological Foundation, organized by Ferguson and assisted by two of the world's most prominent New World (non–Latter-day Saint) archaeologists, Gordon R. Willey and Alfred V. Kidder, the latter of Kaminaljuyu fame. An initial report on Santa Rosa was submitted by the foundation's field director, Dr. Gareth Lowe, with a follow-up report in 1965 by Agustin Delgado. The following represents a summary extracted from Delgado's report. We have added Book of Mormon commentary to Delgado's report.

Santa Rosa had its principal occupation during the Late Preclassic, from 500 BC to 100 BC.

The New World Archaeological Foundation adhered strictly to the norms of investigative research as opposed to making any attempt at Book of Mormon correlations. Although the investigators for the New World Archaeological Foundation were on the payroll of Brigham Young University, a higher percentage of non–Latter-day Saints always worked for the foundation than the percentage of members of the Church. Bruce Warren, Thomas Lee, and Gareth Lowe, who were resident archaeologists for many seasons at Chiapas, were members of the Church. The New World Archaeological Foundation became affiliated with the Church in January of 1961, at which time Elder (President) Howard W. Hunter became the chairman of the board, a position he held for almost thirty years.

Extracts from Delgado's Report of Santa Rosa

The site of Santa Rosa is now under a man-made reservoir along the Grijalva River. However, prior to the river's inundation, the New World Archaeological Foundation conducted archaeological studies of Santa Rosa during the 1958 and 1959 seasons. And a reconnaissance of the upper Grijalva River in the winter of 1956 showed the site of Santa Rosa to be the largest Pre-classic center in the region.

The archaeological report indicates that Santa Rosa had its principal occupation during Late Pre-classic, from 500 BC to 100 BC. This period is referred to as Santa Rosa Period III and is characterized by its advanced architecture, known to be of imposing dimensions in at least a few instances.

Period IV of Santa Rosa, or the Protoclassic era, apparently was an efflorescence of the city, contemporary with similar developments elsewhere in Mesoamerica. At this time, many of the principal structures at Santa Rosa were built, sometimes utilizing cut stone, stucco, and paint. Early Maya polychrome imports mark the close of the period, which began about 100 BC and ended about AD 200. The above dates were arrived at from carbon-14 dating and from comparisons with Chiapa de Corzo Phases VI and VII.

The Santa Rosa V, or Early Classic, Period seems poorly represented at Santa Rosa. Possibly, a reduced population maintained many old traditions, adopting only a few new customs or traits brought from the outside.

The last period or Period VI of Santa Rosa dates from AD 550 to AD 950, at which time Santa Rosa appears to have been abandoned as a ceremonial center.[6]

6. Augustin Delgado, *Excavations at Santa Rosa, Chiapas Mexico*, Papers of the New World Archaeological Foundation, no. 17 (Provo, UT: NWAF, Brigham Young University, 1965), 79–81.

Summary of Archaeological Investigation at Santa Rosa with the Book of Mormon

Period III of Santa Rosa was established as a prominent center in the Grijalva valley lasting from 500 BC to 100 BC. This time period corresponds to the arrival and settlement of the people of Zarahemla, the demise of the Jaredite civilization, and the arrival of Mosiah, who was made king over the land of Zarahemla.

Period IV of Santa Rosa dates from 100 BC to AD 200, labeled above as a period of efflorescence and corresponding to the Nephite occupation with intermediate Lamanite intrusion and Mulekite dissatisfactions. During this time period, we witness the most detailed and concentrated history recorded in the Book of Mormon. The books of Mosiah, Alma, Helaman, and 3 Nephi all fall within Period IV of Santa Rosa.

Period V of Santa Rosa, dating from AD 200 to AD 500, manifests reduced population of the site. The year AD 350 is crucial in Book of Mormon history because that was the year the Nephites made a treaty with the Lamanites in which the Lamanites were given all of the land southward (see Mormon 2:28–29). Zarahemla was in the land southward. Santa Rosa is southward of the Gulf Coast and the Isthmus of Tehuantepec. It was during this same time period that Santa Rosa manifested a decline in population and demonstrated rather distinct Lamanite Maya culture patterns.

It is now time to ask some questions. What happened to Zarahemla? Why didn't it become a Jerusalem? Why didn't it become a Tikal? Why did it get lost and fade away and then get covered over with a reservoir? A few suggestions are as follows:

At 36 BC, or seventy years before Christ visited the Nephites, the Church moved its headquarters from Zarahemla to Bountiful (Helaman 4:6). There was a temple at Zarahemla when they left. They built a new temple at Bountiful where the Savior appeared. The changing of the headquarters from Zarahemla to Bountiful undoubtedly had some effect on the lack of growth at Zarahemla. Think of Nauvoo—one of the largest cities, if not the largest—in Illinois in 1844, and Nauvoo had a temple also. In 1847, the Saints arrived in the Salt Lake Valley and built a new temple. In the year 2002, many Saints returned to Nauvoo to witness the open house and dedication of the rebuilt Nauvoo Temple. One hundred fifty years had passed since the departure of the Saints from Nauvoo, during which time the town did not grow much. It never became a Chicago. Likewise, the city of Zarahemla never became a Tikal.

At 350 AD, the Nephites were driven completely out of the land of Zarahemla, never to return. The city of Zarahemla never regained its stature. Other cities moved to the forefront—cities that developed priestcraft or king-men dynasties, such as Palenque, Uxmal, Tikal, and Copan. Santa Rosa, Chiapa de Corzo, Izapa, El Mirador, and Monte Alban all declined in population. This is the time period when Mormon was calling all the Nephites to gather at the city of Desolation. The year was AD 360, ten years after the treaty: "I did cause my people that they should gather themselves together at the land Desolation, to a city which was in the borders, by the narrow pass which led into the land southward" (Mormon 3:5). The city where they gathered was Desolation, which may have been the ancient city of the Jaredite King Kish, possibly San Lorenzo Tenochtitlan.

What happened to Zarahemla? Why didn't it become a Jerusalem? Why didn't it become a Tikal? Why did it get lost and fade away and then get covered over with a reservoir?

KING NOAH

Noah was the son of Zeniff and the father of Limhi (see Mosiah 11:1). Of these three generations, only Noah did not touch foot on Zarahemla soil. We have a difficult time referring to Noah without calling him "the wicked King Noah." While King Noah was wallowing in wickedness in the land of Nephi, King Benjamin was preaching to the people of Zarahemla and the people of Mosiah who dwelt in the land of Zarahemla (see Mosiah 1:10)—exhorting them to take upon themselves the name of Christ and telling them that when they were in the service of their fellow beings, they were only in the service of their god (see Mosiah 2:17ff.). King Noah taxed the Nephites living among the Lamanites one-fifth of all the Nephites possessed. King Benjamin labored with his own hands to serve the people of Zarahemla so they would not be laden with taxes (see Mosiah 2:14).

Other statements in the Book of Mormon cause us to suspect that not all the people who lived in the land of Zarahemla (Chiapas) were Nephites or Mulekites.

We are told that Noah built many buildings in the land of Shilom. Noah could see the land of Shilom and the land of Shemlon, both of which were in Lamanite lands, from a tower he had built in the land of Lehi-Nephi. Noah caused a great tower to be built north of Shilom at a place that had been a resort for the children of Nephi before they fled out of the land of Nephi under the leadership of King Mosiah.

Although no specific building today is labeled a "Noah building," enough activity appears to have occurred during Noah's time in the land of Nephi to warrant continued and detailed excavation work among the ruins of Kaminaljuyu (proposed city of Nephi) and its surrounding archaeological sites.

King Noah commanded his people to follow him into the wilderness to escape the wrath of the Lamanites. He met his fate, as prophesied by the prophet Abinadi, by being burned to death (see Mosiah 19:20). His own people killed him.

KING BENJAMIN

While Noah was building elaborate buildings in the land of Nephi (Kaminaljuyu), while the prophet Abinadi was calling Noah and his fellow Nephites to repentance, and while Alma, a priest in King Noah's court, was being converted by the prophesying of the prophet Abinadi, King Benjamin was ruling with justice in the land of Zarahemla (Chiapas).

King Benjamin was the son of Mosiah, who had come down from the land of Nephi (Kaminaljuyu) to the land of Zarahemla (Chiapas) and united with the Mulekites. Mosiah became the king of both the Nephites who came with him from the land of Nephi as well as the more numerous Mulekites, or people of Zarahemla, with whom he came in contact. Benjamin was anointed by his father to take Mosiah's place as king over the people of Mosiah and the people of Zarahemla who dwelt in the land of Zarahemla (see Mosiah 1:10).

Other statements in the Book of Mormon cause us to suspect that not all the people who lived in the land of Zarahemla (Chiapas) were Nephites or Mulekites. Remnants of Jaredites (Omni 1:21–23; Mosiah 8:12; Ether 13:21) and perhaps even other people resided among the Nephites and Mulekites. This observation also suggests the possibility of other people's voluntarily coming under the jurisdiction and reign of King Benjamin.

That such is possible can be deduced from the activity that was taking place in Monte Alban and other isolated areas located in the state of Oaxaca during the time of King Benjamin. Monte Alban is located on the opposite side of the Isthmus of Tehuantepec from Chiapas. This location suggests that King Benjamin may have been recognized as king over people who were living in areas other than just the city or land of Zarahemla.

About 130 BC, Benjamin became king over the same people who had been governed by his father, Mosiah. Perhaps Benjamin, as a young boy, traveled from the land of Nephi down to the land of Zarahemla with his father. At any rate, Amaleki, the last record keeper of the small plates of Nephi and a contemporary of Benjamin's father, Mosiah, recognized Benjamin as a just man. As a result, Amaleki's having no seed put Benjamin in charge of the sacred records (see Omni 1:25).

King Benjamin became a defender of his people; and in an account that reminds us of the continual Jewish history in the Old World in relationship to their enemies, the Nephites battled the Lamanites who came into the land of Zarahemla. The account tells us that many thousands of Lamanites were killed under the leadership of King Benjamin (see Words of Mormon 1:11–14; Omni 1:24).

Having established his power to rule, King Benjamin seems to have established himself as the greatest of Nephite kings—much in the same way that David was considered Israel's greatest king.

We probably remember King Benjamin most for his farewell address where he accounted for his service and anointed his son, Mosiah, to be the king. Obviously, Benjamin named his son after his father, as both Benjamin's father and Benjamin's son were named Mosiah.

A cultural setting like we experience at the ruins of Monte Alban gives us an idea of how Benjamin may have addressed his people. The walls of the city form a natural acoustic setting. The temple platforms in Mesoamerica are consistent with Book of Mormon statements such as "I come *up into* the temple" (see Jacob 2:2; Mosiah 1:18). The large central plaza at Monte Alban, the size of seven football fields, is adequate for people to gather with their tents (see chapter 7, "The Zapotec [Mulekite-Nephite] Culture") and hear clearly the words of a speaker.

During this great Jewish ceremonial event, King Benjamin caused his people to take upon themselves the name of Christ, the Messiah who was to be born 120 years from the time of King Benjamin's address. King Benjamin consecrated his son, Mosiah, to be a ruler and a king over his people (see Mosiah 6:3).

King Benjamin seems to have established himself as the greatest of Nephite kings—much in the same way that David was considered Israel's greatest king.

LIMHI, THE SON OF NOAH

While King Benjamin was defending his kingdom and anointing his son Mosiah to succeed him in the land of Zarahemla (Chiapas), Noah was "wine bibbing" in the land of Nephi (Kaminaljuyu). After the death of Noah, the people of Nephi who were still living in Lamanite territory conferred the kingdom on Limhi, the son of Noah. Limhi, not impressed with his father's activities, began to establish peace in the area. Limhi took an oath with the Lamanite king that his Israeli-Nephites would pay one-half of all they raised to the Lamanites to maintain peace. The Lamanites placed guards around the Nephite cities to keep the Nephites from fleeing into the wilderness—like Noah had done and like Mosiah also had done three generations earlier.

A visit to Guatemala, the area we propose as the land of Nephi, immediately causes the visitor to realize what a wilderness looks like. The steep mountains and the deep valleys covered with forests are ideal for a giant game of hide-and-go-seek.

> The steep mountains and the deep valleys of Guatemala are covered with forestation that makes it ideal for a giant game of hide-and-go-seek.

Five major migrations occurred between the land of Nephi and the land of Zarahemla during Limhi's tributary kingship. One of these migrations, although round trip in nature, never reached Zarahemla. This was the migration of what we call the Limhi expedition of forty-three men, which took place about 121 BC. The objective was to make contact with the Nephites living in the land of Zarahemla to appeal to them for assistance in escaping from the Lamanites. The forty-three men never found Zarahemla but traveled through a land of many waters and entered into the land of a civilization that had been destroyed (see Mosiah 8:8; see also chapter 24, "Wilderness Areas," and chapter 26, "Bodies of Water").

ALMA AND HIS MISSIONARY JOURNEY

We learn a lot about the land of Zarahemla from the missionary journeys of Alma. After relinquishing the position of chief judge, Alma set about to place the Church in order. He began in the city of Zarahemla (Santa Rosa). From there, he crossed the river Sidon and went east to the valley of Gideon. He returned to the city of Zarahemla and then went west along the mountains to the city of Melek. From Melek, he traveled three days on the north until he arrived at the city of Ammonihah. After leaving Ammonihah, he was going in the direction of Aaron.

Because the Book of Mormon gives such a detailed description of Alma's travels, we can propose possible locations of the cities he visited. Those cities will be discussed at length in the following pages.

THE CITY OF ZARAHEMLA

After relinquishing the judgment seat, Alma began to set the Church in order beginning in Zarahemla, the capital city, about 83 BC. He spoke to Church members living in Zarahemla—calling them to repentance (see Alma 5:6). The city of Zarahemla apparently received its name from a Mulekite by that same name. The man Zarahemla lived

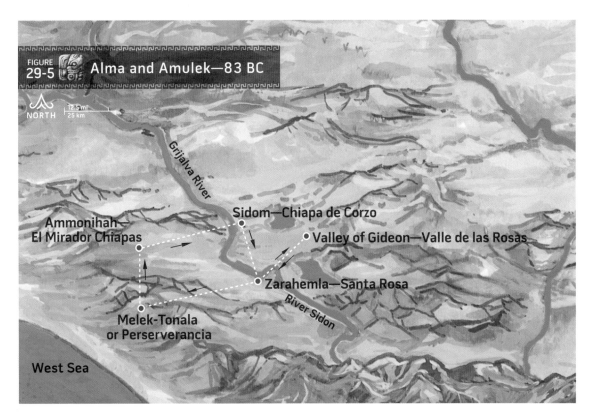

FIGURE 29–5: At 83 BC, the same time that the sons of Mosiah were preaching the gospel in the land of Nephi among the Lamanites, Alma surrendered his position as chief judge and dedicated his time to preaching. This map outlines the places where Alma taught beginning and ending at Zarahemla. Amulek joined Alma at Ammonihah and Sidom.

several generations after Mulek (see Omni 1:14–18). These events indicate that the city was settled sometime between 400 BC–200 BC.

From about 180 BC to approximately 91 BC, Zarahemla served as the capital city of the following Nephite kings: Mosiah, Benjamin, and Mosiah.

From about 91 BC to approximately 51 BC, the city of Zarahemla was the headquarters of both the Nephite judgment seat and the Church of Christ.

The city of Zarahemla fell into the hands of the Lamanites about 51 BC—but for only a short period of time. The city of Zarahemla was the strongest city and was in the center of the land; and yet Coriantumr, head of the Lamanite army, marched in and took possession of the entire city (see Helaman 1:20). In the same year, Moronihah, the son of Moroni, recaptured the city of Zarahemla; and Helaman, the son of Helaman, who was the son of Alma, was chosen to be the chief judge.

From about 50 BC to about 29 BC, the city of Zarahemla continued to operate under judges. An attempt to establish kings again in the land was thwarted. At 36 BC, the Nephites moved their headquarters from Zarahemla to Bountiful (Helaman 4:5–6).

> We learn a lot about the land of Zarahemla from the missionary journeys of Alma.

The chief judge was murdered; and from about 29 BC forward, the people divided themselves into tribes and leaders of tribes (see 3 Nephi 7:3).

Sometime between AD 32 and AD 34, the city of Zarahemla caught fire. This was the time of the great destruction at the death of Christ (see 3 Nephi 8:8; 3 Nephi 8:24). Zarahemla was called a "great city."

About AD 59, twenty-five years after it had burned, the city of Zarahemla was rebuilt (see 4 Nephi 1:8).

From AD 59 to AD 350, the Nephites apparently were still in control of the city of Zarahemla. In the year AD 350, the Lamanites, by treaty, obtained the land and the city of Zarahemla (see Mormon 2:28–29). The Nephites never again ruled in their capital city. The city of Zarahemla became a Lamanite city.

As previously discussed, if the central depression of the state of Chiapas is the land of Zarahemla, then the archaeological site of Santa Rosa is a good candidate for the city of Zarahemla.

THE CITY OF GIDEON

The second leg of Alma's missionary journey was in the city of Gideon, which was in the valley of Gideon. The city was named after that Gideon who was the right-hand man of King Limhi in the land of Nephi and who later was killed by Nehor. The valley of Gideon may have been the area located between Comitan and San Cristobal de las Casas, both modern cities in the state of Chiapas, Mexico. This pleasant valley rises to about six thousand feet above sea level. It is located east of the central depression area of Chiapas. Hence, it is east of the River Grijalva (river Sidon).

It is possible that the greater land of Manti extended to the top of the narrow strip of wilderness.

The Book of Mormon requirement for the valley of Gideon is that it was on the east of the river Sidon and it was *over and upon*—suggesting a higher elevation: "And now it came to pass that when Alma had made these regulations he departed from them, yea, from the church which was in the city of Zarahemla, *and went over upon* the *east of the river Sidon, into the valley of Gideon*, there having been a city built, which was called the city of Gideon, which was in the valley that was called Gideon, being called after the man who was slain by the hand of Nehor with the sword" (Alma 6:7; emphasis added).

We pick up another orientation of the land of Gideon when, some six years later, Alma (ca. 77 BC) was journeying from the land of Gideon southward away to the land of Manti. There he joyfully met the sons of Mosiah returning from a fourteen-year mission among the Lamanites (see Alma 17:1). You will recall that the land of Manti extended to the headwaters of the river Sidon.

These events possibly make the meeting place of Alma and the sons of Mosiah somewhere between the area of Ciudad Cuauhtemoc and Comitan. After dropping down from the mountains of highland Guatemala and then crossing through the Mexico border, travelers come to an area that breaks into a flat plain.

The sons of Mosiah, going toward Zarahemla, could easily have met Alma on his way from the land of Gideon southward to the land of Manti (Alma 17:1). La Libertad, which is an archaeological site located on the wilderness side leading toward the land of Nephi (Guatemala) and which is the proposed city of Manti, is southward of the valley of Gideon. The greater land of Manti possibly extended to the top of the narrow strip of wilderness, which was the dividing line between the land of Nephi and the land of Zarahemla and which was also where the headwaters of the Sidon River are located.

MELEK

After preaching the gospel and setting the Church in order in the land of Gideon, Alma returned to the city of Zarahemla to his home to rest from his labors (see Alma 8:1).

At the beginning of the following year (82 BC), he again picked up his missionary labors and traveled west of the river Sidon, which was also west of the city of Zarahemla, to the land of Melek. Melek Apparently was located near the mountains on the west, or up into the mountains, as the scripture states: "Alma departed from thence [city of Zarahemla] and took his journey over into the land of Melek, on the *west of the river Sidon, on the west by the borders of the wilderness*" (Alma 8:3; emphasis added).

As discussed in earlier chapters, the term "wilderness" in the New World refers to both forested mountain country and jungles. People came from their homes located all along the mountains west of Zarahemla to listen to Alma and to be baptized. This conference possibly included the members of the Church who lived both in the mountains and along the coast from Soconusco to Tonala. People of the Izapa culture, where the Tree of Life Stone discussed earlier was discovered, may have been invited to this portion of Alma's conferences. Izapa was a thriving culture during Alma's time period (see chapter 9, "The Izapa [Jaredite-Nephite-Lamanite] Culture," and chapter 15, "Christ—The Tree of Life").

The city of Melek was where the converted Lamanites (people of Ammon—Anti-Nephi-Lehies) settled after they departed out of the land of Jershon. The place they were originally given was located near the east sea (Caribbean—Atlantic side) near the city of Mulek. Melek, on the other hand, was located near the west sea (Gulf of Tehuantepec—Pacific side; see Alma 27:22 and 35:13). Having lived in three different places in two years, Guatemala, Belize, and western Chiapas, they contributed to that long war movement by allowing their young sons to become stripling warriors. The parents did this, even though they had taken an oath not to go to war anymore and had buried their weapons of war some ten to fifteen years earlier. However, their young sons had not taken the oath (see Alma 24:19; Alma 53:11–22).

The city of Melek was where the converted Lamanites (people of Ammon—Anti-Nephi-Lehies) settled after they departed out of the land of Jershon.

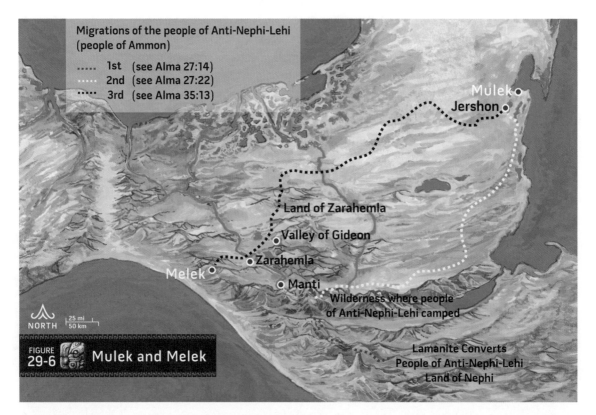

Migrations of the people of Anti-Nephi-Lehi
(people of Ammon)

..... 1st (see Alma 27:14)
..... 2nd (see Alma 27:22)
..... 3rd (see Alma 35:13)

Muleko
Jershon o

Land of Zarahemla
Valley of Gideon
o Zarahemla
Melek o
o Manti
Wilderness where people
of Anti-Nephi-Lehi camped

Lamanite Converts
People of Anti-Nephi-Lehi
Land of Nephi

NORTH   25 mi / 50 km

FIGURE
29-6   Mulek and Melek

FIGURE 29–6: Although the city names of Mulek and Melek sound similar and basically have the same meaning, they are mountains apart. Mulek was located on the shores of the east sea and was close to the city of Bountiful (Alma 52:16–27). Melek, on the other hand, was located near the west sea, near the day-and-a-half fortification line. Mulek was a Mulekite city where Amalickiah and Ammoron tried to establish a kingship and is proposed to be the archaeological site of Cerros, Belize. Cerros (Mulek) is close to Laman Ayin, our candidate for the land of Jershon where the converted Lamanites first settled. Melek is where the people of Ammon moved after leaving the land of Jershon (Alma 35:13). The lines indicate the trail of the converted Lamanites from Guatemala to Belize to Tonala, Chiapas.

TYPES AND SHADOWS

The story of the stripling warriors has a types-and-shadows application. In this respect, Joseph Allen writes:

My hands moved slowly down the wall of the Vietnam Veterans Memorial located in Washington, D.C., until I came to the name of Chris Munson. My mind went back to the time when Chris was a senior in high school and I was his seminary teacher. I had driven him home, and we sat in front of his house until midnight talking about the opportunity he would soon have of going on a mission. A few years later, upon his return from his mission, he married a beautiful girl in the temple for time and eternity, and then he was inducted into the military. At the wall, I reflected on how privileged I was to have spoken at both his mission farewell and his farewell from this life.

Chris was a fine young man, and like the sons of Helaman, he did not doubt. He had been taught by his mother and his father; therefore, he obeyed and observed to perform every word of command with exactness. Because of his exceedingly great faith, he believed in a just God, and he believed that whoever would not doubt would be preserved by His marvelous power.

Let's take another look at those great stripling warriors of Helaman who fought in the land of Zarahemla. The scripture states, "There was not one soul of them who did perish; yea, and neither one soul among them who had not received many wounds" (Alma 57:25).

Not one of those two thousand (2,060) young Lamanites was killed. It is probably this reason that caused Mormon to choose this story to put in his account. Although it is rare, one Utah battalion returned from Iraq without losing any of its members. But notice that the scripture says "not one soul did perish." Because of the Atonement of Christ, it is as if death does not exist—neither for the two thousand striplings nor for Chris Munson, nor for us. "O death, where is thy sting? O grave, where is thy victory?" (1 Corinthians 15:55; see also Alma 22:14). And then we read the follow-up statement that all the young soldiers of Helaman had received many wounds.

As we go through this battle of life, although we die, we will live again; and although we sin and receive many wounds, we can be forgiven, all because of our Savior Jesus Christ—if we will have faith, without doubting, and learn to obey every command.

> Not one of those two thousand (2,060) young Lamanites was killed. It is probably this reason that caused Mormon to choose this story to put in his account.

AMMONIHAH

Three days' journey on the north of the land of Melek were the city and the land of Ammonihah. The city of Ammonihah had the distinction of being the most wicked city in the land of Zarahemla during Alma's time period. The leading people of the city of Ammonihah said: "Behold, we know that thou art Alma; and we know that thou art high priest over the church which thou hast established in many parts of the land, according to your tradition; and we are not of thy church, and we do not believe in such foolish traditions" (Alma 8:11).

In Ammonihah, Alma met Amulek, who had been prepared by the Lord to receive Alma and accept the gospel. Prior to his conversion, he was both a wealthy man and a leading man of the community. After his conversion, he was rejected by his own family. The people who were converted by Alma and Amulek were either burned to death or ostracized from the community. The books of those who believed in the coming of Christ were burned. Alma and Amulek were cast into prison. They were convicted on the same trumped-up charges for which the Jews of Jerusalem convicted Christ—that is, "treason against the law and blasphemy against God" (see Alma 14:5). Finally, Alma and Amulek were cast into prison, starved, and reviled. An earthquake shook down the prison walls. Alma and Amulek were commanded to depart out of the city of Ammonihah. Zeezrom, who had been a chief contender against Alma and Amulek and who was subsequently converted, had already been stoned and driven out of the community.

Alma had earlier prophesied that the wicked city of Ammonihah would be destroyed at the hands of the Lamanites (see Alma 9:18). We place the location of Ammonihah at the western end of the central depression of Chiapas. This location allowed the Lamanites to move up along the Pacific coast and drop over into Ammonihah.

EL MIRADOR, CHIAPAS

This simple dirt mound stands as a monument to a wicked people who said, "How can this city be destroyed?"

Today, there is an ancient archaeological mound at the crossroads near the town of Pomposo Castellanos located in the municipality of Cintalapa, which dates to the Preclassic Period. Driving northward along the coast from Tapachula to Arriaga on our tours and then proceeding north for about twenty-five miles, we arrive at the site of the mound. The mound is referred to as El Mirador (not to be confused with the Peten, Guatemala, El Mirador). The New World Archaeological Foundation did some preliminary excavations at the site.

We propose the area of the municipality of Cintalapa to be where the ancient city of Ammonihah was located. Today, this simple dirt mound stands as a monument to a wicked people who said, "How can this city be destroyed?"

CHAMULA NATIVES

More than a hundred thousand Chamula natives live in the mountains of Chiapas. They are small people and, for the most part, are very poor. The manner of dress of the women consists primarily of blue shawls and black skirts. The men normally wear white cotton shawls. They raise sheep, chickens, and pigs and grow a variety of fruits and vegetables. They speak their own native tongue but are taught Spanish in the local school. Teachers who have received government support for their education are sent to the villages for a two- or three-year assignment. The men are allowed to have more than one wife if they can support them. The society is very tight and socially interrelated.

The Chamula are subject to the Mexican government, but they also have an internal political system. The religion of the Chamula is Catholicism, mingled with their own traditions. A Catholic priest arrives at the village every two weeks to perform the rites of baptism, communion, and marriage. For the most part, however, individual prayers are recited as the Chamula worshipers sit or kneel on the church floor that is covered with pine nettles. A church in the distance was burned in the early part of the twentieth century when the pine nettles caught fire. When asked why they put the nettles on the floor, their answer is always the same: "It has always been done."

FIGURE 29–7: The village of San Juan Chamula, called the Alps of Mexico, is located in the Chiapas Mountains and is home to the Chamula natives. Like the natives of Guatemala, the Chamula still dress in their traditional clothing. They live in the area where, in recent years, conflicts with the central government of Mexico have arisen. Although they are basically Catholic in name, they maintain that they incorporate their native ceremonies with those of Catholicism. (Photo courtesy of Merrill C. Oaks)

SAN JUAN CHAMULA

About ten miles from the city of San Cristobal de las Casas, Chiapas, is a native village named San Juan Chamula. The Chamula who live in and around San Juan Chamula are steeped in the traditions of their fathers. One of these traditions is very similar to what is recorded in the Book of Mormon when Alma and Amulek taught the gospel of Christ at the city of Ammonihah. Those who were converted to the Church were either burned or cast out of the village. When Alma and Amulek arrived at the city of Sidom, they found the converted Church members, whom the people of Ammonihah had cast out and ostracized.

The same tradition exists today in the Chamula environment. The Spaniards and Catholicism conquered the Chamula by force in the sixteenth century; and Catholicism still reigns supreme. So when Protestantism entered among the Chamula people in the latter part of the nineteenth century, any Chamula who accepted the new religion was cast out of the community and, in many cases, had a hand or a finger cut off to mark the offender so he or she could not return. The Protestant converts wandered into the city of San Cristobal. Like Amulek and the people of Ammonihah, Chamula Protestants are rejected by those who were once their friends and also by their fathers and kindred (see Alma 15:16).

CITY/LAND OF SIDOM (ZACTUN: LAND OF WHITE STONE)

The converted Saints who were cast out of the city of Ammonihah went to the land of Sidom: "And it came to pass that Alma and Amulek were commanded to depart out of that city [Ammonihah]; and they departed, and came out even into the *land of Sidom*; and behold, there they found all the people who had departed out of the land of Ammonihah, who had been cast out and stoned, because they believed in the words of Alma" (Alma 15:1; emphasis added).

> The name Sidom is associated with white stone.

The city of Chiapa de Corzo is a strong candidate for the city/land of Sidom where the ostracized Saints fled in the first century BC. It is also the place where Zeezrom was healed as a result of a blessing given by Alma and Amulek: "And then Alma cried unto the Lord saying: O Lord our God, have mercy on this man, and heal him according to his faith which is in Christ. . . . And Alma baptized Zeezrom unto the Lord; and he began from that time forth to preach unto the people. And Alma established a church in the land of Sidom" (Alma 15:10, 12–13). The city of Chiapa de Corzo is located about ten miles east of Tuxtla Gutierrez. It is approximately thirty miles northwest of the inundated archaeological site of Santa Rosa. As noted previously, Santa Rosa is a candidate for the city of Zarahemla. The Grijalva River (river Sidon) flows past the city of Chiapa de Corzo and then turns north through the Sumidero Canyon. One of the most pleasant experiences on our tours consists of the boat trip we take through this majestic canyon.

Evidence points to the Grijalva River as being the river Sidon identified in the Book of Mormon. Some people propose the Usumacinta River to be a candidate for the river Sidon. However, the lack of archaeological evidence and the geographical structure disqualify the Usumacinta basin as a serious contender for Sidon (see also chapter 20, "The Land Southward").

FIGURE 29–8: A natural formation caused by water creates an image of a Christmas tree where the Grijalva River passes through the majestic limestone Sumidero Canyon near Tuxtla Gutierrez, Chiapas, Mexico. (Photo courtesy of Merrill C. Oaks)

The city of Chiapa de Corzo is situated in an area consisting of white limestone. John Sorenson proposes a correlation between the city of Sidom in the Book of Mormon and the area around Chiapa de Corzo. He writes: "The impressive archaeological site of Chiapa de Corzo seems to be Sidom. During several ancient periods it was the largest city in Chiapas, with many dependent towns and villages in its nearby network. It would have been a rich and crucial target for the Lamanite leader Coriantumr, since it and its zone were the 'most capital' part of the entire river basin (Helaman 1:27). As a focal

Exploring the Lands of the Book of Mormon

FIGURE 29–9: A crocodile sunbathes along the banks of the Grijalva River. (Photo courtesy of Cortney Boice)

point for trade and the ceremonial center for the entire lower part of the central depression, it would also be the logical place to which refugees from Ammonihah like Alma and Amulek would gravitate."[7]

Furthermore, and probably most important, the old name of Chiapa de Corzo was Zactun, which means "white stone." The area around, which includes a plasterboard factory, is made of white limestone. The entrance to the majestic Sumidero Canyon, through which the Grijalva River passes, is by the city of Chiapa de Corzo (Zactun) and is almost pure white limestone. The words *zac* (white) and *tun* (stone) in the Maya language have the same meaning as *Sidom*, the name of the city where Alma and Mulek blessed Zeezrom. The name *Sidom* is also associated with white stone. Mount Sidom, located near the Dead Sea and close to where the ancient cities of Sodom and Gomorrah were located, is composed of a core of solid white rock salt in an area of white limestone. In fact, the entire region around the Dead (salt) Sea is composed of limestone caves. This is the area where the Dead Sea scrolls were discovered. *Ma-sada(m)*, the last stronghold of the Jews against the Romans, is a mountain of limestone

The archaeological site of Chiapa de Corzo, which dates to the Preclassic Book of Mormon time period, was excavated by the New World Archaeological Foundation in the 1960s. The oldest Maya long count that has been discovered to this date was discovered at Chiapa de Corzo. It dates to the early part of December 36 BC. New information suggests that this date may have a direct tie-in with events recorded in Helaman 4:3–6.

7. John L. Sorenson, *An Ancient American Setting for the Book of Mormon* (Salt Lake City: Deseret Book and Foundation for Ancient Research and Mormon Studies, 1985), 205.

If the Lamanites took control of Chiapa de Corzo in 36–30 BC, the outcome suggests a movement of the Church (Nephite) headquarters from Zarahemla to Bountiful. The Nephite record reports that the Savior appeared at Bountiful, not Zarahemla.

CITY/LAND OF NOAH (LAND OF THE VULTURES AND SERPENTS)

The city of Noah is not mentioned in Alma's missionary journey. Ocozocoautla, the proposed city of Noah, is a town about twenty miles west of Chiapa de Corzo (proposed city of Sidom) and twenty-five miles east of Cintalapa, the area proposed as the land of Ammonihah.

The word *Ocozocoautla* in the Nahuatl language means "land of vultures and serpents," and it is the entrance way into the Selva del Ocote, which is located north and west from Santa Rosa (city of Zarahemla) and whose name literally means "forests of the vultures." As stated earlier, *Tehuantepec*, of which the forests of Ocote are a part, means "wilderness of wild beasts," the same as given in Alma 2:37–38: "They [Amlicites and Lamanites] were slain and driven, until they were scattered on the west, and on the north, until they had reached the wilderness, which was called Hermounts; and it was that part of the wilderness which was infested by wild and ravenous beasts. And it came to pass that many died in the wilderness of wounds and were devoured by those beasts, and also the vultures of the air; and their bones have been found, and have been heaped upon the earth."

As mentioned in chapter 24, "Wilderness Areas," this is a prophecy wherein Mormon compares the scattering and destruction of a remnant of Israel (Amlicites and Lamanites) to a prophecy about the scattering and gathering of Israel throughout the world.

From the information in the Book of Mormon, Noah clearly is close to Ammonihah. The Lamanite army had at one point destroyed the city of Ammonihah—only to discover during a later attack that Moroni had subsequently fortified the city. The Lamanites then proceeded toward Noah: "Therefore they retreated into the wilderness, and took their camp and marched towards the *land of Noah*, supposing that to be the next best place to come against the Nephites" (Alma 49:12; emphasis added).

CITY OF AARON

After being rejected from Ammonihah, Alma took his journey toward the city that was called Aaron (see Alma 8:13). Aaron is also mentioned in relation to the eastern cities of Moroni and Nephihah (see Alma 50:14; see also chapter 24, "Wilderness Areas").

We do not have enough information from the Alma missionary statement to locate Aaron, and the logic does not hold up to place Aaron along the Grijalva River when the Alma 50:14 statement is taken into consideration.

As a result, either two cities were called Aaron or the statement that Alma was headed toward Aaron indicates that he was headed for the Peten (east wilderness) to

> The word *Ocozocoautla* in the Nahuatl language means "land of vultures and serpents."

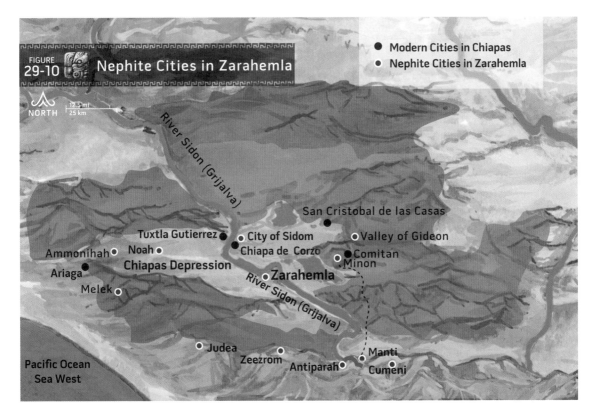

FIGURE 29–10: A number of identifiable archaeological sites are located in the state of Chiapas, Mexico, in correlation with cities in the Book of Mormon that date to the same time period. Some comparative studies are compelling, whereas others are still speculative. The city of Minon was located between the land of Manti and the valley of Gideon. The city of Ammonihah was three days' travel from Melek. The city of Noah was between Ammonihah and Sidom. And Sidom has a name correlation that helps identify it as a Nephite city in the land of Zarahemla.

further his missionary activities, a place where he subsequently went when he and two of his sons, three of the sons of Mosiah, and Amulek and Zeezrom went to teach the gospel to the Zoramites (see Alma 31:6).

THE CITY/LAND OF MANTI

The city/land of Manti was discussed earlier. The location of the land of Manti is mentioned in relation to the headwaters of the river Sidon: "through the borders of Manti, by the head of the river Sidon" (Alma 22:27). "[The Lamanites] took their journey round about in the wilderness, away by the head of the river Sidon, that they might come into the land of Manti and take possession of the land" (Alma 43:22; see also Alma 50:11 and 56:25 for information about the head of the river Sidon).

The archaeological site of La Libertad, located at the base of the narrow strip of wilderness, is a candidate for the city of Manti. On our tours, as we cross the border at

La Mesilla, Guatemala, the land opens up into a valley. A few miles down the road, the traveler can observe the narrow-looking mountain range behind.

THE CITY/LAND OF MINON

The city of Comitan, Mexico, fits nicely in the geographical configuration to be the city of Minon.

The land of Minon was located above the city of Zarahemla and appears to be between the land of Manti and the valley of Gideon. Minon is mentioned in a battle in which Alma, who was the first chief judge, was involved about 87 BC: "Behold, we followed the camp of the Amlicites, and to our great astonishment, in the land of *Minon*, above the land of Zarahemla, in the course of the land of Nephi, we saw a numerous host of the Lamanites; and behold the Amlicites have joined them. And it came to pass that the people of Nephi took their tents, and departed out of the valley of Gideon towards their city, which was the city of Zarahemla" (Alma 2:24, 26; emphasis added).

The city of Comitan, Mexico, fits nicely in the geographical configuration to be the city of Minon. Comitan is within a thirty-five-mile radius in different directions from all three proposed cities of Manti, Gideon, and Zarahemla.

SUMMARY

In this chapter, we have provided information and dialogue that establish the Chiapas depression area of the state of Chiapas, Mexico, as the land of Zarahemla where the people of Zarahemla (Mulekites) settled and where Mosiah with a group of Nephites entered into the Chiapas valley in the second century BC. Mosiah and his people traveled a distance of about three hundred miles from the land/city of Nephi (Kaminaljuyu).

FIGURE 29–11: Many exotic birds live in the Chiapas and Guatemala mountains. (Photo courtesy of Cortney Boice)

They crossed over the only mountain range in all of the Americas that extends from a sea on the east to a sea on the west.

We have analyzed and proposed several cities and geographical places that were located in the land of Zarahemla as determined from the Book of Mormon. We have looked at pottery movements, elevation criteria, directional requirements, archaeological dates of the sites, and name correlations and have presented several name correlations in relationship to their meaning, location, and dating. These include the river Sidon ("fish waters" or "fishery"), Forest of Vultures, wilderness of wild beasts, and city of Sidom (Zactun, or white stone city).

In addition, we have presented information that disqualifies the Usumacinta River and the archaeological sites along that river as legitimate candidates for the geography and time period of the Nephite occupation in the land southward.

Finally, we have introduced some spiritual types and shadows to illustrate the depth and grandeur of the Book of Mormon and the supreme ability of Mormon to weave a spiritual message into the historical account.

FIGURE 29–12: As visitors stand on top of the Olmec archaeological site of La Venta, they can see the state of Chiapas, which is the land southward and which the Jaredites preserved as a place to hunt wild animals. Forty percent of the wild animals in the entire country of Mexico live in Chiapas. (Photo courtesy of Sheryl Lee Wilson)

CHAPTER 30

The Maya Classic Period and the Nephite Apostasy

And the angel said unto me: Behold these shall dwindle in unbelief. (1 Nephi 12:22)

P rior to arriving in the promised land, the prophet Nephi saw in vision that his descendants would be overpowered by the seed of his brethren, and then the descendants of his brethren would dwindle in unbelief. He saw that "after they had dwindled in unbelief they became a dark, and loathsome, and a filthy people, full of idleness and all manner of abominations" (1 Nephi 12:23).

Almost a thousand years later, Mormon, who was a descendant of this same Nephi, reaffirmed that prophecy and then recorded the beginning of its fulfillment when he wrote that "this people shall be scattered, and shall become a dark, a filthy, and a loathsome people, beyond the description of that which ever hath been amongst us, yea, even that which hath been among the Lamanites, and this because of their unbelief

OPPOSITE: The beginning of the Maya Classic Period correlates to the same time period as the Nephite apostasy. The Maya Early Classic Period, beginning at AD 250, is designated by its massive building programs, and the Book of Mormon confirms that same activity: "They did still continue to build up churches unto themselves, and adorn them with all manner of precious things. And thus did two hundred and fifty years pass away" (4 Nephi 1:41). This picture shows the pagan Chac Mul god and its hook nose protruding from the main pyramid at Uxmal. (Photo courtesy of Sheryl Lee Wilson)

and idolatry. For behold, the Spirit of the Lord hath already ceased to strive with their fathers; and they are without Christ and God in the world" (Mormon 5:15–16).

Nephi wrote his prophecy shortly after 600 BC; Mormon wrote his about AD 380. In AD 401, after the Lamanites had hunted down the Nephites, Moroni, the son of Mormon, also wrote about the apostasy and the beginning of the Maya Classic Period: "And there are none that do know the true God save it be the disciples of Jesus, who did tarry in the land until the wickedness of the people was so great that the Lord would not suffer them to remain with the people" (Mormon 8:10). But the apostasy really began two hundred years earlier when many priests and false prophets arose, built up many churches, and did all manner of iniquity (see 4 Nephi 1:34).

> The great apostasy began in the New World at the same time as it began in the Old World. And the activities were the same.

Not surprisingly, the great apostasy in the Book of Mormon correlates in detail to the time period when the apostasy began in Mesoamerica. The activities of the wicked priests referred to in 4 Nephi and the activities of the Maya priests of the same time period are identical.

MAYA CLASSIC PERIOD OR NEPHITE APOSTASY

Many people who have traveled with us to Mexico and Guatemala throughout the years are frustrated to stand in front of the awe-inspiring Temple of Kukulcan at Chichen Itza, now labeled as one of the seven wonders of the world, or the picturesque ruins of Tulum overlooking the enchanting, turquoise waters of the Caribbean and suddenly realize that these ruins are post–Book of Mormon ruins. The Temple of Kukulcan dates to AD 1000, and the majority of the buildings of Tulum date even later in the Postclassic Period. Sometimes we might have difficulty understanding why the beginning of the

FIGURE 30–1: The Postclassic Maya ruins of Tulum postdate the Book of Mormon by several hundred years. Tulum has been popularized by the emergence of Cancun as a major resort. As a result, the daily arrival of large cruise ships at Cozumel has allowed millions of people to visit these ruins. Some Latter-day Saints return from their visit to Tulum erroneously thinking that a connection exists between the pagan rites that prevailed at Tulum with the ancient religious practices of the Nephites. (Photo courtesy of Sheryl Lee Wilson)

Exploring the Lands of the Book of Mormon

apostasy in the Book of Mormon is also the beginning of the Classic Period among the Maya.

However, upon thinking through the details, we need not feel that the situation is strange at all. A society that divorces itself from God almost always ends up worshiping the works of its own hands. The Tower of Babel is one example.

Neither should the concept seem strange when we visit the great cathedrals throughout the world, including Mexico, whose walls glitter with the gold and the unseen blood of its builders who were under bondage to wicked priests.

And why should it seem strange that Satan would work both sides of the ocean in building buildings to get gain: "And they began to be divided into classes; and they began to build up churches unto themselves to get gain, and began to deny the true church of Christ" (4 Nephi 1:26).

The great apostasy began in the New World at the same time as it began in the Old World. And the activities were the same. By the time we finish reading the small book of 4 Nephi, we are aware that the apostasy was well on its way by the year AD 320. The apostasy was well rooted in the Old World by AD 325, as indicated by the activities at Nice where God was reduced to a "spirit without body, parts, and passions."

And finally, we must seriously consider the prophetic message of the Nephite apostasy and the Maya Classic Period. It literally may serve as a prototype of the winding-up scenes in these latter days as the war waged by Satan against Christ escalates to complete fulfillment.

The following comparisons will illustrate the early history of the great apostasy in Mesoamerica and in the Book of Mormon.

THE EARLY CLASSIC/APOSTASY PERIOD (AD 200–AD 350)

The year AD 201 marked the beginning of the great apostasy in Mesoamerica. By AD 350, the light of the gospel had become so dim that a spiritual darkness covered the land for the next fifteen hundred years.

1. Priests Wore Elaborate Clothing Beginning at AD 201

And now, in this two hundred and first year there began to be among them those who were lifted up in pride, such as the wearing of costly apparel, and all manner of fine pearls, and of the fine things of the world. (4 Nephi 1:24)

No place tells the story of the apostasy in Mesoamerica better than at the Maya ruins of Uxmal in Yucatan, Mexico. However, Uxmal is not the only place. We need only to look at the stone monuments and the written codices to realize that the priests controlled everything. The archaeological record illustrates how the priests who wore the elaborate and costly apparel looked. Such apparel became a mark of class distinction.

We need only to look at the stone monuments and the written codices to realize that the priests controlled everything.

FIGURE 30–2: The Maya Classic Period and the Nephite apostasy were identifiable by the wickedness and dictatorial nature of the Maya priests. Shown here is the depiction of a Maya priest dating to that time. (Photo courtesy of Cortney Boice)

FIGURE 30–3: An elite hierarchy, which had its beginning at the same time king-men arose in the Book of Mormon, surfaced again at the beginning of the Maya Classic Period (AD 250). They wore elaborate clothing, and they controlled the religious, social, and economic lives of the people. Shown here is a display in the Maya Room depicting the Maya caste system. (Photo from the National Museum of Anthropology, Mexico City, courtesy of Blake Joseph Allen)

In 4 Nephi, we are told that there were those who were "lifted up in pride, such as the wearing of costly apparel."

Although the principles associated with pride and costly apparel are a valid caution, in a historical context, it was the Maya priests who adorned themselves with items that were forbidden to the common person, such as elaborate quetzal feathered headdresses and jade ornaments as represented on the walls of buildings, gold bracelets and necklaces such as those discovered at Tomb 7 at Monte Alban, and, as Mormon states, all manner of fine pearls, reminiscent of pearls discovered in the tomb of the seventh-century priest, Pacal, of Palenque.

2. An Elite Hierarchy Whose Roots Date to the First Century BC Ruled

Beginning about AD 200, an elite hierarchy who had its beginning in the first century BC began to exercise control over the people. The archaeological record at Uxmal states: "During this period [Early Classic—AD 200–AD 350], the dominant group was a *hereditary elite which emerged in the last century before Christ*. Its authority extended throughout all aspects of social life, but in particular they were representatives or mediators between the community and the divine or supernatural forces, utilizing magical/religious means. This group controlled the knowledge of the times, much of which, in order to maintain a relationship with the direct production of the people, determined social behavior."[1]

This "hereditary elite" is undoubtedly the same people who are called "king-men," or "those of high birth," in the Book of Mormon. These king-men rose up in the "last century before Christ" (67 BC): "Now those who were in favor of kings were *those of high birth*, and they sought to be kings; and they were supported by those who sought power and authority over the people" (Alma 51:8; emphasis added).

1. Alfredo Barrera Rubio, *Official Guide: Uxmal*, trans. Helen Jones-Perrott de Mandri (Mexico, DF: Instituto Nacional de Antropologia e Historia, 1985), 32; emphasis added.

3. They Began to Build up Many Churches and to Adorn Them

The Book of Mormon is very specific on the subject of building churches to get gain. In the last half of 4 Nephi, the church-building activity is mentioned four times.

> And they began to *build up churches* unto themselves to get gain, and began to deny the true church of Christ. (4 Nephi 1:26; emphasis added)
>
> And it came to pass that when two hundred and ten years had passed away there were *many churches* in the land; yea, there were *many churches* which professed to know the Christ, and yet they did deny the more parts of his gospel. (4 Nephi 1:27; emphasis added)
>
> Nevertheless, the people did harden their hearts, for they were led by many priests and false prophets to *build up many churches*, and to do all manner of iniquity. (4 Nephi 1:34; emphasis added)
>
> And they did still continue to *build up churches* unto themselves, and *adorn them with all manner of precious things*. And thus did two hundred and fifty years pass away, and also two hundred and sixty years. (4 Nephi 1:41; AD 245; emphasis added)

Again, the archaeological record at Uxmal explains the same type of activity as outlined in 4 Nephi. This massive building program began in Mesoamerica at AD 200 and continued for more than five centuries.

Architecture was developed during this period and in particular a local architectonic style. The structures generally reflect a predominant use of massive

This massive building program began in Mesoamerica at AD 200 and continued for more than five centuries.

FIGURE 30–4: The Maya Classic ruins of Chicanna illustrate the manner in which the buildings were adorned as described by Mormon: "They began to build up churches unto themselves to get gain, and began to deny the true Church of Christ" (4 Nephi 1:26). And they adorned them "with all manner of precious things" (4 Nephi 1:41). (Photo courtesy of Sheryl Lee Wilson)

stone to create an *impressive exterior aspect* with little concern for the practical use of interior spaces. This tendency served to reinforce the visual and symbolic elements of a structural ideology which reflected the dominant social structures prevalent in everyday life.

It is evident that a great part of the collective force was concentrated in *building constructions* which were not directly concerned with productivity.[2]

2. Rubio, *Official Guide: Uxmal*, 32–33; emphasis added.

The manner in which the Classic Maya adorned their churches is represented in the Classic Maya ruins of the Quadrangle of the Nunnery and in many other places, such as Chicanna, Campeche, as shown in figure 30–4.

4. The Priests Controlled All Major Activities

In Mesoamerica, the priests controlled the religious, social, and commercial activities of the people. The book of 4 Nephi describes the situation as follows:

[The people] did receive all manner of wickedness, and did administer that which was sacred unto him to whom it had been forbidden because of unworthiness. (4 Nephi 1:27)

And again, there was another church which denied the Christ; and they did persecute the true church of Christ. (4 Nephi 1:29)

[The people] did exercise power and authority over the disciples of Jesus who did tarry with them, and they did cast them into prison. (4 Nephi 1:30)

Exploring the Lands of the Book of Mormon

[They] did harden their hearts, for they were led by *many priests and false prophets*. (4 Nephi 1:34; emphasis added)

[And] the wicked part of the people began again to build up the secret oaths and combinations of Gadianton. (4 Nephi 1:42; AD 261)

[And] there were none that were righteous save it were the disciples of Jesus. And gold and silver did they lay up in store in abundance, *and did traffic in all manner of traffic*. (4 Nephi 1:46; AD 301; emphasis added)

We may say that nothing is wrong with practicing free enterprise and having a year's food supply, or more, stored in our basements. But it's not the same thing. The Mesoamerica archaeological record drives home the problem. The thing that was wrong with laying up "in store in abundance" and "trafficking" in all manner of traffic is that priests controlled everything. We can only imagine the "religious" and "social" means the priests employed to control the profits. The Uxmal account states: "This period runs from AD 200–AD 1000 and has been called the period of the Theocratic States Monopoly by the virtue of the fact that the *high priests controlled and monopolized the main activities of the social and economic life* of the population, encompassing even the simple ritualism, symbolism and beliefs.[3]

3. Rubio, *Official Guide: Uxmal*, 32; emphasis added.

Summary of the Early Classic/Apostate Period

By the year AD 321, which is the last date recorded in 4 Nephi, both the Nephite Maya and the Lamanite Maya were proud and vain. The Lord instructed Ammaron to hide up the records that were sacred. A few years thereafter, Mormon began to write the history of the Nephite people.

In the year AD 350, the Lamanites and Gadianton robbers made a treaty with the wicked Nephites wherein the Nephites lost all their territory south of the narrow neck of land (see Mormon 2:28–29). The apostasy was well defined in the Book of Mormon; the Classic Period was well established in Mesoamerica. *They are the same thing.*

MAYA CLASSIC/NEPHITE DISPERSION (AD 250–AD 900)

The beginning of the Maya Classic Period and the Nephite apostasy period paved the way for the beginning of a fluorescent period in Mesoamerica. The AD 350 treaty, referred to in Mormon 2:28–29, made it possible for trade activity throughout Mesoamerica. We should observe that the treaty was not just a treaty between the Lamanites and the Nephites. Rather, it was a treaty that the Nephites made, or were compelled to make, by the combined forces of the Lamanites and the robbers of Gadianton.

We proposed in chapter 8, "The Teotihuacan Culture," that around AD 350, the society in the valley of Mexico was controlled by a combination of "robbers," or "wealthy businessmen," and the clergy. These groups had the military strength to back them up.

The apostasy was well defined in the Book of Mormon; the Classic Period was well established in Mesoamerica. *They are the same thing.*

The situation may not be much different today where the drug smugglers form a secret combination for profit with heads of governments.

From AD 350 to AD 900, a great deal of trade activity occurred throughout Mesoamerica. You will recall the 4 Nephi 1:46 statement, which dates to about AD 301, to the effect that they "did traffic in all manner of traffic."

By AD 400, strong trade agreements had been reached between the administrators living in the Mexico valley (Teotihuacan) and the administrators who lived in Guatemala.

On the outskirts of the city of Huehuetenango, in Guatemala, are the Postclassic Maya ruins of Zaculeu. These ruins apparently served as the last outpost for centuries previous to AD 900. Even today, the Guatemala military outpost is nearby. Of interest here is a map that is located in the small museum at the site of Zaculeu. This map illustrates the trading activity that occurred throughout Mesoamerica and that passed through this military outpost.

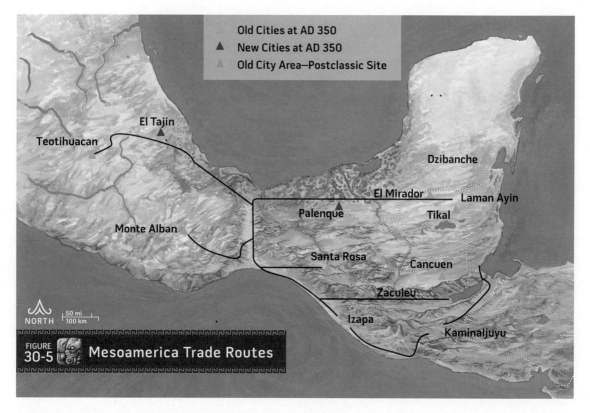

FIGURE 30–5: Toward AD 400, an increase in trade activity began to occur throughout Mesoamerica. This activity corresponds to the treaty recorded in Mormon 2:28–29. The Teotihuacan style of architecture is recognizable in places like Tikal and Kaminaljuyu. All trade activity passed through the top of the Isthmus of Tehuantepec, the area controlled by the Nephites until their destruction at AD 385.

For the reader to understand the ever-changing field of historical geography, we will repeat here what was written in 1989 in the first edition of *Exploring the Lands of the Book of Mormon* with a follow-up of what we have written in the second edition of *Exploring the Lands*, published in 2008.

[1989]: From AD 322 to AD 400, the Nephites were in constant battle with the Lamanites. For some reason, the "robbers," or the administrators at Teotihuacan, did not seem to be directly involved in the last wars of the Nephites and the Lamanites. The Book of Mormon record does say, however, that the Gadianton robbers who were among the Lamanites "did infest the land" (see Mormon 1:18).[4]

[2008]: The AD 350 treaty and the AD 385 destruction of the Nephites paved the way for the extended Mesoamerican trade activity that began at Teotihuacan in the early part of the fourth century AD. In fact, the activities described on Stela 31 of Tikal identify Teotihuacan as a dominating factor in the final destruction of the Nephite nation.[5]

Observe the wars that were fought between the Nephites and the Lamanites beginning at about AD 322. The wars were fought on both sides of the Isthmus of Tehuantepec (narrow neck).

4. Joseph L. Allen, *Exploring the Lands of the Book of Mormon* (Orem, UT: S. A. Publishers, 1989), 394.

5. Joseph Lovell Allen and Blake Joseph Allen, *Exploring the Lands of the Book of Mormon* (Orem, UT: Book of Mormon Tours and Research Institute, 2008), 212.

About AD 322

And it came to pass in this year there began to be a war between the Nephites . . . and the Lamanites. (Mormon 1:8)

The Lamanites withdrew their design, and there was peace settled in the land; and peace did remain for the space of about four years. (Mormon 1:12)

About AD 326

In that same year there began to be a war again between the Nephites and the Lamanites. (Mormon 2:1)

AD 327

The Lamanites did come upon us with exceedingly great power. (Mormon 2:3)

And it was one complete revolution throughout all the face of the land. (Mormon 2:8)

Each Book of Mormon group had in excess of forty thousand soldiers fighting each other in the AD 327 battle. Magic art and witchcraft, signs of the great apostasy, were

Magic art and witchcraft, signs of the great apostasy, were rampant in the land.

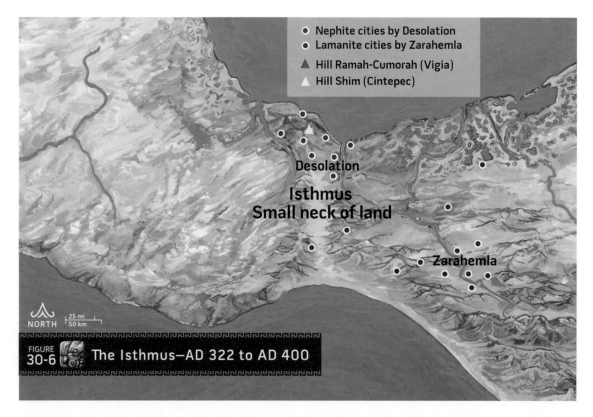

Legend:
- Nephite cities by Desolation
- Lamanite cities by Zarahemla
- ▲ Hill Ramah-Cumorah (Vigia)
- △ Hill Shim (Cintepec)

Desolation

Isthmus
Small neck of land

Zarahemla

NORTH 25 mi / 50 km

FIGURE 30-6 The Isthmus—AD 322 to AD 400

FIGURE 30–6: A careful reading of the events leading up to the demise of the Nephite nation shows that the Nephites never left the area around the narrow neck of land. They were fighting for their "wives, and their children, and their houses, and their homes" (Mormon 2:23). "It was one complete revolution throughout all the face of the land" (Mormon 2:8).

rampant in the land (see Mormon 2:10). History does not change much. Revolutions in the Central American countries have been common throughout modern history.

> Up to this time, all the battles had taken place around the narrow neck of land.

AD 345

The Nephites did begin to flee before the Lamanites. (Mormon 2:16)

The Lamanites drove the Nephites to the city of Jashon, which was near the hill Shim, where Ammaron hid the records. Prior to this, the battles had been fought in the city of Angola and in the lands of David and Joshua (see Mormon 2:4–6).

AD 346

We did contend with an army of thirty thousand against an army of fifty thousand. (Mormon 2:25)

Exploring the Lands of the Book of Mormon

Mormon had urged the Nephites to fight with all their energies—to fight for "their wives, and their children, and their houses, and their homes" (see Mormon 2:23).

AD 350

We did get the lands of our inheritance divided. (Mormon 2:28)

Up to this time, all the battles had taken place around the narrow neck of land.

AD 360

The king of the Lamanites sent an epistle unto me, which gave unto me to know that they were preparing to come again to battle against us. (Mormon 3:4)

The Nephites had gathered together at the city of Desolation, which was by the narrow pass that led into the land southward. They drove the Lamanites back in the AD 360 battle. The city of Desolation was on the northward side of the Isthmus of Tehuantepec and, from what we can now ascertain, was probably the ancient Olmec city of San Lorenzo Tenochtitlan.

AD 362

They did come down again to battle. And we did beat them again. (Mormon 3:8)

Notice that the Lamanites came *down* to battle. In the perspective of the terrain in and around the Isthmus of Tehuantepec, the Lamanites marched down from the state of Chiapas to battle the Nephites by the coast, by the states of Tabasco and Veracruz.

AD 363

The Nephites did go *up* with their armies to battle against the Lamanites, out of the land Desolation. (Mormon 4:1; emphasis added)

In this battle, the Nephites lost possession of the city of Desolation and then fled to the neighboring city of Teancum, which was by the seashore. The city of Desolation was by the narrow passage (see Mormon 4:3).

AD 364

The Lamanites did come against the city Teancum. (Mormon 4:7)

The Nephites defeated the Lamanites in this battle and then went to battle again and retook the city of Desolation. Worth mentioning here is the point that when we take into consideration the great trade and building activity that was just beginning

> The city of Desolation was on the northward side of the Isthmus of Tehuantepec and, from what we can now ascertain, was probably the ancient Olmec city of San Lorenzo Tenochtitlan.

to develop in Mesoamerica, these wars were both politically and economically motivated. The Nephites were literally in the way of the only major trade route between Mexico and Guatemala, as they lived on both sides of the Isthmus of Tehuantepec. Before an adequate trade relationship could be established with Mexico, the Lamanites in Guatemala (land southward) needed to get rid of the tenacious Nephites.

AD 366

> The Lamanites came again upon the Nephites to battle. (Mormon 4:10)

The Lamanites were really angry now. In fact, they were "crazy angry." They defeated the Nephites and recaptured the city of Desolation and captured the city of Teancum. They took Nephite women and children as prisoners and offered them up as sacrifices to their idol gods (see Mormon 4:13–14).

This occasion is the first time that human sacrifice is mentioned in the Book of Mormon. The Lamanites had already become a dark and filthy and loathsome people. The practice of human sacrifice continued for the next twelve hundred years—right through the Dark Ages and up to the time of the conquest of Mexico.

AD 367

> The Nephites [were] angry because the Lamanites had sacrificed their women and their children . . . [and] they did beat again the Lamanites and drive them out of their lands. (Mormon 4:15)

AD 375

> And in this year they did come down against the Nephites with all their powers; and they were not numbered because of the greatness of their numbers. (Mormon 4:17)

Another great battle was fought at the city of Desolation, and Mormon states that from this time forth, the Nephites did not gain power over the Lamanites. The Lamanites defeated the Nephites at both the cities of Desolation and Boaz. Mormon transferred the records from the hill Shim to the Nephite hill Cumorah. The Lamanites again sacrificed to their idol gods the women and children of the Nephites (see Mormon 4:18–23).

You will recall the traditions of the ancient Mexicans wherein they would hunt down and sacrifice people of fair skins (see chapter 12, "Bernardino de Sahagun").

Between AD 375 and AD 380, other battles were fought. The Nephites were able to maintain some of their cities.

Human sacrifice is first mentioned in the Book of Mormon in AD 366. The practice of human sacrifice continued for the next twelve hundred years.

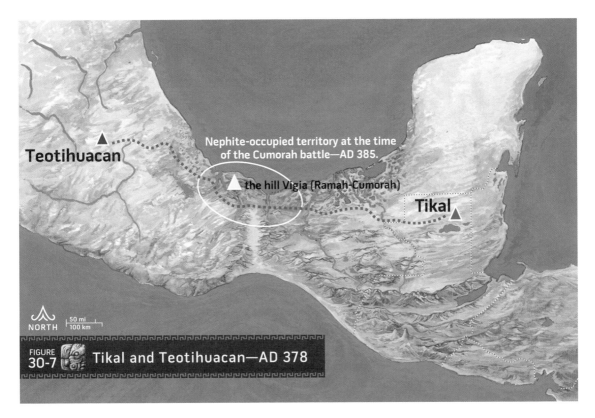

FIGURE 30–7: Amidst the AD 375 to AD 380 Nephite-Lamanite battles, an army from Teotihuacan passed through Nephite territory and entered into Tikal where they killed the standing Lamanite King (Jaguar Paw). Yax Nuun Ayiin, the son of the Teotihuacan dictator Spearthrower Owl, was placed on the throne at Tikal. The circle represents Nephite-occupied territory from AD 310 to AD 385. The Nephites were surrounded on both sides. Their destiny was fixed.

AD 380

The Lamanites did come again against us to battle, and we did stand against them boldly; but it was all in vain, for so great were their numbers. (Mormon 5:6)

Mormon quotes the prophecy that the time would come when the Lamanites would be scattered and would become a dark and filthy and loathsome people (see Mormon 5:15).

The Lord promised Lehi that "this land should be kept as yet from the knowledge of other nations" and that as long as the people would keep the commandments, they would be "kept from all other nations" (2 Nephi 1:8–9).

The Lord, as always, kept His promise. The Americas were preserved until spiritual darkness totally covered the continent. The Americas were preserved until the Spaniards waltzed into Mexico in the sixteenth century.

> The Lord, as always, kept His promise. The Americas were preserved until spiritual darkness totally covered the continent.

On January 16, AD 378, Teotihuacan (the Gadianton society) violated the AD 350 treaty with the Nephites and the Lamanites, and the dictator from Teotihuacan sent his young son with a powerful military escort to Tikal. The Tikal leader was killed, and the Gadianton society then controlled both sides of the Isthmus of Tehuantepec. These events occurred less than two years before the AD 380 date and seven years prior to the Cumorah battle (see chapter 8, "The Teotihuacan Culture"; see also chapter 27, "Hills and Valleys"). The Nephites may have even welcomed the arrival of the foreigners from Mexico, allowing them to pass through their land. The Mexicans (Teotihuacanos) were led by the ferocious Siyaj K'ak' (Fire Is Born), and perhaps the Nephites had hopes that they would destroy their mortal enemies, the Lamanites. However, once Spearthrower Owl gained control over Tikal, there was no longer any reason to be an ally with the Nephites. They were literally in the way.

> Mormon told Moroni that he had some sacred records to give to him. These records consisted of the Jaredite records that had been sealed up.

AD 385

[And] they came to battle against us, and every soul was filled with terror because of the greatness of their numbers. (Mormon 6:8)

Mormon considered this battle to be the last struggle of his people. He called it the "great and tremendous battle at Cumorah" (Mormon 8:2). The Nephites lost 230,000 soldiers in this battle, which, in essence, was the defining battle of the downfall of the Nephite nation.

Between AD 385 and AD 400

My beloved son, I write unto you again, that ye may know that I am yet alive; but I write somewhat of that which is grievous.

For behold, I have had a sore battle with the Lamanites, in which we did not conquer. (Moroni 9:1–2)

Mormon wrote to his son Moroni and mentioned an account of another battle with the Lamanites. This battle was after the battle at Cumorah and prior to AD 400 (see Mormon 8:5–6).

In this same letter to his son, Moroni, Mormon recounted the atrocities of both the Lamanites and the Nephites. He specifically mentioned the manner in which the Nephites at Moriantum robbed the virtue of the Lamanite women, tortured and killed them, and then, as a token of bravery, devoured their flesh like wild beasts (see Moroni 9:9–10).

The name of the place of Moriantum and the continuing wars of the Lamanites with the Nephites after the great battle at Cumorah suggest that both Mormon and Moroni were still living around the narrow neck of land. This assumption is further verified by

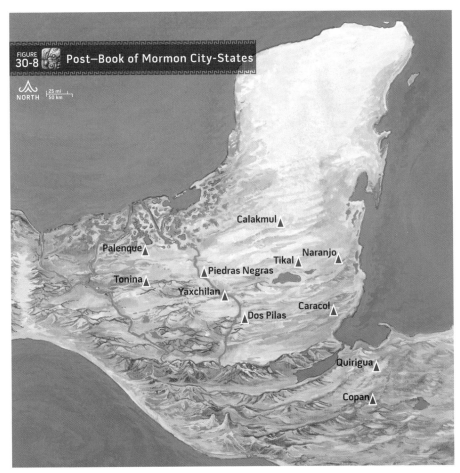

FIGURE 30–8: A new surge of city-states such as Palenque, Copan, and Calakmul arose following the demise of the Nephites. A 2000 book titled *Chronicle of the Maya Kings and Queens: Deciphering the Dynasties of the Ancient Maya*, by Simon Martin and Nikolai Grube, outlines the dynasties of eleven of these city-states dating from ca. AD 250 to ca. AD 900, as shown on this map.

the statements that many Nephites had escaped into the south countries and that many had deserted over to the Lamanites (see Moroni 9:24).

Mormon also told Moroni that he, Mormon, had some sacred records to give to him. These may have been the records of the Jaredites (see Moroni 9:24).

The Book of Mormon record closes with Moroni stating that "I wander whithersoever I can for the safety of mine own life" (see Moroni 1:3).

From this point on, we are working with the traditional history of Mexico and the archaeological records of Mesoamerica. They both bear witness of a society that was steeped in mysticism and idolatry during the Classic Maya Period, AD 250–AD 900.

The priests were in total control during this period of time, and a zealous building program continued for most of the Classic Period. An example of the vanity of the priests during this period is the AD 600 Temple of Pacal at Palenque, Chiapas. The pomp and ceremony associated with the burial of Pacal are representative of the apostasy that prevailed throughout Mesoamerica (see chapter 6, "The Maya [Lamanite-Nephite] Culture").

Once Teotihuacan gained control of the land southward, a hierarchy of kings and queens began to rule throughout the Maya kingdom. Once the Nephites were destroyed, the Maya priests had control of the Isthmus of Tehuantepec. As discussed earlier, both the Mulekite and Jaredite ancestries may have been a significant part of the Maya priest hierarchy during the Classic Period (AD 250–AD 900).

The writings of Ixtlilxochitl provide us with a history of the people called Toltecs (Tultecas), who were dispersed from their homeland beginning at AD 387. Their home-land was the area around the Isthmus of Tehuantepec, the same area proposed as the homeland of the Nephites, who date to the same time period. A correlation was proposed earlier in *Exploring the Lands of the Book of Mormon* between the early Tultecas and the Nephites.[6] Some of the dates recorded by Ixtlilxochitl during the Maya Classic Period are interesting, as they deal with the dispersion of the Tultecas.

6. Alfredo Chavero, *Obras Historicas de Don Fernando de Alva Ixtlilxochitl*, Tomo 1 (Mexico, DF: Editora National, 1965), 27–28, and chapter 11, "Fernando de Alva Ixtlilxochitl," in this text.

AD 344

The dispersion of the Nephites from the lands of their inheritance may be compared to the Jewish diaspora from Jerusalem. The initial dispersion, according to Ixtlilxochitl, began in AD 344, which is the beginning of the wars between the Lamanites and Nephites described above. The Tulteca dispersion carried them along the coast of Baja, California. They escaped both into the north and into the south.[7]

7. Chavero, *Obras Historicas de Don Fernando de Alva Ixtlilxochitl*, 56.

AD 556

Some of the dispersed Tultecas may have established their headquarters in a place called Tula. This Tula was probably named after the ancient Tula. The Tula that Ixtlilxochitl is referring to here should not be confused with Tula, Hidalgo, which subsequently became the capital of the warring Toltecs from AD 900 to AD 1200.[8]

8. Chavero, *Obras Historicas de Don Fernando de Alva Ixtlilxochitl*, 29.

AD 778

Ixtlilxochitl recorded a date of AD 778 wherein he gave the date of the death of a king by the name of Huetzin. He discussed the manner of government that was set down by the people's forefathers. He says that "these kings were tall of body and white and had beards like the Spaniards." For that reason, when Cortez and his men came, they were considered to be of this lineage.[9]

9. Chavero, *Obras Historicas de Don Fernando de Alva Ixtlilxochitl*, 33.

AD 830

Izaccaltzin, the father of Topiltzin, began to rule at Tula, Hidalgo. Tula, Hidalgo, is just north of Mexico City. Topiltzin was named Topiltzin Quetzalcoatl and has been confused with the deity or symbolism of Quetzalcoatl that dates back to the time of Christ (see chapter 14, "The White God Quetzalcoatl").

AD 935

The year AD 935 is considered to be the year that Topiltzin Quetzalcoatl was born at Tula, Hidalgo. In the information leading up to the birth of Topiltzin, Ixtlilxochitl discusses such things as human sacrifice, priestcraft, and marriage. The Toltecs continued to wear long white tunics. In one war, although difficult to believe, 3,200,000 people reportedly were killed on one side and 2,400,000 were killed on the other side.[10]

Throughout Mesoamerica, as the story is told in the archaeological data, many of the great city centers began to be abandoned. The priestcraft society had worn out its welcome. The flickering candle had gone out. The dark years, as prophesied by the Book of Mormon prophets, had spread throughout all of Mesoamerica.

THE POSTCLASSIC PERIOD (AD 900–AD 1519)

The Postclassic Period in Mesoamerica is labeled as a result of the decline of many of the great city centers. Both Teotihuacan and Monte Alban had fallen by AD 750. Tikal and Uxmal endured in fine fashion until about AD 900. But all in all, the power and glory of Mesoamerica had died.

In addition to the Maya cultures that still maintained control east and south of the Isthmus of Tehuantepec, two major civilizations came to power in the Mexico valley. The first was the Toltecs, who reigned from approximately AD 900 to AD 1200. The second was the great Aztec nation that ruled throughout Mesoamerica from AD 1325 to AD 1521.

1. The Toltec Era (AD 900–AD 1200)

The Toltec era is best known for the tenth-century leader Topiltzin Quetzalcoatl. A detailed analysis was given about Topiltzin in chapter 14, "The White God Quetzalcoatl."

Many historians have assigned the qualities of the deity Quetzalcoatl to Topiltzin. Topiltzin, as mentioned above, was born at Tula, Hidalgo, about AD 935.

The Toltec ruins of Tula are located about forty-five minutes' driving time north of Mexico City. When the archaeologists first discovered these ruins, they felt they had discovered the ancient Tula in legend. The exploration work uncovered a Postclassic civilization.

Legend allows us to follow Topiltzin from Tula, after his defeat, to Cholula in the state of Puebla. He finally ended up in the Yucatan. The north section of the ruins of Chichen Itza are structures that date to the tenth century AD and are Toltec buildings. These include the Temple of the Warriors, the Ball Court, the Temple of the Eagles, the Temple of the Serpents, and the Temple of Kukulcan. *Kukulcan* is the Maya word for *Quetzalcoatl*, or feathered serpent.

The warring Toltec nation began to decline by AD 1200, and this decline set the stage for the coming of the barbaric Aztec nation.

10. Chavero, *Obras Historicas de Don Fernando de Alva Ixtlilxochitl*, 57.

The dispersion of the Nephites from the lands of their inheritance may be compared to the Jewish diaspora from Jerusalem.

FIGURE 30–9: The apostasy was universal in nature. The Maya priests controlled the religious, social, and commercial activity in Maya territory. The Teotihuacanos ruled supreme in the Mexico region. Religious symbols such as the wind god Quetzalcoatl and the rain god Tlaloc were part of the apostate culture. (Photo from the Teotihuacan Room at the National Museum of Anthropology in Mexico City, courtesy of George and Audrey DeLange)

FIGURE 30–10: At the time of the Spanish conquest, the Aztec priests reportedly could rip out the heart of the victim with one swoop of the obsidian knife. The heart, still beating, would be held up as an offering to the sun god. The act of human sacrifice is mentioned toward the close of the Book of Mormon—dating to the Maya Classic Period. (Photo from the Aztec Room of the National Museum of Anthropology, courtesy of Blake Joseph Allen)

2. The Aztec Era (AD 1325–AD 1519)

Most people are somewhat familiar with the great Aztec nation. The Aztecs are the late-comers on the Mesoamerican scene and, as such, are vastly removed from the Book of Mormon time period. The legends surrounding the establishment of their sacred city called Tenochtitlan (Mexico City) revolve around a prophecy of their ancient prophet, Huitzilopochtli. Two hundred years prior to the time of the Spanish conquest, this prophet told them, "When you see an eagle standing on a cactus with a serpent in its mouth, that is where you are to establish my sacred city."

They saw the eagle all right. Sure enough, it was standing on a cactus, and it had a serpent in its mouth. The only problem was that the cactus was in the middle of a lake. Therefore, Mexico City was literally built on a lake in a valley seventy-two hundred feet above sea level. To this very day, the symbol of the eagle standing on the cactus with a serpent in its mouth serves as the national emblem on Mexico's flag and on the Mexican peso.

A great deal of literature has been written about the Aztec culture. As a result, we will provide just a few historical facts.

When the Spaniards arrived in Mexico in the year 1519, the conquest of Mexico began. The story of the conquest is an amazing one. A handful of soldiers, about four hundred, conquered one of the most ferocious and bloodthirsty nations of all time, the Aztecs. Historians have proposed a number of reasons for the Spaniards being able to accomplish such a feat. Some of these reasons are the following:

1. Cortez was a conqueror. Once the Spaniards arrived on the shores of Veracruz, Cortez ordered the ships to be burned. There was no turning back.
2. The Spaniards had military advantages in the forms of horses and gunpowder.
3. Cortez gained the confidence of other native tribes who were enemies to the Aztecs. The Aztecs were hated by other indigenous nations because these nations were under bondage to the Aztecs. Human sacrifice was the order of the day, and the purpose of war was to capture soldiers to sacrifice to the Sun God, whom the Aztecs believed thrived on human blood.
4. Cortez gained the services of an interpreter by the name of Dona Marina, also called La Malinche, a native of royal birth. She had learned Spanish from a ship-wrecked sailor. She served Cortez well—so well, in fact, that to this day anyone who betrays another, like Marina betrayed her country by being an interpreter, is called a *Malinche*, which is a nickname for *Marina*.
5. Some historians say that Montezuma II, who was the emperor of Mexico at the time of the conquest, believed that Cortez was either Quetzalcoatl or that the Spaniards were the sons of Quetzalcoatl returning.

Constance Irwin writes: "It is one of fate's poorer ironies that Quetzalcoatl, to whom the Mexicans attributed their culture, was even for an hour confused with Cortes who destroyed it—'beheaded a culture as the passer-by sweeps off the head of a sunflower.'"[11]

Bernal Diaz, a soldier in the army of Cortez, recorded his feelings as they entered Mexico for the first time: "Gazing on such wonderful sights, we did not know what to say, or whether what appeared before us was real, for on the one side, on the land, there were great cities, and in the lake ever so many more, and the lake itself was crowded with canoes, and in the Causeway were many bridges at intervals, and in front of us stood the great city of Mexico, and we—we did not even number four hundred soldiers."[12]

The conquest was finalized two years later in the year 1521 when the army of Cortez captured the nephew of the then-dead Montezuma. His name was Cuauhtemoc. Upon his capture, he is reported to have said: "I have surely done my duty in defense of my City, and I can do no more and I come by force and a prisoner into your presence and into your power, take that dagger that you have in your belt and kill me at once with

11. Constance Irwin, *Fair Gods and Stone Faces: Ancient Seafarers and the New World's Most Intriguing Riddle* (New York: St. Martin's Press, 1963), 12.

12. Bernal Diaz, *The Discovery and Conquest of Mexico—1517–1521*, edited from the only exact copy of the original manuscript by Genaro Garcia, translated by A. P. Maudslay, copyright 1956 by Farrar, Straus and Giroux (New York: The Noonday Press, 1972), 192.

FIGURE 30–11: The cycle of poverty has existed for centuries in Mesoamerica as reflected here by two Guatemala women. The wage of $2 a day for a laborer in the fields of Guatemala goes toward the two daily meals of corn and tortillas. (Photo courtesy of Cortney Boice)

it." And when he said this, he wept tears and sobbed, and other great Lords whom he had brought with him also wept.[13]

Cuauhtemoc was only eighteen years old, and he was the emperor of Mexico. Both Montezuma and Cuitlauac, who preceded Cuauhtemoc, had been killed. Today, the heroes in Mexico are not the conquering Spaniards; they are the native warriors like Cuauhtemoc.

Historians estimate that over two million people lived in Mexico City at the time of the conquest. Today, over twenty-six million people live there. Some estimations report that over 85 percent of the people have native blood running through their veins.

13. Diaz, *The Discovery and Conquest of Mexico*, 452.

SPANISH CONQUEST AND COLONIAL PERIOD (AD 1519–AD 1820)

For the next three hundred years, the Mexican people did not fare a whole lot better. After the conquest, three specific groups of people lived in Mexico:

1. The viceroys, or the government administrators. They were people of royal blood who were born on royal Spanish soil. Only those born on "royal soil" could officiate in a top governmental role.
2. The Creoles, or those of mixed Spanish and Mexican blood who had been born in Mexico. As time went on, they became the second and third generations; and because they could not hold a governmental administrative position, they were given large tracts of land. This system became known as the hacienda system, and it endured until the Mexican revolution of 1910.
3. The natives were the third group; they represented the majority, yet they were not allowed to officiate or to own land. They were, in many ways, treated worse than the slaves in the United States.

Perhaps a fourth group should be mentioned—the Catholic fathers. They administered the sacraments to all three of the above groups. It was Father Miguel Hidalgo who, at the town of Delores in the state of Hidalgo, named in his honor, gave the "shout of Delores." This was a rally cry that gathered natives together to rid themselves from the bondage of Spain.

Exploring the Lands of the Book of Mormon

The seeds of Mexican independence had begun. The date of the "shout of Delores" was September 16, 1810. Eleven more years elapsed before independence was gained, but September 16 is the day the Mexicans celebrate as their independence day.

Before we conclude this chapter, we need to mention that the three hundred years under Spanish domination also meant three hundred years under domination of the Catholic Church. And the Catholic Church domination continued for another forty years after the independence.

Historians are not kind to the activities of the Catholic Church during the 340 years from the time of the conquest in 1521 to the disenfranchisement of the Catholic Church in 1857.

The Catholic Church owned one-half of the wealth of the country. The Spanish fathers brought about the conversion of the native people at all costs. Great cathedrals were built in every village. During the course of the 340 years, the system became corrupt.

Nevertheless, the Catholic fathers brought with them a book that "proceedeth out of the mouth of a Jew" (see 1 Nephi 13:23). That book is the Bible. And although "many plain and precious things" had been taken out of it, it set the stage for the restoration of the gospel of Jesus Christ and paved the way for the record that contains the "fulness of the gospel" to be taken to the seed of Lehi. That book is the Book of Mormon.

Historians estimate that over two million people lived in Mexico City at the time of the conquest. Today, over twenty-six million people live there.

FIGURE 30–12: Nephi prophesied that God's covenant people would be scattered and smitten. Catholicism replaced the pagan rites of the native people of Mesoamerica and controlled the social, spiritual, and economic lives of the people for over three hundred years. Cathedrals, such as the one shown here from Mitla, Oaxaca, were built with the stones from the ancient buildings. (Photo courtesy of Sheryl Lee Wilson)

CHAPTER 31

The Restoration in Mesoamerica

as Foretold in the Book of Mormon

In the latter days, when our seed shall have dwindled in unbelief, yea, for the space of many years, . . . then shall the fulness of the gospel of the Messiah come . . . from the Gentiles unto the remnant of our seed. (1 Nephi 15:13)

ephi was "caught away in the Spirit of the Lord . . . into an exceeding high mountain" where he witnessed the future history of his people (see 1 Nephi 11:1; see also 1 Nephi 11–15).

He witnessed, in vision, the birth, ministry, Crucifixion, and Resurrection of Christ.

He witnessed the great destruction in his land at the time of the Crucifixion of Christ in Jerusalem.

He witnessed the appearance of the Savior of the world to His people, the Nephites, the fulfillment of which is recorded in the book of 3 Nephi in the Book of Mormon.

OPPOSITE: One of the steeples of the Guatemala City Temple shows the statue of the angel Moroni. This temple was dedicated December 14–16, 1984, and is located in the area proposed in *Exploring the Lands of the Book of Mormon* as the ancient city of Nephi. (Photo courtesy of Cortney Boice)

He witnessed the destruction of his people, the Nephites, by the seed of his brethren, the Lamanites, in the fourth generation after Christ. The fulfillment of this prophecy is recorded in the third from the last book in the Book of Mormon.

He witnessed the great apostasy in his land, as the seed of his father Lehi became a "dark, and loathsome, and a filthy people, full of idleness and all manner of abominations" (1 Nephi 12:23). Part of this history had already taken place at the close of the Book of Mormon. The rest of the fulfillment of this prophecy continued right up to the Spanish conquest (see chapter 30, "The Maya Classic Period and the Nephite Apostasy").

He witnessed the coming of Columbus and the coming of the Pilgrims. And he saw the Spaniards conquer and scatter his seed and the seed of his brethren, the remnant of Jacob.

> The conquest of Mexico in 1521 brought about a marriage of two vastly different and distinct cultures.

He witnessed the coming of the Catholic fathers and the establishment of Christianity among his father's descendants. He saw the remnant of Jacob placed in a spiritual bondage for another three hundred years following the conquest.

He witnessed the War of Independence in America, as his seed and the seed of his brethren fought for independence against the Mother Gentiles of Europe.

He witnessed the restoration of the gospel and the coming forth of his record among the Gentiles who lived in the United States of America.

He witnessed the sacred Book of Mormon record return to his people, the remnant of Jacob, as Latter-day Saint missionaries from the Gentile nation of the United States took the gospel to the seed of his brethren in Mesoamerica and in other parts of the Americas.

He witnessed the wickedness in the world prior to the Second Coming of Christ and the millennium. He saw wars and rumors of wars. He saw earthquakes, famines, and pestilences.

He witnessed the gospel taken to the Jews and the return of the lost tribes of Israel. He saw The Church of Jesus Christ of Latter-day Saints as it became a worldwide church.

He witnessed the coming forth of the sealed portion of the Book of Mormon and all the events recorded therein foretelling the Second Coming of Christ and the ushering in of the millennium.

Who can dispute the things that are yet to come to pass when so many of the events that were prophesied by the great prophet Nephi six hundred years prior to the birth of Christ have already come to pass?

OVERVIEW

The purpose of this concluding chapter of *Exploring the Lands of the Book of Mormon* is to analyze briefly the history of Mexico and Central America as they appear to correspond with the prophecies outlined in the Book of Mormon.

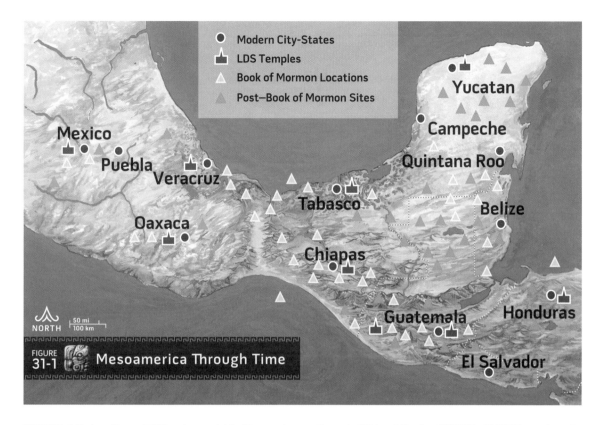

FIGURE 31–1: Modern cities and LDS temples now dot the Mesoamerica map. The ancient history dating from 2600 BC to AD 1500 is complex and intriguing. Sprinkled among the remains of cities representing powerful dynasties is the saga of the remnants of God's covenant people—a saga that is told as if someone were crying from the dust, a saga that bears witness of Jesus Christ who visited His other sheep in a nethermost part of His vineyard, a saga that is still unfolding today in books, customs, artifacts, and geography. Although a great deal of information has come forth since the publication of the Book of Mormon in 1830, we are still exploring the lands of the Book of Mormon.

The conquest of Mexico in 1521 brought about a marriage of two vastly different and distinct cultures. Spain introduced a new language, Spanish, and a new religion, Catholicism. For the most part, however, the customs and the traditions of the people did not change significantly. Many of these customs and traditions are still observable today in such things as food, family relationships, religious ceremonies, work ethics, and manner of dress and native languages.

Mexico and Guatemala are basically indigenous native cultures. As mentioned earlier, more than 85 percent of the Mexican people have an indigenous heritage. About 10 percent of the population is still considered full-blooded natives. That number increases to 50 percent in the country of Guatemala. If you ask a Mexican where he or she descended from, you do not expect a United States answer of England, Denmark, or even Spain. Mexicans simply respond, "Soy Mexicano"—I am Mexican. They have a deep pride in their country, their flag, their families, and their heritage.

Mexico has a population of over a hundred million people. Guatemala's population is about twelve million. At the time of this writing, 2008, approximately 1.5 million Latter-day Saints are living in Mexico and Guatemala. Amazingly, that is about one million more members than lived in these countries when we published the first edition of *Exploring the Lands of the Book of Mormon* in 1989.

The Church of Jesus Christ of Latter-day Saints dedicated its one hundredth stake in Mexico early in 1989. In 2005, the Church had 289 stakes and 83 districts there for a total of 372 stakes and districts. About half that many reside in Central America, with about twenty stakes in Guatemala City, the ancient city of Nephi. Latter-day Saint officials note that the Church is adding a thousand new members each month in Mexico City alone. And in the city of Huehuetenango, ancient land of the Gadianton band, with a population of fifty thousand people, four stakes of the Church are found.

We like to call these developments "geography by their fruits." Throughout this book, *Exploring the Lands of the Book of Mormon*, we have shown how we can trace civilizations by language, pottery, archaeology, architecture, geography, customs, agriculture, traditions, religious practices, historical parallels, elevations, distances, and directions. We will now discuss "geography by faith and prophecy." In that respect, the Book of Mormon prophesies that Mesoamericans will be brought "to the knowledge of their fathers in the latter days, and also to the knowledge of my covenants, saith the Lord" (2 Nephi 3:12).

The results of faith and prophecy are also manifested in the construction of latter-day temples. However, before we talk about temples, we will take a look at the modern history of Mesoamerica in relation to the Book of Mormon.

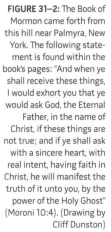

FIGURE 31–2: The Book of Mormon came forth from this hill near Palmyra, New York. The following statement is found within the book's pages: "And when ye shall receive these things, I would exhort you that ye would ask God, the Eternal Father, in the name of Christ, if these things are not true; and if ye shall ask with a sincere heart, with real intent, having faith in Christ, he will manifest the truth of it unto you, by the power of the Holy Ghost" (Moroni 10:4). (Drawing by Cliff Dunston)

MEXICO GAINS HER INDEPENDENCE AND THE GOSPEL IS RESTORED (AD 1820 TO 1846)

In December of the year 1820, Agustin de Iturbide was commissioned by the Spanish viceroy to crush the remaining rebel forces whose intent was to gain their independence from Spain.

Earlier that same year, in the spring of 1820, a young boy by the name of Joseph Smith, whose home was in Manchester County, New York, prayed unto God, asking which of all the churches of the time was true.

Iturbide was a native Mexican. Instead of crushing the rebels, he joined with them and became their leader. Under his leadership, they defeated the Spanish; and in September of 1821, Iturbide rode into Mexico City and placed himself as head of an independent Mexican nation. The last Spanish viceroy recognized Mexico's independence, and the Spanish soldiers went home to Spain.

In answer to his prayer, Joseph Smith was visited by God the Father and His Son, Jesus Christ. The young boy prophet was told that none of the Churches in existence at that time was true.

On October 24, 1824, the Mexican Congress adopted a constitution that made Mexico a republic. The Constitution of Mexico was patterned after the Constitution of the United States of America. The Mexican Constitution was called the Constitution of the United States of Mexico. The Constitution of the United States of America was drafted under the direction of the Lord. Therefore, we can conclude that the Constitution of the United States of Mexico was also drafted under the direction of the Lord: "And for this purpose have I established the Constitution of this land, by the hands of wise men whom I raised up unto this very purpose, and redeemed the land by the shedding of blood" (D&C 101:80).

On September 21, 1823, a personage who identified himself as Moroni told the eighteen-year-old Prophet Joseph Smith that some ancient records were deposited in a hill near the Smith home. For four consecutive years, Joseph Smith went to the hill where he received instruction from the personage who is called the angel Moroni, the same person who, in mortality, had buried the records fourteen hundred years earlier. On September 22, 1827, Joseph Smith took the records from the hill and, by the gift and power of God, translated them into English. The first copies of the translated record, called the Book of Mormon, were published. Joseph Smith had been raised up for that purpose as foretold in the record: "And blessed be he that shall bring this thing to light; for it shall be brought out of darkness unto light, according to the word of God; yea, it shall be brought out of the earth, and it shall shine forth out of darkness, and come unto the knowledge of the people; and it shall be done by the power of God" (Mormon 8:16).

"Geography by their fruits" is how geography helps identify the remnants of the Nephites, Jaredites, and Lamanites.

FIGURE 31–3: Benito Pablo Juarez Garcia was born on March 21, 1806, in a high mountain village in the state of Oaxaca, Mexico. He is revered by Mexicans as one of their greatest political figures—a man with great moral courage and honesty. He served as governor of Oaxaca and as president of the country of Mexico. He died on July 18, 1872. (Photo courtesy of Merrill C. Oaks)

THE MEXICAN-AMERICAN WAR AND MORMON MIGRATIONS (1846 TO 1900)

The United States and Mexico went to war in 1846. The United States annexed the state of Texas, which was still in Mexican territory.

In that same year, 1846, the Mormons who had been driven out of Nauvoo, Illinois, spent the winter at a place they called Winter Quarters, Nebraska. Some of the Mormon men joined the war and served in the Mormon Battalion on the side of the United States.

The United States defeated Mexico; and, in a treaty signed on February 2, 1848, Mexico gave up the territory that now constitutes the states of Arizona, Nevada, California, and Utah, as well as parts of Wyoming, Colorado, and New Mexico.

The Saints arrived in Mexican territory in July of 1847. Within a few months, it was declared a territory of the United States. The place where they settled was called Deseret by the Mormons and consisted of what is now Utah and parts of Nevada.

Mexico struggled to create a stable government. Benito Juarez, a full-blooded Zapotec from the state of Oaxaca, was elected president of Mexico in the year 1858. A year earlier, he was instrumental in drafting laws that brought about the separation of the Catholic Church and the government.

Benito Juarez and Joseph Smith were the same age. Joseph Smith was born in December of 1805. Benito Juarez was born in March of 1806, three months' difference.

The French invaded Mexico in 1861; and, in 1864, they placed Maximillian as emperor of Mexico. Juarez defeated Maximillian three years later; and, in 1867, the

Benito Juarez and Joseph Smith were the same age.

Exploring the Lands of the Book of Mormon

FIGURE 31–4: The Tuxtla Gutierrez, Chiapas Temple was dedicated March 12, 2000. It is located in what is proposed in *Exploring the Lands of the Book of Mormon* as the ancient land of Zarahemla. Several temples have been built in the ancient lands of the Book of Mormon, all of which bear witness of the growth of the Church of Jesus Christ in that land of promise. On December 16, 2006, a temple was announced to be built in Quetzaltenango, Guatemala. This temple will serve an area in which 90 percent of the people are native to the land and will be near the place proposed as the land of Helam in the Book of Mormon (Mosiah 23:4–19). (Photo courtesy of Cortney Boice)

French withdrew from Mexico. The famous Cinco de Mayo celebration is celebrated in honor of Juarez as a result of his initially holding off the French invasion.

Meanwhile, the Latter-day Saints under the direction of Brigham Young began to colonize other parts in the West. They subsequently established colonies in western Canada and northern Mexico.

Brigham Young died on August 29, 1877, five years after the death of Benito Juarez. John Taylor became the third President of The Church of Jesus Christ of Latter-day Saints and served until his death ten years later in 1887.

During the time that Mexico was under the rule of the French and the time that the Latter-day Saints were caught in a war of persecution over polygamy, the United States was engaged in the greatest internal battle of its history, the Civil War. The Saints had been driven out of Missouri in the winter of 1837–38. During the Civil War (1861–65), some of the bloodiest battles were fought in Missouri.

Wilford Woodruff was a year younger than Benito Juarez and two years younger than the Prophet Joseph Smith, who was killed in 1844. Wilford Woodruff, the fourth President of The Church of Jesus Christ of Latter-day Saints, lived to the age of ninety-one years. He died in 1898. President Woodruff issued the Manifesto in 1890, which instructed Latter-day Saints to discontinue the practice of contracting any marriage forbidden by the law of the land (see Doctrine and Covenants Official Declaration—1). He also performed the endowments for many historical figures. Two Mexicans were on the list: Benito Juarez and his wife, Maria.

In the year 1885, Mormons began migrating into Mexico. A party of seventy people led by William McClellan arrived at the Mexican town of Casas Grande, which is located about three hours of driving time southwest of El Paso, Texas. Subsequently, eight colonies were established in Mexico. Today, only two Mormon colonies remain in Mexico—Colonia Dublan and Colonia Juarez. The Mormon colonies, consisting of

In the St. George Temple, President Wilford Woodruff oversaw the temple endowments of many historical figures, including two Mexicans: Benito Juarez and his wife, Maria.

FIGURE 31–5: The faith and conviction of the people who live in the ancient lands of the Nephites, Jaredites, Mulekites, and Lamanites represent a sprinkling of the remnant of Jacob among the people. For the most part, their patriarchal blessings seem to designate them as coming from the lineage of Joseph through Ephraim and Manasseh. The children shown here are now growing up speaking three languages: Spanish, English, and their native Maya language. (Photo courtesy of Merrill C. Oaks)

Utah emigrants, have successfully provided the leadership for the early growth of the Church in Mexico. From the time a remnant of Saints went into Mexico, several General Authorities have been called from the Mormon colonies in Mexico, including Antoine R. Ivins, Marion G. Romney, Waldo Call, Erin Call, Robert Whetten, and others.

Over a hundred people from the two wards have served as mission presidents and in other general Church leadership capacities. The Mormon colonies were a driving force for education development in the state of Chihuahua. The Juarez Stake was organized on December 9, 1895.[1] As a result of the faithfulness of those who have served in that part of the Lord's vineyard, a temple that serves only two stakes and two districts was dedicated in Colonia Juarez on March 6, 1999.

1. Agricol Lozano Herrera, *Historia del Mormonismo en Mexico* (Mexico: Editorial Zarahemla, 1983), 4.

MEXICO AND THE CHURCH OF JESUS CHRIST OF LATTER-DAY SAINTS IN THE TWENTIETH CENTURY (AD 1900 TO 1950)

Porfirio Diaz had ruled Mexico with an iron hand for thirty-three years. The Mexican revolution, which began in 1910 and terminated in 1920, had for its objectives to uproot feudalism in the country. The result ended in the downfall of the Diaz regime, the breakdown of the hacienda system, the distribution of land to the masses, and a statement against foreign intervention.

Latter-day Saints who lived in the Mormon colonies felt the pressure, and many left never to return again. Sister Camilla Eyring Kimball was thirteen years old when her family left the colonies as refugees. She writes:

> The trip to the border at El Paso was only about 150 miles, but the train went at a snail's pace and stopped every few miles. We traveled all day and all night. Finally, just as dawn was breaking, we crawled slowly across the Rio Grande and

"The trip to the border at El Paso was only about 150 miles, but the train went at a snail's pace and stopped every few miles."

—Camilla Eyring Kimball

were greeted by the sight of the Stars and Stripes. A great shout went up from all the refugees. That sight brought a thrill that is revived in me every time I return to the United States and see the flag again. After a harrowing experience we felt safe once more.

The kind people of El Paso met us at the depot and took us in automobiles (only the second time I'd ridden in one) out to a big lumberyard, where they improvised shelter for the refugees.[2]

Rey L. Pratt, who is still remembered and loved by the early Mexican members of the Church, began his service as mission president on September 29, 1907, at the age of thirty-one. He announced to the Mexican people, "The day of the Lamanite has arrived."[3]

By the year 1913, Mexico had 1,204 members of the Church and sixteen branches, in addition to the Juarez Branch. But the Mexican revolution slowed the work and caused the American members to leave. The native members were also in great danger during this time period. As mentioned earlier, two young Mexican members were killed by federal soldiers at the town of San Marcos, Hidalgo. The townspeople were responsible for their deaths, as they told the federal troops that the Mormons were associated with foreigners.

The following account tells of two other Mexican missionaries, Andres Gonzalez and his companion, as reported by his grandson, Clate W. Mask, currently a member of the Second Quorum of the Seventy:

You Can't Kill Us!

During the political turmoil of the Mexican Revolution of 1910–15, two Mormon missionaries were preaching the gospel near Mexico City where they were arrested and sent before a firing squad. Elder Andres C. Gonzalez, remembering Abinadi before King Noah, told the man in charge, "You can't kill us!" Taking off his hat, he then explained that if they did execute two innocent servants of God that not only would their souls be in serious jeopardy with their Maker one day, but their very lives would be at the mercy of President Francisco Madero, the President of the Republic of Mexico, for killing two men who had an important message to deliver to him.

An Official Presidential Proclamation

Taking the safe course, the soldiers took their prisoners to the Presidential Palace so they could deliver their message. They obtained an audience with the President of Mexico, taught him the gospel for two hours, and presented him with a copy of the Book of Mormon. After an amicable discussion, President

2. Caroline Eyring Miner and Edward L. Kimball, *Camilla: A Biography of Camilla Eyring Kimball* (Salt Lake City: Deseret Book, 1980), 31.

3. Herrera, *Historia del Mormonismo en Mexico*, 48.

Elder Andres C. Gonzalez, remembering Abinadi before King Noah, told the man in charge, "You can't kill us!"

Madero gave the missionaries an official Presidential proclamation authorizing them and the Church to preach the gospel in Mexico, unmolested.

Historical Event

Years later, President Agricol Lozano Herrera, the first native stake president in Mexico, said, "This letter [written by Madero] is an event that never should be forgotten." Unfortunately, President Madero was assassinated shortly thereafter in the fury of the revolution and the LDS missionaries were expelled from Mexico in 1914. Years later, Elder Gonzalez had President Madero's temple work performed in the Mesa, Arizona Temple.

After his mission, my grandfather, Elder Andres C. Gonzalez returned to northern Mexico only to find that his wife (whom he had married two years before his mission) and the other Saints had fled the Mormon colonies in "the exodus." After locating his sweetheart, Minnie, in Tucson, they established their home in El Paso, Texas where they were able to help provide food and shelter for many years to countless Spanish-speaking Saints as they sometimes sacrificed nearly all their possessions and made their way to Mesa, Arizona to receive their temple blessings.[4]

4. Clate Mask, "Insights into the 'Lamanite Curse,'" *The Book of Mormon Archaeological Digest* 4, no. 1 (2002): 1.

Of necessity, the Mexican Mission headquarters had to be located in El Paso from 1919 to 1930. The mission included El Paso, Mexico, and parts of Arizona, New Mexico, and Colorado. Rey Pratt returned to Mexico City in 1921 as mission president.

In 1926, Mormon missionaries were again expelled from Mexico. At the time, the Mexican Mission had 3,882 members.[5]

5. Herrera, *Historia del Mormonismo en Mexico*, 54.

A PERIOD OF GROWTH IN THE CHURCH; MEXICO ENTERS THE FREE WORLD (1950 TO 2010)

Joseph Allen writes: "In 1956, when I was a young missionary in Argentina, my Grandfather Hancock, who was in his seventies, served as a missionary in Mexico. The mission extended from El Paso to Panama. Mexico still had only one stake, the Juarez Stake in the Mormon colonies."

In 1961, Harold Brown, one of the greatest leaders of the Church among the Mexican people, became the president of the first Mexican stake outside the Mormon colonies. He subsequently became the first temple president of the Mexican Temple, with his wife serving as matron. The kindness of Harold and Leanore has reached multitudes of members of the Church both in and out of Mexico.

The first non-Anglo stake president in the Church in these latter days was Agricol Lozano Herrera, who was set apart to be president of the second Mexico City stake in 1967. The prophecy was and continues to be fulfilled: the gospel was taken to "the remnant of Jacob by way of the Gentiles" (see 1 Nephi 15:17). Another book at another time could only touch the surface of the great faith and love of individual people who are of the seed of Father Lehi.

Prior to the death of Agricol Lozano Herrera, following a lifetime of faithful service to the Church, he served as the president of the Mexico City Temple. For many years, the Church operated in Mexico as an educational institution using the name of the Mutual Improvement Association, and Elder Lozano was the legal entity. As an attorney, Agricol Lozano Herrera was instrumental in the Church's becoming officially organized as *Le Iglesia de Jesucristo de los Santos de los Ultimos Dias* when, in the year 1993, he took a delegation of Mexican diplomats to Salt Lake City when approval was given.

The conversions and faith of Latter-day Saints who live in the ancient land of the Book of Mormon are legion. Bishop Rosas and his wife of Mexico City raised thirteen children in a small apartment on the roof of a building where he worked as an elevator operator. Daniel Mitch, of Maya descent, was the first convert in Patzicia, Guatemala, and today there are seventeen families, all members of the Church, who are his descendants. There is a stake of the Church at Patzicia, Chilmaltenango, the place described in *Exploring the Lands of the Book of Mormon* as the land of Ishmael where Ammon taught the gospel to the Lamanites.

Subsequently, three more stakes were organized in Mexico City; and then, in 1973, Elder Howard W. Hunter and Elder Thomas Fyans organized sixteen stakes in one weekend in Mexico City from the existing five stakes. As mentioned earlier, that number increased to a hundred stakes throughout the country of Mexico by the year 1989. And, as of the year 2005, there were over five hundred stakes and districts in Mexico and Central America.

The temple in Mexico City was dedicated on December 2, 3, and 4, 1983, and subsequently underwent a fourteen-month renovation. The temple in Guatemala was dedicated in 1985. The first president of the Guatemala Temple was John F. O'Donnal. While we have been working on the second edition of *Exploring the Lands of the Book of Mormon*, another temple is being built in Honduras, and a temple has been announced to be built in Quetzaltenango. When the latter is dedicated, it will represent the most native temple in the Church, as 90 percent of the temple district is composed of members of Maya descent. It will be only five miles from the village of Almolonga, a land of pure water, described in *Exploring the Lands of the Book of Mormon* as the land of Helam, where Alma and his small group of Christians lived for twenty-five years in the second century BC.

And then another miracle happened. From March 9, 1999, to April 28, 2004, eleven temples were built and dedicated in Mexico, and when added to the temples in Mexico City, Guatemala City, Honduras, and Quetzaltenango, the total reaches fifteen temples, manifesting the great vision and tireless efforts of the great administrator and prophet, Gordon B. Hinckley.

The conversions and faith of Latter-day Saints who live in the ancient land of the Book of Mormon are legion.

Elder Howard W. Hunter and Elder Thomas Fyans organized sixteen stakes in one weekend.

And then another miracle happened. From March 9, 1999, to April 28, 2004, eleven temples were built and dedicated in Mexico.

Following is a list that shows the dedication dates and the numbers of stakes and districts that, at the time of this writing, feed into each temple in Mexico, Guatemala, and Honduras:

Mexico City Mexico Temple
Dedicated December 2, 1983
78 Stakes
6 Districts

Guatemala City Guatemala Temple
Dedicated December 14, 1984
88 Stakes
43 Districts

Colonia Juarez Chihuahua Mexico Temple
Dedicated March 6, 1999
2 Stakes
2 Districts

Ciudad Juarez Mexico Temple
Dedicated February 26, 2000
10 Stakes
1 District

Hermosillo Sonora Mexico Temple
Dedicated February 27, 2000
11 Stakes
5 Districts

Oaxaca Mexico Temple
Dedicated March 11, 2000
6 Stakes
3 Districts

Tuxtla Gutierrez Mexico Temple
Dedicated March 12, 2000
6 Stakes
3 Districts

Tampico Mexico Temple
Dedicated May 20, 2000
11 Stakes
2 Districts

Villahermosa Mexico Temple
Dedicated May 21, 2000
8 Stakes
2 Districtss

Merida Mexico Temple
Dedicated July 8, 2000
12 Stakes
2 Districts

Veracruz Mexico Temple
Dedicated July 9, 2000
9 Stakes
1 District

Guadalajara Mexico Temple
Dedicated April 29, 2001
21 Stakes
6 Districts

Monterry Mexico Temple
Dedicated April 28, 2002
27 Stakes
7 Districts

Tegucigalpa Honduras Temple
Announced June 9, 2006
Groundbreaking June 9, 2007

Quetzaltenango Guatemala Temple
Announced December 16, 2006

Guatemala City Temple

Veracruz, Mexico Temple

Words cannot begin to explain the blessings that have come about as a result of latter-day temples dotting the landscape of the ancient land where Nephi, Alma, and Mormon walked. Nor can words describe the prophecy yet to be fulfilled of the Savior's Second Coming as outlined as a shadow in His visit to the ancient Nephites.

During the first part of the twenty-first century, we witnessed a modern miracle with members of the Church who traveled with us to the areas of the ancient Nephites, Lamanites, Mulekites, and Jaredites. We observed the joy of the Saints throughout the land. We were in Merida the day the statue of Moroni was erected; we were at Oaxaca during the open house; and we were at Tuxtla Gutierrez, located in the ancient land of Zarahemla, during the time its temple was dedicated.

FIGURE 31–6: Brother Pablo Choc has been a long-time member of the Church. He is from the village of Patzicia, Chilmaltenango, Guatemala. A number of his family members, including his wife, were killed in the 1976 Guatemala earthquake. An American Fork artist, Inez Hoggard, captured the features of Brother Choc and donated the picture to him on her trip to Mexico and Guatemala.

Nine of the fifteen temples are located in the area of Mesoamerica, the land of the Book of Mormon. The majority of native Americans also live in this same area. Of an estimated thirty-one million indigenous people on the American continent, less than two million live in the United States. We refer to this population statistic as "geography by prophecy":

> For there are many promises which are extended to the Lamanites; for it is because of the traditions of their fathers that caused them to remain in their state of ignorance; therefore the Lord will be merciful unto them and prolong their existence in the land.
>
> And at some period of time they will be brought to believe in his word, and to know of the incorrectness of the traditions of their fathers; and many of them will be saved, for the Lord will be merciful unto all who call on his name. (Alma 9:16–17)

The scripture rings loudly and clearly: "And they shall assist my people, the remnant of Jacob, and also as many of the house of Israel as shall come, that they may build a city, which shall be called the New Jerusalem" (3 Nephi 21:23).

Blake Allen writes:

The following story is regarding an event that took place at the Montufar Ward, where the first chapel was built in Guatemala. Two of my boys were with me, and they were asked to help with the sacrament. After the services, a sister in the ward came up to me and, taking hold of my hands and with tears in her eyes, said something like, "I want to thank you and your people for all you have done, for bringing the gospel to us, for sending your sons and daughters to bring us the Book of Mormon." I assumed she was a new member of the Church and asked her when she had been baptized. She said, "Twenty-six years ago."

The Book of Mormon contains one prophecy that is repeated at least two times, once by Mormon and once by the Savior Himself. It was given earlier by the Savior to Isaiah. It is also recorded in the book of Micah (see Isaiah 5:29 and Micah 5:8). It talks about the gathering of Israel, and it is dualistic in nature. It is written in the Hebrew parallel style of poetry. It is important. Regarding the last days, Micah writes:

> And the remnant of Jacob
>> shall be among the Gentiles
>> in the midst of many people
>>> as a lion among the beasts of the forest,
>>> as a young lion among the flocks of sheep:
>>>> who, if he go through both treadeth down,
>>>> and teareth in pieces, and none can deliver. (Micah 5:8)

Of an estimated thirty-one million indigenous people on the American continent, less than two million live in the United States.

In speaking to the Nephites on the subject of the scattering and gathering of Israel and specifically regarding the Gentiles and this land being a land of their inheritance, Christ said:

> And the Father hath commanded me that I should give unto you this land, for your inheritance.
> And I say unto you, that if the Gentiles do not repent after the blessings which they shall receive, after they have scattered my people—
> Then shall ye, who are a remnant of the house of Jacob, go forth among them; and ye shall be in the midst of them who shall be many; and ye shall be among them as a lion among the beasts of the forest, and as a young lion among the flocks of the sheep, who, if he goeth through both treadeth down and teareth in pieces, and none can deliver. . . .
> And I will gather my people together as a man gathereth his sheaves into the floor. (3 Nephi 20:14–18)

Then, in the next chapter, Christ repeats the same prophecy (3 Nephi 21:12). He is speaking to the Gentiles who live among Native Americans on the American continent: "But if they will repent and hearken unto my words, and harden not their hearts, I will establish my church among them" (see 3 Nephi 21:12–24).

We read in 3 Nephi 22:3 that the seed of Jacob will inherit the land of the Gentiles and make the desolate cities to be inhabited. Mormon follows the same theme when he writes to the Gentiles that if they do not repent and humble themselves, "a remnant of the seed of Jacob shall go forth among you as a lion, and tear you in pieces, and there is none to deliver" (Mormon 5:24).

FIGURE 31–7: Blake Joseph Allen is the coauthor of *Exploring the Lands of the Book of Mormon* and is a professional tour director. Here he is shown discussing the historical events related to Mesoamerica and the Book of Mormon.

Joseph Allen writes: "I have spent one-fourth of my life among the remnant of Jacob. I have spent the other three-fourths of my life among the remnant of Jacob also. That is, I have spent a lot of time traveling throughout and living in the ancient lands of the Nephites, Lamanites, and Mulekites whose ancestors are a remnant of Jacob and Joseph. I have spent most of my life in the United States where members of the Church are a remnant of Jacob and Joseph."

Therefore, we propose that the above prophecies reflect both a physical (temporal) and a spiritual meaning. We live in a day and age where there is much wickedness in the United States as well as in other parts of the world. We also live in a day and age in which many people cross the border into the United States, some legal and others illegal. It may well be that this Mesoamerican remnant of Jacob is a political representative of the scriptures above. However, we believe that the spiritual fulfillment of the above is that the lions and the young lions are the members of the Church reflected in the young missionaries, remnants of Jacob and Joseph, who go throughout the world gathering the seed of Israel and who "treadeth down and teareth apart" the false doctrines of Satan and his followers. We see the result as a type and a shadow of the gathering.

SUMMARY

This book, *Exploring the Lands of the Book of Mormon*, has been written with the idea in mind of helping readers grasp a deeper feeling for the history, language, culture, and geography of the Book of Mormon. Throughout this text, we have compiled a lengthy list of place names and locations that have linguistic, geographical, or historical correlations with the Book of Mormon. They include Jerusalem, Red Sea, Valley of Lemuel, Nahom, Old World Bountiful (Dophar), the many waters (oceans), sea east and sea west, Lehi, Sariah, Laman, Nephi, Noah, Limhi, Mocum, Onihah, Mormon, Helam,

Hermounts, Sidom, Sidon, narrow pass through the Isthmus of Tehuantepec (course of the beasts), Gulf of Mexico, narrow neck (Isthmus of Tehuantepec), King Kish, hill Shim, land among many waters, waters of Ripliancum, land of Cumorah, hill Ramah/Cumorah, city of Lib, fortified cities, city of Mulek, mountains of Lachoneus, narrow strip of wilderness, east wilderness, Bountiful, and Desolation.

As stated, some of the areas that have been presented as Book of Mormon lands are to be considered as tentative, but others manifest compelling evidence that negates a tentative approach.

After careful, thoughtful, and intellectual and spiritual considerations, and to the best of our ability, we hereby make the following declarations.

First, we know the following to be true:

1. The Book of Mormon is true scripturally and historically.
2. Joseph Smith is a prophet of God who translated that "most correct of books."
3. Jesus Christ is the author of our salvation as testified in that same sacred record.
4. We are led by living prophets who teach and encourage us to read and study daily from the pages of The Book of Mormon: Another Testament of Jesus Christ.

Second, we declare the following to be true to the best of our ability:

1. The historical and geographical New World background of the Book of Mormon took place in Mesoamerica.
2. The Olmecs and the Jaredites are the same people.
3. The Frankincense Trail is the path Lehi followed from Jerusalem to Dhofar, Oman.
4. Izapa is the area of first inheritance.
5. Kaminaljuyu (Guatemala) is the area of the ancient city of Nephi.
6. Lake Atitlan is the waters of Mormon.
7. Almolonga, Quetzaltenango, is the land of Helam.
8. The narrow strip of wilderness is a narrow mountain range.
9. The Isthmus of Tehuantepec is the small neck of land.
10. The Chiapas valley is the land of Zarahemla.
11. The Peten and Belize are the east wilderness of Zarahemla.
12. The hill Ramah/Cumorah and the hill Shim are located in the Tuxtla Mountains of Veracruz.
13. The land among many waters and the waters of Ripliancum are identifiable as outlined in *Exploring the Lands of the Book of Mormon*.
14. Teotihuacan and Tikal played major roles in the downfall of the Nephites.
15. The Nephite apostasy and the Maya Classic Period are of the same origin and describe the same people and events.
16. The origin of the name *Quetzalcoatl* is directly associated with the Savior.

> Some of the areas that have been presented as Book of Mormon lands are to be considered as tentative, but others manifest compelling evidence.

17. Mormon and other Nephite writers use the historical record to emphasize spiritual points; the result is called "dualism" or "types and shadows."
18. The landing areas of the Jaredites and the Nephites were on the Pacific side near the Gulf of Tehuantepec, and the landing site of the Mulekites was on the Atlantic side by the Gulf of Mexico.

Furthermore, we believe that the king-men of the first century BC and the Maya priests of the second century AD are of Mulekite descent.

We believe that prophecy of things to come is couched in the historical message of the Book of Mormon.

We believe that the Nephites and Lamanites are the same people and that their skin color was basically the same, having the same DNA if we could test it today, and that the skin color, as mentioned in the Book of Mormon, is related more to the pureness or darkness of the soul as opposed to the actual skin color, although allowance must also be made for differences of skin pigmentation.

We believe in a direct correlation between what we read historically about the ancient Maya during the Book of Mormon time period and what we read about the Nephites and the Lamanites in the Book of Mormon. We further believe that correlation justifies our speaking of the Nephite Maya and the Lamanite Maya as a legitimate way of distinguishing the two groups at the beginning of the Maya Classic Period.

We believe that the day and a half's journey represents a defensive line and does not run from sea to sea. Furthermore, we think it represents a concept of man's journey through life.

We believe that Izapa Stela 5, Altar 10 at Kaminaljuyu, and Tikal Stela 31 all contain engravings that are pertinent to our understanding and confirmation of the historicity of the Book of Mormon.

We believe that Moroni traveled by foot from Veracruz, Mexico, to Palmyra, New York, where he deposited the few plates his father had given him along with the Jaredite sealed portion in a hill near where Joseph Smith's family subsequently settled.

There are many things we do not know. For example, we do not know the precise location of many places, such as the cities of Gid, Omner, Lehi, Morianton, Aaron, Nephihah, Manti, Antionum, Middoni, Shemlon, hill Riplah, waters of Sebus, and other places where very little evidence is given in the Book of Mormon.

May we continue to move forward in our study and understanding of the Book of Mormon. And may the time speedily come, as prophesied, "that the words of the book which were sealed shall be read upon the house tops . . . by the power of Christ; and [then] all things shall be revealed unto the children of men which ever have been among the children of men, and which ever will be even unto the end of the earth" (2 Nephi 27:11).

We believe that prophecy of things to come is couched in the historical message of the Book of Mormon.

Selected Bibliography

Acosta, Jose de. *Historia Natural y Moral de las Indias, en Que se Tratan las Cosas Notables del Ciclo, Elementos, Metales, Plantas, y Animales de Ellos; y los Ritos, Ceremonias, Leyes, Gobierno de los Indios*. Seville: n.p., 1590.

Alcala, Ermilo Solis. *Diccionario Espanol-Maya*. Prologo del Lic. Antonio Mediz Bolio. Ochil, Yucatan, 1949.

Alexander, David and Pat Alexander, Editors. *Eerdmans Handbook to the Bible*. Grand Rapids, MI: William B. Eerdmans, 1974.

Allen, Joseph L. "A Comparative Study of Quetzalcoatl, the Feathered-Serpent God of Meso-America, with Jesus Christ, the God of the Nephites." Unpublished PhD Dissertation, Brigham Young University, 1970.

Allen, Joseph L. "Horses." *The Book of Mormon Archaeological Digest*. Vol. 2, No. 6. 2000, 1.

Allen, Joseph L. "King-men in Belize." *Explorations in the Book of Mormon*. Orem, UT: Book of Mormon Tours, 1999, 111–17.

Allen, Joseph L. "Mormon's Epistle to Yax Ayin." *Book of Mormon Archaeological Digest*. Vol. 3, No. 2. June 2001, 1–5.

Allen, Joseph L. *Sacred Sites: Searching for Book of Mormon Lands*. American Fork, UT: Covenant Communications, 2003.

Alonzo, Gualberto Zapata. *Una Vision Del Mundo Maya: Y Resena de las Culturas Olmeca, Totonaca, Zapoteca, Mixteca, Teotihuacana, Tolteca, y Azteca*. Mexico: Talleres de Mario Esquiliano, 1979.

Anales de Cauhtitlan y Leyenda de los Soles en Codice Chimalpopoca. Edited and translated by Primo F. Valazquez. Mexico: Institute of Historic Investigations, National University, 1945.

Anderson, Arthur O. and Charles E. Dibble, Translator. *Historia General de las Cosas de Nueva Espana: Florentine Codex, by Fray Bernardino de Sahagun.* 12 Volumes. Santa Fe: The School of American Research and the University of Utah, 1950.

Armillas, Pedro. "La Serpiente Emplumada," *Cuadernos Americanos,* February 1947, 161–78.

Atlas Cartografico Historico: Mexico. Mexico: Instituto Nacional Geografia e Informatica, 1988.

Bancroft, Hubert H. *The Native Races.* Volume 3, *Myths and Languages.* San Francisco: A. L. Bancroft, 1883.

Barnstone, Willis, Translator. *Mexico, Before Cortes: Art, History, Legend.* Garden City, NY: Doubleday, 1963.

Bartra, Agusti. *Quetzalcoatl.* Mexico: Fondo de Cultura Economica, 1960.

Beatriz, de la Fuente. *Las Cabezas Colosales Olmecas.* Mexico: Fondo de Cultura Economica, 1975.

Behrens, Helen. *The Virgin and the Serpent-God.* Mexico: Editorial Progreso, 1964.

Benitez, Fernando. *La Ciudad de Mexico: 1325–1982.* Spain: Salvat Mexicana de Ediciones, 1982.

Benson, Elizabeth P., Editor. *The Olmec and Their Neighbors: Essays in Memory of Matthew W. Stirling.* Michael D. Coe and David Grove, organizers. Washington, DC: Dumbarton Oaks Research Library and Collections, 1981.

Benson, Ezra Taft. "Cleansing the Inner Vessel." *Ensign,* May 1986, 4–7.

Beristain, Jose Maria de Souza. *Biblioteca Hispano-American-Septemtrional,* p. 58, as cited by Chavero 1965, Prologo, p. 5.

Bernal, Ignacio. *El Valle de Oaxaca: Guia Official.* Mexico: Instituto Nacional de Antropologia e Historia, 1992.

Bernal, Ignacio. *Guia Official: Teotihuacan.* Mexico: Instituto Nacional de Antropologia e Historia, 1985.

Bernal, Ignacio. *The Mexican National Museum of Anthropology.* Translated by Carolyn B. Czitrom. Great Britain: Harrold and Sons, 1972.

Bernal, Ignacio. *Official Guide: Oaxaca Valley.* Translated by Helen Jones-Perrott de Mandri. Mexico: Instituto Nacional de Antropologia e Historia, 1985 and 1988.

Biart, Lucien. *The Aztecs: Their History, Manners, and Customs.* Translated by J. L. Garner. Chicago: A. C. McClurg, 1887.

Bierhorst, John. *A Nahuatl-English Dictionary and Concordance to the Cantares Mexicanos.* Stanford, CA: Stanford University Press, 1985.

Blom, Frans. *The Conquest of Yucatan.* Boston: Houghton Mifflin Company, 1936.

Blom, Frans. "Tribes and Temples." *Tulane University Middle American Research Series,* Publication No. 1, Vol. 1. New Orleans, 1926, p. 29.

Brewer, Stewart W. "The History of an Idea: The Scene on Stela 5 from Izapa, Mexico, as a Representation of Lehi's Vision of the Tree of Life. *Journal of Book of Mormon Studies*. Vol. 8, No. 1, 1999, 13–21.

Brinton, Daniel G. *American Hero Myths*. Philadelphia: H. C. Watts, 1882.

Brown, Kenneth L. "The Valley of Guatemala—A Highland Port of Trade." *Teotihuacan and Kaminaljuyu: A Study in Prehistoric Culture Contact*. Edited by W. T. Sanders and J. W. Michels.

Burland, C. A. *The Gods of Mexico*. London: Eyre and Spottiswoods, 1967.

Bushnell, Geoffrey H. S. *Ancient Arts of the Americas*. New York: F. A. Praeger, 1965.

Cannon, George Q., Editor. "Editorial Thoughts—The Book of Mormon Geography." *The Juvenile Instructor*. Vol. 25, No. 1, January 1, 1890, 18–19.

Caso, Alfonso. *El Pueblo del Sol*. Mexico: Fondo de Cultura Economica, 1953.

Castanon, Felix Angulo. *Cholula*. Puebla: Inprehscl, 1977.

Cervantes, Maria Antonieta. *National Antrophological Museum*. Spain: Ediciones Americanas Escudo de Oro, 1976.

Chavero, Alfredo. *Obras Historicas de Don Fernando de Alva Ixtlilxochitl*. Tomo I. Mexico: Editora Nacional, 1965.

Cheesman, Paul R. *Early America and the Book of Mormon: A Photographic Essay of Ancient America*. Salt Lake City: Deseret Book, 1972.

Cheesman, Paul R. *Book of Mormon Lands: A Photographic Essay*. Salt Lake City: Blaine T. Hudson, 1978.

Cheesman, Paul R. *The World of the Book of Mormon*. Salt Lake City: Deseret Book, 1978.

Cheesman Paul R. and Barbara W. Hutcins. *Pathways to the Past: A Guide to the Ruins of Mesoamerica*. Bountiful, UT: Horizon Publishers, 1984.

Cheesman, Paul R. *These Early Americans: External Evidences of the Book of Mormon*. Salt Lake City: Deseret Book, 1974.

Cheesman, Paul R. *The Keystone of Mormonism: Little Known Truths about the Book of Mormon*. Salt Lake City: Deseret Book, 1973.

Cheesman, Paul R. *Great Leaders of the Book of Mormon*. Provo, UT: Promised Land Publications, 1973.

Cheesman, Paul R. *Early America and the Polynesians*. Provo, UT: Promised Land Publications, 1975.

Chonay, P. Dionisio Jose, Translator. Adrian Recinos, Introduction and Notes. *Titulo de los Senores de Totonicapan*. Guatemala: Direccion General de Antropologia e Historia, 1980.

Christensen, Ross T., Compiler and Editor. *Progress in Archaeology*. Provo, UT: Brigham Young University, 1963.

Christensen, Ross T. "Stela 5—Izapa: A Review of Its Study as the 'Lehi Tree of Life Stone.'" *Newsletter and Proceedings of the Society for Early Historic Archaeology*. No. 156, March 1984.

Christensen, Ross T., Editor. *U.A.S. Newsletter*, No. 66. May 7, 1960. Now SEHA—Society for Early Historic Archaeology.

Christensen, Ross T., Editor. *U.A.S. Newsletter*. No. 67. July 7, 1960. Now SEHA—Society for Early Historic Archaeology.

Christenson, Allen J. "Chiasmus in Mayan Texts." *Ensign*, October 1988, 28–31.

Christenson, Allen J., Editor and Translator. *Popul Vuh: The Mythic Sections—Tales of First Beginnings from the Ancient K'iche'—Maya*. Provo, UT: Foundation for Ancient Research and Mormon Studies, 2000.

Clark, John E. "A New Artistic Rendering of Izapa Stela 5: A Step toward Improved Interpretation." *Journal of Book of Mormon Studies*. Vol. 8, No. 1, 1999, 23–33.

Clark, John E. "Archaeology and Cumorah Questions." *Journal of Book of Mormon Studies*. Vol. 13, Nos. 1–2, 146–51.

Clavijero, P. *Historia Antigua de Mexico*, Volume 1, p. 37, as cited by Chavero 1965, Prolog, p. 5.

Coe, Michael D. *America's First Civilization*. New York: American Heritage; Distributed by Van Nostrand, Princeton, NJ, 1968.

Coe, Michael D. *Breaking the Maya Code*. New York: Thames and Hudson, 1992.

Coe, Michael D. *The Maya*. Fourth edition. New York: Thames and Hudson, 1987.

Coe, Michael D. *Mexico*. New York: Frederick A. Praeger, 1962.

Coe, Michael D. *Mexico*. Revised and enlarged edition. London: Thames and Hudson, 1984.

Coe, Michael D. and Richard A. Diehl. *In the Land of the Olmec*. Austin: University of Texas Press, 1980.

Coe, Sophie D., Translator. *Maya Hieroglyphic Codices*. Translated from the Russian. New York: Institute for Mesoamerica Studies, 1982.

Coe, William R. *Tikal: A Handbook of the Ancient Maya Ruins*. Philadelphia: University Museum of the University of Pennsylvania, 1967, Third Edition, 1970.

Cogolludo, Diego Lopez. *Historia de Yucatan*. 2 Volumes. Third Edition. Merida: n.p., 1867–68.

Cornyn, John Hubert. *The Song of Quetzalcoatl*. Second Edition. Translated from the Aztec. Yellow Springs, OH: Antioch Press, 1931.

Covarrubias, Miguel. *Indian Art of Mexico and Central America*. New York: Alfred A. Knopf, 1957.

Cross, Frank Moore. "The Phoenician Inscription from Brazil: A Nineteenth-Century Forgery." *Orientalia*, Vol. 37, 1968, 437–60

Cross, Frank Moore. "Phoenicians in Brazil?" *Biblical Archaeological Review*, Vol. 5, No. 1, January/February 1979, 36–43.

Davies, Nigel. *The Ancient Kingdoms of Mexico*. London: Allen Lane, Penguin Books, 1982.

Delgado, Agustin. *Archaeological Research at Santa Rosa, Chiapas and in the Region of Tehuantepec*. New World Archaeological Foundation Papers Nos. 17 and 18. Provo, UT: NWAF, Brigham Young University, 1965.

Diaz, Bernal. *The Discovery and Conquest of Mexico—1517–1521*. Edited from the only exact copy of the original manuscript by Genaro Garcia. Translated by A. P. Maudslay. New York: Noonday Press, 1972.

Diaz-Bolio, Jose. *La Serpienta Emplumada: eje de Culturas*. Third Edition. Merida, Yucatan: Registro de Cultura Yucateca, 1964.

Doctrine and Covenants. First published in 1833 as the Book of Commandments. Salt Lake City: The Church of Jesus Christ of Latter-day Saints, 1981.

Drucker, Phillip. "Ceramic Sequences at Tres Zapotes, Veracruz, Mexico." *Bureau of American Ethnology Bulletin*, No. 140. Washington, DC: U.S. Government Printing Office, 1943.

Duran, Diego. *Book of the Gods and Rites and the Ancient Calendar*. Translated and edited by Fernando Horcasitas and Doris Heyden. Norman: University of Oklahoma Press, 1971.

Duran, Fray Diego. *Historia de las Indias de Nueva Espana y Islas de la Tierra Firme*. La prepara y de a luz Angel Ma. Garibay K., 2 vols. Mexico: Editoria Porrua, 1967.

Duran, Diego. *Ritos y Fiestas de los Antiquos Mexicanos*. Mexico: Editorial Innovacion, 1980.

Edmonson, Munro, *The Book of the Year: Middle American Calendrical Systems*. Salt Lake City: University of Utah Press, 1988.

Ferguson, Thomas S. and Milton R. Hunter, *Ancient America and the Book of Mormon*. Salt Lake City: Deseret Book, 1950.

Ferguson, Thomas S. *Cumorah—Where?* Independence, MO: Press of Zion's Printing & Publishing Co., 1947.

Ferguson, Thomas S. *One Fold and One Shepherd*. Salt Lake City: Deseret News Press, 1958.

Flannery, Kent V. and others. "Farming Systems and Political Growth in Oaxaca." *Science*, Vol. 158, 1967, 445.

Florescano, Enrique. "La Serpiente Emplumada, Tlaloc, y Quetzalcoatl," *Cuadernos Americanos,* March–April 1964, 121–66.

Folan, William J. *Chichen Itza*. Mexico: Ediciones Orto, 1978.

Fong, Charlene R., Translator. *Yucatan and the Mayas: Merida-Uxmal-Chichen Itza-Palenque*. Mexico: Ediciones Alducin, 1983.

Fuente, Beatriz. *Los Hombres de Piedra: Escultura Olmeca*. Mexico: Universidad Nacional Autonoma de Mexico, 1977.

Galbraith, David B., D. Kelly Ogden, and Andrew C. Skinner. *Jerusalem: The Eternal City*. Salt Lake City: Deseret Book, 1996.

Gamiz, Abel. *Quetzalcoatl*. Mexico: Sociadad Folklorica de Mexico, 1941.

Garfias, Luis M. *The Mexican Revolution: A Historic Politico-Military Compendium*. Mexico: Ediciones Lara, 1979.

Gendrop, Paul. *Arte Prehispanico en Mesoamerica*. Mexico: Editorial Trillas, 1979.

Girard, Rafael. *Los Mayas, Su Civilizacion: Su Historia Sus Vinculaciones Coneinentales*. Mexico: Libro Mexico, 1966.

Givens, Terryl L. *By the Hand of Mormon: The American Scripture That Launched a New World Religion*. New York: Oxford University Press, 2002.

Godfrey, Kenneth A. "The Zelph Story." Paper No. GOD-89. Provo, UT: Foundation for Ancient Research and Mormon Studies, 1989.

Goetz, Delia. *Title of the Lords of Totonicapan*. Translated from the Quiche text into Spanish by Dionisio Jose Chonay; English version by Delia Goetz. Norman: University of Oklahoma Press, 1953.

Goetz, Delia and Sylvanus G. Morley. *Popul Vuh: The Sacred Book of the Ancient Quiche Maya*. English version from the translation of Adrian Recinos. Norman: University of Oklahoma Press, 1950.

Golden, Charles and Andrew Scherer. "Border Problems: Recent Archaeological Research along the Usumacinta River." *The PARI Journal* 7, no. 2, Fall 2006: 7–13.

Gordon, C. H. "The Authenticity of the Phoenician Text from Parahyba." *Orientalia* 37, 1968: 75–80.

Grover, Mark L. "El Titulo de Totonicapan." In A. Dean Larsen, Editor. *A Gallimaufry of Acquisitions*. Provo, UT: Friends of the Brigham Young University Library, 1991.

Guemes, Lina O. *National History Museum: Castle of Chapultepec*. Mexico: Ediciones Orto, 1980.

Gugliotta, Guy. "Maya Rise and Fall." *National Geographic Magazine* 212, no. 2, August 2007: 68–109.

Hadlock, David, "The Language of My Father." *Book of Mormon Archaeological Digest*. Winter 2003, 1–2.

Hammond, Fletcher. *Geography of the Book of Mormon*. Salt Lake City: Utah Printing Co., 1959.

Hansen, L. Taylor. *He Walked the Americas*. Amherst, WI: Amherst Press, 1963.

Hanson, Paul M. *Jesus Christ among the Ancient Americans*. Independence, MO: Herald Publishing House, 1945.

Hauck, F. Richard. *Deciphering the Geography of the Book of Mormon*. Salt Lake City: Deseret Book, 1988.

Hay, Clarence L. and others. *The Maya and Their Neighbors*. New York: D. Appleton-Century Co., 1940.

Helfritz, Hans. *Mexican Cities of the Gods: An Archaeological Guide*. New York: Frederick A. Praeger, 1970.

Herman, Paul. *Conquest by Man*. Translated from the German by Michael Bullock. New York: Harper, 1954.

Herrera, Agricol Lozano. *Historia del Mormonismo en Mexico*. Mexico: Editorial Zarahemla, 1983.

Hewett, Edgar Lee. *Ancient Life in Mexico and Central America*. New York: The Bobbs-Merrill Co., 1936.

Hield, Charles R, "The God Quetzalcoatl." *Saints' Herald*, March 1970, 53.

Hilton, Lynn M. and Hope Hilton. *In Search of Lehi's Trail*. Salt Lake City: Deseret Book, 1976.

Honore, Pierre. *In Quest of the White God*. Translated from the German by Oliver Coburn and Ursula Lehrburger. Great Britain: Hutchinson and Co., 1963.

Huber, Jay H. "Lehi's 600-Year Prophecy and the Birth of Christ." Preliminary Report No. HUB l-82. Provo, UT: Foundation for Ancient Research and Mormon Studies, 1982.

Huff, Sandy. *How to Compute Maya Dates: A Simple, Step-by-Step Guide to Reading Dates on Stele, Lintels and Other Maya Monuments*. Safety Harbor, FL: The Author, 1982.

Hunter, Milton R. *Christ in Ancient America: Archaeology and the Book of Mormon II*. Salt Lake City: Deseret News Press, 1959–68.

Hunter, Milton R. and Thomas Stuart Ferguson. *Ancient America and the Book of Mormon*. Oakland, CA: Kolob Book Company, 1950.

Hyman, David S. *Pre-Columbian Cements: A Study of the Calcareous Cements in Prehispanic Mesoamerican Building Construction*. Baltimore: Johns Hopkins University, 1970.

Irwin, Constance. *Fair Gods and Stone Faces: Ancient Seafarers and the New World's Most Intriguing Riddle*. New York: St. Martin's Press, 1963.

Ixtlilxochitl, Don Fernando de Alva. *Obras Historicas*. ed. Alfredo Chavero, 2 vols. Mexico: Editors Nacional, 1965.

Ixtlilxochitl, Fernando de Alva. *Obras Historicas*. Tomo I Edicion, estudio introductorio y un appendice documental por Edmundo O'Gorman. Mexico: Universidad Nacional Autonoma de Mexico, 1985.

Jackson, Kent P., Editor. *Studies in the Scriptures, Vol. 7: 1 Nephi to Alma 29*. Salt Lake City: Deseret Book, 1987.

Jakeman, M. Wells. "The Complex "Tree-of-Life" Carving on Izapa Stela 5: A Reanalysis and Partial Interpretation." *BYU Archaeology and Ethnohistory*. No. 4, 1958.

Jakeman, M. Wells. *The Origins and History of the Mayas*. Los Angeles: Research Publishing, 1945.

Jakeman, M. Wells. "Unusual Tree-of-Life Sculpture from Ancient Central America." *University Archaeological Society Newsletter*. No. 4, 1953, 26–49.

Josephus. Translated by William Whiston. Grand Rapids, MI: Kregel Publications, 1960.

Journal of Discourses, by Brigham Young, President of The Church of Jesus Christ of Latter-day Saints, His Two Counselors, and the Twelve Apostles. 26 Volumes. Liverpool: S. W. Richards, 1854–86. Reprinted in 1966 in Salt Lake City.

Karttunen, Frances. *An Analytical Dictionary of Nahuatl*. Austin: University of Texas Press, 1983.

Keatinge, Richard W. *Peruvian Prehistory: An Overview of Pre-Inca and Inca Society*. Cambridge: Cambridge University Press, 1988.

Kelley, David H. "A Cylinder Seal from Tlatlilco." *American Antiquity*. Volume 31, No. 5, 1966, 744.

Kelley, David H. *Deciphering the Maya Script*. Austin: University of Texas Press, 1976.

Kidder, Alfred V., Jesse D. Jennings, and Edwin M. Shook. *Excavations at Kaminaljuu, Guatemala*. Washington, DC: Carnegie Institution of Washington, 1946).

Kimball, Heber C. "Emigration—The Saints Warned to Repent or Judgments Will Come upon Them." September 28, 1856, Discourse, Salt Lake City, *Journal of Discourses*. Volume 4, 105–10. Liverpool: S. W. Richards, 1857. Reprinted in 1966 in Salt Lake City.

Kimball, Spencer W. Brigham Young University Faculty Address, September 12, 1967.

Kingsborough, Lord. *Antiquities of Mexico: Comprising Facsimiles of Ancient Mexican Paintings and Hieroglyphics*. Nine Volumes. London: Henry G. Bohn, 1848.

Knorozov, Yurii V. *Ancient Writing of Central America*. Unpublished. Translated from *Sovietskaya Etnografiya*. Volume 3, 1952, 100–18.

Knorozov, Yurii. *Maya Hieroglyphic Codices*. Translated from the Russian by Sophie D. Coe. Publication No. 8. Institute for Mesoamerican Studies, State University of New York at Albany. Albany: Institute for Mesoamerican Studies, 1982.

Krickburg, Walter. *Las Antiguas Culturas Mexicanas*. Translated from the German by Sita Garst and Jasmin Reuter. Mexico: Fondo de Cultura Economica, 1964.

Labastille, A. "The Quetzal: Fabulous Bird of Maya Land." *National Geographic Magazine*. Vol. 135, No. 1, January 1969, 140–48.

Landa, Diego de. *Relacion de las Cosas de Yucatan*. Edited with notes by Alfred M. Tozzer. Papers of the Peabody Museum of American Archaeology and Ethnology, Harvard University, Vol. 18. Cambridge, MA: The Museum, 1941.

"Latter-day Temples." *Ensign*, Vol. 2, No. 1, January 1972, 33.

Lawrence, D. H. *The Plumed Serpent*. Great Britain: The Chaucer Press, 1926.

Layton, Lynn C. "An 'Ideal' Book of Mormon Geography." *Improvement Era*. Vol. 41, No. 7, July 1938, 394–95, 439.

Lee, Harold B. "Mexico and Central America Area." General Conference Report. Salt Lake City: The Church of Jesus Christ of Latter-day Saints, 1972.

Lefgren, John C. *April Sixth*. Salt Lake City: Deseret Book, 1980.

Leonard, Johnathan Norton. *Ancient America*. New York: Time, 1967.

Leon-Portilla, Miguel. *Historia de Mexico*. Vol. 3. Mexico: Salvat Editores de Mexico, 1974.

Leon-Portilla, Miguel. *Los Antiguos Mexicanos a Traves de sus Cronicas y Cantares*. Mexico: Fondo de Cultura Economica, 1961.

Leon-Portilla, Miguel. *Quetzalcoatl*. Mexico: Fondo de Cultura Economica, 1968.

Lizana, Bernardo de. *Historia de Yucatan, Devocionario de Nuestra Senora de Izmal y Conquista Espiritual*. Mexico: n.p., 1893.

Los Hombres de Piedra: Escultura Olmeca. Mexico: Universidad Nacional Autonoma de Mexico, 1977.

Lowe, Gareth W. *Archaeological Exploration of the Upper Grijalva River, Chiapas, Mexico*. Papers of the New World Archaeological Foundation, No. 2. Provo, UT: NWAF, Brigham Young University, 1959.

Lowe, Gareth W. "Desarrollo y Function del Incensario en Izapa." *Estudios de Cultura Maya*. Volume 5, 53–64. Mexico: Universidad Nacional Autonoma de Mexico. 1965.

Lowe, Gareth W., Thomas A. Lee Jr., and Eduardo Martinez Espinosa. *Izapa: An Introduction to the Ruins and Monuments*. Papers of the New World Archaeological Foundation, No. 31. Provo, UT: NWAF, Brigham Young University, 1982.

Luckert, Karl W. *Olmec Religions: A Key to Middle America and Beyond*. Norman: University of Oklahoma Press, 1976.

Ludlow, Daniel H. *A Companion to Your Study of the Book of Mormon*. Salt Lake City: Deseret Book, 1976.

Marcus, Joyce. "Zapotec Writing." *Scientific American*. Vol. 242, No. 2, February 1980, 50–64.

Martin, Simon and Nikolai Grube. *Chronicle of the Maya Kings and Queens: Deciphering the Dynasties of the Ancient Maya*. London: Thames and Hudson, 2000.

Martinez, Maria del Carmen Rodriguez, et al. "Did the Olmec Know How to Write." *Science*, Vol. 313, No. 5793, September 15, 2006, 1537.

Matheny, Ray T. "An Early Maya Metropolis Uncovered, El Mirador." *National Geographic*, Vol. 172, No. 3, September 1987, 316–39.

Matheny, Ray T. and Deanne L. Gurr. "Ancient Hydraulic Techniques in the Chiapas Highlands." *American Scientist*. July–August 1979, 441.

Matthews, Robert J. "Notes on 'Lehi's Travels.'" *BYU Studies*. Vol. 12, No. 3, Spring 1972, 312–14.

McGavin, E. Cecil and Willard Bean. *The Geography of the Book of Mormon*. Salt Lake City: Bookcraft, 1949.

Menzies, James S. and others. *Christ in America*. Independence: Herald Publishing House, 1965.

Miner, Alan. "Did the Nephites Know of Lehi's Dream?" *The Book of Mormon Archaeological Digest*. Vol. 2, No. 4, 1999, 5–12.

Moctezuma, Eduardo Matos. *The Great Temple: Official Guide*. Mexico: Impresora Formal, 1985.

Moll, Roberto Garcia. *Las Ruinas de Palenque: Xupa y Finca Encanto*. Mexico: Instituto Nacional de Antropologia e Historia, 1923.

Monson, Thomas S. "Go for It." *Ensign*. Vol. 19, No. 5, May 1989, 43–46.

Monteflor, Eugenio P. *Pictorial Archaeology*. Mexico: Editur, 1983.

Morley, Sylvanus Griswold. *The Ancient Maya*. Revised by George W. Brainerd. Third Edition. Stanford, CA: Stanford University Press, 1956.

Morley, Sylvanus G. *An Introduction to the Study of the Maya Hieroglyphs*. New York: Dover Publications, 1975.

Myths of the New World: A Treatise on the Symbolism and Mythology of the Red Race of America. Philadelphia: David McKay, 1896.

National Geographic. Vol. 148, No. 6, December 1975; Vol. 169, No. 4, April 1986. Vol. 172, No. 3, September 1987; Vol. 176, No. 4, October 1989.

Nibley, Hugh. *Since Cumorah: The Book of Mormon in the Modern World*. Salt Lake City: Deseret Book, 1967.

Norman, V. Garth. "Astronomical Orientations of Izapa Sculptures." Unpublished Master's Thesis, Brigham Young University, 1980.

Norman, V. Garth. *Book of Mormon—Mesoamerican Geography: History Study Map*. American Fork, UT: ARCON with Ancient America Foundation, 2008.

Norman, V. Garth, *Izapa Sculpture*. Part 1: Album. Papers of the New World Archaeological Foundation, No. 30. Provo, UT: NWAF, 1973.

Norman, V. Garth. *Izapa Sculpture*. Part 2: Text. Papers of the New World Archaeological Foundation, No. 30. Provo, UT: NWAF, 1976.

Norman, V. Garth. "Joseph Smith and the Beginning of Book of Mormon Archaeology: Did the Prophet Joseph Smith in 1842 Locate Book of Mormon Lands in Middle America?" *Meridian Magazine*. 2003, www.meridianmagazine.com/ideas (accessed March 12, 2007).

Norman, V. Garth. "Tree of Life Stone Under Attack: New FARMS Drawing Creating Temporary Confusion." *Book of Mormon Archaeological Digest*. Vol. 2, No. 4, 1999, 1, 7–8, 13–14.

Nuttall, Zelia, Editor. *The Codex Nuttall: A Picture Manuscript from Ancient Mexico*. New York: Dover Publications, 1975.

The Oaxaca Valley: Official Guide. Fifth Edition in English. Mexico: Instituto Nacional de Antropologia e Historia, 1973.

Ochoa, Lorenzo and Marcia Castro. *Archeological Guide of the Park—Museum of La Venta*. Villahermosa: Tabasco State Government, 1986.

Ochoa, Lorenzo, Coordinator. *Olmecas y Mayas en Tabasco: Cinco Acercamientos*. Villahermosa: Gobierno del Estado de Tabasco, 1985.

O'Gorman, Edmundo. *Fernando de Alva Ixtlilxochitl: Obras Historicas*. Tomo I. Edicion, estudio introductoio y un appendice documental por Edmundo O'Gorman. Mexico: Universidad Nacional Autonoma de Mexico, 1985.

Ogden, D. Kelly. "Answering the Lord's Call." *Studies in Scripture, Volume 7: 1 Nephi to Alma 29*. Edited by Kent P. Jackson. Salt Lake City: Deseret Book, 1987.

Palacios, Enrique Juan and Miguel O. de Mandizabal. *Quetzalcoatl y la Irradiacion de su Cultura en el Antiguo Territorio Mexicano*. Mexico: Museo National de Arqueologia, 1921.

Palmer, David A. "Cumorah." In Daniel H. Ludlow, ed., *Encyclopedia of Mormonism*. New York: Macmillan, 1992, 1:346–47.

Palmer, David A. *In Search of Cumorah: New Evidences for the Book of Mormon from Ancient Mexico*. Bountiful, UT: Horizon Publishers, 1981.

Palmer, David A. "A Study of Mesoamerican Religious Symbolism." *SEHA Newsletter*, 103, No. 61, 1967, Brigham Young University, Provo, Utah.

Palmer, David A. "A Survey of Pre-1830 Historical Sources Relating to the Book of Mormon." *BYU Studies*. Vol. 17, No. 1, 1976, 101.

Parkes, Henry Bamford. *A History of Mexico*. Boston: Houghton Mifflin Company, 1969.

Parque—Museo de La Venta. Villahermosa: Gobierno del Estado de Tabasco, 1985.

Parry, Donald W. *The Book of Mormon Text Reformatted According to Parallelistic Patterns*. Provo, UT: Foundation for Ancient Research and Mormon Studies, 1992.

The Pearl of Great Price. First published in 1851. Salt Lake City: The Church of Jesus Christ of Latter-day Saints, 1981.

Penafiel, Antonio. *Nombres Geograficos de Mexico*. Edicion Primigenia, 1885; Segunda Edicion, 1977. Mexico: Litoimpresores, 1977.

Perez-Acevedo, Roberto. *Encuentro con Quetzalcoatl*. La Habana, Cuba: n.p., 1958.

Peterson, Frederick A. *Ancient Mexico: An Introduction to the Pre-Hispanic Cultures*. New York: Putnam, 1959.

Pina, Roman. *Bonampak*. Mexico: Instituto Nacional de Antropologia e Historia, 1961.

Potter, George D. "An Alternative Model for the Jaredite Trail." The Nephi Project, Bear River, Utah, www.nephiproject.com.

Potter, George D. "Did the Jaredites Land in Peru?" The Nephi Project, Bear River, Utah, www.nephi project.com.

Potter, George D. "A New Candidate in Arabia for the 'Valley of Lemuel.'" *Journal of Book of Mormon Studies*. Vol. 8, No. 1, 1999, 54–63.

Pratt, John P. "The Restoration of Priesthood Keys on Easter 1836; Part 1: Dating the First Easter." *Ensign*, Vol. 15, No. 6, June 1985, 59–68.

Pratt, Orson. "America a Choice Land—Its Aborigines." December 27, 1868, Salt Lake City. *Journal of Discourses*. Volume 12, 338–346. Liverpool: S. W. Richards, 1869. Reprinted in 1966 in Salt Lake City.

Pratt, Orson. "Nephite America—The Day of God's Power—The Shepherd of Israel." February 11, 1872, Salt Lake City. *Journal of Discourses*. Volume 14, 321–35. Liverpool: S. W. Richards, 1869. Reprinted in 1966 in Salt Lake City.

Prescott, Guillermo. *La Conquista del Peru*. Third Edition. Buenos Aires: Editorial Atlantida, 1956.

Prescott, William H. *History of the Conquest of Mexico*. Vol. 2. New York: John W. Lovell Co., 1843.

Prescott, William H. *The Conquest of Mexico*. Garden City: Doubleday, 1937.

Priddis, Venice. *The Book and the Map: New Insights into Book of Mormon Geography*. Salt Lake City: Bookcraft, 1975.

Puleston, Dennis E. and Donald W. Callender Jr. "Defensive Earthworks at Tikal." *Expedition*. Vol. 9, No. 3, Spring 1967, 40–48.

Quincy, Josiah. "Joseph Smith at Nauvoo." *Figures of the Past from the Leaves of Old Journals*. Boston: Roberts Brothers, 1883, 376–400.

Ramirez, J. Fernanco. *Pregrinacion Mexicana*. Vargas Rea, Editor. Mexico: Biblioteca Aportacion Historica, 1945.

Recinos, Adrian, Translator. Introduction and Notes. *Memorial de Solola Anales de Los Cakchiquele*. Guatemala: Direccion General de Antropologia y Historia, 1980.

Recinos, Adrian and Delia Goetz. *The Annals of the Cakchiquels*. Translated from the Cakchiquel Maya. Norman: University of Oklahoma Press, 1953.

Reeve, Rex C. Jr. "Hill Cumorah." In Dennis L. Largey, ed. *Book of Mormon Reference Companion*. Salt Lake City: Deseret Book, 2003, 222–24

Reynolds, George and Janne M. Sjodahl. *Commentary on the Book of Mormon*. Volume 1. Salt Lake City: Deseret Press, 1976.

Reynolds, George. *The Story of the Book of Mormon*. Salt Lake City: Jos. Hyrum Parry, 1888.

Richards, Franklin D. and James A. Little. *A Compendium of the Doctrines of the Gospel*. Salt Lake City: F. D. Richards and J. A. Little, 1886.

Riding, Alan. *Distant Neighbors: A Portrait of the Mexicans*. New York: Random House, 1984.

Roberts, B. H. *New Witnesses for God*. Volumes 1-2. Salt Lake City: Deseret News, 1909.

Roys, Ralph L. *The Book of Chilam Balam of Chumayel*. Norman: University of Oklahoma Press, 1967.

Rubio, Alfredo Barrera. *Official Guide: Uxmal*. Trans. Helen Jones-Perrot de Mandri. Mexico: Instituto Nacional de Antropologia e Historia, 1985.

Ruz, Alberto. *Chichen Itza: Official Guide*. Mexico: Instituto Nacional de Antropologia, 1973.

Ruz, Alberto. *Official Guide from Palenque*. Mexico: Instituto Nacional de Antropologia e Historia, 1978.

Ruz, Alberto. *The Mayas*. Mexico: Salvat Mexicana de Ediciones, 1983.

Ruiz, Fernando Medina. *Mayan Culture: Basic Facts*. Translated by Gillian Glass. Mexico: Panorama Editorial, 1985.

Saenz, Caesar A. *Quetzalcoatl*. Mexico: Instituto Nacional de Antropologia, 1962.

Sahagun, Fray Bernardino de. *Historia General de las Cosas de Nueva Espana: Florentine Codex*. 12 volumes. Edited and translated to English by Arthur O. Anderson and Charles E. Dibble. Santa Fe, NM: The School of American Research and the University of Utah, 1950 ff.

Sanderlin, George. Translator. *Bertolome de las Casas: A Selection of His Writings*. New York: Alfred A. Knopf, 1971.

Schaeffer, Phillip. *Lake Atitlan*. Guatemala: Phillip Schaeffer Productions, 1974.

Schele, Linda. *Maya Glyphs: The Verbs*. Austin: University of Texas Press, 1982.

Schele, Linda and David Freidel. *A Forest of Kings: The Untold Story of the Ancient Maya*. New York: William Morrow and Company, 1990.

Schele, Linda and David Stuart. *The Mayan Languages and the Writing System*. Unpublished; undated. Based on data from T. S. Kaufman, 1969.

Schele, Linda. *Workbook in Maya Hieroglyphics*. Unpublished. Texas, 1987.

Schoonmaker, Rachel. "Lehi's Journey Still Sparks Interest: BYU Students Relive the Trek." *LDS Church News*. January 2, 1988, 11, 13.

Sejourne, Laurette. *Burning Water*. Published in Spanish 1957. Translated to the English by the author and Irene Nicholson. London: Thames and Hudson, 1957.

Sejourne, Laurette. *El Universo de Quetzalcoatl*. Mexico: Fondo de Cultura Economica, 1962.

Seler, Eduard. "Die Alten Bewohner der Landschaft Michuacan." *Gesammelte Abhandiungen,* Vol. 3, 33–156. Berlin, 1908.

Sharer, Robert J. *The Ancient Maya*, 5th ed. Stanford: Stanford University Press, 1994.

Shook, Edwin M. and A. V. Kidder. *Mound E-III-3, Kaminaljuyu, Guatemala*. Carnegie Institute of Washington, Publication 396, Contribution 53, 1952.

Silverberg, Robert. *Mound Builders of Ancient America: The Archaeology of a Myth*. Athens, OH: Ohio University Press, 1968.

Skousen, Royal. *Analysis of Textual Variants of the Book of Mormon*. Provo, UT: Foundation for Ancient Research and Mormon Studies, Brigham Young University, 2004.

Skousen, Royal, Editor. *The Original Manuscript of the Book of Mormon*. Provo, UT: Foundation for Ancient Research and Mormon Studies, 2001.

Skousen, Royal. *The Printer's Manuscript of the Book of Mormon,* 2 parts. Provo, UT: Foundation for Ancient Research and Mormon Studies, 2002.

Skousen, Royal. "Towards a Critical Edition of the Book of Mormon." *BYU Studies.* Vol. 30, No. 1, Winter 1990, 42–69.

Smith, Joseph Jr., Translator. *The Book of Mormon: Another Testament of Jesus Christ.* 1981. First published in 1830. Salt Lake City: The Church of Jesus Christ of Latter-day Saints.

Smith, Joseph Jr. *Documentary History of the Church.* Volume 1, Second Edition Revised. Salt Lake City: Deseret Book, 1964.

Smith, Joseph Jr. *Documentary History of the Church.* Volume 2, Fourth Edition. Salt Lake City: Deseret Book, 1965.

Smith, Lucy Mack. *The History of Joseph Smith by His Mother.* American Fork, UT: Covenant Communications, 2004.

Smith, Robert F. *It Came to Pass in the Bible and the Book of Mormon.* Provo, UT: Foundation for Ancient Research and Mormon Studies, 1983.

Solana, Nelly Guiterrez and Daniel G. Schavelzon. *Corpus Bibliografico de la Cultura Olmeca.* Mexico: Universidad Nacional Autonoma de Mexico, 1980.

Sorenson, John L. *An Ancient American Setting for the Book of Mormon.* Salt Lake City: Deseret Book and Foundation for Ancient Research and Mormon Studies, 1985.

Sorenson, John L. "The Years of the Jaredites." Provo, UT: The Foundation for Ancient Research and Mormon Studies, 1969.

Soustelle, Jacques. *The Olmecs: The Oldest Civilization in Mexico.* Translated from the French by Helen R. Lane. Garden City, NY: Doubleday, 1984.

Spence, Lewis. *The Gods of Mexico.* New York: Frederick A. Stokes, 1923.

Sperry, Sidney B. *Book of Mormon Compendium.* Salt Lake City: Bookcraft, 1968.

Stephens, John Lloyd. *Incidents of Travel in Central America, Chiapas and Yucatan.* 2 Volumes. Illustrations by Frederick Catherwood. First published in 1841. New York: Dover Publications, 1969.

Stevenson, Joseph Grant. "The Life of Edward Stevenson, Member of the First Council of Seventy, Friend of the Prophet Joseph Smith and the Three Witnesses." Unpublished MA Thesis, Brigham Young University, 1955.

Stirling, Matthew W. "Discovering the New World's Oldest Dated Work of Man." *National Geographic,* Vol. 76, 1939, 183–218.

Stirling, Matthew W. "Early History of the Olmec Problem." *Dumbarton Oaks Conference on the Olmec.* Washington, DC: 1968, 1–8.

Stirling, Matthew W. "Expedition Unearths Buried Masterpieces of Carved Jade." *National Geographic,* Vol. 80, 1941, 277–302.

Stirling, Matthew W. "La Venta's Green Stone Tigers." *National Geographic,* Vol. 84, 1943, 321–32.

Stirling, Matthew W. "On the Trail of La Venta Man." *National Geographic*, Vol. 91, 1947, 137–72.

Stirling, Matthew W. *Stone Monuments of the Rio Chiquito, Veracruz, Mexico.* Bulletin 157. Washington, DC: Smithsonian Institution, Bureau of American Ethnology, 1955, 1–24.

Stirling, Matthew W. "The Olmec, Artists in Jade." In *Essays in Pre-Columbian Archaeology.* Edited by S. K. Lothrop. Cambridge, MA: Harvard University Press, 1946, 42–59.

Stout, Walter M. *Harmony in Book of Mormon Geography.* Las Vegas, NV: Walter M. Stout, 1950.

Stuart, David. "'The Arrival of Strangers': Teotihuacan and Tollan in Classic Maya History." In *Mesoamerica's Classic Heritage: From Teotihuacan to the Aztecs.* Edited by David Carrasco, Linda Jones, and Scott Sessions. Boulder, CO: University of Colorado, 2000, 465–513.

Stuart, George E. and Gene S. Stuart. *Discovering Man's Past in the Americas.* Washington, DC: National Geographic Society, 1969.

Taylor, John. *The Mediation and Atonement.* Salt Lake City: Deseret News, 1882.

Thomas, Cyrus. *Report on the Mound Explorations of the Bureau of Ethnology.* Washington, DC: Smithsonian Institution Press, 1985.

Thompson, J. Eric S. *Civilization of the Mayas.* Chicago: Field Museum of National History, 1942.

Thompson, J. Eric S. *A Correlation of the Mayan and European Calendars.* Chicago Natural History Museum of Anthropology Series. Vol. 17. Chicago: Field Museum of Natural History, 1927.

Thompson, J. Eric S. *Maya Hieroglyphic Writing: An Introduction.* Norman: University of Oklahoma Press, 1932, 1960, 1971.

Thompson, J. Eric S. *Maya History and Religion.* Norman: University of Oklahoma Press, 1970.

Thompson, J. Eric S. *The Rise and Fall of Maya Civilization.* Second Edition. Norman: University of Oklahoma Press, 1966.

The Times and Seasons. Volumes 1–6, 1839–46, Nauvoo, Illinois. Editors: November 1839–December 1840, E. Robinson and D. C. Smith; January–August 2, 1841, D. C. Smith (with R. B. Thompson, May–August 1841); August 16, 1841–February 1, 1842, E. Robinson (with G. Hills, February 1, 1842); February 15–October 1842, Joseph Smith; November 1842–February 15, 1846, John Taylor. Publisher varies: November 1839–December 1840, Robinson and Smith; January–August 2, 1841, D. C. Smith; August 16, 1841–February 1842, E. Robinson; March–October 1842, Joseph Smith; November 1842–February 15, 1846, John Taylor. Salt Lake City: Modern Microfilm Co., 1963.

Torquemada, Juan de. *Monarchia Indiana*. Vol. 1, as translated and condensed in Hubert Howe Bancroft, *Myths and Languages*, Vol. 3 of *The Native Races*. San Francisco: A. L. Bancroft, 1883.

Torre, Concepcion de la and Antonio Perez Elias. *El Tajin: Official Guide*. Mexico: Instituto Nacional de Antropologia e Historia, 1976.

Tozzer, Alfred M., Editor of Translation. *Landa's Relacion de las Cosas de Yucatan*. Papers of the Peabody Museum of American Archaeology and Ethnology, Harvard University, Vol. 18. Cambridge, MA: The Museum, 1941.

Treat, Raymond. "Wheat and Barley: Problem or Opportunity." *The Zarahemla Record*. September 1978, 7.

Tula: Official Guide. Mexico: Instituto Nacional de Antropologia, 1968.

Un Palacio en la Ciudad de los Dioses-Teotihuacan. Mexico: Instituto Nacional de Antropologia e Historia, 1959.

Vaillant, George C. *The Aztecs of Mexico*. American Museum of Natural History Science Series. Garden City, NY: Doubleday, Doran and Co., 1941.

The Virgin and the Serpent-God. Mexico: Editorial Orogreso, 1966.

Vogt, Jorge A. Summary and Appraisal. *Desorrollo Cultural de Los Mayas*. Edited by Evon Z. Vogt and Alberto Ruz, 409–47. Mexico: Universidad Nacional Autonoma de Mexico, 1971.

Von Hagen, Victor W. *The Ancient Sun Kingdoms of the Americas*. Cleveland: World Publishing Company, 1957.

Warren, Bruce W. "Jaredite King Name Discovered." *Explorations in the Book of Mormon*. Orem, UT: Book of Mormon Tours, 1999, 9–13.

Warren, Bruce W. "1 Ben 6 Mak: Part Two." *Book of Mormon Archaeological Digest*. Vol. 2, No. 3, 1999, 1, 4–5, 13.

Warren, Bruce W. and Thomas S. Ferguson. *The Messiah in Ancient America*. Provo, UT: Book of Mormon Research Foundation, 1987.

Washburn, J. Nile. *Book of Mormon Geography for Sunday School Teachers and Others*. Unpublished.

Washburn, J. Nile. *Book of Mormon Lands and Times*. Bountiful, UT: Horizon Publishers, 1974.

Waters, Frank. *Book of the Hopi*. New York: Penguin Books, 1977.

Webster, Noah. *An American Dictionary of the English Language*. New York: S. Converse, 1828. Facsimile of first edition by the Foundation for American Christian Education.

Welch, John W., Editor. *Chiasmus in Antiquity: Structures, Analyses, Exegisis*. Hildesheim: Gerstenberg, 1981.

Welch, John W. "Chiasmus in the Book of Mormon." Reprint No. WEL-69. Provo, UT: Foundation for Ancient Research and Mormon Studies, 1969.

Wellington, Richard and George Potter. "Lehi's Trail from the Valley of Lemuel to Nephi's Harbor." The Nephi Project, Bear River, Utah, www.nephi project.com.

Wicke, Charles and others. *Mesoamerican Notes*. Nos. 5–8. Mexico: Department of Anthropology, Mexico City College, 1957–66.

Widstoe, John A. "Is Book of Mormon Geography Known?" In *A Book of Mormon Treasury*. Salt Lake City: Bookcraft, 1959.

Wilhelm, John. *Guide to Mexico City*. 16th edition. Mexico: Ediciones Tolteca, 1975.

Wilkie, James W. *The Mexican Revolution: Federal Expenditure and Social Change Since 1910*. 2nd Edition. Berkeley and Los Angeles: University of California Press, 1970.

Wilkinson, Ernest L. and W. Cleon Skousen. *Brigham Young University: A School of Destiny*. Provo, UT: Brigham Young University Press, 1976.

Willard, Theodore Arthur. *The City of the Sacred Well*. New York: Century Company, 1926.

Wirth, Diane E. *A Challenge to the Critics: Scholarly Evidences of the Book of Mormon*. Bountiful, UT: Horizon Publishers, 1986.

Wirth, Diane E. *Discoveries of the Truth*. Santa Clara, CA: Vanguard Graphics, 1978.

Wirth, Diane E. *Parallels, Mesoamerican and Ancient Middle Eastern Traditions*. St. George, UT: Stonecliff Publishing, 2003.

Wirth, Diane E. "Quetzalcoatl, the Maya Maize God, and Jesus Christ." *Journal of Book of Mormon Studies*. Vol. 11, No. 1, 2002, 4–15.

Wirth, Diane E. "A Review by Diane E. Wirth," *Book of Mormon Archaeological Digest*. Vol 2, No. 4, 1999, 5, 11.

Yorgason, Blaine M., Bruce W. Warren, and Harold Brown. *New Evidences of Christ in Ancient America*. Provo, UT: Stratford Books, 1999.

Young, Brigham. "Trying to Be Saints, etc." June 17, 1877 Discourse, Farmington, Utah. *Journal of Discourses*. Vol. 19, 36–45. Liverpool: S. W. Richards, 1857. Reprinted in 1966 in Salt Lake City.

Zabre, Alfonso Teja. *Historia de Mexico*. Mexico: Ediciones Botas, 1961.

Scripture References

Index

You can easily determine the corresponding chapter number and chapter title for any page number by consulting the "index to page numbers" at the bottom of every odd-numbered page. The first column contains the continuous page numbers for a chapter, the second column contains the chapter number, and the third column contains the chapter title. In the index, slash marks between numbers indicate chapter divisions.

Abbreviations: BofM = Book of Mormon; MA = Mesoamerica

Aaron: 48

City of (Alma 50:14; land southward; land of Zarahemla; associated with city of Moroni near the east sea): 158 / 393 / 420 / 615, 618 / 745, 762, 772 / 815

Jaredite king: 120

Lamanite king (Mormon 2:9; led army of 44,000; AD 336): 700, 705–6

Son of Mosiah (ca. 100 BC; missionary to land of Mormon): 402–3, 422, 425 / 485 / 630, 640–43 / 735–37, 739–40

Abaj Takalik (ah BAH tahk ah LEEK; Maya/Olmec site in Guatemala): 65 / 570

Abinadi (Nephi prophet; suffered martyr's death by fire; ca 150 BC): viii, xix / 42 / 74 / 107 / 356 / 426 / 471 / 562 / 577–78, 585, 593 / 637–38 / 676 / 722, 728 / 755, 760 / 807

Abinadom (Nephite historian; son of Chemish; 279– BC): 721 / 746

Ablom, city of (Ether 9:3; Jaredite city by the seashore; land northward): 379, 395 / 436 / 696

Abrea, Angel (LDS Church Missionary Department): 717

Acapulco (ah kah POOL koh; resort city in Mexico): 120 / 208–9 / 431, 438, 446 / 633

Acayucan (ah kah YOO kahn; modern city in Veracruz, Mexico): 121 / 233 / 458, 464–65 / 549 / 622 / 633, 670 / 685, 699

Adena: 465 / 715

Afterlife: 305–6

Agosh, plains of (Ether 14:15–16; Jaredite site; land northward): 395

Agriculture/agricultural: 88, 97 / 120 / 145 / 197 / 227 / 322, 326 / 358–59, 361, 364 / 540 / 580 / 670 / 649, 656 / 700 / 723–25, 734

Agrinier, Pierre (archaeologist, New World Archaeological Foundation): 388

Aguas Azules (waterfalls in state of Chiapas): 541

Aguateca (Maya site; potential site for Nephihah): 618

Alexander, David (editor, Bible handbook): 69

Alexander, Pat (editor, Bible handbook): 69

Al Kunfidah (Nahom; Old World site associated with Lehi): 522

Allen, Blake Joseph (author; photographer): viii–ix, xi–xiii, xix, xxi–xxvii / 23 / 29, 40–41 / 55 / 87, 94 / 121 / 221 / 321 / 382 / 724 / 745 / 780, 794 / 811, 813

Allen, Blake J. II (contributor to project): xv

Allen, Brent J. (author; foreword): xiii

Allen, Jessica: ix / 399

Allen, Johannah (contributor to project): xv

Allen, Joseph Lovell (author): viii, xi–xiii, xix, xxi, xxiii–xxvii / 1 / 23–24 / 55–56 / 86–87 / 106, 116 / 166, 168 / 206 / 221, 239, 242–43 / 257–58 / 267 / 285 / 311–12, 315, 318, 331 / 335 / 363 / 371–72, 390, 393, 397 / 522 / 595, 609, 618–19 / 698 / 766 / 785 / 808, 813

Allen, Nathan T. (photographer): xv / 94, 375

Allen, Todd B. (tour director): xv, xxv / 334, 350

Allen, Troy R. (contributor to project): xv

Allred, Verle and Alyce (tour participants): xviii

Alma:

Nephite prophet (Mosiah 17:2; Alma the elder; priest of Noah; baptizes at Waters of Mormon; flees to land of Helam; flees to Zarahemla; founder of Church; 173–91 BC): xix / 11, 13 / 29 / 74 / 88 / 167 / 242 / 340 / 363 / 389, 394 / 425 / 471, 484 / 562, 564–65 / 568–69, 572, 577–82, 592–93 / 637–39, 641–46, 648–52, 657 / 676–79, 682 / 719, 711, 742 / 749, 755–56, 760 / 809

Son of Alma (Alma the younger; first chief judge; ca. 100–73 BC): 11 / 29, 37–38, 42 / 165 / 230, 242 / 247 / 304–5 / 337, 339–40 / 354, 362, 364 / 393 / 413, 420, 426 / 447 / 519 / 588–89 / 625 / 651–55, 657 / 679–80 / 737–38 / 745, 762–65, 767–72, 774 / 811

Valley of (a day's travel north of the city of Helam): 87–88 / 562 / 569, 579, 581–82, 593 / 650 / 675–78 / 743

Almaraz, Ramon (author; Teotihuacan): 196

Almolonga (ahl moh LOHN gah; village in Quetzaltenango, Guatemala; proposed land of

Helam; a land of pure water): 86–87 / 147 / 221 / 579–81 / 639, 645, 648–50, 673 / 743 / 809, 814

Altar 10 (also called Stela 10, Kaminaljuyu, Guatemala): 65 / 155–56 / 719, 725–29, 743 / 815

Alta Verapaz (archaeological site; Guatemala; near the headwaters of the Grijalva/Usumacinta Rivers): 663

Altun Ha (ahl TOON hah; Maya archaeological site in Belize): 143 / 596, 618

Alvarado (modern city in Veracruz, Mexico, near the Papaloapan water basin): 128 / 465 / 672

Alvarado, Pedro de (Spanish conqueror of Guatemala): 251

Amaleki (Nephite record keeper; ca. 130 BC): 8 / 471 / 562 / 721, 733 / 746, 761

Amalekites (Nephite dissenters): 640 / 737

Amalickiah (Nephite traitor; ca. 70 BC): 94 / 159 / 444, 451–52 / 605–8, 618, 622 / 632–33 / 706, 709 / 766

Amaron (Nephite record keeper; son of Omni): 145 / 721 / 746

Amatitlan, valley of (ah mah teet LAHN; valley and lake south of Guatemala City): 734

Amlici (Nephite dissenter; ca. 87 BC): 651–52

Amlicites (Nephite dissenters who desire a king): 379 / 651–52 / 679–80 / 772, 774

Ammaron (Nephite record keeper; gives responsibility for all plates to Mormon; ca. AD 306): 44 / 186 / 683–84, 695–96, 698–99 / 766 / 783, 786

Ammon (son of Mosiah; missionary to Lamanites; ca. 100 BC): 10 / 53 / 130 / 402–3 / 561–62, 564 / 569, 575–77, 582 / 588 / 624 / 640–41, 646–48, 665 / 733–34, 736–37, 740–42 / 755–56 / 809

People of (converted Lamanites; also known as Anti-Nephi-Lehies): 210 / 588 / 619, 624 / 635, 658 / 765–66

Ammonihah:

City of (Alma 8:6; 16:1–2; western end of the central depression of Chiapas; near cities of Melek, Noah, and Aaron; destroyed by Lamanites): 29, 43 / 156 / 247–48 / 393 / 412–13, 420 / 588 / 598–600 / 657 / 745, 762–63, 767–73

Land of (three days' journey on the north of the land of Melek; west of the river Sidon): 47 / 271 / 353 / 412–13 / 588 / 598 / 767, 770, 772

Ammoron *(Nephite dissenter; brother of Amalickiah; descendant of Zoram who came with Lehi; ca. 66–61 BC):* 94 / 605, 607–8, 617 / 632–33, 637

Amnihu, hill *(Alma 2:15; land southward; on east of river Sidon):* 651–52

Amulek *(missionary companion of Alma the younger; ca. 82–74 BC):* 29 / 247 / 305 / 366 / 413, 426 / 588 / 763, 767–71, 773

Amulon:
    City of (land southward): 394 / 720, 740, 742
    Land of (land southward; in greater land of Nephi; between Nephi and Zarahemla; department of Quetzaltenango, Guatemala): 394 / 720, 742, 743
    Priest of King Noah: 29 / 250 / 484 / 581 / 640 / 677 / 737, 742

Anderson, Arthur O. *(translator of Florentine Codex, writings of Sahagun):* 7 / 206 / 285 / 311 / 537

Anthon, Charles *(professor consulted by Martin Harris about the Book of Mormon translation):* 90

Angostura Dam *(dam on Grijalva River, Chiapas, Mexico):* 680 / 757

Annals of the Cakchiquels *(native document from Iximche):* 250–51, 256–57 / 540 / 645

Antigua *(ahn TEEG hwah; tourist city in Guatemala):* 647 / 733, 741

And it came to pass: 23–25, 27–28, 50–51 / 167

And then it came to pass: 26–27

Angola, city of *(Mormon 2:4; land southward):* 395 / 786

Ani-Anti, city of *(Alma 21:11; land southward; Lamanite city in land of Nephi):* 393–94 / 737, 739–40

Anti-Nephi-Lehi *(Lamanite brother of Lamoni):* 413, 425 / 563–64 / 635 / 765

Antiomno *(Lamanite king; first century BC):* 741

Antionum, land of *(Alma 31:3; land southward; southwestern Belize):* 624 / 658 / 815

Antiparah, city of *(Nephite city):* 393 / 620 / 745

Antipus *(Nephite commander; ca. 65 BC):* 620 / 682

Apostasy:
    New World: 58–59, 77, 79–80 / 161 / 199, 206–7 / 233 / 312, 331 / 726 / 777–97 / 800, 814
    Old World: 58 / 208 / 331 / 506–8 / 779

Archaeologist: 26, 33 / 64, 73 / 86, 91–93, 101 / 107, 109–12, 115, 117–19, 122, 124, 126, 132 / 135, 137–38, 140, 142, 144, 165–66 / 174, 176, 178, 182, 184–85 / 197 / 236–38 / 146–49 / 271 / 303 / 310, 317, 319 / 334, 339 / 354, 358, 360 / 380, 387–89 / 427 / 432, 460 / 501 / 536 / 550 / 598, 601–2, 611 / 688, 698, 703, 712 / 723, 726 / 737 / 757–58 / 793

Archaeology/archaeological:
    Aaron: 420
    Altun Ha: 618
    Atitlan, Lake: 485 / 639, 641, 643 / 738–39
    Becan: 139 / 487 / 601, 609 / 699
    Belize: 618
    Bolivia: 2 / 167
    Bonampak: 472, 487
    Book of Mormon: xxiii / 17–18, 20–21 / 30, 52 / 66, 73 / 85–86, 91, 94 / 116–17, 126 / 135, 138, 140, 146–47, 163 / 204, 210 / 227 / 246 / 360 / 386, 388–89, 395 / 447 / 470 / 502 / 544 / 602, 611 / 723 / 750
    Brigham Young University: 45
    Catemaco, Lake: 117
    Cerro de Oro: 645
    Cerros: 94, 139 / 601, 604–5, 608–10 / 766
    Chiapa de Corzo: 139 / 489 / 699 / 745 / 770–71
    Chiapas depression: 657 / 649, 756, 773
    Chiapas, state of: 229
    Chichen Itza: 64 / 91, 93 / 139 / 371
    Chiutinamit: 645
    Cholula: 140
    Chukumuk: 645

La Venta: 68 / 105–6, 108, 110–11, 114–15, 118 / 463, 465 / 775

Maya: 4 / 29 / 135, 137, 139–40, 143, 153, 159, 162, 165 / 247 / 421, 427

Mesoamerica: 12, 14, 20 / 29, 33, 52 / 56–57, 59, 66, 73, 79, 83 / 85, 90–91 / 122, 131 / 138, 140 / 146–47, 161, 163–64 / 235 / 242 / 246 / 303 / 310, 319 / 359–60 / 374, 387, 380, 387–89, 395 / 422 / 462 / 470, 476 / 497, 502, 507 / 544 / 598, 602, 609, 618 / 673 / 698, 701 / 779, 783, 791, 793

Mexico, country of: 2 / 167

Mexico, state of: 213 / 447, 450

Mitla: 91 / 139

Monte Alban: 76 / 85, 91 / 139 / 172–73, 175–80, 182–83, 185–86 / 433 / 476 / 536 / 573 / 751–53

Monte Alto: 735

Mulekites: 16 / 151, 165 / 534, 540–41, 544–45 / 651 / 751

Narrow pass: 551

Nephihah: 420

Nephites: 16 / 57 / 86 / 135, 137, 164–65 / 183 / 525, 540, 544 / 651, 667 / 710 / 751

New York Cumorah: 702, 713, 717

Oaxaca, state of: 177 / 447, 450

Palenque: 4 / 26 / 92–93 / 139–40 / 166 / 371 / 472

Papaloapan water basin: 117

Peru: 2 / 167 / 372

Pomoca: 541

Puebla, state of: 447, 450

Pusilha: 618

Guatemala: 78

Quirigua: 4 / 371

Moroni: 484

San Jose Mogote: 67 / 174 / 461

San Lorenzo: 12 / 68 / 115, 132 / 463, 465

Santa Rosa: 483 / 654 / 680 / 749, 757–58, 764, 770

Tabasco, state of: 121 / 464

Tenochtitlan: 96

Tehuantepec, Isthmus of: 545

Teotihuacan: 79 / 91, 93 / 138 /193, 204, 208, 210 / 455, 464 / 699

Tierra Blanca: 541

Tikal: 55, 75 / 94 / 139 / 487 / 601, 611 / 698–99, 710

Tonala: 411–12 / 633

Tonina: 371

Tours to: 95

Tres Zapotes: 68 / 116–17 / 219 / 463, 465 / 672 / 681, 688

Tula: 289

Tulum: 139 / 371

Uaxactun: 487

Usumacinta River: 661, 663–64 / 770, 775

Uxmal: 4 / 78 / 93 / 139–40, 163 / 371 / 487 / 544 / 781

Veracruz, state of: 121 / 447, 464

Vigia, Hill: 116–17 / 688–89, 691

Xochicalco: 208

Yucatan: 64, 78 / 91 / 448

Zarahemla, land of: 542

Architecture/architectural: 24 / 67, 78 / 100–1, 103 / 139, 147, 155–56, 161, 168 / 178, 186 / 200–1, 206 / 320 / 712 / 724, 729 / 758 / 781, 784 / 802

Armillas, Pedro (author; Quetzalcoatl): 317

Asay, David C. (chairman of Book of Mormon Archaeological Forum): xvii

Aston, Warren (author; Lehi's travels in Old World): 517, 524

Astronomy: 21 / 287 / 354 / 468

Atitlan, Lake (ah teet LAHN; borders of the land of Nephi; likely candidate for the waters of Mormon): 58 / 86–87 /160 / 256, 259 / 392 / 454 / 467–68, 471, 485 / 529 / 578–81 / 638–46, 648–49, 673 / 711 / 725, 728, 733, 737–39, 741, 743 / 756–57 / 814

Atlantic Ocean: 89, 102 / 275 / 282, 293 / 392 / 403–6, 418 / 431, 436, 458 / 470, 479 / 498–99, 501 / 529, 534, 537–38, 541 / 548, 554, 556–57 / 577 / 598, 615 / 628–29, 665, 673 / 699 / 720 / 765 / 815

Aztec: xxix–xxx / 30, 43–44, 46 / 59–62, 80–81 / 96–97, 99, 101 / 137 / 173 / 193–94, 203, 206, 208 / 218, 236 / 259 / 268, 273, 276 / 282, 284–85, 293 / 295–96, 298 / 309–10, 315–16, 319, 321, 326, 329 / 428, 456, 462 / 502 / 583 / 648, 670 / 699 / 793–95

Calendar: 59–62 / 124 / 273 / 455

B

Babylonians: 8 / 69–73 / 180, 182 / 206 / 255 / 504 / 516, 533–38 / 750

Balam (Jaredite/Maya word; also Balaam): 43, 48 / 133 / 705

Balderas, Celia (translator): xviii

Bancroft, Hubert Howe (author; native races): 90 / 252 / 321, 324

Baptism:

BofM: 302–3 / 311 / 650 / 676

MA: 283 / 302–3 / 309, 311, 323 / 309, 311, 323 / 768

Barrier: 89, 103 / 128 / 413 / 550–51, 556, 558 / 599–601 / 667

Bartra, Agusti (author; Quetzalcoatl): 319

Batres, Leopoldo (first director of Teotihuacan restoration): 196

Beans: 120 / 147 / 197, 199 / 256 / 354, 358–59 (neas), 361 / 721, 723–24, 735

Becan (bay KAHN; Maya archaeological site in Campeche, Mexico): 94–95 / 139 / 360 / 467, 471–72, 474, 477, 484, 486–87 / 601–2, 603, 609–10 / 664 / 699 /

Belief: 281, 285, 288/ 306 / 316, 330 / 355 / 726, 728 / 783

Belize: 5 / 41, 45 / 94–95, 98 / 137, 143, 153, 158–60 / 202 / 215 / 307 / 389, 392–93 / 405–6, 416–18, 420 / 440, 443, 448, 454 / 467, 471–72, 474, 477, 484, 486–87 / 569 / 595–98, 602, 605, 608–10, 618–21, 623 / 632, 635, 637 / 699, 710 / 720, 730 / 748, 765–66 / 814

Benjamin (Nephite king; land of Zarahemla; second century BC): xix / 28 / 76 / 146, 156 / 230, 242 / 561 / 613 / 721–22 / 755, 760–63

Benjamin Cluff Expedition: 217 / 382–83

Benson, Ezra Taft (thirteenth President of The Church of Jesus Christ of Latter-day Saints, 1985–94): 15 / 398–99

Bering Strait: 148–49

Bernal, Ignacio (Mexican archaeologist): xv / 67 / 98 / 174, 183, 186–87, 189 / 238 / 511 / 751, 754

Berrett, Richard and JoAn (tour participants): xviii

Black, Don (tour participant): xvii

Blom, Frans (archaeologist; author; Maya): xvii / 111 / 258, 260–61 / 369

Boaz, city of (Nephite city, land northward): 395 / 464 / 788

Boice, Cortney (photographer): xv / 147, 160 / 353, 359, 363 / 454 / 472, 474, 490 / 549–50, 556, 560, 563 / 578 / 613 / 640, 649, 651, 668 / 675, 711 / 719, 725, 733–34, 742–43 / 745, 752, 771, 774 / 780, 796 / 799, 805

Bolivia: 2 /167 / 702

Bonampak (boh nahm PAHK; Maya archaeological site in Chiapas): 472, 487 / 596

Books of Chilam Balam: 250, 257 / 305

Borders:
By the seashore: 405, 417, 419, 423 / 443, 458 / 527 / 570 / 597, 603, 606, 608, 615–16, 618, 621–22 / 670 / 681, 695

By the east sea: 418 / 637

By the west sea: 632–33

Of the city of Ammonihah: 598

Of the east sea: 415 / 620–21

Of the Lamanites: 405 / 484–85 / 617 / 639 / 742

Of the land: 578, 582, 589 / 638–39, 642 / 655, 670 / 735, 737

Of the land Bountiful: 204, 208 / 445–46 / 480 / 553 / 633, 670

Of the land by the west sea: 632

Of the land Desolation: 444 / 551–52 / 621 / 634

Of the land of Manti: 657, 659

Of the land of Mormon: 485

Of the land of Moroni: 617

Of the land of Nephi: 578 / 635, 641–42

Of the land of the Lamanites: 640–41

Of the land of Zarahemla: 405, 412–13 / 564

Of the Nephites: 620

Of the Red Sea: 520

Of the seashore: 158 / 404–5, 419–20, 423 / 552 / 572 / 598, 616, 620 / 629, 655, 664

Of the waters of Mormon: 645

Of the wilderness: 404, 423 / 572–73, 588–90 / 629, 654–55, 664–65 / 765

Bountiful:
City of (Alma 52:17, 39; 53:3–4; 3 Nephi 11:1; in land of Bountiful; land southward; northward and inland from the city of Mulek, which was on the eastern seashore within a day's march of Bountiful; possibly Dzibanche or Kohunlich): 95 / 167 / 285–86 / 379, 397 / 445 / 477 / 504 / 602–5, 603–5, 609–10, 612–15 / 623–25 / 685 / 759, 763, 766, 772

Country/state of: 307 / 419 / 477, 480 / 615 /

Land of (Alma 22:31; 63:5; 3 Nephi 3:23; land southward; southern Yucatan Peninsula): 48 / 129 / 157, 159 / 180 / 104 / 267, 276 / 307 / 310, 321 / 406–12, 415, 415, 421–25 / 435, 438, 443–46, 449, 451, 457 / 467, 470, 472, 476–77, 480–81, 491 / 537–38, 540 / 549, 553–55 / 586, 588, 590–91 / 602, 605, 609, 612–15, 620, 624–25 / 630–31, 633, 635, 660, 670 / 731 / 745, 749 / 814

Old World: 496, 507, 509–10 / 515, 518–19, 521–25 / 813

Bourbourg, Brasseur de (publisher of the Troanus Codex, which is part of the Madrid Codex): 248, 256 / 296

Brass plates: 33, 39 / 469 / 533 / 685

Call, Erin (retired, Second Council of Seventy, The Church of Jesus Christ of Latter-day Saints): 806

Call, Waldo (formerly a member of the Quorum of the Seventy, The Church of Jesus Christ of Latter-day Saints): 806

Campeche (kahm PAY chay; state in Mexico): 5 / 93–94 / 150, 167 / 362 / 419 / 440, 444–45, 448, 451, 458 / 467–68, 472, 477, 488 / 529, 536–37, 539–41 / 551–52 / 574–75, 588 / 621 / 666–67, 673 *Bay of:* 74 / 150, 155 / 540–41, 545 / 605 / 655

Cancun (kahn KOON; Maya name of resort city in Mexico): xix / 44 / 57 / 194 / 299 / 477 / 778

Cannon, George Q. (former member of First Presidency, The Church of Jesus Christ of Latter-day Saints): 381–82

Caracol (kahr ah KOHL; Maya site in northern Belize): 618, 620

Carcass (also carcase; types and shadows; parable of the carcass): 584–86

Cardinal directions: xxv / 360–61 / 391 / 430 / 628

Caribbean: 56–57 / 89, 102 / 152, 158, 160 / 310 / 379, 392 / 406, 420 / 443 / 595, 605, 608, 615, 620, 623 / 631, 635, 637 / 765 / 778

Casas, San Bartolome de las (Spanish priest in sixteenth century): xviii / 257–59

Casas, San Cristobal de las (city in mountains of Chiapas, Mexico): 238 / 295

Caso, Alfonso (Mexican archaeologist; discoverer of Monte Alban): xvii / 92 / 109 / 176, 178 / 249 / 324 / 384

Castro, Marcia (author; La Venta): 150 / 540–41

Catemaco, Lake (kah tay MAH koh; village and lake in Veracruz, Mexico): 44 / 117 / 668–69 / 686

Catherwood, Frederick (artist and companion of John Lloyd Stephens): xvii / 4–5 / 86–88, 90 / 166 / 213 / 371, 374–75, 396 / 491–92 / 557–58, 565 / 572

Catholic Church: 31 / 80 / 163 / 189–90 / 197 / 258, 261 / 275 / 282–83, 285 / 295–96 / 454 / 769 / 797 / 801, 804

Causeway: 259 / 300 / 601 / 795

Ceiba tree (SAY bah; name of national tree of Guatemala): 215, 222 / 342

Cement: 3 / 200, 210, 212–13 / 354–56, 367 / 693

Central America: xvi / 4–5 / 82 / 87, 91 / 216–18, 220 / 251, 254 / 267 / 293 / 325 / 375–76, 382–83, 386, 388 / 414 / 445, 458 / 493 / 580 / 628, 649–50, 666 / 702 / 733 / 786 / 800, 802, 809

Ceren (archaeological site in El Salvador covered by volcanic dust ca. AD 500): 354

Cerro de Oro (small volcanic hill on borders of Lake Atitlan, Guatemala): 645 / 738–39

Cerros (SETR ohs; Spanish word for hills; site in Belize; possibly the city of Mulek): 94–95 / 139, 152, 159 / 389 / 601, 603–10, 615 / 766

Chamula natives: 588 / 768–69

Chan Balam (son of Pacal at Palenque): 23

Chan, Roman Pina (Mexican archaeologist): 237 / 320

Chapultepec (chah POOL tay pekh; Nahuatl name of park in Mexico City): 13 / 30, 46

Chavero, Alfredo (author of works of Ixtlilxochitl): 258 / 263–67, 279 / 327 / 792–93

Chavin people: 372 / 492 / 501–2

Cheesman, Paul (retired Brigham Young University religion professor; tour participant): xviii / 388

Chemish (book of Omni): 421 / 746

Chetumal (chay too MAHL; city and state in Mexico): 443 / 605, 609

Chiapa de Corzo (chee AH pah day KOR soh; city and site in Chiapas, Mexico): 58, 63, 65 / 92 / 139, 143, 150, 153, 156–57, 159, 164 / 489 / 541 / 613 / 651, 653, 663 / 699 / 745, 752, 758–59, 770–72

Chiapas (chee AH pahs; name of state in Mexico):
4–5 / 28, 45–46 / 58–59, 63, 74, 76 / 86, 89, 92–93,
97, 102 / 112, 132 / 135, 143, 149–50, 153–56 / 172–
73, 177, 183, 185 / 195 / 217–18, 228–30, 235–37 /
259 / 306–7 / 333 / 353, 357–59, 362 / 380, 387,
390, 392 / 404–7, 409–10, 415–17 / 434–35, 438,
440, 446, 448, 454, 458, 463–64 / 467, 471–73,
475, 477, 482, 484, 486, 490 / 504 / 527, 529, 531–
32, 536–37, 540–41, 543, 545 / 549, 556, 558–60,
562–63, 565 / 568–69, 572–73, 577, 579–80, 587–
88, 591 / 596–97, 613, 619 / 650, 653–54, 656–57,
663, 668, 670 / 675, 679, 683, 699–701, 705, 709,
712 / 730 / 747–48, 750–51, 753–54, 756–58, 760–
62, 764–65, 769–70, 773–75 / 787 / 805
Central depression: 150 / 217 / 390 / 411–12 /
462 / 471 / 541 / 573, 590 / 596–97 / 596–97 /
653–54, 656 / 680 / 737 / 748, 752, 756, 764, 768,
771, 774
Mountains: 410 / 449, 462–63, 474, 481 / 541 /
587–88, 590 / 666 / 679 / 768, 774
Valley: 204 / 565 / 574 / 650–53, 656, 658, 661–
62 / 737 / 748–49, 752, 754, 774 / 814
Wilderness: 112–14 / 659

Chiasmus: xvi / 35, 38–41, 51 / 241 / 253 / 334, 341,
350 / 422–23, 424
Chicanna (chee kah NAH): 782
*Chichen Itza (chee CHEN eet SAH; Maya name
of village and site):* 23, 31, 43–44, 48 / 59, 64 /
91–93 / 139, 141, 167 / 203 / 299–300, 303 / 315,
320, 325, 331 / 354–55, 368–68 / 371, 384 / 479 /
778, 793
*Chichicastenango (chee chee kahs tay NAHN goh;
Nahuatl name of city in Guatemala; place
where* Popol Vuh *was discovered):* 30, 37 / 251 /
363 / 529 / 642 / 733
*Chichimeca (chee chee MAY kah; ancient tribal
name in Mesoamerica):* 265, 267, 269–73, 279 /
286 / 460
Chichimecatl (chee chee may KAH tl): 47 / 270–72
*Chicuasen Dam (chee kwah SEHN; man-made dam
along the Grijalva River):* 541 / 654
Chile (CHEE lay; country in South America): 376,
378, 396 / 500 / 526, 530
*Chimaltenango (chee mahl tay NAHN goh;
Nahuatl name of city in Guatemala):* xx / 358 /
647, 673 / 732, 736, 741

Chiutinamit (chee oo teen ah MEET; ancient Maya city at Lake Atitlan): 641, 645 / 738–39

Choc, Pablo (early LDS Church member from Patzicia, Guatemala): 741 / 811

Cholula (choh LOO lah; large pyramid in Cholula, Puebla): 101, 103 / 140 / 199, 202–3 / 273–77 / 325–26, 329–30 / 447–48, 455, 464–65 / 550 / 793

Christ: viii, xi, xv, xix, xxii, xvii / 28, 38–40, 42 / 56, 61, 65, 69, 81 / 133 / 156 / 206–8 / 240, 242–43 / 275–77 / 282, 286–88 / 304 / 311–13, 321–22, 324–29 / 333–51 / 356, 367 / 401, 425–26 / 493 / 504–5, 510 / 519 / 592–93 / 611, 614 / 640–41, 646, 648, 669–70 / 677, 692–93, 703–4, 706 / 739 / 759–61, 767, 769–70 / 788–79, 781, 792 / 800, 802–3, 812–15

Advent of: 271, 273 / 285 / 329 / 348, 350 / 592 / 739 / 800

Appearance in New World: 76–77 / 95 / 159–60 / 185–86 / 206 / 267, 276–77 / 287–88 / 310–12, 313, 318–19, 321, 324, 327, 330 / 357, 369 / 377, 397 / 402 / 447 / 588–89 / 605, 610–11, 613–14 / 625 / 635, 670 / 685, 695, 707 / 751, 759, 767, 772 / 801, 810

Ascension of: 77 / 273 / 285 / 670

Atonement: 39, 42 / 242 / 334–35, 338, 342–44, 348 / 506 / 523 / 649 / 677 / 767

Baptism of: 2

Birth of: 2 / 56, 61, 69, 71–72, 76 / 82 / 159 / 184–85 / 211 / 232 / 273, 278 / 322–23, 327 / 354, 357 / 376 / 449, 452 / 532 / 549 / 589–90 / 676 / 751 / 799–800

Crucifixion of: 75 / 159 / 218 / 269 / 304 / 329 / 452–53, 455, 464 / 482–83, 485 / 611, 617 / 640, 644 / 711 / 720, 737–38 / 799

Death of: 16 / 56, 76–77, 82 / 184–85 / 232 / 266, 269–70, 273, 278–79 / 304 / 318, 328–29 / 379, 394 / 419 / 456 / 472 / 590 / 611–12 / 641, 643 / 682 / 751, 764

Resurrection: 2 / 76 / 277 / 319, 325, 331 / 611–12 / 648 / 739 / 799

Tree of Life: 333–51

Words of: 583

Christensen, Ross T. (LDS archaeologist, deceased): 236–37

Christenson, Allen J. (translator of Popol Vuh*):* xvii / 37–38 / 252–53 / 728, 743

Christianity: 31 / 257 / 292 / 296 / 310, 316, 323–24, 329–30 / 800

Chukumuk (choo koo MOOK; ancient Maya city at Lake Atitlan): 645 / 738–39

Church:

  BofM: 185–86 / 282 / 480 / 777–79, 781–82 / 813

  MA: 77 / 298 / 768 / 803

Church of Christ: 37 / 156, 162–63 / 185 / 562 / 578, 593 / 612–13 / 637–38, 650, 652, 654 / 676–77 / 735 / 759, 762–65, 767, 769–70, 772 / 779, 781–82

Church of Jesus Christ of Latter-day Saints: x–xii, xv, xix, xxii / 5, 15, 20–21 / 38 / 56, 58, 63 / 90 / 110, 117, 129 / 137, 140–42, 156, 167 / 179, 189–90 / 223, 235, 237–40, 242 / 253–54, 257 / 303–4 / 337 / 360 / 371, 374–76, 381–85, 387–88, 392, 394, 396–99 / 500–2, 507–8 / 532 / 548, 559 / 577, 593 / 647, 649, 662 / 676, 678, 686–87, 690, 702–3, 714–15, 717 / 758 / 800, 802, 805–13

Cintalapa (seen tah LAH pah; city in western Chiapas): 768, 772

Cintepec, Hill (seen tay PAYK; hill near Lake Catemaco, Veracruz; possibly hill Shim): 44, 46 / 117 / 685–86, 699

Ciudad Cuauhtemoc (see oo dahd kwah oo TAY mohk; ancient ruler of Tenochtitlan; also a city): 88 / 582 / 656 / 677, 679 / 764

Clark, Chad (photographer): xv / 639

Clark, John E. (LDS archaeologist): xvii / 45 / 235, 241–42 / 336–40, 345 / 388 / 717

Clavijero, Francesco Saverio (author, Mesoamerica): 263

Coriantumr *(last surviving Jaredite from battle at the hill Ramah):* 10–11, 17 / 109, 119–20, 126–30, 133 / 149 / 180 / 301, 304–5 / 434 / 533, 536 / 670–72 / 681 / 746–47, 750–51, 763, 770

Corihor, *land of/valley of (Jaredite locations in land northward):* 395 / 676, 681

Corn:

> BofM: 166 / 358–59 / 742
>
> MA: 24, 44 / 120 / 146 / 197, 218, 229, 240 / 256 / 315 / 358–59, 361, 369 / 581 / 610 / 685, 693, 699 / 721, 723–24, 735–36 / 796

Corn hill *(Cintepec):* 44 / 685

Cornyn, John Hubert *(author; Quetzalcoatl):* 315

Corozal *(koh roh ZAHL; Maya site in northern Belize):* 389 / 609

> Bay of: 605

Cortez: 60 / 90 / 248, 251, 259 / 274, 279 / 285, 293 / 296 / 792, 795

Cortez Codex: 248

Costa Rica: 137 / 253 / 467

Costly apparel: 162 / 185 / 357 / 779–80

Course of the beasts *(trail of Tehuantepec):* 227, 229 / 459 / 473–74 / 814

Covarrubias, Miguel *(Mexican archaeologist):* xvii / 109

Cowdery, Oliver *(scribe for Joseph Smith; one of the Book of Mormon Three Witnesses):* ix, xxxv / 247 / 605

Cross: 304–5 / 311, 315, 328–29

Cross, Frank Moore *(author; Paraiba stone):* 538–39

Cross, Temple of the *(Palenque, Chiapas):* 38, 40, 49, 51 / 68 / 118–19 / 304

Cubit: 66 / 241 / 268 / 334, 350 / 432 / 529

Cuauhtemoc *(kwah TAY mohk; Aztec ruler of Tenochtitlan; also a city):* 80 / 283–84 / 795–96

Cuchumatanes *(koo choo mah TAH nays; mountain range, Guatemala/Chiapas):* 89, 102 / 392 / 404, 418–19 / 468 / 532 / 556–61, 563 / 590 / 650, 656, 664 / 677 / 737

Cuello *(Maya archaeological site in Belize):* 143

Cuicuilco *(kwee KWEEL koh; archaeolgical site in Mexico City):* 455, 464

Culebro, Carlos *(Mesoamericanist; Izapa):* 235

Cumeni, city of *(Alma 56:13–14; land southward; land of Zarahemla):* 393 / 620 / 745

Culture/cultural:

> Aztec: 30 / 59 / 99 / 137 / 203 / 326 / 648 / 795
>
> Book of Mormon: xii / 15 / 38, 50 / 56 / 89, 101 / 129 / 141–42, 166–67 / 182 / 215, 241 / 306 / 368 / 387, 396 / 422 / 465 / 475, 477, 481 / 532, 544 / 590 / 645 / 715 / 725, 729 / 748 / 813
>
> Criterion for Book of Mormon research: viii, xi–xii, xxiii, xxvii / 2–3, 15, 19–21 / 39 / 89, 96, 103 / 113 / 142 / 166 / 246, 260 / 281, 292 / 295 / 368 / 372–73 / 422 / 564 / 734
>
> El Tajin: 693
>
> Hebrew: 35, 37 / 179, 185 / 247 / 350
>
> Inca: 372
>
> Izapa: 93, 96–97, 99–100, 103 / 150 / 215, 218–19 / 226, 235–39 / 334, 339 / 765
>
> Jaredites: 10, 15 / 86, 96, 103 / 105–33 / 146 / 178–80, 185 / 226, 272 / 432–33 / 499 / 747, 757
>
> Lamanites: 8, 16 / 29 / 103 / 137, 142, 165 / 298 / 397 / 468–69, 489 / 499 / 721, 723 / 752, 759
>
> Maya: 11 / 28–29, 43, 51 / 96, 100–3 / 109 / 135, 137, 140, 142, 144, 148, 150–52, 165–66 / 185 / 218, 231 / 247, 251 / 295–96, 199 / 391 / 468–69, 472, 474 / 540 / 596, 598 / 710 / 727 / 749, 759 / 793–94
>
> Mesoamerica: 5, 16, 20 / 28, 50 / 56–57, 66, 76 / 89, 92, 96–97, 101 / 111, 115, 129 / 135–36, 142, 148–49, 164, 166 / 200, 209 / 226 / 281–82, 284 / 311–12, 315, 317–21, 324, 329–30 / 354, 358, 364, 368 / 372–73, 392, 395–96, 421–22 / 465 / 477 / 540–41 / 590 / 753 / 795 / 800–1
>
> Middle East: 242 / 522

731–33, 735–36, 739, 743 / 745–51, 753–59, 761–65, 770–72, 774 / 779, 781, 783 / 801, 809, 815

AD 250–500 (Early Classic): 7–8, 12–13, 15–16 / 38, 45, 51 / 55, 58–59, 77–80 / 91–93, 95, 97–100 / 112, 115 / 135–37, 140–41, 144, 147, 150, 152, 155–57, 159, 161–64, 168 / 172–73, 176, 185–89 / 193–94, 196, 199–202, 206–9, 211–12 / 218–19, 226, 229, 232–34 / 266, 270, 275, 278–79 / 291 / 300 / 330 / 354, 358, 363 / 395 / 409–10, 414 / 430, 441–42, 456–60 / 468, 472, 476, 487–89, 492 / 496, 505 / 552 / 609, 613 / 653, 660, 662, 664, 670, 672 / 683–84, 687, 89, 691–96, 698–702, 703–13, 715 / 722, 724 / 748–49, 751–54, 759, 764 / 777–81, 783–92 / 801

AD 500–700 (Middle Classic): 8 / 26–28, 38, 40, 51 / 58, 78–79 / 91–93, 95, 97–100 / 137, 141, 147, 152, 157, 159, 163–64, 167 / 172–73, 176, 187, 189 / 193–94, 196–97, 200–2, 211 / 226, 234, 266, 275, 337 / 354, 363 / 414 / 492 / 526 / 715 / 722, 729 / 753, 758 / 783–84, 791–92 / 801

AD 700–900 (Late Classic): 8 / 24, 38, 51 / 58–59, 78–79 / 91–93, 95, 97–98, 100 / 137, 140–41, 147, 152, 157, 159, 163–64 / 172, 188–90 / 193–94, 196, 201–3, 212 / 226, 234 / 249, 266, 275 / 303 / 354–55, 363 / 414 / 492 / 715 / 722, 729 / 753, 758 / 783–84, 791–93 / 801

AD 900–1200 (Early Postclassic): 58, 80 / 91, 96–97, 101 / 137, 141, 163 / 203 / 226, 234 / 249–50, 257 / 266, 273, 275 / 289 / 312, 319, 330 / 414 / 715 / 722, 729 / 758 / 778, 783, 792–93 / 801

AD 1200–1500 (Late Postclassic): 5 / 30, 37 / 56–58, 60, 80 / 91, 96–97, 101 / 110 / 137 / 193–94, 203 / 249, 257 / 266, 275 / 297 / 340 / 356 / 414 / 514 / 699 / 722, 793–94, 796

AD 1500–1800 (Colonial): 30 / 56, 59–60, 65, 74, 80 / 91, 96, 101 / 122 / 137 / 193–94, 201, 203 / 247, 251–55, 257–58 / 263–67, 275 / 281, 284–85, 292 / 295–97, 307 / 327 / 362 / 414 / 537 / 684, 690 / 699 / 722 / 795–97 / 800, 803, 806

AD 1800–Present (Modern): 1–5, 7, 14–16, 19 / 23, 26, 28, 32, 34–36, 38, 45–47, 49 / 56, 60, 62–64, 66, 68–69, 72, 74, 78, 80, 82 / 86–87, 89–93, 95–96, 98, 103 / 106, 109–14, 116–19, 121–22, 126, 129 / 137, 140, 143, 146, 148, 150–52, 164, 167–68 / 176, 178–80, 183, 189–91, 196–97, 201–2, 206, 211 / 215–17, 219, 221, 226, 230, 235–39, 241–42 / 247–49, 252–60 / 263–65, 267–68, 275 / 285 / 295–97, 304 / 310–13, 315, 317–20 / 322, 324–29, 333, 335–38, 341–42, 345 / 354, 359–60, 364 / 371, 374, 378–91, 393–98 / 405, 412, 427 / 430, 432, 454, 461–62 / 472, 477, 483, 490–93 / 496, 500–1, 504, 508–9 / 515–17, 522–23, 528, 530–31, 537–41, 544 / 548, 551, 555, 557, 561, 565 / 572, 580, 582 / 595, 598, 602, 605, 609, 612–13 / 630, 639–41, 643, 649–50, 656, 662, 664, 668, 670, 672 / 678, 684, 686–88, 690, 698, 702–4, 713–17 / 720–23, 725–28, 738, 741 / 751, 753–54, 757–59 / 777, 781, 785, 791–92, 795–97 / 799, 801–11

DeMarest, Arthur (archaeologist; Punta de Chiminov): 602

Desolation:

City of (Mormon 3:5–7; Ether 10:17–18; land northward, San Lorenzo, Veracruz): 79 / 115 / 188–89 / 233 / 395 / 456–60, 464–65 / 487, 489 / 552 / 587 / 622 / 668, 670 / 684–85, 695, 697, 699, 701 / 759 / 787–88

Land of (Alma 22:31–32; 63:5; Helaman 3:3–7; land northward, Veracruz, Mexico): xxvi / 48 / 79 / 98 / 115, 129 / 154, 159, 164 / 180, 188–89 / 204, 208 / 379, 383, 395 / 408–12, 422–25 / 429–30, 435, 437–42, 444–46, 448, 456–61, 464–65 / 476, 480–81, 488–89 / 496, 498 / 537, 540 / 549, 551–55 / 586, 588, 590–91 / 621 / 630, 633–34, 666, 670 / 695, 701 / 731 / 747, 749, 752, 759 / 787 / 814

Diaz, Bernal (soldier in army of Cortez; historian): 80 / 90 / 257, 259 / 296 / 795–96

Diaz, Porfirio (president of Mexico, 1877–80 and 1884–1911): xviii / 265 / 806

Dibble, Charles E. (translator of Florentine Codex; see Anderson, Arthur O.): 7 / 206 / 285 / 311

Diego, Juan (Aztec peasant; vision of Virgin Mary): 281, 283–84

Direction:

Altering Book of Mormon directions: 361 / 421 / 564

Altering map directions: 16 / 361 / 391–92 / 421 / 477

Bountiful: 625

Cardinal: 360–61 / 391 / 430 / 628

Criterion for Book of Mormon research: 16, 20 / 128 / 360 / 373 / 430, 447, 462 / 558, 563 / 569 / 774 / 802

Day and a half's journey: 412

East sea: 629–30

East wilderness: 596 / 603

Grijalva River: 654, 658, 663 / 680

Hermounts, wilderness of: 583

Izapa to Kaminaljuyu: 531

Jershon, land of: 635

Lake Atitlan to Almolonga: 639, 645, 649

Land among many waters: 666

Lehi's colony in Old World: 513, 517, 519–23

Maya orientation: 360–61 / 426 / 529

E

Sea (Atlantic Ocean [Caribbean] by Honduras and Belize): xxv / 102 / 153, 158 / 340 / 392 / 403, 405, 412, 415, 417–20, 423–24 / 443 / 477, 484 / 502 / 555 / 596, 598, 615–16, 620–21 / 628–30, 635–37, 673 / 765–66

Sea to the west: 417 / 596 / 635

Sea to the west sea: xxiii / 412 / 502 / 554 / 630

To the west sea: xxv / 411 / 435 / 476 / 549, 554–55 / 630

Wilderness (Alma 50:7; also known as the east wilderness of Zarahemla; Peten jungle of Guatemala and Belize): xxiii / 45 / 65 / 94 / 152–53, 155–56, 158 / 340 / 356, 360 / 416–18, 420 / 440, 442–44 / 470, 472, 484, 486 / 568–69, 592 / 595–625 / 631–33, 637, 643, 658, 660 / 748–49, 772 / 814

Edmonson, Munro (author): 62, 69, 727

El Baul (archaeological site in Guatemala): 143 / 236 / 570 / 735

El Cayo (small archaeological site along Usumacinta River): 664

El Chichonal (volcano near Villahermosa, Tabasco, Mexico): 454 / 483

El Kinel (small archaeological site along Usumacinta River): 664

Elevation:

Antigua/Chimaltenango: 741

Book of Mormon: 154

Chiapas depression: 573 / 656 / 756

Criterion for Book of Mormon research: 20 / 500 / 558 / 774 / 802

Gideon/Minon/Zarahemla: 678, 680 / 764

Guatemala City/Kaminaljuyu/Nephi: 6 / 573 / 720 / 756

Guatemala highlands: 724

Jerusalem/Red Sea: 515

Mexico City: 6

Mexico valley: 197

Middoni/Ishmael/Antigua, Guatemala: 647 / 742

Nephi, city/land of: 502 / 549, 556, 560, 563 / 572, 577 / 747, 748

Oaxaca, Mexico: 98 / 177

Quetzaltenango, Guatemala, to Mexico border: 572 / 656

San Cristobal de las Casas: 541

Santa Rosa/Zarahemla; Guatemala/land of
Nephi: 757

Tapachula: 218

Zarahemla: 563 / 572, 577 / 747, 748 / 757

Ellsworth, Randall (missionary; Guatemala): 741

**El Mirador (ehl mee da DOHR; Spanish; "lookout"
name of sites):** 93, 95 / 139–40, 150–53, 164 /
389 / 412 / 480, 487–89 / 541 / 596–97, 601, 609,
615, 625 / 699, 705 / 759, 768

El Peru (archaeological site in Peten, Guatemala):
708

**El Salvador (country in Central America; also part
of Mesoamerica):** 5 / 96, 98 / 120 / 137 / 217,
230 / 354, 365 / 384, 390 / 405, 407 / 467 / 499 /
527 / 630, 641 / 720

**El Tajin (ehl tah HEEN; Classic site near Poza
Rica, Veracruz):** 662 / 693, 707, 709, 712

**Emiliana Zapata (small archaeological site along
the Usumacina River):** 150

Enos (Nephite record beeper): 145 / 682 / 721, 724

Escobedo, Hector (archaeologist, Piedras Negras):
662

**Espinosa, Eduardo Martinez (archaeologist,
Izapa):** 216, 219, 226, 229–31, 239

**Esquintla (aays KWINT lah; modern city in
Guatemala):** 570 / 732

Ether (Jaredite prophet): 130

F

Farnsworth, Dewey (LDS author): 388

**Feathered serpent (associated with Quetzalcoatl
deity):** xxix / 106–7, 133 / 276 / 289 / 309, 312,
315–18, 319, 325 / 343 / 367 / 793

**Ferguson, Thomas Stuart (LDS author;
Mesoamericanist):** xvi, xviii / 1 / 117 / 235 /
264–65 / 285 / 341 / 386–88, 397 / 640–41 /
688 / 757

Ferguson, Tom and Jennifer (tour participants):
xviii / back cover

**Fideo (small archaeological site along the
Usumacinta River):** 664

**Filthy water(symbol from Lehi's tree-of-life
vision):** 240 / 347

**Fire Is Born (name of fourth-century military
leader from Teotihuacan):** 707–9 / 790

**First Crocodile (name of fourth-century young
king at Tikal who came from Teotihuacan):** 55 /
202 / 241 / 698, 705, 709, 711

Flannery, Kent V. (Mesoamerican scholar): xvii

Flocks: 165 / 227 / 324 / 473–74 / 564 / 578, 580 /
637–39, 642, 645, 647–48, 657 / 812

Flood: 37 / 56, 61, 67–67 / 122, 124–25 / 247, 252–
54 / 267–68, 273, 279 / 432 / 502 / 743

**Florentine Codex (also known as the writings of
Bernardino Sahagun):** 206 / 285 / 309, 329

Florescano, Enrique (author, Quetzalcoatl): 312,
316, 320–21, 324

Forest:
BofM: 13 / 113 / 485 / 682–83 / 743 / 762, 765,
772, 774 / 812
MA: 5 / 41 / 150 / 365 / 406 / 435 / 462 / 527 /
567, 570 / 663

Forest of Mormon: 13 / 485 / 578 / 637–39, 642,
645 / 682

Forsyth, Donald W. (Mesoamerican scholar): xvii

**Foundation for Ancient Research and Mormon
Studies (FARMS):** xvi / 25, 32, 35–36, 38 / 117 /
241–42 / 253 / 359, 364 / 390 / 461 / 477 / 496 /
630 / 688, 716 / 721, 727 / 771

Fountain: 335, 347 / 523

Frankincense Trail (Old World; Lehi's colony):
243 / 515–17, 519, 524–25 / 814

Freidel, David (Mesoamerican archaeologist):
xvii / 94 / 152 / 605–8 / 704, 708 / 726

Frye, Kevin (print broker): xv

Fuente, Beatriz de la (archaeologist): 90 / 115 / 376

762, 765–66, 768–69, 774 / 778, 784, 788, 796 / 801–2, 805, 812

Guatemala City: 6 / 74 / 86, 92–93 / 143–44, 147, 155, 160 / 194, 201, 211 / 217, 220–21, 223, 225, 232, 234, 236 / 259 / 358 / 390 / 470–71, 486 / 529, 531 / 556–58, 560, 565 / 570, 572–64, 577–80, 582 / 628, 639, 642, 647, 668 / 679 / 720–23, 729–31, 733, 735, 737, 741 / 753, 756 / 799, 802, 809–10, 814

Guerrero (geh DETR oh; state in Mexico): 5 / 96 / 120 / 173 / 301 / 430, 446 / 499 / 550

Gugliotta, Guy (author; Maya): 704, 708

Guzman, Eulalia (author; Izapa): 236

H

Hacienda system: 796 / 806

Hadlock, David (LDS author; contributor to project): xv / 34, 42

Hagoth (Alma 63:4–9, origin of shipping in Salina Cruz, Oaxaca): 204, 208–9 / 279 / 382 / 445–46, 452 / 480 / 553 / 632–33

Hales, Stephen (Stephen Hales Creative; designer): xv

Hamblin, William (LDS author and researcher): 34

Hansen, Beverly (contributor to project): xvi

Hansen, Richard D. (Mesoamerican scholar): xvii

Hanson, Norman and Jane (tour participants): xviii

Harris, Martin (one of the Book of Mormon Three Witnesses): ix / 3 / 90

Hauck, F. Richard (LDS archaeologist; Mesoamericanist): xvii / 117–18 / 215 / 390 / 462 / 477 / 688

Hebrew: 25, 32–37, 40, 43, 47, 49, 50–51 / 144 / 182 / 242 / 341, 344, 350 / 390 / 520, 535, 538 / 634, 651 / 746, 751 / 812

Hebrew parallelism: 37, 40–41 / 241 / 334, 341 / 408, 422 / 452 / 506 / 812

Heimerdinger, Chris (tour participant): xviii

Helam:

City of: 720, 740

Convert from among people of Noah (Mosiah 18:12–14; ca. 147 BC): 676

Land of (Mosiah 23:1–5, 19; land southward; land of pure water; Almolonga): 87 / 221 / 250 / 394 / 569, 577, 579–81 / 645, 648–50, 673 / 676–78 / 720, 742–43 / 755–56 / 805, 809, 813–14

Helaman: xix / 38, 42 / 215, 230, 242 / 354, 356, 362 / 393 / 445, 448, 452 / 529 / 601, 620 / 660 / 676 / 745, 763, 767

Helfritz, Hans (author; Zapotecs): 191

Henning, Paul (early Mormon Mayanist): 382–83

Hermounts, wilderness of (Alma 2:36–38; wilderness of Tehuantepec; wilderness of wild beasts): 13 / 45–47 / 462 / 468 / 569, 582–84, 588 / 651–52, 663 / 682 / 772 / 814

Herod: 71–72, 76

Herrera, Agricol Lozano (lawyer; LDS Church leader in Mexico): xviii / 806–9

Heshlon, plains of (Ether 13:28; Jaredite location): 395

Heth (Jaredite king and city): 395

Hewett, Edgar Lee (author; Mesoamerica): 326

Hidalgo (state in Mexico): 5 / 59 / 140 / 288 / 792

Hidalgo, Miguel (Catholic priest during Mexican independence): 80 / 796

Hield, Charles (author, Reorganized Church of Jesus Christ of Latter Day Saints, now Community of Christ): 319

Highland Guatemala: 28, 43–44 / 87, 102 / 144, 146, 149–51, 156 / 183 / 250–51, 253, 255–56 / 357, 359 / 392 / 403–5, 416–18, 421 / 478, 484 / 540, 543, 545 / 556, 565 / 568–69, 573, 577, 579 / 596, 598, 617 / 630, 635, 637, 646, 648, 655–57, 667 / 675, 683 / 721, 723–25, 730, 742–43 / 764

Highland Maya: 5 / 29 / 151 / 230 / 408, 419 / 447, 452 / 529

Hilton, Lynn M. and Hope (LDS authors): 517, 519–20, 522–23

Himni (son of Mosiah; missionary to Lamanites; ca. 100 BC): 402–3

Hinckley, Gordon B. (fifteenth President of The Church of Jesus Christ of Latter-day Saints, 1995–2008): 398 / 717 / 809

Historical parallels: 598 / 802

History/historical: vii–viii, xi–xii, xix, xxiii, xxv–xxvii / 2–3, 10, 15, 19–21 / 28, 31–32, 38 / 56–58, 66–67, 74, 80, 83 / 85, 89, 96, 103 / 122, 124 / 128–31 / 137, 141–42, 152–53, 160 / 204, 206, 213 / 227–28, 234, 241 / 245–46 / 249, 252–55, 257–58, 260 / 263–64, 266, 269–70, 272–73 / 281, 285, 288–89, 292 / 296–98 / 310, 313, 316, 326–27 / 334 / 363, 368–69 / 372–74, 376, 381–86, 388–89, 392–93, 396–97 / 401, 412, 422, 426 / 429, 432, 445, 456 / 470, 492 / 498, 500–4, 506–7 / 513, 523, 529, 532, 534, 541–42, 544 / 547–48, 564 / 572, 577, 589–91 / 601, 605, 607, 613, 620, 624–25 / 636, 645, 661–63, 666–67, 673 / 675, 683, 691, 693–94, 698, 700–1, 706, 709, 712–13, 716 / 719,

729 / 746, 754, 759, 775 / 779–80, 783–84, 791–92, 795 / 800–1, 813–15

Hoggard, Inez (artist): 811

Hoglund, Boyd (photographer): xv / 513, 518, 521, 524, 542

Honduras (country in Central America, anciently part of Mesoamerica): 5 / 44 / 59 / 92, 98 / 137, 144, 160 / 310 / 403, 405, 407 / 454 / 467, 491 / 618 / 635 / 705 / 720, 730 / 809

Honore, Pierre (author; Quetzalcoatl): 328

Hopewell (native tribe in eastern United States): 96 / 465 / 715

Hopis (native tribe in Arizona): 502

Horse: 292 / 299 / 362, 368 / 570 / 795

Hourglass model: xxii–xxiv / 390–91

Houston, Stephen (Mesoamerican archaeologist; linguist): xvii / 662

Howard, F. Burton (Emeritus General Authority, First Council of the Seventy, The Church of Jesus Christ of Latter-day Saints): 254–55

Huastec: 428

Huatulco (wah TOOL koh; resort city in the state of Oaxaca, Mexico): 209 / 279

Huehue Tlapallan (*WAY way it lah PAH yahn; region in Tuxtla Mountains, Veracruz*): 67 / 268

Huehuetenango (*way way tay NAHN goh; Nahuatl; very old city in Guatemala*): 30 / 86, 88, 90, 102 / 146 / 221, 223 / 486 / 558–61 / 573, 582, 590 / 656 / 677–78 / 737, 742 / 756 / 784 / 802

Hueyapan (*way YAH pahn; Nahuatl; very large waters*): 46 / 112, 128 / 268 / 672

Huitzilopochtli (*hweet zee loh POKHT lee; Aztec leader, fourteenth century*): 60 / 794

Human sacrifice: 80 / 301 / 788, 793–95

Hunsaker, Brett (*news reporter*): 225

Hunter, Howard W. (*fourteenth President of The Church of Jesus Christ of Latter-day Saints, 1994–95*): xvi / 235 / 387, 397 / 758

Hunter, Milton R. (*former member of the First Council of the Seventy, now deceased*): xvi / 1 / 264 / 327, 330

Hurricane: 107, 124–25 / 160 / 268–69, 273, 275 / 328 / 454 / 640, 643–44

I

Incas (*natives of Peru*): 142 / 372 / 492 / 501, 502

Infant baptism: 302–3

Inquisition, Catholic: 80 / 246, 261 / 282 / 296

Inscriptions, Temple of: 26–27 / 271

Irwin, Constance (*author*): 310–11, 320, 324, 326–28 / 795

Ishmael: 10 / 39, 43 / 135 / 348 / 496 / 513, 516, 520–21, 532, 535 / 646–47

City of (*Alma 17:19; Chimaltenango; Iximche*): 393–94 / 647 / 720, 732, 740–41

Land of: 250 / 638, 641, 646–47 / 731, 736, 740–43 / 809

Isthmus (*see Tehuantepec, Panama, and Darian*)

Iturbide, Agustin de (*Native Mexican military leader; ca. 1820*): 803

Ivins, Anthony (*former General Authority, The Church of Jesus Christ of Latter-day Saints*): 383 / 806

Iximche (*ee SHEEM chay; Maya; corn trees; Guatemala*): 251 / 736

Ixtacihuatl (*volcanic mountain in Mexico*): 199

Ixtlilxochitl, Fernando de Alva (*eesht leel shoh CHEE tl; Nahuatl; sixteenth-century Spanish chronicler*): xviii / 9 / 32, 47 / 66–67, 69, 76 / 107, 109, 119, 122, 124–25, 127, 130 / 182 / 247, 255, 257–58, 260 / 263–79 / 310–11, 316, 327–29 / 354, 364 / 381, 387 / 432–33, 448, 453, 455, 460 / 483 / 497–98, 504, 510 / 537–38 / 670 / 693 / 792–93

Izamal (*Maya ruins in the Yucatan*): 371

Izapa (*ee SAH pah; Maya site near Pacific Ocean in Chiapas, Mexico; probably the Nephite landing site and land of fathers' first inheritance*): 333–51 / 445 / 469, 479 / 525, 530 / 570 / 625 / 633, 663 / 699 / 814

Archaeology of: 144 / 216, 228, 232, 235–39 / 333–34 / 726

Crossroads: 216, 219, 234

Culture of: 100 / 215, 235–37 / 334, 339 / 765

Dating of: 94, 100 / 121 / 143–44, 150, 155–56 / 226–32, 234–35, 238, 242 / 633

Geography of: 99, 103 / 216, 218, 220, 238

History of: 143 / 226, 230–33, 236, 238 / 528 / 759

Judea, city of: 100 / 215

Landing site of Lehi: 215–16, 219, 230 / 406 / 525, 527–28, 530–32 / 570–71 / 814

Language, spoken: 150 / 237

Language, written: 28

Location of: 93, 97, 99–100 / 144, 156 / 215–21, 227, 230, 232, 234, 239 / 445 / 532 / 654

Mesoamerica role: 96 / 150, 153 / 218, 228–30, 232–34, 236–38 / 392 / 663 / 705

Monuments: 28, 38–39, 45 / 93, 97, 100 / 144, 155–56 / 215, 219, 221–22, 226, 231, 234–35, 237–42 / 333–51 / 528, 531 / 726 / 815

Olmecs, connection to: 120–21 / 144 / 227–28, 231–32, 237–38 / 499

Peoples of: 216, 219, 227–34, 236, 240 / 499 / 532 / 765

Population: 100 / 164

Traveling to and from: 217–18, 220–21, 232

J

Jackson, Kent P. (Religion professor, Brigham Young University): 517

Jacob: xvii

City of (wicked Lamanite city; probably in land northward; destroyed at great destruction; possibly Teotihuacan): 394 / 429, 453, 455 / 486

Father of twelve tribes: 137 / 255 / 507 / 532, 538–40 / 592 / 663 / 725, 743 / 750 / 800, 806, 808, 811–13

Nephite apostate (ca. 64 BC; of Zoramite sect; king-man in Mulek): 603–4, 608

Nephite apostate (ca. AD 29–30; chosen king by secret combination; led dissenters to northernmost part of land, possibly Teotihuacan): 197, 202, 210–12 / 395 / 431, 437, 452, 455 / 706–7, 709

Jacobugath, city of (city of followers of Jacob, Nephite apostate who led followers to northernmost part of land; probably in land northward; possibly in Mexico valley): 211–12 / 394 / 429, 452–53, 455

Jaguar: 1, 13 / 43, 46, 48 / 98 / 106, 124 / 176, 182 / 432, 434, 463 / 474–75 / 595 / 705 / 743

Jaguar of the Mountains (meaning of the word Mormon): 12–13 / 683–84, 694

Jaguar Paw (Maya ruler at Tikal; fourth century AD): 705–6, 708–9 / 789

Jakeman, M. Wells (first director of Archaeology Department, Brigham Young University; see also Stela 5, Izapa): xvi / 45 / 93 / 215, 236–38, 241 / 265 / 285 / 333–38, 341, 343, 347 / 372, 385–87, 390 / 595 / 661 / 757

Jared (founder and leader of Jaredites): 49 / 122 / 268, 270 432, 460 / 495–96, 500, 504, 506–10 / 696 / 746

Jaredites (descendants of Jared and his family and friends; New World Olmecs): 105–33 / 495–511 / 533, 536 / 574 / 665 / 716 / 806, 811, 815

Arrival in New World (Ether 6:12; Omni 1:21–22; near Salina Cruz, Oaxaca; Pacific coast): 16 / 66–67 / 122 / 255 / 263, 268, 271, 274–75 / 379, 384 / 433 / 495–500, 504–5 / 525–26, 534 / 815

Dating of: xxiii / 11, 15 / 52 / 57–58, 65–69 / 83, 86 / 107, 112, 115, 119, 123, 131 / 174, 185 / 226–27 / 268 / 433, 461 / 467 / 495–97, 499, 501

Destruction of: xxii / 10–11 / 52–53 / 68–69 / 86 / 111, 118, 124–27, 129–30, 131 / 180 / 201 / 232 / 267, 270–73, 275 / 378–79, 388–89 / 429–30, 433–34, 443, 447, 450 / 472 / 496, 507 / 537 / 586–87 / 666–67, 671–72 / 681, 685–86, 690, 702, 704, 713 / 747, 750–51, 759

Hill Ramah/Vigia (see also Cumorah, hill): 53 / 111, 117–18, 131 / 275 / 389 / 465 / 671–72 / 683, 686–87, 690, 701

History of: 10, 13, 17 / 52–53 / 68 / 123–24, 131 / 185 / 226–27, 229 / 255 / 270, 272–73 / 302 / 395 / 427 / 461 / 469, 473, 475 / 496–97, 504–6, 510 / 525–26 / 606 / 666 / 683, 692–93, 702, 704, 713 / 746–47, 750 / 815

Language of: 11 / 32–33, 52 / 122–23, 132 / 143, 146 / 255 / 275 / 433 / 506 / 750

Last battle: 53 / 69 / 116, 117, 126, 129, 131 / 275 / 372, 384, 389, 396 / 429, 434, 450 / 687–88, 691, 712–13, 715, 717

Mother culture: 10 / 105, 110, 119, 129, 131 / 149 / 302 / 430 / 497, 499

Mulekites, association with: 10–11 / 52 / 69 / 172, 180, 182, 185 / 275 / 461 / 499–500 / 537, 544 / 746–47, 750–51, 757

Names: 11, 43, 45, 48–49, 51 / 64, 68 / 115, 118, 132 / 182 / 299, 301 / 430 / 476 / 509

Nephites, influence on: 11, 33, 51–53 / 98 / 109, 120, 133 / 182 / 227–29, 231 / 499–500 / 561 / 746–47, 751, 757

Olmecs, correlation with: xxiii / 105–33 / 44, 52 / 58, 65, 67–69, 73 / 96 / 109, 112, 115–18, 122–24, 126–27, 128–33 / 146, 149 / 179–80 / 226, 229–30, 232, 237 / 268, 271–73 / 430, 432–33, 439 / 499–500 / 554 / 575 / 663 / 685–86, 690, 716 / 750 / 814

Spanish chronicles: 67, 69 / 109 / 255

Territory of: 10–11, 13 / 44, 53 / 68–69, 73 / 98, 103 / 106, 116–18, 121–22, 128–29, 131–32 / 173–74, 178, 180, 185 / 218, 226–27, 229, 231–32, 237 / 268, 271–74 / 379, 381, 395 / 409 / 429–33, 439, 447, 456, 462–64 / 468–69, 473–75 / 496–500, 502–3, 507 / 537–38 / 554 / 561 / 568, 575, 586–87 / 628, 655, 663, 666–67, 669, 671 / 676, 681, 685–86, 697, 712, 716 / 747, 775

Tower of Babel, origination at: 10 / 66–67 / 109, 122–23, 131 / 263, 265–68, 270 / 432 / 495–96 / 681–82 / 746

Jarom (Nephite record keeper between Enos and Omni): 146 / 721, 724

Jashon, city of (Mormon 2:17; Nephite city in land of Desolation; land northward; near hill Shim): 395 / 696 / 786

Jeddah (city in Saudi Arabia, proposed where Nephi broke his bow): 519–20

Jenkins, Marion and Mary Jo (tour participants): xviii

Jennings, Jesse D. (archaeologist; Kaminaljuyu): 93 / 722–23

Jeppson, Brad (Stephen Hales Creative): xiii

Jershon, land of (Alma 27:22–26; 28:1; 31:3; land southward; northern Belize; possibly Lamanai): 588 / 605, 624 / 635, 658–59 / 765–66

Jerusalem: 811, 814

City of (Alma 21:2; Lamanite city in the land of Nephi; possibly at waters of Mormon/Lake Atitlan): 393–94 / 453 / 483–85 / 640–41, 643–45 / 720, 737–40

Land of (Alma 21:1; near the borders of the land of Mormon; land southward): 640–41, 643 / 737–38, 741

Old World: 8–9 / 33–34, 39, 48, 51–53 / 55, 61, 68–73, 75 / 145, 147 / 177, 179 / 196–97 / 231, 243 / 323, 325, 327 / 334 / 353, 366 / 376, 379 / 496 / 513–18, 522–23, 533–35, 538, 543–44 / 584, 590 / 611 / 646 / 685 / 721–22, 734 / 746, 750, 759, 767 / 792 / 799, 813

Jews: 8 / 25, 33–35, 42 / 55, 66, 73 / 142, 145, 147 / 179–80, 182, 185 / 247 / 267 / 302 / 327 / 366 / 448 / 475, 491, 493 / 529, 533, 538, 542 / 585 / 608 / 646 / 693, 704 / 746, 755, 761, 767, 771 / 792, 797 / 800

Jones, Wendell (tour participant): xviii

Jordan (Middle East area possibly traversed by Lehi): 243 / 516–17, 525, 534 / 567

Jordan River: 515–16

Joseph of Egypt: xix / 9–10 / 480 / 529, 532, 534–36, 543, 44 / 750 / 813

Josephus (Jewish historian): 71 / 263

Josh, city of (3 Nephi 9:10; probably in land southward; burned during great destruction): 394 / 453 / 483, 486

Joshua:

  City of (not named in the Book of Mormon; probably in land of Desolation; land northward): 395

  Land of (Mormon 2:6; in borders west by the seashore; probably land Desolation; land northward): 786

Juarez, Benito (nineteenth-century Zapotec president of Mexico): 97–98 / 189–91 / 804–5

Juchitan (hoo chee TAHN; city and site in Oaxaca, Mexico; in the narrow pass): 458

Judea, city of (Alma 56:9; Nephite city; possibly Izapa): 100 / 215 / 393 / 445 / 528 / 620

Judge: 158 / 204, 209 / 413 / 437, 445–46, 448–49 / 475, 480–81 / 588–89 / 601, 613, 621 / 651–54 / 680, 706, 709 / 762–64, 774

Jungle: 5–6 / 91 / 151–52, 156, 158, 166 / 194, 201 / 239 / 299 / 310 / 344 / 415, 417–18 / 467–68, 473–74 / 567 / 595–96, 610, 615, 619 / 666 / 683, 708 / 765

K

Kabah (kah BAH; Maya site in the Yucatan): 371

Kaminaljuyu (cah mee NAHL hoo YOO; Maya; hills of dead; probably the city of Nephi; Guatemala City): 58–59, 65, 74, 79 / 92–94, 96 / 139, 143–46 / 201, 211 / 234, 236 / 390 / 470, 479, 487 / 499 / 531 / 559 / 570–73, 577 / 638, 640–41, 645, 663 / 699, 705–6, 708, 712 / 719–26, 727, 729, 732, 737–39, 743 / 747–48, 750, 752, 757, 760, 762, 774 / 784 / 814–15

Keatinge, Richard W. (author; Inca history): 16

Kelley, David H. (Mesoamerican archaeologist): xvii / 148

Kidder, Alfred V. (archaeologist; Kaminaljuyu): xvii / 93 / 722–23 / 757

Kimball, Camilla Eyring (LDS refuge from Mormon colonies during the Mexican revolution): 806

Kimball, Edward L. (LDS author): 807

Kimball, Heber C. (early leader in The Church of Jesus Christ of Latter-day Saints): 713–14

Kimball, Spencer W. (twelfth President of The Church of Jesus Christ of Latter-day Saints, 1973–85): 397

King:

Aaron: 700, 705–6

Amalickiah: 94 / 159 / 452 / 606

Ammoron: 94 / 607–8, 617 / 632

Anti-Nephi-Lehi: 563 / 635

Benjamin: 28 / 146, 156 / 561 / 613 / 722 / 755, 760–63

Book of Mormon: 98 / 197 / 312 / 338 / 606, 608 / 638, 651 / 705 / 723, 728 / 781

Christ: 565

Coriantumr: 73 / 180 / 461 / 536 / 747, 750–51

Jacob: 210–12 / 431, 452, 455 / 706–7

Jaguar Paw: 705, 709 / 789

Jared: 270 / 495 / 746

Jaredite/Olmec: 35, 43, 45, 48 / 64, 73 / 98 / 105, 115, 118–19, 132–33 / 182 / 272 / 299, 301 / 340 / 436, 461 / 496, 498, 509 / 606

Kish: 49, 51 / 68 / 115, 119, 132–33 / 320 / 501 / 686 / 759 / 813

Laman: 29, 45 / 97 / 250

Laman Ayin: 202 / 710

Lamanite: 45, 55 / 157 / 189 / 202, 212 / 402–3, 409–11, 422–23, 425 / 559–60 / 569, 577–78 / 628–30, 632, 635–39, 646–48, 704 / 731–33, 740–42 / 749, 755–56, 762 / 787

Lamoni: 45 / 152–53, 158 / 486 / 620 / 648 / 705 / 740

Lib: 113, 132 / 435 / 469

Limhi: 53 / 65 / 130 / 156 / 275 / 389 / 474 / 561 / 575 / 665 / 682 / 716, 728–29, 742 / 755, 764

Mesoamerica: 47 / 72 / 94 / 152, 158–59 / 252, 255 / 264, 270–73 / 317–20, 330 / 337 / 605–8 / 701, 708 / 723, 726–28, 792

Mosiah: 8–10 / 61, 73, 76 / 88 / 123 / 136, 147, 155, 158 / 183–85 / 425 / 471 / 534, 543–44 / 565 / 571, 573, 575, 581, 593 / 662 / 677 / 731 / 746–47, 749–51, 755, 759–61, 763

Nebuchadnezzar: 72–73 / 535

Nephi: 52 / 72 / 97 / 229 / 469

Nephite: 158 / 544 / 607 / 727 / 761, 763

Noah: 29 / 65 / 156 / 364 / 426 / 471, 484 / 577–80 / 638, 641, 645–46, 676, 679, 705 / 719, 726–29, 734–35, 739, 742 / 755, 760 / 807

Old Testament: 69–73 / 523

Pacal: 23, 26–27

Pahoran: 708

Spearthrower Owl: 706, 708–9

Tubaloth: 608

Yax Nuun Ayiin: 55 / 202, 212 / 340, 430 / 698, 705–6, 709–10 / 789

Zedekiah: 8–9 / 69–73 / 182 / 376 / 496 / 516, 533–35, 543 / 608 / 796

Zeniff: 728 / 755

King-men: 78 / 94 / 158–59 / 197 / 543 / 606–8 / 707 / 759 / 780–81 / 815

Kingsborough, Lord (British historian): 247 / 265 / 329 / 381

Kinichna (kee neech NAH; Maya site in Chetumal, Mexico; near Dzibanche and Kuhunlich; possibly associated with city of Bountiful complex): 95 / 625

Kish (Ether 1:18–19; Jaredite king; name on Temple of the Cross at Palenque): 11 / 46, 49, 51 / 68 / 113, 115, 118–19, 132–33 / 320 / 501 / 686 / 759 / 814

Kishkumen (Helaman 6:18, 24; cofounder of Gadianton robbers): 133

Kishkumen, city of (3 Nephi 9:10; possibly located along Chiapas-Guatemala border; destroyed by fire in great destruction): 394 / 453 / 483, 486

Knorozov, Yurii V. (Russian scientist who solved the Maya code): xvii / 247, 257

Kohunlich (koh hoon LEECH; Maya site in Quintana Roo, Mexico; neighbor to Dzibanche and Kinichna; possibly associated with the city of Bountiful): 95 / 487 / 605, 608–9, 612, 615, 624–25

Kopp, Irene (tour participant): xviii

Korihor (Alma 30; an antichrist): 354

Krickburg, Walter (author): 317

Kuk Balam (ancestor of Pacal; Palenque; contemporary of Moroni): 135

Kukulcan (koo kool KAHN; Maya word for "feathered serpent" or "Quetzalcoatl"): xxix / 315, 320 / 793

Kukulcan, Temple of (at Chichen Itza): 141 / 312, 315, 320 / 778

Kumen (Maya name; one of twelve Nephite disciples): 46–47

L

Labastille, A. (author; quetzal bird): 310

La Blanca (Olmec/Maya site along the Pacific coast of Guatemala): 236 / 570

Labna (Maya site in the state of Yucatan, Mexico): 371

Lacandone Mountains (see also Lacanha): 47–48 / 159 / 449–50 / 472 / 587, 590–91

Lacandones: 591

Lacanha (Maya name meaning waters of Lacandone; perhaps area where Nephites gathered to defend against the Gadianton robbers; land southward; between the center land of Zarahemla bordering on Desolation and Bountiful; 3 Nephi 3:23–24): 47–48 / 159 / 450

Lachoneus:
 Chief judge of Zarahemla (3 Nephi 1:1; AD 1): 47–48, 89 / 159 / 232 / 449–50 / 480–81 588–90 / 591–92 / 709
 Maya name: 46 / 159 / 450
 Mountains of (probably in Chiapas, Mexico): 814
 Wilderness of (3 Nephi 3:23; land of Zarahemla, between the land of Zarahemla and the land Bountiful): 569, 589, 591

La Farge, Oliver (archaeologist; Olmec): 111

Laguna de Terminos (also called the Bay of Campeche): 74

Lagunes, Augustin Acosta (author, Olmecs): 105

La Libertad (lah lee behr TAHD; archaeological site, Chiapas, Mexico; at the base of the narrow strip of wilderness; near the Grijalva River; possibly the city of Manti): 656, 658 / 765, 773

Lake Atitlan: (see Atitlan, Lake)

Laman:
 City of (3 Nephi 9:10; probably in land southward; burned in great destruction): 394 / 453 / 483, 486
 King of the Lamanites (Mosiah 24:3–4): 29
 Lamanite king (Mosiah 7:21; ca. 200 BC): 250
 Maya name correlation: 45–46 / 55 / 139, 153 / 202, 212 / 241 / 621 / 710 / 813
 River (1 Nephi 2:8; Old World river that empties into the Red Sea): 517–20 / 567 / 710
 Son of Lehi (ca. 600 BC): 7 / 39, 52 / 71, 74 / 97 / 144–45 / 229 / 344–46 / 405 / 469, 486 / 495 / 514 / 516, 526

Lamanai (lah mah NIGH; Maya archaeological site in Belize): 45 / 92 / 152–53, 158–59 / 487–87 / 581 / 596–97, 601, 620–21 / 699, 710

Laman Ayin (lah MAHN ah YEEN; archaeological site in Belize; possibly associated with the title of "Laman"): 45 / 139, 153 / 202 / 241 / 621 / 710 / 766

Lamanites: 135–69 / 568–69 / 716 / 765 / 806–7, 809, 811, 813
 Arrival in New World: 52–53 / 156 / 496 / 726
 Dating of: 7–8, 13, 16 / 51 / 58, 65, 79 / 100 / 135, 137, 146, 157 / 187 / 752
 Gadianton robbers: 79 / 163 / 188 / 211 / 234 / 442 / 694, 699, 701, 706, 709 / 753, 783, 785, 790
 History of: 7–8 / 53 / 58, 77 / 97 / 131 / 137, 142, 152, 157 / 229 / 250 / 271–72 / 339 / 375 / 402 / 467 / 495 / 528, 532 / 549 / 569 / 640, 646 / 678–79, 705 / 740 / 811
 Jaredites, connections to: 53 / 229 / 271–72 / 299 / 499
 Lamanite Maya: 29, 33, 51 / 164 / 186 / 218, 233 / 369 / 427 / 468–69 / 549–50 / 622 / 689, 705, 709, 712, 716 / 759 / 783 / 815
 Language of: 29, 33, 48, 51–52 / 146, 157 / 245, 250
 Last battle at Cumorah/Vigia: 13 / 55 / 111, 117 / 168–69 / 189 / 279 / 300 / 456, 459 / 488 / 687, 689, 691, 715, 717
 Maya, correlation with: 7–8 / 97 / 135–38, 142, 157, 167, 165, 169 / 357 / 468 / 549 / 815
 Nature of: 7 / 52 / 80 / 97 / 135–38, 142, 145, 152–53, 165, 168 / 186, 188 / 234 / 272 / 357 / 423, 425 / 528 / 647 / 777, 788, 790 / 800
 Nephites, relationships with: 7, 12–13 / 29, 33, 45, 51–52, 55–56, 77, 79–80 / 94, 97, 102, 135–37, 142, 145, 152–53, 156–58, 163–64, 167 / 186, 188–89 / 210–11 / 218, 229, 234 / 250 / 275, 279 / 301, 306 / 369 / 377, 395 / 406–7, 411–13, 415, 423–24 / 430, 453–36, 441–42, 445, 456–57 / 472, 476, 484,

488–89 / 528 / 547, 549–50, 560, 562–64 / 576, 581, 593 / 596, 607, 609, 613, 619 / 630–32, 635, 647, 651, 657 / 676–77, 680, 692–94, 696, 700–1, 704 / 728–29, 741–42 / 752, 755–56, 759–60, 762–64, 766, 772 / 778, 783, 788, 790 / 815

Skin color: 136 / 469 / 788–89 / 800, 815

Territory of: 8 / 45 / 79 / 100, 102 / 131 / 135–36, 138, 146, 152–53, 156, 158, 162–64, 167 / 171, 188–89 / 210 / 218–19, 233–34 / 306 / 377, 381, 383, 393–94 / 402–7, 411–12, 415–20, 423, 425 / 430, 436–37, 441–43, 445–47 / 468, 470, 472, 476–76, 484–85, 488, 493 / 527–28, 532 / 549, 556 / 570, 572, 574, 586, 588–91, 593 / 595–96, 598, 603, 605–6, 608, 613, 615–16, 624 / 630–32, 636–41, 643, 646, 650, 652, 655, 658, 660 / 687, 694, 701, 706, 709, 712, 716 / 719, 731–32, 734–37 / 745, 752–53, 755, 759–62, 764, 766, 768

Warfare: 45, 52–53 / 55, 61 / 94 / 117 / 145, 152–53, 158, 164, 168–69 / 187–89 / 279 / 300–1 / 368 / 393 / 406, 412–13, 415 / 430, 435–36, 442, 444–45, 451, 456–59 / 488–89 / 549–50, 552, 554, 559 / 582–83, 590 / 595–606, 613, 616–20, 623 / 632–33, 637, 651–52, 655, 658–60, 663–65,

668, 670, 672 / 676, 680, 690–93, 695–97, 699, 701–2, 704–7, 709–10 / 735 / 761, 763, 768, 772, 774 / 778, 785–92 / 800

Writing, among: 28–29, 33, 51 / 157

La Mesilla (Guatemala border crossing between Guatemala and Mexico): 88 / 582 / 656 / 678 / 774

Lamoni (Lamanite king converted by Ammon; first century BC; brother of Anti-Nephi-Lehi): 45 / 152–53, 158 / 425 / 486 / 564 / 620 / 647–48 / 705 / 740–42

Land:

Among many waters (Mosiah 8:7–11; lagoons between Campeche and Tabasco, Mexico): xxvi / 111 / 439 / 468, 472 / 540 / 561 / 574–75 / 663, 665–68, 673 / 814

North: 8 / 37 / 154 / 171 / 437, 440, 447–48, 450–51 / 477–78, 482 / 513, 529, 533, 536, 539–40

Northward: xxii / 7, 10, 12–13, 17 / 68, 73, 75, 79 / 99, 102 / 109, 113, 123–34, 129 / 151, 153–54, 159–60, 162, 164, 167, 169 / 171–72, 178, 180, 182–83 / 197, 204, 208–12 / 218, 229, 232–34 / 267, 271, 273, 275–76, 279 / 376, 378–79, 384–85,

392, 395–96 / 408–16, 418, 424–25 / 429–65 /
467–69, 472, 474–80, 482, 485–88, 491–92 / 496,
502 / 533, 537, 540, 543 / 547–54 / 577, 586–88,
590 / 618, 620–21 / 628, 630–34, 643, 660, 663,
669–71 / 676, 684, 690, 694–95, 697, 699–700 /
745–48, 752–53

Of first inheritance: 156 / 216, 230 / 469 / 527–28,
530 / 571 / 685 / 721, 726, 731 / 756 / 814

Of many waters: 167 / 540 / 627–28, 665, 668 /
690 / 748, 762

Of many waters, rivers, and fountains: 540 / 665,
668, 673 / 686

Of pure water: 221 / 579–80, 593 / 628, 639, 648–
49, 673 / 676, 678, 690 / 809

Of the Nephites (Alma 53:6; included the land of
Zarahemla, the east wilderness of Zarahemla, and
the land of Bountiful): 605 / 792

South: 8 / 37 / 154 / 171 / 447–48, 450 / 477–78,
482 / 513, 529, 533, 539–40

Southward: xxii / 7–8, 12, 17 / 53 / 68, 73, 75,
79 / 91, 100, 102 / 113, 115, 123–24, 129 / 149, 151,
153–54, 157, 159–60, 163–64, 168–69 / 180, 188 /
211 / 218, 227, 230, 232–34 / 270, 276 / 307 / 376,
378, 384, 392, 396 / 408–11, 414–15, 419, 424–25 /
429–30, 432, 434–35, 437, 442–43, 446–48,
450–54, 456–59, 461–65 / 467–93 / 502 / 529 /
547–49, 551–54 / 577, 586–88, 590 / 630–31,
633–34, 660, 662–63, 669 / 682, 684, 693–95, 697,
700–1, 710 / 745, 749, 751–53, 759, 775 / 787–88,
792

Which was northward (Alma 63:4–9; Helaman
3:3–7; Teotihuacan; Mexico valley): 99 / 195,
204, 208–10, 212 / 355 / 379–80, 395 / 418 / 431,
436–37, 439–40, 443, 445–47, 464 / 551 / 621 /
631, 660, 672–73

Landa, Diego de (Dee YAY goh day LAHN dah; first
bishop of the Yucatan): xviii / 24, 31–32 / 248,
257–58, 260–61 / 270 / 282 / 295–307 / 320 /
345 / 353

Language:

Book of Mormon: xxv / 3, 16, 19–21 / 26, 33, 38,
43–45, 47, 50, 53 / 146 / 226 / 246 / 394 / 417–18 /
554–55 / 598 / 640, 643–44

Criterion for Book of Mormon research: xxiii, xxv,
xxvii / 2–3, 14–16, 19–21 / 37, 39, 45, 51 / 103 /
147 / 245–46 / 372, 394–95 / 417, 421–22 / 490 /
502 / 564 / 568 / 642–43, 645 / 712 / 748–49 /
802, 813

Egyptian: 33–34, 52 / 144

English: 35, 37 / 103 / 252, 256 / 264 / 619 / 687 /
806

Hebrew: 32–34, 51–52 / 144

Inca: 142 / 501–2

Jaredite/Olmec: 10–11 / 32–33, 43, 48, 51–53 /
67 / 96 / 105–6, 109, 122–23, 132 / 146 / 226 / 268,
270, 275 / 432–33, 439 / 495, 501, 503–4, 506,
508 / 750

Lamanite: 29, 51–52 / 146, 157 / 245, 250

Latin: 12 / 33 / 251, 253, 257 / 284–85 / 303

Mam: 536 / 563 / 582 / 656

Maya: 4, 12–13 / 24, 26, 28–32, 37, 43–46, 48, 51,
53 / 62–63, 68, 74 / 95, 103 / 133 / 137, 142–43,
147, 150, 157 / 246, 253, 256–57 / 297, 301, 303,
306 / 320 / 583 / 639, 645, 651, 668 / 698, 709 /
736, 739 / 749, 771 / 806

Mesoamerica: 2, 15–16 / 28–30, 32, 43, 46–47,
50–52 / 62 / 86, 103 / 143–44, 146–47, 156 / 245,
250, 252 / 263–64 / 282, 288, 292 / 295, 298,
305 / 372, 392, 394–95 / 490 / 502 / 514 / 598 /
639, 643 / 749, 751, 754 / 800

Mixe-Zoque: 150 / 226, 237

Mulekite: 9, 11 / 33 / 68 / 130 / 155 / 171, 179, 184 /
533 / 746, 750–51

Nahuatl/Aztec: 12–13 / 30, 44, 46 / 128 / 193 /
236 / 284–85 / 297 / 638 / 739 / 800, 806

Nephite: 9, 11–13 / 25, 29, 32–33, 37, 51–53 / 130 /
146, 155–57 / 184 / 245, 250 / 275 / 514 / 663 /
731 / 746, 750–51

Spanish: 30–32 / 103 / 252, 257 / 282, 284–85 /
297 / 638 / 739 / 801, 806

Tzutuhil: 643, 645 / 739

Yucatec: 32 / 143

Zapotec: 32 / 171, 191

Large and spacious field: 335

Larsen, Jeff *(contributor to project):* xvi

LaSalle, Tawni *(contributor to project):* xvi

La Tecnica *(small archaeological site along the*
Usumacinta River): 664

La Venta *(Olmec archaeological site; famous for*
giant stone heads; land of Desolation; land
northward; proposed Jaredite city of Lib):

City of Lib: 110, 115 / 462 / 554

Dating of: 95 / 109, 113

Giant stone heads and monuments: 95 / 108, 111,
114–15, 118, 121–22, 124 / 321 / 433–34 / 495 / 685

Olmec archaeological site: 68 / 95 / 106, 108,
110–11, 112–15, 118, 120–22, 127 / 230, 232 / 320 /
433–35, 462–63, 465 / 472 / 502 / 554 / 663,
668 / 681, 685, 688, 715 / 775

Outdoor museum in Villahermosa (Parque de La
Venta): 105–6, 108, 111, 114, 118 / 215 / 321 / 474 /
540

Law of Moses: viii / 42 / 324 / 401, 426 / 513 / 611 /
645

Layton, Lynn C. *(LDS author):* 384–85

Lechmann, Vreni *(tour participant):* 586

Lee, Harold B. *(eleventh President of The Church*
of Jesus Christ of Latter-day Saints, 1972–73):
47

Lee, Thomas A. Jr. *(LDS archaeologist, New World*
Archaeological Foundation): xvii / 216, 219, 226,
229–31, 235, 238–39 / 388 / 758

Lefgren, John *(author):* 71–72

Lehi: 10–11 / 34, 37, 39–40, 45, 48, 51–53 / 58, 61,
69–72, 74 / 135, 154 / 171, 191 / 215–16, 218–19,
227, 230, 236–38, 240–43 / 255–56 / 313, 315 /
333–50 / 376, 378–79, 390, 395 / 405–6, 427 /
448 / 469, 472, 477–78, 486 / 495–96, 500,
506–7, 509 / 513–35 / 570–72, 582, 590 / 603,
614, 616–17, 622, 624 / 659 / 676, 683, 699, 713 /
719, 721–22, 726 / 746, 750 / 789, 797 / 800, 809,
813–14

City of: 158 / 393 / 419–20 / 603, 609, 618, 620–23 / 815

Land of (Alma 50:15; land southward; central Belize along the seashore): 37 / 171 / 443, 447 / 477 / 616, 620–21

Valley of: 516

Lehi-Nephi:

City of (Mosiah 9:8, 15; same as the city of Nephi; Guatemala City; Kaminaljuyu): 559–60 / 638–39 / 720, 731–32, 734

Land of: 74 / 448 / 561 / 575–76 / 720, 731, 733 / 755–56, 760

Lemuel: 39 / 71, 74 / 144–45 / 344–46, 349 / 405 / 469 / 514, 516, 526 / 676

City of: 394 / 732, 735–36

Valley of: 334 / 514–17, 519–20 / 813

Leonard, Jonathan Norton (author; Quetzalcoatl): 317

Leon-Portilla, Miguel (author; Quetzalcoatl): 317

Lerdo: 436

Liahona: 42 / 354 / 507, 509 / 515, 519, 526

Lib: 48

City of (Jaredite city in land northward; probably La Venta, Tabasco): 110, 113, 115 / 395 / 462 / 500 / 814

King Lib (Ether 10:18–21; son of Kish; about 1000 BC): 113, 119, 132 / 435, 462 / 469 / 587

Limhi: 10 / 53 / 65, 74 / 129–30 / 156 / 275 / 340 / 389 / 425 / 471, 474 / 504 / 560–62, 565 / 568, 574–75, 582, 592–93 / 638, 665–66 / 676–79, 682 / 719, 722, 726–29, 733, 742 / 749, 755, 760, 762, 764 / 813

Limhi expedition: 10 / 52 / 68–69 / 111, 124, 129–30 / 232 / 272, 275 / 340 / 439 / 472 / 504–5 / 540 / 560–62 / 568–69, 574–75, 577 / 627, 663, 665–67, 673 / 679 748, 755, 762

Limited geographic model: xvi, xxiii / 384 / 480 / 757

Limited Tehuantepec theory: 386

Lindsay, Jeff (Internet Mesoamericanist): 717

Linguistic: 20 / 42 / 96, 100, 103 / 137, 143, 166 / 350 / 372–73 / 401 / 502, 507 / 673 / 743 / 813

Liquor: 364 / 562

Little, James A. (LDS author): 530

Los Encuentros (los ayn KWEN trohs; Spanish; crossroads in Guatemala): 642 / 737

Lothrop, Samuel (archaeologist): 640

Lowe, Gareth W. (LDS archaeologist, New World Archaeological Foundation): xvii / 216, 219, 226, 229–31, 235, 237–39 / 387 / 757–58

Lowland:

Guatemala: 102 / 149 / 357 / 405, 418 / 556 / 569, 572 / 595–96, 598 / 656, 657 / 730

Jungle: 28 / 356 / 393 / 472 / 595, 611

Maya: 5 / 28–29, 48 / 145 / 408, 419 / 441, 447–48, 450, 452 / 601 / 712

Lowlands: 5–6 / 28–29, 48 / 102 / 145, 147, 150–51 / 194 / 477 / 541

Ludlow, Daniel (author, retired professor of Religion, Brigham Young University; tour participant): xviii, xxii / 554–55

Lund, Gerald (tour participant): xviii

Lund, John L. and Bonnie (tour participants): xvii / 688

M

Macabilero: 664

Madrid Codex: 248

Magdalena River: 383

Maler, Teoberto (Mesoamerican acholar): xvii

Mam, land of: 74 / 536, 541

Language: 32 / 143 / 536 / 563 / 656

People: 582 / 656

Mani (Maya village in the Yucatan where records were burned in the sixteenth century): 24, 31 / 261 / 296, 298–300, 307

Manti:

> City of (Alma 17:1; Alma 22:27; located at the base of the mountains in which the river Sidon begins; Ciudad Cuauhtemoc; La Libertad): 393 / 656, 658, 663 / 745, 765, 773, 774 / 815
>
> Land of (extends to the top of the mountain where the headwaters of the river Sidon begin): 404–5, 423 / 614, 616, 620 / 655–56, 658–59, 661, 663–64 / 679 / 764–65, 773–74

Many days: 111 / 215 / 439 / 469, 472 / 520, 525–26, 528, 540 / 570–71, 574, 576 / 666 / 737, 742 / 756

Many waters: 111 / 167 / 298 / 439 / 468, 472 / 509, 510–11 / 521, 524, 540 / 561 / 574–75 / 627–28, 665 / 813

Marina, Dona (sixteenth-century interpreter for Cortez): 795

Martin, Simon (author; Mayanist): xvii / 26 / 211 / 430 / 662 / 704, 707–8 / 791

Martinez, Maria del Carmen Rodríguez (author; Olmec): 118 / 501

Mask, Clate W. (Second Quorum of the Seventy, The Church of Jesus Christ of Latter-day Saints; tour director): xvii–xviii / 808

Matheny, Ray T. (LDS archaeologist, Brigham Young University): xvii / 93 / 140, 150–51 / 389–90

Matthews, Peter (Mesoamerican scholar): xvii

Maudslay, A. P. (archaeologist): 90 / 795

Maya (MAH yah; modern name given to natives): 135–69 / 258 / 295–99 / 310 / 600, 602, 658 / 700, 706 / 809

> Alphabet: 32, 48 / 257–58 / 296–97
>
> Calendar: 60–64, 66 / 125 / 147–49 / 237 / 245 / 297 / 498 / 531 / 726
>
> Correlation with Nephites/Mulekites/Lamanites: 6–8, 12 / 29, 33, 37, 51 / 58, 61, 77, 80 / 97 / 135, 145, 157–58, 160, 165 / 179, 185 / 237 / 298 / 343 / 468, 491 / 562 / 599, 608 / 641 / 758 / 815
>
> Culture: 4–5 / 28 / 60–62 / 96, 100, 103 / 111 / 137–38, 140, 144, 148, 151–52 / 201 / 215, 218, 231 / 247, 256, 259–61 / 295–96, 299, 306 / 335, 345 / 361, 363 / 391 / 607 / 728 / 793
>
> Geography: 218
>
> Glyphs: 23–24, 26–28, 32, 35, 37, 50–51 / 55, 62–63, 68 / 85, 103 / 112, 115, 118, 132–33 / 137, 167 / 178 / 202 / 241 / 246, 257 / 264, 271 / 297 /

338, 340, 342, 350 / 372, 390 / 491 / 706, 708, 710 / 727, 729

History of: 30–32, 37 / 59 / 90, 97 / 109–10, 118, 131 / 136, 143, 148–49, 151, 157, 159, 162 / 173 / 228, 231 / 246–48, 258, 261, 293 / 296–300, 304 / 360, 369 / 702, 709–10 / 727 / 792

Language: 12–13 / 23–24, 26, 28, 30–32, 37, 43–46, 48–51 / 62–63, 68, 74 / 94–96, 103 / 132–33 / 137, 142–44, 147, 150 / 246, 256 / 297–98, 301, 305–6 / 583 / 641, 645, 651, 668 / 698, 709 / 736, 739 / 771

Mountains: 619, 658

Names/words: xxxv / 11–13 / 24, 26, 43–51 / 62, 94–95 / 132–33 / 298, 305–6 / 312, 315, 320 / 394 / 485 / 583 / 618 / 645, 648, 651, 668 / 699, 705, 708–11 / 736, 739 / 771

Sites: 4 / 43, 45 / 57, 63, 65, 78, 79 / 91–93, 95 / 132 / 138–39, 143, 145, 151–52, 156, 168 / 231, 233 / 299 / 354 / 371, 375 / 412, 421 / 476, 480, 483, 486–87, 489 / 541, 544 / 596, 599, 602–5, 605, 608, 612, 615, 620 / 656 / 732 / 745, 766 / 778–79, 782, 784

Spanish conquest: 24, 30–32, 51 / 97 / 162 / 246, 261 / 293 / 296 / 316

Territory of: xxx / 5–6, 8 / 25, 28–30, 32, 37 / 57, 75 / 96–99 / 102–3 / 137–38, 142–44, 150–51, 153–55, 157, 159–63, 166, 168 / 173 / 195, 201–2 / 218–19, 231, 233–34 / 250–51 / 282 / 296–300, 307 / 414, 421 / 432 / 487 / 549 / 595, 597, 599, 601, 619 / 701, 708 / 749 / 793–94

Traditions: 218 / 357, 360–61 / 412, 426–27 / 607 / 727

Writing: 26, 28–29, 32–33, 35, 37–38, 40, 51 / 133 / 144, 149 / 179 / 248, 258, 261 / 296–97 / 380 / 749

Mayapan (mah yah PAHN; ancient Maya tribe and site in the Yucatan): 13 / 299–300, 303

Maximillian (emperor of Mexico, 1832–67; toppled by Benito Juarez; subsequently executed): 191 / 804

Mazatlan (may zaht LAHN; resort city in Mexico): 465

McAffee, Ralph and Ann (tour participants): xviii

Medina, Jose Toribio (biographer; Ixtlilxochitl): 263

Medicine: 286 / 365

Melek:

    City of (Alma 8:3, 6; 35:13; Perservancia, near Tonala, Chiapas): 393 / 412 / 657 / 745, 762, 765–66, 773

    Land of (Alma 8:3; west of the river Sidon, on the west by the borders of the wilderness): 413 / 588–89 / 654 / 765, 767

Melgar, J. M. (author; Olmecs): 110

Mendoza, Wendy (contributor to project): xvi

Merida (MEHD ee dah; Spanish; capital of state of Yucatan): 23–24 / 101 / 300, 303, 305 / 544 / 810–11

Mesoamerica (may soh ah MEHD ee kah; Spanish, denoting area and time): xvii, xxi, xxiii, xxvi / 131 / 135–69 / 171–91 / 318 / 369 / 374, 388, 395 / 491 / 500–1, 508 / 534, 536 / 613 / 683, 687, 690, 705, 711–12 / 743 / 746, 758, 761 / 810–11

    Agriculture: 218 / 693

    Animals: 13 / 303 / 312 / 474

    Archaeology: 12, 20 / 38 / 67, 74–75, 78, 79 / 85–103 / 138, 152 / 187, 190 / 195, 210, 213 / 234–36 / 246 / 336–37 / 354, 356, 363 / 372, 374, 380, 384, 389–90 / 476 / 544 / 598, 602 / 643 / 692–93, 698 / 726 / 781, 783

    Bodies of water: 627–73

    Calendar: 56, 59–62, 64, 66 / 125 / 147–49, 155–56 / 229–30, 232, 236–38 / 245, 247, 258 / 726

    Climate: 6 / 42 / 120 / 356, 365 / 454 / 610 / 667

    Culture: 5–6, 11, 13–16, 20 / 33, 37, 53 / 66–67, 69, 73–74, 77–80 / 90–92, 96, 98, 101, 103 / 109–11, 115–18, 121–22, 124 / 142, 149, 156 / 185 / 194, 203, 209 / 226 / 246 / 325 / 364 / 372, 392, 396 / 422 / 465 / 782

295 / 309, 313, 315, 323, 325 / 361–62 / 376, 381,
384, 386 / 405, 409–10, 412, 415, 427 / 432, 458,
461, 464–65 / 475, 477, 481, 483, 490 / 507, 510 /
529, 536 / 557–58 / 580, 582, 588 / 596, 615 / 650,
656, 668 / 688, 691–92, 700, 702, 706, 710, 716 /
769, 775 / 778–79, 788, 790, 795–96 / 800–9
Altiplano: 195 / 442, 446 / 499
Archaeology of: 86, 90, 96
Border of: 88 / 221–22 / 293 / 529 / 572, 580,
582 / 605, 624 / 633, 656–57 / 677, 679 / 720 /
756, 764
City: 6 / 30 / 55, 59–60, 79–80 / 91–92, 96,
98–99 / 109 / 167 / 172–74 / 193–95, 200, 203–4,
208–11 / 217, 220, 234 / 258–59 / 264, 270 / 281,
283–85, 288–89, 293 / 295–96 / 309, 312 / 356,
362, 365 / 372 / 431, 436, 438, 452, 454–55 /
586 / 615 / 673 / 700–1, 708 / 753 / 792–96 /
802–3, 807–10
Conquest of: 5 / 59, 80–81 / 97 / 182, 191 / 201,
208, 210 / 259 / 265 / 285, 292–93 / 296, 298 /
311 / 362 / 596 / 699 / 788, 795–96 / 801
East coast: 431
Geography of: 414
Gulf Coast of: xxiii / 5 / 74 / 96, 98 / 106, 113, 114,
118, 120–24, 126–30, 132 / 155, 167 / 179, 182, 185 /
236–37 / 430–32, 435, 437–39, 443, 450, 461,
464 / 496–99, 504 / 537–38 / 548 / 568, 574–75,
587 / 666 / 750–51, 753, 759
Gulf of: xxv / 44 / 67, 74 / 102 / 106–7, 112,
120–21 / 182 / 195, 210 / 217, 220, 226–27, 232 /
273–76 / 395 / 410, 414, 416 / 434, 436, 447, 457–
63, 465 / 469, 471, 473 / 498 / 529, 537, 540–41,
545 / 551–54 / 617–18 / 628, 630–31, 634, 655,
659, 666–67, 670–73 / 680–81, 686, 689–90, 715 /
814–15
History: 97, 102 / 293 / 312
Independence: 80–81 / 803
Preconquest: 257, 264, 266

State of: 5 / 258 / 445—47, 450–51, 464 / 477 /
550 / 615
Valley of: 5 / 30 / 58, 60 / 96, 98, 101 / 164 / 187 /
193–95, 197, 199–201, 203–5, 208–13 / 258 / 267 /
284 / 295 / 315 / 355–56 / 395 / 431, 437, 443–44,
446–47, 451–52, 464–65 / 548, 551 / 621 / 672–
73 / 699–700, 708, 712 / 753 / 783–84, 793–94
West coast: 431, 446–47, 451 / 527, 530 / 630, 633
Written language: 85, 103
**Michaels, Joseph W. (author and archaeologist,
Kaminaljuyu Project, Pennsylvania State
University):** 722–25
Michoacan (state in Mexico): 5 / 454
Middoni:
City of (Alma 20:3–8, 28; Antigua): 393–94 /
647 / 720, 732, 736, 740–41 / 815
Land of: 731, 736, 740–42
Midian (Alma 24:5; Guatemala): 393–94 / 517
**Minatitlan (mee nah teet LAHN; Nahuatl name;
city in Mexico):** 12 / 115 / 271 / 462 / 670
Miner, Alan (LDS Mesoamericanist): xvii / 339 /
396
Miner, Caroline Eyring (LDS author): 807
Minon:
City of (Alma 2:24; Comitan, Chiapas): 678 / 745,
774
*Land of (above the city of Zarahemla; close to the
valley of Gideon and in the course of the land of
Nephi; between the land of Manti and the valley
of Gideon):* 652, 658 / 680 / 774
Miracle: 288 / 311, 323–24
**Miraflores style (mee dah FLOHR ays; pottery
style; Kaminaljuyu, Guatemala):** 640–41 / 738 /
757
**Misol Ha (MEE sol HAH; Maya; waterfalls near
Palenque):** 627
Missouri: 156 / 374 / 508 / 577 / 686, 716 / 805

Mitla (MEET lah; village and site in Oaxaca, Mexico): 58–59 / 91–92 / 139 / 171, 188, 190 / 355–56 / 797

Mixe-Zoque (native language of Mexico): 150 / 226, 237

Mixtec (MEESH tehk (native language of Mexico; name of people in state of Oaxaca): 32 / 80 / 98–99 / 172 / 247–49 / 428, 453, 455

Mocum, city of (Maya name; proposed underwater site at Lake Atitlan): 46 / 394 / 453 / 483, 485 / 641, 643–45 / 737, 739–40 / 813

Monarquia Indiana (history of Mexico written by Juan de Torquemada): 258

Monetary system: 38 / 147, 165 / 366, 368

Money: 234 / 353, 365, 368

Monte Alban (MOHN tay ahl BAHN; Spanish site name; Oaxaca): 58–59, 65, 69, 75–76, 79 / 85, 91–92, 98 / 139, 164, 167 / 171–91 / 197, 201, 203 / 354 / 384 / 443, 447, 461, 465 / 476 / 536–37, 542–43 / 573 / 750–53, 759, 761 / 793

Monte Alto (Preclassic site south of Guatemala City): 735

Montezuma (Moctezuma) (emperor of Mexico at the time of the Spanish conquest): 60, 80 / 208 / 329–30 / 699 / 795–96

Moreno, Ayax (artist): 241 / 336–40, 345

Morley, Sylvanus G. (archaeologist, Chichen Itza): xvii / 64 / 91 / 110 / 252 / 384

Morelia (city in the state of Michoacan, Mexico): 451

Morelos (state in Mexico): 5 / 258 / 550

Morgan, Verl F. (artist): xv / 310

Moriancumer (brother of Jared): 506

Morianton: 11 / 49 / 437, 443 / 551–52 / 620–21 / 672 / 790

City of: 393 / 603, 603, 620–23 / 815

Land of (Alma 50:25, 36; 51:26; land southward; central Belize): 620–21

Mormon: viii, xix, xxii / 1, 10, 12–13, 17 / 38, 41–42, 44, 46 / 61–62, 65, 76–77, 79–80, 83 / 98 / 107, 115–16, 128 / 135–36, 141–42, 154, 159, 161–62, 164, 167 / 172, 178, 186–89 / 202, 207, 211 / 233–34, 243 / 246 / 271–72 / 282, 291 / 299, 302–3 / 355–56, 359–62, 369 / 377–78, 392, 395 / 401–3, 407, 409–10, 412, 415, 417–18, 422, 424–26 / 430,

436–37, 441, 451–53, 456–57, 460 / 467, 474, 479, 487, 489 / 495, 504 / 513, 527 / 549–53, 555–56, 563–65 / 568–69, 577, 583–84, 586–87, 591–92 / 599, 602, 604–5, 609, 615, 618, 620 / 630, 634–35, 640, 643, 646, 648–49, 657, 660, 664–65, 668, 670–73 / 677, 683–86, 690–96, 698–707, 709–10 / 738, 743 / 752, 759, 767, 772, 775 / 777–78, 780, 782–83, 787–91 / 811–13, 815

Land of (land southward): 484–85 / 578 / 637–43, 644 / 676, 682 / 720, 731, 737–39, 741, 743 / 755–56

Waters of (Mosiah 18:4–5, 7–8, 30; land southward, Lake Atitlan): 12 / 29, 44 / 87 / 363 / 392, 394 / 468–69, 471, 484–85, 491 / 562 / 569, 577–81, 593 / 628, 637–42, 645–46, 646, 648–49, 651, 673 / 676, 682 / 736–37, 739–40 / 756–57 / 814

Moron: 46, 48–49 / 172 / 395

City of (first capital city of the Jaredites; land northward): 44 / 98 / 173, 176 / 429 / 436 / 498–99

Land of (Ether 7:5–6; land northward; valley of Oaxaca): 98 / 172, 182 / 381 / 434–36, 461 / 511 / 754

Moroni: ix, xix / 3, 10, 13–14, 17 / 33, 35, 39, 41, 44–45 / 66 / 79 / 94 / 107, 122, 124 / 135, 142, 146, 153, 158, 168 / 189 / 201–2 / 215, 227, 230 / 267, 271, 279 / 281 / 300–3 / 360, 368 / 377, 393 / 413, 416–18 / 433, 440–445, 456, 460–61, 463 / 472, 484, 486 / 495–97, 504–7, 510 / 513 / 552, 561 / 595–96, 603 / 763 / 778, 790–91

Angel: 799, 803, 811

City of (Alma 50:13; land southward; southern Belize by the seashore; sank into the sea in the great destruction): 158 / 393–94 / 419–20 / 453 / 483–84 / 603, 609, 615–18, 620–21, 623 / 636, 640, 643 / 748, 772

Land of (Alma 51:22; land southward, in the borders by the seashore off the coast of Belize): 614–17

Military leader, 100 BC: 603–4, 606–9, 616–17, 619–21, 623–24 / 658–59, 663 / 708 / 745, 748–49, 772

Son of Mormon, AD 400: 671 / 681, 684, 686–87, 691–93, 696, 702–6, 709–10, 713–14, 717 / 815

Moronihah: 484 / 608–9, 613 / 763

City of: 43 / 158 / 393–94 / 453, 455 / 483–84 / 682

Mosiah: xix / 8–10 / 65, 68, 73, 76 / 88, 98 / 130 / 136, 145, 147, 154–56 / 172, 178–79, 183–85 / 218, 230, 241–42 / 272 / 306 / 340, 348 / 425 / 470–71, 477, 486, 491 / 504, 506 / 528, 531–34, 543–45 / 558–59, 561–62, 564 / 569, 571–73, 575–76, 581–82, 593 / 612 / 662 / 677, 685, 705 / 719, 721–22, 725, 731–32, 737 / 746–51, 753, 755, 75963, 774

Mosiah, people of: 75

Mother culture: 10 / 105, 109–10, 118, 131 / 430

Mound B-V-6 (Kaminaljuyu, Guatemala): 723

Mound J, Monte Alban: 65 / 184–85 / 354 / 751

Mountain:

BofM: 12–13, 16 / 88 / 404–5, 407, 413 / 449 / 471, 473–74 / 527 / 561 / 567, 590 / 655, 657–59, 664–65 / 675, 682–83 / 719, 749, 756, 762, 764–66 / 814

MA: 5 / 38, 44, 46, 48–49 / 88–89, 98, 101–2 / 114, 116, 119, 128 / 143, 159 / 173, 184–85, 189–90 / 194, 210 / 223 / 256, 259 / 267–69 / 298 / 310 / 353, 357, 359 / 377, 385, 392 / 405–5, 407, 410–12, 417–19 / 434–35, 454, 458, 462 / 467, 471, 474, 483, 486 / 530, 536, 541 / 547, 549–50, 556–57, 559–61, 564–65 / 568, 571, 576, 580–81, 587 / 608, 619 / 641, 650–51, 654–56, 666, 668 / 679, 683, 685, 688–89 / 720, 726, 735 / 752 / 804

Mulek:

City of (Alma 52:2; 51:26; 52:17, 27–34; in land southward; northern Belize on the eastern seashore in the east wilderness of Zarahemla; within a day's march of Bountiful; north of Moroni, Lehi,

Morianton, Omner, and Gid; possibly Cerros):
94–95 / 393 / 444, 448 / 602–5, 608–9, 614–15,
618, 622–25 / 765–66 / 814

Land of (Helaman 6:10, land north): 37 / 171 /
412 / 447, 477 / 539 / 614

*Son of Zedekiah (Mosiah 25:2; Helaman 6:10, 21;
leader of Mulekites):* 8, 10–11 / 37, 52 / 68, 72–73,
76 / 137, 153–55 / 171, 180, 183 / 348 / 379 / 439,
447–48 / 477–78 / 496 / 532–36, 538–40, 542–
43 / 746, 762, 771

Mulekites: 171–91 / 496 / 532–33 / 651 / 746, 750 /
806, 811, 813

*Arrival in New world (Omni 1:15–16, 21; Alma
22:30; Rio Panuco north of Veracruz; Atlantic
Ocean):* 10 / 52 / 68, 72–75 / 130 / 153 / 172,
179–80, 182 / 272, 274–75 / 384 / 408–10, 424 /
429, 438–39, 447–48, 461 / 476 / 496 / 533–34,
536–40, 543, 545 / 586–87 / 750, 758 / 815

Dating of: 69, 72–73 / 130 / 153 / 171, 178–79, 185 /
230 / 275 / 540 / 750

History of: 8 / 69 / 130–31 / 178, 180, 182, 185 /
230 / 302 / 529, 534 / 569 / 746, 750

Jaredites, connections to: 10–11 / 149, 151 / 178–
80, 182, 185 / 272, 275 / 461 / 477 / 499 / 533–34,
544–45 / 746–47, 751, 757

Lamanites, connections to: 138, 165 / 172

Language of: 11 / 33, 51 / 130 / 171, 179, 184 / 533 /
663 / 746

Maya, connections to: 153–54, 165 / 815

Migrations: 8 / 74–76 / 151, 153–54 / 172, 180,
183 / 230 / 409, 424 / 448 / 476 / 529, 533–34,
536, 538–39, 541, 543, 545, 569, 588 / 750

Names: 11 / 651 / 762

Nephites, merger with: 11 / 76 / 155, 165 / 183–
85 / 230 / 272 / 443 / 471 / 533–34, 543–45 /
651 / 707 / 745–47, 751, 755, 757, 760

People: 9 / 68 / 171, 182, 184 / 471 / 533, 542 /
586 / 759, 761

Territory of: 8 / 52 / 68–69, 74–76 / 138, 149, 151,
153–54 / 172, 177–80, 183, 185 / 230, 232 / 275 /
408 / 430, 438–39, 447–48 / 529, 533, 540 / 555 /
569, 586, 588 / 655 / 747, 750–51, 766, 774

Murray, Don and Peggy (tour participants): xviii

N

Nahom (place where Ishmael died; ancient burial valley in Yemen): 515, 518, 520–25 / 813

Nahuatl (NAH oo ah tl; name of Aztec language): xix–xxx / 13 / 30, 44, 46 / 112, 128 / 193 / 268, 278 / 284–85, 288, 292 / 317, 320, 326, 329 / 414 / 462 / 583 / 651 / 685, 699 / 772

Narrow mountain range (see also narrow strip of wilderness and Cuchumatanes): 89, 102 / 404 / 547, 549, 556–58, 560, 564 / 572, 577

Narrow neck of land (Alma 22:32; Ether 10:20; Isthmus of Tehuantepec; see also small neck of land): xvi, xxii / 8, 16–17 / 46 / 74–75 / 102 / 113, 123, 128, 131 / 162, 168 / 172 / 204, 208, 211 / 217–19 / 375, 381, 383–84, 392–93, 395–96 / 419, 424–25 / 429, 432, 435, 439, 440, 445, 456–57, 459, 462, 464–65 / 467–69, 471, 480, 487–88, 490, 492–93 / 500 / 514, 526 / 547–55 / 633, 651, 666, 668–69 / 683–84, 689, 692, 694–701, 703, 707, 712 / 747–48 / 783, 785–87, 790 / 814

Narrow passage (Mormon 2:29; route between east and west mountains through the Isthmus of Tehuantepec): 79 / 102 / 115 / 163–64, 167 / 188 / 218, 233–34 / 271 / 413, 416 / 430, 442, 444–45, 456–60, 464 / 469, 472–73, 480, 488–89 / 502 / 547–55 / 587 / 621 / 632–34, 670 / 684–85, 694–95, 697, 700–1 / 752, 759 / 787 / 814

Narrow path: 335 / 425 / 547

Narrow strip of wilderness (Alma 22:27; possibly the Cuchumatanes mountain range in Mexico and Guatemala): 86, 89, 102–3 / 131 / 392–93 / 401, 404–5, 407, 410, 418, 423–25, 425 / 440 / 468–71 / 500, 502 / 532 / 547–48, 556, 558–61, 563–65 / 572–73 / 628–29, 636, 643, 650, 655, 657–58, 663–65 / 749, 765, 773 / 814

National Museum of Anthropology: 55, 59, 68 / 113 / 167 / 173, 179, 187 / 193, 195, 200 / 362, 365 / 372, 382 / 586 / 780, 794

Nauvoo (LDS settlement on the Mississippi River): 14 / 90 / 374 / 508 / 577 / 755, 759 / 804

Navas, Sergio (tour operator): xviii

Nebuchadnezzar (king of Babylon, ca. 600 BC): 70–73 / 535

Needham, Joseph (author): 148

Neeley, Keith (photographer): 116

Nelson, Fred W. (presented paper in honor of Thomas Stuart Ferguson at a symposium of the Society for Early Historic Archaeology): 387

Nehor (Jaredite name; Nephite apostate; ca. 91 BC): 395 / 764

Nephi: xix / 6–7 / 33–34, 39–40, 42, 45, 47, 52–53 / 71–72, 74, 80–81 / 97 / 137, 144–45, 154, 167 / 171, 190 / 227–29, 234, 241 / 282 / 298, 304 / 311, 315, 326 / 333–36, 340–45, 348 / 354, 356 / 402 / 448, 452 / 469, 474, 478 / 495–96 / 513, 516, 518–20, 522–26, 529, 534, 542–43 / 569–71, 577, 582 / 613–14, 624 / 665 / 683, 699, 713 / 721, 724–26, 729 / 750 / 777–78, 797 / 799–800, 811, 813

City of (2 Nephi 5:5–8; Mosiah 7:1–8; Guatemala City; Kaminaljuyu): 74 / 145, 147, 155 / 228, 236 / 246 / 394 / 390–91, 394 / 406 / 470, 474, 477, 485 / 500 / 531 / 560 / 570–73, 577–82 / 612, / 638–39, 641–42, 645, 647, 662, 668 / 676, 678–79, 706 / 719–21, 723, 729, 731–32, 736, 741 / 748–50, 756–57, 760, 774 / 799, 802, 814

Land of (Alma 22:27; Guatemala): xxvi / 6, 8, 10, 17 / 53 / 74–76 / 131 / 136, 145, 147, 154, 156, 167 / 178, 183 / 227, 230, 232–33 / 246, 250 / 307 / 358, 364 / 390–92, 394–95 / 401–5, 407–8, 410, 413–14, 417–19, 421, 423–25 / 435–36, 441, 443 / 467–72, 476, 478, 484, 486, 491 / 502, 504 / 527–28, 531–32, 540, 543 / 547–49, 556–65 / 569–78, 580, 582–83, 590, 593 / 596–98, 605, 612–13, 617 / 627–31, 635, 638, 641–43, 645–46, 646, 652, 655–58, 660, 666 / 675, 678–80, 685, 712 / 719–43 / 745, 747–48, 750, 755–57, 760–65, 774

Large plates of: 630, 671 / 684, 691, 696

O

Oaks, Merrill C. and Jo (photographer; tour participants): xv, xviii / 81 / 93 / 105, 117 / 143, 146, 165 / 172–73, 189 / 196, 200 / 245, 256, 259 / 357, 365–66, 368 / 559 / 567, 588, 591, 593 / 611, 623, 625, / 627, 642, 644, 646, 666, 669 / 689, 704 / 723–24, 735, 738 / 769–70 / 804, 806

Oaxaca (wah HAH kah; city and state in Mexico): xxx / 365 / 780

City of: 67, 79 / 98 / 172–74, 177, 179, 187, 190 / 195, 208 / 364 / 436 / 502 / 536 / 615 / 752 / 810–11

Mountains: 189–90 / 353 / 458 / 547, 550 / 672

State of: 5 / 28, 32 / 65, 67 / 91, 96, 98 / 120–21 / 150, 167 / 171–73, 178, 182, 189–91 / 279 / 356 / 430, 435, 438, 443, 447, 450–51, 453–54, 458, 461 / 477 / 497–99, 511 / 536 / 550 / 615 / 632 / 750, 761 / 804

Valley of: 5 / 32 / 92, 98 / 171–74, 176–80, 182–83, 185, 187, 189–91 / 197, 201 / 220, 226, 237 / 248–49 / 274 / 434, 437, 461, 465 / 497–99, 504 / 542 / 573 / 751, 753–54

Ochoa, Lorenzo (author on Olmec and Maya): 114 / 150 / 540–41

Ocosingo (oh koh SEEN goh; city in Chiapas, Mexico): 449 / 541 / 591

Ocozocoautla (oh koh zoh koh AHT lah; city in Chiapas, Mexico): 583 / 772

O'Donnal, John F. (early LDS Church leader in Guatemala): 809

Ogden, Kelly (Religion professor/author, Brigham Young University): 197 / 515–16

O'Gorman, Edmundo (published the writings of Ixtlilxochitl): 264–65

Ohio: 156 / 374 / 465 / 483 / 508 / 577 / 686, 713

Old World: 34, 37, 39, 44 / 58 / 133 / 148, 163 / 241 / 331 / 334, 343 / 461 / 495, 498, 504 / 532 / 567 / 681–82 / 750, 761

Olmec (OHL mayk; modern name given to ancient inhabitants; probably the Jaredite; Spanish Olmeca): xxiii / 5–6, 11 / 44, 52 / 58, 65, 68–69 / 92, 95–96, 98–99, 100, 103 / 105–33 / 219, 236

Climate: 120

Connections to Izapa: 120–21 / 144 / 228, 231–32, 236–38

Correlation with Jaredites: 73 / 115, 117–18, 123, 128, 131–32 / 432–33 / 500 / 554, 562 / 575 / 663 / 685–86, 690, 712, 716 / 814

Culture: 113, 115, 121–22, 129, 131 / 143 / 226 / 272

Dating: 110, 112–13, 118–19, 128, 131 / 176 / 226, 231 / 340 / 432 / 467 / 499 / 725

Destruction of: 115, 120, 124, 127, 131 / 167 / 230, 232

History of: 105, 116, 122–24 / 131, 138 / 226, 230–32 / 268, 272–73 / 302 / 498, 499

Influence of: 98 / 120–21, 131, 133 / 149, 153 / 179–80, 182, 185 / 179–80, 182, 185 / 236 / 461 / 541 / 606 / 751, 753–54

Language of: 105 / 146

Monuments: 105, 110, 112, 114–16, 118, 121–22, 133 / 144 / 181 / 231, 235 / 263 / 321 / 340 / 432–33 / 495, 498–99 / 537 / 685

Mother culture: 131 / 497, 501

Names of: 126, 133 / 340

Sites: 114–15, 121 / 176, 179, 181 / 219, 232, 236–37 / 268 / 340 / 428, 432, 435, 458, 462 / 537 / 554 / 575 / 670 / 688, 699 / 775 / 787

Territory of: xxiii / 6, 11 / 75 / 99 / 107, 114, 120, 123, 131 / 149–50, 153 / 172, 179, 182 / 219, 226–27, 232, 236–37 / 271, 273 / 302 / 430–31, 435, 439, 460 / 497, 500 / 537–38 / 554 / 587 / 618 / 663 / 685–86, 715 / 753

Writing: 119, 132–33 / 501

Olmec Museum: 105 / 365

Oman (site near the Arabian Sea): 243 / 510 / 515–16, 521–23, 525 / 567

Omer *(Ether 1:29–30; early Jaredite king):* 379 /
436 / 496 / 696

Omner:

City of *(Alma 51:26; land southward; central
Belize along the seashore):* 393 / 603, 609, 618,
622–23 / 813

Son of Mosiah: 402–3

Omni *(Jarom 1:15; Nephite record keeper; ca. 361
BC):* 146 / 721, 724 / 746

Onihah, city of *(3 Nephi 9:7; city probably at Lake
Atitlan; destroyed in the great destruction):* 44,
46, 49 / 394 / 453 / 483, 485 / 641, 643–45 / 737,
739, 740 / 813

Orellana, Rafael Aapia *(author; Izapa):* 236

Oveson, Stephen B. and Dixie R. *(tour participants):* xviii

P

Paanchi *(Helaman 1:3; son of Pahoran; ca. 52 BC):*
43–44, 46

Pacal *(pah KAHL; Maya ruler at Palenque):* 23,
26–27, 40 / 92 / 133 / 135, 166 / 271 / 337 / 711 /
780, 791

Pacific:

Coast: 136, 143, 149–50 / 208 / 215–16, 221,
226–27, 236, 239 / 263, 274 / 405, 416 / 437, 458 /
501 / 527, 531 / 570 / 632 / 765, 768 / 815

Corridor: 216, 234 / 436 / 548

Ocean: 89, 102 / 173 / 217, 220 / 271 / 348 / 377,
392 / 403–4, 405, 411–12, 418 / 431, 445, 462 /
471, 479–80 / 497–99, 504–5, 510 / 526, 529, 534,
537 / 553–54, 556–57 / 577 / 628–31, 633, 635,
648, 663, 665, 673 / 699 / 720

Pacumeni *(Helaman 1:3; son of Paharon; ca. 52
BC):* 43–44, 46

Pahoran *(Alma 50:39–40; third Nephite chief
judge; ca. 68 BC):* 43–44, 46 / 158 / 544 / 606–7,
616, 619 / 708–9

Palenque *(pah LAYN kay; Maya site name,
Chiapas):* 4 / 26, 38, 48–49, 51 / 59, 68, 79 / 86,
90, 92–93 / 132 / 139–41, 166–68, 169 / 213 / 238 /
271 / 304 / 321 / 337 / 443 / 472, 481, 492 / 501 /

541 / 557 / 578, 591 / 625 / 627, 661–62 / 686, 705, 707, 711–12 / 759 / 780, 791

Palmer, David A. (LDS author; hill Cumorah): xvi / 115–16, 132–33 / 211 / 275 / 390 / 630 / 688–89, 717

Palmyra (village in upstate New York where Hill Cumorah is located): 117 / 505 / 686, 688, 692, 703, 713 / 802, 815

Panajachel (pah nah hah CHAYL; village by Lake Atitlan, Guatemala): 165 / 639, 643 / 738–39

Panama: 381, 383 / 808

Isthmus of: xxii / 376, 378, 384, 396 / 492 / 526 / 548

Pan-American Highway: 221 / 565 / 582

Panuco (also known as Potonchan; possibly area where the Mulekites landed): 274 / 537–38

Papaloapan water basin (pah pah loh AH pahn; Nahuatl for water basin/butterfly; also called Hueyapan, which means very large waters; see Ripliancum): 113, 117, 128 / 210 / 434–35, 438, 458, 465 / 671–73 / 681, 687, 690

Paraiba stone: 538–39

Pardo, Ledus-Lara (Mexican author): 264

Paredon (pay ray DOHN; village along Pacific coast in Chiapas): 411–13, 424 / 633

Paris Codex (discovered in the Paris Library): 248

Parrish, Alan K. (tour participant): xviii

Parry, Donald W. (LDS author): 36

Passover: 76–77 / 95 / 513 / 610–12

Patzicia (paht see SEE ah; native village in Guatemala): 245 / 483 / 647 / 736, 741 / 809, 811

Patzun (village between Guatemala City and Lake Atitlan): 741

Pendergast, David (archaeologist): 152

Perez, Israel (LDS Church leader, Guatemala): xviii / 223–24 / 253

Pericutin (pay dee koo TEEN; modern city covered by volcanic eruption): 454

Perry, David and Julie (tour participants): xviii

Peru: 142, 167 / 372, 388, 394 / 492–93 / 500–3, 507 / 526, 530 / 574 / 666 / 702

Peten (pay TEHN; department in Guatemala):

Department of: 5 / 41, 43, 45 / 74 / 93, 95 / 140, 143, 150–51, 158 / 201 / 217 / 307 / 320 / 353, 357 / 390, 392 / 404–5, 412, 416–17, 420 / 440–41, 444–45, 448 / 471, 477, 482, 484, 487 / 499 / 543 / 597, 605, 611, 618–19, 623 / 632, 637, 650 / 683, 699–701, 705–6, 708, 710, 712 / 731 / 768, 772

East wilderness: 45 / 156, 158 / 416–18, 420 / 444 / 543 / 567, 588 / 596, 598, 620 / 772 / 814

Jungle: 28, 44 / 93 / 151–52, 156, 158 / 201 / 393 / 415, 417–18 / 472, 474 / 595–96, 598, 602, 615, 617–19 / 709 / 748

Rainforest: 41 / 150 / 406 / 567 / 596–97 / 730

Peterson, Frederick A. (author; Mesoamerica): 318

Peterson, Mark and Nancy (tour participants): xvi

Petlecalco, Helaman (tour operator): xviii

Phoenicians: 8 / 73 / 538–39

Piedras Negras (pee AY drahs NAY grahs; Classic Maya site on the Usumacinta River): 219 / 661–62, 664

Place of entrance: 599–601

Place of their fathers' first inheritance: 136 / 395 / 405–6, 423 / 527–28, 531–32 / 570

Place where the sea divides the land (Ether 10:20; Gulf of Mexico): 102 / 113, 123 / 276 / 432, 462 / 469 / 547, 552, 554 / 628, 634, 669–71, 673

Plan of salvation: 422, 424–27 / 592–93

Plates of brass (relates to Old Testament through Jeremiah; Lehi brought them to the New World): 9 / 516 / 746

Pomoca (Preclassic site in the middle Usumacinta basin): 150

Popocatepetl (poh poh kah tay PAY tl; Nahuatl, volcanic mountain in Mexico): 199 / 454

Popol Vuh (poh poohl VOOH; Maya ancient record): 37–38 / 251–54, 256–57 / 338, 340 / 363 / 529 / 645 / 743

Potonchan (also known as Panuco; possibly area where the Mulekites landed; see also Panuco): 274–75 / 538

Potter, George (LDS Old World investigator): 500, 509 / 517–18, 523–24

Pottery: 16, 20 / 148, 155 / 172, 178 / 266 / 303 / 362 / 380 / 564 / 639, 641, 643–44, 663–64 / 737–39 / 757, 774 / 802

Pratt, John P. (LDS researcher, astronomer): 72, 76

Pratt, Orson (early LDS Church leader and Apostle): 376, 378–81, 384 / 686

Pratt, Parley P. (early LDS Church leader and Apostle; brother to Orson): 586 / 716

Pratt, Rey L. (early LDS Church leader to Mexico): 807–8

Preconquest: 257 / 264, 266

Priest:
    BofM: viii / 29, 42 / 77–78 / 97 / 140, 152, 162 / 185–87 / 197, 201, 207 / 250 / 343 / 426 / 471 / 562 / 577, 593 / 638, 645–46, 646, 652 / 676, 679 / 727–28, 742 / 755, 760, 767 / 778–79, 781, 783 /
    Catholic: 31–32, 51 / 80 / 196, 204 / 247, 255, 257–59 / 273 / 281–84, 288, 292–93 / 295 / 768

MA: 77 / 97 / 140 / 152, 159, 161–63 / 185 / 246, 257 / 277 / 386–87 / 311, 315, 317, 319, 324, 328–29 / 337, 344–45 / 355 / 487–88 / 539, 544 / 707 / 778–80, 782–83, 791–92, 794 / 815

Priestcraft: 201 / 298 / 759 / 775

Proskouriakoff, Tatiana (archaeologist; Mayanist): xvii / 238 / 710

Puebla:
    City of: 274 / 448, 464 / 615
    State of: 5 / 140 / 173, 182 / 258 / 275 / 430, 447–48, 450, 454–55, 465 / 550 / 615 / 793
    Mountains of: 434

Puerto Vallarta (resort city in Mexico): 633

Puleston, Dennis E. (archaeologist, see also defensive earthworks): 598–601

Pusilha (Maya archaeological site): 158 / 618, 620

Pyramid of the Moon (see also Teotihuacan): 167 / 193, 196, 198–200, 203–6 / 290

Pyramid of the Sun (see also Teotihuacan): 167 / 193, 195–99, 203–6, 210 / 290 / 384

Q

Quadrangle of the Nunnery (see also Uxmal; Maya ruins of Uxmal): 24 / 782

Quarter where no man had been (Ether 2:5; location encountered by Jaredites): 508 / 522

Quetzal (KAYT sahl; revered bird in Mesoamerica): xv / 1 / 30 / 200, 206 / 290 / 304 / 309–10, 320 / 336, 341 / 365 / 780

Quetzalcoatl (kayt sahl koh AH tl; Nahuatl, feathered serpent; used for deity; possible name associated with Christ in Mesoamerica): xvi, xxix / 16 / 40 / 55–56 / 133 / 193, 196, 199–200, 206–8 / 258, 260 / 265, 273–78 / 285–89 / 309–31 / 334–36, 338 / 367 / 448, 455 / 670 / 792–95 / 814

Quetzalcoatl, Temple of (see also Teotihuacan): 200, 206–7 / 312, 329

Quetzaltenango (kayt sahl tay NAHN goh; Nahuatl, Maya city in Guatemala): xx / 30 / 86–88 / 221, 224 / 570, 572, 581–82 / 642, 648–49, 656–57 / 679 / 731, 733, 740, 743 / 756 / 805, 809, 814

Quiche (kee CHAY; Maya language dialect, Guatemala): 32, 37 / 74 / 165 / 251–56 / 363 / 376 / 529, 540 / 638

Quinametzin (keen ah MAYT zeen; ancient tribe named by Ixtlilxochitl): 106, 109, 127 / 182 / 265, 268–73

Quincy, Josiah (author; wrote about Joseph Smith): 3–4

Quintana Roo (state of Mexico): 5 / 59 / 92, 95 / 440, 444–45, 448 / 467, 472, 477 / 605, 609, 612, 620

Quirarte, Jacinto (iconographist; dealt with art and iconography at Izapa): 238

Quirigua (kee ree GWAH; Maya site in Guatemala): 4 / 90 / 371 / 491–93

R

Radiocarbon dating (also called carbon-14 dating): xxiii, xxv, xxvii / 56, 69, 83 / 112, 118 / 178 / 196 / 390, 394 / 613 / 715 / 758

Radzik, Francois (LDS author in Germany): xvii / 584

Rainy season (May to October): 6 / 24 / 220 / 356, 358–59 / 551 / 653 / 700 / 735

Ramah, hill (Ether 15:11; Mormon 6:2–6; scene of Jaredite final destruction; same hill as Nephite hill Cumorah; Hill Vigia; near Santiago, Veracruz): 17 / 53 / 113, 116–17, 127, 129, 131 / 182 / 219 / 389, 392–93, 395–96, 429, 436, 465 / 500, 502, 507 / 622 / 628, 671–72, 681, 683, 686–87, 690, 692, 694, 697–98, 701–2, 716–17 / 814

Rawlings, Jay and Elaine (tour participants): xviii

Recinos, Adrian (translator of the Spanish version of the Popol Vuh*):* 74 / 252, 256 / 540–41

Red Sea: 243 / 376 / 496 / 513–17, 519–20, 523–24, 533, 539 / 675–76 / 813

Reeve, Rex Jr. (tour participant): xviii / 717

Reformed Egyptian (language used in writing on the plates for the Book of Mormon): 23, 25, 32–33, 52–53

Remnant: 53 / 129–30 / 137 / 190 / 218, 227, 229, 236 / 275 / 427 / 456 / 474 / 507 / 561 / 592 / 713 / 725 / 760–61, 772 / 799–801, 806, 808, 811–13

Restoration: 797 / 799–815

Resurrection, of mankind: 82 / 196 / 290 / 305–6 / 315, 328 / 344–45, 349–50

Reynolds, George (LDS author): 380–81, 384

Richards, Brett (participant in tour group; killed by bandits): 221–22, 225

Richards, Franklin D. (former Apostle, The Church of Jesus Christ of Latter-day Saints, 1821–99): 530

S

7 / 196, 204, 206 / 255, 257–58, 260 / 281–93 / 295 / 309, 311, 325, 328–29 / 353–54 / 475 / 537–38

Salina Cruz (city in the state of Oaxaca, Mexico): 431 / 557 / 633

Sam (son of Lehi; brother of Nephi): 39, 53 / 241 / 343–44 / 514, 516

Samuel the Lamanite (Helaman 13–15; Lamanite prophet; ca. 6 BC): xix / 56 / 207 / 357 / 472

San Andres Tuxtla (village in the state of Veracruz, Mexico): 110

San Antonio (village at Lake Atitlan): 259 / 739

San Bartolo (Preclassic Maya site in Peten, Guatemala): 75 / 390 / 597

San Cristobal de las Casas (city in the state of Chiapas, Mexico): 238 / 387 / 449 / 481 / 541 / 591 / 654 / 764, 769

Sanders, William T. (author and archaeologist, Kaminaljuyu Project, Pennsylvania State University): 722–25

San Jose Mogote (archaeological site in Oaxaca, Mexico): 58, 67 / 174 / 461, 465 / 511

San Juan Chamula (native village near San Cristobal de las Casas, Chiapas, Mexico): 353 / 769

San Lorenzo (ancient Olmec site in Veracruz, Mexico; possibly the Jaredite city of Kish): 12 / 58, 68 / 95 / 114–15, 120–22, 132–33 / 230, 232 / 320 / 432, 435, 458, 462–65 / 502 / 554 / 670 / 681, 685, 699 / 759 / 787

San Lucas Toliman Volcano (volcano at Lake Atitlan): 739

San Marcos (village at Lake Atitlan): 739 / 807

San Pedro Volcano (volcano at Lake Atitlan): 711 / 738–39

Santa Caterina (village at Lake Atitlan): 739

Santa Rosa (archaeological site in Chiapas, Mexico; proposed site of the city of Zarahemla):

75 / 483 / 572 / 653–54, 662 / 680 / 749, 752, 757–59, 762, 764, 770, 772

Santiago Atitlan (village at Lake Atitlan): 485 / 643–45 / 738–39

Santiago Atitlan Volcano (see also Lake Atitlan): 739

Santiago Tuxtla (city in Veracruz by the Hill Vigia; see also Ramah and Cumorah): 116–17 / 368 / 554 / 688, 691

Sariah (wife of Lehi): 219, 227, 240–41 / 340, 344, 346 / 514, 516 / 813

Saudi Arabia: 500 / 515 / 567 / 676

Savill, Marshall (museum curator; originated the term "Olmec"): 111

Schele, Linda (twentieth-century Mayanist, artist, author, and educator): xvii / 26, 28, 37 / 92, 94 / 166 / 252 / 97 / 605–8 / 704, 708 / 726

Scherer, Andrew (author): 664

Scribes: 29 / 63 / 248–49 / 327

Sea east (see also east sea): 89, 103 / 360 / 380 / 401, 403–5, 418–19, 423–25 / 554, 556–57 / 572 / 598 / 628–31, 634, 655, 664 / 813

Sea south to the sea north: 380 / 479 / 634

Sea west (see also west sea): 89, 103 / 360 / 380 / 401, 403–5, 418–19, 423–25 / 554, 556–57 / 572 / 628–32, 634, 655, 664 / 813

Sea west to the sea east: 479 / 634

Sebus, waters of (land southward; land of Nephi): 628, 646–48, 673 / 815

Seibal (Maya site; possibly site of Nephihah): 618

Sejourne, Laurette (twentieth-century Mexican author and educator): xvii / 310–11, 313, 316, 321, 324–26

Serpent:
  BofM: 94 / 113 / 186 / 227–28 / 349–50 / 367 / 473–75 / 587 / 670 / 772
  Brazen: 133 / 312, 321 / 360
  MA: 60 / 132–33 / 141 / 171, 188 / 200, 206–8 / 276–77 / 287 / 303–4 / 309–10, 312, 320–21, 326,

331 / 336, 338, 341, 343 / 355, 360, 367 / 434, 463 / 468 / 670 / 794

Sharer, Robert J. (Maya author): 26

Shem:

City of: 395

Land of: 457

Shemlon:

City of: 394 / 720, 732, 734–35 / 815

Land of (Mosiah 10:7; 20:1–5; Guatemala): 734–36 / 760

Shiblom (Mormon 6:14; Nephite military leader): 120, 125–26, 133 / 268

Shiblon (Jaredite name; second son of Alma; ca. 74 BC): 11 / 43, 48 / 209 / 437, 446

Shilom:

City of (Mosiah 9:8; 11:12; Guatemala City): 394 / 518–19 / 559 / 577 / 638 / 720, 732–33

Land of: 732–34, 736 / 755–56, 760

Shilton, Tom and Lorraine (tour participants): xviii

Shim, hill (Mormon 1:3; 2:17; Ether 9:3; probably Hill Cintepec near Lake Catemaco): 44, 46 / 117 / 186 / 383, 393, 395 / 429, 436, 457, 460,

465 / 504, 509 / 622 / 681, 683–86, 689–91, 695–701 / 786, 788 / 814

Shimnilom (Alma 23:8; city in land of Nephi): 394 / 732, 735–36

Shiz (Ether 14:17; Jaredite military leader): 43 / 126–29 / 434 / 671–72 / 681 / 747

Shook, Edwin M. (archaeologist; Kaminaljuyu): xvii / 93 / 722–23

Shout of Delores (1810 cry of freedom from Spain originating in Hidalgo, Mexico): 797

Shule: 11 / 43, 46, 49

Valley of: 395 / 676, 681

Shum: 44 / 366

Sidom:

City of (Alma 15:1, 3, 13; Chiapa de Corzo; formerly Zactun): 46 / 393 / 745, 763, 769–74 / 814

Land of: 614 / 770

Sidon:

Head of the river: 404, 406, 418, 423 / 620 / 631, 655–56, 658, 660, 664 / 773

Headwaters of the river: 410 / 556 / 632, 650, 655, 658, 661, 663 / 764–65, 773

River (Alma 2:27; 6:7; 8:3; Grijalva River): 46 /
73–74 / 153, 167 / 379, 383, 390, 393 / 404, 413 /
448 / 468–69 / 538 / 574, 588–89 / 620 / 628,
650–61, 663–65, 673 / 679–80 / 748, 752, 762,
764–65, 770, 774 / 814

Sierra de las Minas (mountains in Mexico; see also
narrow strip of wilderness): 102 / 559 / 619 /
656

Sierra Madres (mountain range in Mexico): 102 /
403 / 556–57

Silverberg, Robert (author; Mound Builders): 16 /
715

Siyaj Chan K'awiil: 711

Siyaj K'ak' (YAHK KAH AHK; see Fire Is Born;
military leader, Teotihuacan, AD 378): 707–10 /
790

Skin color: 136 / 327

Skinner, Andrew B. (LDS author): 197

Skousen, Phil (photographer): xv / 27 / 157 / 216,
240 / 272 / 295 / 527 / 641, 673

Skousen, Royal (LDS researcher and author): 359,
364 / 605

Skousen, W. Cleon (LDS author and educator):
217 / 382

Small neck of land (see also narrow neck of land,
Isthmus of Tehuantepec): 102 / 378 / 414, 423–
24, 426 / 435, 437, 459 / 469, 473, 476 / 547–49 /
630 / 814

Smith, Joseph Jr. (prophet; translator of the Book
of Mormon; founder of The Church of Jesus
Christ of Latter-day Saints): ix, xvi, xix, xxxv /
3–5, 14, 19 / 28, 35 / 81 / 90–91 / 168 / 189–90 /
213 / 218 / 247 / / 364, 367 / 371, 374–77, 398 /
490–91, 493 / 505, 507 / 530–31 / 563 / 577,
585–86 / 630, 672 / 676, 684, 686–87, 692–93,
713–17 / 803–5, 814–15

Smith, Langdon (archaeological investigator): 703

Smith, Lucy Mack (mother of Joseph Smith Jr.):
364

Smoking Frog (nickname of fourth-century military leader, see also Siyaj K'ak'): 708

Society for Early Historic Archaeology (organization sponsored by Brigham Young University):
235 / 387

Soconusco (soh koh NOOS koh; fertile valley along
Pacific coast in Chiapas): 136 / 216–17 / 527,
531–32 / 765

Solola (municipal department in Guatemala, see
also Lake Atitlan): 256 / 485 / 639, 642–43 / 731,
737–38

Sons of Helaman: 181 / 340 / 393 / 589 / 620, 624 /
632 / 767

Sons of Mosiah: 153, 158 / 340 / 393–94 / 402, 413 /
476, 484–85 / 527–28 / 562–63 / 582 / 624 /
630, 635, 639–44, 646, 651 / 679–80 / 720, 722,
735–38 / 763–65, 773

Sorenson, John L. (LDS author; anthropologist; retired professor from Brigham Young
University): xvii, xxiii / 4–5 / 32 / 117–18 /
390–91 / 461–62 / 477, 483 / 496 / 630 / 688 /
721 / 770–71

Sotuta (Maya village in the Yucatan, Mexico):
299–300

South America: xiii, xxii / 17 / 217, 219 / 325 / 376–
84, 388–89, 396 / 422 / 468, 480, 493 / 526, 530 /
555 / 577

South wilderness: 10 / 74 / 153–54 / 180 / 409–10,
424 / 476 / 540–41, 543 / 568–69, 586–88 / 655,
657, 664 / 746, 748

Spain: 80–82 / 196 / 247–48, 255, 257–58 / 264,
267 / 282, 285, 293 / 295, 302 / 693, 704 / 796 /
801, 803

Spanish chroniclers (sixteenth-century writers/
historians): xviii / 106, 126 / 255, 257–59 / 281 /
316 / 464 / 537–38

Spanish chronicles (written works of the sixteenth-
century Spanish writers/historians): 6 / 30,

47 / 56, 66–67 / 124 / 257 / 285 / 316 / 381, 387 /
464 / 476, 482 / 510 / 543

Spanish conquest: xxvii / 30 / 56, 60, 80 / 91, 97 /
160 / 171, 188 / 231 / 246, 251, 254, 256–58 / 267 /
282–83, 293 / 295, 300, 303 / 366, 368–69 / 414 /
491 / 563 / 701–2 / 741, 743 / 789, 794 / 800

*Spearthrower Owl (fourth-century dictator at
Teotihuacan; also called Spearthrower Shield):*
202, 211–12 / 662 / 706–7, 709–10 / 789–90

*Spearthrower Shield (also called Spearthrower
Owl):* 706, 708–9

Spence, Lewis (author): 318, 326

*Sperry, Sidney B. (LDS author; former Religion
professor, Brigham Young University):* xvi /
388–89

Stacey, Darrell and Loretta (tour participants):
xviii

Star: 311, 323, 329

Stela: 55, 64 / 95 / 142, 148 / 241 / 433 / 815

*Stela 5 (monument at Izapa; known as the Tree of
Life Stone):* xvi / 28, 38, 39, 45 / 93, 100 / 150,
155–56 / 215, 219, 221–22, 231, 235–37, 239–41 /
333–51 / 472 / 528 / 815 /

Stela 24 (monument at Chiapa de Corzo): 150,
155–56

Stela 31 (monument at Tikal): 55 / 155–57, 168 /
202, 212 / 340 / 692, 698, 704–6, 708–11 / 785 /
815

*Stephens, John Lloyd (author; explorer; labeled
"the father of Mesoamerican archaeology"):*
xvii / 86–90 / 140–41 / 213 / 218 / 371, 374–76,
396 / 490–93 / 557–58, 561, 565 / 572, 574, 580–
81 / 650, 655 / 678

Stirling, Matthew (Maya archaeologist): xvii / 95 /
109–10, 112–13, 116, 118 / 219, 235 / 268 / 333

Stoddard, Mary O. (photographer): xv / 81 / 243

Stoddard, Ted D. (editor of Exploring the Lands
of the Book of Mormon; *professor emeritus,
Brigham Young University):* xv, xxi, xxvii / 53 /
86–87 / 117

Stone box: 4 / 328 / 367 / 388 / 692–93

Stripling warriors: 765–67

Stuart, David (Maya scholar and author): xvii /
26 / 202 / 704, 706, 708–10, 712

Sumidero Canyon (canyon on Grivalja River):
590 / 651 / 680 / 770–71

V

215, 228 / 321 / 433 / 471 / 541 / 659, 667 / 680 / 810

Volcano/volcanic: 74 / 87 / 160 / 232 / 454 / 483 / 638, 640–41, 643–44, 649–50 / 690, 711 / 725, 733–34, 739

Von Hagen, Victor W. (author): 325

Vultures: 583–86 / 772, 774

W

Warren, Bruce (LDS archaeologist, author, educator): xi, xvii / 49 / 68, 73, 77 / 117–18, 132–33 / 235, 238 / 285 / 341 / 354 / 380, 388, 390 / 536 / 611–12 / 640–41 / 726–27, 741 / 758

Washburn, J. Niles (LDS author; tour participant): xviii / 384–85

Webster, David (Maya archaeologist; see defensive earthworks): xvii / 94 / 360

Welch, John W. (LDS author, researcher): xvi / 390

Wellington, Richard (LDS author): 524

West, Jack (LDS author): 388

Weapons:
 BofM: 68 / 124, 126 / 145 / 226 / 368 / 389 / 413 / 432, 434 / 604, 623 / 658 / 748, 765
 MA: 275 / 365, 368

Weights and measures: 146–47 / 353, 365–66 / 645

West sea (Pacific Ocean west of Chiapas and Oaxaca): 102 / 204, 208 / 340 / 392 / 403, 405, 411–12, 415–16, 418–20, 423–26 / 445–47, 451 / 477, 480 / 502 / 547, 553 / 589 / 628–30, 632–33, 635–37, 660, 663, 673 / 765–66

West sea, south: 589 / 632–33

Whetten, Robert (former General Authority, The Church of Jesus Christ of Latter-day Saints): 806

Whitmer, David (one of the Book of Mormon Three Witnesses): ix

Widtsoe, John A. (member of the Quorum of the Twelve Apostles, The Church of Jesus Christ of Latter-day Saints, 1921–52): 385, 397

Wilcox, S. Michael (tour participant): xviii

Wilderness:
 BofM: 8–10, 12–13 / 34, 38, 45–46 / 69, 73–74 / 88 / 111, 113, 123 / 136–37, 145, 166–67 / 183 / 227, 230, 243 / 270 / 312–13, 321 / 344 / 404–7, 410, 420, 423–24 / 432, 435–36, 439, 441, 461–62 / 469, 472, 475–76 / 506, 508–10 / 514–16, 519–25, 527–28, 533, 540, 543 / 554, 558–59, 562, 564 / 567–93 / 599, 603, 617, 624 / 629, 641, 644–45, 648, 652, 655–56, 658, 665, 669 / 676–77, 682–83 / 737, 742–43 / 745–46, 748, 755–56, 760, 762, 765, 772–74
 MA: 13 / 38, 44, 46, 48 / 113–14 / 221, 228 / 410, 414 / 434 / 467, 471–74 / 541, 543 / 556–59, 561, 563, 565 / 567–93 / 663, 668 / 677, 683 / 772

Wilkinson, Ernest L. (president of Brigham Young University, 1951–71): 217 / 383

Willard, Joseph (LDS author; contributor to project): xvi / 726

Willey, Gordon R. (archaeologist): 757

Williams, Frederick G. (early LDS Church leader): 163, 166 / 530–31

Williams, Ryan (contributor to project): xvi

Wilson, Sheryl Lee (photographer): xv / 57, 78 / 85, 93, 95 / 110–11, 115, 121, 128 / 140–41, 153, 169 / 171, 174, 176, 179, 181, 184, 187–88 / 263, 276 / 297, 303 / 320, 331 / 355, 367 / 433, 435 / 495, 499, 511 / 542 / 581, 592 / 595, 602, 603, 612, 621 / 670 / 685, 711 / 721 / 775 / 777–78, 782, 797

Wirth, Diane E. (LDS author, Mayanist): xvii / 148–49 / 335, 339

Woodruff, Wilford (fourth President of The Church of Jesus Christ of Latter-day Saints, 1889–98): 189 / 375 / 805

Wooley, Mont and Mary (tour participants): xviii

Workman, Margaret (tour participant): xviii

Yucatec (YOO kah tehk; a member of the Maya people of the Yucatan Peninsula; a Maya language spoken by the Yucatec): 24, 26 / 32, 48, 50 / 143

Z

Zaachila (sah ah CHEE lah; Zapotec site near Oaxaca, Mexico): 179

Zaculeu (sah koo LAY oo; Maya site near Huehuetenango in highland Guatemala): 563 / 656 / 784

Zactun (SAHK toon; Maya name for the archaeological site of Chiapa de Corzo; has the same meaning as Sidom in Alma 15:1–3): 358 / 745, 770–71

Zancudero (sahn koo DAY roh; small Preclassic settlement along the Usumacinta River): 664

Zapatista (sah pah TEES tah; revolutionary group in modern Mexico; name derived from Emiliano Zapata and the Mexican Revolution of 1910–19): 89 / 143 / 449 /

Zapotec (sah poh TEHK; native culture core in the valley of Oaxaca, Mexico; native language of Oaxaca valley): 5–6 / 32 / 75, 79–80 / 91–92, 96, 98–101, 103, 107 / 171, 174, 177–80, 182, 185, 188–91 / 293 / 355–56 / 428 / 804

Zarahemla:

City of (Alma 5:2; 6:1, 4, 7; probably the site of Santa Rosa in the Chiapas central depression): 65, 73 / 89 / 153, 158, 161, 167 / 197 / 391, 393–94 / 425 / 453 / 470, 477, 480, 483–84, 487, 491, 493 / 500, 504 / 540 / 560–62 / 572–73, 579–80, 582 / 597, 607, 612–14, 617, 620 / 632, 652–54, 661–62, 664–66 / 678–80 / 721 / 745, 748, 750, 756–57, 759, 761–65, 770, 772, 774

Land of (Omni 1:12–13; Mosiah 24:23–25; Chiapas, Mexico): 8, 10, 12, 17 / 47–48, 53 / 74–76 / 86, 88–89, 97, 102–3 / 131 / 136, 145, 151, 154–59, 162 / 180, 183, 185 / 204, 208–10 / 219, 227, 230, 232–33 / 272 / 356 / 378, 380, 382–83, 389–93 / 401, 404–15, 417–21, 423, 425 / 435–40, 442–43, 445, 448–49, 456–57, 462 / 467–78, 480–81, 483–84, 486–87, 490–91 / 502 / 527, 532–34, 538, 540–42 / 547–49, 556–60, 562–65 / 568–77, 579–82, 588, 590, 590–93 / 595–97, 602–5, 603, 605, 608–9, 612–14, 616–20, 624–25 / 627–32, 635–36, 639, 642, 650–52, 654–58, 660, 662, 664–67, 673 / 675–80, 685, 699–701, 706, 709, 712 / 719, 721, 730–31, 733, 736, 742 / 745–75 / 805, 811, 814

Leader of Mulekites: 9–10 / 68, 76 / 130 / 154–55 / 184 / 496 / 533, 543 / 576 / 597 / 746, 762

People of: 9–10 / 33 / 68, 73–76 / 109 / 137, 153, 155 / 180, 184 / 272 / 424 / 476–77 / 496 / 532–33, 536–37, 543, 545 / 586 / 651 / 746–48, 750–51, 758, 760, 774

Zedekiah (last king of Judah; ca 600 BC; father of Mulek): 8 / 37, 47 / 69–73 / 171, 182 / 376 / 447 / 477 / 496 / 516, 533–36, 539, 543 / 608 / 746

Zeezrom (Lawyer in city of Ammonihah; ca 82 BC): 768, 770–71, 773

City of (in land southward; near city of Zarahemla): 393

Land of (in land southward; associated with land of Zarahemla): 620 / 745

Zelph (white Lamanite in Mormon myth story): 715–16

Zemnarihah (leader of Gadianton robbers; ca. AD 21): 451–52

Zeniff (first king of Nephites who led a group back to the land of Nephi; ca. 200 BC): 340 / 358–59 / 389 / 471 / 559–60, 562 / 574, 582 / 612 / 638, 666 / 719, 722, 724, 728, 731–33 / 755–56, 760

Zenos (prophet of Israel; allegory of Zenos contained on brass plates): 216 / 531

Zerahemna (Lamanite military leader; ca. 74 BC): 659